China's Provinces and Populations

Eric Croddy

China's Provinces and Populations

A Chronological and Geographical Survey

Springer

Eric Croddy
Astoria, OR, USA

ISBN 978-3-031-09164-3 ISBN 978-3-031-09165-0 (eBook)
https://doi.org/10.1007/978-3-031-09165-0

This Springer imprint is published by the registered company Springer Nature Switzerland AG
The registered company address is: Gewerbestrasse 11, 6330 Cham, Switzerland

IN MEMORIAM
Mei-ying Lin (林美英), a woman
of boundless strength and love.

Preface

The goal of this book is to provide a chronological sketch of China's populations, including the Republic of China (Taiwan), from the earliest of times to the twenty-first century. Each province and major provincial-level city are listed in alphabetical order, with maps sketched to show the main administrative regions (as of 2020).

Note on romanization: except for historical references and transliteration used on Taiwan (Republic of China), the mainland Chinese pinyin system is used throughout. In the case of Taiwan, where the Wade-Giles romanization system is still used (in various guises), well-known names such as Taiwanese President Tsai Ing-wen (蔡英文 *cài yīngwén*) and the capital, Taipei City (臺北市 *táiběi shì*), are used throughout, followed by their pinyin pronunciations. For research into Chinese history, and especially where older naming systems are used in English (such as "Chou-k'ou-tien" for Zhoukoudian 周口店 *zhōukǒudiàn*), there are a number of excellent online resources to convert between pinyin and Wade-Giles, including the University of Chicago's "Wade-Giles to Pinyin Conversion Table" (available online),[1] among many others.

Note that some towns and cities have changed their names throughout the centuries, and, more recently, may have changed in status from town to county, to districts, cities, etc. For mainland China, this compendium will use "county" for *xian* (縣), "town" for *zhen* (鎮), and township for *xiang* (鄉). In addition, even while it seems rather redundant, it makes more sense to render Yixian (易縣) as Yixian county, and not "Yi county." Likewise, for a district such as (Shanxi) Kuangqu (礦區), we render this as Kuangqu [mining] district.

Astoria, OR, USA — Eric Croddy

[1] University of Chicago library, East Asia, https://www.lib.uchicago.edu/about/directory/departments/eastasia/find/wade-giles-pinyin-conversion-table/; accessed 16 January 2022.

Contents

Chapter 1
Introduction to China's Provinces and Populations: A Chronological Survey

Abstract Covering a historical view of China's documented and estimated populations, beginning from pre-history to modern times (including results of China's Seventh National Census in 2020), the introduction also covers events in the past and present that could affect Chinese population numbers. Beginning with the very first human settlements, including those of the legendary periods before recorded history, archeological finds, and ancient documentary evidence of population surveys, such as the seminal survey conducted on 2 CE (Eastern Han), a narrative provides possible explanations for growth (or loss) of populations, China's one-child policy, and the modern development of mainland China's household registration (*hukou*) system. Tabular data includes life expectancy in China, past and present, household sizes from early twentieth century and now; the role of male-female preferences in traditional Chinese society and its modern manifestations; and summaries of major events that resulted in large numbers of unnatural deaths during China's turbulent periods.

Introduction: China's Provinces and Populations

Prehistory

Generally speaking, the consensus has been that modern human beings (*Homo sapiens*) first evolved in Africa about 200,000 years ago. Up until recently, the "Out of Africa" thesis proposed that *Homo sapiens* first emerged from Africa, entering the Eurasian landmass about 60,000 years ago. Recent discoveries, however, have pushed this migration date out further, perhaps to 100,000 (or more) years before present.

Excavations in Hunan province revealed *H. sapiens* having lived in southern China about 100,000 years ago, further substantiating the theory that modern humans migrated out of Africa much longer ago than previously thought. First reported in autumn 2011, one such find is located at the Fuyan cave (福岩洞 *fúyándòng*, previously referred to by locals as Houbeishan Cave (後背山洞

E. Croddy, *China's Provinces and Populations*,
https://doi.org/10.1007/978-3-031-09165-0_1

hòubèishāndòng), in Daoxian County (道縣 *dàoxiàn*). Here, a total 47 human teeth were uncovered and examined, these being dated to an estimated range of between 80,000 and 120,000 years ago. Previously, the oldest known migrations of *H. sapiens* to northern Asia and Europe had been judged to be no older than about 50,000 years.

Chinese researchers have discovered additional *H. sapiens* fossils dating back to about 100,000 years: "Xujiajiao Man" (許家窨人 *xǔjiājiàorén*), uncovered in the area of Shanxi province, Yanggao County (陽高縣 *yánggāoxiàn*). In addition, so-called "Maba Man" (馬壩人 *mǎbàrén*) was uncovered in the vicinity of Maba Town in Qujiang District, Shaoguan City, Guangdong Province (韶關市曲江區 *sháoguānshì qūjiāngqū*). Finally, Chinese researchers excavated teeth and lower mandible of a modern human found at the (literally) "Mulan Mountain *Homo sapiens* Cave" (木欖山智人洞 *mùlǎnshān zhìréndòng*) in Jiangzhou District, Chongzuo City, Guangxi Province (崇左市江洲區 *chóngzuǒ shì jiāngzhōu qū*). These human fossils have been preliminarily dated to 106–116 thousand years ago (Cai et al. 2017).

For different periods ranging about 8000 years ago, archeologists have named various Neolithic and bronze periods communities as "cultures" (文化 *wénhuà*), a general term that can describe a great range of human activity, ancient (prewritten) as well as modern. The more important ones in China are below, roughly in chronological order:

*Peiligang Culture (*裴李崗文化 **péilǐgāng wénhuà***)*

Dating back about 8000 years ago, the Peligang Culture was named after initial discoveries made in the late 1970s in Henan Province, Xinzheng City, Peiligang Village (新鄭市裴李崗村 *xīnzhèngshì péilǐgǎngcūn*). Among these finds include the famous Jiahu site, which showed prototypical writing (not dissimilar from Chinese script), musical instruments (flute made from bone), and beer/wine making. These were found in the eponymous Jiahu Village (賈湖村 *jiǎhúcūn*) in Wuyang County, Luohe City, Henan Province (漯河市舞陽縣 *luòhéshì wǔyángxiàn*).

*Yangshao Culture (*仰韶文化 **yǎngsháo wénhuà***)*

Typified by discoveries excavated in Yangshao village, Mianchi County, Sanmenxia City, Henan Province (三門峽市澠池縣仰村 *sānménxiáshì miǎnchíxiàn yǎngsháocūn*), the Yangshao Culture is among the first Chinese Neolithic cultures to have been discovered and studied (1921). Characterized by its decorative pottery, Yangshao sites include the famous Banpo Village (半坡村 *bànpōcūn*) in Baqiao District, Xi'an City, Shaanxi Province (西安市灞橋區 *xī'ānshì bàqiáoqū*).

*Hongshan Culture (*紅山文化 **hóngshān wénhuà***)*

Found in various sites in today's northern Hebei, Liaoning, and Inner Mongolia, Japanese researchers first discovered remnants of this culture dating back to 4700 BCE. Hongshan Culture is famous for its many carved jade items such as curiously-shaped "pig dragons" (豬龍 *zhūlóng*). Key representative Hongshan relics were found in Xinglonggou Village, Chifeng City, Inner Mongolia (赤峰市興隆溝村 *chìfēngshì xīnglónggōucūn*), and the Niuheliang site (牛河梁遺址 *niúhéliángyízhǐ*) in Chaoyang City, Liaoning Province (朝陽市 *liáoníngshěng cháoyángshì*).

*Dawenkou Culture (*大汶口文化 **dàwènkǒu wénhuà***)*

Also found in northern Anhui and Jiangsu provinces, this culture is named after the site in Daiyue District, Shandong Province (岱岳區 *dàiyuèqū*). Lasting from about 4100–2600 BCE, in addition to evidence of complex drinking ceremonies evinced by numerous vats, jars, and pitchers, the Dawenkou Culture is especially remarkable for ritualized burials reflecting hierarchical social structures. The Longshan Culture (see below) followed the Dawenkou, and is considered to have inherited at least some of these traditions.

*Longshan Culture (*龍山文化 **lóngshān wénhuà***)*

The Longshan Culture (3000–1900 BCE) is especially known for its black pottery, jade, and oracle bone inscriptions. It was first uncovered in 1928 in Longshan township (now a subdistrict), Jinan City, Shandong Province (龍山街道 *lóngshān jiēdào*). Related Longshan artifacts have also been uncovered in Henan (near Luoyang), Shanxi and Shaanxi.

*Liangzhu Culture (*良渚文化 **liángzhǔ wénhuà***) ca. 3300–2100 BCE*

Named for a site in today's Liangzhu Subdistrict, Yuhang District, Hangzhou City, Zhejiang Province (余杭區良渚街道 *yúhángqū liángzhǔ jiēdào*), the Liangzhu Culture exhibits a spectacular array of Neolithic jade work and pottery. First studied in 1936, the Liangzhu site also marked the first methodological excavation this far south in China. Paused during China's devastating years of invasion and civil war (1937–1949), archeological surveys resumed in the 1950s. Liangzhu Culture extended as far as northern Zhejiang and Shanghai, with many Neolithic sites found near Taihu Lake, Jiangsu Province. Famously, the "King of *cong* (*ts'ung*)" was found at one site in Fanshan Mountain (反山 *fǎnshān*), a spectacular cylindrical jade vessel (琮 *cóng*) weighing 6.5 kg.

*Majiayao Culture (*馬家窯文化 **mǎjīayáo wénhuà***)*

Originally named after the excavation site in Majiayao Village, Lintao County, Gansu Province (馬家窯村 *mǎjiāyáocūn*), evidence of Neolithic Majiayao Culture (3100–2700 BCE) has also been found in the eastern part of Qinghai Province. In addition to specimens dated to the Neolithic, Majiayao Culture demonstrated some of the earliest evidence of Chinese bronze-age technology.

*Qijia Culture (*齊家文化 **qíjiā wénhuà***)*

In 1923 the Swedish archeologist Johan Gunnar Andersson made the initial discoveries of a bronze age site located in Guanghe County, Gansu Province (廣河縣 *guǎnghéxiàn*). Stretching across Shaanxi, Qinghai, Ningxia, and Inner Mongolia, the so-called Qijia Culture (2400–1900 BCE) featured horse rearing, as well as the manufacture of intricate bronze and copper mirrors.

*Erlitou Culture (*二里頭文化 **erlĭtóu wénhuà***)*

The Erlitou culture (二里頭 *èrlĭtóu*, ca. 1750–1350 BCE) represents the first veritable state polity in ancient China. (Whether or not it also represents an unbroken link to the legendary Xia Dynasty is still controversial). The main sites of discovery are located in Erlitou Village, Zhaizhen Township, Luoyang City, Henan Province (翟鎮二里頭村 *zháizhèn èrlĭtóu cūn*).

*Erligang Culture (*二里岡文化 **èrlĭgǎng wénhuà***)*

Excavations in the 1950s first revealed what appeared to be a Bronze-age Shang Dynasty capital in Erligang, near Zhengzhou City, (鄭州市 *zhèngzhōu shì*), Henan Province, dated approximately 1600–1400 BCE). With fortified walls and evidence of ritualized burials, there are also signs of political stratification indicating a state-like entity.

Estimating Ancient Chinese Populations

According to a summary of Chinese populations throughout history, about five thousand years ago China was home to an estimated 1,000,000 people. A second breakthrough in population growth occurred during 5000–2000 BCE, increasing to about 10 million individuals. (These prehistorical numbers are of course are the result of best estimates and informed speculation).

*The Xia Dynasty: Yao, Shun and Yu (*堯 **Yáo,** 舜 **Shùn,** 禹 **Yǔ*)***

Tradition has it that, during the time of the Yao emperor (堯 *yáo*; ca. 2300 BCE), his people were populated across four main areas:

- Dingtao District (定陶區 *dìngtáoqū*), comprising modern-day Shandong Province and Tangxian County (唐縣 *tángxiàn*), Hebei Province;
- Taiyuan (太原 *tàiyuán*), Shanxi Province;
- A region that includes Linfen City (臨汾市 *línfénshì*), southwest Shanxi Province; and
- Today's Yuncheng City (運城市 *yùnchéngshì*), Shanxi Province.

Under the Shun (舜 *Shùn*; ca. 2200 BCE), descendants of the Yu clan (虞氏 *yúshì*) were said to have occupied both Henan and Shandong of today. Finally, the Yu (禹 *yǔ*, ca. 2150 BCE) clan settled the central Henan area, expanding to the southwest part of Shanxi province. During about this same time, the San Miao (三苗 *sānmiáo*) people occupied the southern part of Henan and northern Hubei provinces. As far as the archeological record is concerned, at about 2000 BCE there was human activity as far west as the Xinjiang Lop Nor region (羅布淖爾 *luóbùnàoěr*).

Chinese scholarship (going back to ca. 300 CE) determined that, at one point during the legendary reign of Yu the Great (大禹 *dà yǔ*), the population of China was precisely 13,553,923 people. This would have been during the (mythical?) Xia (夏 *xià*) Dynasty (ca. 2070–1600 BCE). By the Erlitou period, dating approximately 1900–1500 BCE, Chinese historians estimate that China had a population of 11,372,000 people. The scholar Yuan Zu (袁祖 *yuán zǔ*), however, believes the imprecise number of 10,000,000, is nonetheless more accurate (Yuan and Peimin 2007a).

Based on the Chinese historical record, during the Zhou Dynasty (周 *zhōu*), in the years spanning 1115–1079 BCE, the population was said to have been slightly higher at 13,714,923. In about 680 BCE, an enumeration arrived at 11,841,923 individuals in China. During the Spring-Autumn and Warring States (ca. 450–221 BCE), modern historians believe China expanded to some 8.4 million square kilometers, with a population of at least 35,000,000 people.

Counting People in Ancient China

China claims to have been the very first country to carry out population surveys (Yang 1995). In nearly all cases, and certainly throughout most of Chinese history until the twentieth century, there was no formal census. Indeed, to paraphrase the German scholar Otto Franke, despite China's best attempts to take detailed surveys, it is a hopeless task to accurately ascertain its ancient populations. Even so, as early as the Shang Dynasty (ca. 1600 BCE), China's early rulers were known to have recorded "registered persons" (登人 *dēngrén*) but details are nonetheless scanty. The first reference to a veritable census in China was recorded by Zuo Qiuming (左丘明 *zuǒ qiūmíng*; 556–451 BCE) in the "Discourse on States: Qi" (國語·齊語 *guóyǔ qíyǔ*). Zuo Qiuming, who was known to Confucius as a contemporary, noted that China conducted a "citizen survey of Taiyuan" (料民於太原 *liàomín yú tàiyuán*) in the Zhouxuan (周宣 *zhōuxuān*) Year 39 (789 BCE). There was also another systematic enumeration of the population in the Spring-Autumn period (ca. 771–476 BCE) that was formally instituted by the time of the Warring States (475–221 BCE).

China's First Unification and Political Administration

> The PRC still carries on the tradition of China's ancient autocracy, directly controlling its people by means of the household registry, record keeping, and the communal *baojia* mechanisms. Every city, town, village, and every family, every individual, all are all woven into a watertight network of the administrative state. –Zheng Yi, *Red Memorial* (Zheng 1993)

As the novelist and historian Zheng Yi pointed out (quoted above), the Qin Dynasty (221–206 BCE) introduced a centralized bureaucracy that, *mutatis mutandis*, has essentially been used to administer China's geography ever since. Historical records reveal a detailed household registry census was performed (ca. 200 BCE) during the self-same Qin dynastic period, as in the example below:

> Responding on house of five: Head of household, wife, children, servant, relatives, looms, domesticated animals.
>
> 1. House: Residential, one building, two rooms, each have doors, indoors covered with tile, large wooden furniture; ten mulberry bushes outside.
> 2. Wife: Said to be deceased, not counted.
> 3. Children: Elder daughter, not married. Son, ~ 5′5″ in height.
> 4. Servant
> 5. Relative: small girl
> 6. (Loom): (Not recorded)
> 7. (Animal): One dog. (Yuan and Peimin 2007a)

Chinese officials carried out numerous population tallies under the unifying force of the Qin (221–206 BCE), but the earliest (and probably most complete) enumeration was in the year 2 CE (Eastern Han) that counted 57,671,400 persons distributed across 12,366,470 households. As they are today, back then the major population centers in ancient China included modern-day Hebei, Shandong, and Henan provinces. This prototypical census was relatively detailed and precise, as shown by the type of information collected and compiled in Donghai Prefecture (東海郡 *dōnghǎi jùn*), located in today's southwestern Shandong Province:

Census: Donghai Prefecture, Western Han Dynasty (ca. 2 CE)

Total Households: 266,290
Overall population: 1,397,343
Males: 706,064
Females: 688,132
80 years or older: 33,871
Six years age and below: 262,589
90 years and older: 11,670. (Yuan 2007)

Based on documentary evidence from the aforementioned census, historians have reconstructed the population of China in 2 CE down the level of prefectures and major cities (see Fig. 1.1 and Table 1.1). Consider, for example, Jingzhaoyin (京兆尹 *jīngzhàoyǐn*, in today's central Shaanxi Province) that fell within the boundaries

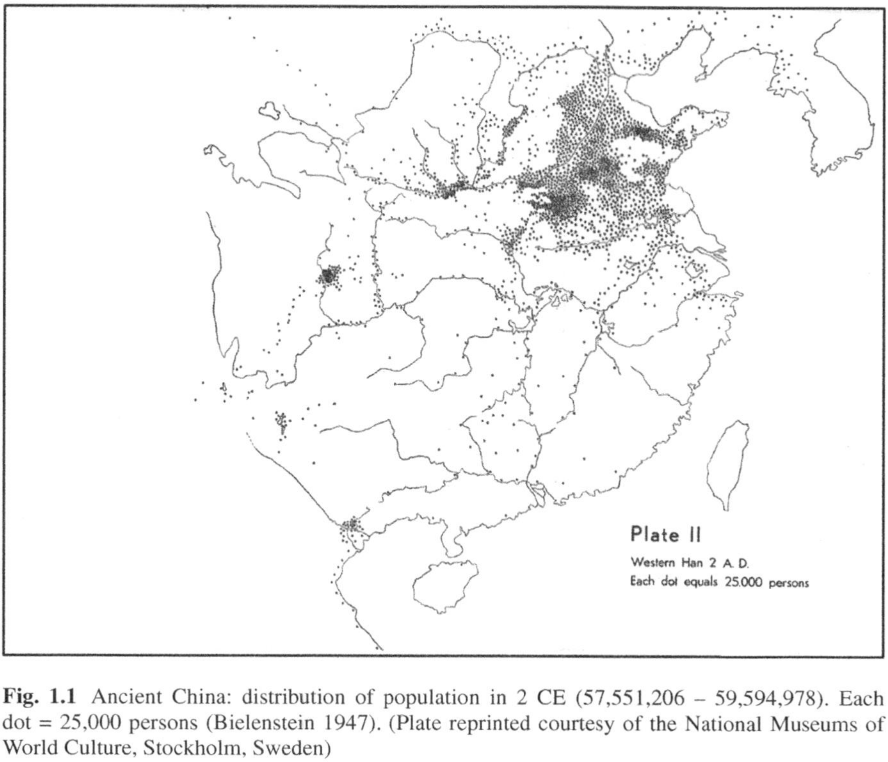

Fig. 1.1 Ancient China: distribution of population in 2 CE (57,551,206 – 59,594,978). Each dot = 25,000 persons (Bielenstein 1947). (Plate reprinted courtesy of the National Museums of World Culture, Stockholm, Sweden)

Table 1.1 Western Han (206 BCE – 8 CE) population estimates of Chinese regions (Yang 1995)

Western Han (206 BCE – 8 CE)	Approximate modern-day provinces/ regions	Counties	Population
司隸部 *sīlìbù*	Shaanxi Xi'an, Shanxi, northern Henan	132	6,682,602
豫州刺史部 *yùzhōu cìshĭbù*	Northern Henan and northern Anhui	102	6,944,353
冀州刺史部 *jìzhōu cìshĭbù*	Hebei	129	5,177,462
兗州刺史部 *yănzhōu cìshĭbù*	Western Shandong, northern Henan	115	7,877,431
徐州刺史部 *xúzhōu cìshĭbù*	Southern Shandong, northern Jiangsu	138	5,241,242
青州刺史部 *qīngzhōu cìshĭbù*	Northeast Shandong	119	4,191,341
荊州刺史部 *jīngzhōu cìshĭbù*	Hubei and Hunan	115	3,597,258
揚州刺史部 *yángzhōu cìshĭbù*	Anhui Hefei, Zhejiang, Jiangxi and Fujian	93	3,206,213
益州刺史部 *yìzhōu cìshĭbù*	Northern Sichuan, northwest Hubei, southwest Shaanxi	128	4,784,214
涼州刺史部 *liángzhōu cìshĭbù*	Gansu	115	1,282,013
並州刺史部 *bìngzhōu cìshĭbù*	Central Inner Mongolia, Shanxi	90	450,432
幽州刺史部 *yōuzhōu cìshĭbù*	Northeast Hebei, Liaoning, southern Jilin Province, and northern Korea	162	880,667
朔方刺史部 *shuòfāng cìshĭbù*	Central Inner Mongolia, Shaanxi	84	1,673,450
交趾刺史部 *jiāozhĭ cìshĭbù*	Northern Vietnam, Guangxi and Guangdong	55	1,372,290
Total		**1577**	**57,671,401**

of the Sili Bu sector (司隸部 *sīlìbù*). Comprising 12 counties, Jingzhaoyin had 682,468 people, while the capital of Chang'an (today's Xi'an) had a population of 246,200. Taiyuan (today's capital of Shanxi Province) during that time was administered within the larger Taiyuan ("commandery") Prefecture (太原郡 *tàiyuánjùn*), consisting of 21 counties and had a total population of 680,488. For its part, Kuaiji Prefecture (會稽郡 *kuàijījùn*), with 26 counties, had an estimated headcount of over 1.3 million. China's northeast Liaodong Prefecture had a population of 272,539 (18 counties). And the western Jiuquan Prefecture (酒泉郡 *jiŭquánjùn*), located in modern-day Gansu Province, had 18,137 households (equating to about 76,726 people), while neighboring Dunhuang Jun Prefecture (six counties) had a total population of 38,335. Or, consider the case of Nanhai Prefecture (南海郡 *nánhăijùn*) in the south, which formed the majority of today's Guangdong Province: during the Western Han (2 CE), records indicate Nanhai Prefecture had 94,253 people across six counties.

By 140 CE, Nanhai Prefecture grew to seven cities with an estimated population of 250,282. This dramatic increase was due to immigration patterns of ancient China, including a great number of people fleeing south to escape turmoil in the north, as well exiled government officials and others who were branded as political malcontents. At this time, in the western region of China, Jiuquan Prefecture had 12,706 households, and Dunhuang's population had dropped down to 29,170. (Fig. 1.2 shows China's population distribution of this period.)

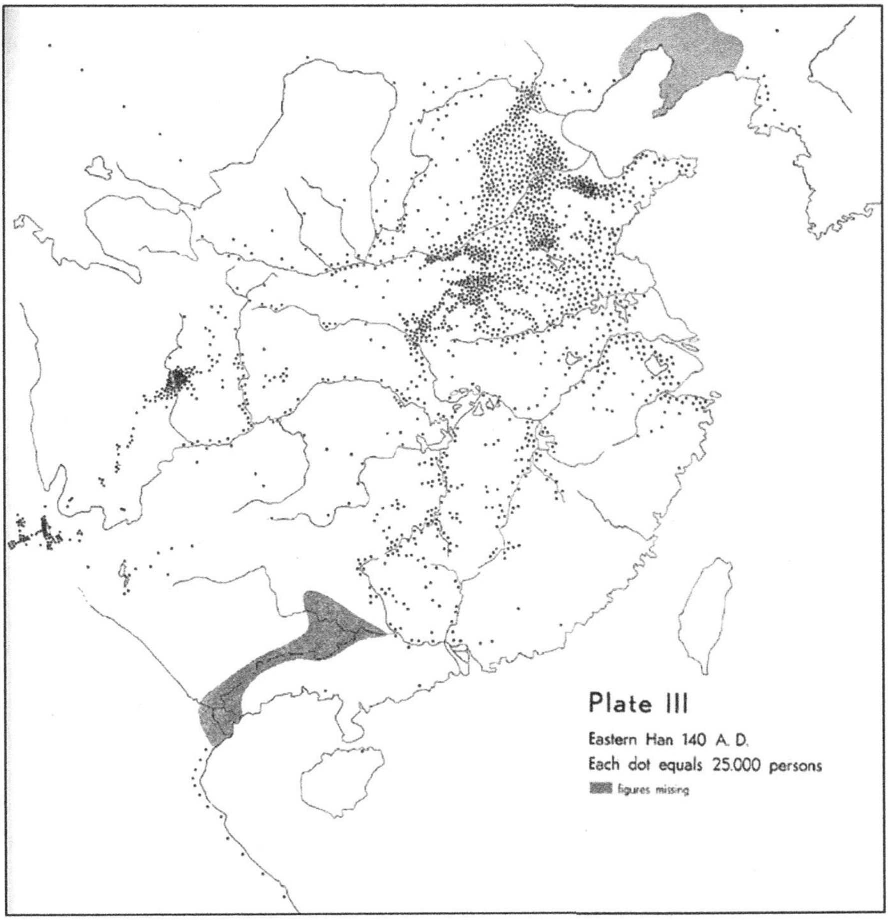

Fig. 1.2 Ancient China: distribution of population, 140 CE. Population estimate range: 48,000,000–49,150,220. Each dot = 25,000 persons (Bielenstein 1947). (Plate reprinted courtesy of The National Museums of World Culture, Stockholm, Sweden)

Importance of the Census for the Ancient Chinese State(s)

The Eastern Han philosopher Xu Gan (徐幹 *xú gàn*; 170–217 CE) emphasized that tallying the size of the population was fundamental to the nation-state:

> If to rule the state requires the successful accomplishment of many and varied tasks, in order to accomplish these things, this requires the service of people. Such work is all within the confines of numbers of people, and thus the population is the foundation of the kingdom. (Yang 1995)

Xu Gan's explanation shows that, more than anything else, these regular surveys were designed to count households and numbers of people in order to tax, divvy up land, determine officials' salaries, maintain political order, as well as enlist military age males, and (notoriously) to round up corvée labor for the emperors' many construction projects.

Data Collection in Dunhuang, 416 CE

Intriguingly, we have an example of the kind of details Chinese officials of the Western Liang (西涼 *xīliáng* 400–421 CE) were looking for when counting their populations, found on a piece of parchment that had since been repurposed for a Buddhist scripture. In a region that encompassed today's Gansu and Xinjiang provinces, in 416 CE a survey collected the following data on a household in Dunhuang county, Dunhuang commandery (敦煌郡 *dūnhuángjùn*) in today's Turpan city (吐魯番市 *xīnjiāng shěng tǔlǔfān shì*), Xinjiang. The text (Bielenstein 1947) reads as follows:

兵裴保年六十六 (*bīng péibǎo nián liùshíliù*)	Soldier; (name) Pei Bao; (age) 66
妻袁年六十三 (*qī yuán nián liùshísān*)	Wife, (name) Yuan (age) 63
息男金年卅九 (*xī nán jīn nián sàjiǔ*)	Son, (name) Jin (age) 39
金男弟隆年卅[?]四 (*jīn nándì nián sà?sì*)	Jin's younger brother, (name) Long, (age) 34 (probably)[a]
金妻張年卅六 (*jīn qī zhāng nián sàliù*)	Jin's wife, (name) Zhang, (age) 36
隆妻蘇年廿二 (*long qī sū nián niàn'èr*)	Long's wife (name) Su, (age) 22
金息男養年二 (*jīn xī nán yǎng nián'èr*)	Jin's son (name) Yang, (age) 2
居趙羽 [塢] (*jū zhàoyǔ* [*wù*])	Residence: Zhao Yu's [rampart that is, a walled area that was built by a certain Zhao Yu.]

[a]A small hole in the original manuscript made the number difficult to discern

In summary, this survey tallied the number of two adult males (丁男二 *dīngnán èr*), including a mature son (次男 *cìnán*) and one little boy (小男一 *xiǎonán yī*); three females (女口 *nǚkǒu*); and a total number (7) of inhabitants 凡口 (*fánkǒu*). Due to his relatively advanced age of 66, the elder (and veteran) Pei Bao was excluded from the final total, having already aged out of military service.

Sui (581 CE) and Tang (618 CE) Dynastic Transition

Considered (quite rightly) to be one of China's most glorious time periods, the rulers of the Tang Dynasty nonetheless took some time before conducting a proper census of its sovereign territories. Adding to the uncertainty of population figures during this time were bureaucratic confusion over what records were still viable following one dynasty to another, shifting populations, and widespread chaos following the massive unrest of the Anlushan rebellion (安史之亂 *ānshǐ zhīluàn*) in 755–763 CE. As such, because of the inherent problems in administrating census (even under "normal" circumstances), such numbers (e.g., exactly 52,919,309 people in 755 CE) probably should be seen as minimum estimates. (Fig. 1.3 shows the Tang population distribution as of 742 CE).

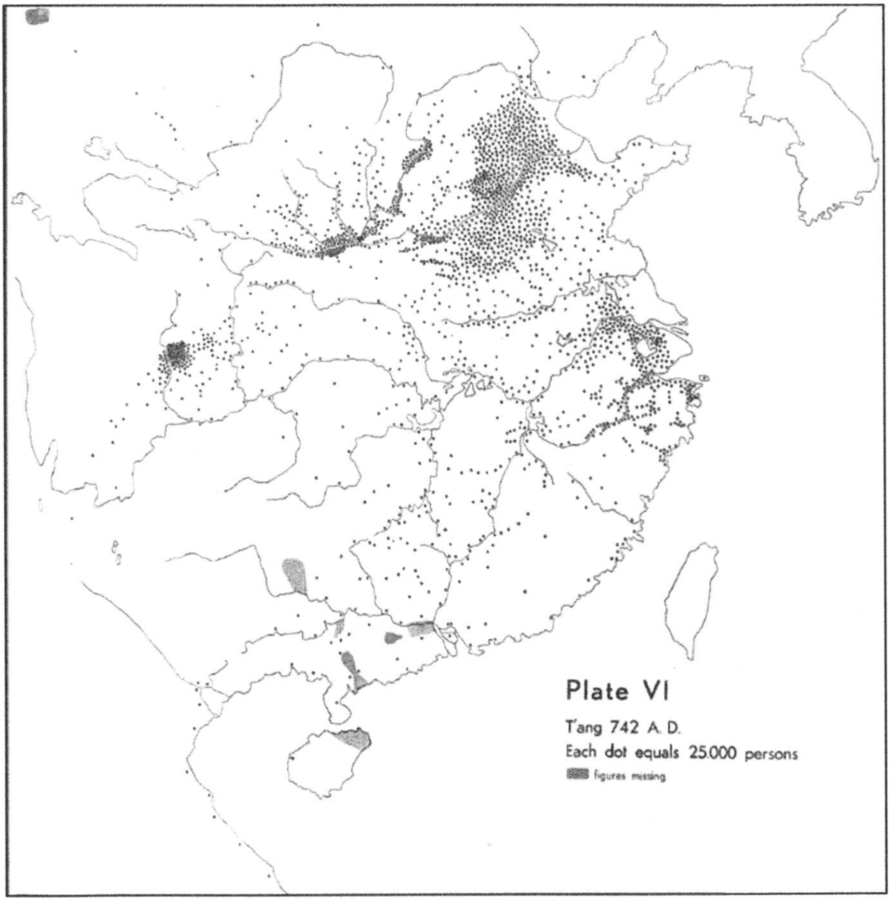

Fig. 1.3 China: distribution of population as of 742 CE (48,089,800), Tang Dynasty (Bielenstein 1947). Each dot = 25,000 persons. (Shaded Areas Indicate Lack of Available Data. Plate reprinted courtesy of The National Museums of World Culture, Stockholm, Sweden)

Ming Dynastic Surveys

Centuries later, in 1370 (when the last of the remaining Yuan Dynasty fell, and the Ming began) another document showed how surveys of households were being conducted. The form begins with a description of the household, location, and short summary (ter Haar 2013):

一戶張得肆, (*yīhù zhāng désì*):
"One household, (that of) Zhang Desi;"

係嘉興府崇德縣梧桐鄉 (*xì jiāxīngfǔ, chóngdé xiàn, wútóng xiāng*):
"[Located] in Wutong village, Chongde county, Jiaxingfu" [i.e., modern-day Tongxiang city, Jiaxing municipality, Zhejiang province 浙江省嘉興市桐鄉市 *zhèjiāng sheng jiāxīng shì tóngxiāng shì*];

二十九都貽字圍, 本戶計今四口. (*èrshíjiǔ dū yí zì wéi, běnhù jì jīn sìkǒu*):
"The twenty-ninth subdivision[1] rampart enclosure, (marked by the) character "Yi," this household having, at present, four people [literally: four mouths]";

男子二口: 成丁壹: 本身, 年三十四歲; (*nánzǐ èr kǒu: chéng dīng yī: běnshēn, nián sānshísì suì*):
"Two males: adult male, one: the aforementioned, 34 years of age;"

不成丁壹口: 男阿狗, 一歲. (*bùchéng dīng yī kǒu: nán āgǒu, yī suì*):
"Young person, one: male, "Ah Gou" ['pup'], one year of age.[2]"

婦女二口: 妻宋大娘, 年二十六歲; 女阿勝, 年四歲. (*fùnǚ èr kǒu: qī sòng dàniáng nián èrshíliù suì; nǚ āshèng, nián sìsuì*):
"Females, two: Wife, Madame Song, 26 years of age; girl 'Ah Sheng,' four years old.";

事產: 民田, 三畝五分一厘; 房屋, 壹間壹廈. (*shìchǎn: míntián, sān mǔ wǔ fēn yī lí; fángwū, yījiān, yīshà*):
"Real estate: land, 3.501 *mu* (a little more than half acre); One room house, one foyer."

After being stamped for approval and acceptance, the head of household (Zhang Desi), inscribed in his own hand what amounted to an "X" for a signature, as he was most likely illiterate. This type of document was emblematic of how the Ming, at least through the end of the 1300s, signaled a new, reinvigorated effort to conduct a proper enumeration of people within the empire (minus "barbarians," and those located in areas that were nearly impossible to safely travel for imperial bureaucrats). However, the Chinese "census" eventually became less and less reliable, both in terms of how it was conducted, and the quality of the numbers that were being compiled. Eventually, going into the later Ming and the Qing dynasties, instead of counting households 戶 (*hù*) and people 口 (*kǒu* = "mouths"), able-bodied men and heads of household (property) were subsequently counted in units of *ding* 丁 (*dīng*). Because the long-standing goal of Chinese enumerations was to find adult males (roughly 16 years of age to about 65) that could fight, work on public projects, and be taxed, eventually the *ding* became primarily a tax-surveying instrument. By the end of the 1600s, a contemporary official complained:

[1] The character 都 (*dū*) usually means a city or larger section; in older China, it was often used as a subdivision administrative unit within a county.

[2] Ages in China usually began at one year beginning at birth.

> Evasions and omissions in population registration are common throughout the country and by no means confined to the southeast. Yet there are reasons why such fraudulent practices are most serious in the southeast. During the early years of the dynasty..., labor services were apportioned according to the ding, the assessment of which had to be very careful. Later on [the ding assessment] was no longer based exclusively on the ding but partially on the land tax.... South of the Yangtze (Changjiang river) there is no longer actual population registration, as labor services are largely borne by the land. (Ho 1959)

Thus, historians have since struggled to reconstruct Chinese populations from the Ming to the Qing (and following the 1911 revolution). How many people does a *ding* represent? Depending on the source or context, it could range from about four to six people, some falling within the middle average of those two (i.e., 5.5 per *ding*). Such is how the total populations could be estimated. However, as the pre-eminent scholar on the issue concluded,

> To sum up the official Chinese population data of the past five centuries, it may be said that the more useful ones are those of the Ming [Taizu 太祖 *tàizǔ*; i.e., Emperor Hongwu 洪武帝 *hóngwǔdì*] period (1368–1398); of the period 1776–1850; and, of the census year 1953. The data of the period 1741–1775, while highly defective, may be of some help. The century between 1851 and 1949, despite the availability of various figures, is practically a demographer's vacuum. (Ho 1959)

Downward Pressures on Ancient Chinese Populations

Given the major problems in obtaining accurate population numbers throughout China's history, determining major changes in the numbers of recorded people is similarly challenging, especially when trying to ascribe discrete causes to shifting population numbers. Nonetheless, throughout China's ancient history, precipitous declines in population have been attributed to the wartime killing and the capture of civilians (for labor) and POWs following major warfare. During the Han-Xiongnu wars (133 BCE – 89 CE), the Lulin (綠林 *lǜlín*) peasant revolts (17 CE), and the Red Eyebrow (赤眉 *chìméi*) rebellion in the following year, there was nearly almost non-stop conflict from 25 – 36 CE. As is true throughout world history elsewhere, even more than the disruption and devastation brought about by military conflict, it was the resulting famine and disease that often took its far greater share of human life. For example, beginning in 19 CE, northeast China was gripped with severe famine. The histories recount that the

> The people of Qing (青 *qīng*) and Xu (徐 *xú*) prefectures [in modern-day Shandong province] abandoned their villages, scattered to the winds... the old and weak die on the road, while the stronger ones became brigands. (Yuan and Peimin 2007b)

Furthermore, "barbarian" Xiongnu attacks in ca. 23 CE led to widespread chaos and misery, with battlefield deaths in the tens of thousands in Qingzhou (青州 *qīngzhōu*; northeast Shandong); Xuzhou (徐州 *xúzhōu*, approximately Jiangsu Province today; Jingzhou (荊州 *jīngzhōu*; Hubei and Hunan provinces); and Chu (楚 *chǔ*, today's Xuzhou City area). Warfare broke an already fragile agricultural economy:

due to the state's emphasis on the war effort, crop fields could not be attended, leading to famine, epidemics, and often cannibalism. For example, going back to what Sun Zi (the purported author of the *Art of War*) noted was common practice in his day (ca. 500 BCE), crops raised on land that could support the local population were exacted by the state to raise funds for war horses. In this maelstrom of hostility, any semblance of law and order on the roads was no longer observed, and "even rich people couldn't protect themselves, while the poor had no means to sustain their mere existence…" (Yang 1995). Famine and disease ineluctably took their toll in the wartime chaos, and the numbers of households reportedly fell by half. The years 26 – 27 CE typified the desperation and widespread misery of the common people during this tumultuous period:

> [There were] three great famines…; cities and suburbs were emptied, bones scattered in the fields…. Hundreds starved to death, and resorted to cannibalism; five pints of beans is all you would get in exchange for a pound of gold. The roads were severed, and piled-up goods couldn't make it to their destinations. Soldiers all resorted to eating nuts and fruit. (Yang 1995)

Based on the aforementioned census in 2 CE, the entire population of China was cut at least in half.

Even when the major wars ended, natural disasters and smaller-scale revolts in China continued to dramatically increase mortality. In 38 CE, an epidemic struck Kuaiji Prefecture (會稽郡 *kuàijījùn*; modern-day Jiangsu and Zhejiang provinces), killing tens of thousands in this region alone. Indeed, Chinese history is replete with such episodes of a dramatic decrease in population, usually following every major flood, drought, locust swarm and the like, resulting in horrific famine, cannibalism, and the sudden desolation of entire communities.

In other times, once the dust had settled, the return of political normalcy and relative peace led to a resurgence in populations, such as during the Shundi (順帝 *shùndì*) court period (126–144 CE). Previously, in the Western Han period (ca. 2 CE), Ba Prefecture (巴郡 *bājùn*, now roughly today's Chongqing City), had a population of 708,148. Following a survey and mapping of Ba Prefecture in 154 CE, it was more than double that, consisting of 14 counties with a total population of 1,875,435.

Natural disasters, famine, and pestilence also likely contributed to the fall of China's population from ca. 105–125 CE. For example, in 107 there were 18 earthquakes across China, 28 major storms with rain and hail. In 119 China recorded some 50 earthquakes and a plague in Kuaiji. The years 124–125 CE brought nearly two dozen earthquakes, 36 hailstorms, and famine (大疾 *dàjí*) in the imperial capital city. In the beginning of the Xiandi Xingping (獻帝興平 *xiàndì xìngpíng*) reign (194 CE), three extensive droughts led to massive inflated prices for food grains, resulting in widespread starvation and cannibalism, the latter being a tragic occurrence that continued through the mid-twentieth century.

In contrast to the glorified era of the previous Han, which maintained a unified polity for nearly four hundred years, the balkanization of China that followed was typified by war, disease and famine, bringing population numbers down to their lowest levels in centuries. As the historian Yi-Fu Tuan put it, "Life had little worth around the end of the second and third centuries" (Tuan 2008). And one must also consider the large numbers of desperate people who fled various parts of the empire for their own safety, as well as the breakdown in official functions, all leading to an undercounting (or in some cases overcounting) of people. The Xiongnu barbarian rebellion in Shanxi Province (304 CE) brought about a series of violent campaigns that scattered millions of Han Chinese, many of them deciding to flee towards the south. During the time of the Yongjia revolt (or literally, disaster: 永嘉之窩 *yǒngjiā zhīwō*; 307–311), when the Wu Hu (五胡 *wǔhú*) barbarian tribes sacked Luoyang (311), the calamity of war dramatically reduced population numbers in northern China. By ca. 325 CE, up to seven-tenths of its upper classes fled south of the Yangtze (長江 *chángjiāng*) River.

Song Dynasty Populations

With the relative prosperity of the Song Dynasty (960–1279), China's population grew to about 60,000,000. It was during this time (1125) that the metropolis of Kaifeng (then known as Bianjing; 汴京 *biànjīng*) was besieged by the invading Jurchen (女真 *nǚzhēn*). During this so-called Jingkang Incident (靖康之亂 *jìngkāng zhīluàn*) some five million Chinese moved south. As this migration proceeded, the Jurchen, Mongolians and other "barbarian" minorities took their place in China's central plains.

Populations in the Age of the Mongols

The Mongol invasions of China must have led to massive population drop-offs, but actual numbers are difficult to match up with the historical record. Estimates vary, but serious scholars have cited the figure of 18 million people who were slaughtered by Mongolian armies, and this is not counting the many more who perished from famine and disease. For example, in the year 1223, the Southern Song empire had a population of 76,810,000. When combined with the Jin State (金國 *jīn guó*) to the north, the total population was well north of 100 million. Following the extinction of the Southern Song in 1279 by the Mongolians, a comprehensive Yuan Dynasty census recorded a population of 58,834,711 (Li 2012).

Urbanization During the Ming, and Increase of Population During the Qing

During the Ming Dynasty, the economics of the times contributed to its urbanization, spurred on by the growth of sophisticated market centers. The selling of textiles, such as cotton cloth, found home in the following cities of the Jiangnan region (south of the Yangtze): Songjiang (now within Shanghai), Suzhou (Jiangsu Province) and Hangzhou (Zhejiang Province). By 1393, Songjiang had a population of 1,219,937, and Suzhou had 2,355,030 people. As mercantilism and city dwellers formed metropolitan communities, the density of their populations also increased. In 1393, the population density of Nanjing (Nanzhili 南直隸 *nánzhílì*) reached a peak of nearly 48 people per square kilometer (Yang 1995).

Dramatic growth in China's population can be especially seen from the first large-scale population survey conducted during the Qing Dynasty in 1652, which arrived at a figure of 144,838,580 persons, then later totaling more than double that by 1834 to 401,008,574. Scholars of China's populations throughout history have suggested, with good rationale, that introduction of hardier, draught-resistant crops, such as corn (maize) in ca. 1574, and particularly the sweet potato (番薯 *fānshǔ* "foreign potato"), was instrumental in providing vital food supplies to support such a growth in population (Ho 1959).While it is certain that having a more reliable source of calories should help to explain the surge in China's population during the Qing, scholarship since has cast doubt on this simplistic cause and effect. First, the widespread promotion of the sweet potato in China, for example, really only took hold by the mid-nineteenth century. And others have noted it was not an increase in agricultural production per se, but more efficient food distribution systems and an improved supporting infrastructure that really played crucial roles. Finally, the historical record seems to support the conclusion that it was the *growth in population* that promoted more tilling of new crops such as corn and potatoes—rather than the reverse (Li 1982).

Deaths Caused by the Taiping Rebellion (1851–1864)

The question of how many lives were lost during the tumult of the Taiping Rebellion (1851–1864) is answered by a large range of estimates, from 11 to 70 million, possibly more. Complicating the problem is the unreliability of Qing census data. Undaunted, scholars specializing in this period of history examined the five provinces impacted the most by the Taiping Rebellion. After adding up their populations as of 1851 (170,366,348), they compared these with later populations as of 1911 (104,808,294). Assuming that their populations should have achieved a general increase (under ordinary circumstances), the number of people lost during the Taiping Rebellion begins at 65,000,000. Extrapolating from this, by 1864 (the end of the Taiping Rebellion) the population of those self-same provinces should have been about 177,000,000, arriving at a total number of unusual deaths at 87 million. Other historians estimated a staggering 100,000,000 lives lost during this time (Hua and Hongjun 2007). Regardless of the actual figure, in terms of orders of magnitude, the calamity that befell upon China during the Taiping Rebellion likely ranks equivalent alongside the massive numbers of Chinese deaths caused by the Japanese invasion of China (1937–45), approximately 11 million; the Chinese Civil War (1945–1949), from 6 to 20 million; the Great Leap Forward (1958–61), at least 37 million dead; and the Cultural Revolution (1966–1976), about 1.5 million were killed—*combined.*

China's Civil War Dead (1945–1949)

The violent struggle between the ruling party of the Republic of China (ROC), the Kuomintang (Nationalists) and the Chinese Communist Party (CCP) was an ongoing state of affairs, especially beginning in 1927, which ultimately resulted in the defeat of the KMT in 1949. Numbers of dead from fighting as well as civilian deaths (e.g., famine and disease) generally range from one to six million during the Chinese Civil War of 1945–1949 (Proske 2008). R. J. Rummel of the University of Hawaii counts no fewer than 6,194,000 having died during the internecine conflict from all causes (Rummel 2002). According to official numbers published in mainland China, compiling data from July 1946 to June 1950, the communist forces "wiped out" some 8,070,000 KMT forces, and three million civilians died. Not to be outdone, numbers provided from a history of the Chinese communist field armies during the civil war period claimed the CCP forces "annihilated" 10,658,000 KMT forces. In both figures above, it is unclear as to what "wiped out" or "annihilated" really mean, but all told, mainland Chinese estimates tally some 20,000,000 dead, including both sides of the war and civilians (Xin 2011).

The Great Proletarian Cultural Revolution (1966–1976)

As for the Cultural Revolution (CR, 1966–1976), its death toll was not nearly as high as previous chaotic episodes in China's history. Nonetheless, knowledgeable sources believe that one-and a half to two million dead is a conservative estimate. It is also worthy to note that, when one includes all of the people who suffered during the excesses of the 10-year CR, to include false accusations, victims of "struggle sessions," and generally horrific means of persecution, over 100,000,000 Chinese citizens were adversely impacted.

Life Expectancy: Ancient and Modern

Taking sample of life expectancy estimates from various times in the ancient world, it is commonplace to find numbers ranging from 20–35 (early human settlements), to 36 years of age (Sweden, mid-eighteenth century), and under 50 on average in the United States (early 1900s). For China, when also taking infant mortality into account (common to all civilizations before the advent of modern medicine), a similar picture can be found in these surveys (see Table 1.2).

We are *not* to conclude from such averages of life expectancy that few (if any) lived to very old age. Even from the earliest period of China's history, a significant number of people lived well past the age of 35, as famously evinced by Confucius who died at about age 71 (479 BCE). Table 1.3 shows estimated ages of death for a Yangshao Culture (ca. 5000–3000 BCE) burial site.

A couple of millennia later, Table 1.4 shows a sample of ages and sex distribution from the Shang Dynasty.

Table 1.2 Life expectancy from ancient to modern China (Tspweb 2020)

Time period	Average life expectancy, China[a]
Xia (夏 *xià*) and Shang (商 *shāng*) ca. 2000–1000 BCE	18
Zhou (周 *zhōu*) and Qin (秦 *qín*) ca. 1000–250 BCE	20
Han (漢 *hàn*) ca. 200 BCE – 200 CE	20
Tang (唐 *táng*) ca. 600–900 CE	27
Song (宋 *sòng*) ca. 900–1300 CE	30
Qing (清 qīng) 1600–1900 CE	33
Nationalist, Republic of China (民國 *mínguó*) ca. 1912–1945	35
People's Republic of China (ca. late 1950s)	57
1981	68
1985	69

[a]Averages include the factor of infant mortality

Table 1.3 Yangshao Culture (仰韶文化 yǎngsháo wénhuà) ca. 5000–3000 BCE, Burial Site, Age Distributions (Yuan and Peimin 2007a)

Sex	Infant-child (0–12 years)	Young-mature adults (13–35)	Middle-aged (36–50)	Elderly (50+)	(General adult age)	Subtotal
Male	0	49	30	1	10	90
Female	2	45	10	1	7	65
Sex Indeterminate	33	7	0	1	5	46
Total	35	101	40	3	22	201

Table 1.4 Age and sex distributions from a Shang Dynasty Cemetery, ca. 1200 BCE (Yuan and Peimin 2007a)

Years of age	15–24	25–35	36–44	45–50	>50	Total
No. Males	10	14	16	6	7	53
No. Females	13	7	7	1	1	29
Total number	23	21	23	7	8	82
Percentage	~28	~25.5	~28	~8.5	~10	100

Chinese Life Expectancy in the Twenty-First Century

In 2020, not surprisingly, those living in the wealthier and more developed parts of mainland China statistically live longer than poorer, less-developed provinces. With an overall average life expectancy of about 75 years of age across the PRC, the highest numbers are recorded in places like Shanghai City (80.3) and Guangdong Province (76.5), and lower in Qinghai (70.0) and Tibet (Xizang): 68.2 (Everyone's Library 2021). As for the Republic of China (Taiwan), its Ministry of the Interior published data in 2020 that found an average life expectancy nationwide at 81.3, with the highest (84.1) in Taipei City (臺北市 *táiběi shì*); about 82 years of age in Hsinchu City (新竹市 *xīnzhú shì*); and the lowest in eastern Taitung County (臺東縣 *táidōng xiàn*): 76.5.

China's One-Child Policy

During the early period of the People's Republic of China (PRC) in the 1950s, Chinese communists believed a larger population (about 550 million at the time) was quite advantageous. Thus, the initial Chinese Communist Party (CCP) line on birth control was neither kind nor subtle, considering it "a means of slaughtering the people without drawing blood" (Chai 1977). In fact, Maoist political forces halted the implementation of a birth control program in 1958. Party stalwarts firmly opposing birth control was none other than Hu Yaobang, who, in the heady early stages of the Great Leap Forward (1958 – 1962), said:

> We Marxists believe that for the sake of the health of our people and the welfare of the next generation, planned parenthood should be promoted. However, a large population is a good, and not an undesirable thing. A larger population means greater manpower. This is simple logic: the force of 600 million liberated people is tens of thousands more powerful than a nuclear explosion. Such a force is capable of creating wonders which our enemies cannot even imagine. Facts since the Great Leap Forward movement have sufficiently proved this point. (Chai 1977)

As we have already seen, the Great Leap Forward (1958–1962) proved to be a monumental disaster, with as many as 45 million people having died from starvation. As a consequence, birth control was reinstated in China (albeit with little fanfare) in 1962. But just as one Maoist mass movement interrupted this key policy initiative, yet another came along to delay Chinese efforts at family planning. The chaos of the Cultural Revolution (1966–1976) tore the country apart. Only after that tumult were efforts renewed to address China's growing population. A strict, one-child policy was finally implemented in late 1979, which was more widely and officially promulgated in the early 1980s. This, unfortunately, led to a horrific series of mass campaigns that included forced abortions and sterilization, while the tradition of favoring males ineluctably led to widespread female infanticide. According to Steven Mosher, in the years following the institution of the one-child policy hundreds of thousands of newly-born girls were killed or abandoned. Mosher concludes:

> When China's geriatric leaders, then led by the diminutive septuagenarian Deng Xiaoping, embarked upon the one-child-per-couple policy in 1979, they did not imagine that they were remaking their country in their own demographic image. But—with China's population rapidly ageing and its sex ratio even more skewed in favor of men—this is exactly what is happening. The face of China is slowly coming to resemble the Politburo of the Chinese Communist Party, that is to say, it will be grey and overwhelmingly male. (Mosher 2011)

Sensing the demographic trends were not in China's favor, and after some relaxation in the one-child policy in 2013, the Chinese government officially changed its policy to allow families to have two children in October 2015, and further relaxed the restriction to three in 2020. But according to the Chinese demographer Liang Zhongtang, it is likely far too late for this to make a meaningful impact upon China's greying population trend (Buckley 2015). As has been the case for industrializing countries around the world, average sizes of households have continued to fall, as seen in Table 1.5.

Table 1.5 Average sizes of households in China: 1910[a] and 2010 compared (Mi et al. 1997)

Area/province (historical and modern equivalents)	Number of households (1910)	Number of individuals (1910)	Average household size (1910)	Number of households (2010)	Number of individuals (2010)	Average household size (2010)
Zhili (Hebei) 直隸 *zhílì*)	5,721,623	29,505,773	5.16	20,395,116	68,538,709	3.36
Jiangsu (江蘇 *jiāngsū*)	5,385,427	26,165,638	4.86	24,381,782	71,685,839	2.94
Anhui (安徽 *ānhuī*)	3,141,184	16,229,052	5.17	18,861,956	56,493,891	3.00
Shandong (山東 *shāndōng*)	5,380,277	31,047,430	5.77	28,630,609	88,979,305	3.11
Shanxi (山西 *shānxī*)	2,001,776	10,149,469	5.07	10,330,207	33,484,131	3.24
Henan (河南 *hénán*)	4,661,566	26,894,945	5.77	25,928,729	90,028,072	3.47
Shaanxi (陜西 *shǎnxī*)	1,605,342	8,071,792	5.03	10,718,563	34,462,115	3.22

(continued)

Table 1.5 (continued)

Area/province (historical and modern equivalents)	Number of households (1910)	Number of individuals (1910)	Average household size (1910)	Number of households (2010)	Number of individuals (2010)	Average household size (2010)
Gansu (甘肅 *gānsù*)	908,040	4,699,494	5.18	6,900,369	24,052,594	3.49
Fujian (福建 *fújiàn*)	2,379,139	12,534,842	5.27	11,206,317	33,397,663	2.98
Zhejiang (浙江 *zhèjiāng*)	3,891,277	17,997,858	4.63	18,854,021	49,425,543	2.62
Jiangxi (江西 *jiāngxī*)	3,439,843	16,725,685	4.89	11,542,527	42,181,417	3.65
Hubei (湖北 *húběi*)	4,938,625	23,941,688	4.85	16,695,121	52,745,625	3.16
Hunan (湖南 *húnán*)	4,288,164	21,712,203	5.06	18,625,710	61,911,446	3.32
Sichuan (四川 *sìchuān*)	9,190,377	52,859,128	5.75	25,794,161	76,207,174	2.95
Guangdong (廣東 *guǎngdōng*)	5,052,418	28,058,658	5.55	28,630,609	88,979,305	3.11
Guangxi (廣西 *guǎngxī*)	1,381,572	7,239,437	5.24	13,151,404	43,970,320	3.34
Yunnan (雲南 *yúnnán*)	1,549,381	7,174,884	4.62	12,339,961	43,626,674	3.54
Guizhou (貴州 *guìzhōu*)	1,771,533	8,503,054	4.80	10,558,461	33,571,308	3.18
Fengtian (奉天 *fèngtiān*; Modern-day Liaoning)	1,650,573	10,696,004	6.48	14,994,046	41,755,874	2.78
Jilin (吉林 *jílín*)	739,461	5,393,744	7.20	8,998,492	26,457,769	2.94
Heilongjiang (黑龍江 *hēilóngjiāng*)	245,957	1,858,792	7.56	13,000,088	36,884,039	2.84
Xinjiang (新疆 *xīnjiāng*)	465,880	2,149,654	4.61	6,705,607	20,802,249	3.10
Qinghai (青海 *qīnghǎi*)	67,355	311,520	4.63	1,529,039	5,284,525	3.46
Tibet (西藏 *xīzàng*)	293,244	1,357,722	4.63	670,838	2,837,769	4.23
Total	**70,430,432**	**372,563,555**	**5.29**	**401,934,196**	**1,239,981,250**	**3.09**

[a]Data compiled from 1909–1910 survey

The average household size in the PRC according to the 2020 census was 2.62 compared to 3.09 in 2010 (NBS 2021). Of note, the closest simulacrum to mainland China in terms of culture and social patterns, the Republic of China (ROC) on Taiwan, has had a similar pattern of shrinking household size, but of course without a one-child policy. For example, Taiwan in 1961 had an average household of 5.6 in 1961, 3.9 in 1991, 2.9 in 2010, and most recently holding at 2.9 in 2020. The legacy of the one-child policy notwithstanding, like the majority of nations where industrialization and modernization continue apace, Chinese families are having fewer children than in the past. With a slowing down in overall population growth in China (as shown in the recent 2020 census), the Chinese state has responded by allowing an increase in the number of children per family from two (in late 2015) to now three. Even so, the initial reaction on Chinese social media to this policy change was lukewarm: given the demands of a modernizing economy, complete with long working hours, commuting, and increased living expenses among them, many Chinese are not keen on having large numbers of children.

China's Male Dominated Society 4.1

> Parent's attitudes toward children are such that they congratulate each other when it is a boy, and kill it if it is a girl… (This is because) they are considering their later convenience and calculating their long-term interests. Han Feizi (韓非子 *hán fēizǐ*), legalist philosopher, d. 233 BCE (Kinney 1993)

China's emphasis on males at the expense of female children has its roots in pre-Qin history. Starting from the very pinnacle of ancient Chinese social strata, boys were favored because only men could really hope to become nobles and otherwise occupy prominent positions. The spiritual tradition of worshiping one's ancestors, primarily male, and the custom that daughters were essentially lost to another family clan upon marriage, all made male births preferable. Consequently, girls were more often than not considered more of a burden than a bundle of joy. Especially for the poor, simply having one more child, including males that would divide up ever shrinking inheritances meant that infanticide was distressingly common (Gernet 1962). Depending upon the exigencies, usually (but not always) dire poverty and food privation, boys were neither spared from being killed postpartum, either from drowning (溺殺 *nìshā*), or abandoning (棄殺 *qìshā*) the newly born to the elements. However, other factors, such as birth on an inauspicious day, or merely presenting with an anomalous physical attribute may have resulted in the killing of a newborn. The *Zuozhuan* (左傳 *zuǒzhuàn*), a record of China during the years 722–468 BCE, for example, relates that a daughter was condemned to exposure because of her hairy, red-toned appearance (Kinney 1993). By the Eastern Han, the Taiping Classic (太平經 *tàipíngjīng*), a collection of Daoist texts, laments: "We have lost our way—many denigrating girls, even committing infanticide, placing girls beneath that of boys."[3] In the *Account of Minister Yu Yan* (虞延傳 *yúyán zhuàn*), ca. 70 CE, a mother

[3] "今天下失道以來, 多賤女子, 而反賊殺之, 令使女子少於男."

had no choice but to abandon her newly born girl to a ditch. This was because she was already raising an infant son, and this was the only way to ensure his survival. Although it was nominally forbidden to commit infanticide in ancient China, punishments were not particularly severe. Qin dynastic law (ca. 210 BCE), for example, merely called for "tattooing and grain-pounding [a form of community labor]" for the "unauthorized killing of an infant"[4] (Kinney 1993).

In the twelfth century CE, the general practice in Fujian province was "if a man should have numerous sons, he brings up no more than four and keeps no more than three daughters. He claims that he has not the means for bringing up more." Infanticide, using the euphemism "bathing the infant," was most often practiced by drowning the baby soon as s/he was delivered. This and other means of infanticide were finally made illegal in 1138, and the Song authorities established a child services system that would take care of children who were born to poverty-stricken parents. Nonetheless, and although the establishment of orphanages had been well in place by the Qing Dynasty, in seventeenth century China the practice of infanticide commonly occurred "regardless if they were poor, or whether a child was a girl or boy"[5] (Yang 1995).

Still, because most victims of infanticide in China were females, in addition to limiting family sizes (averaging about 5 to 5.8 during the Han period, for example), this also put a rate-limiting check on future population growth (Kinney 1993). "In other words," according to two modern China scholars, infanticide was "the functional equivalent of family planning" (Lavely and Bin Wong 1998).

Such were the extremes that Chinese society took in favoring sons over daughters. In addition to the increased earning power in agriculture of males over females, spiritual (patriarchal ancestor worship), as well as property inheritance and propagating the family name, Confucianism also called upon males to support their parents in old age. Conversely, giving birth to daughters meant that, inevitably, they would be married off to join other families and were of less value.

A classic anecdote highlights this continued bias throughout Chinese history: In the late nineteenth century, the revolutionary Dr. Sun Yat-sen had a medical practice in Maui, Hawaii, and administered smallpox vaccines to a local Chinese-American family. He charged the boy two dollars, but only one dollar for the young daughter. When she asked him why, he replied, "because you are a girl (Ma Lum and Lum 1999)." This prejudice against girls in older Chinese societies was such that often they were given no unique names. And if they did deign to name them, their monikers often expressed disappointment at not having been born male, such as "too many" (太多 *tàiduō*) or "little mistake" (小錯 *xiǎocuò*). In older China, foreign missionaries observed villagers naming boys a girl's name in order to fool malevolent ghosts who would otherwise take their sons (Watson 1986). A comparison of sex ratios in 1910 (pre-revolution) and modern (2010–2020) China is shown in Table 1.6. Some demographic studies have estimated much larger male/female

[4] "擅殺子黥為城旦舂其子."

[5] "無論貧者溺, 即不貧者亦溺; 無論生女溺, 即生男溺."

ratios in China, especially in recent decades (Poston et al. 2011a). Nonetheless, the numbers in Table 1.6 (below) are based on official Chinese statistics, one from the ROC (Nationalist) era, and later national PRC census figures.

The ratio of males over females in the PRC is decidedly higher than those of other advanced East Asian countries, where, arguably, the societal norms that favor boys over girls are just as prevalent. For example, China, with an overall average ration of 105.07 males to 100 females, is considerably more lopsided than the Republic of Korea (100.84), the Republic of China on Taiwan (where it is the reverse, slightly favoring females 98.76), as well as Japan (95.41) (Knoema.com 2020).

But the numbers only tell part of the story. Table 1.6 (below) only represents an average of male/female ratios across all cohorts. As they age (55 and older), the numbers of females begin to roughly match those of living males, and increasingly become the dominant cohort as they further age. Critically, for females in China who in the key marriage and childbearing years (beginning at the legal marital age of 20 to about 30), and those right on the cusp (upper teens), the ratio is much more imbalanced in favor of males, based on 2020 census data (Table 1.7).

Table 1.6 Male-female population ratios: 1910, and 2010, 2020: selected provincial regions (Mi et al. 1997; CSP 2010; NBS 2021)

China province/region	Males per 100 females (1910)	Males per 100 females (2000)	Males per 100 females (2010)	Males per 100 females (2020)
Zhili 直隸 *zhílì* (modern-day Hebei)	119.8	103.6	102.8	102.0
Jiangsu 江蘇 *jiāngsū*	111.3	100.5	102.5	103.1
Anhui 安徽 *ānhuī*	123.1	106.6	103.4	103.9
Shandong 山東 *shāndōng*	117.3	102.5	102.3	102.7
Shanxi 山西 *shānxī*	135.5	107.2	105.6	104.0
Henan 河南 *hénán*	111.5	106.5	102.0	100.6
Shaanxi 陝西 *shǎnxī*	120.0	107.2	106.9	104.8
Gansu 甘肅 *gānsù*	109.8	107.6	104.4	103.1
Fujian 福建 *fújiàn*	128.9	106.3	106.0	106.9
Zhejiang 浙江 *zhèjiāng*	118.5	105.5	105.7	109.0
Jiangxi 江西 *jiāngxī*	125.6	108.2	106.7	106.6
Hunan 湖南 *húnán*	127.3	109.0	105.8	104.8
Sichuan 四川 *sìchuān*	130.1	105.2	103.1	102.2
Yunnan 雲南 *yúnnán*	114.1	107.0	107.9	107.2
Guizhou 貴州 *guìzhōu*	119.9	108.5	106.3	104.5
Fengtian 奉天 *fèngtiān* (modern-day Liaoning)	117.6	104.0	102.5	99.7
Jilin 吉林 *jílín*	132.0	104.9	102.7	99.7
Heilongjiang 黑龍江 *hēilóngjiāng*	120.8	104.5	102.8	100.3

Table 1.7 Male-female population ratios by age groups, 2020 census data (NBS 2021)

Age group	Male (percentage)	Female (percentage)	Ratio (female = 100)
Total	51.24	48.76	104.8
0–4	2.91	2.62	110.98
5–9	3.41	3.00	113.71
10–14	3.24	2.81	115.03
15–19	**2.77**	**2.39**	**116.12**
20–24	**2.81**	**2.50**	**112.51**
25–29	**3.42**	**3.10**	**110.24**
30–34	4.53	4.28	105.97
35–39	3.61	3.41	105.93
40–44	3.38	3.21	105.10
45–49	4.13	3.97	103.85
50–54	4.33	4.26	101.74
55–59	3.60	3.59	100.46
60–64	2.62	2.59	100.98
66–69	2.58	2.67	96.47
70–74	1.71	1.80	95.03
75–79	1.05	1.17	89.48
80+	1.08	1.46	74.27

Even more striking are statistics from sex ratios at birth (SRB) data. For the years 1982, 1990, 2000, 2010, and 2020, the respective ratios of male births over females in China were 107.63, 111.45, 119.92, 121.21, and 111.30. In addition, Mainland Chinese population researchers found discrepancies after comparing male births from 1980–2000, with an average of 112.91 in favor of males, to the 2020 census numbers which returned a value of only 108.9. As far as they can determine, a significant portion of this difference has simply been the underreporting of female births by couples who, having wished for boys but had girls instead. Constrained by the erstwhile one-child policy, they either hid these births or abandoned their newborn girls via unregistered adoptions. Today (2022), with the recent allowance for three children in the PRC, it is anticipated that this will alleviate such disparities (Li and Jiang 2021).

There still remains, however, the rather tricky societal problem that China will likely continue to struggle with, that is, having too many eligible males for marriage and too few females. Such unmarried men, called "bare branch bachelors" (光棍兒漢 *guānggùn'ér hàn*), face a bleak prospect, having little or no opportunity to start a family of their own. And this "marriage squeeze" is likely to worsen in the near future. According to the US Census Bureau, by 2040 Chinese men aged 30–50 will outnumber women in the 25–45 age group by 30 million (Eberstadt 2021).

Women in Positions of Political Power

While no doubt a consequence of numerous and complex factors, it is nonetheless surprising how few roles in China's political hierarchy are occupied by women. Mao Zedong may have famously said that "women hold up half the sky,"[6] but as of 2021, the highest-ranking deliberative body, the Politburo Standing Committee of the Chinese Communist Party (CCP), had no women in its seven-member ranks. Of the 25 politburo members, one is female. In the PRC State Council (10), one woman Sun Chunlan (孫春蘭 *sūn chūnlán*) serves as vice premier. Of the China's National People's Conference (nearly 3000 members) a quarter of the NPC is made up of women. Overall, of 3827 top ranking cadres in China, less than 6% are women.[7]

From Peasants to Urbanites

Throughout her history, China's population has mostly been rural. Going back to the Han (206 BCE – 220 CE), Chinese peasants are variously estimated to have comprised from 80% to 90% of the overall population, and continued to form the majority by the late twentieth century. In 1979, just after Deng Xiaoping formally instated the "reform and opening up" (改革開放 *gǎigékāifàng*), the Chinese Communist Party reported an estimated 200–250 million (mostly rural) were poverty stricken, a tacit admission that the Maoist economy had been a failure. But with the growth of China's economy, there were significant migrations of rural peasants to China's cities in the 1980s and 1990s. Even so, in 1996, less than 20% of China's population were estimated to live in urban areas. However, China's statist economic policy continued to encourage moving rural populations to the cities, so that by 2011 the Chinese government estimated that, for the first time, more of its people were urbanized (~691 million) than rural (~657 million). As counting and quantifying these and other vital population data became more and more vital, China had by this time conducted modern, decennial censuses, steadily improving upon its first in 1953 (Table 1.8).

---

[6] "婦女能頂半邊天 *fùnǚ néngdǐng bàn biāntiān*." In August 1958, as the Great Leap Forward and communalization was on its way, Zhu Danhua, wife of Mao Zedong's brother, Mao Zemin, cited the experiences of Jiangxi province's Xiushui County (修水縣 *xiūshuǐ xiàn*) in the promotion of women and their valuable role in national production. After she used the idiom during an all-nation's women's conference, Hu Yaobang picked it up, adding that "women not only hold up half the sky in the battlelines of production, but should also be considered half the sky for all social activity. (婦女不僅是生產戰線的邊天，應是整個社會活動的半邊天 *fùnǚ bùjǐn shì shēngchǎn zhànxiàn de biāntiān, yīngshì zhěnggè shèhuìhuódòng de bàn biāntiān*.) The next day, the *People's Daily* carried the story, emphasizing the Xiushui County's achievements in "women holding up half the sky." It was not long after this that Mao Zedong spoke of the saying to the entire country.

[7] Data from table compiled by Lu Fang, social media posting by Victor Shih, 31 August 2021.

Table 1.8 Modern Mainland Chinese Censuses: 1953–2020 (CSP 2010; NBS 2021)[a]

Province/city	Population (1953)	Population (1964)	Population (1982)	Population (1990)	Population (2000)	Population (2010)	Population (2020)
Beijing	2,768,149	7,568,495	9,230,687	10,819,414	13,569,194	19,612,368	21,893,095
Tianjin[b]	2,693,831	N/A	7,764,141	8,785,427	9,848,731	12,938,224	13,866,009
Hebei	35,984,644	45,687,781	53,005,876	61,082,755	66,684,419	71,854,202	74,610,235
Shanxi	14,314,485	18,015,067	25,291,389	28,758,846	32,471,242	35,712,111	34,915,616
Inner Mongolia	6,100,104	12,348,638	19,274,279	21,456,518	23,323,347	24,706,321	24,049,155
Liaoning	18,545,147	26,946,200	35,721,693	39,459,694	41,824,412	43,746,323	42,591,407
Jilin	11,290,073	15,668,663	22,560,053	24,659,790	26,802,191	27,462,297	24,073,453
Heilongjiang	11,897,309	20,118,271	32,665,546	35,215,932	36,237,576	38,312,224	31,850,088
Shanghai	6,204,417	10,816,458	11,859,748	13,341,852	16,407,734	23,019,148	24,870,895
Rehe (Jehol)[c]	5,160,822	N/A	N/A	N/A	N/A	N/A	N/A
Jiangsu	41,252,192	44,504,608	60,521,114	67,056,812	73,043,577	78,659,903	84,748,016
Zhejiang	22,865,747	28,318,573	38,884,603	41,446,015	45,930,651	54,426,891	64,567,588
Anhui	30,343,637	31,241,657	49,665,724	56,181,005	58,999,948	59,500,510	61,027,171
Fujian	13,142,721	16,757,223	25,931,106	30,048,275	34,097,947	36,894,216	41,540,086
Jiangxi	16,772,865	21,068,019	33,184,827	37,710,177	40,397,598	44,567,475	45,188,635
Shandong	48,876,548	55,519,038	74,419,054	84,392,104	89,971,789	95,793,065	101,527,453
Henan	44,214,594	50,325,511	74,422,739	85,534,200	91,236,854	94,023,567	99,365,519
Hubei	27,789,693	33,709,344	47,804,150	53,970,501	59,508,870	57,237,740	57,752,557
Hunan	33,226,954	37,182,286	54,008,851	60,657,992	63,274,173	65,683,722	66,444,864
Guangdong	34,770,059	42,800,849	59,299,220	62,829,741	85,225,007	104,303,132	126,012,510
Guangxi	19,560,822	20,845,017	36,420,960	42,244,884	43,854,538	46,026,629	50,126,804
Hainan[d]	N/A	N/A	N/A	6,556,831	7,559,035	8,671,518	10,081,232
Chongqing[e]	N/A	N/A	N/A	N/A	30,512,763	28,846,170	32,054,159
Sichuan	62,303,999	67,956,490	99,713,310	107,218,310	82,348,296	80,418,200	83,674,866
Guizhou	15,037,310	17,140,521	28,552,997	32,391,051	35,247,695	34,746,468	38,562,148

(continued)

Province/city	Population (1953)	Population (1964)	Population (1982)	Population (1990)	Population (2000)	Population (2010)	Population (2020)
Yunnan	17,472,737	20,509,525	32,553,817	36,972,587	42,360,089	45,966,239	47,209,277
Xizang (Tibet)	N/A	1,251,225	1,892,393	2,196,029	2,616,329	3,002,166	3,648,100
Xizang (Tibet) and Qamdo (Changdu)	1,273,969	N/A	N/A				
Xikang[f]	3,381,064	N/A	N/A	N/A	N/A	N/A	N/A
Overseas Chinese	11,743,320	N/A	N/A	N/A	N/A	N/A	N/A
Paracel Is.	N/A	N/A	N/A	1245	N/A	N/A	N/A
Shaanxi	15,881,281	20,766,915	28,904,423	32,882,286	35,365,072	37,327,378	39,528,999
Gansu	12,928,102	12,630,569	19,569,261	22,371,085	25,124,282	25,575,254	25,019,831
Qinghai	1,676,534	2,145,604	3,895,706	4,456,952	4,822,963	5,626,722	5,923,957
Ningxia[g]	N/A	N/A	3,895,578	4,655,445	5,486,393	6,301,350	7,202,654
Xinjiang	4,873,608	7,270,067	13,081,681	15,156,883	18,459,511	21,813,334	25,852,345
Military forces	N/A	5,469,145[h]	4,238,210	3,199,100	2,498,600	2,300,000	2,000,000
Undetermined place of residency	N/A	N/A	N/A	N/A	N/A	4,649,985	N/A
Total	**601,938,035**	**723,070,269**	**1,031,882,509**	**1,133,709,738**	**1245,110,826**	**1,339,724,852**	**1,411,778,724**

[a]Additional numbers and statistics, including tabulated Excel spreadsheets can be found at China Statistics Press, http://www.stats.gov.cn/tjsj/pcsj/rkpc/6rp/indexce.htm. In addition, localized census data reporting, while incomplete in some areas, can also be found at this excellent site/aggregator and database: Honghei Statistical Public Reporting Database: https://tjgb.hongheiku.com/. For extensive spreadsheets on Taiwan census data (in Chinese), to include breakdowns of officially recognized indigenous peoples, see Republic of China (Taiwan) Ministry of the Interior, https://ws.moi.gov.tw

[b]Counted as part of Hebei province in the 1964 census

[c]Dissolved in 1955, shared among Hebei, Liaoning, Tianjin, and Nei Mengu (Inner Mongolia)

[d]Made a province officially in 1988; prior to that, Hainan Island was part of Guangdong province

[e]Previously subordinate to Sichuan province, made a provincial-level city in 1997

[f]Later merged into Sichuan and then Tibet, 1955, 1965, resp

[g]Established in 1958

[h]Extrapolated by subtracting provincial totals from overall total

The PRC conducted its first official (if not fully complete) census in 1953, with direct contact enumeration of 574,205,940, and, using indirect counting, adding another 27,732,095, for a total of 601,938,035. (Subtracting Taiwan gives us a total of 594,346,737). Reportedly, Chinese census officials then found it difficult if not impossible to survey more remote areas such as Tibet and Qamdo (Changdu 昌都 *chāngdū*). In other respects, as China's first two census efforts were imbued with Maoist, mass movement energy, helping to expedite the gathering of demographic data across the rest of the country. The second census recorded a total of 720,370,269 for China in 1964, including Taiwan, and 694,581,759 (not including Taiwan, Hong Kong, Macao, and overseas Chinese).

No doubt due to the chaos of the Cultural Revolution (1966–1976), it would be 18 more years before a nation-wide census was conducted in 1982. This time, unlike the previous two efforts in 1953 and 1964, and because China had begun its "reform and opening up" phase (1978), the CCP looked to conduct a more vigorous census, adopting international standards and assistance from foreign countries. With the Deng Xiaoping leadership now demanding better numbers, making an accurate count was considered especially important for economic policy planning.

As it happens, China's most recent decennial 2020 census shows a continued slowing of its population growth (see Table 1.7). From 1990 (1,133,682,501)[8] to 2000 (1245,110,826), there was an increase of 9.83%. It increased 7.60% from 2000 to 2010 (1,339,724,852), and finally slowed to a 5.4% increase in 2020 (1,411,778,724). Foretelling an ever-aging demographic, it was this slowing down of population growth that moved the Chinese authorities to revise the limit of two children to three (see also above).

China's Household Registration System (*Hukou*)

For more than half a century, the *hukou* (household registration) system in China has segregated the rural and urban populations, initially in geographical terms, but more fundamentally in social, economic, and political terms. It is the foundation of China's divisive dualistic socioeconomic structure and the country's two classes of citizenship. Under this system, some 700–800 million people are in effect treated as second-class citizens, deprived of the opportunity to settle legally in cities and of access to most of the basic welfare and state-provided services enjoyed by regular urban residents. To an individual, *hukou* status is an important ascribed attribute in determining one's social and economic circumstances. The existence of such an overt discriminatory state institution is starkly incompatible with a rapidly modernizing China, aspiring to great power status—Kam Wing Chan (Chan 2010).

[8] Official final tally, slightly different from accumulated populations in table (1990), a difference of 27,237 people.

Population Data: Permanent *Hukou* (Household Registered) Residents

Unlike the typical census conducted on a decennial basis, permanent registered populations *huji renkou* (戶籍人口 *hùjí rénkǒu*) or shortened to simply *hukou* (戶口 *hùkǒu*) in the PRC are tallied up in the China's household registry system, which became fully in force by 1958. The permanent registry records family members, births, deaths, marriages, divorces, etc., establishing for every individual a particular place of origin. It is worth noting that the overall population totals in the permanent registered household data are lower than those in the nation-wide census, e.g., 1,404,420,000 versus the 2020 census result of 1,411,778,724, a difference of nearly 7,360,000. One can speculate that this is due to a number of factors, including the rounding of numbers in published *hukou* data. And, significantly, population statistics listed in the tables following each provincial entry are compiled by the China's Ministry of Public Security (公安部 *gōng'ānbù*) from about 2 years prior. Thus there a lag in reporting of updated registered *hukou* data when compared to decennial census figures.

The Household Registry (*Hukou*) System: Background

Although it has roots going back to ancient China, modern China's household registry marks its informal beginnings on 12 August 1950, when the Chinese Communist Party's public security apparatus internally published a draft "Special Provisional Measures on Population Management." In 1952, on the heels of the standoff between China and the west during the Korean War, there was a brief interlude of economic recovery, where grain production increased nearly 45% over 3 years prior. But this would not be nearly enough. It was believed that the only way to accumulate enough foodstuffs to support industrialization was to change the nature of private agricultural economy (Zhao 2004). A devoted adherent of Stalin, Mao Zedong was keen to follow the Soviet model of exploiting the peasantry to fuel a modern, socialist industrial state. Thus, the course was set for the collectivization of agriculture. Ten years later, this would lead to further impoverishment (if that were even possible) of the average Chinese citizen, especially peasants in the countryside, bringing painful starvation and death for tens of millions in the Great Leap Forward (1958 – 1962).

In September 1953, Liang Shuming (梁漱溟 *liáng shùmíng*), an intellectual who had conducted extensive field work in the modernization and improvement of rural communities during the prior Nationalist era, had a spirited conversation with Mao Zedong. Liang Shuming pointed out that, dependent as the CCP was on farmers in the remote villages, as lives improved in the cities jobs would become more and more desirable in the urban sector. City dwellers would live in relative comfort, peasants would find themselves in a life of the hardscrabble earth—a so-called "heaven-hell" schism. What, then, was to stop the countryside from emptying out and moving into the major cities? Mao Zedong bristled at such "thoroughly reactionary thinking" that "shattered the unified base of workers and peasants." Despite Mao's seeming reluctance to divide the labor force in such a way, by 1954 China had essentially carried this policy out by categorizing people based on their urban or rural status. On 31 July 1955, at Central Committee meeting that gathered provincial, municipal, and autonomous region representatives, Mao Zedong underscored that, unless the "problem of the cooperative transformation of agriculture" is resolved, there will be no solution to the long-term issue of supplying necessary food and raw materials. Critically, "our socialist industrialization undertaking will be met with immense difficulties, and we will have no way to complete it." Furthermore, in his famous "On Ten Major Relationships (論十大關係 *lùnshídà guānxì*)" of April 1956, Mao Zedong laid it on the line: "Heavy industry is the focus of our national construction…. But if there isn't enough food and other daily necessities, there won't even be a way to feed the workers, never mind developing heavy industry (Zhao 2004)."

Cementing a new policy of keeping the peasants on the farms and out of the cities, on 18 December 1957 the CCP central government issued, rather matter-of-factly, its "Directive on the prevention of unbridled [lit. blind] rural population outflows." One of its key passages reads:

> Our national socialist construction policy is based upon prioritizing first and foremost the development of heavy industry, developing this in tandem with agriculture, the latter occupying a key role in our national socialist construction. Mass outflows of the farming population not only diminishes the agricultural workforce, putting an obstacle in the path of consolidating the development of agricultural production and farming cooperatives, but will also make for an increase in the unemployed population, creating no end to troubles in every aspect of work in the cities. (Zhao 2004)

But Chinese peasants were nonetheless soon flooding into the cities, not just looking for better jobs but in desperate search of food. Mao Zedong's rabid approach to collectivizing agriculture led to crop failures and famine in the countryside. And although the household registry system prior to 1958 allowed for a certain freedom of movement, on 9 January of that year the central government issued the strict PRC Household Registration Ordinance.[9] Under this enforced system, China's citizens categorized *de jure* as either "Agricultural household individual (農業戶口 *nóngyè hùkǒu*)" or "Non-agricultural household individual (非農業戶口 *fēinóngyè hùkǒu*[10])," these classifications stamped in large, red characters in the upper left of their *hukou* registry card. Fatefully, the ability of peasants to move anywhere else was now strictly prohibited. For as the Great Leap Forward (GLF) was now well underway, the fates of millions were now sealed. As Yang Jisheng explains,

> All agricultural products, including foodstuffs, cotton, and cooking oil, were procured for marketing by the state, and all goods needed for daily life were supplied to urban and rural

[9] 中華人民共和國戶口登記條例 *zhōnghuárénmín gònghéguó hùkǒu dēngjì tiáolì.*

[10] In the registry card format, the "household type" line below the stamp was formally (in smaller, bold black font) "Non] Agricultural family household individual" ([非]農業家庭戶口 [*fēi*] *nóng yè jiā tíng hù kǒu.*)

> residents through a system of state-issued ration coupons. These coupons could be exchanged for goods only in the locality where one was registered under the household registration system (*hukou*). Likewise, under the *hukou* system, peasants were allowed to engage only in agricultural labor, and could leave their villages only with permission from production team heads. The labor and lives of peasants were thus tightly restricted within the confines of political authority. If an error in policy prevented the collective from supplying daily necessities, peasants had no other recourse. (Yang 2008)

Trapped in a collective with its own communal canteen, when the food stopped the peasants had nowhere else to turn. At least 37 million people starved to death during the years 1958–1962.

By 1978, there was a partial relaxation of the strict rules regarding migration. Despite initial reforms, Chinese citizens are still separated under urban and rural distinctions, not to mention other identities to include their ethnic nationality (Han versus Kazakh, etc.,) education status, etc., filled out in the *hukou* registration. Each is record kept "Under the supervision of the Ministry of Public Security of P.R.C. [sic],"[11] with a copy held in the local public security office. With the assumption of Xi Jinping to power over the CCP and China, reforming and improving the hukou registration system was made a key note area of emphasis in January 2013.

When comparing figures from the decennial census, one finds major disparities between the "typical" residential populations (常住人口 *chángzhù rénkǒu*) and those found in the permanent registered (戶籍人口 *hùjí rénkǒu*) data. In those places where there is real or perceived opportunity for advancement, career opportunities, and better standards of life (e.g., Beijing, Shanghai), their census populations at any given time are likely to be greater than their permanent registered residents. Poorer, less developed provinces (e.g., Anhui), will generally have a higher number of permanent registered population than their typical resident census population. For example, Shanghai, based on the 2020 census, recorded a residential population (常住人口 *chángzhù rénkǒu*) of 24,870,895. In contrast, the permanent, registered (戶籍人口 *hùjí rénkǒu*) data from the same year for Shanghai was 14,620,000. Conversely, Guizhou province had a typical residential population as defined under the 2020 census of 38,562,148, but a permanent hukou registry of 45,290,000 (see Table 1.9 for a provincial listing). Each demonstrates the nature of China's "floating populations (流動人口 *liúdòng rénkǒu*)," reflecting the mass movements of peoples from poorer, less developed regions, to find a better economic future (not to mention more generous social services).

---

[11] 中華人民共和國公安部制 *zhōnghuárénmíngònghéguó gōngānbù zhì.*

Table 1.9 Permanent registered (Hukou) populations, mainland China, compiled from 2012, 2016 and 2020 (MCA 2020)

City/province	2012	2016	2020
Beijing	12,620,000	13,000,000	13,740,000
Tianjin	9,900,000	9,960,000	10,820,000
Hebei	72,980,000	75,200,000	77,310,000
Shanxi	34,740,000	35,010,000	35,340,000
Inner Mongolia	24,530,000	24,600,000	24,410,000
Liaoning	42,520,000	42,450,000	41,920,000
Jilin	27,240,000	27,020,000	26,090,000
Heilongjiang	38,430,000	38,110,000	35,740,000
Shanghai	14,120,000	14,400,000	14,620,000
Jiangsu	74,670,000	76,490,000	78,320,000
Zhejiang	47,480,000	47,980,000	50,000,000
Anhui	68,250,000	69,050,000	70,830,000
Fujian	35,300,000	35,790,000	38,610,000
Jiangxi	46,940,000	48,040,000	50,260,000
Shandong	95,360,000	95,800,000	100,960,000
Henan	108,000,000	109,320,000	114,440,000
Hubei	61,490,000	61,650,000	61,730,000
Hunan	70,690,000	71,320,000	73,270,000
Guangdong	85,220,000	86,360,000	95,020,000
Guangxi	53,310,000	53,780,000	56,590,000
Hainan	8,960,000	9,020,000	9,250,000
Chongqing	33,030,000	33,430,000	34,040,000
Sichuan	90,010,000	90,970,000	91,210,000
Guizhou	41,890,000	41,340,000	45,290,000
Yunnan	45,280,000	45,760,000	47,690,000
Xizang	2,940,000	3,100,000	3,320,000
Shaanxi	38,740,000	39,260,000	40,230,000
Gansu	27,120,000	27,130,000	27,830,000
Qinghai	5,500,000	5,660,000	5,870,000
Ningxia	6,430,000	6,590,000	6,840,000
Xinjiang	21,640,000	22,260,000	22,830,000
Total	**1,345,330,000**	**1,359,850,000**	**1,404,420,000**

Chinese Populations from Ancient Times Until Today

Table 1.10 (below) provides best estimates of Chinese populations going back to about 2100 BCE. For post-1949 data, populations do not include Taiwan, and, wherever it was possible to parse out, numbers from Taiwan-administered off shore islands (Jinmen and Matsu) were subtracted.

Table 1.10 Chinese populations from 2100 BCE through 2015 (Yang 1995; Ho 1959; Yuan 2007; Yuan and Peimin 2007a, b; NBS 2021)

Xia Dynasty 夏代 *xiàdài* (2100–1600 BCE)	Population
2100 BCE	13,553,923
Shang Dynasty 商代 *shāngdài* (1600–1050 BCE)	
1105–1057 BCE	13,714,923
Zhou Dynasty 周代 *zhōudài* (1046–256 BCE)	
684 BCE	11,841,923
Qin Dynasty 秦代 *qíndài* (221–206 BCE)	
221 BCE	25,000,000–40,000,000
Han Dynasty 漢代 *hàndài* (206 BCE – 220 CE)	
Western/Former Han 西漢/前漢 *xīhàn/qiánhàn* (206 BCE – 9 CE)	
129 BCE	36,000,000
91 BCE	32,000,000
67 BCE	40,000,000
2 CE	57,551,206–59,594,978
Eastern Han/Later Han 東漢/後漢 *dōnghàn/hòuhàn* (25–220 CE)	
25	28,000,000
30	22,539,292
57	21,007,820
75	34,125,021–36,305,694
88	43,356,367
105	53,256,229
125	48,690,789–49,690,789
136	53,869,588
139	53,869,588–60,747,009
140	48,000,000–49,150,220
144	49,730,550
145	49,524,183
146	47,566,772
156	50,066,856–56,486,586
157	56,486,856
184	55,000,000
217	15,000,000
Six Dynasties Period 六朝 *liùcháo* (220–589 CE)	
Three Kingdoms 三國時代 *sānguó shídài* (220–265 CE)	
220	23,000,000
221	900,000
240	2,400,000
263	4,432,881
Jin Dynasty 晉朝 *jìncháo* (265–420)	
280	16,163,863–24,000,000
282	22,620,000
318	12,400,000
345	30,000,000

(continued)

Table 1.10 (continued)

Xia Dynasty 夏代 *xiàdài* (2100–1600 BCE)	Population
370	9,987,935
Northern and Southern Dynasties 南北朝 *nánběicháo* (386–589)	
464	4,685,501–5,174,074
520	25,000,000–30,000,000
534	22,300,000
564	20,006,886–22,000,000
577	20,006,880
580	9,009,604
Sui Dynasty 隋代 *suídài* (581–618)	
581	22,272,768
606	46,019,956
609	46,019,956–50,320,000
Tang Dynasty 唐代 *tángdài* (618–906)	
624	15,373,921
639	12,350,000
652	20,900,000
680	11,841,923
705	37,140,000
726	41,419,712
732	45,431,265
733	43,200,000
734	46,285,161
739	48,143,609
740	48,142,609
742	48,089,800
754	52,880,488
755	52,919,309
760	16,990,386
764	34,000,000
780	40,000,000–53,500,000
807	45,000,000
820	47,280,000
839	50,000,000
845	51,000,000
887	43,000,000
Song Dynasty 宋代 *sòngdài* (960–1270)	
Northern Song 北宋 *běisòng* (960–1127)	
976	32,500,000
997	39,944,498
1006	42,400,000
1034	58,800,000
1041	59,858,326
1053	61,672,600

(continued)

Table 1.10 (continued)

Xia Dynasty 夏代 *xiàdài* (2100–1600 BCE)	Population
1066	77,500,000
1083	86,100,000
1094	85,132,486
1097	106,700,000
1102	90,648,308
1106	106,800,000
1110	93,469,568
1122	112,764,193
1109	100,000,000
1122	93,470,000
1126	100,000,000
Southern Song 南宋 *nánsòng* (1127–1279)	
1141	32,800,000
1161	36,250,000
1162	49,862,930–56,500,000
1175	55,268,020
1187	44,705,086
1187	44,705,086
1190	45,447,900
1195	48,490,400
1200	110,000,000
1207	53,532,151
1218	81,600,000
1223	76,810,000
1264	35,600,000
1279	55,276,000
Yuan Dynasty 元代 *yuándài* (1279–1368)	
1281	58,830,000
1290	58,834,711–61,601,225
1291	59,848,964–60,491,230
1294	53,654,337
1330	59,510,000–67,445,338
Ming Dynasty 大明/明朝 *dàmíng/míngcháo* (1368–1644)	
1381	59,873,305
1393	60,545,812
1403	66,598,337
1404	50,950,470
1412	65,377,633
1457	54,338,476
1464	60,499,330
1479	71,850,132
1500	155,000,000
1566	165,300,000

(continued)

Table 1.10 (continued)

Xia Dynasty 夏代 *xiàdài* (2100–1600 BCE)	Population
1573	150,000,000
Qing Dynasty 大清/清朝 *dàqīng*/*qīngcháo* (1644–1912)	
1652	144,838,580
1661	191,376,520
1721	150,362,838
1731	167,049,469
1741	143,410,559
1742	159,801,551
1743	164,454,616
1744	166,808,604
1745	169,922,127
1746	171,896,773
1747	171,896,773
1748	177,495,039
1749	177,495,039
1750	179,538,540
1751	181,811,359
1752	182,857,277
1753	183,678,259
1754	184,504,493
1755	185,612,881
1756	186,615,514
1757	190,348,328
1758	191,672,808
1759	194,791,859
1760	196,837,977
1761	198,214,555–228,153,439
1762	200,472,461
1763	204,209,828
1764	205,591,017
1765	206,693,224
1766	208,095,796
1767	209,839,546
1768	210,837,502
1769	212,023,042
1770	213,613,163
1771	214,600,356
1772	216,467,258
1773	218,743,315
1774	221,027,224
1775	264,561,355
1776	268,238,181
1777	270,863,760

(continued)

Table 1.10 (continued)

Xia Dynasty 夏代 *xiàdài* (2100–1600 BCE)	Population
1778	242,695,618
1779	275,042,916
1780	277,554,413
1781	279,816,070
1782	281,822,675
1783	284,733,785
1784	286,331,307
1785	288,863,974
1786	291,102,486
1787	292,429,018
1788	294,852,189
1789	297,717,496
1790	301,487,114
1791	304,354,160
1792	307,467,279
1793	310,497,210
1794	313,281,795
1795	296,968,968
1796	275,662,044
1797	271,333,544
1798	290,982,980
1799	293,283,179
1800	295,273,311–340,000,000
1801	297,501,548–335,211,520
1802	299,749,770
1803	302,250,673
1804	304,461,284
1805	332,181,403
1806	335,309,469
1807	338,062,439
1808	350,291,724
1809	352,900,024
1810	345,717,214
1811	358,610,039
1812	361,691,431–362,447,183
1813	336,451,672
1814	316,574,895
1815	326,574,895
1816	328,814,957
1817	331,330,433
1818	348,820,037
1819	351,260,545
1820	353,377,694

(continued)

Table 1.10 (continued)

Xia Dynasty 夏代 *xiàdài* (2100–1600 BCE)	Population
1821	355,540,258
1822	372,457,539
1823	375,153,122
1824	374,601,132
1825	379,885,340
1826	380,287,007
1827	383,696,095
1828	386,531,513
1829	390,500,650
1830	394,784,681
1831	395,821,092
1832	397,132,659
1833	398,942,036
1834	401,008,574
1835	403,052,086
1836	404,901,448
1837	406,984,114
1838	409,038,799
1839	410,850,639
1840	412,814,828
1841	413,457,311
1842	416,118,189
1843	417,239,097
1844	419,441,336
1845	421,342,730
1846	423,121,129
1847	425,106,201
1848	426,928,854
1849	428,420,667
1850	429,931,034
1851	432,164,047
1887	377,636,000
1901	450,000,000
1910	435,000,000
Republic of China (ROC) 中華民國 *zhōnghuá mínguó* (1912–1949)[a]	
1912	341,423,867–377,673,423
1919	452,600,000
1923	438,373,680–444,968,000
1926	485,500,000
1928	441,849,148
1933	444,486,537
1936	479,084,651
1939	517,568,000

(continued)

Table 1.10 (continued)

Xia Dynasty 夏代 *xiàdài* (2100–1600 BCE)	Population
1944	454,666,000
1946	455,592,000
1947	454,880,279
1949	540,000,000
People's Republic of China 中華人民共和國 *zhōnghuá rénmín gònghéguó*	
1953	594,346,737
1964	694,581,759
1978	962,590,000
1982	1,008,175,289
1990	1,133,682,501 (Does not include Taiwan, Hong Kong and Macao.)
2000	1,265,830,000 (Does not include Taiwan, Hong Kong and Macao.)
2010	1,339,724,852 (Does not include Taiwan, Hong Kong and Macao.)
2020	1,411,778,724 (Does not include Taiwan, Hong Kong and Macao.)

[a]Officially, the Republic of China (ROC) on Taiwan remains to this day

China's Ethnic Nationalities 4.2

During the first two decades of the Republic of China (ROC) following the 1911 revolution, China flew a national five-color flag that promoted the concept of "Five Races under One Union" (五族共和 *wǔzú gònghé*). With simple, horizontal stripes, from top to bottom each color represented each of the major ethnic groups: the Han (red), Manchu (yellow), Mongolian (blue), Hui (white), and Tibetan (black). Following the communist takeover in 1949, the PRC has since employed a red flag with one large yellow star, accompanied by four smaller ones, leading to the popular idea that this continues the tradition of displaying China's five major ethnic minorities (Poston et al. 2011b). However, the meaning of the new Chinese flag is actually in keeping with staid, Marxist ideology: while the background of red represents (naturally) the communist revolution, the large star symbolizes CCP leadership, with the four smaller stars representing the working, peasantry, petit-bourgeoisie and national bourgeoisie classes (Tsang 1968).

In 2020, according to the PRC's national census, there were 56 (including Han Chinese) ethnic groups identified in mainland China. Data on Chinese ethnic minority populations during selected years are below, based on official PRC government statistics (Table 1.11).

Table 1.11 Mainland Chinese official Ethnic Groups (NBS 2021)

Chinese	English/initialism	2000	2010	2020
漢族 *hàn zú*	Han/HA	1,137,386,112	1,220,844,520	1,284,446,389
蒙古族 *měnggǔ zú*	Mongol/MG	5,813,947	5,981,840	6,290,204
回族 *huí zú*	Hui/HU	9,816,805	10,586,087	11,377,914
藏族 *zàng zú*	Tibetan/ZA	5,416,021	6,282,187	7,060,731
維吾爾族 *wéiwúěr zú*	Uyghur/UG	8,399,393	10,069,346	11,774,538
苗族 *miáo zú*	Miao/MH	8,940,116	9,426,007	11,067,929
彝族 *yí zú*	Yi/YI	7,762,272	8,714,393	9,830,327
壯族 *zhuàng zú*	Zhuang/ZH	16,178,811	16,926,381	19,568,546
布依族 *bùyī zú*	Bouyei/BY	2,971,460	2,870,034	3,576,752
朝鮮族 *cháoxiǎn zú*	Chosen/CS	1,923,842	1,830,929	1,702,479
滿族 *mǎn zú*	Man/MA	10,682,262	10,387,958	10,423,303
侗族 *dòng zú*	Dong/DO	2,960,293	2,879,974	3,495,993
瑶族 *yáo zú*	Yao/YA	2,637,421	2,796,003	3,309,341
白族 *bái zú*	Bai/BA	1,858,063	1,933,510	2,091,543
土家族 *tǔjiā zú*	Tujia/TJ	8,028,133	8,353,912	9,587,732
哈尼族 *hāní zú*	Hani/HN	1,439,673	1,660,932	1,733,166
哈薩克族 *hāsàkè zú*	Kazakh/KZ	1,250,458	1,462,588	1,562,518
傣族 *dǎi zú*	Dai/DA	1,158,989	1,261,311	1,329,985
黎族 *lí zú*	Li/LI	1,247,814	1,463,064	1,602,104
傈僳族 *lìsù zú*	Lisu/LS	634,912	702,839	762,996
佤族 *wǎ zú*	Va/VA	396,610	429,709	430,977
畲族 *shē zú*	She/SH	709,592	708,651	746,385
拉祜族 *lāhù zú*	Lahu/LH	453,705	485,966	499,167
水族 *shuǐ zú*	Sui/SU	406,902	411,847	495,928
東鄉族 *dōngxiāng zú*	Dongxiang/DX	513,805	621,500	774,947
納西族 *nàxī zú*	Naxi (Nakhi)/NX	308,839	326,295	323,767
景頗族 *jǐngpō zú*	Jingpo/JP	132,143	147,828	160,471
柯爾克孜族 *kēěrkèzī zú*	Kyrgyz/KG	160,823	186,708	204,402
土族蒙古爾 *tǔ zú ménggǔ'ěr*	Tu/TU	241,198	289,565	281,928
達斡爾族 *dáwòěr zú*	Daur/DU	132,394	131,992	132,299
仫佬族 *mùlǎo zú*	Mulao/ML	207,352	216,257	277,233
羌族 *qiāng zú*	Qiang/QI	306,072	309,576	312,981
布朗族 *bùlǎng zú*	Blang/BL	91,882	119,639	127,345
撒拉族 *sǎlá zú*	Salar/SL	104,503	130,607	165,159
毛南族 *màonán zú*	Maonan/MN	107,166	101,192	124,092
仡佬族 *gēlǎo zú*	Gelao/GL	579,357	550,746	677,521
錫伯族 *xíbó zú*	Xibe/XB	188,824	190,481	191,911
阿昌族 *āchāng zú*	Achang/AC	33,936	39,555	43,775
普米族 *pǔmǐ zú*	Pumi/PM	33,600	42,861	45,012
塔吉克族 *tǎjíkè zú*	Tajik/TA	41,028	51,069	50,896

(continued)

Table 1.11 (continued)

Chinese	English/initialism	2000	2010	2020
怒族 *nù zú*	Nu/NU	28,759	37,523	36,575
烏茲別克族 *wūzībiékè zú*	Uzbek/UZ	12,370	10,569	12,742
俄羅斯族 *éluōsī zú*	Russ/RS	15,609	15,393	16,136
鄂溫克族 *èwēnkè zú*	Ewenki/EW	30,505	30,875	34,617
德昂族 *déáng zú*	Deang/DE	17,935	20,556	22,354
保安族 *bǎo'ān zú*	Bonan/BO	16,505	20,074	24,434
裕固族 *yùgù zú*	Yugur (Yughur)/YG	13,719	14,378	14,706
京族 *jīng zú*	Gin/GI	22,517	28,199	33,112
塔塔爾族 *tǎtǎěr zú*	Tatar/TT	4890	3556	3544
獨龍族 *dúlóng zú*	Derung/DR	7426	6930	7310
鄂倫春族 *èlúnchūn zú*	Oroqen/OR	8196	8659	9168
赫哲族 *hèzhé zú*	Hezhen/HZ	4640	5354	5373
門巴族 *ménbā zú*	Monba/MB	8923	10,561	11,143
珞巴族 *luòbā zú*	Lhoba/LB	2965	3682	4237
基諾族 *jīnuò zú*	Jino/JN	20,899	23,143	26,025
高山族 *gāoshān zú*	Gaoshan/GS	4461	4009	3479

China's Muslim Populations 4.6

Going back to China's first major trading relationships with the outside world in the 600s and 700s CE, their entrée being key trading ports along the southeast coast (to include Fujian and Guangdong provinces), Muslims have played an important role in Chinese history and politics ever since. Integration into Chinese society continued during the Mongolian (Yuan) dynastic regime, during which time there was also great increase in the number of Muslims in China, but they only began to enjoy fuller acceptance by Ming officialdom in ca. 1400 (Poston et al. 2011b). Largely because of the geographical location of the Silk Road and its major oases that supported overland logistics with Europe, the majority of Chinese Muslims have traditionally occupied China's northwest territories. For example, using the land route from Afghanistan in his mission to find "Cathay" (which turned out to be China, but this had yet to be fully determined), the intrepid Portuguese traveler Bento de Góis (d. 1607) spent much of his explorative journey in what is now Xinjiang province. At that time (1603), however, it was not in Ming-controlled China he was travelling but various Islamic fiefdoms (Cronin 1984). This state of affairs continued until China, under the Manchu Qing, finally was able to take control of the "new frontier" province in 1759 (Poston et al. 2011b).

In broad strokes, China's Muslims of today can be categorized in two major groups, comprising some 90 percent of all Muslims living in mainland China today: the Turkic (e.g., Uyghur), mostly populating the aforementioned northwest provinces of China; and the Hui (ethnically related to the Chinese), with sizeable portion also inhabiting China's northwest (about 47 percent), as well as across the remaining mainland Chinese provinces (Ma 2014). Confusingly, especially as it was for Western missionaries such as Matteo Ricci, S.J. (d. 1610), the older Chinese term "Hui-Hui" (回回 *huíhuí*) could also refer to other monotheistic religions in China, namely the very small population of Jews and Nestorian Christians (Laven 2011).

The Hui (回 *huí*)

With their origins going back to the apex of the Tangut Empire in the thirteenth century, many Hui are represented in the eponymously-named Ningxia Hui Autonomous Region (寧夏回族自治區 *níngxià huízú zìzhìqū*). While many trace their roots from Central Asia during the 1200s, the Hui also hail from the first "Mohammedans" from the Middle East (e.g., Persia) who arrived in China for trade in ca. eighth century. They also include the Hui mercantilists who lived in modern-day Xi'an City, which continues to have a thriving Muslim Quarter and hosts the Grand Mosque (西安大清真寺 *xī'ān dàqīngzhēnsì* first built in 742).

Ethnically and linguistically, the Hui in China are largely indistinguishable from Han Chinese, unlike the Turkic Uyghur Muslims whose physical appearance and language are immediately apparent. While this may have helped the Hui to enjoy more tolerable treatment from the CCP, recently the Chinese authorities in the last few years (2018–2022) have been taking repressive measures against the Hui as well, padlocking mosques, stripping away traditional Islamic symbols (e.g., calligraphy) and restricting activities such as the traditional call to prayer (Myers 2019). Much of these recent anti-Muslim measures can be traced to CCP Chairman and President Xi Jinping's directive in 2015 to "Sinicize Islam in our country," laid out in more detailed form with China's (official state) Islamic Association of China having issued the "2018–2022 Five-Year Planning Outline for Upholding Our Nation's Path for Islam's Sinicization.[12]" (IAC 2019).

Turkic and Other Muslim Ethnic Nationalities

Numbering roughly the same in total number as the Hui, the Uyghur ethnic group forms the other major share of Muslims living in China, and nearly all live in the Xinjiang Uyghur Autonomous Region (新疆維吾爾自治區 *xīnjiāng wéiwúěr zìzhìqū*). The persecution and repression of the Uyghur Muslims in China has been of great concern by the world community of nations since the early 2000s (and is also addressed in the chapter on Xinjiang). The Uyghurs are of Turkic (Altay Mountain) origin, with their literary form written in Arabic. Some 99.8% (2010 data) of all Uyghurs live in Xinjiang province and are mostly engaged in agriculture

[12] "堅持我國伊斯蘭教中國化方向 五年工作規劃綱要 (2018–2022)."

(Ma 2014). Listed in decreasing numbers and in terms of total percentage of Muslim minorities in China are the remaining eight officially recognized ethnic groups in China:

- **Kazakh** (哈薩克族 *hāsàkè zú*): The third largest Muslim group in China, Kazakhs originated from the Wusun (烏孫 *wūsūn*) people, a nomadic tribe that followed Genghis Khan in his western expeditions (thirteenth century) towards Russia, but then later returned to China. The Kazakhs (哈薩克族 *hāsàkè zú*) numbered over 1.5 million as of 2020.
- **Dongxiang** (東鄉族 *dōngxiāng zú*): Ethnically Mongolian, the Dongxiang refer to themselves as Sarta (撒爾塔 sā'ěrtǎ), and with a population of about 775 thousand form the fourth largest Muslim group in China.
- **Kirgiz** (Kyrgyz; 柯爾克孜族 *kē'ěrkèzī zú*): numbering over 204,000 (2020). As their name would indicate, the Kyrgyz ethnic group originated from modern-day Kyrgyzstan, parts of which were once then ruled by the Tang (Poston et al. 2011b).
- The **Salar** (撒拉族 *sǎlá zú*), with more than 165,000, are believed to have originated from Central Asia in ca. thirteenth century, and now mostly inhabit Qinghai province, with the remainder populating Xinjiang and Gansu.
- The **Tajiki** (塔吉克族 *tǎjíkè zú*) ancestors were of the Pamir, Eastern Iran, and numbering over 50,000 individuals they are the only recognized Muslim group in China that are classified as Shi'ite (as opposed to the vast majority who are Sunni), in this case, Ismaili Shi'a (Poston et al. 2011b).
- Of Mongolian heritage, the **Bonan** (保安族 *bǎo'ān zú*) numbered about 24,000 in 2020, and mostly inhabit Gansu province.
- **Uzbek** (Ozbek 烏茲別克族 *wūzībiékè zú*): Originating from Uzbekistan[13] and currently (2020) with just under 13,000 individuals, the Ozbeks mostly live in western Xinjiang. The Ozbeks first arrived in ca. fourteenth century (Yuan Dynasty) to conduct trade with the Chinese.
- **Tatar** (塔塔爾族 *tǎtǎ'ěr zú*) with just over 3500 in 2020, the Tatar nomadic tribe has origins going back to the Tang Dynasty (ca. seventh century CE). Although the smallest in terms of their numbers as an ethnic group, they are overrepresented in positions of government leadership and professional classes. As a consequence, they are economically much better off than the average Muslim living in China (Poston et al. 2011b).

Because the Chinese government does not officially provide statistics regarding numbers of Chinese citizens who actually practice Islam, we must rely upon informed estimates, and then extrapolating these from the large percentage of nationalities listed in China (below) who are known to be Muslim. Poston et al. estimated about 23 million Muslims lived in China in 2008 (Poston et al. 2011b), approximately the same number as of 2010 (Ma 2014). According to more recent estimates, however, in 2022 there may be as many as 28 million Muslims in China (WPR 2022).

---

[13] Referred to by locals as Özbekistan.

The Zhuang: Fastest Growing Ethnic Minority Population

Of China's large ethnic groups, the Zhuang minority experienced among the most rapid increase in population from 2010–2020. In an effort to explain (at least in part) the increase of 15.6% in population for the Zhuang nationality from 2010–2020, Chinese governmental media (May 2021) claimed this was the result of positive "all-around development" of the country having benefited ethnic minority groups (Cui 2021).

Religious Affiliations: Mainland China

Although the mainland Chinese government has, especially within recent years, become more and more uncomfortable addressing the issue of religion of all kinds across China, there are reliable data collected by the prestigious Peking University. According to research in 2011 by its Institute of Social Science Survey (sic), the religious affiliations of China's population were apportioned as Table 1.12 below.

Provincial Shorthand Characters

Finally, especially when approaching the study of mainland Chinese provinces and major cities, it is very helpful to memorize or at least become familiar with the one-character initialisms used in China when referring to provinces and major cities, especially when using Chinese language atlases (Table 1.13).

Table 1.12 Chinese religious affiliations survey, 2011; Mainland China (RMZX 2022)

Religion	Adherents	Percentage
No religion	700,680,000	52.2
Popular/Folklore	294,320,000	21.9
Buddhist	244,130,000	18.2
Christian	68,410,000	5.1
Islam	24,690,000	1.8%
Other[a]	9,080,000	0.7
Hindu	20,000	<0.1
Judaism	<10,000	<0.1

[a]Includes Daoists, and other religions, including those practiced among foreign registered residents in China: Baha'i, Jainism (耆那教 qínàjiào), Sikh, Shinto, etc.

Table 1.13 Chinese provinces and shorthand descriptors

Province/city	Shorthand character	Simplified	Pinyin
Beijing	京	京	*Jīng*
Tianjin	津	津	*jīn*
Shanghai	滬; less common: 申	沪; 申	*lú; shēn*
Chongqing	渝	渝	*yú*
Hebei	冀	冀	*jì*
Shanxi	晉	晋	*jìn*
Liaoning	遼	辽	*liáo*
Jilin	吉	吉	*jí*
Heilongjiang	黑	黑	*hēi*
Jiangsu	蘇	苏	*sū*
Zhejiang	浙	浙	*zhè*
Anhui	皖	皖	*wǎn*
Fujian	閔	闽	*mǐn*
Jiangxi	贛	赣	*gàn*
Shandong	魯	鲁	*lǔ*
Henan	豫	豫	*yù*
Hubei	鄂	鄂	*è*
Hunan	湘	湘	*xiāng*
Guangdong	粵	粤	*yuè*
Hainan	瓊	琼	*qióng*
Sichuan	川	川	*chuān*
Guizhou	黔; 貴	黔; 贵	*qián; guì*
Yunnan	滇; 雲	滇; 云	*diān; yún*
Shaanxi	陝; 秦	陕; 秦	*shǎn; qín*
Gansu	甘; 隴	甘; 陇	*gān; lǒng*
Qinghai	青	青	*qīng*
Tibet	藏	藏	*zàng*
Guangxi	桂	桂	*guì*
Inner Mongolia	蒙	蒙	*měng*
Ningxia	寧	宁	*níng*
Xinjiang	新	新	*xīn*
Hong Kong	港	港	*Gang*
Macao (Macau)	澳	澳	*ào*

References

Bielenstein, Hans. 1947. *The census of China during the period 2-742 A.D.* Vol. 19, 125–163. Stockholm: Museum of Far Eastern Antiquities.

Buckley, Chris. 2015. China ends one-child policy, allowing families two children. *New York Times*, October 29. https://www.nytimes.com/2015/10/30/world/asia/china-end-one-child-policy.html.

Cai, Yanjun, Xiaoke Qiang, Xulong Wang, et al. 2017. The age of human remains and associated fauna from Zhiren cave in Guangxi, Southern China. *Quaternary International* 434 (A): 84–91.

Chai, Sunglin. 1977. *Population and population policy in mainland China*. Taipei: Asia and the World Forum Monograph Series, No.6.

Chan, Kam Wing. 2010. The household registration system and migrant labor in China: Notes on a debate. *Population and Development Review* 36 (2): 357–364.

China Statistics Press (CSP). 2010. *Tabulation on the 2010 population census of the People's Republic of China*. http://www.stats.gov.cn/tjsj/pcsj/rkpc/6rp/indexce.htm. Accessed 1 Sept 2021.

Cronin, Vincent. 1984. *The wise man from the west: Matteo Ricci and his mission to China*. San Francisco: Ignatius Press.

Cui, Jia. 2021. Ethnic minority population sees significant rapid growth. *China Daily* (Hong Kong), May 12. https://www.chinadailyhk.com/article/167195?showpdf=true.

Eberstadt, Nicholas. 2021. The China Challenge: A demographic predicament will plague the mainland for decades. *Discourse*, June 9. https://www.discoursemagazine.com/culture-and-society/2021/06/09/the-china-challenge-a-demographic-predicament-will-plague-the-mainland-for-decades/.

Everyone's Library. 2021. [In 2020, the average life expectancy of 31 provinces and municipalities in China: What did you find?] 个人图书馆. 2020年我国31省直辖市人均寿命排行如下从中你发现了什么? http://www.360doc.com/content/21/0406/19/28279891_970896106.shtml. Accessed 6 Jan.

Gernet, Jacques. 1962. *Daily life in China: On the eve of the Mongol invasion, 1250–1276*. Stanford: Stanford University Press.

Ho, Ping-ti. 1959. *Studies on the population of China, 1368–1953*. Cambridge, MA: Harvard University Press.

Hua, Qiang, and Cai Hongjun. 2007. [*China's population loss during the Taiping rebellion: State and society in the late Qing Dynasty*]. China Academy of Social Sciences and Policy Research Office, Suzhou University Academy of Social Sciences. Suzhou: Social Science Documentary Press. 华强, 蔡宏俊. 太平天国时期中国人口损失问题, 晚清国家与社会. 中国社科院近代史所政治史研究室, 苏州大学社会学院. 苏州: 社会科学文献出版社.

Kinney, Anne Behnke. 1993. Infant abandonment in early China. *Early China* 18: 107–138.

Knoema.com. *World data atlas*. 2020. Male to female ratio of the total population. 2022. https://knoema.com/atlas/topics/Demographics/Population/Male-to-female-ratio. Accessed 1 Sept 2021.

Lavely, William, and R. Bin Wong. 1998. Revising the Malthusian narrative: The comparative study of population dynamics in late Imperial China. *Journal of Asian Studies* 57 (3): 714–748.

Laven, Mary. 2011. *Mission to China: Matteo Ricci and the Jesuit encounter with the East*. London: Faber and Faber.

Li, Lillian M. 1982. Introduction: Food, famine, and the Chinese. *The Journal of Asian Studies* 41 (4): 687–707.

Li, Sha. 2012. [*China's population through history: Yuan Dynasty*]. Beijing: People's Press. 李莎. 中國人口通史:元代卷. Vol. 9. 北京: 人民出版社.

Li, Mei, and Quanbao Jiang. 2021. Overestimated SRB and missing girls in China. *Frontiers in Sociology*, October 26. https://www.frontiersin.org/articles/10.3389/fsoc.2021.756364/full.

Ma, Zhengliang. 2014. [Analysis of Chinese Muslim population trends]. *Journal of Guizhou University Art Edition* (sic). 馬正亮. 中國穆斯林人口發展分析. 貴州大學學報 (社會科學版) 32(3): 98–106.

Ma Lum, Yansheng, and Raymond Mun Kong Lum. 1999. *Sun Yat-Sen in Hawaii*. University of Hawaii Press.

Mi, Hong, Li Shuzhuo, Hu Ping, and Wang Qiong. 1997. [Two household population surveys in the late Qing Dynasty and early Republic of China]. *Historical Research*. 米红, 李树茁, 胡平, 王琼. 清末民初的两次户口人口调查. 历史研究 1: 58–72.

Ministry of Civil Affairs (MCA), People's Republic of China. 2020. [*County/township administration handbook*]. Beijing: China Statistics Press. 中華人民共和國民政部, 中華人民共和國, 鄉鎮行政區劃簡冊.

Mosher, Steven W. 2011. *Population control: Real costs, illusory benefits*. New Brunswick: Transaction Publishers.

Myers, Steven Lee. 2019. A crackdown on Muslims is spreading beyond Xinjiang. *The New York Times*, September 23. Section A, p. 8.

National Bureau of Statistics (NBS), People's Republic of China. 2001. [Year 2000 fifth national census report, Issue No. 2.] 2000. 年第五次全国人口普查主要数据公报 (第二号). 2 April. http://www.gov.cn/gongbao/content/2001/content_60741.htm.

———. 2021. [Report of the Seventh All-National Census]. May 19. 第七次全国人口普查公报. http://www.stats.gov.cn/ztjc/zdtjgz/zgrkpc/dqcrkpc/ggl/202105/t20210519_1817697.html.

Poston, Dudley L., Jr., Eugenia Conde, and Bethany DeSalvo. 2011a. China's unbalanced sex ratio at birth: Millions of excess bachelors and societal implications. *Vulnerable Children and Youth Studies* 6 (4): 314–320.

Poston, Dudley L., Jr., Wadha Saeed Khamis Alnuaimi, and Li Zhang. 2011b. The social demography of China's Muslims. *Modern China Studies* 18 (1): 14–72.

Proske, Dirk. 2008. *Catalogue of risks: Natural, technical, social and health risks*. Berlin: Springer.

Remen Zixun (RMZX). 2022. [*How many people are religious in China now? Are there statistics on how many people there are in each religion?*]. 热门资讯. 现在中国有多少人信教?每个宗教有多少人数有这方面的统计吗. http://www.yinzdian.com/z/12764.html. Accessed 16 Apr 2022.

Rummel, R. J. China's bloody century. 2002. https://hawaii.edu/powerkills/CHINA.CHAP1.HTM.

ter Haar, Barend J. 2013. Divine violence to uphold moral values: The casebook of an emperor Guan temple in Hunan Province 1851–1852. In *Law and empire: Ideas, practices, actors*, ed. Jeroen Duindam, Jill Harries, Caroline Humfress, and Nimrod Hurvitz, 313–338. Leiden: Brill.

Tsang, Chiu-Sam. 1968. *Society, schools & progress in China*. Toronto: Pergamon Press.

Tspweb. 2020. [*How to calculate life expectancy in ancient times*]. 古代人均寿命怎么算的. 调色盘网络. https://www.tspweb.com/key/. Accessed 6 Jan 2022.

Tuan, Yi-Fu. 2008. *A Historical geography of China*. New Brunswick: Aldine Transaction.

Watson, Rubie S. 1986. The named and the nameless: Gender and person in Chinese society. *American Ethnologist* 13 (4): 619–631.

World Population Review (WPR). 2022. *Muslim population by country: 2022*. https://worldpopulationreview.com/country-rankings/muslim-population-by-country. Accessed 14 Apr 2022.

Xin, Lijian. 2011. [Xin Lijian: How many abnormal deaths were there in China after 1945?]. *Chinaweek*. May 6. 信力建: 1945 年后中国有多少人非正常死亡. https://www.china-week.com/html/5977.htm.

Yang, Zihui. 1995. [*China's historical population statistical data research*]. Beijing: Reform Press. 楊子慧, 中國歷代人口統計資料研究. 北京: 改革出版社.

Yang, Jisheng. 2008. *Tombstone: The great Chinese famine, 1958–1962*. New York: Farrar, Straus and Giroux.

Yuan, Zuliang. 2007. [China's population through history: Qin to Western Han]. Beijing: People's Press. 袁祖亮. 中國人口通史: 秦西漢卷. Vol. 3. 北京:人民出版社.

Yuan, Zuliang, and Jiao Peimin. 2007a. [*China's population through history: Beginning Qin*]. Beijing: People's Press. 袁祖亮, 焦培民. 中國人口通史:先秦卷. Vol. 2, 北京: 人民出版社.

———. 2007b. [*China's population through history: Eastern Han*]. Beijing: People's Press. 袁祖亮, 焦培民. 中國人口通史: 東漢卷. Vol. 4. 北京:人民出版社.

Zhao, Wenyuan. 2004. [Historical reasons why China changed the system of free migration of *hukou* in 1958.] *Historiography Monthly*. No. 10. 趙文遠. 1958年中國改變戶口自由遷移制度的歷史原因. 史學月刊 (10).

Zheng, Yi. 1993. [Red memorial]. Taipei: Huashi Publications. 鄭義. 紅色紀念碑. 台北: 華視叢書.

Chapter 2
Anhui Province

Abstract The chapter on Anhui Provinces starts with some of the oldest hominids to have appeared in China, including *Homo erectus*, continuing with Anhui populations throughout the centuries to the present. While cities and towns in Anhui province appear in the oldest of China's recorded literature, its current borders are relatively recent, created in the first few decades of the Qing dynasty. It is fortuitous that Anhui Province is the first chapter of this survey, as it features a striking example of China's "floating populations." In this case, the usual resident populations of Anhui typically are far lower than the *hukou* (family registered) population. This is due to the fact that, year after year, official Anhui registered (*hukou*) citizens spend most if not all of their lives in other Chinese provinces and cities, mostly for economic opportunities. With regard to the latter, data are provided on Anhui's current economic standing when compared with 31 other mainland Chinese provinces and cities, and concludes with *hukou* registered populations down to the district/county level.

E. Croddy, *China's Provinces and Populations*,
https://doi.org/10.1007/978-3-031-09165-0_2

Anhui Province (Anhwei; 安徽省 *ānhuī shěng*): Abbreviation 皖 (*wǎn*) (Fig. 2.1)

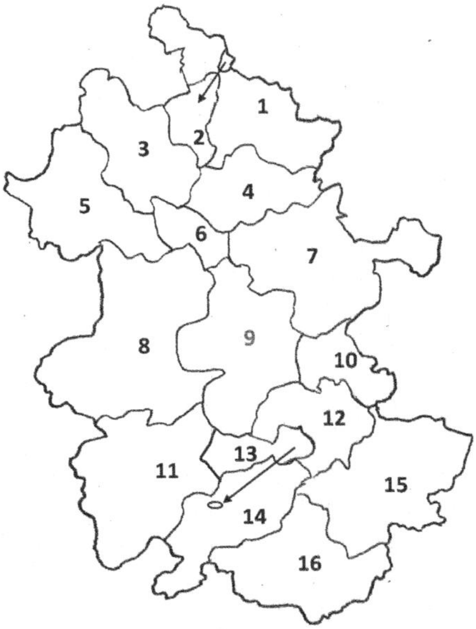

	Population, Anhui Province (2020)
1. 宿州市 **Suzhou City**	**5,324,476**
2. 淮北市 **Huaibei City**	**1,970,265**
3. 亳州市 **Bozhou City**	**4,996,844**
4. 蚌埠市 **Bengbu City**	**3,296,408**
5. 阜陽市 **Fuyang City**	**8,200,264**
6. 淮南市 **Huainan City**	**3,033,528**
7. 滁州市 **Chuzhou City**	**3,987,054**
8. 六安市 **Lu'an City**[1]	**4,393,699**
9. 合肥市 **Hefei City**	**9,369,881**
10. 馬鞍山市 **Ma'anshan City**	**2,159,930**
11. 安慶市 **Anqing City**	**4,165,284**
12. 蕪湖市 **Wuhu City**	**3,644,420**
13. 銅陵市 **Tongling City**	**1,311,726**
14. 池州市 **Chizhou City**	**1,342,764**
15. 宣城市 **Xuancheng City**	**4,165,284**
16. 黃山市 **Huangshan City**	**1,330,565**

Fig. 2.1 Anhui province: major subdivisions (Provincial Capital: Hefei City). (Drawn by the Author after People's Republic of China, Ministry of Civil Affairs, MCA 2020)

General Impressions

Landlocked in China's east (華東 *huádōng*), Anhui Province straddles the northern and southern regional geography of the PRC, its territory intersecting both the Huai (淮 *huái*) and the Yangtze (長江 *chángjiāng*) Rivers. The name of Anhui is simply a combination of two major cities, **An**qing 安慶 and the legacy place name **Hui**zhou 徽州, now a district in Huangshan City. The old Chinese moniker for Anhui, 水墨徽州 (*shuǐmò huīzhōu*), reflects one of its many historical legacies, notably Anhui's famous black ink used in classical monochrome paintings. Anhui also brings to the Chinese mind its own architecture, ancestral temples, stylized arched bridges, ornate carvings, and lake-side communities all dating back centuries. These impressions, along with Anhui's famous Huangshan and Tianzhu Mountain scenic regions, are commonly-known features for both Chinese and world travelers alike. Indeed, the Ming dynasty travel writer, Xu Xiake (徐霞客 *xú xiákè*; d.1641) famously said that, "once you've seen the Huangshan mountains, you really don't need bother visiting all five of China's spectacular peaks."[1] For all of its bucolic attributes, Anhui province also has a general reputation for being generally poor, and infamous for its mostly unfertile soil. Noted one modern observer of Chinese societies throughout history, "It was always considered a misery to be born in Anhui (Lee 2005)."

Formally named in 1667, in terms of China's modern provincial administration Anhui province is a relatively recent entity. Even so, Anhui's counties have provenance going back for many centuries. For example, historical records trace the origins of Yixian county (黟縣 *yīxiàn*, population 76,211) to the third century BCE.

Prehistory

In the early 1980s, Chinese investigators uncovered numerous specimens of *Homo erectus*, including that of a young male, in Hexian County (和縣 *héxiàn*), Longtandong Cave (龍潭洞 *lóngtán dòng*). Similar in many ways to that of Peking Man (albeit with some important differences), Hexian Man may be over 190,000 years old.

Evidence of Neolithic settlements in Qianshan County (潛山縣 *qiánshān xiàn*), Xuejiagang (薛家崗 *xuējiāgāng*), date back nearly six thousand years ago. The Dawenkou Culture (大汶口文化 *dàwènkǒu wénhuà* 5000–2500 BCE), which featured advanced pottery and sophisticated social structures has also been found in Anhui Province.

---

[1] "五嶽歸來不看山黃山歸來不看岳" *wǔyuèguīlái, bùkànshān, huángshānguīlái, bùkàn yuè.*

Earliest Chinese Civilization

Tradition has it that Tang (i.e., Cheng Tang 成湯 *chéng tāng*), founder of the Shang dynasty (sixteenth to eleventh centuries BCE) had established a capital for a short time in today's Bozhou City (亳州市 *bòzhōu shì*). Subsequently, the modern-day region of Anhui in those ancient times became an important political center. Its State of Wan (皖國 *wǎnguó*) came into prominance during the Spring Autumn Period (ca. 771 to 476 BCE), thus the short character abbreviation for Anhui: Wan (皖 *wǎn*).

From 493–447 BCE (Eastern Zhou period), Zhoulai (州來 *zhōulái*), near modern day Shouxian county (壽縣 *shòuxiàn*, population), was the center of the Cai State (蔡國 *cài guó*). The sophistication of the Cai culture was evinced by the discovery in the late 1950s of five bronze tallies (金節 *jīnjié*). These ancient fiduciary instruments were dated to 323 BCE, and are believed to have been originally produced in Shouchun (壽春 *shòuchūn*). These E' Jun Qi (鄂君啟 *è'jūnqǐ*) tallies were inscribed on a cylinder in old Chinese script, enabling the bearer (usually a merchant) to travel about without having to pay tolls. (In essence, this was an ancient Chinese version of the modern "E-Z Pass" on specified toll routes throughout the State of Chu). During the Song dynasty (960–1280), the Anhui region was also well known as a source of minted coinage (von Falkenhausen 2005). Eventually, the powerful State of Chu (ca. 241–223 BCE) had moved its capital in Shouchun today's Shouxian County (壽縣 *shòuxiàn*). Upon being attacked by 600,000 Qin dynasty troops, however, the kingdom of Chu fell.

In 210 BCE, the administratively harsh methods of the Qin dynasty made already difficult life even more miserable for many of its subjects. Exerting a fiat policy of corvée labor and mandatory military service, these pressures contributed to peasant rebellions. During these harsh and difficult times, two individuals in particular, Chen Sheng (陳勝 *chén sheng*, d. 208 BCE) and Wu Guang (吳廣 *wú guǎng*) were faced with an untenable situation. Just when it was their turn to become pressed into active duty, regional flooding prevented them from traveling to their muster point, and, under the punitive rules of the day, they faced execution. Realizing that they had nothing to lose, Chen Sheng and Wu Guang led 900 local farmers in Daze County (大澤縣 *dàzé xiàn*), southwest of today's Anhui Suzhou City (宿州市 *sùzhōu shì*), to rebel against Qin tyranny. In their offensive against the Qin, this hard scrabble army is described in the ancient histories as having "raised a stick as a banner" (揭竿为旗 *jiēgān wèiqí*), and is the source of the Chinese idiom "rise to rebellion" (揭竿而起 *jiēgān érqǐ*). A series of subsequent peasant rebellions and pitched battles across a large swath of China's central plan ultimately led to the downfall of the Qin.

The ultimate battle occurred in December 202 BCE, when Liu Bang (劉邦 *liú bāng*) defeated Xiang Yu (項羽 *Xiàng Yǔ*) at the Battle of Gaixia (垓下之戰 *gāixià zhīzhàn*) in modern-day Guzhen County (固鎮縣 *gùzhèn xiàn*), leading to the establishment of the Han dynasty (206 BCE – 220 CE). Xiang Yu himself committed suicide during his last stand at Wujiang River (烏江 *wūjiāng*) in today's Hexian county (和縣 *héxiàn*), Anhui province.

During the Han dynasty, the Eastern Ou State (東甌國 *dōng'ōu guó*) had expanded into Lujiang Prefecture (盧江郡 *lújiāng jùn*), today's Shucheng County (舒城縣 *shūchéng xiàn*). Towards the end of the Han, the warlord Yuan Shu (袁術 *yuán shù*) occupied Shouchun (壽春 *shòuchūn*), in today's Shouxian County (壽縣 *shòuxiàn*), and used it as his main base of operations. He died of illness in 199 CE, not long after declaring himself emperor. Famed warlord Cao Cao (曹操 *cáo cāo*), the Duke of Wei (魏公 *wèi gōng*), who was originally from Bozhou (亳州 *bòzhōu*), took control of Shouchun. During his wars with the State of Wu (吳國 *wú guó*), in 214 CE, Cao Cao dispatched his lieutenant Zhang Liao (張遼 *zhāng liáo*) to battle, who famously defended Hefei during the Xiaoyao Ford Battle (逍遙津之戰 *xiāoyáojīnzhīzhàn*) against Sun Quan (孫權 *sūn quán*).

Through the Tang dynasty, the Anhui region was relatively prosperous. Emperor Wen of Sui (隋文帝 *suíwéndì*, r. 581–604) promoted economic development throughout the region that included modern-day Anhui Province. During the interregnum between Emperor Yang of Sui (隋煬帝 *suíyángdì*; 610 CE) and the Tang dynasty, however, this region was beset by bloody conflict. The An Lushan rebellion (安史之亂 *ānshǐzhīluàn*; ca. 755 CE) led to widespread destruction throughout China, but none more so than in the region north of the Huai River in today's Anhui. Towards the end of the Tang dynasty, in ca. 875, Anhui was further impacted by the chaos that ensued during the Huang Chao uprising (黃巢起義 *huángcháo qǐyì*).

After Northern Song and the rise of the Jin (金 *jīn*; or Liao) dynasty in the north, the Huai river region, including northern Anhui Province today, formed the border between the growing Jin to the north, and the retreating southern Song (ca. 1130). Advocating the Sinicization of the Jin, the Jurchen Prince Wan Yanliang (完顏亮 *wán yánliàng*), later known as Emperor Hailing Wang (海陵王 *hǎi língwáng*) initially achieved some success against the Song, but was ultimately defeated in 1161 during the battle of Ma'anshan (馬鞍山採石大戰 *mǎ'ān shān cǎishídàzhàn*).

Following the Mongolian invasion, both the Jin and Song were now under the dominance of the Mongolian Yuan dynasty by 1276, which included all of the Anhui region. When the Taizu (Zhu Yuanzhang 朱元璋 *zhū yuánzhāng*) founded the Ming dynasty in 1368, from this point forward Anhui and Jiangsu belonged to one of six centrally managed prefectures generally termed Zhili (直隸 *zhílì* or "direct administration.") During this period of imperial rule, seven governing entities (prefectures) in the Ming Dynasty were established in the Anhui region, four of these being south of the Changjiang (Yangtze) river:

- Huizhou Prefecture (徽州府 *huīzhōu fǔ*)
- Ningguo Prefecture (寧國府 *níngguó fǔ*)
- Taiping Prefecture (太平府 *tàipíng fǔ*), and
- Chizhou Prefecture (池州府 *chízhōu fǔ*)

Governance under the Ming included two regions north of the Changjiang river bank, which included Anqing (安慶府 *ānqìng fǔ*) and Luzhou (廬州府 *lúzhōu fǔ*) prefectures, both located in today's Hefei City. Finally, the entire Huai river area was governed by Fengyang (鳳陽府 *fèngyáng fǔ*), home of the Ming dynasty emperor Zhu Yuanzhang. Meanwhile, Wuhu Prefecture (蕪湖府 *wúhú fǔ*) developed into a prosperous economic center. When the Yongle emperor established Beijing as the capital (ca. 1420), the Anhui region of today and its environs were formally designated a southern administrative area, i.e., Nanzhili (南直隸 *nánzhí lì*).

China's Modern Ice Age

As evinced by London's Thames River "Frost Fairs" first held in 1608, early seventeenth century Europe experienced a "little ice age." These freakishly cold episodes led to misery in England. On the other end of the planet, China was also seriously impacted by this intemperate weather. In the latter part of the Ming dynasty, crop failures were legion. The Ming emperor, unable (or unwilling) to take appropriate action, helped spark the various peasant up-risings, such as the one in that occurred in the Anhui region (1632).

After the invading Qing armies occupied Nanjing, the Nanzhili region in 1645 was renamed Jiangnan Province. In 1667, Jiangnan was separated into Anhui and Jiangsu provinces. At that time, Anhui Province had its capital in Anqing. The Anhui region was brought to near economic ruin as the Taiping Rebellion (太平天國 *tàipíng tiānguó*: "Heavenly Kingdom," 1850–1864) began its occupation of Nanjing. Pitched battles in the region forced large numbers of refugees to flee southern Anhui by 1860. Cao Shuji, a preeminent scholar of Chinese demographics throughout history, has compared the calamity of the Taiping and its impact on the population in the Anhui region to those deaths recorded as a result of the Great Leap Forward (official dates: 1958–1961) in Table 2.1).

Following the end of the Taiping conflict (1865), an influx of immigrants to Anhui from Henan and Hubei significantly transformed the demographic and cultural landscape.

Anhui finally declared its independence from the Qing in November 1911. After the Japanese surrender, the Republic of China (ROC) moved the capital of Anhui at Anqing to its current Hefei City in 1946. For a short time beginning in ca. 1948, Anhui was divided into north and south: Wanbei (皖北 *wǎnběi*) and Wannan (皖南 *wǎnnán*), respectively.

More adjustments in Anhui provincial geography were made in 1952: Wuyuan County (婺源縣 *wùyuán xiàn*) was drawn into Jiangxi Province, while Xutai (盱胎縣 *xūtāi xiàn*) and Sigong (泗洪縣 *sìhóng xiàn*) counties were included within the boundaries of Jiangsu. The latter province swapped Xiaoxian (蕭縣 *xiāo xiàn*) and Dangshan (碭山縣 *dàngshān xiàn*) counties, and these were made subordinate to Anhui province.

As seen above, Mao Zedong's disastrous Great Leap Forward (GLF, 1958–1962) led to an estimated 6.3 million deaths in Anhui Province, the highest number of all provinces in China. The ravages of the GLF also wrecked Anhui's agricultural sector, which hitherto had been known as China's "Iron Rice Bowl" (鐵飯碗 *tiěfànwǎn*).

Table 2.1 Unnatural deaths during Taiping Rebellion (1850–1864) and Great Leap Forward (1958–1961) compared (Cao 2005)

Prefecture	Modern equivalent	Population (1851)	Wartime deaths[a], Taiping Rebellion (1850–1864)	Population (1958)	Famine deaths, Great Leap Forward (1958–1961)
Lujiangfu 廬江府 *lújiāng fǔ*	Lujiang County 廬江縣 *lújiāng xiàn*	4,165,000	765,000	4,990,000	1,160,000
Hezhou 和州 *hézhōu*	Hexian County 和縣 *héxiàn*	502,000	(N/A)	751,000	193,000
Chuzhou 滁州 *chúzhōu*	Chuzhou City 滁州市 *chúzhōu shì*	704,000	458,000	845,000	111,000
Sizhou 泗州 *sìzhōu*	Sixian County 泗縣 *sìxiàn*	1,842,000	696,000	2,195,000	253,000
Fengyangfu 鳳陽府 *fèngyáng fǔ*	Fengyang County 鳳陽縣 *fèngyáng xiàn*	5,113,000	1,669,000	6,623,000	1,500,000
Yingzhoufu 潁州府 *yǐngzhōu fǔ*	Fuyang City 阜陽市 *fùyáng shì*	4,670,000	(N/A)	8,261,000	1,945,000
Lu'anzhou 六安州 *lù'ān zhōu*	Lu'an City 六安市 *lù'ān shì*	1,682,000	651,000	1,513,000	238,000
Anqingfu 安慶府 *ānqìng fǔ*	Anqing City 安慶市 *ānqìng shì*	6,400,000	3,600,000	3,398,000	330,000
Chizhoufu 池州府 *chízhōu fǔ*	Chizhou City 池州市 *chízhōu shì*	3,220,000	2,800,000	1,096,000	20,000
Taipingfu 太平府 *tàipíng fǔ*	Ma'anshan City, Wuhu City 馬鞍山市, 蕪湖市 *mǎ'ānshān shì, wúhú shì*	1,730,000	1,300,000	1,528,000	96,000
Guangdezhou 廣德州 *guǎngdé zhōu*	Guangde County廣德縣 *guǎngdé xiàn*	643,000	601,000	474,000	72,000
Ningguofu 寧國府 *níngguó fǔ*	Ningguo City 寧國市 *níngguó shì*	4,000,000	3,232,000	1,716,000	370,000
Huizhoufu 徽州府 *huīzhōu fǔ*	Huangshan City, Jixi County and Jiangxi province's Wuyuan County 黃山市, 績溪縣, 江西省婺源縣 *huángshān shì, jìxī xiàn, jiāngxī sheng, wùyuán xiàn*	2,715,000	2,092,000	1,070,000	18,000
Total		**37,386,000**	**17,864,000**	**34,460,000**	**6,306,000**

[a]Also includes deaths due to famine, illness, etc.

Floating Populations: Residential and Permanent (*Hukou*)

According to the People's Republic of China (PRC) national census in 2010, Anhui's resident (typical) population (常住人口 *chángzhù rénkǒu*) was 59,500,468. But looking at the permanent (戶籍人口 *hùjí rénkǒu*, i.e., registered with the Ministry of Public Security), the number was significantly higher, 68,406,000. Why the disparity?

The main distinction between the two categories is that permanent (戶籍人口 *hùjí rénkǒu*) populations are those who are officially listed in the local *hukou* registry. Usual residents (常住人口 *chángzhù rénkǒu*), on the other hand, are included in the net total, unofficially registered, but otherwise live, work, and study in a given area for 6 months or more out of a year. In more rapidly developing regions in China we see large shifts between these two populations, with many more registered (常住 *chángzhù*; nonpermanent) versus permanently registered (戶籍 *hùjí*) citizens. For example, in 2010 Beijing City had a permanent registered population of about 12,842,000 people. However, when including all residents, including temporary and migrant workers, students, etc., this figure ballooned to some 20 million people. In Anhui, however, there are usually far more *permanent* residents than the total number of residents that typically live there. This is a reflection of the fact that, while its economy is doing relatively well, Anhui still lags behind other regions of China. It is not surprising, then, that millions of Anhui citizens, mostly from the rural areas, routinely move to other, more dynamic economies in China to find work. For example, in 2005 there may have been as many as two million Anhui migrant workers in Shanghai City alone (Chen and Wu 2006). From a survey in 2014, nearly eight and a half million Anhui permanent residents emigrated to work in other provinces and cities, notably Zhejiang, Guangdong, and Shanghai. With a family registered (*hukou*) population of 70,830,000 in 2020, once can compare this number with the 2020 census (typical residential population, 常住人口 *chángzhù rénkǒu*) of 61,027,171. Thus, over nine million Anhui-registered individuals were somewhere else, living, working, studying, etc., and doing so for extended periods of time.

And it seems to always have been thus. Long ago, Anhui was already known for having produced two types of successful activities, most often for young men: commercial business or academics. There really hasn't been any other option. As a consequence, and because such professions lend themselves to leaving the province for work, Anhui men have a reputation for being on the road and away from home for long stretches of time, including a significant number of teenagers who also travel to other provinces in search of work. Therefore the plaintive lament of the Anhui housewife has been "married her whole life, but together as a couple for only three-and-a-half years; ten years a wife, but nine of those apart."[2] For those in the less arable areas of Anhui, especially those in and around Xiuning (休寧 *xiūníng*), they turned their efforts primarily to mercantilism, and Anhui merchants have ever been famous for their business acumen. Indeed, two expressions reflect the nature of the Anhui people over the centuries. One, is to be clever in business, with superior accounting skills: an "Anhui abacus" (徽算盤 *huī suànpán*). Another saying reflects the stereotype of a hardworking, no-nonsense type that is willing to do what it takes to make a living: a work horse, or, in the Chinese, an "Anhui camel" (徽駱駝 *huīluòtuó*).

Like most of traditional China, Anhui once was an agricultural-led economy. Today, there is still much work to be done in Anhui's agricultural sector, and it receives its own fair share of guest workers from other, even less-developed regions. Thus, while about 9.6 million people departed Anhui in 2010 for various reasons, about 717,000 from other provinces migrated to Anhui for work in that year (Qiao and Yanchun 2013). Today, however, with a growing industrial base and large coal reserves, by 2018 Anhui's agricultural sector contributed no more than 9% to its overall economy. Still viewed as China's rural heartland, modern Anhui is nonetheless densely populated, with about 500 people per square kilometer, and ten of its cities having a population of more than three million people. Its capital, Hefei City (合肥市 *héféi shì*) has a population of over 9 million, and Fuyang City (阜陽市 *fùyáng shì*) has a population of over eight million individuals.

One of China's fastest growing economies, as of 2020, Anhui has shown to be economically competitive by any measure, ranked eleventh of mainland China's 31 provinces and major cities in terms of gross domestic product (GDP), amounting to nearly USD $60.2 billion. In terms of per capita income, Anhui ranked thirteenth in 2020 with an average of $4670 per person, a 6% increase over 2019 (Zhang 2021) (Tables 2.2, 2.3 and Fig. 2.2).

Table 2.4 (below) shows the *hukou* (family registered) populations based on PRC Ministry of Civil Affairs data. (Districts listed directly under major cities are government seats, as are those in parentheses). One can compare these data with the census (usual residential populations based on 2010 and 2020 censuses in Tables 2.2 and 2.3 (below):

[2] "一世夫妻三年半, 十年夫妻九年空" *yīshìfūqī sānniánbàn, shíniánfūqī jiǔniánkōng*).

Table 2.2 Anhui province population (Residential 常住人口 chángzhù rénkǒu). (NBS 2021)

City/region	Population (2010)	Population (2020)
Hefei City 合肥市 *héféi shì* [abbrev. 盧 *lú*; 合 *hé*]	5,702,000	9,369,881
Suzhou City 宿州市 *sùzhōu shì*	5,353,000	5,324,476
Huaibei City 淮北市 *huáiběi shì*	2,114,000	1,970,265
Bozhou City 亳州市 *bózhōu shì*	4,851,000	4,996,844
Bengbu City 蚌埠市 *bèngbù shì*	3,164,000	3,296,408
Fuyang City 阜陽市 *fùyáng shì*	7,600,000	8,200,264
Huainan City 淮南市 *huáinán shì*	2,334,000	3,033,528
Chuzhou City 滁州市 *chúzhōu shì*	3,938,000	3,987,054
Lu'an City[a] 六安市 *lù'ān shì*	5,612,000	4,393,699
Anqing City 安慶市 *ānqìng shì* [abbrev. 宜 *yí*]	5,311,000	4,165,284
Ma'anshan City 馬鞍山市 *mǎ'ānshān shì*	1,366,000	2,159,930
Wuhu City 蕪湖市 *wúhú shì*	2,263,000	3,644,420
Tongling City 銅陵市 *tónglíng shì*	724,000	1,311,726
Chizhou City 池州市 *chízhōu shì*	1,403,000	1,342,764
Xuancheng City 宣城市 *xuānchéng shì*	2,533,000	4,165,284
Huangshan City 黃山市 *huángshān shì*	1,359,000	1,330,565
Chaohu City 巢湖市 *cháohú shì*	3,873,000	N/A[b]
Total	**59,501,000**	**61,027,171**

[a]六 in this placename is pronounced *lù*

[b]City was dissolved and parceled out among Hefei, Wuhu and Ma'anshan cities in 2011

Table 2.3 Anhui province cities and their subordinate sectors (NBS 2021)

Cities and subordinate sectors, population (2020 census)	Subordinate district, city and county populations (2020)	Total population (2020)
Hefei City 合肥市 ***héféi shì* [abbrev.** 盧 ***lú***; 合 ***hé***]		**9,369,881**
Shushan District 蜀山區 *shǔshān qū*	1,047,150	
Luyang District 廬陽區 *lúyáng qū*	697,293	
Yaohai District 瑤海區 *yáohǎi qū*	862,043	
Baohe District 包河區 *bāohé qū*	1,217,469	
Chaohu City 巢湖市 *cháohú shì* (includes Chaokai District 巢開區 *chákāi qū*)	727,162	
Changfeng County長豐縣 *chángfēng xiàn*	783,982	
Feidong County 肥東縣 *féidōng xiàn*	884,792	
Feixi County 肥西縣 *féixī xiàn*	967,508	
Lujiang County 廬江縣 *lújiāng xiàn*	888,238	
Suzhou City 宿州市 ***sùzhōu shì***		**5,324,476**
Yongqiao District 埇橋區 *yǒngqiáo qū*	1,766,285	
Dangshan County 碭山縣 *dàngshān xiàn*	765,564	
Xiaoxian County 蕭縣 *xiāoxiàn*	1,054,597	
Lingbi County 靈璧縣 *língbì xiàn*	974,720	

(continued)

Table 2.3 (continued)

Cities and subordinate sectors, population (2020 census)	Subordinate district, city and county populations (2020)	Total population (2020)
Sixian County 泗縣 *sìxiàn*	763,310	
Huaibei City 淮北市 ***huáiběi shì***		**1,970,265**
Xiangshan District 相山區 *xiāngshān qū*	548,934	
Duji District 杜集區 *dùjí qū*	239,692	
Lieshan District 烈山區 *lièshān qū*	249,237	
Suixi County 濉溪縣 *suīxī xiàn*	932,402	
Bozhou City 亳州市 ***bózhōu shì***		**4,996,844**
Qiaocheng District 譙城區 *qiáochéng qū*	1,537,231	
Woyang County 渦陽縣 *wōyáng xiàn*	1,170,719	
Mengcheng County 蒙城縣 *mēngchéng xiàn*	1,101,640	
Lixin County 利辛縣 *lìxīn xiàn*	1,187,254	
Bengbu City 蚌埠市 ***bèngbù shì***		**3,296,408**
Bengshan District 蚌山區 *bèngshān qū*	171,045	
Longzihu District 龍子湖區 *lóngzǐhú qū*	216,875	
Yuhui District 禹會區 *yǔhuì qū*	325,814	
Huaishang District 淮上區 *huáishàng qū*	283,872	
Huaiyuan County 懷遠縣 *huáiyuǎn xiàn*	935,335	
Wuhe County 五河縣 *wǔhé xiàn*	523,351	
Guzhen County 固鎮縣 *gùzhèn xiàn*	501,449	
Gaoxin District 高新區 *gāoxīn qū*	61,850	
Jingkai District 經開區 *jīngkāi qū*	276,637	
Fuyang City 阜陽市 ***fùyáng shì***		**8,200,264**
Yingzhou District 潁州區 *yǐngzhōu qū*	992,347	
Yingdong District 潁東區 *yǐngdōng qū*	538,187	
Yingquan District 潁泉區 *yǐngquán qū*	598,004	
Jieshou City 界首市 *jièshǒu shì*	650,870	
Linquan County 臨泉縣 *línquán xiàn*	1,658,442	
Taihe County 太和縣 *tàihé xiàn*	1,379,982	
Funan County 阜南縣 *fùnán xiàn*	1,183,602	
Yingshang County 潁上縣 *yǐngshàng xiàn*	1,198,830	
Huainan City 淮南市 ***huáinán shì***		**3,033,528**
Tianjia'an District 田家庵區 *tiánjiā'ān qū*	730,078	
Datong District 大通區 *dàtōng qū*	165,671	
Xiejiaji District 謝家集區 *xièjiājí qū*	221,589	
Bagongshan District 八公山區 *bāgōngshān qū*	118,221	
Panji District 潘集區 *pānjí qū*	326,077	
Fengtai County 鳳台縣 *fèngtái xiàn*	633,385	
Shouxian County 壽縣 *shòuxiàn*	838,507	
Chuzhou City 滁州市 ***chúzhōu shì***		**3,987,054**
Langya District 瑯琊區 *lángyá qū*	268,430	

(continued)

Table 2.3 (continued)

Cities and subordinate sectors, population (2020 census)	Subordinate district, city and county populations (2020)	Total population (2020)
Nanqiao District 南譙區 *nánqiáo qū*	348,762	
Chuzhou Jingkai District 滁州經開區 *chúzhōu jīngkāiqū*	141,870	
Suchu Gaoxin District 蘇滁高新區 *sūchú gāoxīnqū*	23,609	
Tianchang City 天長市 *tiāncháng shì*	603,780	
Lai'an County 來安縣 *lái'ān xiàn*	416,048	
Quanjiao County 全椒縣 *quánjiāo xiàn*	395,633	
Dingyuan County 定遠縣 *dìngyuǎn xiàn*	671,361	
Fengyang County 鳳陽縣 *fèngyáng xiàn*	631,934	
Mingguang City 明光市 *míngguāng shì*	485,627	
Lu'an City[a] 六安市 ***lù'ān shì***		**4,393,699**
Jin'an County 金安縣 *jīn'ān xiàn*	829,236	
Yu'an District 裕安區 *yù'ān qū*	923,301	
Yeji District 葉集區 *yèjí qū*	216,229	
Huoqiu County 霍邱縣 *huòqiū xiàn*	944,985	
Shucheng County 舒城縣 *shūchéng xiàn*	697,250	
Jinzhai County 金寨縣 *jīnzhài xiàn*	496,501	
Huoshan County 霍山縣 *huòshān xiàn*	286,197	
Anqing City 安慶市 ***ānqìng shì* [abbrev.** 宜***yí*]**		**4,165,284**
Daguan District 大觀區 *dàguān qū*	214,112	
Yingjiang District 迎江區 *yíngjiāng qū*	253,694	
Yixiu District 宜秀區 *yíxiù qū*	196,672	
Anqing City Jingkai District 安慶市經開區 *ānqìng shì jīngkāiqū*	140,015	
Tongcheng City 桐城市 *tóngchéng shì*	593,629	
Huaining County 懷寧縣 *huáiníng xiàn*	496,683	
Qianshan City 潛山市 *qiánshān shì*	441,224	
Taihu County 太湖縣 *tàihú xiàn*	430,465	
Susong County 宿松縣 *sùsōng xiàn*	612,586	
Wangjiang County 望江縣 *wàngjiāng xiàn*	462,367	
Yuexi County 岳西縣 *yuèxī xiàn*	323,837	
Ma'anshan City 馬鞍山市 ***mǎ'ānshān shì***		**2,159,930**
Yushan District 雨山區 *yǔshān qū*	355,986	
Huashan District 花山區 *huāshān qū*	450,983	
Bowang District 博望區 *bówàng qū*	158,483	
Dangtu County 當塗縣 *dāngtú xiàn*	446,991	
Hanshan County 含山縣 *hánshān xiàn*	336,588	
Hexian County 和縣 *héxiàn*	410,899	
Wuhu City 蕪湖市 ***wúhú shì***		**3,644,420**

(continued)

Table 2.3 (continued)

Cities and subordinate sectors, population (2020 census)	Subordinate district, city and county populations (2020)	Total population (2020)
Jiujiang District 鳩江區 *jiūjiāng qū*	540,487	
Yijiang District 弋江區 *yìjiāng qū*	422,620	
Wanzhi District 灣沚區 *wānzhǐ qū*[b]	344,016	
Sanshan Economic Development Zone 三山經濟開發區 *sānshān jīngjìkāifāqū*	184,553	
Economic and Technical Development Zone 經濟技術開發區 *jīngjìjìshù kāifāqū*	181,034	
Jinghu District 鏡湖區 *jìnghú qū*	478,658	
Fanchang County 繁昌縣 *fánchāng xiàn*	243,907	
Nanling County 南陵縣 *nánlíng xiàn*	431,148	
Wuwei County 無為縣 *wúwéi xiàn*	817,997	
Tongling City 銅陵市 ***tónglíng shì***		**1,311,726**
Tongguan District 銅官區 *tóngguān qū*	450,949	
Jiaoqu District 郊區 *jiāoqū*	164,233	
Yi'an District 義安區 *yìān qū*	227,493	
Zongyang County 樅陽縣 *zōngyáng xiàn*	469,051	
Chizhou City 池州市 ***chízhōu shì***		**1,342,764**
Guichi District 貴池區 *guìchí qū*	615,274	
Dongzhi County 東至縣 *dōngzhì xiàn*	398,414	
Shitai County 石台縣 *shítái xiàn*	80,612	
Qingyang County 青陽縣 *qīngyáng xiàn*	248,464	
Xuancheng City 宣城市 ***xuānchéng shì***		**2,500,063**
Xuanzhou District 宣州區 *xuānzhōu qū*	671,209	
Ningguo 寧國市 *níngguó shì*	384,644	
Langxi County 郎溪縣 *lángxī xiàn*	311,513	
Guangde County 廣德縣 *guǎngdé xiàn*	499,132	
Jingxian County 涇縣 *jīngxiàn*	275,837	
Jingde County 旌德縣 *jīngdé xiàn*	112,368	
Jixi County 績溪縣 *jìxī xiàn*	138,784	
Xuancheng Economic Development Zone (宣城市經開區 *shìjīng kāiqū*)	106,576	
Huangshan City 黃山市 ***huángshān shì***		**1,330,565**
Tunxi District 屯溪區 *túnxī qū*	291,188	
Huangshan District 黃山區 *huángshān qū*	146,942	
Huizhou District 徽州區 *huīzhōu qū*	96,162	
Shexian County 歙縣 *shèxiàn*	362,962	
Xiuning County 休寧縣 *xiūníng xiàn*	211,456	
Yixian County 黟縣 *yīxiàn*	76,211	
Qimen County 祁門縣 *qímén xiàn*	145,644	
Total		**61,027,171**

[a]六 here is pronounced *lù*

[b]Wuhu county was dissolved, forming Wanzhi district in 2020

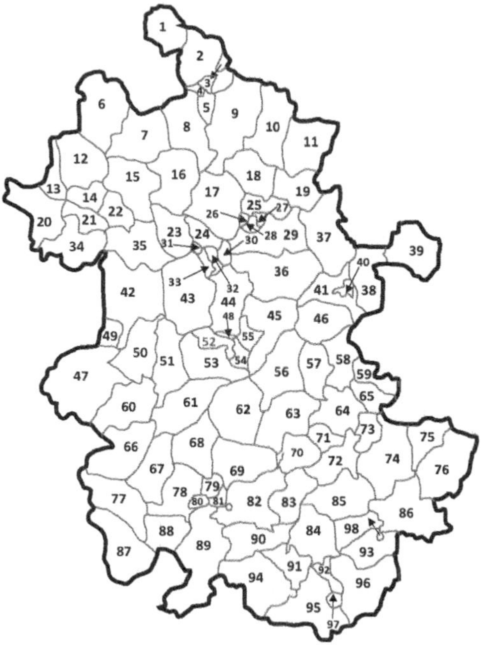

1. Dangshan County
2. Xiaoxian County
3. Duji District
4. Xiangshan District
5. Lieshan District
6. Qiaocheng District
7. Guoyang County
8. Suixi County
9. Yongqiao District
10. Lingbi County
11. Sixian County
12. Taihe County
13. Jieshou City
14. Yingquan District
15. Lixin County
16. Mengcheng County
17. Huaiyuan County
18. Guzhen County
19. Wuhe County
20. Linquan County
21. Yingzhou District
22. Yingdong District
23. Fengtai County
24. Panji District
25. Huaishang District
26. Yuhui District
27. Longzihu District
28. Bengshan District
29. Fengyang County
30. Datong District
31. Bagongshan District
32. Tianjia'an District
33. Xiejiaji District
34. Funan County
35. Yingshan County
36. Dingyuan County
37. Mingguan City
38. Lai'an County
39. Tianchang City
40. Langya District
41. Nanqiao District
42. Huoqiu County
43. Shouxian County
44. Changfeng County
45. Feidong County
46. Quanjiao County
47. Jinzhai County
48. Luyang District
49. Yeji District
50. Yu'an District
51. Jin'an District
52. Shushan District
53. Feixi County
54. Baohe District
55. Yaohai District
56. Chaohu City
57. Hanshan County
58. Hexian County
59. Ma'anshan City: Huashan, Yushan and Bowang Districts
60. Huoshan County
61. Shucheng County
62. Lujiang County
63. Wuwei City
64. Wuhu City
65. Dangtu County
66. Yuexi County
67. Qianshan County
68. Tongcheng City
69. Zongyang County
70. Tongling City
71. Fanchang County
72. Nanling County
73. Wuhu County
74. Xuanzhou District
75. Langxi County
76. Guangde City
77. Taihu County
78. Huaining County
79. Yixiu District
80. Daguan District
81. Yingjiang District
82. Guichi District
83. Qingyang County
84. Huangshan District
85. Jingxian County
86. Ningguo City
87. Susong County
88. Wangjiang County
89. Dongzhi County
90. Shitai County
91. Yixian County
92. Huizhou District
93. Jixi County
94. Qimen County
95. Xiuning County
96. Shexian County
97. Tunxi District
98. Jingde County

Fig. 2.2 Anhui province: subdistricts (Capital city governmental seat: Shushan district). (Map Drawn by the Author, after People's Republic of China, Ministry of Civil Affairs, MCA 2020)

Anhui Province 安徽省 *ānhuī sheng* (Abbreviation: 皖 *wǎn*)

Provincial Capital: Hefei City

Table 2.4 Anhui province: permanent registered (户籍人口 hùjí rénkǒu) populations (MCA 2020)

Name (government seat)	Traditional	Simplified	Population (2012)	Population (2016)	Population (2020)	Area (km^2)
Anhui province	安徽省	安徽省	**68,250,000**	**69,050,000**	**70,830,000**	**139,615**
Hefei City	合肥市	合肥市	7,450,000	7,310,000	7,580,000	11,496
Shushan District (Sanli'an Subdistrict)	蜀山區 (三李庵街道)	蜀山区 (三里庵街道)	1,020,000	1,040,000	990,000	643
Luyang District (Bozhoulu Subdistrict)	廬陽區 (亳州路街道)	庐阳区 (亳州路街道)	610,000	460,000	500,000	139
Yaohai District (Mingguanglu Subdistrict)	瑤海區 (明光路街道)	瑶海区 (明光路街道)	900,000	590,000	670,000	247
Baohe District (Luogang Subdistrict)	包河區 (駱崗街道)	包河区 (骆岗街道)	820,000	510,000	660,000	316
Chaohu City (Woniushan Subdistrict)	巢湖市 (臥牛山街道)	巢湖市 (卧牛山街道)	780,000	890,000	860,000	2082
Changfeng County (Shuihu Town)	長豐縣 (水湖鎮)	长丰县 (水湖镇)	630,000	770,000	780,000	1835
Feidong County (Dianbu Town)	肥東縣 (店埠鎮)	肥东县 (店埠镇)	860,000	1,070,000	1,080,000	2191
Feixi County (Shangpai Town)	肥西縣 (上派鎮)	肥西县 (上派镇)	860,000	790,000	840,000	1695
Lujiang District (Lucheng Town)	廬江縣 (廬城鎮)	庐江县 (庐城镇)	970,000	1,190,000	1,210,000	2,348
Suzhou City	宿州市	宿州市	6,430,000	6,510,000	6,570,000	9787
Yongqiao District (Yongqiao Subdistrict)	埇橋區 (埇橋街道)	埇桥区 (埇桥街道)	1,880,000	1,880,000	1,920,000	2868
Dangshan County (Dangcheng Town)	碭山縣 (碭城鎮)	砀山县 (砀城镇)	1,000,000	1,000,000	1,000,000	1193
Xiaoxian County (Longcheng Town)	蕭縣 (龍城鎮)	萧县 (龙城镇)	1,440,000	1,430,000	1,400,000	1885
Lingbi County (Lingcheng Town)	靈璧縣 (靈城鎮)	灵璧县 (灵城镇)	1,240,000	1,260,000	1,290,000	2054
Sixian County (Sicheng Town)	泗縣 (泗城鎮)	泗县 (泗城镇)	940,000	940,000	960,000	1787
Huaibei City	淮北市	淮北市	2,210,000	2,170,000	2,180,000	2732
Xiangshan District (Xiangnan Subdistrict)	相山區 (相南街道)	相山区 (相南街道)	410,000	410,000	420,000	135

(continued)

Table 2.4 (continued)

Name (government seat)	Traditional	Simplified	Population (2012)	Population (2016)	Population (2020)	Area (km^2)
Duji District (Gaoyue Subdistrict)	杜集區 (高岳街道)	杜集区 (高岳街道)	340,000	340,000	300,000	230
Lieshan District (Yangzhuang Subdistrict)	烈山區 (楊莊街道)	烈山区 (杨庄街道)	350,000	350,000	320,000	380
Suixi County (Suixi Town)	濉溪縣 (濉溪鎮)	濉溪县 (濉溪镇)	1,110,000	1,070,000	1,130,000	1987
Fuyang City	阜陽市	阜阳市	10,120,000	10,360,000	10,710,000	9775
Yingzhou District (Qinghe Subdistrict)	潁州區 (清河街道)	颍州区 (清河街道)	730,000	820,000	890,000	599
Yingdong District (Hedong Subdistrict)	潁東區 (河東街道)	颍东区 (河东街道)	640,000	660,000	670,000	674
Yingquan District (Zhongshi Subdistrict)	潁泉區 (中市街道)	颍泉区 (中市街道)	700,000	730,000	740,000	641
Jieshou City (Dongcheng Subdistrict)	界首市 (東城街道)	界首市 (东城街道)	790,000	790,000	830,000	666
Linquan County (Chengguan Town)	臨泉縣 (城關鎮)	临泉县 (城关镇)	2,200,000	2,250,000	2,300,000	1818
Taihe County (Chengguan Town)	太和縣 (城關鎮)	太和县 (城关镇)	1,710,000	1,750,000	1,770,000	1820
Funan County (Lucheng Town)	阜南縣 (鹿城鎮)	阜南县 (鹿城镇)	1,660,000	1,610,000	1,730,000	1698
Yingshang County (Shencheng Town)	潁上縣 (慎城鎮)	颍上县 (慎城镇)	1,690,000	1,750,000	1,780,000	1859
Bozhou City	亳州市	亳州市	6,020,000	6,220,000	6,570,000	8429
Qiaocheng District (Huaxilou Subdistrict)	譙城區 (花戲樓街道)	谯城区 (花戏楼街道)	1,620,000	1,660,000	1,680,000	2226
Woyang County (Chengguan Subdistrict)	渦陽縣 (城關街道)	涡阳县 (城关街道)	1,500,000	1,610,000	1,700,000	2107
Mengcheng County (Chengguan Subdistrict)	蒙城縣 (城關街道)	蒙城县 (城关街道)	1,320,000	1,350,000	1,450,000	2091
Lixin County (Chengguan Town)	利辛縣 (城關鎮)	利辛县 (城关镇)	1,580,000	1,610,000	1,730,000	2005
Bengbu City	蚌埠市	蚌埠市	3,620,000	3,650,000	3,840,000	5912

(continued)

Table 2.4 (continued)

Name (government seat)	Traditional	Simplified	Population (2012)	Population (2016)	Population (2020)	Area (km²)
Bengshan District (Tianqiao Subdistrict)	蚌山區 (天橋街道)	蚌山区 (天桥街道)	2280,000	280,000	340,000	83
Longzihu District (Jiefang Subdistrict)	龍子湖區 (解放街道)	龙子湖区 (解放街道)	230,000	230,000	170,000	162
Yuhui District (Jincheng Community)	禹會區 (金城社區)	禹会区 (金城社区)	240,000	340,000	360,000	313
Huaishang District (Xiaobengbu Town)	淮上區 (小蚌埠鎮)	淮上区 (小蚌埠镇)	170,000	250,000	280,000	351
Huaiyuan County (Chengguan Town)	懷遠縣 (城關鎮)	怀远县 (城关镇)	1,340,000	1,260,000	1,330,000	2212
Wuhe County (Chengguan Town)	五河縣 (城關鎮)	五河县 (城关镇)	730,000	660,000	690,000	1428
Guzhen County (Chengguan Town)	固鎮縣 (城關鎮)	固镇县 (城关镇)	630,000	630,000	660,000	1363
Huainan City	淮南市	淮南市	2,450,000	3,440,000	3,900,000	5650
Tianjia'an District (Gongyuan Subdistrict)	田家庵區 (公園街道)	田家庵区 (公园街道)	540,000	620,000	580,000	256
Datong District (Datong Subdistrict)	大通區 (大通街道)	大通区 (大通街道)	190,000	190,000	190,000	350
Xiejiaji District (Pingshan Subdistrict)	謝家集區 (平山街道)	谢家集区 (平山街道)	340,000	330,000	310,000	276
Bagongshan District (Xingzhuangzi Subdistrict)	八公山區 (新莊孜街道)	八公山区 (新庄孜街道)	170,000	180,000	150,000	148
Panji District (Tianji Subdistrict)	潘集區 (田集街道)	潘集区 (田集街道)	450,000	400,000	460,000	590
Fengtai County (Chengguan Town)	鳳台縣 (城關鎮)	凤台县 (城关镇)	760,000	690,000	810,000	1044
Shouxian County (Shouchun Town)	壽縣 (壽春鎮)	寿县 (寿春镇)	1,370,000	1,030,000[a]	1,400,000	2986
Chuzhou City	**滁**州市	**滁**州市	4,500,000	4,520,000	4,540,000	13,398
Langya District (Fenghuang Community)	瑯琊區 (鳳凰社區)	琅琊区 (凤凰街道)	270,000	290,000	280,000	161
Nanqiao District (Beimen Community)	南譙區 (北門社區)	南谯区 (北門社区)	270,000	250,000	280,000	1238

(continued)

Table 2.4 (continued)

Name (government seat)	Traditional	Simplified	Population (2012)	Population (2016)	Population (2020)	Area (km^2)
Mingguang City (Mingguang Subdistrict)	明光市 (明光街道)	明光市 (明光街道)	650,000	640,000	640,000	2335
Tianchang City (Tianchang Subdistrict)	天長市 (天長街道)	天长市 (天长街道)	630,000	630,000	630,000	1770
Lai'an County (Xin'an Town)	來安縣 (新安鎮)	来安县 (新安镇)	500,000	500,000	490,000	1481
Quanjiao County (Xianghe Town)	全椒縣 (襄河鎮)	全椒县 (襄河镇)	460,000	460,000	450,000	1572
Dingyuan County (Dingcheng Town)	定遠縣 (定城鎮)	定远县 (定城镇)	970,000	980,000	980,000	2891
Fengyang County (Fucheng Town)	鳳陽縣 (府城鎮)	凤阳县 (府城镇)	750,000	770,000	790,000	1950
Ma'anshan city	馬鞍山市	馬鞍山市	2,280,000	2,290,000	2,290,000	4042
Yushan District (Yushan Subdistrict)	雨山區 (雨山街道)	雨山区 (雨山街道)	270,000	260,000	260,000	164
Huashan District (Huoli Subdistrict)	花山區 (霍里街道)	花山区 (霍里街道)	270,000	380,000	380,000	176
Bowang District (Bowang Town)	博望區 (博望鎮)	博望区 (博望镇)	N/A	190,000	190,000	351
Dangtu County (Gushu Town)	當塗縣 (姑孰鎮)	当涂县 (姑孰镇)	650,000	470,000	480,000	995
Hanshan County (Huanfeng Town)	含山縣 (環峰鎮)	含山县 (环峰镇)	440,000	440,000	450,000	1037
Hexian County (Liyang Town)	和縣 (歷陽鎮)	和县 (历阳镇)	540,000	550,000	540,000	1319
Wuhu City	蕪湖市	芜湖市	3,840,000	3,830,000	3,890,000	5987
Jiujiang District (Guandou Subdistrict)	鳩江區 (官陡街道)	鸠江区 (官陡街道)	360,000	570,000	600,000	820
Yijiang District (Liminlu Subdistrict)	弋江區 (利民路街道)	弋江区 (利民路街道)	230,000	220,000	200,000	154
Sanshan District (Sanshan Subdistrict)	三山區 (三山街道)	三山区 (三山街道)	180,000	190,000	200,000	319
Jinghu District (Xingjiashan Community)	鏡湖區 (邢家山社區)	镜湖区 (邢家山社区)	470,000	460,000	460,000	121
Wuhu County (Wanzhi Town)	蕪湖縣 (灣沚鎮)	芜湖县 (湾沚镇)	350,000	350,000	350,000	667

(continued)

Table 2.4 (continued)

Name (government seat)	Traditional	Simplified	Population (2012)	Population (2016)	Population (2020)	Area (km²)
Fanchang County (Fanyang Town)	繁昌縣 (繁陽鎮)	繁昌县 (繁阳镇)	280,000	280,000	280,000	560
Nanling County (Jishan Town)	南陵縣 (籍山鎮)	南陵县 (籍山镇)	550,000	550,000	550,000	1263
Wuwei City (Wucheng Town)	無為縣 (無城鎮)	无为县 (无城镇)	1,420,000	1,210,000	1,210,000	2042
Tongling City	銅陵市	铜陵市	740,000	170,000	1,710,000	3008
Tongguanshan District (Wusong Community)[b]	銅官山區 (五松社區)	铜官山区 (五松社区)	270,000	N/A	N/A	(30)
Tongguan District (Wumushan Community)	銅官區 (烏木山社區)	铜官区 (乌木山社区)	N/A	370,000	360,000	95
Shizishan District (Lixin Community)[c]	獅子山區 (立新社區)	狮子山区 (立新社区)	100,000	N/A	N/A	(53)
Jiaoqu District (Qiaonan Subdistrict)	郊區 (橋南街道)	郊区 (桥南街道)	70,000	80,000	80,000	260
Tongling County (Wusong Town)	銅陵縣 (五松鎮)	铜陵县 (五松镇)	290,000	N/A	N/A	(876)
Yi'an District (Wusong Town)	義安區 (五松鎮)	义安区 (伍松镇)	N/A	290,000	290,000	845
Zongyang County (Zongyang Town)	樅陽縣 (樅陽鎮)	枞阳县 (枞阳镇)	970,000	960,000	970,000	1808
Anqing City	安慶市	安庆市	6,140,000	5,360,000	5,280,000	13,528
Daguan District (Dekuanlu Subdistrict)	大觀區 (德寬路街道)	大观区 (德宽路街道)	270,000	270,000	260,000	204
Yingjiang District (Yingchenglu Subdistrict)	迎江區 (宜城路街道)	迎江区 (宜城路街道)	210,000	320,000[d]	210,000	207
Yixiu District (Dalongshan Town)	宜秀區 (大龍山鎮)	宜秀区 (大龙山镇)	250,000	280,000	270,000	414
Tongcheng City (Wenchang Subdistrict)	桐城市 (文昌街道)	桐城市 (文昌街道)	750,000	750,000	750,000	1572
Huaining County (Gaohe Town)	懷寧縣 (高河鎮)	怀宁县 (高河镇)	690,000	700,000	710,000	1276
Qianshan City (Meicheng Town)	潛山市 (梅城鎮)	潜山市 (梅城镇)	580,000	580,000	580,000	1688
Taihu County (Jinxi Town)	太湖縣 (晉熙鎮)	太湖县 (晋熙镇)	560,000	570,000	580,000	2040

(continued)

Table 2.4 (continued)

Name (government seat)	Traditional	Simplified	Population (2012)	Population (2016)	Population (2020)	Area (km^2)
Susong County (Fuyu Town)	宿松縣 (孚玉鎮)	宿松县 (孚玉镇)	830,000	850,000	870,000	2394
Wangjiang County (Huayang Town)	望江縣 (華陽鎮)	望江县 (华阳镇)	630,000	630,000	640,000	1357
Yuexi County (Tiantang Town)	岳西縣 (天堂鎮)	岳西县 (天堂镇)	400,000	410,000	410,000	2372
Huangshan City	黃山市	黄山市	1,480,000	1,480,000	1,490,000	9807
Tunxi District (Yudong Subdistrict)	屯溪區 (昱東街道)	屯溪区 (昱东街道)	170,000	180,000	210,000	249
Huangshan District (Gantang Town)	黃山區 (甘棠鎮)	黄山区 (甘棠镇)	160,000	160,000	160,000	1669
Huizhou District (Yansi Town)	徽州區 (岩寺鎮)	徽州区 (岩寺镇)	100,000	100,000	100,000	424
Shexian County (Huicheng Town)	歙縣 (徽城鎮)	歙县 (徽城镇)	490,000	480,000	470,000	2236
Xiuning County (Haiyang Town)	休寧縣 (海陽鎮)	休宁县 (海阳镇)	270,000	280,000	270,000	2125
Yixian County (Biyang Town)	黟縣 (碧陽鎮)	黟县 (碧阳镇)	100,000	90,000	90,000	847
Qimen County (Qishan Town)	祁門縣 (祁山鎮)	祁门县 (祁山镇)	190,000	190,000	190,000	2257
Lu'an City	六安市	六安市	7,040,000	5,770,000	5,890,000	15,452
Jin'an County (Zhongshi Subdistrict)	金安縣 (中市街道)	金安区 (中市街道)	860,000	840,000	880,000	1669
Yu'an District (Pingqiao Township)	裕安區 (平橋鄉)	裕安区 (平桥乡)	1,000,000	1,030,000	1,040,000	1908
Yeji District (Yeji Town)	葉集區 (葉集鎮)	叶集区 (叶集镇)	N/A	170,000	280,000	573
Huoqiu County (Chengguan Town)	霍邱縣 (城關鎮)	霍邱县 (城关镇)	1,790,000	1,700,000	1,640,000	3239
Shucheng County (Chengguan Town)	舒城縣 (城關鎮)	舒城县 (城关镇)	990,000	1,000,000	1,000,000	2110
Jinzhai County (Meishan Town)	金寨縣 (梅山鎮)	金寨县 (梅山镇)	660,000	670,000	680,000	3919
Huoshan County (Hengshan Town)	霍山縣 (衡山鎮)	霍山县 (衡山镇)	370,000	360,000	360,000	2044
Chizhou City	池州市	池州市	1,610,000	1,620,000	1,620,000	8272
Guichi District (Chiyang Subdistrict)	貴池區 (池陽街道)	贵池区 (池阳街道)	660,000	670,000	670,000	2432
Dongzhi County (Yaodu Town)	東至縣 (堯渡鎮)	东至县 (尧渡镇)	550,000	550,000	550,000	3256

(continued)

Table 2.4 (continued)

Name (government seat)	Traditional	Simplified	Population (2012)	Population (2016)	Population (2020)	Area (km²)
Shitai County (Renli Town)	石台縣 (仁里鎮)	石台县 (仁里镇)	110,000	110,000	110,000	1403
Qingyang County (Rongcheng Town)	青陽縣 (蓉城鎮)	青阳县 (蓉城镇)	290,000	290,000	290,000	1181
Xuancheng City	宣城市	宣城市	2,780,000	2,810,000	2,790,000	12,340
Xuanzhou District (Xilin Subdistrict)	宣州區 (西林街道)	宣州区 (西林街道)	860,000	870,000	860,000	2533
Ningguo City (Xijin Subdistrict)	寧國市 (西津街道)	宁国市 (西津街道)	390,000	390,000	380,000	2447
Langxi County (Jianping Town)	郎溪縣 (建平鎮)	郎溪县 (建平镇)	340,000	340,000	350,000	1105
Guangde County (Taozhou Town)	廣德縣 (桃州鎮)	广德县 (桃州镇)	510,000	520,000	520,000	2165
Jingxian County (Jingchuan Town)	涇縣 (涇川鎮)	泾县 (泾川镇)	350,000	360,000	350,000	2059
Jingde County (Jingyang Town)	旌德縣 (旌陽鎮)	旌德县 (旌阳镇)	150,000	150,000	150,000	905
Jixi County (Huayang Town)	績溪縣 (華陽鎮)	绩溪县 (华阳镇)	180,000	180,000	170,000	1126

[a]"103 萬"; possibly a typo
[b]In 2015, merged with Shizishan to form Tongguan district
[c]Dissolved 3 December 2015
[d]Possibly a typo

References

Cao, Shuji. 2005. [Population deaths and their causes in China from 1959 to 1961]. *Chinese Population Studies*. 曹树基. 1959–1961 年中国的人口死亡及其成因. 中国人口科学. No.1. http://ww2.usc.cuhk.edu.hk/PaperCollection/Details.aspx?id=4016.

Chen, Guidi, and Chuntao Wu. 2006. *Will the boat sink the water? The life of China's peasants*. New York: Public Affairs.

Lee, Khoon Choy. 2005. *Pioneers of modern China: Understanding the inscrutable Chinese*. Singapore: World Scientific.

Ministry of Civil Affairs (MCA), People's Republic of China. 2020. [*County/township administration handbook*]. Beijing: China Statistics Press. 中華人民共和國民政部, 中華人民共和國, 鄉鎮行政區劃簡冊.

National Bureau of Statistics (NBS), People's Republic of China. 2021. [Report of the seventh all-national census]. May 19, 2021. 第七次全国人口普查公报. http://www.stats.gov.cn/ztjc/zdtjgz/zgrkpc/dqcrkpc/ggl/202105/t20210519_1817697.html/.

Qiao, Xiaochun, and Huang Yanchun. 2013. [China's situation with cross-provincial floating populations]. *Population & Development*. 喬曉春, 黃衍華. 中國跨省流動人口狀況. 人口與發展 19(1): 13–28.

von Falkenhausen, Lothar. 2005. The E Jun Qi metal tallies. In *Text and ritual in early China*, ed. Martin Kern, 79–123. Seattle: University of Washington Press.

Zhang, Shunan. 2021. [The 2020 per capita income list of residents in various provinces: Shanghai is the richest, and it has risen sharply]. Finance.people.com. January 22. 张澍楠. 2020年各省份居民人均收入榜: 上海最有钱, 这地涨得猛. http://finance.people.com.cn/n1/2021/0122/c1004-32008733.html.

Chapter 3
Beijing City

Abstract Today's center of modern China's political power was, at various times, also the central place of authority in its imperial past, known by different names throughout the centuries. Called 'Cambaluc' by Marco Polo during its Mongol Yuan dynastic rule, this was also a formative time in terms of modern Beijing's urban character, notably the characteristic *hutong* neighborhoods. Invaded by various foreign peoples even before the arrival of European colonial powers, Beijing is now a bustling powerhouse, with the weight of the all-powerful Chinese Communist Party (CCP) at its core, but also carrying impressive weight in terms of economic growth and modern, high-tech industry. In contrast to other, relatively backward provinces in China, the residential population of Beijing is nearly ten million more than its officially-registered (*hukou*) citizens: nearly 22 million according to the 2020 census. With a registered household (*hukou*) population of 13,740,000 in 2020, this highlights the fact that many of Beijing's usual residents are part of China's "floating population."

E. Croddy, *China's Provinces and Populations*,
https://doi.org/10.1007/978-3-031-09165-0_3

Beijing City (Peking; 北京市 *běijīng shì*): Abbreviation 京 (*jīng*) (Fig. 3.1)

Beijing City Population (2020):

1.	**Yanqing District**	**345,671**
2.	**Huairou District**	**441,040**
3.	**Miyun District**	**527,683**
4.	**Changping District**	**2,269,487**
5.	**Shunyi District**	**1,324,044**
6.	**Pinggu District**	**457,313**
7.	**Mentougou District**	**392,606**
8.	**Shijingshan District**	**567,851**
9.	**Haidian District**	**3,133,469**
10.	**Xicheng District**	**1,106,214**
11.	**Dongcheng District**	**708,829**
12.	**Chaoyang District**	**3,452,460**
13.	**Tongzhou District**	**1,840,295**
14.	**Fangshan District**	**1,312,778**
15.	**Fengtai District**	**2,019,764**
16.	**Daxing District**	**1,993,59**

Fig. 3.1 Major Beijing districts. (Drawn by the Author, after People's Republic of China, Ministry of Civil Affairs, MCA 2020)

Beijing: General Impressions

Over a span of three thousand years, Beijing began as a small village into an international, metropolitan, and political powerhouse that we now recognize today. The Beijing dialect, sharp and full of words that end with the classic "er" (兒 *ér*) sound, may be classic, but it is not represented across the rest of mainland China even where standard mandarin is largely spoken.

In addition to being the seat of Chinese Communist Party (CCP) power, one thinks of Beijing's classic hutongs: quaint, narrow streets and alleys that intersect throughout China's history. And, while the number of streets and allies that are considered part of the hutong system number some 1300, the conventional wisdom among Beijing residents is that there are "360 famous Hutongs, and a seemingly endless number of not-so-famous ones."[1]

The doggerel below gives a sense:

胡同歌 (*hútóng gē*) **Song of the Hutong**

胡同胡同, 北京勝景 (*hútóng hútóng, běijīng shèngjǐng*).
Hutong, Hutong, the splendor of Beijing.
元朝初現, 明清益興 (*yuáncháo chūxiàn, míngqīng yìxìng*).
First appeared in the Yuan and Chao dynasties, flourished in the Ming and the Qing;
民族文化, 古都風情 (*mínzú wénhuà, gǔddū fēngqíng*).
A people's culture, the sentiment of the old Capitol.
內涵深邃, 魅力無窮 (*nèihán shēnsuì, mèilì wúqióng*).
It's interior deep, its charm unrivaled.
京韵京俗, 盡在其中 (*jīngyùn jīngsú, jìnzài qízhōng*).
Operatic or plain custom, it has it all.
胡同胡同, 妙若天成 (*hútóng hútóng, miàoruò tiānchéng*).
Hutong, wonders nonpareil.
縱橫交織, 長寬制定 (*zònghéng jiāozhī, chángkuān zhìdìng*).
Crisscrossing network, arranged long and wide;
院稱四合, 路相連通 (*yuànchēng sìhé, lùxiāng liántōng*).
The traditional courtyards and interconnected lanes;
高門顯貴, 陋宅百姓 (*gāomén xiǎnguì, lòuzhái bǎixìng*).
Imposing majestic gates, humble abodes of the *hoi polloi*.
同住胡同, 宛如親朋 (*tóngzhù hútóng, wǎnrú qīnpéng*).
Like friends, they all reside in the Hutong,
胡同胡同, 巧取其名 (*hútóng hútóng, qiǎoqǔ qímíng*).
Hutong, your name captivates.
羅圈, 拐棒, 如狀如形 (*luóquān, guǎibàng, rúzhuàng rúxíng*).
Shaped both bowed and bent;
劉海, 秦老, 因人因姓 (*liúhǎi, qínlǎo, yīnrén yīnxìng*).
The eponymous Liuhai and Qinlao;
錢糧, 察院, 衙署官廳 (*qiánliáng, cháyuàn, yáshǔ guāntīng*).
The Qianliang, Chayuan and Yamen courts;
裱褙, 演樂, 巧匠能工 (*biǎobèi, yǎnlè, qiǎojiàng, nénggōng*).
Pictures, paintings, performers, skillful craftsmen.
胡同胡同, 沐雨櫛風 (*hútóng, hútóng, mùyǔ jiéfēng*).
Hutong, rain, sleet or snow;

---

[1] 有名胡同三百六, 無名胡同似牛毛 *yǒumíng hútóng sānbǎiliù, wúmíng hútóng sì niúmáo.*

代有變遷, 無盡無終 (*dàiyǒu biànqiān, wújìn wúzhōng*).
Generations change and move, endlessly.
崇雅鄙俗, 改號更名 (*chóngyǎ bǐsú, gǎihào gèngmíng*).
Haute couture, Vaudeville, numbers and the names change.
通街展路, 消形滅踪 (*tōngjiē zhǎnlù, xiāoxíng mièzōng*).
Through the opening and expansion of roads, traces are swept away.
並大化小, 新非舊容 (*bìngdà huàxiǎo, xīnfēi jiùróng*).
The large changes to small, out with the old, in with the new.
胡同胡同, 煥然新生 (*hútóng hútóng, huànrán xīnshēng*).
Hutong, you are suddenly all anew.
坑洼塵泥, 一掃而淨 (*kēngwā chénní, yīsǎo érjìng*).
The gutters and dust have all been cleaned.
現代設施, 層出不窮 (*xiàndài shèshī, céngchū bùqióng*).
Modern structures, floors ascending above.
可窺歷史, 可察民風 (*kěkuī lìshǐ, kěchá mínfēng*).
You can see into history, and observe the people's character.
雖多變化, 遠播名聲 (*suīduō biànhuà, yuǎnbō míngshēng*).
Despite all the changes, and the sounds off in the distance;
善加開發, 栽梧引風 (*shànjiā kāifā, zāiwú yǐnfēng*).
Progress and development, the willows draw the wind.
按圖索驥, 游人鐘情 (àntú suǒjì, yóurén zhōngqíng).
Follow the path and regale in the delight of the traveler. (Anon. 1997)

Owing to its Yuan dynasty roots, the word hutong itself (胡同 *hútóng*) is derived from the Mongolian word for a water well, *hottog*, which became Sinicized as (衚衕 *hútòng*). As referenced in the poem above, the hutongs feature the rectangular shaped 四合院 (*sìhéyuàn*) "four-facing courtyard" residences, and the alleyways interconnecting these traditional structures developed into a thriving community of their own. Many of these hutongs, however, are more and more slated to be demolished for modern urban development projects.

Beijing City has been its own provincial-level, self-administered municipality since the fifteenth century (CE). Shanghai, Chongqing and Tianjin cities also share this provincial-level status. The center of Chinese modern political power, namely, the Chinese Communist Party (CCP), is headquartered in Beijing City at Zhongnanhai (中南海 *zhōngnánhǎi*) in Xicheng District (西城區 *xīchéng qū*).

Prehistory

The name and spelling of "Peking" is a throwback to its pronunciation by Westerners based upon a southern Mandarin Chinese patois. 'Peking Man' (*Homo erectus pekinensis*) was famously discovered from a cave site southwest Beijing (Fangshan district 房山區 *fángshān qū*), and a museum is dedicated to the site at Zhoukoudian (周口店 *zhōukǒudiàn*). Unfortunately, the original specimens of Peking man originally unearthed in the 1920s were lost in the beginning of World War II. The eminent anthropologist Kwang-chih Chang (張光直 *Zhāng Guāngzhí*) described the historical events surrounding the loss of Peking Man fossils:

> Although Peking fell to Japanese invaders in 1937, scientists at the Cenezoic Laboratory of the Geological Survey of China were able to continue study at [Zhoukoudian] until 1939. Then, in 1941, decision was reached between the [Chongqing] and American authorities to transport these fossils to the United States for safekeeping, and they were crated and moved to a warehouse in [Qinhuangdao], a small port city northeast of Peking, into the custody of the U.S. Marines. Just at this time Pearl Harbor was attacked. In the resultant confusion the fossils disappeared either form the warehouse or together with a sunken ship and have never been heard of since. (Chang 1977)

Based on more recent dating techniques, analysis now shows Peking Man may have lived some 780,000 years ago. Early on, the (justifiably) sensational nature of the Zhoukoudian excavations led some researchers, both foreign and Chinese, to believe modern humans in China developed *sui generis* (Yen 2014). However, genetic studies have since shown that all peoples of the world (i.e., *Homo sapiens*) derive from a single ancestral line of humans, having migrated from northeast Africa about 60,000 years ago (Meredith 2011).

Early Human Inhabitation

Evidence of clannish social structures going back about 18,000 years at Zhoukoudian includes the discovery in 1930 of a hominid skull in called "Upper Cave Man" (Shandingdong Man 山頂洞人 *shāndǐngdòngrén*). Decades later, some influential researchers in the People's Republic of China (PRC) were determined to show that Upper Cave Man proved the direct nexus between the oldest hominids (*Homo erectus*) in China and modern Chinese (*Homo sapiens*). Indeed, they claimed a "continuous nature between them, the yellow race, and contemporary Chinese people." However, the skull found the upper cave at Zhoukoudian, variously dated back eleven thousand years ago, demonstrated "no continuity between Peking Man and modern Chinese," and, as discussed above, was most likely a modern immigrant from Africa via the Middle East and/or Southeast Asia (Stautman 2001).

Among the oldest known examples of nascent agriculture, to include evidence of millet and its processing with stone tools have been found at Donghulin village (東胡林村 *dōnghúlín cūn*), at Zhaitang Town (齋堂鎮 *zhāitáng zhèn*) in Mentougou District (門頭溝區 *méntóugōu qū*). Evidence of human inhabitation and millet cultivation in this region has been dated to approximately 9.5 to 10 thousand years ago (Yang et al. 2012).

Beijing: Ancient to Modern Populations

The official history of Beijing marks its origins to 1045 BCE. However, depending upon the specific era and dynastic reign, Beijing has had over 20 different names throughout China's history. Its origins begin with a Shang-Zhou dynastic reference to a state called Ji (薊 *jì*) in the eleventh century BCE, its capital being Jicheng City (薊城*jìchéng*). This walled metropolis was located in present-day Guang'anmen (廣安門 *guǎng'ānmén*), in today's Xicheng District. During the Zhou Dynasty (about seventh century BCE), a locality based in today's Liulihe Township (琉璃河鄉 *liúlíhé xiāng*) served as the capital, which later grew to absorb Ji (薊 *jì*) as part of the northern Yan (北燕 *běiyàn*). The state of Yan grew towards the Bohai Gulf, extending through modern-day Liaoning, Jilin, and Heilongjiang provinces. During approximately the Warring States period (ca. 300 BCE), the Yan state capital occupied today's northwest region of Beijing, an area comprising of "over 2000 li [about a thousand kilometers], several hundred thousand men at arms, seven hundred war chariots, six thousand cavalry, and grain stores to last ten years." From this we can extrapolate a civilian population of over 100,000. The Yan state lasted until about 222 BCE, when it was destroyed during the foundation of the Qin 秦 (*qín*) Dynasty under the First Emperor, Shih Huang Ti (i.e., Shihuangdi 始皇帝 *shǐhuángdì*).

Under the Qin 秦 (*qín*), Beijing of today was centered within parts of northeastern commanderies (郡 *jùn*), with Jixian County (薊縣*jìxiàn*) as the seat of Guangyang Prefecture (廣陽郡 *guǎngyáng jùn*). Guangyang and Jixian remained largely intact throughout the Western Han (西漢 *xīhàn*) from ca. 202 BCE – 8 CE, but now within the much larger prefecture of Youzhou 幽州 (*yōuzhōu*), its full title being 幽州刺史部 (*yōuzhōu cìshǐbù*): "Youzhou Inspection Circuit." (刺史 *cìshǐ* was an old term for a provincial governor). By the Eastern Han, Guangyang Prefecture was drawn within borders more closely to that of modern-day Beijing. At this time (ca. 140 CE), its county seat of Jixian had a population of 280,600. By 281 CE, Guangyang was renamed the state of Yan (燕國 *yànguó*), and later renamed again Yan Prefecture (燕郡 *yànjùn*) in 327 CE. Yet another name for the area that includes today's Beijing city (plus parts of Hebei and Tianjin city) was Zhuo Prefecture (琢郡 *zhuójùn*) in 612 CE. By the Tang dynasty, Youzhou-subordinate Jicheng City was further subdivided into a smaller county of over 60,000 people (781 CE).

In 938 CE, the Emperor Taizong of Liao (太宗耶律德光 *tàizōngyé lǜdéguāng*) elevated You Prefecture into a provincial capital, and by 1012 the Liao changed the name to Xijin Prefecture (析津府 *xījīnfǔ*), drawn within the larger administrative sector of Nanjing Dao (南京道 *nánjīngdào*). Then, a district called Yanjing (燕京 *yànjīng*) became the progenitor of modern Beijing. By 1113, this area was named Nanjing (南京 *nánjīng*). Confusingly, Nanjing means "southern capital," as opposed to the modern-day Beijing which means "northern capital." The reason for this is that the northern-based peoples, the Khitan (契丹*qìdān*), who invaded China and established the Liao (遼*liáo*) dynasty (ca. 1000 CE), saw this capital city as being "southern" from their own (northern) geographic perspective.[2] In the event, the larger Nanjing area had at this time a population of about 583,000, while the Yanjing urban city district had 158,000 people.

[2] Parenthetically, the name of this nomadic tribe, the Khitan (probably a related Mongolian group) is where Russian and other languages derive their term for China (Китай = Khitai), and is the etymological root for the old English name for China, 'Cathay.'

Thus, China's history is typified by various "barbarian" peoples, with their origins stretching across Eurasian steppes who frequently contested with rival Chinese dynastic groups. This was especially true in the case of Beijing and its environs. In the twelfth century, yet one more northern ethnic group came to rule, the Jurchens (女真 *nǚzhēn*). These Tungusic tribes have their ethnic origins in Tunguska in the eastern part of Russian Siberia, its southernmost representatives inhabiting modern-day Ha'erbin (Harbin City) in "Manchuria." (Manchurians, or Manzu 滿族*mǎnzú*, still form the fourth largest ethnic minority in China.)

When the Prince of Hailing (海陵王 *hǎilíng wáng*), the fourth Jin emperor, declared that Yanjing be expanded, he established a true "capital" in today's Beijing called "Zhongdu" (中都 *zhōngdū*, "Central Capital") in 1153. At the same time, Xijin Prefecture (析津府 *xījīnfǔ*) was changed to Daxing Prefecture (大興府 *dàxīngfǔ*). The region formerly known as Yanjing subsequently became the political, economic, and cultural center of northern China. One source posits that, in 1207, Zhongdu had a population of 400,000. However, according to researchers Chen Xibo and Han Guanghui, in 1207 the population of the main Zhongdu district was home to 839,576 individuals (Chen and Guanghui 2008). If one wants to locate the origins of the Jin dynasty capital of Zhongdu today, one starts at the densely-populated Xicheng District (西城區 *xīchéng qū*). Historical remnants of the original Jin Dynasty (金中都 *jīnzhōngdū*) walls and other historical artifacts are on display at the Beijing Liao and Jin Dynasty City Wall Museum,[3] located near Beijing's Fengtai district.

Conquered by the Mongols

Despite having an impressive wall fortification, stretching about 28 km surrounding the city with ramparts of about 12 meters in height, the capital Zhongdu ultimately fell to a Mongolian siege (1215–1216). This led to large-scale slaughter and starvation of its inhabitants. One source memorably described the Mongolian sacking of Zhongdu thusly:

> By the summer of 1215 there were reports of cannibalism, and in June the Jin commander abandoned his post and fled to join the [Jurchen] emperor in Kaifeng. The city surrendered soon afterwards, and was thoroughly sacked and burned. A disinterested and therefore unbiased eyewitness reported several months later that the bones of the slaughtered formed white mountains, and the soil was still greasy with human fat. (Turnbull 2003)

By 1272, and with the formal establishment of the Yuan dynasty under Kublai Khan, the capital was renamed (in Chinese) the "Great Capital Circuit" (大都路 (*dàdūlù*) or simply "Dadu" (大都 *dàdū* or Daidu). This magnificent city (population of about 900,000) made a big impression upon the Venetian itinerant Marco Polo. In the Mongolian language it was known as Khanbaliq (汗八里 *hànbālǐ*, "City of Khan"), and was thus rendered 'Cambaluc,' per Marco Polo's contemporary account (ca. 1290):

[3] 北京遼金城垣博物館 *běijīng liáojīn chéngyuán bówùguǎn.*

> You must know that for three months of the year, to wit December, January and February, the Great [Khan] resides in the capital city of Cathay, which is called CAMBALUC, [and which is at the north-eastern extremity of the country]. In that city stands his great Palace, and now I will tell you what it is like. It is enclosed all round by a great wall forming a square, each side of which is a mile in length; that is to say, the whole compass thereof is four miles. This you may depend on; it is also very thick, and a good ten paces in height, whitewashed and loopholed all round. (Polo, 1993)

By 1349, Dadu had grown to a population of 834,000. With the ascendence of the Ming dynasty, in 1368 the city was renamed Beiping (北平 *běipíng*). At that time the city had a population of about one million (Gao 2003). However, this was also a period of repeated uprisings (having begun with devastating floods in 1351), open warfare, and general mayhem, leading to massive civilian losses (mostly by flight or violence we are unsure). Beiping in ca. 1375 dropped to a total population of 143,000 (this included military personnel). After moving from Nanjing (that is, in the south) to establish the new capital in Beiping (now called Jingshi 京師 *jīngshī*) in 1421, its population began to increase dramatically. In 1629 Beijing had a population of about 700,000, but once again this fell dramatically to 515,000 during the end of the Ming and beginning of the Qing Dynasty (1647).

The Death of Matteo Ricci, S.J. in Beijing—And His Legacy 4.10

Although he was not the only Christian missionary making inroads into China, Matteo Ricci (Chinese name 利瑪竇 *lì mǎdòu*), an Italian Jesuit who first began converting Chinese souls in Guangdong province in 1583, is among the most famous. Like other missionaries of that time, in an attempt to gain favor and access to a closed-off empire, Ricci gave the mandarins in charge knowledge of recent Western scientific and technological developments. Although Ricci's Chinese interlocutors were nonetheless disappointed that he had no secret alchemical knowledge, such as the ability to turn cinnabar (mercury) into silver, Ricci made quite a splash, notably with his excellent cartography skills. Indeed, until Ricci published his first Chinese-language map in 1584, China was largely ignorant of the rest of the world, especially that of the geography of places that Europe had catalogued with its most recent travels of exploration. This included the wider view of the Earth's spherical shape, its main land and water masses, the five continents, even down to the basic descriptions of foreign countries (Ch'en and Ricci 1939). Matteo Ricci used this and other means to extend his missionary work from the relative backwaters of southern China, and, ultimately, secure a meeting with the Emperor Wanli (萬曆帝 *wànlì dì*; r. 1572–1620) himself in Beijing.

Unfortunately, during the key years during which Ricci sought approval for travel to Peking, there was a foreign policy crisis underway that made it even more difficult for foreigners. From 1592–1598, the Japanese warlord Toyotomi Hideyoshi (豊臣秀吉 *xìnchén xiùjí*) had undertaken his invasion of neighboring Korea, making China worry that it could be next on the Daimyo's list. The Ming empire had no time for Westerners who, for all it knew, could be the source of all kinds of intrigue. But Ricci never gave up on his efforts to reach the imperial palace, and Ricci made perilous riverine journeys along the imperial canal. using it to travel from Hangzhou to Beijing. Much to his chagrin and frustration (not to mention his own financial savings), Ricci saw that the empire's canals were monopolized by unscrupulous, imperial eunuch navigators (Laven 2011). Finally arriving in Beijing in 1601, and having been given permission to enter the imperial palace, he still was unable to gain a personal audience with the Wanli Emperor. However, in one sense Ricci did make his physical presence known: a six-panel reproduction of his Map of the World, each section measuring some six feet was put on display inside the imperial palace (Spence 1984). Ricci died in Beijing on May 11, 1610.

Ricci's reputation is, justifiably, one of an enlightened, diplomatic, and indefatigable man of letters, courageously exploring the hitherto unknown world of Ming dynastic lands, while sharing *terra incognita* of the outer world with the Chinese. In translating languages back and forth, not only religious texts but philosophical, mathematical, and geographical publications, Ricci is also remembered by Chinese scholars with great respect and admiration. (A small but important example, Ricci is singularly responsible for latinizing the name 'Confucius' from the Chinese 孔夫子 *kǒngfūzǐ*). Following Ricci's death in China, no less than the governor of Beijing wrote the following as his epitaph: "To he who came to China, attracted by our justice system, and to the author of so many books." As Mary Laven succinctly concludes: "For the rulers of China, Ricci was to become the acceptable face of the west" (Laven 2011).

However, one also must confront the practical limits of his legacy: while the literati (scholar-officials) were quite amazed by Ricci's erudite knowledge of the Chinese classics as well as his scientific acumen, not all were convinced of Ricci's brilliance or motives, notably late Ming scholars such as Wei Jun (魏濬 *wèi jùn*; b. 1553), who complained that his Map of the World put China.

> not in the center but slightly to the west and inclined to the north. This is altogether far from the truth, for China should be in the center of the world, which we can prove by the single fact that we can see the North Star resting at the zenith of the heaven at midnight. How can China be treated like a small unimportant country, and placed slightly to the north as in this map? (Ch'en and Ricci 1939)

China's views of Ricci's and his foreign ideas got even worse by the Manchu Qing dynasty. Among the influential, educated elite in the eighteenth century, Ricci's purported knowledge of the outside world was lambasted as nonsense. A Qing dynasty imperial-sponsored compendium of knowledge said that Ricci's "description of the five continents is nothing more than a wild fabulous story, and his other statements of similar nature are probably copied from some other source without proper acknowledgement" (Ch'en and Ricci 1939). Thus, much of what Ricci tried to import to the Chinese, something as secular as the most recent estimations of the charted world, was corrupted by local Chinese scholars and was eventually lost in time. Following the Manchu invasion decades later (ca. 1644+), China would continue to remain insular, xenophobic, and refractive to Western concepts, critically in those areas that could have strengthened the Chinese state. Slow to modernize and to take an objective stock of what was happening outside its walls, China ultimately paid the cost, not the least of which being the humiliating foreign invasions of the nineteenth century.

Foreign Occupation of Peking: A Chapter in China's "National Humiliation"

It is difficult to imagine now, but China's venal and weakly-organized imperial structure of the Qing during the Second Opium War was such that two colonial powers, England and France, were able to essentially occupy Beijing (including the Forbidden City) in 1860. Infamously, the foreign invaders also burned down the Summer Palace (頤和園 *yíhéyuán*). This shameful episode underscored two major factors: the rapaciousness of foreign colonial powers in their treatment of China, but also the woefully corrupt and inept imperial court that was unable (or unwilling) to put up a sufficient defense. It is then more understandable that, under such baleful leadership, a relatively small uprising over a thousand miles to the south was able to successfully overthrow the Qing dynasty in 1911.

Revolutionary China

In 1910, the year before the Chinese revolution against the Qing dynasty, Beijing had a population of 812,336. A couple of years later, no doubt due to societal disruptions and civilian flight, Beijing had a population of 725,000. In 1925, due to an expansion of Beijing's territory, the population increased further to 1,266,148. Finally, after the Chinese Communist Party (CCP) came to power in 1949, the PRC capital was officially changed to Beijing, with a population numbering 2,030,986.

The Walls of Beijing

In 1949, when the CCP gained control, Beijing still possessed its inner and outer city walls dating back to the Ming dynasty (ca. 1400 CE). To allow for road and subway construction, Mao Zedong ordered the destruction of these historic treasures, and nearly all were demolished in the mid- and late-1950s. As to his original motivations for the tearing down of centuries-old ramparts, Mao Zedong's own words suffice. Referring to Zhang Xiruo (張奚若 *zhāng xīruò*), a minister of education who famously opposed the destruction of Beijing's city walls, Mao Zedong responded to criticisms during the Nanning conference in January 1958:

> Zhang Xiruo criticizes me for 'delusions of grandeur, eager for quick success and instant benefit, disparaging the past and having blind faith in the future.' … If we don't despise the past and believe in the future, what hope can we have? … As for having no love of antiquities, this is a question of favoring advancement or backwardness. Antiquities are somewhat backward, aren't they? What comes later typically supersedes what came before, rather than the other way around. It's not that antiquities can't be appreciated, just not too much. When Beijing dismantled its decorative archways and knocked holes in the city walls, Zhang Xiruo bawled his head off—this is a political issue. (Yang 2012)

Today, remnants of the 500-year old fortifications still survive, including the Ming City Wall Ruins Park, in Dongcheng District (東城區 *dōngchéng qū*).

Beijing: Political and Economic Powerhouse

From 1949–1951, Beijing's central and neighboring sectors were literally reduced to numbers on a map, simply named "District No. 1" through "District No. 16" (第十六區 *dìshíliùqū*, etc.). By 1955, some of the now more familiar Beijing wards were mapped and renamed, such as Haidian and Fengtai. Commensurate with its status as China's modern, post-civil war capital, Beijing City's borders expanded dramatically from 1955 onward. Most of Beijing's territorial growth expanded northward at the expense of Hebei province, crossing the Shahe River (PRC 2001).

During the 1950s, Soviet advisors actively promoted Beijing as an industrial base. While still holding on to state-owned heavy industries, the rapid growth of Beijing's economy really took off from 1978 onward, the fastest rate continuing through the early 1990s. Today, in addition to legacy "rust belt" state owned enterprises, as well as defense and aerospace concerns, Beijing's northwest region is also considered the Silicon Valley of the PRC. With the powerful influence of being the country's political and cultural center, it is no wonder that Beijing ranks up there with Shanghai in terms of economic might, both cities representing more than $1.6 trillion in national industrial output. And whereas Shanghai ranks tenth in gross domestic product (GDP) out of mainland China's 31 provinces and major cities, Beijing is 13th at US $56 billion (2020). It is noteworthy that Beijing is second overall (behind Shanghai) in terms of per capita income, approximately USD $10,800 (Zhang 2021).

The Future Jing-Jin-Ji (京津冀 *jīng-jīn-jì*) Regional Mega-Project

In March 2014, China announced an initiative that would incorporate areas including Beijing Tianjin and Hebei:

> President Xi Jinping, head of the leading group for overall reform, called for integrated and coordinated development of Beijing and the two neighboring provincial areas during a symposium after listening to work reports delivered by officials from Beijing, Tianjin and Hebei province… (Zhao and Zheng 2014)

The ultimate goal of the Jing-Jin-Ji—that is, Jing = 京, i.e., Beijing; Jin = 津 i.e., Tianjin; and Ji = 冀 i.e., Hebei—project is to develop a northern, regional economic hub analogous to the southern China economic model that began in the 1980s. The combined areas of the Jing-Jin-Ji region will include a population well above 130 million. This announcement of this planned "megalopolis" in 2014 spurred rumors that the Hebei provincial city of Baoding would eventually become an "auxiliary capital." In the event, with Tianjin City being combined with Beijing, along with the addition of Hebei Province's Baoding, Langfang, Tangshan, Shijiazhuang, Cangzhou, Qinhuangdao, Chengde, Zhangjiakou, Hengshui, Xingtai, and Hantan cities, the envisioned geographical area will include some 218,000 square kilometers—roughly the size of Hunan Province. Early conceptual plans aim to have much of the Jing-Jin-Ji Region (京津冀區域 *jīng-jīn-jì qūyù*) fully integrated by 2030.

The phenomenal growth of Beijing can be seen in tables below, starting with background data from 1990 (Table 3.1), census results from 2010 and 2020 (Table 3.2), and detailed subdistrict data is also provided in Table 3.3. One can also compare the census numbers with the family registered (*hukou*) data in Table 3.4.

Table 3.4 shows the *hukou* (family registered) populations based on PRC Ministry of Civil Affairs data. (Districts listed directly under major cities are government seats, as are those in parentheses). One can compare these data with the census (usual residential populations based on 2010 and 2020 censuses in Tables 3.2 and 3.3.

Table 3.1 Census (Residential 常住人口 chángzhù rénkǒu) data for Beijing City, 1990 (NBS 2001)

Beijing city district and counties: 1990	Population
Dongcheng District 東城區 *dōngchéng qū*	606,203
Xicheng District 西城區 *xīchéng qū*	755,813
Chongwen District 崇文區 *chóngwén qū*	417,651
Xuanwu District 宣武區 *xuānwǔ qū*	556,877
Chaoyang District 朝陽區 *cháoyáng qū*	1,448,441
Fengtai District 豐台區 *fēngtái qū*	789,151
Shijingshan District 石景山區 *shíjǐngshān qū*	308,811
Haidian District 海澱區 *hǎidiàn qū*	1,442,776
Mentougou District 門頭溝區 *méntóugōu qū*	270,343
Fangshan District 房山區 *fángshān qū*	766,360
Changping County 昌平縣 *chāngpíng xiàn*	433901
Shunyi County 順義縣 *shùnyì xiàn*	548,345
Tongxian County 通縣 *tōngxiàn*	602,597
Daxing County 大興縣 *dàxìng xiàn*	523,603
Pinggu County 平谷縣 *pínggǔ xiàn*	386,234
Huairou County 懷柔縣 *huáiróu xiàn*	261,448
Miyun County 密雲縣 *mìyún xiàn*	426,454
Yanqing County 延慶縣 *yánqìng xiàn*	274,406
Total	**10,819,414**

Table 3.2 Census (Residential 常住人口 *chángzhù rénkǒu*) data, Beijing, 2010 and 2020 (NBS 2021)

Beijing city districts	Population (2010)	Population (2020)
Dongcheng District 東城區 *dōngchéng qū*	919,000	708,829
Xicheng District 西城區 *xīchéng qū*	1,243,000	1,106,214
Chaoyang District 朝陽區 *cháoyáng qū*	3,545,000	3,452,460
Fengtai District 豐台區 *fēngtái qū*	2,112,000	2,019,764
Shijingshan District 石景山區 *shíjǐngshān qū*	616,000	567,851
Haidian District 海澱區 *hǎidiàn qū*	3,281,000	3,133,469
Mentougou District 門頭溝區 *méntóugōu qū*	290,000	392,606
Fangshan District 房山區 *fángshān qū*	945,000	1,312,778
Tongzhou District 通州區 *tōngzhōu qū*	1,184,000	1,840,295
Shunyi District 順義區 *shùnyì qū*	877,000	1,324,044
Changping District 昌平區 *chāngpíng qū*	1,661,000	2,269,487
Daxing District 大興區 *dàxìng qū*	1,365,000	1,993,591
Huairou District 懷柔區 *huáiróu qū*	373,000	441,040
Pinggu District 平谷區 *pínggǔ qū*	416,000	457,313
Miyun District 密雲區 *mìyún qū*	468,000	527,683
Yanqing District 延慶區 *yánqìng qū*	317,000	345,671
Total	**19,612,000**	**21,893,095**

Table 3.3 Population data of Beijing and subordinate districts (NBS 2021)

Cities and subordinate sectors, population (2020 census)	Subordinate subdistrict populations (2020)	Total population (2020)
Dongcheng District 東城區 ***dōngchéng qū***		**708,829**
Donghuamen Subdistrict 東華門街道 *dōnghuámén jiēdào*	38,090	
Jingshan Subdistrict 景山街道 *jǐngshān jiēdào*	25,374	
Jiaodaokou Subdistrict 交道口街道 *jiāodàokǒu jiēdào*	31,951	
Andingmen Subdistrict 安定門街道 *āndìngmén jiēdào*	32,173	
Beixinqiao Subdistrict 北新橋街道 *běixīnqiáo jiēdào*	55,449	
Dongsi Subdistrict 東四街道 *dōngsì jiēdào*	33,670	
Chaoyangmen subdistrict 朝陽門街道 *zhāoyángmén jiēdào*	30,473	
Jianguomen subdistrict 建國門街道 *jiànguómén jiēdào*	33,094	
Dongzhimen Subdistrict 東直門街道 *dōngzhímén jiēdào*	46,712	
Hepingli Subdistrict 和平里街道 *hépínglǐ jiēdào*	102,227	
Qianmen Subdistrict 前門街道 *qiánmén jiēdào*	9081	

(continued)

Table 3.3 (continued)

Cities and subordinate sectors, population (2020 census)	Subordinate subdistrict populations (2020)	Total population (2020)
Chongwenmenwai Subdistrict 崇文門外街道 *chóngwénménwài jiēdào*	44,545	
Donghuashi Subdistrict 東花市街道 *dōnghuāshì jiēdào*	47,864	
Longtan Subdistrict 龍潭街道 *lóngtán jiēdào*	53,930	
Tiyuguanlu Subdistrict 體育館路街道 *tǐyùguǎnlù jiēdào*	31,977	
Tiantan Subdistrict 天壇街道 *tiāntán jiēdào*	27,429	
Yongdingmen Subdistrict 永定門街道 *yǒngdìngmén jiēdào*	64,790	
Xicheng District 西城區 ***xīchéng qū***		**1,106,214**
Desheng Subdistrict 德勝街道 *déshèng jiēdào*	116,338	
Shichahai Subdistrict 什刹海街道 *shíchàhǎi jiēdào*	75,447	
Xichang Anjie Subdistrict 西長安街街道 *xīchángānjiē jiēdào*	36,645	
Dashilan (Dashilar) Subdistrict 大柵欄街道 *dàshílànr jiēdào*	28,985	
Tianqiao Subdistrict 天橋街道 *tiānqiáo jiēdào*	34,427	
Xinjiekou Subdistrict 新街口街道 *xīnjiēkǒu jiēdào*	84,866	
Jinrongjie Subdistrict 金融街街道 *jīnróngjiē jiēdào*	54,849	
Chunshu Subdistrict 椿樹街道 *chūnshù jiēdào*	27,417	
Taoranting Subdistrict 陶然亭街道 *táorántíng jiēdào*	42,231	
Zhanlanlu Subdistrict 展覽路街道 *zhǎnlǎnlù jiēdào*	114,831	
Yuetan Subdistrict 月壇街道 *yuètán jiēdào*	97,771	
Guang'anmennei Subdistrict 廣安門內街道 *guǎng'ānménnèi jiēdào*	60,318	
Niujie Subdistrict 牛街街道 *niújiē jiēdào*	51,410	
Baizhifang Subdistrict 白紙坊街道 *báizhǐfāng jiēdào*	82,022	
Guang'anmenwai Subdistrict 廣安門外街道 *guǎng'ānménwài jiēdào*	198,657	
Chaoyang District 朝陽區 ***cháoyáng qū***		**3,452,460**
Jianwai Subdistrict 建外街道 *jiànwài jiēdào*	36,414	
Chaowai Subdistrict 朝外街道 *zhāowài jiēdào*	33,212	
Hujialou Subdistrict 呼家樓街道 *hūjiālóu jiēdào*	53,018	
Sanlitun Subdistrict 三里屯街道 *sānlǐtún jiēdào*	32,347	
Zuojiazhuang Subdistrict 左家莊街道 *zuǒjiāzhuāng jiēdào*	70,245	
Xiangheyuan Subdistrict 香河園街道 *xiānghéyuán jiēdào*	43,002	
Hepingjie Subdistrict 和平街街道 *hépíngjiē jiēdào*	81,180	
Anzhen Subdistrict 安貞街道 *ānzhēn jiēdào*	57,016	
Yayuncun (Asian Games Village) Subdistrict 亞運村街道 *yàyùncūn jiēdào*	67,745	

(continued)

Table 3.3 (continued)

Cities and subordinate sectors, population (2020 census)	Subordinate subdistrict populations (2020)	Total population (2020)
Xiaoguan Subdistrict 小關街道 *xiǎoguān jiēdào*	61,966	
Jiuxianqiao Subdistrict 酒仙橋街道 *jiǔxiānqiáo jiēdào*	63,910	
Maizidian Subdistrict 麥子店街道 *màizǐdiàn jiēdào*	30,143	
Tuanjiehu Subdistrict 團結湖街道 *tuánjiéhú jiēdào*	32,091	
Liulitun Subdistrict 六里屯街道 *liùlǐtún jiēdào*	75,229	
Balizhuang Subdistrict 八里莊街道 *bālǐzhuāng jiēdào*	98,084	
Shuangjing Subdistrict 雙井街道 *shuāngjǐng jiēdào*	93,962	
Jinsong Subdistrict 勁松街道 *jìnsōng jiēdào*	103,316	
Panjiayuan Subdistrict 潘家園街道 *pānjiāyuán jiēdào*	100,272	
Fatou Subdistrict 垡頭街道 *fátóu jiēdào*	78,952	
Nanmofang Region 南磨房地區 *nánmófáng dìqū*	127,268	
Gaobeidian Region 高碑店地區 *gāobēidiàn dìqū*	109,631	
Jiangtai Region 將台地區 *jiāngtái dìqū*	53,714	
Taiyangying Region 太陽營地區 *tàiyángyíng dìqū*	86,935	
Datun Subdistrict 大屯街道 *dàtún jiēdào*	132,457	
Wangjing Subdistrict 忘京街道 *wàngjīng jiēdào*	146,220	
Xiaohongmen Region 小紅門地區 *xiǎohóngmén dìqū*	83,675	
Shibalidian Region 十八里店地區 *shíbālǐdiàn dìqū*	178,177	
Pingfang Region 平房地區 *píngfáng dìqū*	85,581	
Dongfeng Region 東風地區 *dōngfēng dìqū*	63236	
Aoyuncun (Olympic Village) Subdistrict 奧運村街道 *àoyùncūn jiēdào*	109,688	
Laiguangying Region 來廣營地區 *láiguǎngyíng dìqū*	163,970	
Changying Region 常營地區 *chángyíng dìqū*	113,891	
Sanjianfang Region 三間房地區 *sānjiānfáng dìqū*	109,672	
Guanzhuang Region 管莊地區 *guǎnzhuāng dìqū*	93,273	
Jinzhan Region 金盞地區*jīnzhǎn dìqū*	82,756	
Sunhe Region 孫河地區 *sūnhé dìqū*	31,288	
Cuigezhuang Region 崔格莊地區 *cuīgézhuāng dìqū*	107,029	
Dongba Region 東壩地區 *dōngbà dìqū*	124,163	
Heizhuanghu Region 黑莊戶地區 *hēizhuānghù dìqū*	49,983	
Dougezhuang Region 豆各莊地區 *dòugèzhuāng dìqū*	53,766	
Wangsiying Region 王四營地區 *wángsìyíng dìqū*	54,679	
Donghu Subdistrict 東湖街道 *dōnghú jiēdào*	62,467	
Shoudu (Capital) Airport Subdistrict 首都機場街道 *shǒudūjīcháng jiēdào*	16,837	
Fengtai District 豐台區 *fēngtái qū*		**2,019,764**

(continued)

Table 3.3 (continued)

Cities and subordinate sectors, population (2020 census)	Subordinate subdistrict populations (2020)	Total population (2020)
You'anmen Subdistrict 右安門街道 *yòuānmén jiēdào*	73,499	
Taipingqiao Subdistrict 太平橋街道 *tàipíngqiáo jiēdào*	74,275	
Xiluoyuan Subdistrict 西羅園街道 *xīluóyuán jiēdào*	83,815	
Dahongmen Subdistrict 大紅門街道 *dàhóngmén jiēdào*	177,946	
Nanyuan Subdistrict 南苑街道 *nányuàn jiēdào*	61,926	
Donggaodi Subdistrict 東高地街道 *dōnggāodì jiēdào*	42,705	
Dongtiejiangying Subdistrict 東鐵匠營街道 *dōngtiějiàngyíng jiēdào*	152,873	
Lugouqiao (Marco Polo Bridge) Subdistrict 盧溝橋街道 *lúgōuqiáo jiēdào*	223,304	
Fengtai Subdistrict 豐台街道 *fēngtái jiēdào*	137,290	
Xincun Subdistrict 新村街道 *xīncūn jiēdào*	204,697	
Changxindian Subdistrict 長辛店街道 *chángxīndiàn jiēdào*	85,636	
Yungang Subdistrict 雲崗街道 *yúngǎng jiēdào*	34,537	
Fangzhuang Region 方莊地區 *fāngzhuāng dìqū*	74,999	
Wanpingcheng Region 宛平城地區 *wǎnpíngchéng dìqū*	46,208	
Majiapu Subdistrict 馬家堡街道 *mǎjiāpù jiēdào*	111,470	
Heyi Subdistrict 和義街道 *héyì jiēdào*	40,108	
Lugouqiao (Marco Polo Bridge) Region 盧溝橋地區 *lúgōuqiáo dìqū*	112,087	
Huaxiang Region 花鄉地區 *huāxiāng dìqū*	119,171	
Nanyuan Region 南苑地區 *nányuàn dìqū*	59,408	
Changxindian Town 長辛店鎮 *chángxīndiàn zhèn*	44,358	
Wangzuo Town 王佐鎮 *wángzuǒ zhèn*	59,452	
Shijingshan District 石景山區 ***shíjǐngshān qū***		**567,851**
Babaoshan Subdistrict 八寶山街道 *bābǎoshān jiēdào*	61,211	
Laoshan Subdistrict 老山街道 *lǎoshān jiēdào*	40,023	
Bajiao Subdistrict 八角街道 *bājiǎo jiēdào*	110,929	
Gucheng Subdistrict 古城街道 *gǔchéng jiēdào*	67,685	
Pingguoyuan Subdistrict 蘋果園街道 *píngguǒyuán jiēdào*	97,543	
Jindingjie Subdistrict 金頂街街道 *jīndǐngjiē jiēdào*	67,734	
Guangning Subdistrict 廣寧街道 *guǎngníng jiēdào*	14,684	
Wulituo Subdistrict 五里坨街道 *wǔlǐtuó jiēdào*	41,248	
Lugu Subdistrict 魯谷街道 *lǔgǔ jiēdào*	66,794	
Haidian District 海澱區 ***hǎidiàn qū***		**3,133,469**
Wanshoulu Subdistrict 萬壽路街道 *wànshòulù jiēdào*	121,453	

(continued)

Table 3.3 (continued)

Cities and subordinate sectors, population (2020 census)	Subordinate subdistrict populations (2020)	Total population (2020)
Yongdinglu Subdistrict 永定路街道 *yǒngdìnglù jiēdào*	90,879	
Yangfangdian Subdistrict 羊坊店街道 *yángfāngdiàn jiēdào*	120,302	
Ganjiakou Subdistrict 甘家口街道 *gānjiākǒu jiēdào*	117,946	
Balizhuang Subdistrict 八里莊街道 *bālǐzhuāng jiēdào*	133,400	
Zizhuyuan Subdistrict 紫竹院街道 *zǐzhúyuàn jiēdào*	129,367	
Beixiaguan Subdistrict 北下關街道 *běixiàguān jiēdào*	146,366	
Beitaipingzhuang Subdistrict 北太平莊街道 *běitàipíngzhuāng jiēdào*	163,920	
Xueyuanlu Subdistrict 學院路街道 *xuéyuànlù jiēdào*	226,315	
Zhongguancun Subdistrict 中關村街道 *zhōngguāncūn jiēdào*	130,672	
Haidian Subdistrict 海澱街道 *hǎidiàn jiēdào*	123,191	
Qinglongqiao Subdistrict 青龍橋街道 *qīnglóngqiáo jiēdào*	84,221	
Qinghe Subdistrict 清河街道 *qīnghé jiēdào*	147,395	
Huayuanlu Subdistrict 花園路街道 *huāyuánlù jiēdào*	139,362	
Xisanqi Subdistrict 西三旗街道 *xīsānqí jiēdào*	157,643	
Malianwa Subdistrict 馬連洼街道 *mǎliánwā jiēdào*	119,022	
Tiancunlu Subdistrict 田村路街道 *tiáncūnlù jiēdào*	108,088	
Shangdi Subdistrict 上地街道 *shàngdì jiēdào*	67,139	
Wanliu Region (Haidian Village) 萬柳地區 *wànliǔ dìqū* (海澱村 *hǎidiàn cūn*)	2022	
Dongsheng Region 東昇地區 *dōngshēng dìqū*	58,151	
Puguang Subdistrict 曝光街道 *pùguāng jiēdào*	86,181	
Wenquan Region 溫泉地區 *wēnquán dìqū*	69,165	
Sijiqing Region 四季青地區 *sìjìqīng dìqū*	162,700	
Xibeiwang Region 西北旺地區 *xīběiwàng dìqū*	164,795	
Sujiatuo Region 蘇家坨地區 *sūjiātuó dìqū*	78,235	
Shangzhuang Region 上莊地區 *shàngzhuāng dìqū*	71,554	
Mentougou District 門頭溝區 ***méntóugōu qū***		**392,606**
Dayu Subdistrict 大峪街道 *dàyù jiēdào*	87,097	
Chengzi Subdistrict 城子街道 *chéngzǐ jiēdào*	44,644	
Dongxinfang Subdistrict 東辛房街道 *dōngxīnfáng jiēdào*	36,076	
Datai Subdistrict 大台街道 *dàtái jiēdào*	3728	
Wangping Town 王平鎮 *wángpíng zhèn*	7013	
Yongding Town 永定鎮 *yǒngdìng zhèn*	106,112	
Longquan Town 龍泉鎮 *lóngquán zhèn*	52,072	

(continued)

Table 3.3 (continued)

Cities and subordinate sectors, population (2020 census)	Subordinate subdistrict populations (2020)	Total population (2020)
Tanzhesi Town 潭柘寺鎮 *tánzhèsì zhèn*	11,053	
Junzhuang Town 軍莊鎮 *jūnzhuāng zhèn*	16,128	
Yanchi Town 雁翅鎮 *yànchì zhèn*	5160	
Zhaitang Town 齋堂鎮 *zhāitáng zhèn*	7486	
Qingshui Town 清水鎮 *qīngshuǐ zhèn*	6,025	
Miaofengshan Town 妙峰山鎮 *miàofēngshān zhèn*	10,012	
Fangshan District 房山區 ***fángshān qū***		**1,312,778**
Chengguan Subdistrict 城關街道 *chéngguān jiēdào*	121,242	
Xinzhen Subdistrict 新鎮街道 *xīnzhèn jiēdào*	10,681	
Xiangyang Subdistrict 向陽街道 *xiàngyáng jiēdào*	19,142	
Dongfeng Subdistrict 東風街道 *dōngfēng jiēdào*	22,556	
Yingfeng Subdistrict 迎風街道 *yíngfēng jiēdào*	34,721	
Xingcheng Subdistrict 星城街道 *xīngchéng jiēdào*	21,663	
Liangxiang Region 良鄉地區 *liángxiāng dìqū*	24,317	
Zhoukoudian Region 周口店地區 *zhōukǒudiàn dìqū*	41,868	
Liulihe Region 琉璃河地區 *liúlíhé dìqū*	66,787	
Gongchen Subdistrict 拱辰街道 *gǒngchén jiēdào*	214,662	
Xilu Subdistrict 西潞街道 *xīlù jiēdào*	75,903	
Yancun Town 閻村鎮 *yáncūn zhèn*	77,621	
Doudian Town 竇店鎮 *dòudiàn zhèn*	96,184	
Shilou Town 石樓鎮 *shílóu zhèn*	32,131	
Changyang Town 長陽鎮 *chángyáng zhèn*	241,691	
Hebei Town 河北鎮 *héběi zhèn*	18,895	
Changgou Town 長溝鎮 *chánggōu zhèn*	22,002	
Dayouwo Town 大石窩鎮 *dàshíwō zhèn*	31,000	
Zhangfang Town 張坊鎮 *zhāngfāng zhèn*	18,299	
Shidu Town 十渡鎮 *shídù zhèn*	9132	
Qinglonghu Town 青龍湖鎮 *qīnglónghú zhèn*	52,319	
Hancunhe Town 韓村河鎮 *háncūnhé zhèn*	37,435	
Xiayunling Township 霞雲嶺鄉 *xiáyúnlǐng xiāng*	4885	
Nanwo Township 南窩鄉 *nánwō xiāng*	3190	
Fozizhuang Township 佛子莊鄉 *fózǐzhuāng xiāng*	6183	
Da'anshan Township 大安山鄉 *dà'ānshān xiāng*	2871	
Shijiaying Township 史家營鄉 *shǐjiāyíng xiāng*	3364	
Puwa Township 蒲洼鄉 *púwā xiāng*	2074	
Tongzhou District 通州區 ***tōngzhōu qū***		**1,840,295**
Yuqiao Subdistrict 玉橋街道 *yùqiáo jiēdào*	115,813	
Beiyuan Subdistrict 北苑街道 *běiyuàn jiēdào*	108,840	
Zhongcang Subdistrict 中倉街道 *zhōngcāng jiēdào*	66,803	
Tongyun Subdistrict 通運街道 *tōngyùn jiēdào*	49,613	
Xinhua Subdistrict 新華街道 *xīnhuá jiēdào*	37,286	
Luyuan Subdistrict 潞源街道 *lùyuán jiēdào*	8472	

(continued)

Table 3.3 (continued)

Cities and subordinate sectors, population (2020 census)	Subordinate subdistrict populations (2020)	Total population (2020)
Yongshun Town 永順鎮 *yǒngshùn zhèn*	304,781	
Liyuan Town 梨園鎮 *líyuán zhèn*	285,445	
Majuqiao Town 馬駒橋鎮 *mǎjūqiáo zhèn*	175,794	
Taihu Town 台湖鎮 *táihú zhèn*	151,735	
Songzhuang Town 宋莊鎮 *sòngzhuāng zhèn*	145,247	
Zhangjiawan Town 張家灣鎮 *zhāngjiāwān zhèn*	127,992	
Lucheng Town 潞城鎮 *lùchéng zhèn*	69,288	
Huoxian[a] Town 漷縣鎮 *huǒxiàn zhèn*	68,466	
Xiji Town 西集鎮 *xījí zhèn*	46,678	
Yongledian Town 永樂店鎮 *yǒnglèdiàn zhèn*	43,308	
Yujiage Huizu (Hui) Township 于家各回族鄉 *yújiāgèhuízú xiāng*	34,734	
Shunyi District 順義區 ***shùnyì qū***		**1,324,044**
Shengli Subdistrict 勝利街道 *shènglì jiēdào*	46,494	
Guangming Subdistrict 光明街道 *guāngmíng jiēdào*	70,609	
Renhe Region 仁和地區 *rénhé dìqū*	67,391	
Houshayu Region 後沙峪地區 *hòushāyù dìqū*	74,841	
Tianzhu Region 天竺地區 *tiānzhú dìqū*	32,979	
Yangzhen Region 楊鎮地區 *yángzhèn dìqū*	64,578	
Niulanshan Region 牛欄山地區 *niúlánshān dìqū*	54,687	
Nanfaxin Region 南法信地區 *nánfǎxìn dìqū*	54,195	
Mapo Region 馬坡地區 *mǎpō dìqū*	38,547	
Shiyuan Subdistrict 石園街道 *shíyuán jiēdào*	68,302	
Konggang Subdistrict 空港街道 *kōnggǎng jiēdào*	99,297	
Shuangfeng Subdistrict 雙豐街道 *shuāngfēng jiēdào*	68,176	
Wangquan Subdistrict 旺泉街道 *wàngquán jiēdào*	94,415	
Gaoliying Town 高麗營鎮 *gāolìyíng zhèn*	80,840	
Liqiao Town 李橋鎮 *lǐqiáo zhèn*	97,059	
Lisui Town 李遂鎮 *lǐsuì zhèn*	22,538	
Nancai Town 南彩鎮 *náncǎi zhèn*	73,163	
Beiwu Town 北務鎮 *běiwù zhèn*	13,980	
Dasungezhuang Town 大孫各莊鎮 *dàsūngèzhuāng zhèn*	23,712	
Zhangzhen Town 張鎮 *zhāngzhèn*	24,795	
Longwantun Town 龍灣屯鎮 *lóngwāntún zhèn*	14,212	
Dalin Town 木林鎮 *mùlín zhèn*	34,114	
Beixinying Town 北小營鎮 *běixiǎoyíng zhèn*	42,805	
Beishicao Town 北石槽鎮 *běishícáo zhèn*	15,109	
Zhaoquanying Town 趙全營鎮 *zhàoquányíng zhèn*	47,206	
Changping District 昌平區 ***chāngpíng qū***		**2,269,487**
Chengbei Subdistrict 城北街道 *chéngběi jiēdào*	228,561	
Nankou Region 南口地區 *nánkǒu dìqū*	82,146	

(continued)

Table 3.3 (continued)

Cities and subordinate sectors, population (2020 census)	Subordinate subdistrict populations (2020)	Total population (2020)
Machikou Region 馬池口地區 *mǎchíkǒu dìqū*	87,506	
Shahe Region 沙河地區 *shāhé dìqū*	294,408	
Chengnan Subdistrict 城南街道 *chéngnán jiēdào*	88,963	
Dongxiaokou Region 東小口地區 *dōngxiǎokǒu dìqū*	85,874	
Tiantong Yuanbei Subdistrict 天通苑北街道 *tiāntōngyuànběi jiēdào*	142,707	
Tiantong Yuannan Subdistrict 天通苑南街道 *tiāntōngyuànnán jiēdào*	116,529	
Huoying Subdistrict 霍營街道 *huòyíng jiēdào*	93,545	
Huilongguan Subdistrict 回龍觀街道 *huílóngguān jiēdào*	166,074	
Longzeyuan Subdistrict 龍澤園街道 *lóngzéyuán jiēdào*	181,906	
Shigezhuang Subdistrict 史各莊街道 *shǐgèzhuāng jiēdào*	64,910	
Yangfang Town 陽坊鎮 *yángfāng zhèn*	26,470	
Xiaotangshan Town 小湯山鎮 *xiǎotāngshān zhèn*	80,273	
Nanshao Town 南邵鎮 *nánshào zhèn*	65,403	
Cuicun Town 崔村鎮 *cuīcūn zhèn*	24,630	
Baishan Town 百善鎮 *bǎishàn zhèn*	36,546	
Beiqijia Town 北七家鎮 *běiqījiā zhèn*	308,907	
Xingshou Town 興壽鎮 *xīngshòu zhèn*	34,139	
Liucun Town 流村鎮 *liúcūn zhèn*	18,139	
Shisanling Town 十三陵鎮 *shísānlíng zhèn*	34,085	
Yanshan Town 延壽鎮 *yánshòu zhèn*	7766	
Daxing District 大興區 ***dàxìng qū***		**1,993,591**
Xingfeng Subdistrict 興豐街道 *xīngfēng jiēdào*	79,851	
Linxiaolu Subdistrict 林校路街道 *línxiàolù jiēdào*	81,389	
Qingyuan Subdistrict 清源街道 *qīngyuán jiēdào*	147,810	
Yizhuang Town 亦莊鎮 *yìzhuāng zhèn*	108,255	
Huangcun Town 黃村鎮 *huángcūn zhèn*	176,890	
Jiugong Town 舊宮鎮 *jiùgōng zhèn*	189,300	
Xihongmen Town 西紅門鎮 *xīhóngmén zhèn*	179,974	
Yinghai Town 瀛海鎮 *yínghǎi zhèn*	102,463	
Guanyinsi Subdistrict 觀音寺街道 *guānyīnsì jiēdào*	111,225	
Tiangongyuan Subdistrict 天宮院街道 *tiāngōngyuàn jiēdào*	87,415	
Gaomidian Subdistrict 高米店街道 *gāomǐdiàn jiēdào*	99,959	
Qingyundian Town 青雲店鎮 *qīngyúndiàn zhèn*	69,612	
Caiyu Town 採育鎮 *cǎiyù zhèn*	54,690	
Anding Town 安定鎮 *āndìng zhèn*	30,764	
Lixian Town 禮賢鎮 *lǐxián zhèn*	40,930	

(continued)

Table 3.3 (continued)

Cities and subordinate sectors, population (2020 census)	Subordinate subdistrict populations (2020)	Total population (2020)
Yufa Town 榆垡鎮 *yúfá zhèn*	71,812	
Panggezhuang Town 龐各莊鎮 *pánggèzhuāng zhèn*	74,912	
Beizangcun Town 北藏村鎮 *běizàngcūn zhèn*	35,391	
Weishanzhuang Town 魏善莊鎮 *wèishànzhuāng zhèn*	46,661	
Changziying Town 長子營鎮 *chángzǐyíng zhèn*	34,588	
Beijing National Biotechnology Industry Base 北京國家生物醫藥產業基地 *běijīng guójiā shēngwù yīyào chǎnyè jīdì*	10,201	
National New Media Industry Base 國家新媒體產業基地 *guójiā xīnméitǐ chǎnyè jīdì*	9827	
Daxing International Airport (Daxing section) 大興國際機場 *dàxīng guójìjīchǎng*	1527	
Beijing Economic and Technology Development Zone 北京經濟技術開發區 *běijīng jīngjìjìshù kāifāqū*	148,145	
Huairou District 懷柔區 ***huáiróu qū***		**441,040**
Quanhe Subdistrict 泉河街道 *quánhé jiēdào*	78,632	
Longshan Subdistrict 龍山街道 *lóngshān jiēdào*	74,596	
Huairou Region 懷柔地區 *huáiróu dìqū*	41,990	
Yanqi Region 雁棲地區 *yànqī dìqū*	38,483	
Miaocheng Region 廟城地區 *miàochéng dìqū*	40,883	
Beifang Town 北房鎮 *běifáng zhèn*	33,712	
Yangsong Town 楊宋鎮 *yángsòng zhèn*	31,270	
Qiaozi Town 橋梓鎮 *qiáozǐ zhèn*	25,076	
Huaibei Town 懷北鎮 *huáiběi zhèn*	22,487	
Tanghekou Town 湯河口鎮 *tānghékǒu zhèn*	5445	
Bohai Town 渤海鎮 *bóhǎi zhèn*	12,702	
Jiuduhe Town 九渡河鎮 *jiǔdùhé zhèn*	12,533	
Liulimiao Town 琉璃廟鎮 *liúlímiào zhèn*	4312	
Baoshan Town 寶山鎮 *bǎoshān zhèn*	6246	
Changxiaoying Manchu Township 長哨營滿族鄉 *chángshàoyíng mǎnzú xiāng*	5378	
Labagoumen Manchu Township 喇叭溝門滿族鄉 *lǎbāgōumén mǎnzú xiāng*	4034	
Beijing Yanqi Economic Development Zone 北京雁棲經濟開發區 *běijīng yànqī jīngjì kāifāqū*	3261	
Pinggu District 平谷區 ***pínggǔ qū***		**457,313**
Binhe Subdistrict 濱河街道 *bīnhé jiēdào*	50,541	
Xinggu Subdistrict 興谷街道 *xīnggǔ jiēdào*	61,949	
Tangyang Region 漁陽地區 *yúyáng dìqū*	62,694	
Yukou Region 峪口地區 *yùkǒu dìqū*	28,385	
Mafang Region 馬坊地區 *mǎfāng dìqū*	29,601	

(continued)

Table 3.3 (continued)

Cities and subordinate sectors, population (2020 census)	Subordinate subdistrict populations (2020)	Total population (2020)
Jinhaihu Region 金海湖地區 *jīnhǎihú dìqū*	25,376	
Donggaocun Town 東高村鎮 *dōnggāocūn zhèn*	28,406	
Nandulehe Town 南獨樂河鎮 *nándúlèhé zhèn*	18,847	
Dahuashan Town 大華山鎮 *dàhuáshān zhèn*	15,209	
Xiagezhuang Town 夏各莊鎮 *xiàgèzhuāng zhèn*	26,185	
Machangying Town 馬昌營鎮 *mǎchāngyíng zhèn*	16,794	
Wangxinzhuang Town 王辛莊鎮 *wángxīnzhuāng zhèn*	30,586	
Daxingzhuang Town 大興莊鎮 *dàxīngzhuāng zhèn*	23,739	
Liujiadian Town 劉家店鎮 *liújiādiàn zhèn*	7155	
Zhenluoying Town 鎮羅營鎮 *zhènluóyíng zhèn*	7610	
Huangsongyu Township 黃松峪鄉 *huángsōngyù xiāng*	5062	
Xiong'erzhai Township 熊兒寨鄉 *xióng'érzhài xiāng*	2859	
Miyun District 密雲區 ***mìyún qū***		**527,683**
Gulou Subdistrict 鼓樓街道 *gǔlóu jiēdào*	154,739	
Guoyuan Subdistrict 果園街道 *guǒyuán jiēdào*	88,764	
Tanying Region 檀營地區 *tányíng dìqū*	15,466	
Miyun Town 密雲鎮 *mìyún zhèn*	20,392	
Xiwengzhuang Town 溪翁莊鎮 *xīwēngzhuāng zhèn*	20,438	
Xitiangezhuang Town 西田各莊鎮 *xītiángèzhuāng zhèn*	33,702	
Shilipu Town 十里堡鎮 *shílǐbǎo zhèn*	29,824	
Henanzhai Town 河南寨鎮 *hénánzhài zhèn*	24,155	
Jugezhuang Town 巨各莊鎮 *jùgèzhuāng zhèn*	22,032	
Mujiayu Town 穆家峪鎮 *mùjiāyù zhèn*	23,084	
Taishitun Town 太師屯鎮 *tàishītún zhèn*	22,388	
Gaoling Town 高嶺鎮 *gāolǐng zhèn*	9967	
Bulaotun Town 不老屯鎮 *bùlǎotún zhèn*	12,705	
Fengjiayu Town 馮家峪鎮 *féngjiāyù zhèn*	4485	
Gubeikou Town 古北口鎮 *gǔběikǒu zhèn*	7170	
Dachengzi Town 大城子鎮 *dàchéngzǐ zhèn*	9443	
Dongshaoqu Town 東邵渠鎮 *dōngshàoqú zhèn*	9495	
Beizhuang Town 北莊鎮 *běizhuāng zhèn*	5993	
Xinchengzi Town 新城子鎮 *xīnchéngzǐ zhèn*	6528	
Shicheng Town 石城鎮 *shíchéng zhèn*	4014	
Beijing Miyun Economic Development Zone 北京密雲經濟開發區 *běijīng mìyún jīngjì kāifāqū*	2899	
Yanqing District 延慶區 ***yánqìng qū***		**345,671**
Yanqing Town 延慶鎮 *yánqìng zhèn*	54,790	
Xiangshuiyuan Subdistrict 香水園街道 *xiāngshuǐyuán jiēdào*	48,251	

(continued)

Table 3.3 (continued)

Cities and subordinate sectors, population (2020 census)	Subordinate subdistrict populations (2020)	Total population (2020)
Baiquan Subdistrict 百泉街道 *bǎiquán jiēdào*	36,013	
Kangzhuang Town 康莊鎮 *kāngzhuāng zhèn*	32,815	
Rulin Subdistrict 儒林街道 *rúlín jiēdào*	28,230	
Zhangshanying Town 張山營鎮 *zhāngshānyíng zhèn*	24,259	
Yongning Town 永寧鎮 *yǒngníng zhèn*	23,483	
Jiuxian Town 舊縣鎮 *jiùxiàn zhèn*	17,676	
Shenjiaying Town 沈家營鎮 *shěnjiāyíng zhèn*	16,661	
Dayushu Town 大榆樹鎮 *dàyúshù zhèn*	16,166	
Badaling Town 八達嶺鎮 *bādálǐng zhèn*	10,024	
Jingzhuang Town 井莊鎮 *jǐngzhuāng zhèn*	9500	
Qianjiadian Town 千家店鎮 *qiānjiādiàn zhèn*	6273	
Xiangying Township 香營鄉 *xiāngyíng xiāng*	6019	
Liubinbu Township 劉斌堡鄉 *liúbīnbǎo xiāng*	4497	
Sihai Town 四海鎮 *sìhǎi zhèn*	4343	
Dazhuangke Township 大莊科鄉 *dàzhuāngkē xiāng*	4202	
Zhenzhuquan Township 珍珠泉鄉 *zhēnzhūquán xiāng*	2469	

[a] 漷 usually read *kuò*

Beijing City (京) and Subdistricts

Table 3.4 Beijing city: permanent registered (戶籍人口 hùjí rénkǒu) populations, 2012, 2016, and 2020 (MCA 2020)

Name	Traditional	Simplified	Population (2012)	Population (2016)	Population (2020)	Area (km^2)
Beijing City (Capitol)	北京市	北京市	12,620,000	13,000,000	13,740,000	17,000
Dongcheng District (Jingshan Subdistrict)	東城區 (景山街道)	東城区 (景山街道)	960,000	970,000	970,000	42
Xicheng District (Jinrongjie Subdistrict)	西城區 (金融街道)	西城区 (金融街道)	1,350,000	1,390,000	1,460,000	51
Chaoyang District (Chaowai Subdistrict)	朝陽區 (朝外街道)	朝阳区 (朝外街道)	1,900,000	1,980,000	2,120,000	455
Fengtai District (Fengtai Subdistrict)	豐台區 (豐台街道)	丰台区 (丰台街道)	1,060,000	1,100,000	1,150,000	306
Shijingshan District (Lugu Subdistrict)	石景山區 (魯谷街道)	石景山区 (鲁谷街道)	360,000	37,000	39,000	84
Haidian District (Haidian Subdistrict)	海澱區 (海澱街道)	海澱區 (海澱街道)	2,220,000	2,320,000	2,360,000	431
Mentougou District (Dayu Subdistrict)	門頭溝 (大峪街道)	门头沟 (大峪街道)	250,000	250,000	250,000	1451

(continued)

Table 3.4 (continued)

Name	Traditional	Simplified	Population (2012)	Population (2016)	Population (2020)	Area (km²)
Fangshan District (Gongchen Subdistrict)	房山區 (拱辰街道)	房山區 (拱辰街道)	770,000	780,000	830,000	1990
Tongzhou District (Beiyuan Subdistrict)	通州區 (北苑街道)	通州区 (北苑街道)	660,000	680,000	790,000	906
Shunyi District (Shengli Subdistrict)	順義區 (勝利街道)	顺义区 (胜利街道)	580,000	590,000	640,000	1020
Changping District (Chengbei Subdistrict)	昌平區 (城北街道)	昌平区 (城北街道)	530,000	560,000	630,000	1344
Daxing District (Xingfeng Subdistrict)	大興區 (興豐街道)	大兴区 (兴丰街道)	600,000	620,000	720,000	1036
Huairou District (Longshan Subdistrict)	懷柔區 (龍山街道)	怀柔区 (龙山街道)	280,000	280,000	290,000	2123
Pinggu District (Binhe Subdistrict)	平谷區 (濱河街道)	平谷區 (滨河街道)	400,000	400,000	410,000	950
Miyun District (Gulou Subdistrict)	密雲區 (鼓樓街道)	密云区 (鼓楼街道)	430,000	430,000	440,000	2229
Yanqing District (Rulin Subdistrict	延慶區 (儒林街道)	延庆区 (儒林街道)	280,000	280,000	290,000	1994

References

Anon. 1997. *Beijing street and hutong maps*. Beijing: China Map Publishers.

Ch'en, Vincent, and Matteo Ricci. 1939. Matteo Ricci's contribution to, and influence on, geographical knowledge in China. *Journal of the American Oriental Society* 59 (3): 325–359.

Chang, Kwang-chih. 1977. *The archeology of ancient China*. 3rd ed. New Haven: Yale University Press.

Chen, Xibo, and Han Guanghui. 2008. [A preliminary analysis of the development, evolution and spatial distribution characteristics of the Zhongdu Lu urban agglomeration in the Jin Dynasty]. 陈喜波, 韩光辉. 试析金代中都路城市群的发展演变及其空间分布特征. 中国历史地理论丛. *Journal of Chinese Historical Geography* 23(1): 25–33. http://www.iqh.net.cn/users/uploadfiles/2008528/20085289118_32478.pdf.

Gao, Shouxian. 2003. [Research on the urban population of Beijing in the Ming Dynasty]. *Beijing City University Journal*. 高寿仙. 明代北京城市人口数额研究. 北京城市学院学报 (4): 32–36. https://www.bcu.edu.cn/bcuxbxb/.

Laven, Mary. 2011. *Mission to China: Matteo Ricci and the Jesuit encounter with the East*. London: Faber and Faber.

Meredith, Martin. 2011. *Born in Africa: The quest for the origins of human life*. New York: Public Affairs.

Ministry of Civil Affairs (MCA), People's Republic of China. 2020. [*County/township administration handbook*]. Beijing: China Statistics Press. 中華人民共和國民政部, 中華人民共和國, 鄉鎮行政區劃簡冊.

National Bureau of Statistics (NBS), People's Republic of China. 2001. [Year 2000 fifth national census report, issue no. 2]. 2000 年第五次全国人口普查主要数据公报 (第二号). March 28. http://www.gov.cn/gongbao/content/2001/content_60740.htm.

———. 2021. [Report of the seventh all-national census]. May 19. 第七次全国人口普查公报. http://www.stats.gov.cn/ztjc/zdtjgz/zgrkpc/dqcrkpc/ggl/202105/t20210519_1817697.html.

People's Republic of China (PRC). 2001. *Administrative division reform atlas, 1949–1999*. Beijing: China Map Publishers.

Polo, Marco. 1993. *The travels of Marco Polo: The complete Yule-Cordier edition*. Vol. I. New York: Dover Publications.

Spence, Jonathan D. 1984. *The memory palace of Matteo Ricci*. New York: Elisabeth Sifton Books/Viking.

Stautman, Barry. 2001. Peking Man and the politics of paleoanthropological nationalism in China. *Journal of Asian Studies* 60 (1): 95–124.

Turnbull, Stephen. 2003. *Genghis Khan & the Mongol conquests, 1190–1400*. Oxford: Osprey Publishing.

Yang, Jisheng. 2012. *Tombstone*. New York: Farrar, Straus and Giroux.

Yang, Xiaoyan, Zhiwei Wan, Linda Perry, et al. 2012. Early millet use in northern China. *Proceedings of the National Academy of Sciences* 109 (10): 3726–3730. https://www.pnas.org/content/109/10/3726.

Yen, Hsiao-pei. 2014. Evolutionary Asiacentrism, Peking Man, and the origins of Sinocentric ethno-nationalism. *Journal of the History of Biology* 47 (4): 585–625.

Zhang, Shunan. 2021. [The 2020 per capita income list of residents in various provinces: Shanghai is the richest, and it has risen sharply]. Finance.people.com. January 22. 张澍楠. 2020年各省份居民人均收入榜: 上海最有钱, 这地涨得猛. http://finance.people.com.cn/n1/2021/0122/c1004-32008733.html.

Zhao, Yinan, and Zheng Jinran. 2014. Beijing-Tianjin-Hebei region's coordinated development. *China Daily*. February 28. https://www.pressreader.com/hong-kong/china-daily/20140228/281599533417506.

Chapter 4
Chongqing City

Abstract The history of Chongqing (once known to the West as "Chunking") harkens back to the original Ba Kingdom, dating to the early Zhou (ca. 1000 BCE) dynastic period. Poetically described by arguably China's most famous poet, Du Fu, Chongqing City is notable for a number of features, not the least of which being its very large population of just over 32 million, as well as its spicy hot pot cuisine. Like Tianjin, Shanghai, and Beijing, Chongqing is politically a provincial-level city. Once the wartime capital under the Nationalists in World War II, having suffered aerial bombing as did other Chinese population centers, the southwestern metropolis of Chongqing has variously been called a mountain city, as well as a city of fog and bridges, among other nicknames. This chapter addresses its current economic status to include gross domestic product (GDP) and per capita income (USD $4800 in 2020), and as such Chongqing is ranked 17th and 11th, respectively, among China's provinces and major cities. This chapter also provides 2020 census data for Chongqing City down to the county and district levels, followed by tabular data showing official household registered (*hukou*) population numbers.

E. Croddy, *China's Provinces and Populations*,
https://doi.org/10.1007/978-3-031-09165-0_4

Chongqing City (重慶市 *chóngqìng shì*): Abbreviation 渝 (*yú*) (Fig. 4.1)

Chongqing City Population (2020)

1. Chengkou County	197,497
2. Kaizhou District	1,203,306
3. Yunyang County	929,034
4. Wuxi County	388,685
5. Fengjie County	744,836
6. Wushan County	462,462
7. Liangping District	645,315
8. Wanzhou District	1,564,449
9. Dianjiang County	650,694
10. Zhongxian County	720,976
11. Shizhu Tujia Autonomous County	389,001
12. Tongnan District	688,115
13. Hechuan District	1,245,294
14. Beibei District	834,887
15. Yubei District	2,191,493
16. Changshou District	692,960
17. Fengdu County	557,374
18. Rongchang District	668,997
19. Dazu District	834,592
20. Tongliang District	685,729
21. Bishan District	756,022
22. Shapingba District	1,477,345
23. Jiangbei District	719,134
24. Nan'an District	1,197,639
25. Yuzhong District	588,717
26. Banan District	1,178,856
27. Dadukou District	421,904
28. Jiulongpo District	1,526,821
29. Yongchuan District	1,148,896
30. Jiangjin District	1,359,611
31. Nanchuan District	572,362
32. Fuling District	1,115,016
33. Wulong District	356,748
34. Pengshui Miao and Tujia Autonomous County	530,599
35. Qianjiang District	487,281
36. Qijiang District	1,011,334
37. Youyang Tujia and Miao Autonomous County	607,338
38. Xiushan Tujia and Miao Autonomous County	496,194

Fig. 4.1 Chongqing: subdistricts (City Governmental Seat: Yuzhong District). (Drawn by the author, after People's Republic of China, Ministry of Civil Affairs, MCA 2020)

Chongqing City: General Impressions

First off, one is impressed by the sheer numbers of people who live in the larger incorporated Chongqing, a provincial-level city. According to the most recent (7th, 2020) PRC-wide census, Chongqing City had a population of 32,054,159 (NBS 2021). Chongqing is also among a number Chinese cities that, along with the rest of the nation, is experiencing a rapidly ageing population. In fact, Chinese media has focused on Chongqing in particular, reporting a "deep ageing" trend where at least 14% of its population are 64 years or older (Shao 2021).

At the gastronomical level, Chongqing brings to mind the fiery hot and spicy hot pot dish (火鍋 *huǒguō*). In addition to hot chili peppers, this soup delicacy features Sichuan pepper corns (花椒 *huājiāo*), balancing the pain of capsaicin (辣 *là*) with the tongue-numbing effects (麻 *má*) of the pepper, ergo making it *mala* (麻辣 *málà*). As famous for its spicy hot pot cuisine, Chongqing is infamous for its wickedly hot summer weather. As such, it is known as one of the "three furnaces' (三大火爐 *sāndà huǒlú*), the other cities being Wuhan and Nanjing.

Chinese abbreviations and names for Chongqing include Ba (巴 *bā*), Yu (渝 *yú*), as well as Shancheng ("Mountain City" 山城 *shānchéng*), and Yudu (渝都 *yúdū*), the latter a reference to an older name of the Jialing (嘉陵江 *jiālíng jiāng*) River tributary, Yushui (渝水 *yúshuǐ*) (CBT 1999). Other monikers include the "misty" or "foggy" capital (霧都 *wùdū*), and Qiaodu ("Bridge Capital" 橋都 *qiáodū*) for its famed traditional bridge structures. Famously the gateway to the Yangtze (長江 *Chángjiāng*) river and the Three Gorges, Chongqing City was first widely known to the west as "Chunking" when it was the Republic of China (ROC) wartime capital in the war against Japan (1937–1945).

Prehistory of Ba (See Also Sichuan Province)

Evidence of the Neolithic Tongliang Culture (銅梁文化 *tóngliáng wénhuà*) was found at the Zhang'ertang (張二塘 *zhāng'èrtáng*) site in Tongliang District. This includes stone scrapers, flint flakes and choppers, all dating back at least 20,000 years ago. Some of these tools and their manufacture resemble that of the Guanyindong culture (觀音洞文化 *guānyīndòng wénhuà*) in Guizhou Province (Olsen 1987).

Ancient oracle bone scripts (see also Henan Province) relate that the "Ba" (巴方 *bāfāng*) people lived during the reign of the Wu Ding (武丁 *wǔdīng*) emperor in the Shang Dynasty (ca. 1200 BCE). In one such ancient divination (卜 *bǔ*) of a turtle shell (plastron), for example, an inscription asked if it would be propitious for Wu Ding's allied General Zhi Guo (沚聝 *zhǐ guó*) to attack the Ba (伐巴方 *fábāfāng*) (Keightley 1978). There is speculation that the origins of the ideograph Ba (巴 *bā*) depicted a form of ritual dance performed by the Ba people.

Chinese historical sources hold that the later Kingdom of Ba (巴國 *bāguó*) goes back to the time of the early Zhou (1046–256 BCE). Its capital was Jiangzhou (江州 *jiāngzhōu*, which is now modern-day Yuzhong District (渝中區 *yúzhōng qū*). The neighboring Shu (蜀 *shǔ*, modern-day Sichuan) and Ba states often interacted with each other, sometimes peacefully, other times in sanguineous conflict. Linguistic experts consider the modern-day Tujia (土家族 *tǔjiā zú*) ethnic minority in China (numbering about eight million) to have originated from the ancient Ba (Brassett et al. 2006).

The State of Qin (秦國 *qínguó*), encroaching upon the territory of both the Shu (蜀 *shǔ*) and Ba states in 441 BCE, further increased its economic and military might. In 316 BCE, the strategist Zhang Yi (張儀 *zhāng yí*) of the Qin finally conquered the Ba state, establishing 2 years later Ba Prefecture (巴郡 *bājùn*). Its capital was built at Jiangzhou (Zhong 1993).

During in the Western Han period (ca. 2 CE), Ba Prefecture (巴郡 *bājùn*, roughly occupying today's Chongqing City), had a population then of 708,148. Following a survey and mapping of Ba Prefecture in 154 CE, Ba Prefecture had 14 counties with a recorded population of 1,875,435 (Yang 1995). By the Three Kingdoms era (三國 *sānguó*), in ca. 262 CE, parts of Sichuan and Chongqing were all administered under the northern Yizhou state (益州). In the beginning of the Sui (隋 *suí*) Dynasty (ca. 600 CE), Ba Prefecture's name was changed to Yuzhou (渝州 *yúzhōu*), from which the modern abbreviation character for Chongqing, Yu (渝 *yú*), is derived.

Du Fu's Meanderings

Arguably China's most famous poet, Du Fu (杜甫 *dù fǔ*), perambulated through modern-day Chongqing during the chaos of the Anshi Rebellion (安史之亂 *ānshǐzhī luàn*, ca. 755–763). Among the places Du Fu lived while in Chongqing included modern-day Yuzhou, as well as Zhongxian (忠縣 *zhōng xiàn*), Yunyang (雲陽縣 *yúnyáng xiàn*), and Fengjie (奉節縣 *fèngjié xiàn*) counties, which were then part of Kuizhou Prefecture (夔州 *kuízhōu*). During his 2 years in Fengjie, Du Fu wrote nearly 400 poems, including "Singing My Feelings on Traces of the Past" (766). The opening lines are evocative of the times in which he lived as well as the surrounding geography, the nearby Three Gorges:

> Split apart from the northeast at the edge of dust and war,
> Drifting along the southwest between Earth and Heaven.
> By the Three Gorges' towers and terraces, I linger for days and months … (Owen 2016)

In the Song dynasty, as of 1111 CE the name Yuzhou had been changed to Gongzhou (恭州 *gōngzhōu*) (Tan 1996). Then, at the beginning of year 1189, Zhao Dun (趙惇 *zhào dūn*), the third son of Xiaozong emperor, was enthroned as Prince of Gong (恭王 *gōngwáng*). A month later, to mark the occasion, the state of Gongzhou was renamed Chongqing, the shortened form of 雙重喜慶 (*shuāngchóng xǐqìng*), i.e., "double (重) celebration (慶)". For centuries afterward Chongqing remained a Sichuan provincial entity.

Chongqing's Modern History

Chongqing was subject to British encroachments in the late nineteenth century. Under the Chefoo Convention,[1] known as the Yantai Convention in Chinese (煙臺條約 *yāntái tiáoyuē*), in 1876 China and Britain resolved the controversy surrounding the murder of the British diplomat and explorer Augustus Raymond Margary. Known in Chinese as "Dian'an" (滇案 *diān àn*) after the abbreviation character 滇 (*diān*) for Yunnan where the incident occurred, this treaty gave British diplomatic privileges in Chongqing. Renewing this agreement in 1890, the British promoted Chongqing as a key inland port facility due to its access to the Yangtze (長江 *chángjiāng*) river. A year later Chongqing was formally opened as a key transportation hub. Highlighting its continued strategic importance, after China was defeated in the first Sino-Japanese War (1895), terms of the Treaty of Shimonoseki (known in Chinese as 馬關條約 *mǎguāntiáoyuē*) opened Chongqing to Japanese trade. As its economic importance grew, so did its population. Table 4.1 gives a sense of Chongqing's population growth from the nineteenth to mid-twentieth centuries:

Table 4.1 Chongqing populations compared: 1812 and 1953 (Cao 2003)

City/county/district	Population (1812)	Population (1953)
Chongqing City 重慶市 *chóngqìng shì*	N/A[a]	1,772,486
Baxian County 巴縣 *bāxiàn*	218,779	879,378
Jiangjin 江津 *jiāngjīn*	199,115	971,838
Changshou 長壽 *chángshòu*	154,023	543,095
Yongchuan 永川 *yǒngchuān*	107,702	501,044
Rongchang 榮昌 *róngchāng*	93,598	431,029
Qijiang 綦江 *qíjiāng*	108,215	570,617
Nanchuan 南川 *nánchuān*	149,562	390,196
Tongliang 銅梁 *tóngliáng*	297,264	512,491
Hezhou 合州 *hézhōu*	187,357	959,326
Fuzhou 涪州 *fúzhōu*	260,746	798,710
Dazu 大足 *dàzú*	117,561	504,523
Bishan 璧山 *bìshān*	151,022	387,979
Dingyuan 定遠 *dìngyuǎn*	168,823	436,946
Jiangbei 江北 *jiāngběi*	152,039	719,134
Total	**2,365,806**	**10,605,941**

[a]Chongqing was a governing entity as 重慶府 in 1812, composed of the subordinate counties listed

[1]"Chefoo" was the English corruption of Zhifu by British expats who lived in the residential district within Yantai City, Zhifu District 芝罘區 (*zhīfú qū*), now with a population of about 680,000. China used Yantai as the geographical reference instead.

Wartime Capital

As the Republic of China (ROC) wartime capital from 1937–1945 ("Chunking"), an influx of Kuomingdang (KMT) officials and refugees led to dramatic fluctuations in population throughout the 1930s and 1940s (see Table 4.2). While this was happening, the Japanese military adopted a strategy to cripple the will of Chinese resistance, carrying out terror bombing raids against Chongqing from February 1938 to December 1944. Flying from Wuhan and Yichang (Hebei Province), Japanese bombers struck targets in Wanzhou, Zhongxian, Fengdu, Fuling, and Changshou, among others. According to a study published in 2015, Chongqing recorded a total of 32,829 casualties as a direct result of bombing, 16,376 of these fatal (CCRGWL 2017). Among the districts in Chongqing, Youyang County (酉陽縣 *yǒuyáng xiàn*) was hardest hit in terms of civilian casualties during the Sino-Japanese War.

Chongqing's Role in China's Cold War

At the nadir of Sino-Soviet relations, Mao Zedong put all of China under war footing, with particular focus on civil defense programs. Because of its strategic position, Chongqing was selected as a key "Third Line" city. From 1964–1968, some 270,000 laborers were brought into Chongqing from Shanghai, Jiangsu, and regions across the northeast of China (Manchuria) to work on this project. One result of this

Table 4.2 Historical Chongqing city population data (CCRGWL 2017)

Year	Households	Chongqing City population (total)
1931	322,981	1,863,424
1932	452,538	2,299,572
1933	189,752	1,367,730
1934	710,319	3,896,321
1935	1,518,818	8,019,487
1936	1,358,737	7,707,114
1937	1,502,421	9,055,106
1938	1,194,969	7,459,816
1939	1,355,580	8,114,271
1940	1,152,172	7,520,872
1941	1,579,464	9,513,581
1942	1,588,541	9,705,448
1943	1,576,383	9,265,552
1944	1,614,689	9,496,046
1945	1,450,432	8,929,345
1946	1,673,969	8,467,221

Third Line of construction was the concentration of armaments factories in and around Chongqing City. During the tumult of the Cultural Revolution (1966–1976), rivaling rebel factions fought pitched battles against each other in Chongqing, this violence exacerbated by ready access to military arms, artillery, and even naval gunboats (Dikötter 2016). As Mao Zedong encouraged country-wide chaos, beginning in 1967 there were thousands of armed assaults in Chongqing during the Cultural Revolution, including the firing of over 10,000 artillery shells. Large sections of key port facilities were destroyed in the Chaotianmen subdistrict (朝天門街道 *cháotiānmén jiēdào*), and some 180,000 refugees fled Chongqing City to Chengdu, Sichuan Province (MacFarquhar and Schoenhals 2006).

Chongqing as Provincial-Level City

Having been established as a municipality since 1929, Chongqing City was later placed under Sichuan Province's jurisdiction in 1954. Then, in 1997, Chongqing once again became its own provincial level, metropolitan entity, bringing in Wanxian (萬縣市 *wànxiàn shì*), Fuling (涪陵市 *fúlíng shì*) cities, as well as the Qianjiang region (黔江地區 *qiánjiāng dìqū*). Today, as a provincial-level city, Chongqing City continues to be a key economic hub in China's southwest. In terms of gross domestic product (GDP) during the vaunted 2007–2020 "urban-rural overall plan" (重慶市城鄉總體規畫 *chóngqìng shì chéngxiāng zǒngtǐ guīhuà*) Chongqing grew from about USD $64 billion in 2007, to nearly $389 billion in 2020. As such, Chongqing City was ranked 17th in terms of overall GDP among mainland China's 31 provinces and major cities. For per capita income, Chongqing City ranks eleventh at about USD $4800 (Zhang 2021) (Table 4.3).

Table 4.3 Chongqing population (Residential 常住人口 chángzhù rénkǒu) census data (CCBS 2021)

City/county/district	Population (2010)	Population (2020)
Chongqing City 重慶市 ***chóngqìng shì***	**28,846,170**	**32,054,159**
一小時經濟圈 **(One-hour economic circle)[a]**	**1,764,490**	**N/A[b]**
Wanzhou District 萬州區 *wànzhōu qū*	1,563,050	1,564,449
Fuling District 涪陵區 *fúlíng qū*	1,066,714	1,115,016
Yuzhong District 渝中區 *yúzhōng qū*	630,090	588,717
Dadukou District 大渡口區 *dàdùkǒu qū*	301,042	421,904
Jiangbei District 江北區 *jiāngběi qū*	738,003	925,800
Shapingba District 沙坪壩區 *shāpíngbà qū*	1,000,013	1,477,345
Jiulongpo District 九龍坡區 *jiǔlóngpō qū*	1,084,419	1,526,821
Nan'an District 南岸區 *nán'àn qū*	759,570	1,197,639
Beibei District 北碚區 *běibèi qū*	680,360	834,887
Qijiang District 綦江區 *qíjiāng qū*	1,056,817	1,011,334
Qijiang District not including the Wansheng (Economic) Development District [綦江 (不含萬盛)][c]	801,017	775,509

(continued)

Table 4.3 (continued)

City/county/district	Population (2010)	Population (2020)
Wansheng Economic Development District 萬盛經開區	255,800	235,825
Dazu District 大足區 *dàzú qū*	721,359	834,592
Yubei District 渝北區 *yúběi qū*	1,345,410	2,191,493
Banan District 巴南區 *bānán qū*	918,692	1,178,856
Qianjiang District 黔江區 *qiánjiāng qū*	445,012	487,281
Changshou District 長壽區 *chángshòu qū*	770,009	692,960
Jiangjin District 江津區 *jiāngjīn qū*	1,233,149	1,359,611
Hechuan District 合川區 *héchuān qū*	1,293,028	1,245,294
Yongchuan District 永川區 *yǒngchuān qū*	1,024,708	1,148,896
Nanchuan District 南川區 *nánchuān qū*	534,329	572,362
Bishan District 璧山區 *bìshān qū*	586,034	756,022
Tongliang District 銅梁區 *tóngliáng qū*	600,086	685,729
Tongnan District 潼南區 *tóngnán qū*	639,985	688,115
Rongchang District 榮昌區 *róngchāng qū*	661,253	668,997
Kaizhou District 開州區 *kāizhōu qū*	1,160,336	1,203,306
Liangping District 梁平區 liángpíng qū	687,525	645,315
Chengkou County 城口縣 *chéngkǒu xiàn*	192,967	197,497
Fengdu County 豐都縣 *fēngdū xiàn*	649,182	557,374
Dianjiang County 墊江縣 *diànjiāng xiàn*	704,458	650,694
Wulong District 武隆縣 *wǔlóng xiàn*	351,038	356,748
Zhongxian County 忠縣 *zhōngxiàn*	751,424	720,976
Yunyang County 雲陽縣 *yúnyáng xiàn*	912,912	929,034
Fengjie County 奉節縣 *fèngjié xiàn*	834,259	744,836
Wushan County 巫山縣 *wūshān xiàn*	495,072	462,462
Wuxi County 巫溪縣 *wūxī xiàn*	414,073	388,685
Shizhu Tujia Autonomous County 石柱土家族自治縣 *shízhù tǔjiāzú zìzhìxiàn*	415,050	389,001
Xiushan Tujia and Miao Autonomous County 秀山土家族苗族自治縣 *xiùshān tǔjiāzú miáozú zìzhìxiàn*	501,590	496,194
Youyang Tujia and Miao Autonomous County 酉陽土家族苗族自治縣 *yǒuyáng tǔjiāzú miáozú zìzhìxiàn*	578,058	607,338
Pengshui Miao and Tujia Autonomous County 彭水苗族土家族自治縣 *péngshuǐ miáozú tǔjiāzú zìzhìxiàn*	545,094	530,599
Total	**28,846,200**	**32,054,159**

[a]This includes: Yuzhong District (渝中區); Dadukou District (大渡口區); Jiangbei District (江北區); Shapingba District (沙坪壩區); Jiulongpo District (九龍坡區); Nan'an District (南岸區); Beibei District (北碚區); Yubei District (渝北區); Banan District (巴南區); Zhoubian District County (周邊區縣) Fuling District (涪陵區) Changshou District (長壽區); Jiangjin District (江津區); Hechuan District (合川區); Yongchuan District (永川區); Nanchuan District (南川區); Qijiang District (綦江區); Dazu District (大足區); Bishan District (璧山區); Tongliang District (銅梁區); Rongchang District (榮昌區); and Tongnan District (潼南區)

[b]A figure was not provided in the official 2020 (7th) national census

[c]A figure was not provided in the official 2020 (7th) national census

Based on the subdistrict data for 2020 (Table 4.4), one is struck by the large numbers of people living in a relatively small administrative district, such as Wanmu Town (萬木鎮 *wànmù zhèn*), home to over 14,000 individuals. Table 4.5 shows the *hukou* (family registered) populations based on PRC Ministry of Civil Affairs. (Districts listed directly under major cities are government seats, as are those in parentheses). One can compare these data with the census (usual residential populations based on 2010 and 2020 censuses in Table 4.3.

Table 4.4 Chongqing city: population data of subordinate sectors (CCBS 2021)

Selected data, cities and subordinate sectors, population (2020 census)[a]	Subordinate subdistrict populations (2020)	Total population (2020)
Fuling District 涪陵區 *fúlíng qū*		**1,115,016**
Dunren Subdistrict 敦仁街道 *dūnrén jiēdào*	87,279	
Chongyi Subdistrict 崇義街道 *chóngyì jiēdào*	160,835	
Lizhi Subdistrict 荔枝街道 *lìzhī jiēdào*	227,587	
Jiangbei Subdistrict 江北街道 *jiāngběi jiēdào*	22,364	
Jiangdong Subdistrict 江東街道 *jiāngdōng jiēdào*	48,672	
Lidu Subdistrict 李渡街道 *lǐdù jiēdào*	17,847	
Longqiao Subdistrict 龍橋街道 *lóngqiáo jiēdào*	26,088	
Baitao Subdistrict 白濤街道 *báitāo jiēdào*	42,311	
Ma'an Subdistrict 馬鞍街道 *mǎ'ān jiēdào*	147,853	
Nantuo Town 南沱鎮 *nántuó zhèn*	16,259	
Qingyang Town 青羊鎮 *qīngyáng zhèn*	12,189	
Baisheng Town 百勝鎮 *bǎishèng zhèn*	21,947	
Zhenxi Town 珍溪鎮 *zhēnxī zhèn*	42,183	
Qingxi Town 清溪鎮 *qīngxī zhèn*	19,537	
Jiaoshi Town 焦石鎮 *jiāoshí zhèn*	19,816	
Mawu Town 馬武鎮 *mǎwǔ zhèn*	20,518	
Longtan Town 龍潭鎮 *lóngtán zhèn*	27,837	
Linshi Town 藺市鎮 *lìnshì zhèn*	28,708	
Xinmiao Town 新妙鎮 *xīnmiào zhèn*	31,715	
Shituo Town 石沱鎮 *shítuó zhèn*	16,729	
Yihe Town 義和鎮 *yìhé zhèn*	24,786	
Luoyun Township 羅雲鄉 *luóyún xiāng*	9881	
Damu Township 大木鄉 *dàmù xiāng*	2380	
Wulingshan Township 武陵山鄉 *wǔlíngshān xiāng*	4518	
Dashun Township 大順鄉 *dàshùn xiāng*	13,297	
Zengfu Township 增福鄉 *zēngfú xiāng*	8842	
Tongle Township 同樂鄉 *tónglè xiāng*	13,038	
Dadukou District 大渡口區 *dàdùkǒu qū*		**421,904**
Xinshancun Subdistrict 新山村街道 *xīnshāncūn jiēdào*	36,266	
Yuejincun Subdistrict 躍進村街道 *yuèjìncūn jiēdào*	41,475	

(continued)

Table 4.4 (continued)

Selected data, cities and subordinate sectors, population (2020 census)[a]	Subordinate subdistrict populations (2020)	Total population (2020)
Jiugongmiao Subdistrict 九宮廟街道 *jiŭgōngmiào jiēdào*	29,863	
Qiezixi Subdistrict 茄子溪街道 *qiézĭxī jiēdào*	31,938	
Chunhuilu Subdistrict 春暉路街道 *chūnhuīlù jiēdào*	109,360	
Baqiao Town 八橋鎮 *bāqiáo zhèn*	116,013	
Jiansheng Town 建勝鎮 *jiànshèng zhèn*	29,017	
Tiaodeng Town 跳蹬鎮 *tiàodēng zhèn*	27,972	
Jiangbei District 江北區 ***jiāngběi qū***		**925,800**
Huaxinjie Subdistrict 華新街街道 *huáxīnjiē jiēdào*	84,947	
Jiangbeicheng Subdistrict 江北城街道 *jiāngběichéng jiēdào*	10,533	
Shimahe Subdistrict 石馬河街道 *shímăhé jiēdào*	200,467	
Dashiba Subdistrict 大石壩街道 *dàshíbà jiēdào*	119,135	
Cuntan Subdistrict 寸灘街道 *cùntān jiēdào*	67,186	
Guanyinqiao Subdistrict 觀音橋街道 *guānyīnqiáo jiēdào*	193,455	
Wulidian Subdistrict 五里店街道 *wŭlĭdiàn jiēdào*	112,338	
Guojiatuo Subdistrict 郭家沱街道 *guōjiātuó jiēdào*	20,039	
Tieshanping Subdistrict 鐵山坪街道 *tiěshānpíng jiēdào*	41,541	
Yuzui Town 魚嘴鎮 *yúzuĭ zhèn*	51,796	
Fusheng Town 復盛鎮 *fùshèng zhèn*	17,237	
Wubao Town 五寶鎮 *wŭbăo zhèn*	7126	
Qijiang District 綦江區 ***qíjiāng qū***		**775,407**
Gunan Subdistrict 古南街道 *gŭnán jiēdào*	97,841	
Wenlong Subdistrict 文龍街道 *wénlóng jiēdào*	187,629	
Sanjiang Subdistrict 三江街道 *sānjiāng jiēdào*	30,310	
Xinsheng Subdistrict 新盛街道 *xīnshèng jiēdào*	9102	
Tonghui Subdistrict 通惠街道 *tōnghuì jiēdào*	59,115	
Shijiao Town 石角鎮 *shíjiăo zhèn*	29,318	
Dongxi Town 東溪鎮 *dōngxī zhèn*	49,001	
Ganshui Town 趕水鎮 *gănshuĭ zhèn*	36,439	
Datong Town 打通鎮 *dătōng zhèn*	42,592	
Shihao Town 石壕鎮 *shíháo zhèn*	30,072	
Yongxin Town 永新鎮 *yŏngxīn zhèn*	35,651	
Sanjiao Town 三角鎮 *sānjiăo zhèn*	22,345	
Longsheng Town 隆盛鎮 *lóngshèng zhèn*	18,691	
Guofu Town 郭扶鎮 *guōfú zhèn*	24,708	
Zhuantang Town 篆塘鎮 *zhuàntáng zhèn*	14,401	
Dingshan Town 丁山鎮 *dīngshān zhèn*	6955	

(continued)

Table 4.4 (continued)

Selected data, cities and subordinate sectors, population (2020 census)[a]	Subordinate subdistrict populations (2020)	Total population (2020)
Anwen Town 安穩鎮 *ānwěn zhèn*	32,199	
Fuhuan Town 扶歡鎮 *fúhuān zhèn*	20,796	
Yongcheng Town 永城鎮 *yǒngchéng zhèn*	12,869	
Zhongfeng Town 中峰鎮 *zhōngfēng zhèn*	9596	
Hengshan Town 橫山鎮 *héngshān zhèn*	5777	
Dazu District 大足區 ***dàzú qū***		**834,592**
Longgang Subdistrict 龍崗街道 *lónggǎng jiēdào*	88,330	
Tangxiang Subdistrict 棠香街道 *tángxiāng jiēdào*	150,488	
Longtanzi Subdistrict 龍灘子街道 *lóngtānzǐ jiēdào*	17,023	
Shuanglu Subdistrict 雙路街道 *shuānglù jiēdào*	40,575	
Tongqiao Subdistrict 通橋街道 *tōngqiáo jiēdào*	29,758	
Zhifeng Subdistrict 智鳳街道 *zhìfèng jiēdào*	27,786	
Longshui Town 龍水鎮 *lóngshuǐ zhèn*	112,170	
Baoding Town 寶頂鎮 *bǎodǐng zhèn*	15,037	
Zhong'ao Town 中敖鎮 *zhōng'áo zhèn*	35,360	
Sanqu Town 三驅鎮 *sānqū zhèn*	30,722	
Baoxing Town 寶興鎮 *bǎoxīng zhèn*	17,534	
Yulong Town 玉龍鎮 *yùlóng zhèn*	14,978	
Shima Town 石馬鎮 *shímǎ zhèn*	17,452	
Shiwan Town 拾萬鎮 *shíwàn zhèn*	14,565	
Huilong Town 回龍鎮 *huílóng zhèn*	13,260	
Jinshan Town 金山鎮 *jīnshān zhèn*	12,900	
Wangu Town 萬古鎮 *wàngǔ zhèn*	37,108	
Guoliang Town 國梁鎮 *guóliáng zhèn*	10,178	
Yongxi Town 雍溪鎮 *yōngxī zhèn*	17,154	
Zhuxi Town 珠溪鎮 *zhūxī zhèn*	29,947	
Longshi Town 龍石鎮 *lóngshí zhèn*	10,952	
Youting Town 郵亭鎮 *yóutíng zhèn*	32,443	
Tieshan Town 鐵山鎮 *tiěshān zhèn*	16,721	
Gaosheng Town 高升鎮 *gāoshēng zhèn*	13,534	
Jijia Town 季家鎮 *jìjiā zhèn*	11,392	
Gulong Town 古龍鎮 *gǔlóng zhèn*	4774	
Gaoping Town 高坪鎮 *gāopíng zhèn*	12,451	
Qianjiang District 黔江區 ***qiánjiāng qū***		**487,281**
Chengdong Subdistrict 城東街道 *chéngdōng jiēdào*	105,248	
Chengnan Subdistrict 城南街道 *chéngnán jiēdào*	54,520	
Chengxi Subdistrict 城西街道 *chéngxī jiēdào*	49,848	
Zhengyang Subdistrict 正陽街道 *zhèngyáng jiēdào*	32,701	

(continued)

Table 4.4 (continued)

Selected data, cities and subordinate sectors, population (2020 census)[a]	Subordinate subdistrict populations (2020)	Total population (2020)
Zhoubai Subdistrict 舟白街道 *zhōubái jiēdào*	47,196	
Fengjia Subdistrict 馮家街道 *féngjiā jiēdào*	18,085	
Apengjiang Town 阿蓬江鎮 *ā'péngjiāng zhèn*	14,210	
Shihui Town 石會鎮 *shíhuì zhèn*	9,999	
Heixi Town 黑溪鎮 *hēixī zhèn*	10,035	
Huangxi Town 黃溪鎮 *huángxī zhèn*	7746	
Lishui Town 黎水鎮 *líshuǐ zhèn*	6749	
Jinxi Town 金溪鎮 *jīnxī zhèn*	7024	
Mala Town 馬喇鎮 *mălă zhèn*	9822	
Zhuoshui Town 濯水鎮 *zhuóshuǐ zhèn*	15,245	
Shijia Town 石家鎮 *shíjiā zhèn*	7036	
Echi Town 鵝池鎮 *échí zhèn*	5883	
Xiaonanhai Town 小南海鎮 *xiǎonánhǎi zhèn*	5080	
Lin'e Town 鄰鄂鎮 *lín'èzhèn*	7115	
Baishi Town白石鎮 *báishí zhèn*	8471	
Zhongtang Town 中塘鎮 *zhōngtáng zhèn*	9648	
Shaba Town 沙壩鎮 *shābà zhèn*	9380	
Pengdong Town 蓬東鎮 *péngdōng zhèn*	5404	
Shanling Township 杉嶺鄉 *shānlǐng xiāng*	4889	
Taiji Township 太極鄉 *tàijí xiāng*	6138	
Shuitian Township 水田鄉 *shuǐtián xiāng*	4740	
Baitu Township 白土鄉 *báitǔ xiāng*	3354	
Jindong Township 金洞鄉 *jīndòng xiāng*	5459	
Wuli Township 五里鄉 *wǔlǐ xiāng*	5922	
Shuishi Township 水市鄉 *shuǐshì xiāng*	5351	
Xinhua Township 新華鄉 *xīnhuá xiāng*	4983	
Jiangjin District 江津區 ***jiāngjīn qū***		**1,359,611**
Jijiang Subdistrict 幾江街道 *jījiāng jiēdào*	148,012	
Degan Subdistrict 德感街道 *dégǎn jiēdào*	85,291	
Shuangfu Subdistrict 雙福街道 *shuāngfú jiēdào*	182,176	
Dingshan Subdistrict 鼎山街道 *dǐngshān jiēdào*	123,819	
Shengquan Subdistrict 聖泉街道 *shèngquán jiēdào*	46,964	
Youxi Town 油溪鎮 *yóuxī zhèn*	49,664	
Wutan Town 吳灘鎮 *wútān zhèn*	23,530	
Shimen Town 石門鎮 *shímén zhèn*	27,813	
Zhuyang Town 朱楊鎮 *zhūyáng zhèn*	18,918	
Shima Town 石蟆鎮 *shímá zhèn*	61,462	
Yongxing Town 永興鎮 *yǒngxīng zhèn*	26,197	
Tanghe Town 塘河鎮 *tánghé zhèn*	10,652	
Baisha Town 白沙鎮 *báishā zhèn*	115,446	

(continued)

Table 4.4 (continued)

Selected data, cities and subordinate sectors, population (2020 census)[a]	Subordinate subdistrict populations (2020)	Total population (2020)
Longhua Town 龍華鎮 *lónghuá zhèn*	23,055	
Lishi Town 李市鎮 *lǐshì zhèn*	55,345	
Ciyun Town 慈雲鎮 *cíyún zhèn*	17,669	
Caijia Town 蔡家鎮 *càijiā zhèn*	35,141	
Zhongshan Town 中山鎮 *zhōngshān zhèn*	13,867	
Jiaping Town 嘉平鎮 *jiāpíng zhèn*	12,549	
Bailin (Bolin) Town 柏林鎮 *bǎilín zhèn*	20,696	
Xianfeng Town 先鋒鎮 *xiānfēng zhèn*	46,468	
Luohuang Town 珞璜鎮 *luòhuáng zhèn*	84,363	
Jiasi Town 賈嗣鎮 *jiǎsì zhèn*	20,335	
Xiaba Town 夏壩鎮 *xiàbà zhèn*	9292	
Xihu Town 西湖鎮 *xīhú zhèn*	29,293	
Dushi Town 杜市鎮 *dùshì zhèn*	20,967	
Guangxing Town 廣興鎮 *guǎngxīng zhèn*	7512	
Simianshan Town 四面山鎮 *sìmiànshān zhèn*	8138	
Zhiping Town 支坪鎮 *zhīpíng zhèn*	28,241	
Siping Town 四屏鎮 *sìpíng zhèn*	6736	
Nanchuan District 南川區 ***nánchuān qū***		**572,362**
Dongcheng Subdistrict 東城街道 *dōngchéng jiēdào*	83,856	
Nancheng Subdistrict 南城街道 *nánchéng jiēdào*	105,292	
Xicheng Subdistrict 西城街道 *xīchéng jiēdào*	101,799	
Nanping Town 南平鎮 *nánpíng zhèn*	30,143	
Shuijiang Town 水江鎮 *shuǐjiāng zhèn*	44,703	
Shentong Town 神童鎮 *shéntóng zhèn*	6168	
Mingyu Town 鳴玉鎮 *míngyù zhèn*	8903	
Daguan Town 大觀鎮 *dàguān zhèn*	19,469	
Xinglong Town 興隆鎮 *xīnglóng zhèn*	15,529	
Taipingchang Town 太平場鎮 *tàipíngcháng zhèn*	8742	
Baisha Town 白沙鎮 *báishā zhèn*	5726	
Shiqiang Town 石墻鎮 *shíqiáng zhèn*	5744	
Lixianghu Town 黎香湖鎮 *líxiānghú zhèn*	5234	
Muliang Town 木涼鎮 *mùliáng zhèn*	5663	
Nanzhushan Town 楠竹山鎮 *nánzhúshān zhèn*	6533	
Shixi Town 石溪鎮 *shíxī zhèn*	9441	
Minzhu Town 民主鎮 *mínzhǔ zhèn*	6411	
Fushou Town 福壽鎮 *fúshòu zhèn*	6743	
Hetu Town 河圖鎮 *hétú zhèn*	4804	
Shilian Town 石蓮鎮 *shílián zhèn*	3224	
Qianfeng Town 乾豐鎮 *qiánfēng zhèn*	4610	

(continued)

Table 4.4 (continued)

Selected data, cities and subordinate sectors, population (2020 census)[a]	Subordinate subdistrict populations (2020)	Total population (2020)
Qilong Town 騎龍鎮 *qílóng zhèn*	4873	
Lengshuiguan Town 冷水關鎮 *lěngshuǐguān zhèn*	5959	
Zhongqiao Township 中橋鄉 *zhōngqiáo xiāng*	5927	
Fengyan Township 峰岩鄉 *fēngyán xiāng*	5260	
Dayou Town 大有鎮 *dàyǒu zhèn*	10,156	
Hexi Town 合溪鎮 *héxī zhèn*	5382	
Qingyuan Town 慶元鎮 *qìngyuán zhèn*	6761	
Guhua Town 古花鎮 *gǔhuā zhèn*	6135	
Jinshan Town 金山鎮 *jīnshān zhèn*	7403	
Toudu Town 頭渡鎮 *tóudù zhèn*	4680	
Delong Town 德隆鎮 *délóng zhèn*	4392	
Sanquan Town 三泉鎮 *sānquán zhèn*	10,894	
Shanwangping Town 山王坪鎮 *shānwángpíng zhèn*	5803	
Tongliang District 銅梁區 ***tóngliáng qū***		**685,729**
Bachuan Subdistrict 巴川街道 *bāchuān jiēdào*	141,804	
Dongcheng Subdistrict 東城街道 *dōngchéng jiēdào*	145,652	
Nancheng Subdistrict 南城街道 *nánchéng jiēdào*	81,945	
Pulü Subdistrict 蒲呂街道 *púlǚ jiēdào*	24,472	
Jiuxian Subdistrict 舊縣街道 *jiùxiàn jiēdào*	25,653	
Tuqiao Town 土橋鎮 *tǔqiáo zhèn*	11,066	
Erping Town 二坪鎮 *èrpíng zhèn*	6071	
Shuikou Town 水口鎮 *shuǐkǒu zhèn*	4598	
Anju Town 安居鎮 *ānjū zhèn*	16,523	
Baiyang Town 白羊鎮 *báiyáng zhèn*	6573	
Pingtan Town 平灘鎮 *píngtān zhèn*	25,961	
Xiaolin Town 小林鎮 *xiǎolín zhèn*	6096	
Shuangshan Town 雙山鎮 *shuāngshān zhèn*	5945	
Hufeng Town 虎峰鎮 *hǔfēng zhèn*	23,182	
Shiyu Town 石魚鎮 *shíyú zhèn*	10,723	
Fuguo Town 福果鎮 *fúguǒ zhèn*	8275	
Qinglong Town 慶隆鎮 *qìnglóng zhèn*	6795	
Shaoyun Town 少雲鎮 *shǎoyún zhèn*	15,103	
Weixin Town 維新鎮 *wéixīn zhèn*	8164	
Gaolou Town 高樓鎮 *gāolóu zhèn*	4915	
Damiao Town 大廟鎮 *dàmiào zhèn*	14,493	
Weilong Town 圍龍鎮 *wéilóng zhèn*	12,737	
Huaxing Town 華興鎮 *huáxīng zhèn*	7236	
Yongjia Town 永嘉鎮 *yǒngjiā zhèn*	18,162	

(continued)

Table 4.4 (continued)

Selected data, cities and subordinate sectors, population (2020 census)[a]	Subordinate subdistrict populations (2020)	Total population (2020)
Anxi Town 安溪鎮 *ānxī zhèn*	5437	
Xihe Town 西河鎮 *xīhé zhèn*	9668	
Lüfeng Town 侶俸鎮 *lǚfèng zhèn*	25,211	
Taiping Town 太平鎮 *tàipíng zhèn*	13,269	
Rongchang District 榮昌區 ***róngchāng qū***		**668,997**
Changyuan Subdistrict 昌元街道 *chāngyuán jiēdào*	160,316	
Changzhou Subdistrict 昌州街道 *chāngzhōu jiēdào*	155,705	
Guangshun Subdistrict 廣順街道 *guǎngshùn jiēdào*	29,710	
Shuanghe Subdistrict 雙河街道 *shuānghé jiēdào*	31,167	
Anfu Subdistrict 安富街道 *ānfù jiēdào*	33,750	
Fenggao Subdistrict 峰高街道 *fēnggāo jiēdào*	24,779	
Ronglong Town 榮隆鎮 *rónglóng zhèn*	22,223	
Renyi Town 仁義鎮 *rényì zhèn*	29,653	
Panlong Town 盤龍鎮 *pánlóng zhèn*	40,254	
Wujia Town 吳家鎮 *wújiā zhèn*	27,862	
Zhisheng Town 直升鎮 *zhíshēng zhèn*	8669	
Wanling Town 萬靈鎮 *wànlíng zhèn*	9000	
Qingsheng Town 清升鎮 *qīngshēng zhèn*	11,181	
Qingjiang Town 清江鎮 *qīngjiāng zhèn*	8009	
Guchang Town 古昌鎮 *gǔchāng zhèn*	11,600	
Hebao Town 河包鎮 *hébāo zhèn*	23,614	
Guansheng Town 觀勝鎮 *guānshèng zhèn*	9708	
Tonggu Town 銅鼓鎮 *tónggǔ zhèn*	8817	
Qingliu Town 清流鎮 *qīngliú zhèn*	7945	
Yuanjue Town 遠覺鎮 *yuǎnjué zhèn*	6724	
Longji Town 龍集鎮 *lóngjí zhèn*	8291	
Kaizhou District 開州區 ***kāizhōu qū***		**1,203,306**
Hanfeng Subdistrict 漢豐街道 *hànfēng jiēdào*	127,220	
Wenfeng Subdistrict 文峰街道 *wénfēng jiēdào*	103,081	
Yunfeng Subdistrict 雲楓街道 *yúnfēng jiēdào*	137,811	
Zhendong Subdistrict 鎮東街道 *zhèndōng jiēdào*	18,125	
Fengle Subdistrict 豐樂街道 *fēnglè jiēdào*	20,986	
Baihe Subdistrict 白鶴街道 *báihè jiēdào*	34,126	
Zhaojia Subdistrict 趙家街道 *zhàojiā jiēdào*	46,265	
Dade Town 大德鎮 *dàdé zhèn*	28,772	
Zhen'an Town 鎮安鎮[b] *zhèn'ān zhèn*	15,330	
Houba Town 厚壩鎮 *hòubà zhèn*	15,156	
Jinfeng Town 金峰鎮 *jīnfēng zhèn*	10,578	

(continued)

Table 4.4 (continued)

Selected data, cities and subordinate sectors, population (2020 census)[a]	Subordinate subdistrict populations (2020)	Total population (2020)
Wenquan Town 温泉鎮 *wēnquán zhèn*	30,183	
Guojia Town 郭家鎮 *guōjiā zhèn*	26,883	
Baiqiao Town 白橋鎮 *báiqiáo zhèn*	9449	
Heqian Town 和謙鎮 *héqiān zhèn*	17,289	
Heyan Town 河堰鎮 *héyàn zhèn*	19,578	
Dajin Town 大進鎮 *dàjìn zhèn*	28,037	
Tanjia Town 譚家鎮 *tánjiā zhèn*	12,070	
Dunhao Town 敦好鎮 *dūnhǎo zhèn*	30,175	
Gaoqiao Town 高橋鎮 *gāoqiáo zhèn*	19,539	
Jiulongshan Town 九龍山鎮 *jiǔlóngshān zhèn*	27,092	
Tianhe Town 天和鎮 *tiānhé zhèn*	9808	
Zhonghe Town 中和鎮 *zhōnghé zhèn*	35,027	
Yihe Town 義和鎮 *yìhé zhèn*	18,290	
Linjiang Town 臨江鎮 *línjiāng zhèn*	72,796	
Zhuxi Town 竹溪鎮 *zhúxī zhèn*	25,311	
Tieqiao Town 鐵橋鎮 *tiěqiáo zhèn*	37,688	
Nanya Town 南雅鎮 *nányǎ zhèn*	23,348	
Wushan Town 巫山鎮 *wūshān zhèn*	13,954	
Yuexi Town 岳溪鎮 *yuèxī zhèn*	40,735	
Changsha Town 長沙鎮 *chángshā zhèn*	45,400	
Nanmen Town 南門鎮 *nánmén zhèn*	32,461	
Qukou Town 渠口鎮 *qúkǒu zhèn*	10,411	
Manyue Town 滿月鎮 *mǎnyuè zhèn*	7909	
Xuebaoshan Town 雪寶山鎮 *xuěbǎoshān zhèn*	6563	
Guanmian Township 關面鄉 *guānmiàn xiāng*	4959	
Maliu Township 麻柳鄉 *máliǔ xiāng*	14,306	
Zishui Township 紫水鄉 *zǐshuǐ xiāng*	12,561	
Sanhui Township 三匯鄉 *sānhuì xiāng*	10,161	
Wutong Township 五通鄉 *wǔtōng xiāng*	3873	
Dianjiang County 墊江縣 *diànjiāng xiàn*		**650,694**
Guixi Subdistrict 桂溪街道 *guìxī jiēdào*	117,226	
Guiyang Subdistrict 桂陽街道 *guìyáng jiēdào*	110,107	
Xinmen Town 新民鎮 *xīnmín zhèn*	23,326	
Shaping Town 沙坪鎮 *shāpíng zhèn*	28,986	
Zhoujia Town 周嘉鎮 *zhōujiā zhèn*	24,558	
Pushun Town 普順鎮 *pǔshùn zhèn*	17,453	
Yong'an Town 永安鎮 *yǒng'ān zhèn*	17,789	
Gao'an Town 高安鎮 *gāoān zhèn*	40,824	
Gaofeng Town 高峰鎮 *gāofēng zhèn*	16,975	
Wudong Town 五洞鎮 *wǔdòng zhèn*	14,149	
Chengxi Town 澄溪鎮 *chéngxī zhèn*	37,878	

(continued)

Table 4.4 (continued)

Selected data, cities and subordinate sectors, population (2020 census)[a]	Subordinate subdistrict populations (2020)	Total population (2020)
Taiping Town 太平鎮 *tàipíng zhèn*	21,953	
Heyou Town 鶴游鎮 *hèyóu zhèn*	10,311	
Pingshan Town 坪山鎮 *píngshān zhèn*	27,997	
Yantai Town 硯台鎮 *yàntái zhèn*	22,429	
Caohui Town 曹回鎮 *cáohuí zhèn*	15,238	
Gangjia Town 杠家鎮 *gàngjiā zhèn*	15,023	
Baojia Town 包家鎮 *bāojiā zhèn*	9990	
Baijia Town 白家鎮 *báijiā zhèn*	13,552	
Yongping Town 永平鎮 *yǒngpíng zhèn*	8032	
Sanxi Town 三溪鎮 *sānxī zhèn*	7923	
Peixing Town 裴興鎮 *péixīng zhèn*	8635	
Huangsha Town 黄沙鎮 *huángshā zhèn*	12,197	
Changlong Town 長龍鎮 *chánglóng zhèn*	16,784	
Shahe Township 沙河鄉 *shāhé xiāng*	4865	
Dashi Township 大石鄉 *dàshí xiāng*	6494	
Wulong District 武隆區 ***wǔlóng qū***		**356,748**
Fengshan Subdistrict 鳳山街道 *fèngshān jiēdào*	68,193	
Furong Subdistrict 芙蓉街道 *fúróng jiēdào*	57,202	
Xiannüshan Subdistrict 仙女山街道 *xiānnǚshān jiēdào*	12,424	
Yangjiao Subdistrict 羊角街道 *yángjiǎo jiēdào*	18,029	
Baima Town 白馬鎮 *báimǎ zhèn*	25,389	
Jiangkou Town 江口鎮 *jiāngkǒu zhèn*	19,296	
Huolu Town 火爐鎮 *huǒlú zhèn*	20,836	
Yajiang Town 鴨江鎮 *yājiāng zhèn*	15,615	
Changba Town 長壩鎮 *chángbà zhèn*	14,601	
Pingqiao Town 平橋鎮 *píngqiáo zhèn*	13,508	
Tongzi Town 桐梓鎮 *tóngzǐ zhèn*	8905	
Heshun Town 和順鎮 *héshùn zhèn*	7613	
Shuanghe Town 雙河鎮 *shuānghé zhèn*	8207	
Fenglai Town 鳳來鎮 *fènglái zhèn*	8810	
Miaoya Township 廟埡鄉 *miàoyà xiāng*	6876	
Shiqiao Miaozu Tujiazu (Miao and Tujia) Township 石橋苗族土家族鄉 *shíqiáo miáozú tǔjiāzú xiāng*	6694	
Huangying Township 黃鶯鄉 *huángyīng xiāng*	5497	
Canggou Township 滄溝鄉 *cānggōu xiāng*	6428	
Wenfu Miaozu Tujiazu (Miao and Tujia) Township 文復苗族土家族鄉 *wénfù miáozú tǔjiāzú xiāng*	5456	
Tudi Township 土地鄉 *tǔdì xiāng*	4506	
Baiyun Township 白雲鄉 *báiyún xiāng*	4602	

(continued)

Table 4.4 (continued)

Selected data, cities and subordinate sectors, population (2020 census)[a]	Subordinate subdistrict populations (2020)	Total population (2020)
Houping Miaozu Tujiazu (Miao and Tujia) Township 後坪苗族土家族鄉 *hòupíng miáozú tǔjiāzú xiāng*	4644	
Jiekou Miaozu Gelaozu (Miao and Gelao) Township 潔口苗族仡佬族鄉 *jiékǒu miáozú qìlǎozú xiāng*	4270	
Jielong Township 接龍鄉 *jiēlóng xiāng*	3529	
Zhaojia Township 趙家鄉 *zhàojiā xiāng*	2938	
Dadonghe Township 大洞河鄉 *dàdònghé xiāng*	2678	
Yunyang County 雲陽縣 ***yúnyáng xiàn***		**929,034**
Shuangjiang Subdistrict 雙江街道 *shuāngjiāng jiēdào*	106,247	
Qinglong Subdistrict 青龍街道 *qīnglóng jiēdào*	146,722	
Renhe Subdistrict 人和街道 *rénhé jiēdào*	11,274	
Panlong Subdistrict 盤龍街道 *pánlóng jiēdào*	6499	
Longjiao Town 龍角鎮 *lóngjiǎo zhèn*	7236	
Guling Town 故陵鎮 *gùlíng zhèn*	4767	
Hongshi Town 紅獅鎮 *hóngshī zhèn*	5784	
Luyang Town 路陽鎮 *lùyáng zhèn*	6178	
Nongba Town 農壩鎮 *nóngbà zhèn*	5894	
Quma Town 渠馬鎮 *qúmǎ zhèn*	3632	
Huangshi Town 黄石鎮 *huángshí zhèn*	5854	
Bayang Town 巴陽鎮 *bāyáng zhèn*	10,188	
Shashi Town 沙市鎮 *shāshì zhèn*	11,274	
Yuquan Town 魚泉鎮 *yúquán zhèn*	6499	
Fengming Town 鳳鳴鎮 *fèngmíng zhèn*	7236	
Baoping Town 寶坪鎮 *bǎopíng zhèn*	4767	
Nanxi Town 南溪鎮 *nánxī zhèn*	5784	
Shuangshi Town 雙土鎮 *shuāngtǔ zhèn*	6178	
Sangping Town 桑坪鎮 *sāngpíng zhèn*	5894	
Jiangkou Town 江口鎮 *jiāngkǒu zhèn*	3632	
Gaoyang Town 高陽鎮 *gāoyáng zhèn*	5854	
Ping'an Town 平安鎮 *píng'ān zhèn*	10,188	
Yunyang Town 雲陽鎮 *yúnyáng zhèn*	11,274	
Yun'an Town 雲安鎮 *yún'ān zhèn*	6499	
Qixia Town 棲霞鎮 *qīxiá zhèn*	7236	
Shuanglong Town 雙龍鎮 *shuānglóng zhèn*	4767	
Nixi Town 泥溪鎮 *níxī zhèn*	5784	
Biaocao Town 蔈草鎮 *biāocǎo zhèn*	6178	
Yanglu Town 養鹿鎮 *yǎnglù zhèn*	5894	
Shuikou Town 水口鎮 *shuǐkǒu zhèn*	3632	
Yanping Town 堰坪鎮 *yànpíng zhèn*	5854	
Longdong Town 龍洞鎮 *lóngdòng zhèn*	10,188	

(continued)

Table 4.4 (continued)

Selected data, cities and subordinate sectors, population (2020 census)[a]	Subordinate subdistrict populations (2020)	Total population (2020)
Houye Town 後葉鎮 *hòuyè zhèn*	11,274	
Yaoling Town 耀靈鎮 *yàolíng zhèn*	6499	
Dayang Town 大陽鎮 *dàyáng zhèn*	7236	
Wailang Township 外郎鄉 *wàiláng xiāng*	4767	
Xinjin Township 新津鄉 *xīnjīn xiāng*	5784	
Pu'an township 普安鄉 *pǔ'ān xiāng*	6178	
Donglu Township 洞鹿鄉 *dònglù xiāng*	5894	
Shimen Township 石門鄉 *shímén xiāng*	3632	
Shangba Township 上壩鄉 *shàngbà xiāng*	5854	
Qingshui Tujia Autonomous Township 清水土家族自治鄉 *qīngshuǐ tǔjiāzú zìzhìxiāng*	10,188	
Fengjie County 奉節縣 ***fèngjié xiàn***		**744,836**
Yong'an Subdistrict 永安街道 *yǒng'ān jiēdào*	182,983	
Kuizhou Subdistrict[c] 夔州街道 *kuízhōu jiēdào*	N/A	
Yufu Subdistrict 魚復街道 *yúfù jiēdào*	67,360	
Kuimen Subdistrict 夔門街道 *kuímén jiēdào*	19,620	
Baidi Town 白帝鎮 *báidì zhèn*	18,750	
Caotang Town 草堂鎮 *cǎotáng zhèn*	21,840	
Fenhe Town 汾河鎮 *fénhé zhèn*	14,609	
Kangle Town 康樂鎮 *kānglè zhèn*	22,579	
Dashu Town 大樹鎮 *dàshù zhèn*	10,873	
Zhuyuan Town 竹園鎮 *zhúyuán zhèn*	28,513	
Gongping Town 公平鎮 *gōngpíng zhèn*	31,737	
Zhuyi Town 朱衣鎮 *zhūyī zhèn*	19,099	
Jiagao Town 甲高鎮 *jiǎgāo zhèn*	25,465	
Yangshi Town 羊市鎮 *yángshì zhèn*	8300	
Tuxiang Town 吐祥鎮 *tǔxiáng zhèn*	37,971	
Xinglong Town 興隆鎮 *xīnglóng zhèn*	39,829	
Qinglong Town 青龍鎮 *qīnglóng zhèn*	13,702	
Xinmen Town 新民鎮 *xīnmín zhèn*	17,943	
Yongle Town 永樂鎮 *yǒnglè zhèn*	17,396	
Anping Town 安坪鎮 *ānpíng zhèn*	22,020	
Wuma Town 五馬鎮 *wǔmǎ zhèn*	20,771	
Qinglian Town 青蓮鎮 *qīnglián zhèn*	16,571	
Yanwan Township 岩灣鄉 *yánwān xiāng*	3086	
Pingan Township 平安鄉 *píng'ān xiāng*	9883	
Hongtu Township 紅土鄉 *hóngtǔ xiāng*	10,471	
Shigang Township 石崗鄉 *shígǎng xiāng*	11,718	
Kangping Township 康坪鄉 *kāngpíng xiāng*	5586	
Taihe Tujiazu Township 太和土家族鄉 *tàihé tǔjiāzú xiāng*	8157	

(continued)

Table 4.4 (continued)

Selected data, cities and subordinate sectors, population (2020 census)[a]	Subordinate subdistrict populations (2020)	Total population (2020)
Hefeng Township 鶴峰鄉 *hèfēng xiāng*	9935	
Fengping Township 馮坪鄉 *féngpíng xiāng*	11,431	
Changan Tujiazu Township 長安土家族鄉 *cháng'ān tǔjiāzú xiāng*	7267	
Longqiao Tujiazu Township 龍橋土家族鄉 *lóngqiáo tǔjiāzú xiāng*	6519	
Yunwu Tujiazu Township 雲霧土家族鄉 *yúnwù tǔjiāzú xiāng*	2852	
Wushan County 巫山縣 ***wūshān xiàn***		**462,462**
Gaotang Subdistrict 高唐街道 *gāotáng jiēdào*	135,588	
Longmen Subdistrict 龍門街道 *lóngmén jiēdào*	17,142	
Miaoyu Town 廟宇鎮 *miàoyǔ zhèn*	31,472	
Dachang Town 大昌鎮 *dàchāng zhèn*	31,633	
Futian Town 福田鎮 *fútián zhèn*	25,536	
Longxi Town 龍溪鎮 *lóngxī zhèn*	12,362	
Shuanglong Town 雙龍鎮 *shuānglóng zhèn*	14,076	
Guanyang Town 官陽鎮 *guānyáng zhèn*	9628	
Luoping Town 騾坪鎮 *luópíng zhèn*	21,248	
Baolong Town 抱龍鎮 *bàolóng zhèn*	15,302	
Guandu Town 官渡鎮 *guāndù zhèn*	35,525	
Tonggu Town 銅鼓鎮 *tónggǔ zhèn*	12,302	
Wuxia Town 巫峽鎮 *wūxiá zhèn*	27,298	
Hongchun Township 紅椿鄉 *hóngchūn xiāng*	3277	
Liangping Township 兩坪鄉 *liǎngpíng xiāng*	9766	
Quchi Township 曲尺鄉 *qūchǐ xiāng*	7121	
Jianping Township 建平鄉 *jiànpíng xiāng*	5350	
Daxi Township 大溪鄉 *dàxī xiāng*	4315	
Jinping Township 金坪鄉 *jīnpíng xiāng*	1909	
Pinghe Township 平河鄉 *pínghé xiāng*	6466	
Dangyang Township 當陽鄉 *dāngyáng xiāng*	4015	
Zhuxian Township 竹賢鄉 *zhúxián xiāng*	2719	
Sanxi Township 三溪鄉 *sānxī xiāng*	11,205	
Peishi Township 培石鄉 *péishí xiāng*	4302	
Duping Township 篤坪鄉 *dǔpíng xiāng*	10,424	
Dengjia Township 鄧家鄉 *dèngjiā xiāng*	2481	
Xiushan Tujia and Miao Autonomous County 秀山土家族苗族自治縣 ***xiùshān tǔjiāzú miáozú zìzhìxiàn***		**496,194**
Zhonghe Subdistrict 中和街道 *zhōnghé jiēdào*	103,387	
Wuchang Subdistrict 烏場街道 *wūcháng jiēdào*	48,205	

(continued)

Table 4.4 (continued)

Selected data, cities and subordinate sectors, population (2020 census)[a]	Subordinate subdistrict populations (2020)	Total population (2020)
Pingkai Subdistrict 平凱街道 *píngkǎi jiēdào*	45,552	
Guanzhuang Subdistrict 官莊街道 *guānzhuāng jiēdào*	25,978	
Qingxichang Town 清溪場鎮 *qīngxīcháng zhèn*	45,392	
Aikou Town 隘口鎮 *àikǒu zhèn*	12,055	
Rongxi Town 溶溪鎮 *róngxī zhèn*	13,793	
Longchirongxi 龍池鎮 *lóngchí zhèn*	24,139	
Shidi Town 石堤鎮 *shídī zhèn*	10,305	
E'rong Town 峨溶鎮 *é'róng zhèn*	14,307	
Hong'an Town 洪安鎮 *hóngān zhèn*	16,416	
Yajiang Town 雅江鎮 *yǎjiāng zhèn*	10,185	
Shiye Town 石耶鎮 *shíyé zhèn*	8046	
Meijiang Town 梅江鎮 *méijiāng zhèn*	30,127	
Lanqiao Town 蘭橋鎮 *lánqiáo zhèn*	11,784	
Gaotian Town 膏田鎮 *gāotián zhèn*	6819	
Xikou Town 溪口鎮 *xīkǒu zhèn*	9314	
Miaoquan Town 妙泉鎮 *miàoquán zhèn*	5355	
Songnong Town 宋農鎮 *sòngnóng zhèn*	4370	
Liren Town 里仁鎮 *lǐrén zhèn*	7176	
Zhongling Town 鍾靈鎮 *zhōnglíng zhèn*	13,946	
Xiaoxi Town 孝溪鄉 *xiàoxī xiāng*	6424	
Haiyang Township 海洋鄉 *hǎiyáng xiāng*	4158	
Daxi Township 大溪鄉 *dàxī xiāng*	4025	
Yongdong Township 湧洞鄉 *yǒngdòng xiāng*	4580	
Zhongping Township 中平鄉 *zhōngpíng xiāng*	5491	
Cenxi Township 岑溪鄉 *cénxī xiāng*	4865	
Youyang Tujia and Miao Autonomous County 酉陽土家族苗族自治縣 ***yǒuyáng tǔjiāzú miáozú zìzhìxiàn***		**607,338**
Taohuayuan Subdistrict 桃花源街道 *táohuāyuán jiēdào*	67,589	
Zhongduo Subdistrict 鐘多街道 *zhōngduō jiēdào*	79,729	
Longtan Town 龍潭鎮 *lóngtán zhèn*	65,311	
Mawang Town 麻旺鎮 *máwàng zhèn*	35,018	
Youchou Town 酉酬鎮 *yǒuchóu zhèn*	18,031	
Daxi Town 大溪鎮 *dàxī zhèn*	12,985	
Xinglong Town 興隆鎮 *xīnglóng zhèn*	11,327	
Heishui Town 黑水鎮 *hēishuǐ zhèn*	12,782	
Dingshi Town 丁市鎮 *dīngshì zhèn*	20,369	
Gongtan Town 龔灘鎮 *gōngtān zhèn*	15,009	
Lixi Town 李溪鎮 *lǐxī zhèn*	22,487	

(continued)

Table 4.4 (continued)

Selected data, cities and subordinate sectors, population (2020 census)[a]	Subordinate subdistrict populations (2020)	Total population (2020)
Ganxi Town 泔溪鎮 *gānxī zhèn*	11,174	
Youshuihe Town 酉水河鎮 *yǒushuǐhé zhèn*	10,450	
Cangling Town 蒼嶺鎮 *cānglǐng zhèn*	9938	
Xiaohe Town 小河鎮 *xiǎohé zhèn*	9781	
Banxi Town 板溪鎮 *bǎnxī zhèn*	13,720	
Tushi Town 塗市鎮 *túshì zhèn*	11,715	
Tonggu Town 銅鼓鎮 *tónggǔ zhèn*	16,463	
Wufu Town 五福鎮 *wǔfú zhèn*	8460	
Wanmu Town 萬木鎮 *wànmù zhèn*	14,108	
Nanyaojie Town 南腰界鎮 *nányāojiè zhèn*	12,828	
Keda Township 可大鄉 *kědà xiāng*	8708	
Pianbai (Pianbo) Township 偏柏鄉 *piānbǎi xiāng*	9310	
Daye Township 木葉鄉 *mùyè xiāng*	5918	
Maoba Township 毛壩鄉 *máobà xiāng*	6879	
Huatian Township 花田鄉 *huātián xiāng*	4682	
Houping Township 後坪鄉 *hòupíng xiāng*	8271	
Tianguan Township 天館鄉 *tiānguǎn xiāng*	7740	
Yiju Township 宜居鄉 *yíjū xiāng*	11,505	
Liangzeng Township 兩罾鄉 *liǎngzēng xiāng*	7691	
Banqiao Township 板橋鄉 *bǎnqiáo xiāng*	6210	
Guanqing Township 官清鄉 *guānqīng xiāng*	7872	
Chetian Township 車田鄉 *chētián xiāng*	5168	
Yudi Township 腴地鄉 *yúdì xiāng*	5952	
Qingquan Township 清泉鄉 *qīngquán xiāng*	5006	
Miaoxi Township 廟溪鄉 *miàoxī xiāng*	9562	
Langping Township 浪坪鄉 *làngpíng xiāng*	6444	
Shuangquan Township 雙泉鄉 *shuāngquán xiāng*	7435	
Nanmu Township 楠木鄉 *nánmù xiāng*	3711	
Pengshui Miao and Tujia Autonomous County 彭水苗族土家族自治縣 ***péngshuǐ miáozú tǔjiāzú zìzhìxiàn***		**530,599**
Hanjia Subdistrict 漢葭街道 *hànjiā jiēdào*	123,500	
Shaoqing Subdistrict 紹慶街道 *shàoqìng jiēdào*	71,400	
Dianshui Subdistrict 靛水街道 *diànshuǐ jiēdào*	27,400	
Baojia Town 保家鎮 *bǎojiā zhèn*	42,000	
Yushan Town 鬱山鎮 *yùshān zhèn*	22,700	
Gaogu Town 高谷鎮 *gāogǔ zhèn*	12,100	
Sangzhe Town 桑柘鎮 *sāngzhè zhèn*	19,000	
Lujiao Town 鹿角鎮 *lùjiǎo zhèn*	7500	
Huangjia Town 黄家鎮 *huángjiā zhèn*	7700	
Puzi Town 普子鎮 *pǔzǐ zhèn*	15,800	

(continued)

Table 4.4 (continued)

Selected data, cities and subordinate sectors, population (2020 census)[a]	Subordinate subdistrict populations (2020)	Total population (2020)
Longshe Town 龍射鎮 *lóngshè zhèn*	12,600	
Lianhu Town 連湖鎮 *liánhú zhèn*	13,700	
Wanzu Town 萬足鎮 *wànzú zhèn*	2700	
Ping'an Town 平安鎮 *píng'ān zhèn*	7400	
Changsheng Town 長生鎮 *chángshēng zhèn*	4600	
Xintian Town 新田鎮 *xīntián zhèn*	14,900	
Anzi Town 鞍子鎮 *ānzǐ zhèn*	8100	
Taiyuan Town 太原鎮 *tàiyuán zhèn*	6300	
Longxi Town 龍溪鎮 *lóngxī zhèn*	7900	
Meiziya Town 梅子埡鎮 *méizǐyà zhèn*	7500	
Datong Town 大同鎮 *dàtóng zhèn*	5100	
Yandong Township 岩東鄉 *yándōng xiāng*	3300	
Luming Township 鹿鳴鄉 *lùmíng xiāng*	11,200	
Ditang Township 棣棠鄉 *dìtáng xiāng*	6800	
Sanyi Township 三義鄉 *sānyì xiāng*	3900	
Lianhe Township 聯合鄉 *liánhé xiāng*	6100	
Shiliu Township 石柳鄉 *shíliǔ xiāng*	5600	
Zoumai Township 走馬鄉 *zǒumǎ xiāng*	9300	
Lutang Township 蘆塘鄉 *lútáng xiāng*	4200	
Qiaozi Township 喬梓鄉 *qiáozǐ xiāng*	6400	
Zhufo Township 諸佛鄉 *zhūfó xiāng*	7100	
Tonglou Township 桐樓鄉 *tónglóu xiāng*	3000	
Shangan Township 善感鄉 *shàngǎn xiāng*	3700	
Shuanglong Township 雙龍鄉 *shuānglóng xiāng*	2500	
Shipan Township 石盤鄉 *shípán xiāng*	1500	
Daya Township 大埡鄉 *dàyà xiāng*	2500	
Runxi Township 潤溪鄉 *rùnxī xiāng*	6200	
Langxi Township 朗溪鄉 *lǎngxī xiāng*	3600	
Longtang Township 龍塘鄉 *lóngtáng xiāng*	3900	

[a]Population data on several subdistricts unavailable as of January 2022
[b]At the decennial census time (2020), Zhenan Town had not yet been changed to Zhenan subdistrict
[c]Data for Kuizhou was not available as it had not been officially established; its data is found within Yong'an subdistrict (above)

Table 4.5 shows the *hukou* (family registered) populations based on PRC Ministry of Civil Affairs data. (Districts listed directly under major cities are government seats, as are those in parentheses). One can compare these data with the census (usual residential populations based on 2010 and 2020 censuses in Table 4.3.

Chongqing City (渝) and Subdistricts

Table 4.5 Permanent registered (戶籍人口 *hùjí rénkǒu*) populations (MCA 2020)

Name	Traditional	Simplified	Population (2012)	Population (2016)	Population (2020)	Area (km^2)
Chongqing City	重慶市	重庆市	33,030,000	33,430,000	34,040,000	82,370
Yuzhong District (Qixinggang Subdistrict)	渝中區 (七星崗街道)	渝中区 (七星岗街道)	570,000	560,000	500,000	23
Dadukou District (Xinshancun Subdistrict)	大渡口區 (新山村街道)	大渡口区 (新山村街道)	240,000	240,000	270,000	103
Jiangbei District (Cuntan Subdistrict)	江北區 (寸灘街道)	江北区 (寸滩街道)	550,000	570,000	620,000	221
Shapingba District (Qinjiagang Subdistrict)	沙坪壩區 (覃家崗街道)	沙坪坝区 (覃家岗街道)	790,000	800,000	860,000	396
Jiulongpo District (Yangjiaping Subdistrict)	九龍坡區 (楊家坪街道)	九龙坡区 (杨家坪街道)	820,000	860,000	950,000	431
Nan'an District (Tianwen Subdistrict)	南岸區 (天文街道)	南岸区 (天文街道)	610,000	640,000	740,000	262
Beibei District (Beiwenquan Subdistrict)	北碚區 (北溫泉街道)	北碚区 (北温泉街道)	640,000	630,000	640,000	751
Qijiang District (Gunan Subdistrict)	綦江區 (古南街道)	綦江区 (古南街道)	1,220,000	1,210,000	1,200,000	2747
Dazu District (Tangxiang Subdistrict)	大足區 (棠香街道)	大足区 (棠香街道)	1,010,000	1,040,000	1,070,000	1434
Yubei District (Shuangfengqiao Subdistrict)	渝北區 (雙鳳橋街道)	渝北区 (双凤桥街道)	1,020,000	1,110,000	1,370,000	1457
Ba'nan District (Longzhouwan Subdistrict)	巴南區 (龍州灣街道)	巴南区 (龙洲湾街道)	880,000	900,000	930,000	1823
Wanzhou District (Chenjiaba Subdistrict)	萬州區 (陳家壩街道)	万州区 (陈家坝街道)	1,730,000	1,750,000	1,740,000	3453
Fuling District (Lizhi Subdistrict)	涪陵區 (荔枝街道)	涪陵区 (荔枝街道)	1,160,000	1,170,000	1,150,000	2941
Qianjiang District (Chengxi Subdistrict)	黔江區 (城西街道)	黔江区 (城西街道)	540,000	550,000	560,000	2390

(continued)

Table 4.5 (continued)

Name	Traditional	Simplified	Population (2012)	Population (2016)	Population (2020)	Area (km²)
Changshou District (Fengcheng Subdistrict)	長壽區 (鳳城街道)	长寿区 (凤城街道)	900,000	910,000	890,000	1421
Jiangjin District (Jijiang Subdistrict)	江津區 (幾江街道)	江津区 (几江街道)	1,490,000	1,500,000	1,490,000	3216
Hechuan District (Nanjinjie Subdistrict)	合川區 (南津街街道)	合川区 (南津街街道)	1,550,000	1,560,000	1,530,000	2343
Yongchuan District (Zhongshanlu Subdistrict)	永川區 (中山路街道)	永川区 (中山路街道)	1,120,000	1,130,000	1,140,000	1579
Nanchuan District (Dongcheng Subdistrict)	南川區 (東城街道)	南川区 (东城街道)	670,000	680,000	690,000	2589
Tongnan District (Guilin Subdistrict)	潼南區 (桂林街道)	潼南区 (桂林街道)	940,000	950,000	950,000	1585
Tongliang District (Bachuan Subdistrict)	銅梁區 (巴川街道)	铜梁区 (巴川街道)	840,000	840,000	850,000	1341
Rongchang District (Changyuan Subdistrict)	榮昌區 (昌元街道)	荣昌区 (昌元街道)	830,000	840,000	850,000	1077
Bishan District (Bicheng Subdistrict)	璧山區 (璧城街道)	璧山区 (璧城街道)	630,000	640,000	650,000	915
Dianjiang County (Guixi Town)	墊江縣 (桂溪鎮)	垫江县 (桂溪街道)	960,000	970,000	970,000	1517
Wulong District (Xiangkou Town)	武隆區 (巷口鎮)	武隆区 (巷口镇)	410,000	410,000	410,000	2892
Fengdu County (Sanhe Subdistrict)	豐都縣 (三合街道)	丰都县 (三合街道)	840,000	840,000	820,000	2899
Chengkou County (Gecheng Subdistrict)	城口縣 (葛城街道)	城口县 (葛城街道)	250,000	250,000	250,000	3289
Liangping District (Liangshan Subdistrict)	梁平區 (梁山街道)	梁平区 (梁山街道)	910,000	920,000	930,000	1888
Kaizhou District (Hanfeng Subdistrict)	開州區 (漢豐街道)	开州区 (汉丰街道)	1,630,000	1,660,000	1,690,000	3964

(continued)

Table 4.5 (continued)

Name	Traditional	Simplified	Population (2012)	Population (2016)	Population (2020)	Area (km^2)
Wuxi County (Baiyang [Boyang] Subdistrict)	巫溪縣 (柏楊街道)	巫溪县 (柏杨街道)	530,000	540,000	540,000	4015
Wushan County (Wuxia Town)	巫山縣 (高唐街道)	巫山县 (高唐街道)	630,000	640,000	630,000	2955
Fengjie County (Yong'an Subdistrict)	奉節縣 (永安街道)	奉节县 (永安街道)	1,050,000	1,070,000	1,060,000	4098
Yunyang County (Shuangjiang Subdistrict)	雲陽縣 (雙江街道)	云阳县 (双江街道)	1,340,000	1,340,000	1,340,000	3636
Zhongxian County (Zhongzhou Subdistrict)	忠縣 (忠州街道)	忠县 (忠州街道)	1,000,000	1,010,000	990,000	2187
Shizhu Tujiazu (Tujia) Autonomous County (Nanbin Town)	石柱土家族自治縣 (南賓鎮)	石柱土家族自治县 (南宾镇)	540,000	550,000	550,000	3014
Pengshui Miaozu Tujiazu (Miao and Tujia) Autonomous County (Hanjia Subdistrict)	彭水苗族土家族自治縣 (漢葭街道)	彭水苗族土家族自治县 (汉葭街道)	680,000	690,000	700,000	3897
Youyang Tujiazu Miaozu (Tujia and Miao) Autonomous County (Taohuayuan Subdistrict)	酉陽土家族苗族自治縣 (桃花源街道)	酉阳土家族苗族自治县 (桃花源街道)	840,000	840,000	850,000	5168
Xiushan Tujiazu Miaozu (Tujia and Miao) Autonomous County (Zhonghe Subdistrict)	秀山土家族苗族自治縣 (中和街道)	秀山土家族苗族自治县 (中和街道)	650,000	660,000	670,000	2453

References

Brassett, Cecilia, Philip Brassett, and Lu. Meiyan. 2006. *The Tujia language*, Languages of the World/455. München: Lincom Europa.

Cao, Shuji. 2003. [Population of Sichuan separate prefectures in mid-Qing dynasty – Looking at 1812 data]. *Chinese Economic History Research*. 曹树基. 清代中期四川分府人口: 以 1812 年数据为心. 中国经济史研究. 1: 92–105.

Chongqing Bureau of Transportation (CBT). 1999. [Successes of China's fifty years of transportation: Volume on Chongqing]. People's Transportation Press. 重庆交通局. 中国交通五十年成就: 重庆卷. 重庆: 人民交通出版社.

Chongqing City Bureau of Statistics (CCBS). 2021. [Report on Chongqing City, seventh national census, issue no. 2]. 重庆市第七次全国人口普查公报, 第二号. May 13. http://tjj.cq.gov.cn/zwgk_233/fdzdgknr/tjxx/sjjd_55469/202105/t20210513_9277501.html.

Chongqing City Research Group on Wartime Losses (CCRGWL). 2017. [*Investigation report on casualties and property losses in Chongqing during the anti-Japanese War*]. June 24. Chinese Communist Party History Net. 重庆市抗战损失调研课题组. 重庆市抗日战争时期人口伤亡和财产损失调研报告. 中国共产党历史网. https://www.krzzjn.com/show-627-51707.html.

Dikötter, Frank. 2016. *The cultural revolution: A people's history, 1962–1976*. New York: Bloomsbury Press.

Keightley, David N. 1978. *Sources of Shang history: The oracle-bone inscriptions of Bronze Age China*. Berkeley: University of California Press.

MacFarquhar, Roderick, and Michael Schoenhals. 2006. *Mao's last revolution*. Cambridge, MA: The Belknap Press of Harvard, Harvard University Press.

Ministry of Civil Affairs (MCA), People's Republic of China. 2020. [County/township administration handbook]. Beijing: China Statistics Press. 中華人民共和國民政部, 中華人民共和國, 鄉鎮行政區劃簡冊.

Olsen, John W. 1987. Recent developments in the upper Pleistocene prehistory of China. In *The Pleistocene old world: Regional perspectives*, ed. Olga Soffer, 135–146. New York: Plenum Press.

Owen, Steven. 2016. *The poetry of Du Fu*, 4(17). Boston: Walter de Gruyte Inc.

Shao, Yi. 2021. [44% of China's population is nearly 'aging deeply']. *Epoch Times*. September 10. 邵亦. 四成四中国人口近 '深度老龄化.' https://www.epochtimes.com/gb/21/9/10/n13223305.htm.

Tan, Qixiang, ed. 1996. *The historical atlas of China*. Vol. VI. Beijing: China Cartographic Publishing House.

Yang, Zihui. 1995. [China's historical population statistical data research]. Beijing: Reform Press. 楊子慧. 中國歷代人口統計資料研究. 北京: 改革出版社.

Zhang, Shunan. 2021. [The 2020 per capita income list of residents in various provinces: Shanghai is the richest, and it has risen sharply]. Finance.people.com. January 22. 张澍楠. 2020年各省份居民人均收入榜: 上海最有钱, 这地涨得猛. http://finance.people.com.cn/n1/2021/0122/c1004-32008733.html.

Zhong, Yongling. 1993. [*Educational Gazette of Shizhong District*]. Editorial Committee of *Educational Journal of Shizhong District, Chongqing*. Chongqing: Sichuan Literature and Art Publishing House. 钟永玲. 重庆市市中区教育志编委会. 重庆市市中区教育志. 重庆: 四川文艺出版社.

Chapter 5
Fujian Province

Abstract Originally referred to as the land of the *Min* (e.g., 閩國 *mǐnguó*), Fujian has also been known to the western world as 'Fukkien.' Fueled by cross-strait ties and increased trade in recent decades, Fujian Province, located along China's south-eastern coast, has enjoyed a resurgence. Figuring prominently in China's historical interactions with the outside world, Fujian Province also has played a very influential role in the political development of the Republic of China (Taiwan). With its own distinctive dialect, a close version of which is also popularly spoken in Taiwan, Fujian's dynamism and role in mercantile trade has allowed it to reach its economic potential. It is ranked seventh in both gross domestic product (GDP) and per capita income when compared with mainland China's 31 provinces and major cities. In addition to official *hukou* (registered household) population data, this chapter provides results of the national 2020 census for Fujian Province at the county and district level.

E. Croddy, *China's Provinces and Populations*,
https://doi.org/10.1007/978-3-031-09165-0_5

Fujian (Fukkien) Province (福建 *fújiàn*): Abbreviation 閩 (*mǐn*) (Fig. 5.1)

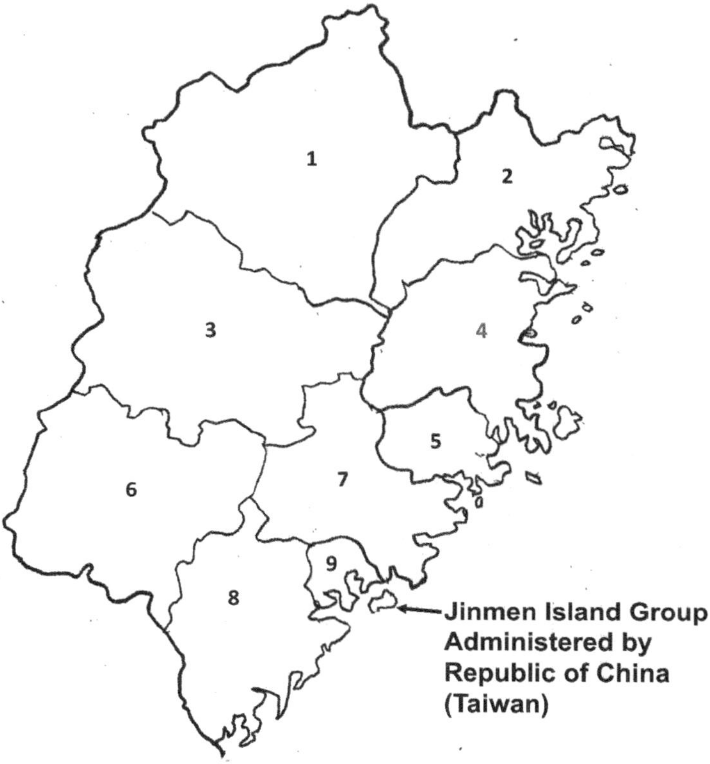

Fujian Province Population (2020)

1.	Nanping City	2,680,465
2.	Ningde City	3,146,789
3.	Sanming City	2,486,450
4.	Fuzhou City	8,291,268
5.	Putian City	3,210,714
6.	Longyan City	2,723,637
7.	Quanzhou City	8,782,285
8.	Zhangzhou City	5,054,328
9.	Xiamen (Amoy) City	5,163,970

Fig. 5.1 Fujian Province: subdistricts (Provincial Capital: Fuzhou City). (Drawn by the Author after People's Republic of China, Ministry of Civil Affairs, MCA 2020)

Fujian (福建 *fújiàn*) Province: General Impressions

For the Chinese, if there was one thought that comes to mind about Fujian province it is that everywhere you look in the capital of Fuzhou City are Banyan trees. Thus the moniker, "Banyan Tree Capital" (榕樹之都 *róngshùzhī dū*). Said to have been cultured as a means of flood control during the northern Song dynasty (ca. 1100 CE), there is an "Emperor Banyan" tree in the national forest of Fuzhou city said to be over a thousand years old. And the fabled history of foresting in Fujian doesn't stop here, as we will see in the case of Quanzhou City (below). Fujian probably gets its name from merging names of two previous prefectures: Fuzhou (福州 *fúzhōu*) and Jianning county (建寧縣 *jiànníng xiàn*). The short character abbreviation for Fujian is Min (閩 *mǐn*). This brings to mind the belief that Min (閩 *mǐn*) is in fact originally derived from the character barbarian (蠻 *mán*), due both to the similar shape of the Chinese ideographs, as well as the prevailing chauvinistic view of the Chinese imperial court when it came to these "uncivilized" populations. During the late period of the Tang (ca. 700 CE), a contemporary noted that the people of Fujian could not speak the Chinese dialect, that some were cave-dwellers, and many other locals lived along the water in makeshift boats (Ebrey 2010).

This long tradition of Fujian having its own unique identity, such as its own distinctive Hokkien (Min; Fujianese; *hokkiàn oē*) dialect has had long-lasting effects, including how the outside world has viewed China throughout history. For example, Fujian's Special Economic Zone (SEZ) has long been known to the West as "Amoy," which is based on the Hokkien pronunciation of its name, versus the official mandarin Chinese Xiamen (廈門 *xiàmén*). Hokkien is still widely spoken in Fujian and is a close variant of Taiwanese dialect (台灣閩南語 *táiwān mǐnnányǔ*).

English Words from Chinese Dialects

The English word "tea" itself is actually of Chinese origin, specifically Hokkien dialect: Tea (*chá* 茶, in Mandarin) is pronounced *te* ("tay") in the Min language (close to modern Spanish, *té*). When encountered by westerners, namely the Dutch who traded in the southern city of Xiamen, they learned this word from the locals. Eventually spelled in English "tea," back then it rhymed with "tay" (as in "Yeats.") (Wilkinson 2012). Other words of Hokkien dialect that found their way into early English usage include

- Pekoe 白毫 (*pe'h-hô*) tea variety
- Cumsha(w) (金沙 "gold sand"), meaning a gratuity, bribe, to hustle something;
- Ketchup (茄汁 *kiô-chiap*); and
- Possibly the English pronunciation of 'kow-tow' (磕頭 *khàu-thâu*) (Chew 2013)

Fujian Prehistory

In Fujian's coastal Pingtan, the Neolithic Keqiutou (殼丘頭 *kéqiūtóu*; ca. 6000 BCE) site shows evidence of primitive farming, stone tools and pottery. The presence of numerous shells and other evidence also indicated this to have been a largely maritime-based society.

First excavated in 1954, the Tanshishan (曇石山 *tánshí shān*) site (dated 5500–4000 years ago) in Minhou County (閩侯縣 *mǐnhóu xiàn*) included a number of tools, including made of sea shells, as well as sophisticated pottery. And the bronze-age Huangtulun (黄土崙 *huángtǔlún*) site, also in Minhou (dated to 1325 BCE) also featured highly-stylized ceramic pottery (Jiao 2007).

A historical document that dates as far back as ca. 400 BCE, the *Shanhai Jing* (山海經 *shānhǎi jīng*, the *Classic of Mountains and Seas*, serves as a sometimes reliable, and other times mythological, survey of China. Describing China's southeast coastal area which included modern-day Fujian, the *Shanhai Jing* had this to say: "The Ou (甌 *ōu*) people [probably referring to Yue people or related group] live close to the sea (甌居海中 *ōujū hǎizhōng*). The Min [Fujian region] is water, to its northwest are mountains; when one speaks of the Min (閩 *mǐn*) one is talking about a place in both the mountains and sea." The ancient treatise *Zhouli* (周禮 *zhōulǐ* or the Rites of Zhou) pejoratively described these southern Chinese people as "barbarians (蠻 *mán*)" but also included them as belonging to the Seven Min (七閩 *qīmǐn*)." (Lin 2018).

From ca. 770–475 BCE in the Spring Autumn (春秋 *chūnqiū*) period, the northern part of the Seven Min existed within the larger State of Yue (越國 *yuèguó*). In the 35th year of King Xian of Zhou (周顯王 *zhōuxiǎn wáng*) reign (334 BCE), the State of Chu defeated the Yue, and the latter's extended imperial family was forced to move to the coast, while their homeland became a tribute state to the Chu. The Yue descendants eventually found their way to the Min, or so the histories tell us, and unified the Seven Min groups.

The Qin Dynasty's unification of China administered the Fujian area under the Min Central Prefecture (閩中郡 *mǐnzhōngjùn*). Liu Bang of the Han dynasty (202 BCE) gave King Gou Jian's successor, Wu Zhu (無諸 *wú zhū*), the kingship of the State of Minyue (閩越國 *mǐnyuèguó*). The Minyue capital was located at Dongye (東冶 *dōngyě*), with a defensive redoubt established in Wuyishan (武夷山 *wǔyíshān*). When the State of Minyue set upon a more expansionist policy, the Han dynasty (110 BCE) conducted a punitive military campaign in response, occupying its capital and destroying the national palace. With the end of the Minyue, its peoples scattered to the Changjiang and Huainan regions. In the beginning of the Eastern Han (196 CE) an official county magistrate was established in today's Fuzhou City. From about 220–560 CE, modern-day Fujian was composed of Jian'an Prefecture (建安 *jiàn'ān*), divided into three subprefectures:

- Jin'an (晉安 *jìn'ān*)
- Jian'an (建安), and
- Nan'an (南安 *nán'ān*)

By this time (ca. 600 CE), some of the more commonly found Chinese (Han) family names arrived in Fujian, to include the more commonly found Lin (林 *lín*), Huang (黄 *huáng*), Chen (陳 *chén*), Zheng (鄭 *zhèng*), Zhan (詹 *zhān*), Qiu (邱 *qiū*), He (何 *hé*), and Hu (胡 *hú*).

In 733 CE, Fuzhou (福州 *fúzhōu*) and Jianzhou (建州 *jiànzhōu*) prefectures, located within the jurisdiction of Jiangnan Dongdao (江南東道 *jiāngnán dōngdào*) were administered by a military commissioner (經略使 *jīngluèshǐ*), and later named a Fujian Inspectorate (福建觀察使 *fújiàn guāncháshǐ*). For a short time thereafter, Fuzhou was drawn within the small State of Yin (殷國 *yīnguó*). Later, from 909–943 CE, Fujian existed as the Min State (閩國 *mǐnguó*), with Fuzhou as the capital. In the Song dynasty (ca. 960), a province-like entity called Fujian (福建路 *fújiàn lù*) administered six subordinate prefectures:

- Fuzhou (福州 *fúzhōu*)
- Jianzhou (建州 *jiànzhōu*)
- Quanzhou (泉州 *quánzhōu*)
- Nanjian Zhou (南劍州 *nánjiàn zhōu*)
- Zhangzhou (漳州 *zhāngzhōu*)
- Tingzhou (汀州 *tīngzhōu*)

There were also two military subdistricts (prefectures): Shaowu (邵武軍 *shàowǔ jūn*) and Xinghua (興化軍 *xìnghuà jūn*).

The City Known as 'Zaitun'

By the Song dynastic period, Muslim merchants knew Quanzhou by the name 'Zaitun,' leading some to believe the word satin is derived (Arabic *zaitūnī*). The name Zaitun itself, however, was probably a corruption of Quanzhou's nickname that it had already earned in the tenth century, "Citong City" (刺桐城 *cìtóng chéng*). This was because of the many Citong trees (*Erythrina variegate*; 刺桐 *cìtóng*) planted there. In the year 1120, the governor of Quanzhou claimed his city had some 500,000 residents (Schottenhammer 2010).

Because Fujian had six prefectures and two military-led entities, the region later earned the moniker "Eight Min" (八閩 *bāmǐn*). By the Yuan dynasty it had been renamed Fujian Haiyoudao (福建海右道 *fújiàn hǎiyòudào*: "Fujian, on the right, ocean side"). Finally, in the Ming dynasty, Fujian was formally named a province (福建省 *fújiàn shěng*), which was then converted to a Fujian Provincial Administration (福建布政使司 *fújiàn bùzhèng shǐsī*). In 1278 a Yuan Central Administered Prefecture was established at Quanzhou, then moving to Fuzhou 3 years later. Although still reliant on imported foodstuffs, notably rice, Fujian's favorable trading location as well as its various industries led to dramatic increase in household population during the Tang to the Southern Song periods (see Table 5.1 below):

Table 5.1 Numbers of households in Fujian: ca. 700–1200 (Elvin 1973)

Date (circa).	Fujian-based households
713	115,311
742	95,586
806	74,467
976	467,808
1068	992,087
1078	1,044,235
1131	1,330,000
1208	1,599,214

In ca. 1400, due to its location and its growing maritime infrastructure, Fujian was the staging point for China's "maritime silk road." The city of Quanzhou was the naval port staging area for the eunuch Zheng He (鄭和 *zhèng hé*) and his famous international maritime expeditions (1405–1433). By the 1500s, so-called Japanese pirates, derisively called the *Wokou* (倭寇 *wōkòu* "dwarf brigands") had become a real problem, constantly raiding the burgeoning maritime trade centers off China's coast. However, these pirates were more often than not *Chinese* privateers, often operating out of Japanese-held bases. Thus the epithet *Wokou*, used to denigrate the Japanese, was really a political expedient to obscure the fact that powerful Fujian-based Chinese families were very much a part of the piracy business (Dardess 2012).

Contact with Europe

In ca. 1518, the Portuguese sailor Jorge Mascaranhas sailed north to the prefecture of Quanzhou (then Quanzhoufu 泉州府; "Chwanchao-fû.") Years later, after a trade-based relation-ship was established, the port was referred to in the West as the Portuguese-Chinese trading port of Zaytun (Zaitun)-Quanzhou. But the Portuguese were generally unwelcome: Their sometimes savage behavior resulted in local Chinese retaliation, leading to the massacre (1549) of a Portuguese settlement in Quanzhou. As one historian put it:

> For this ill fortune the Portuguese had chiefly themselves to thank. Truculant and lawless, regarding all Eastern peoples as legitimate prey, they were little if any better than the contemporary Japanese pirates who pillaged the Chinese coasts. The Ming authorities can scarcely be censured for treating them as free-booters. (Latourette 1967)

Dealing with Pirates

During the later Ming dynasty, the Chinese Emperor Jiajing (嘉靖 *jiājìng* 1521–1567) was at wits end when it came to dealing with the "*Wokou*" pirates. Finding the situation intolerable, and taking the most extraordinary step available, the Ming court put a kibosh on all seaborne trade. This naturally led to a fast decline not only international commerce but, more importantly, a precipitous fall in tax revenue for the Ming government. This blanket prohibition on maritime trade was finally relaxed by the following Ming emperor, Longqing (隆慶 *lóngqìng*; 1567–1572). The only remaining prohibition was on official trade with the Japanese, which would be exploited by the Portugal merchants who served as middlemen (Shi 2006).

With the capture of the Ming dynasty Emperor Long Wu (隆武帝 *lóngwǔ dì*) in Fuzhou on 6 October 1646 by the Qing, a young scion of the powerful Zheng family, later named Zheng Chenggong (鄭成功 *zhèng chénggong*; also known as Koxinga) led armed struggles against both the Qing dynasty and the Dutch East India Company. Operating out of Xiamen and Taiwan, and just after wresting Taiwan island (Formosa) from Dutch control, Koxinga died in 1662 at the age of 37 (probably of malaria but syphilis is also suspected). But the Zheng family continued to hold power in the region, and from 1662–1683 it encouraged a large migration of Chinese from the southeastern coast of China to move to Formosa (Taiwan). Administered under a Ming dynasty-styled regime, Taiwan continued to develop its agriculture while promoting Confucian education. In the 22nd year of the Kangxi (康熙 *Kāngxī*) reign of the Qing dynasty (1683), Admiral Shi Lang (施琅 *shī láng*) conquered Taiwan, making it the first time that China had de facto control over the island. Before then, Taiwan was variously known as the Barbarian State (夷洲 *yízhōu*) and Liu Qiu (琉球 *liúqiú*), among others. (See also chapter on Republic of China, Taiwan). Fujian Province officially was now under the direct rule of the Qing government.

The mid-nineteenth century Opium Wars foreshadowed the eventual decline of the Qing dynasty. In defeat, China lost its sovereignty of selected areas to the European powers, especially its key trading ports. Under threat of continued naval bombardment, the British concluded the Treaty of Nanjing (ratified by Queen Victoria on 28 December 1842). Among its provisions included the "Opening of five ports to trade and residence of British consuls and merchants and their families: Canton [Guangzhou], Amoy (Xiamen), Foochow (Fuzhou), Ningpo (Ningbo), and Shanghai."

In the face of such foreign aggression, and emblematic of China's loss of territorial sovereignty, Fuzhou became one of the key areas for China's nativist Self-Strengthening Movement (自強運動 *zìqiáng yùndòng*). Under this banner and led by the modernizer Zuo Zongtang (左宗棠 *zuǒ zōngtáng*), the Qing built the Foochow (Fuzhou) Dockyard in 1866. With the establishment of a maritime academy, Fuzhou became the cradle of the China's first modern navy (Hsü 2000).

Fujian Self-Funded Development

Due to various historical and geographic reasons, a great number of overseas Chinese (about seven million) have Fujian provincial heritage (only Guangdong has a higher number.) These familial connections (關係 *guānxì*) helped to provide a key source of capital investment in Fujian, as well as monetary remittances to relatives still living in Fujian after the establishment of the People's Republic of China (PRC). However, in contrast to its dynamic mercantile and commercially-successful past, under Mao Zedong in the 1950s and 1960s Beijing provided a mere trifle of financial investment for Fujian. Largely neglected to the point of contempt, Fujian's economy during this time showed negative growth. It is not surprising, then, that by the time Deng Xiaoping announced his opening and reform initiative in 1978 Fujian province was among the poorest in China. The introduction of market forces in the subsequent decades would change all of that. In 1984, with the establishment of Xiamen (Amoy) as a Special Economic Zone (SEZ), Fujian's economic development led the country. Highlighting the critical role of investment by overseas Chinese expatriates, Deng Xiaoping remarked that, of the five richest overseas Chinese that year, three were originally from Fujian Province. Continuing in this trend, then Fujian Governor Xi Jinping (2000–2002; currently, and for a very long time in the future China's president) also encouraged Taiwanese investors to do business in Fujian. Now among the wealthiest of all China's provinces, Fujian continues to prosper, especially with the formalization of direct trade with Taiwan, especially since 2008. As of 2020, Fujian province ranked seventh overall in terms of gross domestic product (GDP) out of 31 provinces and major cities in mainland China (USD $683 billion), and seventh with a per capita income of $5785 (Zhang 2021).

In 2010, Fujian province had total population (including permanent and non-permanent residents) of 36,894,216; in 2015, 38,340,000; and in 2020, 41,540,086 (see Table 5.2) below. Compared to the permanent (hukou) registered population (see Table 5.4) of 38,610,000, this suggests a significant number of Chinese from other regions move to Fujian for work, study, etc. (Fig. 5.2).

Table 5.4 (below) shows the *hukou* (family registered) populations based on PRC Ministry of Civil Affairs data. (Districts listed directly under major cities are government seats, as are those in parentheses). One can compare these data with the census (usual residential populations based on 2010 and 2020 censuses in Tables 5.2 and 5.3 (below):

Table 5.2 Fujian province census (Residential 常住人口 chángzhù rénkǒu) Data (FPBS 2021)

City	Population (2010)	Population (2020)
Fuzhou City 福州市 *fúzhōu shì*	7,115,370	8,291,268
Xiamen (Amoy) City 廈門市 *xiàmén shì*	3,531,347	5,163,970
Longyan City 龍岩市 *lóngyán shì*	2,559,545	2,723,637
Nanping City 南平市 *nánpíng shì*	2,645,549	2,680,465
Ningde City 寧德市 *níngdé shì*	2,821,996	3,146,789
Putian City 莆田市 *pútián shì*	2,778,508	3,210,714
Quanzhou City 泉州市 *quánzhōu shì*	8,128,530	8,782,285
Sanming City 三明市 *sānmíng shì*	2,503,388	2,486,450
Zhangzhou City 漳州市 *zhāngzhōu shì*	4,809,983	5,054,328
Total	**36,894,216**[a]	**41,540,086**

[a]The statistical spreadsheet from 2010 holds 36,894,217

1. Pucheng County
2. Guangze County
3. Wuyishan City
4. Songxi County
5. Zhenghe County
6. Zhouning County
7. Shouning County
8. Fu'an City
9. Zherong County
10. Fuding City
11. Shaowu City
12. Jianyang District
13. Jian'ou City
14. Pingnan County
15. Jiaocheng District
16. Xiapu County
17. Jianning County
18. Taining County
19. Jiangle County
20. Shunchang County
21. Yanping District
22. Gutian County
23. Luoyuan County
24. Ninghua County
25. Qingliu County
26. Mingxi County
27. Sanyuan District
28. Meilie District
29. Shaxian County
30. Youxi County
31. Minqing County
32. Minhou County
33. Pu'an District
34. Lianjiang County
35. Gulou District
36. Jinmen County (Administered by Republic of China, Taiwan)
37. Mawei District
38. Changting County
39. Liancheng County
40. Yong'an City
41. Datian County
42. Dehua County
43. Yongtai County
44. Changle City
45. Wuping County
46. Shanghang County
47. Xinluo District
48. Zhangping City
49. Yongchun County
50. Xianyou County
51. Chengxiang County
52. Hanjiang District
53. Fuqing City
54. Pingtan County
55. Licheng District
56. Xiuyu District
57. Yongding District
58. Nanjing County
59. Hua'an County
60. Anxi County
61. Nan'an City
62. Licheng District
63. Luojiang District
64. Quangang District
65. Fengze District
66. Hui'an County
67. Xiangcheng District
68. Changtai County
69. Longwen District
70. Tong'an District
71. Jimei District
72. Xiang'an City
73. Pujiang City
74. Shishi City
75. Huli District
76. Siming District
77. Pinghe County
78. Haicang District
79. Longhai City
80. Zhao'an County
81. Yunxiao County
82. Zhangpu County
83. Dongshan County

Fig. 5.2 Fuzhou province subdistricts (Capital Government Seat: Gulou District). (Drawn by the Author after People's Republic of China, Ministry of Civil Affairs, MCA 2020)

Table 5.3 Fujian province: population data of cities and their subordinate sectors (FPBS 2021)

Cities and subordinate sectors, population (2020 census)	Subordinate district, city and county populations (2020)	Total population (2020)
Fuzhou City 福州市 ***fúzhōu shì***		**8,291,268**
Gulou District 鼓樓區 *gŭlóu qū*	669,090	
Taijiang District 台江區 *táijiāng qū*	411,819	
Cangshan District 倉山區 *cāngshān qū*	1,142,991	
Mawei District 馬尾區 *măwĕi qū*	290,554	
Jin'an District 晉安區 *jìn'ān qū*	789,775	
Fuqing City 福清市 *fúqīng shì*	1,390,487	
Changle City 長樂市 *chánglè shì*	790,262	
Minhou County 閩侯縣 *mĭnhóu xiàn*	988,200	
Lianjiang County 連江縣 *liánjiāng xiàn*	639,498	
Luoyuan County 羅源縣 *luóyuán xiàn*	255,214	
Minqing County 閩清縣 *mĭnqīng xiàn*	256,181	
Yongtai County 永泰縣 *yŏngtài xiàn*	281,216	
Pingtan County 平潭縣 *píngtán xiàn*[a]	385,981	
Xiamen (Amoy) City 廈門市 ***xiàmén shì***		**5,163,970**
Siming District 思明區 *sīmíng qū*	1,073,315	
Haicang District 海滄區 *hăicāng qū*	582,519	
Huli District 湖里區 *húlĭ qū*	1,036,974	
Jimei District 集美區 *jímĕi qū*	1,036,987	
Tong'an District 同安區 *tóngān qū*	855,920	
Xiang'an District 翔安區 *xiángān qū*	578,255	
Longyan City 龍岩市 ***lóngyán shì***		**2,723,637**
Xinluo District 新羅區 *xīnluó qū*	841,745	
Zhangping City 漳平市 *zhāngpíng shì*	253,394	
Changting County 長汀縣 *chángtīng xiàn*	397,470	
Yongding District 永定區 *yŏngdìng qū*	325,880	
Shanghang County 上杭縣 *shàngháng xiàn*	376,392	
Wuping County 武平縣 *wŭpíng xiàn*	278,238	
Liancheng County 連城縣 *liánchéng xiàn*	250,518	
Nanping City 南平市 ***nánpíng shì***		**2,680,465**
Yanping District 延平區 *yánpíng qū*	454,605	
Zhaowu City 昭武市 *zhāowŭ shì*	273,721	
Wuyishan City 武夷山市 *wŭyíshān shì*	259,668	
Jian'ou City 建甌市 *jiàn'ōu shì*	434,451	
Jianyang District 建陽區 *jiànyáng qū*	340,843	
Shunchang County 順昌縣 *shùnchāng xiàn*	179,064	
Pucheng County 浦城縣 *pŭchéng xiàn*	297,719	
Guangze County 光澤縣 *guāngzé xiàn*	130,294	
Songxi County 松溪縣 *sōngxī xiàn*	130,867	
Zhenghe County 政和縣 *zhènghé xiàn*	179,413	
Ningde City 寧德市 ***níngdé shì***		**3,146,789**
Jiaocheng District 蕉城區 *jiāochéng qū*	623,840	

(continued)

Table 5.3 (continued)

Cities and subordinate sectors, population (2020 census)	Subordinate district, city and county populations (2020)	Total population (2020)
Fu'an City 福安市 *fú'ān shì*	609,779	
Fuding City 福鼎市 *fúdǐng shì*	553,132	
Shouning County 壽寧區 *hòuníng qū*	177,960	
Xiapu County 霞浦縣 *xiápǔ xiàn*	475,936	
Zherong County 柘榮縣 *zhèróng xiàn*	92,989	
Pingnan County 屏南縣 *píngnán xiàn*	139,815	
Gutian County 古田縣 *gǔtián xiàn*	323,771	
Zhouning County 周寧縣 *zhōuníng xiàn*	149,567	
Putian City 莆田市 *pútián shì*		**3,210,714**
Chengxian District 城厢區 *chéngxiāng qū*	547,422	
Hanjiang District 涵江區 *hánjiāng qū*	479,605	
Licheng District 荔城區 *lìchéng qū*	673,935	
Xiuyu District 秀嶼區 *xiùyǔ qū*	486,713	
Bei'an (North Shore) Economic Development Zone 北岸經濟開發區 *běi'àn jīngjì kāifāqū*	83,977	
Meizhou Island 湄洲島 *méizhōu dǎo*	33,994	
Xianyou County 仙游縣 *xiānyóu xiàn*	905,068	
Quanzhou City 泉州市 *quánzhōu shì*		**8,782,285**
Fengze District 豐澤區 *fēngzé qū*	698,557	
Licheng District 鯉城區 *lǐchéng qū* (includes the Licheng High-Technology Industrial Development Zone)	428,361	
Licheng District 鯉城區 *lǐchéng qū* (minus the High Technology Industrial Development Zone, below)	396,112	
Licheng High-Technology Industrial Zone 鯉城高新技術產業開發區 *lǐchéng gāoxīnjìshù chǎnyè kāifāqū*	32,249	
Luojiang District 洛江區 *luòjiāng qū*	247,172	
Quangang District 泉港區 *quángǎng qū*	354,296	
Shishi City 石獅市 *shíshī shì*	685,930	
Jinjiang City 晉江市 *jìnjiāng shì*	2,061,551	
Nan'an City 南安市 *nán'ān shì*	1,517,514	
Hui'an County 惠安縣 *huì'ān xiàn* (Includes the Quanzhou Taiwanese Investment Zone)	1,030,626	
Hui'an County 惠安縣 *huì'ān xiàn* (minus the Quanzhou Taiwanese Investment Zone)	781,397	
Quanzhou Taiwanese Investment Zone 泉州台商投資區 *quánzhōu táishāng tóuzīqū*	249,229	
Anxi County 安溪縣 *ānxī xiàn*	1,003,599	
Yongchun couny 永春縣 *yǒngchūn xiàn*	422,531	
Dehua County 德化縣 *déhuà xiàn*	332,148	
Sanming City 三明市 *sānmíng shì*		**2,486,450**
Meilie District 梅列區 *méiliè qū*	220,115	

(continued)

Table 5.3 (continued)

Cities and subordinate sectors, population (2020 census)	Subordinate district, city and county populations (2020)	Total population (2020)
Sanyuan District 三元區 *sānyuán qū*	187,936	
Yong'an City 永安市 *yǒng'ān shì*	344,793	
Mingxi County 明溪縣 *míngxī xiàn*	98,930	
Qingliu County 清流縣 *qīngliú xiàn*	118,029	
Ninghua County 寧化縣 *nínghuà xiàn*	261,579	
Datian County 大田縣 *dàtián xiàn*	299,513	
Youxi County 尤溪縣 *yóuxī xiàn*	341,638	
Shaxian County 沙縣 *shāxiàn*	250,503	
Jiangle County 將樂縣 *jiānglè xiàn*	144,943	
Taining County 泰寧縣 *tài'níng xiàn*	104,071	
Jianning County 建寧縣 *jiànníng xiàn*	114,400	
Zhangzhou City 漳州市 *zhāngzhōu shì*		**5,054,328**
Longwen District 龍文區 *lóngwén qū*	301,883	
Xiangcheng District 薌城區 *xiāngchéng qū*	638,060	
Longhai City 龍海市 *lónghǎi shì*	952,000	
Yunxiao County 雲霄縣 *yúnxiāo xiàn*	411,558	
Zhangpu County 漳鋪縣 *zhāngpū xiàn*	847,535	
Zhao'an County 詔安縣 *zhào'ān xiàn*	560,969	
Changtai County 長泰縣 *chángtài xiàn*	228,235	
Dongshan County 東山縣 *dōngshān xiàn*	219,511	
Nanjing County 南靖縣 *nánjìng xiàn*	305,259	
Pinghe County 平和縣 *pínghé xiàn*	455,042	
Hua'an County 華安縣 *huá'ān xiàn*	134,276	

[a]Pingtan was omitted from the census listing, likely an oversight: without Pingtan county, population of Fuzhou city only adds up to 7,905,287; remaining residential population of Pingtan county is 385,981, making for total 8,291,268

Fujian Province (閩 *mǐn*)

Provincial Capital: Fuzhou

Table 5.4 Fujian province: permanent registered (戶籍人口 *hùjí rénkǒu*) populations (MCA 2020)

Name	Traditional	Simplified	Population (2012)	Population (2016)	Population (2020)	Area (km^2)
Fujian province	福建省	福建省	35,300,000	35,790,000	38,610,000	122,870
Fuzhou city	福州市	福州市	6,460,000	6,560,000	7,030,000	11,788
Gulou District (Dongjie subdistrict)	鼓樓區 (東街街道)	鼓楼区 (东街街道)	580,000	580,000	580,000	35
Taijiang District (Houzhou subdistrict)	台江區 (後洲街道)	台江区 (后洲街道)	330,000	330,000	320,000	18

(continued)

Table 5.4 (continued)

Name	Traditional	Simplified	Population (2012)	Population (2016)	Population (2020)	Area (km^2)
Cangshan District (Cangqian subdistrict)	倉山區 (倉前街道)	仓山区 (仓前街道)	460,000	480,000	600,000	142
Mawei District (Luoxing subdistrict)	馬尾區 (羅星街道)	马尾区 (罗星街道)	160,000	170,000	180,000	281
Jin'an district (Yuefeng town)	晉安區 (岳峰鎮)	晋安区 (岳峰镇)	350,000	370,000	420,000	567
Fuqing City (Yuping subdistrict)	福清市 (玉屏街道)	福清市 (玉屏街道)	1,280,000	1,290,000	138,000	1518
Changle City (Wuhang subdistrict)	長樂市 (吳航街道)	长乐市 (吴航街道)	690,000	690,000	750,000	658
Minhou County (Ganzhe subdistrict)	閩侯縣 (甘蔗街道)	闽侯县 (甘蔗街道)	650,000	650,000	690,000	2136
Lianjiang County (Fengcheng subdistrict)	連江縣 (鳳城街道)	连江县 (凤城街道)	630,000	640,000	680,000	1168
Luoyuan County (Fengshan subdistrict)	羅源縣 (鳳山街道)	罗源县 (凤山街道)	260,000	260,000	270,000	1187
Minqing County (Meicheng town)	閩清縣 (梅城鎮)	闽清县 (梅城镇)	310,000	320,000	330,000	1466
Yongtai County (Zhangcheng town)	永泰縣 (樟城鎮)	永泰县 (樟城镇)	360,000	370,000	390,000	2241
Pingtan County (Tancheng town)	平潭縣 (潭城鎮)	平潭县 (潭城镇)	400,000	410,000	450,000	371
Nanping city	南平市	南平市	3,140,000	3,140,000	3,200,000	26,312
Yanping District (Ziyun subdistrict)	延平區 (紫雲街道)	延平区 (紫云街道)	500,000	500,000	500,000	2660
Zhaowu City (Zhaoyang subdistrict)	昭武市 (昭陽街道)	邵武市 (昭阳街道)	310,000	300,000	310,000	2851
Wuyishan City (Chong'an subdistrict)	武夷山市 (崇安街道)	武夷山市 (崇安街道)	230,000	230,000	250,000	2814
Jian'ou City (Ou'ning subdistrict)	建甌市 (甌寧街道)	建瓯市 (瓯宁街道)	540,000	540,000	550,000	4200
Jianyang District (Tancheng subdistrict)	建陽區 (潭城街道)	建阳区 (潭城街道)	340,000	350,000	360,000	3387

(continued)

Table 5.4 (continued)

Name	Traditional	Simplified	Population (2012)	Population (2016)	Population (2020)	Area (km²)
Shunchang County (Shuangxi subdistrict)	順昌縣 (雙溪街道)	顺昌县 (双溪街道)	230,000	240,000	240,000	1985
Pucheng County (Nanpu subdistrict)	浦城縣 (南浦街道)	浦城县 (南浦街道)	430,000	430,000	430,000	3383
Guangze County (Hangchuan town)	光澤縣 (杭川鎮)	光泽县 (杭川镇)	160,000	160,000	160,000	2240
Songxi County (Songyuan subdistrict)	松溪縣 (松源街道)	松溪县 (松源街道)	160,000	160,000	170,000	1043
Zhenghe County (Xiongshan subdistrict)	政和縣 (熊山街道)	政和县 (熊山街道)	230,000	230,000	240,000	1749
Sanming city	三明市	三明市	2,720,000	2,750,000	2,890,000	23,191
Meilie District (Liexi subdistrict)	梅列區 (列西街道)	梅列区 (列西街道)	140,000	140,000	150,000	353
Sanyuan District (Chengguan subdistrict)	三元區 (城關街道)	三元区 (城关街道)	140,000	140,000	140,000	807
Yong'an City (Yanxi subdistrict)	永安市 (燕西街道)	永安市 (燕西街道)	320,000	330,000	330,000	2942
Mingxi County (Xuefeng town)	明溪縣 (雪峰鎮)	明溪县 (雪峰镇)	120,000	120,000	120,000	1708
Qingliu County (Longjin town)	清流縣 (龍津鎮)	清流县 (龙津镇)	150,000	150,000	160,000	1825
Ninghua County (Cuijiang town)	寧化縣 (翠江鎮)	宁化县 (翠江镇)	360,000	360,000	380,000	2407
Datian County (Junxi town)	大田縣 (均溪鎮)	大田县 (均溪镇)	370,000	370,000	420,000	2294
Youxi County (Chengguan town)	尤溪縣 (城關鎮)	尤溪县 (城关镇)	420,000	420,000	450,000	3463
Shaxian County (Fenggang subdistrict)	沙縣 (鳳崗街道)	沙县 (凤岗街道)	250,000	260,000	270,000	1815
Jiangle County (Guyong town)	將樂縣 (古鏞鎮)	将乐县 (古镛镇)	170,000	180,000	190,000	2246
Taining County (Shancheng town)	泰寧縣 (杉城鎮)	泰宁县 (杉城镇)	130,000	130,000	140,000	1540
Jianning County (Suicheng town)	建寧縣 (濉城鎮)	建宁县 (濉城鎮)	150,000	150,000	160,000	1791

(continued)

Table 5.4 (continued)

Name	Traditional	Simplified	Population (2012)	Population (2016)	Population (2020)	Area (km^2)
Putian city	莆田市	莆田市	3,220,000	3,300,000	3,600,000	3895
Chengxian District (Xialin subdistrict)	城廂區 (霞林街道)	城厢区 (霞林街道)	380,000	390,000	430,000	502
Hanjiang District (Handong subdistrict)	涵江區 (涵東街道)	涵江区 (涵东街道)	430,000	440,000	450,000	752
Licheng District (Zhenhai subdistrict)	荔城區 (鎮海街道)	荔城区 (镇海街道)	500,000	520,000	600,000	271
Xiuyu District (Hushi town)	秀嶼區 (笏石鎮)	秀屿区 (笏石镇)	830,000	850,000	960,000	519
Xianyou County (Licheng subdistrict)	仙游縣 (鯉城街道)	仙游县 (鲤城街道)	1,080,000	1,100,000	1,170,000	1851
Quanzhou city	泉州市	泉州市	6,860,000	6,930,000	7,550,000	10,864
Fengze District (Fengze subdistrict)	豐澤區 (豐澤街道)	丰泽区 (丰泽街道)	220,000	220,000	270,000	108
Licheng District (Jiangnan subdistrict)	鯉城區 (江南街道)	鲤城区 (江南街道)	260,000	250,000	270,000	54
Luojiang District (Wan'an subdistrict)	洛江區 (萬安街道)	洛江区 (万安街道)	180,000	180,000	200,000	382
Quangang District (Shanyao subdistrict)	泉港區 (山腰街道)	泉港区 (山腰街道)	380,000	390,000	420,000	306
Shishi City (Hubin subdistrict)	石獅市 (湖濱街道)	石狮市 (湖滨街道)	320,000	320,000	350,000	160
Jinjiang City (Luoshan subdistrict)	晉江市 (羅山街道)	晋江市 (罗山街道)	1,070,000	1,070,000	1,180,000	642
Nan'an City (Ximei subdistrict)	南安市 (溪美街道)	南安市 (溪美街道)	1,500,000	1,520,000	1,660,000	1985
Hui'an county (Luocheng town)	惠安縣 (螺城鎮)	惠安县 (螺城镇)	960,000	970,000	1,040,000	481
Anxi County (Fengcheng town)	安溪縣 (鳳城鎮)	安溪县 (凤城镇)	1,090,000	1,120,000	1,220,000	3057
Yongchun couny (Taocheng town)	永春縣 (桃城鎮)	永春县 (桃城镇)	560,000	570,000	610,000	1457

(continued)

Table 5.4 (continued)

Name	Traditional	Simplified	Population (2012)	Population (2016)	Population (2020)	Area (km²)
Dehua County (Xunzhong town)	德化縣 (潯中鎮)	德化县 (浔中镇)	320,000	320,000	350,000	2232
Jinmen County[a]	金門縣	金门县	N/A	N/A	N/A	N/A
Xiamen (Amoy) city	廈門市 (副省級)	厦门市 (副省级)	1,790,000	1,910,000	2,410,000	1516
Siming District (Xiagang subdistrict)	思明區 (廈港街道)	思明区 (厦港街道)	630,000	670,000	810,000	75
Haicang District (Haicang subdistrict)	海滄區 (海滄街道)	海沧区 (海沧街道)	120,000	140,000	210,000	176
Huli District (Heshan subdistrict)	湖里區 (禾山街道)	湖里区 (禾山街道)	220,000	250,000	340,000	72
Jimei District (Jimei subdistrict)	集美區 (集美街道)	集美区 (集美街道)	210,000	210,000	310,000	183
Tong'an district (Xiangping subdistrict)	同安區 (祥平街道)	同安区 (祥平街道)	320,000	330,000	390,000	658
Xiang'an district (Xindian town)	翔安區 (新店鎮)	翔安区 (新店镇)	290,000	310,000	360,000	352
Zhangzhou city	漳州市	漳州市	4,740,000	4,820,000	5,210,000	12,608
Longwen District (Buwen town)	龍文區 (步文鎮)	龙文区 (步文镇)	130,000	130,000	160,000	124
Xiangcheng District (Dongputou subdistrict)	薌城區 (東鋪頭街道)	芗城区 (东铺头街道)	430,000	440,000	470,000	265
Longhai City (Shima subdistrict)	龍海市 (石碼街道)	龙海市 (石码街道)	800,000	830,000	900,000	1115
Yunxiao County (Yunling town)	雲霄縣 (雲陵鎮)	云霄县 (云陵镇)	440,000	440,000	470,000	1069
Zhangpu County (Sui'an town)	漳鋪縣 (綏安鎮)	漳浦县 (绥安镇)	840,000	870,000	940,000	1999
Zhao'an county (Nanzhao town)	詔安縣 (南詔鎮)	诏安县 (南诏镇)	600,000	610,000	680,000	1247
Changtai County (Wu'an town)	長泰縣 (武安鎮)	长泰县 (武安镇)	200,000	200,000	210,000	913
Dongshan County (Xipu town)	東山縣 (西埔鎮)	东山县 (西埔镇)	210,000	210,000	220,000	244

(continued)

Table 5.4 (continued)

Name	Traditional	Simplified	Population (2012)	Population (2016)	Population (2020)	Area (km^2)
Nanjing County (Shancheng town)	南靖縣 (山城鎮)	南靖县 (山城镇)	350,000	350,000	360,000	1988
Pinghe County (Xiaoxi town)	平和縣 (小溪鎮)	平和县 (小溪镇)	580,000	580,000	620,000	2329
Hua'an county (Huafeng town)	華安縣 (華豐鎮)	华安县 (华丰镇)	160,000	160,000	170,000	1315
Longyan city	龍岩市	龙岩市	2,950,000	2,980,000	3,190,000	19,052
Xinluo District (Dongcheng subdistrict)	新羅區 (東城街道)	新罗区 (东城街道)	480,000	490,000	550,000	2679
Zhangping City (Jingcheng subdistrict)	漳平市 (菁城街道)	漳平市 (菁城街道)	280,000	280,000	300,000	2976
Changting County (Tingzhou town)	長汀縣 (汀州鎮)	长汀县 (汀州镇)	510,000	510,000	550,000	3100
Yongding District (Fengcheng town)	永定區 (鳳城鎮)	永定区 (凤城镇)	480,000	490,000	500,000	2224
Shanghang County (Linjiang town)	上杭縣 (臨江鎮)	上杭县 (临江镇)	500,000	500,000	530,000	2859
Wuping County (Pingchuan town)	武平縣 (平川鎮)	武平县 (平川镇)	370,000	380,000	400,000	2638
Liancheng County (Lianfeng town)	連城縣 (蓮峰鎮)	连城县 (莲峰镇)	330,000	330,000	350,000	2576
Ningde city	寧德市	宁德市	3,390,000	3,430,000	3,540,000	13,644
Jiaocheng District (Jiaobei subdistrict)	蕉城區 (蕉北街道)	蕉城区 (蕉北街道)	440,000	460,000	510,000	1664
Fu'an City (Chengbei subdistrict)	福安市 (城北街道)	福安市 (城北街道)	650,000	650,000	670,000	1880
Fuding City (Tongshan subdistrict)	福鼎市 (桐山街道)	福鼎市 (桐山街道)	580,000	580,000	600,000	1526
Shouning County (Aoyang town)	壽寧區 (鰲陽鎮)	寿宁县 (鳌阳镇)	270,000	270,000	270,000	1424
Xiapu County (Songcheng subdistrict)	霞浦縣 (松城街道)	霞浦县 (松城街道)	530,000	540,000	550,000	1716
Zherong County (Shuangcheng town)	柘榮縣 (雙城鎮)	柘荣县 (双城镇)	100,000	110,000	110,000	544

(continued)

Table 5.4 (continued)

Name	Traditional	Simplified	Population (2012)	Population (2016)	Population (2020)	Area (km^2)
Pingnan County (Gufeng town)	屏南縣 (古峰鎮)	屏南县 (古峰镇)	190,000	190,000	190,000	1458
Gutian County (Chengdong subdistrict)	古田縣 (城東街道)	古田县 (城东街道)	430,000	430,000	430,000	2385
Zhouning County (Shicheng town)	周寧縣 (獅城鎮)	周宁县 (狮城镇)	200,000	200,000	210,000	1047

[a]Administered by Taiwan (ROC)

References

Chew, Phyllis Ghim-Lian. 2013. *A sociolinguistic history of early identities in Singapore: From colonialism to nationalism*. New York: Palgrave Macmillan.

Dardess, John W. 2012. *Ming China, 1368–1644: A concise history of a resilient empire*. Boulder: Rowman & Littlefield.

Ebrey, Patricia Buckley. 2010. *The Cambridge illustrated history of China*. 2nd ed. New York: Cambridge University Press.

Elvin, Mark. 1973. *The pattern of the Chinese past: A social and economic interpretation*. Stanford: Stanford University Press.

Fujian Province Bureau of Statistics (FPBS). 2021. [Fujian Province: Sixth census data report, 2020, second issue]. January 5. 福建省第七次全国人口普查公报, 第二号. January 5. http://tjj.sm.gov.cn/ztzl/d7crkpc/zlxz_0103/202105/t20210525_1667313.htm.

Hsü, Immanuel C.Y. 2000. *The rise of modern China*. 6th ed. New York: Oxford University Press.

Jiao, Tianlong. 2007. *The Neolithic of Southeast China: Cultural transformation and regional interaction on the coast*. Youngstown/New York: Cambria Press.

Latourette, Kenneth Scott. 1967. *The Chinese: Their history and culture*. New York: The Macmillan Company.

Lin, Tingshui. 2018. [Some recommendations for the study of Fujian history]. Sohu.com. December 22. 林汀水. 对福建史研究的几点建议. https://www.sohu.com/a/281455311_99900054.

Ministry of Civil Affairs (MCA), People's Republic of China. 2020. [County/township administration handbook]. Beijing: China Statistics Press. 中華人民共和國民政部, 中華人民共和國, 鄉鎮行政區劃簡冊.

Schottenhammer, Angela. 2010. Transfer of *xiangyao* 香藥 from Iran and Arabia to China – A reinvestigation of entries in the *Youyang zazu* 酉陽雜俎 (863). In *Aspects of the maritime silk road: From the Persian Gulf to the East China Sea*, ed. Ralph Kauz, 117–149. Wiesbaden: Harrassowitz Verlag.

Shi, Zhihong. 2006. China's overseas trade policy and its historical results. In *Intra-Asian trade and the world market*, ed. A.J.H. Latham and Heita Kawakatsu, 4–23. New York: Routledge.

Wilkinson, Endymion. 2012. *Chinese history: A new manual*. Cambridge, MA: Harvard University Press.

Zhang, Shunan. 2021. [The 2020 per capita income list of residents in various provinces: Shanghai is the richest, and it has risen sharply]. Finance.people.com. January 22. 张澍楠. 2020年各省份居民人均收入榜: 上海最有钱, 这地涨得猛. http://finance.people.com.cn/n1/2021/0122/c1004-32008733.html.

Chapter 6
Gansu Province

Abstract Archeological excavations show human habitation in Gansu Province going back at least 20,000 years, and the progenitors of the Zhou and Qin are also said to have hailed from this region. Today, Gansu Province brings immediate imagery of the oases that formed the central network of the Silk Road, connecting ancient China with the European continent. It also conjures the grottoes of Dunhuang City, where a treasure trove of documents and religious art span the centuries, and these materials are still being mined for historical gems today. The western province also served as an essential defensive stronghold for successive Chinese empires, while also being a modern staging area for China's burgeoning space and ballistic missile programs. Among the most diverse of Chinese provinces when it comes to the representation of its 56 official ethnic nationalities, Gansu is relatively poor, and consistently ranks near the bottom of China's overall economic development and per capita income when compared to the mainland's 31 provinces and major cities.

E. Croddy, *China's Provinces and Populations*,
https://doi.org/10.1007/978-3-031-09165-0_6

Gansu Province (甘肃省 *gānsù shěng*): Abbreviations (甘 *gān*; 隴 *lǒng*) (Fig. 6.1)

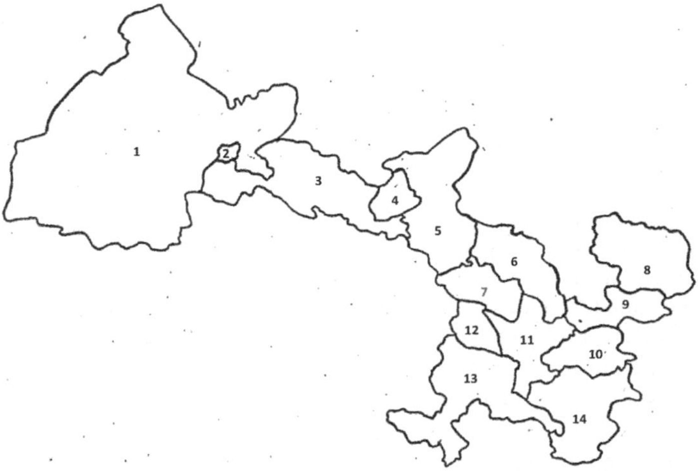

Gansu ProvincePopulation (2020)

1.	**iuquan City**	**1,055,706**
2.	**Jiayuguan City**	**312,663**
3.	**Zhangye City**	**1,131,016**
4.	**Jinchang City**	**438,026**
5.	**Wuwei City**	**1,464,955**
6.	**Baiyin City**	**1,512,110**
7.	Lanzhou City	4,359,446
8.	**Qingyang City**	**2,179,716**
9.	**Pingliang City**	**1,848,607**
10.	**Tianshui City**	**2,984,659**
11.	**Dingxi City**	**2,524,097**
12.	**Linxia Hui Autonomous Prefecture**	**2,109,750**
13.	**Gannan Tibetan Autonomous Prefecture**	**691,808**
14.	**Longnan City**	**2,407,272**

Fig. 6.1 Gansu province: major cities (Provincial Capital: Lanzhou City). (Map drawn by the Author, after People's Republic of China, Ministry of Civil Affairs, MCA 2020)

Gansu (甘肃 *gānsù*) Province: General Impressions

As the doorway to the Silk Road, Gansu province conjures images of western border defenses, barren deserts, and cliff-hewn grottos with vast holdings ancient manuscripts. There is also the spirit of literary pursuit, as embodied in the long-standing serial publication *Reader* (讀者 *dúzhě*) that began (1981) in Lanzhou City. Gansu also brings to mind a bowl of beef soup with hand-stretched noodles (牛肉麵 *niúròu miàn*). As a major staging area for China's scientific and strategic military programs going back to the late 1950s, Gansu's Jiuquan City (酒泉市 *jiǔquán shì*) hosts China's first rocket launch development center, as well as a key test site for nuclear-capable ballistic missiles.

Gansu Prehistory

Late Pleistocene archeological studies of eastern Gansu's Dadiwan site (大地灣遺址 *dàdìwān yízhǐ*) in Qin'an County (秦安縣 *qín'ān xiàn*), Tianshui City (天水市 *tiānshuǐ shì*), show human activity dated about 32,000–18,000 years ago (Bettinger et al. 2010). Tradition has it that this is where the legendary founding Emperor, Fuxi (伏羲 *fúxī*) was born. Residues at the Dadiwan excavation show evidence of millet (*Panicum miliaceum* and *Setaria italica*) having been grown and milled there about 7500 years ago. Additional evidence of early forms of agriculture dating as far back as 5800–5300 BCE in eastern Gansu Province include small-scale millet farming, as well as stone implements and kilned pottery. A representative of Yangshao Culture (仰韶文化 *yǎngsháo wénhuà*; ca. 5000–3000 BCE), the aforementioned Dadiwan shows evidence of an organized society, having built large domiciles, and domesticating dogs and swine for meat. Copper tools related to Machang (馬廠文化 *mǎchǎng wénhuà*) and Majiayao (馬家窰文化 *mǎjiā yáowénhuà*) cultures, dating back to 3000–2000 BCE, have also been unearthed in Lintao County (臨洮縣 *líntáo xiàn*). (Qiu 1996).

Zhou and Qin dynasty ancestors are said to have their origins in eastern Gansu Province. During the Shang dynastic period, the regions of today's Gansu were populated by the Qiang (羌方 *qiāngfāng*) and Quanrong (犬戎 *quǎnróng*) tribal communities. King Wen of Zhou (周文王 *Zhōuwén Wáng*; 1152–1056 BC) was able to defeat the Xirong (西戎 *xī róng*, i.e., "the Rong people of the west") and the Hunyi (混夷 *hùn yí*) barbarian tribes, successfully fighting his way into modern Gansu Province's Lingtai County (靈台縣 *língtái xiàn*). At this early stage of China's history, the area of today's Gansu was still largely populated by non-Chinese clans, including the Qiang (羌 *qiāng*), who lived in both Gansu and Shaanxi provinces. The aforementioned King Wen also battled the local Mi tribe (密國 *mì guó*), also in modern-day Lingtai, as well as the State of Gong (共國 *gòngguó*) in Jingchuan County (涇川縣 *jīngchuān xiàn*). During the Spring-Autumn era (771–476 BCE), the Gansu region was occupied by both the State of Qin and the Xirong people. The Western Rong (i.e., 西戎 *xīróng*) mainly inhabited the following areas:

- Mianzhu (綿諸 *miánzhū*), near Tianshui City
- Guirong (邽戎 *guīróng*) in southwest Tianshui
- Jirong (冀戎 *jìróng*; in today's Gangu county)
- Yiqurong (義渠 戎 *yìqúróng*), which equates approximately to Liupanshan of today
- Di (翟 *dí*), today's Lintao county and
- Huan (獂 *huán*) in northern Longxi County (隴西縣 *lǒngxī xiàn*)

Even after the founding of the Qin State (770 BCE), multiple attempts to subjugate the Rong clans all but failed. However, the Qin State, later led by Duke Wu (秦武公 *qín wǔgōng*, 697–678 BCE) had managed to expand into the aforementioned counties, establishing Gui (邽縣 *guīxiàn*) and Ji (冀縣 *jìxiàn*) counties in modern-day Maiji district (麥積區 *màijī qū*), and Gangu County (甘谷縣 *gāngǔ xiàn*), respectively.

The Shajing culture (沙井文化 *shājǐng wénhuà*), which is named after Shajingcun village (沙井村 *shājǐngcūn*) located in Minqin County (民勤縣 *mínqín xiàn*) was first studied in 1923, and is dated approximately during the Spring Autumn period. Indeed, carbon-14 dating supports a time frame of 780–560 BCE. Human skeletons found there were Mongoloid in morphology, and its fortification structures (earthen wall) and agricultural tools all showed the Shajing people to have been a permanent (versus nomadic) settlement. By 280 BCE, under the Qin (秦 *qín*), Longxi prefecture (隴西郡 *lǒngxī jùn*) was established, and from which the character (隴 *lǒng*) abbreviation for Gansu is derived. Ten years later, its Northern Prefecture (北地郡 *běidì jùn*) was created, an area covering modern-day Ningxia and Shaanxi provinces. After the unification of China by the Qin dynasty (221–206 BCE), and with its famed centralized administrative system put well into place, both Longxi and Beidi prefectures remained. Longxi was governed from the capital Didao (狄道 *dídào*) in modern-day northeast Lintao county, while Beidi prefecture had its ruling center in Yiqu (義渠 *yìqú*), located in today's southwest Ningxian County (寧縣 *níngxiàn*).

Expanding into the west, and building upon victories against the Xiongnu, the Han dynasty (121 BCE) established two prefectures ("commanderies") at Wuwei (武威郡 *wǔwēi jùn*) and Jiuquan (酒泉郡 *jiǔquán jùn*). A decade later, additional prefectures were named, splitting existing commanderies into Zhangye, Jiuquan, and Dunhuang, all falling under the general administrative region of the Liangzhou Inspectorate (涼州刺史部 *liángzhōu cìshǐbù*). The borders of this geographical administrative region looked very much like Gansu province of today.

For several centuries afterward, while maintaining their prefectural status, the aforementioned places were governed under two auspices, namely the Guanlong (關隴諸郡 *guānlǒngzhū jùn*) and Hexi (河西諸郡 *héxīzhū jùn*) prefectural groups (ca. 612 CE). In the Tang (741 CE), Gansu Province of today primarily existed within the borders of Longyoudao, Eastern Region (隴右道東部 *lǒngyòudào dōngbù*) that was divided into prefectural states (州 *zhōu*) with names that are familiar today (from west to east):

- Shazhou (沙州 *shāzhōu*), including Dunhuang (敦煌 *dūnhuáng*)
- Guazhou (瓜州 *guāzhōu*) so named due to its famed honeydew melons
- Suzhou (肅州 *sùzhōu*), including Jiuquan (酒泉 *jiǔquán*)
- Ganzhou (甘州 *gānzhōu*)
- Liangzhou (涼州 *liángzhōu*)
- Lanzhou (蘭州 *lánzhōu*); and
- Qinzhou (秦州 *qínzhōu*)

During the Tang Dynasty, Ganzhou and Suzhou were neighboring prefectures, and their names later combined to form Gansu, as the modern province is known today. The chaos that resulted from the An Lushan Rebellion (安史之亂 *ānshǐzhī luàn*; 755–763) provided the Tibetans an opportunity to make their move on the western territories, and they laid siege to Ganzhou, Liangzhou, Suzhou, Guazhou, and Shazhou, among others. In 1111 CE, Ganzhou would be occupied by the Tangut empire, the Xixia (黨項族西夏 *dǎngxiàngzú xīxià* 1038–1227). Gansu Province (甘肅行省 *gānsù xíngshěng*) was later formally established by the Yuan dynasty (ca. 1330), its borders extending into modern-day Inner Mongolia and Ningxia Province. Centuries later, Shaanxi Province was incorporated a large swath of territory in western China, which then included today's Gansu province (ca. 1582). During the Qing dynasty, the population of the Gansu region was recorded at 273,292 in 1685, and reached 8,870,504 by 1765 (LHCCGP 1995). Later in the Qing, Gansu Province (1884) encompassed the following prefectural entities:

- Lanzhou (蘭州府 *lánzhōu fǔ*)
- Pingliang (平涼府 *píngliáng fǔ*)
- Gongchang (鞏昌府 *gǒngchāng fǔ*)
- Qingyang (慶陽府 *qìngyáng fǔ*)
- Ningxia (寧夏府 *níngxià fǔ*)
- Xining (西寧府 *xīníng fǔ*)
- Liangzhou (涼州府 *liángzhōu fǔ*)
- Ganzhou (甘州府 *gānzhōu fǔ*)

As well as the following prefectures:

- Jingzhou (涇州 *jīngzhōu*)
- Guyuanzhou (固原州 *gùyuán zhōu*)
- Jiezhou (階州 *jiēzhōu*)
- Qinzhou (秦州 *qínzhōu*)
- Suzhou (肅州 *sùzhōu*) and
- Anxizhou (安西州 *ānxīzhōu*) (Table 6.1)

Table 6.1 Populations in Gansu, Ningxia and Qinghai Provinces: 1820 and 1908 (Shi 2000)

Prefecture/State entity (Modern-day province)	1820	1908
Lanzhou (Gansu) 蘭州府 *lánzhōu fǔ*	2,694,991	547,636
Gongchang (Gansu) 鞏昌府 *gǒngchāng fǔ*	1,895,260	658,894
Pingliang (Gansu) 平涼府 *píngliáng fǔ*	2,340,323	427,036[a]
Qingyang (Gansu) 慶陽府 *qìngyáng fǔ*	1,272,823	158,362
Ningxia 寧夏府 (Ningxia) *níngxià fǔ*	1,392,815	230,802
Ganzhou (Gansu) 甘州府 *gānzhōu fǔ*	813,615	249,789
Liangzhou (Gansu) 涼州府 *liángzhōu fǔ*	1,504,498	583,557
Xining (Qinghai) 西寧府 *xīníng fǔ*	708,829	367,115
Jingzhou (Gansu) 涇州 *jīngzhōu*	837,730	229,919
Qinzhou (Gansu) 秦州 *qínzhōu*	868,948	1,058,026
Suzhou (Gansu) 肅州 *sùzhōu*	452,063	161,703
Anxi (Gansu) 安西州 *ānxī zhōu*	77,873	38,139
Total	**15,238,974**	**5,093,680**

[a]Also includes population in Guyuan, Ningxia

The Dunhuang City Grottoes: Treasure Trove of Historical Documents

In ca. 1895, a Daoist practitioner by the name of Wang Yuanlu (王圓籙 *wáng yuánlù*) was living rent free in a cave among the temple grottoes in Dunhuang (敦煌莫高窟 *dūnhuáng mògāokū*). In 1900, his helper, only known since by his surname (楊 *yáng*), stumbled across a cache of ancient documents in what is now called Cave 16. What they found was a library of priceless documents, numbering about 50,000 in all, dating back to the fifth century CE. This treasure trove of historical writings had been sealed (for unclear reasons) in ca. 1000 CE (Wilkinson 2015). In addition to those Chinese language documents found in the Dunhuang haul, there were also numerous foreign manuscripts, to include: Arabic, Uyghur, Tangut (Xixia), Sanscrit, Tibetan, Gupta, Mongolian, and even a Hebrew prayer, composed by an itinerant merchant who wrote it on his way to China via Babylon (Mikanowski 2013).

In the mid-1930s the Republic of China (ROC) drew the provincial lines that brought together Shaanxi and Gansu Provinces (陝甘省 *shǎngān shěng*). With the expansion of the Chinese Communist Party in November 1934, however, Gansu became the seat of the Shaan-Gan (Shaanxi-Gansu) Border Area Soviet Government,[1] with its command headquarters in Liyuanbao (荔原堡 *lìyuán bǎo*), Huachi County (華池縣 *huáchí xiàn*). In July 1937, CCP territory was expanded to the Shaanxi-Gansu-Ningxia border region government.[2] Following the complete

[1]陝甘邊區蘇維埃政府 *shǎngānbiānqū sūwéi'āi zhèngfǔ.*

[2]陝甘寧邊區政府 *shǎngānníng biānqū zhèngfǔ.*

"liberation" of China in August 1949, Gansu was made into a prefectural governmental entity.[3]

Great Leap Forward Years (1958–1961) and the "Tongwei Incident"

Even remote Gansu could not escape the ravages of Mao Zedong's Great Leap Forward (GLF) disaster (1958–1962). During the latter period, some 666,700 people died from starvation in Gansu alone. And while Henan's Xinyang City suffered greatly, where a million or more people died during the GLF, Yang Jisheng reports that the case of Gansu's Tongwei County (通渭縣 *tōngwèi xiàn*) was even worse in terms of percentage of population. Counting those who starved to death (78,462), and the surfeit of births as a result of the famine, ultimately its population was reduced by nearly a third (Yang 2012).

Yumen's Missile Silos

China's strategic rocket forces, formerly known as the People's Liberation Army (PLA) Second Artillery, now known as the PLA Strategic Rocket Forces (PLARF), have continued to grow and modernize apace since their establishment in 1966. In 2021, academics at the Middlebury Institute of International Studies in Monterey, California, found what appear to be PLARF ballistic missile launch silos, located roughly 50 kilometers west of Yumen City. Based on commercial satellite imagery, there appear to be as many as one hundred silos having been constructed in and around this area, possibly for the mobile DF-41 intercontinental ballistic missile (ICBM) system. Similarly constructed silos have also been seen in imagery at PLARF training site located in Jilantai, Alxa Left Banner (阿拉善左旗 *ālāshàn zuǒqí*), Inner Mongolia. In the case of the Yumen site(s), it is unknown if these are meant for training or are intended to be used as operational launch sites for PLARF nuclear missiles (Fung 2021.)

Modern Gansu: Economics and Population

Compared to the average per capita income (USD $6370) in regions such as Beijing, Shanghai and Zhejiang that have benefited from recent economic development, in 2014 the per capita income in Gansu Province was nearly half of that (US $3567). By 2020, Gansu remained near the bottom of China's 31 provinces and major cities

[3] 甘肅行政公署 *gānsù xíngzhènggōngshǔ.*

in terms of gross domestic product (GDP) of about US $140.2 billion, and absolute bottom in per capita income (US $3162) in 2020 (Zhang 2021).

During mainland China's 2011–2015 12th Five-Year Plan, the number of poor people in Gansu numbered about eight million. Beginning in 2013, the Chinese government took an initiative to improve the lot of some 224,000 households, focusing on those who live in remote and infertile regions, and where in some places water can only be brought in by pack mule. As of early 2016, some 1,116,000 people in those desolate areas had been moved closer to urban living, some now having modern conveniences to include running water toilets for the first time in their lives. That said, it is unclear how many of these relocations were truly "voluntary" (PRCGN 2016).

In 2015, Gansu province had a population of about 26 million. A more precise figure, 26,099,500, can be found for Gansu's resident (including non-permanent) population for 2016. Given a permanent (戶籍人口 *hùjí rénkǒu*) population of about 27,130,000, this shows a net deficit due to 'floating populations' (about 1% of total) regularly leave Gansu for work elsewhere. Following this trend, Gansu's resident population dropped over 2% from 2010–2020 (census data) (Tables 6.2 and 6.3).

Table 6.2 Gansu Province: census data (Residential 常住人口 chángzhù rénkǒu) 2010 and 2020 (GPBS 2021)

City/prefecture	Population (2010)	Population (2020)
Jiuquan City 酒泉市 *jiǔquán shì*	1,095,947	1,055,706
Jiayuguan City 嘉峪關市 *jiāyùguān shì*	231,853	312,663
Zhangye City 張掖市 *zhāngyè shì*	1,199,515	1,131,016
Jinchang City 金昌市 *jīnchāng shì*	464,050	438,026
Wuwei City 武威市 *wǔwēi shì*	1,815,054	1,464,955
Baiyin City 白銀市 *báiyín shì*	1,708,751	1,512,110
Lanzhou City 蘭州市 *lánzhōu shì* [abbrev. 皋 *gāo*; 蘭 *lán*]	3,616,163	4,359,446
Dingxi City 定西市 *dìngxī shì*	2,698,622	2,524,097
Longnan City 隴南市 *lǒngnán shì*	2,567,718	2,407,272
Tianshui City 天水市 *tiānshuǐ shì*	3,262,548	2,984,659
Pingliang City 平涼市 *píngliàng shì*	2,068,033	1,848,607
Qingyang City 慶陽市 *qìngyáng shì*	2,211,191	2,179,716
Linxia Hui Autonomous Prefecture 臨夏回族自治州 *línxià huízú zìzhìzhōu*	1,946,677	2,109,750
Gannan Tibetan Autonomous Prefecture 甘南藏族自治州 *gānnán zāngzú zìzhìzhōu*	689,132	691,808
Total	25,575,254	25,019,831

Table 6.3 Gansu province: population data of cities and their subordinate sectors (GPBS 2021)

Cities and subordinate sectors, population (2020 census)	Subordinate district, city and county populations (2020)	Total population (2020)
Jiuquan City 酒泉市 ***jiǔquán shì***		**1,055,706**
Suzhou District 肅州區 *sùzhōu qū*	455,611	
Yumen City 玉門市 *yùmén shì*	137,736	
Dunhuang City 敦煌市 *dūnhuáng shì*	185,231	
Jinta County 金塔縣 *jīntǎ xiàn*	121,766	
Guazhou County 瓜州縣 *guāzhōu xiàn*	129,299	
Subei Mengguzu (Mongol) Autonomous County 肅北蒙古族自治縣 *sùběi měnggǔzú zìzhìxiàn*	15,093	
Akesai Hasakezu (Aksai; Aksay Kazakh) Autonomous County 阿克塞哈薩克族自治縣 *ākèsāi hāsàkè zúzìzhìxiàn*	10,970	
Jiayuguan City 嘉峪關市 ***jiāyùguān shì***		**312,663**
Zhangye City 張掖市 ***zhāngyè shì***		**1,131,016**
Ganzhou District 甘州區 *gānzhōu qū*	519,096	
Minle County 民樂縣 *mínlè xiàn*	192,476	
Linze County 臨澤縣 *línzé xiàn*	115,946	
Gaotai County 高台縣 *gāotái xiàn*	125,705	
Shandan County 山丹縣 *shāndān xiàn*	150,031	
Sunan Yuguzu (Yughur) Autonomous County 肅南裕固族自治縣 *sùnán yùgùzú zìzhìxiàn*	27,762	
Jinchang City 金昌市 ***jīnchāng shì***		**438,026**
Jinchuan District 金川區 *jīnchuān qū*	260,385	
Yongchang County 永昌縣 *yǒngchāng xiàn*	177,641	
Wuwei City 武威市 ***wǔwēi shì***		**1,464,955**
Liangzhou District 涼州區 *liángzhōu qū*	885,277	
Minqin County 民勤縣 *mínqín xiàn*	178,470	
Gulang County 古浪縣 *gǔlàng xiàn*	250,177	
Tianzhu Zangzu (Bairi Tibetan) Autonomous County 天祝藏族自治縣 *tiānzhù zāngzú zìzhìxiàn*	151,031	
Baiyin City 白銀市 ***báiyín shì***		**1,512,110**
Baiyin District 白銀區 *báiyín qū*	337,645	
Pingchuan District 平川區 *píngchuān qū*	200,869	
Jingyuan County 靖遠縣 *jìngyuǎn xiàn*	373,050	
Huining County 會寧縣 *jìngyuǎn xiàn*	401,581	
Jingtai County 景泰縣 *jǐngtài xiàn*	198,965	
Lanzhou City 蘭州市 ***lánzhōu shì*** **[abbrev. 皋 *gāo*; 蘭 *lán*]**		**4,359,446**
Chengguan District 城關區 *chéngguān qū*	1,484,016	
Qilihe District 七里河區 *qīlǐhé qū*	712,271	
Xigu District 西固區 *xīgù qū*	407,010	

(continued)

Table 6.3 (continued)

Cities and subordinate sectors, population (2020 census)	Subordinate district, city and county populations (2020)	Total population (2020)
Anning District 安寧區 *ānníng qū*	439,566	
Honggu District 紅古區 *hónggǔ qū*	143,795	
Yongdeng County 永登縣 *yǒngdēng xiàn*	285,549	
Gaolan County 皋蘭縣 *gāolán xiàn*	125,157	
Yuzhong County 榆中縣 *yúzhōng xiàn*	473,882	
Lanzhou New District 蘭州新區 *lánzhōu xīnqū*	288,200	
Dingxi City 定西市 ***dìngxī shì***		**2,524,097**
Anding District 安定區 *āndìng qū*	422,383	
Tongwei County 通渭縣 *tōngwèi xiàn*	323,648	
Lintao County 臨洮縣 *líntáo xiàn*	480,149	
Zhangxian County 漳縣 *zhāngxiàn*	167,309	
Minxian County 岷縣 *mínxiàn*	425,627	
Weiyuan County 渭源縣 *wèiyuán xiàn*	277,608	
Longxi County 隴西縣 *lǒngxī xiàn*	427,373	
Longnan City 隴南市 ***lǒngnán shì***		**2,407,272**
Wudu District 武都區 *wǔdū qū*	546,616	
Chengxian County 成縣 *chéngxiàn*	241,587	
Tanchang[a] County 宕昌縣 *tànchāng xiàn*	254,944	
Kangxian County 康縣 *kāngxiàn*	162,418	
Wenxian County 文縣 *wénxiàn*	196,906	
Xihe County 西和縣 *xīhé xiàn*	351,069	
Lixian County 禮縣 *lǐxiàn*	424,135	
Liangdang County 兩當縣 *liǎngdāng xiàn*	39,709	
Huixian County 徽縣 *huīxiàn*	189,888	
Tianshui City 天水市 ***tiānshuǐ shì***		**2,984,659**
Qinzhou District 秦州區 *qínzhōu qū*	656,689	
Maiji District 麥積區 *màijī qū*	556,102	
Qingshui County 清水縣 *qīngshuǐ xiàn*	240,597	
Qin'an County 秦安縣 *qín'ān xiàn*	416,337	
Gangu County 甘谷縣 *gāngǔ xiàn*	506,801	
Wushan County 武山縣 *wǔshān xiàn*	363,727	
Zhangjiachuan Huizu (Hui) Autonomous County 張家川回族自治縣 *zhāngjiāchuān huízú zìzhìxiàn*	244,406	
Pingliang City 平涼市 ***píngliàng shì***		**1,848,607**
Kongtong District 崆峒區 *kōngtóng qū*	504,265	
Jingchuan County 涇川縣 *jīngchuān xiàn*	222,210	
Lingtai County 靈台縣 *língtái xiàn*	156,224	
Chongxin County 崇信縣 *chóngxìn xiàn*	82,138	
Huating City 華亭市 *huátíng shì*	182,449	

(continued)

Table 6.3 (continued)

Cities and subordinate sectors, population (2020 census)	Subordinate district, city and county populations (2020)	Total population (2020)
Zhuanglang County 莊浪縣 *zhuānglàng xiàn*	335,864	
Jingning County 靜寧縣 *jìngníng xiàn*	365,637	
Qingyang City 慶陽市 ***qìngyáng shì***		**2,179,716**
Xifeng District 西峰區 *xīfēng qū*	513,856	
Qingcheng County 慶城縣 *qìngchéng xiàn*	235,154	
Huanxian County 環縣 *huánxiàn*	304,687	
Huachi County 華池縣 *huáchí xiàn*	119,346	
Heshui County 合水縣 *héshuǐ xiàn*	135,908	
Zhengning County 正寧縣 *zhèngníng xiàn*	173,243	
Ningxian County 寧縣 *níngxiàn*	336,316	
Zhenyuan County 鎮原縣 *zhènyuán xiàn*	361,206	
Linxia Hui Autonomous Prefecture 臨夏回族自治州 ***línxià huízú zìzhìzhōu***		**2,109,750**
Linxia City 臨夏市 *línxià shì*	355,968	
Linxia County 臨夏縣 *línxià xiàn*	322,628	
Kangle County 康樂縣 *kānglè xiàn*	255,955	
Yongjing County 永靖縣 *yǒngjìng xiàn*	180,650	
Guanghe County 廣河縣 *guǎnghé xiàn*	260,596	
Hezheng County 和政縣 *hézhèng xiàn*	204,529	
Dongxiangzu (Sarta) Autonomous County 東鄉族自治縣 *dōngxiāngzú zìzhìxiàn*	290,034	
Jishishan Bao'anzu Dongxiangzu Salazu (Bonan, Sarta, and Salar) Autonomous County 積石山保安族東鄉族撒拉族自治縣 *jīshíshān bǎoānzú dōngxiāngzú sālāzú zìzhìxiàn*	239,930	
Gannan Tibetan Autonomous Prefecture 甘南藏族自治州 ***gānnán zāngzú zìzhìzhōu***		**691,808**
Hezuo City 合作市 *hézuò shì*	112,173	
Lintan County 臨潭縣 *líntán xiàn*	127,387	
Zhuoni (Jonê) County 卓尼縣 *zhuóní xiàn*	95,387	
Zhouqu (Zhugqu) County 舟曲縣 *zhōuqū xiàn*	125,367	
Diebu (Têwo) County 迭部縣 *diébù xiàn*	52,192	
Maqu County 瑪曲縣 *mǎqū xiàn*	57,076	
Luqu County 碌曲縣 *lùqū xiàn*	35,871	
Xiahe (Sangqu) County 夏河縣 *xiàhé xiàn*	86,355	

[a]Elsewhere 宕 is usually read *dàng*

Gansu Province: Ethnic Groups

Gansu has an impressive diversity of ethnic (non-Han) peoples, the Hui forming the largest percentage (about 50 percent) of all minority groups (see Tables 6.4, 6.5 and Fig. 6.2):

Table 6.4 Breakdown of major Gansu Ethnic Groups by percentage of population (1953–2000)

Gansu province Ethnic Groups	1953	1964	1982	1990	2000
Hui (Moslem) 回族 (*huízú*)	60.17	62.09	61.55	58.99	53.89
Tibetan 藏族 (*zàngzú*)	21.25	20.15	19.58	19.76	20.15
Sarta 東鄉族 (*dōngxiāng zú*)	16.14	14.47	15.70	16.79	20.55
Tu 土族/(Monguor) 蒙古爾 (*ménggŭ'ĕdr*)	0.55	0.80	0.81	1.15	1.38
Yugur 裕固族 (*yùgù zú*)	0.40	0.59	0.66	0.64	0.59
Bonan 保安族 (*băoān zú*)	0.51	0.53	0.54	0.57	0.68

Sources: Gansu Provincial Government Website; Chinese Wikipedia (https://zh.wikipedia.org)

Table 6.5 Detailed Ethnic minority breakdown, Gansu Province (1990, 2000)

Ethnic Group	Pinyin	Population (1990)	Population (2000)
Han Chinese 漢族	*hànzú*	20,510,000	22,930,000
Minority Ethnic Population 少數民族	*shăoshù mínzú*	1,856,000	2,199,000
Tibetan 藏族	*zàngzú*	367,006	443,228
Hui (Moslem) 回族	*huízú*	1,095,668	1,184,930
Tu 土族/(Monguor) 蒙古爾	*tŭzú/ménggŭ'ĕr*	21,397	30,338
Salar 撒拉族	*sālā zú*	6740	11,784
Mongol 蒙古族	*ménggŭ zú*	8135	15,774
Manchu 滿族	*măn zú*	16,701	17,285
Sarta 東鄉族	*dōngxiāng zú*	311,902	451,622
Tujia 土家族	*tŭjiā zú*	608	1341
Zhuang 壯族	*zhuàng zú*	867	1308
Miao 苗族	*miáo zú*	359	1509
Bonan 保安族	*băoān zú*	10,555	15,170
Yi 彝族	*yí zú*	108	1722
Kazakh 哈薩克族	*hāsàkè zú*	3146	3963
Bai 白族	*bái zú*	97	272
Korean 朝鮮族	*cháoxiăn zú*	560	1565
Bouyei 布依族	*bùyī zú*	75	768
Uyghur 維吾爾族	*wéiwúĕr zú*	943	2132
Yao 瑶族	*yáo zú*	73	228
Yugur 裕固族	*yùgù zú*	11,801	12,962

(continued)

Table 6.5 (continued)

Ethnic Group	Pinyin	Population (1990)	Population (2000)
Dong 侗族	*dòng zú*	108	1722
Li 黎族	*lí zú*	22	58
Xibe 錫伯族	*xībó zú*	373	312
Qiang 羌族	*qiāng zú*	60	64
Klau 仡佬族	*gēlǎo zú*	4	30
She 畲族	*shē zú*	44	201
Russian 俄羅斯族	*éluōsī zú*	38	55
Nakhi 納西族	*nàxī zú*	17	28
Dai 傣族	*dǎi zú*	13	13
Sui 水族	*shuǐ zú*	10	88
Dauer 達斡爾族	*dáwò'ěr zú*	51	115
Lisu 傈僳族	*lìsù zú*	3	115
Gaoshan 高山族	*gāoshān zú*	15	55
Wa 佤族	*wǎ zú*	2	143
Hani 哈尼族	*hāní zú*	26	40
Mulao 仫佬族	*mùlǎo zú*	4	30
Hezhen 赫哲族	*hèzhé zú*	0	21
Gin 京族	*jīng zú*	1	7
Maonan 毛南族	*máonán zú*	5	77
Lahu 拉祜族	*lāhù zú*	0	10
Ewenki/Evenks 鄂溫克族	*èwēnkè zú*	10	16
Nu 怒族	*nù zú*	0	7
Jingpo 景頗族	*jǐngpǒ zú*	0	11
Monba 門巴族	*ménbā zú*	1	24
Kyrgyz 柯爾克孜族	*kē'ěrkèzī zú*	13	13
Derung 獨龍族	*dúlóng zú*	0	37
Tajik 塔吉克族	*tǎjíkè zú*	2	99
Pumi 普米族	*pǔmǐ zú*	0	11
Blang 布朗族	*bùlǎng zú*	0	9
Tatar 塔塔爾族	*tǎtǎěr zú*	1	186
Uzbek 烏孜別克族/烏茲別克族	*wūzībiékè zú*	6	18
Oroqen 鄂倫春族	*èlúnchūn zú*	3	10
Deang 德昂族	*déáng zú*	0	7
Jino 基諾族	*jīnuò zú*	0	1
Achang 阿昌族	*āchāng zú*	0	1
Lhoba 珞巴族	*luòbā zú*	0	0
Recently registered Chinese citizens		8	5
Other as of yet unrecognized minority groups		N/A	34
Provincial total population		22,370,000	25,120,000

Sources: Gansu Provincial Government Website; Chinese Wikipedia (https://zh.wikipedia.org/)

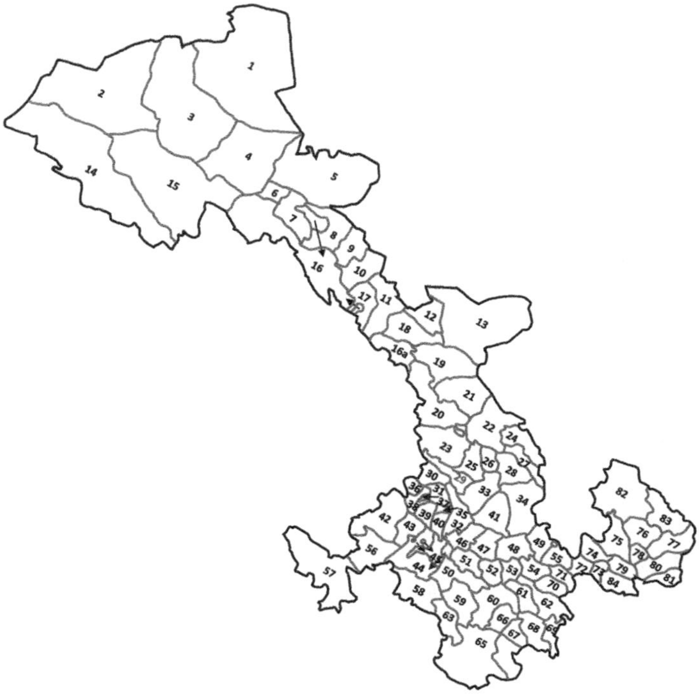

1. (Belongs to Subei Mongolian Autonomous County)
2. Dunhuang City
3. Guazhou County
4. Yumen City
5. Jinta County
6. Jiayuguan City
7. Jiuquan City
8. Gaotai County
9. Linze County
10. Ganzhou District
11. Shandan County
12. Jinchuan District
13. Minqin County
14. Akesai (Aksai) Kazakh Autonomous County
15. Subei Mongolian Autonomous County
16. Sunan Yugu (Yughur) Autonomous County

16a. (Belongs to Sunan Yugu (Yuhgur) Autonomous County

17. Minle County
18. Yongchang County
19. Liangzhou District
20. Tianzhu Tibetan Autonomous County
21. Gulang County
22. Jingtai County
23. Yongdeng County
24. (Under Jingyuan County jurisdiction)
25. Gaolan County
26. Baiyin District
27. Pingchuan District
28. Jingyuan County
29. Lanzhou City
30. Yongjing County
31. Dongxiang (Sarta) Autonomous County
32. Lintao County
33. Yuzhong County
34. Huining County
35. Guanghe County
36. Jishishan Bao'an Dongxiang Sala (Bonan, Sarta, and Salar) Autonomous County
37. Linxia City
38. Linxia County
39. Hezheng County
40. Kangle County
41. Anding County
42. Xiahe County
43. Hezuo City
44. Zhuoni County
45. Lintan County
46. Weiyuan County
47. Longxi County
48. Tongwei County
49. Jingning County
50. Minxian County
51. Zhangxian County
52. Wushan County
53. Ganyu County
54. Tai'an County
55. Zhuanglang County
56. Luqu County
57. Maqu County
58. Diebu County
59. Tanchang County
60. Lixian County
61. Qinzhou District
62. Mianji District
63. Zhouqu County
64. Wenxian County
65. Wudu District
66. Xihe County
67. Chengxian County
68. Huixian County
69. Liangdang County
70. Qingshui County
71. Zhangjiachuan Hui Autonomous County
72. Huating County
73. Chongxin County
74. Kongtong District
75. Zhenyuan County
76. Qingcheng County
77. Heshui County
78. Xifeng District
79. Jingchuan County
80. Ningxian County
81. Zhengning County
82. Huanxian County
83. Huachi County
84. Lingtai County

Fig. 6.2 Gansu Province subdivisions (Provincial Capital: Lanzhou City). (Map drawn by the Author, after People's Republic of China, Ministry of Civil Affairs, MCA 2020)

Table 6.6 (below) shows the *hukou* (family registered) populations based on PRC Ministry of Civil Affairs data. (Districts listed directly under major cities are government seats, as are those in parentheses). One can compare these data with the census (usual residential populations based on 2010 and 2020 censuses in Tables 6.2 and 6.3 (above):

Gansu Province (Abbreviations: 甘 *gān* and 隴 *lǒng*)

Provincial Capital: Lanzhou

Table 6.6 Gansu Province: permanent registered (戶籍人口 hùjí rénkǒu) populations (MCA 2020)

Name	Traditional	Simplified	Population (2012)	Population (2016)	Population (2020)	Area (km^2)
Gansu Province	甘肅省	甘肃省	27,120,000	27,130,000	27,830,000	430,000
Lanzhou City	蘭州市	兰州市	3,230,000	3,220,000	3,280,000	13,083
Chengguan District (Zhangyelu Subdistrict)	城關區 (張掖路街道)	城关区 (张掖路街道)	940,000	930,000	950,000	222
Qilihe District (Xihu Subdistrict)	七里河區 (西湖街道)	七里河区 (西湖街道)	470,000	470,000	470,000	420
Xigu District (Fulilu Subdistrict)	西固區 (福利路街道)	西固区 (福利路街道)	330,000	330,000	320,000	383
Anning District (Anningxilu Subdistrict)	安寧區 (安寧西路街道)	安宁区 (安宁西路街道)	220,000	200,000	210,000	86
Honggu District (Haishiwan Town)	紅古區 (海石灣鎮)	红古区 (海石湾镇)	140,000	140,000	140,000	519
Yongdeng County (Chengguan Town)	永登縣 (城關鎮)	永登县 (城关镇)	520,000	530,000	540,000	5652
Gaolan County (Shidong Town)	皋蘭縣 (石洞鎮)	皋兰县 (石洞镇)	180,000	180,000	200,000	2556
Yuzhong County (Chengguan Town)	榆中縣 (城關鎮)	榆中县 (城关镇)	430,000	440,000	460,000	3245
Jiayuguan Minor Revision (Kiayükwan) City	嘉峪市	嘉峪市	190,000	200,000	210,000	2935
Jinchang City	金昌市	金昌市	450,000	460,000	450,000	8927
Jinchuan District (Guangzhoulu Subdistrict)	金川區 (廣州路街道)	金川区 (广州路街道)	200,000	210,000	210,000	3060
Yongchang County (Chengguan Town)	永昌縣 (城關鎮)	永昌县 (城关镇)	250,000	250,000	240,000	5867
Baiyin City	白銀市	白银市	1,800,000	1,750,000	1,820,000	21,210

(continued)

Table 6.6 (continued)

Name	Traditional	Simplified	Population (2012)	Population (2016)	Population (2020)	Area (km^2)
Baiyin District (Renminlu Subdistrict)	白銀區 (人民路街道)	白银区 (人民路街道)	290,000	280,000	290,000	1372
Pingchuan District (Xingpinglu Subdistrict)	平川區 (興平路街道)	平川区 (兴平路街道)	210,000	210,000	210,000	2126
Jingyuan County (Wulan Town)	靖遠縣 (烏蘭鎮)	靖远县 (乌兰镇)	480,000	470,000	500,000	5790
Huining County (Huishi Town)	會寧縣 (會師鎮)	会宁县 (会师镇)	580,000	560,000	580,000	6439
Jingtai County (Yitiaoshan Town)	景泰縣 (一條山鎮)	景泰县 (一条山镇)	240,000	230,000	240,000	5483
Tianshui City	天水市	天水市	3,680,000	3,690,000	3,720,000	14,431
Qinzhou District (Dacheng Subdistrict)	秦州區 (大城街道)	秦州区 (大城街道)	680,000	690,000	700,000	2442
Maiji District (Daobei Subdistrict)	麥積區 (道北街道)	麦积区 (道北街道)	620,000	620,000	620,000	3480
Qingshui County (Yongqing Town)	清水縣 (永清鎮)	清水县 (永清镇)	320,000	330,000	330,000	2012
Qin'an County (Xingguo Town)	秦安縣 (興國鎮)	秦安县 (兴国镇)	620,000	610,000	590,000	1602
Gangu County (Daxiangshan Town)	甘谷縣 (大像山鎮)	甘谷县 (大像山镇)	630,000	630,000	640,000	1573
Wushan County (Chengguan Town)	武山縣 (城關鎮)	武山县 (城关镇)	460,000	460,000	470,000	2011
Zhangjiachuan Huizu (Hui) Autonomous County (Zhangjiachuan Town)	張家川回族自治縣 (張家川鎮)	张家川回族自治县 (张家川镇)	350,000	350,000	370,000	1311
Wuwei City	武威市	武威市	1,910,000	1,860,000	1,890,000	33,328
Liangzhou District (Dongdajie Subdistrict)	涼州區 (東大街街道)	凉州区 (东大街街道)	1,020,000	1,000,000	1,040,000	5081
Minqin County (Sanlei Town)	民勤縣 (三雷鎮)	民勤县 (三雷镇)	280,000	270,000	270,000	15,907
Gulang County (Gulang Town)	古浪縣 (古浪鎮)	古浪县 (古浪镇)	400,000	380,000	380,000	5103
Tianzhu Zangzu (Bairi Tibetan) Autonomous County (Huazangsi Town)	天祝藏族自治 (華藏寺鎮)	天祝藏族自治县 (华藏寺镇)	210,000	210,000	210,000	7147

(continued)

Table 6.6 (continued)

Name	Traditional	Simplified	Population (2012)	Population (2016)	Population (2020)	Area (km^2)
Jiuquan City	酒泉市	酒泉市	990,000	1,010,000	1,020,000	189,997
Suzhou District (Xibei Subdistrict)	肅州區 (西北街道)	肃州区 (西北街道)	400,000	410,000	420,000	3386
Yumen City (Yumen Town)	玉門市 (玉門鎮)	玉门市 (玉门镇)	140,000	140,000	160,000	13,389
Dunhuang City (Shazhou Town)	敦煌市 (沙州鎮)	敦煌市 (沙州镇)	140,000	140,000	140,000	31,200
Jinta County (Jinta Town)	金塔縣 (金塔鎮)	金塔县 (金塔镇)	150,000	150,000	150,000	18,800
Guazhou County (Yuanquan Town)	瓜州縣 (淵泉鎮)	瓜州县 (渊泉镇)	120,000	130,000	130,000	24,100
Subei Mengguzu (Mongol) Autonomous County (Dangchengwan Town)	肅北蒙古族自治縣 (黨城灣鎮)	肃北蒙古族自治县 (党城湾镇)	10,000	10,000	10,000	66,748
Akesai Hasakezu (Aksai; Aksay Kazakh) Autonomous County (Hongliuwan Town)	阿克塞哈薩克族自治縣 (紅柳灣鎮)	阿克塞哈萨克族自治县 (红柳湾镇)	30,000	30,000	10,000	32,374
Zhangye City	張掖市	张掖市	1,310,000	1,320,000	1,310,000	40,826
Ganzhou District (Nanjie subdistrict)	甘州區 (南街街道)	甘州区 (南街街道)	520,000	520,000	510,000	4240
Minle County (Hongshui Town)	民樂縣 (洪水鎮)	民乐县 (洪水镇)	240,000	250,000	270,000	3687
Linze County (Shahe Town)	臨澤縣 (沙河鎮)	临泽县 (沙河镇)	150,000	150,000	150,000	2729
Gaotai County (Chengguan Town)	高台縣 (城關鎮)	高台县 (城关镇)	160,000	160,000	160,000	4312
Shandan County (Qingquan Town)	山丹縣 (清泉鎮)	山丹县 (清泉镇)	200,000	200,000	200,000	5402
Sunan Yuguzu (Yughur) Autonomous County (Hongwansi Town)	肅南裕固族自治縣 (紅灣寺鎮)	肃南裕固族自治县 (红湾寺镇)	40,000	40,000	40,000	20,456
Qingyang City	慶陽市	庆阳市	2,610,000	2,620,000	2,700,000	27,119
Xifeng District (Nanjie Subdistrict)	西峰區 (南街街道)	西峰区 (南街街道)	360,000	370,000	390,000	996
Qingcheng County (Qingcheng Town)	慶城縣 (慶城鎮)	庆城县 (庆城镇)	290,000	290,000	290,000	2673
Huanxian County (Huancheng Town)	環縣 (環城鎮)	环县 (环城镇)	350,000	350,000	360,000	9236

(continued)

Table 6.6 (continued)

Name	Traditional	Simplified	Population (2012)	Population (2016)	Population (2020)	Area (km^2)
Huachi County (Rouyuan Town)	華池縣 (柔遠鎮)	华池县 (柔远镇)	130,000	130,000	140,000	3776
Heshui County (Xihuachi Town)	合水縣 (西華池鎮)	合水县 (西华池镇)	170,000	170,000	180,000	2976
Zhengning County (Shanhe Town)	正寧縣 (山河鎮)	正宁县 (山河镇)	240,000	240,000	240,000	1329
Ningxian County (Xinning Town)	寧縣 (新寧鎮)	宁县 (新宁镇)	550,000	550,000	560,000	2633
Zhenyuan County (Chengguan Town)	鎮原縣 (城關鎮)	镇原县 (城关镇)	520,000	520,000	530,000	3500
Pingliang City	平涼市	平凉市	2,300,000	2,320,000	2,340,000	11,169
Kongtong District (Xijiao Subdistrict)	崆峒區 (西郊街道)	崆峒区 (西郊街道)	510,000	510,000	520,000	1936
Jingchuan County (Chengguan Town)	涇川縣 (城關鎮)	泾川县 (城关镇)	350,000	350,000	360,000	1409
Lingtai County (Zhongtai Town)	靈台縣 (中台鎮)	灵台县 (中台镇)	230,000	230,000	230,000	2038
Chongxin County (Jinping Town)	崇信縣 (錦屏鎮)	崇信县 (锦屏镇)	100,000	100,000	100,000	852
Huating City (Donghua Town)	華亭市 (東華鎮)	华亭市 (东华镇)	180,000	190,000	190,000	1183
Zhuanglang County (Shuiluo Town)	莊浪縣 (水洛鎮)	庄浪县 (水洛镇)	440,000	450,000	450,000	1558
Jingning County (Chengguan Town)	靜寧縣 (城關鎮)	静宁县 (城关镇)	490,000	490,000	480,000	2193
Dingxi City	定西市	定西市	3,010,000	2,970,000	3,040,000	20,330
Anding District (Yongdinglu Subdistrict)	安定區 (永定路街道)	安定区 (永定路街道)	470,000	470,000	470,000	4225
Tongwei County (Pingxiang Town)	通渭縣 (平襄鎮)	通渭县 (平襄镇)	450,000	430,000	440,000	2899
Lintao County (Taoyang Town)	臨洮縣 (洮陽鎮)	临洮县 (洮阳镇)	540,000	530,000	520,000	2851
Zhangxian County (Wuyang Town)	漳縣 (武陽鎮)	漳县 (武阳镇)	210,000	210,000	210,000	2164
Minxian County (Minyang Town)	岷縣 (岷陽鎮)	岷县 (岷阳镇)	480,000	480,000	500,000	3500
Weiyuan County (Qingyuan Town)	渭源縣 (清源鎮)	渭源县 (清源镇)	350,000	340,000	350,000	2034
Longxi County (Gongchang Town)	隴西縣 (鞏昌鎮)	陇西县 (巩昌镇)	510,000	510,000	520,000	2657
Longnan City	隴南市	陇南市	2,810,000	2,810,000	2,880,000	27,838
Wudu District (Chengguan Town)	武都區 (城關鎮)	武都区 (城关镇)	580,000	580,000	610,000	4642

(continued)

Table 6.6 (continued)

Name	Traditional	Simplified	Population (2012)	Population (2016)	Population (2020)	Area (km^2)
Chengxian County (Chengguan Town)	成縣 (城關鎮)	成县 (城关镇)	260,000	260,000	260,000	1678
Tanchang[a] County (Chengguan Town)	宕昌縣 (城關鎮)	宕昌县 (城关镇)	300,000	300,000	310,000	3315
Kangxian County (Chengguan Town)	康縣 (城關鎮)	康县 (城关镇)	200,000	200,000	200,000	2968
Wenxian County (Chengguan Town)	文縣 (城關鎮)	文县 (城关镇)	250,000	240,000	250,000	5002
Xihe County (Hanyuan Town)	西和縣 (漢源鎮)	西和县 (汉源镇)	430,000	430,000	450,000	1862
Lixian County (Chengguan Town)	禮縣 (城關鎮)	礼县 (城关镇)	520,000	530,000	540,000	4264
Liangdang County (Chengguan Town)	兩當縣 (城關鎮)	两当县 (城关镇)	50,000	50,000	50,000	1408
Huixian County (Chengguan Town)	徽縣 (城關鎮)	徽县 (城关镇)	220,000	220,000	230,000	2699
Linxia Huizu (Hui) Autonomous Prefecture	臨夏回族自治州	临夏回族自治州	2,090,000	2,170,000	2,410,000	8169
Linxia City (Chengnan Subdistrict)	臨夏市 (城南街道)	临夏市 (城南街道)	230,000	240,000	270,000	89
Linxia County (Hanji Town)	臨夏縣 (韓集鎮)	临夏县 (韩集镇)	390,000	400,000	430,000	1213
Kangle County (Fucheng Town)	康樂縣 (附城鎮)	康乐县 (附城镇)	270,000	270,000	300,000	1083
Yongjing County (Liujiaxia Town)	永靖縣 (劉家峽鎮)	永靖县 (刘家峡镇)	200,000	200,000	210,000	1864
Guanghe County (Chengguan Town)	廣河縣 (城關鎮)	广河县 (城关镇)	240,000	260,000	300,000	538
Hezheng County (Chengguan Town)	和政縣 (城關鎮)	和政县 (城关镇)	200,000	210,000	240,000	960
Dongxiangzu (Sarta) Autonomous County (Suonanba Town)	東鄉族自治縣 (鎖南壩鎮)	东乡族自治县 (锁南坝镇)	310,000	330,000	370,000	1512
Jishishan Bao'anzu Dongxiangzu Salazu (Bonan, Sarta, and Salar) Autonomous County (Chuimatan Town)	積石山保安族東鄉族撒拉族自治縣 (吹麻灘鎮)	积石山保安族东乡族撒拉族自治县 (吹麻滩镇)	250,000	260,000	280,000	910
Gannan Zangzu (Tibetan) Autonomous Prefecture	甘南藏族自治州	甘南藏族自治州	730,000	740,000	750,000	38,521

(continued)

Table 6.6 (continued)

Name	Traditional	Simplified	Population (2012)	Population (2016)	Population (2020)	Area (km^2)
Hezuo City (Jianmuke'er Subdistrict)	合作市 (堅木克爾街道)	合作市 (坚木克尔街道)	90,000	90,000	90,000	2670
Lintan County (Chengguan Town)	臨潭縣 (城關鎮)	临潭县 (城关镇)	160,000	160,000	160,000	1557
Zhuoni (Jonê) County (Liulin Town)	卓尼縣 (柳林鎮)	卓尼县 (柳林镇)	110,000	110,000	110,000	5420
Zhouqu (Zhugqu) County (Chengguan Town)	舟曲縣 (城關鎮)	舟曲县 (城关镇)	140,000	140,000	140,000	3010
Diebu (Têwo) County (Dianga Town)	迭部縣 (電尕鎮)	迭部县 (电尕镇)	60,000	60,000	60,000	5148
Maqu County (Nima Town)	瑪曲縣 (尼瑪鎮)	玛曲县 (尼玛镇)	50,000	50,000	50,000	10,190
Luqu County (Ma'ai Town)	碌曲縣 (瑪艾鎮)	碌曲县 (玛艾镇)	30,000	40,000	40,000	4260
Xiahe (Sangqu) County (Labuleng [Labrang] Town)	夏河縣 (拉卜楞鎮)	夏河县 (拉卜楞镇)	90,000	90,000	90,000	6266

[a]Elsewhere宕 is usually read *dàng*

References

Bettinger, Robert L., Loukas Barton, Christopher Morgan, et al. 2010. The transition to agriculture at Dadiwan, People's Republic of China. *Current Anthropology* 51 (5): 703–714.

Fung, John. 2021. Satellite images reveal China's new missile silos. *Newsweek*. July 1. https://www.newsweek.com/satellite-images-reveal-nearly-120-new-missile-silos-china-1605969#slideshow/1835518.

Gansu Province Bureau of Statistics (GPBS). 2021. [Communiqué of the seventh national census of Gansu Province, second issue]. May 18. 甘肃省第七次全国人口普查公报, 第二号. http://tjj.gansu.gov.cn/tjj/c109465/202105/18d7185cc69f4cb6bc4047a5ab0b3449.shtml.

Local History Compilation Committee of Gansu Province (LHCCGP). 1995. *Gansu Gazette*. Gansu People's Press. 甘肃省志, 甘肃省地方史志编纂委员会, 甘肃人民出版社.

Ministry of Civil Affairs (MCA), People's Republic of China. 2020. [County/township administration handbook]. Beijing: China Statistics Press. 中華人民共和國民政部, 中華人民共和國, 鄉鎮行政區劃簡冊.

People's Republic of China Government Net (PRCGN). 2016. [1.116 million poor people in Gansu have been relocated]. 甘肃111.6万贫困人口实现易地搬迁. 中国政府网. https://www.sohu.com/a/59922600_119038. Accessed 31 Dec 2021.

Qiu, Lianghui. 1996. Metallurgical technology in ancient China. In *Chinese studies in the history and philosophy of science and technology*, ed. Fan Dainian and Robert S. Cohen, 219–241. Boston: Kluwer Academic Publishers.

Shi, Zhixin. 2000. [Economic stagnation and population decline in Gansu at the end of the Qing Dynasty]. *Researches in Chinese Economic History*. 石志新. 清末甘肃地区经济凋敝和人口锐减. 中国经济史研究. 2: 79–86.

Wilkinson, Edymion. 2015. *Chinese history: A new manual*. Cambridge, MA: Harvard University Press.

Yang, Jisheng. 2012. *Tombstone: The Great Chinese Famine, 1958–1962*. Trans. Stacy Mosher and Guo Jian. New York: Farrar, Straus and Giroux.

Zhang, Shunan. 2021. [The 2020 per capita income list of residents in various provinces: Shanghai is the richest, and it has risen sharply]. Finance.people.com. January 22. 张澍楠. 2020年各省份居民人均收入榜: 上海最有钱, 这地涨得猛. http://finance.people.com.cn/n1/2021/0122/c1004-32008733.html.

Chapter 7
Guangdong Province

Abstract Guangdong, China's most populous and, arguably, its most dynamic province, was a key conduit for business with the outside world in the nineteenth century via its capital of Guangzhou City ("Canton"). Once considered a southern backwater for disgraced imperial bureaucrats and other undesirables, Guangdong has since developed into a province of unique and prosperous character. In addition to having played a key role in mercantile trade internationally, not to mention the ignoble trade in opium, Guangzhou was home to the violent uprising of the Taiping Rebellion in the mid-nineteenth century. Then, 50 years later, led by Guangdong's most famous son, Sun Yat-sen, the province was the springboard for the 1911 revolution that overthrew millennia of imperial rule and created modern China. Now an economic powerhouse, Guangdong Province famously served as a key test base for free enterprise and capitalism, helping to bring mainland China out of a moribund, Maoist quagmire into a modern, world-class superpower. Furthermore, the dynamism of Guangdong is reflected in the patterns and growth of its population: with an official *hukou* family registered population of just over 95 million, and a resident population of over 126 million (based on the 2020 census), a significant number of China's "floating population" is to be found amongst Guangdong's economically vibrant cities, notably Shenzhen.

E. Croddy, *China's Provinces and Populations*,
https://doi.org/10.1007/978-3-031-09165-0_7

Guangdong Province (廣東省 *guǎngdōng shěng*): Abbreviation 粤 (*yuè*) (Fig. 7.1)

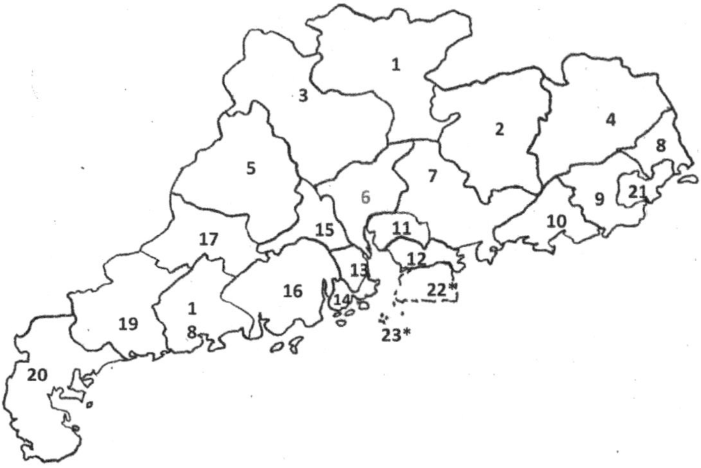

		Population (2020):
1.	Shaoguan City	2,855,131
2.	Heyuan City	2,837,686
3.	Qingyuan City	3,969,473
4.	Meizhou City	3,873,239
5.	Zhaoqing City	4,113,594
6.	Guangzhou City	18,676,605
7.	Huizhou City	6,042,852
8.	Chaozhou City	2,568,387
9.	Jieyang City	5,577,814
10.	Shanwei City	2,672,819
11.	Dongguan City	10,466,625
12.	Shenzhen City	17,560,061
13.	Zhongshan City	4,418,060
14.	Zhuhai City	2,439,585
15.	Foshan City	9,498,863
16.	Jiangmen City	4,798,090
17.	Yunfu City	2,383,350
18.	Yangjiang City	2,602,959
19.	Maoming City	6,174,050
20.	Zhanjiang City	6,981,236
21.	Shantou City	5,502,031
22.	*[Hong Kong]	* See Hong Kong
23.	*[Macao (Aomen)]	* See Macao

Fig. 7.1 Guangdong Province major cities (Provincial Capital: Guangzhou City). Drawn by the Author after People's Republic of China, Ministry of Civil Affairs. (MCA 2020)

Guangdong Province: General Impressions

Guangdong Province (廣東省 *guǎngdōng shěng*) has also been known as "Kwangtung." But especially since the 1800s, it was really its capital city of Guangzhou (廣州市 *guǎngzhōu shì*) or "Canton" that represented "China" to much of the western world.

Today, an economic powerhouse and densely populated, Guangdong rose to prominence quite late in the Chinese empire. Distant from the power and authority of the imperial court geographically as well as culturally, Guangdong has had relative autonomy for most of China's history. As a result, its people have a reputation for going their own way.

It is worth reflecting upon the critical role Guangdong province, specifically, the city of Guangzhou (Canton) played in how westerners formed their early impressions of China and the Chinese people. Because the traditional Chinese imperial court placed restrictions upon where trade and even interactions with "foreigners" could take place, Guangzhou and its treaty ports played an essential role in the transfer of goods and culture between China and the west. Thus, for nearly a century or more, this uniquely southern Chinese culture was very much overrepresented when it came to how outsiders viewed China. Consequently, when the larger Western world was exposed to Chinese culture in the 1800s, "Canton" was most often the interface between Europe and China. Furthermore, many of the first major waves of Chinese immigrants to the outside world beginning in the mid-nineteenth century were originally from Guangdong, in many instances from one particular city or region. This includes those who founded "Chinatowns" in the United States and elsewhere, many tracing their lineage from Taishan City (台山市 *táishān shì*), for example, and who speak its unique regional dialect (Toisan).

Due to its close geographical and linguistic relationship with the formerly free city of Hong Kong, as well as its early exposure to western political ideas, the political and economic dynamism of Guangdong province preceded that of the rest of mainland China. This is in contrast to the past centuries when Guangdong, and the southern region of China generally, were regarded as a hostile, snake-ridden backwater, populated mostly by barbarians, banished imperial mandarins, as well as other undesirables. But in the modern era, the people of Guangdong played an instrumental role in no less than the making of modern China. After all, were it not for the leadership of the Cantonese, notably Sun Yat-sen (as well as countless overseas Chinese from Guangdong), there likely would have been no overthrow of the sclerotic Qing monarchy (1911), and no founding of a democratic Republic of China (ROC). Even more importantly for the modern era, it was Guangdong that led China out of its self-imposed dark ages, eschewing the bankrupt policies of Maoist, anti-capitalist dogma and building a market-based economy that now rivals every country on earth.

Pleistocene Guangdong

Of the more celebrated archeological finds after China's "liberation" in 1949, Guangdong-based investigators uncovered "Maba Man" (馬壩猿人 *mǎbà yuán-rén*), based upon a humanoid skull that dates back to about 130,000 BCE (Guldin 1994). The original site is located in Shiziyan (狮子岩 *shīziyán*), Maba town, Shaoguan City, Qujiang District (曲江區馬壩鎮 *qūjiāng qū, mǎbà zhèn*).

Before the unification by the Qin dynasty, the region of Guangdong was part of the larger Yue (or 'Hundred Yue' 百越 *bǎiyuè*) people, considered by earlier Chinese empires as "an unhealthy, malaria-ridden region, covered with dense tangled forests so infested with savage beasts, [where] only escaped criminals or banished people would go…" (Snow 2004).

*The Yue (*越 **yuè***)*

While the Yue can describe a number of peoples populating regions from Guangxi in the south to Zhejiang in the north, the Guangdong-North Vietnam area was collectively named the "Southern Yue (南越 *nányuè*)." The general description of the Southern Yue peoples and their customary ways are described in the Huainanzi (淮南子 *huáinánzi*), an ancient text that recorded discussions held in the Huainan Court:

> To the south of the Nine Passes [九疑 *jiǔyí*, i.e., Hunan], their activities on dry land are few, while tasks on the water are many. So the people cut their hair and tattoo their bodies in order to resemble scaly creatures (民人被發文身, 以像鱗蟲 *mínrén bèi fā wénshēn, yǐ xiàng línchóng*). They wear short pants, not trousers, in order to make swimming easier. And they have short sleeves in order to make poling their boats easier. This is how they are (Brindley 2015).

In 214 BCE, and only after protracted struggle with the recalcitrant Yue locals did the Qin dynasty finally conquer the southern region. The Qin established a South Seas Prefecture (南海郡 *nánhǎi jùn*), encompassing a geographic entity roughly the size of what Guangdong Province is today. But even so, the restless Yue managed to stay independent from the rest of unified China. In 204 BCE, for example, the ruggedly individualist Nan Yue (Southern Yue 南越 *nányuè*) Kingdom was established under a former Qin official, Zhao Tuo (趙佗 *zhào tuó*).

The territory later controlled by King Wu of the Southern Yue (南越武王 *nányuèwǔwáng*) extended down south to northern Vietnam of today. With its capital at Panyu (番禺 *pānyù*), located in modern-day Guangzhou City, this kingdom survived for 93 years until its defeat during the Han (111 BCE). From this time onward, the region was divided into seven prefectures (commanderies). The "History of the Former Han" (ca. 111 CE; 漢書 *hànshū*)[1] describes these conquered lands as Yang

[1] 西南夷兩粵朝鮮傳 *xīnán yíliǎngyuèzhāo zhuàn*.

Yue (揚粵 *yángyuè*), encompassing modern-day Guilin, Nanhai (Guangdong), and Xiangjun Prefecture (象郡 *xiàngjùn*, now modern-day western Guangxi and north-central Vietnam). Today, the Yue (粵 *yuè*) ideograph describes both Guangxi and Guangdong provinces, as well as the Cantonese people and their language. In sum, this was a land "populated by banished miscreants, as well as various Yue peoples, all mixed together." (Snow 2004).

During the Han dynasty, China controlled not only today's Guangdong province but also north central Vietnam, then known as Rinan Prefecture (日南郡 *rìnán jùn*), extending far south as Thua Thien-Hue in modern-day Vietnam (Thừa Thiên-Huế: 承天- 化 *chéng tiānhuà*, just north of Da Nang). The History of the Later Han (後漢書 *hòuhànshū*) describes the flourishing growth of Rinan Prefecture as of ca. 100 CE, which then had 18,263 households and a population by then of 100,676 people. During this period, an overarching administrative region in the south was called the Jiaozhi Inspectorate (交阯刺史部 *jiāozhǐ cìshǐbù*). The latter controlled not only Nanhai (南海郡 *nánhǎi jùn*) and Hepu (合浦郡 *hépǔ jùn*) prefectures (which basically occupied Guangdong province of today), but also north-central Vietnam. The other prefectures were:

- Jiaozhi 交阯郡 *jiāozhǐ jùn*
- Jiuzhen (九真郡 *jiǔzhēn jùn*)
- Rinan (日南郡 *rìnán jùn*)
- Yulin (郁林郡 *yùlín jùn*) and
- Cangwu (蒼梧郡 *cāngwú jùn*)

Centered around present-day Hanoi in northern Vietnam, Jiaozhi Prefecture (交阯郡 *jiāozhǐ jùn*) was a major trade route for western commerce, including merchants as far back as the Roman Empire. In 226 CE, according to the Liangshu (梁書 *liáng shū*) documents that date back to 636 CE, a Roman ("Daqin" 大秦 *dàqín*) trader presented himself at the Jiaozhi capital. Impressed by this distinguished visitor from across the seas, the local governor sent him northward to meet with Sun Quan (孫權 *sūn quán*), the emperor of the Wu Kingdom (吳國 *wúguó*), tasking the foreigner to describe to the imperial court in some detail about his homeland (Liu 2015).

During this time, while governing the same prefectures as before, during in the Eastern Han (25–220 CE) the Jiaozhi Inspectorate changed its name to Jiaozhou Inspectorate (交州刺史部 *jiāozhōu cìshǐbù*). A large portion of Guangdong today, including its capital at Panyu (番禺 *pānyù*) was governed under Nanhai Prefecture (南海郡 *nánhǎi jùn*). By 262 CE, Jiaozhou added two districts dividing the south: Gaoliang (高涼郡 *gāoliáng jùn*) and Zhuyai (朱崖郡 *zhūyái jùn*[2]) prefectures. The latter two, along with Nanhai and Hepu, extended across the region of today's Guangdong province. A larger Guangzhou state (廣州) was created (281 CE) under the Western Jin (西晉 *xījìn*). Despite the many subsequent dynastic changes, the basic territorial limits of the Guangzhou state that included the regions of modern-day Guangxi and Guangdong provinces were largely preserved for centuries. In

[2] Also read *zhūyá jùn*.

500 CE, the southern peninsula of Guangdong was then known as Yuezhou (粤州 *yuèzhōu*).

Going into the first millennium, Han Chinese migrated to Guangdong in ever greater numbers, with a significant increase during the tumult of the An Lushan rebellion (also known as the Anshi Chaos 安史之亂 *ānshǐ zhī luàn*) in ca. 755. During the Han dynasty, Guangdong had a population of about 960,000. By the Tang (ca. 800 CE) the Guangdong region—known then as Lingnan (嶺南 *lǐngnán*)—reached a population of over two-and-a-half million.

A number of renaming and redistricting measures then took place. By the Five Dynasties and Ten Kingdoms period (ca. 943 CE) the Nan Han (南漢 *nánhàn*) region was established. With its capital at Xingwang Prefecture (興王府 *xìngwáng fǔ*), Nan Han governed modern-day Guangxi, Guangdong and Hainan island (the latter having its capital at Yazhou 崖洲 *yázhōu*). The Song dynasty (997 CE) established a Guangnan Donglu (廣南東路 *guǎngnán dōnglù*) administrative zone. Finally, the Ming dynasty (May 1369) officially named Guangdong a province (廣東行省 *guǎngdōng xíngshěng*), with its capital in Guangzhou Prefecture (廣州府 *guǎngzhōu fǔ*).

Canton: Historic Maritime Trade Center

The first major international mercantile zone in China was Guangzhou City (Canton), the main port of call for not only European but Indian, Persian, and Arabian commerce. As early as the Zhou (beginning early twelfth century BCE), historical documents listed eight different foreign countries were trading with China, all employing Canton as a mercantile entrepôt (Hirth 1885).

Global Trade with the Arabs and Rome

The old histories also tell us about the first trade with Arabic peoples by way of southern China:

> Every year the king of the country of [Dashi] 大食 [*dàshí*, i.e., the Arabs of the Khalif empire] who is styled Su-Tan [蘇丹 *sūdān*, i.e., Sultan] sends tribute-bearers…they do not drink wine. At the beginning of the Yen-hsi period [延熹 *yánxī*, A.D. 158–67]…the ruler of this country sent an embassy who, from outside the territory of Jihnan [i.e., Rinan prefecture日南郡] came to offer rhinoceros horns, ivory, and tortoise-shell, this being the first direct communication with China (Hirth 1885).

In dealing with peoples from the Roman Empire, called Daqin (大秦 *dàqín*) by the Chinese, China at least knew of the Roman province of Syria, and that its capital was Antioch (安都 *āndū*). The *Weishu* (魏書 *wèishū*), a chronicle of fourth–sixth century China, plainly states that "Daqin, also known as Lixuan, has its capital city in Andu."[3] When receiving trade representatives from Daqin, in addition to other routes, the Weishu tells us that "there is also connection by water with the principalities of Yi-chou (益州 *yìzhōu*) and Yung-ch'ang (永昌 *yǒngchāng*)," the latter two prefectures making up modern-day Yunnan province:

> [A]nd after the road from [Daqin] had been performed from the north of the sea by land, another road was tried which followed the sea to the south and connected with the north of the outer barbarians at the seven principalities of Chiao-chih [Jiaozhi; 交趾, i.e., Cochinchina]...There was also a water-road leading through to [Yizhou] and [Yongchang] prefectures (Hirth 1885).

First arriving in about 620 CE, Moslem merchants practiced their faith in Canton, Yangzhou (Jiangsu) and Quanzhou (Fujian province). The Muslim population that resided in Canton referred to the city as Khanfu. The burgeoning commercial relationship, however, was interrupted with significant violence, when a large rabble, probably consisting of both Arabs and Persians, blockaded and sacked Canton in 758. With the local government impotent (the governor was on the run), these pirates went on to steal whatever food and valuables they could find, burning down a number of local villages before taking flight to sea (Benn 2002). Despite such occasional disruptions, the quantity of trade with foreigners increased to the point that by the 800s (Tang dynasty) the Fujianese city of Quanzhou, already a trading port for centuries with Japan and Korea, was being utilized to handle commerce from overseas. It is also during that this time that China was first introduced to opium from Arab commerce. In fact, the Chinese word for opium likely is derived from the Arabic *afiyun*, which was then transliterated into the Chinese (鴉片 *yāpiàn*). (Dikötter, Laaman and Zhou 2004).

As the Tang dynasty fell into chaos, the Huang Chao (黄巢 *huángcháo*) rebellion led to an attack on Khanfu (i.e., Guangzhou) in ca. 877, where in addition to local Chinese, reportedly some 120,000 Muslims, Jews, Christians and Zoroastrians were massacred. With the advent of the Song (960), some sort of normalcy made it possible for international trade to resume, both at Canton and Quanzhou. By the end of the 900 s, the Chinese authorities monopolized all trade with foreign nations. According to the historian Chong Su See:

> Sometime during the years 976-983 the government undertook to control it entirely, and independent trading without official sanction was severely punished, the offender being branded on the face and banished to some island of the ocean. Shortly after this, all importers of foreign aromatics and articles of value, such as jewels, ivory, rhinoceros' horn, amber, ebony, coral and the like, were required by law to deposit such merchandise in the government storehouses… trade in aromatics, jewels, etc., was prejudicial to China, for it caused a constant drain on the metallic currency of the empire, more particularly copper cash. [It became] so serious by the middle 12th century that various measures were taken by the Government to check it, such as the imposition of restrictions on foreign trade. The above rule applied not only to the various ports of entry into China, but also to Kiauchi (交阯 *jiāozhǐ*, capital near Hanoi), which at that time was integral to the kingdom (See 1919).

---

[3] 大秦國, 一名黎軒, 都安都城 *dàqínguó, yīmíng líxuān dū āndūchéng*.

Throughout the Tang and Song dynastic periods, Chinese foreign commerce had developed to the point that an official trading administration and service was established in 971, revamping a Canton Inspectorate of Maritime Trade (市舶使 *shìbóshǐ*, Overseas Trade Commissioner), and creating a full-on customs organization in 999. By the twelfth century, the Chinese authorities restricted such trade to only Canton and Quanzhou.

Trade with Portugal in the Sixteenth Century

During the reign of Zheng De (正德 *zhèng dé*; 1505–1521), foreigners from the west, called Fahlanki (Franks), who said they had tribute, abruptly entered the Bogue (on the Canton River), and by their tremendously loud guns, shook the place near and far. — Chong Su See, *The Foreign Trade of China* (See 1919).

Tracing Portugal's initial excursions to southern China back to ca. 1520, we find the first uses of the placename "Canton." While 'Canton' is itself derived from the Portuguese *Cantão*, it is unclear exactly how this name was first contrived. What appears most likely is, such as it was in the case of the name 'Hong Kong' from the British experience, 'Canton' is yet another case of foreign (mis)interpretations upon meeting Chinese locals. The Portuguese, in their first trade visits to China, probably heard people in Guangzhou (using local dialect) refer to the larger province of Guangdong, and this was transliterated as *Cantão*. (They may have also heard "Guangzhou," as in the port city, which would have sounded something like *gwong-zau* in Cantonese dialect). In a likely mix up, the Portuguese traders took "Guangdong" to mean the place where they were actually engaged in commerce, that is, Guangzhou, the latter since being referred to now as *Cantão*. This was then later corrupted in some fashion into the English 'Canton' (Ren 2004).

By the early 1500s, trade between Chinese in Guangzhou and the Portuguese (sailing from its colony in Malacca) was quite lively, and introduced a number of items to both sides. For example, this route brought hot chili peppers (capsicum) to China (Simoons 1991). From their earliest encounters, the Portuguese described the Chinese as "people of great skill, and on par with ourselves, but of uglier aspect, with little bits of eyes…" Still, the Portuguese were overall favorably impressed by the Chinese, if contemporary accounts (ca. 1525) of Guangdong province are any indication:

> This province has thirteen cities and seven *chenos* (i.e., towns, 鎮 *zhèn*), which are large cities that do not bear the name of cities; it has one hundred walled towns besides other walled places…. [T]here is under the sun nothing so prepared as this, and with people without number, and thickly populated on those borders where there are rivers (and where there are none it is not so populous, not by a fifth), of every sort of craftsman of every mechanical office, I mean carpenters, caulkers, smiths, stone masons, tilers, sawyers, carvers: in fine that there is a superabundance of the things that are necessary for the service of the king and of his fortresses, and from hence may be taken every year four or five thousand men without causing any lack in the country (Ferguson 1902).

And trade was profitable:

> During this last year [1515] some of our Portuguese made a voyage to China. They were not permitted to land; for they say 'tis against their custom to let foreigners enter their dwellings. But they sold their goods at great gain, and they say there is as great profit taking spices to China as in taking them to Portugal.... (Ferguson 1902)

The Portuguese also noticed that local Chinese magistrates from a certain province, such as Guangdong, were not allowed to serve in the same province, and that China had a regimented official-scholar examination system that determined someone's future career.

While substantive trade benefited both sides, Portuguese behavior was often predatory and brigandish. For example, in ca. 1519, Simão de Andrade first offended the Cantonese by carrying out his own execution of a sailor at a gallows that had been hastily and ostentatiousy built in clear view. Then, after Simão de Andrade set sail for Malacca, the people of Guangzhou learned that he had kidnapped local Chinese children, taking them away to be sold as slaves. Tensions between the Chinese and Europeans of all stripes also occurred, but often it was the Portuguese who earned the old Chinese epithet of the "foreign devil" (番鬼 *fānguǐ*).

Matteo Ricci, S.J., in Guangdong (1583–1592)

Not typical "foreign devils," the Catholic Jesuit missionaries Michele Ruggieri and Matteo Ricci gained permission from the local Chinese magistrate to start up their mission in Zhaoqing (肇慶; "Shiuhing"), 110 kilometers west of Canton (Guangzhou). At this time, a western observer estimated Zhaoqing to have some 50,000 households, or three times the size of Seville (Spence 1984). But after having found their sea legs in Zhaoqing, a local power shift forced the Jesuits to leave in 1589, this time moving to Shaozhou (韶州 *sháozhōu*; now Shaoguan 韶關 *sháoguān*), also in Guangdong province. Ricci believed the latter's population was twice that of Zhaoqing (Cronin 1984). Subjected there to local insult, both verbal and physical, Ricci was forced to move his mission yet again in 1592, leaving Guangdong for Nanchang, Jiangxi province.

Qing Dynasty (1644+) and Foreign Trade

During the Qing dynasty, the Kangxi emperor, in 1685, allowed foreigners access to Chinese ports, and later (1733) the Yongzheng emperor wanted Macao (Macau) to be the exclusive sole point of foreign trade entry. But he died in 1735 before his plans could be fully enacted. In order to assert more control over the barbarians, and also as a means to funnel tax income through a single source, the next Qing emperor declared in 1757 that all (non-Russian) foreign trade would be exclusively conducted (一口通商 *yīkǒu tōngshāng*) at Canton port (Guangzhou).

Nineteenth Century Canton

Describing Guangzhou in ca. 1840, a foreign contemporary wrote that

> Canton stands upon the north bank of the Chookeang [珠江 *zhūjiāng*] or Pearl River about sixty miles in-land from the 'great sea'. It is one of the oldest cities in the southern provinces, and second to no other in importance in the empire, except Pekin, where the emperor holds his court. It is the great commercial emporium for China, and the only port where foreign trade is permitted. It is not very large in extent, the whole circuit of the walls not extending probably six miles; but it is densely populated, and in the suburbs, including the river population, contain as many inhabitants as the city proper (Langdon 1842).

The Opium Trade

Largely confined at this time to the Taiwan Strait and Guangdong, the smoking of opium in China (mixed with tobacco, called *madak)* had continued despite a 1729 edict prohibiting this practice by the Yongzheng Emperor. As related by a later account in the 1820s:

> It is needless to say that the opium trade was prohibited by Imperial edicts as well as by proclamations of the Canton authorities. The Chinese who dealt in "foreign mud" (洋土 *yángtǔ*) were threatened even with capital punishment, but so perfect a system of bribery existed (with which foreigners had nothing whatever to do) that the business was carried on with ease and regularity (Hunter 1882).

Infamously, much of the trade conducted by the west to China in the nineteenth century included British opium, harvested from its plantations in India. In a desperate move to tamp down the ravages of the opium trade, the Qing dynasty authorities expanded the already restricted foreign trade areas in Canton (Guangzhou) out to more than 50 miles south to Lintin Island (Lingding; now Nei Lingding Dao 内伶仃島 *nèilíngdīng dǎo*) in 1820 (Dikötter et al. 2004). But now the Qing government was out of patience, and in 1839 the Chinese forced the British to relinquish some 20,000 chests of opium.

As Jonathan Spence described the event:

> As for the opium, the Chinese officials spent days disposing of it, mixing it in pots with lime and—after first apologizing to the spirits of the waters—flushing it out to sea. When all the opium was handed over, the British were allowed to leave Canton, and most other foreigners did the same (Spence 1996).

In response, the British returned with gunboats. In 1841 the British navy had defeated the poorly equipped Chinese in Canton, capturing its western forts in May. China ceded Hong Kong to the British that year, and in August 1842, when the British threatened Nanjing, China ultimately surrendered. This led to a notorious succession of costly and humiliating reparations that China was forced to pay, including the loss of its own sovereignty.

At about this time, a western observer estimated the city of Canton (Guangzhou)—"including the village of Fo Shan (佛山 *fóshān*) which may be termed the Manchester of China"—had a population between and 2 million. This same observer also noted a substantial number, on the order of about 40,000 sampans on the river representing a "population of more than 200,000 souls." (Langdon 1842).

For those who lived on land, their domiciles were described this way:

> The houses are but one story high. A few of them are of wood or stone; many, belonging to the poorer classes, of mud, and with but a single apartment; but the largest portion of bricks. The dwellings of those in easy circumstances contain various well-furnished apartments, the walls of which are generally ornamented with carvings, pictures, and various scrolls, inscribed with moral maxims from Confucius and other sages. The houses of the wealthy are often furnished in a style of great magnificence, and the occupants indulge in the most luxurious habits. Official personages, however, for the most part set a commendable example of simplicity and economy in their manner of living. The doors have no plates to tell who the occupant of the mansion is, but cylindrical lanterns are hung up by the sides of the gates of all houses of consequence, with the names and titles of the owners inscribed, so as to be read either by day or night, when the lanterns are lighted (Langdon 1842).

This same chronicler noted that in Canton there were 67,000 cloth and silk manufacturing, 4,200 cobblers and "an army of barbers numbering 7,300!" (Langdon 1842).

Home of the Taiping Rebellion

A memorial from the eighteenth century described Guangdong province in this way:

> The population of [Guangdong] is dense. The rice produced in this province is not sufficient for the people to eat. They always rely upon [Guangxi] and Hunan to sell and transport rice for relief (Elvin 1973).

Born (1814) into this environment, Hong Xiuquan (洪秀全 *Hóng Xiùquán*), a Hakka, and his family lived in Guanlubu Village (官禄布村 *guānlùbù cūn*), in modern-day Huadu District (花都區 *huādū qū*). Then a relatively new county, it was populated by about 14,000 people. Based on a fever dream, Hong Xiuquan (who had been baptized as a Christian) soon believed he was the son of God. Having moved from Canton to Guangxi province, in 1851 Hong Xiuquan and his fellow God-worshippers (拜上帝教 *bàishàngdì jiào*) went to battle against Qing military forces in Jintian (today's Guiping City 桂平市 *guìpíng shì*). The war raged until 1864., the Taiping Rebellion leading to the deaths of at least 11 to 30 million lives. Some scholars believe this number should be much higher, as many as 70 million to an incredible 100 million deaths (Hua and Hongjun 2007).

During about this same time (approximately 1855–1868) in Guangdong, a conflict raged between imperial loyalists composed of Hakka (客家人 *kèjiārén*) minority and the locals (本土 *běntǔ*), since referred to as the Punti-Hakka Clan Wars (punti being the Cantonese dialect for locals), or in Chinese 土客械鬥 (*tǔkè xièdǒu*). Taking place largely in the Taishan (台山 *táishān*, or in dialect *Toi Shan*), and the Siyi (四邑 sìyì or *Sze Yup*) regions, the general consensus is that about 1 million people died during the conflict. One source suggests that tens of thousands of Hakka killed in retribution for their overrepresentation in the Taiping Rebellion (1851–1864).[4] However, the latter claim is contradicted by the famous historian and authority on the Hakka, Lo Hsiang-lin (羅香林 *luó xiānglín*), who found no records substantiating this claim.[5] This story may have been conflated with what occurred in Guangdong province (the Punti-Hakka Clan Wars), in which both sides suffered enormous casualties, although the Hakka were particularly hard hit (Constable 1994).

The Cantonese Diaspora of the Nineteenth Century

In order to escape hardscrabble poverty, large numbers of Chinese emigrants of the nineteenth century left seeking work in the newly industrializing world. Many of the migrations were ultimately due to widespread violence in the countryside surrounding Canton, such as that caused by the Punti-Hakka Clan Wars (above), and revolts of the "Red Turbans" (secret societies in revolt against the Qing government) in 1854. Such turmoil led to widespread destruction and misery especially in areas such as Xiangshan (香山 *xiāngshān*), Xinhui (新會 *xīnhuì*), and Taishan (台山 *táishān*, formerly known as Xinning 新寧 *xīnníng*) counties. In the government-led reprisals, some 70,000 executions were carried out in Canton and up to 1 million were killed in the rural areas. The result was a mass exit for young men, not just for labor but for their very lives. According to an official local history of Xinning (later Taishan) in late nineteenth century:

> Ever since the disturbances caused by the Red [Turban] bandits and the Hakka bandits, dealings with foreigners have increased greatly. The able-bodied go abroad. The fields are clogged with weeds. . . Daughters are often drowned rather than raised. (Mei 1979).

Yee Fong Toy

Many overseas Chinese shared the same county (if not local village) back home. And not only might they share home towns but family names as well. Chinese having the same surname often congregated in benevolent, eponymous associations ("Tongs," i.e., Cantonese pronunciation of a hall, 堂 *táng*), usually in "Chinatowns" around the world. One such famous Tong in North America is the Yee Fong Toy Association (余風采堂; mandarin: *yú fēngcǎi táng*). This familial surname of Yee (余; mandarin: *yú*) is said to date back to a personage of some renown in the

---

[4] The Hakka Wikipedia page states: "In retaliation for establishing the Taiping Heavenly Kingdom, the Qing Dynasty military massacred the Hakkas, killing 30,000 of the Hakkas daily during the height of the anti-Hakka mass-killing operation."

[5] I am grateful to Allen Yuan (袁易), for passing me this important information. Personal communication, 9 January 2022.

Northern Song dynasty, Yee Chung-Sheung (余忠襄; mandarin: *yú zhōngxiāng*), who lived 1000 — 1064 CE, and was originally born in the Qujiang District (區江 *qūjiāng*) of Shaozhou (now Shaoguan City). Because of Yee Chung-Sheung's famed literary skills and impeccable demeanor, he was labeled by his contemporary admirers with the sobriquet of Fong Toy (風采; mandarin: *fēngcǎi*), meaning someone of "graceful bearing" (Yee 2007). Coincidentally, it is more than possible that the Jesuit Matteo Ricci had occasion to see the ceremonial gateway that was built (1497) in Yee Chung-Sheung's honor in Shaozhou (Shaoguan).

As it happens, the majority of people in the worldwide Chinese diaspora named Yee (余 *yú*) can trace their familiar origins to the old "four counties" in Guangdong, traditionally called Szeyup (四邑; mandarin: *sìyì*):

- Sunwui 新會 (*xīnhuì*)
- Hoiping 開平 (*kāipíng*)
- Toisan 台山 (*táishān*)
- Yunping 恩平 (*ēnpíng*)

The largest emigrations from the Szuyup region to North America, notably California, coincided with building the transcontinental railroad in ca. 1870. Some three-quarters of Chinese who founded and lived in San Francisco's Chinatown, for example, called Taishan their home (Min 2009). For California in general, a great number of Chinese immigrants also originated from these counties located in Guangdong's Pearl River region (Mei 1979):

- Bo-on 寶安 (*bǎo'ān*), later made into Shenzhen City;
- Punyu 番禺 (*pānyù*)
- Namhoi 南海 (*nánhǎi*)
- Shuntak 順德 (*shùndé*) and
- Heungshan 香山 (xiāngshān), now Zhongshan

Nearly 70% of Chinese who migrated to Southeast Asia, usually looking for work were from Guangdong province, including a large representation from the city of Chaozhou (潮州市 *cháozhōu shì*). And while other provinces, notably Fujian, also contributed to large Chinese migrations nearly all of those who wound up in the Americas (north and south) as well as the West Indies were also from Guangdong Province.

In ca. 1850, when Hawaii drew people from around the world for whaling and sandlewood (the old Chinese name for Hawaii is "Sandlewood Fragant Hills" 檀香山 *tánxiāngshān*), Chinese began arriving to the islands in numbers. Because Guangdong's Xiangshan bordered Macao, many Chinese from that county found it convenient to gain passage on European commercial boats that used the island peninsula as a regular port of call (Wu and Lamley 2010). Thus, large numbers of Cantonese immigrants from Heungshan (Xiangshan) found themselves making a living in Hawaii, such as cutting and raising sugar cane. Among these Xiangshan Chinese families included a future revolutionary named Sun Wen, later more widely known as Sun Zhongshan. It was in Hawaii especially that fellow immigrants from his home county provided financial support to the Chinese revolution, and its standard bearer, Sun Zhongshan or Dr. Sun Yat-sen.

Dr. Sun Yat-Sen (孫逸仙 sūn yìxiān)

The father of revolutionary China, Sun Yat-sen (usually known as 孫中山 *sūn zhōngshān*) was born on 12 November 1866 in (then) Xianshan Prefecture, Cuiheng Village (香山縣翠亨村 *xiāngshān xiàn, cuìhēng cūn*). In his later revolutionary career, Sun Yat-sen was largely on the run from the Qing authorities. As a result, Sun Yat-sen conducted many of his operations abroad and under various aliases. One of the names he chose was while he was in Japan, Kikori Nakayama, or in Japanese Kanji, 中山樵 (Mandarin: *zhōngshān qiáo*). This is the origin of his *nomme de guerre*, Sun Zhongshan. (In his honor, the Republic of China changed the name of Xiangshan county to Zhongshan in 1925). Living overseas to escape the reach of Manchu agents, the relatively safe haven of Hawaii was key to Sun Yat-sen's open and clandestine operations. It was during his travels in the United States (Denver, Colorado) that Sun Yat-sen learned of the 1911 successful overthrow of the Qing dynasty. Today, he is celebrated both on mainland China as well as Taiwan.

Guangdong in the 1980s as Special Economic Zone

Deng Xiaoping famously conducted a "southern tour" in 1992, extolling the success of Guangdong's Special Economic Zones (SEZs) that were established in the early 1980s, these being Zhuhai, Shenzhen, Shantou, Guangzhou and Zhanjiang. Acknowledging that capitalism was essential for China's modernization (contra Mao Zedong), Deng Xiaoping brought back a pragmatic phrase he used in the early sixties, to wit: "It doesn't matter whether it's tan or black, so long as it catches rats, it's a good cat." When Deng Xiaoping first used the idiom in late June 1962 it was in reference to the efforts to ameliorate the ravages of the Great Leap Forward with the introduction of "responsibility fields" (責任田 *zérèntián*). These personal farming plots allowed peasants to not just feed themselves, but also earn extra incomes (Lanteigne 2005).[6] Increased economic development led to more opportunities for work, with a concomitant increase in population in Guangzhou (Table 7.1) as well as other cities Table 7.2).

[6] "不管黑猫黄猫，能逮住老鼠就是好猫" *bùguǎn hēimāo huángmāo, néng dǎizhù lǎoshǔ jiùshì hǎomāo.*

Table 7.1 Guangzhou (Canton) city population: 1990–2020. (PGGM 2021)

District/County	Population 1990	Population 2010	Population 2020
Dongshan District 東山區 *dōngshān qū*	545,136	N/A[a]	N/A
Liwan District 荔灣區 *lìwān qū*	554,589	898,204	1,238,305
Yuexiu District 越秀區 *yuèxiù qū*	441,316	1,157,277	1,038,643
Haizhu District 海珠區 *hǎizhū qū*	776,679	1,558,663	1,819,037
Tianhe District 天河區 *tiānhé qū*	430,153	1,432,431	2,241,826
Fangcun District 芳村區 *fāngcūn qū*	167,803	N/A[b]	N/A
Baiyun District 白雲區 *báiyún qū*	828,245	2,222,658	3,742,991
Huangpu District 黃埔區 *huángpǔ qū*	191,272	457,930	1,264,447
Huadu District 花都區 *huādū qū*	511,061	945,053	1,642,360
Conghua District 從化區 *cónghuà qū*	422,695	593,415	717,684
Zengcheng District增城區 *zēngchéng qū*	645,468	1,036,731	1,466,331
Panyu District 番禺區 *pānyù qū*	785,526	1,764,869	2,658,397
Nansha District 南沙區 *nánshā qū*	N/A	259,899	846,584
Menggang District 夢崗區 *mènggǎng qū*	N/A	373,670	N/A[c]
Total	**6,299,943**	**12,700,800**	**18,676,605**

[a]District dissolved in (2005)
[b]District was combined with Liwan in (2005)
[c]District dissolved in (2014)

Table 7.2 Guangdong population data for 2000, 2010, and 2020 (Residential 常住人口 *chángzhù rénkǒu*). (PGGM 2021)

City	Population (2000, rounded)	Population (2010)	Population (2020)
Guangzhou City (Canton) 廣州市 *guǎngzhōu shì* [abbrev. 穗 *suì*]	9,943,000	12,700,800	18,676,605
Shenzhen City 深圳市 *shēnzhèn shì* [abbrev. 鵬 *péng*]	7,008,400	10,357,938	17,560,061
Qingyuan City 清遠市 *qīngyuǎn shì*	3,147,700	3,698,394	3,969,473
Shaoguan City 韶關市 *sháoguān shì*	2,735,100	2,826,612	2,855,131
Heyuan City 河源市 *héyuán shì*	2,265,200	2,953,019	2,837,686
Meizhou City 梅州市 *méizhōu shì*	3,802,000	4,240,139	3,873,239
Chaozhou City 潮州市 *cháozhōu shì*	2,402,200	2,669,844	2,568,387
Zhaoqing City 肇慶市 *zhàoqìng shì*	3,371,400	3,918,085	4,113,594
Yunfu City 雲浮市 *yúnfú shì*	2,152,900	2,360,128	2,383,350
Foshan City 佛山市 *fóshān shì* [abbrev. 禪 *chán*]	5,337,900	7,194,311	9,498,863
Dongguan City 東莞市 *dōngguǎn shì*	6,445,700	8,220,237	10,466,625
Huizhou City 惠州市 *huìzhōu shì*	3,216,300	4,597,002	6,042,852
Shanwei City 汕尾市 *shànwěi shì*	2,453,100	2,935,717	2,672,819
Jieyang City 揭陽市 *jiēyáng shì*	5,237,400	5,877,025	5,577,814
Shantou City 汕頭市 *shàntóu shì*	4,671,100	5,391,028	5,502,031
Zhanjiang City 湛江市 *zhànjiāng shì*	6,072,900	6,993,304	6,981,236
Maoming City 茂名市 *màomíng shì*	5,239,700	5,817,753	6,174,050
Yangjiang City 陽江市 *yángjiāng shì*	2,170,400	2,421,812	2,602,959
Jiangmen City 江門市 *jiāngmén shì*	3,950,300	4,448,871	4,798,090
Zhongshan City 中山市 *zhōngshān shì*	2,363,500	3,120,884	4,418,060
Zhuhai City 珠海市 *zhūhǎi shì*	1,235,600	1,560,229	2,439,585
Total	**86,420,000**	**104,303,132**	**126,012,510**

A Model All Its Own: Shenzhen City

Owing to the COVID-19 pandemic, there is more than an even chance that the reader may have used a surgical mask produced by the BYD (比亞迪 *bǐyàdí*) Precision Manufacture Co. Ltd., located in Longgang District (population nearly 4 million), in Shenzhen City. Not only was BYD the largest surgical mask manufacturer in the world, it is a significant world player in electronic vehicles (to include hybrids), selling nearly 32,000 in the single month of May 2021 (Cox 2021). It is all the more remarkable that in late 1978 Shenzhen City did not even exist.

As author Richard Hu observed, Shenzhen City and its great success can be distilled into three main factors: timing, location, and its people (Hu 2021). Before its creation as a municipality in 1979, few Chinese would have heard of Shenzhen, a small area historically known by locals as "deep ditch village" (深圳墟 *shēnzhèn xū*) dating back to 1410 (Hu 2021). Created in 1979 out of Bao'an County (寶安縣 *bǎo'ān xiàn*), just north to the border of Hong Kong, Shenzhen is now held to be the premier model of China's Special Economic Zones (SEZs). When it got its start as a new model for economic development, Shenzhen (2,020 KM^2) had a population of over 314,000 people (the figure often seen of 30,000 likely is that of its smaller, old market town). Ultimately it was free enterprise that allowed the hardworking people of Shenzhen (with the assistance of numerous overseas Chinese also from the region) to create this spectacular success story (Juan 2020).

And the impetus for Shenzhen's rapid economic development had as much to do with geography than the wisdom of Chinese leadership. Having just been released from military prison in 1977 (following the end of the Cultural Revolution), Deng Xiaoping visited Guangdong that following year. One of the most obvious concerns on the ground was the fact that a Chinese peasant made one hundred times less than his farming counterpart in the British colony of Hong Kong, which led to thousands of Guangdong citizens to escape the PRC to the "West." Deng Xiaoping is rightly credited with having finally come to the realization that something had to be done. And although the phrase "reform and opening up" (改革開發 *gǎigékāifā*) was instituted in late 1978, intransigence among the Marxist (and Maoist) party faithful often impeded progress in empowering the SEZs at the local level. In the case of Shenzhen, having been formally designated an SEZ in August 1980, it took more than just the dynamism of local leadership to overcome national objections to capitalism. In a symbolic gesture, Deng Xiaoping made his first "Southern Tour" of the SEZs in 1984, deliberately making Shenzhen his first visit on his itinerary (Juan 2020). Having made his point, Shenzhen could carry on with unfettered enterprise, harnessing the mind power and initiative of the southern Chinese people, and making extraordinary economic gains ever since. From its relatively humble beginnings in 1979 to 2017, Shenzhen City recorded an average yearly growth rate in gross domestic product (GDP) of over 22%, nearly 12% annual growth in employment, leading to an increase in population of 10% on average from year to year. From a demographic perspective writ large, Richard Hu also notes that Shenzhen is very much a migrant city, with a 2020 population of 17.5 million people, but a registered (*hukou*) population of only 5 million (Hu 2021).

Judging by population growth alone across Guangdong Province, the results of China's reform and opening up since 1978 and free trade zones have been just as astonishing. Guangdong had a population of about 34,770,000 when Deng Xiaoping officially announced the need for reforms. By 1984, 4 years after Deng Xiaoping's economic reforms, Guangdong had a population of about 60 million; in 1990 almost 63 million, and, in 2000, Guangdong had a population of some 85,225,000. Indeed, between the years 1990 and 2000, nearly 20% of all population growth in the PRC was in Guangdong.

And Guangdong's population growth has shown no signs of slowing. With over 104,303,000 individuals in 2010, Guangdong remained the fastest growing province in terms of population in 2020 (126,012,000), with an overall increase of nearly 21%. The huge disparity in resident (census) of over 126 million, and the permanent resident (*hukou*) of 95,020,000 underscores the attractiveness of Guangdong for Chinese immigrating from other provinces for a better, and hopefully prosperous life. Ranked sixth in terms of per capita income in 2020 (USD $6,380), Guangdong continues to lead all Chinese provinces in terms of gross domestic product (GDP) (Zhang 2021) (Table 7.3).

The growth in Guangdong's population over the past decade can be readily seen in Table 7.2 (above); below (Table 7.4) is a detailed breakdown according to 2020 census data:

Table 7.5 (below) shows the *hukou* (family registered) populations based on PRC Ministry of Civil Affairs data. (Districts listed directly under major cities are government seats, as are those in parentheses). One can compare these data with the census (usual residential populations based on 2010 and 2020 censuses in Tables 7.2 and 7.3 (below):

Table 7.3 Top five Chinese Provinces and cities in terms of Gross Domestic Product (GDP), 2017–2020 (USD = 6.43 yuan). (China News Net 2021)

Province/City	2017	2018	2019	2020
Guangdong	1.397 trillion	1.513 trillion	1.674 trillion	1.722 trillion
Jiangsu	1.336 trillion	1.440 trillion	1.549 trillion	1.597 trillion
Shandong	1.130 trillion	1.189 trillion	1.105 trillion	1.137 trillion
Zhejiang	805.10 billion	873.98 billion	969.70 billion	1.005 trillion
Henan	699.66 billion	747.37 billion	843.84 billion	855.32 billion

Table 7.4 Guangdong Province: population data of cities and their subordinate sectors. (GPSB 2021)

Cities and subordinate sectors, population (2020 census)	Subordinate district, city and county populations (2020)	Total population (2020)
Guangzhou City (Canton) 廣州市 ***guǎngzhōu shì* [abbrev.** 穗 ***suì*]**		**18,676,605**
Yuexiu District 越秀區 *yuèxiù qū*	1,038,643	
Liwan District 荔灣區 *lìwān qū*	1,238,305	
Haizhu District 海珠區 *hǎizhū qū*	1,819,037	
Tianhe District 天河區 *tiānhé qū*	2,241,826	
Baiyun District 白雲區 *báiyún qū*	3,742,991	
Huangpu District 黃埔區 *huángpǔ qū*	1,264,447	
Panyu District 番禺區 *pānyú qū*	2,658,397	
Huadu District 花都區 *huādū qū*	1,642,360	
Nansha District 南沙區 *nánshā qū*	846,584	
Zengcheng City 增城區 *zēngchéng qū*	1,466,331	
Conghua District 從化區 *cónghuà qū*	717,684	
Shenzhen City 深圳市 ***shēnzhèn shì* [abbrev.** 鵬 ***péng*]**		**17,560,061**
Futian District 福田區 *fútián qū*	1,553,225	
Luohu District 羅湖區 *luóhú qū*	1,143,801	
Nanshan District 南山區 *nánshān qū*	1,795,826	
Bao'an District 寶安區 *bǎo'ān qū*	4,476,554	
Longgang District 龍崗區 *lónggǎng qū*	3,979,037	
Yantian District 鹽田區 *yántián qū*	214,225	
Longhua District 龍華區 *lónghuá qū*	2,528,872	
Pingshan District 坪山區 *píngshān qū*	551,333	
Guangming District 光明區 *guāngmíng qū*	1,095,289	
Dapeng New District 大鵬新區 *dàpéng xīnqū*	156,236	
Shenzhen-Shanwei Special Cooperation Zone 深汕特別合作區 *shēnshàn tèbié hézuòqū*	65,633	
Qingyuan City 清遠市 ***qīngyuǎn shì***		**3,969,473**
Qingcheng District 清城區 *qīngchéng qū*	1,119,901	
Qingxin District 清新區 *qīngxīn qū*	618,523	
Yingde City 英德市 *yīngdé shì*	941,325	
Lianzhou City 連州市 *liánzhōu shì*	377,220	
Fogang County 佛岡縣 *fógāng xiàn*	315,502	
Yangshan County 陽山縣 *yángshān xiàn*	367,175	
Lianshan Zhuangzu Yaozu (Zhuang and Yao) Autonomous County 連山壯族瑤族自治縣 *liánshān zhuàngzú yáozú zìzhìxiàn*	95,136	
Liannan Yaozu (Yao) Autonomous County 連南瑤族自治縣 *liánnán yáozú zìzhìxiàn*	134,691	
Shaoguan City[a] 韶關市 ***sháoguān shì***		**2,855,131**

(continued)

Table 7.4 (continued)

Cities and subordinate sectors, population (2020 census)	Subordinate district, city and county populations (2020)	Total population (2020)
Zhenjiang District 湞江區 *zhēnjiāng qū*	364,319	
Wujiang District 武江區 *wǔjiāng qū*	373,686	
Qujiang District 曲江區 *qūjiāng qū*	290,455	
Lechang City 樂昌市 *lèchāng shì*	383,498	
Nanxiong City 南雄市 *nánxióng shì*	353,916	
Shixing County 始興縣 *shǐxīng xiàn*	198,060	
Renhua County 仁化縣 *rénhuà xiàn*	186,009	
Wengyuan County 翁源縣 *wēngyuán xiàn*	322,482	
Xinfeng County 新豐縣 *xīnfēng xiàn*	195,430	
Ruyuan Yaozu (Yao) Autonomous County 乳源瑤族自治縣 *rǔyuán yáozú zìzhìxiàn*	187,276	
Heyuan City 河源市 ***héyuán shì***		**2,837,686**
Yuancheng District 源城區 *yuánchéng qū*	703,607	
Zijin County 紫金縣 *zǐjīn xiàn*	551,095	
Longchuan County 龍川縣 *lóngchuān xiàn*	595,471	
Lianping County 連平縣 *liánpíng xiàn*	285,224	
Heping County 和平縣 *hépíng xiàn*	353,903	
Dongyuan County 東源縣 *dōngyuán xiàn*	348,386	
Meizhou City 梅州市 ***méizhōu shì***		**3,873,239**
Meijiang District 梅江區 *méijiāng qū*	435,616	
Xingning City 興寧市 *xīngníng shì*	779,411	
Meixian District 梅縣區 *méixiàn qū*	556,735	
Dapu County 大埔縣 *dàpǔ xiàn*	330,948	
Fengshun County 豐順縣 *fēngshùn xiàn*	478,731	
Wuhua County 五華縣 *wǔhuá xiàn*	916,961	
Pingyuan County 平遠縣 *píngyuǎn xiàn*	190,482	
Jiaoling County 蕉嶺縣 *jiāolǐng xiàn*	184,355	
Chaozhou City 潮州市 ***cháozhōu shì***		**2,568,387**
Xiangqiao District 湘橋區 *xiāngqiáo qū*	575,795	
Chao'an District 潮安區 *cháo'ān qū*	1,017,036	
Raoping County 饒平縣 *ráopíng xiàn*	817,442	
Fengxi District 楓溪區 *fēngxī qū*	158,114	
Zhaoqing City肇慶市 ***zhàoqìng shì***		**4,113,594**
Duanzhou District 端州區 *duānzhōu qū*	602,402	
Dinghu District 鼎湖區 *dǐnghú qū*	209,116	
Gaoyao District 高要區 *gāoyào qū*	741,591	
Sihui City 四會市 *sìhuì shì*	526,457	
Guangning County 廣寧縣 *guǎngníng xiàn*	408,112	
Huaiji County 懷集縣 *huáijí xiàn*	805,117	
Fengkai County 封開縣 *fēngkāi xiàn*	374,848	

(continued)

Table 7.4 (continued)

Cities and subordinate sectors, population (2020 census)	Subordinate district, city and county populations (2020)	Total population (2020)
Deqing County 德慶縣 *déqìng xiàn*	331,438	
Zhaoqing High Technology Industrial Development Zone 肇慶高新技術產業開發區 *zhàoqìng gāoxīnjìshù chǎnyè kāifāqū*	114,453	
Yunfu City 雲浮市 ***yúnfú shì***		**2,383,350**
Yuncheng District 雲城區 *yúnchéng qū*	408,537	
Luoding City 羅定市 *luódìng shì*	936,931	
Yun'an District 雲安區 *yún'ān qū*	235,390	
Xinxing County 新興縣 *xīnxīng xiàn*	430,831	
Yu'nan County 郁南縣 *yùnán xiàn*	371,661	
Foshan City 佛山市 ***fóshān shì*** **[abbrev.** 禪 ***chán*]**		**9,498,863**
Chancheng District 禪城區 *chánchéng qū*	1,330,262	
Nanhai District 南海區 *nánhǎi qū*	3,667,247	
Shunde District 順德區 *shùndé qū*	3,229,090	
Sanshui District 三水區 *sānshuǐ qū*	803,226	
Gaoming District 高明區 *gāomíng qū*	469,038	
Dongguan City 東莞市 ***dōngguǎn shì***		**10,466,625**
Dongcheng Subdistrict Office 東城街道辦事處 *dōngchéng jiēdào bànshìchǔ*	597,192	
Nancheng subdistrict Office 南城街道辦事處 *nánchéng jiēdào bànshìchǔ*	418,288	
Wanjiang Subdistrict Office 萬江街道辦事處 *wànjiāng jiēdào bànshìchǔ*	328,856	
Guancheng Subdistrict Office 莞城街道辦事處 *guānchéng jiēdào bànshìchǔ*	173,957	
Shijie Town 石碣鎮 *shíjié zhèn*	282,255	
Shilong Town 石龍鎮 *shílóng zhèn*	144,762	
Chashan Town 茶山鎮 *cháshān zhèn*	219,333	
Shipai Town 石排鎮 *shípái zhèn*	235,194	
Qishi Town 企石鎮 *qǐshí zhèn*	169,396	
Hengli Town 橫瀝鎮 *hénglì zhèn*	278,858	
Qiaotou Town 橋頭鎮 *qiáotóu zhèn*	207,294	
Xiegang Town 謝崗鎮 *xiègǎng zhèn*	106,152	
Dongkeng Town 東坑鎮 *dōngkēng zhèn*	187,877	
Changping Town 常平鎮 *chángpíng zhèn*	444,894	
Liaobu Town寮步鎮 *liáobù zhèn*	513,090	
Zhangmutou Town 樟木頭鎮 *zhāngmùtóu zhèn*	173,875	
Dalang Town 大郎鎮 *dàláng zhèn*	556,778	
Huangjiang Town 黃江鎮 *huángjiāng zhèn*	283,426	
Qingxi Town 清溪鎮 *qīngxī zhèn*	344,303	

(continued)

Table 7.4 (continued)

Cities and subordinate sectors, population (2020 census)	Subordinate district, city and county populations (2020)	Total population (2020)
Tangxia Town 塘廈鎮 *tángshà zhèn*	629,016	
Fenggang Town 鳳崗鎮 *fènggǎng zhèn*	417,430	
Dalingshan Town 大嶺山鎮 *dàlǐngshān zhèn*	366,101	
Chang'an Town 長安鎮 *cháng'ān zhèn*	807,391	
Humen Town 虎門鎮 *hǔmén zhèn*	838,144	
Houjie Town 厚街鎮 *hòujiē zhèn*	550,087	
Shatian Town 沙田鎮 *shātián zhèn*	210,175	
Daojiao Town 道滘鎮 *dàojiào zhèn*	159,502	
Hongmei Town 洪梅鎮 *hóngméi zhèn*	65,325	
Mayong Town 麻湧鎮 *máyǒng zhèn*	182,416	
Wangniudun Town 望牛墩鎮 *wàngniúdūn zhèn*	86,960	
Zhongtang Town 中堂鎮 *zhōngtáng zhèn*	196,890	
Gaobu Town 高埗鎮 *gāobù zhèn*	169,923	
Songshanhu Science and Technology Industrial Park 松山湖科技產業園 *sōngshānhú kējì chǎnyèyuán*	120,765	
Huizhou City 惠州市 ***huìzhōu shì***		**6,042,852**
Huicheng District 惠城區 *huìchéng qū*	155,793	
Huiyang District 惠陽區 *huìyáng qū*	959,750	
Boluo County 博羅縣 *bóluó xiàn*	1,210,878	
Huidong County 惠東縣 *huìdōng xiàn*	1,018,076	
Longmen County 龍門縣 *lóngmén xiàn*	319,183	
Dayawan District 大亞灣區 *dàyàwān qū*	444,387	
Zhongkai District 仲愷區 *zhòngkǎi qū*	531,785	
Shanwei City 汕尾市 ***shànwěi shì***		**2,672,819**
Chengqu District 城區 *chéngqū*	394,593	
Lufeng City 陸豐市 *lùfēng shì*	1,221,634	
Haifeng County 海豐縣 *hǎifēng xiàn*	736,791	
Luhe County 陸河縣 *lùhé xiàn*	249,242	
Honghaiwan 紅海灣 *hónghǎi wān*	56,366	
Overseas Chinese Management District 華僑管理區 *huáqiáo guǎnlǐqū*	14,193	
Jieyang City 揭陽市 ***jiēyáng shì***		**5,577,814**
Rongcheng District 榕城區 *róngchéng qū*	537,212	
Jiedong District 揭東區 *jiēdōng qū*	931,719	
Puning City 普寧市 *pǔníng shì*	1,998,619	
Jiexi County 揭西縣 *jiēxī xiàn*	674,829	
Huilai County 惠來縣 *huìlái xiàn*	1,040,779	
Jieyang Airport Economic Zone 揭陽空港經濟區 *jiēyáng kōnggǎng jīngjìqū*	394,656	
Shantou (Swatow) City 汕頭市 ***shàntóu shì***		**5,502,031**

(continued)

Table 7.4 (continued)

Cities and subordinate sectors, population (2020 census)	Subordinate district, city and county populations (2020)	Total population (2020)
Jinping District 金平區 *jīnpíng qū*	777,024	
Haojiang District 濠江區 *háojiāng qū*	269,471	
Longhu District 龍湖區 *lónghú qū*	630,749	
Chaoyang District 潮陽區 *cháoyáng qū*	1,654,276	
Chaonan District 潮南區 *cháonán qū*	1,231,638	
Chenghai District 澄海區 *chénghǎi qū*	874,444	
Nan'ao County 南澳縣 *nán'ào xiàn*	64,429	
Zhanjiang City 湛江市 ***zhànjiāng shì***		**6,981,236**
Chikan District 赤坎區 *chìkǎn qū*	390,300	
Xiashan District 霞山區 *xiáshān qū*	536,424	
Potou District坡頭區 *pōtóu qū*	337,723	
Mazhang District 麻章區 *mázhāng qū*	326,154	
Wuchuan City 吳川市 *wúchuān shì*	907,354	
Lianjiang City 廉江市 *liánjiāng shì*	1,363,470	
Leizhou City雷州市 *léizhōu shì*	1,321,091	
Suixi County 遂溪縣 *suìxī xiàn*	824,608	
Xuwen County 徐聞縣 *xúwén xiàn*	633,258	
Zhanjiang Economic and Technological Development Zone 湛江經濟技術開發區 *zhànjiāng jīngjìjìshù kāifāqū*	340,854	
Maoming City 茂名市 ***màomíng shì***		**6,174,050**
Maonan District 茂南區 *màonán qū*	1,035,411	
Dianbai District 電白區 *diànbái qū*	1,503,737	
Huazhou City 化州市 *huàzhōu shì*	1,291,668	
Xinyi City 信宜市 *xìnyí shì*	1,014,577	
Gaozhou City 高州市 *gāozhōu shì*	1,328,657	
Yangjiang City 陽江市 ***yángjiāng shì***		**2,602,959**
Jiangcheng District 江城區 *jiāngchéng qū*	637,984	
Yangchun City 陽春市 *yángchūn shì*	875,896	
Yangxi County 陽西縣 *yángxī xiàn*	434,076	
Yangdong District 陽東區 *yángdōng qū*	478,299	
Zhanjiang High technology Industry Development Zone 湛江高新技術產業開發區 *zhànjiāng gāoxīn jìshù chǎnyè kāifāqū*	62,328	
Hailing District 海陵區 *hǎilíng qū*	78,376	
Jiangmen City 江門市 ***jiāngmén shì***		**4,798,090**
Pengjiang District 蓬江區 *péngjiāng qū*	853,007	
Jianghai District 江海區 *jiānghǎi qū*	364,964	
Xinhui District 新會區 *xīnhuì qū*	909,277	
Enping City 恩平市 *ēnpíng shì*	483,907	
Taishan City 台山市 *táishān shì*	907,744	

(continued)

Table 7.4 (continued)

Cities and subordinate sectors, population (2020 census)	Subordinate district, city and county populations (2020)	Total population (2020)
Kaiping City 開平市 *kāipíng shì*	748,777	
Heshan City 鶴山市 *hèshān shì*	530,684	
Zhongshan City 中山市 ***zhōngshān shì***		**4,418,060**
Shiqi Subdistrict 石岐街道 *shíqí jiēdào*	257,472	
Dongqu Subdistrict 東區街道 *dōngqū jiēdào*	213,948	
Zhongshangang Subdistrict 中山港街道 *zhōngshāngǎng jiēdào*	289,518	
Xiqu Subdistrict 西區街道 *xīqū jiēdào*	133,078	
Nanqu Subdistrict 南區街道 *nánqū jiēdào*	90,270	
Wuguishan Subdistrict 五桂山街道 *wǔguìshān jiēdào*	46,049	
Xiaolan Town 小欖鎮 *xiǎolǎn zhèn*	513,726	
Huangpu Town 黄圃鎮 *huángpǔ zhèn*	187,775	
Mingzhong Town 民眾鎮 *mínzhòng zhèn*	112,345	
Dongfeng Town 東鳳鎮 *dōngfèng zhèn*	201,023	
Dongsheng Town 東升鎮 *dōngshēng zhèn*	266,863	
Guzhen Town 古鎮鎮 *gǔzhèn zhèn*	230,405	
Shaxi Town 沙溪鎮 *shāxī zhèn*	223,625	
Tanzhou Town 坦洲鎮 *tǎnzhōu zhèn*	382,445	
Gangkou Town 港口鎮 *gǎngkǒu zhèn*	140,134	
Sanjiao Town 三角鎮 *sānjiǎo zhèn*	126,294	
Henglan Town 横欄鎮 *hénglán zhèn*	200,522	
Nantou Town 南頭鎮 *nántóu zhèn*	158,234	
Fusha Town 阜沙鎮 *fùshā zhèn*	73,381	
Nanlang Town 南朗鎮 *nánlǎng zhèn*	101,589	
Sanxiang Town 三鄉鎮 *sānxiāng zhèn*	234,853	
Banfu Town 板芙鎮 *bǎnfú zhèn*	95,876	
Dayong Town 大湧鎮 *dàyǒng zhèn*	99,763	
Shenwan Town 神灣鎮 *shénwān zhèn*	38,872	
Zhuhai City 珠海市 ***zhūhǎi shì***		**2,439,585**
Xiangzhou District 香洲區 *xiāngzhōu qū*	1,124,126	
Doumen District 斗門區 *dǒumén qū*	608,899	
Jinwan District 金灣區 *jīnwān qū*	301,507	
Hengqin Xinqu 横琴新區 *héngqín xīnqū*	43,618	
Zhuhai High Technology Industry Development Zone 珠海高新技術產業開發區 *zhūhǎi gāoxīn jìshù chǎnyè kāifāqū*	207,151	
Baoshui District 保税區 *bǎoshuì qū*	4,493	
Wanshan District 萬山區 *wànshān qū*	4,929	
Zhuhai Gaolan Port Economic Zone 珠海高欄港經濟區 *zhūhǎi gāolángǎng jīngjìqū*	144,862	

[a]Includes the Shaoguan New District (韶關新區 *sháoguān xīnqū*) with a population of 71,235

Guangdong Province (粵 *yuè*) (Fig. 7.2)

Provincial Capital: Guangzhou

Table 7.5 Guangdong Province: permanent registered (戶籍人口 *hùjí rénkǒu*) populations. (MCA 2020)

Name	Traditional	Simplified	Population (2012)	Population (2016)	Population (2020)	Area (Sq. Km)
Guangdong Province	廣東省	广东省	85,220,000	86,360,000	95,020,000	174,246
Guangzhou City	廣州市	广州市	8,050,000	8,230,000	9,280,000	7,436
Yuexiu District (Beijing Subdistrict)	越秀區 (北京街道)	越秀区 (北京街道)	1,170,000	1,170,000	1,180,000	33
Liwan District (Jinhua Subdistrict)	荔灣區 (金花街道)	荔湾区 (金花街道)	710,000	710,000	750,000	62
Haizhu District (Jianghai Subdistrict)	海珠區 (江海街道)	海珠区 (江海街道)	950,000	980,000	1,060,000	91
Tianhe District (Tianyuan Subdistrict)	天河區 (天園街道)	天河区 (天园街道)	770,000	800,000	940,000	96
Baiyun District (Jingtai Subdistrict)	白雲區 (景泰街道)	白云区 (景泰街道)	830,000	860,000	1,030,000	796
Huangpu District (Luogang Subdistrict)	黃埔區 (蘿崗街道)	黄埔区 (萝岗街道)	200,000	400,000	530,000	484
Panyu District (Shiqiao Subdistrict)	番禺區 (市橋街道)	番禺区 (市桥街道)	1,000,000	810,000	990,000	530
Huadu District (Xinhua Subdistrict)	花都區 (新華街道)	花都区 (新华街道)	660,000	680,000	780,000	969
Nansha District (Huangge Town)	南沙區 (黃閣鎮)	南沙区 (黄阁镇)	150,000	370,000	440,000	784
Luogang District (Luogang Subdistrict)[a]	蘿崗區 (蘿崗街道)	萝岗区 (萝岗街道)	190,000	N/A	N/A	(393)
Zengcheng City (Licheng Subdistrict)	增城區 (荔城街道)	增城区 (荔城街道)	840,000	850,000	950,000	1,616
Conghua District (Jiekou Subdistrict)	從化區 (街口街道)	从化区 (街口街道)	580,000	600,000	630,000	1,975
Qingyuan City	清遠市	清远市	4,140,000	4,050,000	4,430,000	19,265
Qingcheng District (Dongcheng Subdistrict)	清城區 (東城街道)	清城区 (东城街道)	660,000	650,000	750,000	1,334

(continued)

Table 7.5 (continued)

Name	Traditional	Simplified	Population (2012)	Population (2016)	Population (2020)	Area (Sq. Km)
Qingxin District (Taihe Town)	清新區 (太和鎮)	清新区 (太和镇)	690,000	670,000	720,000	2,353
Yingde City (Yingcheng Subdistrict)	英德市 (英城街道)	英德市 (英城街道)	1,110,000	1,090,000	1,190,000	5,671
Lianzhou City (Lianzhou Town)	連州市 (連州鎮)	连州市 (连州镇)	530,000	510,000	550,000	2,665
Fogang County (Shijiao Town)	佛岡縣 (石角鎮)	佛冈县 (石角镇)	330,000	320,000	350,000	1,271
Yangshan County (Yangcheng Town)	陽山縣 (陽城鎮)	阳山县 (阳城镇)	540,000	530,000	580,000	3,450
Lianshan Zhuangzu Yaozu (Zhuang and Yao) Autonomous County (Jitian Town)	連山壯族瑤族自治縣 (吉田鎮)	连山壮族瑶族自治县 (吉田镇)	120,000	120,000	120,000	1,218
Liannan Yaozu (Yao) Autonomous County (Sanjiang Town)	連南瑤族自治縣 (三江鎮)	连南瑶族自治县 (三江镇)	160,000	160,000	180,000	1,303
Shaoguan City	韶關市	韶关市	3,290,000	3,260,000	3,370,000	18,398
Zhenjiang District (Donghe Subdistrict)	湞江區 (東河街道)	浈江区 (东河街道)	360,000	350,000	320,000	562
Wujiang District (Xinhua Subdistrict)	武江區 (新華街道)	武江区 (新华街道)	260,000	260,000	280,000	720
Qujiang District (Maba Town)	曲江區 (馬壩鎮)	曲江区 (马坝镇)	320,000	310,000	310,000	1,666
Lechang City (Lecheng Subdistrict)	樂昌市 (樂城街道)	乐昌市 (乐城街道)	530,000	510,000	530,000	2,384
Nanxiong City (Xiongzhou Subdistrict)	南雄市 (雄州街道)	南雄市 (雄州街道)	470,000	470,000	490,000	2,402
Shixing County (Taiping TOWN)	始興縣 (太平鎮)	始兴县 (太平镇)	250,000	250,000	260,000	1,861
Renhua County (Danxia subdistrict)	仁化縣 (丹霞街道)	仁化县 (丹霞街道)	230,000	230,000	240,000	2,318
Wengyuan County (Longxian Town)	翁源縣 (龍仙鎮)	翁源县 (龙仙镇)	400,000	400,000	420,000	2,171
Xinfeng County (Fengcheng Subdistrict)	新豐縣 (豐城街道)	新丰县 (丰城街道)	250,000	260,000	270,000	2,015

(continued)

Table 7.5 (continued)

Name	Traditional	Simplified	Population (2012)	Population (2016)	Population (2020)	Area (Sq. Km)
Ruyuan Yaozu (Yao) Autonomous County (Rucheng Town)	乳源瑤族自治縣 (乳城鎮)	乳源瑶族自治县 (乳城镇)	220,000	220,000	230,000	2,299
Heyuan City	河源市	河源市	3,580,000	3,560,000	3,730,000	15,644
Yuancheng District (Shangcheng Subdistrict)	源城區 (上城街道)	源城区 (上城街道)	310,000	290,000	330,000	365
Zijin County (Zicheng town)	紫金縣 (紫城鎮)	紫金县 (紫城镇)	810,000	830,000	860,000	3,621
Longchuan County (Laolong Town)	龍川縣 (老隆鎮)	龙川县 (老隆镇)	970,000	960,000	990,000	3,093
Lianping County (Yuanshan Town)	連平縣 (元善鎮)	连平县 (元善镇)	400,000	400,000	410,000	2,274
Heping County (Yangming Town)	和平縣 (陽明鎮)	和平县 (阳明镇)	520,000	530,000	560,000	2,286
Dongyuan County (Xiantang Town)	東源縣 (仙塘鎮)	东源县 (仙塘镇)	570,000	550,000	590,000	4,005
Meizhou City	梅州市	梅州市	5,150,000	5,200,000	5,480,000	15,925
Meijiang District (Jinshan Subdistrict)	梅江區 (金山街道)	梅江区 (金山街道)	320,000	360,000	360,000	571
Xingning City (Xingtian Subdistrict)	興寧市 (興田街道)	兴宁市 (兴田街道)	1,170,000	1,180,000	1,180,000	2,107
Meixian District (Chengjiang Town)	梅縣區 (程江鎮)	梅县区 (程江镇)	630,000	590,000	620,000	2,503
Dapu County (Huliao Town)	大埔縣 (湖寮鎮)	大埔县 (湖寮镇)	540,000	550,000	560,000	2,470
Fengshun County (Tangkeng Town)	豐順縣 (湯坑鎮)	丰顺县 (汤坑镇)	690,000	700,000	740,000	2,710
Wuhua County (Shuizhai Town)	五華縣 (水寨鎮)	五华县 (水寨镇)	1,310,000	1,330,000	1,520,000	3,226
Pingyuan County (Dazhe Town)	平遠縣 (大柘鎮)	平远县 (大柘镇)	260,000	260,000	270,000	1,381
Jiaoling County (Jiaocheng Town)	蕉嶺縣 (蕉城鎮)	蕉岭县 (蕉城镇)	230,000	230,000	230,000	957
Chaozhou City	潮州市	潮州市	2,600,000	2,630,000	2,760,000	3,098
Xiangqiao District (Fengxin Subdistrict)	湘橋區 (鳳新街道)	湘桥区 (凤新街道)	350,000	500,000	520,000	321
Chao'an District (Anbu Town)	潮安區 (庵埠鎮)	潮安区 (庵埠镇)	1,240,000	1,100,000	1,170,000	1,093
Raoping County (Huanggang Town)	饒平縣 (黃岡鎮)	饶平县 (黄冈镇)	1,010,000	1,030,000	1,070,000	1,684

(continued)

Table 7.5 (continued)

Name	Traditional	Simplified	Population (2012)	Population (2016)	Population (2020)	Area (Sq. Km)
Shantou (Swatow) City	汕頭市	汕头市	5,240,000	5,310,000	5,690,000	2,123
Jinping District (Shipaotai Subdistrict)	金平區 (石砲台街道)	金平区 (石炮台街道)	750,000	750,000	740,000	102
Haojiang District (Dahao Subdistrict)	濠江區 (達濠街道)	濠江区 (达濠街道)	280,000	280,000	300,000	168
Longhu District (Jinxia Subdistrict)	龍湖區 (金霞街道)	龙湖区 (金霞街道)	400,000	410,000	460,000	101
Chaoyang District (Wenguang Subdistrict)	潮陽區 (文光街道)	潮阳区 (文光街道)	1,660,000	1,690,000	1,840,000	678
Chaonan District (Xiashan Subdistrict)	潮南區 (峽山街道)	潮南区 (峡山街道)	1,330,000	1,360,00	1,480,000	596
Chenghai District (Chenghua Subdistrict)	澄海區 (澄華街道)	澄海区 (澄华街道)	750,000	750,000	790,000	367
Nan'ao County (Houzhai Town)	南澳縣 (後宅鎮)	南澳县 (后宅镇)	70,000	70,000	80,000	111
Jieyang City	揭陽市	揭阳市	6,630,000	6,730,000	7,050,000	5,269
Rongcheng District (Xinxing Subdistrict)	榕城區 (新興街道)	榕城区 (新兴街道)	700,000	710,000	1,000,000	337
Jiedong District (Quxi Subdistrict)	揭東區 (曲溪街道)	揭东区 (曲溪街道)	1,290,000	1,310,000	1,120,000	694
Puning City (Liushabei Subdistrict)	普寧市 (流沙北街道)	普宁市 (流沙北街道)	2,330,000	2,380,000	2,470,000	1,620
Jiexi County (Hepo Subdistrict)	揭西縣 (河婆街道)	揭西县 (河婆街道)	980,000	980,000	990,000	1,365
Huilai County (Huicheng Town)	惠來縣 (惠城鎮)	惠来县 (惠城镇)	1,330,000	1,350,000	1,480,000	1,253
Shanwei City	汕尾市	汕尾市	3,460,000	3,470,000	3,630,000	4,957
Chengqu District (Xiangzhou Subdistrict)	城區 (香洲街道)	城区 (香洲街道)	520,000	500,000	500,000	404
Lufeng City (Donghai Subdistrict)	陸豐市 (東海街道)	陆丰市 (东海街道)	1,770,000	1,810,000	1,920,000	1,777
Haifeng County (Haicheng Town)	海豐縣 (海城鎮)	海丰县 (海城镇)	830,000	810,000	850,000	1,771
Luhe County (Hetian Town)	陸河縣 (河田鎮)	陆河县 (河田镇)	340,000	350,000	350,000	1,005
Huizhou City	惠州市	惠州市	3,380,000	3,410,000	3,810,000	11,159

(continued)

Table 7.5 (continued)

Name	Traditional	Simplified	Population (2012)	Population (2016)	Population (2020)	Area (Sq. Km)
Huicheng District (Longfeng Subdistrict)	惠城區 (龍豐街道)	惠城区 (龙丰街道)	880,000	930,000	1,120,000	1,410
Huiyang District (Danshui Subdistrict)	惠陽區 (淡水街道)	惠阳区 (淡水街道)	460,000	450,000	520,000	1,262
Boluo County (Luoyang Town)	博羅縣 (羅陽鎮)	博罗县 (罗阳镇)	850,000	840,000	920,000	2,795
Huidong County (Pingshan Subdistrict)	惠東縣 (平山街道)	惠东县 (平山街道)	840,000	840,000	890,000	3,397
Longmen County (Longcheng Subdistrict)	龍門縣 (龍城街道)	龙门县 (龙城街道)	350,000	350,000	360,000	2,295
Dongguan City	東莞市	东莞市	1,820,000	1,860,000	2,320,000	2,512
Shenzhen City (subprovincial City)	深圳市	深圳市	2,600,000	2,990,000	4,980,000	2,019.95
Futian District (Shatou Subdistrict)	福田區 (沙頭街道)	福田区 (沙头街道)	660,000	750,000	1,160,000	96
Luohu District (Huangbei Subdistrict)	羅湖區 (黃貝街道)	罗湖区 (黄贝街道)	470,000	520,000	670,000	86
Nanshan District (Nantou Subdistrict)	南山區 (南頭街道)	南山区 (南头街道)	550,000	650,000	1,020,000	193
Bao'an District (Xin'an Subdistrict)	寶安區 (新安街道)	宝安区 (新安街道)	480,000	560,000	640,000	396.69
Longgang District (Longcheng Subdistrict)	龍崗區 (龍城街道)	龙岗区 (龙城街道)	390,000	460,000	850,000	682.58
Yantian District (Haishan Subdistrict)	鹽田區 (海山街道)	盐田区 (海山街道)	50,000	50,000	80,000	67
Longhua District[b] (Guanlan Subdistrict)	龍華區 (觀瀾街道)	龙华区 (观澜街道)	N/A	N/A	380,000	175.58
Pingshan District[b] (Pingshan Subdistrict)	坪山區 (坪山街道)	坪山区 (坪山街道)	N/A	N/A	80,000	167
Guangming District[c] (Guangming Subdistrict)	光明區 (光明街到)	光明区 (光明街道)	N/A	N/A	80,000	156.1
Zhuhai City	珠海市	珠海市	1,050,000	1,060,000	1,270,000	1,696
Xiangzhou District (Meihua Subdistrict)	香洲區 (梅華街道)	香洲区 (梅华街道)	570,000	590,000	720,000	536

(continued)

Table 7.5 (continued)

Name	Traditional	Simplified	Population (2012)	Population (2016)	Population (2020)	Area (Sq. Km)
Doumen District (Jing'an Town)	斗門區 (井岸鎮)	斗门区 (井岸镇)	340,000	340,000	380,000	625
Jinwan District (Sanzao Town)	金灣區 (三竈鎮)	金湾区 (三灶镇)	140,000	130,000	170,000	535
Zhongshan City	中山市	中山市	1,490,000	1,520,000	1,770,000	1,770
Jiangmen City	江門市	江门市	3,930,000	3,910,000	3,990,000	9,554
Pengjiang District (Huanshi Subdistrict)	蓬江區 (環市街道)	蓬江区 (环市街道)	470,000	480,000	510,000	320
Jianghai District (Jiaotou Subdistrict)	江海區 (窖頭街道)	江海区 (滘头街道)	160,000	160,000	170,000	111
Xinhui District (Huicheng Subdistrict)	新會區 (會城街道)	新会区 (会城街道)	750,000	750,000	760,000	1,387
Enping City (Encheng Subdistrict)	恩平市 (恩城街道)	恩平市 (恩城街道)	500,000	500,000	500,000	1,698
Taishan City (Taicheng Subdistrict)	台山市 (台城街道)	台山市 (台城街道)	990,000	980,000	970,000	3,296
Kaiping City (Changsha Subdistrict)	開平市 (長沙街道)	开平市 (长沙街道)	690,000	680,000	690,000	1,659
Heshan City (Shaping Subdistrict)	鶴山市 (沙坪街道)	鹤山市 (沙坪街道)	370,000	360,000	380,000	1,083
Foshan City	佛山市	佛山市	3,700,000	3,790,000	4,370,000	3,875
Chancheng District (Zumiao Subdistrict)	禪城區 (祖廟街道)	禅城区 (祖庙街道)	600,000	610,000	680,000	158
Nanhai District (Guicheng Subdistrict)	南海區 (桂城街道)	南海区 (桂城街道)	1,190,000	1,230,000	1,480,000	1,077
Shunde District (Ronggui Subdistrict)	順德區 (容桂街道)	顺德区 (容桂街道)	1,230,000	1,250,000	1,450,000	806
Sanshui District (Xinan Subdistrict)	三水區 (西南街道)	三水区 (西南街道)	390,000	400,000	440,000	874
Gaoming District (Hecheng Subdistrict)	高明區 (荷城街道)	高明区 (荷城街道)	290,000	300,000	320,000	960
Zhaoqing City	肇慶市	肇庆市	4,220,000	4,270,000	4,500,000	15,006
Duanzhou District (Chengdong Subdistrict)	端州區 (城東街道)	端州区 (城东街道)	360,000	360,000	410,000	152

(continued)

Table 7.5 (continued)

Name	Traditional	Simplified	Population (2012)	Population (2016)	Population (2020)	Area (Sq. Km)
Dinghu District (Kengkou Subdistrict)	鼎湖區 (坑口街道)	鼎湖区 (坑口街道)	150,000	150,000	170,000	512
Gaoyao District (Nan'an Subdistrict)	高要區 (南岸街道)	高要区 (南岸街道)	770,000	790,000	820,000	2,071
Sihui City (Dongcheng Subdistrict)	四會市 (東城街道)	四会市 (东城街道)	440,000	450,000	470,000	1,258
Guangning County (Nanjie Town)	廣寧縣 (南街鎮)	广宁县 (南街镇)	570,000	570,000	590,000	2,459
Huaiji County (Huaicheng Town)	懷集縣 (懷城鎮)	怀集县 (怀城镇)	1,050,000	1,060,000	1,110,000	3,573
Fengkai County (Jiangkou Town)	封開縣 (江口鎮)	封开县 (江口镇)	500,000	510,000	520,000	2,723
Deqing County (Decheng Subdistrict)	德慶縣 (德城街道)	德庆县 (德城街道)	380,000	380,000	410,000	2,258
Yunfu City	雲浮市	云浮市	2,830,000	2,880,000	3,010,000	7,778
Yuncheng District (Yuncheng Subdistrict)	雲城區 (雲城街道)	云城区 (云城街道)	300,000	320,000	340,000	777
Luoding City (Luocheng Subdistrict)	羅定市 (羅城街道)	罗定市 (罗城街道)	1,210,000	1,230,000	1,290,000	2,328
Yun'an District (Ludu Town)	雲安區 (六都鎮)	云安区 (六都镇)	330,000	330,000	340,000	1,185
Xinxing County (Xincheng Town)	新興縣 (新城鎮)	新兴县 (新城镇)	470,000	480,000	490,000	1,522
Yu'nan County (Ducheng Town)	郁南縣 (都城鎮)	郁南县 (都城镇)	520,000	520,000	540,000	1,966
Yangjiang City	陽江市	阳江市	2,820,000	2,820,000	3,000,000	8,006
Jiangcheng District (Nan'en Subdistrict)	江城區 (南恩街道)	江城区 (南恩街道)	680,000	680,000	720,000	666
Yangchun City (Chuncheng Subdistrict)	陽春市 (春城街道)	阳春市 (春城街道)	1,140,000	1,150,000	1,220,000	4,055
Yangxi County (Zhigong Town)	陽西縣 (織簣鎮)	阳西县 (织簣镇)	510,000	510,000	550,000	1,455
Yangdong District (Dongcheng Town)	陽東區 (東城鎮)	阳东区 (东城镇)	490,000	480,000	510,000	1,830
Maoming City	茂名市	茂名市	7,470,000	7,480,000	8,110,000	11,345

(continued)

Table 7.5 (continued)

Name	Traditional	Simplified	Population (2012)	Population (2016)	Population (2020)	Area (Sq. Km)
Maonan District (Zhanqian Subdistrict)	茂南區 (站前街道)	茂南区 (站前街道)	830,000	840,000	890,000	526
Maogang District[a] (Nanhai Subdistrict)	茂港區 (南海街道)	茂港区 (南海街道)	500,000	N/A	N/A	(372)
Huazhou City (Dongshan Subdistrict)	化州市 (東山街道)	化州市 (东山街道)	1,610,000	1,620,000	1,770,000	2,404
Xinyi City (Dongzhen Subdistrict)	信宜市 (東鎮街道)	信宜市 (东镇街道)	1,400,000	1,360,000	1,490,000	3,081
Gaozhou City (Panzhou Subdistrict)	高州市 (潘州街道)	高州市 (潘州街道)	1,700,000	1,690,000	1,830,000	3,389
Dianbai District (Shuidong Town)	電白區 (水東鎮)	电白区 (水东镇)	1,430,000	1,970,000	2,120,000	1,945
Zhanjiang City	湛江市	湛江市	7,780,000	7,850,000	8,480,000	11,692
Chikan District (Nanqiao Subdistrict)	赤坎區 (南橋街道)	赤坎区 (南桥街道)	240,000	240,000	260,000	79
Xiashan District (Gongnong Subdistrict)	霞山區 (工農街道)	霞山区 (工农街道)	390,000	400,000	430,000	129
Potou District (Nantiao Subdistrict)	坡頭區 (南調街道)	坡头区 (南调街道)	390,000	400,000	430,000	562
Mazhang District (Mazhang Town)	麻章區 (麻章鎮)	麻章区 (麻章镇)	510,000	520,000	560,000	878
Wuchuan City (Meilu Subdistrict)	吳川市 (梅菉街道)	吴川市 (梅菉街道)	1,100,000	1,110,000	1,220,000	848
Lianjiang City (Luozhou Subdistrict)	廉江市 (羅州街道)	廉江市 (罗州街道)	1,680,000	1,710,000	1,850,000	2,543
Leizhou City (Leicheng Subdistrict)	雷州市 (雷城街道)	雷州市 (雷城街道)	1,690,000	1,690,000	1,840,000	3,025
Suixi County (Suicheng Town)	遂溪縣 (遂城鎮)	遂溪县 (遂城镇)	1,050,000	1,050,000	1,110,000	2,023
Xuwen County (Xucheng Subdistrict)	徐聞縣 (徐城街道)	徐闻县 (徐城街道)	730,000	730,000	780,000	1,605

[a]Dissolved in February (2014)
[b]Formally established 7 January (2017)
[c]Formally established May (2018)

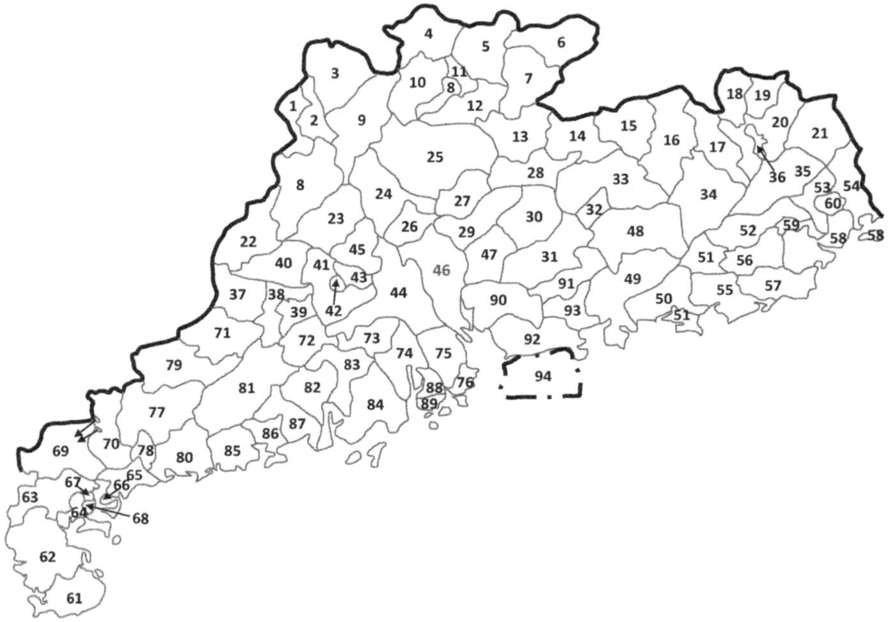

1. Lianshan Zhuang and Yao Autonomous County
2. Liannan Yao Autonomous County
3. Lianzhou City
4. Lechang City
5. Renhua County
6. Nanxiong City
7. Shixing County
8. Wujiang District
9. Yangshan County
10. Ruyuan Yao Autonomous County
11. Zhanjiang District
12. Qujiang District
13. Wengyuan County
14. Lianping County
15. Heping County
16. Longchuan County
17. Xingning City
18. Pingyuan County
19. Jiaoling County
20. Meixian District
21. Dapu County
22. Fengkai County
23. Guangning County
24. Qingxin District
25. Yingde City
26. Qingcheng District
27. Fogang County
28. Xinfeng County
29. Conghua District
30. Longmen County
31. Boluo County
32. Yuancheng District
33. Dongyuan County
34. Wuhua County
35. Fengshun County
36. Meijiang District
37. Yunan County
38. Yun'an District
39. Yuncheng District
40. Deqing County
41. Gaoyao District
42. Duanzhou District
43. Dinghu District
44. Foshan City
45. Sihui City
46. Guangzhou City
47. Zengcheng District
48. Zijin County
49. Huidong County
50. Haifeng County
51. Luhe County
52. Jiexi County
53. Hu'an District
54. Raoping County
55. Lufeng City
56. Puning City
57. Huilai County
58. Shantou City
59. Rongcheng District
60. Chaozhou City
61. Xuwen County
62. Leizhou City
63. Suixi County
64. Mazhang District
65. Wuchuan City
66. Potou District
67. Chikan District
68. Xiashan District
69. Lianjiang City
70. Huazhou City
71. Luoding County
72. Xinxing County
73. Heshan City
74. Jiangmen City
75. Zhongshan City
76. Xiangzhou District
77. Gaozhou City
78. Maonan District
79. Xinyi City
80. Dianbai District
81. Yangchun City
82. Enping City
83. Kaiping City
84. Taishan City
85. Yangxi County
86. Jiangcheng District
87. Yangdong District
88. Doumen District
89. Jinwan District
90. Dongguan City
91. Huicheng District
92. Shenzhen City
93. Huiyang District
94. (Hong Kong)

Fig. 7.2 Guangzhou Province subdistricts (Capital Government Seat: Guangzhou City). Drawn by the Author after People's Republic of China, Ministry of Civil Affairs. (MCA 2020)

References

Benn, Charles. 2002. *China's golden age: Everyday life in the Tang Dynasty*. New York: Oxford University Press.

Brindley, Erica Fox. 2015. *Ancient China and the Yue: Perceptions and identities on the southern frontier, c. 400 BCE – 50 CE*. Cambridge: Cambridge University Press.

China News Net. 2021. *The GDP of 31 provinces in 2020 is released! Anhui's ranking*, 30 January. 31省份2020年GDP出炉!安徽排名. 中国新闻网. 30 January 2021. https://www.sohu.com/a/447712301_391398

Constable, Nicole. 1994. *Christian souls and Chinese spirits: A Hakka community in Hong Kong*. Berkeley: University of California Press.

Cox, Nick. 2021. BYD auto has strong drivers for greatly increased revenues and profits. *Seeking Alpha*. 23 June. https://seekingalpha.com/article/4436264-byd-auto-stock-strong-drivers-for-greatly-increased-revenues-and-profits

Cronin, Vincent. 1984. *The wise man from the West: Matteo Ricci and his mission to China*. San Francisco: Ignatius Press.

Dikötter, Frank, Lars Laamann, and Zhou Xun. 2004. *Narcotic culture: A history of drugs in China*. London: Hurst & Company.

Elvin, Mark. 1973. *The pattern of the Chinese past: A social and economic interpretation*. Stanford: Stanford University Press.

Ferguson, Donald. 1902. *Letters from Portuguese captives in Canton, written in 1534 & 1536*. Bombay: Education Society's Steam Press.

Guangdong Province Statistical Bureau (GPSB). 2021. *Communiqué of the seventh national census of Guangdong Province*, 28 May. 广东省第七次全国人口普查公报. http://stats.gd.gov.cn/dqcrkpc/index.html.

Guldin, Gregory Eliyu. 1994. *The saga of anthropology in China: From Malinowski to Moscow to Mao*. Armonk: M.E. Sharpe.

Hirth, Friedrich. 1885. *China and the Roman orient: Researches into their ancient and mediaeval relations, as represented in old Chinese records*. Hong Kong: Kelly & Walsh.

Hu, Richard. 2021. *The Shenzhen phenomenon: From fishing village to global knowledge city*. New York: Routledge.

Hua, Qiang, and Cai Hongjun. 2007. *China's population loss during the Taiping rebellion*. Beijing: Social Sciences Literature Press. 华强, 蔡宏俊. 太平天国时期中国人口损失问题. 北京: 社会科学文献出版社.

Hunter, William C. 1882. *The 'Fan Kwae' at Canton before treaty days, 1825–1844*. London: Kegan Paul, Trench &.

Juan, Du. 2020. *The Shenzhen experiment: The story of China's Instant City*. Cambridge, MA: Harvard University Press.

Langdon, William B. 1842. *Ten thousand things relating to China and the Chinese; an epitome of the genius, government, history, literature, agriculture, arts, trade, manners, customs, and social life of the people of the celestial empire*. London: Hyde Park Corner.

Lanteigne, Marc. 2005. *China and international institutions: Alternate paths to global power*. New York: Routledge.

Liu, Zunyue. 2015. "Made in Italy" branding in China. PhD dissertation. Università degli Studi di Genova.

Mei, June. 1979. Socioeconomic origins of emigration: Guangdong to California, 1850–1882. *Modern China* 5(4): 463–501.

Min, Zhou. 2009. *Contemporary Chinese America: Immigration, ethnicity, and community transformation*. Philadelphia: Temple University Press.

Ministry of Civil Affairs (MCA). 2020. *People's Republic of China. [County/township administration handbook]*. Beijing: China Statistics Press. 中華人民共和國民政部, 中華人民共和國, 鄉鎮行政區劃簡冊.

People's Government of Guangzhou municipality (PGGM). 2021. *Guangzhou seventh national population census communiqué (no. 6): urban, rural population and floating Population*. 4 July. 广州市第七次全国人口普查公报，第六号. 城乡人口和流动人口情况. http://www.gz.gov.cn/zwgk/sjfb/tjgb/content/post_7286220.html

Ren, Jiyu. 2004. *International Chinese studies*. 10th ed. Zhengzhou: Henan University Press. 任繼愈. 國際漢學. 鄭州:河南教育出版社出.

See, Chong Su. 1919. *The foreign trade of China. Doctoral Dissertation*. New York: Columbia University.

Simoons, Frederick J. 1991. *Food in China: A cultural and historical inquiry*. Ann Arbor: CRC Press.

Snow, Don. 2004. *Cantonese as written language: The growth of a written Chinese vernacular*. Hong Kong: Hong Kong University Press.

Spence, Jonathan D. 1984. *The memory palace of Matteo Ricci*. New York: Elisabeth Sifton Books/Viking.

———. 1996. *God's Chinese son: The Taiping heavenly kingdom of Hong Xiuquan*. New York: W. W. Norton.

Wu, David Y. H., and Harry J. Lamley. 2010. The Hawai'i Chinese: Their experience and identity over two centuries. In *Chinese America: History & Perspectives – The Journal of the Chinese Historical Society of America* (special issue), 1–12.

Yee, Yen Ock. 2007. *Fung Toy*. Detroit Yee Fung Toy Family Association Website. https://detroit-yeefungtoy.weebly.com/fung-toy.html

Zhang, Shunan. 2021. *The 2020 per capita income list of residents in various provinces: Shanghai is the richest, and it has risen sharply*. Finance.people.com. 22 January. 张澍楠. 2020年各省份居民人均收入榜：上海最有钱，这地涨得猛. http://finance.people.com.cn/n1/2021/0122/c1004-32008733.html

Chapter 8
Guangxi Zhuang Autonomous Region

Abstract While its name suggests the province has some sort of autonomy, that is, the Guangxi Zhuang Autonomous Region, it is basically just another province directly ruled from Beijing but having a significant Zhuang ethnic minority population (nearly one-third of its total). Like its neighboring Guangdong Province, going back centuries the Guangxi region had long been considered difficult territory and populated by "southern barbarians." Lush, green, and with picturesque scenery, Guangxi has a history that indeed begins with a modicum of independence from central imperial rule, but, inevitably, became a part of the Qin empire, with more and more Han Chinese occupying this southern region by ca. 210 BCE. In the nineteenth century, Guangxi was heavily impacted by the chaotic and lethal Taiping Rebellion. Later, during Mao's Cultural Revolution, Guangxi's Binyang County was the site of an ugly social outbreak of violence that included human cannibalism. And unlike Guangdong Province, Guangxi is among the poorest of mainland China's provinces and major cities, with a per capita income ranking 25th out of 31 mainland China's provinces and major cities.

E. Croddy, *China's Provinces and Populations*,
https://doi.org/10.1007/978-3-031-09165-0_8

Guangxi Zhuang Autonomous Region (廣西壯族自治區 *guǎngxī zhuàngzú zìzhìqū* (Zhuang Language: *Gvangjsih Bouxcuengh Swcigih*)

Guangxi Provincial Abbreviation 桂 (guì) *(Fig. 8.1)*

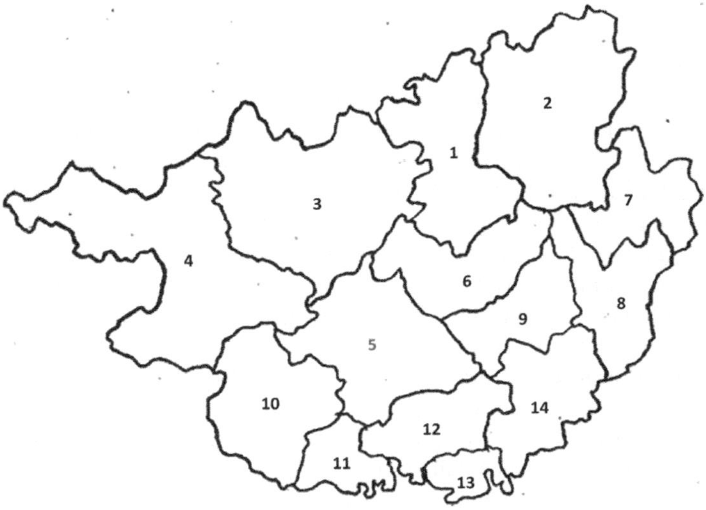

		Population (2020)
1.	Liuzhou City	4,157,934
2.	Guilin City	4,931,137
3.	Hechi City	3,417,945
4.	Baise City	3,571,505
5.	Nanning City	8,741,584
6.	Laibin City	2,074,611
7.	Hezhou City	2,007,858
8.	Wuzhou City	2,820,977
9.	Guigang City	4,316,202
10.	Chongzuo City	2,088,692
11.	Fangchenggang City	1,046,068
12.	Qinzhou City	3,302,238
13.	Beihai City	1,853,227
14.	Yulin City	5,796,766

Fig. 8.1 Guangxi Zhuang Autonomous Region, Major Cities (Provincial Capital: Nanning City). (Map drawn by the Author, after People's Republic of China, Ministry of Civil Affairs, MCA 2020)

Guangxi Province: General Impressions

The character abbreviation for Guangxi is Gui (桂 *guì*), i.e., cassia, or Chinese cinnamon, and this name is the basis for many place names in the province. Guangxi Province is home to some of the most breathtaking scenery in the world, and is especially famous for its picturesque mountain ranges, having been depicted in many classical Chinese paintings throughout the centuries. The capital of Guangxi province, Nanning City (南寧市 *nánníng shì*) is typified by its strikingly green flora. In fact, it has been characterized as "one half greenery, one half buildings." (Shang-Ch'i 2017). It is also home to numerous poisonous snakes, a well-known threat going back to ancient times and which remain a problem today. In the late twentieth century, for example, Pingle County (平樂縣 *pínglè xiàn*; population 450,000) averaged nearly a dozen cases of snake-bite per 100,000 people (Zhao 1993).

As the name of the region indicates, the Guangxi Zhuang Autonomous Region is home to the Zhuang (壯族 *zhuàng zú*) ethnic group, making up about 35% of the population, in addition to many other minority groups. However, as is the case of any of mainland China's "Autonomous" regions, counties, districts, etc., there is no question that ultimate power of decision for the people in these areas is held by the leadership of the Chinese Communist Party in Zhongnanhai, Beijing (Table 8.1).

Table 8.1 Guangxi Ethnic populations (GPBS 2021)

Ethnic Group	Population	Percentage	Locations of major presence in Guangxi Province
Han 漢族 *hànzú*	27,020,000	61%	Southeastern Guangxi
Zhuang 壯族 *zhuàngzú*	15,200,000	35%	Nanning, Liuzhou, Chongzuo, Baise (Bose), Laibin, Hechi, Guigang, Fangchenggang, Qinzhou
Yao 瑶族 *yáozú*	1,470,000	~3%	Liuzhou, Guilin, Hezhou, Baise, Hechi, Laibin; Gongcheng, Jinxiu, Fuchuan, Bama, and Du'an autonomous counties.
Miao 苗族 *miáozú*	460,000	<1%	Rongshui, Longlin, Sanjiang, Ziyuan, Xilin, Longsheng, Nandan
Dong, Kam 侗族 *dòngzú*	300,000	<1%	Sanjiang, Longsheng Rongshui
Mulam 仫佬族 *mùlǎozú*	170,000	<1%	Luocheng, Yizhou, Liucheng
Maonan, Anan; 毛南族 *máonánzú*	74,000	<1%	Huanjiang
Hui (Muslim) 回族 *huízú*	33,000	<1%	Guilin, Liuzhou, Nanning, Baise (Bose); Lingchuan, Luzhai and Yongfu counties
Bouyei 布依族 *bùyīzú*	21,000	<1%	(Wide distribution)
Gin 京族 *jīngzú*	20,000	<1%	Wanweidao; Wutoudao, Shanxindao
Sui 水族 *shuǐzú*	15,000	<1%	Nandan, Yizhou, Rongshui, Huanjiang, Du'an, Xing'an, Hechi City, Jinchengjiang district
Yi, Lolo 彝族 *yízú*	~10,000	<1%	Longllin, Napo, Xilin
Manchu 满族 *mǎnzú*	~9500	<1%	Rongshui, Yizhou, Huanjiang, Nandan

Prehistoric Guangxi

If Yunnan Province holds a place for the oldest known hominid specimen ever found (*Homo erectus Yuanmouensis*, ~1.7 million years), Guangxi is known for having uncovered the oldest known *Homo sapiens* in southern China. So-called "Liujiang Man" was discovered in 1958 by farmers at the Tongtianyan (通天岩 *tōngtiānyán*) cave in Liujiang District (柳江區 *liǔjiāng qū*). (Coward 2013). Liujiang man lived about 68,000 years ago, but may be even older.

Neolithic sites in Guangxi, dating back roughly to 8000–5000 BCE, are exemplified by the Dingsishan Culture (*dǐngsīshān* 頂螄山) found in Yongning District, Pumiao Town (邕寧區蒲廟鎮 *yōngníng qū, púmiào zhèn*). Pottery, cowries, shaped stone tools and complex burial rites were in evidence among these ancient riverine communities. Other remnants of Dengsishan Culture have also been excavated at the Baozitou (豹子頭 *bàozitóu*) site in Nanning City (南寧市 *nánníng shì*), these artifacts dating back to about 8000–7000 BCE. Millenia later, indigenous communities were also producing intricately-carved stone shovels about 4,000 years ago in and around Guangxi province (GTIA 2004).

Dating to about 1000 BCE, evidence of an advanced social structure was found among burial sites in southern Guangxi. An indigenous bronze age culture (ca. 1000 BCE) includes the Yuanlongpo (元龍坡 *yuánlóngpō*) site discovered in 1985, located in Wuming County, Matou Town (武鳴縣馬頭鎮 *wǔmíng xiàn, mǎtóu zhèn*) (von Falkenhausen 1999).

Traditionally, in this region of the so-called Southern Barbarians (南蠻 *nánmán*), the aboriginal people of Guangxi were known as the Baiyue (百越 or 百粵 *bǎiyuè*), or more specifically the Ou Yue (甌越 *ōu yuè*) and Luo Yue (雒越 *luò yuè*), who lived in modern-day Guangxi and northern Vietnam. The Zhuang (壯; also 僮, both pronounced *zhuàng*) minority are believed to have descended from the original Yue (越 *yuè*) peoples going back many centuries.

For much of China's ancient history, the region of the south was governed by the Kingdom of Chu (楚國 *chǔguó*), which, under the rule of King Wei (ca. 330 BCE), occupied a large part of China. According to the histories (史記 *shǐjì*), his contemporary Su Qin (蘇秦 *sū qín*) informed King Wei of the following:

> The Kingdom of Chu is expansive, and under its heavens its King is nonpareil in his sagacity. The Kingdom stretches for more than five thousand miles, from Qianzhong and Wujun [eastern border of Sichuan] to the west, and Xiazhou (Hubei) and Haiyang (Jiangsu) to the east; Dongting and Cangwu (蒼梧 *cāngwú*) Guangxi) to the south, and to the north Xing mountain (Henan) and Huanyang [郇陽 *huányáng*, modern-day Shaanxi Province, Xunyang county 陜西省旬陽縣 *shǎnxī sheng, xúnyáng xiàn*]. With a million soldiers and a thousand chariots, and ten thousand horses, you also have provisions to last ten years. This is where you dominate all others. (Zhao 2015)

Despite its constant attempts to resist Sinicization, the Guangxi region eventually became a significant part of the Chinese empire with its unification under the Qin (ca. 214 BCE). Table 8.2 shows how the area which includes modern-day Guangxi was named and administered over the centuries: 4.8.

Table 8.2 Administrative Regions Governing Guangxi Province over history (Guangxi 2021)

Era/Time period	Names of regions administering modern-day Guangxi
Ca. 2000–402 BCE	Nanman[a]
Warring States 403–221 BCE	Cangwu (under the Chu Kingdom)
Qin Dynasty 221–202 BCE	Guilin and Xiang Prefectures
Han Dynasty (202 BCE) to Three Kingdoms (ca. 265 CE)	Jiaozhi and Yulin Prefectures
Three Kingdoms 220–581	Guangzhou
Sui Dynasty	Lingnan Prefectures
Tang Dynasty 618–902	Lingnan Prefecture
Five Dynasties & Ten Kingdoms 902–960	Nanhan
Song Dynasty 960–1271	Guangnan Xilu
Yuan Dynasty 1271–1368	Huguang Xingsheng
Ming Dynasty 1368–1644	Guangxi Provincial Administration
Qing Dynasty 1644 – Republic of China (1911–1949)	Guangxi Prefecture
People's Republic of China (1949+)	Guangxi Zhuang Autonomous Region

[a]Literally "Southern Barbarians" (南蠻 *nánmán*)

Unified Under Qin (221–206 BCE)

Unified under the Qin, Han Chinese began to arrive in modern-day Guangxi by 214 BCE. At that time it was administered under Xiang (象郡 *xiàng jùn*) and Guilin (桂林郡 *guìlín jùn*) prefectures, the latter forming parts of today's Guizhou province. From the northern Han Chinese perspective, in ca. 100 BCE the "Southern Barbarian" (南蠻 *nánmán*) region was home to a particular ethnic group referred to as the Li (俚 *lǐ*). According to the Record of the Later Han, in then Nanman Chronicles: "In Jiuzhen, Rinan, and Hepu, the latter regions were occupied by the barbarian Li, comprising 65 cities." (Zhang 2002.)[1] These lands included modern-day northern Vietnam, administered by Chinese prefectures, Rinan (日南郡 *rìnán jùn*) and Jiuzhen (九真郡 *jiǔzhēn jùn*), as well as Hepu (合浦郡 *hépǔ jùn*) that formed the southern parts of today's Guangxi and Guangdong provinces. In addition to southeast regions, the Li people were found distributed across the following places in modern Guangxi province during the Three Kingdoms era (三國 *sānguó*; ca. 200 CE):

- Cangwu (蒼梧 *cāngwú*), today's Wuzhou City (梧州市 *wúzhōushì*)
- Yulin (鬱林 *yùlín*), now Guiping City (桂平市 *guìpíngshì*)
- Ningpu (寧浦 *níngpǔ*), modern-day Hengxian county (橫縣 *héngxiàn*), Nanning City (南寧市 *nánníng shì*)

---

[1]"九真, 日南, 合浦蠻里皆應之, 凡略六十五城" *jiǔzhēn, rìnán, hépǔ, mánlǐ jiē yìng zhī, fánluè liùshíwǔ chéng*.

The first appearance of the name "Guangxi" for this geographic area appeared in ca. 1330 during the Yuan dynasty. Officially under the administration of the "Guangxi Two River Circuit Pacification Commission" (廣西兩江道宣慰司 *guǎngxī liǎngjiāngdào xuānwèisī*), this entity governed areas to include modern-day Guangxi province. By 1582, Guangxi province in the Ming dynasty was composed of the following prefectures or administrative areas (*zhou, fu, si*; Table 8.3).

One contemporary observer at this time, the Jesuit Michele Ruggieri, visited Guilin in ca. 1587, reckoning it to have "100,000" hearths, or approximately 500,000 people, if we are to use a base average of 5 persons per household (Laven 2011).

Many of the above administrative entities kept their names and borders throughout the Qing dynasty. While the overall population of China doubled from about 1741–1794 (with an estimated 15% annual growth rate), during this time the population of Guangxi grew from about six million to seven million. This caused the Qianlong emperor to worry about the many hungry mouths to feed in this very poor southern region. By 1851, Guangxi had a population of about 7,800,000, and remained poverty stricken. Exacerbating the issue was an evaluation of silver compared to copper, forcing many of its businesses to go bankrupt. The untold suffering

Table 8.3 Ming Dynasty Guangxi provincial subdistricts, ca. 1582 (Tan 1996)

Anlong Si 安隆司 *ānlóng sī*
Shanglin Si 上林司 *shànglín sī*
Sicheng Zhou 泗城州 *sìchéng zhōu*
Zhen'an Fu 鎮安府 *zhèn'ān fǔ*
Guishun Zhou 歸順州 *guīshùn zhōu*
Qingyuan Fu 慶遠府 *qìngyuǎn fǔ*
Tianzhou 田州 *tiánzhōu*
Fengyi Zhou 奉議州 *fèngyì zhōu*
Xiangwu Zhou 向武州 *xiàngwǔ zhōu*
Liuzhou Fu 柳州府 *liǔzhōu fǔ*
Guilin Fu 桂林府 *guìlín fǔ*
Pingle Fu 平樂府 *pínglè fǔ*
Shuwu Fu 屬梧府 *shǔwú fǔ*
Wuzhou Fu 梧州府 *wúzhōu fǔ*
Xunzhou Fu 潯州府 *xúnzhōu fǔ*
Si'en Fu 思恩府 *sī'ēn fǔ*
Nanning Fu 南寧府 *nánníng fǔ*
Taiping Fu 太平府 *tàipíng fǔ*
Siming Fu 思明府 *sīmíng fǔ*
Longzhou 龍州 *lóngzhōu*
Pingxiang Fu 憑祥府 *píngxiáng fǔ*
Siling Zhou 思陵州 *sīlíng zhōu*
Shu'nanning Fu 屬南寧府 *shǔ'nánníng fǔ*

among the people in Guangxi drove many to join the Sanhehui (三合會 *sānhéhuì*) Triad, and motivated them to participate in a rebellion against the Qing government. Already by fall 1850, the leader of the Taiping Heavenly Kingdom, Hong Xiuquan (洪秀全 *hóng xiùquán*), had shored up his base of operations in Jintian (金田), Guiping City (桂平市 *guìpíng shì*) in the larger Guigang City (貴港市 *guìgǎng shì*) area. On September 25, 1851, following skirmishes with Qing military forces, Hong Xiuquan's forces captured the walled city of Yong'an (now Yong'an Township 永安鄉 *yǒng'ān xiāng*). The Taiping Rebellion would go on to cause the death of tens of millions over the next 13 years.

Republican China

From the mid-1920s, Guangxi was essentially ruled by a military junta during China's difficult transition from empire to Republic of China (ROC; 中華民國 *zhōnghuá mínguó*). Under the leadership of the very capable Li Zongren (李宗仁 *Lǐ Zōngrén*), Bai Chongxi (白崇禧 *bái chóngxī*), and Huang Shaohong (黃紹竑 *huáng shàohóng*), in early 1924 the "United Guangxi Army for Bandit Pacification in the Gui (region)" (廣西定桂討賊聯軍 *guǎngxī dìngguì tǎozéi liánjūn*) was formed. By 1944, Guangxi province had enlisted some one million men to fight the Japanese Imperial Army, ranking among the highest per capita in terms of military participation among China's provinces. Li Zongren remained *de facto* ruler of Guangxi until the end of World War II. By this time, however, the leader of the ROC nationalists Chiang Kai-shek, had essentially cashiered Li Zongren, appointing him to a ceremonial post in charge of northern-most provinces (e.g., Hebei) and cities (e.g., Beiping, Tianjin).

It is important here to note that, throughout China's history, the largest ethnic minority, the Zhuang people, were often marginalized and constantly pushed ever further into Guangxi's inhospitable hinterland. In the 1920s, having been alienated by the predatory Han Chinese, the Zhuang formed an alliance with the early Chinese Communist Party uprisings led by Deng Xiaoping (Becker 2000). After occupying Guangxi in December 1949, the CCP reestablished Guangxi province, incorporating within it some of Guangdong-subordinate Qinzhou City (欽州市 *qīnzhōu shì*) and Lianzhou (廉州 *liánzhōu*), while making Huaiji County (懷集縣 *huáijí xiàn*) part of Guangdong.

On 5 March 1958, the People's Republic of China (PRC) formally designated the province as the Guangxi Zhuang Autonomous Region (廣西僮族自治區 *guǎngxī zhuàngzú zìzhìqū*), later changing to the Guangxi Zhuang Autonomous Region (廣西壯族自治區 *guǎngxī zhuàngzú zìzhìqū*) in 1965.

Guangxi, the Cultural Revolution, and Cannibalism

The novelist Zheng Yi, having fled China after the persecution of students and demonstrators after Tiananmen (4 June 1989), later revealed to the west that Guangxi experienced horrific violence during the Cultural Revolution (1966–1976). This resulted in a massive social spasm that included over 100,000 politically-motivated deaths. In one example, Binyang County (賓陽縣 *bīnyáng xiàn*), Zheng Yi recounts that in late July 1968,

> Throughout the entire county, 3681 people were beaten or persecuted to death. Among them, fifty-one were state-level cadres, 27 state workers, 75 workers in collective units, 87 teachers, and 3441 were either peasants or township residents…. One hundred seventy families suffered the loss of a spouse and children. Fourteen families were totally wiped out. (Zheng 1996)

One particularly egregious episode of mass social unrest occurred during the Cultural Revolution (CR) in Guangxi's Shanglin County, Sanli District (上林縣三里區 *shànglínxiàn, sānlǐqū*). During these the heady days of the CR, a large group exhorted to agitate against a "handful of class enemies" on 17 August 1968. After some ten thousand people gathered there, an orgy of violence followed, leading to the beating deaths of 167 people. Noteworthy amidst the political violence was the practice of cannibalism in Guangxi during this time, involving thousands of people eating hundreds of their "class enemy" victims. While cannibalism had been an ancient tradition among the Zhuang ethnic minority, the proximal inspiration for this horrific practice during the CR was the hate-filled atmosphere sparked by Mao Zedong and his allies in Beijing. This barbarous activity was further fueled by resentment of average citizens towards lower-level CCP cadres (Zheng 1996).

Modern Guangxi Populations and Economy

In contrast to the more developed and prosperous provinces such as neighboring Guangdong, Guangxi has *more* permanently registered (戶口 *hùkǒu*) population on paper (e.g., 49,367,000 in 2010) than the total resident (常住 *chángzhù*) population (46,023,000). This is on account of China's "floating populations" (流動人口 *liúdòng rénkǒu*), temporary emigrants from Guangxi (about 4,185,000) that spend significant periods of their lives in other parts of China for work, study, etc. (Qiao and Yanchun 2013). In 2020, according to provincial statistics, Guangxi had a total (including nonpermanent) population of 50,126,800, and a permanent registered *hukou* population of 56,590,000.

The economic incentive to leave Guangxi for other opportunities in other Chinese provinces and cities are reflected in the relatively low per capita income (ranked 25th out of 31 and major cities) of USD $3820 (2020) (Zhang 2021). Nonetheless, based on the recent census, the residential population of Guangxi increased about 9% from 2010 to 2020 (Fig. 8.2 and Tables 8.4, 8.5).

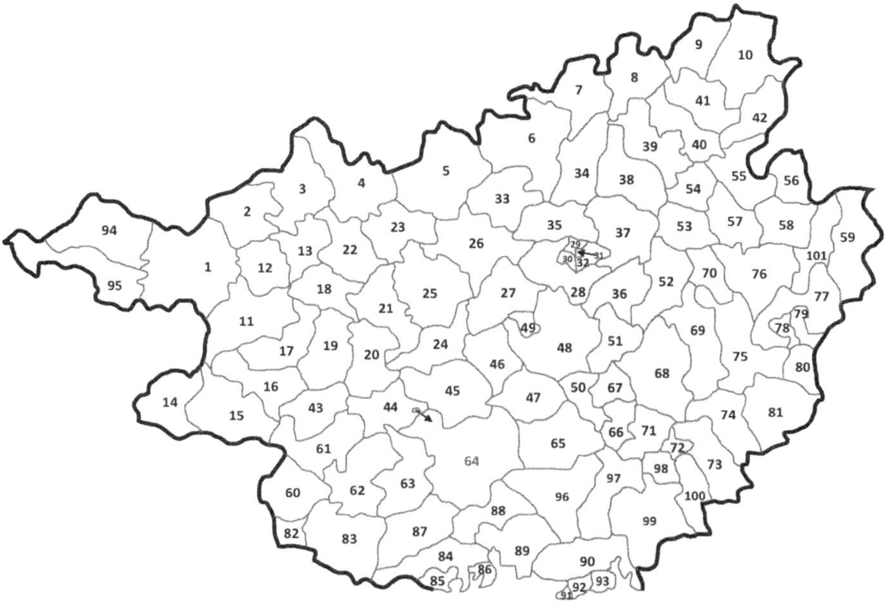

1. Tianlin County
2. Leye County
3. Tian'e County
4. Nandan County
5. Huanjiang Maonan Autonomous County
6. Rongshui Miao Autonomous County
7. Sanjiang Dong Autonomous County
8. Longsheng Gezu (Various Ethnic Groups) Autonomous County
9. Ziyuan County
10. Quanzhou County
11. Youjiang District
12. Lingyun County
13. Fengshan County
14. Napo County
15. Jingxi County
16. Debao County
17. Tianyang District
18. Bama Yao Autonomous County
19. Tiandong County
20. Pingguo City
21. Dahua Yao Autonomous County
22. Donglan County
23. Jinchengjiang District
24. Mashan County
25. Du'an Yao Autonomous County
26. Yizhou District
27. Xincheng County
28. Liujiang District
29. Liubei District
30. Liunan District
31. Chengzhong District
32. Yufeng District
33. Luocheng Mulao Autonomous County
34. Rong'an County
35. Liucheng County
36. Xiangzhou County
37. Luzhai County
38. Yongfu County
39. Lingui District
40. Lingchuan County
41. Xing'an County
42. Guanyang County
43. Tiandeng County
44. Long'an County
45. Wuming County
46. Shanglin County
47. Binyang County
48. Xingbin District
49. Heshan City
50. Qintang District
51. Wuxuan County
52. Jinxiu Yao Autonomous County
53. Lipu City
54. Yangshuo County
55. Gongcheng Yao Autonomous County
56. Fuchuan Yao Autonomous County
57. Pingle Count y
58. Zhongshan County
59. Babu District
60. Longzhou County
61. Daxin County
62. Jiangzhou District
63. Fusui County
64. Nanning City
65. Hengxian County
66. Gangnan District
67. Gangbei District
68. Guiping City
69. Pingnan County
70. Mengshan County
71. Xingye County
72. Yulin City
73. Beiliu City
74. Rongxian County
75. Tengxian County
76. Zhaoping County
77. Cangwu County
78. Changzhou District
79. Wanxiu District
80. Longxu District
81. Cenxi City
82. Pingxiang City
83. Jingxi City
84. Fangcheng District
85. Dongxing City
86. Gangkou District
87. Shangsi County
88. Qinbei District
89. Qinnan District
90. Hepu County
91. Haicheng District
92. Yinhai District
93. Qinshangang District
94. Longlin Various Ethnic Minorities Autonomous County
95. Xilin County
96. Lingshan County
97. Pubei County
98. Fumian District
99. Bobai County
100. Luchuan County
101. Pinggui County

Fig. 8.2 Guangxi province subdistricts (Capital Government Seat: Nanning City). (Map drawn by the Author, after People's Republic of China, Ministry of Civil Affairs, MCA 2020)

Table 8.4 Guangxi province (residential 常住人口 *chángzhù rénkǒu*) population (Yangguang Net 2021)

City	Name in Zhuang Dialect	Population (2010)	Population (2020)
Baise (Bose) City 百色市 *bǎisè shì*	*Baksaek Si*	3,466,800	3,571,505
Hechi City 河池市 *héchí shì*	*Hozciz Si*	3,369,200	3,417,945
Liuzhou City 柳州市 *liǔzhōu shì*	*Liujcouh Si*	3,758,700	4,157,934
Guilin City 桂林市 *guìlín shì*	*Gveilinz Si*	4,748,000	4,931,137
Hezhou City 賀州市 *hèzhōu shì*	*Hohcouh Si*	1,954,100	2,007,858
Chongzuo City 崇左市 *chóngzuǒ shì*	*Cungzcoj Si*	1,994,300	2,088,692
Nanning City 南寧市 *nánníng shì* [abbrev. 邕 *yōng*]	*Namzningz Si*	6,661,600	8,741,584
Laibin City 來賓市 *láibīn shì*	*Leizbingz Si*	2,099,700	2,074,611
Guigang City 貴港市 *guìgǎng shì*	*Gveigangj Si*	4,118,800	4,316,202
Wuzhou City 梧州市 *wúzhōu shì*	*Ngouzcouh Si*	2,882,200	2,820,977
Fangchenggang City 防城港市 *fángchénggǎng shì*	*Fangzcwngzgangj Si*	866,900	1,046,068
Qinzhou City 欽州市 *qīnzhōu shì*	*Ginhcouh Si*	3,079,700	3,302,238
Beihai City 北海市 *běihǎi shì*	*Baekhaij Si*	1,539,300	1,853,227
Yulin City 玉林市 *yùlín shì*	*Yoglinz Si*	5,487,400	5,796,766
Total		**46,026,600**	**50,126,804**

Table 8.5 Guangxi province: population data of cities and their subordinate sectors (GPBS 2021)

Cities and subordinate sectors, population (2020 census)	Subordinate district, city and county populations (2020)	Total population (2020)
Baise (Bose) City 百色市 ***bǎisè shì***		**3,571,505**
Youjiang District 右江區 *yòujiāng qū*	472,086	
Tianyang District 田陽區 *tiányáng qū*	308,785	
Tiandong County 田東縣 *tiándōng xiàn*	352,007	
Pingguo City 平果市 *píngguǒ shì*	455,643	
Debao County 德保縣 *débǎo xiàn*	269,758	
Jingxi City 靖西市 *jìngxī shì*	489,163	
Napo County 那坡縣 *nàpō xiàn*	171,781	
Lingyun County 淩雲縣 *língyún xiàn*	188,194	
Leye County 樂業縣 *lèyè xiàn*	146,397	
Xilin County 西林縣 *xīlín xiàn*	142,098	
Tianlin County 田林縣 *tiánlín xiàn*	244,828	
Longlin Gezu (various ethnic minorities) Autonomous County 隆林各族自治縣 *lónglín gèzú zìzhìxiàn*	350,765	
Hechi City 河池市 ***héchí shì***		**3,417,945**
Jinchengjiang District 金城江區 *jīnchéngjiāng qū*	372,251	
Yizhou City 宜州市 *yízhōu shì*	549,359	
Nandan County 南丹縣 *nándān xiàn*	275,554	

(continued)

Table 8.5 (continued)

Cities and subordinate sectors, population (2020 census)	Subordinate district, city and county populations (2020)	Total population (2020)
Tian'e County 天峨縣 *tiān'é xiàn*	143,155	
Fengshan County 鳳山縣 *fèngshān xiàn*	169,845	
Donglan County 東蘭縣 *dōnglán xiàn*	219,549	
Bama Yaozu (Yao) Autonomous County 巴馬瑤族自治縣 *bāmǎ yáozúzìzhì xiàn*	236,152	
Du'an Yaozu (Yao) Autonomous County 都安瑤族自治縣 *dū'ān yáozú zìzhìxiàn*	538,061	
Dahua Yaozu (Yao) Autonomous County 大化瑤族自治縣 *dàhuà yáozú zìzhìxiàn*	365,001	
Luocheng Mulaozu (Mulao) Autonomous County 羅城仫佬族自治縣 *luóchéng mùlǎozú zìzhìxiàn*	272,672	
Huanjiang Maonanzu (Maonan) Autonomous County 環江毛南族自治縣 *huánjiāng máonánzú zìzhìxiàn*	276,076	
Liuzhou City 柳州市 ***liǔzhōu shì***		**4,157,934**
Liubei District 柳北區 *liǔběi qū*	484,765	
Chengzhong District 城中區 *chéngzhōng qū*	243,638	
Yufeng District 魚峰區 *yúfēng qū*	668,961	
Liunan District 柳南區 *liǔnán qū*	617,925	
Liujiang District 柳江區 *liǔjiāng qū*	503,772	
Liucheng County 柳城縣 *liǔchéng xiàn*	314,242	
Luzhai County 鹿寨縣 *lùzhài xiàn*	337,298	
Rong'an County 融安縣 *róngān xiàn*	253,360	
Sanjiang Dongzu (Dong) Autonomous County 三江侗族自治縣 *sānjiāng dòngzú zìzhìxiàn*	321,538	
Rongshui Miaozu (Miao) Autonomous County 融水苗族自治縣 *róngshuǐ miáozú zìzhìxiàn*	412,455	
Guilin City 桂林市 ***guìlín shì***		**4,931,137**
Xiangshan District 象山區 *xiàngshān qū*	286,872	
Diecai District 疊彩區 *diécǎi qū*	202,875	
Xiufeng District 秀峰區 *xiùfēng qū*	161,066	
Qixing District 七星區 *qīxīng qū*	387,304	
Yanshan District 雁山區 *yànshān qū*	132,639	
Yangshuo County 陽朔縣 *yángshuò xiàn*	273,124	
Lingui County 臨桂縣 *língui xiàn*	555,109	
Lingchuan County 靈川縣 *língchuān xiàn*	472,776	
Quanzhou County 全州縣 *quánzhōu xiàn*	565,696	
Xing'an County 興安縣 *xīng'ān xiàn*	307,043	
Yongfu County 永福縣 *yǒngfú xiàn*	228,646	
Guanyang County 灌陽縣 *guànyáng xiàn*	208,412	
Ziyuan County 資源縣 *zīyuán xiàn*	139,212	

(continued)

Table 8.5 (continued)

Cities and subordinate sectors, population (2020 census)	Subordinate district, city and county populations (2020)	Total population (2020)
Pingle County 平樂縣 *pínglè xiàn*	340,921	
Lipu City 荔浦市 *lìpǔ shì*	334,527	
Longsheng Gezu (Various national minorities) Autonomous County 龍勝各族自治縣 *lóngshèng gèzú zìzhìxiàn*	139,483	
Gongcheng Yaozu (Yao) Autonomous County 恭城瑤族自治縣 *gōngchéng yáozú zìzhìxiàn*	245,532	
Hezhou City 賀州市 ***hèzhōu shì***		**2,007,858**
Babu District 八步區 *bābù qū*	655,994	
Pinggui District 平桂區 *píngguì qū*	404,161	
Zhaoping County 昭平縣 *zhāopíng xiàn*	330,116	
Zhongshan County 鐘山縣 *zhōngshān xiàn*	351,057	
Fuchuan Yaozu (Yao) Autonomous County 富川瑤族自治縣 *fùchuān yáozú zìzhìxiàn*	266,530	
Chongzuo City 崇左市 ***chóngzuǒ shì***		**2,088,692**
Jiangzhou District 江州區 *jiāngzhōu qū*	435,438	
Pingxiang City 憑祥市 *píngxiáng shì*	129,843	
Fusui County 扶綏縣 *fúsuí xiàn*	408,921	
Daxin County 大新縣 *dàxīn xiàn*	282,563	
Tiandeng County 天等縣 *tiānděng xiàn*	280,473	
Ningming County 寧明縣 *níngmíng xiàn*	319,386	
Longzhou County 龍州縣 *lóngzhōu xiàn*	232,068	
Nanning City 南寧市 ***nánníng shì*** **[abbrev. 邕 *yōng*]**		**8,741,584**
Qingxiu District 青秀區 *qīngxiù qū*	1,124,334	
Xingning District 興寧區 *xīngníng qū*	615,486	
Jiangnan District 江南區 *jiāngnán qū*	989,823	
Xixiangtang District 西鄉塘區 *xīxiāngtáng qū*	1,643,819	
Liangqing District 良慶區 *liángqìng qū*	587,618	
Yongning District 邕寧區 *yōngníng qū*	332,280	
Wuming District 武鳴區 *wǔmíng qū*	683,826	
Hengxian County 橫縣 *héngxiàn*	896,099	
Binyang County 賓陽縣 *bīnyáng xiàn*	801,407	
Shanglin County 上林縣 *shànglín xiàn*	359,323	
Long'an County 隆安縣 *lóng'ān xiàn*	325,140	
Mashan County 馬山縣 *mǎshān xiàn*	382,430	
Laibin City 來賓市 ***láibīn shì***		**2,074,611**
Xingbin District 興賓區 *xīngbīn qū*	925,377	
Heshan City 合山市 *héshān shì*	98,938	
Xiangzhou County 象州縣 *xiàngzhōu xiàn*	281,846	
Wuxuan County 武宣縣 *wǔxuān xiàn*	340,312	

(continued)

Table 8.5 (continued)

Cities and subordinate sectors, population (2020 census)	Subordinate district, city and county populations (2020)	Total population (2020)
Xincheng County 忻城縣 *xīnchéng xiàn*	297,825	
Jinxiu Yaozu (Yao) Autonomous County 金秀瑤族自治縣 *jīnxiù yáozú zìzhìxiàn*	130,313	
Guigang City 貴港市 ***guìgǎng shì***		**4,316,262**
Gangbei District 港北區 *gǎngběi qū*	760,633	
Gangnan District 港南區 *gǎngnán qū*	516,598	
Qintang District 覃塘區 *tántáng qū*	423,747	
Guiping City 桂平市 *guìpíng shì*	1,511,011	
Pingnan County 平南縣 *píngnán xiàn*	1,104,273	
Wuzhou City 梧州市 ***wúzhōu shì***		**2,820,977**
Changzhou District 長洲區 *chángzhōu qū*	299,344	
Wanxiu District 萬秀區 *wànxiù qū*	271,989	
Longxu District 龍墟區 *lóngxū qū*	288,482	
Cenxi City 岑溪市 *cénxī shì*	724,364	
Cangwu County 蒼梧縣 *cāngwú xiàn*	276,766	
Tengxian County 藤縣 *téngxiàn*	795,612	
Mengshan County 蒙山縣 *mēngshān xiàn*	164,420	
Fangchenggang City 防城港市 ***fángchénggǎng shì***		**1,046,068**
Gangkou District 港口區 *gǎngkǒu qū*	244,280	
Fangcheng District 防城區 *fángchéng qū*	390,961	
Dongxing City 東興市 *dōngxīng shì*	216,053	
Shangsi County 上思縣 *shàngsī xiàn*	194,774	
Qinzhou City 欽州市 ***qīnzhōu shì***		**3,302,238**
Qinnan District 欽南區 *qīnnán qū*	679,692	
Qinbei District 欽北區 *qīnběi qū*	720,442	
Lingshan County 靈山縣 *língshān xiàn*	1,218,140	
Pubei County 浦北縣 *pǔběi xiàn*	683,964	
Beihai City 北海市 ***běihǎi shì***		**1,853,227**
Haicheng District 海城區 *hǎichéng qū*	527,895	
Yinhai District 銀海區 *yínhǎi qū*	315,196	
Tieshangang District 鐵山港區 *tiěshāngǎng qū*	145,943	
Hepu County 合浦縣 *hépǔ xiàn*	864,193	
Yulin City 玉林市 ***yùlín shì***		**5,796,766**
Yuzhou District 玉州區 *yùzhōu qū*	908,121	
Fumian District 福綿區 *fúmián qū*	318,709	
Beiliu City 北流市 *běiliú shì*	1,211,637	
Xingye County 興業縣 *xīngyè xiàn*	508,344	
Rongxian County 容縣 *róngxiàn*	654,916	
Luchuan County 陸川縣 *lùchuān xiàn*	804,427	
Bobai County 博白縣 *bóbái xiàn*	1,390,612	

Table 8.6 (below) shows the *hukou* (family registered) populations based on PRC Ministry of Civil Affairs data. (Districts listed directly under major cities are government seats, as are those in parentheses). One can compare these data with the census (usual residential populations based on 2010 and 2020 censuses in Tables 8.4 and 8.5 (above):

Guangxi Zhuang Autonomous Region (桂)

Provincial Capital: Nanning

Table 8.6 Guangxi: permanent registered (戶籍人口 *hùjí rénkǒu*) populations (MCA 2020)

Name	Traditional	Simplified	Population (2012)	Population (2016)	Population (2020)	Area (km²)
Guangxi Zhuang Autonomous Region	廣西壯族自治區	广西壮族自治区	53,310,000	53,780,000	56,590,000	237,438
Nanning City	南寧市	南宁市	7,070,000	7,140,000	7,710,000	22,341
Qingxiu District (Changtang Town)	青秀區 (長塘鎮)	青秀区 (长塘镇)	610,000	630,000	770,000	872
Xingning District (Xingdong Subdistrict)	興寧區 (興東街道)	兴宁区 (兴东街道)	300,000	300,000	350,000	751
Jiangnan District (Jiangnan Subdistrict)	江南區 (江南街道)	江南区 (江南街道)	450,000	460,000	540,000	1154
Xixiangtang District (Hengyang Subdistrict)	西鄉塘區 (衡陽街道)	西乡塘区 (衡阳街道)	770,000	760,000	810,000	1298
Liangqing District (Dashatian Subdistrict)	良慶區 (大沙田街道)	良庆区 (大沙田街道)	240,000	250,000	310,000	1379
Yongning District (Pumiao Town)	邕寧區 (蒲廟鎮)	邕宁区 (蒲庙镇)	340,000	350,000	370,000	1255
Wuming District (Chengxiang Town)	武鳴區 (城廂鎮)	武鸣区 (城厢镇)	680,000	690,000	720,000	3378
Hengxian County (Hengzhou Town)	橫縣 (橫州鎮)	横县 (横州镇)	1,200,000	1,210,000	1,270,000	3464
Binyang County (Binzhou Town)	賓陽縣 (賓州鎮)	宾阳县 (宾州镇)	1,050,000	1,040,000	1,060,000	2299
Shanglin County (Dafeng Town)	上林縣 (大豐鎮)	上林县 (大丰镇)	490,000	490,000	500,000	1869
Long'an County (Chengxiang Town)	隆安縣 (城廂鎮)	隆安县 (城厢镇)	400,000	410,000	420,000	2277
Mashan County (Baishan Town)	馬山縣 (白山鎮)	马山县 (白山镇)	540,000	550,000	580,000	2345
Guilin City	桂林市	桂林市	5,190,000	5,220,000	5,380,000	27,809

(continued)

Table 8.6 (continued)

Name	Traditional	Simplified	Population (2012)	Population (2016)	Population (2020)	Area (km^2)
Xiangshan District (Nanmen Subdistrict)	象山區 (南門街道)	象山区 (南门街道)	230,000	240,000	240,000	88
Diecai District (Beimen Subdistrict)	疊彩區 (北門街道)	叠彩区 (北门街道)	140,000	140,000	150,000	52
Xiufeng District (Lijun Subdistrict)	秀峰區 (麗君街道)	秀峰区 (丽君街道)	110,000	110,000	110,000	54
Qixing District (Lidong Subdistrict)	七星區 (漓東街道)	七星区 (漓东街道)	200,000	200,000	220,000	83
Yanshan District (Yanshan Town)	雁山區 (雁山鎮)	雁山区 (雁山镇)	80,000	70,000	70,000	288
Yangshuo County (Yangshuo Town)	陽朔縣 (陽朔鎮)	阳朔县 (阳朔镇)	310,000	320,000	330,000	1428
Lingui County (Lingui Town)	臨桂縣 (臨桂鎮)	临桂区 (临桂镇)	490,000	490,000	520,000	2202
Lingchuan County (Lingchuan Town)	靈川縣 (靈川鎮)	灵川县 (灵川镇)	380,000	380,000	390,000	2287
Quanzhou County (Quanzhou Town)	全州縣 (全州鎮)	全州县 (全州镇)	820,000	830,000	850,000	4021
Xing'an County (Xing'an Town)	興安縣 (興安鎮)	兴安县 (兴安镇)	380,000	380,000	390,000	2344
Yongfu County (Yongfu Town)	永福縣 (永福鎮)	永福县 (永福镇)	280,000	280,000	290,000	2806
Guanyang County (Guanyang Town)	灌陽縣 (灌陽鎮)	灌阳县 (灌阳镇)	290,000	290,000	300,000	1837
Ziyuan County (Ziyuan Town)	資源縣 (資源鎮)	资源县 (资源镇)	170,000	180,000	180,000	1954
Pingle County (Pingle Town)	平樂縣 (平樂鎮)	平乐县 (平乐镇)	450,000	450,000	460,000	1919
Lipu County (Licheng Town)	荔浦縣 (荔城鎮)	荔浦县 (荔城镇)	380,000	380,000	N/A	1759
Lipu City[a] (Licheng Town)	荔浦市 (荔城鎮)	荔浦市 (荔城镇)	N/A	N/A	380,000	1759
Longsheng Gezu (Various national minorities) Autonomous County (Longsheng Town)	龍勝各族自治縣 (龍勝鎮)	龙胜各族自治县 (龙胜镇)	180,000	180,000	170,000	2538
Gongcheng Yaozu (Yao) Autonomous County (Gongcheng Town)	恭城瑤族自治縣 (恭城鎮)	恭城瑶族自治县 (恭城镇)	300,000	300,000	300,000	2149
Liuzhou City	柳州市	柳州市	3,730,000	3,720,000	3,900,000	18,652
Liubei District (Que'ershan Subdistrict)	柳北區 (雀兒山街道)	柳北区 (雀儿山街道)	340,000	340,000	350,000	302

(continued)

Table 8.6 (continued)

Name	Traditional	Simplified	Population (2012)	Population (2016)	Population (2020)	Area (km^2)
Chengzhong District (Chengzhong Subdistrict)	城中區 (城中街道)	城中区 (城中街道)	130,000	140,000	170,000	78
Yufeng District (Qilin Subdistrict)	魚峰區 (麒麟街道)	鱼峰区 (麒麟街道)	230,000	330,000	410,000	473
Liunan District (Tanxi Subdistrict)	柳南區 (潭西街道)	柳南区 (潭西街道)	340,000	340,000	360,000	164
Liujiang District (Labao Town)	柳江區 (拉堡鎮)	柳江區 (拉堡镇)	560,000	550,000	530,000	2538
Liucheng County (Dapu Town)	柳城縣 (大埔鎮)	柳城县 (大埔镇)	410,000	410,000	410,000	2114
Luzhai County (Luzhai Town)	鹿寨縣 (鹿寨鎮)	鹿寨县 (鹿寨镇)	500,000	410,000	410,000	2960
Rong'an County (Chang'an Town)	融安縣 (長安鎮)	融安县 (长安镇)	330,000	320,000	330,000	2905
Sanjiang Dongzu (Dong) Autonomous County (Guyi Town)	三江侗族自治縣 (古宜鎮)	三江侗族自治县 (古宜镇)	380,000	380,000	400,000	2454
Rongshui Miaozu (Miao) Autonomous County (Rongshui Town)	融水苗族自治縣 (融水鎮)	融水苗族自治县 (融水镇)	510,000	500,000	520,000	4664
Wuzhou City	梧州市	梧州市	3,260,000	3,290,000	3,520,000	12,582
Changzhou District (Datang Subdistrict)	長洲區 (大塘街道)	长洲区 (大塘街道)	150,000	160,000	190,000	378
Wanxiu District (Chengnan Subdistrict)	萬秀區 (城南街道)	万秀区 (城南街道)	160,000	320,000	300,000	439
Longxu District[b] (Longxu Town)	龍墟區 (龍圩鎮)	龙圩区 (龙圩镇)	N/A	270,000	310,000	971
Dieshan District (Jiaozui Subdistrict)	蝶山區 (角嘴街道)	蝶山区 (角嘴街道)	200,000	N/A	N/A	313
Cenxi City (Cencheng Town)	岑溪市 (岑城鎮)	岑溪市 (岑城镇)	900,000	920,000	970,000	2783
Cangwu County (Shiqiao Town)	蒼梧縣 (石橋鎮)	苍梧县 (石桥镇)	600,000	360,000	410,000	2784
Tengxian County (Tengzhou Town)	藤縣 (藤州鎮)	藤县 (藤州镇)	1,030,000	1,040,000	1,120,000	3946

(continued)

Table 8.6 (continued)

Name	Traditional	Simplified	Population (2012)	Population (2016)	Population (2020)	Area (km²)
Mengshan County (Mengshan Town)	蒙山縣 (蒙山鎮)	蒙山县 (蒙山镇)	220,000	220,000	220,000	1281
Guigang City	貴港市	贵港市	5,240,000	5,300,000	5,610,000	10,596
Gangbei District (Guicheng Subdistrict)	港北區 (貴城街道)	港北区 (贵城街道)	660,000	660,000	720,000	806
Gangnan District (Jiangnan Subdistrict)	港南區 (江南街道)	港南区 (江南街道)	670,000	670,000	700,000	1225
Qintang District (Qintang Town)	覃塘區 (覃塘鎮)	覃塘区 (覃塘镇)	570,000	580,000	610,000	1502
Guiping City (Xishan Town)	桂平市 (西山鎮)	桂平市 (西山镇)	1,880,000	1,920,000	2,030,000	4074
Pingnan County (Pingnan Town)	平南縣 (平南鎮)	平南县 (平南镇)	1,460,000	1,470,000	1,540,000	2989
Yulin City	玉林市	玉林市	6,740,000	7,140,000	7,330,000	12,839
Yuzhou District (Yucheng Subdistrict)	玉州區 (玉城街道)	玉州区 (玉城街道)	1,010,000	740,000	700,000	464
Fumian District[c] (Fumian Town)	福綿區 (福綿鎮)	福绵区 (福绵镇)	N/A	530,000	440,000	787
Beiliu City (Lingcheng Subdistrict)	北流市 (陵城街道)	北流市 (陵城街道)	1,370,000	1,430,000	1,540,000	2457
Xingye County (Shinan Town)	興業縣 (石南鎮)	兴业县 (石南镇)	750,000	750,000	760,000	1487
Rongxian County (Rongzhou Town)	容縣 (容州鎮)	容县 (容州镇)	810,000	830,000	870,000	2257
Luchuan County (Wenquan Town)	陸川縣 (溫泉鎮)	陆川县 (温泉镇)	1,040,000	1,070,000	1,110,000	1551
Bobai County (Bobai Town)	博白縣 (博白鎮)	博白县 (博白镇)	1,760,000	1,790,000	1,900,000	3836
Qinzhou City	欽州市	钦州市	3,870,000	3,910,000	4,150,000	10,783
Qinnan District (Shuidong Subdistrict)	欽南區 (水東街道)	钦南区 (水东街道)	650,000	600,000	650,000	2517
Qinbei District (Changtian Subdistrict)	欽北區 (長田街道)	钦北区 (长田街道)	750,000	810,000	870,000	2195
Lingshan County (Lingcheng Town)	靈山縣 (靈城街道)	灵山县 (灵城街道)	1,560,000	1,580,000	1,680,000	3550
Pubei County (Xiaojiang Subdistrict)	浦北縣 (小江街道)	浦北县 (小江街道)	910,000	920,000	950,000	2521
Beihai City	北海市	北海市	1,660,000	1,680,000	1,780,000	3337

(continued)

Table 8.6 (continued)

Name	Traditional	Simplified	Population (2012)	Population (2016)	Population (2020)	Area (km²)
Haicheng District (Zhongjie Subdistrict)	海城區 (中街街道)	海城区 (中街街道)	290,000	290,000	320,000	140
Yinhai District (Yintan Town)	銀海區 (銀灘鎮)	银海区 (银滩镇)	150,000	150,000	180,000	423
Tieshangang District (Nankang Town)	鐵山港區 (南康鎮)	铁山港区 (南康镇)	170,000	180,000	190,000	394
Hepu County (Lianzhou Town)	合浦縣 (廉州鎮)	合浦县 (廉州镇)	1,050,000	1,060,000	1,100,000	2380
Fangchenggang City	防城港市	防城港市	910,000	920,000	990,000	6227
Gangkou District (Yuzhouping Subdistrict)	港口區 (漁洲坪街道)	港口区 (渔洲坪街道)	130,000	130,000	140,000	401
Fangcheng District (Zhuhe Subdistrict)	防城區 (珠河街道)	防城区 (珠河街道)	410,000	410,000	450,000	2427
Dongxing City (Dongxing Town)	東興市 (東興鎮)	东兴市 (东兴镇)	130,000	140,000	150,000	590
Shangsi County (Siyang Town)	上思縣 (思陽鎮)	上思县 (思阳镇)	240,000	240,000	250,000	2809
Chongzuo City	崇左市	崇左市	2,430,000	2,450,000	2,520,000	17,331
Jiangzhou District (Jiangnan Subdistrict)	江州區 (江南街道)	江州区 (江南街道)	360,000	360,000	380,000	2918
Pingxiang City (Pingxiang Town)	憑祥市 (憑祥鎮)	凭祥市 (凭祥镇)	110,000	110,000	120,000	645
Fusui County (Xinning Town)	扶綏縣 (新寧鎮)	扶绥县 (新宁镇)	450,000	450,000	460,000	2841
Daxin County (Taocheng Town)	大新縣 (桃城鎮)	大新县 (桃城镇)	370,000	370,000	390,000	2747
Tiandeng County (Tiandeng Town)	天等縣 (天等鎮)	天等县 (天等镇)	440,000	440,000	460,000	2165
Ningming County (Chengzhong Town)	寧明縣 (城中鎮)	宁明县 (城中镇)	430,000	440,000	440,000	3704
Longzhou County (Longzhou Town)	龍州縣 (龍州鎮)	龙州县 (龙州镇)	270,000	270,000	270,000	2311
Baise (Bose) City	白色市	白色市	4,050,000	4,110,000	4,210,000	36,206
Youjiang District (Baicheng Subdistrict)	右江區 (百城街道)	右江区 (百城街道)	350,000	350,000	N/A	3717

(continued)

Table 8.6 (continued)

Name	Traditional	Simplified	Population (2012)	Population (2016)	Population (2020)	Area (km²)
Tianyang District[d] (Tianzhou Town)	田陽區 (田州鎮)	田阳区 (田州镇)	N/A	N/A	330,000	2373
Tianyang District (Tianzhou Town)	田陽縣 (田州鎮)	田阳县 (田州镇)	350,000	350,000	330,000	2373
Tiandong County (Pingma Town)	田東縣 (平馬鎮)	田东县 (平马镇)	430,000	430,000	440,000	2816
Pingguo County (Matou Town)	平果縣 (馬頭鎮)	平果县 (马头镇)	510,000	510,000	N/A	2485
Pingguo City[e] (Matou Town)	平果市 (馬頭鎮)	平果市 (马头镇)	N/A	N/A	460,000	2485
Debao County (Chengguan Town)	德保縣 (城關鎮)	德保县 (城关镇)	370,000	370,000	370,000	2575
Jingxi City (Xinjing Town)	靖西市 (新靖鎮)	靖西市 (新靖镇)	640,000	660,000	660,000	3232
Napo County (Chengxiang Town)	那坡縣 (城廂鎮)	那坡县 (城厢镇)	210,000	210,000	220,000	2231
Lingyun County (Sicheng Town)	淩雲縣 (泗城鎮)	凌云县 (泗城镇)	210,000	220,000	230,000	2053
Leye County (Tongle Town)	樂業縣 (同樂鎮)	乐业县 (同乐镇)	170,000	170,000	180,000	2633
Xilin County (Bada Town)	西林縣 (八達鎮)	西林县 (八达镇)	150,000	160,000	160,000	2963
Tianlin County (Leli Town)	田林縣 (樂里鎮)	田林县 (乐里镇)	250,000	260,000	270,000	5577
Longlin Gezu (various ethnic minorities) Autonomous County (Xinzhou Town)	隆林各族自治縣 (新州鎮)	隆林各族自治县 (新州镇)	410,000	420,000	440,000	3551
Hechi City	河池市	河池市	4,190,000	4,200,000	4,330,000	33,494
Jinchengjiang District (Jinchengjiang Subdistrict)	金城江區 (金城江街道)	金城江区 (金城江街道)	340,000	340,000	35,000	2340
Yizhou District (Qingyuan Town)	宜州區 (慶遠鎮)	宜州区 (庆远镇)	660,000	660,000	670,000	3869
Nandan County (Chengguan Town)	南丹縣 (城關鎮)	南丹县 (城关镇)	310,000	310,000	330,000	3902
Tian'e County (Liupai Town)	天峨縣 (六排鎮)	天峨县 (六排镇)	170,000	170,000	180,000	3196
Fengshan County (Fengcheng Town)	鳳山縣 (鳳城鎮)	凤山县 (凤城镇)	210,000	210,000	220,000	1743
Donglan County (Donglan Town)	東蘭縣 (東蘭鎮)	东兰县 (东兰镇)	300,000	300,000	310,000	2435

(continued)

Table 8.6 (continued)

Name	Traditional	Simplified	Population (2012)	Population (2016)	Population (2020)	Area (km^2)
Bama Yaozu (Yao) Autonomous County (Bama Town)	巴馬瑤族自治縣 (巴馬鎮)	巴马瑶族自治县 (巴马镇)	280,000	280,000	300,000	1966
Du'an Yaozu (Yao) Autonomous County (Anyang Town)	都安瑤族自治縣 (安陽鎮)	都安瑶族自治县 (安阳镇)	700,000	710,000	730,000	4092
Dahua Yaozu (Yao) Autonomous County (Dahua Town)	大化瑤族自治縣 (大化鎮)	大化瑶族自治县 (大化镇)	460,000	460,000	480,000	2754
Luocheng Mulaozu (Mulao) Autonomous County (Dongmen Town)	羅城仫佬族自治縣 (東門鎮)	罗城仫佬族自治县 (东门镇)	380,000	380,000	390,000	2639
Huanjiang Maonanzu (Maonan) Autonomous County (Si'en Town)	環江毛南族自治縣 (思恩鎮)	环江毛南族自治县 (思恩镇)	380,000	380,000	380,000	4558
Laibin City	來賓市	**来宾**市	2,600,000	2,600,000	2,690,000	13,386
Xingbin District (Chengdong Subdistrict)	興賓區 (城東街道)	兴宾区 (城东街道)	1,080,000	1,100,000	1,140,000	4404
Heshan City (Lingnan Town)	合山市 (嶺南鎮)	合山市 (岭南镇)	140,000	140,000	140,000	365
Xiangzhou County (Xiangzhou Town)	象州縣 (象州鎮)	象州县 (象州镇)	370,000	360,000	370,000	1919
Wuxuan County (Wuxuan Town)	武宣縣 (武宣鎮)	武宣县 (武宣镇)	440,000	440,000	460,000	1705
Xincheng County (Chengguan Town)	忻城縣 (城關鎮)	忻城县 (城关镇)	420,000	410,000	430,000	2522
Jinxiu Yaozu (Yao) Autonomous County (Jinxiu Town)	金秀瑤族自治縣 (金秀鎮)	金秀瑶族自治县 (金秀镇)	150,000	150,000	160,000	2471
Hezhou City	賀州市	**贺**州市	2,330,000	2,320,000	2,460,000	11,855
Babu District (Babu Subdistrict)	八步區 (八步街道)	八步区 (八步街道)	1,050,000	1,050,000	750,000	3,504

(continued)

Table 8.6 (continued)

Name	Traditional	Simplified	Population (2012)	Population (2016)	Population (2020)	Area (km^2)
Pinggui District (Xiwan Subdistrict)	平桂區 (西灣街道)	平桂区 (西湾街道)	N/A	N/A	460,000	2022
Zhaoping County (Zhaoping Town)	昭平縣 (昭平鎮)	昭平县 (昭平镇)	440,000	440,000	450,000	3274
Zhongshan County (Zhongshan Town)	鍾山縣 (鍾山鎮)	钟山县 (钟山镇)	520,000	510,000	450,000	1483
Fuchuan Yaozu (Yao) Autonomous County (Fuyang Town)	富川瑤族自治縣 (富陽鎮)	富川瑶族自治县 (富阳镇)	320,000	320,000	340,000	1572

[a]Lipu county made a city in 2018
[b]Established March 2013
[c]Established June 2013
[d]Made a district in 2019
[e]Pingguo county made a city in November 2019

References

Becker, Jasper. 2000. *The Chinese*. New York: The Free Press.

Coward, Fiona. 2013. Ancestral migration patterns. In *Introductory readings in anthropology*, ed. Hilary Callan, Brian Street, and Simon Underdown, 190–194. New York: Berghahn.

Guangxi. 2021. *Wikipedia* (Chinese). https://zh.wikipedia.org/wiki. Accessed 21 Dec 2021.

Guangxi Province Bureau of Statistics (GPBS). 2021. [Bulletin of the main data of the seventh national census in Guangxi]. May 27. 广西第七次全国人口普查主要数据公报. https://tjgb.hongheiku.com/10283.html.

Guangxi Team of the Institute of the Archaeology (GTIA), Cultural Heritage Team of Guangxi Zhuang Autonomous Region and Nanning City Museum. 2004. The Baozitou shellmidden site in Nanning, Guangxi. *Chinese Archeology* 4 (1): 57–62.

Laven, Mary. 2011. *Mission to China: Matteo Ricci and the Jesuit encounter with the East*. London: Faber and Faber.

Ministry of Civil Affairs (MCA), People's Republic of China. 2020. [*County/township administration handbook*]. Beijing: China Statistics Press. 中華人民共和國民政部, 中華人民共和國, 鄉鎮行政區劃簡冊.

Qiao, Xiaochun, and Huang Yanchun. 2013. [China's situation with cross-provincial floating populations]. *Population & Development*. 喬曉春, 黃衍華. 中國跨省流動人口狀況. 人口與發展. 19(1): 13–28.

Shang-Ch'i Guide. 2017. [Backpacking in China: The most complete collection of self-guided travel for China, 2018]. Taipei: Shang-Ch'i Shitai Publishing. 2018 最完整的中國自助旅遊全集. 台北: 上奇時代.

Tan, Qixiang, ed. 1996. *The historical atlas of China*. Vol. VII. Beijing: China Cartographic Publishing House.

von Falkenhausen, Lothar. 1999. The waning of the bronze age: Material culture and social developments, 770–481 B.C. In *The Cambridge history of ancient China: From the origins of civi-*

lization to 221 B.C, ed. Michael Loewe and Edward L. Shaughnessy, 450–544. New York: Cambridge University Press.

Yangguang Net. 2021. [The main data of the seventh national census in Guangxi released]. 央广网. 广西第七次全国人口普查主要数据公布. May 13. https://www.163.com/dy/article/G9T5TG120514R9NP.html.

Zhang, Qizhi. 2002. [History of Qin, Han, Wei, Jin, Southern and Northern Dynasties]. Taipei, Republic of China: Wunan Book Publishing Company. 張豈之. 秦汉魏晋南北朝史. 中華民國: 五南圖書出版公司.

Zhang, Shunan. 2021. [The 2020 per capita income list of residents in various provinces: Shanghai is the richest, and it has risen sharply]. Finance.people.com. January 22. 张澍楠. 2020年各省份居民人均收入榜: 上海最有钱, 这地涨得猛. http://finance.people.com.cn/n1/2021/0122/c1004-32008733.html.

Zhao, Ermi. 1993. Terrestrial poisonous snakes in China. In *Toxin-related diseases: Poisons originating from plants, animals and spoilage*, ed. Anthony T. Tu, 355–388. Andover: Intercept.

Zhao, Dingxin. 2015. *The Confucian-legalist state: A new theory of Chinese history*. New York: Oxford University Press.

Zheng, Yi. 1996. *Scarlet Memorial: Tales of Cannibalism in Modern China*. Ed. and Trans. T.P. Sym. Boulder: Westview Press.

Chapter 9
Guizhou Province

Abstract Home to a number of archeological excavations showing hominid activity about a hundred thousand years ago, Guizhou is endowed with spectacular karst and tree-lined ravines (as depicted in many classic Chinese landscape paintings). As a provincial entity, its names had changed throughout history, and took the Ming dynasty (ca. fifteenth century) to finally settle upon its current name. While rich in its bucolic scenery and local culture, Guizhou has long had a reputation for being poor and having inclement weather. With a noticeable growth in population during the Qing dynasty (ca. seventeenth century), today, except for the lucrative tobacco crop, Maotai liquor, and the tourism industry, and despite a continuing improvement in its growth domestic product, Guizhou remains among the poorest of mainland China's 31 provinces and major cities. As of 2020, Guizhou's per capita income ranks 29th out of mainland China's 31 provinces and major cities. Like its neighboring Guangxi, Guizhou has a large number of ethnic nationalities, the largest percentage of these being the Buyi (Bouyei) people.

E. Croddy, *China's Provinces and Populations*,
https://doi.org/10.1007/978-3-031-09165-0_9

Guizhou Province (貴州省 *guìzhōu shěng*): Abbreviations 貴 (*guì*); 黔 (*qián*) (Fig. 9.1)

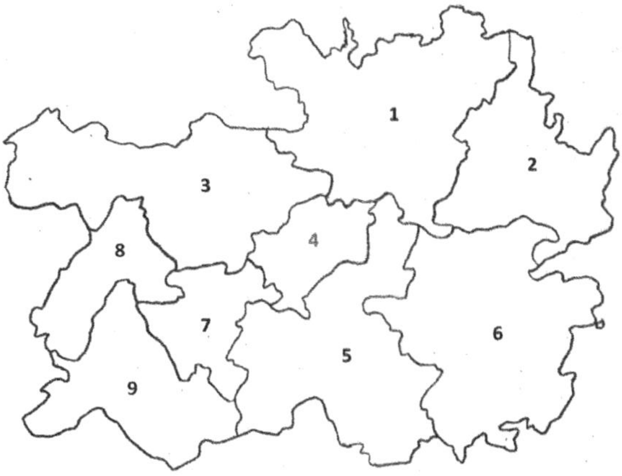

Guizhou Population (2020)

1.	**Zunyi City**	**6,606,675**
2.	**Tongren City**	**3,298,468**
3.	**Bijie City**	**6,899,636**
4.	Guiyang City	5,897,018
5.	**Qiannan Buyei and Miao Autonomous Region**	**3,494,385**
6.	**Qiandongnan Miao and Dong Autonomous Prefecture**	**3,758,622**
7.	**Anshun City**	**2,470,630**
8.	**Liupanshui City**	**3,031,602**

Fig. 9.1 Guizhou province: Major cities and Prefectures (Provincial Capital: Guiyang City). (Map drawn by the author, after People's Republic of China, Ministry of Civil Affairs (MCA 2020))

Guizhou Province: General Impressions

Shorthand characters for Guizhou province include Qian (黔 *qián*) and Gui (貴 *guì*). The initialism Qian (黔 *qián*) is found in the Chinese idiom, "one trick pony," the Guizhou donkey that was found to have only one effective technique (黔驢技窮 *qiánlǘ jìqióng*).

One immediately thinks of Guizhou's scenic views as captured in classical Chinese paintings: winding ravines closely banked by striking karst precipices, winding roads and misty-green, terraced rice fields. Guizhou's rain forest-like climate, such as that found in Guizhou's capital of Guiyang, inspires the expression "No three days of clear weather" (天無三日晴 *tiānwú sānrì qíng*). The province's hot and humid weather perhaps is in keeping with its penchant for spicy cuisine (Shang-Ch'i 2017).

Prehistoric Guizhou

Paleolithic sites, such as the Guanyindong (觀音洞 *guānyīndòng*) cave deposits in Qianxi County (黔西縣 *qiánxīxiàn*), are replete with manmade tools and animal fossils. The Guanyindong site has been dated somewhere between 57,000 and 115,000 years ago. Discovered in 1964, some 3000 artifacts were found. A relatively high percentage of the flint specimens at this Guanyindong Culture (觀音洞文化 *guānyīndòng wénhuà*) site were, by all appearances, finished tools, which was not typical for the Chinese Paleolithic of this time period. Showing many similarities with the Guangyindong culture, the Wangjiayuanzi site, in Caohai southbank, Wangjiayuanzi Village (草海南岸王家院子村 *cǎohǎinán'àn wángjiāyuànzicūn*) was excavated in 1982.

Other Chinese Paleolithic sites of note in Guizhou include:

- Laoya Cave (老鴉洞 *lǎoyādòng*), located in Bijie City, Qixing district (畢節市七星區 *bìjié shì qīxīng qū*); dated approximately 18,000 years ago;
- Ma'anshan Mountain (馬鞍山 *mǎ'ān shān*) in Tongzi County (桐梓縣 *tóngzǐ xiàn*), dated about 15,000–18,000 years ago;
- Pudingchuan Cave (普定穿洞 *pǔdìngchuān dòng*) in Anshun City, Puding County (安順市普定縣 *ānshùn shì pǔdìng xiàn*), dated ca. 8000–16,000 years ago;
- Baiyanjiao Cave (白岩脚洞 *báiyánjiǎodòng*), Puding County, estimated 12,000–16,000 years old;
- Xingyi Maomao Cave (興義貓貓洞 *xìngyì māomāo dòng*) Xingyi City, Dingxiao Town (興義市頂效鎮 *xìngyì shì dǐngxiào zhèn*), dated 10,000–15,000 years ago;
- Xiaohui Cave (硝灰洞 *xiāohuī dòng*), Liupanshui City (六盤水市 *liùpánshuǐ shì*), Zhongshan District (鐘山區 *zhōngshān qū*); about 50,000 years old
- Panxian Big Cave (盤縣大洞 *pánxiàndàdòng*), Panzhou City (盤州市 *pánzhōu shì*), dated 130,000–300,000 years ago;
- Yanhui Cave (岩灰洞 *yánhuī dòng*) Tongzi County (桐梓縣 *tóngzǐ xiàn*) Jiuba Town (九壩鎮 *jiǔbà zhèn*), 113,000–181,000 years old;
- Bianbiandong Cave (扁扁洞 *biǎnbiǎn dòng*), Bijie City, Qixing District, Haizijie Town (海子街鎮 *hǎizijiē zhèn*), 130,000–170,0000 years ago

While the Gaomiao Culture (高廟文化 *gāomiào wénhuà*), dated about 5800–4800 BCE, has mostly been found in Hunan Province (e.g., a site located in Hongjiang City, Anjiang Town 洪江市安江鎮 *hóngjiāngshì, ānjiāngzhèn*), there is further evidence of Gaomiao Culture located in southwestern Guizhou (Flad and Chen 2013).

Ancient to Modern

Following the unification of China under the Qin (221 BCE), the landmass of today's Guizhou was once parceled among the Ba and Shu prefectures (巴郡 *bājùn*; 蜀郡 *shǔjùn*), both comprising modern-day Sichuan; Qiongdu (邛都 *qióng dū*), and Yelang (夜郎 *yè láng*); as well as Qianzhong (黔中郡 *qián-zhōng jùn*) and Xiangjun prefectures (象郡 *xiàng jùn*).

In a recent discovery (2015), researchers uncovered 1800 year-old Han Dynasty (206–220 CE) remains at the Huangjinwan site (黄金灣遺址 *huángjīnwān yízhǐ*), located in Xishui County (習水縣 *xíshuǐ xiàn*). Notably, and an archaeological first of such vintage, the tomb's funerary objects included two chicken eggs, along with porcelain and animal bones. By 262 CE, in the Three Kingdoms period, as part of the larger southern Yizhou (益州 *yìzhōu*), Guizhou was then called Zangke Prefecture (牂柯郡 *zāngkē jùn*; also known as 牂牁 *zānggē*).

During the Tang, in ca. 740 CE, we find the formal name of an administrative area called Qianzhong Dao (黔中道 *qiánzhōng dào*). Its capital was Chizhou (敕州 *chìzhōu*), which was located in modern-day Guiyang City. China's historical atlas shows a Qianzhou Inspectorate (黔州觀察使 *qiánzhōu guānchá shǐ*) in ca. 820 CE, its borders roughly describing those of modern-day Guizhou Province. During the Song Dynasty, a Chizhou prefectural document of 974 CE includes a description of a "far away Guizhou," and is reportedly the first known historical reference to the name. Another source relates that the first recorded reference to the name Guizhou dates much later to 1119 CE. Other less credible (and more convoluted) explanations suggest that, due to the fact that transportation was exorbitantly expensive in the southern region, the character (貴 *guì*) was given to the area meaning "treasure, high cost." Yet another has it that a name of the region was originally the Luo Clan Ghost State (羅氏鬼國 *luóshì guǐguó*), but then the very inauspicious ghost (鬼 *guǐ*) character was changed to the homonym (and much more auspicious) "gui" (貴 *guì*).

We can be sure, however, that during the Yuan dynasty, in ca. 1330, a place name of Guizhou was definitively used to describe modern-day Guiyang, located within the Bafanshun Pacification Commission (八番順元宣慰司 *bāfānshùn yuánxuānwèisī*) under Huguang Province (湖廣行省 *húguǎng xíngshěng*). But it took the Ming dynasty formation of a Guizhou Provincial Administration Commission (貴州承宣布政使 *guìzhōuchéngxuānbù zhèngshǐ*) in 1413 which formally gave Guizhou Province its current name.

In about the sixteenth century, Guizhou's population increased 260,000–328,781. But the most rapid growth in population occurred during the Qing Dynasty, with an increase from 307,000 in 1749 to 525,000 by ca. 1800 (*Guizhou* 2002). More immigrants hailing from Sichuan and Hunan increased Guizhou's population further by the nineteenth century. From the historical map, Guizhou in 1820 was divided into prefectures (Fu, Zhou) and Ting (廳 *tīng*) administrative districts, their names (below) of which being similar to those cities and counties of today (Table 9.1):

Guizhou declared its independence from the Qing dynasty in November 1911. According to the Republic of China census of 1912, Guizhou had a population of 9,665,227, and 11,470,099 in 1918. By 1928, Guizhou had a population of 12,691,900 (Lu and Teng 2000).

Following their disastrous "soviet" experience in Jiangxi, and hounded by KMT armies, Chinese Communist Party (CCP) forces fled westward during the so-called Long March. Later, a pivotal CCP meeting was held in January 1935 at Zunyi, in which Mao Zedong was able to solidify his stamp on the party apparatus, eliminating opposition from the so-called "internationalists." During the Sino-Japanese War (1937–1945), coastal populations moved inland to Guizhou for safety. In the years following the communist revolution, Guizhou had a population of 14,164,000 (1949) and 14,172,000 in 1950 (GPLCCC 2013).

Maotai Liquor

Named after Maotai Town (茅台鎮 *máotáizhèn*), in Zunyi City (遵義市 *zūnyìshì*), Renhuai City (仁懷市 *rénhuáishì*), China's famous Maotai liquor has been described thusly:

Table 9.1 Qing Dynasty Guizhou Prefectures, 1820. (Tan 1996)

Zunyi 遵義府 *zūnyì fǔ*
Si'nan 思南府 *sīnán fǔ*
Songtao 松桃廳 *sōngtáo tīng*
Dading 大定府 *dàdìng fǔ*
Tongren 銅仁府 *tóngrén fǔ*
Pingyue 平越州 *píngyuè zhōu*
Shiqian 石阡府 *shíqiān fǔ*
Sizhou 思州府 *sīzhōu fǔ*
Guiyang 貴陽府 *guìyáng fǔ*
Zhenyuan 鎮遠府 *zhènyuǎn fǔ*
Pu'an 普安廳 *pǔ'ān tīng*
Anshun 安順府 *ānshùn fǔ*
Du'yun 都匀府 *dūyún fǔ*
Liping 黎平府 *lípíng fǔ*
Xingyi 興義府 *xìngyì fǔ*

> This [jiu 酒 *jiǔ*] – Chinese for "beverage alcohol" – is distilled seven times in traditional pot stills and collected in large jars, which are sealed with lotus leaves and clay, capped with ceramic covers, and allowed to slumber undisturbed for many years. The resulting liquor – moutai or mao-tai – is pale amber, quite strong, and tastes like the bottom of Bluto Blutarsky's laundry hamper (Wondrich 2007).

The locality of Guizhou's Maotai town has been celebrated in China for 2000 years for being home to many literati, but more famously for wine (beer), and liquor. The famed historian Sima Qian (司馬遷 *sīmǎ qiān*) memorialized that the Hanwu Emperor (漢武帝 *hànwǔdì*) himself praised the region for its distilled alcoholic beverages (ca. 135 BCE). A regional method of using fermented grains to make wine (or perhaps closer to a beer) dates back to 1108 (Song dynasty). But the original Maotai liquor production that we are more familiar with today can be traced to 1704 (Qing Dynasty), which included Maochun (茅春 *máochūn*), Maotai Shaochun (茅台燒春 *máotái shāochūn*) and Huisha Maotai (回沙茅台 *huíshā máotái*) liquors. While there may have been as many as 20 or more Maotai factories operating in the nineteenth century, these original and antique distilleries were reportedly destroyed during the Taiping Rebellion (ca. 1860). Having secured a gold medal at the 1915 Panama-Pacific Exposition in San Francisco, Maotai has since earned global fame. During the Maoist craze of the 1950s, Maotai was also caught up in the swell of ever-increasing production quotas during the Great Leap Forward (1958–1962). Named a "satellite launch" site, its maniacal quota was to "produce tens of thousands of tons." Achieving a production run of 283 tons in 1957, by 1960 Maotai recorded some 912 tons of liquor. But to procure enough starch to ferment this amount led to the forced confiscation of 100,000 kilos of grain from the neighboring area of Tongren City in 1960. In that year alone, this "procurement" led to massive starvation in Tongren City's Sinan County (思南縣 *sīnán xiàn*), causing its population to drop by 51,000. In Meitan County (湄潭縣 *méitán xiàn*), the forced requisition of grain from peasants (along the lines of Stalin's confiscation of food from the "kulaks") led to the death of 122,000 people during the first 5 months of 1960 (Yang 2008).

Modern-Day Guizhou

Home to nearly 50 different ethnic groups, Guizhou is a relative latecomer in terms of economic development. Traditionally (and justifiably) regarded as a remote and poverty-stricken part of the Chinese empire, Guizhou has traditionally been regarded as a place with the "three nothings": "No three days of clear weather, no three miles of level land, and no one with three taels of silver." (Hsieh and Hsieh 1995).

As of 2020, Guizhou had an estimated 6,230,000 people who were categorized as being poor, a condition the Chinese government aimed to ameliorate with targeted social programs for the 13th five-year plan (2016–2020). In 2015, (see Table 9.2) Guizhou Province broke the gross domestic production (GDP) value of 1050 trillion Yuan (Renminbi).

Following continued economic growth since China's 1978 economic reforms, in 2015 Guizhou ranked near bottom (25th) in terms of GDP when compared to other provinces. However, by 2020 Guizhou had steadily made gains (see Table 9.3), ranking now 20th, although its per capita income was still near at the bottom (29th out of 31) at US $3390 (Zhang 2021).

Table 9.2 Guizhou Province Gross Domestic Product (GDP) 2011–2020. (Zhang 2021)

Year	GDP in Yuan (billion)	GDP in billion US Dollars; exchange one USD = 6.45 yuan
2011	600	93.0
2012	700	108.5
2013	800	124.0
2014	900	139.5
2015	1050	162.8
2016	1173	182.5
2017	1354	210.6
2018	1481	230
2019	1677	260
2020	1783	276

Table 9.3 Gross Domestic Product (GDP) rankings of Chinese Provinces (2020). (China News Net 2021)

Province/city	2020 GDP in Yuan	GDP in US Dollars (billions)[a]
Guangdong	11,076,094,000,000	1722
Jiangsu	10,270,000,000,000	1597
Shandong	7,312,900,000,000	1137
Zhejiang	6,461,300,000,000	1005
Henan	5,499,707,000,000	855
Sichuan	4,859,876,000,000	756
Fujian	4,390,389,000,000	683
Hubei	4,344,346,000,000	676
Hunan	4,178,149,000,000	650
Shanghai City	3,870,058,000,000	602
Anhui	3,868,060,000,000	601
Hebei	3,620,600,000,000	563
Beijing	3,610,260,000,000	561
Shaanxi	2,618,186,000,000	407
Jiangxi	2,569,150,000,000	400
Liaoning	2,511,500,000,000	390
Chongqing	2,500,279,000,000	389
Yunnan	2,450,000,000,000	381

(continued)

Table 9.3 (continued)

Province/city	2020 GDP in Yuan	GDP in US Dollars (billions)[a]
Guangxi	2,215,669,000,000	344
Guizhou	**1,782,656,000,000**	**277**
Shanxi	1,765,193,000,000	274
Neimengu (Inner Mongolia)	1,736,000,000,000	270
Tianjin	1,408,373,000,000	219
Xinjiang	1,379,758,000,000	214
Heilongjiang	1,369,850,000,000	213
Jilin	1,231,132,000,000	191
Gansu	901,670,000,000	140
Hainan	553,239,000,000	86
Ningxia	392,055,000,000	61
Qinghai	300,592,000,000	47
Tibet (Xizang)	190,274,000,000	30

[a]Exchange rate 2021: one USD = 6.43 yuan; rounded

Nearly 40% of Guizhou's population (based on the 2000 census) fall into officially-recognized ethnic minority groups. The Buyi (Bouyei), a Thai-related people, are among the largest represented in Guizhou Province. In 2000, Guizhou's main cash crop was tobacco, and remains a key agricultural product, earning 1.24 billion (US dollars) in 2015 (GGP 2016).

Rapid Urbanization

The population (both registered and nonpermanent) of Guizhou as of 2015 was 35,295,000 (the latter figure is lower than registered *hukou* numbers, reflecting a net decrease due to "floating populations" who live outside Guizhou Province). Based on official statistics, of this population 14,827,400 were living in towns and cities, while 20,467,600 lived in rural villages. The number of people who had transitioned to an urban environment from 2010 to 2015 increased by 42%, heralded as exceeding the goals of the 12th five-year plan. Using registered (戶籍人口 *hùjírénkǒu*) population figures (43,254,900 in 2014), the non-farming population of Guizhou in 2010 was 6,760,700, increasing 16% to 7,092,200 by 2014 (Yao 2016).

Census figures for 2010 and 2020 are provided in Table 9.4 (below), followed by a detailed breakdown by subdistricts for the most recent 2020 census (Table 9.5 and Fig. 9.2).

Table 9.6 (below) shows the *hukou* (family registered) populations based on PRC Ministry of Civil Affairs data. (Districts listed directly under major cities are government seats, as are those in parentheses). One can compare these data with the census (usual residential populations based on 2010 and 2020 censuses in Tables 9.4 and 9.5 (below).

Table 9.4 Population (Residential 常住人口 *chángzhù rénkǒu*) data for Guizhou Province. (GPSB 2021)

City/region	Population 2010	Population 2020
Guiyang City 貴陽市 *guìyáng shì* [abbrev. 築 *zhú*]	4,324,561	5,897,018
Liupanshui City 六盤水市 *liùpánshuǐ shì*	2,851,180	3,031,602
Zunyi City 遵義 *zūnyì shì*	6,127,009	6,606,675
Anshun City 安順市 *ānshùn shì*	2,297,339	2,470,630
Tongren City 銅仁市 *tóngrén shì*	3,092,365	3,298,468
Qianxinan Buyei and Miao Autonomous Region 黔西南布依族苗族自治州 *qiánxī'nán bùyīzú miáozú zìzhìzhōu*	2,805,857	3,015,112
Bijie City 畢節市 *bìjíe shì*	6,536,370	6,899,636
Qiandongnan Miao and Dong Autonomous Region 黔東南苗族侗族自治州 *qiándōngnán miáozú dòngzú zìzhìzhōu*	3,480,626	3,758,622
Qiannan Buyei and Miao Autonomous Region 黔南布依族苗族自治州 *qiánnán bùyīzú miáozú zìzhìzhōu*	3,231,161	3,494,385
Total	**34,746,468**	**38,562,148**

Table 9.5 Guizhou Province: Population data of cities and their subordinate sectors. (GPSB 2021)

Cities and subordinate sectors, population (2020 census)	Subordinate district, city and county populations (2020)	Total population (2020)
Guiyang City 貴陽市 ***guìyáng shì* [abbrev.** 築 ***zhú*]**		**5,897,018**
Wudang District 烏當區 *wūdāng qū*	336,363	
Nanming District 南明區 *nánmíng qū*	1,047,792	
Yunyan District 雲岩區 *yúnyán qū*	1,056,819	
Huaxi District 花溪區 *huāxī qū*	966,276	
Baiyun District 白雲區 *báiyún qū*	456,250	
Guanshanhu District 觀山湖區 *guānshānhú qū*	642,634	
Qingzhen City 清鎮市 *qīngzhèn shì*	629,088	
Kaiyang County 開陽縣 *kāiyáng xiàn*	343,871	
Xiuwen County 修文縣 *xiūwén xiàn*	288,090	

(continued)

Table 9.5 (continued)

Cities and subordinate sectors, population (2020 census)	Subordinate district, city and county populations (2020)	Total population (2020)
Xifeng County 息烽縣 *xīfēng xiàn*	219,835	
Liupanshui City 六盤水市 ***liùpánshuǐ shì***		**3,031,602**
Zhongshan District 鐘山區 *zhōngshān qū*	674,249	
Panzhou City 盤州市 *pánzhōu shì*	1,074,073	
Liuzhi Special Zone 六枝特區 *liùzhī tèqū*	536,873	
Shuicheng County 水城縣 *shuǐchéng xiàn*	746,407	
Zunyi City 遵義 ***zūnyì shì***		**6,606,675**
Huichuan District 匯川區 *huìchuān qū*	627,721	
Honghuagang District 紅花崗區 *hónghuāgǎng qū*	971,337	
Bozhou District[a] 播州區 *bōzhōu qū*	761,491	
Chishui City 赤水市 *chìshuǐ shì*	247,287	
Renhuai City 仁懷市 *rénhuái shì*	655,300	
Tongzi County 桐梓縣 *tóngzǐ xiàn*	529,471	
Suiyang County 綏陽縣 *suíyáng xiàn*	379,677	
Zheng'an County 正安縣 *zhèng'ān xiàn*	396,159	
Fenggang County 鳳岡縣 *fènggāng xiàn*	304,156	
Meitan County 湄潭縣 *méitán xiàn*	372,865	
Yuqing County 余慶縣 *yúqìng xiàn*	223,952	
Xishui County 習水縣 *xíshuǐ xiàn*	584,947	
Daozhen Gelaozu Miaozu (Gelao and Miao) Autonomous County 道真仡佬族苗族自治縣 *dàozhēn yìlǎozú miáozú zìzhìxiàn*	243,846	
Wuchuan Gelaozu Miaozu (Gelao and Miao) Autonomous County 務川仡佬族苗族自治縣 *wùchuān yìlǎozú miáozú zìzhìxiàn*	308,466	
Anshun City 安順市 ***ānshùn shì***		**2,470,630**
Xixiu District 西秀區 *xīxiù qū*	870,441	
Pingba District 平壩區 *píngbà qū*	347,060	
Puding County 普定縣 *pǔdìng xiàn*	376,285	
Guanling Buyizu Miaozu (Buyei and Miao) Autonomous County 關嶺布依族苗族自治縣 *guānlǐng bùyīzú miáozú zìzhìxiàn*	283,497	
Zhenning City Buyizu Miaozu (Buyei and Miao) Autonomous County 鎮寧布依族苗族自治縣 *zhènníng bùyīzú miáozú zìzhìxiàn*	299,696	
Ziyun Miaozu Buyizu (Miao and Buyei) Autonomous County 紫雲苗族布依族自治縣 *zǐyún miáozú bùyīzú zìzhìxiàn*	293,651	
Tongren City 銅仁市 ***tóngrén shì***		**3,298,468**
Bijiang District 碧江區 *bìjiāng qū*	442,076	
Wanshan District 萬山區 *wànshān qū*	160,624	

(continued)

Table 9.5 (continued)

Cities and subordinate sectors, population (2020 census)	Subordinate district, city and county populations (2020)	Total population (2020)
Jiangkou County 江口縣 *jiāngkǒu xiàn*	184,764	
Shiqian County 石阡縣 *shíqiān xiàn*	297,086	
Sinan County 思南縣 *sīnán xiàn*	457,745	
Dejiang County 德江縣 *déjiāng xiàn*	393,596	
Yuping Dongzu (Dong) Autonomous County 玉屏侗族自治縣 *yùpíng dòngzú zìzhìxiàn*	150,457	
Yinjiang Tujiazu (Tujia) Autonomous County 印江土家苗族自治縣 *yìnjiāng tǔjiā miáozú zìzhìxiàn*	294,490	
Yanhe Tujiazu (Tujia) Autonomous County 沿河土家族自治縣 *yánhé tǔjiāzú zìzhìxiàn*	429,893	
Songtao Miaozu (Miao) Autonomous County 松桃苗族自治縣 *sōngtáo miáozú zìzhìxiàn*	487,737	
Qianxinan Buyei and Miao Autonomous Region 黔西南布依族苗族自治州 ***qiánxī'nán bùyīzú miáozú zìzhìzhōu***		**3,015,112**
Xingyi City 興義市 *xīngyì shì*	1,004,132	
Xingren City 興仁市 *xīngrén shì*	425,770	
Pu'an County 普安縣 *pǔ'ān xiàn*	242,958	
Qinglong County 晴隆縣 *qínglóng xiàn*	234,162	
Zhenfeng County 貞豐縣 *zhēnfēng xiàn*	307,313	
Wangmo County 望謨縣 *wàngmó xiàn*	235,243	
Ceheng County 冊亨縣 *cèhēng xiàn*	189,709	
Anlong County 安龍縣 *ānlóng xiàn*	375,825	
Bijie City 畢節市 ***bìjíe shì***		**6,899,636**
Qixingguan District 七星關區 *qīxīngguān qū*	1,305,066	
Dafang County 大方縣 *dàfāng xiàn*	857,578	
Qianxi County 黔西縣 *qiánxī xiàn*	732,008	
Jinsha County 金沙縣 *jīnshā xiàn*	544,033	
Zhijin County 織金縣*zhījīn xiàn*	815,661	
Nayong County 納雍縣 *nàyōng xiàn*	716,703	
Hezhang County 赫章縣 *hèzhāng xiàn*	648,471	
Weining Yizu Huizu Miaozu (Yi, Hui and Miao) Autonomous County 威寧彝族回族苗族自治縣 *wēiníng yízú huízú miáozú zìzhìxiàn*	1,280,116	
Qiandongnan Miao and Dong Autonomous Region 黔東南苗族侗族自治州 ***qiándōngnán miáozú dòngzú zìzhìzhōu***		**3,758,622**
Kaili City 凱里市 *kǎilǐ shì*	709,057	
Huangping County 黃平縣 *huángpíng xiàn*	244,125	
Shibing County 施秉縣 *shībǐng xiàn*	125,518	
Sansui County 三穗縣 *sānsuì xiàn*	162,798	

(continued)

Table 9.5 (continued)

Cities and subordinate sectors, population (2020 census)	Subordinate district, city and county populations (2020)	Total population (2020)
Zhenyuan County 鎮遠縣 *zhènyuǎn xiàn*	189,715	
Cen'gong County 岑鞏縣 *céngǒng xiàn*	168,441	
Tianzhu County 天柱縣 *tiānzhù xiàn*	273,588	
Jinping County 錦屏縣 *jǐnpíng xiàn*	155,182	
Jianhe County 劍河縣 *jiànhé xiàn*	188,507	
Taijiang County 台江縣 *táijiāng xiàn*	122,861	
Liping County 黎平縣 *lípíng xiàn*	412,813	
Rongjiang County 榕江縣 *róngjiāng xiàn*	297,572	
Congjiang County 從江縣 *cóngjiāng xiàn*	313,887	
Leishan County 雷山縣 *léishān xiàn*	124,835	
Majiang County 麻江縣 *májiāng xiàn*	131,081	
Danzhai County 丹寨縣 *dānzhài xiàn*	138,642	
Qiannan Buyei and Miao Autonomous Region 黔南布依族苗族自治州 ***qiánnán bùyīzú miáozú zìzhìzhōu***		**3,494,385**
Duyun City 都匀市 *dānyún xiàn*	529,688	
Fuquan City 福泉市 *fúquán shì*	297,899	
Libo County 荔波縣 *lìbō xiàn*	154,896	
Guiding County 貴定縣 *guìdìng xiàn*	250,146	
Weng'an County 翁安縣 *wēng'ān xiàn*	395,536	
Dushan County 獨山縣 *dúshān xiàn*	264,266	
Pingtang County 平塘縣 *píngtáng xiàn*	234,417	
Luodian County 羅甸縣 *luódiàn xiàn*	257,551	
Changshun County 長順縣 *chángshùn xiàn*	201,540	
Longli County 龍里縣 *lónglǐ xiàn*	236,221	
Huishui County 惠水縣 *huìshuǐ xiàn*	395,878	
Sandu Shuizu (Sui) Autonomous County 三都水族自治縣 *sāndū shuǐzú zìzhìxiàn*	276,347	

[a]Established in 2016

1. Chishui City
2. Xishui County
3. Tongzi County
4. Suiyang County
5. Zheng'an County
6. Daozhen Mulao and Miao Autonomous County
7. Wuchuan Mulao and Miao Autonomous County
8. Meitan County
9. Fenggang County
10. Dejiang County
11. Yanhe Tujia Autonomous County
12. Weining Zang and Hui Autonomous County
13. Zhongshan District
14. Hezhang County
15. Qixingguan District
16. Nayong County
17. Dafang County
18. Jinsha County
19. Renhuai City
20. Bozhou District
21. Huichuan District
22. Honghuagang District
23. Sinan County
24. Yinjiang Tujia and Miao Autonomous County
25. Songtao Miao Autonomous County
26. Shuicheng County
27. Liuzhi Tiqu (Special Region)
28. Zhijin County
29. Dafang County
30. Xifeng County
31. Kaiyang County
32. Fuquan City
33. Weng'an County
34. Huangping County
35. Yuqing County
36. Shiqian Count y
37. Shibing County
38. Cengong County
39. Jiangkou County
40. Bijiang District
41. Wanshan District
42. Zhenhuan County
43. Yuping Dong Autonomous County
44. Panxian County
45. Pu'an County
46. Qinglong County
47. Guanling Yi and Miao Autonomous County
48. Puding County
49. Zhenning Buyi (Bouyei) and Miao Autonmous County
50. Xixiu District
51. Pingba District
52. Qingzhen City
53. Xiuwen Count y
54. Guanshanhu District
55. Baiyun District
56. Huaxi District
57. Nanming District
58. Wudang District
59. Yunyan District
60. Longli County
61. Guiding County
62. Majiang County
63. Kaili City
64. Taijiang County
65. Jianhe County
66. Sansui County
67. Tianzhu County
68. Jinping County
69. Xingyi City
70. Xingren City
71. Zhenfeng County
72. Ziyun Miao an d Buyi (Bouyei) Autonomous County
73. Changshun County
74. Huishui County
75. Duyun City
76. Danzhai County
77. Leishan County
78. Liping County
79. Anlong County
80. Ceheng County
81. Wangmou County
82. Luodian Count y
83. Pingtang County
84. Dushan County
85. Libo County
86. Sandu Shui (Sui) Autonomous County
87. Rongjiang County
88. Congjiang County

Fig. 9.2 Guizhou Province: Subdistricts (Capital City Governmental Seat: Wudang District). (Map drawn by the author, after People's Republic of China, Ministry of Civil Affairs (MCA 2020))

Guizhou Province (黔 *qián*) and Gui (貴 *guì*)

Provincial Capital: Guiyang

Table 9.6 Guizhou Province: Permanent registered (戶籍人口 *hùjí rénkǒu*) populations. (MCA 2020)

Name	Traditional	Simplified	Population (2012)	Population (2016)	Population (2020)	Area (Sq. Km)
Guizhou Province	貴州省	贵州省	41,890,000	41,340,000	45,290,000	176,161.4
Guiyang City	貴陽市	贵阳市	3,730,000	3,750,000	4,180,000	8035
Wudang District (Shunxin Community)	烏當區 (順新社區)	乌当区 (顺新社区)	320,000	190,000	220,000	686
Nanming District (Xinhua Community)	南明區 (新華社區)	南明区 (新华社区)	560,000	550,000	640,000	271
Yunyan District (Guiwu Community)	雲岩區 (貴烏社區)	云岩区 (贵乌社区)	650,000	640,000	660,000	94
Huaxi District (Guizhu Community)	花溪區 (貴築社區)	花溪区 (贵筑社区)	330,000	490,000	520,000	964
Baiyun District (Hongyun Community)	白雲區 (紅雲社區)	白云区 (红云社区)	200,000	190,000	230,000	270
Guanshanhu District[a] (Shijicheng Community)	觀山湖區 (世紀城社區)	观山湖区 (世纪城社区)	N/A	180,000	310,000	309
Qingzhen City (Hongxin Community)	清鎮市 (紅新社區)	清镇市 (红新社区)	510,000	500,000	540,000	1302
Kaiyang County (Chengguan Town)	開陽縣 (城關鎮)	开阳县 (城关镇)	430,000	440,000	450,000	2026
Xiuwen County (Longchang Town)	修文縣 (龍場鎮)	修文县 (龙场镇)	310,000	310,000	330,000	1076
Xifeng County (Yongjing Town)	息烽縣 (永靖鎮)	息烽县 (永靖镇)	260,000	260,000	270,000	1037
Liupanshui City	六盤水市	六盘水市	3,200,000	3,230,000	3,490,000	9914
Zhongshan District (Fenghuang Subdistrict)	鐘山區 (鳳凰街道)	钟山区 (凤凰街道)	500,000	500,000	490,000	487
Panzhou City (Yizi Subdistrict)	盤州市 (亦資街道)	盘州市 (亦资街道)	1,180,000	1,190,000	1,290,000	4057

(continued)

Table 9.6 (continued)

Name	Traditional	Simplified	Population (2012)	Population (2016)	Population (2020)	Area (Sq. Km)
Liuzhi Special Zone (Pingzhai Town)	六枝特區 (平寨鎮)	六枝特区 (平寨镇)	690,000	700,000	740,000	1792
Shuicheng County (Lanba Town)	水城縣 (濫壩鎮)	水城县 (滥坝镇)	830,000	840,000	970,000	3578
Zunyi City	遵義市	遵义市	7,630,000	7,720,000	8,130,000	30,763
Huichuan District (Dalianlu Subdistrict)	匯川區 (大連路街道)	汇川区 (大连路街道)	350,000	360,000	560,000	1479.69
Honghuagang District (Zhongzhuang Town)	紅花崗區 (忠莊鎮)	红花岗区 (忠庄镇)	510,000	510,000	800,000	1405.72
Bozhou District (Nanbai Town)	播州區 (南白鎮)	搏州区 (男白镇)	N/A	N/A	870,000	2501
Chishui City (Shizhong Subdistrict)	赤水市 (市中街道)	赤水市 (市中街道)	310,000	310,000	320,000	1801
Renhuai City (Zhongshu Subdistrict)	仁懷市 (中樞街道)	仁怀市 (中枢街道)	660,000	680,000	720,000	1788
Zunyi County[b] (Nanbai Town)	遵義縣 (南白鎮)	遵义县 (南白镇)	1,200,000	1,210,000	N/A	(4104)
Tongzi County (Loushanguan Town)	桐梓縣 (婁山關鎮)	桐梓县 (娄山关镇)	700,000	730,000	750,000	3190
Suiyang County (Yangchuan Town)	綏陽縣 (洋川鎮)	绥阳县 (洋川镇)	540,000	550,000	570,000	2566
Zheng'an County (Fengyi Town)	正安縣 (鳳儀鎮)	正安县 (凤仪镇)	640,000	640,000	660,000	2595
Fenggang County (Longquan Town)	鳳岡縣 (龍泉鎮)	凤冈县 (龙泉镇)	430,000	430,000	450,000	1883
Meitan County (Chacheng Subdistrict)	湄潭縣 (茶城街道)	湄潭县 (茶城街道)	490,000	490,000	510,000	1845
Yuqing County (Baini Town)	余慶縣 (白尼鎮)	余庆县 (白泥镇)	300,000	300,000	310,000	1630
Xishui County (Donghuang Town)	習水縣 (東皇鎮)	习水县 (东皇镇)	710,000	720,000	770,000	3128
Daozhen Gelaozu Miaozu (Gelao and Miao) Autonomous County (Yuxi Town)	道真仡佬族苗族自治縣 (玉溪鎮)	道真仡佬族苗族自治县 (玉溪镇)	340,000	340,000	350,000	2156

(continued)

Table 9.6 (continued)

Name	Traditional	Simplified	Population (2012)	Population (2016)	Population (2020)	Area (Sq. Km)
Wuchuan Gelaozu Miaozu (Gelao and Miao) Autonomous County (Duru Town)	務川仡佬族苗族自治縣 (都濡鎮)	务川仡佬族苗族自治县 (都濡镇)	450,000	450,000	480,000	2773
Anshun City	安順市	安顺市	2,800,000	2,860,000	3,040,000	9269
Xixiu District (Dongguan Subdistrict)	西秀區 (東關街道)	西秀区 (东关街道)	870,000	880,000	930,000	1705
Pingba District (Anping Subdistrict)	平壩區 (安平街道)	平坝区 (安平街道)	350,000	360,000	380,000	999
Puding County (Chengguan Town)	普定縣 (城關鎮)	普定县 (城关镇)	460,000	480,000	510,000	1092
Guanling Buyizu Miaozu (Buyei and Miao) Autonomous County (Guansuo Subdistrict)	關嶺布依族苗族自治縣 (關索街道)	关岭布依族苗族自治县 (关索街道)	370,000	380,000	410,000	1468
Zhenning City Buyizu Miaozu (Buyei and Miao) Autonomous County (Chengguan Town)	鎮寧布依族苗族自治縣 (城關鎮)	镇宁布依族苗族自治县 (城关镇)	380,000	390,000	410,000	1721
Ziyun Miaozu Buyizu (Miao and Buyei) Autonomous County (Songshan Town)	紫雲苗族布依族自治縣 (松山鎮)	紫云苗族布依族自治县 (松山镇)	370,000	380,000	410,000	2284
Bijie City	畢節市	毕节市	8,330,000	7,430,000	9,300,000	26,852
Qixingguan District (Mayuan Subdistrict)	七星關區 (麻園街道)	七星关区 (麻园街道)	1,480,000	510,000	1,670,000	3412
Dafang County (Hongqi Subdistrict)	大方縣 (紅旗街道)	大方县 (红旗街道)	1,080,000	1,100,000	1,210,000	3502
Qianxi County (Liancheng Subdistrict)	黔西縣 (蓮城街道)	黔西县 (莲城街道)	910,000	950,000	1,010,000	2554

(continued)

Table 9.6 (continued)

Name	Traditional	Simplified	Population (2012)	Population (2016)	Population (2020)	Area (Sq. Km)
Jinsha County (Guchang Subdistrict)	金沙縣 (鼓場街道)	金沙县 (鼓场街道)	670,000	660,000	710,000	2528
Zhijin County (Wenteng Subdistrict)	織金縣 (文騰街道)	织金县 (文腾街道)	1,090,000	1,130,000	1,240,000	2867
Nayong County (Yongxi Subdistrict)	納雍縣 (雍熙街道)	纳雍县 (雍熙街道)	940,000	980,000	1,060,000	2448
Hezhang County (Chengguan Town)	赫章縣 (城關鎮)	赫章县 (城关镇)	770,000	660,000	870,000	3245
Weining Yizu Huizu Miaozu (Yi, Hui and Miao) Autonomous County (Haibian Subdistrict)	威寧彝族回族苗族自治縣 (海邊街道)	威宁彝族回族苗族自治县 (海边街道)	1,390,000	1,440,000	1,550,000	6296
Tongren City	銅仁市	铜仁市	4,210,000	4,260,000	4,440,000	18,002
Bijiang District (Shizhong Subdistrict)	碧江區 (市中街道)	碧江区 (市中街道)	290,000	300,000	330,000	1002
Wanshan District (Wanshan Town)	萬山區 (萬山鎮)	万山区 (万山镇)	150,000	150,000	170,000	849
Jiangkou County (Shuangjiang Subdistrict)	江口縣 (雙江街道)	江口县 (双江街道)	240,000	240,000	250,000	1869
Shiqian County (Tangshan Town)	石阡縣 (湯山鎮)	石阡县 (汤山镇)	410,000	410,000	420,000	2172
Sinan County (Sitang Subdistrict)	思南縣 (思唐街道)	思南县 (思唐街道)	670,000	670,000	680,000	2231
Dejiang County (Yushui Subdistrict)	德江縣 (玉水街道)	德江县 (玉水街道)	520,000	530,000	550,000	2072
Yuping Dongzu (Dong) Autonomous County (Pingxi Town)	玉屏侗族自治縣 (平溪鎮)	玉屏侗族自治县 (平溪镇)	150,000	150,000	170,000	516
Yinjiang Tujiazu (Tujia) Autonomous County (E'ling Town)	印江土家苗族自治縣 (峨嶺鎮)	印江土家族苗族自治县 (峨岭镇)	430,000	440,000	450,000	1961

(continued)

Table 9.6 (continued)

Name	Traditional	Simplified	Population (2012)	Population (2016)	Population (2020)	Area (Sq. Km)
Yanhe Tujiazu (Tujia) Autonomous County (Heping Town)	沿河土家族自治縣(和平鎮)	沿河土家族自治县(和平镇)	650,000	660,000	690,000	2469
Songtao Miaozu (Miao) Autonomous County (Liaogao Town)	松桃苗族自治縣(蓼皋鎮)	松桃苗族自治县(蓼皋镇)	700,000	710,000	730,000	2861
Qiandongnan Miaozu Dongzu (Miao and Dong) Autonomous Prefecture	黔東南苗族侗族自治州	黔东南苗族侗族自治州	4,530,000	4,610,000	4,810,000	30,399
Kaili City (Dashizi Subdistrict)	凱里市(大十字街道)	凯里市(大十字街道)	490,000	550,000	570,000	1570
Huangping County (Xinzhou Town)	黃平縣(新州鎮)	黄平县(新州镇)	380,000	380,000	390,000	1668
Shibing County (Chengguan Town)	施秉縣(城關鎮)	施秉县(城关镇)	170,000	170,000	180,000	1544
Sansui County (Bagong Town)	三穗縣(八弓鎮)	三穗县(八弓镇)	220,000	220,000	230,000	1036
Zhenyuan County (Wuyang Town)	镇远县 (㵲阳镇)	鎮遠縣 (㵲陽鎮)	270,000	270,000	280,000	1878
Cen'gong County (Siyang Town)	岑鞏縣(思暘鎮)	岑巩县(思旸镇)	230,000	230,000	240,000	1487
Tianzhu County (Fengcheng Town)	天柱縣(鳳城鎮)	天柱县(凤城镇)	400,000	410,000	420,000	2201
Jinping County (Sanjiang Town)	錦屏縣(三江鎮)	锦屏县(三江镇)	230,000	230,000	240,000	1597
Jianhe County (Gedong Town)	劍河縣(革東鎮)	剑河县(革东镇)	250,000	260,000	270,000	2165
Taijiang County (Taigong Town)	台江縣(台拱鎮)	台江县(台拱镇)	160,000	160,000	170,000	1078
Liping County (Defeng Subdistrict)	黎平縣(德鳳街道)	黎平县(德凤街道)	520,000	530,000	570,000	4439
Rongjiang County (Guzhou Town)	榕江縣(古州鎮)	榕江县(古州镇)	350,000	360,000	380,000	3316

(continued)

Table 9.6 (continued)

Name	Traditional	Simplified	Population (2012)	Population (2016)	Population (2020)	Area (Sq. Km)
Congjiang County (Bingmei Town)	從江縣 (丙妹鎮)	从江县 (丙妹镇)	340,000	350,000	380,000	3245
Leishan County (Danjiang Town)	雷山縣 (丹江鎮)	雷山县 (丹江镇)	150,000	150,000	160,000	1219
Majiang County (Xingshan Town)	麻江縣 (杏山鎮)	麻江县 (杏山镇)	210,000	170,000	170,000	958
Danzhai County (Longquan Town)	丹寨縣 (龍泉鎮)	丹寨县 (龙泉镇)	160,000	170,000	180,000	938
Qiannan Buyizu Miaozu (Buyei and Miao) Autonomous Prefecture	黔南布依族苗族自治州	黔南布依族苗族自治州	4,050,000	4,050,000	4,240,000	26,195
Duyun City (Guanghuilu Subdistrict)	都匀市 (廣惠路街道)	都匀市 (广惠路街道)	490,000	480,000	500,000	2278
Fuquan City (Jinshan Subdistrict)	福泉市 (金山街道)	福泉市 (金山街道)	330,000	330,000	340,000	1691
Libo County (Yuping Subdistrict)	荔波縣 (玉屏街道)	荔波县 (玉屏街道)	170,000	180,000	180,000	2432
Guiding County (Jinan Subdistrict)	貴定縣 (金南街道)	贵定县 (金南街道)	290,000	290,000	300,000	1631
Weng'an County (Yongyang Subdistrict)	翁安縣 (雍陽街道)	瓮安县 (雍阳街道)	470,000	470,000	490,000	1974
Dushan County (Baiquan Town)	獨山縣 (百泉鎮)	独山县 (百泉镇)	350,000	350,000	360,000	2442
Pingtang County (Pingzhou Town)	平塘縣 (平舟鎮)	平塘县 (平舟镇)	320,000	320,000	340,000	2816
Luodian County (Longping Town)	羅甸縣 (龍坪鎮)	罗甸县 (龙坪镇)	340,000	340,000	360,000	3010
Changshun County (Changzhai Town)	長順縣 (長寨鎮)	长顺县 (长寨镇)	260,000	260,000	270,000	1555
Longli County (Guanshan Subdistrict)	龍里縣 (冠山街道)	龙里县 (冠山街道)	220,000	220,000	240,000	1518
Huishui County (Lianjiang Subdistrict)	惠水縣 (漣江街道)	惠水县 (涟江街道)	450,000	450,000	470,000	2464
Sandu Shuizu (Sui) Autonomous County (Sanhe Town)	三都水族自治 縣 (三合街道)	三都水族自治县 (三合街道)	360,000	360,000	380,000	2384

(continued)

Table 9.6 (continued)

Name	Traditional	Simplified	Population (2012)	Population (2016)	Population (2020)	Area (Sq. Km)
Qianxinan Buyizu Miaozu (Buyei and Miao) Autonomous Prefecture	黔西南布依族苗族自治州	黔西南布依族苗族自治州	3,400,000	3,490,000	3,650,000	16,805
Xingyi City (Huangcaoba Subdistrict)	興義市(黃草壩街道)	兴义市(黄草坝街道)	810,000	830,000	890,000	2911
Xingren City (Chengbei Subdistrict)	興仁市(城北街道)	兴仁市(城北街道)	510,000	540,000	570,000	1785
Pu'an County (Panshui Town)	普安縣(盤水鎮)	普安县(盘水镇)	330,000	340,000	350,000	1429
Qinglong County (Liancheng Town)	晴隆縣(蓮城鎮)	晴隆县(莲城镇)	330,000	340,000	350,000	1327
Zhenfeng County (Mingu Subdistrict)	貞豐縣(珉谷街道)	贞丰县(珉谷街道)	400,000	410,000	430,000	1512
Wangmo County (Pingdong Subdistrict)	望謨縣(平洞街道)	望谟县(平洞街道)	320,000	320,000	330,000	3006
Ceheng County (Zhelou Town)	冊亨縣(者樓鎮)	册亨县(者楼镇)	240,000	240,000	250,000	2597
Anlong County (Qifeng Subdistrict)	安龍縣(棲鳳街道)	安龙县(栖凤街道)	460,000	470,000	490,000	2238

[a]Formally established in November 2012
[b]Dissolved in March 2016, establishing Bozhou district

References

China News Net. 2021. [*The GDP of 31 provinces in 2020 is released! Anhui's ranking*], 30 January. 31省份2020年GDP出炉!安徽排名. 中国新闻网. https://www.sohu.com/a/447712301_391398.

Flad, Rowan K., and Pochan Chen. 2013. *Ancient central China: centers and peripheries along the Yangzi River*. New York: Cambridge University Press.

Government of Guizhou Province (GGP). 2016. [*Last year, the average income of tobacco farmers in Guizhou Province was 59,000 yuan, and tobacco leaves have become the 'golden leaves' for poverty alleviation*], 4 January. 去年贵州省烟农户均收入5.9万元 烟叶成为脱贫'黄金叶'. http://61.243.4.193:8088/eportal/ui?pageId=597466&articleKey=604720&columnId=595286.

Guizhou Provincial Local Chronicles Compilation Committee (GPLCCC). 2013. *Gazetteer of Guizhou Province*, Vol. 14. Guizhou: Guizhou People's Publishing House. 贵州省志, 贵州省地方志编纂委员会, 贵州人民出版社出版发行.

Guizhou Provincial Statistical Bureau (GPSB 2021). 2021. [*Communiqué of the seventh national census of Guizhou Province, issue no. 2*], 28 May. 贵州省第七次全国人口普查公报, 第二号. http://www.guizhou.gov.cn/xwdt/tzgg/202105/t20210528_68308660.html.

[Guizhou through history]. 2002. Beijing: Modern China Publishing. 贵州通史. 北京: 当代中国出版社. 2002.

Hsieh, Chiao-min, and Jean Kan Hsieh. 1995. *China: A provincial atlas*. New York: Macmillan Publishing.

Lu, Yu, and Teng Zezhi. 2000. [*China's population through history*], Vol. 2. Shandong: Shandong People's Publishing. 路遇, 滕泽之. 中国人口通史. 山东: 山东人民出版社.

Ministry of Civil Affairs (MCA), People's Republic of China. 2020. [*County/township administration handbook*]. Beijing: China Statistics Press. 中華人民共和國民政部, 中華人民共和國, 鄉鎮行政區劃簡冊.

Shang-Ch'i Guide. 2017. [*Backpacking in China: The most complete collection of self-guided travel for china, 2018*]. Taipei: Shang-Ch'i Shitai publishing. 2018 最完整的中國自助旅遊全集. 台北: 上奇時代.

Tan, Qixiang, ed. 1996. *The historical atlas of China*. Vol. VIII. Beijing: China Cartographic Publishing House.

Wondrich, David. 2007. The taste of booze in China. *Esquire*, 21 December. https://www.esquire.com/food-drink/drinks/a1834/esq0104-jan-fooddrink/.

Yang, Jisheng. 2008. *Tombstone: the great Chinese famine, 1958–1962*. New York: Farrar, Straus and Giroux.

Yao, Dong. 2016. [The urbanization of Guizhou province is advancing rapidly: In 2015, the urbanization rate reached 42.01%]. *Guizhou Capital City News*. 姚东. 贵州省城镇化快速推进 2015年城镇化率达42.01%. 贵州都市报. 17 March. http://www.ciudsrc.com/webdiceng.php?id=99237. Accessed 21 Sept 2021.

Zhang, Shunan. 2021. [*The 2020 per capita income list of residents in various provinces: Shanghai is the richest, and it has risen sharply*]. Finance.people.com, 22 January. 张澍楠. 2020年各省份居民人均收入榜: 上海最有钱, 这地涨得猛. http://finance.people.com.cn/n1/2021/0122/c1004-32008733.html.

Chapter 10
Hainan (Island) Province

Abstract Once linked by land to mainland China in its geological past, Hainan Province was long ago inhabited by the local Li people. With signs of inhabitation going back to about 6000 BCE, eventually Hainan became a part of the Chinese empire, with a Han dynasty garrison established there in ca. 100 BCE. Like all of China's provinces and major cities, and despite being an island province, Hainan was severely affected by the ravages of Mao's Great Leap Forward in the late 1950s. Now a popular destination for holiday makers, complete with beaches and world-class golf courses, the island province of Hainan is also home to China's most advanced space launch vehicle programs. Hainan also serves administratively over China's (heavily contested) claims in the South China Sea, the so-called "nine-dash line" that covers some two million square kilometers. In addition to economic data, this chapter includes Hainan populations over time, as well as an up-to-date naming of China's claims in the South China Sea and their western equivalents.

E. Croddy, *China's Provinces and Populations*,
https://doi.org/10.1007/978-3-031-09165-0_10

Hainan Province (海南省 *hǎinán shěng*): Abbreviation 瓊 (*qióng*) (Fig. 10.1)

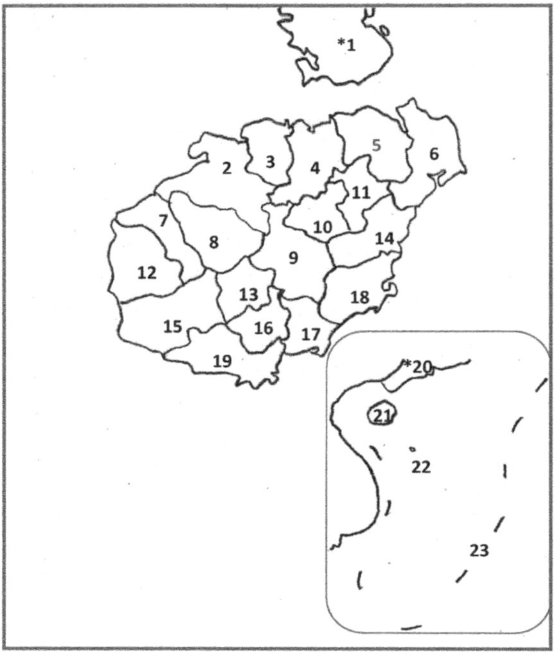

		Population (2020)
1.	*Guangdong Province (Zhanjiang City)	(See Guangdong).
2.	Danzhou City	954,259
3.	Lingao County	420,594
4.	Chengmai County	497,593
5.	Haikou City	2,873,358
6.	Wenchang City	560,894
7.	Changjiang Li Autonomous County	232,124
8.	Baisha Li Autonomous County	164,699
9.	Qiongzhong Li and Miao Autonomous County	179,586
10.	Tunchang County	255,335
11.	Ding'an County	284,690
12.	Dongfang City	444,458
13.	Wuzhishan City	112,269
14.	Qionghai City	528,238
15.	Ledong Li Autonomous County	464,435
16.	Baoting Li and Miao Autonomous County	156,108
17.	Lingshui Li Autonomous County	420,594
18.	Wanning City	545,992
19.	Sanya City	1,031,396
20.	*Guangdong Province	(See Guangdong)
21.	Sanya City	
22.	Sansha City	2,333
23.	People's Republic of China (PRC) "nine-dash" claims	N/A

Fig. 10.1 Hainan Island: Major cities and counties (Provincial Capital: Haikou City). (Drawn by the author after People's Republic of China, Ministry of Civil Affairs (MCA 2020))

Hainan Province: General Impressions

The shorthand character for Hainan is Qiong (瓊 *qióng*), a throwback to the name of an older prefecture on the island. (The PRC officially named a Hainan provincial government on 26 April 1988.) An island province located in the South China Sea, and as with the southernmost regions of China, Hainan had long been considered primitive and dangerous, inhabited by hostile natives, poisonous snakes, and wracked with disease, a "region of tropical miasmic plagues." (瘴癘地區 *zhànglì dìqū*). Throughout China's imperial past, when officials and otherwise troublesome intellectuals offended the court, these malcontents were often sent off to the southern boondocks, and the southern Lingnan region (to include Guangxi, Guangdong and Hainan) was often their (final) destination. For example, Hainan is where the Song poet Su Shi (蘇軾 sū shì) was unceremoniously dispatched in ca. 1100 CE. But nowadays, when it comes to modern Hainan island, one thinks more often of swaying coconut palm trees along the beaches (椰林海灘 *yēlín hǎitān*), sprawling golf courses, a new, advanced space launch center (Wenchang), and Hainan traditional opera (瓊劇 *qióngjù*).

Prehistory

Approximately 20,000 years ago, during the glacial period, Hainan Island was linked to both mainland China (e.g., Guangxi Province) and Vietnam by land, then separated by water about six thousand years in the past. It is highly likely (although difficult to prove with certainty) that the Li (Hlai) people who lived in Hainan four millennia ago were its very first inhabitants, probably a result of south-to-north migrations from Southeast Asia. While many of Hainan's more recent populations trace their origins back to Fujian province (ca. 1000 BCE), mitochondrial DNA testing of the Li (黎族 *lízú*) people showed them related to mainland Chinese in Guangxi (Peng et al. 2011). The Li ethnic group represents the largest segment (>15%) of Hainan's minority population (1,172,181 in 2000, and 1,395,400 in 2009.) Other ethnic groups (non-Han) include Miao and Zhuang ethnic minorities (each less than 1% total).

Neolithic specimens of pottery shards and stone ware have been found dating back to 6000–3000 BCE in southeast Hainan at the Yingdun (英墩 *yīngdūn*) site in Haitang District (海棠區 *hǎitángqū*), as well as Qiaoshan Mountain (橋山 *qiáoshān*) and Lianziwan Bay (蓮子灣 *liánziwān*) in Lingshui County (陵水縣 *língshuǐ xiàn*).

From about 110–46 BCE, the Han dynasty court had established a garrison at Zhuya prefecture (珠崖郡 *zhūyá jùn*), located near modern-day Haikou City. During the same time, another prefectural entity on the northeastern part of Hainan was named Dan'er Prefecture (儋耳郡 *dàn'ěr jùn*). By 46 BCE, however, the Han decided to abandon Hainan due to its excessive administrative and logistical costs. During the Eastern Han (25–220 CE), Hainan Island was named Zhuya State (朱崖

洲 *zhūyá zhōu*), but as of ca. 500 CE it was still not a fully-administered part of the empire. By the Tang Dynasty (631 CE), the imperial court had established Qiongzhou (瓊州 *qióng zhōu*) Prefecture, located near Haikou City (海口市 *hǎikǒu shì*). Thus the modern-day shortened character for Hainan (瓊 *qióng*). As of 741 CE, Hainan was divided into four main prefectures:

- Yazhou (崖州 *yázhōu*)
- Wan'anzhou 萬安州 (*wàn'ānzhōu*)
- Zhenzhou 振州 (*zhènzhōu*) and
- Danzhou (儋州 *dànzhōu*)

The first major wave of Han Chinese migration from the mainland to Hainan occurred during the Song dynasty, increasing the island's overall population to about 160,000. By the time of the Northern Song (1111 CE), Qiongzhou was placed under the jurisdiction of the Guangnan West Circuit (廣南西路 *guǎngnán xīlù).* By the Ming Dynasty (ca. 1400), Hainan was home to nearly 300,000 people (CPU 1988). During the Yuan (ca. 1330), an inspectorate was established for Hainan called Yiweisi (宜慰司 *yíwèisī*). Centuries later, subordinate to Guangdong Province in the Qing Dynasty (ca. 1820), Hainan was named Qiongzhou Prefecture (瓊州府 *qióngzhōufǔ*).

Still administered by Guangdong province after the 1911 revolution, the Republic of China (ROC) established a Qiongya (瓊崖 *qióngyá*) Special Region in the 1930s. After the war with Japan, the ROC renamed Qiongya the Hainan Special Administrative Region[1] in August 1947. Following the Chinese civil war, the People's Republic of China (PRC) wrested control of Hainan from Kuomingtang (KMT) forces in spring of 1950, placing it under Guangdong's jurisdiction.

Even after "liberation" by the Chinese Communist Party (CCP), poor living conditions had long been the norm in Hainan. According to the Chinese Red Cross in 1952, Ledong County, with a population then of 15,989 recorded 489 deaths, and had a mortality rate of 30%, while, in Baisha county, of the 556 births only 232 infants survived (Hua 1982). Maoist social and economic policies in the late 1950s made life on Hainan even more unbearable. Because it was still under the jurisdiction of Guangdong Province, data are scarce on the precise number of deaths that occurred in Hainan during the manmade famine of the Great Leap Forward (1958–1962). However, Hainan certainly lost at least tens of thousands to not only hunger and disease, but also to horrific violence. In Changjiang County during 1958 there were 61,704 people suffering from edema due to malnutrition, and 17,850 people died. During the first 8 months of 1960, at least 358 people died from unnatural causes, 73 committed suicide, eight were beaten to death, and eleven died from food poisoning at Chenghua County's Ruixi commune[2] (Li 2002).

Table 10.1 shows Hainan historical population data. Census data, which includes both permanent and normal residents (常住人口 *chángzhùrénkǒu*), are shown in

[1] 海南特別行政區 *hǎinán tèbiéxíngzhèngqū*.

[2] 澄化縣瑞溪公社 *chénghuà xiàn ruìxīgōngshè*.

Table 10.1 Hainan population data: Ancient to modern. (MCSEB 1993; HPBS 2021)

Year	Hainan population (estimate)
110 BCE	115,000
1393	298,000
1774	1,180,000
1835	1,250,900
1928	2,190,000–2,200,000
1947	2,120,000
1950	2,281,200–2,468,200
1951	2,531,100
1952	2,594,000
1953	2,656,900–2,671,919
1954	2,731,100
1955	2,778,500
1956	2,855,300
1957	2,908,100
1958	3,027,900
1959	3,116,000
1960	3,000,000–3,170,500
1961	3,265,300
1962	3,351,800
1963	3,432,400
1964	3,470,445–3,533,300
1965	3,657,900
1966	3,776,600
1967	3,851,600
1968	3,964,900
1969	4,108,500
1970	4,288,900
1971	4,545,000
1972	4,679,500
1973	4,794,900
1974	4,877,700
1975	4,968,200
1976	5,051,500
1977	5,163,600
1978	5,284,500
1979	5,403,000
1980	5,525,300
1981	5,607,700
1982	5,713,800
1983	5,806,600

(continued)

Table 10.1 (continued)

Year	Hainan population (estimate)
1984	5,893,100
1985	5,975,100
1986	6,056,300
1987	6,150,800
1988	6,268,500
1989	6,392,000
1990	6,557,482–6,627,700
1991	6,741,300
1992	6,860,000
1993	7,010,000
1994	7,110,000
1995	7,240,000
1996	7,340,000
1997	7,430,000
1998	7,530,000
1999	7,620,000
2000	7,890,000
2001	7,960,000
2002	8,030,000
2003	8,110,000
2004	8,180,000
2005	8,280,000
2006	8,360,000
2007	8,450,000
2008	8,540,000
2009	8,640,000
2010	8,671,518
2020	10,081,232

(Table 10.2). A more detailed breakdown of Hainan populations by subordinate districts are presented in Table 10.3. The official registered (*hukou*) number (戶籍人口 *hùjírénkǒu*) was 8,359,000 in 2010, and had risen to 9,250,000 by ca. 2020 (see Table 10.5 below).

Today, Hainan is regionally (if not globally) famous for its scenery, beaches, and neatly manicured golf courses. Hainan is also host to China's South Sea Fleet at Sanya as well as an important People's Liberation Army Navy Air Force (PLANAF) base at Lingshui (陵水黎族自治縣 *língshuǐ lízú zìzhìxiàn*). On 1 April 2001, a PLANAF fighter jet accidentally collided with a United States Navy EP-3E reconnaissance aircraft, which had to make an emergency landing on Lingshui airfield.

Table 10.2 Hainan Province residential population (常住人口 *chángzhù rénkǒu*) census data. (HPBS 2021)

City	Population (2010)	Population (2020)
Haikou City 海口市 *hǎikǒu shì*	2,046,189	2,873,358
Sanya City 三亞市 *sānyà shì*	685,408	1,031,396
Danzhou City 儋州市 *dānzhōu shì*	932,362	954,259[a]
Sansha City[b] 三沙市 *sānshā shì*	N/A	2333
Qionghai City 瓊海市 *qiónghǎi shì*	483,217	528,238[c]
Wanning City 萬寧市 *wànníng shì*	545,597	545,992
Wuzhishan City 五指山市 *wǔzhǐshān shì*	104,122	112,269
Dongfang City 東方市 *dōngfāng shì*	408,309	444,458
Wenchang Cit y文昌市 *wénchāng shì*	537,428	560,894
Lingao County 臨高縣 *lín'gāo xiàn*	427,873	420,594
Chengmai County 澄邁縣 *chéngmài xiàn*	467,161	497,593
Ding'an County 定安縣 *dìng'ān xiàn*	284,616	284,690
Tunchang County 屯昌縣 *túnchāng xiàn*	256,931	255,335
Changjiang Li Autonomous County 昌江黎族自治縣 *chāngjiāng lízú zìzhìxiàn*	223,839	232,124
Baisha Li Autonomous County 白沙黎族自治縣 *báishā lízú zìzhìxiàn*	167,918	164,699
Qiongzhong Li and Miao Autonomous County 瓊中黎族苗族自治縣 *qióngzhōng lízú miáozú zìzhìxiàn*	174,076	179,586
Lingshui Li Autonomous County 陵水黎族自治縣 *língshuǐ lízú zìzhìxiàn*	320,468	372,511
Baoting Li and Miao Autonomous County 保亭黎苗族自治縣 *bǎotíng lízú miáozú zìzhìxiàn*	146,684	156,108
Ledong Li Autonomous County 樂東黎族自治縣 *lèdōng lízú zìzhìxiàn*	458,876	464,435
Xisha (西沙群島 *xīshā qúndǎo*), Spratly (Nansha 南沙群島 *nánshā qúndǎo*) and Zhongsha (中沙群島 *zhōngshā qúndǎo*)	444	N/A[d]
Total	**8,671,518**	**10,081,232**

[a]Includes 洋浦 *yángpǔ*

[b]Includes Xisha (西沙群島 *xīshā qúndǎo*), Spratly (Nansha 南沙群島 *nánshā qúndǎo*) and Zhongsha (中沙群島 *zhōngshā qúndǎo*)

[c]Does not include deployed military personnel

[d]See Sansha City which includes Xisha 西沙群島 *xīshā qúndǎo*), Spratly (Nansha 南沙群島 *nánshā qúndǎo*) and Zhongsha 中沙群島 *zhōngshā qúndǎo*)

The new Wenchang Satellite Launch Center (文昌衛星發射中心 *wénchāng wèixīng fāshè zhōngxīn*) in Wencheng city became fully operational when it successfully launched a Long March 7 (長征七號) on 25 June 2016. Wenchang is outfitted and geographically well-suited to launch China's heaviest rocket launch vehicle, the Long March 5 (長征五號 *chángzhēng wǔhào*), which was successfully launched in November 2016.

Table 10.3 Hainan Province: Population data of cities and their subordinate sectors. (HPBS 2021)

Selected cities and subordinate sectors, population (2020 census)[a]	Subordinate district, city and county populations (2020)	Total population (2020)
Haikou City 海口市 ***hǎikǒu shì***		**2,873,358**
Longhua District 龍華區 *lónghuá qū*	797,684	
Xiuying District 秀英區 *xiùyīng qū*	567,108	
Qiongshan District 瓊山區 *qióngshān qū*	655,553	
Meilan District 美蘭區 *měián qū*	853,013	
Sanya City 三亞市 ***sānyà shì***		**1,031,396**
Jiyang District 吉陽區 *jíyáng qū*	447,322	
Haitang District 海棠區 *hǎitáng qū*	113,481	
Tianya District 天涯區 *tiānyá qū*	353,698	
Yazhou District 崖州區 *yázhōu qū*	116,895	
Baisha Li Autonomous County 白沙黎族自治縣 ***báishā lízú zìzhìxiàn***		**164,699**
Yacha Town 牙叉鎮 *yáchā zhèn*	49,027	
Qifang Town 七坊鎮 *qīfāng zhèn*	37,847	
Bangxi Town 邦溪鎮 *bāngxī zhèn*	14,413	
Da'an Town 打安鎮 *dǎ'ān zhèn*	15,612	
Xishui Township 細水鄉 *xìshuǐ xiāng*	4891	
Yuanmen Township 元門鄉 *yuánmén xiāng*	5539	
Nankai Township 南開鄉 *nánkāi xiāng*	4197	
Fulong Township 阜龍鄉 *fùlóng xiāng*	4627	
Qingsong Township 青松鄉 *qīngsōng xiāng*	7657	
Jinbo Township 金波鄉 *jīnbō xiāng*	7927	
Rongbang Township 榮邦鄉 *róngbāng xiāng*	12,962	
Qiongzhong Li and Miao Autonomous County 瓊中黎族苗族自治縣 ***qióngzhōng lízú miáozú zìzhìxiàn***		**179,586**
Yinggen Town 營根鎮 *yínggēn zhèn*	55,646	
Wanling Town 灣嶺鎮 *wānlǐng zhèn*	27,449	
Limushan Town 黎母山鎮 *límǔshān zhèn*	34,598	
Heping Town 和平鎮 *hépíng zhèn*	11,665	
Changzheng Town 長征鎮 *chángzhēng zhèn*	9901	
Hongmao Town 紅毛鎮 *hóngmáo zhèn*	10,295	
Zhongping Town 中平鎮 *zhōngpíng zhèn*	11,509	
Diaoluoshan Township 吊羅山鄉 *diàoluóshān xiāng*	7254	
Shang'an Township 上安鄉 *shàngān xiāng*	5974	
Shiyun Township 什運鄉 *shíyùn xiāng*	4774	
Limushan Forestry Area 黎母山林場 *límǔshān línchǎng*	521	

[a]Data on some counties not available as of 14 January 2022

Hainan's Population and Economy

Given its relatively small population and limited industrial base, Hainan province has a relatively modest gross domestic product (GDP), although it has continued to increase over the last decade, registering USD $163 billion in 2015, and $277 billion in 2020. In percentage terms, its population has increased at a rapid pace from 2010 to 2020 (about 16%). While the per capita income on Hainan ranks low in mainland China at $4340 in 2020, this was an increase of 6% over the year prior (Zhang 2021).

China's (and Taiwan's) Contested Claims in the South China Sea

Going back to 1946, the Republic of China (ROC) has claimed islands, shoals and reefs spanning some two million square kilometers in the South China Sea (SCS). Today, not without controversy, the People's Republic of China (PRC) has been doubling down on these claims, building upon and expanding its occupied islets in the Paracel and Spratly islands. Technically, the ROC (Taiwan) also makes the same claim on the region, but not with the same vehemence (nor with the extent of newly-built military infrastructure) of the mainland Chinese government.

We will not address the merits (or lack thereof) of China's argument for sovereignty in the SCS, but chart out how the PRC officially names and administers these islands (at least on paper). While the region offers substantial natural resources, including fisheries and potential petroleum reserves, China's main interest in securing the South China Sea has a great deal to do with maintaining its strategic sea lines of communication (Fig. 10.2).

On 21 June 2012, the PRC state council renamed and changed the administrative status of the Paracel (Xisha 西沙群島 *xīshā qúndǎo*), Spratly (Nansha 南沙群島 *nánshā qúndǎo*) and Macclesfield Bank (Zhongsha 中沙群島 *zhōngshā qúndǎo* including Scarborough Reef) island groups, putting these under the jurisdiction of Hainan province's Sansha City (三沙市 *sānshā shì*), the latter's government being located on Woody Island (永興島 *yǒngxìng dǎo*). China has built, reclaimed, and established military outposts on the following islands in the Spratlys:

- Cuarteron Reef 華陽礁 (*huáyáng jiāo*)
- Fiery Cross Reef 永署礁 (*yǒngshǔ jiāo*)
- Hughes Reef 東門礁 (*dōngmén jiāo*)
- Subi Reef 渚碧礁 (*zhǔbì jiāo*)
- Johnson Reef 赤瓜礁 (*chìguā jiāo*)
- Mischief Reef 美濟礁 (*měijì jiāo*)
- Gaven Reef 南薰礁 (*nánxūn jiāo*)

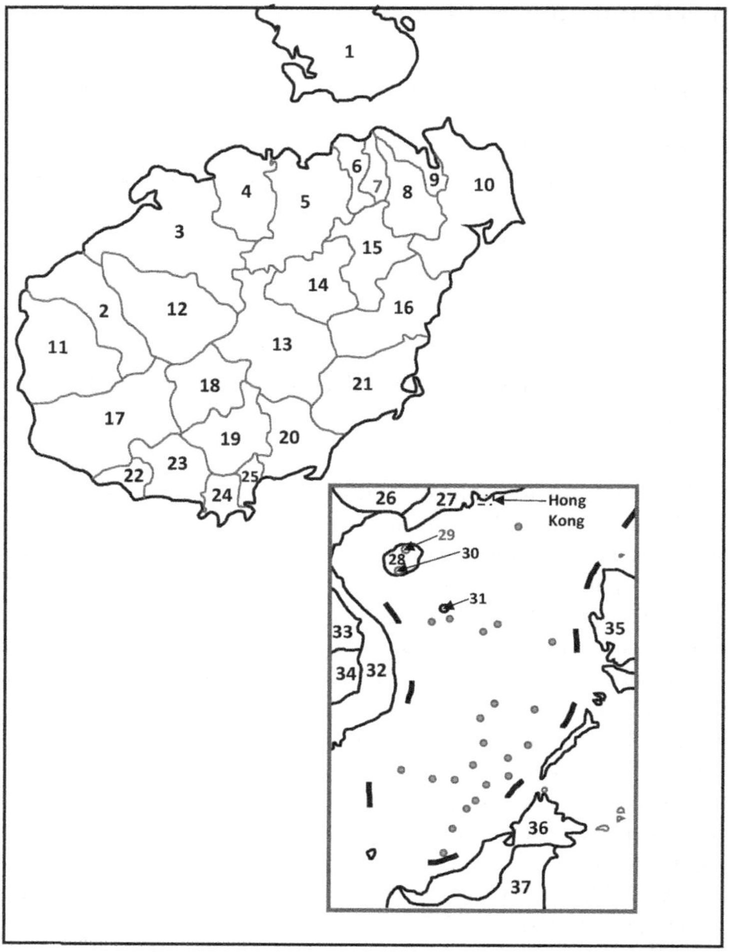

1. Guangdong Province
2. Changjiang Li Autonomous County
3. Danzhou City
4. Lingao County
5. Chengmai County
6. Xiuying District
7. Longhua District
8. Qiongshan District
9. Meilan District
10. Wenchang City
11. Dongfang City
12. Baisha Li Autonomous County
13. Qiongzhong Li and Miao Autonomous County
14. Tunchang County
15. Ding'an County
16. Qionghai City
17. Ledong Li Autonomous County
18. Wuzhishan City
19. Baoting Li and Miao Autonomous County
20. Lingshui Li Autonomous County
21. Wanning City
22. Yazhou District
23. Tianya District
24. Jiyang District
25. Haitang District
26. Guangxi Zhuang Autonomous Region
27. Guangdong Province
28. Hainan Province
29. Haikou City
30. Sanya City
31. Sansha City
32. Vietnam
33. Laos
34. Cambodia
35. Phillippines
36. Malaysia
37. Indonesia

Fig. 10.2 Hainan Province subordinate districts (Government Seat: Longhua District). (Drawn by the author after People's Republic of China, Ministry of Civil Affairs (MCA 2020))

Table 10.4 (below) provides Chinese-English names for South China Sea islands and atolls that China (and Taiwan, incidentally) claim to be sovereign territory:

Table 10.5 (below) shows the *hukou* (family registered) populations based on PRC Ministry of Civil Affairs data. (Districts listed directly under major cities are government seats, as are those in parentheses). One can compare these data with the census (usual residential populations based on 2010 and 2020 censuses in Tables 10.2 and 10.3 (above).

Table 10.4 Chinese claimed islands/reefs in the Paracel Island Group

Island name	Chinese (traditional)	Simplified	Pinyin
Siamese Shoal	西門暗沙	西门暗沙	*xīmén ànshā*
Bankok Shoal	本固暗沙	本固暗沙	*běngù ànshā*
Magpie Shoal	美濱暗沙	美滨暗沙	*měibīn ànshā*
Carpenter Shoal	魯班暗沙	鲁班暗沙	*lǔbān ànshā*
Oliver Shoal	中北暗沙	中北暗沙	*zhōngběi ànshā*
Pygmy Shoal	比微暗沙	比微暗沙	*bǐwēi ànshā*
Egeria Bank	隱磯灘	隐矶滩	*yǐnjī tān*
Howard Shoal	武勇暗沙	武勇暗沙	*wǔyǒng ànshā*
Learmonth Shoal	濟猛暗沙	济猛暗沙	*jìměng ànshā*
Plover Shoal	海鳩暗沙	海鸠暗沙	*hǎijiū ànshā*
Addington Patch	安定連礁	安定连礁	*āndìng liánjiū*
Smith Shoal	美溪暗沙	美溪暗沙	*měixī ànshā*
Bassett Shoal	布德暗沙	布德暗沙	*bùdé ànshā*
Balfour Shoal, Balfour, Banc	波洑暗沙	波洑暗沙	*bōfú ànshā*
Parry Shoal	排波暗沙	排波暗沙	*páibō ànshā*
Cawston Shoal	過淀暗沙	过淀暗沙	*guòdiàn ànshā*
Penguin Reef	排洪灘	排洪滩	*páihóng tān*
Taojing Ansha, Tancred Shoal	濤靜暗沙	涛静暗沙	*tāojìng ànshā*
Combe Shoal	控湃暗沙	控湃暗沙	*kòngpài ànshā*
Cathay Shoal	華夏暗沙	华夏暗沙	*huáxià ànshā*
Hardy Patches	石塘連礁	石塘连礁	*shítáng ànshā*
Finger Palm Shoal	指掌暗沙	指掌暗沙	*zhǐzhǎng ànshā*
Margesson Shoal	南扉暗沙	南扉暗沙	*nánfēi ànshā*
Walker Shoal	漫步暗沙	漫步暗沙	*mànbù ànshā*
Phillips Shoal	樂西暗沙	乐西暗沙	*lèxī ànshā*
Payne Shoal	屏南暗沙	屏南暗沙	*píngnán ànshā*
ROC: Democracy Reef (PRC: Scarborough Reef)	民主礁 (黃岩島)	黄岩岛 (民主礁)	*huángyán dǎo/mínzhǔ jiāo*
South rock	南岩	南岩	*Nányán*
North rock	北岩	北岩	*Běiyán*
Constitution shoal	憲法暗沙	宪法暗沙	*xiànfǎ ànshā*
Yitong Ansha	一統暗沙	一统暗沙	*yītǒng ànshā*
Shenhu Ansha	神狐暗沙	神狐暗沙	*shénhú ànshā*
Middle south shoal	中南暗沙	中南暗沙	*zhōngnán ànshā*

(continued)

Table 10.4 (continued)

Island name	Chinese (traditional)	Simplified	Pinyin
Chinese claimed islands and reefs in the Spratly Group (Nansha)			
Two Islands; North Danger Reef; N. Danger Cay	雙子群礁	双子群礁	*shuāngzǐ qúnjiāo*
North Reef	貢士礁	贡士礁	*gòngshì jiāo*
North East Cay	北子島	北子岛	*běizǐ dǎo*
Shira Reef	北外沙洲	北外沙洲	*běiwài shāzhōu*
South-west cay	南子島	南子岛	*nánzǐ dǎo*
South Reef	奈羅礁	奈罗礁	*nàiluó jiāo*
Sabine Patches	東南暗沙	东南暗沙	*dōngnán ànshā*
Day Shoal	東北暗沙	东北暗沙	*dōngběi ànshā*
Iroquois Ridge	北子暗沙	北子暗沙	*běizǐ ànshā*
Trident Shoal	永登暗沙	永登暗沙	*yǒngdēng ànshā*
Lys Shoal	樂斯暗沙	乐斯暗沙	*lèsī ànshā*
Thitu Island and Reefs; Thitu Reef	中業群礁	中业群礁	*zhōngyè qúnjiāo*
Thitu reef	鐵峙礁	铁峙礁	*tiězhì jiāo*
Thitu trough	鐵峙水道	铁峙水道	*tiězhì shuǐdào*
Meijiu Jiao	梅九礁	梅九礁	*méijiǔ jiāo*
Thitu Island	中業島	中业岛	*zhōngyè dǎo*
Tiexian Jiao	鐵線礁	铁线礁	*tiěxiàn jiāo*
Subi Reef	渚碧礁	渚碧礁	*zhǔbì jiāo*
Loaita Bank and Reefs	道明群礁	道明群礁	*dàomíng qúnjiāo*
Shuanghuang Shazhou	雙黃沙礁	双黄沙洲	*shuānghuáng shāzhōu*
Loaita Island	南鑰島	南钥岛	*nányuè dǎo*
Lankiam Cay	楊信沙洲	杨信沙洲	*yángxìn shāzhōu*
Kugui Jiao	庫歸礁	库归礁	*kùguī jiāo*
Chang Tan	長灘	长滩	*cháng tān*
Menzies Reef	蒙自礁	蒙自礁	*méngzì tān*
Tizzard Bank and Reefs	鄭和群礁	郑和群礁	*zhènghé qúnjiāo*
Taiping Dao, Itu Aba Island[a]	太平島	太平岛	*tàipíng dǎo*
Sandy Cay	敦謙沙洲	敦谦沙洲	*dūnqiān shāzhōu*
Petley Reef	舶蘭礁	舶兰礁	*bólán jiāo*
Eldad Reef	安達礁	安达礁	*āndá jiāo*
Namyit Island	鴻庥島	鸿庥岛	*hóngxiū dǎo*
Gaven Reef	南薰礁	南薰礁	*nánxūn jiāo*
Discovery Small Reef	小現礁	小现礁	*xiǎoxiàn jiāo*
Discovery Great Reef	大現礁	大现礁	*dàxiàn jiāo*
Western or Flora Temple Reef	福祿寺礁	福禄寺礁	*fúlùsì jiāo*
Corn Wallis Reef	康樂礁	康乐礁	*kānglè jiāo*

(continued)

Table 10.4 (continued)

Island name	Chinese (traditional)	Simplified	Pinyin
Union Banks and Reef, Union Tablemount	九章群礁	九章群礁	*jiǔzhāng qúnjiāo*
Sin Cowe Island	景宏島	景宏岛	*jǐnghóng dǎo*
Edmund Reef	南門礁	南门礁	*nánmén jiāo*
McKennan Reef	西門礁	西门礁	*xīmén jiāo*
Hughes Reef	東門礁	东门礁	*dōngmén jiāo*
Hallet Reef	安樂礁	安乐礁	*ānlè jiáo*
Holiday Reef	長線礁	长线礁	*chángxiàn jiāo*
Empire Reef	主權礁	主权礁	*zhǔquán jiāo*
Whitsum Reef	牛軛礁	牛轭礁	*niú'è jiāo*
Ross Reef	染青東礁	染青东礁	*rǎnqīng dōngjiāo*
Grierson Reef	染青沙洲	染青沙洲	*rǎnqīng shāzhōu*
Bamford Reef	龍蝦礁	龙虾礁	*lóngxiā jiāo*
Tetley Reef	扁參礁	扁参礁	*biǎnshēn jiāo*
Jones Reef	漳溪礁	漳溪礁	*zhāngxī jiāo*
Higgen Reef	屈原礁	屈原礁	*qūyuán jiāo*
Lansdowne Reef	瓊礁	琼礁	*qióng jiāo*
Johnson Reef	赤瓜礁	赤瓜礁	*chìguā jiāo*
Collins Reef	鬼喊礁	鬼喊礁	*guǐhǎn jiāo*
Loveless Reef	華礁	华礁	*huá jiāo*
Gent Reef	吉陽礁	吉阳礁	*jíyáng jiāo*
Fancy Wreck Shoal	泛愛暗沙	泛爱暗沙	*fàn'ài ànshā*
Genges South Reef	伏波礁	伏波礁	*fúbō jiāo*
Fiery Cross Reef	永署礁	永暑礁	*yǒngshǔ jiāo*
Daulle Shoal	逍遙暗沙	逍遥暗沙	*xiāoyáo ànshā*
Irving Reef	火艾礁	火艾礁	*huǒ'ài jiāo*
West York Island	西月島	西月岛	*xīyuè dǎo*
Mahuan Dao, Nanshan Island	馬歡島	马欢岛	*mǎhuān dǎo*
Flat Island	費信島	费信岛	*fèixìn dǎo*
Third Thomas Reef	和平暗沙	和平暗沙	*hépíng ànshā*
Hopkins Reef	火星礁	火星礁	*huǒxīng jiāo*
Nares Reef	大淵灘	大渊滩	*dàyuān tān*
Jackson Atoll	五方礁	五方礁	*wǔfāng jiāo*
Hamspoon Reef	五方尾	五方尾	*wǔfāngwěi*
Petch Reef	五方南	五方南	*wǔfāngnán*
Deane Reef	五方西	五方西	*wǔfāngxī*
Hoare Reef	五方北	五方北	*wǔfāngběi*
Dickinson Reef	五方頭	五方头	*wǔfāngtóu*
Shinko Shoal	潯江暗沙	浔江暗沙	*xúnjiāng ànshā*

(continued)

Table 10.4 (continued)

Island name	Chinese (traditional)	Simplified	Pinyin
Hardy Reef	半路礁	半路礁	*bànlù jiāo*
Southern Bank or Southern Shoal	南方淺灘	南方浅滩	*nánfāng qiǎntān*
Pennsylvania S. Reef	東坡礁	东坡礁	*dōngpō jiāo*
Brown Bank	棕灘	棕滩	*zōng tān*
Bao Tan	寶灘	宝滩	*bǎo tān*
Foulerton Reef	東華礁	东华礁	*dōnghuá jiāo*
Bin Jiao	彬礁	彬礁	*bīn jiāo*
Amy Douglas Bank	安塘灘	安塘滩	*āntáng tān*
Amy Douglas Reef	安塘礁	安塘礁	*āntáng jiāo*
Iroquois Reef	鱟藤礁	鲎藤礁	*hòuténg jiāo*
Baker Reef	鞏珍礁	巩珍礁	*gǒngzhēn jiāo*
Reed Bank/Tablemount	禮樂灘	礼乐滩	*lǐyuè tān*
Marie Louise Bank	雄難礁	雄南礁	*xióngnán jiāo*
Pennsylvania North Reef	陽明礁	阳明礁	*yángmíng jiāo*
North Reef	禮樂南礁	礼乐南礁	*lǐyuè nánjiāo*
Wood Bank	紫灘	紫滩	*zǐ tān*
Lord Auckland Shoal	莪蘭暗沙	莪兰暗沙	*élán ànshā*
Carnatic Shoal	紅石暗沙	红石暗沙	*hóngshí ànshā*
Fairie Queen	仙后灘	仙后滩	*xiānhòu tān*
Templier Bank or Templer Bank	忠孝灘	忠孝滩	*zhōngxiào tān*
Leslie Bank	勇士灘	勇士滩	*yǒngshì tān*
Sandy Shoal	神仙暗沙	神仙暗沙	*shénxiān ànshā*
Seahorse Shoal or Routh Bank	海馬灘	海马滩	*hǎimǎ tān*
Ganges North Reef	北恆礁	北恒礁	*běihéng jiāo*
Ganges Reef	恆礁	恒礁	*héng jiāo*
Pennsylvania South Reef	孔明礁	孔明礁	*kǒngmíng jiāo*
Livock Reef	三角灘	三角礁	*sānjiǎo jiāo*
Hopps Reef	祿沙礁	禄沙礁	*lùshā jiāo*
South Mischief Reef	美濟礁	美济礁	*měijì jiāo*
Alicia Annie Reef	仙娥礁	仙娥礁	*xiān'é jiāo*
First Thomas Shoal	信義礁	信义礁	*xìnyì jiāo*
Investigator Northeast Shoal	海口礁	海口礁	*hǎikǒu jiāo*
Half Moon Shoal	半月礁	半月礁	*bànüè jiāo*
Royal Captain Shoal	艦長礁	舰长礁	*jiànzhǎng jiāo*
Second Thomas Reef	仁愛礁	仁爱礁	*rén'ài jiāo*
Sabina Reef	仙賓礁	仙宾礁	*xiānbīn jiāo*
Zhongshan Jiao	鐘山礁	钟山礁	*zhōngshān jiāo*
Lixin Jiao	立新礁	立新礁	*lìxīn jiāo*
Boxall Reef	牛車輪礁	牛车轮礁	*niúchēlún jiāo*
Pian Jiao	片礁	片礁	*piàn jiāo*

(continued)

Table 10.4 (continued)

Island name	Chinese (traditional)	Simplified	Pinyin
Bombay Shoal	蓬勃暗沙	蓬勃暗沙	*péngbó ànshā*
Director Reef, Director Rock	指向礁	指向礁	*zhǐxiàng jiāo*
Glasgow Shoal or Glasgow	南樂暗沙	南乐暗沙	*nánlè ànshā*
North East Shoal	校尉暗沙	校尉暗沙	*xiàowèi ànshā*
North Viper Shoal or Seahorse	都護暗沙	都护暗沙	*dūhù ànshā*
South Viper Shoal	保衛暗沙	保卫暗沙	*bǎowèi ànshā*
Commodore Reef	司令礁	司令礁	*sīlìng jiāo*
Galsgow Bank	雙礁	双礁	*shuāng jiāo*
Observation Rock	石龍岩	石龙岩	*shílóngyán*
Madagascar Rock	乙辛石	乙辛石	*yǐxīnshí*
Tennent Reef or Pigeon Reef	無乜礁	无乜礁	*wúmiē jiāo*
Cay Marino	玉諾礁	玉诺礁	*yùnuò jiāo*
Cornwallis South Reef	南華礁	南华礁	*nánhuá jiāo*
Alison Reef	六門礁	六门礁	*liùmén jiāo*
Maralie Reef or Bittern Shoal	石盤仔	石盘仔	*shípánzǎi*
Pearson Reef	畢生礁	毕生礁	*bìshēng jiāo*
Investigator Shoal	榆亞暗沙	榆亚暗沙	*yúyà ànshā*
Erjiao Jiao	二角礁	二角礁	*èrjiǎo jiāo*
Langkou Jiao	浪口礁	浪口礁	*làngkǒu jiāo*
Xiantou Jiao	線頭礁	线头礁	*xiàntóu jiāo*
Southwest Shoal	金吾暗沙	金吾暗沙	*jīnwǔ ànshā*
U.S.S. Plymouth	普寧暗沙	普宁暗沙	*pǔníng ànshā*
Erica Reef	簸箕礁	簸箕礁	*bòjī jiāo*
Ardasier Bank	安渡礁	安渡礁	*āndù tān*
Gloucester Breakers	破浪礁	破浪礁	*pòlàng jiāo*
Dallas Reef	光星礁	光星礁	*guāngxīng jiāo*
Ardasier Reef	光星仔礁	光星仔礁	*guāngxīngzǎi jiāo*
Ardasier Breakers	息波礁	息波礁	*xībō jiāo*
Mariveles Reef	南海礁	南海礁	*nánhǎi jiāo*
Barque Canada Reef	柏礁	柏礁	*bó jiāo*
Lizzie Webber Reef	單柱石	单柱石	*dānzhùshí*
Niaoyudingshi	鳥魚錠石	鸟鱼锭石	*niǎoyúdìngshí*
Amboyne or Amboyna Cay	安波沙洲	安波沙洲	*ānbō shāzhōu*
Stag Shoal	隱遁暗沙	隐遁暗沙	*yǐndùn ànshā*
London Reefs	尹慶群礁	尹庆群礁	*yǐnqìng qúnjiāo*
Cuarteron Reef	華陽礁	华阳礁	*huáyáng jiāo*
East Reef or East London Reef	東礁	东礁	*dōng jiāo*
Central Reef	中礁	中礁	*zhōng jiāo*
West Reef or West London Reef	西礁	西礁	*xī jiāo*
Spratly Island	南威島	南威岛	*nánwēi dǎo*

(continued)

Table 10.4 (continued)

Island name	Chinese (traditional)	Simplified	Pinyin
Ladd Reef	日積礁	日积礁	*rìjī jiāo*
Coronation Bank	康泰灘	康泰滩	*kāngtài tān*
Jubilee Bank	朱應灘	朱应滩	*zhūyìng tān*
Owen Shoal	奧援暗沙	奥援暗沙	*àoyuán ànshā*
Suilang Ansha	碎浪暗沙	碎浪暗沙	*suìlàng ànshā*
Rifleman Bank	南薇灘	南薇滩	*nánwéi tān*
Bombay Castle	蓬勃保	蓬勃堡	*péngbóbǎo*
Johnson Patch	常駿暗沙	常骏暗沙	*chángjùn ànshā*
Kingston Shoal	金盾暗沙	金盾暗沙	*jīndùn ànshā*
Orleana Shoal	奧南暗沙	奥南暗沙	*àonán ànshā*
Prince of Wales Bank	廣雅灘	广雅滩	*guǎngyǎ tān*
Alexandra Bank	人駿灘	人骏滩	*rénjùn tān*
Grainger Bank	李准灘	李准滩	*lǐzhǔn tān*
Prince Consort Bank	西衛灘	西卫滩	*xīwèi tān*
Vanguard Bank	萬安灘	万安滩	*wàn'ān tān*
Swallow Reef	彈丸礁	弹丸礁	*dànwán jiāo*
Royal Charlotte Reef	皇路礁	皇路礁	*huánglù jiāo*
Louisa Reef	南通礁	南通礁	*nántóng jiāo*
North Luconia Shoals	北康暗沙	北康暗沙	*běikāng ànshā*
Friendship Shoal	盟誼暗沙	盟谊暗沙	*méngyì ànshā*
Aitken Reef	義淨礁	义净礁	*yìjìng jiāo*
Hardie Shoal	海康暗沙	海康暗沙	*hǎikāng ànshā*
Buck Reef	法顯暗沙	法显暗沙	*fǎxiǎn ànshā*
Mordy Reef	康西暗沙	康西暗沙	*kāngxī ànshā*
Bei'an Jiao	北安礁	北安礁	*běi'ān jiāo*
Sea-horse Breakers	南安礁	南安礁	*nán'ān jiāo*
Hayes Reef	南屏礁	南屏礁	*nánpíng jiāo*
South Luconia Shoals	南康暗沙	南康暗沙	*nánkāng ànshā*
Connell Reef	隱波暗沙	隐波暗沙	*yǐnbō ànshā*
Stigant Reef	海安礁	海安礁	*hǎi'ān jiāo*
Luconia Breakers	瓊台礁	琼台礁	*qióngtái jiāo*
Richmond Reef	潭門礁	潭门礁	*tánmén jiāo*
Haining Jiao, Herald Reef	海寧礁	海宁礁	*hǎiníng jiāo*
Sterra Blanca	澄平礁	澄平礁	*chéngpíng jiāo*
Comus Shoal	歡樂暗沙	欢乐暗沙	*huānlè ànshā*
James Shoal	曾母暗沙	曾母暗沙	*zēngmǔ ànshā*
Middle Pass	中水道	中水道	*zhōng shuǐdào*
U.S.S. Pigeon Passage	南華水道	南华水道	*nánhuá shuǐdào*

[a]Occupied and administered by Republic of China (Taiwan)

Hainan Province (瓊 *qióng*)

Provincial Capital: Haikou

Table 10.5 Hainan Province: Permanent registered (戶籍人口 *hùjí rénkǒu*) populations. (MCA 2020)

Name	Traditional	Simplified	Population (2012)	Population (2016)	Population (2020)	Area (Sq. Km)
Hainan Province	海南省	海南省	8,960,000	9,020,000	9,250,000	34,000
Haikou City	海口市	海口市	1,610,000	1,630,000	1,780,000	2315
Longhua District (Jinmao Subdistrict)	龍華區 (金貿街道)	龙华区 (金贸街道)	440,000	450,000	490,000	300
Xiuying District (Xiuying Subdistrict)	秀英區 (秀英街道)	秀英区 (秀英街道)	280,000	290,000	340,000	512
Qiongshan District (Fucheng Subdistrict)	瓊山區 (府城街道)	琼山区 (府城街道)	390,000	390,000	400,000	940
Meilan District (Bailong Subdistrict)	美蘭區 (白龍街道)	美兰区 (白龙街道)	500,000	500,000	540,000	563
Sanya City	三亞市	三亚市	570,000	690,000	610,000	1918
Jiyang District[a] (Yingbinlu)	吉陽區 (迎賓路)	吉阳区 (迎宾路)	N/A	240,000	180,000	372
Haitang District[b] (Xinminlu)	海棠區 (新民路)	海棠区 (新民路)	N/A	90,000	80,000	255
Tianya District[c] (Fenghuanglu)	天涯區 (鳳凰路)	天涯区 (凤凰路)	N/A	250,000	260,000	944
Yazhou District[d] (Shuinandadao)	崖州區 (水南大道)	崖州区 (水南大道)	N/A	110,000	100,000	347
Sansha City (Xisha Yongxingdao aka Paracel, Woody Island)	三沙市 (西沙永興島)	三沙市 (西沙永兴岛)	N/A	N/A	630	N/A[e]
Danzhou City (Nada Town)	儋州市 (那大鎮)	儋州市 (那大镇)	1,070,000	1,030,000	1,060,000	3400
County-level administrative units under direct provincial jurisdiction	省直轄縣級行政單位	省直辖县级行政单位				
Wenchang City (Wencheng Town)	文昌市 (文城鎮)	文昌市 (文城镇)	580,000	590,000	600,000	2486
Qionghai City (Jiaji Town)	瓊海市 (嘉積鎮)	琼海市 (嘉积镇)	500,000	500,000	520,000	1692
Wanning City (Wancheng Town)	萬寧市 (萬城鎮)	万宁市 (万城镇)	610,000	620,000	630,000	1883

(continued)

Table 10.5 (continued)

Name	Traditional	Simplified	Population (2012)	Population (2016)	Population (2020)	Area (Sq. Km)
Wuzhishan City (Tongshi Town)	五指山市 (通什鎮)	五指山市 (通什镇)	110,000	110,000	110,000	1130
Dongfang City (Basuo Town)	東方市 (八所鎮)	东方市 (八所镇)	440,000	460,000	460,000	2272
Lingao County (Lincheng Town)	臨高縣 (臨城鎮)	临高县 (临城镇)	490,000	510,000	500,000	1317
Chengmai County (Jinjiang Town)	澄邁縣 (金江鎮)	澄迈县 (金江镇)	560,000	570,000	570,000	2068
Ding'an County (Dingcheng Town)	定安縣 (定城鎮)	定安县 (定城镇)	340,000	340,000	350,000	1196
Tunchang County (Tuncheng Town)	屯昌縣 (屯城鎮)	屯昌县 (屯城镇)	300,000	310,000	310,000	1224
Changjiang Lizu (Li) Autonomous County (Shilu Town)	昌江黎族自治縣 (石碌鎮)	昌江黎族自治县 (石碌镇)	270,000	260,000	260,000	1596
Baisha Lizu (Li) Autonomous County (Yacha Town)	白沙黎族自治縣 (牙叉鎮)	白沙黎族自治县 (牙叉镇)	200,000	200,000	200,000	2117
Qiongzhong Lizu (Li) Autonomous County (Yinggen Town)	瓊中黎族苗族自治縣 (營根鎮)	琼中黎族苗族自治县 (营根镇)	230,000	230,000	220,000	2704
Lingshui Lizu (Li) Autonomous County (Yelin Town)	陵水黎族自治縣 (椰林鎮)	陵水黎族自治县 (椰林镇)	370,000	380,000	390,000	1128
Baoting Lizu (Li) Autonomous County (Baocheng Town)	保亭黎族自治縣 (保城鎮)	保亭黎族苗族自治县 (保城镇)	170,000	170,000	170,000	1161
Ledong Lizu (Li) Autonomous County (Baoyou Town)	樂東黎族自治縣 (抱由鎮)	乐东黎族自治县 (抱由镇)	540,000	540,000	540,000	2763

[a]Established on 12 February 2014
[b]Established on 12 February 2014
[c]Established on 12 February 2014
[d]Established on 12 February 2014
[e]According to the PRC Ministry of Civil Affairs (MCA) 2020 administrative handbook, the surface area of Sansha city is "temporarily unavailable"

References

China People's University (CPU), Qing Historical Research Office. 1988. [*Qing historical communications*]. Beijing: China Social Sciences Press. 中国社会科学院. 清史研究室, 中国人民大学. 清史研究通訊. 北京: 中国社会科学出版社.

Hainan Province Bureau of Statistics (HPBS). 2021. [*The seventh national census communiqué of Hainan Province*]. 海南省第七次全国人口普查公报(第二号), 13 May. http://stats.hainan.gov.cn/tjj/ywdt/xwfb/202105/t20210512_2977770.html.

Hua, Xinzhi. 1982. [The population of the Li nationality in Hainan: A survey on development]. *Population Research*. 华辛芝. 海南黎族人口发: 展情况调查. 人口研究 6 (3): 47–49.

Li, Ruojian. 2002. [The Great Leap Forward and analysis of causes of unusual death in difficult times]. *21st Century Bimonthly Journal*. 李若建. 大躍進與困難時期非正常死亡原因分析. 二十一世紀雙月刊 27: 59–70.

Ministry of Civil Affairs (MCA), People's Republic of China. 2020. [*County/township administration handbook*]. Beijing: China Statistics Press. 中華人民共和國民政部, 中華人民共和國, 鄉鎮行政區劃簡冊.

Modern China Series Editorial Board (MCSEB). 1993. [*Modern China: Hainan*]. Beijing: Modern China Publishing. 丛书编辑委员会. 当代中国, 当代中国的海南. 北京: 当代中国出版社.

Peng, Min-Sheng, Jun-Dong He, Hai-Xin Liu, and Ya-Ping Zhang. 2011. Tracing the legacy of the early Hainan islanders: A perspective from mitochondrial DNA. *BMC Evolutionary Biology* 11 (46): 1–13.

Zhang, Shunan. 2021. [The 2020 per capita income list of residents in various provinces: Shanghai is the richest, and it has risen sharply]. Finance.people.com. 22 January. 张澍楠. 2020年各省份居民人均收入榜: 上海最有钱, 这地涨得猛. http://finance.people.com.cn/n1/2021/0122/c1004-32008733.html.

Chapter 11
Hebei Province

Abstract The modern-day region that is now Hebei Province has long been heavily populated. Indeed, there is evidence of significant communities having been established in Hebei more than 10,000 years ago. Ancient Chinese cultures such as the Erligang that are foundational to the original Shang dynasty (ca. 1750–1100 BCE) can also be found in archeological sites throughout Hebei Province. Today, Hebei Province looks to become part of an even larger populated megalopolis, the planned metropolitan combination of Jing-Jin-Ji (Bejing, Tianjin, Hebei) into one massive entity. Once referred to as a "*zhili*" or directly administered prefecture, Hebei Province has also been considered a region of great strategic importance, notably its major cities that include Zhangjiakou City (formerly known as Kalgan), Baoding City, and Shijiazhuang City. Its borders surrounding the highly-economic developed provincial-level metropolises of Beijing and Tianjin, Hebei ranks about the middle in terms of gross domestic product (GDP) and per capita income when compared to mainland China's 31 provinces and major cities.

E. Croddy, *China's Provinces and Populations*,
https://doi.org/10.1007/978-3-031-09165-0_11

Hebei Province (河北省 *hébĕi shĕng*): Abbreviation 冀 (*jì*) (Fig. 11.1)

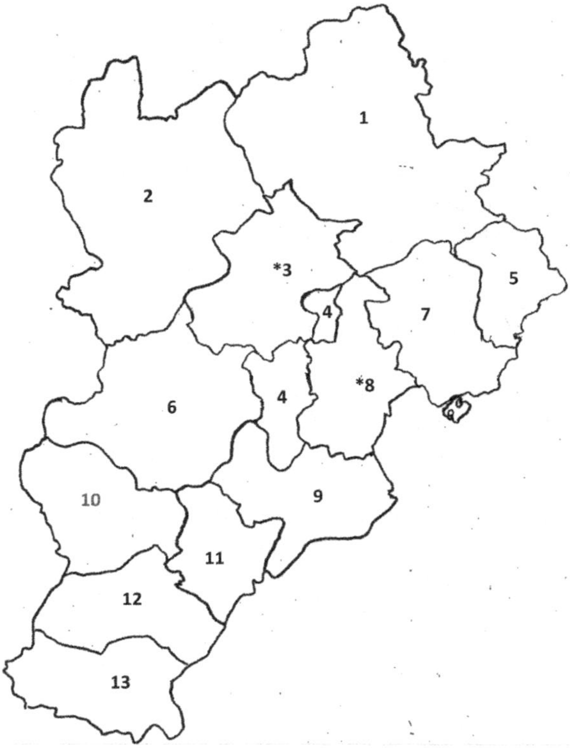

Fig. 11.1 Hebei Province major cities (Provincial Capital: Shijiazhuang City). (Map drawn by the author, after People's Republic of China, Ministry of Civil Affairs (MCA 2020))

	City	Population (2020)
1.	Chengde City	3,354,444
2.	Zhangjiakou City	4,118,908
3.	*Beijing City	(See Beijing)
4.	Langfang City	5,464,087
5.	Qinhuangdao City	3,136,879
6.	Baoding City	9,242,610
7.	Tangshan City	7,717,983
8.	*Tianjin City	(See Tianjin)
9.	Cangzhou City	7,300,783
10.	Shijiazhuang City	10,640,458
11.	Hengshui City	4,212,933
12.	Xingtai City	7,111,106
13.	Handan City	9,413,990

Hebei Province: General Impressions

Hebei Province, previously Romanized "Hopei" or "Ho-pei" (based on older transcriptions) has been a key political, economic, and cultural center throughout China's history. Geographically surrounding the provincial-level cities of Beijing and Tianjin, Hebei Province itself describes a very large area with historically important cities (north to south): Zhangjiakou City (formerly known as Kalgan), Baoding City, and Shijiazhuang City (formerly known as Shimen 石門 *shímén*).

The city of Handan has a residential population of over 9.4 million (based on the 2020 census), and gives us the curious idiom "Learning the Handan walk (學步邯鄲 *xuébù hándān*)." Here, it refers to the story of a boy from the state of Yan who, after arriving in the Zhao capital city of Handan, was amazed by the elegant gait of the people who walked there, and eagerly set about to learn it. However, not only was unsuccessful in learning the Handan walk, he lost his the ability to walk at all, and was forced to crawl back home. Thus it means someone who slavishly copies something but only ends up being the laughing stock.

Some sources and legends have it that (the mythological) Fu Xi (伏羲 *fúxī*), progenitor of the Chinese people, flourished in and around today's Xingtai City (邢台市 *xíngtái shì*), and Xinle City (新樂市 *xīnlè shì*). It is also said that the legendary Yellow Emperor battled his nemesis Chiyou (蚩尤 *Chīyóu*) at modern-day Zhuolu County (涿鹿縣 *zhuōlù xiàn*).

Prehistory

Stories about Fu Xi and his progeny may belong to myth, but fascinating archeological finds in southern Hebei support the notion that this region was host to among China's first organized societies. For example, in 1986, evidence of mankind's earliest agriculture (millet) going back to ca. 9500 BCE was discovered near Nanzhuangtou (南莊頭 *nánzhuāngtóu*) in Xushui County (徐水縣 *xúshuǐ xiàn*) (Chang 1999) Dating back to about 5300 BCE, the Cishan Culture (磁山文化 *císhān wénhuà*) was found in Wu'an City (武安市 *wǔān shì*). This kinship society developed farming tools such as harvesting scythe blades made of stone, as well as woven textiles and crafted pottery (Yuan and Jiao 2007).

In 1973, a later Erligang Culture (二里崗文化 *èrlǐgāng wén-huà*) site (dated ca. 1300 BCE) was found in Hebei at Gaocheng District (藁城區 *gǎochéng qū*), Taixicun Village (台西村 *táixī cūn*). This site has typical Erligang-styled, layered ercengtai (二層臺 *èrcéngtái*) burial shaft arrangements and yaokeng (腰坑 *yāokēng*) sacrificial pits. Along with classic bronze vessel designs, evidence was also found of both human and animal sacrifices (Bagely 1999).

Hebei Province, along with Henan, Shanxi, Shandong and Jiangxi, is also the location of key sites of ancient Chinese culture and civilization going back to the Shang dynasty (about 1750–1100 BCE). For example, a Shang dynasty era ge (戈 *gē*) halberd with an iron blade was unearthed in Gaocheng District during the early 1970s. Thriving in the Spring-Autumn period (ca. 680 BCE), the Shanrong (山戎 *shānróng*) state, populated by a nomadic tribe, had its capital in today's Qian'an City (遷安市 *qiānān shì*). During the Warring States (戰國 *zhànguó*) period (ca. 470 BCE), the northern part of today's Hebei formed the State of Yan (燕國 *yànguó*), while the southern part is where the states of Central Mountain (中山國 *zhōngshān guó*), Zhao (趙國 *zhàoguó*) and Wei (魏國 *wèiguó*) were located. The subsequent encroachment and occupation of major cities by rival states in the region gave Hebei the classic sobriquet "the great region of the Yan and the Zhao" (燕趙大地 *yànzhào dàdì*).

Modern-day Baoding City is the rough border line separating the ancient Yan (燕國) and Zhao (趙國) states. It is for this reason that Hebei has another alternate name, "Yanzhao" (燕趙 *yànzhào*). During the Han (漢 *hàn*) period (202 BCE–220 CE), the southern portion of modern-day Hebei was known as Ji prefecture (冀州 *jìzhōu*), thus today's abbreviated name (冀 jì) for Hebei. It was during this time that the region became more heavily populated, with a population during the Eastern Han (ca. 200 CE) of 5,949,637 individuals (Yuan and Jiao 2007). Some of the more sensational archaeological discoveries found in Hebei Province also include a sepulcher dating to the Western Han at a Mancheng District (滿城區 *mǎnchéng qū*) excavation in 1968, complete with burial suits made entirely of jade which were meant to preserve their bodies.

Going back to the Tang dynasty, administrative areas were delineated using the Huanghe River as a reference during the Zhenguan (貞觀 *zhēngudān*) year (627 CE), thus the name Hebei (河北 *héběi*), i.e., "north of (Yellow) river)." And as the Hebei region formed the front lines against the Khitan (契丹 *qìdān*) barbarians to the north, its geographical location was strategically important. During the Song (960–1279), Hebei hosted 300,000 troops in response to this threat. By the Yuan dynasty (ca. 1280), modern Hebei was directly subordinated to the capital (Dadu) as a "provincial secretariat" (中書省 *zhōngshū shěng*), and was referred to as a northern subordinate area, Beizhili (北直隸 *běizhílì*).

Ming Dynasty Agriculture in Hebei

The late Ming dynasty scholar and polymath, Xu Guangqi (徐光啟 *xú guāngqǐ*; Latinized: Paulus, 1562–1633), encouraged wet-rice cultivation in more northern areas to include Hebei, and in doing so brought about a veritable watershed in Chinese agriculture. This likely helped to support and encourage a burgeoning population in the Hebei region from the Ming to Qing dynasties (see Table 11.1).

During the Qing dynasty, Hebei's government, in the person of the viceroy (直隸總督 *zhílì zǒngdū*), was located in modern-day Baoding City in 1730. In the later

Table 11.1 Historical population data for Hebei Province. (Spence 1999)

1573	4,625,000
1685	3,297,000
1749	13,933,000
1767	16,691,000
1776	20,291,000
1790	23,497,000

Qing, Tangshan City built its first railway and the first modern coal mining concern, running between Beijing and Zhangjiakou. Under the leadership of engineer Zhan Tianyou (詹天佑 *Zhān Tiānyòu*; also known as Tien Yow Jeme, b. 1861, Guangdong), this railroad was the first ever designed and built by the Chinese. Through the late 1920s, Hebei was still referred to as a "directly controlled" province, Zhili (直隸 *zhílì*).

The Hebei provincial city of Zhangjiakou (once known as Kalgan, from the Mongolian *halha* for "mart," and also referred to as "Beijing's northern gate") has long been considered the strategic gateway to the capital. In September 1945, for example, as Chinese Nationalists (Guomingdang, or KMT under Chiang Kai-shek) and the Chinese Communist Party (CCP) struggled for position, Joseph Stalin called for Chinese communist forces to hold Kalgan as a check against the KMT (Dikötter 2013).

The 1976 Tangshan Earthquake

Early in the morning (3:42 local) on 28 July 1976, a 7.5 magnitude earthquake struck Tangshan City, resulting in one of the deadliest natural disasters every recorded. Following a mere several seconds, at least 242,769 people died, representing nearly a quarter of Tangshan City's population at the time, with 164,851 injured and some 5,300,000 homes toppled (Yao and Jiang 2006). Some later estimates have even doubled that number. Jolting a swath through Tangshan Fengnan District (豐南區 *fēngnán qū*), the epicenter was located along Jixiang Road (吉祥路 *jíxiáng lù*) in Lunan District (路南區 *lùnán qū*), causing severe damage across an area of nearly 50 square kilometers. The temblor leveled older style, brick single-level houses, but neither were steel-reinforced high-rise structures spared. The Tangshan earthquake was even felt throughout northeast China, from northern Heilongjiang Province's Manzhouli City (滿洲里市 *mǎnzhōulǐ shì*), south to central Henan Province, east to the Bohai Gulf, and as far west as Ningxia's mountain range. Mao Zedong, at that time quite infirm and in the late stages of amyotrophic lateral sclerosis (Lou Gehrig's disease), read the reports of the disaster from his sick bed. He died about 1 month later.

Hebei's Capital: Past and Future Developments

Within recent decades, Hebei's capital city has shifted from Baoding (population about 12 million), to Tianjin, then finally to Shijiazhuang where it remains today. This may again change in the near future, however. In an initiative announced by President Xi Jinping in 2014, Hebei Province will be the "Ji" (冀 *jì*, the common abbreviation for Hebei) in a future united Jing-Jin-Ji (Be**jing**, Tian**jin**, Hebei) megalopolis development plan. There also has been talk that Baoding, by dint of its location, continued economic development, and its key role as a regional hub, may eclipse Shijiazhuang City, and perhaps once again be restored as the alternate capital to Beijing.

In 2016, Hebei's population (to include non-permanent residents) was 74,700,500 people, a 1% increase from the year prior (74,249,200). Modest growth was seen overall from 2010 to 2020 (Table 11.2). Coming in at 12th of 31 mainland China's provinces and modern cities in terms of gross domestic product (USD $563 billion) in 2020, the per capita income for Hebei province was ranked 17th at $4,220 (Zhang 2021).

Table 11.4 (below) shows the *hukou* (family registered) populations based on PRC Ministry of Civil Affairs data. (Districts listed directly under major cities are government seats, as are those in parentheses). One can compare these data with the census (usual residential populations based on 2010 and 2020 censuses in Tables 11.2 and 11.3 (below).

Table 11.2 Hebei Province residential population (常住人口 *chángzhù rénkǒu*) data. (HPBS 2021)

Hebei Province cities	Population (2010)	Population (2020)
Shijiazhuang City 石家莊市 *shíjiāzhuāng shì* [abbrev. 石 *shí*]	10,163,788	10,640,458
Tangshan City 唐山市 *tángshān shì*	7,577,284	7,717,983
Qinhuangdao City 秦皇島市 *qínhuángdǎo shì*	2,987,605	3,136,879
Handan City 邯鄲市 *hándān shì*	9,174,679	9,413,990
Xingtai City 邢台市 *xíngtái shì*	7,104,114	7,111,106
Baoding City 保定市 *bǎodìng shì*	11,194,379	9,242,610
Zhangjiakou City 張家口市 *zhāngjiākǒu shì*	4,345,491	4,118,908
Chengde City 承德市 *chéngdé shì*	3,473,197	3,354,444
Cangzhou City 滄州市 *cāngzhōu shì*	7,134,053	7,300,783
Langfang City 廊坊市 *lángfāng shì*	4,358,839	5,464,087
Hengshui City 衡水市 *héngshuǐ shì*	4,340,773	4,212,933
Dingzhou City 定州市 *dìngzhōu shì*	N/A	1,095,986
Xinji City 辛集市 *xīnjí shì*	N/A	594,628
Xiong'an Xinqu (New District)[a] 雄'安新區 *xióngān xīnqū*	N/A	1,205,440
Total	71,854,202	**74,610,235**

[a]Xi Jinping's personal project, the Xiong'an "City of the Future" was founded in 2017, and reportedly some 160,000 construction workers moved there since to build key infrastructure projects. Via reporting by Xifang Yang (楊希璠), China Correspondent for *Die Zeit*, social media post, January 27, 2022

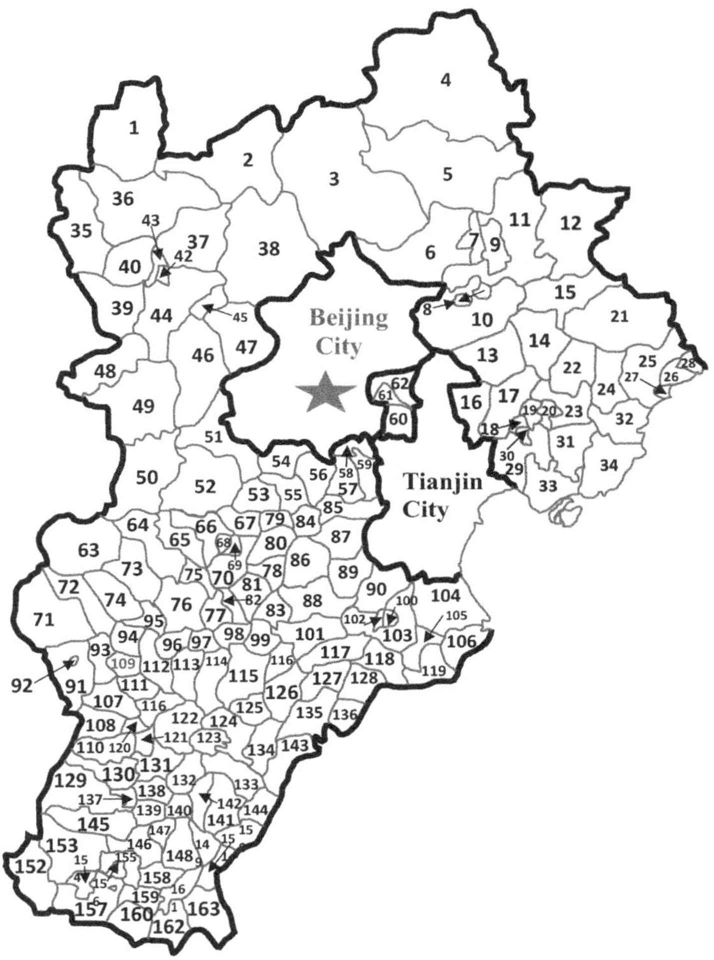

1. Kangbao County
2. Guyuan County
3. Fengning Manchu Autonomous County
4. Weichang Manchu and Mongolian Autonomous County
5. Longhua County
6. Luanping County
7. Shuangluan District
8. Yingshou Yingzi Kuangqu (Mining District)
9. Shuangqiao District
10. Xinglong County
11. Chengde County
12. Pingquan City
13. Zunhua City
14. Qianxi County
15. Kuancheng Manchu Autonomous County
16. Yutian County
17. Fengrun District
18. Lubei District
19. Kaiping District
20. Guye District
21. Qinglong Manchu Autonomous County
22. Qian'an City
23. Luanzhou City
24. Lulong County
25. Funing District
26. Haigang District
27. Beidaihe District
28. Shanhaiguan strict

Fig. 11.2 Hebei Province: Subdistricts (Capital City Governmental Seat: Chang'an District). (Map drawn by the author, after People's Republic of China, Ministry of Civil Affairs (MCA 2020)

29. Fengnan District
30. Lunan District
31. Luannan County
32. Changli County
33. Caofeidian District
34. Laoting County
35. Shangyi County
36. Zhangbei County
37. Chongli County
38. Chicheng County
39. Huai'an County
40. Wanquan County
41. Xuanhua District
42. Qiaodong District
43. Qiaoxi District
44. Xuanhua District
45. Xiahuayuan District
46. Zhuolu County
47. Huailai County
48. Yangyuan County
49. Jixian County
50. Laiyuan County
51. Laishui County
52. Yixian County
53. Dingxing County
54. Zhuozhou City
55. Gaobeidian City
56. Gu'an County
57. Yongqing County
58. Guangyang District
59. Anci District
60. Xianghe County
61. Dachang Hui Autonomous County
62. Sanhe City
63. Fuping County
64. Tangxian County
65. Shunping County
66. Mancheng District
67. Xushui District
68. Jingxiu District
69. Lianchi District
70. Qingyuan District
71. Pingshan County
72. Lingshou County
73. Quyang County
74. Xingtang County
75. Wangdu County
76. Dingzhou City
77. Anguo City
78. Gaoyang County
79. Rongcheng County
80. Anxin County
81. Lixian County
82. Boye County
83. Suning County
84. Xiongxian County
85. Bazhou City
86. Renqiu City
87. Wen'an County
88. Hejian City
89. Dacheng County
90. Qingxian County
91. Jingxing County
92. Jingxing Kuangqu (mining district)
93. Luquan District
94. Zhengding County
95. Xinle City
96. Wuji County
97. Shenze County
98. Anping County
99. Raoyang County
100. Xinhua District
101. Songxian County
102. Yunhe District
103. Cangxian County
104. Huanghua City
105. Mengcun Hui Autonomous County
106. Haixing County
107. Yuanshi County
108. Zanghuang County
109. Chang'an District
110. Lincheng County
111. Luancheng City
112. Gaocheng District
113. Puzhou City
114. Xinji City
115. Shenzhou City
116. Wuqiang County
117. Botou City
118. Nanpi County
119. Yanshan County
120. Gaoyi County
121. Baixiang County
122. Ningpu County
123. Xinhe County
124. Jizhou City
125. Taocheng District
126. Wuyi County
127. Fucheng County
128. Dongguang County
129. Xingtai County
130. Neiqiu County
131. Longyao County
132. Julu County
133. Nangong City
134. Zaoqiang County
135. Jingxian County
136. Wuqiao County
137. Qiaodong and Qiaoxi Districts
138. Renxian County
139. Nanhe County
140. Pingxiang County
141. Weixian County
142. Guangzong County
143. Gucheng County
144. Qinghe County
145. Shahe City
146. Yongnian County
147. Jize County
148. Quzhou County
149. Qiuxian County
150. Linxi County
151. Guantao County
152. Shexian County
153. Wu'an County
154. Fengfeng Kuangqu (mining district)
155. Fuxing District
156. Hanshan District
157. Cixian County
158. Feixian County
159. Cheng'an County
160. Linzhang County
161. Guangping County
162. Weixian County
163. Daming County

Fig. 11.2 (continued)

Table 11.3 Hebei Province: Population data of cities and their subordinate sectors. (HPBS 2021)

Cities and subordinate sectors, population (2020 census)	Subordinate district, city and county populations (2020)	Total population (2020)
Shijiazhuang City 石家莊市 ***shíjiāzhuāng shì* [abbrev.** 石 ***shí*]**		**11,235,086**
Chang'an District 長安區 *cháng'ān qū*	1,059,572	
Qiaoxi District 橋西區 *qiáoxī qū*	979,646	
Xinhua District 新華區 *xīnhuá qū*	802,057	
Yuhua District 裕華區 *yùhuá qū*	771,255	
Jingxing Kuangqu (mining) District 井陘礦區 *jǐngxíngkuàng qū*	77,015	
Xinji City 辛集市 *xīnjí shì*	594,628	
Gaocheng District 藁城區 *gǎochéng qū*	741,068	
Jinzhou City 晉州市 *jìnzhōu shì*	507,959	
Xinle City 新樂市 *xīnlè shì*	478,529	
Luquan District 鹿泉區 *lùquán qū*	588,279	
Jingxing County 井陘縣 *jǐngxíng xiàn*	250,898	
Zhengding County 正定縣 *zhèngdìng xiàn*	549,321	
Luancheng District 欒城區 *luánchéng qū*	378,689	
Xingtang County 行唐縣 *xíngtáng xiàn*	376,627	
Lingshou County 靈壽縣 *língshòu xiàn*	309,121	
Gaoyi County 高邑縣 *gāoyì xiàn*	178,368	
Shenze County 深澤縣 *shēnzé xiàn*	215,806	
Zanhuang County 贊皇縣 *zànhuáng xiàn*	242,549	
Wuji County 無極縣 *wújí xiàn*	451,377	
Pingshan County 平山縣 *píngshān xiàn*	423,333	
Yuanshi County 元氏縣 *yuánshì xiàn*	392,710	
Zhaoxian County 趙縣 *zhàoxiàn*	505,366	
Shijiazhuang High Technology Industrial Development Zone 石家莊高新技術產業開發區 shíjiāzhuāng gāoxīnjìshù chǎnyè kāifāqū	304,675	
Shijiazhuang Xunhuan Chemical Industrial Park Area 石家莊循環化工園區 *shíjiāzhuāng xúnhuán huàgōngyuán qū*	56,147	
Tangshan City 唐山市 ***tángshān shì***		**7,717,983**
Lubei District 路北區 *lùběi qū*	784,667	
Lunan District 路南區 *lùnán qū*	334,204	
Guye District 古冶區 *gǔyě qū*	317,932	
Kaiping District 開平區 *kāipíng qū*	279,432	
Fengrun District 豐潤區 *fēngrùn qū*	800,740	
Fengnan District 豐南區 *fēngnán qū*	552,532	
Caofeidian District 曹妃甸區 *cáofēidiàn qū*	352,069	
Zunhua City 遵化市 *zūnhuà shì*	707,047	
Qian'an City 遷安市 *qiān'ān shì*	776,752	

(continued)

Table 11.3 (continued)

Cities and subordinate sectors, population (2020 census)	Subordinate district, city and county populations (2020)	Total population (2020)
Luanzhou City[a] 灤州市 *luánzhōu shì*	520,102	
Luannan County 灤南縣 *luánnán xiàn*	508,538	
Laoting County 樂亭縣 *làotíng xiàn*	389,198	
Qianxi County 遷西縣 *qiānxī xiàn*	365,615	
Yutian County 玉田縣*yùtián xiàn*	664,906	
Lutai Economic and Technology Development Zone 蘆台經濟技術開發區 *lútái jīngjì jìshù kāifāqū*	43,558	
Hangu Management District 漢沽管理區 *hàngū guǎnlǐqū*	52,550	
Tangshan High Technology Industrial Development Zone 唐山高新技術產業開發區 *tángshān gāoxīnjìshù chǎnyè kāifāqū*	169,923	
Tangshan Seaport Economic Development Zone 唐山海港經濟開發區 *tángshān hǎigǎngjīngjì kāifāqū*	98,218	
Qinhuangdao City 秦皇島市 ***qínhuángdǎo shì***		**3,136,879**
Haigang District 海港區 *hǎigǎng qū*	1,024,876	
Shanhaiguan District 山海關區 *shānhǎiguān qū*	164,989	
Beidaihe District 北戴河區 *běidàihé qū*	130,104	
Changli County 昌黎縣 *chānglí xiàn*	487,989	
Funing District 撫寧區 *fǔníng qū*	291,211	
Lulong County 盧龍縣 *lúlóng xiàn*	333,942	
Qinglong Manzu (Manchu) Autonomous County 青龍滿族自治縣 *qīnglóng mǎnzú zìzhìxiàn*	431,138	
Qinhuangdao Economic and Technology Development Zone 秦皇島經濟技術開發區 *qínhuángdǎo jīngjìjìshù kāifāqū*	197,898	
Handan City 邯鄲市 ***hándān shì***		**9,413,990**
Congtai District 叢台區 *cóngtái qū*	572,175	
Hanshan District 邯山區 *hánshān qū*	614,303	
Fuxing District 復興區 *fùxīng qū*	319,980	
Fengfeng Kuangqu (mining) District 峰峰礦區 *fēngfēng kuàngqū*	429,245	
Wu'an City 武安市 *wǔ'ān shì*	811,631	
Linzhang County 臨漳縣 *línzhāng xiàn*	589,003	
Cheng'an County 成安縣 *chéng'ān xiàn*	401,052	
Daming County 大名縣 *dàmíng xiàn*	726,396	
Shexian County 涉縣 *shèxiàn*	379,559	
Cixian County磁縣 *cíxiàn*	440,728	
Feixiang District 肥鄉區 *féixiāng qū*	372,265	
Yongnian County 永年區 *yǒngnián qū*	851,227	

(continued)

Table 11.3 (continued)

Cities and subordinate sectors, population (2020 census)	Subordinate district, city and county populations (2020)	Total population (2020)
Qiuxian County 邱縣 *qiūxiàn*	210,998	
Jize County 雞澤縣 *jīzé xiàn*	297,425	
Guangping County 廣平縣 *guǎngpíng xiàn*	264,025	
Guantao County 館陶縣 *guǎntáo xiàn*	307,912	
Weixian County 魏縣 *wèixiàn*	796,806	
Quzhou County 曲周縣 *qūzhōu xiàn*	463,727	
Jinan New District 冀南新區 *jìnán xīnqū*	271,097	
Handan Economic and Technology Development Zone 邯鄲經濟技術開發區 *hándān jīngjìjìshù kāifāqū*	294,436	
Xingtai City 邢台市 ***xíngtái shì***		**7,111,106**
Xiangdu District 襄都區 *xiāngdū qū*	362,857	
Xindu District 信都區 *xìndū qū*	798,770	
Nangong City 南宮市 *nángōng shì*	396,718	
Shahe City 沙河市 *shāhé shì*	431,746	
Lincheng County 臨城縣 *línchéng xiàn*	199,793	
Neiqiu County 內丘縣 *nèiqiū xiàn*	258,260	
Bai(bo)xiang County 柏鄉縣 *bǎixiāng xiàn*	168,761	
Longyao County 隆堯縣 *lóngyáo xiàn*	480,447	
Renze District 仁澤區 *rénzé qū*	342,869	
Nanhe County 南和縣 *nánhé xiàn*	350,384	
Ningjin County 寧晉縣 *níngjìn xiàn*	745,389	
Julu County 巨鹿縣 *jùlù xiàn*	346,007	
Xinhe County 新河縣 *xīnhé xiàn*	134,095	
Guangzong County 廣宗縣 *guǎngzōng xiàn*	280,063	
Pingxiang County 平鄉縣 *píngxiāng xiàn*	323,675	
Weixian County 威縣 *wēixiàn*	496,230	
Qinghe County 清河縣 *qīnghé xiàn*	421,582	
Linxi County 臨西縣 *línxī xiàn*	326,968	
Xingtai Economic Development Zone 邢台經濟開發區 *xíngtái jīngjì kāifāqū*	182,585	
Xingdong New District 邢東新區 *xíngdōng xīnqū*	63,367	
Baoding City保定市 ***bǎodìng shì***		**9,242,610**
Jingxiu District 競秀區 *jīngxiù qū*	522,813	
Lianchi District 蓮池區 *liánchí qū*	913,541	
Zhuozhou City 琢州市 *zhuózhōu shì*	667,678	
Anguo City 安國市 *ānguó shì*	363,091	
Gaobeidian City 高碑店市 *gāobēidiàn shì*	532,731	
Mancheng District 滿城區 *mǎnchéng qū*	391,359	
Qingyuan District 清苑區 *qīngyuàn qū*	625,246	

(continued)

Table 11.3 (continued)

Cities and subordinate sectors, population (2020 census)	Subordinate district, city and county populations (2020)	Total population (2020)
Yixian County 易縣 *yìxiàn*	485,536	
Xushui District 徐水區 *xúshuǐ qū*	604,275	
Laiyuan County 淶源縣 *láiyuán xiàn*	248,890	
Dingxing County 定興縣 *dìngxīng xiàn*	512,765	
Shunping County 順平縣 *shùnpíng xiàn*	269,678	
Tangxian County 唐縣 *tángxiàn*	505,849	
Wangdu County 望都縣 *wàngdū xiàn*	233,790	
Laishui County 淶水縣 *láishuǐ xiàn*	315,753	
Gaoyang County 高陽縣 *gāoyáng xiàn*	318,986	
Quyang County 曲陽縣 *qūyáng xiàn*	573,975	
Fuping County 阜平縣 *fùpíng xiàn*	194,004	
Boye County 博野縣 *bóyě xiàn*	225,065	
Lixian County 蠡縣 *lǐxiàn*	488,152	
Baoding High Technology Industrial Development Zone 保定高新技術產業開發區 *bǎodìng gāoxīnjìshù chǎnyè kāifāqū*	96,301	
Baigou Xincheng 白溝新城 *báigōu xīnchéng*	153,132	
Zhangjiakou City 張家口市 ***zhāngjiākǒu shì***		**4,118,908**
Qiaoxi District 橋西區 *qiáoxī qū*	279,033	
Qiaodong District 橋東區 *qiáodōng qū*	279,616	
Xuanhua District 宣化區 *xuānhuà qū*	542,358	
Xiahuayuan District 下花園區 *xiàhuāyuán qū*	64,216	
Zhangbei County 張北縣 *zhāngběi xiàn*	308,880	
Kangbao County 康保縣 *kāngbǎo xiàn*	138,205	
Guyuan County 沽源縣 *gūyuán xiàn*	160,995	
Shangyi County 尚義縣 *shàngyì xiàn*	104,247	
Yuxian County 蔚縣 *yùxiàn*	411,824	
Yangyuan County 陽原縣 *yángyuán xiàn*	205,773	
Huai'an County 懷安縣 *huáiān xiàn*	179,949	
Wanquan District 萬全區 *wànquán qū*	216,795	
Huailai County 懷來縣 *huáilái xiàn*	348,746	
Zhuolu County 涿鹿縣 *zhuōlù xiàn*	294,013	
Chicheng County 赤城縣 *chìchéng xiàn*	197,919	
Chongli District 崇禮區 *chónglǐ qū*	105,501	
Zhangjiakou Economic and Technology Development Zone 張家口經濟技術開發區 *zhāngjiākǒu jīngjìjìshù kāifāqū*	257,331	
Chabei Management District 察北管理區 *cháběi guǎnlǐqū*	16,915	
Saibei Management District 塞北管理區 *sāiběi guǎnlǐqū*	6,592	

(continued)

Table 11.3 (continued)

Cities and subordinate sectors, population (2020 census)	Subordinate district, city and county populations (2020)	Total population (2020)
Chengde City 承德市 ***chéngdé shì***		**3,354,444**
Shuangqiao District 雙橋區 *shuāngqiáo qū*	358,431	
Shuangluan District 雙灤區 *shuāngluán qū*	187,361	
Yingshouyingzi Kuangqu (mining) District 鷹手營子礦區 *yīngshǒuyíngzǐ kuàngqū*	54,730	
Chengde County 承德縣 *chéngdé xiàn*	340,579	
Xinglong County 興隆縣 *xīnglóng xiàn*	271,628	
Pingquan City 平泉市 *píngquán shì*	399,378	
Luanping County 灤平縣 *luánpíng xiàn*	268,647	
Longhua County 隆化縣 *lónghuà xiàn*	347,707	
Fengning Manchu Autonomous County 豐寧滿族自治縣 *fēngníng mǎnzú zìzhìxiàn*	326,353	
Kuancheng Manzu (Manchu) Autonomous County 寬城滿族蒙古族自治縣 *kuānchéng mǎnzú ménggǔzú zìzhìxiàn*	240,579	
Weichang Manzu (Manchu) Autonomous County 圍場滿族蒙古族自治縣 *wéicháng mǎnzú ménggǔzú zìzhìxiàn*	423,676	
Chengde High Technology Industrial Development Zone 承德高新技術產業開發區 *chéngdé gāoxīnjìshù chǎnyè kāifāqū*	135,375	
Cangzhou City 滄州市 ***cāngzhōu shì***		**7,300,783**
Yunhe District 運河區 *yùnhé qū*	511,086	
Xinhua District 新華區 *xīnhuá qū*	253,222	
Botou City 泊頭市 *bótóu shì*	573,842	
Renqiu City 任丘市 *rènqiū shì*	816,401	
Huanghua City 黃驊市 *huánghuá shì*	484,313	
Hejian City 河間市 *héjiān shì*	795,198	
Cangxian County 滄縣 *cāngxiàn*	626,011	
Qingxian County 青縣 *qīngxiàn*	420,878	
Dongguang County 東光縣 *dōngguāng xiàn*	340,288	
Haixing County 海興縣 *hǎixīng xiàn*	189,273	
Yanshan County 鹽山縣 *yánshān xiàn*	411,356	
Suning County 肅寧縣 *sùníng xiàn*	341,919	
Nanpi County 南皮縣 *nánpí xiàn*	347,473	
Wuqiao County 吳橋縣 *wúqiáo xiàn*	217,986	
Xianxian County 獻縣 *xiànxiàn*	568,418	
Mengcun Hui Autonomous County 孟村回族自治縣 *mèngcūn huízú zìzhìxiàn*	203,507	
Bohai New District 渤海新區 *bóhǎi xīnqū*	153,135	
Cangzhou Economic Development Zone 滄州經濟開發區 *cāngzhōu jīngjì kāifāqū*	31,524	

(continued)

Table 11.3 (continued)

Cities and subordinate sectors, population (2020 census)	Subordinate district, city and county populations (2020)	Total population (2020)
Cangzhou High Technology Industrial Development Zone 滄州高新技術產業開發區 *cāngzhōu gāoxīnjìshù chǎnyè kāifāqū*	14,953	
Langfang City 廊坊市 ***lángfāng shì***		**5,464,087**
Guangyang District 廣陽區 *guǎngyáng qū*	538,798	
Anci District 安次區 *āncì qū*	479,826	
Bazhou City 霸州市 *bàzhōu shì*	743,226	
Sanhe City 三河市 *sānhé shì*	965,075	
Gu'an County 固安縣 *gù'ān xiàn*	576,344	
Yongqing County 永清縣 *yǒngqīng xiàn*	384,767	
Xianghe County 香河縣 *xiānghé xiàn*	449,038	
Dacheng County 大城縣 *dàchéng xiàn*	481,902	
Wen'an County 文安縣 *wén'ān xiàn*	544,778	
Dachang Hui Autonomous County 大廠回族自治縣 *dàchǎng huízú zìzhìxiàn*	171,366	
Langfang Economic and Technology Development Zone 廊坊經濟技術開發區 *lángfāng jīngjìjìshù kāifāqū*	128,967	
Hengshui City 衡水市 ***héngshuǐ shì***		**4,212,933**
Taocheng District 桃城區 *táochéng qū*	608,586	
Jizhou City 冀州市 *jìzhōu shì*	304,854	
Shenzhou City 深州市 *shēnzhōu shì*	482,289	
Zaoqiang County 棗強縣 *zǎoqiáng xiàn*	365,640	
Wuyi County 武邑縣 *wǔyì xiàn*	265,962	
Wuqiang County 武強縣 *wǔqiáng xiàn*	176,672	
Raoyang County 饒陽縣 *ráoyáng xiàn*	254,613	
Anping County 安平縣 *ānpíng xiàn*	327,496	
Gucheng County 故城縣 *gùchéng xiàn*	444,493	
Jingxian County 景縣 *jǐngxiàn*	463,949	
Fucheng County 阜城縣 *fùchéng xiàn*	293,877	
Hengshui High Technology Industrial Development Zone 衡水市高新技術產業開發區 *héngshuǐshì gāoxīnjìshù chǎnyè kāifāqū*	144,731	
Binhu New District 濱湖新區 *bīnhú xīnqū*	79,771	
Dingzhou City 定州市 ***dìngzhōu shì***		**1,095,986**
Xinji City 辛集市 ***xīnjí shì***		**594,628**
Xiongan Xinqu (New District) 雄安新區 ***xióngān xīnqū***		**1,205,440**
Xiongxian County 雄縣 *xióngxiàn*	478,553	
Rongcheng County 容城縣 *róngchéng xiàn*	273,164	
Anxin County 安新縣 *ānxīn xiàn*	453,723	

[a]Luanxian County was renamed Luanzhou City in September 2018

Hebei Province (冀 *jì*)

Provincial Capital: Shijiazhuang

Table 11.4 Hebei Province: Permanent registered (戶籍人口 *hùjí rénkǒu*) populations. (MCA 2020)

Name	Traditional	Simplified	Population (2012)	Population (2016)	Population (2020)	Area (Sq. Km)
Hebei Province	河北省	河北省	72,980,000	75,200,000	77,310,000	187158.9
Shijiazhuang City	石家莊市	石家庄市	9,900,000	10,560,000	10,450,000	14,530
Chang'an District (Yucai Subdistrict)	長安區 (育才街道)	长安区 (育才街道)	430,000	710,000	650,000	138
Qiaodong District[a] (Zhongshandonglu Subdistrict)	橋東區 (中山東路街道)	桥东区 (中山东路街道)	380,000	N/A	N/A	(43)
Qiaoxi District (Zhentou Subdistrict)	橋西區 (振頭街道)	桥西区 (振头街道)	510,000	870,000	670,000	69
Xinhua District (Gexin Subdistrict)	新華區 (革新街道)	新华区 (革新街道)	490,000	660,000	500,000	97
Yuhua District (Yuxing Subdistrict)	裕華區 (裕興街道)	裕华区 (裕兴街道)	530,000	570,000	640,000	101
Jingxing Kuangqu (mining) District (Kuangshi [mining] City Subdistrict)	井陘礦區 (礦市街道)	井陉矿区 (矿市街道)	100,000	100,000	90,000	76
Xinji City (Xinji Town)	辛集市 (辛集鎮)	辛集市 (辛集镇)	620,000	630,000	640,000	951
Gaocheng District (Lianzhou Town)	藁城區 (廉州鎮)	藁城区 (廉州镇)	790,000	810,000	860,000	836
Jinzhou City (Jinzhou Town)	晉州市 (晉州鎮)	晋州市 (晋州镇)	540,000	550,000	580,000	619
Xinle City (Changshou Subdistrict)	新樂市 (長壽街道)	新乐市 (长寿街道)	490,000	510,000	520,000	525
Luquan District (Huolu Town)	鹿泉區 (獲鹿鎮)	鹿泉区 (获鹿镇)	390,000	400,000	440,000	603
Jingxing County (Weishui Town)	井陘縣 (微水鎮)	井陉县 (微水镇)	330,000	330,000	330,000	1381
Zhengding County (Zhending Town)	正定縣 (正定鎮)	正定县 (正定镇)	470,000	490,000	510,000	468
Luancheng District (Luancheng Town)	欒城區 (欒城鎮)	栾城区 (栾城镇)	350,000	330,000	360,000	326
Xingtang County (Longzhou Town)	行唐縣 (龍州鎮)	行唐县 (龙州镇)	440,000	460,000	460,000	1025
Lingshou County (Lingshou Town)	靈壽縣 (靈壽鎮)	灵寿县 (灵寿镇)	330,000	340,000	350,000	1066

(continued)

Table 11.4 (continued)

Name	Traditional	Simplified	Population (2012)	Population (2016)	Population (2020)	Area (Sq. Km)
Gaoyi County (Gaoyi Town)	高邑縣 (高邑鎮)	高邑县 (高邑镇)	190,000	200,000	200,000	222
Shenze County (Shenze Town)	深澤縣 (深澤鎮)	深泽县 (深泽镇)	260,000	260,000	260,000	296
Zanhuang County (Zanhuang Town)	贊皇縣 (贊皇鎮)	赞皇县 (赞皇镇)	260,000	270,000	280,000	1210
Wuji County (Wuji Town)	無極縣 (無極鎮)	无极县 (无极镇)	510,000	530,000	540,000	524
Pingshan County (Pingshan Town)	平山縣 (平山鎮)	平山县 (平山镇)	480,000	500,000	500,000	2648
Yuanshi County (Huaiyang Town)	元氏縣 (槐陽鎮)	元氏县 (槐阳镇)	420,000	440,000	440,000	675
Zhaoxian County (Zhaozhou Town)	趙縣 (趙州鎮)	赵县 (赵州镇)	590,000	600,000	620,000	674
Zhangjiakou City	張家口市	张家口市	4,670,000	4,910,000	4,650,000	36,303
Qiaoxi District (Xinhuajie Subdistrict)	橋西區 (新華街街道)	桥西区 (新华街街道)	240,000	320,000	240,000	217.52
Qiaodong District (Hongqilou Subdistrict)	橋東區 (紅旗樓街道)	桥东区 (红旗楼街道)	280,000	410,000	290,000	385.27
Xuanhua District (Jianguojie Subdistrict)	宣化區 (建國街街道)	宣化区 (建国街街道)	320,000	390,000	610,000	2013.69
Xiahuayuan District (Chengzhen Subdistrict)	下花園區 (城鎮街道)	下花园区 (城镇街道)	70,000	70,000	60,000	315
Xuanhua County[b] (Zhangjiakou City Xuanhua District)	宣化縣 (張家口市宣化區)	宣化县 (张家口市宣化区)	310,000	280,000	N/A	(2057)
Zhangbei County (Zhangbei Town)	張北縣 (張北鎮)	张北县 (张北镇)	380,000	360,000	380,000	3863
Kangbao County (Kangbao Town)	康保縣 (康保鎮)	康保县 (康保镇)	280,000	280,000	270,000	3365
Guyuan County (Pingdingbu Town)	沽源縣 (平定堡鎮)	沽源县 (平定堡镇)	230,000	220,000	230,000	3388
Shangyi County (Nanhaoqian Town)	尚義縣 (南壕塹鎮)	尚义县 (南壕堑镇)	190,000	190,000	190,000	2601
Yuxian County (Yuzhou Town)	蔚縣 (蔚州鎮)	蔚县 (蔚州镇)	490,000	500,000	500,000	3220
Yangyuan County (Xicheng Town)	陽原縣 (西城鎮)	阳原县 (西城镇)	280,000	280,000	270,000	1849
Huai'an County (Chaigoubu Town)	懷安縣 (柴溝堡鎮)	怀安县 (柴沟堡镇)	250,000	250,000	240,000	1698

(continued)

Table 11.4 (continued)

Name	Traditional	Simplified	Population (2012)	Population (2016)	Population (2020)	Area (Sq. Km)
Wanquan District (Kongjiazhuang Town)	萬全區 (孔家莊鎮)	万全区 (孔家庄镇)	230,000	220,000	230,000	1128.16
Huailai County (Shacheng Town)	懷來縣 (沙城鎮)	怀来县 (沙城镇)	350,000	360,000	370,000	1801
Zhuolu County (Zhuolu Town)	涿鹿縣 (涿鹿鎮)	涿鹿县 (涿鹿镇)	350,000	350,000	350,000	2802
Chicheng County (Chicheng Town)	赤城縣 (赤城鎮)	赤城县 (赤城镇)	290,000	300,000	290,000	5287
Chongli District (Xiwanzi Town)	崇禮區 (西灣子鎮)	崇礼区 (西湾子镇)	130,000	130,000	130,000	2324.1
Chengde City	承德市	承德市	3,720,000	3,790,000	3,820,000	39,719
Shuangqiao District (Zhonghualu Subdistrict)	雙橋區 (中華路街道)	双桥区 (中华路街道)	370,000	380,000	390,000	667
Shuangluan District (Yuanbaoshan Subdistrict)	雙灤區 (元寶山街道)	双滦区 (元宝山街道)	140,000	150,000	150,000	452
Yingshouyingzi Kuangqu (mining) District (Tiebeilu Subdistrict)	鷹手營子礦區 (鐵北路街道)	鹰手营子矿区 (铁北路街道)	70,000	70,000	60,000	148
Chengde County (Xiabancheng Town)	承德縣 (下板城鎮)	承德县 (下板城镇)	420,000	420,000	430,000	3648
Xinglong County (Xinglong Town)	興隆縣 (興隆鎮)	兴隆县 (兴隆镇)	320,000	330,000	330,000	3123
Pingquan City (Pingquan Town)	平泉市 (平泉鎮)	平泉市 (平泉镇)	470,000	480,000	480,000	3294
Luanping County (Luanping Town)	灤平縣 (灤平鎮)	滦平县 (滦平镇)	310,000	320,000	330,000	2993
Longhua County (Anzhou Subdistrict)	隆化縣 (安州街道)	隆化县 (安州街道)	440,000	440,000	450,000	5473
Fengning Manchu Autonomous County (Dage Town)	豐寧滿族自治縣 (大閣鎮)	丰宁满族自治县 (大阁镇)	400,000	410,000	410,000	8765
Kuancheng Manzu (Manchu) Autonomous County (Kuancheng Town)	寬城滿族蒙古族自治縣 (寬城鎮)	宽城满族自治县 (宽城镇)	250,000	250,000	260,000	1936
Weichang Manzu (Manchu) Autonomous County (Weichang Town)	圍場滿族蒙古族自治縣 (圍場鎮)	围场满族蒙古族自治县 (围场镇)	530,000	540,000	540,000	9220
Qinhuangdao City	秦皇島市	秦皇岛市	2,880,000	2,910,000	3,000,000	7813

(continued)

Table 11.4 (continued)

Name	Traditional	Simplified	Population (2012)	Population (2016)	Population (2020)	Area (Sq. Km)
Haigang District (Jianshedajie Subdistrict)	海港區 (建設大街街道)	海港区 (建设大街街道)	650,000	780,000	840,000	713
Shanhaiguan District (Lunan Subdistrict)	山海關區 (路南街道)	山海关区 (路南街道)	140,000	150,000	150,000	193
Beidaihe District (Shanxi Subdistrict)	北戴河區 (西山街道)	北戴河区 (西山街道)	70,000	120,000	130,000	155
Changli County (Changli Town)	昌黎縣 (昌黎鎮)	昌黎县 (昌黎镇)	560,000	530,000	560,000	1212
Funing District (Funing Town)	撫寧區 (撫寧鎮)	抚宁区 (抚宁镇)	490,000	350,000	350,000	1069
Lulong County (Lulong Town)	盧龍縣 (盧龍鎮)	卢龙县 (卢龙镇)	420,000	420,000	420,000	961
Qinglong Manzu (Manchu) Autonomous County (Qinglong Town)	青龍滿族自治縣 (青龍鎮)	青龙满族自治县 (青龙镇)	550,000	560,000	570,000	3510
Tangshan City	唐山市	唐山市	7,340,000	7,410,000	7,580,000	13,869
Lubei District (Qiaotun Subdistrict)	路北區 (喬屯街道)	路北区 (乔屯街道)	690,000	590,000	900,000	168
Lunan District (Xueyuan Nanlu Subdistrict)	路南區 (學院南路街道)	路南区 (学院南路街道)	240,000	370,000	350,000	118
Guye District (Jinghua Subdistrict)	古冶區 (京華街道)	古冶区 (京华街道)	360,000	360,000	340,000	249
Kaiping District (Kaiping Subdistrict)	開平區 (開平街道)	开平区 (开平街道)	330,000	250,000	250,000	251
Fengrun District (Taipinglu Subdistrict)	豐潤區 (太平路街道)	丰润区 (太平路街道)	920,000	920,000	760,000	1290
Fengnan District (Xugezhuang Subdistrict)	豐南區 (胥各莊街道)	丰南区 (胥各庄街道)	540,000	520,000	540,000	1262
Caofeidian District (Tanghai Town)	曹妃甸區 (唐海鎮)	曹妃甸区 (唐海镇)	N/A	210,000	210,000	1281
Zunhua City (Zunhua Town)	遵化市 (遵化鎮)	遵化市 (遵化镇)	730,000	750,000	760,000	1509
Qian'an City (Yongshun Subdistrict)	遷安市 (永順街道)	迁安市 (永顺街道)	720,000	740,000	780,000	1227
Luanzhou City (Luanhe Subdistrict)	灤州市 (灤河街道)	滦州市 (滦河街道)	550,000	560,000	570,000	1027
Luannan County (Youyilu Subdistrict)	灤南縣 (友誼路街道)	滦南县 (友谊路街道)	580,000	570,000	570,000	1482

(continued)

Table 11.4 (continued)

Name	Traditional	Simplified	Population (2012)	Population (2016)	Population (2020)	Area (Sq. Km)
Laoting County (Le'an Subdistrict)	樂亭縣 (樂安街道)	乐亭县 (乐安街道)	490,000	490,000	450,000	1417
Qianxi County (Xingcheng Town)	遷西縣 (興城鎮)	迁西县 (兴城镇)	380,000	390,000	400,000	1439
Yutian County (Wuzhong Subdistrict)	玉田縣 (無終街道)	玉田县 (无终街道)	670,000	690,000	710,000	1165
Langfang City	廊坊市	廊坊市	4,200,000	4,330,000	4,790,000	6420
Guangyang District (Jiefangdao Subdistrict)	廣陽區 (解放道街道)	广阳区 (解放道街道)	460,000	410,000	500,000	384
Anci District (Yinhenanlu Subdistrict)	安次區 (銀河南路街道)	安次区 (银河南路街道)	350,000	360,000	380,000	578
Bazhou City (Bazhou Subdistrict)	霸州市 (霸州鎮)	霸州市 (霸州镇)	620,000	630,000	660,000	802
Sanhe City (Dingshengdongdajie Subdistrict)	三河市 (鼎盛東大街街道)	三河市 (鼎盛东大街街道)	540,000	600,000	730,000	634
Gu'an County (Gu'an Town)	固安縣 (固安鎮)	固安县 (固安镇)	430,000	460,000	520,000	703
Yongqing County (Yongqing Town)	永清縣 (永清鎮)	永清县 (永清镇)	390,000	390,000	410,000	761
Xianghe County (Shuyang Town)	香河縣 (淑陽鎮)	香河县 (淑阳镇)	320,000	340,000	370,000	448
Dacheng County (Pingshu Town)	大城縣 (平舒鎮)	大城县 (平舒镇)	480,000	500,000	540,000	897
Wen'an County (Wen'an Town)	文安縣 (文安鎮)	文安县 (文安镇)	490,000	520,000	550,000	1037
Dachang Hui Autonomous County (Dachang Town)	大廠回族自治縣 (大廠鎮)	大厂回族自治县 (大厂镇)	120,000	120,000	130,000	176
Baoding City	保定市	保定市	11,620,000	11,860,000	12,080,000	22,135
Xinshi District (Xianfeng Subdistrict)	新市區 (先鋒街道)	新市区 (先锋街道)	460,000	N/A	N/A	(139)
Jingxiu District (Xianfeng Subdistrict)	競秀區 (先鋒街道)	竞秀区 (先锋街道)	N/A	500,000	510,000	139
Beishi District (Wusilu Subdistrict)	北市區 (五四路街道)	北市区 (五四路街道)	320,000	N/A	N/A	(74)
Nanshi District (Lianmeng Subdistrict)	南市區 (聯盟路街道)	南市区 (联盟路街道)	280,000	N/A	N/A	(99)

(continued)

Table 11.4 (continued)

Name	Traditional	Simplified	Population (2012)	Population (2016)	Population (2020)	Area (Sq. Km)
Lianchi District (Mancheng Town)	蓮池區 (滿城鎮)	莲池区 (满城镇)	N/A	700,000	630,000	173
Dingzhou City (Nancheng District neighborhood)	定州市 (南城區街道)	定州市 (南城区街道)	1,210,000	1,230,000	1,240,000	1283
Zhuozhou City (Shuangta Subdistrict)	琢州市 (雙塔街道)	涿州市 (双塔街道)	650,000	660,000	700,000	751
Anguo City (Qizhou Town)	安國市 (祁州鎮)	安国市 (祁州镇)	410,000	420,000	410,000	486
Gaobeidian City (Xinghualu Subdistrict)	高碑店市 (興華路街道)	高碑店市 (兴华路街道)	610,000	570,000	630,000	618
Mancheng District (Mancheng Town)	滿城區 (滿城鎮)	满城区 (满城镇)	410,000	400,000	410,000	629
Qingyuan District (Qingyuan Town)	清苑區 (清苑鎮)	清苑区 (清苑镇)	650,000	640,000	690,000	867
Yixian County (Yizhou Town)	易縣 (易州鎮)	易县 (易州镇)	350,000	580,000	580,000	2534
Xushui District (Ansu Town)	徐水區 (安肅鎮)	徐水区 (安肃镇)	220,000	580,000	630,000	723
Laiyuan County (Laiyuan Town)	淶源縣 (淶源鎮)	涞源县 (涞源镇)	590,000	360,000	290,000	2448
Dingxing County (Dingxing Town)	定興縣 (定興鎮)	定兴县 (定兴镇)	590,000	600,000	610,000	714
Shunping County (Puyang Town)	順平縣 (蒲陽鎮)	顺平县 (蒲阳镇)	590,000	320,000	320,000	711
Tangxian County (Renhou Town)	唐縣 (仁厚鎮)	唐县 (仁厚镇)	340,000	600,000	600,000	1417
Wangdu County (Wangdu Town)	望都縣 (望都鎮)	望都县 (望都镇)	270,000	270,000	270,000	370
Laishui County (Laishui Town)	淶水縣 (淶水鎮)	涞水县 (涞水镇)	280,000	360,000	360,000	1658
Gaoyang County (Gaoyang Town)	高陽縣 (高陽鎮)	高阳县 (高阳镇)	270,000	350,000	360,000	495
Anxin County (Anxin Town)	安新縣 (安新鎮)	安新县 (安新镇)	440,000	460,000	470,000	728
Xiongxian County (Xiongzhou Town)	雄縣 (雄州鎮)	雄县 (雄州镇)	570,000	390,000	400,000	514
Rongcheng County (Rongcheng Town)	容城縣 (容城鎮)	容城县 (容城镇)	610,000	270,000	280,000	314
Quyang County (Hengzhou Town)	曲陽縣 (恆州鎮)	曲阳县 (恒州镇)	530,000	630,000	660,000	1084
Fuping County (Fuping Town)	阜平縣 (阜平鎮)	阜平县 (阜平镇)	320,000	230,000	230,000	2496

(continued)

Table 11.4 (continued)

Name	Traditional	Simplified	Population (2012)	Population (2016)	Population (2020)	Area (Sq. Km)
Boye County (Boye Town)	博野縣 (博野鎮)	博野县 (博野镇)	270,000	270,000	270,000	331
Lixian County (Liwu Town)	蠡縣 (蠡吾鎮)	蠡县 (蠡吾镇)	380,000	540,000	550,000	652
Cangzhou City	滄州市	沧州市	7,330,000	7,460,000	7,830,000	13,488
Yunhe District (Shuiyuesi Subdistrict)	運河區 (水月寺街道)	运河区 (水月寺街道)	290,000	320,000	350,000	138
Xinhua District (Jianshebeijie Subdistrict)	新華區 (建設北街街道)	新华区 (建设北街街道)	250,000	230,000	230,000	89
Botou City (Jiefang Subdistrict)	泊頭市 (解放街道)	泊头市 (解放街道)	600,000	620,000	630,000	1009
Renqiu City (Xinhualu Subdistrict)	任丘市 (新華路街道)	任丘市 (新华路街道)	840,000	870,000	900,000	1012
Huanghua City (Huaxi Subdistrict)	黃驊市 (驊西街道)	黄骅市 (骅西街道)	540,000	470,000	580,000	1545
Hejian City (Yingzhou Town)	河間市 (瀛洲鎮)	河间市 (瀛州镇)	810,000	840,000	900,000	1333
Cangxian County (Cangzhou City Xinhua District)	滄縣 (滄州市新華區)	沧县 (沧州市新华区)	690,000	710,000	740,000	1520
Qingxian County (Qingzhou Town)	青縣 (清州鎮)	青县 (清州镇)	410,000	420,000	440,000	968
Dongguang County (Dongguang Town)	東光縣 (東光鎮)	东光县 (东光镇)	370,000	370,000	380,000	711
Haixing County (Suji Town)	海興縣 (蘇基鎮)	海兴县 (苏基镇)	230,000	230,000	240,000	919
Yanshan County (Yanshan Town)	鹽山縣 (鹽山鎮)	盐山县 (盐山镇)	460,000	480,000	500,000	795
Suning County (Suning Town)	肅寧縣 (肅寧鎮)	肃宁县 (肃宁镇)	350,000	360,000	370,000	516
Nanpi County (Nanpi Town)	南皮縣 (南皮鎮)	南皮县 (南皮镇)	380,000	390,000	400,000	790
Wuqiao County (Sangyuan Town)	吳橋縣 (桑園鎮)	吴桥县 (桑园镇)	290,000	280,000	280,000	583
Xianxian County (Leshou Town)	獻縣 (樂壽鎮)	献县 (乐寿镇)	600,000	640,000	660,000	1173
Mengcun Hui Autonomous County (Mengcun Town)	孟村回族自治縣 (孟村鎮)	孟村回族自治县 (孟村镇)	220,000	230,000	230,000	387
Hengshui City	衡水市	衡水市	4,410,000	4,360,000	4,560,000	8758

(continued)

Table 11.4 (continued)

Name	Traditional	Simplified	Population (2012)	Population (2016)	Population (2020)	Area (Sq. Km)
Taocheng District (Zhonghuadajie Subdistrict)	桃城區 (中華大街街道)	桃城区 (中华大街街道)	490,000	410,000	650,000	563
Jizhou City (Jizhou Town)	冀州市 (冀州鎮)	冀州市 (冀州镇)	370,000	370,000	340,000	878
Shenzhou City (Shenzhou Town)	深州市 (深州鎮)	深州市 (深州镇)	570,000	570,000	570,000	1245
Zaoqiang County (Zaoqiang Town)	棗強縣 (棗強鎮)	枣强县 (枣强镇)	400,000	400,000	410,000	905
Wuyi County (Wuyi Town)	武邑縣 (武邑鎮)	武邑县 (武邑镇)	330,000	330,000	320,000	832
Wuqiang County (Wuqiang Town)	武強縣 (武強鎮)	武强县 (武强镇)	220,000	220,000	220,000	443
Raoyang County (Raoyang Town)	饒陽縣 (饒陽鎮)	饶阳县 (饶阳镇)	290,000	290,000	290,000	572
Anping County (Anping Town)	安平縣 (安平鎮)	安平县 (安平镇)	330,000	330,000	340,000	496
Gucheng County (Zhengkou Town)	故城縣 (鄭口鎮)	故城县 (郑口镇)	510,000	530,000	530,000	941
Jingxian County (Jingzhou Town)	景縣 (景州鎮)	景县 (景州镇)	540,000	550,000	550,000	1188
Fucheng County (Fucheng Town)	阜城縣 (阜城鎮)	阜城县 (阜城镇)	360,000	360,000	350,000	695
Xingtai City	邢台市	邢台市	7,330,000	7,570,000	7,970,000	12,143
Qiaodong District (Nanchangjie Subdistrict)	橋東區 (南長街街道)	桥东区 (南长街街道)	330,000	460,000	480,000	63
Qiaoxi District (Gangtielu Subdistrict)	橋西區 (鋼鐵路街道)	桥西区 (钢铁路街道)	390,000	400,000	420,000	99
Nangong City (Fenggang Subdistrict)	南宮市 (鳳崗街道)	南宫市 (凤岗街道)	480,000	490,000	510,000	861
Shahe City (Dalian Subdistrict)	沙河市 (褡褳街道)	沙河市 (褡裢街道)	490,000	430,000	460,000	859
Xingtai County (Xingtai City Qiaodong District)	邢台縣 (邢台市橋東區)	邢台县 (邢台市桥东区)	390,000	350,000	360,000	1848
Lincheng County (Lincheng Town)	臨城縣 (臨城鎮)	临城县 (临城镇)	210,000	220,000	220,000	797
Neiqiu County (Neiqiu Town)	內丘縣 (內丘鎮)	内丘县 (内丘镇)	280,000	290,000	300,000	788

(continued)

Table 11.4 (continued)

Name	Traditional	Simplified	Population (2012)	Population (2016)	Population (2020)	Area (Sq. Km)
Baixiang County (Baixiang Town)	柏鄉縣 (柏鄉鎮)	柏乡县 (柏乡镇)	200,000	200,000	210,000	268
Longyao County (Longyao Town)	隆堯縣 (隆堯鎮)	隆尧县 (隆尧镇)	520,000	540,000	570,000	749
Renxian County (Rencheng Town)	任縣 (任城鎮)	任县 (任城镇)	350,000	370,000	390,000	431
Nanhe County (Heyang Town)	南和縣 (和陽鎮)	南和县 (和阳镇)	350,000	370,000	400,000	405
Ningjin County (Fenghuang Town)	寧晉縣 (鳳凰鎮)	宁晋县 (凤凰镇)	790,000	780,000	860,000	1032
Julu County (Julu Town)	巨鹿縣 (巨鹿鎮)	巨鹿县 (巨鹿镇)	390,000	410,000	430,000	631
Xinhe County (Xinhe Town)	新河縣 (新河鎮)	新河县 (新河镇)	170,000	180,000	180,000	366
Guangzong County (Guangzong Town)	廣宗縣 (廣宗鎮)	广宗县 (广宗镇)	310,000	320,000	340,000	504
Pingxiang County (Zhonghualu Subdistrict)	平鄉縣 (中華路街道)	平乡县 (中华路街道)	330,000	340,000	370,000	406
Weixian County (Mingzhou Town)	威縣 (洺州鎮)	威县 (洺州镇)	580,000	620,000	650,000	994
Qinghe County (Gexianzhuang Town)	清河縣 (葛仙莊鎮)	清河县 (葛仙庄镇)	400,000	420,000	450,000	500
Linxi County (Linxi Town)	臨西縣 (臨西鎮)	临西县 (临西镇)	370,000	380,000	390,000	542
Handan City	邯鄲市	邯郸市	9,650,000	10,040,000	10,580,000	12,066.18
Congtai District (Congxi Subdistrict)	叢台區 (叢台西街道)	丛台区 (丛台西街道)	360,000	370,000	820,000	387
Hanshan District (Huomo Subdistrict)	邯山區 (火磨街道)	邯山区 (火磨街道)	360,000	420,000	760,000	415.98
Fuxing District (Shengliqiao Subdistrict)	復興區 (勝利橋街道)	复兴区 (胜利桥街道)	260,000	310,000	370,000	243.35
Fengfeng Kuangqu (mining) District (Linshui Town)	峰峰礦區 (臨水鎮)	峰峰矿区 (临水镇)	510,000	510,000	480,000	353
Wu'an City (Wu'an Town)	武安市 (武安鎮)	武安市 (武安镇)	780,000	810,000	850,000	1806
Handan County[c] (Nanbao Township)	邯鄲縣 (南堡鄉)	邯郸县 (南堡乡)	420,000	320,000	N/A	(339)

(continued)

Table 11.4 (continued)

Name	Traditional	Simplified	Population (2012)	Population (2016)	Population (2020)	Area (Sq. Km)
Linzhang County (Lintan Town)	臨漳縣 (臨潭鎮)	临漳县 (临漳镇)	680,000	730,000	760,000	742
Cheng'an County (Cheng'an Town)	成安縣 (成安鎮)	成安县 (成安镇)	420,000	440,000	470,000	482
Daming County (Daming Town)	大名縣 (大名鎮)	大名县 (大名镇)	850,000	920,000	940,000	1053
Shexian County (Ping'an Subdistrict)	涉縣 (平安街道)	涉县 (平安街道)	400,000	410,000	430,000	1509
Cixian County (Cizhou Town)	磁縣 (磁州鎮)	磁县 (磁州镇)	690,000	650,000	480,000	716.25
Feixiang District (Feixiang Town)	肥鄉區 (肥鄉鎮)	肥乡区 (肥乡镇)	370,000	390,000	410,000	503
Yongnian County (Linmingguan Town)	永年區 (臨洺關鎮)	永年区 (临洺关镇)	1,020,000	1,080,000	970,000	898
Qiuxian County (Xinmatou Town)	邱縣 (新馬頭鎮)	邱县 (新马头镇)	240,000	250,000	260,000	449
Jize County (Jize Town)	雞澤縣 (雞澤鎮)	鸡泽县 (鸡泽镇)	290,000	310,000	340,000	336
Guangping County (Guangping Town)	廣平縣 (廣平鎮)	广平县 (广平镇)	280,000	300,000	310,000	314
Guantao County (Guantao Town)	館陶縣 (館陶鎮)	馆陶县 (馆陶镇)	340,000	350,000	360,000	456
Weixian County (Weicheng Town)	魏縣 (魏城鎮)	魏县 (魏城镇)	930,000	990,000	1,040,000	864
Quzhou County (Quzhou Town)	曲周縣 (曲周鎮)	曲周县 (曲周镇)	450,000	480,000	530,000	677

[a]Dissolved in September 2014
[b]Dissolved and incorporated into Xuanhua district in 2016
[c]Dissolved in 2016

References

Bagley, Robert. 1999. Shang archaeology. In *The Cambridge history of ancient China: From the origins of civilization to 221 B.C*, ed. Michael Loewe and Edward L. Shaughnessy, 123–231. New York: Cambridge University Press.

Chang, Kwang-chih. 1999. China on the eve of the historical record. In *The Cambridge history of ancient China: From the origins of civilization to 221 B.C*, ed. Michael Loewe and Edward L. Shaughnessy, 37–73. New York: Cambridge University Press.

Dikötter, Frank. 2013. *The tragedy of liberation: A history of the Chinese revolution: A history of the Chinese revolution, 1945–57*. New York: Bloomsbury Press.

Hebei Province Bureau of Statistics (HPBS). 2021. [*Communiqué of the seventh national population census of Hebei Province, Issue No. 2*]. 河北省第七次全国人口普查公报 (第二号), 19 May. http://tjj.hebei.gov.cn/res/hetj.

Ministry of Civil Affairs (MCA), People's Republic of China. 2020. [*County/township administration handbook*]. Beijing: China Statistics Press. 中華人民共和國民政部, 中華人民共和國, 鄉鎮行政區劃簡冊.

Spence, Jonathan D. 1999. *The search for modern China*. New York: W. W. Norton & Company.

Yao, Xuerong, and Jiang Changsheng. 2006. [Bibliography and analysis of geoscience research on the Tangshan earthquake]. *Recent Developments in World Seismology*. 姚雪绒, 蒋长胜. 唐山地震的地学研究文献目录及分析.国际地震动态 7 (331): 145–176.

Yuan, Zuliang, and Jiao Peimin. 2007. [*China's population through history: Eastern Han*]. Beijing: People's Press. 袁祖亮主, 焦培民著. 中國人口通史: 東漢卷, Vol. 4. 北京: 人民出版社.

Zhang, Shunan. 2021. [The 2020 per capita income list of residents in various provinces: Shanghai is the richest, and it has risen sharply]. Finance.people.com. 22 January. 张澍楠. 2020年各省份居民人均收入榜: 上海最有钱, 这地涨得猛. http://finance.people.com.cn/n1/2021/0122/c1004-32008733.html.

Chapter 12
Heilongjiang Province

Abstract Capping China's furthest northeast, Heilongjiang conjures images of snowy mountains, grasslands, and (seasonally) frozen bodies of water. The now extinct species of human known as *Homo longi* was originally discovered in Heilongjiang's capital of Harbin (Ha'erbin). Inhabited by early Wuji and Shushen clans, the Mohe people in particular gave tribute to the Zhou dynastic court in ca. 1000 BCE, and later became the Manchu group of nomadic tribes. Formally established as part of imperial China by the Ming (ca. fourteenth century), and a protectorate by the Qing, Heilongjiang was populated later by Russians, many fleeing pogroms, and their lasting influences can be seen today. Unfortunately, being a border between bellicose Russia and Japan by the time of the Pacific War, the people of Heilongjiang and prisoners of war were subjected to Japanese military depredations, where, among other atrocities, biological and chemical weapons were tested on human subjects. In terms of economic development, Heilongjiang ranks in the bottom ten of mainland China's 31 provinces and major cities, and helps to explain the contraction in Heilongjiang's population growth within recent years.

E. Croddy, *China's Provinces and Populations*,
https://doi.org/10.1007/978-3-031-09165-0_12

Heilongjiang Province (黑龍江): Abbreviation 黑 (*hēi*) (Fig. 12.1)

		Population (2020)
1.	Daxing'anling (Da Hinggan Ling) Prefecture	331,276
2.	Heihe City	1,286,401
3.	Yichun City	878,881
4.	Hegang City	891,271
5.	Jiamusi City	2,156,505
6.	Shuangyashan City	1,208,803
7.	Qiqiha'er City	4,067,489
8.	Suihua City	3,756,167
9.	Qitaihe City	689,611
10.	Jixi City	1,502,060
11.	Daqing City	2,781,562
12.	Ha'erbin (Harbin) City	10,009,854
13.	Mudanjiang City	2,290,208

Fig. 12.1 Heilongjiang province: Major cities (Provincial Capital: Ha'erbin City). (Drawn by the author after People's Republic of China, Ministry of Civil Affairs (MCA 2020))

Heilongjiang Province: General Impressions

Heilongjiang Province (abbreviated 黑 *hēi*) is named after the "Black Dragon River" (黑龍江 *hēilóngjiāng*, also known as the Amur River), which forms a natural border between China and Russia. In China's distant past, Heilongjiang was a sparsely populated wilderness, and only in the Ming dynasty (ca. fourteenth century) did the Chinese empire directly rule over the region (Hsieh and Hsieh 1995).

Known for its fertile soil, the other half of Heilongjiang province is rugged, mountainous terrain. Thus the adage that has long described Heilongjiang: "five parts mountain, one part water, one part grassland, three parts farm fields."[1] (Christofferson 2002) There is also the general moniker of "frozen north" (冰雪北國 *bīngxuě běiguó*), and Heilongjiang has also been called "China's Siberia" because of its severe, cold winter climate. And because of its history and architecture, the capital city of Harbin (Ha'erbin) has been known among Russians as "Moscow of the East," while others in the west refer to Harbin as the "Paris of the East." (Shang-Ch'i 2017). The 2014 film, *Black Coal, Thin Ice* ("Daylight Fireworks"白日焰火 *báirì yànhuǒ*), directed by Diao Yinan (刁亦男 *diāo yìnán*), was filmed in and around Harbin, and won best film that year at the Berlin International Film Festival.

However, as part of China's "rustbelt," Heilongjiang (along with other northern provinces, Jilin and Liaoning), has lost a significant number (6,463,903) of its resident population from 2010 to 2020 (see Table 12.1 below), representing nearly a

Table 12.1 Heilongjiang (Residential 常住人口 *chángzhù rénkǒu*) population data. (HPBS 2021)

City	Population (2010)	Population (2020)
Harbin City 哈爾濱市 (*Hā'ěrbīn shì*)	10,635,971	10,009,854
Qiqihar City 齊齊哈爾市 (*Qíqíhā'ěr shì*)	5,367,003	4,067,489
Mudanjiang City 牡丹江市 (*Mǔdānjiāng shì*)	2,798,723	2,290,208
Jiamusi City 佳木斯市 (*Jiāmùsī shì*)	2,552,097	2,156,505
Daqing City 大慶市 (*Dàqìng shì*)	2,904,532	2,781,562
Jixi City 雞西市 (*Jīxī shì*)	1,862,161	1,502,060
Shuangyashan City 雙鴨山市 (*Shuāngyāshān shì*)	1,462,626	1,208,803
Yichun City 伊春市 (*Yīchūn shì*)	1,148,126	878,881
Qitaihe Cty 七台河市 (*Qītáihé shì*)	920,419	689,611
Hegang City 鶴崗市 (*Hègǎng shì*)	1,058,665	891,271
Heihe City 黑河市 (*Hēihé shì*)	1,673,898	1,286,401
Suihua City 綏化市 (*Suíhuà shì*)	5,416,439	3,756,167
Daxinganling Prefecture 大興安嶺地區 (*Dàxīng'ānlǐng Dìqū*)	511,564	331,276
Total	**38,312,224**	**31,850,088**

[1] "五山一水一草三分田 *wǔshān yīshuǐ yīcǎo sānfēn tián*."

17% drop. Many of these losses were likely due to the attractiveness of the southeastern provinces with more economic opportunities, especially for younger demographics (Leng 2021).

Prehistory

The discovery of an ancient hominid called *Homo longi* (named after the local appellation of the Dragon River (龍江 *lóngjiāng*) revealed a new species of human having lived in northeast China. In 1933, a local found a nearly complete fossilized cranium in a construction site of a bridge over the Songhua river (松花江 *sōnghuā jiāng*) in Harbin. As this was during the Japanese occupation of northern China, the unnamed individual hid his discovery until finally revealing it upon his deathbed. Eighty-five years later, analysis of the fossil showed "Dragon Man" having a large cranium capacity (over 1400 ml), very thick brow ridges, and a bulbous nose. This particular individual is estimated to have been a 50-year-old male, and probably lived at least 140 thousand years ago (Ni et al. 2021).

Insofar as *Homo sapiens* is concerned, going back before the Qin (秦 *qín*), Heilongjiang was originally populated by the Wuji clan (勿吉 *wùjí* meaning "forest"), who were likely related to the Sushen (肅慎 *sùshèn*), a group of hunting clans. The latter were then grouped into the category of the Mohe (靺鞨 *mòhé* or 靺羯 *mòjié*) or the Malgal (Korean reading 말갈). Pejoratively, Mohe (靺鞨 *mòhé*) indicates a barbarian people, at least from the perspective of the more "civilized" southern Chinese. According to the histories, the original Mohe gave their prized hunting bows and arrows as tribute to Zhou Cheng Wang (周成王 *zhōu chéngwáng*), the Zhou King (ca. 1000 BCE). The largest and most influential of the Mohe clan were the "Black Water Mohe" (黑水靺鞨 *hēishuǐ mòhé*), who inhabited the northern portion of Heilongjiang region, saddled between the Changbai Mountains and the Amur (Heilongjiang) River. These "hearty, tough and brave" marauders of the northern regions were among the most feared by the Chinese imperial courts to the south. The ethnic line of the Mohe clan later became known as the Jurched (Jurchen, i.e., Manchu) dynastic group.

Another native people, the Yilou (挹婁 *yìlóu*), rose to prominence in the Han (202 BCE–220 CE) Dynasty. During the Three Kingdoms period (ca. 220–280 CE), the Yilou paid tribute in the form of animal furs to the Kingdom of Wei (魏國 *wèiguó*). At about the same time as the Yilou, in ca. 200 BCE the proto-Korean State of Buyeo (부여 *Buyeo*; 扶餘 *fúyú*) ruled over Heilongjiang, placed under the jurisdiction of Xuantu prefecture (玄菟郡 *xuántù jùn*; Korean 현도군 *Hyondogun*).

In the time of the North South dynasty (南北朝 *nánběicháo*), the aforementioned Wuji (勿吉 *wùjí*), having found their way into Manchuria in 494 CE, came to dominate modern-day Heilongjiang (West 2009). (In older maps, Wuji 勿吉 is transliterated as "Mukri.") During the Sui Dynasty (ca. 600 CE), Heilongjiang was mainly populated by the Mohe clan in its southeast. The Mohe (靺鞨 *mòhé*) had a tributary relationship with another ethnically-related group to the west known as the Shiwei (室韋 *shìwéi*; today there is a Shiwei village, Inner Mongolia, near the Russian border). Following the Tang dynasty's defeat of the Tujue (631 CE), the Black Water Mohe (黑水靺鞨 *hēishuǐ mòhé)* entered into a tributary relationship with the Chinese emperor.

Until challenged by the Tungusic and horse-riding Jurchen, the Liao dynasty of the Greater Khitan Mongols (大契丹國 *dàqìdānguó*) dominated northeast China in the tenth century. The rise of the Jurchen began with the Wanyan tribe (完顏部 *wányán bù*), who lived in the A-Shi River (阿什河 *āshí hé*) area. Under the leadership of the Jurchen Aguda (阿骨打 *āgúdǎ*; Chinese name 完顏旻 *wán-yánmín*), the Jurchen rebelled against the Liao.

Following his victory, Aguda named his rule the Jin (金*jīn* gold) in 1115, with its capital in Huining Prefecture (會寧府 *huìníng fǔ*) near today's Harbin City, Acheng district (阿城區 *āchéng qū*). Following the practice of previous Han Chinese emperors, he had an honorific title ("temple name") Taizu (太祖 *tàizǔ*). Thus, Heilongjiang Province can be rightly considered the birthplace of the Jin (金 *jīn*) dynasty (1115–1234).[2] In about 1150 CE, it made an unsteady truce with the Song, and the Jin dynasty controlled northeast China, including today's Heilongjiang under the Shangjing Lu (上京路 *shàngjīng lù*) administrative region (Ge 2014). After being defeated by the Mongols and the Southern Song, the Yuan dynasty administered today's Heilongjiang split between two provinces, Lingbei (嶺北行省 *lǐngběi xíngshěng*) and Liaoyang (遼陽行省 *liáoyáng xíngshěng*).

The Ming dynasty formally began its rule over regions that include modern-day Heilongjiang and the Wusuli (烏蘇里 *wūsūlǐ*; Ussuri) river region by 1411. Finally, a Heilongjiang protectorate (黑龍江將軍 *hēilóngjiāng jiāngjūn*) was established during the Kangxi reign (1683) of the Qing Dynasty. At this point in its history, because Heilongjiang had vast tracts of land and sparsely populated areas, its potential for growth was immense. While solidifying control of its outlying areas in the face of foreign pressure, as well as for other economic and political reasons, in 1860 the Qing dynasty loosened the restrictions that had forbidden Han Chinese emigration to Heilongjiang. Subsequently, from 1851 to 1911, the population of Heilongjiang rose dramatically, increasing from 200,000 to 1,800,000 individuals (Zhang 2009).

At the beginning of the twentieth century, as the Boxer Rebellion raged in northern China, the resultant turmoil weakened China's control over its boundaries. Foreign powers, notably Russia, saw further opportunities for expansion. The "allied" eight-nation counter-assault against the Boxers in 1900 led Russian troops to attack the Qing banner troops in northern Manchuria. With its more modern weaponry, Russian troops routed the Qing military, leading to the destruction of

[2] Not to be confused with the earlier Jin (晉 *jìn* 265–420) dynasty.

Aihui Distrtict (愛輝區 *àihuī qū*), whereupon Russia occupied Heilongjiang. Defeated by Japan 5 years later, the Russian empire was later forced to concede this territory to the Japanese.

During the last years of the Qing, in Guangxu (光緒 *guāngxù*) year 33 (1907), the protectorate of Heilongjiang was made into an administrative province with its governing capital at Longjiang Prefecture (龍降府 *lóngjiàng fū*), now Qiqihar City (齊齊哈爾城 *qíqíhāěr chéng*). The name Qiqihar comes from a word in a Mongolian group language, Daur (達斡爾 *dáwòěr*), meaning pasture.[3] The capital was transferred to Harbin in 1954.

Russian Influence in Heilongjiang

In the midst of the pogroms of nineteenth century Russia, the Czar incentivized its persecuted Jewish population to move to Manchuria. The extension of the Trans-Siberian railroad made Harbin an important hub, and Russian Jews were offered a new start in a rapidly growing economy. Reaching a population of about 25,000 by 1930, Harbin was home the father of future Israeli Prime Minister (ca. 2006) Ehud Olmert. (The name of the capital of Heilongjiang, Harbin, originates from the Manchurian word for a place to dry out fish nets.) Today, Russian influence remains visible in Harbin. The Glazunov Conservatory of Music, founded in 1925 has been reopened in 2014. Also recently, a Russian-style synagogue, built in the early 1900s in the Daoli District, has also been restored.

Japan's Invasion of Manchuria

Having invaded Manchuria in the 1930s, the Japanese empire not only extracted raw inorganic materials but also conducted horrific chemical and biological warfare experiments in China. Pingfang District (平房區 *píngfángqū*) was the location of the notorious Japanese Unit 731, which performed horrific human experimentation with toxic and infectious agents, *inter alia*, under the cover name of the Kwantung Army Hygiene Water Supply Unit.[4] After the Soviets departed Heilongjiang (but not before dismantling industrial facilities and transporting their loot back to Russia), the Chinese Communist Party (CCP) occupied the province. This territory would turn out to be critical in holding onto Manchuria, using it as a base to further "liberate" the rest of China.

---

[3] Some sources say it means "border."

[4] 関東軍防疫給水部本部 *Kantōgun Bōeki Kyūsuibu Honbu.*

In 1947, bubonic plague hit Harbin, and up to 30,000 people died. While some have blamed this on Japanese biological warfare experiments it had conducted during the war, it is not clear that these can be definitively linked. Plague had long been endemic in Northeast China, with a large outbreak in Manchuria that had earlier impacted Harbin in December 1910 (Wu 1995). It is nonetheless true, however, that the Japanese occupation of China left its public health infrastructure in such terrible and vulnerable shape that outbreaks of disease were inevitable.

Japanese wartime depredations in China also left a toxic legacy in the form of abandoned chemical weapons. In anticipation of the final battles with the Soviet Union near the end of World War II, much of these were buried in Manchuria, to include Heilongjiang and in the following locations:

- Qiqihar, Acheng District (阿城區 *āchéng qū*)
- Bayan County (巴彥縣 *bāyàn xiàn*)
- Fujin City (富錦市 *fùjǐn shì*)
- Shangzhi City (尚志市 *shàngzhì shì*) and
- Sunwu County (孫吳縣 *sūnwú xiàn*)

The disposal of these abandoned chemical weapons, which is being paid for by the Japanese government, continued through 2022.

In 1952, what was previously known as Songjiang Province (松江省 *songjiāng shěng*) was dissolved, and was incorporated into Heilongjiang Province, adding substantial area within its new boundaries. In addition to large mineral deposits, gold among them, and important heavy industries, Heilongjiang is known for its significant petroleum reserves in Daqing City (大慶市 *dàqìng shì*), representing about 25% of all Chinese domestic oil production. As such, Daqing had originally been hailed by Mao Zedong as a model in 1964 for its progress in modernizing and industrialization (Mackerras 2001).

As mentioned at the start, declining economic opportunities in older, heavy industries (e.g. coal, steel) that once dominated Manchuria has meant a recent drop in its population, and among all of China's northernmost provinces this trend is most keenly being felt in Heilongjiang, dropping nearly 17% from 2010 to 2020 (see Table 12.1, census data). In 2020, Heilongjiang had a per capita Gross Domestic Product (GDP) of about USD $213 billion, ranking 25th (just below Xinjiang with a GDP $212 billion) out of mainland China's 31 provinces and major cities. In terms of per capita income ($3,873), Heilongjiang ranked 23rd in 2020 (Zhang 2021).

Table 12.3 (below) shows the *hukou* (family registered) populations based on PRC Ministry of Civil Affairs data. (Districts listed directly under major cities are government seats, as are those in parentheses). One can compare these data with the census (usual residential populations based on 2010 and 2020 censuses in Tables 12.1 (above) and 12.2 (below).

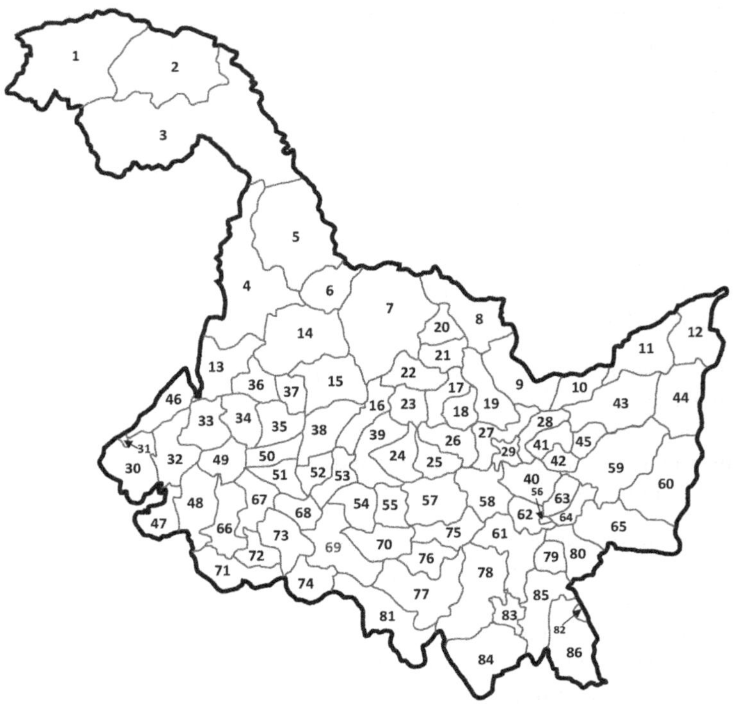

1. Mohe City
2. Tahe County
3. Huma County
4. Nenjiang City
5. Aihui District
6. Sunwu County
7. Xunke County
8. Jiayin County
9. Mengbei County
10. Suibin County
11. Tongjiang City
12. Fuyuan City
13. Nehe City
14. Wudalianchi City
15. Bei'an City
16. Suiling County
17. Yimei District
18. Jinlin District
19. Hegang City
20. Tangwang County
21. Fenglin County
22. Youhao District
23. Wucui District
24. Tieli City
25. Daqingshan County
26. Nancha County
27. Tangyuan County
28. Huachuan County
29. Jiamusi City
30. Longjiang County
31. Nianzishan District
32. Qiqiha'er City
33. Fuyu Count
34. Yi'an County
35. Baiquan County
36. Keshan County
37. Kedong County
38. Hailun City
39. Qing'an County
40. Huanan County
41. Jixian County
42. Shuangyashan City
43. Fujin City
44. Raohe County
45. Youyi County
46. Gannan County
47. Tailai County
48. Du'erbote (Durbod) Mongolian Autonomous County
49. Lindian County
50. Mingshui County
51. Qinggang County
52. Wangkui County
53. Suihua City
54. Bayan County
55. Mulan County
56. Taoshan District
57. Tonghe County
58. Yilan County
59. Baoqing County
60. Hulin City
61. Linkou County
62. Boli County
63. Xinxing District
64. Qiezihe District
65. Mishan City
66. Daqing City
67. Anda City
68. Lanxi County
69. Ha'erbin (Harbin) City
70. Binxian County
71. Zhaoyuan County
72. Zhaozhou County
73. Zhaodong City
74. Shuangcheng District
75. Fangzhen County
76. Yanshou County
77. Shangzhi City
78. Hailin City
79. Jixi City
80. Jidong County
81. Wuchang City
82. Suifenhe City
83. Mudanjiang City
84. Ning'an City
85. Muling City
86. Dongning City

Fig. 12.2 Heilongjiang Province: Subdistricts (Capital City: Ha'erbin). (Drawn by the author after People's Republic of China, Ministry of Civil Affairs (MCA 2020))

Table 12.2 Heilongjiang Province: Population data of cities and their subordinate sectors. (HPBS 2021)

Cities and subordinate sectors, population (2020 census)	Subordinate district, city and county populations (2020)	Total population (2020)
Harbin City 哈爾濱市 ***(hā'ěrbīn shì)***		**10,009,854**
Songbei District 松北區 *sōngběi qū*	413,515	
Daoli District 道里區 *dàolǐ qū*	1,097,430	
Nangang District 南崗區 *nángǎng qū*	1,390,769	
Daowai District 道外區 *dàowài qū*	811,178	
Xiangfang District 香坊區 *xiāngfāng qū*	1,120,185	
Pingfang 平房區 *píngfáng qū*	238,945	
Hulan District 呼蘭區 *hūlán qū*	769,997	
Acheng District 阿城區 *āchéng qū*	500,327	
Shuangcheng District 雙城區 *shuāngchéng qū*	633,880	
Shangzhi City 尚志市 *shàngzhì shì*	463,358	
Wuchang City 五常市 *wǔcháng shì*	724,705	
Yilan County 依蘭縣 *yīlán xiàn*	258,345	
Fangzheng County 方正縣 *fāngzhèng xiàn*	183,789	
Binxian County 賓縣 *bīnxiàn*	444,314	
Bayan County 巴彥縣 *bāyàn xiàn*	420,409	
Mulan County 木蘭縣 *mùlán xiàn*	176,245	
Tonghe County 通河縣 *tōnghé xiàn*	179,828	
Yanshou County 延壽縣 *yánshòu xiàn*	182,275	
Qiqihar City 齊齊哈爾市 ***(qíqīhā'ěr shì)***		**4,067,489**
Jianhua District 建華區 *jiànhuá qū*	332,566	
Longsha District 龍沙區 *lóngshā qū*	355,849	
Tiefeng District 鐵鋒區 *tiěfēng qū*	271,372	
Ang'angxi District 昂昂溪區 *áng'ángxī qū*	67,824	
Fula'erji (Hulan Ergi) District 富拉爾基區 *fùlā'ěrjī qū*	197,424	
Nianzishan District 碾子山區 *niǎnzǐshān qū*	56,533	
Meilisi Dawo'erzu (Daur) District 梅里斯達斡爾族區 *méilǐsī dáwò'ěrzú qū*	125,399	
Nehe City 訥河市 *nèhé shì*	436,906	
Longjiang County 龍江縣 *lóngjiāng xiàn*	414,285	
Yi'an County 依安縣 *yī'ān xiàn*	353,872	
Tailai County 泰來縣 *tàilái xiàn*	249,153	
Gannan County 甘南縣 *gānnán xiàn*	288,203	
Fuyu County 富裕縣 *fùyù xiàn*	224,404	
Keshan County 克山縣 *kèshān xiàn*	255,041	
Kedong County 克東縣 *kèdōng xiàn*	156,983	
Baiquan County 拜泉縣 *bàiquán xiàn*	282,019	

(continued)

Table 12.2 (continued)

Cities and subordinate sectors, population (2020 census)	Subordinate district, city and county populations (2020)	Total population (2020)
Mudanjiang City 牡丹江市 **(*mǔdānjiāng shì*)**		**2,290,208**
Dong'an District 東安區 *dōng'ān qū*	221,194	
Aimin District 愛民區 *àimín qū*	275,436	
Yangming District 陽明區 *yángmíng qū*	190,973	
Xi'an District 西安區 *xī'ān qū*	242,412	
Muling[a] City 穆棱市 *mùlíng shì*	197,065	
Suifenhe City 綏芬河市 *suífēnhé shì*	114,564	
Hailin City 海林市 *hǎilín shì*	292,755	
Ning'an City 寧安市 *níng'ān shì*	322,127	
Dongning City 東寧市 *dōngníng shì*	195,489	
Linkou County林口縣 *línkǒu xiàn*	238,193	
Jiamusi City 佳木斯市 **(*jiāmùsī shì*)**		**2,156,505**
Qianjin District 前進區 *qiánjìn qū*	180,893	
Xiangyang District 向陽區 *xiàngyáng qū*	295,017	
Dongfeng District 東風區 *dōngfēng qū*	121,305	
Jiaoqu District 郊區 *jiāoqū*	265,340	
Tongjiang City 同江市 *tóngjiāng shì*	176,112	
Fujin City 富錦市 *fùjǐn shì*	414,090	
Hua'nan County 樺南縣 *huà'nán xiàn*	286,855	
Huachuan County 樺川縣 *huàchuān xiàn*	145,876	
Tangyuan County 湯原縣 *tāngyuán xiàn*	173,688	
Fuyuan County 撫遠縣 *fǔyuǎn xiàn*	97,329	
Daqing City 大慶市 **(*dàqìng shì*)**		**2,781,562**
Sa'ertu [Sartu] District 薩爾圖區 *sà'ěrtú qū*	327,192	
Longfeng District 龍鳳區 *lóngfèng qū*	290,827	
Ranghulu District 讓胡露區 *rànghúlù qū*	592,603	
Datong District 大同區 *dàtóng qū*	180,266	
Honggang District 紅崗區 *hónggǎng qū*	129,988	
Zhaozhou County 肇州縣 *zhàozhōu xiàn*	306,036	
Zhaoyuan County 肇源縣 *zhàoyuán xiàn*	330,340	
Lindian County 林甸縣 *líndiàn xiàn*	191,238	
Du'erbote Mengguzu (Dorbod Mongol) Autonomous County 杜爾伯特蒙古族自治縣 *dù'ěrbótè měnggǔzú zìzhìxiàn*	199,293	
Daqing High Technology Industry Development Zone 大慶高新技術產業開發區 *dàqìng gāoxīnjìshù chǎnyè kāifāqū*	233,779	
Jixi City 雞西市 **(*jīxī shì*)**		**1,502,060**
Jiguan District 雞冠區 *jīguān qū*	402,345	

(continued)

Table 12.2 (continued)

Cities and subordinate sectors, population (2020 census)	Subordinate district, city and county populations (2020)	Total population (2020)
Hengshan District 恆山區 *héngshān qū*	87,822	
Didao District 滴道區 *dīdào qū*	65,980	
Lishu District 梨樹區 *líshù qū*	39,833	
Chengzihe District 城子河區 *chéngzǐhé qū*	69,951	
Mashan District 麻山區 *máshān qū*	17,301	
Hulin City 虎林市 *hǔlín shì*	267,870	
Mishan City 密山市 *mìshān shì*	339,103	
Jidong County 雞東縣 *jīdōng xiàn*	211,855	
Shuangyashan City 雙鴨山市 **(*shuāngyāshān shì*)**		**1,208,803**
Jianshan District 尖山區 *jiānshān qū*	262,359	
Lingdong District 嶺東區 *lǐngdōng qū*	27,498	
Sifangtai District 四方台區 *sìfāngtái qū*	39,550	
Baoshan District 寶山區 *bǎoshān qū*	72,475	
Jixian County 集賢縣 *jíxián xiàn*	243,945	
Youyi County 友誼縣 *yǒuyì xiàn*	101,080	
Baoqing County 寶清縣 *bǎoqīng xiàn*	331,377	
Raohe County 饒河縣 *ráohé xiàn*	130,519	
Yichun City 伊春市 **(*yīchūn shì*)**		**878,881**
Yimei District[b] 伊美區 *yīměi qū*	173,320	
Jinlin District 金林區 *jīnlín qū*	60,466	
Nancha District 南岔區 *nánchà qū*	82,895	
Youhao District 友好區 *yǒuhǎo qū*	54,302	
Wucui District[c] 烏翠區 *wūcuì qū*	72,259	
Tangwang County 湯旺縣 *tāngwàng xiàn*	33,245	
Tieli City 鐵力市 *tiělì shì*	225,960	
Fenglin County 豐林縣 *fēnglín xiàn*	62,214	
Daqingshan 大箐山縣 *dàqìngshān xiàn*	57,697	
Jiayin County 嘉蔭縣 *jiāyīn xiàn*	56,523	
Qitaihe Cty 七台河市 **(*qītáihé shì*)**		**689,611**
Taoshan District 桃山區 *táoshān qū*	204,111	
Xinxing District 新興區 *xīnxīng qū*	158,418	
Qiezihe District 茄子河區 *qiézǐhé qū*	127,499	
Boli County 勃利縣 *bólì xiàn*	199,583	
Hegang City 鶴崗市 **(*hègǎng shì*)**		**891,271**
Xiangyang District 向陽區 *xiàngyáng qū*	72,867	
Xingshan District 興山區 *xīngshān qū*	21,125	
Gongnong District 工農區 *gōngnóng qū*	136,519	
Nanshan District 南山區 *nánshān qū*	119,662	
Xing'an District 興安區 *xīng'ān qū*	99,013	

(continued)

Table 12.2 (continued)

Cities and subordinate sectors, population (2020 census)	Subordinate district, city and county populations (2020)	Total population (2020)
Dongshan District 東山區 *dōngshān qū*	96,218	
Luobei County 蘿北縣 *luóběi xiàn*	206,072	
Suibin County 綏濱縣 *suíbīn xiàn*	139,795	
Heihe City 黑河市 **(*hēihé shì*)**		**1,286,401**
Aihui District 愛輝區 *àihuī qū*	223,832	
Bei'an City 北安市 *běi'ān shì*	308,237	
Wudalianchi City 五大連池市 *wǔdàliánchí shì*	243,283[d]	
Nenjiang City 嫩江市 *nènjiāng shì*	355,528	
Xunke County 遜克縣 *xùnkè xiàn*	82,134	
Sunwu County 孫吳縣 *sūnwú xiàn*	73,387	
Suihua City 綏化市 **(*suíhuà shì*)**		**3,756,167**
Beilin District 北林區 *běilín qū*	698,025	
Anda City 安達市 *āndá shì*	357,535	
Zhaodong City 肇東市 *zhàodōng shì*	666,532	
Hailun City 海倫市 *hǎilún shì*	480,216	
Wangkui County 望奎縣 *wàngkuí xiàn*	286,848	
Lanxi County 蘭西縣 *lánxī xiàn*	308,684	
Qinggang County 青岡縣 *qīnggāng xiàn*	287,557	
Qing'an County 慶安縣 *qìng'ān xiàn*	260,592	
Mingshui County 明水縣 *míngshuǐ xiàn*	198,271	
Suiling County 綏棱縣 *suílíng xiàn*	211,907	
Daxinganling Prefecture 大興安嶺地區 **(*dàxīng'ānlǐng Dìqū*)**		**331,276**
Huma County 呼瑪縣 *hūmǎ xiàn*	36,362	
Tahe County 塔河縣 *tǎhé xiàn*	51,056	
Mohe City 漠河市 *mòhé shì*	54,036	
Jiagedaqi (Jagdaqi) District 家格達奇區 *jiāgédáqí qū*	137,105	
Songling District 松嶺區 *sōnglǐng qū*	15,996	
Xinlin District 新林區 *xīnlín qū*	20,362	
Huzhong District 呼中區 *hūzhōng qū*	16,359	

[a]Usually 棱 is read *léng* but here *líng* in mainland China
[b]Established in 2019
[c]Established 2019
[d]Includes Fengjing District 風景區 *fēngjǐng qū*

Heilongjiang Province (黑 *hēi*)

Provincial Capital: Ha'erbin

Table 12.3 Heilongjiang Province: Permanent registered (戶籍人口 *hùjí rénkǒu*) populations. (MCA 2020)

Name	中文	Simplified	Population (2012)	Population (2016)	Population (2020)	Area (Sq. Km)
Heilongjiang Province	黑龍江省	黑龙江省	**38,430,000**	**38,110,000**	**35,740,000**	**460,000**
Ha'erbin (Harbin) City	哈爾濱市	哈尔滨市	**9,940,000**	**9,940,000**	**9,520,000**	**53,186**
Songbei District (Songbei Town)	松北區 (松北鎮)	松北区 (松北镇)	200,000	200,000	220,000	736
Daoli District (Fushun Subdistrict)	道里區 (撫順街道)	道里区 (抚顺街道)	710,000	720,000	770,000	479
Nangang District (Dacheng Subdistrict)	南崗區 (大城街道)	南岗区 (大成街道)	1,000,000	1,000,000	1,040,000	192
Daowai District (Daxing Subdistrict)	道外區 (大興街道)	道外区 (大兴街道)	690,000	690,000	650,000	619
Xiangfang District (Xiangfangdajie Subdistrict)	香坊區 (香坊大街街道)	香坊区 (香坊大街街道)	770,000	750,000	740,000	340
Pingfang District (Youxie Subdistrict)	平房區 (友協街道)	平房区 (友协街道)	160,000	160,000	160,000	94
Hulan District (Limin Subdistrict)	呼蘭區 (利民街道)	呼兰区 (利民街道)	620,000	620,000	610,000	2197
Acheng District (Heping Subdistrict)	阿城區 (和平街道)	阿城区 (和平街道)	580,000	580,000	540,000	2445
Shuangcheng District (Shuangcheng Town)	雙城區 (雙城鎮)	双城区 (双城镇)	820,000	820,000	770,000	3112
Shangzhi City (Shangzhi Town)	尚志市 (尚志鎮)	尚志市 (尚志镇)	620,000	620,000	560,000	8891
Wuchang City (Wuchang Town)	五常市 (五常鎮)	五常市 (五常镇)	1,000,000	1,010,000	900,000	7512
Yilan County (Yilan Town)	依蘭縣 (依蘭鎮)	依兰县 (依兰镇)	410,000	410,000	380,000	4616
Fangzheng County (Fangzheng Town)	方正縣 (方正鎮)	方正县 (方正镇)	230,000	230,000	220,000	2969

(continued)

Table 12.3 (continued)

Name	中文	Simplified	Population (2012)	Population (2016)	Population (2020)	Area (Sq. Km)
Binxian County (Binzhou Town)	賓縣 (賓州鎮)	宾县 (宾州镇)	630,000	630,000	570,000	3845
Bayan County (Bayan Town)	巴彥縣 (巴彥鎮)	巴彦县 (巴彦镇)	710,000	710,000	650,000	3135
Mulan County (Mulan Town)	木蘭縣 (木蘭鎮)	木兰县 (木兰镇)	280,000	270,000	250,000	3179
Tonghe County (Tonghe Town)	通河縣 (通河鎮)	通河县 (通河镇)	240,000	250,000	240,000	5675
Yanshou County (Yanshou Town)	延壽縣 (延壽鎮)	延寿县 (延寿镇)	270,000	270,000	250,000	350
Qiqiha'er (Qiqihar) City	齊齊哈爾市	**齐齐哈尔**市	5,700,000	5,580,000	5,300,000	44,287
Jianhua District (Bukui Subdistrict)	建華區 (卜奎街道)	建华区 (卜奎街道)	250,000	260,000	250,000	853
Longsha District (Nanhang Subdistrict)	龍沙區 (南航街道)	龙沙区 (南航街道)	300,000	290,000	280,000	188
Tiefeng District (Longhua Subdistrict)	鐵鋒區 (龍華街道)	铁锋区 (龙华街道)	290,000	290,000	270,000	695
Ang'angxi District (Xinxing Subdistrict)	昂昂溪區 (新興街道)	昂昂溪区 (新兴街道)	80,000	100,000	70,000	1166
Fula'erji (Hulan Ergi) District (Hong'an Subdistrict)	富拉爾基區 (紅岸街道)	富拉尔基区 (红岸街道)	250,000	240,000	210,000	375
Nianzishan District (Fanrong Subdistrict)	碾子山區 (繁榮街道)	碾子山区 (繁荣街道)	80,000	80,000	70,000	357
Meilisi Dawo'erzu (Daur) District (Meilisi Subdistrict)	梅里斯達斡爾族區 (梅里斯街道)	梅里斯达斡尔族区 (梅里斯街道)	170,000	170,000	160,000	1948
Nehe City (Tongjiang Subdistrict)	訥河市 (通江街道)	讷河市 (通江街道)	740,000	730,000	680,000	6664
Longjiang County (Longjiang Town)	龍江縣 (龍江鎮)	龙江县 (龙江镇)	610,000	600,000	580,000	6197
Yi'an County (Yi'an Town)	依安縣 (依安鎮)	依安县 (依安镇)	500,000	490,000	460,000	3780
Tailai County (Tailai Town)	泰來縣 (泰來鎮)	泰来县 (泰来镇)	330,000	300,000	300,000	4061

(continued)

Table 12.3 (continued)

Name	中文	Simplified	Population (2012)	Population (2016)	Population (2020)	Area (Sq. Km)
Gannan County (Gannan Town)	甘南縣 (甘南鎮)	甘南县 (甘南镇)	400,000	390,000	380,000	4384
Fuyu County (Fuyu Town)	富裕縣 (富裕鎮)	富裕县 (富裕镇)	300,000	270,000	280,000	4335
Keshan County (Keshan Town)	克山縣 (克山鎮)	克山县 (克山镇)	500,000	490,000	460,000	3632
Kedong County (Kedong Town)	克東縣 (克東鎮)	克东县 (克东镇)	300,000	300,000	280,000	2083
Baiquan County (Baiquan Town)	拜泉縣 (拜泉鎮)	拜泉县 (拜泉镇)	600,000	580,000	550,000	3569
Heihe City	黑河市	黑河市	1,720,000	1,710,000	1,590,000	68,285
Aihui District (Xing'an Subdistrict)	愛輝區 (興安街道)	爱辉区 (兴安街道)	190,000	190,000	180,000	14,446
Bei'an City (Tiexi Subdistrict)	北安市 (鐵西街道)	北安市 (铁西街道)	470,000	460,000	420,000	7194
Wudalianchi City (Qingshan Subdistrict)	五大連池市 (青山街道)	五大连池市 (青山街道)	360,000	360,000	340,000	9874
Nenjiang City (Nenjiang Town)	嫩江市 (嫩江鎮)	嫩江市 (嫩江镇)	500,000	500,000	470,000	15,109
Xunke County (Qike Town)	遜克縣 (奇克鎮)	逊克县 (奇克镇)	100,000	100,000	100,000	17,344
Sunwu County (Sunwu Town)	孫吳縣 (孫吳鎮)	孙吴县 (孙吴镇)	100,000	100,000	90,000	4318
Daqing City	大慶市	大庆市	2,790,000	2,820,000	2,760,000	21,643
Sa'ertu [Sartu] District (Dong'an Subdistrict)	薩爾圖區 (薩政路)	萨尔图区 (萨政路)	320,000	330,000	380,000	504
Longfeng District (Longfeng Subdistrict)	龍鳳區 (龍政路)	龙凤区 (龙政路)	180,000	190,000	190,000	416
Ranghulu District (Zhongyang Pedestrian Street)	讓胡露區 (中央大街)	让胡路区 (中央大街)	450,000	460,000	480,000	1394
Datong District (Datong Town)	大同區 (大同鎮)	大同区 (大同镇)	250,000	240,000	220,000	2372
Honggang District (Honggang Subdistrict)	紅崗區 (薩大中路)	红岗区 (萨大中路)	130,000	130,000	110,000	625
Zhaozhou County (Zhaozhou Town)	肇州縣 (肇州鎮)	肇州县 (肇州镇)	460,000	470,000	430,000	2445
Zhaoyuan County (Zhaoyuan Town)	肇源縣 (肇源鎮)	肇源县 (肇源镇)	470,000	480,000	440,000	4120
Lindian County (Lindian Town)	林甸縣 (林甸鎮)	林甸县 (林甸镇)	270,000	270,000	250,000	3591

(continued)

Table 12.3 (continued)

Name	中文	Simplified	Population (2012)	Population (2016)	Population (2020)	Area (Sq. Km)
Du'erbote Mengguzu (Dorbod Mongol) Autonomous County (Du'erbote [Dorbod] Town)	杜爾伯特蒙古族自治縣 (杜爾伯特鎮)	杜尔伯特蒙古族自治县 (杜爾伯特镇)	260,000	250,000	240,000	6176
Yichun City	伊春市	伊春市	1,270,000	1,220,000	1,180,000	32,860
Yimei District (Xuri Subdistrict)	伊美區 (旭日街道)	伊美区 (旭日街道)	N/A	N/A	200,000	2756
Yichun District (Xuri Subdistrict)	伊春區 (旭日街道)	伊春区 (旭日街道)	160,000	160,000	N/A	(89)
Jinlin District (Jinshantun Town)	金林區 (金山屯鎮)	金林区 (金山屯镇)	N/A	N/A	90,000	2306
Nancha District (Lianhe Subdistrict)	南岔區 (聯合街道)	南岔区 (联合街道)	130,000	130,000	120,000	3084
Youhao District (Youhao Subdistrict)	友好區 (雙子河街道)	友好区 (双子河街道)	70,000	60,000	80,000	3001
Xilin District (Xilin Subdistrict)	西林區 (西林街道)	西林区 (西林街道)	50,000	50,000	N/A	(381)
Wucui District (Shuguang Subdistrict)	烏翠區 (曙光街道)	乌翠区 (曙光街道)	N/A	N/A	80,000	2379
Cuiluan District (Shuguang Subdistrict)	翠巒區 (曙光街道)	翠峦区 (曙光街道)	50,000	50,000	N/A	(1572)
Xinqing County (Xinqing Subdistrict)	新青縣 (新青街道)	新青县 (新青街道)	50,000	50,000	N/A	(1047)
Meixi District (Meixi Subdistrict)	美溪區 (美溪街道)	美溪区 (美溪街道)	40,000	40,000	N/A	(2264)
Jinshantun District (Fendou Subdistrict)	金山屯區 (奮鬥街道)	金山屯区 (奋斗街道)	50,000	40,000	N/A	(1854)
Wuying District (Wuying Subdistrict)	五營區 (五營街道)	五营区 (五营街道)	40,000	40,000	N/A	(1039)
Wumahe District (Wumahe Subdistrict)	烏馬河區 (烏馬河街道)	乌马河区 (乌马河街道)	30,000	30,000	N/A	(1210)
Tangwanghe District (Henan Subdistrict)	湯旺河區 (河南街道)	汤旺河区 (河南街道)	30,000	30,000	N/A	(2142)

(continued)

Table 12.3 (continued)

Name	中文	Simplified	Population (2012)	Population (2016)	Population (2020)	Area (Sq. Km)
Tangwang County (Tangwanghe Town)	湯旺縣 (湯旺河鎮)	汤旺县 (汤旺河镇)	N/A	N/A	50,000	2142
Dailing District (Dailing Subdistrict)	帶嶺區 (帶嶺街道)	带岭区 (带岭街道)	40,000	40,000	N/A	(1039)
Wuyiling District[a] (Wuyiling Subdistrict)	烏伊嶺區 (烏伊嶺街道)	乌伊岭区 (乌伊岭街道)	20,000	20,000	N/A	(897)
Hongxing District[b] (Hongxing Subdistrict)	紅星區 (紅星街道)	红星区 (红星街道)	30,000	20,000	N/A	(885)
Shangganling District[c] (Hongshan Subdistrict)	上甘嶺區 (紅山街道)	上甘岭区 (红山街道)	20,000	20,000	N/A	(634)
Tieli City (Tieli Town)	鐵力市 (鐵力鎮)	铁力市 (铁力镇)	390,000	370,000	300,000	3776
Fenglin County (Xinqing Town)	豐林縣 (新青鎮)	丰林县 (新青镇)	N/A	N/A	100,000	2971
Daqingshan (Dailing Town)	大箐山縣 (帶嶺鎮)	大箐山县 (带岭镇)	N/A	N/A	90,000	3706
Jiayin County (Chaoyang Town)	嘉蔭縣 (朝陽鎮)	嘉荫县 (朝阳镇)	70,000	70,000	80,000	6739
Hegang City	鶴崗市	**鹤岗**市	1,080,000	1,080,000	1,000,000	14,665
Xiangyang District (Guangming Subdistrict)	向陽區 (光明街道)	向阳区 (光明街道)	100,000	100,000	90,000	8
Xingshan District (Gounan Subdistrict)	興山區 (溝南街道)	兴山区 (沟南街道)	50,000	50,000	40,000	28
Gongnong District (Hongqi Subdistrict)	工農區 (紅旗街道)	工农区 (红旗街道)	170,000	170,000	170,000	12
Nanshan District (Tiexi Subdistrict)	南山區 (鐵西街道)	南山区 (铁西街道)	130,000	130,000	120,000	31
Xing'an District (Xing'an Subdistrict)	興安區 (興安街道)	兴安区 (兴安街道)	140,000	140,000	130,000	254
Dongshan District (Dongshan Subdistrict)	東山區 (東山街道)	东山区 (东山街道)	80,000	80,000	60,000	4220
Luobei County (Fengxiang Town)	蘿北縣 (鳳翔鎮)	萝北县 (凤翔镇)	220,000	220,000	210,000	6768

(continued)

Table 12.3 (continued)

Name	中文	Simplified	Population (2012)	Population (2016)	Population (2020)	Area (Sq. Km)
Suibin County (Suibin Town)	綏濱縣 (綏濱鎮)	绥滨县 (绥滨镇)	190,000	190,000	180,000	3344
Jiamusi City	佳木斯市	佳木斯市	2,530,000	2,480,000	2,330,000	32,470
Qianjin District (Zhanqian Subdistrict)	前進區 (站前街道)	前进区 (站前街道)	160,000	160,000	160,000	16
Xiangyang District (Qiaonan Subdistrict)	向陽區 (橋南街道)	向阳区 (桥南街道)	230,000	220,000	220,000	41
Dongfeng District (Jianguo Subdistrict)	東風區 (建國街道)	东风区 (建国街道)	150,000	150,000	120,000	143
Jiaoqu District (Youyi Subdistrict)	郊區 (友誼街道)	郊区 (友谊街道)	280,000	280,000	260,000	1704
Tongjiang City (Tongjiang Town)	同江市 (同江鎮)	同江市 (同江镇)	180,000	180,000	180,000	6229
Fujin City (Chengguan Subdistrict)	富錦市 (城關街道)	富锦市 (城关街道)	470,000	470,000	450,000	8224
Huanan County (Huanan Town)	樺南縣 (樺南鎮)	桦南县 (桦南镇)	470,000	450,000	410,000	4418
Huachuan County (Yuelai Town)	樺川縣 (悅來鎮)	桦川县 (悦来镇)	220,000	220,000	200,000	2228
Tangyuan County (Tangyuan Town)	湯原縣 (湯原鎮)	汤原县 (汤原镇)	270,000	260,000	240,000	3420
Fuyuan City (Fuyuan Town)	撫遠市 (撫遠鎮)	抚远市 (抚远镇)	100,000	90,000	80,000	6047
Shuangyashan City	雙鴨山市	双鸭山市	1,530,000	1,500,000	1,410,000	22,802
Jianshan District (Tiexi Subdistrict)	尖山區 (鐵西街道)	尖山区 (铁西街道)	230,000	240,000	240,000	118
Lingdong District (Beishan Subdistrict)	嶺東區 (北山街道)	岭东区 (北山街道)	80,000	70,000	60,000	802
Sifangtai District (Zhenxingzhonglu Subdistrict)	四方台區 (振興中路街道)	四方台区 (振兴中路街道)	70,000	70,000	60,000	225
Baoshan District (Hongqi Subdistrict)	寶山區 (紅旗街道)	宝山区 (红旗街道)	130,000	120,000	110,000	750
Jixian County (Fuli Town)	集賢縣 (福利鎮)	集贤县 (福利镇)	320,000	320,000	290,000	2253

(continued)

Table 12.3 (continued)

Name	中文	Simplified	Population (2012)	Population (2016)	Population (2020)	Area (Sq. Km)
Youyi County (Youyi Town)	友誼縣 (友誼鎮)	友谊县 (友谊镇)	130,000	120,000	110,000	888
Baoqing County (Baoqing Town)	寶清縣 (寶清鎮)	宝清县 (宝清镇)	420,000	420,000	400,000	10,001
Raohe County (Raohe Town)	饒河縣 (饒河鎮)	饶河县 (饶河镇)	150,000	140,000	140,000	6765
Qitaihe City	七台河市	七台河市	930,000	920,000	780,000	6221
Taoshan District (Dongjin street)	桃山區 (東進街)	桃山区 (东进街)	200,000	200,000	190,000	74
Xinxing District (Huancheng highway)	新興區 (環城公路)	新兴区 (环城公路)	220,000	220,000	170,000	2003
Qiezihe District (Dong'an street)	茄子河區 (東安街)	茄子河区 (东安街)	150,000	150,000	120,000	1569
Boli County (Boli Town)	勃利縣 (勃利鎮)	勃利县 (勃利镇)	360,000	350,000	300,000	2575
Jixi City	雞西市	鸡西市	1,900,000	1,840,000	1,730,000	22,551
Jiguan District (Hongjunlu Subdistrict)	雞冠區 (紅軍路街道)	鸡冠区 (红军路街道)	340,000	330,000	340,000	148
Hengshan District (Fendou Subdistrict)	恆山區 (奮鬥街道)	恒山区 (奋斗街道)	170,000	160,000	140,000	587
Didao District (Dongxing Subdistrict)	滴道區 (東興街道)	滴道区 (东兴街道)	120,000	110,000	100,000	500
Lishu District (Lishu Subdistrict)	梨樹區 (梨樹街道)	梨树区 (梨树街道)	90,000	80,000	70,000	412
Chengzihe District (Chengzihe Subdistrict)	城子河區 (城子河街道)	城子河区 (城子河街道)	140,000	130,000	110,000	181
Mashan District (Mashan Subdistrict)	麻山區 (麻山街道)	麻山区 (麻山街道)	30,000	30,000	30,000	425
Hulin City (Hulin Town)	虎林市 (虎林鎮)	虎林市 (虎林镇)	290,000	290,000	280,000	9334
Mishan City (Mishan Town)	密山市 (密山鎮)	密山市 (密山镇)	420,000	420,000	400,000	7731
Jidong County (Jidong Town)	雞東縣 (雞東鎮)	鸡东县 (鸡东镇)	300,000	290,000	270,000	3233
Mudanjiang City	牧丹江市	牧丹江市	2,700,000	2,700,000	2,520,000	38,827

(continued)

Table 12.3 (continued)

Name	中文	Simplified	Population (2012)	Population (2016)	Population (2020)	Area (Sq. Km)
Dong'an District (Xin'an Subdistrict)	東安區 (新安街道)	东安区 (新安街道)	190,000	190,000	190,000	581
Aimin District (Xiangyang Subdistrict)	愛民區 (向陽街道)	爱民区 (向阳街道)	230,000	230,000	210,000	437
Yangming District (Yangming Subdistrict)	陽明區 (陽明街道)	阳明区 (阳明街道)	230,000	260,000	220,000	1096
Xi'an District (Xianfeng Subdistrict)	西安區 (先峰街道)	西安区 (先锋街道)	240,000	250,000	240,000	246
Muling City (Bamiantong Town)	穆棱市 (八面通鎮)	穆棱市 (八面通镇)	300,000	290,000	270,000	6247
Suifenhe City (Suifenhe Town)	綏芬河市 (綏芬河鎮)	绥芬河市 (绥芬河镇)	70,000	70,000	70,000	422
Hailin City (Hailin Town)	海林市 (海林鎮)	海林市 (海林镇)	410,000	400,000	370,000	8816
Ning'an City (Ning'an Town)	寧安市 (寧安鎮)	宁安市 (宁安镇)	440,000	440,000	410,000	7227
Dongning City (Dongning Town)	東寧市 (東寧鎮)	东宁市 (东宁镇)	210,000	210,000	200,000	7117
Linkou County (Linkou Town)	林口縣 (林口鎮)	林口县 (林口镇)	380,000	360,000	340,000	6638
Suihua City	綏化市	绥化市	5,870,000	5,770,000	5,250,000	35,211
Beilin District (Dayou Subdistrict)	北林區 (大有街道)	北林区 (大有街道)	900,000	890,000	810,000	2,723
Anda City (Anda Town)	安達市 (安達鎮)	安达市 (安达镇)	520,000	490,000	810,000	3586
Zhaodong City (Zhaodong Town)	肇東市 (肇東鎮)	肇东市 (肇东镇)	980,000	940,000	860,000	4330
Hailun City (Hailun Town)	海倫市 (海倫鎮)	海伦市 (海伦镇)	850,000	840,000	760,000	4667
Wangkui County (Wangkui Town)	望奎縣 (望奎鎮)	望奎县 (望奎镇)	490,000	470,000	440,000	2299
Lanxi County (Lanxi Town)	蘭西縣 (蘭西鎮)	兰西县 (兰西镇)	540,000	540,000	480,000	2499
Qinggang County (Qinggang Town)	青岡縣 (青岡鎮)	青冈县 (青冈镇)	480,000	500,000	450,000	2686
Qing'an County (Qing'an Town)	慶安縣 (慶安鎮)	庆安县 (庆安镇)	410,000	400,000	370,000	5607

(continued)

Table 12.3 (continued)

Name	中文	Simplified	Population (2012)	Population (2016)	Population (2020)	Area (Sq. Km)
Mingshui County (Mingshui Town)	明水縣 (明水鎮)	明水县 (明水镇)	370,000	370,000	330,000	2308
Suiling County (Suiling Town)	綏棱縣 (綏棱鎮)	绥棱县 (绥棱镇)	330,000	330,000	290,000	4506
Daxing'anling (Da Hinggan Ling) Prefecture (Jiagedaqi [Jagdaqi] District)	大興安嶺地區 (加格達奇區)	大兴安岭地区 (加格达奇区)	530,000	510,000	430,000	46,755
Huma County (Huma Town)	呼瑪縣 (呼瑪鎮)	呼玛县 (呼玛镇)	340,000	330,000	290,000	14,285
Tahe County (Tahe Town)	塔河縣 (塔河鎮)	塔河县 (塔河镇)	100,000	90,000	70,000	14,103
Mohe City (Xilinji Town)	漠河市 (西林吉鎮)	漠河市 (西林吉镇)	90,000	90,000	70,000	18,367

[a]Merged into Tangwang county, 29 June 2019
[b]Merged into Fenglin district 29 June 2019
[c]Merged into Youhao district 29 June 2019

References

Christoffersen, Gaye. 2002. The political implications of Heilongjiang's industrial structure. In *Rethinking China's provinces*, ed. John Fitzgerald, 221–246. New York: Routledge.

Ge, Jianxiong. 2014. [*Border regions and their political administration*] 葛劍雄, 疆域與政區. Hong Kong: China Books.

Heilongjiang Province Bureau of Statistics (HPBS). 2021. [*Bulletin of the main data of the seventh national census of Heilongjiang province in 2020*]. 2020年黑龙江省第七次全国人口普查主要数据公报, 27 May. http://tjj.hlj.gov.cn/zxfb/202105/t20210527_87736.html.

Hsieh, Chiao-min, and Jean Kan Hsieh. 1995. *China: A provincial atlas*. New York: Macmillan Publishing.

Leng, Sidney. 2021. China's rust belt population plummeted in last decade, exacerbating regional economic divide. *South China Morning Post*, 14 May. https://www.scmp.com/economy/china-economy/article/3133397/chinas-rust-belt-population-plummeted-last-decade

Mackerras, Colin. 2001. *The new Cambridge handbook of contemporary China*. Cambridge: Cambridge University Press.

Ministry of Civil Affairs (MCA), People's Republic of China. 2020. [*County/township administration handbook*]. Beijing: China Statistics Press. 中華人民共和國民政部, 中華人民共和國, 鄉鎮行政區劃簡冊.

Ni, Xijun, Qiang Ji, Wu Wensheng, et al. 2021. Massive cranium from Harbin in northeastern China establishes a new middle Pleistocene human lineage. *The Innovation* 21: 1–8. https://www.cell.com/the-innovation/pdf/S2666-6758(21)00055-2.pdf.

Shang-Ch'i Guide. 2017. [*Backpacking in China: the most complete collection of self-guided travel for China, 2018*]. Taipei: Shang-Ch'i Shitai Publishing. 2018 最完整的中國自助旅遊全集. 台北: 上奇時代.

West, Barbara A. 2009. *Encyclopedia of the peoples of Asia and Oceania*. New York: Facts on File.
Wu, Yu-lin. 1995. *Memories of Dr. Wu Lien-Teh, Plague fighter*. Singapore: World Scientific.
Zhang, Zheng. 2009. [Immigration within the customs of Heilongjiang in the Qing dynasty and its historical role]. *China Economics Net*, 16 June. 张正. 清代黑龙江的关内移民及其历史作用. 中国经济网. Via https://www.chinanews.com.cn/cul/news/2009/06-16/1735750.shtml. Accessed 31 Dec 2021.
Zhang, Shunan. 2021. [*The 2020 per capita income list of residents in various provinces: Shanghai is the richest, and it has risen sharply*]. Finance.people.com. 22 January. 张澍楠. 2020年各省份居民人均收入榜: 上海最有钱, 这地涨得猛. http://finance.people.com.cn/n1/2021/0122/c1004-32008733.html.

Chapter 13
Henan Province

Abstract Although modern archeology sees Chinese civilizational development as having sprung up from different regions, in a very general sense, one can say that Henan Province is where China, as we know it, basically started. After all, the Confucian texts relate to us that Henan (that is, Yuzhou), was the center of China's ancient nine states. Henan is also where one finds the remnants of the foundational Shang dynasty (ca. sixteenth century BCE), and is where the ancient oracle bones demonstrated the earliest examples of Chinese writing and literature. Today, Henan is one of China's most populated provinces, having reached nearly 100 million people. Routinely subjected to deadly flooding and its resulting miseries throughout its history, it was even deliberately caused in order to fight the Japanese invasion in 1938, leading to the deaths of some 800,000 civilians. With a relatively impressive gross national product in 2020, ranked fifth after Zhejiang Province, its per capita income is nonetheless relatively low, which probably helps to explain why Henan's registered (*hukou*) population is much larger than its residential census figures, demonstrating that a significant number of Henan citizens actually live and work elsewhere.

E. Croddy, *China's Provinces and Populations*,
https://doi.org/10.1007/978-3-031-09165-0_13

Henan Province (河南省 *hénán shěng*): Abbreviation 豫 (*yù*) (Fig. 13.1)

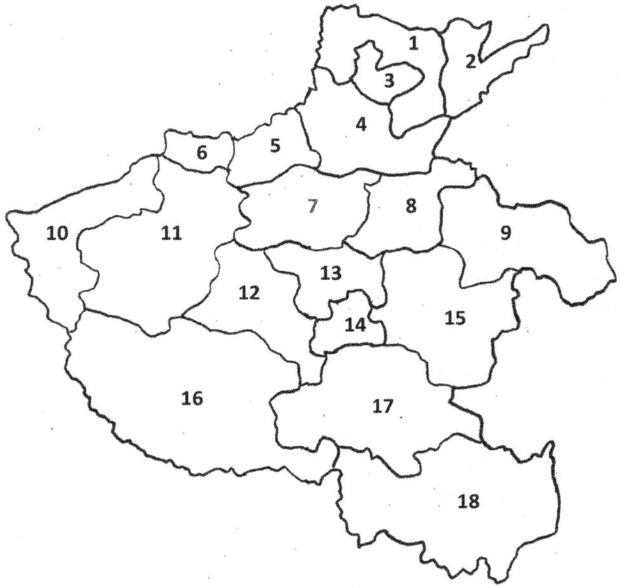

		Population (2020)
1.	Anyang City	5,477,614
2.	Puyang City	3,772,088
3.	Hebi City	1,565,973
4.	Xinxiang City	6,251,929
5.	Jiaozuo City	3,521,078
6.	Jiyuan City	727,265
7.	Zhengzhou City	12,600,574
8.	Kaifeng City	4,824,016
9.	Shangqiu City	7,816,831
10.	Sanmenxia City	2,034,872
11.	Luoyang City	7,056,699
12.	Pingdingshan City	4,987,137
13.	Xuchang City	4,379,998
14.	Luohe City	2,367,490
15.	Zhoukou City	9,026,015
16.	Nanyang City	9,713,112
17.	Zhumadian City	7,008,427
18.	Xinyang City	6,234,401

Fig. 13.1 Henan province major cities (Provincial Capital: Zhengzhou City). (Drawn by the Author after People's Republic of China, Ministry of Civil Affairs (MCA 2020))

Henan Province: General Impressions

Henan is the second most populated of all China's provinces, the most recent (2020) national census recording 99,365,519 residents. Its capital, Zhengzhou City (鄭州市 *zhèngzhōu shì*), has a population of over 12 million. Once referred to as the central state (中州 *zhōngzhōu*), Henan has had other other monikers indicating its centrality: "Central Earth" 中土 (*zhōngtǔ*) and "Central Plain" 中原 (*zhōngyuán*), etc. It is fitting, then, that Henan and the Yellow River (黃河 *huánghé*) that runs through it (the so-called "mother river" 母親河 *mǔqīnhé*) are regarded as the cradle of China's civilization. Henan is indeed home to some of the most important historical sites of China's formative Shang dynasty 商代 (*shāngdài*). In popular culture, Henan conjures images of Chinese classical martial arts, such as the Shaolin temple (少林寺 *shǎolínsì*), located at the center of the five great mountains (五嶽 *wǔ yuè*) in China, Songshan (嵩山 *sōng shān*) (Shang-Ch'i 2017).

The histories tell us that, after 'Yu the Great' (大禹 *dàyǔ*) of the Xia dyasty (夏 *xià*, ca. 2100 BCE) completed his legendary task of controlling the rivers, and thereby reducing the severity of flooding, he divided the central plains into nine states. One of these included Yuzhou (豫州 *yùzhōu)*. The Confucian texts relate that "Henan is to say Yuzhou (豫州), which is in the middle of the nine states."[1] The character Yu (豫 *yù*) for Henan is therefore used as shorthand for Henan Province (e.g., atlases, car license plates, etc.).

Prehistoric Henan

Some of the earliest signs of a sophisticated culture were discovered at the Neolithic Jiahu (賈湖 *jiǎhú*) site, located in Henan Province, Wuyang County (舞陽縣 *wǔyáng xiàn*). In adition to other amazing finds at Jiahu, evidence was found of beer making (醴 *lǐ*) using honey, rice and fruit (McGovern et al. 2004). In 2006, the brew master Sam Calagione (Dogfish Head Craft Brewery) devised a recreation of an ancient liquor that he called "Chateau Jiahu" using ingredients likely used at that time: rice, hawthorn fruit and wildflower honey (McGovern 2009). Even more intriguing are early forms of writing found at the Jiahu site that resemble (although seem to have no clear connection to) Shang Dynasty writing that only appeared several millennial later. These discoveries, as well as the uncovering of musical instruments (e.g., seven-holed flutes) showed a proto-typical Chinese culture that is at least 9000 years old.

Among other Neolithic sites, the most famous is the Yangshao Culture (仰韶文化 *yangsháo wénhuà* 5000–3000 BCE), uncovered in Yangshao village (仰韶村 *yangsháo cūn*), Mianchi County (澠池縣 *miǎnchí xiàn*). This millet-farming and shamanistic culture stretched from modern-day Zhengzhou City out west to Qinghai

[1] "河南曰豫州, 豫州在九州之中" *hénán yuē yùzhōu, yùzhōu zài jiǔzhōu zhī zhōng.*

Province (Chang 1999). Possibly referring to the Yangshao Culture, the Baihutong (白虎通 *báihŭtōng*), a text dated ca. 80 CE, described the level of social and technological progress of a prehistorical “Sui (flint) people” (燧人 *suìrén*). Some claim this legendary Neolithic people lived in today’s Shangqiu City (商丘市 *shāngqiū shì*), Henan Province:

> They drilled wood to make fire; taught people how to cook, cultivated the people favorably; rid poison by avoiding smelly things—these were the Sui (Li 2014).[2]

Henan is also home to important examples of the Longshan culture (ca. 3000–2000 BCE), typified by a new style of gray and black ceramics, showing a well-organized, stratified society. Evidence of copper and bronze smelting were discovered in Henan’s Linru County (since 1988 renamed Ruzhou City 汝州市 *rŭzhōu shì*) and Niuzhai Village (牛寨村 *niúzhài cūn*) in Xiping County (西平縣 *xīpíng xiàn*), respectively. It was also during this time (ca. 2800 BCE) that the legendary Emperor Fuxi–(伏羲 *fúxī*; also known as Tai Hao 太昊 *tàihào* and Pao Xi (庖羲 *páoxī*)—established the capital Chen (陳 *chén*) near today’s Huaiyang (淮陽 *huáiyáng*). Among other accomplishments to his credit, Fuxi “invented the eight (Daoist) trigrams and weaved nets to catch fish.”[3] The grandson of the (also legendary) Yellow Emperor, Zhuan Xu (顓頊 *zhuānxù*; ca. 2500 BCE) and his descendants are said to have united the clans around modern-day Xinzheng City (新鄭市 *xīnzhèng shì*). (Yuan and Peimin 2007).

Among the most important in Chinese archaeology, the Erlitou Culture (二里頭文化 *èrlĭtóu wénhuà*) was discovered at Erlitou Village (翟鎮二里頭村 *zháizhèn èrlĭtóu cūn*), Zhaizhen Town, in Yanshi City (偃師市 *yǎnshī shì*). The Erlitou Culture flourished in today’s Henan and southern Shanxi. The Erlitou excavation revealed bronze foundries, jade, and temple structures with traditional tamped earth (夯土 *hāngtŭ*) foundations. Significantly, these and other artifacts have been radiocarbon dated within the ranges mentioned in historical writings of the Xia dynasty, i.e., 2100–1600 BCE.

Approaching the Center(s) of Chinese Civilization; and Is It Really 5000 Years Old?

Recent archeology no longer views ancient Chinese civilization as having developed primarily in one main central location, but rather from multiple sites throughout the region to include Henan, Shandong, Hubei, and Jiangsu provinces, each having their own sophisticated rites, technologies, and social strata. That said, the eminent scholar Kwang-Chih Chang reminded us that

---

[2] 鑽木燧取火, 教民熟食, 養人利性, 避臭去毒, 謂之燧人也 *zuànmù suì qŭhuŏ, jiàomín shóushí, yǎngrén lìxìng, bìchòu qùdú, wèizhī suìrén yě.*

[3] 作八卦, 結繩為網以漁 *zuò bā guà, jiéshéng wéi wǎng yĭyú.*

> [Henan] still commands our special attention, because it was the earliest to emerge in the archeological record and is by far the most literate and archeologically the richest. It is the civilization of the Shang dynasty, the second historical dynasty—after the [Xia]—but the first that has been archeologically verified (Chang 1977).

Archeological evidence of Shang dynastic culture, generally accepted as ca. sixteenth century BCE, is critical in locating a unified source of Chinese civilization. If one also includes the "legendary" Xia rulers, this pushes the origins further back to 2070 BCE. Even so, the oft-repeated claim that "China has 5000 years of history" and "Five Thousand Years of Chinese Civilization" would seem to fall short by this measure. Based on the archaeological record, however, and assessing the trends and transferring of ideas, technologies, artistic expression found in the earliest of Chinese cultures, Kwang-chih Chang believed that

> [B]y 3000 BC, the Chinese interaction sphere can properly and appropriately be called China, as it became the stage where Chinese history began to play out, with its clearly defined actors, events, motivations, and story lines (Chang 1999).

Oracle Bones and the Shang

Making inscriptions on turtle shells, oxen, sheep scapula, oracle bones were used in ancient times to divine the course of future events. Writings were incised or painted on turtle plastron, then heated. Cracks (卜 *bǔ*) that appear would give an indication of whether or not a course of action would be auspicious. In one example, the following divination asked whether

> This season, the king should *not* follow Wang Cheng (望乘 *wàngchéng*) to attack the Xia Wei (下危 *xiàwéi*) for if he does, we will not perhaps receive assistance in this case. (Keightley 1978)

This was followed by an opposing divination question, proposing that

> This season, the king *should* follow Wang Cheng to attack the Xia Wei for if he does, we *will* receive assistance in this case (Keightley 1978).

It was in Henan Province that a chain of very serendipitous events led to the first discovery and understanding of these oracle bones. In the late nineteenth century, peasants in Anyang City discovered shards of bone and turtle shells that had strange inscriptions on them. Not having any recognizable meaning, the farmers sold them as medicinal "dragon bones" (龍骨 *lónggú*), as they have been used as a pharmaceutical ingredient since 600 BCE. The traditional telling of how these were discovered in the nineteenth century involved some rather fantastic happenstances:

In 1899 Wang Yirong (王懿榮 *wáng yìróng*), the chancellor of the directorate of education (國子監祭酒 *guózi jiānjìjiǔ*), was ill with malaria (or at least had a serious fever). At the time, Wang's houseguest friend and writer of some renown, Liu E (劉鶚 *liú e*), then went to a traditional apothecary to acquire medicine. As Liu watched the pharmacist get ready to pulverize a "dragon bone," he saw that there was some form of writing on it. Now, it just so happened that Liu E was acquainted with ancient Chinese bronze inscriptions, i.e., *jinwen* (金文 *jīnwén*), and he was able to compare these with the writing on the bone fragments (Lee 2008). As soon as Wang Yirong's fever subsided, the two scholars returned to the pharmacist to purchase all of his remaining dragon bones. Wang Yirong surmised that these oracle bones were a vital link to China's ancient past.

Tragically, a year later (1900), Wang Yirong and his wife would commit suicide due to events associated with the Boxer Rebellion. Fortunately, Liu E was able to acquire Wang Yirong's oracle bones in 1902, and published the rubbings of the inscriptions in the following year. Between 1912 and 1916, Liu E compiled three volumes that described the collection in great detail (Shaughnessy 1991). Once a closely held secret due to their intrinsic value, other scholars eventually found access to extensive caches of oracle bones in the village of Xiaotun, Yindu District (殷都區小屯村 *yīndū qū, xiǎotún cūn*). In the late 1930s, researchers found 300 complete tortoise shells, some dating back to ca. 1300 BCE. Since then, over 160,000 such specimens with ancient writing have been collected, the largest of such finds being located at the famous Yinxu Ruins of Yin (殷虛遺址 *yīnxū yízhǐ*) in the Xiaotun area. Put simply: "The Anyang excavations began as an investigation of the source of the oracle bones, but they ended up unearthing a civilization." (Bagley 1999). In this same archeological site, and matching the Shang dynasty chronological royalty were the tombs of the following:

- Wu Ding (武丁 *wǔ dīng*; ca. 1189 BCE
- Zu Geng (祖庚 *zǔ gēng*; 1188–1178 BCE)
- Zu Jia (祖甲 *zǔ jiǎ* 1177–1158 BCE)
- Lin Xin (廩辛 *lǐn xīn*; 1157–1149 BCE)
- Kang Ding (康丁 *kāng dīng*; 1148–1132 BCE)
- Wu Yi (武乙 *wǔ yǐ*; 1131–1171 BCE)
- Wen Ding (文武丁 *wén wǔdīng*; 1116–1106 BCE)
- Di Yi (帝乙 *dì yǐ*; 1105–1087 BCE)

The Shang Dynasty imperial court was centered in and around Xiaotun, its nobility also living in modern-day Xinxiang (新鄉市 *xīnxiāng shì*) and Xingtai cities (邢台市 *xíngtái shì*). More recently (December 2015), next to a sports stadium in downtown Zhengzhou were discovered ancient tombs, pottery kilns, bone tools and animal bones, and these were later identified as dating back to the Shang dynasty (*China News Net* 2015).

Fall of the Shang

King Wu of the Zhou (周武王 *zhōu wǔwáng*) from the west (Shaanxi) invaded the Shang in 1045 BCE, his troops arriving at Muye (牧野 *mùyě*), located south of Anyang in modern-day Qixian County, Zhaoge Subdistrict (淇縣朝歌街道

qíxiànzhāogē jiēdào). The battle led to the defeat of the Shang king, Di Xin (帝辛 *dìxīn*, also known Zhou Xin (紂辛 *zhòuxīn*). According to the Book of Odes (史經 *shǐjīng*), ca. eleventh to seventh century BCE:

The Yin-Shang legions, 殷商之旅, (*yīn shāng zhī lǚ*)
Their battle flags like a forest, 其會如林。(*qí kuài rú lín*)
Were arrayed on the field of Muye. 矢於牧野, (*shǐ yú mùyě*)
"Arise, my lords, 維予侯興。(*wéi yú hóu xìng*)
The Lord on High looks down on you; 上帝臨女, (*shàngdì lín nǚ*)
Have no second thoughts." 無貳爾心。(*wúèr ěr xīn*)
The field of Muye was so broad. 牧野洋洋, (*mù yě yáng yáng*)
The sandal wood chariots were so gleaming. 檀車煌煌, (*tán chē huánghuáng*)
The teams of four were so pounding. 駟騵彭彭。(*sìyuán péngpéng*)
There was the general Shangfu. 維師尚父, (*wéi shī shàngfù*)
He rose as an eagle, 時維鷹揚。(*shí wéi yīng yáng*)
Aiding that King Wu, 涼彼武王, (*liàng bǐ wǔ wáng*)
And attacked the great Shang, 肆伐大商, (*sìfá dàshāng*)
Meeting in the morning, clear and bright. 會朝清明。(*huìcháo qīngmíng*) (Shirokauer and Brown 2012)

In 771 BCE, having fallen under attack by combined barbarian Quan Rong (犬戎 *quǎnróng*) and rival Shen (伸 *shēn*) forces, the Zhou dynasty finally moved its capital to the modern-day region of Henan. But it was not only this conflict but domestic political turmoil, and the ill omen of a large earthquake, that precipitated this sudden departure. The new Zhou eastern capital was established at Chengzhou (成周 *chéngzhōu*) by the prevailing King Ping (周平王 *zhōu píngwáng*) in present day Luoyang (落陽 *luòyáng*). (Hsu 1999).

In the Spring and Autumn Period (722–481 BCE), the subsequent fiefdoms/states occupied the Henan region of today:

- Dai (戴國 *dàiguó*)
- Chen (陳國 *chénguó*)
- Cai (蔡國 *càiguó*)
- Cao (曹國 *cáoguó*)
- Zheng (鄭國 *zhèngguó*)
- Wei (衛國 *wèiguó*) and
- Song (宋國 *sòngguó*)

During this time the Chu state (楚國 *chǔguó*), having achieved hegemony over various states, had established its capital in Danyang (丹陽 *dānyáng*) in today's Xichuan County (淅川縣 *xīchuān xiàn*). Before the unification of China under the Qin, today's Henan Province had regions occupied by the major Warring States (481–221 BCE):

- Wei (魏國 *wèiguó*), capital at Daliang (大梁 *dàliáng*) modern-day Kaifeng
- Zhao (趙國 *zhàoguó*), and
- Han (韓國 *hánguó*; capital at Xinzheng 新鄭 *xīnzhèng*) (Lewis 1999)

These satraps were eliminated by the conquering Qin dynasty, which then adopted a 48-prefecture system with the following administrative areas (Table 13.1):

Table 13.1 Qin dynasty (221–206 BCE) prefectures and modern day Henan province. (Tan 1985)

Prefecture Entity	Prefectural County	Modern Day Henan Area
Sanchuan 三川 *sānchuān*	Luoyang 洛陽 *luòyáng*	East Luoyang City
Yingchuan 潁川 *yǐngchuān*	Yangzhai 陽翟 *yángzhái*	Yuxian county (Yuzhou city 禹州市 *yǔzhōu shì*)
Dongjun 東郡 *dōngjùn*	Puyang 濮陽 *púyáng*	South Puyang City (濮陽市)
Dangjun 碭郡 *dàngjùn*	Qiaoyang 瞧陽 *qiáoyáng*	South Shangqiu City 商丘市 *shāngqiū shì*
Nanyang 南陽 *nányáng*	Wanxian county 宛縣 wǎnxiàn	Nanyang City 南陽市
Chenjun 陳郡 *chénjùn*	Chenxian county 陳縣	Huaiyang county 淮陽縣 *huáiyáng xiàn*
Henei 河内 *hé'nèi*	Huaixian county 懷縣 *huáixiàn*	Southwest Wuzhi county 武陟縣 *wǔzhì xiàn*

Rebellious History

Henan has a reputation for being home to a number of famed peasant rebellions, such as those led by Chen Sheng (陳勝 *chén shèng*) and Wu Guang (吳廣 *wú guǎng*). In 209 BCE, they sparked an uprising in Chenxian County (陳縣 *chénxiàn*) in today's Huaiyang (淮陽 *huáiyáng*). (Hsieh and Hsieh 1995). Henan was also where another rebellion that resulted in the Yellow Turban chaos (黃巾之亂 *huángjīnzhīluàn*) also occurred. The Yellow Turbans suffered a major defeat at Wan (宛 *wǎn*), modern day Wancheng District (宛城區 *wǎnchéng qū*) in Nanyang City (南陽市 *nányáng shì*). The aftermath of the Yellow Turban rebellion, which often involved siege-style warfare, spurred a trend towards strengthening medieval fortresses and cities with hangtu (夯土 *hāngtǔ*) rammed earth and brick in order to protect urban areas. Such was the case of Chancellor Dong Zhuo (董卓 *dǒng zhuó*) who controlled the empire from Luoyang, and who had his own (unsuccessful) run-ins with the Yellow Turbans. Thinking ahead, in 192 CE (the year of his death, as it turned out) he ordered the construction a fortified storage facility called the "Ten Thousand Year Rampart" (萬歲塢 *wànsuìwù*) at Meiwu (郿塢 *méiwù*), located north-east of modern-day Meixian County (眉縣 *méixiàn*), Shaanxi Province. It was reported to have stored 30 years' worth of grain provisions (Elvin 1973).

Throughout the Han dynasty, the name Yuzhou (豫州 *yùzhōu*) was used to refer to the Hunan area. Following various changes to China's geopolitical landscape over the next 100 years, in 494 CE Emperor Xiao Wen (孝文帝 *xiàowén dì*) of the Northern Wei (北魏 *běi wèi*) saw fit to move his capital to modern-day Luoyang ("the place of the nine tripod cauldrons" 九鼎之所 *jiǔdǐng zhīsuǒ*). When the Tang (618–907) court established its capital at Xi'an (Chang'an), Luoyang was made the secondary "Eastern Capital" (東部 *dōngbù*). In 904, Zhu Wen (朱溫 *zhū wēn*; later

Zhu Huang 朱晃 *zhū huǎng*) seized the imperial court and forced them to move back to Luoyang, making it once again the capital.

Origins of the Name 'Saraga' (Saragh) for Luoyang City

History records the presence of a Nestorian Christian community in China during the Tang dynasty (ca. 657 CE). The original Sogdian Christians were from a region in modern-day Uzbekistan (Samarkand) and Tajikistan, and were referred to as the "nine family names of Zhaowu" (昭武九姓 *zhāowǔjiǔxìng*). A stone tablet found in May 2006 in Xi'an, dated 781 CE, describes the organization of the Nestorian Christian community that was populated by the Sogdians who had originally established their church in China. One inscription (written in Syriac) reads in part, "Gabri'el, priest and archdeacon, and head of the Church in Khumdan and Sarag …" (Nicolini-Zani 2013) The Sogdian name *Khumdan* refers China's western capital in Chang'an (modern day Xi'an), while Sarag equates to Luoyang. Thus, westerners in ancient times also knew of Luoyang by its Sanskrit transliteration as Saraga (Saragh).

Kaifeng's Jewish Diaspora

As befitting a major center of culture, Kaifeng was also home to a large Jewish community. Going back to the third century CE, Jewish peoples may have arrived in China due to persecution in Persia, settling along the Silk Road in the fourth century. Especially during Tang Dynasty, Jewish merchants were known to be multilingual, and used bilingual coinage. (Their presence was first widely known to Europeans after being discovered by the Jesuit Matteo Ricci in 1605). In the seventeenth century, Kaifeng was home to about 5000 Jews. After the founding of the People's Republic China (PRC), in 1954 the capital of Henan was moved from Kaifeng to Zhengzhou.

Development of Kaifeng as a Metropolis

The completion of the Grand Canal connecting Kaifeng (560 CE) really put this bustling city on the commercial map. Near the end of Northern Song (ca. 1100 CE), today's Kaifeng, then called Bianliang (汴梁 *biànliáng*), had a population of over 1 million, and was one of the world's most cosmopolitan. Its social and cultural milieu is famously depicted in Zhang Zeduan's (張擇端 *zhāng zéduān* 1085–1145) painting, 'Qingming Festival on the River' (清明上河 *qīngmíng shànghé*). The painting, measuring about 15 feet in width, shows some 500 individuals, detailing the activities of contemporary itinerant merchants, mendicants, and urban administration (Lim 2012).

By 1111, the Northern Song's capital was established in Dongjing City (東京城 *dōngjīng chéng*), and modern-day Henan Province was then administered under the Jingxi Southern Circuit (京西南路 *jīngxī nánlù*), Jingxi Northern Circuit (京西北路 *jīngxī běilù*), and the Kaifeng Governing Circuit (開封府路 *kāifēngfŭ lù*. The grand city of Bianliang (also called Bianjing 汴京) was sacked by northern Jin (金 *jīn*) military forces in 1127, an event since referred to as the Jingkang Incident (靖康事變 *jìngkāng shìbiàn*). After repeated incursions by the Mongols, the Jin (金 *jīn*) dynasty moved the capital from Yanjing (燕京 *yànjīng*, modern-day Beijing) to Kaifeng in 1214, calling it Nanjing (南京 *nánjīng*) or southern capital. Later, Kaifeng became the administrative seat of the 'Henan Jiangbei Secretariat Province' (河南將北等處行中書省 *hénánjiāngběi děngchŭ xíngzhōng shūshěng*). During the Yuan dynasty, a Henan North River Province was created in 1291, which also included Hubei, Anhui, and Jiangsu provinces. Organized into eight Prefectures (府 *fŭ*), Henan's modern-day provincial borders are basically the same as they were in 1368. At the end of the Ming dynasty, over 30 years of war had taken its toll on Henan, but it recovered economically during the Qing under the Kangxi (康熙 *kāngxī*) emperor (ca. 1700). By then it had a much larger population and a well-developed agricultural sector.

Sino-Japanese War and Great Tragedy in Hunan

During Japan's invasion of China, Chiang Kai-shek (蔣介石 *jiăng jièshí*) and his military were nearly always on the defensive. It was not long before Japanese troops had embarked on commandeered trains, and were now making fast progress to Zhengzhou. Alexander von Falkenhausen, a German military advisor to the Nationalists, had earlier recommended that China destroy the Huanghe (Yellow River) dikes to flood the area in order to slow the Japanese army's advance. Later, the same idea was proposed by one of Chiang's own compatriots. In early June 1938, the Nationalist army used explosives to destroy the dikes, flooding not only Henan but Jiangsu and Anhui provinces, causing the death of some 800,000 Chinese civilians (Taylor 2011).

Henan Province and the Great Leap Forward (1958–61)

Henan Province played a prominent and commensurately tragic role in the disastrous Great Leap Forward (GLF). In one of the most detailed and authoritative accounts of the GLP, Yang Jisheng refers to Henan as being the "epicenter of the disaster," largely because its provincial authorities were the standard bearers of

Mao Zedong's maniacal economic and agricultural "development" policies. From 1959 to 1960, for example, of Xinyang's 8.5 million residents, at least 1 million people died of starvation, epitomizing the tragedy not only in terms famine, but also the horrific physical violence perpetrated by the party faithful on Mao Zedong's behalf (Yang 2012).

Henan's Population and Economy

As of the end of 2016, Henan had a permanent registered population (戶籍人口 *hùjí rénkǒu*) of 107,881,400, and a resident (常住人口 *chángzhù rénkǒu*) population of 95,324,200 (net difference of 12,557,200). This deficit reflects the large number of Hunan people spending significant amount of time living and working in other provinces. By 2020, with a resident population (census) of 99,365,519, and hukou population of 114,440,000, the difference grew to just over 15 million (see census data, Table 13.2 and 13.3).

Table 13.2 Henan province residential population (常住人口 *chángzhù rénkǒu*) data. (HPBS 2021)

City	Population (2010)	Population (2020)
Zhengzhou City 鄭州市 *zhèngzhōu shì*	8,626,505	12,600,574
Anyang City 安陽市 *ānyáng shì* [abbrev. 殷 *yīn*; 鄴 *yè*]	5,172,834	5,477,614
Hebi City 鶴壁市 *hèbì shì*	1,569,100	1,565,973
Jiaozuo City 焦作市 *jiāozuò shì*	3,539,860	3,521,078
Kaifeng City 開封市 *kāifēng shì* [abbrev. 汴 *biàn*]	4,676,159	4,824,016
Luohe City 漯河市 *luòhé shì*	2,544,103	2,367,490
Luoyang City 洛陽市 *luòyáng shì* [abbrev. 洛 *luò*]	6,549,486	7,056,699
Nanyang City 南陽市 *nányáng shì* [abbrev. 宛 *wǎn*]	10,263,006	9,713,112
Pingdingshan City 平頂山市 *píngdǐngshān shì*	4,904,367	4,987,137
Puyang City 濮陽市 *púyáng shì* [abbrev. 濮 *pú*]	3,598,494	3,772,088
Sanmenxia City 三門峽市 *sānménxiá shì*	2,233,872	2,034,872
Shangqiu City 商丘市 *shāngqiū shì*	7,362,472	7,816,831
Xinxiang City 新鄉市 *xīnxiāng shì*	5,707,801	6,251,929
Xinyang City 信陽市 *xìnyáng shì*	6,108,683	6,234,401
Xuchang City 許昌市 *xǔchāng shì*	4,307,199	4,379,998
Zhoukou City 周口市 *zhōukǒu shì*	8,953,172	9,026,015
Zhumadian City 駐馬店市 zhùmǎdiàn shì	7,230,744	7,008,427
Jiyuan City 濟源市 *jìyuán shì*	675,710	727,265[a]
Total	**94,023,567**	**99,365,519**

[a]Officially Jiyuan industrial city integrated demonstration zone as of 2020

Table 13.3 Henan province: population data of cities and their subordinate sectors. (HPBS 2021)

Selected cities and subordinate sectors, population (2020 census)[a]	Subordinate district, city and county populations (2020)	Total population (2020)
Zhengzhou City 鄭州市 ***zhèngzhōu shì***		**12,600,574**
Zhongyuan District 中原區 *zhōngyuán qū*	962,642	
Erqi District 二七區 *èrqī qū*	1,061,263	
Guancheng Huizu (Hui) District 管城回族區 *guǎnchéng huízúqū*	819,439	
Jinshui District 金水區 *jīnshuǐ qū*	1,617,541	
Shangjie District 上街區 *shàngjiē qū*	197,399	
Huiji District 惠濟區 *huìjì qū*	555,002	
Xinzheng City 新鄭市 *xīnzhèng shì*	1,172,237	
Dengfeng City 登封市 *dēngfēng shì*	729,332	
Xinmi City 新密市 *xīnmì shì*	826,031	
Gongyi City 鞏義市 *gǒngyì shì*	785,242	
Xingyang City 滎陽市 *xíngyáng shì*	730,135	
Zhongmu County 中牟縣 *zhōngmù xiàn*	702,657	
Zhengzhou Economic and Technology Development Zone 鄭州經濟技術開發區 *zhèngzhōu jīngjìjìshù kāifāqū*	328,812	
Zhengzhou High Technology Industry Development Zone 鄭州高新技術產業開發區 *zhèngzhōu gāoxīnjìshù chǎnyè kāifāqū*	546,226	
Zhengzhou Airport Economy Zone 鄭州航空港經濟綜合實驗區 *zhèngzhōu hángkōnggǎng jīngjì zōnghéshíyànqū*	621,382	
Nanyang City Public Industrial Zone 南陽市官莊工區 *nányángshì guānzhuānggōngqū*	133,342	
Zhengzhou Airport Economy Zone 鄭州航空港經濟綜合實驗區 *zhèngzhōu hángkōnggǎng jīngjì zōnghéshíyànqū*	621,382	
Nanyang City Public Industrial Zone 南陽市官莊工區 *nányángshì guānzhuānggōngqū*	133,342	
Hebi City 鶴壁市 ***hèbì shì***		**1,565,973**
Qibin District 淇濱區 *qíbīn qū*	460,780	
Shancheng District 山城區 *shānchéng qū*	155,449	
Heshan District 鶴山區 *hèshān qū*	62,713	
Xunxian County 濬縣 *jùnxiàn*	624,728	
Qixian County 淇縣 *qíxiàn*	262,303	
Jiaozuo City 焦作市 ***jiāozuò shì***		**3,521,078**
Jiefang District 解放區 *jiěfàng qū*	347,382	
Shanyang District 山陽區 *shānyáng qū*	303,222	
Zhongzhan District 中站區 *zhōngzhàn qū*	107,281	
Macun District 馬村區 *mǎcūn qū*	120,560	
Mengzhou City 孟州市 *mèngzhōu shì*	334,213	

(continued)

Table 13.3 (continued)

Selected cities and subordinate sectors, population (2020 census)[a]	Subordinate district, city and county populations (2020)	Total population (2020)
Qinyang City 沁陽市 *qìnyáng shì*	447,487	
Xiuwu County 修武縣 *xiūwǔ xiàn*	248,585	
Bo'ai County 博愛縣 *bó'ài xiàn*	350,140	
Wuzhi County 武陟縣 *wǔzhì xiàn*	661,341	
Wenxian County 溫縣 *wēnxiàn*	393,838	
Urban-Rural Integration Demonstration Zone 城鄉一體化示範區 *chéngxiāng yītǐhuà shìfànqū*	207,029	
Kaifeng City 開封市 ***kāifēng shì* [abbrev.** 汴 ***biàn*]**		**4,824,016**
Gulou District 鼓樓區 *gǔlóu qū*	136,167	
Longting District 龍亭區 *lóngtíng qū*	156,245	
Shunhe Hui District 順河回族區 *shùnhé huízúqū*	227,864	
Yuwangtai District 禹王台區 *yǔwángtái qū*	124,859	
Xiangfu District[b] 祥符區 *xiángfú qū*	672,139	
Qixian County 杞縣 *qǐxiàn*	932,126	
Tongxu County 通許縣 *tōngxǔ xiàn*	539,222	
Weishi County 尉氏縣 *wèishì xiàn*	839,809	
Urban-Rural Integration Demonstration Zone 城鄉一體化示範區 *chéngxiāng yītǐhuà shìfànqū*	418,307	
Lankao County 蘭考縣 *lánkǎo xiàn*	777,278	
Luohe City 漯河市 ***luòhé shì***		**2,367,490**
Yancheng District 郾城區 *yǎnchéng qū*	505,302	
Yuanhui District 源匯區 *yuánhuì qū*	322,334	
Zhaoling District 召陵區 *zhàolíng qū*	499,051	
Wuyang County 舞陽縣 *wǔyáng xiàn*	447,130	
Linying County 林潁縣 *línyǐng xiàn*	593,673	
Luoyang City 洛陽市 ***luòyáng shì* [abbrev.** 洛 ***luò*]**		**7,056,699**
Xigong District 西工區 *xīgōng qū*	369,165	
Laocheng District 老城區 *lǎochéng qū*	252,165	
Chanhe Huizu (Hui) District 瀍河回族區 *chánhé huízú qū*	222,833	
Jianxi District 澗西區 *jiànxī qū*	509,962	
Jili District 吉利區 *jílì qū*	69,142	
Luolong District 洛龍區 *luòlóng qū*	643,625	
Yanshi City 偃師市 *yǎnshī shì*	545,632	
Mengjin County 孟津縣 *mèngjīn xiàn*	416,845	
Xin'an county 新安縣 *xīn'ān xiàn*	483,375	
Luanchuan County 欒川縣 *luánchuān xiàn*	327,121	
Songxian County 嵩縣 *sōngxiàn*	543,417	
Ruyang County 汝陽縣 *rǔyáng xiàn*	434,770	
Yiyang County 宜陽縣 *yíyáng xiàn*	576,104	
Luoning County 洛寧縣 *luòníng xiàn*	386,124	

(continued)

Table 13.3 (continued)

Selected cities and subordinate sectors, population (2020 census)[a]	Subordinate district, city and county populations (2020)	Total population (2020)
Yichuan County 伊川縣 *yīchuān xiàn*	792,841	
Nanyang City 南陽市 ***nányáng shì* [abbrev.** 宛 ***wǎn*]**		**9,713,112**
Wolong District 臥龍區 *wòlóng qū*	866,748	
Wancheng District 宛城區 *wǎnchéng qū*	873,731	
Dengzhou City 鄧州市 *dèngzhōu shì*	1,247,807	
Nanzhao County[c] 南召縣 *nánzhào xiàn*	545,475	
Fangcheng County 方城縣 *fāngchéng xiàn*	873,731	
Xixia County 西峽縣 *xīxiá xiàn*	450,418	
Zhenping County 鎮平縣 *zhènpíng xiàn*	829,780	
Neixiang County 內鄉縣 *nèixiāng xiàn*	549,068	
Xichuan County 淅川縣 *xīchuān xiàn*	538,569	
Sheqi County 社旗縣 *shèqí xiàn*	561,573	
Tanghe County 唐河縣 *tánghé xiàn*	1,052,978	
Xinye County 新野縣 *xīnyě xiàn*	602,827	
Tong(bo)bai County 桐柏縣 *tóngbǎi xiàn*	375,206	
Urban-Rural Integration Demonstration Zone 城鄉一體化示範區 *chéngxiāng yītǐhuà shìfànqū*	225,116	
Nanyang High Technology Development Zone 南陽高新技術開發區 *nányáng gāoxīnjìshù kāifāqū*	226,911	
Pingdingshan City 平頂山市 ***píngdǐngshān shì***		**4,987,137**
Xinhua District 新華區 *xīnhuá qū*	336,957	
Weidong District 衛東區 *wèidōng qū*	315,705	
Zhanhe District 湛河區 *zhànhé qū*	345,928	
Shilong District 石龍區 *shílóng qū*	43,429	
Wugang City 舞鋼市 *wǔgāng shì*	294,839	
Ruzhou City 汝州市 *rǔzhōu shì*	974,541	
Baofeng County 寶豐縣 *bǎofēng xiàn*	498,157	
Yexian County 葉縣 *yèxiàn*	702,345	
Lushan County 魯山縣 *lǔshān xiàn*	787,109	
Jiaxian County 郟縣 *jiáxiàn*	506,377	
Puyang City 濮陽市 ***púyáng shì* [abbrev. 濮 *pú*]**		**3,772,088**
Hualong District 華龍區 *huálóng qū*	607,028	
Qingfeng County 清豐縣 *qīngfēng xiàn*	592,425	
Nanle County 南樂縣 *nánlè xiàn*	476,557	
Fanxian County 范縣 *fànxiàn*	447,760	
Taiqian County 台前縣 *táiqián xiàn*	323,113	
Puyang County 濮陽縣 *púyáng xiàn*	968,721	
Puyang Economic and Technology Development Zone 濮陽經濟技術開發區 *púyáng jīngjìjìshù kāifāqū*	260,477	
Puyang Industrial Park 濮陽工業園 *púyáng gōngyèyuán*	27,299	

(continued)

Table 13.3 (continued)

Selected cities and subordinate sectors, population (2020 census)[a]	Subordinate district, city and county populations (2020)	Total population (2020)
Urban-Rural Integration Demonstration Zone 城鄉一體化示範區 *chéngxiāng yītǐhuà shìfànqū*	68,708	
Sanmenxia City 三門峽市 ***sānménxiá shì***		**2,034,872**
Hubin District 湖濱區 *húbīn qū*	326,682	
Yima City 義馬市 *yìmǎ shì*	135,819	
Lingbao City 靈寶市 *língbǎo shì*	656,571	
Mianchi County 澠池縣 *miǎnchí xiàn*	310,130	
Shanzhou District 陝州區 *shǎnzhōu qū*	288,538	
Lushi County 盧氏縣 *lúshì xiàn*	317,132	
Shangqiu City 商丘市 ***shāngqiū shì***		**7,816,831**
Liangyuan District 梁園區 *liángyuán qū*	631,325	
Suiyang District 睢陽區 *suīyáng qū*	912,971	
Yongcheng City 永城市 *yǒngchéng shì*	1,256,409	
Yucheng County 虞城縣 *yúchéng xiàn*	972,091	
Minquan County 民權縣 *mínquán xiàn*	746,389	
Ningling County 寧陵縣 *nínglíng xiàn*	562,657	
Suixian County 睢縣 *suīxiàn*	723,771	
Xiayi County 夏邑縣 *xiàyì xiàn*	896,578	
Zhecheng County 柘城縣 *zhèchéng xiàn*	799,213	
Yongcheng City 永城市 *yǒngchéng shì*	1,256,409	
Yudong Integrated Logistics Industrial Collective District 豫東綜合物流產業聚集區 *yùdōng zōnghé wùliúchǎnyè jùjíqū*	139,093	
Shangqiu Economic and Technology Development Zone 商丘經濟技術開發區 *shāngqiū jīngjìjìshù kāifāqū*	176,334	
Xuchang City 許昌市 ***xǔchāng shì***		**4,379,998**
Weidu District 魏都區 *wèidū qū*	400,974	
Jian'an District 建安區 *jiàn'ān qū*	578,598	
Yuzhou City 禹州市 *yǔzhōu shì*	1,109,782	
Changge City 長葛市 *chánggé shì*	710,033	
Dongcheng District 東城區 *dōngchéng qū*	226,085	
Xuchang Economic and Technology Development Zone 許昌商丘經濟開發區 *xǔchāng shāngqiū jīngjìkāifāqū*	69,498	
Yanling County 鄢陵縣 *yānlíng xiàn*	547,411	
Xiangcheng County 襄城縣 *xiāngchéng xiàn*	674,832	
Urban-Rural Integration Demonstration Zone 城鄉一體化示範區 *chéngxiāng yītǐhuà shìfànqū*	62,785	
Zhoukou City 周口市 ***zhōukǒu shì***		**9,026,015**
Chuanhui District[d] 川匯區 *chuānhuì qū*	698,341	

(continued)

Table 13.3 (continued)

Selected cities and subordinate sectors, population (2020 census)[a]	Subordinate district, city and county populations (2020)	Total population (2020)
Xiangcheng City 項城市 *xiàngchéng shì*	973,197	
Fugou County 扶溝縣 *fúgōu xiàn*	553,830	
Xihua County 西華縣 *xīhuá xiàn*	692,846	
Shangshui County 商水縣 *shāngshuǐ xiàn*	960,453	
Taikang County 太康縣 *tàikāng xiàn*	1,152,685	
Dancheng County 鄲城縣 *dānchéng xiàn*	1,057,093	
Huaiyang County 淮陽縣 *huáiyáng xiàn*	1,022,322	
Shenqiu County 沈丘縣 *shěnqiū xiàn*	956,631	
Luyi County 鹿邑縣 *lùyì xiàn*	958,617	
Zhumadian City 駐馬店市 *zhùmădiàn shì*		**7,008,427**
Yicheng District 驛城區 *yìchéng qū*	756,859	
Queshan County 確山縣 *quèshān xiàn*	430,044	
Biyang County 泌陽縣 *bìyáng xiàn*	695,239	
Suiping County 遂平縣 *suìpíng xiàn*	441,370	
Xiping County 西平縣 *xīpíng xiàn*	647,311	
Shangcai County 上蔡縣 *shàngcài xiàn*	1,005,745	
Ru'nan County 汝南縣 *rŭnán xiàn*	612,551	
Pingyu County 平輿縣 *píngyú xiàn*	728,672	
Xincai County 新蔡縣 *xīncài xiàn*	823,829	
Zhengyang County 正陽縣 *zhèngyáng xiàn*	625,123	
Xincai County 新蔡縣 *xīncài xiàn*	823,829	
Zhumadian Economic and Technology Development Zone Economic and Technology Development Zone 駐馬店經濟技術開發區 *zhùmădiàn jīngjìjìshù kāifāqū*	268,864	
Jiyuan City 濟源市 *jìyuán shì*		**727,265**

[a]Not all cities have published subdistrict data as of January 2022
[b]Established out of Kaifeng county on 19 October 2014
[c]Nanzhao county includes data from the Yahe Industrial area
[d]Includes data from the Chuanhui economic technology development zone, urban-rural integration demonstration district, and harbor logistics industrial collective zone

Economically, and especially since 2015, Henan has generally shown a strong a steady showing in terms of gross domestic product (GDP) of in 2020 (USD $855 billion), ranking fifth behind Zhejiang province. In terms of per capita income ($3,860), Henan does not fare well, ranking 24th out of 31 mainland China's provinces and major cities (Zhang 2021).

1. **Linzhou City**
2. **(Subordinat to Anyang County)**
3. **Heshan District**
4. **Shancheng District**
5. **Anyang County**
6. **Tangyang County**
7. **Neihuang County**
8. **Nanle County**
9. **Qingfeng County**
10. **Fanxian County**
11. **Taiqian County**
12. **Huixian City**
13. **Weihui City**
14. **Qixian County**
15. **Qibin District**
16. **Xunxian County**
17. **Huaxian County**
18. **Hualong District**
19. **Puyang County**
20. **Lingbao City**
21. **Hubin District**
22. **Shanxian County**
23. **Mianchi County**
24. **Yima City**
25. **Xin'an County**
26. **Jiyuan City**
27. **Jili District**
28. **Qinyang City**
29. **Boai County**
30. **Jiaozuo City**
31. **Xiuwu County**
32. **Huojia County**
33. **Xinxiang County**
34. **Xinxiang City**
35. **Yanjin County**
36. **Changyuan City**
37. **Lushi County**
38. **Luoning County**
39. **Yiyang County**
40. **Mengjin County**
41. **Luoyang City**
42. **Yanshi City**
43. **Gongyi City**
44. **Mengzhou City**
45. **Shangjie District**
46. **Wenxian County**
47. **Wuzhi County**
48. **Yingyang City**
49. **Zhengzhou City**
50. **Yuanyang County**
51. **Fengqiu County**

Fig. 13.2 Henan province: subdistricts (Capital City: Zhengzhou City). (Drawn by the Author after People's Republic of China, Ministry of Civil Affairs (MCA 2020))

52. Xixia County
53. Luanchuan County
54. Songxian County
55. Yichuan County
56. Ruyang County
57. Dengfeng City
58. Xinmi City
59. Xinzheng City
60. Zhongmu County
61. Kaifeng City
62. Xiangfu District
63. Lankao County
64. Neixiang County
65. Nanzhao County
66. Lushan County
67. Shilong District
68. Ruzhou City
69. Baofeng County
70. Jiaxian County
71. Yuzhou City
72. Changge City
73. Weishi County
74. Tongxu County
75. Qixian County
76. Minquan County
77. Suixian County
78. Ningling County
79. Liangyuan District
80. Yucheng County
81. Pingdingshan City
82. Xiangcheng County
83. Weidu District
84. Xuchang County
85. Yanling County
86. Fugou County
87. Taikang County
88. Zhecheng County
89. Suiyang District
90. Xiayi County
91. Yongcheng City
92. Zhechuan County
93. Zhenping County
94. Wolong District
95. Fangcheng County
96. Yexian County
97. Wuyang County
98. Luohe City
99. Linying County
100. Xihua County
101. Huaiyang District
102. Luyi County
103. Wugang City
104. Xiping County
105. Suiping County
106. Shangcai County
107. Shangshui County
108. Chuanhui District
109. Dancheng County
110. Xiangcheng City
111. Shenqiu County
112. Dengzhou City
113. Xinye County
114. Wancheng District
115. Duqi County
116. Biyang County
117. Yicheng District
118. Runan County
119. Pingyu County
120. Zhengyang County
121. Xincai County
122. Tanghe County
123. Tongbai County
124. Queshan County
125. Pingqiao District
126. Xixian County
127. Huaibin County
128. Shihe District
129. Luoshan County
130. Guangshan County
131. Hengchuan County
132. Gushi County
133. Shangcheng County
134. Xinxian County

Fig. 13.2 (continued)

Table 13.4 shows the *hukou* (family registered) populations based on PRC Ministry of Civil Affairs data. (Districts listed directly under major cities are government seats, as are those in parentheses). One can compare these data with the census (usual residential populations based on 2010 and 2020 censuses in Tables 13.2 and 13.3.

Henan Province (豫 *yù*)

Provincial Capital: Zhengzhou

Table 13.4 Henan province: permanent registered (戶籍人口 *hùjí rénkǒu*) populations. (MCA 2020)

Name	Traditional	Simplified	Population (2012)	Population (2016)	Population (2020)	Area (Sq. Km)
Henan Province	河南省	河南省	108,000,000	109,320,000	114,440,000	166,785
Zhengzhou City	鄭州市	郑州市	7,440,000	7,680,000	8,640,000	7507
Zhongyuan District (Jianshelu Subdistrict)	中原區 (建設路街道)	中原区 (建设路街道)	680,000	710,000	850,000	195
Erqi District (Huaihelu Subdistrict)	二七區 (淮河路街道)	二七区 (淮河路街道)	540,000	560,000	640,000	159
Guancheng Huizu (Hui) District (Beixiajie Subdistrict)	管城回族區 (北下街街道)	管城回族区 (北下街街道)	420,000	450,000	550,000	204
Jinshui District (Dongfenglu Subdistrict)	金水區 (東風路街道)	金水区 (东风路街道)	990,000	1,060,000	1,330,000	242
Shangjie District (Jiyuanlu Subdistrict)	上街區 (濟源路街道)	上街区 (济源路街道)	120,000	120,000	120,000	18
Huiji District (Xincheng Subdistrict)	惠濟區 (新城街道)	惠济区 (新城街道)	190,000	210,000	260,000	206
Xinzheng City (Xinhualu Subdistrict)	新鄭市 (新華路街道)	新郑市 (新华路街道)	700,000	720,000	830,000	873
Dengfeng City (Songyang Subdistrict)	登封市 (嵩陽街道)	登封市 (嵩阳街道)	690,000	700,000	730,000	1220
Xinmi City (Qingpingjie Subdistrict)	新密市 (青屏街街道)	新密市 (青屏街街道)	870,000	870,000	900,000	1001
Gongyi City (Zijinglu Subdistrict)	鞏義市 (紫荊路街道)	巩义市 (紫荆路街道)	820,000	820,000	850,000	1041
Xingyang City (Suohe Subdistrict)	滎陽市 (索河街道)	荥阳市 (索河街道)	650,000	660,000	710,000	955
Zhongmu County (Guanghuijie Subdistrict)	中牟縣 (廣惠街街道)	中牟县 (广惠街街道)	770,000	800,000	890,000	1393

(continued)

Table 13.4 (continued)

Name	Traditional	Simplified	Population (2012)	Population (2016)	Population (2020)	Area (Sq. Km)
Sanmenxia City	三門峽市	三门峡市	2,290,000	2,300,000	2,270,000	10,475
Hubin District (Hubin Subdistrict)	湖濱區 (湖濱街道)	湖滨区 (湖滨街道)	290,000	290,000	290,000	164
Yima City (Qianqiu Subdistrict)	義馬市 (千秋路街道)	义马市 (千秋路街道)	170,000	170,000	160,000	112
Lingbao City (Chengguan Town)	靈寶市 (城關鎮)	灵宝市 (城关镇)	750,000	740,000	750,000	3011
Mianchi County (Chengguan Town)	澠池縣 (城關鎮)	渑池县 (城关镇)	360,000	370,000	360,000	1421
Shanxian County[a] (Daying Town)	陝縣 (大營鎮)	陕县 (大营镇)	340,000	N/A	N/A	(1763)
Shanzhou District (Daying Town)	陝州區 (大營鎮)	陕州区 (大营区)	N/A	350,000	340,000	1763
Lushi County (Chengguan Town)	盧氏縣 (城關鎮)	卢氏县 (城关镇)	380,000	380,000	380,000	4004
Luoyang City	洛陽市	洛阳市	7,050,000	7,100,000	7,400,000	15,492
Xigong District (Wangchenglu Subdistrict)	西工區 (王城路街道)	西工区 (王城路街道)	360,000	340,000	320,000	56
Laocheng District (Xiguan Subdistrict)	老城區 (西關街道)	老城区 (西关街道)	150,000	170,000	170,000	57
Chanhe Huizu (Hui) District (Dongguan Subdistrict)	瀍河回族區 (東關街道)	瀍河回族区 (东关街道)	180,000	180,000	170,000	29
Jianxi District (Hubeilu Subdistrict)	澗西區 (湖北路街道)	涧西区 (湖北路街道)	530,000	540,000	610,000	89
Jili District (Daqinglu Subdistrict)	吉利區 (大慶路街道)	吉利区 (大庆路街道)	70,000	70,000	70,000	80
Luolong District (Kaiyuanlu Subdistrict)	洛龍區 (開元路街道)	洛龙区 (开元路街道)	380,000	660,000	730,000	303
Yanshi City (Shangcheng Subdistrict)	偃師市 (商城街道)	偃师市 (商城街道)	870,000	620,000	630,000	888

(continued)

Table 13.4 (continued)

Name	Traditional	Simplified	Population (2012)	Population (2016)	Population (2020)	Area (Sq. Km)
Mengjin County (Chengguan Town)	孟津縣 (城關鎮)	孟津县 (城关镇)	470,000	470,000	480,000	759
Xin'an County (Chengguan Town)	新安縣 (城關鎮)	新安县 (城关镇)	540,000	530,000	540,000	1160
Luanchuan County (Chengguan Town)	欒川縣 (城關鎮)	栾川县 (城关镇)	340,000	340,000	360,000	2478
Songxian County (Chengguan Town)	嵩縣 (城關鎮)	嵩县 (城关镇)	590,000	610,000	640,000	3009
Ruyang County (Chengguan Town)	汝陽縣 (城關鎮)	汝阳县 (城关镇)	480,000	500,000	530,000	1325
Yiyang County (Chengguan Town)	宜陽縣 (城關鎮)	宜阳县 (城关镇)	710,000	690,000	720,000	1666
Luoning County (Chengguan Town)	洛寧縣 (城關鎮)	洛宁县 (城关镇)	520,000	500,000	510,000	2350
Yichuan County (Chengguan Town)	伊川縣 (城關鎮)	伊川县 (城关镇)	860,000	880,000	930,000	1243
Jiaozuo City	焦作市	焦作市	3,690,000	3,680,000	3,730,000	4072
Jiefang District (Minsheng Subdistrict)	解放區 (民生街道)	解放区 (民生街道)	290,000	300,000	300,000	62
Shanyang District (Xincheng Subdistrict)	山陽區 (新城街道)	山阳区 (新城街道)	280,000	400,000	430,000	67
Zhongzhan District (Lifeng Subdistrict)	中站區 (李封街道)	中站区 (李封街道)	120,000	120,000	110,000	124
Macun District (Macun Subdistrict)	馬村區 (馬村街道)	马村区 (马村街道)	150,000	150,000	140,000	118
Mengzhou City (Huichang Subdistrict)	孟州市 (會昌街道)	孟州市 (会昌街道)	380,000	380,000	380,000	542
Qinyang City (Tanhuai Subdistrict)	沁陽市 (覃懷街道)	沁阳市 (覃怀街道)	500,000	490,000	490,000	623

(continued)

Table 13.4 (continued)

Name	Traditional	Simplified	Population (2012)	Population (2016)	Population (2020)	Area (Sq. Km)
Xiuwu County (Chengguan Town)	修武縣 (城關鎮)	修武县 (城关镇)	310,000	280,000	270,000	722
Boai County (Qinghua Town)	博愛縣 (清化鎮)	博爱县 (清化镇)	450,000	380,000	400,000	492
Wuzhi County (Mucheng Subdistrict)	武陟縣 (木城街道)	武陟县 (木城街道)	740,000	710,000	730,000	860
Wenxian County (Wenquan Town)	溫縣 (溫泉鎮)	温县 (温泉镇)	470,000	470,000	460,000	462
Xinxiang City	新鄉市	新乡市	6,030,000	6,160,000	6,560,000	8629
Weibin District (Jiankanglu Subdistrict)	衛濱區 (健康路街道)	卫滨区 (健康路街道)	240,000	240,000	230,000	52
Hongqi District (Xijie Subdistrict)	紅旗區 (西街街道)	红旗区 (西街街道)	330,000	340,000	390,000	99
Fengquan District (Baoxilu Subdistrict)	鳳泉區 (寶山西路街道)	凤泉区 (宝山西路街道)	140,000	140,000	150,000	115
Muye District (Rongxiaolu Subdistrict)	牧野區 (榮校路街道)	牧野区 (荣校路街道)	310,000	310,000	330,000	80
Weihui City (Chengxiao Township)	衛輝市 (城郊鄉)	卫辉市 (城郊乡)	510,000	520,000	540,000	882
Huixian City (Chengguan Subdistrict)	輝縣市 (城關街道)	辉县市 (城关街道)	830,000	840,000	910,000	2007
Xinxiang County (Xiaoji Town)	新鄉縣 (小冀鎮)	新乡县 (小冀镇)	340,000	350,000	370,000	365
Huojia County (Chengguan Town)	獲嘉縣 (城關鎮)	获嘉县 (城关镇)	420,000	430,000	450,000	473
Yuanyang County (Yanghe Subdistrict)	原陽縣 (陽和街道)	原阳县 (阳和街道)	730,000	760,000	810,000	1339
Yanjin County (Chengguan Town)	延津縣 (城關鎮)	延津县 (城关镇)	490,000	500,000	510,000	946
Fengqiu County (Chengguan Town)	封丘縣 (城關鎮)	封丘县 (城关镇)	780,000	800,000	870,000	1220

(continued)

Table 13.4 (continued)

Name	Traditional	Simplified	Population (2012)	Population (2016)	Population (2020)	Area (Sq. Km)
Changyuan County (Puxi Subdistrict)	長桓縣 (蒲西街道)	长垣县 (蒲西街道)	910,000	930,000	N/A	(1051)
Changyuan City[b] (Puxi Subdistrict)	長桓市 (蒲西街道)	长垣市 (蒲西街道)	910,000	930,000	780,000	1051
Hebi City	鶴壁市	鹤壁市	1,610,000	1,630,000	1,710,000	2299
Qibin District (Dalaidian Subdistrict)	淇濱區 (大賚街道)	淇滨区 (大赉店镇)	260,000	290,000	390,000	295
Shancheng District (Hongqi Subdistrict)	山城區 (紅旗街道)	山城区 (红旗街道)	230,000	210,000	180,000	176
Heshan District (Zhongshanbeilu Subdistrict)	鶴山區 (中山北路街道)	鹤山区 (中山北路街道)	120,000	110,000	90,000	159
Xunxian County (Weixi Subdistrict)	濬縣 (衛溪街道)	浚县 (卫溪街道)	720,000	730,000	750,000	1088
Qixian County (Zhaoge Subdistrict)	淇縣 (朝歌街道)	淇县 (朝歌街道)	280,000	290,000	300,000	581
Anyang City	安陽市	安阳市	5,820,000	5,940,000	6,270,000	7355
Beiguan District (Hongqilu Subdistrict)	北關區 (紅旗路街道)	北关区 (红旗路街道)	250,000	250,000	250,000	59
Wenfeng District (Dongdajie Subdistrict)	文峰區 (東大街街道)	文峰区 (东大街街道)	390,000	410,000	480,000	179
Yindu District (Meiyuanzhuang Subdistrict)	殷都區 (梅園莊街道)	殷都区 (梅园庄街道)	250,000	240,000	230,000	70
Long'an District (Minhanglu Subdistrict)	龍安區 (民航路街道)	龙安区 (民航路街道)	200,000	210,000	220,000	236
Linzhou City (Kaiyuan Subdistrict)	林州市 (開元街道)	林州市 (开元街道)	1,060,000	1,080,000	1,140,000	2046
Anyang County (Anyang City Beiguan District Dengtalu Subdistrict)	安陽縣 (安陽市北關區燈塔路街道)	安阳县 (安阳市北关区灯塔路街道)	1,010,000	1,040,000	1,080,000	1196
Tangyin County (Chengguan Town)	湯陰縣 (城關鎮)	汤阴县 (城关镇)	490,000	500,000	520,000	639

(continued)

Table 13.4 (continued)

Name	Traditional	Simplified	Population (2012)	Population (2016)	Population (2020)	Area (Sq. Km)
Huaxian County (Daokou Town)	滑縣 (道口鎮)	滑县 (道口镇)	1,410,000	1,430,000	1,490,000	1784
Neihuang County (Chengguan Town)	內黃縣 (城關鎮)	内黄县 (城关镇)	760,000	780,000	860,000	1146
Puyang City	濮陽市	濮阳市	4,110,000	4,210,000	4,350,000	4266
Hualong District (Zhongyuanlu Subdistrict)	華龍區 (中原路街道)	华龙区 (中原路街道)	680,000	700,000	750,000	255
Qingfeng County (Chengguan Town)	清豐縣 (城關鎮)	清丰县 (城关镇)	720,000	740,000	760,000	869
Nanle County (Chengguan Town)	南樂縣 (城關鎮)	南乐县 (城关镇)	550,000	560,000	580,000	623
Fanxian County (Chengguan Town)	范縣 (城關鎮)	范县 (城关镇)	580,000	590,000	610,000	610
Taiqian County (Chengguan Town)	台前縣 (城關鎮)	台前县 (城关镇)	400,000	410,000	420,000	454
Puyang County (Chengguan Town)	濮陽縣 (城關鎮)	濮阳县 (城关镇)	1,180,000	1,210,000	1,230,000	1455
Kaifeng City	開封市	开封市	5,360,000	5,470,000	5,600,000	6247
Gulou District (Xiangguosi Subdistrict)	鼓樓區 (相國寺街道)	鼓楼区 (相国寺街道)	160,000	150,000	150,000	58
Longting District (Wuchaomen Subdistrict)	龍亭區 (午朝門街道)	龙亭区 (午朝门街道)	120,000	360,000	380,000	345
Shunhe Hui District (Qingping Subdistrict)	順河回族區 (清平街道)	顺河回族区 (清平街道)	250,000	250,000	240,000	88
Yuwangtai District (Caishi Subdistrict)	禹王台區 (菜市街道)	禹王台区 (菜市街道)	140,000	130,000	130,000	56
Xiangfu District (Chengdong Subdistrict)	祥符區 (城東街道)	祥符区 (城东街道)	N/A	780,000	820,000	1302

(continued)

Table 13.4 (continued)

Name	Traditional	Simplified	Population (2012)	Population (2016)	Population (2020)	Area (Sq. Km)
Jinming District (Shunhe Hui District Songmen Subdistrict)	金明區 (順河回族區宋門街道)	金明区 (顺河回族区宋门街道)	190,000	N/A	N/A	(197)
Qixian County (Chengguan Town)	杞縣 (城關鎮)	杞县 (城关镇)	1,180,000	1,210,000	1,230,000	1258
Tongxu County (Chengguan Town)	通許縣 (城關鎮)	通许县 (城关镇)	670,000	680,000	690,000	767
Weishi County (Chengguan Town)	尉氏縣 (城關鎮)	尉氏县 (城关镇)	980,000	1,000,000	1,030,000	1257
Kaifeng County (Chengguan Town)	開封縣 (城關鎮)	开封县 (城关镇)	780,000	N/A	N/A	(1302)
Lankao County (Chengguan Town)	蘭考縣 (城關鎮)	兰考县 (城关镇)	890,000	910,000	940,000	1116
Shangqiu City	商丘市	商丘市	9,180,000	9,350,000	9,990,000	10,658
Liangyuan District (Pingyuan Subdistrict)	梁園區 (平原街道)	梁园区 (平原街道)	890,000	910,000	910,000	673
Suiyang District (Xincheng Subdistrict)	睢陽區 (新城街道)	睢阳区 (新城街道)	880,000	900,000	970,000	913
Yongcheng City (Xuefeng Subdistrict)	永城市 (雪楓街道)	永城市 (雪枫街道)	1,490,000	1,520,000	1,640,000	2068
Yucheng County (Chengguan Town)	虞城縣 (城關鎮)	虞城县 (城关镇)	1,200,000	1,230,000	1,370,000	1558
Minquan County (Lüzhou Subdistrict)	民權縣 (綠洲街道)	民权县 (绿洲街道)	970,000	980,000	1,020,000	1222
Ningling County (Chengguan Hui Town)	寧陵縣 (城關回族鎮)	宁陵县 (城关回族镇)	670,000	680,000	720,000	786
Suixian County (Chengguan Hui Town)	睢縣 (城關回族鎮)	睢县 (城关回族镇)	880,000	890,000	930,000	920

(continued)

Table 13.4 (continued)

Name	Traditional	Simplified	Population (2012)	Population (2016)	Population (2020)	Area (Sq. Km)
Xiayi County (Chengguan Town)	夏邑縣 (城關鎮)	夏邑县 (城关镇)	1,190,000	1,210,000	1,330,000	1470
Zhecheng County (Chengguan Town)	柘城縣 (城關鎮)	柘城县 (城关镇)	1,010,000	1,030,000	1,110,000	1048
Xuchang City	許昌市	许昌市	4,890,000	4,950,000	5,090,000	4977
Weidu District (Xida Subdistrict)	魏都區 (西大街道)	魏都区 (西大街街道)	410,000	420,000	410,000	67
Jian'an District[c] (Jiangguan Town)	建安區 (將官池鎮)	建安区 (将官池镇)	N/A	N/A	930,000	1002
Yuzhou City (Yingchuan Subdistrict)	禹州市 (潁川街道)	禹州市 (颍川街道)	1,270,000	1,280,000	1,330,000	1472
Changge City (Jianshe Subdistrict)	長葛市 (建設街道)	长葛市 (建设路街道)	760,000	770,000	780,000	650
Xuchang County (Jiangguanchi Town)	許昌縣 (將官池鎮)	许昌县 (将官池镇)	890,000	910,000	N/A	(1002)
Yanling County (Anling Town)	鄢陵縣 (安陵鎮)	鄢陵县 (安陵镇)	680,000	690,000	730,000	866
Xiangcheng County (Chengguan Town)	襄城縣 (城關鎮)	襄城县 (城关镇)	880,000	880,000	910,000	920
Luohe City	漯河市	漯河市	2,780,000	2,740,000	2,680,000	2617
Yancheng District (Chengguan Town)	郾城區 (城關鎮)	郾城区 (城关镇)	520,000	520,000	510,000	413
Yuanhui District (Ganhechen Subdistrict)	源匯區 (干河陳街道)	源汇区 (干河陈街道)	340,000	330,000	310,000	202
Zhaoling District (Zhaizhuang Subdistrict)	召陵區 (翟莊街道)	召陵区 (翟庄街道)	550,000	540,000	530,000	405
Wuyang County (Wuquan Town)	舞陽縣 (舞泉鎮)	舞阳县 (舞泉镇)	610,000	610,000	600,000	776
Linying County (Chengguan Town)	林穎縣 (城關鎮)	临颍县 (城关镇)	760,000	740,000	730,000	821

(continued)

Table 13.4 (continued)

Name	Traditional	Simplified	Population (2012)	Population (2016)	Population (2020)	Area (Sq. Km)
Pingdingshan City	平頂山市	平顶山市	5,400,000	5,460,000	5,700,000	7874
Xinhua District (Shuguangjie Subdistrict)	新華區 (曙光街街道)	新华区 (曙光街街道)	400,000	410,000	420,000	157
Weidong District (Dong'anlu Subdistrict)	衛東區 (東安路街道)	卫东区 (东安路街道)	320,000	320,000	370,000	103
Zhanhe District (Xinhua District Shuguangjie Subdistrict)	湛河區 (新華區曙光街街道)	湛河区 (新华区曙光街街道)	250,000	250,000	270,000	124
Shilong District (Renminlu Subdistrict)	石龍區 (人民路街道)	石龙区 (人民路街道)	60,000	60,000	60,000	35
Wugang City (Yakou Subdistrict)	舞鋼市 (垭口街道)	舞钢市 (垭口街道)	340,000	340,000	340,000	640
Ruzhou City (Meishan Subdistrict)	汝州市 (煤山街道)	汝州市 (煤山街道)	1,070,000	1,090,000	1,180,000	1573
Baofeng County (Chengguan Town)	寶豐縣 (城關鎮)	宝丰县 (城关镇)	530,000	530,000	560,000	722
Yexian County (Jiulong Subdistrict)	葉縣 (九龍街道)	叶县 (九龙街道)	880,000	880,000	880,000	1387
Lushan County (Luyang Subdistrict)	魯山縣 (魯陽街道)	鲁山县 (鲁阳街道)	920,000	940,000	980,000	2406
Jiaxian County (Longshan Subdistrict)	郟縣 (龍山街道)	郏县 (龙山街道)	630,000	530,000	660,000	727
Nanyang City	南陽市	南阳市	11,850,000	12,080,000	12,380,000	26,591
Wolong District (Qiyi Subdistrict)	臥龍區 (七一街道)	卧龙区 (七一街道)	990,000	1,030,000	1,070,000	1007
Wancheng District (Dongguan Subdistrict)	宛城區 (東關街道)	宛城区 (东关街道)	890,000	920,000	950,000	880
Dengzhou City (Huazhou Subdistrict)	鄧州市 (花洲街道)	邓州市 (花洲街道)	1,760,000	1,780,000	1,850,000	2294

(continued)

Table 13.4 (continued)

Name	Traditional	Simplified	Population (2012)	Population (2016)	Population (2020)	Area (Sq. Km)
Nanzhao County (Chengguan Town)	南召縣 (城關鎮)	南召县 (城关镇)	650,000	650,000	690,000	2946
Fangcheng County (Fengrui Subdistrict)	方城縣 (鳳瑞街道)	方城县 (凤瑞街道)	1,100,000	1,130,000	1,180,000	2542
Xixia County (Zijin Subdistrict)	西峽縣 (紫金街道)	西峡县 (紫金街道)	470,000	480,000	490,000	3453
Zhenping County (Nieyang Subdistrict)	鎮平縣 (涅陽街道)	镇平县 (涅阳街道)	1,050,000	1,080,000	1,090,000	1490
Neixiang County (Chengguan Town)	內鄉縣 (城關鎮)	内乡县 (城关镇)	700,000	720,000	720,000	2465
Xichuan County (Longcheng Subdistrict)	淅川縣 (龍城街道)	淅川县 (龙城街道)	810,000	740,000	730,000	2817
Sheqi County (Shedian Town)	社旗縣 (賒店鎮)	社旗县 (赊店镇)	730,000	770,000	770,000	1203
Tanghe County (Binhe Subdistrict)	唐河縣 (濱河街道)	唐河县 (滨河街道)	1,390,000	1,430,000	1,480,000	2497
Xinye County (Hancheng Subdistrict)	新野縣 (漢城街道)	新野县 (汉城街道)	820,000	850,000	850,000	1056
Tongbai County (Chengguan Town)	桐柏縣 (城關鎮)	桐柏县 (城关镇)	490,000	500,000	500,000	1941
Xinyang City	信陽市	信阳市	8,700,000	8,670,000	9,120,000	18,819
Shihe District (Hudong Subdistrict)	浉河區 (湖東街道)	浉河区 (湖东街道)	640,000	640,000	670,000	1783
Pingqiao District (Pingqiao Subdistrict)	平橋區 (平橋街道)	平桥区 (平桥街道)	840,000	850,000	900,000	1889
Xixian County (Qiaolou Subdistrict)	息縣 (譙樓街道)	息县 (谯楼街道)	1,080,000	1,060,000	1,130,000	1836
Huaibin County (Binhu Subdistrict)	淮濱縣 (濱湖街道)	淮滨县 (滨湖街道)	740,000	750,000	820,000	1192

(continued)

Table 13.4 (continued)

Name	Traditional	Simplified	Population (2012)	Population (2016)	Population (2020)	Area (Sq. Km)
Huangchuan County (Dingcheng Subdistrict)	潢川縣 (定城街道)	潢川县 (定城街道)	860,000	840,000	900,000	1638
Guangshan County (Zishui Subdistrict)	光山縣 (紫水街道)	光山县 (紫水街道)	910,000	920,000	940,000	1829
Gushi County (Xiushui Subdistrict)	固始縣 (秀水街道)	固始县 (秀水街道)	1,720,000	1,690,000	1,790,000	2916
Shangcheng County (Chicheng Subdistrict)	商城縣 (赤城街道)	商城县 (赤城街道)	760,000	780,000	800,000	2117
Luoshan County (Chengguan Town)	羅山縣 (城關鎮)	罗山县 (城关镇)	760,000	770,000	79,000	2065
Xinxian County (Xinji Town)	新縣 (新集鎮)	新县 (新集镇)	390,000	370,000	380,000	1554
Zhoukou City	周口市	周口市	12,240,000	12,300,000	12,590,000	11,968
Chuanhui District (Renhejie Subdistrict)	川匯區 (人和街道)	川汇区 (人和街道)	540,000	590,000	640,000	141
Xiangcheng City (Huayuan Subdistrict)	項城市 (花園街道)	项城市 (花园街道)	1,330,000	1,380,000	1,360,000	1083
Fugou County (Chengguan Town)	扶溝縣 (城關鎮)	扶沟县 (城关镇)	770,000	780,000	790,000	1163
Xihua County (Wacheng Subdistrict)	西華縣 (媧城街道)	西华县 (娲城街道)	1,000,000	970,000	970,000	1208
Shangshui County (Xincheng Subdistrict)	商水縣 (新城街道)	商水县 (新城街道)	1,260,000	1,260,000	1,320,000	1325
Taikang County (Chengguan Hui Town)	太康縣 (城關回族鎮)	太康县 (城关回族镇)	1,560,000	1,570,000	1,650,000	1761
Luyi County (Zhenyuan Subdistrict)	鹿邑縣 (真源街道)	鹿邑县 (真源街道)	1,320,000	1,330,000	1,380,000	1248

(continued)

Table 13.4 (continued)

Name	Traditional	Simplified	Population (2012)	Population (2016)	Population (2020)	Area (Sq. Km)
Dancheng County (Xincheng Subdistrict)	鄲城縣 (新城街道)	郸城县 (新城街道)	1,550,000	1,580,000	1,590,000	1490
Huaiyang District (Chengguan Hui Town)	淮陽區 (城關回族鎮)	淮阳区 (城关回族镇)	1,550,000	1,490,000	980,000	1321
Shenqiu County (Dongcheng Subdistrict)	沈丘縣 (東城街道)	沈丘县 (东城街道)	1,360,000	1,350,000	1,360,000	1082
Zhumadian City	駐馬店市	驻马店市	8,860,000	8,990,000	9,640,000	14,974
Yicheng District (Renminjie Subdistrict)	驛城區 (人民街街道)	驿城区 (人民街街道)	670,000	810,000	850,000	886
Queshan County (Panlong Subdistrict)	確山縣 (盤龍街道)	确山县 (盘龙街道)	530,000	530,000	560,000	1667
Biyang County (Gucheng Subdistrict)	泌陽縣 (古城街道)	泌阳县 (古城街道)	1,000,000	910,000	970,000	2789
Suiping County (Quyang Subdistrict)	遂平縣 (灈陽街道)	遂平县 (灈阳街道)	560,000	560,000	580,000	1080
Xiping County (Baicheng Subdistrict)	西平縣 (柏城街道)	西平县 (柏城街道)	870,000	870,000	890,000	1098
Shangcai County (Chongyang Subdistrict)	上蔡縣 (重陽街道)	上蔡县 (重阳街道)	1,510,000	1,530,000	1,600,000	1517
Ru'nan County (Ru'ning Subdistrict)	汝南縣 (汝寧街道)	汝南县 (汝宁街道)	840,000	850,000	900,000	1306
Pingyu County (Guhuai Subdistrict)	平輿縣 (古槐街道)	平舆县 (古槐街道)	980,000	990,000	1,160,000	1285
Xincai County (Gulü Subdistrict)	新蔡縣 (古呂街道)	新蔡县 (古吕街道)	1,100,000	1,120,000	1,250,000	1442
Zhengyang County (Zhenyang Town)	正陽縣 (真陽鎮)	正阳县 (真阳镇)	800,000	820,000	870,000	1904

(continued)

Table 13.4 (continued)

Name	Traditional	Simplified	Population (2012)	Population (2016)	Population (2020)	Area (Sq. Km)
(County-level administrative unit under direct provincial jurisdiction) [省直轄縣級行政單位]	省直轄縣級行政單位	省直辖县级行政单位				
Jiyuan City (Qinyuan Subdistrict)	濟源市 (沁源街道)	济源市 (沁园街道)	680,000	690,000	730,000	1965

[a]Became a district in 2016
[b]County made a city in July 2019
[c]Created out of the dissolution of Xuchang county in 2017

References

Bagley, Robert. 1999. Shang archaeology. In *The Cambridge history of ancient China: From the origins of civilization to 221 B.C.*, ed. Michael Loewe and Edward L. Shaughnessy, 124–231. New York: Cambridge University Press.

Chang, Kwang-chih. 1977. *The archeology of ancient China*. 3rd ed. New Haven: Yale University Press.

———. 1999. China on the eve of the historical record. In *The Cambridge history of ancient China: From the origins of civilization to 221 B.C.*, ed. Michael Loewe and Edward L. Shaughnessy, 37–73. New York: Cambridge University Press.

China News Net. 2015. [*A large group of ancient tombs in the center of Zhengzhou is preliminarily determined to belong to the Shang dynasty*]. 29 December. 郑州市中心现大型古墓群 初步判定属商代. 中国新闻网 http://china.chinadaily.com.cn/shizheng/2015-12/29/content_22852980.htm.

Elvin, Mark. 1973. *The pattern of the Chinese past: A social and economic interpretation*. Stanford: Stanford University Press.

Henan Province Bureau of Statistics (HPBS). 2021. [*Communiqué of the seventh national census of Henan Province*, issue No. 2]. 河南省第七次全国人口普查公报, 第二号. 15 June. http://www.hnadr.org/view/7257.

Hsieh, Chiao-min, and Jean Kan Hsieh. 1995. *China: A provincial atlas*. New York: Macmillan Publishing.

Hsu, Cho-yun. 1999. The spring and autumn period. In *The Cambridge history of ancient China: From the origins of civilization to 221 B.C.*, ed. Michael Loewe and Edward L. Shaughnessy, 545–586. New York: Cambridge University Press.

Keightley, David N. 1978. *Sources of Shang history: The oracle-bone inscriptions of bronze age China*. Berkeley: University of California Press.

Lee, Keekok. 2008. *Warp and weft: Chinese language and culture*. New York: Eloquent Books.

Lewis, Mark Edward. 1999. Warring states political history. In *The Cambridge history of ancient China: from the origins of civilization to 221 B.C.*, ed. Michael Loewe and Edward L. Shaughnessy, 587–650. New York: Cambridge University Press.

Li, Dandan. 2014. [*Physical origins: physics history and physics technology*]. Beijing: China Modern Publishing. 李丹丹, 物理源流: 物理历史与物理科技, 现代出版社.

Lim, Justin Yifu. 2012. *Demystifying the Chinese economy*. New York: Cambridge University Press.

McGovern, Patrick E. 2009. *Uncorking the past: The quest for wine, beer, and other alcoholic beverages*. Berkeley: University of California Press.

McGovern, Patrick E., Juzhong Zhang, Jigen Tang, et al. 2004. Fermented beverages of pre- and proto-historic China. *Proceedings of the National Academy of Science* 101 (51): 17593–17598.

Ministry of Civil Affairs (MCA), People's Republic of China. 2020. [*County/township administration handbook*]. Beijing: China Statistics Press. 中華人民共和國民政部, 中華人民共和國, 鄉鎮行政區劃簡冊.

Nicolini-Zani, Matteo. 2013. Luminous ministers of the Da Qin monastery. In *From the Oxus River to the Chinese shores: Studies on east Syriac Christianity in China and Central Asia*, ed. Li Tang and Dietmar W. Winkler, 141–160. Berlin: Lit Verlag.

Shang-Ch'i Guide. 2017. [*Backpacking in China: The most complete collection of self-guided travel for China, 2018*]. Taipei: Shang-Ch'i Shitai publishing. 2018 最完整的中國自助旅遊全集. 台北: 上奇時代.

Shaughnessy, Edward L. 1991. *Sources of western Zhou history: Inscribed bronze vessels*. Berkeley: University of California.

Shirokauer, Conrad, and Miranda Brown. 2012. *A brief history of Chinese civilization*. 4th ed. Belmont, CA: Wadsworth Cengage Learning.

Tan, Qixiang. 1985. *Concise historical atlas of China*. Beijing: China Cartographic Publishing House.

Taylor, Jay [蔣]. 2011. *The generalissimo: Chiang Kai-shek and the struggle for modern China*. Cambridge: The Belknap Press of Harvard University Press.

Yang, Jisheng. 2012. *Tombstone: The great Chinese famine, 1958–1962*. Trans. Stacy Mosher and Guo Jian. New York: Farrar, Straus and Giroux.

Yuan, Zuliang, and Jiao Peimin. 2007. [*China's population through history: Beginning Qin volume*]. Beijing: People's Press. 袁祖亮主編, 焦培民著, 中國人口通史: 先秦卷, Vol. 2, 北京: 人民出版社.

Zhang, Shunan. 2021. [*The 2020 per capita income list of residents in various provinces: Shanghai is the richest, and it has risen sharply*]. Finance.people.com. 22 January. 张澍楠. 2020年各省份居民人均收入榜: 上海最有钱, 这地涨得猛. http://finance.people.com.cn/n1/2021/0122/c1004-32008733.html.

Chapter 14
Hong Kong

Abstract Having been part of a southern Chinese prefecture since at least the Qin dynasty (ca. 200 BCE), Hong Kong was more than just a small fishing village before the arrival of the British in the mid-nineteenth century. However, there is no denying that the imposition of colonial government and free trade that was promoted in Hong Kong made it the economic power that it is today. Having spoken its own form of Cantonese (and English) for decades, Hong Kong has long had its own special character. Even with its handover to Beijing in 1997, Hong Kong was meant to be a "special administrative region," with the promise of legal protections to its own sovereignty even while being part of China. However, since 2019, Beijing has put more and more pressure upon Hong Kong, making sure that the Chinese Communist Party (CCP) has complete and total control over the population of Hong Kong, to include what is printed or said in Hong Kong media.

E. Croddy, *China's Provinces and Populations*,
https://doi.org/10.1007/978-3-031-09165-0_14

Hong Kong Special Administrative Region (香港特別行政區 *xiānggǎng tèbié xíngzhèngqū*): Abbreviation 港 (*gǎng*) (Fig. 14.1)

	Hong Kong SAR Population (GHKSAR, 2021)	
	(As of mid-2020)	Area (square kms)
New Territories and Islands (新界及離島):	**3,952,800**	**958.44**
1. 北區 North District	318,500	136.46
2. 元朗區 Yuen Long District	646,100	138.48
3. 大埔區 Taipo District	311,200	136.12
4. 屯門區 Tuen Mun District	503,100	84.84
5. 荃灣區 Tsuen Wan District	313,500	61.94
6. 沙田區 Sha Tin District	689,300	68.71
7. 西貢區 Sai Kung District	475,500	129.67
8. 離島區 Islands District	186,600	178.89
9. 葵青區 Kwai Tsing District	508,900	23.34
Kowloon (九龍):	**2,303,100**	**46.95**
10. 深水埗區 Sham Shui Po District	440,500	9.36
11. 油尖旺區 Yau Tsim Mong District	326,600	9.99
12. 九龍城區 Kowloon City District	425,400	10.02
13. 黃大仙 Wong Tai Sin	418,200	9.30
14. 觀塘區 Kwun Tong District	692,400	11.28
Hong Kong Island (香港島):	**1,224,700**	**79.93**
15. 中西區 Central and Western District	239,000	12.55
16. 灣仔區 Wan Chai District	175,000	10.56
17. 東區 Eastern District	542,900	17.99
18. 南區 Southern District	267,900	38.84

Fig. 14.1 Hong Kong Major Districts. (Drawn by the Author after People's Republic of China, Ministry of Civil Affairs (MCA 2020))

Hong Kong: General Impressions

The history of modern Hong Kong can be roughly broken into three parts: (1) 1950s–1997: a busy, dynamic, impossibly crowded, and yet quaint British-Chinese colonial metropolis with local customs and cuisines; (2) 1997–2019: all of the aforementioned, but still a (reasonably) free Hong Kong polis, nominally drawn within the geopolitical sphere of the People's Republic of China (PRC); and (3) June 2020 onward: with the passing of the "National Security Law (香港國家安全法 *xiānggǎng guójiā ānquán fǎ*),"[1] Hong Kong is now essentially a Chinese provincial city, having none of the precious freedoms it once had even under the most restrictive British colonial government. Under its catch-all terms, the wording of the national security law criminalizes "the incitement of state subversion"[2] as well as "national splittism," terrorism, "collusion with foreign forces," and "inciting hatred of the central government and Hong Kong's regional government." (NPC 2021).[3] This was ultimately evinced by the jailing of *Apple Daily* founder and media mogul Jimmy Lai (黎智英 *lí zhìyīng*) in April 2021 for having participated in pro-democracy protests in October 2019 (Pang 2021). The interpretation this new law is so wide that a 40-year-old man (surnamed 梁) was arrested (30 July 2021) for booing the Chinese national anthem during the Summer Olympics. What is more, although cited under a law passed in June 2020 regarding respecting national songs (國歌條例 *guógētiáolì*), carrying a fine of HK$50,000 and potential imprisonment term of 3 years, legal circles in Hong Kong also believed it could also represent a violation of Hong Kong's "National Security Law." (ITN 2021).

Hong Kong's Name Origins

Literally meaning "fragrant harbor" (香港 *xiānggǎng*; Cantonese: *Hēunggóng*), the origins of the name "Hong Kong" describing the *entire* island bloc grouping (i.e., Hong Kong Special Administrative Region) are somewhat convoluted. But as far as the Chinese were concerned, the name of an island called "Hong Kong" could be found in a book titled, *Great Matters of Guangdong* (粵大事 *yuèdàshì*), by Guo Fei (郭棐 *guōfěi*), written sometime during 1573–1619 (Ming dynasty). In Guo Fei's map of the Guangdong coast, one also finds place names to include 赤柱 (*chìzhù*, now also known as Stanley); 黃泥涌 (*huángníyǒng*, now also known as Wong Nai Chung Gap); and (尖沙咀 *jiānshāzuǐ*), known as Tsim Sha Tsui (Liu 2016). Later, Chinese maps (ca. 1820) also showed Hong Kong Tsai (香港仔 *xiānggǎngzǎi*). (Tan 1996).

However, for the outside world, the name "Hong Kong" to describe a small harbor and associated islands came to be known only by the late eighteenth century,

[1] Full name: "Law of the People's Republic of China on Safeguarding National Security in the Hong Kong Special Administrative Region" 中華人民共和國香港特別行政區維護國家安全法 *zhōnghuá rénmín gònghéguó xiānggǎng tèbiéxíngzhèngqū wéihù guójiā ānquán fǎ*.

[2] 煽动颠覆国家政权罪 *shāndòng diānfù guójiā zhèngquán zuì*.

[3] Article 29 (5).

and was specifically mentioned as a regular mooring site for British naval expeditions to China. In 1816, for example, in an account by Captain Basil Hall in command of a "ten-gun brig" in his diplomatic mission to China, his and other ships

> proceeded to the coast of China, there to communicate with Sir George Staunton, chief of the English Factory at Canton [Guangzhou], and with other persons destined to accompany the expedition. The [Chinese] Emperor had already been informed of the intention of the Prince Regent to send a mission to the court of Pekin [Beijing], and his reply was hourly expected. The vessels took in water at Hong Kong, one of the Ladrone Islands, where they awaited the Emperor's answer, which was at length received by an express from the Factory. Full permission was granted by it for the embassy to advance up the coast … (Hall 1828).

This same island would be later be commonly known as Aberdeen to the west. In 1841, when a British delegation visited Aberdeen—that is, Hong Kong island to the locals—they consulted a local guide named Chen Qun (陳群 *chén qún*, it is not clear if it was a man or woman). Chen was among the water-dwelling persons. Back then, they were pejoratively known as Tanka (疍家/蛋家 *dànjiā* = "egg people," named for the shape of their boats). With their own distinctive dialect and maritime way of life, they are now referred to as Shui Sheung Yan (水上人 *shuǐshàngrén*). During the time of early interactions with the British empire, Hong Kong had a population of about 7450, including some 2000 Shui Sheung Yan (Liu 2016). When the foreigners asked Chen the name of the area, s/he responded (in Tanka dialect) something along the lines of "*Hong Kong*," but was probably referring to the site where they stood. Having jotted down the name in English transliteration, the British continued to use the name "Hong Kong," but it now referred to the entire group of islands (Zhou 2011).

Hong Kong Neolithic

On the southernmost part of Hong Kong's Lamma Island (南丫島 *nányā dǎo*), in the Sham Wan bay (深灣 *shēnwān*), researchers during the 1970s discovered nearly two dozen burial sites. The excavations revealed tombs and human skulls showing evidence of human sacrifice, head-hunting and cannibalism. In addition to cremated human remains, researchers also found adzes, stone rings, as well as pottery with roped designs. Covering an area of about eight square kilometers, the Sham Wan Neolithic site and its contents have been dated back to about 3000 BCE.

Later-dated Neolithic sites (2500–1500 BCE) have also been found in Hong Kong, including Yung Long (涌浪 *yǒnglàng*) in Tuen Mun (屯門 *túnmén*) district, where numerous stone implements were uncovered, including adzes, drills, and a boat anchor (Zhou 2011). Researchers found fishing and primitive textile industries—also from the late Neolithic—at Sha Lo Wan (沙螺灣 *shāluówān*) on Lantau Island (大嶼山 *dàyǔshān*). They also uncovered stone implements and pottery (Higham 1996). On the very small island (about one square kilometer) of Ma Wan (馬彎 *mǎwān*), the Tung Wan Tsai (東灣仔 *dōng wān zài*) late Neolithic site was excavated in June 1996. Unearthed were tombs showing elements (such as tools) of both Neolithic and early Bronze age periods.

Approximately 3500 years ago, during the Shang Dynasty (1600–1046 BCE), a new group of people arrived in the modern-day Hong Kong, Zhuhai and Shenzhen areas. This group crafted distinctive etched pottery, and addition to fishing and hunting they also had a primitive agricultural economy. On a 10 square-kilometer site at Yung Long (勇浪 *yǒnglàng*) on Tuen Mun (屯門 *túnmén*), researchers found evidence of this densely-populated community. This clan lived in simple dwellings, with unusually-shaped ash pits, and a variety of tools. It is believed that these early inhabitants used fire pits to char wood in order to make outer boat hulls. In keeping with the maritime technology of that period, the site revealed stone anchors weighing approximately 25–55 pounds (Liu 2012).

Hong Kong, Ancient to Modern

Starting with the Qin dynasty (221–206 BCE), and as it was the case for neighboring areas such as Macao, the islands that form Hong Kong today were administered by Nanhai Prefecture, Panyu County (南海郡番禺縣 *nánhǎi jùn pānyù xiàn*), which is now today's "Old Town District" (老城區 *lǎochéng qū) in Guangzhou*. In the Han Dynasty (ca. 200 CE), the establishment of salt commissioners in the area included Hong Kong, and modern archeology has found evidence of salt making kilns along its coastal areas. In order to defend against salt smuggling, the Han established military garrisons in Lamma Tai Wan Bay (南丫島大灣 *nányā dǎo dàwān*), and Lantau's Pak Mong (白芒 *báimáng*).

During the first reign of the Nanbeichao (南北朝 *nánběicháo*), Liu Song (劉宋 *liú sòng*; 420–479 CE), the famed vagabond Indian monk Beidu (高僧杯渡禪師 *gāosēng bēidù chánshī*) and who famously carried a raft wherever he went, lived in modern-day Tuen Mun, Hong Kong. A nearby landmark, Pui To Shan (杯渡山 *bēidù shān*); aka Qingshan Mountain (青山 *qīngshān* "Castle Peak") was named after him.

Like Macao, modern-day Hong Kong was made subordinate to Bao'an County (寶安縣 *bǎoān xiàn*), and then Dongguan County (東莞縣 *dōngguǎn xiàn*) by the Tang (ca. 700 CE). Tuen Mun Town (屯門鎮 *túnmén zhèn*) was at that time fortified as a military redoubt to help defend the mouth of the vital Pearl River.

Pearls and Salt

During the fractious Five Dynasties and Ten Kingdoms (905–971), the region known as Southern Han (南漢 *nánhàn*) comprised modern-day Guangxi and Guangdong provinces. Tai Po Harbor (大埔海 *dàpǔhǎi*), a stretch of water known today as Tolo Harbor (吐露港 *tǔlùgǎng*) in Hong Kong New Territories was called Meizhu Chi (媚珠池 *mèizhūchí*) on account of the active pearl harvesting that went on there. The pearl industry was so lucrative a whole new governmental entity was created to oversee it: Meichuan City (媚川都 *mèichuān dū*).

In the thirteenth century, salt fields were worked in modern-day Lantau Island, stretching from To Kwa Wan (土瓜灣 *tŭguāwān*) to Tsim Sha Tsui (尖沙咀 *jiānshāzuǐ*), as well as Kowloon (九龍 *jiŭlóng*. (Zhou 2011.) But between the Song dynasty prohibition on allowing officials to participate in conducting private trade, and the Qing dynasty policy of the "Great Clearance" (遷界令 *qiānjièlìng*, aka coastal evacuation order, see also below), the profitable sandalwood, salt, and pearl industries fell further by the wayside, while farming and fishing continued to flourish.

It is perhaps with some irony that, following the Mongolian invasion, in 1278 the 17th Song emperor, Duan Zong (端宗 *duān zōng*) was forced to flee to Guangdong, seeking temporary refuge in Kowloon. This historic event is memorialized at the Kowloon Sung Wong Toi Garden (宋皇臺花園 *sònghuángtái huāyuán*) in Ma Tau Wai (馬頭圍 *mătóuwéi*). Indeed, a good number of Song dynasty notables fled to Hong Kong during the Mongol Yuan reign (1276–1368). (Zhang 2006).

As a means to defend against pirates (and later, European incursions), by 1381 China had built fortresses ("thousand housed redoubts" 千戶所 *qiānhùsuŏ*) in modern-day Shenzhen, including the impressive Dapeng Fortress (大鵬所城 *dàpéngsuŏchéng*). Commissioned by the Ming emperor in 1394, these were also established in what are now the New Northwest Territories (新界東北 *xīnjièdōngbĕi*). In ca. 1600, a Nantou Military District Garrison was placed in charge of six main regions responsible for defense around Hong Kong and environs, such as Fat Tong Mun (佛堂門 *fótáng mén*), Lung Shun Wan (龍船灣 *lóngchuánwān*), and Tai O (大澳 *dàào*). It commanded anywhere form 50–80 war junks, and up to 2500 men-at-arms.

As mentioned earlier, the Qing edict (1661–1669) of the "Great Clearance"—or withdrawing from the coast to deal with anti-Qing holdouts (especially Koxinga; see also chapter on Republic of China, Taiwan) from the Ming dynasty—put an immediate impediment to Hong Kong's economic development. When the order was finally rescinded, the areas of today's New Territories of Hong Kong restored their role as a center for commerce. During this economic recovery, different market places developed into full-fledged urban communities under two main families. Prior to the Opium War, the New Territories' major socioeconomic centers were the old Tai Po (大埔墟 *dàpŭ xū*) and Yuen Long (元朗墟 *yuánlăng xū*) districts, each run by the locally powerful Tang (鄧 *dèng*) family (Zhou 2011). During the Qing dynasty, the Yongzheng emperor (1723–1735) during built additional defenses, including the fortification of Tung Chung (東涌 *dōngchōng*). With the outbreak of the Opium War, and despite increasing the number of cannon placements in Kowloon and other places (at the urging by the local command and Qing official Lin Zexu 林則徐 *lín zéxú*) these artillery pieces were ineffective against British naval firepower. China, defeated, handed Hong Kong over to the British (in perpetuity) under terms of the Treaty of Nanking (Nanjing) on 29 August 1842.

Hong Kong in Modern Times

Unlike the picture drawn by later colonial writers, before the arrival of the British Hong Kong was not just a barren rock, nor was it just sparsely populated with a few itinerant fishermen. Still, much of its modern history owes itself to

British commercially-driven imperialism. In contrast to Macao, whose occupation by Portugal had much to do with being an entry point and operating base for Christian missionaries, Hong Kong started out mainly to serve as a British imperial post to foster trade. One of the many ports in the East to facilitate, among other things, opium, Hong Kong had been utilized by English merchant fleets since at least 1821 (Carroll 2007). In August 1834, the British Superintendent for Trade, Lord William Napier, recommended taking over Hong Kong as a means to establish commercial trade with the Chinese. Regarding the latter suggestion, the English language newspaper, *Canton Register* (and owned by Scottish merchants) opined:

> If the lion's paw is to be put down on any part of the south side of China, let it be Hong Kong; let the lion declare it to be under his guarantee a free port, and in ten years it will be the most considerable mart east of the Cape. The Portuguese made a mistake: They adopted shallow water and exclusive laws. Hong Kong, deep water, and a free port forever (Zhang 2006).

Still, Hong Kong in 1844 did not seem to offer much promise to the British empire, as one contemporary (Robert Montgomery Martin, the imperial treasury officer) said,

> There does not appear to be the slightest probability that, under any circumstances, Hong Kong will ever become a place of trade (Carroll 2007).

Occupied by Britain as a result of the first Opium War (1839–42), on 26 June in 1843 Hong Kong became an official British colony. But ultimately, this process of colonization was mainly the historical result of "a long crusade by British free traders to promote trade with China." (Carroll 2007).

Local Populations

Hong Kong held its first official census in June 1845, counting a total of 23,817 residents (not including garrisoned soldiers). Broken down by origin, native Hong Kong Chinese made up 22,860, European (595), and Indian (362). By about this time, a quarter of foreign businesses in Hong Kong were owned by either Persians (Parsees, by way of Bombay), or Indian Muslims. From 1845 to 1849, about 75% of Indian grown opium was traded through Hong Kong's Victoria Harbor, and opium generated a great majority of government tax revenue until as late as 1941.

A large number of Chinese laborers—called "coolies" from the Chinese "苦力 *(kŭlì)*" for hard labor—flowed through Hong Kong, but the trade in such exploitative labor began to wane towards the 1870s (Zhang 2006).

Hong Kong Immigration During the Taiping Rebellion

When the Taiping Rebellion (1851–1864) tore China apart; thousands fled their villages, many finding safety by relocating to Hong Kong. As a result the population of the colony nearly quadrupled (see Table 14.1):

Table 14.1 Population Growth in Hong Kong during Taiping Rebellion (1851–64). (Zhang 2006)

1851	32,983
1853	39,017
1854	55,715
1855	72,607
1856	71,730
1861[a]	119,321
1866	115,098

[a]Includes population of Kowloon

Unfortunately, the growing density of Hong Kong's population exacerbated the spread of communicable diseases. Adding to the public health and moral contretemps of the times, an industry of kidnapping Chinese girls from poor villages in China to serve as maids or prostitutes prospered in the 1870s. The 1876 census counted 25,000 women in Hong Kong; over 80% of those counted were prostitutes, and, perhaps not surprisingly, the numbers of people infected with syphilis skyrocketed. The urban density of Hong Kong, as well as those communities in Guangdong and the remainder of mainland China were highly vulnerable to the third pandemic of bubonic plague. In 1894, for example, Hong Kong lost 2512 people to the illness (Chen 1992), and 12,506 Hong Kong residents died from plague during 1894–1907 (Cao and Yushang 2006).

June 1898 marked the start of the notorious British lease of the New Territories as a result of the Treaty of Peking that same year. In addition to Hong Kong Island, Britain would control (for 99 years) 365 square miles to include Kowloon and 230 islands in and around the Shenzhen River estuary, notably Lantau Island. The new areas incorporated a population of over 80,000.

A Place for Refugees from Mainland China

Hong Kong's population had often ballooned during times of crisis in neighboring China, and has also fallen precipitously during times of relative peace. For example, if a million (or more) Chinese fled to Hong Kong during the first half of the Sino-Japanese War (1937–1941), the population numbers suggest many of these same refugees returned to China after World War II (Zhang 2006). During Japan's occupation of Hong Kong (beginning Christmas 1941), the immediate step by the Japanese military was to put British Hong Kong citizens into labor camps, where many died under cruel conditions to include torture, while many more Chinese fled Hong Kong *en masse*. Upon the fall of the Kuomingtang (KMT) Nationalists and the founding of the PRC under the Chinese Communist Party (CCP) in 1949, Hong Kong experienced a large influx of Chinese businessmen and others escaping certain requisition of their property and probably their own lives.

During the Great Leap Forward (1959–1962), some 142,000 starving Chinese mainlanders found refuge in Hong Kong, and later, throughout the chaos of the Cultural Revolution (1966–1976), about 244,200 Chinese escaped to the British colony. It is to the credit of the colonial authorities that they were able to accept and incorporate such large numbers, and ultimately these immigrants contributed to the overall economic benefit of Hong Kong (Fung 2004). And despite (or perhaps as a result of) Deng Xiaoping's policy of "reform opening up" (1978+), some 300,000 mainland Chinese sought residency in Hong Kong. Such was the lure of economic opportunities that further increased Hong Kong's population, as seen in the Tuen Men (屯門 *túnmén*) settlement (Table 14.2) and in other major districts (Table 14.3).

When Hong Kong was handed over to the People's Republic of China (PRC) in 1997, some 32 percent of Hong Kong residents were immigrants from mainland China, with a little over 7% having arrived from other countries (Fung 2004). Currently, Hong Kong keeps statistics to include numbers of its citizens that were born in mainland China as well as Taiwan and Macao, these comprising 31% of Hong Kong's population according to the 2016 census (GHKSAR 2016). Table 14.4 provides an overall view of Hong Kong population growth since 1841.

Table 14.2 Tuen Mun population data: 1971–2011. (Liu 2012)

Year	Population
1971	46,361
1976	58,17
1981	126,883
1986	287,539
1991	380,683
1996	463,703
2001	488,831
2006	502,035
2011	487,546

Table 14.3 Regional Hong Kong population distribution by percentage and year. (Zhang 2006)

Region (four main areas):	1911	1921	1931	1961	1971	1981	1986
Hong Kong (香港島)	53	56	49	32	25	24	22
Kowloon (九龍)	12	18	28	23	18	16	13
New Kowloon (新九龍)	3	2	3	27	38	33	30
New Territories (新界)	18	13	12	14	17	26	35
Marine Region (水上)	14	11	8	4	2	1	0.7

Hong Kong Population History

Table 14.4 Hong Kong Populations 1841–2020. (Zhang 2006; GHKSAR 2021)

Year	Population
1841	7450–7545
1842	12,631
1844	19,000
1845	23,817
1846	21,835
1851	32,983
1853	39,017
1854	55,715
1855	72,607
1856	71,730
1861[a]	119,321
1866	115,098
1871	124,198
1872	121,985
1876	139,144
1881	152,858–160,402
1886	181,720
1891	217,936–221,441
1896	239,419
1898	254,400
1900	277,740
1901	290,124–368,987
1902	303,116
1903	317,330
1904	352,487
1905	370,325
1906	318,304–329,038
1907	323,380
1908	329,650
1909	337,160
1910	344,180
1911	456,739–464,277
1912	464,277
1913	489,114
1914	501,304
1915	509,160
1916	528,010–529,010
1917	535,100
1918	561,500
1919	598,100

(continued)

Table 14.4 (continued)

Year	Population
1920	648,150
1921	625,166–686,680
1922	662,200
1923	681,800
1924	799,550
1925	874,420
1926	710,000–874,420
1931	840,473–850,000
1936	988,190
1941	1,639,337
1945	600,000–650,000
1946	1,550,000–1,600,000
1947	1,800,000
1950	2,200,000
1951	2,015,300
1956	2,500,000–2,614,600
1960	3,010,000
1961	3,129,648
1966	3,790,000
1971	3,936,630
1976	4,402,990
1979	5,010,000
1981	5,109,812
1986	5,524,600
1990	5,841,000
1991	5,674,114
1996	6,217,556
2001	6,708,389
2006	6,857,100
2011	7,071,576
2013	7,190,000
2015	7,324,300
2016	7,336,585
2020	7,509,200

[a]Includes population of Kowloon

Population Density

While not the most densely populated city in the world, Hong Kong surely ranks among them. In ca. 2012, the average density was about 6500 people per square kilometer. At the most extreme, Tin Shui Wai New Town (天水圍新市鎮 *tiānshuǐwéi xīnshì zhèn*), New Territories, has about 60,000 persons per square kilometer. Kwun Tong district (觀塘區 *guāntáng qū*), east Kowloon, has upwards of 50,000 per square kilometer (for comparison, crowded New Dehli is less than half that). Kowloon districts with population densities well north of 40,000 people per square kilometer include Wong Tai Sin (黃大仙區 *huángdàxiān qū*), Sham Shui Po (深水埗區 *shēnshuǐbù qū*) and Yau Tsim Mong (油尖旺區 *yóujiānwàng qū*) districts. Finally, those districts with about 30,000 people per square kilometer include New Territories' Fanling (粉嶺 *fěnlǐng*), and those living primarily on boats, i.e., Shui Sheung Yan (水上人 *shuǐshàngrén*) (Harris 2012).

Although ruled by the British (until 1997) with more than a slight authoritarian bent, colonial Hong Kong nonetheless had a decidedly liberal tradition. As Wei-bin Zhang put it in 2006, during British rule,

> The people of Hong Kong had actually enjoyed substantial measures of social, economic, and cultural freedom. The degree of freedom that Hong Kong Chinese people had enjoyed in the colony has never achieved in Mainland China even until today (Zhang 2006).

As such, Hong Kong had considerable freedom and private property rights. These characteristics helped to spur its export-led, market approach to economic policy in the 1970s, making it one of the Asia's "Four Asian Dragons" (along with Taiwan, Singapore and South Korea). Unlike the PRC, then still mired in a socialist and communalistic ideology, Hong Kong grew into an economic and financial powerhouse. What's more, mainland China has long depended upon Hong Kong as a window to the rest of the free world, notably for foreign investment. Even as of 2005, some 40% of direct investment in the PRC originated in Hong Kong. But it was not just financial capital, but also managerial and modern economic skill sets imported from Hong Kong that were critical for China's rapid development after the 1978 economic reforms (Huang and Duncan 1997).

For about two decades since the handover to the PRC in July 1997, Hong Kong remained autonomous. However, despite the agreement that, under the "One Country, Two Systems" rubric Hong Kong should remain as it has been for 50 years, less than a quarter of Hong Kong residents believed that Beijing faithfully honored this commitment. Their misgivings were justified later in 2019, when Beijing set about ensuring its repressive political regime would extend *de facto* and *de jure* to Hong Kong.

Hong Kong Population Trends and Economy

According to its government-supplied statistics, Hong Kong's economy (see Table 14.5) has continued to grow at a healthy 7.6% from 2020 to 2021 (Dodwell 2021). This may be due to the fact that Hong Kong was recovering from a drop in overall GDP during 2019–20:

With a population of 7.5 million people, Hong Kong in 2020 had a larger GDP ($347 billion) than Guangxi province ($344 billion). Its per capita income, however, dwarfs all PRC provinces and major cities (including Macao) at $46,324. Since the

Table 14.5 Hong Kong Gross Domestic Product (GDP): 2016–2020. (Macrotrends 2021)

Year	GDP (USD $billion)	Increase (Decline)
2017	$341.24	6.36%
2018	$361.69	6.00%
2019	$363.02	0.37%
2020	$346.59	(4.53%)

Table 14.6 Hong Kong population data: 2011 and 2020. (GHKSAR 2011; GHKSAR 2021)

Hong Kong Population: Hong Kong Island, Kowloon, and New Territories (Mandarin pronunciation of names) totaled, broken down by their main districts	Population (2006)	Population (2011)	Population (2020)
Hong Kong Island 香港島 *(xiānggang dǎo)* **total:**	**1,268,112**	**1,270,876**	**1,224,700**
Central and Western District中西 *(zhōngxī qū)*	250,064	251,519	239,000
Wan Chai District灣仔區 *(wānzī qū)*	155,196	152,608	175,000
Eastern District東區 *(dōng qū)*	587,690	588,094	542,900
Southern District南區 *(nán qū)*	275,162	278,655	267,900
Kowloon九龍 *(jiǔlóng)* **total:**	**2,019,533**	**2,108,419**	**2,303,100**
Sham Shui Po District 深水埗區 *(shēnshuǐbù qū)*	365,540	380,855	440,500
Yau Tsim Mong District 油尖旺區 *(yóujiānwàng qū)*	280,548	307,878	326,600
Kowloon City District 九龍城區 *(jiǔlóngchéng qū)*	362,501	377,351	425,400
Wong Tai Sin 黃大仙 *(huángdà xiān)*	423,521	420,183	418,200
Kwun Tong District 觀塘區 *(guāntáng qū)*	587,423	622,152	692,400
New Territories and Islands 新界及離島 *(xīnjièjílídǎo)* **total:**	**3,573,635**	**3,691,093**	**3,952,800**
North District 北區 *(běi qū)*	280,730	304,134	318,500
Yuen Long District 元朗區 *(yuánlǎng qū)*	534,192	578,529	646,100
Taipo District 大埔區 *(dàpǔ qū)*	293,542	296,853	311,200
Tuen Mun District 屯門區 *(túnmén qū)*	502,035	487,546	503,100
Tsuen Wan District 荃灣區 *(quánwān qū)*	288,728	304,637	313,500
Sha Tin District 沙田區 *(shātián qū)*	607,544	630,273	689,300
Sai Kung District西貢區 *(xīgòng qū)*	406,442	436,627	475,500
Islands District 離島區 *(lídǎo qū)*	137,122	141,327	186,600
Kwai Tsing District 葵青區 *(kuíqīng qū)*	523,300	511,167	508,900
Total	**6,864,346**	**7,071,576**	**7,480,700**

introduction of the notorious National Security Law, Hong Kong has experienced a net outflow of its population (as of August 2021). Recording a population of 7,394,700 as of June 2021 (see Table 14.6), there has been a net loss of over 860,000 Hong Kong residents, many of these—numbering over 10,000 (Davidson 2021)—finding permanent residence in freer countries such as Taiwan (Kawase 2021).

References

Cao, Shuji, and Li Yushang. 2006. *Plague, wartime and in peace: China's environment and social movement (1230-1960)*. Shandong: Shandong Pictorial Press. 曹树基, 李玉尚. 鼠疫: 战争与和平: 中国的环境与社会变迁 (1230-1960年). 山東: 山東畫報出版社.

Carroll, John Mark. 2007. *A concise history of Hong Kong*. Lanham: Rowman and Littlefield.

Chen, Qian. 1992. *Hong Kong records of old matters, seen and heard*. Hong Kong: Central Plain Publishing. 陳謙. 香港舊事見聞錄. 香港: 中原出版社.

Davidson, Helen. 2021. Number of Hong Kong residents moving to Taiwan nearly doubles in 2020. *The Guardian*. 25 February. https://www.theguardian.com/world/2021/feb/25/number-of-hong-kong-residents-moving-to-taiwan-nearly-doubles-in-2020.

Dodwell, David. 2021. Shaky statistics, absurd quarantine rules: is Hong Kong's economy really on track for recovery? *South China Morning Post*. 13 September. https://www.scmp.com/comment/opinion/article/3148444/shaky-statistics-absurd-quarantine-rules-hong-kongs-economy-really.

Fung, Ho-lup. 2004. The 'right of abode' issue: A test case of "one country, two systems". In *"One country, two systems" in crisis: Hong Kong's transformation since the handover*, ed. Wong Yiu-chung, 97–112. Boulder: Lexington Books.

Government of the Hong Kong Special Administrative Region (GHKSAR), Census and Statistics Department. 2016. *2016 population by-census*. https://www.censtatd.gov.hk/en/data/stat_report/product/B1120098/att/B11200982016XXXXB0100.pdf.

———. 2021. *Land area, mid-year population and population density by district council district (2020)*. https://www.censtatd.gov.hk/en/EIndexbySubject.html?pcode=D5320189&scode=150.

Government of the Hong Kong Special Administrative Region (GHKSAR), Population Census Office Census and Statistics Department. 2011. *Population census: Summary report*. https://www.censtatd.gov.hk/en/data/stat_report/product/B1120055/att/B11200552011XXXXB0100.pdf.

Hall, Basil. 1828. Reviewed work(s): A voyage to the eastern seas in the year 1816; including an account of Captain Maxwell's attack on the batteries at Canton; and notes of an interview with Bonaparte at St Helena, in August, 1817 by Captain Basil Hall. *The North American Review* 26 (59): 514–538.

Harris, Paul G. 2012. *Environmental policy and sustainable development in China: Hong Kong in global context*. Bristol: The Policy Press.

Higham, Charles. 1996. *The bronze age of Southeast Asia (Cambridge World Archaeology)*. New York: Cambridge University Press.

Huang, Yiping, and Ronald Duncan. 1997. Sustainability of rapid growth: Is China the same as the former Soviet Union? In *China's economic growth and transition: Macroeconomic, environmental and social/regional dimensions*, ed. Clement Allan Tisdell and C.H. Chai, 107–136. Commack: Nova Science Publishers.

ITN News. 2021. *Hong Kong man boos China's national anthem while watching the Olympics, and is now a matter of the national security law*. 31 July. 港人看奧運噓中國國歌也涉違國安法. https://news.ltn.com.tw/news/politics/paper/1463971.

Kawase, Kenji. 2021. Hong Kong's population outflow accelerates amid crackdown. *Asia Nikkei*. 13 August. https://asia.nikkei.com/Spotlight/Hong-Kong-security-law/Hong-Kong-s-population-outflow-accelerates-amid-crackdown.

Liu, Zhipeng. 2012. *Four histories of Hong Kong Districts: Tun Men*. Hong Kong: Joint Publishing. 劉智鵬. 香港地區史研究之四:屯門.

Liu, Shuyong. 2016. *A brief history of Hong Kong*. Hong Kong: Joint Publishing. 劉蜀永. 簡明香港史.

Macrotrends. 2021. *Hong Kong GDP: 1960-2021*. https://www.macrotrends.net/countries/HKG/hong-kong/gdp-gross-domestic-product. Accessed 7 Sept 2021.

Ministry of Civil Affairs (MCA), People's Republic of China. 2020. [*County/township administration handbook*]. Beijing: China Statistics Press. 中華人民共和國民政部, 中華人民共和國, 鄉鎮行政區劃簡冊.

National People's Congress (NPC) of the People's Republic of China. 2021. http://www.npc.gov.cn/npc/c30834/202007/3ae94fae8aec4468868b32f8cf8e02ad.shtml. Accessed 31 Dec 2021.

Pang, Jesse. 2021. Jailed HK tycoon Jimmy Lai sentenced to 14 months for Oct. 1 illegal assembly. *Reuters*. 28 May 28. https://www.reuters.com/world/asia-pacific/jailed-hk-media-tycoon-jimmy-lai-faces-new-sentence-over-illegal-assembly-2021-05-28/.

Tan, Qixiang, ed. 1996. *The historical atlas of China, volume 8*. Beijing: China Cartographic Publishing House.

Zhang, Wei-Bin. 2006. *Hong Kong: The pearl made of British mastery and Chinese docile-diligence*. New York: Nova Science Publishers.

Zhou, Zifeng. 2011. *Hong Kong history in photos: Distant past to 1949*. Hong Kong: China Book Company. 周子峰. 圖解香港史: 遠古至一九四九年. 香港: 中華書局.

Chapter 15
Hubei Province

Abstract Literally referring to its location, "north of the (Dongting) lake," Hubei Province is replete with key historical events, such as the famous Battle of Red Cliffs (ca. 200 CE). Its riverine environment has also been the cause of endless suffering for its populations from constant flooding in the region. Still, access to made Wuhan City a key transportation hub, and its nearby Wuchang was the site of the 10 October 1911 Revolution that created the Republic of China, overthrowing the sclerotic Qing Dynasty. Unfortunately, Wuhan, the capital of Hubei Province, having increased its population significantly since 2010, is more widely known now because of the COVID-19 viral outbreak, which likely resulted from research activities related to bat coronaviruses at the Wuhan Institute of Virology. Overall, Hubei's population has not seen much of an increase since 2010, while its census numbers remain smaller (by about four million individuals) than its official household (*hukou*) registry. Hubei's economy has performed well in terms of gross domestic product (ranked 8th), while its per capita income was ranked 17th when compared with mainland China's 31 provinces and major cities.

E. Croddy, *China's Provinces and Populations*,
https://doi.org/10.1007/978-3-031-09165-0_15

Hubei Province (湖北省 *húběi shěng*): Abbreviation 鄂 (*è*) (Fig. 15.1)

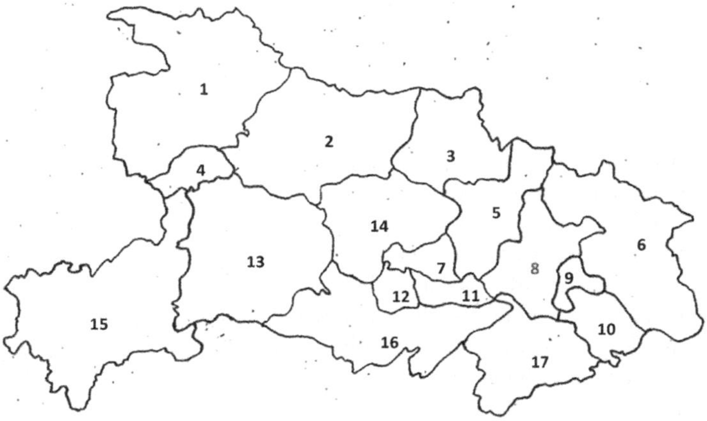

Hubei Province Population (2020)

1.	**Shiyan City**	**3,209,004**
2.	**Xiangyang City**	**5,260,951**
3.	**Suizhou City**	**2,047,923**
4.	**Shennong Jialin Forestry District**	**66,571**
5.	**Xiaogan City**	**4,270,371**
6.	**Huanggang City**	**5,882,719**
7.	**Tianmen City**	**1,158,640**
8.	**Wuhan City**	**12,326,518**
9.	**Ezhou City**	**1,079,353**
10.	**Huangshi City**	**2,469,079**
11.	**Xiantao City**	**1,134,715**
12.	**Qianjiang City**	**886,547**
13.	**Yichang City**	**4,017,607**
14.	**Jingmen City**	**2,596,927**
15.	**Enshi Tujia and Miao Autonomous Prefecture**	**3,456,136**
16.	**Jingzhou City**	**5,231,180**
17.	**Xianning City**	**2,658,316**

Fig. 15.1 Hubei Province Major City Administrations (Provincial Capital: Wuhan City). (Drawn by the author, after People's Republic of China, Ministry of Civil Affairs (MCA 2020))

Hubei Province: General Impressions

Province of a thousand lakes (千湖之省 *qiānhú zhīshěng*). (Shang-Ch'i 2017)

Hubei's capital of Wuhan is now, quite unfortunately, synonymous with the SARS-2 (SARS-CoV-2) variant. Immediately following its outbreak in Wuhan City (ca. December 2019), the virus was then renamed COVID-19 at the urging of China to avoid the negative connotations with its SARS outbreak in 2003 (Enserink 2020). Just 3 days before the start of Spring Festival (25 January 2020), the most important of China's holidays, Chinese authorities sealed off the entire city of Wuhan City (武漢市 *wǔhàn shì*), a metropolis of over 12 million people. In mid-February, the Chinese government had told the entire population of Hubei province (over fifty-seven million) to stay home unless in cases of emergency, and prohibited the use of privately-owned vehicles (BBC 2020). A global pandemic as of 2022, Chinese language media outside the People's Republic of China (PRC) have since referred to the illness as "Wuhan pneumonia (武漢肺炎 *wǔhànfèiyán*)."

Wuhan city has long had a reputation for being literally and figuratively "warm": a reputation for friendliness among its people that reaches familial proportions, and the literal heat: especially beginning in July, it is extremely hot and humid in the summer, and has been compared to being in a steam bath. No wonder it is one of the three "furnaces (火爐 *huǒlú*)" of China, the other two cities being Chongqing and Nanjing.

Reflecting its ancient origins, Hubei is also referred to using its shorthand character "E" (鄂 *è*) (see below). Hubei is named for being north of Dongting Lake (洞庭湖 *dòngtíng hú*), the second largest freshwater lake in China after Poyang Lake (鄱陽湖 *póyáng hú*).

Prehistoric Hubei

In 1970, fossils of an extinct large ape, *Gigantopithicus blacki*, estimated to have weighed around 500 kg and 3 m (nine feet) tall when standing upright, were found at the Dragon Bone Cave (龍骨洞 *lónggúdòng*) in Jianshi County (建始縣 *jiànshǐ xiàn*), Enshi Tujia and Miao Autonomous Prefecture,[1] Hubei Province. This "giant ape" (巨猿 *jùyuán*) lived about 2.6 million to 11,000 years ago. One might wonder if earlier hominids crossed paths with this "Bigfoot." As in the case of oracle bones (see also Henan Province), fossilized teeth of *Gigantopithics blacki* were sometimes found in traditional Chinese medicinal preparations. A jawbone found off Penghu islands, Taiwan, in 2008 showed shared some characteristics with *G. blacki*, but also had hominid features as well (McMenamin 2015).

[1] 恩施土家族苗族自治州 *ēnshītǔjiāzú miáozú zìzhì-zhōu*.

In 2004, during state construction of the railway running from Yichang City (宜昌市 *yíchāng shì*) to Chongqing City's Wanzhou District, (萬州區 *wànzhōu qū*), workers discovered fossils belonging to *Homo sapiens* from the Late Pleistocene, along with numerous mammalian fossils at the nearby Yangjiapo Cave (楊家坡洞 *yángjiāpōdòng*). Amongst the various fossil specimens found were monkeys, Asian Black bear, and fox, *inter alia*.

When one looks at the Yellow River region and the growth of early Chinese social structures, one finds the southernmost examples of the late Neolithic in northern Hubei province. The Qujialing Culture (屈家嶺文化 *qūjiālǐng wénhuà*; ca. 2800 BCE) is typified by findings at the site in Jingshan County (京山縣 *jīngshān xiàn*) as well as Zhongxiang City (鐘祥市 *zhōngxiáng shì*). Extending into modern-day Henan and northern Hunan, the Qujialing Culture featured its own distinctive style of ceramics (Valenstein 1989).

In 1963, evidence of a sophisticated ancient society similar to that found in Henan to the north was later determined to be an example Erligang Culture (二里崗文化 *èrlǐgāng wénhuà*). Dated 1500–1300 BCE, the Panlong Cheng (盤龍城 *pánlóng chéng*) site is located in Wuhan City's Huangpi District (黃陂區 *huángpí qū*). In addition to its classic "two layered platform" (二層臺 *èrcéng tái*) burial shaft arrangements, archeologists also discovered sacrificial pits called yaokeng (腰坑 *yāokēng*). The site also contained jade fragments of bronze-age halberd/spear (戈 *gē*) blades (Bagley 1999).

Going back to the early Zhou (1000 BCE), Hubei's Tonglushan Mountain (銅綠山 *tónglǜ shān*) Daye ("great metal foundry," 大冶 dàyě) has long been famed for its copper mining and metallurgy. Among the most spectacular finds were uncovered in 1978 at (擂鼓墩 *léigǔdūn*) in Suixian county (隨縣 *suíxiàn*), which included 65 orchestral bells, weighing a total of 4400 kilograms, that were associated with the Marquis Yi of Zeng (曾侯乙 *zēng hóuyǐ*) who lived from 477–433 BCE. (Qiu 1996).

Dynastic History

During the Western Zhou (西周 *xīzhōu*, 1046–771 BCE), the State of E (鄂國 *èguó*) flourished near today's Wuhan. By the Spring and Autumn Period (ca. 770 BCE), the State of E (pronounced "uh"), along with a number of other vying kingdoms, were swallowed up by the Chu State (楚國 *chǔguó*). The Chu soon occupied the Han River to the north and the confluence of the Dan River (Henan province) to the southwest. This stretch of area around Xichuan County (淅川縣 *xīchuān xiàn*) was the capital and the very epicenter of Chu culture. The Chu State capital later moved (ca. 700–280 BCE) to Ying (郢 *yǐng*), now Jiangling County (江陵縣 *jiānglíng xiàn*) in Jingzhou City (荊州市 *jīngzhōu shì*). During this time period, the famous statesman Qu Yuan (屈原 *qū yuán*, ca. 300 BCE), was born in the State of Chu, in today's Zigui County (秭歸縣 *zǐguī xiàn*). Qu Yuan, author of, *inter alia*, "Li Sao" ("Sorrow of Parting"離騷 *lísāo*), wrote the famous "Lament for Ying"

(哀郢 *āiyǐng*) memorializing the defeat of the capital of Chu by the Qin (278 BCE). Despondent that his prince would not heed his counsel, Qu Yuan drowned himself in the Miluo River (汨羅江 *mìluó jiāng*). Subsequently, the Dragon Boat Festival (端午節 *duānwǔ jié*) has been a ceremonial recreation of the people's frantic search for Qu Yuan's body. (Duanwu 端午 is the traditional notation for the fifth day of the fifth month in the Chinese lunar calendar). Furthermore, legend has it that commoners threw rice and other foods into the water to distract predatory fish and crabs from consuming Qu Yuan's corpse. The tradition of serving sticky rice (棕子 *zōngzi*) continues as a symbolic part of this holiday. While the life and writings of Qu Yuan are largely authentic, the popular origins of the Dragon Boat festival are improbable. More likely, this tradition had long been performed as part of an old fertility rite, and/or a summer solstice holiday to beseech rain for the growing season (Latourette 1967).

As is the case with Henan Province, Hubei is the drainage for the Changjiang (Yangtze) river, creating a large expanse of marshland (the so-called Dream Cloud Marsh "雲夢澤 *yúnmèngzé*"). It was under the unified Qin that an effort was undertaken to reclaim this marsh for agriculture. Because the previous leader of the Qin, King Zhuangxiang (秦莊襄王 *qín zhuāngxiāng wáng*; 281–247 BCE) had a personal name of Zichu (子楚 *zǐ chǔ*), the very name "Chu" (楚 *chǔ*) had become a taboo word (名諱 *mínghuì*) during this time. Thus, what had been known as Chu was renamed Jingshan, today's Nanzhang County (南漳縣 *nánzhāng xiàn*). From this point onward, what is known as Hubei today was referred to variously as Jingzhou (荊州 *jīngzhōu*) and later Jingchu (荊楚 *jīngchǔ*). The provincial name "Hubei" would not be used until the Song dynasty (ca. 1000 CE), when it became part of the Jinghu Beilu (荆湖北路 *jīnghú běilù*) administrative area, and then finally becoming Hubei Province in the Ming (ca. seventeenth century.)

In 208 CE, at the end of the Han dynasty, the warlord Cao Cao (曹操 *cáo cāo*) attacked Jingzhou (荊州 *jīngzhōu*). His opponent, Liu Bei (劉備 *liú bèi*), finding himself on the defensive, teamed up with the 27-year old military strategist Zhuge Liang (諸葛亮 *zhūgé liàng*) in modern-day Wuhan City. Ably guided by Zhuge Liang's counsel, Liu Bei was able to acquire essential allies, defeating Cao Cao at the Red Cliffs (赤壁 *chìbì*) near Puqi (蒲圻 *púqí*), now Chibi city (赤壁市). (Knechtges and Chang 2014.) Among many other depictions, the battle at Red Cliff was spectacularly depicted in Hong Kong director John Woo's (吳宇森 *wú yǔsēn*) film (2008) of the same name (赤壁 chìbì).

Starting in the Han dynasty (ca. 206 BCE – 220 CE), modern-day Hubei and Hunan were formerly known as Jiangxia Prefecture or commandery (江夏郡 *jiāngxià jùn*), ruled under a Jingzhou Prefectural Governorship (荆州刺使部 *jīngzhōu cìshǐbù*). From about 190 CE to 280 CE, the region, named E'dong (鄂東 *èdōng*), was ruled by the State of Wu (吳國 *wú guó*). Beginning with the Jin Dynasty (晉代 *jìndài*) to about 420 CE, two prefectures were established around modern Hubei: Jingzhou (荆州 *jīngzhōu*) and Yingzhou (郢州 *yǐngzhōu*). Under the Tang (ca. 733 CE), modern-day Hubei province covered Jiangnan Dongdao (江南東道 *jiāngnán dōngdào*), Huainandao (淮南道 *huáinán dào*), Shannan Dongdao (山南

東道 *shānnán dōngdào*) and Qianzhongdao (黔中道 *qiánzhōngdào*). During the Song dynasty (960–1279), Jinghu Beilu (荊湖北路 *jīnghú běilù*), later simplified to Hubei Lu (湖北路 *húběi lù*), established the name of Hubei. Later, under the Song, Hubei was governed under the Jinghu Northern Circuit (荆湖北路 *jīnghú běilù*) and Jingxi Southern Circuit (京西南路 *jīngxī nánlù*). During this period, the Hubei area flourished as a major source of agriculture, with key cash crops being cotton and tea.

The Hubei region fell into ruin with the encroach of the Jurchen Jin (金 *jīn*) and the the sacking of Kaifeng (Bianliang 汴梁 *biàn-liáng* or 汴京 *biànjīng*) in 1127 the so-called Jingkang incident (靖康事變 *jìngkāng shìbiàn*). In 1134, defending against this overwhelming offensive, the famous military hero Yue Fei (岳飛 *yuè fēi*) was put in command at Ezhou Prefecture (鄂州 *èzhōu*) in modern-day Hubei. (Mote 1999).

From 1271 to 1368, the Yuan dynasty established a Huguang Provincial Secretariat,[2] where Hanyang became a governing prefecture (漢陽府 *hànyáng fŭ*). Wuchang (武昌 *wŭchāng*) developed into a significant political, military and agricultural center for the Huguang (湖廣 *húguăng*) area. Having already suffered a serious flood in 1332, Hubei was later devastated by the bubonic plague, likely brought by invading Mongols of the Yuan. Estimates are that five million people, amounting to 90% of the population, perished in the Hubei area (Eaton 2015).

Later in the Ming, Huguang Province (湖廣省 *húguăng shĕng*) was later changed to Huguang Territorial Prefecture (湖廣布政使司 *húguăng bùzhèngshĭsī*). During this time, Hankou Town (漢口鎮 *hànkŏu zhèn*) became one of the four famous cities in China. The Hubei-based city of Macheng (麻城 *máchéng*) became famous for its erudition and scholarship. Said one contemporary Confucian in 1535,

> It is said that throughout the empire that, in terms of literary production, no province can match Hubei, no prefecture in Hubei can match Huangzhou (黃州 huángzhōu), and no county in Huangzhou can match Macheng (Rowe 2007).

In the Qing dynasty (1664), Huguang was split, creating modern-day Hubei province (湖 北省 *húběi sheng*) to its north.

Later, the mid-nineteenth century Opium Wars foisted foreign-controlled concessions at Hankou (漢口 *hànkŏu*), the major port facility in modern-day Wuhan. Now there were German, Russian, French and Japanese legations at Hankou from 1895 to 1898. Hankou eventually merged into Wuhan City. Hubei was also the site of the 10 October Wuchang Uprising (武昌起義 *wŭchāng qĭyì*), the spark that ignited the 1911 revolution. At this time, Dr. Sun Yat-sen was touring the United States (staying at the Brown Palace Hotel, Denver, Colorado), and learned of the revolution only after the fact.

[2] 湖廣等處行中書省 *húguăng dĕng chŭxíng zhōngshūshĕng*.

Building of the Three Gorges Dam (三峽大壩 *sānxiá dàbà*)

Because of flooding that has long been the source of so much human tragedy, the Yellow River (黃河 *huánghé*) truly deserved the moniker "China's Sorrow" (中國憂患 *zhōngguó yōuhuàn*). (Pietz 2015)[3] But the Yangtze (Changjiang 長江 *chángjiāng*) River (to the south) has also been the source of multiple disasters. A historical review of flood events in and around the Three Gorges (to include Hubei, Chongqing and eastern Sichuan areas) are listed in Table 15.1. As a means to finally control the Yangtze (Changjiang) River's occasional meanderings (and inundations), China undertook a massive project to build a hydroelectric dam. The largest hydroelectric generating structure in the world, at a height of 185 m and over 2300 m wide, the Three Gorges Dam project got underway at long last in 1992. Ultimately,

Table 15.1 History of Severe Flooding in the Three Gorges Region. (Zhu et al. 1997)

Date (CE)	Location (Modern day)
293	Hubei province, Zigui county (秭歸縣 *zǐguī xiàn*)
399	Hubei province, Yichang City (宜昌市 *yíchāng shì*)
441	Yangtze river banks (長江沿岸 *chángjiāng yán'àn*)
507	Yangtze river banks
520	Yangtze river banks
653	Chongqing City, Fengjie county (奉節縣 *fèngjié xiàn*)
786	Upper Yangtze river area
831	Eastern Sichuan province
836	Upper Yangtze river area
933	Chongqing City, Fengjie county[a]
968	Yangtze river banks
980	Yangtze river banks
983	Chongqing City, Fengjie county
1001	Eastern Sichuan province
1056	Chongqing City, Fengjie county
1110	Chongqing City, Fengjie county
1118	Chongqing City, Fengjie county
1153	Chongqing City, Zhongxian county (忠縣 *zhōngxiàn*)

(continued)

[3] This may have been originally used by foreign missionaries in ca. mid-nineteenth century. Other monikers such as "悲傷之河 *bēishāngzhīhé*" and "scourge of the sons of the Han" (大漢民族的苦難之源 *dàhànmínzú de kǔnánzhīyuán*) appear to be foreign, and are difficult to find in the original Chinese.

Table 15.1 (continued)

Date (CE)	Location (Modern day)
1172	Chongqing City, Fengjie county
1177	Chongqing City, Fengjie county
1188	Eastern Sichuan/Western Hubei provinces
1194–1224	Eastern Sichuan province
1290	Eastern Sichuan province; Wuhan
1294	Chongqing City, Fengjie county
1310	Hubei province, Zigui county
1332	Yangtze river banks
1349	Yangtze river banks
1371	Chongqing City, Fengjie county
1443	Chongqing City, Fengjie county
1463	Hubei province, Yichang City
1478	Chongqing City, Fengjie county
1509	Hubei province, Yichang City
1511	Chongqing City, Fengjie county
1550	Chongqing City, Wushan county (巫山縣 *wūshān xiàn*)[b]
1560	Hubei province, Zigui county
1612	Hubei province, Badong county (巴東縣 *bādōng xiàn*)
1613	Hubei province, Yichang City
1658	Chongqing City, Fengjie county
1661	Chongqing City, Fengjie county
1672	Hubei province, Badong county
1680	Chongqing City, Fengjie county
1681	Hubei province, Badong county
1700	Hubei province, Yichang City
1761	Hubei province, Yichang City
1788	Hubei province, Yichang City
1789	Hubei province, Badong county
1821	Chongqing City, Wushan county
1822	Chongqing City, Wushan county
1833	Hubei province, Zigui county
1834	Hubei province, Yichang City
1840	Hubei province, Yichang City
1849	Hubei province, Zigui county
1860	Hubei province, Zigui county
1896	Chongqing City, Fengjie county
1905	Hubei province, Yichang City
1954	Hubei province, Yichang City

[a]In the Tang dynasty, the eastern part of Fengjie was called Kuizhou (夔州 *kuízhōu*)
[b]Wushan county shares the border of northeast Hubei province

a huge lake was created behind the Three Gorges Dam, swallowing up the former governing seat of Zigui County (秭歸縣 *zǐguī xiàn*), Guizhou Town (歸州鎮 *guīzhōu zhèn*) in 2003. As a consequence, during the building of the hydroelectric dam, at least 1.3 million people were forced to relocate. In 2009, to those people who had been forced to move from the flooded areas, then Vice-Premier Li Keqiang declared that they had "made immense sacrifice for the construction of the Three Gorges project." That same year, the Three Gorges Dam was fully operational, with a generating output of 22,500 megawatts (2011). (Trouw 2014).

Hubei's Population and Economy

In 2010, Hubei had a permanent registered population (戶籍人口 *hùjí rénkǒu*) of 61,759,720, and a resident (常住人口 *chángzhù rénkǒu*) population of about 57,237,740. The population (including non-permanent, 常住人口 *chángzhù rénkǒu*) of Hubei at the end of 2015 was estimated at 58,515,000. By the 2020 census (see Tables 15.2 and 15.3), Hubei's population (57,752,557) grew just under 1%, with a *hukou* population of 61,730,000. Hubei's gross domestic product (GDP) has grown

Table 15.2 Population (常住人口 chángzhù rénkǒu) Data for Hubei Province. (HPBS 2021)

City/prefecture	Population (2010)	Population (2020)
Wuhan City 武漢市 *wǔhàn shì* [Abbrev. 漢 *hàn*]	9,785,392	12,326,518
Ezhou City 鄂州市 *èzhōu shì*	1,048,672	1,079,353
Huanggang City 黃岡市 *huánggāng shì*	6,162,072	5,882,719
Huangshi City 黃石市 *huángshí shì*	2,429,318	2,469,079
Jingmen City 荊門市 *jīngmén shì*	2,873,687	2,596,927
Jingzhou City 荊州市 *jīngzhōu shì*	5,691,707	5,231,180
Shiyan City 十堰市 *shíyàn shì*	3,340,843	3,209,004
Suizhou City 隨州市 *suízhōu shì*	2,162,222	2,047,923
Xiangyang City 襄陽市 *xiāngyang shì*	5,500,307	5,260,951
Xianning City 咸寧市 *xiánníng shì*	2,462,583	2,658,316
Xiaogan City 孝感市 *xiàogǎn shì*	4,814,542	4,270,371
Yichang City 宜昌市 *yíchāng shì*	4,059,686	4,017,607
Enshi Tujia and Miao Autonomous Prefecture 恩施土家族苗族自治州 *ēnshī tǔjiāzú miáozú zìzhìzhōu*	3,290,294	3,456,136
Tianmen City 天門市 *tiānmén shì*	1,418,913	1,158,640
Qianjiang City 潛江市 *qiánjiāng shì*	946,277	886,547
Xiantao City 仙桃市 *xiāntáo shì*	1,175,085	1,134,715
Shennongjia Forestry District 神農架林區 *shénnóngjià línqū*	76,140	66,571
Total	**57,237,740**	**57,752,557**

Table 15.3 Hubei Province: population data of cities and their subordinate sectors. (HPBS 2021)

Selected cities and subordinate sectors, population (2020 census)[a]	Subordinate district, city and county populations (2020)	Population (2020)
Wuhan City 武漢***wǔhàn shì* [Abbrev.** 漢 ***hàn*]**		**12,326,518**
Jiang'an District 江岸區 *jiāngàn qū*	965,260	
Jianghan District 江漢區 *jiānghàn qū*	647,932	
Qiaokou District 礄口區 *qiáokǒu qū*	666,661	
Hanyang District 漢陽區 *hànyáng qū*	837,263	
Wuchang District 武昌區 *wǔchāng qū*	1,092,750	
Qingshan District 青山區[b] *qīngshān qū*	463,295	
Hongshan District 洪山區 *hóngshān qū*	1,728,811	
Dongxihu District 東西湖區 *dōngxīhú qū*	845,782	
Wuhan Economic and Technology Development District[c] 武漢經濟技術開發區 *wǔhàn jīngjìjìshù kāifāqū*	481,338	
Caidian District 蔡甸區 *càidiàn qū*	554,383	
Jiangxia District 江夏區 *jiāngxià qū*	974,715	
Huangpi District 黃陂區 *huángbēi qū*	1,151,644	
Xinzhou District 新洲區 *xīnzhōu qū*	860,377	
Wuhan Donghu New Technology Development Zone 武漢東湖新技術開發區*wǔhàn dōnghú xīnjìshù kāifāqū*	935,146	
East Lake Scenic Area of Wuhan 武漢東湖風景區 *wǔhàn dōnghú fēngjǐngqū*	121,161	
Ezhou City 鄂州市 ***èzhōu shì***		**1,079,353**
Echeng District 鄂城市 *èchéng shì*	695,697	
Liangzihu District 梁子湖區*liángzǐhú qū*	126,822	
Huarong District 華容區 *huáróng qū*	256,834	
Huanggang City 黃岡市 ***huánggāng shì***		**5,882,719**
Huangzhou District 黃州區 *huángzhōu qū*	456,862	
Macheng City 麻城市 *máchéng shì*	893,654	
Wuxue City 武穴市 *wǔxué shì*	676,264	
Hong'an County 紅安縣 *hóng'ān xiàn*	510,189	
Luotian County 羅田縣 *luótián xiàn*	473,195	
Yingshan County 英山縣 *yīngshān xiàn*	310,180	
Xishui County 浠水縣 *xīshuǐ xiàn*	716,273	
Qichun County 蘄春縣 *qíchūn xiàn*	792,101	
Huangmei County[d] 黃梅縣 *huángméi xiàn*	787,783	
Tuanfeng County 團風縣 *tuánfēng xiàn*	266,218	
Huangshi City 黃石市 ***huángshí shì***		**2,469,079**
Xialu District 下陸區 *xiàlù qū*	215,181	
Huangshigang District 黃石港區 *huángshígǎng qū*	241,589	
Xisaishan District 西塞山區 *xīsāishān qū*	197,217	

(continued)

Table 15.3 (continued)

Selected cities and subordinate sectors, population (2020 census)[a]	Subordinate district, city and county populations (2020)	Population (2020)
Tieshan District 鐵山區 *tiěshān qū*	41,907	
Daye City 大冶市 *dàyě shì*	871,214	
Yangxin County 陽新縣 *yángxīn xiàn*	901,971	
Jingmen City 荊門市 ***jīngmén shì***		**2,596,927**
Dongbao District 東寶區 *dōngbǎo qū*	328,088	
Duodao District 掇刀區 *duōdāo qū*	379,602	
Zhongxiang City 鐘祥市 *zhōngxiáng shì*	868,897	
Shayang County 沙洋縣 *shāyáng xiàn*	395,717	
Jingshan City 京山市 *jīngshān shì*	492,843	
Zhanghe New District 漳河新區 *zhānghé xīnqū*	79,780	
Qujialing Management District 屈家嶺管理區 *qūjiālǐng guǎnlǐqū*	52,000	
Jingzhou City 荊州市 ***jīngzhōu shì***		**5,231,180**
Shashi District 沙市區 *shāshì qū*	504,893	
Jingzhou Economic and Technology Development Zone 荊州經濟技術開發區 *jīngzhōu jīngjìjìshù kāifāqū*	190,084	
Jingzhou District 荊州區 *jīngzhōu qū*	563,398	
Shishou City 石首市 *shíshǒu shì*	473,707	
Honghu City 洪湖市 *hónghú shì*	698,188	
Songzi City 松滋市 *sōngzī shì*	654,762	
Jiangling County 江陵縣 *jiānglíng xiàn*	278,192	
Gong'an County 公安縣 *gōng'ān xiàn*	747,134	
Jianli County 監利縣 *jiānlì xiàn*	1,120,822	
Shiyan City 十堰市 ***shíyàn shì***		**3,209,004**
Maojian District 茅箭區 *máojiàn qū*	498,594	
Zhangwan District 張灣區 *zhāngwān qū*	431,859	
Danjiangkou City[e] 丹江口市 *dānjiāngkǒu shì*	409,940	
Yunyang District 鄖陽區 *yúnyáng qū*	395,222	
Fangxian County 房縣 *fángxiàn*	369,776	
Yunxi County 鄖西縣 *yúnxī xiàn*	371,012	
Zhushan County 竹山縣 *zhúshān xiàn*	346,069	
Zhuxi County 竹溪縣 *zhúxī xiàn*	283,578	
Shiyan Economic and Technology Development Zone 十堰經濟技術開發區 *shíyàn jīngjìjìshù kāifāqū*	102,954	
Suizhou City 隨州市 ***suízhōu shì***		**2,047,923**
Zengdu District 曾都區 *zēngdū qū*	699,475	
Guangshui City 廣水市 *guǎngshuǐ shì*	710,900	
Suixian County 隨縣 *suíxiàn*	637,548	

(continued)

Table 15.3 (continued)

Selected cities and subordinate sectors, population (2020 census)[a]	Subordinate district, city and county populations (2020)	Population (2020)
Xiangyang City 襄陽市***xiāngyang shì***		**5,260,951**
Xiangcheng District 襄城區 *xiāngchéng qū*	475,611	
Fancheng District 樊城區 *fánchéng qū*	632,393	
Xiangzhou District 襄州區 *xiāngzhōu qū*	766,561	
Laohekou City 老河口市 *lǎohékǒu shì*	420,495	
Zaoyang City 棗陽市 *zǎoyáng shì*	888,794	
Yicheng City 宜城市 *yíchéng shì*	469,417	
Nanzhang County 南漳縣 *nánzhāng xiàn*	455,690	
Gucheng County 谷城縣 *gǔchéng xiàn*	483,293	
Baokang County 保康縣 *bǎokāng xiàn*	223,622	
Xiangyang High Technology Industry Development Zone 襄陽高新技術產業開發區 *xiāngyáng gāoxīnjìshù chǎnyè kāifāqū*	304,552	
Dongjin New District 東津新區 *dōngjīn xīnqū*	127,335	
Yuliang Economic Development Zone 魚梁洲經濟開發區 *yúliángzhōu jīngjìkāifāqū*	13,188	
Xianning City咸寧市***xiánníng shì***		**2,658,316**
Xian'an District 咸安區 *xiánān qū*	657,590	
Chibi City 赤壁市*chìbì shì*	470,355	
Jiayu County 嘉魚縣 *jiāyú xiàn*	285,642	
Tongcheng County 通城縣 *tōngchéng xiàn*	426,288	
Chongyang County 崇陽縣 *chóngyáng xiàn*	427,130	
Tongshan County 通山縣 *tōngshān xiàn*	391,311	
Xiaogan City 孝感市***xiàogǎn shì***		**4,270,371**
Xiaonan District[f] 孝南區 *xiàonán qū*	988,479	
Yingcheng City 應城市 *yīngchéng shì*	476,596	
Anlu City 安陸市 *ānlù shì*	498,356	
Hanchuan City 漢川市 *hànchuān shì*	903,296	
Xiaochang County[g] 孝昌縣 *xiàochāng xiàn*	483,367	
Dawu County 大悟縣 *dàwù xiàn*	486,153	
Yunmeng County 雲夢縣 *yúnmèng xiàn*	434,124	
Yichang City 宜昌市 ***yíchāng shì***		**4,017,607**
Xiling District 西陵區 *xīlíng qū*	537,686	
Wujiagang District 伍家崗區 *wǔjiāgǎng qū*	336,294	
Dianjun District 點軍區 *diǎnjūn qū*	101,649	
Xiaoting District 猇亭區 *xiāotíng qū*	68,728	
Yiling District 夷陵區 *yílíng qū*	560,383	
Zhijiang City 枝江市 *zhījiāng shì*	447,378	
Yidu City 宜都市 *yídū shì*	367,374	
Dangyang City 當陽市 *dāngyáng shì*	430,465	

(continued)

Table 15.3 (continued)

Selected cities and subordinate sectors, population (2020 census)[a]	Subordinate district, city and county populations (2020)	Population (2020)
Yuan'an County 遠安縣 *yuǎn'ān xiàn*	181,174	
Xingshan County 興山縣 *xīngshān xiàn*	153,886	
Zigui County 秭歸縣 *zǐguī xiàn*	324,642	
Changyang Tujiazu (Tujia) Autonomous County 長陽土家族自治縣 *chángyáng tǔjiāzú zìzhìxiàn*	336,294	
Wufeng Tujiazu (Tujia) Autonomous County 五峰土家族自治縣 *wǔfēng tǔjiāzú zìzhìxiàn*	171,026	
Enshi Tujia and Miao Autonomous Prefecture 恩施土家族苗族自治州 ***ēnshī tǔjiāzú miáozú zìzhìzhōu***		**3,456,136**
Enshi City 恩施市 *ēnshī shì*	836,781	
Lichuan City 利川市 *lìchuān shì*	750,670	
Jianshi County 建始縣 *jiànshǐ xiàn*	411,622	
Badong County 巴東縣 *bādōng xiàn*	395,376	
Xuan'en County 宣恩縣 *xuān'ēn xiàn*	284,955	
Xianfeng County 咸鳳縣 *xiánfèng xiàn*	318,827	
Laifeng County 來鳳縣 *láifèng xiàn*	283,255	
Hefeng County 鶴峰縣 *hèfēng xiàn*	174,650	

[a]Not all district population data available as of 14 January 2022

[b]Includes the Wuhan Chemical Industry District (武漢化學工業區 *wǔhàn huàxuégōngyè qū*), population 31,477

[c]Includes Hannan District, population 145,103

[d]Includes Longganhu with 27,855 people

[e]Includes population of the Wudang Mountain Tourism Special Economic Zone (武當山旅遊經濟特區 *wǔdāng shānlǚyóu jīngjìtèqū*)

[f]Xiaonan district population includes the high technology development zone and the airport economic zone

[g]Xiaochang population includes the Shuangfengshan travel holiday zone

dramatically since 2015 (USD $462 billion) to $676 billion by 2020, ranked eighth overall out of mainland China's 31 provinces and major cities. In 2020, Hubei's per capita income (ranked 17th) fell 1.5% to $4336 from the year prior (Zhang 2021).

Table 15.4 (below) shows the *hukou* (family registered) populations based on PRC Ministry of Civil Affairs data. (Districts listed directly under major cities are government seats, as are those in parentheses). One can compare these data with the census (usual residential populations based on 2010 and 2020 censuses in Tables 15.2 and 15.3 (above):

1. **Yunxi County**
2. **Yunyang District**
3. **Zhuxi County**
4. **Zhushan County**
5. **Fangxian County**
6. **Zhangwan District**
7. **Maojian District**
8. **Danjiangkou City**
9. **Gucheng County**
10. **Laohekou City**
11. **Xiangcheng District**
12. **Xiangcheng City**
13. **Xiangzhou District**
14. **Zaoyang City**
15. **Suixian County**
16. **Zengdu District**
17. **Guangshui City**
18. **Dawu City**
19. **Hong'an County**
20. **Shennong Jialin District**
21. **Baokang County**
22. **Nanzhang County**
23. **Xuancheng City**
24. **Zhongxiang City**
25. **Jingshan City**
26. **Anlu City**
27. **Xiaochang County**
28. Wuhan City
29. **Huangling District**
30. **Xinzhou District**
31. **Caidian District**
32. **Hannan District**
33. **Jiangxia District**
34. **Yuan'an County**
35. **Dangyang City**
36. **Dongbao District**
37. **Duodao District**
38. **Shayang County**
39. **Tianmen City**
40. **Yingcheng City**
41. **Yunmeng County**
42. **Xiaonan District**
43. **Jianshi County**
44. **Changyang Tujia Autonomous County**
45. **Dianjun District**
46. **Xiling District**
47. **Wujiagang District**
48. **Yidu City**
49. **Xiaoting District**
50. **Macheng City**
51. **Xingshan County**
52. **Badong County**
53. **Zigui County**
54. **Yiling District**
55. **Zhijiang City**
56. **Xingzhou District**
57. **Shashi District**
58. **Qianjiang City**
59. **Xiantao City**
60. **Hanchuan City**
61. **Lichuan City**
62. **Enshi City**
63. **Luotian County**
64. **Tuanfeng County**
65. **Huangzhou District**
66. **Ezhou City**
67. **Wufeng Tujia Autonomous County**
68. **Songzi City**
69. **Gongan County**
70. **Jiangling County**
71. **Huangshi City**
72. **Jianli County**
73. **Honghu City**
74. **Jiayu County**
75. **Huangshan County**
76. **Xishui County**
77. **Chibi City**
78. **Daye City**
79. **Xian'an District**
80. **Qichun County**
81. **Wuxue City**
82. **Huangmei County**
83. **Shishou City**
84. **Toncheng County**
85. **Chongyang County**
86. **Tongshan County**
87. **Yangxin County**

Fig. 15.2 Hubei Province: Subdistricts (Provincial Capital City: Wuhan City). (Drawn by the author, after People's Republic of China, Ministry of Civil Affairs (MCA 2020))

Hubei Province (鄂)

Provincial Capital: Wuhan

Table 15.4 Hubei Province: permanent registered (戶籍人口 hùjí rénkǒu) populations. (MCA 2020)

Name	Traditional	Simplified	Population (2012)	Population (2016)	Population (2020)	Area (Sq. Km)
Hubei Province	湖北省	湖北省	61,490,000	61,650,000	61,730,000	185,750
Wuhan City	武漢市	武汉市	8,350,000	8,210,000	8,840,000	8483
Jiang'an District (Siwei Subdistrict)	江岸區 (四唯街道)	江岸区 (四唯街道)	680,000	690,000	760,000	64
Jianghan District (Beihu Subdistrict)	江漢區 (北湖街道)	江汉区 (北湖街道)	480,000	480,000	510,000	33
Qiaokou District (Hanjiadun Subdistrict)	礄口區 (韓家墩街道)	硚口区 (韩家墩街道)	530,000	530,000	530,000	46
Hanyang District (Qinduankou Subdistrict)	漢陽區 (琴斷口街道)	汉阳区 (琴断口街道)	520,000	530,000	680,000	108
Wuchang District (Jiyuqiao Subdistrict)	武昌區 (積玉橋街道)	武昌区 (积玉桥街道)	1,170,000	1,140,000	1,100,000	81
Qingshan District (Xingouqiao Subdistrict)	青山區 (新溝橋街道)	青山区 (新沟桥街道)	450,000	450,000	460,000	45
Hongshan District (Luonan Subdistrict)	洪山區 (珞南街道)	洪山区 (珞南街道)	810,000	780,000	1,120,000	509
Dongxihu District (Wujiashan Subdistrict)	東西湖區 (吴家山街道)	东西湖区 (吴家山街道)	270,000	270,000	340,000	439
Hannan District (Shamao Subdistrict)	漢南區 (紗帽街道)	汉南区 (纱帽街道)	110,000	110,000	120,000	288
Caidian District (Caidian Subdistrict)	蔡甸區 (蔡甸街道)	蔡甸区 (蔡甸街道)	480,000	470,000	470,000	1094
Jiangxia District (Zhifang Subdistrict)	江夏區 (紙坊街道)	江夏区 (纸坊街道)	740,000	700,000	630,000	2015
Huangpi District (Qianchuan Subdistrict)	黃陂區 (前川街道)	黄陂区 (前川街道)	1,130,000	1,110,000	1,150,000	2261
Xinzhou District (Zhucheng Subdistrict)	新洲區 (邾城街道)	新洲区 (邾城街道)	980,000	950,000	970,000	1500

(continued)

Table 15.4 (continued)

Name	Traditional	Simplified	Population (2012)	Population (2016)	Population (2020)	Area (Sq. Km)
Shiyan City	十堰市	十堰市	3,470,000	3,470,000	3,470,000	23,698
Maojian District (Wudanglu Subdistrict)	茅箭區 (武當路街道)	茅箭区 (武当路街道)	270,000	280,000	300,000	578
Zhangwan District (Chechenglu Subdistrict)	張灣區 (車城路街道)	张湾区 (车城路街道)	260,000	260,000	260,000	652
Danjiangkou City (Junzhoulu Subdistrict)	丹江口市 (均州路街道)	丹江口市 (均州路街道)	460,000	460,000	460,000	3121
Yunyang District (Chengguan Town)	鄖陽區 (城關鎮)	郧阳区 (城关镇)	640,000	620,000	630,000	3863
Fangxian County (Chengguan Town)	房縣 (城關鎮)	房县 (城关镇)	490,000	490,000	480,000	5110
Yunxi County (Chengguan Town)	鄖西縣 (城關鎮)	郧西县 (城关镇)	510,000	520,000	520,000	3509
Zhushan County (Chengguan Town)	竹山縣 (城關鎮)	竹山县 (城关镇)	470,000	470,000	460,000	3586
Zhuxi County (Chengguan Town)	竹溪縣 (城關鎮)	竹溪县 (城关镇)	370,000	370,000	360,000	3279
Xiangyang City	襄陽市	襄阳市	5,920,000	5,940,000	5,920,000	19,626
Xiangcheng District (Zhenwushan Subdistrict)	襄城區 (真武山街道)	襄城区 (真武山街道)	460,000	460,000	460,000	645
Fancheng District (Hanjiang Subdistrict)	樊城區 (漢江街道)	樊城区 (汉江街道)	730,000	770,000	810,000	614
Xiangzhou District (Zhangwan Subdistrict)	襄州區 (張灣街道)	襄州区 (张湾街道)	1,060,000	1,030,000	1,000,000	2306
Laohekou City (Guanghua Subdistrict)	老河口市 (光化街道)	老河口市 (光化街道)	530,000	530,000	520,000	1032
Zaoyang City (Beicheng Subdistrict)	棗陽市 (北城街道)	枣阳市 (北城街道)	1,110,000	1,120,000	1,130,000	3277

(continued)

Table 15.4 (continued)

Name	Traditional	Simplified	Population (2012)	Population (2016)	Population (2020)	Area (Sq. Km)
Yicheng City (Yancheng Subdistrict)	宜城市 (鄢城街道)	宜城市 (鄢城街道)	570,000	570,000	560,000	2115
Nanzhang County (Chengguan Town)	南漳縣 (城關鎮)	南漳县 (城关镇)	590,000	590,000	570,000	3859
Gucheng County (Chengguan Town)	谷城縣 (城關鎮)	谷城县 (城关镇)	590,000	590,000	600,000	2553
Baokang County (Chengguan Town)	保康縣 (城關鎮)	保康县 (城关镇)	280,000	280,000	270,000	3225
Jingmen City	荊門市	荆门市	3,000,000	3,030,000	2,930,000	12,100
Dongbao District (Quankou Subdistrict)	東寶區 (泉口街道)	东宝区 (泉口街道)	380,000	380,000	360,000	1645
Duodao District (Duodaoshi Subdistrict)	掇刀區 (掇刀街道)	掇刀区 (掇刀石街道)	340,000	330,000	300,000	639
Zhongxiang City (Yingzhong Subdistrict)	鐘祥市 (郢中街道)	钟祥市 (郢中街道)	1,040,000	1,080,000	1,050,000	4488
Shayang County (Shayang Town)	沙洋縣 (沙洋鎮)	沙洋县 (沙洋镇)	590,000	590,000	600,000	2044
Jingshan City (Xinshi Town)	京山市 (新市鎮)	京山市 (新市镇)	650,000	650,000	630,000	3284
Xiaogan City	孝感市	孝感市	5,320,000	5,270,000	5,180,000	8941
Xiaonan District (Shuyuan Subdistrict)	孝南區 (書院街道)	孝南区 (书院街道)	960,000	960,000	960,000	1020
Yingcheng City (Chengzhong Subdistrict)	應城市 (城中街道)	应城市 (城中街道)	680,000	670,000	650,000	1103
Anlu City (Fucheng Subdistrict)	安陸市 (府城街道)	安陆市 (府城街道)	640,000	630,000	620,000	1355
Hanchuan City (Xiannüshan Subdistrict)	漢川市 (仙女山街道)	汉川市 (仙女山街道)	1,130,000	1,120,000	1,080,000	1663
Xiaochang County (Huayuan Town)	孝昌縣 (花園鎮)	孝昌县 (花园镇)	670,000	670,000	670,000	1217
Dawu County (Chengguan Town)	大悟縣 (城關鎮)	大悟县 (城关镇)	650,000	640,000	630,000	1979

(continued)

Table 15.4 (continued)

Name	Traditional	Simplified	Population (2012)	Population (2016)	Population (2020)	Area (Sq. Km)
Yunmeng County (Chengguan Town)	雲夢縣 (城關鎮)	云梦县 (城关镇)	590,000	580,000	580,000	604
Huanggang City	黃岡市	**黄冈**市	7,420,000	7,490,000	7,410,000	17,453
Huangzhou District (Chibi Subdistrict)	黃州區 (赤壁街道)	黄州区 (赤壁街道)	370,000	360,000	350,000	353
Macheng City (Longchiqiao Subdistrict)	麻城市 (龍池橋街道)	麻城市 (龙池桥街道)	1,150,000	1,170,000	1,160,000	3599
Wuxue City (Wuxue Subdistrict)	武穴市 (武穴街道)	武穴市 (武穴街道)	770,000	800,000	820,000	1246
Hong'an County (Chengguan Town)	紅安縣 (城關鎮)	红安县 (城关镇)	660,000	660,000	650,000	1796
Luotian County (Fengshan Town)	羅田縣 (鳳山鎮)	罗田县 (凤山镇)	610,000	600,000	600,000	2129
Yingshan County (Wenquan Town)	英山縣 (溫泉鎮)	英山县 (温泉镇)	400,000	400,000	400,000	1449
Xishui County (Qingquan Town)	浠水縣 (清泉鎮)	浠水县 (清泉镇)	1,040,000	1,030,000	1,010,000	1949
Qichun County (Caohe Town)	蘄春縣 (漕河鎮)	蕲春县 (漕河镇)	1,020,000	1,030,000	1,010,000	2398
Huangmei County (Huangmei Town)	黃梅縣 (黃梅鎮)	黄梅县 (黄梅镇)	1,020,000	1,060,000	1,040,000	1701
Tuanfeng County (Tuanfeng Town)	團風縣 (團風鎮)	团风县 (团风镇)	380,000	380,000	370,000	833
Ezhou City	鄂州市	鄂州市	1,080,000	1,100,000	1,110,000	1505
Echeng District (Fenghuang Subdistrict)	鄂城市 (鳳凰街道)	鄂城区 (凤凰街道)	650,000	650,000	660,000	520
Liangzihu District (Taihe Town)	梁子湖區 (太和鎮)	梁子湖区 (太和镇)	180,000	190,000	190,000	525
Huarong District (Huarong Town)	華容區 (華容鎮)	华容区 (华容镇)	250,000	260,000	270,000	460
Huangshi City	黃石市	黄石市	2,590,000	2,610,000	2,730,000	4576
Xialu District (Xinxing Community)	下陸區 (新星社區)	下陆区 (新星社区)	150,000	150,000	160,000	69
Huangshigang District (Guihuawan Community)	黃石港區 (桂花灣社區)	黄石港区 (桂花湾社区)	200,000	200,000	210,000	30

(continued)

Table 15.4 (continued)

Name	Traditional	Simplified	Population (2012)	Population (2016)	Population (2020)	Area (Sq. Km)
Xisaishan District (Linjiang Community)	西塞山區 (臨江社區)	西塞山区 (临江社区)	220,000	230,000	210,000	100
Tieshan District (Sanchalu Community)	鐵山區 (三岔路社區)	铁山区 (三岔路社区)	60,000	50,000	50,000	28
Daye City (Dongyuelu Subdistrict)	大冶市 (東岳路街道)	大冶市 (东岳路街道)	940,000	950,000	1,000,000	1566
Yangxin County (Xingguo Town)	陽新縣 (興國鎮)	阳新县 (兴国镇)	1,020,000	1,030,000	1,110,000	2783
Xianning City	咸寧市	咸宁市	2,920,000	2,990,000	3,050,000	10,019
Xian'an District (Fushan Subdistrict)	咸安區 (浮山街道)	咸安区 (浮山街道)	600,000	620,000	630,000	1502
Chibi City (Chimagang Subdistrict)	赤壁市 (赤馬港街道)	赤壁市 (赤马港街道)	520,000	530,000	530,000	1723
Jiayu County (Yuyue Town)	嘉魚縣 (魚岳鎮)	嘉鱼县 (鱼岳镇)	370,000	370,000	370,000	1017
Tongcheng County (Junshui Town)	通城縣 (雋水鎮)	通城县 (隽水镇)	490,000	500,000	530,000	1,129
Chongyang County (Tiancheng Town)	崇陽縣 (天城鎮)	崇阳县 (天城镇)	470,000	490,000	510,000	1968
Tongshan County (Tongyang Town)	通山縣 (通羊鎮)	通山县 (通羊镇)	470,000	480,000	490,000	2680
Jingzhou City	荊州市	荆州市	6,590,000	6,630,000	6,410,000	14,104
Shashi District (Zhongshanlu Subdistrict)	沙市區 (中山路街道)	沙市区 (中山路街道)	550,000	550,000	530,000	469
Jingzhou District (Xicheng Subdistrict)	荊州區 (西城街道)	荆州区 (西城街道)	580,000	580,000	550,000	1046
Shishou City (Xiulin Subdistrict)	石首市 (繡林街道)	石首市 (绣林街道)	670,000	670,000	620,000	1427
Honghu City (Xindi Subdistrict)	洪湖市 (新堤街道)	洪湖市 (新堤街道)	940,000	940,000	920,000	2519
Songzi City (Xinjiangkou Town)	松滋市 (新江口鎮)	松滋市 (新江口镇)	850,000	850,000	830,000	2235
Jiangling County (Haoxue Town)	江陵縣 (郝穴鎮)	江陵县 (郝穴镇)	410,000	420,000	390,000	1032

(continued)

Table 15.4 (continued)

Name	Traditional	Simplified	Population (2012)	Population (2016)	Population (2020)	Area (Sq. Km)
Gong'an County (Douhudi Town)	公安縣 (斗湖堤鎮)	公安县 (斗湖堤镇)	1,050,000	1,060,000	1,000,000	2258
Jianli County (Rongcheng Town)	監利縣 (容城鎮)	监利县 (容城镇)	1,540,000	1,560,000	1,570,000	3118
Yichang City	宜昌市	宜昌市	3,990,000	3,980,000	3,920,000	21,081
Xiling District (Xiling Subdistrict)	西陵區 (西陵街道)	西陵区 (西陵街道)	420,000	420,000	410,000	90
Wujiagang District (Wujiagang Subdistrict)	伍家崗區 (伍家崗街道)	伍家岗区 (伍家岗街道)	150,000	160,000	190,000	69
Dianjun District (Dianjun Subdistrict)	點軍區 (點軍街道)	点军区 (点军街道)	110,000	100,000	100,000	546
Xiaoting District (Gulaobei Subdistrict)	猇亭區 (古老背街道)	猇亭区 (古老背街道)	50,000	50,000	50,000	118
Yiling District (Xiaoxita Subdistrict)	夷陵區 (小溪塔街道)	夷陵区 (小溪塔街道)	520,000	520,000	520,000	3424
Zhijiang City (Majiadian Subdistrict)	枝江市 (馬家店街道)	枝江市 (马家店街道)	500,000	490,000	480,000	1310
Yidu City (Lucheng Subdistrict)	宜都市 (陸城街道)	宜都市 (陆城街道)	390,000	400,000	390,000	1,357
Dangyang City (Yuyang Subdistrict)	當陽市 (玉陽街道)	当阳市 (玉阳街道)	480,000	490,000	470,000	2159
Yuan'an County (Mingfeng Town)	遠安縣 (鳴鳳鎮)	远安县 (鸣凤镇)	190,000	190,000	190,000	1752
Xingshan County (Gufu Town)	興山縣 (古夫鎮)	兴山县 (古夫镇)	180,000	170,000	170,000	2327
Zigui County (Maoping Town)	秭歸縣 (茅坪鎮)	秭归县 (茅坪镇)	380,000	380,000	370,000	2427
Changyang Tujiazu (Tujia) Autonomous County (Longdanping Town)	長陽土家族自治縣 (龍丹坪鎮)	长阳土家族自治县 (龙舟坪镇)	410,000	410,000	390,000	3430

(continued)

Table 15.4 (continued)

Name	Traditional	Simplified	Population (2012)	Population (2016)	Population (2020)	Area (Sq. Km)
Wufeng Tujiazu (Tujia) Autonomous County (Yuyangguan Town)	五峰土家族自治縣 (漁洋關鎮)	五峰土家族自治县 (渔洋关镇)	210,000	200,000	200,000	2072
Suizhou City	隨州市	**随**州市	2,560,000	2,570,000	2,510,000	9636
Zengdu District (Xicheng Subdistrict)	曾都區 (西城街道)	曾都区 (西城街道)	640,000	640,000	660,000	1379
Guangshui City (Yingshan Subdistrict)	廣水市 (應山街道)	广水市 (应山街道)	940,000	950,000	920,000	2647
Suixian County (Lishan Town)	隨縣 (厲山鎮)	随县 (厉山镇)	980,000	980,000	930,000	5610
(County-level administrative unit under direct provincial jurisdiction)	省直轄縣級行政單位	省直**辖县级**行政**单**位				
Xiantao City (Shazui Subdistrict)	仙桃市 (沙嘴街道)	仙桃市 (沙嘴街道)	1,530,000	1,550,000	1,540,000	2538
Tianmen City (Jingling Subdistrict)	天門市 (竟陵街道)	天门市 (竟陵街道)	1,670,000	1,670,000	1,610,000	2622
Qianjiang City (Yuanlin Subdistrict)	潛江市 (園林街道)	潜江市 (园林街道)	1,020,000	1,030,000	1,010,000	2004
Shennongjia Forestry District (Songbai Town)	神農架林區 (松柏鎮)	神农架林区 (松柏镇)	80,000	80,000	80,000	3253
Enshi Tujiazu Miaozu (Tujia and Miao) Autonomous prefecture	恩施土家族苗族自治州	恩施土家族苗族自治州	3,980,000	4,040,000	4,020,000	24,111
Enshi City (Xiaoduchuan Subdistrict)	恩施市 (小渡船街道)	恩施市 (小渡船街道)	800,000	810,000	810,000	3972
Lichuan City (Duting Subdistrict)	利川市 (都亭街道)	利川市 (都亭街道)	900,000	920,000	920,000	4603
Jianshi County (Yezhou Town)	建始縣 (業州鎮)	建始县 (业州镇)	510,000	510,000	510,000	2666

(continued)

Table 15.4 (continued)

Name	Traditional	Simplified	Population (2012)	Population (2016)	Population (2020)	Area (Sq. Km)
Badong County (Xinling Town)	巴東縣 (信陵鎮)	巴东县 (信陵镇)	490,000	500,000	490,000	3354
Xuan'en County (Zhushan Town)	宣恩縣 (珠山鎮)	宣恩县 (珠山镇)	360,000	360,000	360,000	2730
Xianfeng County (Gaoleshan Town)	咸鳳縣 (高樂山鎮)	咸丰县 (高乐山镇)	380,000	390,000	390,000	2550
Laifeng County (Xiangfeng Town)	來鳳縣 (翔鳳鎮)	来凤县 (翔凤镇)	320,000	330,000	330,000	1344
Hefeng County (Rongmei Town)	鶴峰縣 (容美鎮)	鹤峰县 (容美镇)	220,000	220,000	220,000	2892

References

Bagley, Robert. 1999. Shang archaeology. In *The Cambridge history of ancient China: From the origins of civilization to 221 B.C*, ed. Michael Loewe and Edward L. Shaughnessy, 124–231. New York: Cambridge University Press.

BBC News. 2020. *Coronavirus: China enacts tighter restrictions in Hubei*. 16 February. https://www.bbc.com/news/world-asia-china-51523835

Eaton, Gale. 2015. *A history of civilization in 50 disasters*. Maine: Tilbury House Publishers.

Enserink, Martin. 2020. Update: 'a bit chaotic.' Christening of new coronavirus and its disease name create confusion. *Science*, 12 February. https://www.sciencemag.org/news/2020/02/bit-chaotic-christening-new-coronavirus-and-its-disease-name-create-confusion. https://doi.org/10.1126/science.abb2806.

Hubei Province Bureau of Statistics (HPBS 2021). 2021. [Communiqué of the seventh national population census of Hubei Province, issue no. 2]. 湖北省第七次全国人口普查公报(第二号). 25 May. http://tjj.hubei.gov.cn/tjsj/tjgb/pcgb/qrp/202105/t20210525_3559343.shtml

Knechtges, David R., and Taiping Chang. 2014. *Ancient and early medieval Chinese literature: A reference guide, part III*. Boston: Brill.

Latourette, Kenneth Scott. 1967. *The Chinese: Their history and culture*. New York: The Macmillan Company.

McMenamin, Mark A.S. 2015. *Homo tsaichangensis and Gigantopithecus*. South Hadley: Meanma Press.

Ministry of Civil Affairs (MCA), People's Republic of China. 2020. *County/township administration handbook*. Beijing: China Statistics Press. 中華人民共和國民政部, 中華人民共和國,鄉鎮行政區劃簡冊.

Mote, Frederick W. 1999. *Imperial China 900–1800*. Harvard: Harvard University Press.

Pietz, David A. 2015. *The Yellow River: The problem of water in modern China*. Harvard: Harvard University Press.

Qiu, Lianghui. 1996. Metallurgical technology in ancient China. In *Chinese studies in the history and philosophy of science and technology*, ed. Fan Dainian and Robert S. Cohen, 219–241. Boston: Kluwer Academic Publishers.

Rowe, William T. 2007. *Crimson rain: Seven centuries of violence in a Chinese county*. Stanford: Stanford University Press.

Shang-Ch'i, Guide. 2017. *Backpacking in China: The most complete collection of self-guided travel for China, 2018*. Taipei: Shang-Ch'i Shitai Publishing. 2018 最完整的中國自助旅遊全集. 台北: 上奇時代.

Trouw, Jan. 2014. *The Three Gorges Dam's impact on peasant livelihood: China's project on the Yangtze River*. Norderstedt: Herstellung und Verlag Books on Demand.

Valenstein, Suzanne G. 1989. *A handbook of Chinese ceramics*. New York: Metropolitan Museum of New York.

Zhang, Shunan. 2021. *The 2020 per capita income list of residents in various provinces: Shanghai is the richest, and it has risen sharply*. Finance.people.com. 22 January. 张澍楠. 2020年各省份居民人均收入榜: 上海最有钱, 这地涨得猛. http://finance.people.com.cn/n1/2021/0122/c1004-32008733.html.

Zhu, Cheng, Yu Shiyong, and Lu Chuncheng. 1997. Holocene environmental archaeology and abnormal flood disasters in the Three Gorges of the Yangtze River and Jianghan Plain. *Acta Geographica Sinica*. 朱诚, 于世永, 卢春成. 长江三峡及江汉平原地区全新世环境考古与异常洪涝灾害研究. 地理学报 52(3): 272–275.

Chapter 16
Hunan Province

Abstract On the other side of Hubei, to the south of Dongting lake, is Hunan Province, thus its name "south of the lake" that goes back to the Tang dynasty. Humans have inhabited Hunan going back 18,000 years, and have also been cultivating rice there for some 10,000 years. Often associated with its spicy cuisine, Hunanese cooking has heavily relied upon a relatively recent import from the New World, the chili pepper. Hunan is also home to Mao Zedong, the most consequential ruler of China since Qin Shihuangdi. It was also in Hunan where a significant player, Marshal Peng Dehuai, discovered firsthand the ravages of Mao's disastrous Great Leap Forward (1958–62), and his criticism of Mao Zedong that followed was the proximal cause of the Cultural Revolution (1966–76). Being somewhat remote from the more economically vibrant regions along the southeastern coast, it is for this reason that a significant number of China's "floating populations" from Hunan spend much (if not all) of their lives working and living outside Hunan province. One can infer this based on the discrepancy in numbers between Hubei's census figures and its official household (*hukou*) registered persons.

E. Croddy, *China's Provinces and Populations*,
https://doi.org/10.1007/978-3-031-09165-0_16

Hunan Province (湖南省 *húnán shěng*): Abbreviation 湘 (*xiāng*) (Fig. 16.1)

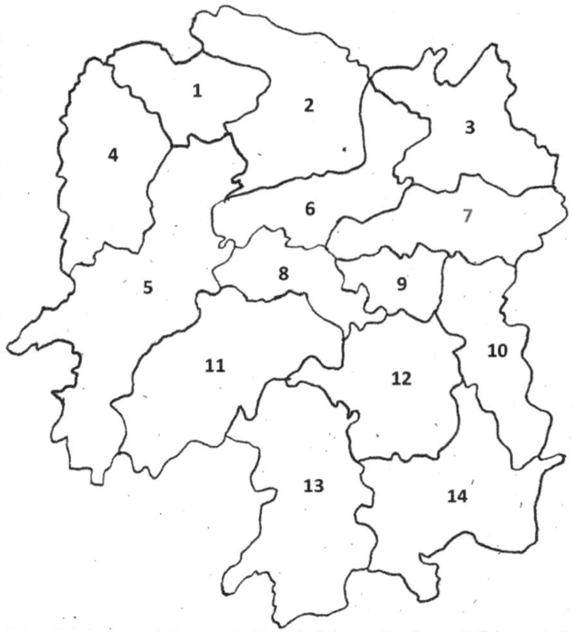

	Hunan Province Population (2020)
1. Zhangjiajie City	1,517,027
2. Changde City	5,279,102
3. Yueyang City	5,051,922
4. Xiangxi Tujia and Miao Autonomous Prefecture	2,488,105
5. Huaihua City	4,587,594
6. Yiyang City	3,851,564
7. Changsha City	10,047,914
8. Loudi City	3,826,996
9. Xiangtan City	2,726,181
10. Zhuzhou City	3,902,738
11. Shaoyang City	6,563,520
12. Hengyang City	6,645,243
13. Yongzhou City	5,289,824
14. Chenzhou City	4,667,134

Fig. 16.1 Hunan province major cities (Provincial Capital: Changsha City). (Drawn by the author, after People's Republic of China, Ministry of Civil Affairs (MCA 2020))

Hunan Province: General Impressions

Just as Hubei is named for its northern location being above a large body of water, Hunan Province (湖南省 *húnán shěng*) derives from being south of Dongting Lake (洞庭湖 *dòngtíng hú*). The shorthand character, 湘 (*xiāng*), is based on the Xiang River that traverses Hunan. In its earlier history, mostly non-Han peoples inhabited Hunan, and many of China's ethnic minorities are represented in the province's autonomous counties and prefectures:

- The Yao (瑶族 *yáozú*), e.g., Jianghua Yao Autonomous County (江華瑤族自治縣 *jiānghuá yáozú zìzhì-xiàn*);
- The Dong (侗族 *dòngzú*), e.g., Xinhuang Dong Autonomous County (新晃侗族自治縣 *xīnhuǎng dòngzú zzhìxiàn*); Tujia (土家族 *tǔjiāzú*) and
- Miao (苗族 *miáozú*), e.g., Enshi Tujia and Miao Autonomous Prefecture (恩施土家族苗族自治州 *ēnshī tǔjiāzú miáozú zìzhìzhōu*)

The birthplace of Mao Zedong (Shaoshan city 韶山市 *sháoshān shì*) and his communist movement, Hunan is also well known for its spicy cuisine. Hunan (especially in the capital of Changsha city) is considered the home of stinky tofu (臭豆腐 *chòu dòufǔ*), a delicacy enjoyed throughout Southeast China and especially in Taiwan.

Prehistoric Rice Farming

Evidence of some of the oldest known rice cultivation in the world was found in Hunan province. Specimens of rice were unearthed in the Yuchanyan cave (玉蟾岩 *yùchányán*; commonly known as Gemadong: 蛤蟆洞 *gémádòng*), located in Shouyan Town (壽雁鎮 *shòuyàn zhèn*), Daoxian County (道縣 *dàoxiàn*). These samples were dated to ca. 8000 BCE. Human occupation has also been dated at Yuchanyan even earlier, as far back as 18,000 years ago (Bar-Yosef 2012).

Excavations at the Bashidang site (八十壋遺址 *bāshí dàngyízhǐ*) in Lixian County (澧縣 *lǐxiàn*) showed evidence of ancient rice cultivation. A sample of 782 grains found there was determined to be 8000 years old (Zhao et al. 2000). Fossils of rice found at the Pengtoushan Mountain (彭頭山 *péngtóushān*) site, also located within Lixian County were originally sewn in ca. 7000 BCE. Intricately designed pottery from the Gaomiao Culture (高廟文化 *gāomiào wénhuà*, ca. 5800–4800 BCE), has been found in Anjiang Town, Hongjiang City (洪江市安江鎮 *hóngjiāng shì, ānjiāng zhèn*). In addition, coincident with the Tangjiagang Culture (湯家崗文化 *tāngjiāgāng wénhuà*), rice fields dated from about 4500 BCE were discovered at Chengtoushan Mountain (城頭山 *chéngtóushān*), Lixian County (Wilkinson 2012).

Hunan: Ancient to Modern

During the Western Zhou (西周 *xīzhōu* 1046–771 BCE), a region known as "Yangyue" (揚越 *yángyuè*) roughly described the area around modern day Hunan Province, which also included modern-day Changsha (長沙 *chángshā*). This region was populated by the so-called "One hundred Yue" (百越 *bǎiyuè*) people and the "One hundred Pu" (百濮 *bǎipú*) clans. The most famous Chinese historian, Sima Qian (ca. 100 BCE 司馬遷 *sīmǎ qiān*), referred to the "Yangyue" when describing the southern part of China. In his section that cites the historical figure, Kong Anguo (孔安國 *kǒng ānguó*), Sima Qian notes that the "Pu (濮) are south of the Jianghan (tributary of the Changjiang) river (Chen 1999)."[1] Before the unification of the Qin Dynasty (秦 *qín*; 221 BCE), Hunan was part of the State of Chu (楚國 *chǔ guó*), its border formed by Jingzhou (荊州 *jīngzhōu*) to the north, Qianzhong Prefecture (黔中郡 *qiánzhōng jùn*) on the east, and Changsha Prefecture (長沙郡 *chángshā jùn*) to its west.

In the time of Emperor Wu of the Han (漢武帝 *hànwǔ dì*; d. 87 BCE), a Jingzhou Prefectural Governorship (荆州刺使部 *jīngzhōu cìshǐbù*) extended across both modern-day Hunan and Hubei provinces. Under its jurisdiction were the State of Changsha (長沙國 *chángshā guó*) in 202 BCE, as well as Wuling (武陵郡 *wǔlíng jùn*), Guiyang (桂陽郡 *guìyáng jùn*), and Lingling (零陵郡 *línglíng jùn*) prefectures. The geography of the State of Changsha closely resembles Hunan's provincial borders of today (Tan 1996).

*Lady Xin Zhui (*辛追 **xīn zhuī***)*

Discovered in 1971 during construction of a hospital near Changsha City, the Mawangdui (馬王堆 *mǎwángduī*) Tombs from the Western Han (206 BCE–24 CE) include some of the most fascinating archeological specimens in all of China. For buried inside was Xin Zhui (辛追 *xīn zhuī*), the wife of Li Cang (利蒼 *lì cāng*), the Marquis of Dai. Amazingly, Lady Xin Zhui's body was found to have been fairly well preserved (or, less charitably, pickled) for some 2200 years:

On 14 December 1972, a team of physicians carried out a necropsy on Xin Zhui, estimated to have been 50 years of age at the time of her death, just over 5 feet in height, and weighing approximately 150 pounds. She was blood type A. Manifesting the resiliency of the human body, the necropsy revealed Xin Zhui had lived with a number of health issues that are typical of humans in more modern times: atherosclerosis, gallstones, tuberculosis, at least three different parasites, spinal disc degeneration, and heavy metal poisoning (lead and mercury). They also found nearly 140 musk melon seeds still undigested in her esophagus and belly. Her corpse still had relatively supple flesh and some flexibility in her limbs. The air-tight

[1] 濮在江漢之南 *púzàijiānghàn zhīnán*.

sepulcher, charcoal-coated coffin, and, critically, the alcohol mixture used to embalm her all contributed to her preservation. In addition, there was also a low pH (high acidity) solution in her coffin that helped retard bacterial growth (Liu-Perkins 2014).

Post-Han Dynasty Hunan Province

During the Western Han, modern-day Hunan was part of Jingzhou Prefecture (荊州 *jīngzhōu*). As of 262 CE, this region encroached upon modern-day Guizhou, Guangxi, Guangdong, and Hubei provinces. Jingzhou remained largely the same in the Western Jin (281 CE), but increased the number of its subordinate prefectures. These also included those districts located south of Dongting Lake (each old prefecture name is followed by modern equivalent, wherever applicable):

- Tianmen Prefecture (天門郡 *tiānmén jùn*; Tianmen city (天門市 *tiānmén shì*)
- Nanping Prefecture (南平郡 *nánpíng jùn*); Changsha (長沙郡 *chángshā*)
- Hengyang Prefecture (衡陽郡 *héngyáng jùn*; Hengyang City 衡陽市 *héngyáng shì*)
- Wuling Prefecture (武陵郡 *wǔlíng jùn*; Wuling District (武陵區 *wǔlíng qū*)
- Shaoling Prefecture (邵陵郡 *shàolíng jùn*)
- Xiangdong Prefecture (湘東郡 *xiāngdōng jùn*)
- Lingling Prefecture (零陵郡 *línglíng jùn*; Lingling District 零陵區 *línglíng qū*) and
- Guiyang Prefecture (桂陽郡 *guìyáng jùn*); Guiyang County (桂陽縣 *guìyáng xiàn*)

This geopolitical arrangement continued under the Sui dynasty, which brought these prefectures (ca. 612) into a Jiang-Han-Yuan-Xiang grouping (江漢沅湘 *jiānghànyuánxiāng*), named after the main rivers that feed into Dongting lake: Changjiang (Yangtze), Hanjiang, Yuanjiang, and Xiangjiang. In 741, under the Tang dynasty, Jiangnan Xidao (江南西道 *jiāngnán xīdào*) included much of this same area, but now many of its prefectures were renamed "zhou" (州 *zhōu*):

- Lizhou (澧州 *lǐzhōu*)
- Hongzhou (洪州 *hóngzhōu*)
- Hengzhou (衡州 *héngzhōu*)
- Chenzhou (郴州 *chēnzhōu*)
- Daozhou (道州 *dàozhōu*)
- Tanzhou (潭州 *tánzhōu*) and
- Yuanzhou (袁州 *yuánzhōu*)

One finds some of these names still today in Hunan province, e.g.,

- Lixian County (澧縣 *lǐxiàn*)
- Hengyang City (衡陽市 *héngyáng shì*)
- Chenzhou City (郴州市 *chēnzhōu shì*)
- Daoxian Countyu (道縣 *dàoxiàn*), among others

Hunan During the Tang Dynasty

The Tang dynasty was challenged on many fronts, as it faced the An Lushan rebellion (755 CE; also known as the Anshi Chaos (安史之亂 *ānshǐ zhī luàn*) from within, military conflict with the Tibetans, and violent encounters with Uyghurs to the west. Facing such challenges, in 763, the Tang essentially militarized the empire, raising up to 750,000 men-in-arms, and created a new provincial administrative system. Provincial leaders essentially became military despots, and the imperial court allowed them substantive autonomy (Benn 2002). In 764, Hunan Dao (湖南道 *húnán dào*) first appeared as a name for the region. The full name for this military administrative governorship was, however, the Hunan Capital, Militia Surveillance and Supervisory Commissioner,[2] simplified to Hunan Supervisory Commissioner, Hunan Guanchashi (湖南觀察使 *húnán guāncháshǐ*). A governorship based in Hengzhou (衡州 *héngzhōu*) was in charge of five prefectural states, namely

- Tanzhou (潭州 *tánzhōu*)
- Shaozhou (邵州 *shàozhōu*)
- Yongzhou (永州 *yǒngzhōu*), and
- Daozhou (道州 *dàozhōu*)

In 769, the central leadership of this region moved to Zhijiang (治江州 *zhìjiāng zhōu*), in modern-day Jiangxi Province (江西省 *jiāngxī shěng*), Jiujiang City (九江市 *jiǔjiāng shì*). In 885, the authority of the Hunan Supervisory Commissioner was raised to that of a formal military governorship (Wu 1994). During the period of the Five Dynasties and Ten Kingdoms (907–960), and after the capture of Hunan by the warlord Ma Yin (馬殷 *mǎ yīn*), a State of Chu was established that included Hunan Province of today, making Changsha Prefecture (長沙府 *chángshā fǔ*) its capital.

In the Northern Song era, the Hunan region of today was drawn within the borders of the Jinghu Southern Circuit (荊湖南路 *jīnghú nánlù*) and Jinghu Northern Circuit (荊湖北路 *jīnghú běilù*). Developing rapidly during this time, this region had a population (see Table 16.1) of some 2,612,300 near the end of the Northern Song (1102). The Mongol Yuan Dynasty (ca. 1300) maintained a provincial capital at Wuhan, Hubei province, under the Huguang Provincial Secretariat,[3] with a Hunan Pacification Commission (宣慰司 *xuānwèisī*) based in Hengzhou.

---

[2] 湖南都團練守捉觀察處置使 *húnándū tuánliàn shǒuzhuō guānchá chǔzhì shǐ.*

[3] 湖廣等處行中書省 *húguǎngděng chùxíngzhōng shūshěng.*

Table 16.1 Hunan Province Population Data. (Population Journal 1999)

Year (CE)	Population, Hunan Area
2	717,400
811	420,000
963	500,000
1102	2,612,300
1816	18,754,259
1840	19,891,000
1949	29,868,300
1953	33,226,954
1964	37,182,286
1982	54,008,851
1990	60,659,754
2000	63,274,173
2010	65,683,722
2020	66,444,864

Hunan Province During the Qing

In 1820, Hunan was divided into various prefectural governorships (zhou 州 and fu 府), some with by now quite familiar names:

- Lizhou (澧州 *lǐzhōu*)
- Yongshun (永順府 *yǒngshùnfǔ*)
- Yuezhou (岳州府 *yuèzhōufǔ*)
- Changde (長德府 *chángdéfǔ*)
- Chenzhou (辰州府 *chénzhōufǔ*)
- Hengzhou (衡州府 *héngzhōufǔ*)
- Yuanzhou (沅州府 *yuánzhōufǔ*)
- Changsha (長沙府 *chángshāfǔ*)
- Baoqing (寶慶府 *bǎoqìng fǔ*)
- Jingzhou (靖州 *jìngzhōu*)
- Guiyang (桂陽州 *guìyáng zhōu*) and
- Chenzhou (郴州 *chēnzhōu*)

Meanwhile, smaller regional prefectural entities were called Ting (廳 tīng), and were grouped along the Sichuan and Guizhou borders to the west:

- Yongsui (永綏廳 *yǒngsuī tīng*)
- Qianzhou (乾州廳 *qiánzhōu tīng*), and
- Fenghuang (鳳凰廳 *fènghuáng tīng*)

The Hunan Military Tradition

The old Chinese saying that "without Hunan, China would have no army" (無湘不成軍 *wúxiāng bùchéngjūn*) came about because, throughout its history, a significant number of China's military officers have been Hunanese. This remained true even after founding of the People's Republic of China (1949). For example, Zeng Guofan (曾國藩 *zēng guófán*), born in modern-day Xiangxiang city (湘鄉市 *xiāngxiāng shì*), famously organized the Xiang (Hunan) Army (湘軍 *xiāngjūn*) when leading the campaigns to suppress the Taiping Rebellion (1850–1864).

Hunan: Reform and Revolution

In 1898, the Hunan provincial governorship distinguished itself as an enthusiastic supporter of the so-called "Hundred Days Reform" movement (戊戌變法 *wùróng biànfă*). Technically lasting 103 days, it was a doomed initiative on the part of the Qing emperor Guangxu (光緒帝 *guāngxù dì*) to get China with the times, especially when it came to defending itself against foreign aggression.

Mao Zedong

More infamously, Mao Zedong (毛澤東 *máo zédōng*) was born 26 December 1893 in Shaoshanchong (韶山沖 *sháoshānchōng*, now Shaoshan city 韶山市 *sháoshān shì*), Hunan province. As a child growing up during the decline of the Qing dynasty, his father was considered a "rich landlord" (土豪 *tǔháo*), the same class of people, relatively well-off but by no means wealthy, that Mao's Chinese Communist Party (CCP) would later prosecute with vehement fury. Isolated and rural, Mao Zedong's Shaoshanchong was then a feudal, pre-capitalist society with nearly unimaginable poverty. In 1911, Mao Zedong left for school in Changsha city, and his first encounter with modernity was described by Alexander V. Pantsov:

> Mao, who lived in Changsha for more than seven years, was overwhelmed by the first city he had ever encountered. Never before had he seen urban streets, two- and three-story houses, and countless junks bobbing on the waves at stone wharves. In the early twentieth century Changsha, with a population over 200,000, was considered one of the best cities in China (Pantsov and Levine 2017).

Based in Hunan province, Mao Zedong led the Autumn Harvest Uprising in September 1927. The shibboleth of his campaign was forthright: "Execute local reactionaries, confiscate their property, burn down their houses, and destroy traffic and communication services." This so-called peasant uprising, meant to defeat both the nationalists (KMT, 國民黨 *guómíndăng*) as well as local power brokers ended in failure, and Mao Zedong was forced to escaped to Jinggangshan (井岡山 *jĭnggāng shān*) in October. He later oversaw the building of a CCP Revolutionary Base in that remote area.

"Great Leap Forward"

Even before the disastrous Great Leap Forward (GLF 1958–1962), as soon as Mao Zedong rose to power in 1949 Hunan soon felt the ravages of collectivization (Becker 1996). Particularly disastrous was the state acquisition and monopoly on grain in late 1953. By January 1954, more than 15% of people living in rural Hunan were going hungry (Dikötter 2013). In late 1958, as the GLF was underway, Peng Dehuai learned for himself. Marshal Peng Dehuai (彭德懷元帥 *péng déhuái yuánshuài*) was one of China's preeminent military leaders and a key supporter of Mao Zedong's adventure in the Korean War (1949–51). In a November 1958 visit to his hometown in Xiangtan County (湘潭縣 xiāngtán xiàn), not far from where Mao Zedong was born, Peng Dehuai quickly learned that grain quotas and production figures were being falsified. But it was the personal tragedies that he witnessed that moved the old soldier, including the following episode. And although some attribute the poem below to Peng Dehuai's own writing, Yang Jisheng reports that it was actually a Red Army disabled veteran and comrade who slipped a piece of paper to Peng Dehuai during his inspection visit. It read:

> Grain scattered on the ground; potato leaves withered;
> Strong young people have left to make steel;
> Only children and old women reap the crops;
> How can they pass the coming year?
> Allow me to raise my voice for the people! (Domes 1985)

Peng Dehuai later paid dearly for his efforts to call attention to the disaster that was already underway in the GLF (Peng Dehuai has since been posthumously rehabilitated).[4] Rightly blamed for the disaster of the years 1958–62, Mao Zedong was politically demoted. In an effort to reclaim total revolutionary power once again, Mao Zedong, using his power-hungry wife Jiang Qing (姜青 *jiāng qīng*) as a conduit, instigated the Cultural Revolution (1966–1976). This most recent spasm of insanity would once again put China into chaos, something that Mao Zedong said he had desired from the beginning in August 1966 (Domes 1977). Here again, Hunan province, led by Hua Guofeng, played an important role in supporting Mao Zedong's latest venture. Having supported Mao Zedong during the GLF, Hua Guofeng also curried favor simply by being a fellow Hunanese (Xu 2014). But although Mao Zedong finally ceded power to him, famously telling Hua Guofeng that "With you in charge, I'm at ease (你辦事, 我放心 *nǐbànshì, wǒfàngxīn*)," the excesses of the Cultural Revolution also caught up to him, and the CCP cashiered Hua Guofeng in favor of Deng Xiaoping in January 1979.

---

[4] 湘潭縣石譚鎮烏石寨 *xiāngtán xiàn, shítán zhèn, wūshí zhài.*

Hunan Cooking: Introduction of the Chili Pepper

With its penchant for piquant spices, not limited to but usually spicy chili peppers, Hunan cuisine is deservedly famous. After the discovery of the new world and its flora, the Portuguese brought chili (capsicum) peppers (辣椒 *làjiāo*) to Europe as well as India. After having seized Malacca in 1511, the Portuguese made great profits trading in spices and other items with southern Chinese, especially in Guangzhou (Canton). (Simoons 1990). By 1542, Portugal was growing chili peppers in quantity on Goa, India. As for the first introduction of chilis into mainland China, there seems to be agreement that it first was likely introduced from three entry points: via Southeast Asia, Northeast (Korea), and Taiwan (by way of the Dutch.) The earliest mention (1591) of chili peppers being imported into China proper was in Hangzhou, Zhejiang province (Dott 2000). However, according to scholar Cao Yu, chili peppers first found favor in China because of their colorful aesthetics, not as a flavor adjunct. They simply looked pretty (Cao 2021). It was only when the people of Guizhou province and in nearby areas, lacking access to affordable salt, began using chili peppers as a condiment, classifying it a "ground-sprouting salt substitute" (土苗用以代鹽 *tǔmiáo yòngyǐ dài yán*) during in the Kangxi-era (1662–1722). From the Qian Long era (1736–1795), Guizhou was using chili peppers in great quantity, exporting them to Zhenxiong (鎮雄 *zhènxióng*) in Yunnan, and then to Chenzhou (辰州 *chénzhōu*) in Hunan. From here, we presume the use of hot chili peppers in cuisine then spread to Sichuan and the rest of China. There is now even a medical term, "Hunan hand," to describe the fulminant irritation of the fingers from excessive contact with capsaicin (the active ingredient in spicy chili).

Hunan: Modern Population and Economy

The population of Hunan province has experienced only a modest increase from 2010–2020 (see Tables 16.2 and 16.3), a little over 1%. The discrepancy in Hunan's 2020 census numbers (66,444,864) and permanent registered (*hukou*) for 2020 (73,270,000) suggests a great number of Hunanese spend significant periods of time outside their home province. In 2020, Hunan had a gross domestic product (GDP) that ranked it ninth (USD $650 billion) among 31 other provinces and other major cities in mainland China. With a per capita income of $4570, Hunan ranked 12th (after Chongqing City). (Zhang 2021).

Table 16.4 shows the *hukou* (family registered) populations based on PRC Ministry of Civil Affairs data. (Districts listed directly under major cities are government seats, as are those in parentheses). One can compare these data with the census (usual residential populations based on 2010 and 2020 censuses in Tables 16.2 and 16.3:

Table 16.2 Population (residential 常住人口 *chángzhù rénkǒu*) data for Hunan province. (HPBS 2021)

City	Population (2010)	Population (2020)
Changsha City 長沙市 *chángshā shì*	7,044,118	10,047,914
Changde City 常德市 *chángdé shì*	5,747,218	5,279,102
Chenzhou City 郴州市 *chēnzhōu shì*	4,581,778	4,667,134
Hengyang City 衡陽市 *héngyáng shì*	7,141,462	6,645,243
Huaihua City 懷化市 *huáihuà shì*	4,741,948	4,587,594
Loudi City 婁底市 *lóudǐ shì*	3,785,627	3,826,996
Shaoyang City 邵陽市 *shàoyáng shì*	7,071,826	6,563,520
Xiangtan City 湘潭市 *xiāngtán shì*	2,748,552	2,726,181
Yiyang City 益陽市 *yìyáng shì*	4,313,084	3,851,564
Yongzhou City 永州市 *yǒngzhōu shì*	5,180,235	5,289,824
Yueyang City 岳陽市 *yuèyáng shì*	5,477,911	5,051,922
Zhangjiajie City 張家界市 *zhāngjiājiè shì*	1,476,521	1,517,027
Zhuzhou City 株洲市 *zhūzhōu shì*	3,855,609	3,902,738
Xiangxi Tujia and Miao Autonomous Prefectures 湘西土家族苗族自治州 *xiāngxī tǔjiāzú miáozú zìzhìzhōu*	2,547,833	2,488,105
Total	**65,683,722**	**66,444,864**

Table 16.3 Hunan province: population data of cities and their subordinate sectors. (HPBS 2021)

Cities and subordinate sectors, population (2020 census)	Subordinate district, city and county populations (2020)	Population (2020)
Changsha City 長沙市 ***chángshā shì***		**10,047,914**
Yuelu District 岳麓區 *yuèlù qū*	1,526,641	
Furong District 芙蓉區 *fúróng qū*	642,010	
Tianxin District 天心區 *tiānxīn qū*	836,157	
Kaifu District 開福區 *kāifú qū*	820,790	
Yuhua District 雨花區 *yǔhuā qū*	1,264,895	
Wangcheng District 望城區 *wàngchéng qū*	890,214	
Liuyang City 瀏陽市 *liúyáng shì*	1,429,384	
Changsha County 長沙縣 *chángshā xiàn*	1,374,491	
Ningxiang County 寧鄉縣 *níngxiāng xiàn*	1,263,332	
Changde City 常德市 ***chángdé shì***		**5,279,102**
Wuling District 武陵區 *wǔlíng qū*	730,970	
Dingcheng District 鼎城區 *dǐngchéng qū*	738,085	
Jinshi City 津市市 *jīnshì shì*	212,739	
Anxiang County 安鄉縣 *ānxiāng xiàn*	427,412	
Hanshou County 漢壽縣 *hànshòu xiàn*	706,249	
Lixian County 澧縣 *lǐxiàn*	721,927	
Linli County 臨澧縣 *línlǐ xiàn*	373,043	
Taoyuan County 桃源縣 *táoyuán xiàn*	809,220	
Shimen County 石門縣 *shímén xiàn*	559,457	
Chenzhou City 郴州市 ***chēnzhōu shì***		**4,667,134**

(continued)

Table 16.3 (continued)

Cities and subordinate sectors, population (2020 census)	Subordinate district, city and county populations (2020)	Population (2020)
Beihu District 北湖區 *běihú qū*	568,778	
Suxian District 蘇仙區 *sūxiān qū*	435,836	
Zixing City 資興市 *zīxīng shì*	322,990	
Guiyang County 桂陽縣 *guìyáng xiàn*	709,372	
Yongxing County 永興縣 *yǒngxīng xiàn*	538,532	
Yizhang County 宜章縣 *yízhāng xiàn*	567,970	
Jiahe County 嘉禾縣 *jiāhé xiàn*	343,169	
Linwu County 臨武縣 *línwǔ xiàn*	322,987	
Rucheng County 汝城縣 *rǔchéng xiàn*	344,617	
Guidong County 桂東縣 *guìdōng xiàn*	160,956	
Anren County 安仁縣 *ānrén xiàn*	351,927	
Hengyang City 衡陽市 ***héngyáng shì***		**6,645,243**
Zhengxiang District 蒸湘區 *zhēngxiāng qū*	478,072	
Yanfeng District 雁峰區 *yànfēng qū*	247,791	
Zhuhui District 珠暉區 *zhūhuī qū*	337,337	
Shigu District 石鼓區 *shígǔ qū*	227,515	
Nanyue District 南岳區 *nányuè qū*	70,370	
Changning City 常寧市 *chángníng shì*	790,676	
Leiyang City 耒陽市 *lěiyáng shì*	1,140,675	
Hengyang County 衡陽縣 *héngyáng xiàn*	888,433	
Hengnan County 衡南縣 *héngnán xiàn*	796,327	
Hengshan County 衡山縣 *héngshān xiàn*	335,704	
Hengdong County 衡東縣 *héngdōng xiàn*	565,423	
Qidong County 祁東縣 *qídōng xiàn*	776,920	
Huaihua City 懷化市 ***huáihuà shì***		**4,587,594**
Hecheng District 鶴城區 *hèchéng qū*	712,584	
Hongjiang City 洪江市 *hóngjiāng shì*	341,706	
Yuanling County 沅陵縣 *yuánlíng xiàn*	510,014	
Chenxi County 辰溪縣 *chénxī xiàn*	407,578	
Xupu County 溆浦縣 *xùpǔ xiàn*	757,797	
Zhongfang County 中方縣 *zhōngfāng xiàn*	233,378	
Huitong County 會同縣 *huìtóng xiàn*	291,067	
Mayang Miaozu (Miao) Autonomous County 麻陽苗族自治縣 *máyáng miáozú zìzhìxiàn*	313,305	
Xinhuang Dongzu (Dong) Autonomous County 新晃侗族自治縣 *xīnhuǎng dòngzú zìzhìxiàn*	220,775	
Zhijiang Dongzu (Dong) Autonomous County 芷江侗族自治縣 *zhǐjiāng dòngzú zìzhìxiàn*	307,661	
Jingzhou Miaozu Dongzu (Miao and Dong) Autonomous County 靖州苗族侗族自治縣 *jìngzhōu miáozú dòngzú zìzhìxiàn*	233,638	
Tongdao Dongzu (Dong) Autonomous County 通道侗族自治縣 *tōngdào dòngzú zìzhìxiàn*	201,047	

(continued)

Table 16.3 (continued)

Cities and subordinate sectors, population (2020 census)	Subordinate district, city and county populations (2020)	Population (2020)
Huaihua City Hongjiang Management Area 懷化市洪江管理區 *huáihuàshì hóngjiāng guǎnlǐqū*	57,004	
Loudi City 婁底市 ***lóudǐ shì***		**3,826,996**
Louxing District 婁星區 *lóuxīng qū*	752,530	
Lengshuijiang 冷水江市 *lěngshuǐ jiāng shì*	329,912	
Lianyuan City 漣源市 *liányuán shì*	862,099	
Shuangfeng County 雙峰縣 *shuāngfēng xiàn*	685,917	
Xinhua County 新化縣 *xīnhuà xiàn*	1,196,538	
Shaoyang City 邵陽市 ***shàoyáng shì***		**6,563,520**
Daxiang County 大祥縣 *dàxiáng xiàn*	362,289	
Shuangqing District 雙清區 *shuāngqīng qū*	317,283	
Beita District 北塔區 *běitǎ qū*	122,658	
Wugang City 武岡市 *wǔgāng shì*	640,181	
Shaodong City 邵東市 *shàodōng shì*	1,038,416	
Shaoyang County 邵陽縣 *shàoyáng xiàn*	752,125	
Xinshao County 新邵縣 *xīnshào xiàn*	612,943	
Longhui County 隆回縣 *lónghuí xiàn*	1,009,778	
Dongkou County 洞口縣 *dòngkǒu xiàn*	675,495	
Suining County 綏寧縣 *suíníng xiàn*	290,664	
Xinning County 新寧縣 *xīnníng xiàn*	513,777	
Chengbu Miaozu (Miao) Autonomous County 城步苗族自治縣 *chéngbù miáozú zìzhìxiàn*	227,911	
Xiangtan City 湘潭市 ***xiāngtán shì***		**2,726,181**
Yuetang District 岳塘區 *yuètáng qū*	483,762	
Yuhu District 雨湖區 *yǔhú qū*	616,130	
Xiangxiang City 湘鄉市 *xiāngxiāng shì*	730,103	
Shaoshan City 韶山市 *sháoshān shì*	103,357	
Xiangtan County 湘潭縣 *xiāngtán xiàn*	792,829	
Yiyang City 益陽市 ***yìyáng shì***		**3,851,564**
Heshan District 赫山區 *hèshān qū*	889,068	
Ziyang District 資陽區 *zīyáng qū*	356,405	
Yuanjiang City 沅江市 *yuánjiāng shì*	567,159	
Nanxian County[a] 南縣 *nánxiàn*	572,367	
Taojiang County 桃江縣 *táojiāng xiàn*	685,596	
Anhua County 安化縣 *ānhuà xiàn*	780,969	
Yongzhou City 永州市 ***yǒngzhōu shì***		**5,289,824**
Lengshuitan District 冷水灘區 *lěngshuǐtān qū*	583,136	
Lingling District 零陵區 *línglíng qū*	563,556	
Dong'an County 東安縣 *dōng'ān xiàn*	490,385	
Daoxian County 道縣 *dàoxiàn*	621,275	
Ningyuan County 寧遠縣 *níngyuǎn xiàn*	684,121	
Jiangyong County 江永縣 *jiāngyǒng xiàn*	235,699	
Lanshan County 藍山縣 *lánshān xiàn*	329,909	

(continued)

Table 16.3 (continued)

Cities and subordinate sectors, population (2020 census)	Subordinate district, city and county populations (2020)	Population (2020)
Xintian County 新田縣 *xīntián xiàn*	343,595	
Shuangpai County 雙牌縣 *shuāngpái xiàn*	157,140	
Qiyang County 祁陽縣 *qíyáng xiàn*	832,813	
Jianghua Yaozu (Yao) Autonomous County 江華瑤族自治縣 *jiānghuá yáozú zìzhìxiàn*	448,195	
Yueyang City 岳陽市 ***yuèyáng shì***		**5,051,922**
Yueyanglou District 岳陽樓區 *yuèyánglóu qū*	980,401	
Junshan District 君山區 *jūnshān qū*	201,634	
Yunxi District 雲溪區 *yúnxī qū*	153,657	
Miluo City 汨羅市 *mìluó shì*	632,246	
Linxiang City 臨湘市 *línxiāng shì*	433,200	
Yueyang County 岳陽縣 *yuèyáng xiàn*	561,888	
Huarong County 華容縣 *huáróng xiàn*	553,800	
Xiangyin County 湘陰縣 *xiāngyīn xiàn*	583,984	
Pingjiang County 平江縣 *píngjiāng xiàn*	951112	
Zhangjiajie City 張家界市 ***zhāngjiājiè shì***		**1,517,027**
Yongding District 永定區 *yǒngdìng qū*	517,595	
Wulingyuan District 武陵源區 *wǔlíng yuán qū*	60,857	
Cili County 慈利縣 *cílì xiàn*	562,493	
Sangzhi County 桑植縣 *sāngzhí xiàn*	376,082	
Zhuzhou City 株洲市 ***zhūzhōu shì***		**3,902,738**
Tianyuan District 天元區 *tiānyuán qū*	478,309	
Hetang District 荷塘區 *hétáng qū*	348,894	
Lusong District 蘆淞區 *lúsōng qū*	307,012	
Shifeng District 石峰區 *shífēng qū*	223,634	
Lukou District[b] 淥口區 *lùkǒu qū*	260,534	
Liling City 醴陵市 *lǐlíng shì*	885,987	
Youxian County 攸縣 *yōuxiàn*	630,427	
Chaling County 茶陵縣 *chálíng xiàn*	491,849	
Yanling County 炎陵縣 *yánlíng xiàn*	160,274	
Xiangxi Tujia and Miao Autonomous Prefectures 湘西土家族苗族自治州 ***xiāngxī tǔjiāzú miáozú zìzhìzhōu***		**2,488,105**
Jishou City 吉首市 *jíshǒu shì*	408,812	
Luxi County 瀘溪縣 *lúxī xiàn*	240,937	
Fenghuang County 鳳凰縣 *fènghuáng xiàn*	315,619	
Huayuan County 花垣縣 *huāyuán xiàn*	249,238	
Baojing County 保靖縣 *bǎojìng xiàn*	238,792	
Guwen County 古文縣 *gǔwén xiàn*	108,798	
Yongshun County 永順縣 *yǒngshùn xiàn*	413,470	
Longshan County 龍山縣 *lóngshān xiàn*	476,439	

[a]Includes population of Datonghu district (大通湖區 *dàtōnghú qū*): 83,100
[b]Formally established in June 2018

1. Longshan County
2. Sangzhi County
3. Wulingyuan District
4. Cili County
5. Shimen County
6. Lixian County
7. Linli County
8. Jinshi City
9. Anxiang County
10. Huarong County
11. Yueyang County
12. Junshan District
13. Yunxi District
14. Yueyanglou District
15. Linxiang City
16. Nanxian County
17. Yuanjiang City
18. Miluo City
19. Pingjiang County
20. Baojing County
21. Yongshun County
22. Yongding District
23. Yuanling County
24. Taoyuan County
25. Dingcheng District
26. Wuling District
27. Dingcheng District
28. Hanshou County
29. Ziyang District
30. Huayuan County
31. Gushou City
32. Guzhang County
33. Anhua County
34. Taojiang County
35. Heshan District
36. Xiangyin County
37. Changsha City
38. Changsha County
39. Liuyang City
40. Fenghuang County
41. Luxi County
42. Chenxi County
43. Xupu County
44. Xinhua County
45. Lengshuijiang City
46. Lianyuan City
47. Louxing District
48. Ningxiang County
49. Xiangxiang City
50. Shaoshan City
51. Xiangtan County
52. Xiangtan City
53. Zhuzhou City
54. Lukou District
55. Liling City
56. Xinhuang Dongzu Autonomous County
57. Mayang Miao Autonomous County
58. Zhijiang Dong Autonomous County
59. Hecheng District
60. Zhongfang County
61. Hongjiang City
62. Dongkou County
63. Longhui County
64. Xinshao County
65. Beita District
66. Shaodong City
67. Shuangqing District
68. Daxiang District
69. Shaoyang County
70. Qidong County
71. Hengyang County
72. Shuangfeng County
73. Hengshan County
74. Zhengxiang District
75. Shigu District
76. Nanyue District
77. Hengdong County
78. Youxian County
79. Yanfeng District
80. Huitong County
81. Suining County
82. Wugang City
83. Xinning County
84. Dong'an County
85. Lengshuitan District
86. Qiyang County
87. Changning City
88. Leiyang City
89. Anren County
90. Chaling County
91. Jingzhou Miao and Dong Autonomous County
92. Tongdao Dong Autonomous County
93. Chengbu Miao Autonomous County
94. Lingling County
95. Shuangpai District
96. Ningyuan County
97. Xintian County
98. Guiyang County
99. Yongxing County
100. Daoxian County
101. Lanshan County
102. Jiahe County
103. Beihu District
104. Zixing City
105. Yanling County
106. Jiangyong County
107. Jianghua Yao Autonomous County
108. Linwu County
109. Yizhang County
110. Rucheng County
111. Guidong County

Fig. 16.2 Hunan province: subdistricts (Provincial Capital City: Changsha City). (Drawn by the author, after People's Republic of China, Ministry of Civil Affairs (MCA 2020))

Hunan Province (湘)

Provincial Capital: Changsha

Table 16.4 Hunan province: permanent registered (戶籍人口 *hùjí rénkǒu*) populations. (MCA 2020)

Name	Traditional	Simplified	Population (2012)	Population (2016)	Population (2020)	Area (Sq. Km)
Hunan Province	湖南省	湖南省	70,690,000	71,320,000	73,270,000	211,833
Changsha City	長沙市	长沙市	6,510,000	6,610,000	7,290,000	11,816
Yuelu District (Wangyue Subdistrict)	岳麓區 (望岳街道)	岳麓区 (望岳街道)	660,000	660,000	820,000	539
Furong District (Dongtundu Subdistrict)	芙蓉區 (東屯渡街道)	芙蓉区 (东屯渡街道)	410,000	410,000	420,000	43
Tianxin District (Qingyuan Subdistrict)	天心區 (青園街道)	天心区 (青园街道)	400,000	400,000	500,000	73
Kaifu District (Furongbeilu Subdistrict)	開福區 (芙蓉北路街道)	开福区 (芙蓉北路街道)	420,000	430,000	510,000	189
Yuhua District (Guitang Subdistrict)	雨花區 (圭塘街道)	雨花区 (圭塘街道)	540,000	560,000	720,000	115
Wangcheng District (Gaotangling Subdistrict)	望城區 (高塘嶺街道)	望城区 (高塘岭街道)	510,000	520,000	590,000	951
Liuyang City (Guankou Subdistrict)	瀏陽市 (關口街道)	浏阳市 (关口街道)	1,410,000	1,440,000	1,490,000	4997
Changsha County (Xingsha Subdistrict)	長沙縣 (星沙街道)	长沙县 (星沙街道)	790,000	810,000	810,000	1997
Ningxiang County (Yutan Subdistrict)	寧鄉縣 (玉潭街道)	宁乡县 (玉潭街道)	1,370,000	1,380,000	1,430,000	2912
Zhangjiajie City	張家界市	张家界市	1,670,000	1,690,000	1,700,000	9534
Yongding District (Xixiping Subdistrict)	永定區 (西溪坪街道)	永定区 (西溪坪街道)	460,000	470,000	480,000	2169
Wulingyuan District (Jundiping Subdistrict)	武陵源區 (軍地坪街道)	武陵源区 (军地坪街道)	50,000	50,000	60,000	398
Cili County (Lingyang Town)	慈利縣 (零陽鎮)	慈利县 (零阳镇)	700,000	700,000	700,000	3492
Sangzhi County (Liyuan Town)	桑植縣 (澧源鎮)	桑植县 (澧源镇)	460,000	470,000	470,000	3475

(continued)

Table 16.4 (continued)

Name	Traditional	Simplified	Population (2012)	Population (2016)	Population (2020)	Area (Sq. Km)
Changde City	常德市	常德市	6,170,000	6,150,000	6,050,000	18,176
Wuling District (Nanping Subdistrict)	武陵區 (南坪街道)	武陵区 (南坪街道)	550,000	600,000	610,000	412
Dingcheng District (Wuling Town)	鼎城區 (武陵鎮)	鼎城区 (武陵镇)	870,000	800,000	790,000	2340
Jinshi City (Xiangyangjie Subdistrict)	津市市 (襄陽街街道)	津市市 (襄阳街街道)	260,000	260,000	230,000	556
Anxiang County (Shenliu Town)	安鄉縣 (深柳鎮)	安乡县 (深柳镇)	600,000	590,000	540,000	1086
Hanshou County (Longyang Town)	漢壽縣 (龍陽鎮)	汉寿县 (龙阳镇)	860,000	860,000	870,000	2091
Lixian County (Liyang Town)	澧縣 (澧陽鎮)	澧县 (澧阳镇)	930,000	930,000	920,000	2075
Linli County (Anfu Town)	臨澧縣 (安福鎮)	临澧县 (安福镇)	450,000	460,000	450,000	1204
Taoyuan County (Zhangjiang Town)	桃源縣 (漳江鎮)	桃源县 (漳江镇)	970,000	980,000	970,000	4442
Shimen County (Chujiang Town)	石門縣 (楚江鎮)	石门县 (楚江镇)	680,000	670,000	670,000	3970
Yiyang City	益陽市	益阳市	4,710,000	4,770,000	4,780,000	12,320
Heshan District (Heshan Subdistrict)	赫山區 (赫山街道)	赫山区 (赫山街道)	900,000	920,000	930,000	1279
Ziyang District (Damatou Subdistrict)	資陽區 (大碼頭街道)	资阳区 (大码头街道)	410,000	420,000	420,000	572
Yuanjiang City (Qionghu Subdistrict)	沅江市 (瓊湖街道)	沅江市 (琼湖街道)	730,000	740,000	740,000	2129
Nanxian County (Nanzhou Town)	南縣 (南州鎮)	南县 (南洲镇)	800,000	800,000	780,000	1327
Taojiang County (Taohuajiang Town)	桃江縣 (桃花江鎮)	桃江县 (桃花江镇)	870,000	880,000	890,000	2068
Anhua County (Leping Town)	安化縣 (樂坪鎮)	安化县 (东坪镇)	1,000,000	1,010,000	1,020,000	4945
Yueyang City	岳陽市	岳阳市	5,640,000	5,600,000	5,690,000	14,858
Yueyanglou District (Wuxingpai Subdistrict)	岳陽樓區 (五星牌街道)	岳阳楼区 (五星牌街道)	670,000	660,000	690,000	408
Junshan District (Liulinzhou Town)	君山區 (柳林洲鎮)	君山区 (柳林洲镇)	250,000	240,000	250,000	627

(continued)

Table 16.4 (continued)

Name	Traditional	Simplified	Population (2012)	Population (2016)	Population (2020)	Area (Sq. Km)
Yunxi District (Yunxi Town)	雲溪區 (雲溪鎮)	云溪区 (云溪镇)	170,000	170,000	170,000	378
Miluo City (Chengjiao Township)	汨羅市 (城郊鄉)	汨罗市 (城郊乡)	750,000	750,000	760,000	1670
Linxiang City (Chang'an Subdistrict)	臨湘市 (長安街道)	临湘市 (长安街道)	520,000	520,000	540,000	1719
Yueyang County (Rongjiawan Town)	岳陽縣 (榮家灣鎮)	岳阳县 (荣家湾镇)	720,000	720,000	730,000	2810
Huarong County (Chengguan Town)	華容縣 (城關鎮)	华容县 (城关镇)	730,000	710,000	710,000	1591
Xiangyin County (Wenxing Town)	湘陰縣 (文星鎮)	湘阴县 (文星镇)	760,000	710,000	710,000	1541
Pingjiang County (Hanchang Town)	平江縣 (漢昌鎮)	平江县 (汉昌镇)	1,070,000	1,090,000	1,120,000	4114
Zhuzhou City	株洲市	株洲市	3,870,000	3,950,000	4,030,000	11,248
Tianyuan District (Songshanlu Subdistrict)	天元區 (嵩山路街道)	天元区 (嵩山路街道)	160,000	240,000	290,000	328
Hetang District (Guihua Subdistrict)	荷塘區 (桂花街道)	荷塘区 (桂花街道)	210,000	210,000	210,000	152
Lusong District (Fengxi Subdistrict)	蘆淞區 (楓溪街道)	芦淞区 (枫溪街道)	190,000	240,000	240,000	217
Shifeng District (Xiangshiling Subdistrict)	石峰區 (響石嶺街道)	石峰区 (响石岭街道)	250,000	250,000	240,000	166
Lukou District[a] (Lukou Town)	淥口區 (淥口鎮)	渌口区 (渌口镇)	N/A	N/A	350,000	1053.69
Liling City (Xishan Subdistrict)	醴陵市 (西山街道)	醴陵市 (西山街道)	1,030,000	1,060,000	1,050,000	2156
Zhuzhou County (Lukou Town)	株洲縣 (淥口鎮)	株洲县 (渌口镇)	460,000	N/A	N/A	(1054)
Youxian County (Lianxing Subdistrict)	攸縣 (聯星街道)	攸县 (联星街道)	780,000	790,000	810,000	2649
Chaling County (Chengguan Town)	茶陵縣 (城關鎮)	茶陵县 (城关镇)	600,000	620,000	650,000	2496
Yanling County (Xiayang Town)	炎陵縣 (霞陽鎮)	炎陵县 (霞阳镇)	190,000	190,000	190,000	2030
Xiangtan City	湘潭市	湘潭市	2,900,000	2,910,000	2,890,000	5005

(continued)

Table 16.4 (continued)

Name	Traditional	Simplified	Population (2012)	Population (2016)	Population (2020)	Area (Sq. Km)
Yuetang District (Wulidui Subdistrict)	岳塘區 (五里堆街道)	岳塘区 (五里堆街道)	350,000	350,000	350,000	206
Yuhu District (Yuhulu Subdistrict)	雨湖區 (雨湖路街道)	雨湖区 (雨湖路街道)	540,000	530,000	510,000	446
Xiangxiang City (Wangchunmen Subdistrict)	湘鄉市 (望春門街道)	湘乡市 (望春门街道)	920,000	920,000	930,000	1966
Shaoshan City (Qingxi Town)	韶山市 (清溪鎮)	韶山市 (清溪镇)	110,000	120,000	120,000	247
Xiangtan County (Yisuhe Town)	湘潭縣 (易俗河鎮)	湘潭县 (易俗河镇)	980,000	990,000	970,000	2140
Hengyang City	衡陽市	衡阳市	7,800,000	7,740,000	8,010,000	15,300
Zhengxiang District (Changhu Township)	蒸湘區 (長湖鄉)	蒸湘区 (长湖乡)	230,000	240,000	280,000	112
Yanfeng District (Yanfeng Subdistrict)	雁峰區 (雁峰街道)	雁峰区 (雁峰街道)	200,000	190,000	190,000	83
Zhuhui District (Guangdonglu Subdistrict)	珠暉區 (廣東路街道)	珠晖区 (广东路街道)	290,000	290,000	290,000	219
Shigu District (Songmu Township)	石鼓區 (松木鄉)	石鼓区 (松木乡)	210,000	200,000	200,000	105
Nanyue District (Zhurong Subdistrict)	南岳區 (祝融街道)	南岳区 (祝融街道)	60,000	60,000	60,000	179
Changning City (Yiyang Subdistrict)	常寧市 (宜陽街道)	常宁市 (宜阳街道)	930,000	910,000	960,000	2048
Leiyang City (Caizichi Subdistrict)	耒陽市 (蔡子池街道)	耒阳市 (蔡子池街道)	1,380,000	1,370,000	1,420,000	2648
Hengyang County (Xidu Town)	衡陽縣 (西渡鎮)	衡阳县 (西渡镇)	1,210,000	1,220,000	1,250,000	2559
Hengnan County (Yunji Town)	衡南縣 (雲集鎮)	衡南县 (云集镇)	1,100,000	1,050,000	1,100,000	2614
Hengshan County (Kaiyun Town)	衡山縣 (開雲鎮)	衡山县 (开云镇)	440,000	440,000	450,000	935
Hengdong County (Chengguan Town)	衡東縣 (城關鎮)	衡东县 (城关镇)	720,000	740,000	760,000	1927
Qidong County (Yuhe Subdistrict)	祁東縣 (玉合街道)	祁东县 (玉合街道)	1,030,000	1,030,000	1,060,000	1871
Chenzhou City	郴州市	郴州市	4,970,000	5,120,000	5,350,000	19,342

(continued)

Table 16.4 (continued)

Name	Traditional	Simplified	Population (2012)	Population (2016)	Population (2020)	Area (Sq. Km)
Beihu District (Luoxian Subdistrict)	北湖區 (駱仙街道)	北湖区 (骆仙街道)	350,000	370,000	410,000	819
Suxian District (Suxianling Subdistrict)	蘇仙區 (蘇仙嶺街道)	苏仙区 (苏仙岭街道)	360,000	370,000	390,000	1340
Zixing City (Tangdong Subdistrict)	資興市 (唐洞街道)	资兴市 (唐洞街道)	370,000	370,000	380,000	2730
Guiyang County (Longtan Subdistrict)	桂陽縣 (龍潭街道)	桂阳县 (龙潭街道)	870,000	900,000	920,000	2958
Yongxing County (Bianjiang Town)	永興縣 (便江鎮)	永兴县 (便江镇)	660,000	680,000	710,000	1980
Yizhang County (Yuxi Town)	宜章縣 (玉溪鎮)	宜章县 (玉溪镇)	600,000	620,000	650,000	2118
Jiahe County (Zhuquan Town)	嘉禾縣 (珠泉鎮)	嘉禾县 (珠泉镇)	390,000	400,000	440,000	699
Linwu County (Shunfeng Town)	臨武縣 (舜峰鎮)	临武县 (舜峰镇)	340,000	360,000	380,000	1383
Rucheng County (Luyang Town)	汝城縣 (盧陽鎮)	汝城县 (卢阳镇)	380,000	390,000	420,000	2401
Guidong County (Oujiang Town)	桂東縣 (漚江鎮)	桂东县 (沤江镇)	210,000	210,000	190,000	1452
Anren County (Yonglejiang Town)	安仁縣 (永樂江鎮)	安仁县 (永乐江镇)	440,000	450,000	470,000	1462
Yongzhou City	永州市	永州市	6,230,000	6,310,000	6,450,000	22,259
Lengshuitan District (Wutong Subdistrict)	冷水灘區 (梧桐街道)	冷水滩区 (梧桐街道)	540,000	550,000	560,000	1217
Lingling District (Xujiajing Subdistrict)	零陵區 (徐家井街道)	零陵区 (徐家井街道)	610,000	610,000	620,000	1964
Dong'an County (Baiyashi Town)	東安縣 (白牙市鎮)	东安县 (白牙市镇)	620,000	630,000	650,000	2204
Daoxian County (Lianxi Subdistrict)	道縣 (濂溪街道)	道县 (濂溪街道)	800,000	830,000	800,000	2448
Ningyuan County (Shunling Subdistrict)	寧遠縣 (舜陵街道)	宁远县 (舜陵街道)	850,000	850,000	900,000	2501
Jiangyong County (Xiaopu Town)	江永縣 (瀟浦鎮)	江永县 (潇浦镇)	270,000	270,000	290,000	1629
Lanshan County (Tafeng Town)	藍山縣 (塔峰鎮)	蓝山县 (塔峰镇)	400,000	400,000	420,000	1798

(continued)

Table 16.4 (continued)

Name	Traditional	Simplified	Population (2012)	Population (2016)	Population (2020)	Area (Sq. Km)
Xintian County (Longquan Town)	新田縣 (龍泉鎮)	新田县 (龙泉镇)	420,000	420,000	450,000	1000
Shuangpai County (Longbo Town)	雙牌縣 (瀧泊鎮)	双牌县 (泷泊镇)	180,000	180,000	180,000	1726
Qiyang County (Changhong Subdistrict)	祁陽縣 (長虹街道)	祁阳县 (长虹街道)	1,040,000	1,060,000	1,050,000	2538
Jianghua Yaozu (Yao) Autonomous County (Tuojiang Town)	江華瑤族自治縣 (沱江鎮)	江华瑶族自治县 (沱江镇)	500,000	510,000	540,000	3234
Shaoyang City	邵陽市	邵阳市	7,890,000	8,060,000	8,280,000	20,822
Daxiang County (Chengnan Subdistrict)	大祥縣 (城南街道)	大祥区 (城南街道)	320,000	320,000	330,000	215
Shuangqing District (Qichezhan Subdistrict)	雙清區 (汽車站街道)	双清区 (汽车站街道)	270,000	280,000	270,000	135
Beita District (Zhuangyuanzhou Subdistrict)	北塔區 (狀元洲街道)	北塔区 (状元洲街道)	90,000	90,000	100,000	84
Wugang City (Yingchunting Subdistrict)	武岡市 (迎春亭街道)	武冈市 (迎春亭街道)	810,000	830,000	840,000	1539
Shaodong City (Dahetang Subdistrict)	邵東市 (大禾塘街道)	邵东市 (大禾塘街道)	1,290,000	1,310,000	1,350,000	1778
Shaoyang County (Tangdukou Town)	邵陽縣 (塘渡口鎮)	邵阳县 (塘渡口镇)	1,020,000	1,040,000	1,060,000	2001
Xinshao County (Niangxi Town)	新邵縣 (釀溪鎮)	新邵县 (酿溪镇)	800,000	810,000	830,000	1762
Longhui County (Taohong Town)	隆回縣 (桃洪鎮)	隆回县 (桃洪镇)	1,190,000	1,230,000	1,290,000	2868
Dongkou County (Dongkou Town)	洞口縣 (洞口鎮)	洞口县 (洞口镇)	850,000	870,000	900,000	2179
Suining County (Changpu Town)	綏寧縣 (長鋪鎮)	绥宁县 (长铺镇)	370,000	370,000	380,000	2917
Xinning County (Jinshi Town)	新寧縣 (金石鎮)	新宁县 (金石镇)	610,000	630,000	650,000	2756
Chengbu Miaozu (Miao) Autonomous County (Rulin Town)	城步苗族自治縣 (儒林鎮)	城步苗族自治县 (儒林镇)	270,000	280,000	280,000	2588
Huaihua City	懷化市	怀化市	5,150,000	5,170,000	5,240,000	27,573

(continued)

Table 16.4 (continued)

Name	Traditional	Simplified	Population (2012)	Population (2016)	Population (2020)	Area (Sq. Km)
Hecheng District (Hongxing Subdistrict)	鶴城區 (紅星街道)	鹤城区 (红星街道)	360,000	370,000	400,000	673
Hongjiang City (Qiancheng Town)	洪江市 (黔城鎮)	洪江市 (黔城镇)	510,000	510,000	500,000	2283
Yuanling County (Yuanling Town)	沅陵縣 (沅陵鎮)	沅陵县 (沅陵镇)	660,000	660,000	640,000	5833
Chenxi County (Chenyang Town)	辰溪縣 (辰陽鎮)	辰溪县 (辰阳镇)	520,000	530,000	540,000	1987
Xupu County (Lufeng Town)	漵浦縣 (盧峰鎮)	溆浦县 (卢峰镇)	900,000	890,000	940,000	3429
Zhongfang County (Zhongfang Town)	中方縣 (中方鎮)	中方县 (中方镇)	280,000	280,000	290,000	1515
Huitong County (Lincheng Town)	會同縣 (林城鎮)	会同县 (林城镇)	360,000	360,000	370,000	2259
Mayang Miaozu (Miao) Autonomous County (Gaocun Town)	麻陽苗族自治縣 (高村鎮)	麻阳苗族自治县 (高村镇)	400,000	410,000	400,000	1566
Xinhuang Dongzu (Dong) Autonomous County (Xinhuang Town)	新晃侗族自治縣 (新晃鎮)	新晃侗族自治县 (新晃镇)	270,000	270,000	260,000	1502
Zhijiang Dongzu (Dong) Autonomous County (Zhijiang Town)	芷江侗族自治縣 (芷江鎮)	芷江侗族自治县 (芷江镇)	390,000	380,000	380,000	2095
Jingzhou Miaozu Dongzu (Miao and Dong) Autonomous County (Quyang Town)	靖州苗族侗族自治縣 (渠陽鎮)	靖州苗族侗族自治县 (渠阳镇)	270,000	270,000	280,000	2208
Tongdao Dongzu (Dong) Autonomous County (Shuangjiang Town)	通道侗族自治縣 (雙江鎮)	通道侗族自治县 (双江镇)	230,000	240,000	240,000	2223
Loudi City	婁底市	**娄**底市	4,320,000	4,350,000	4,550,000	8110

(continued)

Table 16.4 (continued)

Name	Traditional	Simplified	Population (2012)	Population (2016)	Population (2020)	Area (Sq. Km)
Louxing District (Changqing Subdistrict)	婁星區 (長青街道)	娄星区 (长青街道)	460,000	470,000	620,000	429
Lengshuijiang City (Lengshuijiang Subdistrict)	冷水江市 (冷水江街道)	冷水江市 (冷水江街道)	370,000	360,000	370,000	438
Lianyuan City (Lantian Subdistrict)	漣源市 (藍田街道)	涟源市 (蓝田街道)	1,160,000	1,150,000	1,150,000	1912
Shuangfeng County (Yongfeng Town)	雙峰縣 (永豐鎮)	双峰县 (永丰镇)	940,000	950,000	900,000	1711
Xinhua County (Shangmei Town)	新化縣 (上梅鎮)	新化县 (上梅镇)	1,390,000	1,420,000	1,520,000	3620
Xiangxi Tujiazu Miaozu (Tujia and Miao) Autonomous County	湘西土家族苗族自治州	湘西土家族苗族自治州	2,880,000	2,910,000	2,970,000	15,470
Jishou City (Qianzhou Subdistrict)	吉首市 (乾州街道)	吉首市 (乾州街道)	300,000	310,000	310,000	1078
Luxi County (Baisha Town)	瀘溪縣 (白沙鎮)	泸溪县 (白沙镇)	310,000	310,000	320,000	1566
Fenghuang County (Tuojiang Town)	鳳凰縣 (沱江鎮)	凤凰县 (沱江镇)	420,000	420,000	430,000	1734
Huayuan County (Huayuan Town)	花垣縣 (花垣鎮)	花垣县 (花垣镇)	300,000	300,000	310,000	1109
Baojing County (Qianling Town)	保靖縣 (遷陵鎮)	保靖县 (迁陵镇)	300,000	310,000	310,000	1755
Guwen County (Guyang Town)	古文縣 (古陽鎮)	古丈县 (古阳镇)	140,000	140,000	140,000	1286
Yongshun County (Lingxi Town)	永順縣 (靈溪鎮)	永顺县 (灵溪镇)	530,000	530,000	540,000	3812
Longshan County (Min'an Subdistrict)	龍山縣 (民安街道)	龙山县 (民安街道)	580,000	590,000	610,000	3130

[a]Formally established in June 2018

References

Bar-Yosef, Ofer. 2012. From foraging to farming in western and eastern Asia. In *Biodiversity in agriculture: Domestication, evolution, and sustainability*, ed. Paul Gepts, Thomas R. Famula, Robert L. Bettinger, et al., 57–91. New York: Columbia University Press.

Becker, Jasper. 1996. *Hungry ghosts: Mao's secret famine*. New York: Henry Holt and Company.

Benn, Charles D. 2002. *China's golden age: Everyday life in the Tang dynasty*. New York: Oxford University Press.

Cao, Yu. 2021. How the chili pepper conquered China? *Sixth Tone*. https://www.sixthtone.com/news/1007963/how-the-chili-pepper-conquered-china.

Chen, Guosheng. 1999. [Yangyue, I see]. *Tianfu Xinlun*. 陳國勝. 揚越, 我見. 天府新論. No. 1: 96–7.

Dikötter, Frank. 2013. *The tragedy of liberation: A history of the Chinese revolution, 1945–57*. New York: Bloomsbury Press.

Domes, Jürgen. 1977. *China after the cultural revolution: Politics between two party congresses*. Berkeley: University of California Press.

Domes, Jurgen. 1985. *Peng Te-huai: The man and the image*. London: C. Hurst & Company.

Dott, Brian Russell. 2000. *The Chile pepper in China: A cultural biography*. New York: Columbia University Press.

Hunan Province Bureau of Statistics (HPBS). 2021. [*Communiqué of the seventh national census of Hunan Province*, issue no. 6]. 湖南省第七次全国人口普查公报(第六号). 19 May. https://tjj.hunan.gov.cn/hntj/tjfx/tjgb/rkpc/202105/t20210519_19079329.html.

Liu-Perkins, Christine. 2014. *At home in her tomb: Lady Dai and the ancient Chinese treasures of Mawangdui*. Watertown, MA: Charlesbridge.

Ministry of Civil Affairs (MCA), People's Republic of China. 2020. [*County/township administration handbook*], Beijing: China Statistics Press. 中華人民共和國民政部, 中華人民共和國, 鄉鎮行政區劃簡冊.

Pantsov, Alexander V., and Steven I. Levine. 2017. *Mao: The real story*. New York: Simon and Schuster.

Simoons, Frederick J. 1990. *Food in China: A cultural and historical inquiry*. Ann Arbor: CRC Press.

Tan, Qixiang, ed. 1996. *The historical atlas of China*. Vol. II. Beijing: China Cartographic Publishing House.

Wilkinson, Endymion. 2012. *Chinese history: A new manual*. Cambridge, MA: Harvard University Press.

Wu, Xinfu. 1994. [*Hunan throughout history*]. Hunan: Hunan Publishing. 伍新福, 湖南通史: 古代卷, 湖南出版社.

Xu, Guangqiu. 2014. Mao's death and Hua Guofeng's tragedy. In *Evolution of power: China's struggle, survival, and success*, ed. Xiaobing Li and Xiansheng Tian, 61–78. Lanham, MD: Lexington Books.

Zhang, Shunan. 2021. [The 2020 per capita income list of residents in various provinces: Shanghai is the richest, and it has risen sharply]. Finance.people.com. 22 January. 张澍楠. 2020年各省份居民人均收入榜: 上海最有钱, 这地涨得猛. http://finance.people.com.cn/n1/2021/0122/c1004-32008733.html.

Zhao, Dule, Pei Anping, and Zhang Wenxu. 2000. Restudy of ancient cultivated rice from Bashidang Site in Lixian County, Hunan Province. *Chinese Journal of Rice Science*. 中国水稻科学 14(3): 139–143.

Chapter 17
Inner Mongolia

Abstract Spanning across northern China, Inner Mongolia has archeological evidence of a pastoral life, complete with horse riding and rearing, going back over several millennia. As a political entity in the Chinese empire, however, we begin at the Qing dynasty and its founding under the Manchus. With Soviet and Japanese incursions afterward in the early twentieth century, Inner Mongolia finally became part of modern China following the 1945–1949 Chinese civil war. Inner Mongolia's vast grasslands and animal husbandry belie the fact that there are immense mineral deposits that continue to be exploited, notably coal, but also rare earth elements. While these serve as valuable and prosperous industrial base materials, they also pose their own environment risks as well. Of note, the population numbers from the 2020 census and the official (*hukou*) family registered populations are roughly equal to one another, demonstrating there appears to be no large "floating populations" from (or within) Inner Mongolia.

E. Croddy, *China's Provinces and Populations*,
https://doi.org/10.1007/978-3-031-09165-0_17

Inner Mongolia (Nei Menggu) Autonomous Region (內蒙古自治區 *nèimēnggǔ zìzhìqū*): Abbreviation 蒙 (*méng*) (Fig. 17.1)

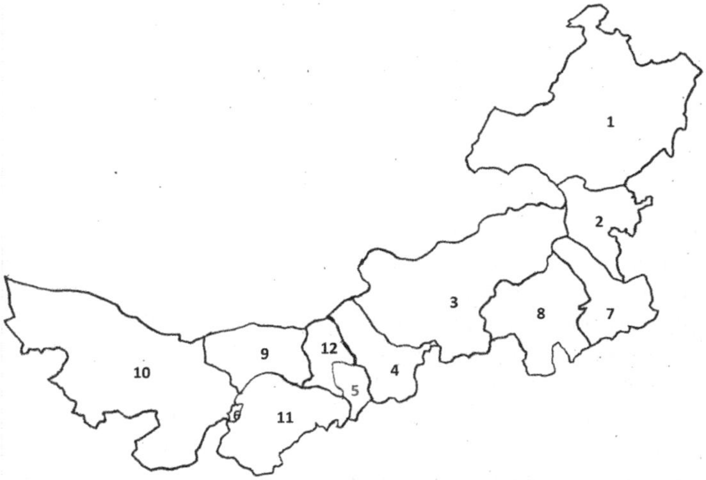

Inner Mongolia Population (2020)

1.	Hu-Lun-Bei-Er (Hulunbuir) City	2,242,875
2.	Xing'an (Hinggan) League	1,416,929
3.	Xilinguolemeng (Xilingol) League	1,107,075
4.	Wulanchabu (Ulanqab) City	1,706,328
5.	Hu-He-Hao-Te (Hohhot) City	3,446,100
6.	Wuhai City	556,621
7.	Tongliao City	2,873,168
8.	Chifeng City	4,035,967
9.	Bayannao'er (Bayan Nur) City	1,538,715
10.	Alashanmeng (Alxa League)	262,361
11.	E'erduosi (Ordos) City	2,153,638
12.	Baotou City	2,709,378

Fig. 17.1 Inner Mongolia major districts (Capital: Hohhot City). (Drawn by the author, after People's Republic of China, Ministry of Civil Affairs (MCA 2020))

Inner Mongolia: General Impressions

Inner Mongolia is a seemingly endless landscape made up of vast green pastures, pocketed here and there with domesticated animals, and interrupted every now and then with modernity. The capital city of Hohhot (Huhehaote city 呼和浩特市 *hūhéhàotè shì*) means "Blue city" in Mongolian, the idea being of immense, azure pure sky (Wright 1995). With a farrago of shifting nomadic clans, alliances, intermixing, and rivalries among disparate ethnicities, a historical sketch of Inner Mongolia (*Neimenggu*) is both convoluted and challenging. However, in sum, both past and present Inner Mongolia, one finds the legacy of three major conquests of China by nomadic, horse-riding peoples. These consisted of various Mongolian and Jurchen (Manchurian) tribes. Mongolians and Manchurians were certainly related to one another in terms of language, culture and social mores. But as they socialized and intermarried with the ethnic Han Chinese majority, they gradually became ever more Sinicized.

The influence of the Mongolian empire across Eurasia was of course immense. For example, the Russian word *denga* (деньга), for money derives from the Mongolian word for stamp, *Tamga*, i.e., to print paper currency, and was first introduced by the khanate of the Golden Horde (thirteenth century CE). Mongolian words that exist in Chinese today include Hutong (胡同 *hútóng*), as in the famous alleyways in Beijing, from water well, *hottog*; the word for station (站 *zhàn*) derives from the Mongolian Jamci, transliterated into old Chinese (站赤 *zhànchì*). And the "Gobi" is from the Mongolian word for desert, *gov*, and transliterated using Chinese characters to mimic its pronunciation, *gebi* (戈壁 *gēbì*).

The formal designations of Inner Mongolia and Outer Mongolia were instituted during the Qing dynasty (1644), when the Manchu, formerly known as the Jurchen, ruled over the Mongolians. The latter referred to Inner Mongolia as *Öbür Monggol*, meaning sunny or southern side of the mountain. China, however, referred to Inner Mongolia based on the Manchurian *dorgi* for "inner", thus (内 *nèi*) in *nèiménggŭ* (内蒙古 *nèiménggŭ*). In other words, China refers to these areas in geographic terms based on its own vantage point: Inner (near) Mongolia and Outer (far) Mongolia. The concept of an Inner and Outer Mongolia, therefore, is distinctly Chinese one, and not Mongolian (Endicott 2012).

Inner Mongolia: Prehistory

Paleolithic discoveries in Inner Mongolia, many of which were uncovered in the 1970s, include numerous rock shard tools at the Dayao village (大窯村 *dàyáocūn*) excavation site, about 30 km northeast of modern-day Hohhot City (呼和浩特市 *hūhéhàotè shì*). These stone implements date back some 20,000 years. Fittingly, given the pastoral- and horse-based culture of the traditional Mongolian steppes, bones and teeth of Mongolian ponies (*Equus przewalskii*) were also found at the

Dayao (大窯文化 *dàyáo wénhuà*) cultural site. These specimens date to about 10,000 years ago. A number of distinctive, square-shaped burial sites appeared during the first millennia BCE throughout the Mongolian region, and continued through about third century BCE. This so-called slab-grave culture seemed to share cultural elements found in southern Siberia (Olsen 1984).

The discovery of artifacts in Hongshanhou (紅山後 *hóngshānhòu*), located in Chifeng City (赤峰市 *chìfēng shì*), Hongshan District (紅山區 *hóngshān qū*), characterize the eponymous Hongshan Culture. Featuring highly stylized jade dragon motifs, sophisticated ritual burial sites, and distinctive pottery, the Hongshan Culture (3000–2500 BCE) is regarded as the first known advanced social structure in northeast China (Liu and Chen 2012).

Inner Mongolia: Recorded History

During the Spring and Autumn period (771–476 BCE), nomadic pastoral life in Mongolia was largely dominated by the Xiongnu (匈奴 *xiōngnú*) and the Donghu ("eastern barbarians" 東胡 *dōnghú*). In 300 BCE, to establish boundary against the Xiongnu, the warring state of Zhao (趙 *zhào*) established a defensive rampart 趙長城 (*zhàochángchéng*) just north of modern-day Hohhot to protect the Yunzhong commandery (雲中郡 *yúnzhōng jùn*). (Gaubatz 1996). In fact, three major Chinese states, the Yan, Zhao, and Qin (燕國 *yànguó*, 趙國 *zhàoguó*, 秦國 *qínguó*) all encroached northward into Mongolian lands at various times. After the Donghu barbarians were defeated (about 300 BCE), China (i.e., the Yan) built the Yanbei Wall (燕北長城 *yànběi chángchéng*) in ca. 280 BCE. This impressive and massive structure spanned some 1200 km, starting just west of today's Zhangjiakou city, stretching north of Aohan Banner (敖漢旗 *áohàn qí*), Inner Mongolia, wrapping around Shenyang and Fushun cities, and winding all the way to Pakch'ŏn (博川 bó chuān) in modern-day North Korea. Under the unifying first emperor of the Qin dynasty, Qin Shi Huang initiated the construction of a Great Wall (萬里長城 *wànlǐ chángchéng*) south of the Yinshan (陰山 *yīnshān*) mountain range that runs through Inner Mongolia and Hebei provinces. Its main purpose was to defend against the "Five Foreigners (barbarians)" (五胡 *wǔhú*) that included the Huns (Xiongnu), Wuhuan (烏桓 *wūhuán*), Xianbei (鮮卑 *xiānbēi* or Xianbi), and other nomadic peoples to the north. In 127 BCE, the Han dynasty established Wuyuan (五原郡 *wǔyuánjùn*) and Shuofang (朔方郡 *shuòfāngjùn*) prefectures. These territories comprised included modern-day Inner Mongolia Bayan Nur (巴彥淖爾市 *bāyànnàoěr shì*), Baotou (包頭 *bāotóu*), and Ordos (鄂爾多斯市 *è'ěrduōsī shì*) cities.

During the "Uprising of the Five Barbarians" (五胡亂華 *Wǔhú luànhuá*), which indeed brought chaos to China (304–316 CE), the Xianbei established the Northern Wei dynasty. The western lands to include the Gobi were controlled by its subordinate Rouran (柔然 *róurán*) Khaganate. In ca. 550 the Eurasian steppes were still dominated by the Rouran, whom were pejoratively called juan-juan (or *ru-ru*) meaning worms (蠕蠕 *rúrú*) by the ethnic Chinese. The Rouran controlled lands from the Turfan Basin (Turpan Depression 吐魯番盆地 *tǔlǔfān péndì*) to northeast Manchuria (bordering modern-day Korea). Another nomadic group, the Hepthalites (White Huns), controlled lands west of the Rouran, from Lake Balkhash (modern day Kazakhstan) to Merv (Turkmenistan) and Afghanistan. China referred to the Hepthalites (sometimes referred to as the Ephthalites) as the Yeda (Chinese term: 嚈噠 *yàndā*). Yet one more nomadic herding people, the Tujue (突厥 *tújué*), or the Turkic Khaganate, originated in the Altai region. The Tujue (Turkic Khaganate) rose to their prominence during the Northern Qi (北齊 *běiqí*; 550–577 CE). Contemporary Chinese wrote of the Tujue in the following way: "They are good equestrians and archers, but cruel by nature." By 552, the Turkic Khaganate usurped the Rouran, dominating essentially all of Mongolia (Xiong 2006).

Tang Dynasty (618–907)

Through the late Tang dynasty (ca. 900), China continued to make some inroads into modern-day Inner Mongolia. These regions were known as Hetao (河套 *hétào*), which included the western Alashan (阿拉善 *ālāshàn*), the eastern Lüliang (呂梁山 *lǚliáng shān*) mountains, and Ordos. But all of this was to end. When the Tang dynasty collapsed, in 907, the Khitan Yelü Abaoji (耶律阿保機 *yēlǜābǎojī*) took over Inner Mongolia. In 916, after the formation of the Khitan State (契丹國 *qìdānguó*), the Liao (遼 *liáo*) dynasty was formally named. During this time its first capital, Shangjing (上京 *shàngjīng*), was founded near today's Inner Mongolia Chifeng City, Bairin Left Banner (巴林左旗 *bālín zuǒqí*).

Another rival nomadic group, the Jurchens (later called the Manchu), defeated the Liao dynasty, and ruled from 1115–1234. It referred to its reign as the Jin (金 *jīn*, from the Jurchen language of a river meaning "gold"). Ultimately, in 1234 the Mongolians would again rise up, combining its armies with the Khitan, Jurchen and even various Han Chinese factions, ultimately defeating the now already Sinicized Jin.

The Mongol Chinggis (aka Genghis) Khan vanquished the Jurched[1] Jin (金 *jīn*) dynasty, establishing the Greater Mongolian State (大蒙古國 *dàménggǔ guó*). In 1271 his grandson, Kublai Khan reigned over the newly named Yuan dynasty. At its apogee (1279), the Mongolian empire not only ruled China (Yuan dynasty), but also extended from modern-day Iran and Russia to the Sea of Japan. With the defeat of the Yuan by the Ming (1368), the Mongols retreated to their homeland steppes.

[1] The English transcription of the Mongolian plural of Jurchen.

Jurchen (Manchu) Rule and the Rise of the Qing Dynasty

In 1593 the Jurchen chief, Nurhači (努爾哈赤 *nŭĕrhāchì*) became the leader of both his tribe and Mongolian rivals. Recalling the earlier Jurchen Jin (金 *jīn*) dynasty (1115–1234), Nurhači declared the founding of the Later Jin (後金 *hòujīn*) in 1616. It was left to his son, Hong Taiji (皇太極 *huángtàijí*; originally from the Mongolian rendering of 皇太子 *huáng tàizi*) to finish the conquest of the Ming. In November 1635, for reasons that are still not altogether clear, Hong Taiji officially coined the term Manju (滿洲 *mănzhōu*) as a means to refer to the Jurchen (女真 *nǚzhēn* or 諸申 *zhūshēn*), to represent his race of people *and* their territory. Endymion Wilkinson believes Hong Taiji adopted the name Manju, even going so far to prohibit any reference to older Jurchen terms, "in order to signal a new beginning" (Wilkinson 2012). For his part, the Manchurian Qian Long (乾隆 *qián lóng*), a later Qing Dynastic emperor, reportedly said that the word Manchu was from the Chinese words Manzhu (滿珠 *mănzhū*), emphasizing that this was an honorific to express the origins of the Jurchen, Mongolian, and Tibetan peoples. Another knowledgeable source reports that *Manjusri*, the Sanskrit for "wonderful luck," was transcribed into (文殊 *wénshū*), and dialectically ended up as Manzhu (Hsü 2000). The English term "Manchuria" likely originates from the nineteenth century Japanese rendering, *Manshū* (滿洲 *mănzhōu*).

After finally defeating the Ming, the Qing dynasty (大清 *dàqīng* 1644–1912) was founded. Although previously meant as a military enlistment system meant only for ethnic Manchurians, in ca. 1670 the Qing dynasty formally instituted the 49-banner (旗 *qí* = flag) territorial administration for Inner Mongolia, allowing Mongol and Chinese to serve in the army ranks (Endicott 2012). These banner names still remain, such as the term "League" or Meng (盟 *méng*) being used for geographical and administrative names. Many of these former Leagues were later converted into larger, provincial-level cities. In 1691, Ulanhot City (烏蘭浩特市 *wūlán hàotè shì*, Mongolian for "Red City") was made the capital (its older name was "Temple of the Royal Prince" (王爺廟 *wángyé miào*). Ulanhot also served for a brief time as the capital of Inner Mongolia from 1947–9.

Revolutionary China

Finally separating it from Inner Mongolia Autonomous Region under Chinese rule, Outer Mongolia was granted independence in 1911. After reverting back to Chinese control (1919–21), Soviet-backed troops invaded Outer Mongolia to defeat White Russian forces in 11 July 1921. The "Mongolian People's Republic" was declared in 1924, albeit only recognized by the Soviet government. The Japanese invasion of China claimed two provinces in 1937: Chahar (察哈爾 *cháhāĕr*) and Suiyuan (綏遠 *suīyuăn*). The capital of the "autonomous" Chahar Province, Kalgan, is from the

Mongolian *halha* for "mart," and is now known as Zhangjiakou (張家口 *zhāngjiākǒu*) in Hebei Province.

In 1953, 4 years after the founding of the People's Republic of China, Zhangjiakou City was the capital of Chahar, Chengde City was the capital of Rehe ("Jehol" 熱河 *rèhé*), and Guisui (歸綏 *guīsuī*) of Suiyuan. Guisui would later (1954) be named Hohhot City (呼和浩特市 *hūhéhàotè shì*) and was later made the capital of Inner Mongolia. By 1955, the modern Inner Mongolian provincial borders were basically shaped the way they are today.

Population Trends and Economy

Inner Mongolia had a population (non-permanent residents, 常住人口 *chángzhù rénkǒu*) of about 24,050,000 as of 2020 (see Table 17.1), contracting nearly 3% since 2010, and a permanent (*hukou*) population of 24,410,000. Ranked 22nd in terms of gross domestic product (GDP) at USD $270 billion out of mainland China's 31 provinces and major cities, but tenth in terms of per capita income with a respectable $4900 (Zhang 2021).

Inner Mongolia is ranked second of all mainland Chinese provinces in coal production (2019), and also leads in terms of rare earths mining. Baotou City represents the largest source of rare earth minerals in all of China, itself a world leader in these special elements (Hui 2021). Developing this source to corner the market led to the

Table 17.1 Inner Mongolia population (residential 常住人口 *chángzhù rénkǒu*) data. (IMBS 2021)

City/League	Population (2010)	Population (2020)
Wu-Lan-Cha-Bu (Ulanqab) City 烏蘭察布市 *wūlánchábù shì*	2,143,590	1,706,328
Xing'an (Hinggan) League 興安盟 *xīngānméng*	1,613,250	1,416,929
Xilinguole (Xilingol) League 錫林郭勒盟 *xīlínguōlèméng*	1,028,022	1,107,075
A-Lashan (Alxa) League 阿拉善盟 *ālāshànméng*	231,334	262,361
E'erduosi (Ordos) City 鄂爾多斯市 *èěrduōsī shì*	1,940,653	2,153,638
Hu-Lun-Bei-Er (Hulunbuir) City 呼倫貝爾市 *hūlúnbèiěr shì*	2,549,278	2,242,875
Bayannao'er (Bayan Nur) City 巴彥淖爾市 *bāyànnàoěr shì*	1,669,915	1,538,715
Wuhai City 烏海市 *wūhǎi shì*	532,902	556,621
Chifeng City 赤峰市 *chìfēng shì*	4,341,245	4,035,967
Tongliao City 通遼市 *tōngliáo shì*	3,139,153	2,873,168
Hu-He-Hao-Te (Hohhot) City 呼和浩特市 *hūhéhàotè shì*	2,866,615	3,446,100
Baotou City 包頭市 *bāotóu shì*	2,650,364	2,709,378
Total	**24,706,321**	**24,049,155**

creation of a new administrative entity, the Baotou Rare Earths and High Technology Industry Development Zone[2] with a recorded (2020 census) population of 184,127 (Table 17.2 and Fig. 17.2).

Table 17.2 Inner Mongolia: population data of cities and their subordinate sectors (IMBS 2021)

Cities and subordinate sectors, population (2020 census)	Subordinate district, city and county populations (2020)	Population (2020)
Wu-Lan-Cha-Bu (Ulanqab) City 烏蘭察布市 ***wūlánchábù shì***		**1,706,328**
Jining District 集寧區 *jíníng qū*	425,059	
Fengzhen City 豐鎮市 *fēngzhèn shì*	195,229	
Zhuozi County 卓資縣 *zhuózī xiàn*	85,648	
Huade County 化德縣 *huàdé xiàn*	95,273	
Shangdu County 商都縣 *shāngdū xiàn*	173,926	
Xinghe County 興和縣 *xīnghé xiàn*	167,881	
Liangcheng County 涼城縣 *liángchéng xiàn*	119,061	
Chaha'eryouyiqianqi (Qahar Right Front Banner; Chahar Youyi Qianqi) 察哈爾右翼前旗 *cháhā'ěr yòuyìqián qí*	125,172	
Chaha'eryouyizhongqi (Qahar Right Middle Banner; Chahar Youyizhongqi) 察哈爾右翼中旗 *cháhā'ěr yòuyìzhōng qí*	86,108	
Chaha'eryouyihouqi (Qahar Right Rear Banner; Chahar Youyihouqi) 察哈爾右翼後期 *cháhā'ěr yòuyìhòu qī*	103,599	
Siziwangqi (Dorbod Banner) 四子王旗 *sìzǐwáng qí*	129,372	
Xing'an (Hinggan) League 興安盟 ***xīngānméng***		**1,416,929**
Wulanhaote (Ulanhot) City 烏蘭浩特市 *wūlánhàotè shì*	356,035	
A'ershan (Arxan) City 阿爾山市 *ā'ěrshān shì*	32,301	
Tuquan County 突泉縣 *tūquán xiàn*	220,668	
Ke'erqinyouyiqianqi (Horqin Right Front Banner; Horqin Youyi Qianqi) 科爾沁右翼前旗 *kē'ěrqìn yòuyìqián qí*	285,392	
Ke'erqinyouyizhongqi (Horqin Right Middle Banner; Horqin Youyi Zhongqi) 科爾沁右翼中旗 *kē'ěrqìn yòuyìzhōng qí*	207,380	
Zhalaiteqi (Jalaid Qi; Jalaid Banner) 扎賚特旗 *zālàitè qí*	315,153	

(continued)

[2] 包頭稀土高新技術產業開發區 (*bāotóu xītǔ gāoxīn jìshù chǎnyè kāifāqū*).

Table 17.2 (continued)

Cities and subordinate sectors, population (2020 census)	Subordinate district, city and county populations (2020)	Population (2020)
Xilinguole (Xilingol) League 錫林郭勒盟 ***xīlínguōlèméng***		**1,107,075**
Xilinhaote (Xilinhot) City 錫林浩特市 *xīlínhàotè shì*	349,953	
Erlianhaote (Erenhot) City 二連浩特市 *èrliánhàotè shì*	75,794	
Duolun (Dolon Nor; Dolonnur) County 多倫縣 *duōlún xiàn*	103,736	
Abagaqi (Abag Qi; Abag Banner; Xin Hot) 阿巴嘎旗 *ābāgā qí*	38,589	
Sunitezuoqi (Sonid Left Banner; Sonid Zuoqi) 蘇尼特左旗 *sūnítèzuǒ qí*	33,643	
Suniteyouqi (Sonid Youqi; Sonid Right Banner; Sonid Youqi) 蘇尼特右旗 *sūnítèyòu qí*	62,402	
Dong Wuzhumuqinqi (East Ujimqin Banner; Dong Ujimqin Qi) 東烏珠穆沁旗 *dōngwūzhūmùqìn qí*	70,610	
Xiwuzhumuqinqi (West Ujimqin Banner; Xi Ujimqin Qi) 西烏珠穆沁旗 *xīwūzhūmùqìn qí*	99,255	
Taipusiqi (Taibus Banner) 太僕寺旗 *tàipūsì qí*	109,370	
Xianghuangqi (Bordered Yellow Banner) 鑲黄旗 *xiānghuáng qí*	27,399	
Zhengxiangbaiqi (Plain and Bordered Banner) 正鑲白旗 *zhèngxiāngbái qí*	42,950	
Zhenglanqi (Xulun Hoh Banner; Plain Blue Banner; Shuluun Huh Banner) 正藍旗 *zhènglán qí*	69,908	
A-Lashan (Alxa) League 阿拉善盟 ***ālāshànméng***		**262,361**
Alashanzuoqi (Alxa Left Banner; Alxa Zuoqi) 阿拉善左旗 *ālāshànzuǒ qí*	176,744	
Alashanyouqi (Alxa Youqi; Alxa Right Banner) 阿拉善右旗 *ālāshànyòu qí*	22,647	
E'jinaqi (Ejin Qi; Ejin Banner) 額濟納旗 *é'jìnà qí*	35,756	
Alashan High Technology Industry Development Zone 阿拉善高新技術產業開發區 *ālāshàn gāoxīnjìshù chǎnyè kāifāqū*	27,214	
E'erduosi (Ordos) City 鄂爾多斯市 ***èěrduōsī shì***		**2,153,638**
Dongsheng District 東勝區 *dōngshèng qū*	574,242	
Kangbashi (Hia Bagx) District 康巴什區 *kāngbāshén qū*	118,796	
Dalateqi (Dalad Banner) 達拉特旗 *dálātè qí*	328,593	
Zhunge'erqi (Junggar Banner) 准格爾旗 *zhǔngé'ěr qí*	359,184	
Etuokeqianqi (Otog Front Banner) 鄂托克前旗 *è'tuōkèqián qí*	92,724	

(continued)

Table 17.2 (continued)

Cities and subordinate sectors, population (2020 census)	Subordinate district, city and county populations (2020)	Population (2020)
Etuokeqi (Otog Banner) 鄂托克旗 *ètuōkè qí*	162,726	
Hangjinqi (Hanggin Qi; Hanggin Banner) 杭錦旗 *hángjǐn qí*	110,824	
Wushenqi (Uxin Banner; Uxin Qi) 烏審旗 *wūshěn qí*	158,566	
Yijinhuoluoqi (Ejin Horo Qi; Ejin Horo Banner) 伊金霍洛旗 *yījīnhuòluò qí*	247,983	
Hu-Lun-Bei-Er (Hulunbuir) City 呼倫貝爾市 ***hūlúnbèiěr shì***		**2,242,875**
Haila'er (Hailar) District 海拉爾區 *hǎilā'ěr qū*	365,012	
Zhalainuo'er District 扎賚諾爾區 *zālàinuò'ěr qū*	84,424	
Manzhouli City 滿洲里市 *mǎnzhōulǐ shì*	150,508	
Zhalantun City 扎蘭屯市 *zālántún shì*	318,933	
Yakeshi City 牙克石市 *yákèshí shì*	256,396	
Genhe City 根河市 *gēnhé shì*	71,437	
E'erguna (Ergun) City 額爾古納市 *é'ěrgǔnà shì*	68,482	
Arongqi (Arun) 阿榮旗 *āróng qí*	257,815	
Xinba'erhuyouqi (New Barag Right Banner; Xin Barag Youqi; Altan Emel) 新巴爾虎右旗 *xīnbā'ěrhǔyòu qí*	38,358	
Xinba'erhuzuoqi (New Barag Left Banner; Xin Barag Zuoqi) 新巴爾虎左旗 *xīnbā'ěrhǔzuǒ qí*	37,007	
Chenba'erhuqi (Old Barag Banner; Bayan Hure) 陳巴爾虎旗 *chénbā'ěrhǔ qí*	50,556	
E'lunchun (Oroqen) Autonomous Banner 鄂倫春自治旗 *è'lúnchūn zìzhìqí*	174,023	
E'wenkezu (Evenk) Autonomous Banner 鄂溫克族自治旗 *è'wēnkèzú zìzhìqí*	141,102	
Molidawa Dawoerzu (Morin Dawa Daur) Autonomous Banner 莫力達瓦斡爾族自治旗 *mòlìdáwǎwò'ěrzú zìzhìqí*	228,822	
Bayannao'er (Bayan Nur) City 巴彥淖爾市 ***bāyànnàoěr shì***		**1,538,715**
Linhe District 臨河區 *línhé qū*	582,206	
Wuyuan County 五原縣 *wǔyuán xiàn*	224,809	
Dengkou County 磴口縣 *dèngkǒu xiàn*	90,196	
Wulateqianqi (Urat/Urad Front Banner; Urad Qianqi) 烏拉特前旗 *wūlātèqián qí*	257,826	
Wulatezhongqi (Urat/Urad Middle Banner; Urad Zhongqi) 烏拉特中旗 *wūlātèzhōng qí*	112,159	
Wulatehouqi (Urat/Urad Rear Banner; Urad Houqi) 烏拉特後旗 *wūlātèhòu qí*	53,946	

(continued)

Table 17.2 (continued)

Cities and subordinate sectors, population (2020 census)	Subordinate district, city and county populations (2020)	Population (2020)
Hangjin Houqi (Hanggin Rear Banner) 杭錦後旗 *hángjǐnhòu qí*	217,573	
Wuhai City 烏海市 ***wūhǎi shì***		**556,621**
Haibowan District 海勃灣區 *hǎibówān qū*	339,155	
Hainan District 海南區 *hǎinán qū*	94,770	
Wuda District 烏達區 *wūdá qū*	122,696	
Chifeng City 赤峰市 ***chìfēng shì***		**4,035,967**
Hongshan District 紅山區 *hóngshān qū*	469,079	
Yuanbaoshan District 元寶山區 *yuánbǎoshān qū*	284,990	
Songshan District 松山區 *sōngshān qū*	706,312	
Ningcheng County 寧城縣 *níngchéng xiàn*	484,397	
Linxi County 林西縣 *línxī xiàn*	186,663	
Aluke'erqinqi (Ar Khorqin Banner) 阿魯科爾沁旗 *ālǔkē'ěrqìn qí*	240,360	
Balin Zuoqi (Bairin Left Banner) 巴林左旗 *bālínzuǒ qí*	277,522	
Balin Youqi (Bairin Right Banner; Bairin Youqi) 巴林右旗 *bālínyòu qí*	155,027	
Keshiketengqi (Hexigten Banner) 克什克騰旗 *kèshénkèténg qí*	186,143	
Wengniuteqi (Ongniud Qi; Ongniud Banner) 翁牛特旗 *wēngniútè qí*	333,970	
Kalaqinqi (Harqin Banner) 喀喇沁旗 *kālǎqìn qí*	262,792	
Aohanqi (Aohan Banner) 敖漢旗 *áohàn qí*	448,712	
Tongliao City 通遼市 ***tōngliáo shì***		**2,873,168**
Ke'erqin (Horqin) District 科爾沁區 *kē'ěrqìn qū*	718,665	
Huolinguole (Holingol) City 霍林郭勒市 *huòlínguōlè shì*	138,676	
Kailu County 開魯縣 *kāilǔ xiàn*	313,364	
Kulunqi (Hure Qi; Hure Banner) 庫倫旗 *kùlún qí*	151,133	
Naimanqi (Naiman Qi) 奈曼旗 *nàimàn qí*	375,312	
Zhaluteqi (Jarud Qi; Jarud Banner) 扎魯特旗 *zālǔtè qí*	251,806	
Ke'erqinzuoyizhongqi (Horqin Left Middle Banner) 科爾沁左翼中旗 *kē'ěrqìnzuǒyìzhōng qí*	399,631	
Ke'erqinzuoyihouqi (Horqin Left Rear Banner) 科爾沁左翼後旗 *kē'ěrqìnzuǒyìhòu qí*	321,438	
Hu-He-Hao-Te (Hohhot) City 呼和浩特市 ***hūhéhàotè shì***		**3,446,100**
Xincheng District 新城區 *xīnchéng qū*	699,672	
Huimin District 回民區 *huímín qū*	436,042	

(continued)

Table 17.2 (continued)

Cities and subordinate sectors, population (2020 census)	Subordinate district, city and county populations (2020)	Population (2020)
Yuquan District 玉泉區 *yùquán qū*	524,573	
Saihan District 賽罕區 *sàihǎn qū*	885,321	
Tuoketuo (Togtoh) County 托克托縣 *tuōkètuō xiàn*	166,192	
Wuchuan County 武川縣 *wǔchuān xiàn*	95,869	
Helinge'er (Horinger) County 和林格爾縣 *hélíngé'ěr xiàn*	162,476	
Qingshuihe County 清水河縣 *qīngshuǐhé xiàn*	76,674	
Tumotezuoqi (Tumed; Tumd Left Banner; Tumd Zuoqi) 土默特左旗 *tǔmòtèzuǒ qí*	263,121	
Hohhot High Technology Industry Development Zone 呼和浩特高新技術產業開發區 *hūhéhàotè gāoxīnjìshù chǎnyè kāifāqū*	136,150	
Baotou City 包頭市 ***bāotóu shì***		**2,709,378**
Kundulun (Hondlon) District 昆都侖區 *kūndūlún qū*	787,681	
Donghe District 東河區 *dōnghé qū*	484,218	
Qingshan District 青山區 *qīngshān qū*	535,128	
Shiguai District 石拐區 *shíguǎi qū*	24,745	
Baiyun'ebo Kuangqu (Bayan Obo mining) District 白雲鄂博礦區 *báiyún'èbó kuàngqū*	22,681	
Jiuyuan District 九原區 *jiǔyuán qū*	245,190	
Guyang County 固陽縣 *gùyáng xiàn*	118,624	
Tumote Youqi (Tumed; Tumd Right Banner; Tumd Youqi) 土默特右旗 *tǔmòtèyòu qí*	237,421	
Da'erhanmaomingan lianheqi (Darhan Muminggan Lianheqi; Darhan United Banner) 達爾罕茂明安聯合旗 *dá'ěrhǎnmàomíngān liánhéqí*	69,563	
Baotou Rare Earths and High Technology Industry Development Zone 包頭稀土高新技術產業開發區 *bāotóu xītǔ gāoxīnjìshù chǎnyè kāifāqū*	184,127	

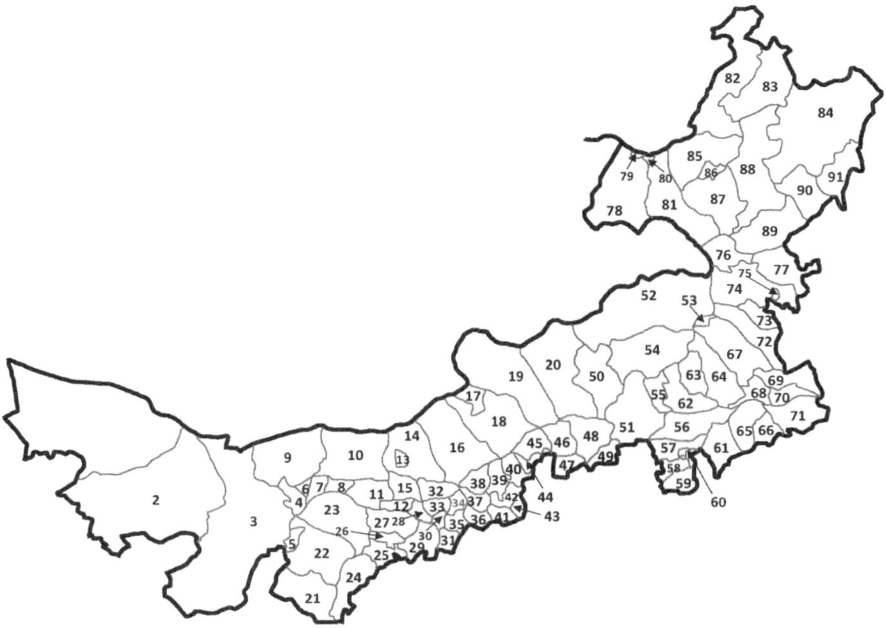

1. **E'jinaqi (Ejin Banner)**
2. **Alashanyouqi (Alxa Right Banner)**
3. **Alashanzuoqi (Alxa Left Banner)**
4. **Dengkou County**
5. **Wuhai City**
6. **Hangjinhouqi (Hanggin Rear Banner)**
7. **Bayannuo'er (Bayan Nur) City**
8. **Wuyuan County**
9. **Wulatehouqi (Urad Rear Banner)**
10. **Wulatezhongqi (Urad Middle Banner)**
11. **Wulateqianqi (Urad Front Banner)**
12. **Baotou City**
13. **Baiyune'bokuangqu (Bayan Obo mining district)**
14. **Da'erhanmaomingan Lianheqi (Darhan United Banner)**
15. **Guyang County**
16. **Siziwangqi (Dorbod Banner)**
17. **Erlianhaote (Erenhot) City**
18. **Suniteyouqi (Sonid Right Banner)**
19. **Sunitezuoqi (Sonid Left Banner)**
20. **Abagaqi (Abag Banner)**
21. **Etuokeqianqi (Otog Front Banner)**
22. **Etuokeqi (Otog Banner)**
23. **Hangjinqi (Hanggin Banner)**
24. **Wushenqi (Uxin Banner)**
25. **Yijinhuoluoqi (Ejin Horo Banner)**
26. **E'erduosi (Ordos) City**
27. **Dalateqi (Dalad Banner)**
28. **Tumoteyouqi (Tumd Right Banner)**
47. **Taibusiqi (Taibus Banner)**
48. **Zhenglanqi (Plain Blue Banner**
49. **Duolun County**
50. **Xilinhaote (Xilinhot) City**
51. **Keshikeshengqi (Hexigten Banner)**
52. **Dongwuzhumuqinqi (East Ujimqin Banner)**
53. **Huolinguole (Holingol) City**
54. **Xiwuzhumuqinqi (West Ujimqin Banner)**
55. **Linxi County**
56. **Wengniuteqi (Ongniud Banner)**
57. **Songshan District**
58. **Kalaqinqi (Harqin Banner)**
59. **Ningcheng County**
60. **Chifeng City: Hongshan District, Yuanbaoshan District**
61. **Aohanqi (Aohan Banner)**
62. **Balinyouqi (Bairin Right Banner)**
63. **Balinzuoqi (Bairin Left Banner)**
64. **Aluke'erqinqi (Ar Khorqin Banner)**
65. **Naimanqi (Naiman Banner)**
66. **Kulunqi (Hure Banner)**
67. **Zhaluteqi (Jarud Banner)**
68. **Kailu County**
69. **Ke'erqinzuoyizhongqi (Horqin Left Middle Banner)**
70. **Ke'erqin (Horqin) District**
71. **Ke'erqinzuoyihouqi (Horqin Left Rear Banner)**
72. **Ke'erqinyouyizhongqi (Horqin Right Middle Banner)**

Fig. 17.2 Inner Mongolia: Subdistricts (Hohhot City's Governmental Center). Drawn by the author, after People's Republic of China, Ministry of Civil Affairs (MCA 2020)

29. Zhunge'erqi (Junggar Banner)
30. Tuoketuo (Togtoh) County
31. Qingshuihe County
32. Wuquan County
33. Tumotezuoqi (Tumd Left Banner)
34. Huhehaote (Hohhot) City (Government Center)
35. Helinge'er (Horinger) County
36. Jingcheng County
37. Zhuozi County
38. Chaha'eryouyizhongqi (Qahar Right Middle Banner)
39. Chaha'eryouyihouqi (Qahar Right Rear Banner)
40. Shangdu County
41. Fengzhen County
42. Chaha'eryouyiqianqi (Qahar Right Front Banner)
43. Xinghe County
44. Huade County
45. Xianghuangqi (Bordered Yellow Banner)
46. Zhengxiangbaiqi (Plain and Bordered Banner)
73. Tuquan County
74. Ke'erqinyouyiqianqi (Horqin Right Front Banner)
75. Wulanhaote (Ulanhot)
76. A'ershan (Arxan) City
77. Zhalaiteqi (Jalaid Banner)
78. Xinba'erhuyouqi (New Barag Banner)
79. Manzhouli City
80. Zhalainuo'er (Jalainur) District
81. Xinba'erhuzuoqi (New Barag Left Banner)
82. E'erguna (Ergun) City
83. Genhe City
84. Elunchun (Oroqen) Autonomous Banner
85. Chenba'erhuqi (Old Barag Banner)
86. Hulunbe'er (Hulunbuir) City
87. Ewenkezu (Evenk) Autonomous Banner
88. Yakeshi City
89. Zhaluntun City
90. Arongqi (Arun Banner)
91. Molidawadawoerzuqi (Morin Dawa Daur Autonomous Banner

Fig. 17.2 (continued)

Table 17.3 shows the *hukou* (family registered) populations based on PRC Ministry of Civil Affairs data. (Districts listed directly under major cities are government seats, as are those in parentheses). One can compare these data with the census (usual residential populations based on 2010 and 2020 censuses in Tables 17.1 and 17.2.

Inner Mongolia (*Nei Menggu*) Autonomous Region (內蒙古自治區)

Prefectural Government: Hu-He-Hao-Te (Hohhot)

Table 17.3 Inner Mongolia: permanent registered (戶籍人口 hùjí rénkǒu) populations (MCA 2020)

Name	Traditional	Simplified	Population (2012)	Population (2016)	Population (2020)	Area (Sq. Km)
Inner Mongolia Autonomous Region	內蒙古自治區	内蒙古自治区	24,530,000	24,600,000	24,410,000	1,961,130
Hu-He-Hao-Te (Huhehaote; Hohhot) City	呼和浩特市	呼和浩特市	2,310,000	2,310,000	2,460,000	17,344
Xincheng District (Chengjisihandajie Subdistrict)	新城區(城吉思汗大街街道)	新城区 (成吉思汗大街街道)	360,000	370,000	420,000	700
Huimin District (Gangtielu Subdistrict)	回民區 (鋼鐵路街道)	回民区 (钢铁路街道)	240,000	240,000	240,000	175
Yuquan District (Zhaojunlu Subdistrict)	玉泉區 (昭君路街道)	玉泉区 (昭君路街道)	200,000	200,000	200,000	207
Saihan District (Zhaowudalu Subdistrict)	賽罕區 (昭烏達路街道)	赛罕区 (昭乌达路街道)	410,000	420,000	520,000	1025
Tuoketuo (Togtoh) County (Shuanghe Town)	托克托縣 (雙河鎮)	托克托县 (双河镇)	210,000	210,000	200,000	1313
Wuchuan County (Kekeyiligeng Town)	武川縣 (可可以力更鎮)	武川县 (可可以力更镇)	180,000	170,000	170,000	4885
Helinge'er [Horinger] County (Chengguan Town)	和林格爾縣 (城關鎮)	和林格尔县 (城关镇)	200,000	200,000	200,000	3401
Qingshuihe County (Chengguan Town)	清水河縣 (城關鎮)	清水河县 (城关镇)	150,000	140,000	140,000	2859
Tumotezuoqi (Tumed; Tumd Left Banner; Tumd Zuoqi] (Chasuqi Town)	土默特左旗 (察素齊鎮)	土默特左旗 (察素齐镇)	360,000	360,000	360,000	2779

(continued)

Table 17.3 (continued)

Name	Traditional	Simplified	Population (2012)	Population (2016)	Population (2020)	Area (Sq. Km)
Baotou City	包頭市	包头市	2,200,000	2,230,000	2,240,000	27,652
Kundulun [Hondlon] District (Shaoxianlu Subdistrict)	昆都侖區 (少先路街道)	昆都仑区 (少先路街道)	490,000	500,000	520,000	301
Donghe District (Hedong Subdistrict)	東河區 (河東街道)	东河区 (河东街道)	430,000	430,000	410,000	470
Qingshan District (Qingfu Town)	青山區 (青福鎮)	青山区 (青福镇)	360,000	370,000	400,000	280
Shiguai District (Shiguai Subdistrict)	石拐區 (石拐街道)	石拐区 (石拐街道)	70,000	70,000	50,000	761
Baiyun'ebo Kuangqu (Bayan Obo mining) District (Tongyang Subdistrict)	白雲鄂博礦區 (通陽街道)	白云鄂博矿区 (通阳道街道)	20,000	20,000	20,000	303
Jiuyuan District (Shahe Subdistrict)	九原區 (沙河街道)	九原区 (沙河街道)	150,000	150,000	170,000	734
Guyang County (Jinshan Town)	固陽縣 (金山鎮)	固阳县 (金山镇)	210,000	210,000	200,000	5025
Tumote Youqi [Tumed; Tumd Right Banner; Tumd Youqi] (Salaqi Town)	土默特右旗 (薩拉齊鎮)	土默特右旗 (萨拉齐镇)	360,000	370,000	360,000	2368
Da'erhanmaomingan lianheqi [Darhan Muminggan Lianheqi; Darhan United Banner] (Bailingmiao Town)	達爾罕茂明安聯合旗 (百靈廟鎮)	达尔罕茂明安联合旗 (百灵庙镇)	110,000	110,000	110,000	17,410
Wuhai City	烏海市	乌海市	440,000	440,000	440,000	1754
Haibowan District (Fenghuangling Subdistrict)	海勃灣區 (鳳凰嶺街道)	海勃湾区 (凤凰岭街道)	220,000	230,000	240,000	529
Hainan District (Lasengzhong Subdistrict)	海南區 (拉僧仲街道)	海南区 (拉僧仲街道)	90,000	90,000	80,000	1005
Wuda District (Binhai Subdistrict)	烏達區 (濱海街道)	乌达区 (滨海街道)	130,000	120,000	120,000	220

Hongshan District (Zhanqian Subdistrict)	紅山區 (站前街道)	红山区 (站前街道)	350,000	360,000	350,000	506
Yuanbaoshan District (Pingzhuangcheng regional Subdistrict)	元寶山區 (平莊城區街道)	元宝山区 (平庄城区街道)	330,000	330,000	320,000	952
Songshan District (Zhenxing Subdistrict)	松山區 (振興街道)	松山区 (振兴街道)	540,000	550,000	600,000	5618
Ningcheng County (Tianyi Town)	寧城縣 (天義鎮)	宁城县 (天义镇)	600,000	610,000	610,000	4305
Linxi County (Linxi Town)	林西縣 (林西鎮)	林西县 (林西镇)	240,000	240,000	230,000	3933
Aluke'erqinqi [Ar Khorqin Banner] (Tianshan Town)	阿魯科爾沁旗 (天山鎮)	阿鲁科尔沁旗 (天山镇)	300,000	300,000	290,000	14,555
Balin Zuoqi [Bairin Left Banner] (Lindong Town)	巴林左旗 (林東鎮)	巴林左旗 (林东镇)	360,000	360,000	340,000	6459
Balin Youqi [Bairin Right Banner; Bairin Youqi] (Daban Town)	巴林右旗 (大板鎮)	巴林右旗 (大板镇)	180,000	180,000	180,000	9837
Keshiketengqi [Hexigten Banner] (Jingpeng Town)	克什克騰旗 (經棚鎮)	克什克腾旗 (经棚镇)	250,000	250,000	250,000	20,673
Wengniuteqi [Ongniud Qi; Ongniud Banner] (Wudan Town)	翁牛特旗 (烏丹鎮)	翁牛特旗 (乌丹镇)	480,000	490,000	480,000	11,882
Kalaqinqi [Harqin Banner] (Jinshan Town)	喀喇沁旗 (錦山鎮)	喀喇沁旗 (锦山镇)	350,000	350,000	350,000	3050
Aohanqi [Aohan Banner] (Xinhui Town)	敖漢旗 (新惠鎮)	敖汉旗 (新惠镇)	600,000	600,000	610,000	8294
Tongliao City	通遼市	通辽市	3,200,000	3,210,000	3,160,000	59,364
Ke'erqin [Horqin] District (Ximen Subdistrict)	科爾沁區 (西門街道)	科尔沁区 (西门街道)	840,000	850,000	840,000	3214
Huolinguole [Holingol] City (Mositai Subdistrict)	霍林郭勒市 (莫斯台街道)	霍林郭勒市 (莫斯台街道)	80,000	80,000	80,000	585

(continued)

Table 17.3 (continued)

Name	Traditional	Simplified	Population (2012)	Population (2016)	Population (2020)	Area (Sq. Km)
Kailu County (Kailu Town)	開魯縣 (開魯鎮)	开鲁县 (开鲁镇)	400,000	400,000	390,000	4488
Kulunqi [Hure Qi; Hure Banner] (Kulun Town)	庫倫旗 (庫倫鎮)	库伦旗 (库伦镇)	180,000	180,000	180,000	4714
Naimanqi [Naiman Qi] (Daqintala Town)	奈曼旗 (大沁他拉鎮)	奈曼旗 (大沁他拉镇)	440,000	450,000	450,000	8120
Zhaluteqi [Jarud Qi; Jarud Banner] (Lubei Town)	扎魯特旗 (魯北鎮)	扎鲁特旗 (鲁北镇)	310,000	310,000	310,000	17,193
Ke'erqinzuoyizhongqi [Horqin Left Middle Banner] (Baokang Town)	科爾沁左翼中旗 (保康鎮)	科尔沁左翼中旗 (保康镇)	540,000	540,000	520,000	9569
Ke'erqinzuoyihouqi [Horqin Left Rear Banner] (Ganqika Town)	科爾沁左翼後旗 (甘旗卡鎮)	科尔沁左翼后旗 (甘旗卡镇)	410,000	400,000	400,000	11,481
Hu-Lun-Bei-Er (Hulunbuir) City	呼倫貝爾市	呼伦贝尔市	2,710,000	2,820,000	2,560,000	262,062
Haila'er [Hailar] District (Zhengyang Subdistrict)	海拉爾區 (正陽街道)	海拉尔区 (正阳街道)	270,000	280,000	290,000	1440
Zhalainuo'er District[a] (Disan Subdistrict)	扎賚諾爾區 (第三街道)	扎赉诺尔区 (第三街道)	N/A	150,000	90,000	279
Manzhouli City (Dongshan Subdistrict)	滿洲里市 (東山街道)	满洲里市 (东山街道)	170,000	170,000	90,000	453
Zhalantun City (Xinghua Subdistrict)	扎蘭屯市 (興華街道)	扎兰屯市 (兴华街道)	430,000	420,000	410,000	16,800
Yakeshi City (Xingong Subdistrict)	牙克石市 (新工街道)	牙克石市 (新工街道)	370,000	350,000	330,000	27,590
Genhe City (Hexi Subdistrict)	根河市 (河西街道)	根河市 (河西街道)	160,000	160,000	130,000	19,659
E'erguna (Ergun) City (Labudalin Subdistrict)	額爾古納市 (拉布大林街道)	额尔古纳市 (拉布大林街道)	80,000	80,000	80,000	28,958
Arongqi [Arun] (Naji Town)	阿榮旗 (那吉鎮)	阿荣旗 (那吉镇)	330,000	330,000	320,000	12,063

Xinba'erhuyouqi [Xin (New) Barag Right Banner; Xin Barag Youqi; Altan Emel] (Alatane'mole Town)	新巴爾虎右旗 (阿拉坦額莫勒鎮)	新巴尔虎右旗 (阿拉坦额莫勒镇)	40,000	40,000	40,000	24,839
Xinba'erhuzuoqi [Xin (New) Barag Left Banner; Xin Barag Zuoqi] (Amugulang [Amgalang] Town)	新巴爾虎左旗 (阿木古郎鎮)	新巴尔虎左旗 (阿木古郎镇)	40,000	40,000	40,000	22,000
Chenba'erhuqi [Chen (Old) Barag Banner; Bayan Hure] (Bayankuren Town)	陳巴爾虎旗 (巴彥庫仁鎮)	陈巴尔虎旗 (巴彦库仁镇)	60,000	60,000	60,000	18,634
E'lunchun [Oroqen] Autonomous Banner (Alihe Town)	鄂倫春自治旗 (阿里河鎮)	鄂伦春自治旗 (阿里河镇)	280,000	270,000	250,000	59,880
E'wenkezu [Evenk] Autonomous Banner (Bayantuohai [Bayan Tohoi] Town)	鄂溫克族自治旗 (巴彥托海鎮)	鄂温克族自治旗 (巴彦托海镇)	140,000	140,000	140,000	19,111
Molidawa Dawoerzu [Morin Dawa Daur] Autonomous Banner (Ni'erji Town)	莫力達瓦斡爾族自治旗 (尼爾基鎮)	莫力达瓦达斡尔族自治旗 (尼尔基镇)	340,000	330,000	320,000	10,356
E'erduosi (Ordos) City	鄂爾多斯市	鄂尔多斯市	1,530,000	1,530,000	1,620,000	86,873.55
Dongsheng District (Tianjiao Subdistrict)	東勝區 (天驕街道)	东胜区 (天骄街道)	260,000	260,000	300,000	2526
Kangbashi [Hia Bagx] District (Binhe Subdistrict)	康巴什區 (濱河街道)	康巴什区 (滨河街道)	N/A	N/A	40,000	372.55
Dalateqi [Dalad Banner] (Gongye Subdistrict)	達拉特旗 (工業街道)	达拉特旗 (工业街道)	360,000	360,000	370,000	8241
Zhunge'erqi [Junggar Banner] (Xinglong Subdistrict)	准格爾旗 (興隆街道)	准格尔旗 (兴隆街道)	310,000	310,000	330,000	7551
Etuokeqianqi [Otog Front Banner] (Aolezhaoqi Town)	鄂托克前旗 (敖勒召其鎮)	鄂托克前旗 (敖勒召其镇)	80,000	80,000	80,000	12,221

(continued)

Table 17.3 (continued)

Name	Traditional	Simplified	Population (2012)	Population (2016)	Population (2020)	Area (Sq. Km)
Etuokeqi [Otog Banner] (Wulan [Ulan] Town)	鄂托克旗 (烏蘭鎮)	鄂托克旗 (乌兰镇)	100,000	100,000	100,000	20,367
Hangjinqi [Hanggin Qi; Hanggin Banner] (Xini Town)	杭錦旗 (錫尼鎮)	杭锦旗 (锡尼镇)	150,000	140,000	140,000	18,814
Wushenqi [Uxin Banner; Uxin Qi] (Galutu Town)	烏審旗 (嘎魯圖鎮)	乌审旗 (嘎鲁图镇)	110,000	110,000	120,000	11,674
Yijinhuoluoqi [Ejin Horo Qi; Ejin Horo Banner] (Aletengxire [Altan Xiret] Town)	伊金霍洛旗 (阿勒騰席熱鎮)	伊金霍洛旗 (阿勒腾席热镇)	160,000	170,000	180,000	5487
Wu-Lan-Cha-Bu (Wulanchabu; Ulanqab) City	烏蘭察布市	乌兰察布市	2,880,000	2,870,000	2,710,000	54,795
Jining District (Xintilu Subdistrict)	集寧區 (新體路街道)	集宁区 (新体路街道)	300,000	320,000	310,000	418
Fengzhen City (Beicheng regional Subdistrict)	豐鎮市 (北城區街道)	丰镇市 (北城区街道)	340,000	340,000	310,000	2704
Zhuozi County (Zhuozishan Town)	卓資縣 (卓資山鎮)	卓资县 (卓资山镇)	220,000	220,000	200,000	3119
Huade County (Changshun Town)	化德縣 (長順鎮)	化德县 (长顺镇)	180,000	180,000	160,000	2527
Shangdu County (Qitai Town)	商都縣 (七台鎮)	商都县 (七台镇)	350,000	340,000	330,000	4304
Xinghe County (Chengguan Town)	興和縣 (城關鎮)	兴和县 (城关镇)	330,000	330,000	320,000	3519
Liangcheng County (Daihai Town)	涼城縣 (岱海鎮)	凉城县 (岱海镇)	250,000	250,000	230,000	3451
Chaha'eryouyiqianqi [Qahar Right Front Banner; Chahar Youyi Qianqi] (Tuguiwula Town)	察哈爾右翼前旗 (土貴烏拉鎮)	察哈尔右翼前旗 (土贵乌拉镇)	250,000	230,000	220,000	2734

Chaha'eryouyizhongqi [Qahar Right Middle Banner; Chahar Youyizhongqi] (Kebu'er [Hobor] Town)	察哈爾右翼中旗 (科布爾鎮)	察哈尔右翼中旗 (科布尔镇)	250,000	230,000	200,000	4200
Chaha'eryouyihouqi [Qahar Right Rear Banner; Chahar Youyihouqi] (Baiyinchagan Town)	察哈爾右翼後期 (白音察干鎮)	察哈尔右翼后旗 (白音察干镇)	220,000	220,000	210,000	3803
Siziwangqi [Dorbod Banner] (Wulanhua Town)	四子王旗 (烏蘭花鎮)	四子王旗 (乌兰花镇)	220,000	210,000	210,000	24,016
Bayannao'er (Bayan Nur) City	巴**彥淖**爾市	巴彦**淖尔**市	1,860,000	1,870,000	1,740,000	66,263
Linhe District (Jiefang Subdistrict)	臨河區 (解放街道)	临河区 (解放街道)	560,000	560,000	520,000	2354
Wuyuan County (Longxingchang Town)	五原縣 (隆興昌鎮)	五原县 (隆兴昌镇)	300,000	300,000	280,000	2493
Dengkou County (Bayangaole Town)	磴口縣 (巴彥高勒鎮)	磴口县 (巴彦高勒镇)	120,000	120,000	110,000	4167
Wulateqianqi [Urat/Urad Front Banner; Urad Qianqi] (Wulashan Town)	烏拉特前旗 (烏拉山鎮)	乌拉特前旗 (乌拉山镇)	340,000	340,000	330,000	7476
Wulatezhongqi [Urat/Urad Middle Banner; Urad Zhongqi] (Hailiutu Town)	烏拉特中旗 (海流圖鎮)	乌拉特中旗 (海流图镇)	140,000	150,000	140,000	23,096
Wulatehouqi [Urat/Urad Rear Banner; Urad Houqi] (Bayinbaolige Town)	烏拉特後旗 (巴音寶力格鎮)	乌拉特后旗 (巴音宝力格镇)	70,000	70,000	60,000	24,925
Hangjin Houqi [Hanggin Rear Banner] (Shanba Town)	杭錦後旗 (陝壩鎮)	杭锦后旗 (陕坝镇)	330,000	330,000	290,000	1752
Xing'an (Hinggan) League	興安盟	兴安盟	1,680,000	1,680,000	1,640,000	59,815
Wulanhaote (Ulanhot) City (Heping Subdistrict)	烏蘭浩特市 (和平街道)	乌兰浩特市 (和平街道)	320,000	320,000	320,000	2728

(continued)

Table 17.3 (continued)

Name	Traditional	Simplified	Population (2012)	Population (2016)	Population (2020)	Area (Sq. Km)
A'ershan (Arxan) City (Wenquan Subdistrict)	阿爾山市 (溫泉街道)	阿尔山市 (温泉街道)	50,000	50,000	50,000	7409
Tuquan County (Tuquan Town)	突泉縣 (突泉鎮)	突泉县 (突泉镇)	310,000	310,000	300,000	4800
Ke'erqinyouyiqianqi [Horqin Right Front Banner; Horqin Youyi Qianqi] (Ke'erqin [Horqin] Town)	科爾沁右翼前旗 (科爾沁鎮)	科尔沁右翼前旗 (科尔沁镇)	340,000	340,000	330,000	17,428
Ke'erqinyouyizhongqi [Horqin Right Middle Banner; Horqin Youyi Zhongqi] (Bayanhushu [Bayan Huxu] Town)	科爾沁右翼中旗 (巴彥呼舒鎮)	科尔沁右翼中旗 (巴彦呼舒镇)	260,000	260,000	250,000	15,613
Zhalaiteqi [Jalaid Qi; Jalaid Banner] (Yinde'er [Inder] Town)	扎賚特旗 (音德爾鎮)	扎赉特旗 (音德尔镇)	400,000	400,000	390,000	11,837
Xilinguolemeng (Xilingol) League	錫林郭勒盟	**锡**林郭勒盟	1,000,000	1,020,000	1,040,000	199,882
Xilinhaote (Xilinhot) City (Xiritala Subdistrict)	錫林浩特市 (希日塔拉街道)	锡林浩特市 (希日塔拉街道)	170,000	180,000	190,000	14,780
Erlianhaote (Erenhot) City (Wulan Subdistrict)	二連浩特市 (烏蘭街道)	二连浩特市 (乌兰街道)	30,000	30,000	30,000	4013
Duolun (Dolon Nor; Dolonnur) County (Duolunnao'er Town)	多倫縣 (多倫淖爾鎮)	多伦县 (多伦淖尔镇)	110,000	110,000	110,000	3864
Abagaqi [Abag Qi; Abag Banner; Xin Hot] (Bieligutai [Biligtai] Town)	阿巴嘎旗 (別力古台鎮)	阿巴嘎旗 (别力古台镇)	40,000	50,000	40,000	27,474
Sunitezuoqi [Sonid Left Banner; Sonid Zuoqi] (Mandulatu Town)	蘇尼特左旗 (滿都拉圖鎮)	苏尼特左旗 (满都拉图镇)	30,000	30,000	30,000	34,240

Suniteyouqi [Sonid Youqi; Sonid Right Banner; Sonid Youqi] (Saihantala [Saihan Tal] Town)	蘇尼特右旗 (賽漢塔拉鎮)	苏尼特右旗 (赛汉塔拉镇)	70,000	70,000	70,000	22,455
Dong Wuzhumuqinqi [East Ujimqin Banner; Dong Ujimqin Qi] (Wuliyasitai [Uliastai] Town)	東烏珠穆沁旗 (烏里雅斯太鎮)	东乌珠穆沁旗 (乌里雅斯太镇)	80,000	80,000	80,000	45,575
Xiwuzhumuqinqi [West Ujimqin Banner; Xi Ujimqin Qi] (Balaga'ergaole [Bayan Ul Hot] Town)	西烏珠穆沁旗 (巴拉嘎爾高勒鎮)	西乌珠穆沁旗 (巴拉嘎尔高勒镇)	80,000	80,000	80,000	22,459
Taipusiqi [Taibus Banner] (Baochang Town)	太僕寺旗 (寶昌鎮)	太仆寺旗 (宝昌镇)	210,000	210,000	210,000	3426
Xianghuangqi [Bordered Yellow Banner] (Xinbaolage [Xin Bulag] Town)	鑲黃旗 (新寶拉格鎮)	镶黄旗 (新宝拉格镇)	30,000	30,000	30,000	5137
Zhengxiangbaiqi [Plain and Bordered Banner] (Ming'antu Town)	正鑲白旗 (明安圖鎮)	正镶白旗 (明安图镇)	70,000	70,000	70,000	6253
Zhenglanqi [Xulun Hoh Banner; *Plain Blue Banner; Shuluun* Huh Banner] (Shangdu Town)	正藍旗 (上都鎮)	正蓝旗 (上都镇)	80,000	80,000	80,000	10,206
Alashanmeng (Alxa League)	阿拉善盟	阿拉善盟	180,000	190,000	190,000	270,244
Alashanzuoqi [Alxa Left Banner; Alxa Zuoqi] (Bayanhaote [Bayan Hot] Town)	阿拉善左旗 (巴彥浩特鎮)	阿拉善左旗 (巴彦浩特镇)	140,000	140,000	150,000	80,412
Alashanyouqi [Alxa Youqi; Alxa Right Banner] (Badanjilin Town)	阿拉善右旗 (巴丹吉林鎮)	阿拉善右旗 (巴丹吉林镇)	20,000	30,000	30,000	75,226
E'jinaqi [Ejin Qi; Ejin Banner] (Dalaihubu [Dalaihob] Town)	額濟納旗 (達來呼布鎮)	额济纳旗 (达来呼布镇)	20,000	20,000	20,000	114,606

[a]Formally established in 8 March 2013

References

Endicott, Elizabeth. 2012. *A history of land use in Mongolia: The thirteenth century to the present*. New York: Palgrave and Macmillan.

Gaubatz, Piper Rae. 1996. *Beyond the great wall: Urban form and transformation on the Chinese frontiers*. Stanford: Stanford University Press.

Hsü, Immanuel C.Y. 2000. *The rise of modern China*. 6th ed. New York: Oxford University Press.

Hui, Mary. 2021. China's rare earth hub is rolling out massive subsidies to fix the industry's Achilles heel. *Quartz*. 15 July. https://qz.com/2031940/chinas-rare-earth-hub-baotou-introduces-massive-subsidies/.

Inner Mongolia Bureau of Statistics (IMBS). 2021. [*Communiqué of the seventh national census of Inner Mongolia Autonomous Region*]. 内蒙古自治区第七次全国人口普查公报. 20 May. http://tj.nmg.gov.cn/tjyw/tjgb/202105/t20210526_1596844.html.

Liu, Li, and Xingcan Chen. 2012. *The archaeology of China: From the late paleolithic to the early bronze age*. New York: Cambridge University Press.

Ministry of Civil Affairs (MCA), People's Republic of China. 2020. [*County/township administration handbook*]. Beijing: China Statistics Press. 中華人民共和國民政部, 中華人民共和國, 鄉鎮行政區劃簡冊.

Olsen, Stanley J. 1984. The early domestication of the horse in North China. *Archaeology* 37 (1): 62–63.

Wilkinson, Endymion. 2012. *Chinese history: A new manual*. Cambridge, Massachusetts: Harvard University Press.

Wright, H.E. 1995. *Global climates since the last glacial maximum*. Minneapolis: University of Minnesota Press.

Xiong, Victor Cunrui. 2006. *Emperor Yang of the Sui dynasty: His life, times, and legacy*. New York: State University of New York Press.

Zhang, Shunan. 2021. [*The 2020 per capita income list of residents in various provinces: Shanghai is the richest, and it has risen sharply*]. Finance.people.com. 22 January. 张澍楠. 2020年各省份居民人均收入榜: 上海最有钱, 这地涨得猛. http://finance.people.com.cn/n1/2021/0122/c1004-32008733.html.

Chapter 18
Jiangsu Province

Abstract Jiangsu Province, referred to as the "land of fish and rice," with origins going back to the Wu Kingdom that was advised by Sun Tzu (Sun Zi) himself, is now a densely populated, dynamic region. And commerce has long been in Jiangsu's bailiwick, long famed for a wealthy merchant class going back at least to the Song dynasty (ca. 960 CE). Having thrived economically through the Ming dynasty (ca. 1370), Jiangsu (and its surrounding regions) suffered greatly during the tumult of the Taiping Rebellion (ca. 1860), and its capital, Nanjing (Nanking), was razed by Japanese military depredations in World War II, including wanton massacre and rape. Today, Jiangsu's economy ranks well above the top five provinces and major cities in mainland China, as well as per capital income of about USD $6750. It is not surprising, therefore, that significant numbers of Jiangsu residents are represented in China's "floating populations," with a registered household (*hukou*) population of about 78 million, and a 2020 census figure of about 84 million.

E. Croddy, *China's Provinces and Populations*,
https://doi.org/10.1007/978-3-031-09165-0_18

Jiangsu Province (江蘇省 *jiāngsū shěng*): Abbreviation 蘇 (*sū*) (Fig. 18.1)

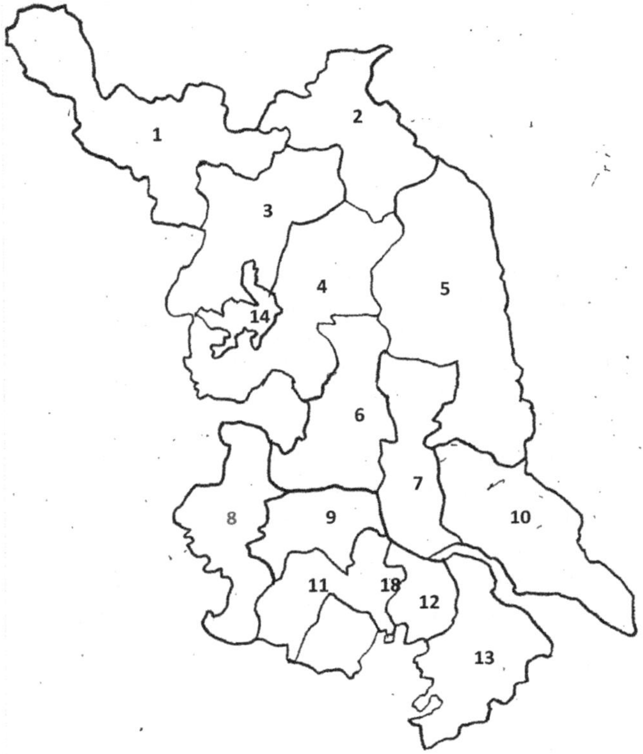

Jiangsu Population (2020)

1.	Xuzhou City	9,083,790
2.	Lianyungang City	4,599,360
3.	Suqian City	4,986,192
4.	Huai'an City	4,556,230
5.	Yancheng City	6,709,629
6.	Yangzhou City	4,559,797
7.	Taizhou City	4,512,762
8.	Nanjing City	9,314,685
9.	Zhendddjiang City	3,210,418
10.	Nantong City	7,726,635
11.	Changzhou City	5,278,121
12.	Wuxi City	7,462,135
13.	Suzhou City	12,748,262

Fig. 18.1 Jiangsu province major cities (Provincial Capital: Nanjing City). (Drawn by the author, after People's Republic of China, Ministry of Civil Affairs (MCA 2020))

Jiangsu Province: General Impressions

With about 1000 km of coastal area, Jiangsu has long been known for its fecund agriculture and seafood, thus the "land of fish and rice" (魚米之鄉 *yúmǐ zhī xiāng*). This saying is from China's venerable historian, Sima Qian (司馬遷 *Sīmǎ qiān*), who described both Jiangsu and Zhejiang areas as being sparsely populated, but fertile "with rice and fish soup (飯稻羹魚 *fàndào gēngyú*)." As for its capital, Nanjing, the Song dynasty scholar Wang Anshi (王安石 *wáng ānshí*; d. 1086 CE) waxed nostalgic: "The old events of the Six Dynasties have flowed away with the stream, but the withered grasses are still darkly emerald."[1]

Jiangsu Province is named from combining **Jiang**ning (江寧 ***jiāng** níng*) and **Su**zhou (蘇州 ***sū** zhōu*). Formally established in 1667, the Jiangsu region had been known as Wu (吳 *wú*), from the ancient state of Wu (吳國 *wúguó*), and is the name of the regional Wu Chinese dialect that also includes Shanghaiese (滬語 *hùyǔ*).

Jiangnan's Origins in Wu

The old histories (ca. third century BCE) relate: "*Jiangnan*, is to say, Yangzhou (揚州 *yángzhōu*)." In modern times Jiangnan still refers to this geographic terrain. For example, the writer Henry Liu (劉宜良 *liú yíliáng*) used the penname "Jiangnan." While of Taiwanese citizenship, he was originally born in Jingjiang City (靖江市 *jìngjiāng shì*), Jiangsu Province. Because of his criticism of Republic of China (Taiwan) President Chiang Ching-Kuo, Henry Liu was assassinated in 15 October 1984 in Daly City, California. (Kaplan 1992).

The State (or Kingdom) of Wu had its own tradition going back at least to the Zhou (eleventh century BCE). The histories (Sima Qian) tell us that Taibo (泰伯 *tài bó*), the eldest son of Zhou Tai Wang (周泰王 *zhōu tài wáng*) and the leader of the Zhou people, established the Wu territory after fleeing southward to the area around Jiangsu. In 585 BCE, Wu Shoumeng (吳壽夢 *wú shòumèng*), personal name Ji Cheng (姬乘 *jī chéng*), declared himself King of Wu. The Kingdom of Wu (吳國 *wúguó*), also called Gouwu (勾吳 *gōuwú* "Kouwu" in older English transliterations), was located in and around today's Suzhou (蘇州 *sūzhōu*).

The great Chinese military strategist Sun Wu (孫武 *sūn wǔ*), known more popularly as Sun Tzu (孫子 *sūn zi*), was purportedly an advisor (modern day strategic consultant in military affairs) to King Wu Helu (吳王闔閭 *wúwáng hélǘ*; reigned 514–496 BCE). In 1972, the historical record of this story was found on bamboo strips unearthed at Western Han tombs (dated ca. third century BCE to first century CE) in Yinqueshan (銀雀山 *yínquèshān*), Shandong province. Among the amazing finds were both volumes of *Art of War* (孫子兵法 *sūnzi bīngfǎ*), attributed to Sun Tzu, and the second *Art of War* supposedly written by Sun Tzu's descendent, Sun Bin (孫臏 *sūn bìn*). As for Sun Tzu and his discussions with King

[1] 六朝舊事流水, 但寒煙衰草凝綠 *liùcháo jiùshì liúshuǐ, dàn hányān shuāicǎo nínglǜ.*

He Lü of Wu,[2] these did not only include military affairs but civil administration and tax codes as well. After hearing what Sun Tzu had to say about these matters using historical examples, King Wu replied: "Excellent—the Way of the True King is to love the people generously." (Sun-Tzu 1993) Said to have been in no small part due to the strategic counsel of Sun Tzu, the Kingdom of Wu became one of the original "Five Hegemons" during the Spring-Autumn period, conquering its rivals to include the Yue (越 *yuè*) in 494 BCE. For, according to the histories,

> The Wu Kingdom demolished the Kingdom of Chu to the west, entered its capital of Ying, all the while deterring the Qi and Jin (晉 *jìn*) kingdoms to the north. The Kingdom of Wu became prominent among the other states, with Sun Tzu for his part contributing to its might (Ctext.org, 2021).

After a sordid series of events, however, the Yue Kingdom turned the tables and defeated the State of Wu in 473 BCE. In turn, the major State of Chu (楚 *chŭ*) demolished the Yue in 333 BCE. The Qin dynasty (221 BCE) unified the existing six states of China but the people chafed under its despotic rule. In 209 BCE, military officers serving in the north against the Xiongnu "barbarians," Chen Sheng (陳勝 *chén shèng*) and Wu Guang (吳廣 *wú guăng*) fought back against their masters by leading peasant rebellions. In September of that year, Xiang Liang (項梁 *xiàng liáng*) Xiang Yu (項羽 *xiàng yŭ*) and Liu Bang (劉邦 *liú bāng*) instigated mass uprisings in present day Jiangsu, Suzhou City (蘇州市 *sūzhōu shì*) and Peixian County (沛縣 *pèixiàn*). Xiang Yu, originally from today's Suqian City, Sucheng district (宿遷市宿城區 *sùqiān shì sùchéng qū*), struck against modern day Suzhou (Tong 2011). After internecine struggles, Liu Bang, who also hailed from Jiangsu, eventually became emperor and founder of the long-lasting Han dynasty (206 BCE–220 CE). The Han became arguably the most resplendent of all China's dynastic eras.

During this time, the Jiangsu region was divided in two prefectural areas, Yangzhou (揚州 *yángzhōu*) and Xuzhou (徐州 *xúzhōu*). The Han historian, Sima Qian (司馬遷 *sīmă qiān*; ca. 100 BCE), described the area that includes the Jiangsu region as being sparsely populated but was also

> [W]here people eat rice and drink fish soup (飯稻羹魚 *fàndàogēngyú*) and farmers essentially employed slash and burn agricultural techniques. The place is fertile and suffers no famine. Hence in the south of the [Changjiang] and the Huai (淮河 *huáihé*) rivers, there are neither hungry nor frozen people, nor a family which holds a thousand gold (Jacobs, 1999).

The Jiangsu region began to rise in prominence during the Three Kingdoms period (220–280 CE). The Eastern Wu (東吳 *dōngwú*) included the area of modern day Huainan City (淮南市 *huáinán shì*), with its capital at Jianye (建業 *jiànyè*), today's Nanjing City (南京市 *nánjīng shì*). The Eastern Wu was conquered by the Jin (晉 *jìn*)[3] dynasty (265–420 CE), and in 313 CE, the Jin renamed the Jianye capital Jiankang (建康 *jiànkāng*). Following the downfall of the Eastern Jin (414), its erstwhile nobility fled for safety to a walled redoubt known as the "Eastern Mansions"

[2] 吳王闔廬 *wú wáng hélú*; aka 吳王闔閭 *wú wáng hélǘ*.

[3] Not to be confused with the later Jin (金 *jīn* = Gold) dynasty.

(Dongfu 東府 *dōngfǔ*) in today's Yangzhou, located about 60 km northeast of modern-day Nanjing City (Steinhardt, 2013).

The Huaihe (淮河 *huáihé*) River to the north of Jiangsu formed a natural, front-line border for the Southern and Northern Dynasties (南北朝 *nánběi cháo*; 420–589). Jiankang (Nanking or Nanjing today) was then a vital economic, cultural, political, and military center. Until the unification of the Sui dynasty (589), Jiankang remained the capital of China's Southern Dynasties: The Song (宋 *sòng*), Qi (齊 *qí*), Liang (梁 *liáng*), and the Chen (陳 *chén*).

Having reunified China, the Emperor Yang of the Sui (隋煬帝 *suí yángdì*) expanded upon the Great Canal (大運河 *dàyùnhé*) in 610, linking the north and south, spurring the economic development of Jiangdu (江都 *jiāngdū*) and Shanyang (山陽 *shānyáng*), the latter being modern-day Huai'an district (淮安區 *huái'ān qū*). Under control by the Tang, in 892 Yang Xingmi (楊行密 *yáng xíngmì*) established his self-styled State of Wu (吳國) at Yangzhou. The Southern Tang (南唐 *nántáng*), led by Li Bian (李昪 lǐ biàn) of Xuzhou, in today's Jiangsu Province, made his capital at Jiangning (江寧 *jiāngníng*).

Growth of Commerce

As of 960 CE (Song dynasty), the wealthy merchant class quickly developed, particularly in the Suzhou and Yangzhou commercial centers. The Song established regional administrative sectors, designated as Lu (路 *lù*) "circuit," loosely translated here as prefecture, i.e., Jiangnan Donglu (江南東路 *jiāngnán dōnglù*), Liangzhe Xilu (兩浙西路 *liǎngzhè xīlù*), Huainan Donglu (淮南東路 *huáinán dōnglù*), and Jingdong Xilu (京東西路 *jīngdōng xīlù*). Today's Jiangsu capital, Nanjing, was named Jiangning Prefecture (江寧府 *jiāngníng fǔ*).

In the time of the Jurchen Jin (金 *jīn*) dynasty, the Huaihe River formed the boundary between the Jin and Southern Song in 1127. As the Yuan Mongols took control, two areas split the region into two governorships, Huainan Donglu (east) and Huainan Xilu (west) in 1279. The region of Jiangsu supplied successive dynasties with agricultural goods, including rice, and remained a key economic center throughout the Mongol Yuan (1271–1368), the Ming (1368–1644), and Qing (through 1911) dynasties.

From the beginning of the Ming (1368), the capital was established at Nanjing. But in order to better address and confront threat from the Mongols, the Ming moved the capital to Beijing in 1421. The collective areas of Jiangsu, Anhui and Shanghai governments were centrally administered as part of southern Nan Zhili (南直隸 *nánzhílì*). Later, Qing dynastic forces, after occupying Yangzhou and Nanjing, captured the Southern Ming Hongguang (弘光 *hóngguāng*) emperor, changing the Nanzhili name to Jiangnan Province. It was then formally designated Jiangsu Province in 1667, splitting Jiangsu from Anhui, with the capital located in Suzhou until the end of the Qing dynasty. As did much of its regional neighbors, the cataclysm of the Taiping Rebellion (1851–1864) heavily impacted Jiangsu Province.

Comparing populations of Jiangsu counties from before and after the (see Table 18.1) conflict helps to illustrate this tragic part of China's history.

After the revolution of 1911, the Republic of China (ROC) made Nanjing its capital. Previously administered by Jiangsu Province, both Nanjing and Shanghai were made independent municipalities in 1927.

Nanjing Massacre

Among the most perfidious and notorious of Japanese imperial military atrocities occurred in Nanjing (Nanking), the capital of the Republic of China under the Nationalists. Following Japan's full-on invasion of China, even as Chiang Kai-shek pleaded with Stalin to help fight the Japanese, Nanjing fell and some 70,000 ROC soldiers were dead. Beginning in December 1937, Japanese troops carried out a three-month campaign targeting civilians, turning Nanjing into an abattoir. Raping women and killing everyone in sight, foreign observers recounted the following:

> Death was frequent penalty for the slightest resistance on the part of a victim or the members of her family who sought to protect her. Even girls of tender years and old women were raped in large numbers throughout the city, and many cases of abnormal and sadistic behavior in connection with these rapings [sic] occurred. Many women were killed after the fact and their bodies mutilated. Approximately 20,000 cases of rape occurred within the city during the first month of occupation. (Lu 2012)

In all, perhaps as many as 300,000 people died during the Rape of Nanking (Nanjing). Due to its loss to the Japanese, the ROC capital was subsequently moved to Wuhan, and then to Chongqing (Chunking) for safety.

Table 18.1 Selected Jiangsu County Populations Before and After the Taiping Rebellion (Yang, 1995)

Jiangsu provincial county	Year (before and during Taiping Rebellion)	Population	Year (after Taiping Rebellion)	Population
Jiading County 嘉定縣	1813	436,466	1864	223,131
Jurong County 句容縣	1809	306,968	1900	79,053
Wujiang County 吳江縣	1820	304,057	1864	113,653
Qingpu County 青浦縣	1810	332,164	1865	208,870
Changre County 常熱縣	1820	377,918	1865	213,532
Zhaowen County 昭文縣	1820	260,839	1865	185,571
Wuxi County 無錫縣	1830	339,549	1865	72,052
Jinkui County 金匱縣	1830	258,934	1865	138,008
Jiangyin County 江陰縣	1839	564,603	1876	176,603
Lishui County 溧水縣	1847	185,143	1878	30,847
Gaochun County 高淳縣	1847	188,930	1869	55,159
Dantu County 丹徒縣	1859	331,713	1867	107,611

After "Liberating" Nanjing in 1949, the Chinese Communist Party (CCP) divided Jiangsu into north and south: Subei (蘇北 *sūběi*), with its government in Taizhou (泰州市 *tàizhōu shì*), and Sunan (蘇南 *sūnán*), administered by Wuxi City (無錫市 *wúxī*). (The name Wuxi is actually not Han Chinese in origin, but rather a transcription from the Yue 越 *yuè* language). On 15 November 1952, the Chinese central government approved the dissolution of Subei (蘇北) and Sunan (蘇南), restoring Jiangsu Province. On 1 January 1953, the CCP formally made Nanjing City the governing entity for Jiangsu. In 1958, ten counties were redistricted under Shanghai City jurisdiction, while dissolving the Songjiang Special Zone (宋江專區 *sòngjiāng zhuānqū*):

- Jiading (嘉定 *jiādìng*)
- Baoshan (寶山 *bǎoshān*)
- Shanghai (上海 *shànghǎi*)
- Chuansha (川沙 *chuānshā*)
- Qingpu (青浦 *qīngpǔ*)
- Nanhui (南匯 *nánhuì*)
- Fenghe (奉賀 *fènghè*)
- Songjiang (宋江 *sòngjiāng*
- Jinshan (金山 *jīnshān*) and
- Chongming (崇明 *chóngmíng*)

On 28 May 1959, the CCP declared the formation of the Shanghai municipal government, detaching it from Jiangsu and establishing Shanghai as a provincial-level city.

Jiangsu in Modern Times

During the 1980s and early 1990s, as China's southern economic zones (SEZs) proceeded to develop quite rapidly (e.g., Guangdong), overall economic development in Jiangsu Province was relatively slow. But southern Jiangsu cities (e.g., Wuxi and Suzhou) were able to leverage their links with Shanghai, helping them to spur on progress. Especially from 1993–1997, Jiangsu successfully emphasized agricultural development, consumer goods manufacturing, and fostered its own export-driven markets.

Jiangsu Economy and Population

In recent years (2015–2020), Jiangsu has maintained the second highest gross domestic product (GDP) among mainland China's 31 provinces and major cities, the first being Guangdong (Table 18.2).

Jiangsu remains among the most densely populated province in all of China, at about 755 persons per square kilometer, with a number of districts (see Table 18.4) having more than 1 million residents. Its continuing increase population (see Table 18.3), like its economic growth, continues to be among the higher among China's provinces, increasing 7.7% in 2020 over 10 years prior. The per capita income of Jiangxi ranked fifth in 2020 at $6748 (Zhang 2021) (Fig. 18.2).

Table 18.2 Top five Chinese provinces, Gross Domestic Product (GDP): 2015 and 2020. (21st Century 2016; Zhang, 2021)

Province/ City	2015 GDP in Yuan	GDP in US Dollars (billion)	2020 GDP in Yuan	GDP in US Dollars (billion)
Guangdong	7,281,255,000,000	1132.4	11,076,094,000,000	1722
Jiangsu	7,011,640,000,000	1090.5	10,270,000,000,000	1597
Shandong	6,300,230,000,000	980.0	7,312,900,000,000	1137
Zhejiang	4,288,600,000,000	667.0	6,461,300,000,000	1005
Henan	3,701,025,000,000	575.6	5,499,707,000,000	855

Table 18.3 Jiangsu Province population (residential 常住人口 *chángzhù rénkǒu*) data. (JPBS 2021)

City	Population (2010)	Population (2020)
Nanjing City 南京市 *nánjīng shì* [abbrev. 寧 *níng*]	8,004,680	9,314,685
Changzhou City 常州市 *chángzhōu shì*	4,591,972	5,278,121
Huai'an City 淮安市 *huái'ān shì*	4,799,889	4,556,230
Lianyungang City 連雲港市 *liányúngǎng shì* [abbrev 連 *lián*]	4,393,914	4,599,360
Nantong City 南通市 *nántōng shì*	7,282,835	7,726,635
Suqian City 宿遷市 *sùqiān shì* [abbrev. 宿 *sù*]	4,715,553	4,986,192
Suzhou City 蘇州市 *sūzhōu shì* [abbrev. 蘇 *sū*]	10,465,994	12,748,262
Taizhou City 泰州市 *tàizhōu shì*	4,618,558	4,512,762
Wuxi City 無錫市 *wúxī shì*	6,372,624	7,462,135
Xuzhou City 徐州市 *xúzhōu shì*	8,580,500	9,083,790
Yancheng City 鹽城市 *yánchéng shì*	7,260,240	6,709,629
Yangzhou City 揚州市 *yángzhōu shì*	4,459,760	4,559,797
Zhenjiang City 鎮江市 *zhènjiāng shì*	3,160,384	3,210,418
Total	**78,659,903**	**84,748,016**

Table 18.4 Jiangsu Province: population data of cities and their subordinate sectors. (JPBS 2021)

Cities and subordinate sectors, population (2020 census)	Subordinate district, city and county populations (2020)	Population (2020)
Nanjing City 南京市 ***nánjīng shì*** **[abbrev.** 寧 ***níng*****]**		**9,314,685**
Xuanwu District 玄武區 *xuánwǔ qū*	537,825	
Qinhuai District 秦淮區 *qínhuái qū*	740,809	
Jianye District 建鄴區 *jiànyè qū*	534,257	
Gulou District 鼓樓區 *gǔlóu qū*	940,387	
Pukou District 浦口區 *pǔkǒu qū*	1,171,603	
Luhe District 六合區 *lùhé qū*	946,563	
Qixia District 棲霞區 *qīxiá qū*	987,835	
Yuhuatai District 雨花台區 *yǔhuātái qū*	608,780	
Jiangning District 江寧區 *jiāngníng qū*	1,926,117	
Lishui District 溧水區 *lìshuǐ qū*	491,336	
Gaochun County 高淳區 *gāochún qū*	429,173	
Changzhou City 常州市 ***chángzhōu shì***		**5,278,121**
Xinbei District 新北區 *xīnběi qū*	883,125	
Zhonglou District 鍾樓區 *zhōnglóu qū*	658,537	
Tianning District 天寧區 *tiānníng qū*	668,906	
Wujin District[a] 武進區 *wǔjìn qū*	1,277,487	
Jintan District 金壇區 *jīntán qū*	505,081	
Liyang City 溧陽市 *lìyáng shì*	785,902	
Jiangsu Changzhou Economic Development Zone 江蘇常州經濟開發區 *jiāngsū chángzhōu jīngjì kāifāqū*	419,893	
Huai'an City 淮安市 ***huái'ān shì***		**4,556,230**
Huai'an District 淮安區 *huáiān qū*	785,272	
Huaiyin District 淮陰區 *huáiyīn qū*	748,971	
Qingjiangpu District 清江浦區 *qīngjiāngpǔ qū*	594,524	
Jinhu County 金湖縣 *jīnhú xiàn*	289,456	
Xutai County 盱眙縣 *xūtāi xiàn*	607,211	
Hongze County 洪澤縣 *hóngzé xiàn*	285,097	
Lianshui County 漣水縣 *liánshuǐ xiàn*	829,699	
Huai'an Economic Development Zone 淮安經濟開發區 *huái'ān jīngjì kāifāqū*	416,180	
Lianyungang City 連雲港市 ***liányúngǎng shì*** **[abbrev** 連 ***lián*****]**		**4,599,360**
Lianyun District 連雲區 *liányún qū*	292,762	
Haizhou District 海州區 *hǎizhōu qū*	918,005	
Ganyu District 贛榆區 *gànyú qū*	1,003,844	
Guanyun County 灌雲縣 *guànyún xiàn*	725,047	
Donghai County 東海縣 *dōnghǎi xiàn*	1,047,357	
Guannan County 灌南縣 *guànnán xiàn*	612,345	
Nantong City 南通市 ***nántōng shì***		**7,726,635**

(continued)

Table 18.4 (continued)

Cities and subordinate sectors, population (2020 census)	Subordinate district, city and county populations (2020)	Population (2020)
Chongchuan District 崇川區 *chóngchuān qū*	1,183,740	
Tongzhou District 通州區 *tōngzhōu qū*	1,258,739	
Haimen City 海門市 *hǎimén shì*	991,782	
Qidong City 啟東市 *qǐdōng shì*	967,313	
Rugao City 如皋市 *rúgāo shì*	1,238,448	
Rudong County 如東縣 *rúdōng xiàn*	880,006	
Hai'an County 海安縣 *hǎi'ān xiàn*	874,334	
Nantong Economic and Technology Development Zone 南通經濟技術開發區 *nántōng jīngjìjìshù kāifāqū*	332,273	
Suqian City 宿遷市 ***sùqiān shì* [abbrev.** 宿 ***sù*]**		**4,986,192**
Sucheng District 宿城區 *sùchéng qū*	845,147	
Suyu District 宿豫區 *sùyù qū*	588,520	
Shuyang County 沭陽縣 *shùyáng xiàn*	1,674,978	
Siyang County 泗陽縣 *sìyáng xiàn*	829,562	
Sihong County 泗洪縣 *sìhóng xiàn*	858,740	
Suqian Economic and Technology Development Zone 宿遷經濟技術開發區 *sùqiān jīngjìjìshù kāifāqū*	189,245	
Suzhou City 蘇州市 ***sūzhōu shì* [abbrev.** 蘇 ***sū*]**		**12,748,262**
Gusu District 姑蘇區 *gūsū qū*	924,083	
Huqiu District[b] 虎丘區 *hǔqiū qū*	832,499	
Wuzhong District 吳中區 *wúzhōng qū*	1;388,972	
Xiangcheng District 相城區 *xiāngchéng qū*	891,055	
Wujiang District 吳江區 *wújiāng qū*	1,545,023	
Kunshan City 昆山市 *kūnshān shì*	2,092,496	
Taicang City 太倉市 *tàicāng shì*	831,113	
Changshu(shou) City 常熟市 *chángshú shì*	1,677,050	
Zhangjiagang City 張家港市 *zhāngjiāgǎng shì*	1,432,044	
Suzhou Industrial Park 蘇州工業園區 *sūzhōu gōngyèyuánqū*	1,133,927	
Taizhou City 泰州市 ***tàizhōu shì***		**4,512,762**
Hailing District 海陵區 *hǎilíng qū*	577,016	
Gaogang District 高港區 *gāogǎng qū*	258,590	
Jiangyan District 姜堰區 *jiāngyàn qū*	668,408	
Jingjiang City 靖江市 *jìngjiāng shì*	663,408	
Taixing City 泰興市 *tàixīng shì*	994,445	
Xinghua City 興化市 *xīnghuà shì*	1,128,204	
泰州醫藥高新技術產業開發區 Taizhou Medical Technology Industry Development Zone ("China Medical City") *tàizhōu yīyào gāoxīnjìshù chǎnyè kāifāqū*	222,691	

(continued)

Table 18.4 (continued)

Cities and subordinate sectors, population (2020 census)	Subordinate district, city and county populations (2020)	Population (2020)
Wuxi City 無錫市 ***wúxī shì***		**7,462,135**
Liangxi District 梁溪區 *liángxī qū*	985,465	
Binhu District 濱湖區 *bīnhú qū*	592,984	
Xinwu District 新吳區 *xīnwú qū*	720,215	
Huishan District 惠山區 *huìshān qū*	893,675	
Xishan District 錫山區 *xīshān qū*	882,387	
Jiangyin City 江陰市 *jiāngyīn shì*	1,779,515	
Yixing City 宜興市 *yíxīng shì*	1,285,785	
Wuxi Economic Development Zone 無錫經濟開發區 *wúxī jīngjì kāifāqū*	322,109	
Xuzhou City 徐州市 ***xúzhōu shì***		**9,083,790**
Yunlong District 雲龍區 *yúnlóng qū*	471,566	
Gulou District 鼓樓區 *gǔlóu qū*	425,143	
Jiawang District 賈汪區 *jiǎwāng qū*	453,555	
Quanshan District 泉山區 *quánshān qū*	619,784	
Tongshan District 銅山區 *tóngshān qū*	1,237,760	
Pizhou City 邳州市 *pīzhōu shì*	1,462,563	
Xinyi City 新沂市 *xīnyí shì*	969,922	
Suining County 睢寧縣 *suīníng xiàn*	1,088,553	
Peixian County 沛縣 *pèixiàn*	1,462,563	
Fengxian County 豐縣 *fēngxiàn*	935,200	
Xuzhou Economic and Technology Development Zone 徐州經濟技術開發區 *xúzhōu jīngjìjìshù kāifāqū*	381,407	
Yancheng City 鹽城市 ***yánchéng shì***		**6,709,629**
Tinghu District 亭湖區 *tínghú qū*	798,003	
Yandu District 鹽都區 *yándū qū*	832,584	
Dongtai City 東台市 *dōngtái shì*	888,410	
Dafeng City 大豐市 *dàfēng shì*	645,603	
Sheyang County 射陽縣 *shèyáng xiàn*	759,403	
Funing County 阜寧縣 *fùníng xiàn*	794,036	
Binhai County 濱海縣 *bīnhǎi xiàn*	820,084	
Xiangshui County 響水縣 *xiǎngshuǐ xiàn*	459,156	
Jianhu County 建湖縣 *jiànhú xiàn*	609,346	
Yancheng Economic and Technology Development Zone 鹽城經濟技術開發區 *yánchéng jīngjìjìshù kāifāqū*	103,004	
Yangzhou City 揚州市 ***yángzhōu shì***		**4,559,797**
Hanjiang District 邗江區 *hánjiāng qū*	726,906	
Guangling District 廣陵區 *guǎnglíng qū*	542,305	
Jiangdu District 江都區 *jiāngdū qū*	926,577	
Yizheng City 儀徵市 *yízhēng shì*	532,571	

(continued)

Table 18.4 (continued)

Cities and subordinate sectors, population (2020 census)	Subordinate district, city and county populations (2020)	Population (2020)
Gaoyou City 高郵市 *gāoyóu shì*	709,572	
Baoying County 寶應縣 *bǎoyīng xiàn*	682,219	
Yangzhou Economic and Technology Development Zone 揚州經濟技術開發區 *yángzhōu jīngjìjìshù kāifāqū*	238,785	
Yangzhou City Ecological Technology New City ("Yangzhou Biodiverse and Sci-Tech City") 揚州市生態科技新城 *yángzhōu shìshēngtàikējì xīnchéng*	66,355	
Shugang Shouxihu Scenery District 蜀岡瘦西湖風景名勝區 *shǔgāng shòuxīhú fēngjǐng míngshèngqū*	134,507	
Zhenjiang City 鎮江市 *zhènjiāng shì*		**3,210,418**
Jingkou District 京口區 *jīngkǒu qū*	355,757	
Runzhou District 潤州區 *rùnzhōu qū*	239,892	
Dantu District 丹徒區 *dāntú qū*	347,264	
Yangzhong City 揚中市 *yángzhōng shì*	315,462	
Danyang City 丹陽市 *dānyáng shì*	988,900	
Jurong City 句容市 *jùróng shì*	639,266	
Zhenjiang New District 鎮江新區 *zhènjiāng xīnqū*	263,813	
Zhenjiang High Technology Industry Development Zone 鎮江高新技術產業開發區 *zhènjiāng gāoxīnjìshù chǎnyè kāifāqū*	60,064	

[a]Does not include the Changzhou economic development zone
[b]Includes the high technology industry development zone

Table 18.5 shows the *hukou* (family registered) populations based on PRC Ministry of Civil Affairs data. (Districts listed directly under major cities are government seats, as are those in parentheses). One can compare these data with the census (usual residential populations based on 2010 and 2020 censuses in Tables 18.3 and 18.4.

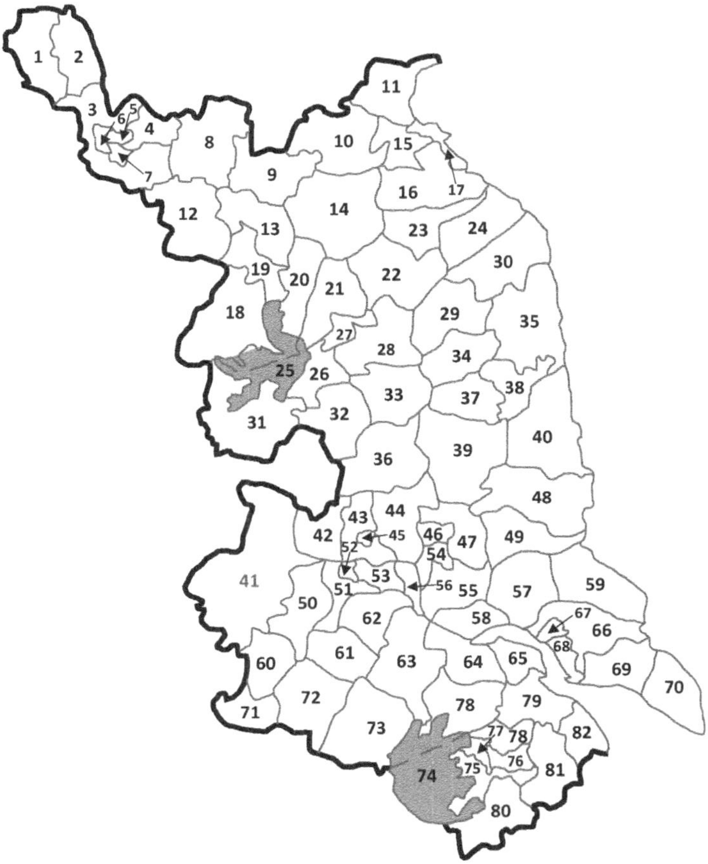

1. Fengxian County
2. Peixian County
3. Tongshan District
4. Jiawang District
5. Gulou District
6. Quanshan District
7. Yunlong District
8. Pizhou City
9. Xinyi City
10. Donghai County
11. Ganyu District
12. Suining County
13. Suyu District
14. Shuyang County
15. Haizhou District
16. Guanyun County
17. Lianyun District
18. Sihong County
19. Sucheng District
20. Siyang County
21. Huaiyin District
22. Lianshui County
23. Guannan County
24. Xiangshui County
25. Hongze Hu (Lake)
26. Hongze County
27. Qingjiangpu District
28. Huai'an District
29. Funing County
30. Binhai County
31. Xuyi County
32. Jinhu County
33. Baoying County
34. Jianhu County
35. Sheyang County
36. Gaoyou City
37. Yandu District
38. Tinghu District
39. Xinghua City
40. Dafeng District
41. Nanjing City
42. Yizheng City
43. Qianjiang District
44. Hanjiang District
45. Guangling District
46. Hailing District
48. Jiangyan District
48. Dongtai City
49. Hai'an County
50. Jurong City
51. Dantu District
52. Runzhou District
53. Jingkou District
54. Gaogang District
55. Taixing City
56. Yangzhong City
57. Rugao City
58. Jingjiang City
59. Rudong County
60. Lishui District
61. Jintan District
62. Danyang City
63. Changzhou City
64. Jiangyin City
65. Zhangjiagang City
66. Tongzhou District
67. Gangzha District
68. Chongchuan District
69. Haimen City
70. Qidong City
71. Gaochun District
72. Liyang City
73. Yixing City
74. Taihu (Lake)
75. Wuzhong District
76. Gusu District
77. Huqiu District
78. Xiangcheng District
79. Changshu City
80. Wujiang District
81. Kunshan City
82. Taicang City

Fig. 18.2 Jiangsu Province: subdistricts (Provincial Capital: Nanjing City). (Drawn by the author, after People's Republic of China, Ministry of Civil Affairs (MCA 2020))

Jiangsu Province (蘇 *sū*)

Provincial Capital: Nanjing

Table 18.5 Jiangsu Province: permanent registered (戶籍人口 *hùjí rénkǒu*) populations. (MCA 2020)

Name	Traditional	Simplified	Population (2012)	Population (2016)	Population (2020)	Area (Sq. Km)
Jiangsu Province	江蘇省	江苏省	74,670,000	76,490,000	78,320,000	102,378
Nanjing City	南京市	南京市	6,320,000	6,390,000	6,970,000	6586
Xuanwu District (Meiyuan Xincun Subdistrict)	玄武區 (梅園新村街道)	玄武区 (梅园新村街道)	510,000	510,000	470,000	75
Baixia District (Wulaocun Subdistrict)	白下區 (五老村街道)	白下区 (五老村街道)	460,000	N/A	N/A	(26)
Qinhuai District (Wulaocun Subdistrict)	秦淮區 (五老村街道)	秦淮区 (五老村街道)	250,000	710,000	690,000	49
Jianye District (Mochouhu Subdistrict)	建鄴區 (莫愁湖街道)	建邺区 (莫愁湖街道)	240,000	260,000	380,000	83
Gulou District (Ninghailu Subdistrict)	鼓樓區 (寧海路街道)	鼓楼区 (宁海路街道)	660,000	960,000	920,000	53
Xiaguan District (Yuejianglou Subdistrict)	下關區 (閱江樓街道)	下关区 (阅江楼街道)	310,000	N/A	N/A	(28)
Pukou District (Jiangpu Subdistrict)	浦口區 (江浦街道)	浦口区 (江浦街道)	560,000	590,000	740,000	911
Luhe District (Xiongzhou Subdistrict)	六合區 (雄州街道)	六合区 (雄州街道)	890,000	890,000	930,000	1471
Qixia District (Yaohua Subdistrict)	棲霞區 (堯化街道)	栖霞区 (尧化街道)	430,000	430,000	510,000	395
Yuhuatai District (Yuhua Subdistrict)	雨花台區 (雨花街道)	雨花台区 (雨花街道)	230,000	240,000	300,000	132
Jiangning District (Dongshan Subdistrict)	江寧區 (東山街道)	江宁区 (东山街道)	940,000	950,000	1,120,000	1563
Lishui District (Yongyang Town)	溧水區 (永陽鎮)	溧水区 (永阳镇)	410,000	420,000	440,000	1064
Gaochun County (Chunxi Town)	高淳區 (淳溪鎮)	高淳区 (淳溪镇)	430,000	430,000	450,000	790
Xuzhou City	徐州市	徐州市	9,730,000	9,900,000	10,450,000	11,258

(continued)

Table 18.5 (continued)

Name	Traditional	Simplified	Population (2012)	Population (2016)	Population (2020)	Area (Sq. Km)
Yunlong District (Daguozhuang Subdistrict)	雲龍區 (大郭莊街道)	云龙区 (大郭庄街道)	310,000	310,000	370,000	118
Gulou District (Pailou Subdistrict)	鼓樓區 (牌樓街道)	鼓楼区 (牌楼街道)	480,000	490,000	630,000	68
Jiawang District (Daquan Subdistrict)	賈汪區 (大泉街道)	贾汪区 (大泉街道)	510,000	510,000	520,000	834
Quanshan District (Kuishan Subdistrict)	泉山區 (奎山街道)	泉山区 (奎山街道)	600,000	610,000	630,000	108
Tongshan District (Tongshan Subdistrict)	銅山區 (銅山街道)	铜山区 (铜山街道)	1,290,000	1,340,000	1,330,000	1909
Pizhou City (Donghu Subdistrict)	邳州市 (東湖街道)	邳州市 (东湖街道)	1,790,000	1,800,000	1,940,000	2088
Xinyi City (Xin'an Subdistrict)	新沂市 (新安街道)	新沂市 (新安街道)	1,040,000	1,070,000	1,130,000	1571
Suining County (Suicheng Town)	睢寧縣 (睢城鎮)	睢宁县 (睢城镇)	1,330,000	1,370,000	1,440,000	1767
Peixian County (Hanyuan Subdistrict)	沛縣 (漢源街道)	沛县 (汉兴街道)	1,220,000	1,230,000	1,240,000	1349
Fengxian County (Zhongyangli Subdistrict)	豐縣 (中陽里街道)	丰县 (中阳里街道)	1,160,000	1,170,000	1,210,000	1446
Lianyungang City	連雲港市	连云港市	4,970,000	5,070,000	5,340,000	7614
Xinpu District[a] (Pudong Subdistrict)	新浦區 (浦東街道)	新浦区 (浦东街道)	460,000	N/A	N/A	(462)
Lianyun District (Haizhouwan Subdistrict)	連雲區 (海州灣街道)	连云区 (海州湾街道)	240,000	250,000	250,000	797
Haizhou District (Xinpu Subdistrict)	海州區 (新浦街道)	海州区 (新浦街道)	230,000	670,000	790,000	700
Ganyu District (Qingkou Town)	贛榆區 (青口鎮)	赣榆区 (青口镇)	1,130,000	1,160,000	1,200,000	1514
Guanyun County (Yishan Town)	灌雲縣 (伊山鎮)	灌云县 (伊山镇)	1,000,000	1,020,000	1,040,000	1538
Donghai County (Niushan Subdistrict)	東海縣 (牛山街道)	东海县 (牛山街道)	1,150,000	1,180,000	1,250,000	2037

(continued)

Table 18.5 (continued)

Name	Traditional	Simplified	Population (2012)	Population (2016)	Population (2020)	Area (Sq. Km)
Guannan County (Xin'an Town)	灌南縣 (新安鎮)	灌南县 (新安镇)	760,000	790,000	820,000	1028
Suqian City	宿遷市	宿迁市	5,470,000	5,600,000	5,910,000	8462
Sucheng District (Xiangli Subdistrict)	宿城區 (項里街道)	宿城区 (项里街道)	890,000	920,000	1,110,000	854
Suyu District (Yuxin Subdistrict)	宿豫區 (豫新街道)	宿豫区 (豫新街道)	710,000	720,000	660,000	1237
Shuyang County (Shucheng Subdistrict)	沭陽縣 (沭城街道)	沭阳县 (沭城街道)	1,830,000	1,870,000	1,980,000	2299
Siyang County (Zhongxing Town)	泗陽縣 (眾興鎮)	泗阳县 (众兴镇)	1,020,000	1,040,000	1,070,000	1378
Sihong County (Qingyang Town)	泗洪縣 (青陽鎮)	泗洪县 (青阳镇)	1,020,000	1,050,000	1,100,000	2694
Huai'an City	淮安市	淮安市	5,380,000	5,480,000	5,610,000	10,047
Qinghe District[b] (Fuqian Subdistrict)	清河區 (府前街道)	清河区 (府前街道)	370,000	410,000	N/A	(143)
Qingpu District[c] (Chengnan Township)	清浦區 (城南鄉)	清浦区 (城南乡)	320,000	N/A	N/A	(277)
Huai'an District (Huaicheng Town)	淮安區 (淮城鎮)	淮安区 (淮城镇)	1,180,000	1,190,000	1,150,000	1452
Huaiyin District (Wangying Town)	淮陰區 (王營鎮)	淮阴区 (王营镇)	910,000	910,000	910,000	1264
Qingjiangpu[d] District (Chengnan Township)	清江浦區 (城南鄉)	清江浦区 (城南乡)	N/A	N/A	900,000	420
Jinhu County (Licheng Town)	金湖縣 (黎城鎮)	金湖县 (黎城镇)	360,000	360,000	350,000	1344
Xutai County (Xucheng Town)	盱眙縣 (盱城鎮)	盱眙县 (盱城镇)	770,000	780,000	800,000	2497
Hongze County (Gaoliangrun Subdistrict)	洪澤縣 (高良澗街道)	洪泽县 (高良涧街道)	380,000	390,000	370,000	1394
Lianshui County (Liancheng Town)	漣水縣 (漣城鎮)	涟水县 (涟城镇)	1,090,000	1,110,000	1,130,000	1676
Yancheng City	鹽城市	盐城市	8,160,000	8,230,000	8,250,000	16,972
Tinghu District (Yulong Subdistrict)	亭湖區 (毓龍街道)	亭湖区 (毓龙街道)	870,000	950,000	1,020,000	815

(continued)

Table 18.5 (continued)

Name	Traditional	Simplified	Population (2012)	Population (2016)	Population (2020)	Area (Sq. Km)
Yandu District (Xindu Subdistrict)	鹽都區 (新都街道)	盐都区 (新都街道)	760,000	720,000	710,000	1047
Dongtai City (Dongtai Town)	東台市 (東台鎮)	东台市 (东台镇)	1,130,000	1,140,000	1,100,000	3221
Dafeng City (Dazhong Town)	大豐市 (大中鎮)	大丰市 (大中镇)	730,000	730,000	710,000	3059
Sheyang County (Hede Town)	射陽縣 (合德鎮)	射阳县 (合德镇)	970,000	970,000	950,000	2855
Funing County (Xincheng Subdistrict)	阜寧縣 (新城街道)	阜宁县 (新城街道)	1,100,000	1,110,000	1,120,000	1439
Binhai County (Dongkan Town)	濱海縣 (東坎鎮)	滨海县 (东坎镇)	1,180,000	1,200,000	1,230,000	1915
Xiangshui County (Xiangshui Town)	響水縣 (響水鎮)	响水县 (响水镇)	610,000	610,000	620,000	1461
Jianhu County (Tanghe Subdistrict)	建湖縣 (塘河街道)	建湖县 (塘河街道)	810,000	800,000	780,000	1160
Yangzhou City	揚州市	扬州市	4,630,000	4,580,000	4,590,000	6592
Hanjiang District (Hanshang Subdistrict)	邗江區 (邗上街道)	邗江区 (邗上街道)	740,000	700,000	760,000	641
Guangling District (Wenhe Subdistrict)	廣陵區 (汶河街道)	广陵区 (汶河街道)	490,000	500,000	490,000	335
Jiangdu District (Xiannü Town)	江都區 (仙女鎮)	江都区 (仙女镇)	1,070,000	1,070,000	1,040,000	1330
Yizheng City (Zhenzhou Town)	儀徵市 (真州鎮)	仪征市 (真州镇)	600,000	590,000	590,000	902
Gaoyou City (Gaoyou Subdistrict)	高郵市 (高郵街道)	高邮市 (高邮街道)	820,000	820,000	810,000	1922
Baoying County (Anyi Town)	寶應縣 (安宜鎮)	宝应县 (安宜镇)	910,000	900,000	890,000	1462
Taizhou City	泰州市	泰州市	5,050,000	5,060,000	5,030,000	5788
Hailing District (Chengzhong Subdistrict)	海陵區 (城中街道)	海陵区 (城中街道)	570,000	570,000	600,000	305
Gaogang District (Kou'an Subdistrict)	高港區 (口岸街道)	高港区 (口岸街道)	260,000	260,000	260,000	334
Jiangyan District[e] (Luotang Subdistrict)	姜堰區 (羅塘街道)	姜堰区 (罗塘街道)	N/A	790,000	780,000	928

(continued)

Table 18.5 (continued)

Name	Traditional	Simplified	Population (2012)	Population (2016)	Population (2020)	Area (Sq. Km)
Jingjiang City (Jingcheng Subdistrict)	靖江市 (靖城街道)	靖江市 (靖城街道)	670,000	670,000	660,000	656
Taixing City (Jichuan Subdistrict)	泰興市 (濟川街道)	泰兴市 (济川街道)	1,200,000	1,200,000	1,180,000	1170
Xinghua City (Zhaoyang Town)	興化市 (昭陽鎮)	兴化市 (昭阳镇)	1,560,000	1,570,000	1,560,000	2395
Nantong City	南通市	南通市	7,630,000	7,650,000	7,630,000	8001
Chongchuan District (Hongqiao Subdistrict)	崇川區 (虹橋街道)	崇川区 (虹桥街道)	680,000	670,000	700,000	221
Gangzha District (Yongxing Subdistrict)	港閘區 (永興街道)	港闸区 (永兴街道)	190,000	190,000	200,000	134
Tongzhou District (Jinsha Town)	通州區 (金沙鎮)	通州区 (金沙镇)	1,250,000	1,260,000	1,260,000	1166
Haimen City (Haimen Subdistrict)	海門市 (海門街道)	海门市 (海门街道)	1,000,000	1,000,000	1,000,000	939
Qidong City (Huilong Town)	啟東市 (匯龍鎮)	启东市 (汇龙镇)	1,120,000	1,120,000	1,110,000	1208
Rugao City (Rucheng Subdistrict)	如皋市 (如城街道)	如皋市 (如城街道)	1,410,000	1,420,000	1,420,000	1492
Rudong County (Juegang Town)	如東縣 (掘港鎮)	如东县 (掘港镇)	1,050,000	1,050,000	1,020,000	1733
Hai'an County (Hai'an Town)	海安縣 (海安鎮)	海安县 (海安镇)	930,000	940,000	930,000	1108
Zhenjiang City	鎮江市	镇江市	2,710,000	2,720,000	2,710,000	3847
Jingkou District (Zhengdonglu Subdistrict)	京口區 (正東路街道)	京口区 (正东路街道)	510,000	500,000	500,000	341
Runzhou District (Qilidian Subdistrict)	潤州區 (七里甸街道)	润州区 (七里甸街道)	250,000	250,000	240,000	130
Dantu District (Yicheng Subdistrict)	丹徒區 (宜城街道)	丹徒区 (宜城街道)	280,000	290,000	290,000	611
Yangzhong City (Sanmao Subdistrict)	揚中市 (三茅街道)	扬中市 (三茅街道)	280,000	280,000	280,000	331
Danyang City (Yunyang Subdistrict)	丹陽市 (雲陽街道)	丹阳市 (云阳街道)	810,000	810,000	810,000	1047

(continued)

Table 18.5 (continued)

Name	Traditional	Simplified	Population (2012)	Population (2016)	Population (2020)	Area (Sq. Km)
Jurong City (Chongming Subdistrict)	句容市 (崇明街道)	句容市 (崇明街道)	580,000	590,000	590,000	1387
Changzhou City	常州市	常州市	3,600,000	3,680,000	3,820,000	4374
Xinbei District (Hehai Subdistrict)	新北區 (河海街道)	新北区 (河海街道)	450,000	540,000	600,000	509
Zhonglou District (Beigang Subdistrict)	鍾樓區 (北港街道)	钟楼区 (北港街道)	360,000	420,000	430,000	142
Tianning District (Lanling Subdistrict)	天寧區 (蘭陵街道)	天宁区 (兰陵街道)	380,000	460,000	480,000	154
Qishuyan District[f] (Lucheng Subdistrict)	戚墅堰區 (潞城街道)	戚墅堰区 (潞城街道)	80,000	N/A	N/A	(32)
Wujin District (Hutang Town)	武進區 (湖塘鎮)	武进区 (湖塘镇)	1,000,000	920,000	970,000	1057
Jintan District (Xicheng Subdistrict)	金壇區 (西城街道)	金坛区 (西城街道)	550,000	550,000	550,000	976
Liyang City (Licheng Town)	溧陽市 (溧城鎮)	溧阳市 (溧城镇)	780,000	790,000	790,000	1535
Wuxi City	無錫市	无锡市	4,660,000	5,630,000	4,970,000	4628
Chong'an District[g] (Chong'ansi Subdistrict)	崇安區 (崇安寺街道)	崇安区 (崇安寺街道)	190,000	N/A	N/A	(16)
Liangxi District[h] (Chong'ansi Subdistrict)	梁溪區 (崇安寺街道)	梁溪区 (崇安寺街道)	N/A	950,000	780,000	72
Beitang District[i] (Beidajie Subdistrict)	北塘區 (五河街道)	北塘区 (五河街道)	250,000	N/A	N/A	(31)
Binhu District (Lihu Subdistrict)	濱湖區 (蠡湖街道)	滨湖区 (蠡湖街道)	780,000	700,000	530,000	628
Xinwu District[j] (Xin'an Subdistrict)	新吳區 (新安街道)	新吴区 (新安街道)	N/A	560,000	370,000	220
Huishan District (Yanqiao Subdistrict)	惠山區 (堰橋街道)	惠山区 (堰桥街道)	420,000	430,000	490,000	325
Xishan District (Dongting Subdistrict)	錫山區 (東亭街道)	锡山区 (东亭街道)	410,000	700,000	460,000	399

(continued)

Table 18.5 (continued)

Name	Traditional	Simplified	Population (2012)	Population (2016)	Population (2020)	Area (Sq. Km)
Jiangyin City (Chengjiang Subdistrict)	江陰市 (澄江街道)	江阴市 (澄江街道)	1,210,000	1,210,000	1,260,000	987
Yixing City (Yicheng Subdistrict)	宜興市 (宜城街道)	宜兴市 (宜城街道)	1,070,000	1,080,000	1,080,000	1997
Suzhou City	蘇州市	苏州市	6,390,000	6,480,000	7,040,000	8488
Gusu District[k] (Sujin Subdistrict)	姑蘇區 (蘇錦街道)	姑苏区 (苏锦街道)	N/A	750,000	730,000	83
Huqiu District (Shishan Subdistrict)	虎丘區 (獅山街道)	虎丘区 (狮山街道)	690,000	740,000	950,000	335
Wuzhong District (Changqiao Subdistrict)	吳中區 (長橋街道)	吴中区 (长桥街道)	600,000	610,000	680,000	2043
Xiangcheng District (Yuanhe Subdistrict)	相城區 (元和街道)	相城区 (元和街道)	380,000	390,000	430,000	490
Wujiang District[l] (Binhu Subdistrict)	吳江區 (濱湖街道)	吴江区 (滨湖街道)	N/A	800,000	840,000	1238
Kunshan City (Yushan Town)	昆山市 (玉山鎮)	昆山市 (玉山镇)	710,000	740,000	900,000	932
Taicang City (Loudong Subdistrict)	太倉市 (婁東街道)	太仓市 (娄东街道)	470,000	470,000	490,000	823
Changshu City (Yushan Town)	常熟市 (虞山鎮)	常熟市 (虞山镇)	1,070,000	1,070,000	1,070,000	1276
Zhangjiagang City (Yangshe Town)	張家港市 (楊舍鎮)	张家港市 (杨舍镇)	910,000	910,000	930,000	990

[a]Merged with Haizhou district in 2014
[b]Merged with Qingjiangpu district in July 2016
[c]Merged with Qingjiangpu district in July 2016
[d]Established July 2016
[e]Made a district in 2012
[f]Merged with Wujin district in 2012
[g]Dissolved in 2016
[h]Established in 2015
[i]Dissolved in 2015
[j]Established in 2015
[k]Established October 2012
[l]Established October 2012

References

21st Century Economic Reports. 2016. [*2016 GDP data ranking and growth forecast of China's provinces and cities*]. 2016年中国各省市 GDP 数据排名及增速预测. 21世纪经济报道. 16 February. https://m.phbang.cn/general/154671.html.

Ctext.org. 2021. Sima Qian. [Records of the grand historian] *Shi Ji*. Chapter 65: 史記. Chinese Text Project.

Jacobs, Bruce J. 1999. Uneven development: Prosperity and poverty in Jiangsu Province. In *The political economy of China's provinces: competitive and comparative advantage*, ed. Hans Hendrischke and Feng Chongli, 113–150. New York: Routledge.

Jiangsu Province Bureau of Statistics (JPBS). 2021. [*Bulletin of the main data of the seventh national census of Jiangsu Province in 2020*]. 10 April. 江苏省2020年第七次全国人口普查主要数据公报. http://tj.jiangsu.gov.cn/col/col80064/index.html

Kaplan, David E. 1992. *Fires of the dragon: politics, murder and the Kuomintang*. New York: Atheneum.

Lu, Suping, ed. 2012. *A dark page in history: The Nanjing massacre and post-massacre social conditions reported in British diplomatic dispatches, admiralty documents, and U.S. Naval intelligence reports*. Lanham, MD: University Press of America.

Ministry of Civil Affairs (MCA), People's Republic of China. 2020. [*County/township administration handbook*]. Beijing: China Statistics Press. 中華人民共和國民政部, 中華人民共和國, 鄉鎮行政區劃簡冊.

Steinhardt, N. 2013. China. In *The Oxford handbook of cities in world history*, ed. Peter Clark. Oxford: Oxford University Press.

Sun-Tzu. 1993. *The art of war: The first English translation incorporating the recently discovered Yin-ch'üeh-shan texts, translated, with an introduction and commentary, by Roger T. Ames*. New York: Ballantine Books.

Tong, Hui. 2011. [*A complete collection of historical knowledge that you must know*]. Jiangxi: Baihuazhou Literature and Art Publishing House. 同辉. 不可不知的历史常识大全集. 江西: 百花洲文艺出版社.

Yang, Zihui. 1995. [*China's historical population statistical data research*]. Beijing: Reform Press. 楊子慧. 中國歷代人口統計資料研究. 北京: 改革出版社.

Zhang, Shunan. 2021. [*The 2020 per capita income list of residents in various provinces: Shanghai is the richest, and it has risen sharply*]. Finance.people.com. 22 January. 张澍楠. 2020年各省份居民人均收入榜: 上海最有钱, 这地涨得猛. http://finance.people.com.cn/n1/2021/0122/c1004-32008733.html.

Chapter 19
Jiangxi Province

Abstract Like Jiangsu, Jiangxi Province is classically known as a place rich with rice and fish, but added to that a tradition of literary excellence as well. Some of the oldest evidence of rice cultivation anywhere has been found in modern-day Jiangxi. Key archeological excavations in Jiangxi have also helped to challenge the previous concept of a central node from which Chinese civilization grew (e.g., Henan), showing a much more complex model of China's social and cultural development. Located near China's largest fresh water lake, Poyang, and connected to key waterways, Jiangxi became famous for a number of products, nowadays remembered for its Jingdezhen porcelain that continues to be manufactured today. It is also the site of the Chinese Communist Party's Nanchang uprising, as well as the official birthplace of the modern military in mainland China, the People's Liberation Army (PLA). Jiangxi's economy nowadays ranks roughly in the middle of mainland China's 31 provinces and major cities. As a consequence, there are a significant number of Jiangxi residents that have decided to live and work in other, more prosperous and dynamic areas in China.

E. Croddy, *China's Provinces and Populations*,
https://doi.org/10.1007/978-3-031-09165-0_19

Jiangxi Province (江西省 *jiāngxī shěng*): Abbreviation 赣 (*gàn*) (Fig. 19.1)

		Population (2020)
1.	Jiujiang City	4,600,276
2.	Nanchang City	6,255,007
3.	Jingdezhen City	1,618,979
4.	Shangrao City	6,491,088
5.	Yingtan City	1,154,223
6.	Yichun City	5,007,702
7.	Pingxiang City	1,804,805
8.	Xinyu City	1,202,499
9.	Fuzhou City	3,614,866
10.	Ji'an City	4,469,176
11.	Ganzhou City	8,970,014

Fig. 19.1 Jiangxi Province Major Cities (Provincial Capital Nanchang City). (Drawn by the author, after People's Republic of China, Ministry of Civil Affairs. (MCA 2020))

Jiangxi Province: General Impressions

Nearly three-quarters of the soil in Jiangxi is red, and as the Chinese Communist Party (CCP) says, this is from the blood of over 250,000 martyrs in the province who sacrificed themselves for the revolution (Shang-Ch'i 2017). Traditionally, Jiangxi is known as "the land of literary excellence, white cranes, fish and rice."[1] (For a general outline of Jiangxi's history see Table 19.1 below).

Table 19.1 Outline of Jiangxi History. (Tan 1985)

Era	Jiangxi regional state and name(s)
Xia dynasty (夏 *xià*) 2070 BCE-1600 BCE	San Miao (三苗 *sānmiáo*)
Shang dynasty (商 *shāng*) 1600 BCE-1046 BCE	Yu Yue, Yang Yue (於越；揚越 *yúyuè*; *yángyuè*)
Zhou (周 *zhōu*) 1046 BCE-256 BCE	Ai Guo (艾國 *àiguó*); Yan Guo (雁國 *yànguó*)
Spring and Autumn (春秋 *chūnqiū*) 722 BCE-403 BCE	Baiyue, State of Chu, State of Wu (百越; 楚國; 吳國 *bǎiyuè*; *chǔguó*; *wú guó*)
Qin dynasty (秦 *qín*) 221 BCE-206 BCE	Jiujiang and Lujiang Prefectures (九江郡; 廬江郡 *jiǔjiāng jùn*; *lújiāng jùn*)
Han dynasty (漢 *hàn*) 202 BCE-220 CE	Yuzhang Prefecture (豫章郡 *yùzhāng jùn*)
Three Kingdoms (三國 *sānguó*) 220 CE-280 CE	Yuzhang, Luling Prefectures (豫章郡; 廬陵郡 *yùzhāng jùn*; *lúlíng jùn*)
Jin dynasty (晉 *jìn*) 265 CE-420 CE	Jiang State (江州 *jiāngzhōu*)
South-North dynasties (南北朝 *nánběi cháo*) 420 CE-581 CE	Jiang State (江州 *jiāngzhōu*)
Sui dynasty (隋 *suí*) 581 CE-618 CE	Yuzhang, Jiujiang, Poyang, Yichun, Luling, Linchuan and Nankang Prefectures (豫章郡, 九江郡, 鄱陽郡, 宜春郡, 廬陵郡, 臨川郡, 南康郡 *yùzhāng jùn; jiǔjiāng jùn; póyáng jùn; yíchūn jùn; lúlíng jùn; línchuān jùn; nánkāng jùn*)
Tang dynasty (唐 *táng*) 618 CE-907 CE	Jiangnan Western Prefecture (江南西道 *jiāngnán xīdào*)[a]
Five Dynasties and Ten Kingdoms (五代十國 *wǔdài shíguó*) 902 CE-960 CE	Southern Tang (Nan Tang南唐 *nántáng*)
Song Dynasty (宋 *sòng*) 960-1270	Jiangnan Western State (江南西路 *jiāngnán xīlù*)
Yuan Dynasty (元 *yuán*) 1271-1368	Jiangxi Administered Prefecture (江西行省 *jiāngxī xíngshěng*)[b]
Ming Dynasty (明 *míng*) 1368-1644	Jiangxi Administration Section (江西布政使司 *jiāngxī bùzhèng shǐsī*)
Qing Dynasty (清 *qīng*) 1644-1912	Jiangxi Province (江西省 *jiāngxī shěng*)

[a]Snap shot as of second year of Zongzhang (總章二年), 669 CE
[b]About the seventeenth year of the Yuan (元十七年), 1280 CE

[1] "文章節義之邦, 白鶴魚米" *wénzhāng jiéyì zhī bang, báihè yúmǐ.*

Jiangxi Province (江西省 *jiāngxī shěng*) has the short name character Gan (贛 *gàn*) after the Gan River (贛江 *gàn jiāng*). The Gan River (along with the Fuhe (撫河 *fǔhé*), Xinjiang (信江 *xìnjiāng*), Pojiang (鄱江 *pójiāng*), and Xiushui (修水 *xiūshuǐ*) rivers) feeds into China's largest fresh water lake, Poyang Hu (鄱陽湖 *póyáng hú*). Another stylistic reference to Jiangxi therefore includes "Ganpo" (贛鄱 *gànpó*).

Prehistoric Jiangxi

Excavations at Xianrendong Cave (仙人洞 *xiānrén dòng*) and the Diaotonghuan (吊桶環 *diàotǒnghuán*) caves in Jiangxi, Wannian County (萬年縣 *wànnián xiàn*) reveal human activity going back some 14,000–12,000 years ago. These sites showed not only pottery making, some of the oldest found in all of China, but also among the earliest rice cultivation in China (Blench et al. 2005).

Limestone caves, located at the foot of Huaiyushan (懷玉山 *huáiyù shān*) Mountain, also yielded large amounts of polished stone and animal bone tools. Chinese historians categorize these findings as representative of the Xianrendong age (10,000–7000 BCE). Similar evidence of this type of human activity were also found in Hunan, Daoxian county, and Hebei's Baoding City, Xushui County.

In 1989, an important archeological excavation revealed bronze and jade specimens dating back to the Shang (ca. 1200 BCE) in Xingan County (新干縣 *xīngān xiàn*). This, along with other finds such as one at Sanxingdui (三星堆 *sānxīngduī*) in Sichuan (1986) challenged the centrality of Chinese civilization as being primarily centered in the central plain (i.e., Henan). This has since led historians to adjust their approach to China, now seen as having "multiple centers of innovation jointly ancestral to Chinese civilization." (Bagley 1999).

After the unification of China by the Qin (秦 *qín*), in 223 BCE today's Jiangxi was administered by two governing entities, the major one being Jiujiang Prefecture centered at Shouchun (壽春 *shòuchūn*) in today's Anhui Province. During the Taizu (太祖 *tàizǔ*) year (ca. 202 BCE), a Yuzhang Prefecture (豫郡 *yùzhāng jùn*) was established, named after the old name of the Gan River, Yuzhang Jiang (豫章江 *yùzhāngjiāng*). This entity governed Nanchang (南昌 *nánchāng*), its name being a shortened portmanteau of prosperous south (昌大南疆 *chāngdà nánjiāng*), and flourishing southern border area (南方昌盛 *nánfāng chāngshèng*).

Home of the First Organized Taoist (Daoist) Sect

Said to have had over three thousand followers in his lifetime, Master Zhang (張天師 *zhāng tiānshī*) or Zhang Daoling (張道陵 *zhāng dàolíng*, 34–156 CE) was the founder of the original Daoist movement, "Way of the Five Pecks of Rice" (五斗米道 *wǔdòumǐdào*) after the grain to the each of his followers gave to his school. In 90

CE, he practiced alchemy at Longhushan (龍虎山 *lónghŭ shān*; Dragon Tiger Mountain), located in Guixi City (貴溪市 *guìxī shì*), Jiangxi Province. Tradition has it that he died in Hanzhong (Shaanxi Province) at the tender age of 122 (although tradition has it he actually became immortal).

Yuzhang Prefecture (豫章郡 *yùzhāng jùn*)

According the Han Geography Records (漢書˙地理志 *hànshū dìlǐzhì*), in the second year, CE, Yuzhang Prefecture had 67,642 households and a total population of about 352,000 individuals. With the expansion of use of iron for farming tools, and a burgeoning copper mine industry, Nanchang became a major source of coin minting. (Sun 2006). In 464 CE, however, due to conflict and famine, the regional population of modern-day Jiangxi dropped to 330,000 (Hsieh and Hsieh 1995).

Jiangnan Xidao (江南西道 *jiāngnánxīdào*): Progenitor to Jiangxi

In ca. 630, under the Tang Emperor Taizong (太宗 *tàizōng*), China was divided into ten major regions (*Dao*), Jiangxi belonging to Jiangnan Dao (江南道 *jiāngnándào*). His successor, Xuanzong (玄宗 *Xuánzōng*), in 733, added to this regional inspectorate (監察區 *jiānchácqū*) the following prefectures (州 *zhōu*) and their modern equivalents under the Jiangnan Xidao region (江南西道 *jiāngnánxīdào*). The core prefectures (below) eventually became Jiangxi province, its name derived from the Jiang and Xi of 江南西道 ***jiāng**nán**xī**dào*:

- Qianzhou (虔州 *qiánzhōu*) today's Ganzhou, thus the abbreviated character 虔 (*qián*)
- Hongzhou (洪州 *hóngzhōu*), which included today's Nanchang City (南昌市 *nánchāng shì*)
- Raozhou (饒州 *ráozhōu*), todays' Shangrao City (上饒市 *shàngráo shì*)
- Jizhou (吉州 *jízhōu*), modern-day Ji'an City (吉安市 *jí'ān shì*)
- Jiangzhou (江州 *jiāngzhōu*) back then included today's Jiujiang City 九江市 (*jiŭjiāng shì*). Its older city name was Xunyang (潯陽 *xúnyáng*), thus the abbreviated character for Jiujiang (潯 *xún*)
- Yuanzhou (袁州 *yuánzhōu*), modern-day Yichun City (宜春市 *yíchūn shì*)
- Fuzhou (撫州 *fŭzhōu*), today's Fuzhou City (撫州市 *fŭzhōu shì*)

Located near Poyang Lake, Raozhou (饒州 *ráozhōu*), now Shangrao City, has recently attracted a large number of tourists because of its scenery. Shangrao's Wuyuan County (婺源縣 *wùyuán xiàn*), for example, has been lauded in China as having some of its most picturesque farm-village sites, and even China's "last remaining 'Shangrila.'" Tracing its roots back to the Zhou, Jiangxi's Shangrao city during the Tang was designated a prefecture called Raozhou (饒州 *ráozhōu*).

By ca. 800 CE, the Jiangxi area had a rapidly developing economy and was soon one of China's most prosperous areas, taking the lead in terms of agriculture, handicrafts, porcelain, as well as being home to a significant number of reknowned scholars. On the eighth year (943 CE) of Jintianfu (晉天福八年 *jìntiānfú bānián*) during the Five Dynasties and Ten Kingdoms (五代十國 *wǔdàishí guó*) era, a larger, prefecture-level state of Southern Tang (南唐 *nántáng*) included Jiangxi Province of today, extending through modern Anhui and Jiangsu to the Yellow Sea. In the northern Song (ca. 1100 CE), the Jiangxi region grew to a population of 4,445,547 (Hsieh and Hsieh 1995). Under the Mongols (Yuan), formally establishing Jiangxi Branch Secretariat (江西等處行中書省 *jiāngxī děngchǔ xíngzhōng shūshěng*) in 1277, its northern sectors formed much of today's Jiangxi province, including the following "circuits" (路 *lù*) and one subordinate prefecture (州 *zhōu*):

- 龍興路 (*lóngxīnglù*)
- 吉安路 (*jíānlù*)
- 南康路 (*nánkānglù*)
- 贛州路 (*gànzhōulù*)
- 建昌路 (*jiànchānglù*)
- 江州路 (*jiāngzhōulù*)
- 南安路 (*nánānlù*)
- 瑞州路 (*ruìzhōulù*)
- 袁州路 (*yuánzhōulù*)
- 臨江路 (*línjiānglù*)
- 撫州路 (*fǔzhōulù*)
- 南奉州 (*nánfèngzhōu*)

During the Ming Dynasty (1368), much of Jiangxi's administration was left the same as it was during the prior Yuan, with thirteen governing (府 *fǔ*) districts (including 78 subordinate counties). Many of these place names are recognizable in today's Jiangxi Province:

- Nanchang (南昌 *nánchāng*)
- Ruizhou (瑞州 *ruìzhōu*)
- Raozhou (饒州 *ráozhōu*)
- Nankang (南康 *nánkāng*)
- Jiujiang (九江 *jiǔjiāng*)
- Guangxin (廣信 *guǎngxìn*)
- Fuzhou (撫州 *fǔzhōu*)
- Jianchang (建昌 *jiànchāng*)
- Ji'an (吉安 *jí'ān*)
- Yuanzhou (袁州 *yuánzhōu*)
- Linjiang (臨江 *línjiāng*) and
- Ganzhou (贛州 *gànzhōu*)

By ca. 1400, this prefecture's borders shrank to dimensions that are much closer to that of modern-day Jiangxi Province.

Late Sixteenth Century Nanchang: Visit by Matteo Ricci, S.J. 4.10

Local politics in the south of China ultimately forced the Jesuit missionaries Michele Ruggieri and Matteo Ricci to leave Guangdong province. Using the highly efficient (if sometimes dangerous) inland riverways, after about 2 weeks of traveling on water, in 1595 the Jesuits arrived at Nanchang (referred to by its old name of 豫章 *yùzhāng*). Ricci reckoned Nanchang to have been a city double the size of Florence (Laven 2011). Upon their journeys northward, Jesuits were pleased to see that the locals did not treat them with the hostility they were used to in southern China. Seeking individuals who had the clout and funds to help him in his missionary work, they found that this was a city populated by many relatives of the imperial family, and, what's more, Ricci's reputation preceded him. Ricci also had his own impressions of Nanchang, noting that while not the most resplendent, it was famous for its great number of literati who took on government roles (Lo 2006). Having been warmly received there by the Prince Jian'an (建安王 *jiàn'ān wáng*; aka Qian Zhaizi 乾齋子 *qián zhāizǐ*), Ricci later recounted, "That which [the prince] valued most were two books with plates after our fashion, with a map of Japan very fine and firm. One of them contained a 'Description of the Whole World,' with other maps of Europe, Asia, Africa, Americas, and [Magellanica, i.e., the as of yet uncharted southern continent], together with diagrams of the nine spheres and the four elements, and other things mathematical never before seen in this country, and all with explanations in their writings" (Ch'en and Ricci 1939). As he worked on the means to gain approval for travel to Beijing and an audience with the emperor, it was in Nanchang that Ricci regaled his hosts with his prodigious, photographic memory, reciting whole passages of Chinese characters without using notes. Eventually, after about 3 years, Ricci would move on from Nanchang, travelling further north in order to reach the capital, Beijing.

Jiangxi Through the Qing

Jiangxi largely held on to the older Ming style of governance during the Qing dynasty (1644–1910). The riverine transport connections to Guangdong and the wider Yangtze (長江 *chángjiāng*) region brought continued prosperity to Jiangxi, with Jingdezhen, famed for its porcelain, being officially labeled one of China's four great cities. The other three great cities were Zhuxian Town (朱仙鎮 *zhūxiān zhèn*), Hunan Province (famed for printing, Spring Festival posters); Hankou Town

(漢口鎮 *hànkǒu zhèn*), Hubei Province (known as a mercantile center); and Foshan Town (佛山鎮 *fóshān zhèn*), Guangdong Province (well regarded for its fine handicrafts).

Taiping Rebellion and Its Aftermath

Caught between rebels and the Hunan Army, the devastation wrought by the Taiping Rebellion (1850–64) took a serious toll on Jiangxi Province. As a consequence, during 1853–1873, the population of Jiangxi lost nearly seven million people.

Nanchang Uprising

On 1 August 1927, the CCP carried out the Nanchang Uprising (南昌起義 *nánchāng qǐyì*), at the eponymous capital city. The date of the Nanchang uprising also marks China's establishment of the People's Liberation Army (PLA), which is also why the characters "1 August" (八一 *bayī*) appear on its flag. Aiming now to conquer other provinces, the revolutionary campaign ultimately led to disaster for CCP forces later that fall, as they were soundly defeated by the Nationalists in Guangdong at Shantou City (Swatow 汕頭市 *shàntóu shì*).

Under Mao Zedong's leadership, the CCP built its model and nascent army at the Jinggangshan Mountain (井岡山 *jǐnggāng shān*) Revolutionary Base. This rugged terrain had long been occupied by rebellions and brigands throughout China's history, Mao Zedong himself deeming it "an excellent base for a mobile army." It was at nearby Ciping (茨坪 *cípíng*) that the CCP scored a significant victory against the Nationalists in summer 1928. To this day, PLA leadership makes visits to Jinggangshan to pay homage to the founding spirit of China's military.

Beginning on 7 November 1931, until finally being routed by the Nationalists Fifth Encirclement Campaign in autumn of 1934, the CCP had established a Chinese Soviet Republic[2] based in Ruijin (瑞金 *ruìjīn*), complete with its own currency. One of the most valuable materials in the province was its large stores of tungsten, a strategic metal that has plays an enormously important role in the making of modern armaments. While the Chinese communists used a variety of ways to support itself financially, including selling opium, profits from sales of tungsten greatly helped support the CCP. The conflict between the Chinese Jiangxi Soviet and Nationalist forces resulted in large numbers of deaths, causing locals to flee the area, and reducing the population from 18,720,000 in 1931 to 15,560,000 by 1936 (Halliday and Chang 2005).

[2] 中華蘇維埃共和國 *zhōnghuá sūwéiāi gònghéguó*.

Some geopolitical changes were made to Jiangxi borders after the founding of the PRC. For example, in 1957 an area of Qiaotou (橋頭 *qiáotóu*), formerly Suichuan county (遂川縣 *suìchuān xiàn*), was redrawn into Hunan Province, Guidong county (桂東縣 *guìdōng xiàn*).

Jingdezhen: from pottery to helicopters: While sources differ, it is recorded in the Qing dynasty's Fuliang County Records (浮梁縣志 *fúliáng xiàn zhì*) that Jingdezhen, once called Xinping, had a porcelain industry going back to the Han dynasty. Indeed, it was said that Xinping's ceramics "prospered in the Song and Yuan dynasties, and prospered in the Ming and Qing." A contemporary observer, Wang Shimao (王世茂 *wáng shìmào*; 1536–1588) described the scene of the pottery industry in Jingdezhen[3]:

> Tens of thousands of pestles shake the ground with their noise. The heavens are a-light with the glare from the fires, so that one cannot sleep at night. The place has been called in jest "The Town of Year-round Thunder and Lightning." (Elvin 1973)

Arguably the most famous ceramic in all of China is Song porcelain (宋瓷 *songcí*) that was produced during that time at Jingdezhen. While porcelain production continued through the Ming dynasty, the Qing invasion from Manchuria (ca. 1644) resulted in the destruction of the Jingdezhen kilns. Nonetheless, the Jingdezhen pottery industry continues to thrive in modern times, and generates large numbers of ceramic products. Since 1969, Jingdezhen has also hosted the Chinese helicopter manufacturer, Changhe Aircraft Industries Corporation[4] (CAIC), its primary customer being the PLA.

Jiangxi Economy and Population in 2020

In 2015, Jiangxi province had a gross domestic production (GDP) valued at USD $259 billion, and by 2020 ranked 15th in GDP ($400 billion) out of mainland China's 31 provinces and major cities. Jiangxi ranked 14th in terms of per capita income (USD $4,357) in 2020 (Zhang 2021). Jiangxi's population only grew incrementally (1.4%) over 2010–2020 (see Tables 19.2 and 19.3). With a *hukou* (permanent registered) of 50,260,000, a substantial disparity (over five million) compared to the 2020 census (45,188,635), indicates a large number of Jiangxi natives live and work in other China's provinces and cities.

Table 19.5 (below) shows the *hukou* (family registered) populations based on PRC Ministry of Civil Affairs data. (Districts listed directly under major cities are government seats, as are those in parentheses). One can compare these data with the census (usual residential populations based on 2010 and 2020 censuses in Tables 19.3 and 19.4 (below):

---

[3] Mark Elvin, *The Pattern of the Chinese Past: A Social and Economic Interpretation*, Stanford: Stanford University Press, 1973, p285.

[4] 昌河飛機工業 *chānghéfēijīgōngyè*.

Table 19.2 Historical Population Data for Jiangxi Province. (Yang 1995)

Western year	Total population
2 CE	352,000
1491	6,549,800
1843	26,500,000
1853	24,500,000
1873	17,700,000
1909–11	16,977,000
1928	20,322,800
1947	12,725,200
1949	13,140,000
1950	15,680,000
1953	16,772,865
1964	21,068,019
1978	31,828,000
1982	33,184,827
1990	37,710,281
1998	41,912,100
2001	41,857,700
2007	43,684,100
2010	44,567,475
2020	45,188,635

Table 19.3 Jiangxi Provincial Residential (常住人口 *chángzhù rénkǒu*) Population Data. (JPBS 2021)

City	Population (2010)	Population (2020)
Nanchang City 南昌市 *nánchāng shì* [abbrev. 昌 *chāng*; 洪 *hóng*]	5,042,565	6,255,007
Fuzhou City 撫州市 *fǔzhōu shì*	3,912,312	3,614,866
Ganzhou City 贛州市 *gànzhōu shì* [abbrev. 虔 *qián*]	8,368,440	8,970,014
Ji'an City 吉安市 *jí'ān shì*	4,810,340	4,469,176
Jingdezhen City 景德鎮市 *jǐngdézhèn shì*	1,587,477	1,618,979
Jiujiang City 九江市 *jiǔjiāng shì* [abbrev. 潯 *xún*]	4,728,763	4,600,276
Pingxiang City 萍鄉市 *píngxiāng shì*	1,854,510	1,804,805
Shangrao City 上饒市 *shàngráo shì*	6,579,714	6,491,088
Xinyu City 新余市 *xīnyú shì* [abbrev. 渝 *yú*]	1,138,873	1,202,499
Yichun City 宜春市 *yíchūn shì*	5,419,575	5,007,702
Yingtan City 鷹潭市 *yīngtán shì*	1,124,906	1,154,223
Total	**44,567,475**	**45,188,635**

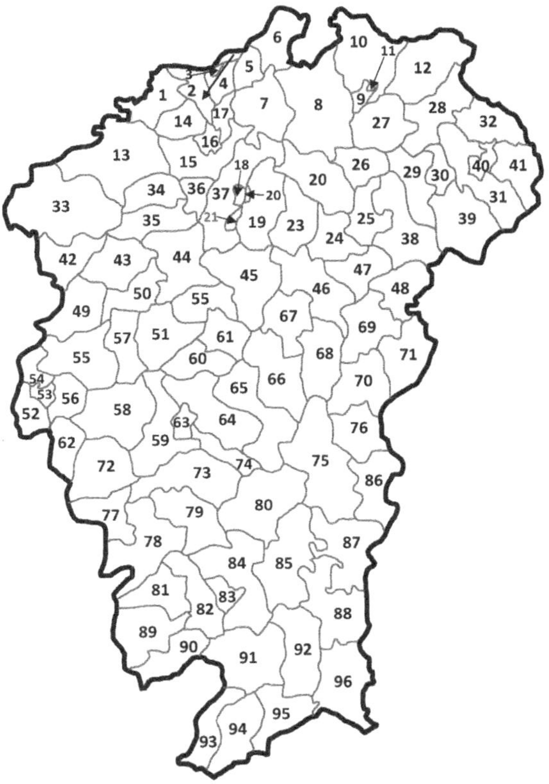

1. Ruichang City
2. Chaisang District
3. Xunyang District
4. Lianxi District
5. Hukou County
6. Pengze County
7. Duchang County
8. Poyang County
9. Changjiang District
10. Fuliang County
11. Zhushan District
12. Wuyuan County
13. Wuning County
14. De'an County
15. Yongxiu County
16. Gongqingcheng City
17. Lushan City
18. Qingshanhu District
19. Nanchang County
20. Donghu District
21. Honggutan District
22. Yugan County
23. Jinxian County
24. Dongxiang County
25. Yuehu District
26. Wannian County
27. Leping City
28. Dexing City
29. Yiyang County
30. Hengfeng County
31. Guangxin District
32. Yushan County
33. Xiushui County
34. Jing'an County
35. Fengxin County
36. Anyi County
37. Xinjian District
38. Guixi City
39. Chuanshan County
40. Xinzhou District
41. Guangfeng County
42. Tonggu County
43. Yifeng County
44. Gao'an City
45. Fengcheng City
46. Linchuan District
47. Jinxi County
48. Zixi County
49. Wanzai County
50. Shanggao County
51. Yushui District
52. Xiangdong District
53. Anyuan District
54. Shangli County
55. Yuanzhou District
56. Luxi County
57. Fenyi County
58. Anfu County
59. Ji'an County
60. Xiajiang County
61. Xingan County
62. Lianhua County
63. Jizhou District
64. Jishui County
65. Yongfeng County
66. Le'an County
67. Chongren County
68. Yihuang County
69. Nancheng County
70. Nanfeng County
71. Lichuan County
72. Yongxin County
73. Taihe County
74. Qingyuan District
75. Ningdu County
76. Guangchang County
77. Jinggangshan City
78. Suichuan County
79. Wan'an County
80. Xingguo County
81. Shangyou County
82. Nankang District
83. Zhanggong District
84. Ganxian District
85. Yudu County
86. Shicheng County
87. Ruijin City
88. Huichang County
89. Chongyi County
90. Dayu County
91. Xinfeng County
92. Anyuan County
93. Quannan County
94. Longnan County
95. Dingnan County
96. Xunwu County

Fig. 19.2 Jiangxi Province: Subdistricts (Capital City Governmental Seat: Honggutan District). (Drawn by the author, after People's Republic of China, Ministry of Civil Affairs. (MCA 2020))

Table 19.4 Jiangxi Province: Population Data of Cities and Their Subordinate Sectors. (JPBS 2021)

CITIES AND SUBORDINATE SECTORS, POPULATION (2020 CENSUS)	Subordinate district, city and county populations (2020)	Population (2020)
Nanchang City 南昌市 ***nánchāng shì* [abbrev.** 昌 ***chāng*;** 洪 ***hóng*]**		**6,255,007**
Honggutan District 紅谷潭區 *hónggǔtán qū*	555,755	
Donghu District 東湖區 *dōnghú qū*	421,690	
Xihu District 西湖區 *xīhú qū*	485,161	
Qingyunpu District 青雲譜區 *qīngyúnpǔ qū*	349,074	
Qingshanhu District 青山湖區 *qīngshānhú qū*	1,307,366	
Nanchang County 南昌縣 *nánchāng xiàn*	1,452,502	
Xinjian District 新建區 *xīnjiàn qū*	810,614	
Anyi County 安義縣 *ānyì xiàn*	252,591	
Jinxian County 進賢縣 *jìnxián xiàn*	620,524	
Fuzhou City 撫州市 ***fǔzhōu shì***		**3,614,866**
Linchuan District 臨川區 *línchuān qū*	1,102,421	
Nancheng County南城縣 *nánchéng xiàn*	286,260	
Lichuan County 黎川縣 *líchuān xiàn*	205,205	
Nanfeng County 南豐縣 *nánfēng xiàn*	271,888	
Chongren County 崇仁縣 *chóngrén xiàn*	302,181	
Le'an County 樂安縣 *lè'ān xiàn*	307,909	
Yihuang County 宜黃縣 *yíhuáng xiàn*	201,127	
Jinxi County 金溪縣 *jīnxī xiàn*	95,826	
Zixi County 資溪縣 *zīxī xiàn*	253,828	
Dongxiang County 東鄉縣 *dōngxiāng xiàn*	383,846	
Guangchang County 廣昌縣 *guǎngchāng xiàn*	204,375	
Ganzhou City 贛州市 ***gànzhōu shì* [abbrev.** 虔 ***qián*]**		**8,970,014**
Zhanggong District 章貢區 *zhānggòng qū*	1,123,276	
Ruijin City 瑞金市 *ruìjīn shì*	613,894	
Nankang District南康區 *nánkāng qū*	888,474	
Ganxian District 贛縣區 *gànxiàn qū*	576,310	
Xinfeng County 信豐縣 *xìnfēng xiàn*	673,763	
Dayu County 大余縣 *dàyú xiàn*	264,995	
Shangyou County 上猶縣 *shàngyóu xiàn*	268,557	
Chongyi County 崇義縣 *chóngyì xiàn*	177,831	
Anyuan County 安遠縣 *ānyuǎn xiàn*	346,435	
Longnan County 龍南縣 *lóngnán xiàn*	319,166	
Dingnan County 定南縣 *dìngnán xiàn*	209,914	
Quannan County 全南縣 *quánnán xiàn*	169,503	
Ningdu County 寧都縣 *níngdū xiàn*	702,394	
Yudu County 于都縣 *yúdū xiàn*	905,439	
Xingguo County 興國縣 *xīngguó xiàn*	715,149	

(continued)

Table 19.4 (continued)

CITIES AND SUBORDINATE SECTORS, POPULATION (2020 CENSUS)	Subordinate district, city and county populations (2020)	Population (2020)
Huichang County 會昌縣 *huìchāng xiàn*	451,513	
Xunwu County 尋烏縣 *xúnwū xiàn*	280,219	
Shicheng County 石城縣 *shíchéng xiàn*	283,182	
Ji'an City 吉安市 ***jí'ān shì***		**4,469,176**
Jizhou District 吉州區 *jízhōu qū*	402,669	
Qingyuan District 青原區 *qīngyuán qū*	240,730	
Jinggangshan City 井岡山市 *jǐnggāngshān shì*	155,976	
Ji'an County 吉安縣 *jí'ān xiàn*	469,513	
Jishui County 吉水縣 *jíshuǐ xiàn*	421,849	
Xiajiang County 峽江縣 *xiájiāng xiàn*	149,954	
Xingan County 新幹縣 *xīn'gān xiàn*	286,077	
Yongfeng County 永豐縣 *yǒngfēng xiàn*	388,464	
Taihe County 泰和縣 *tàihé xiàn*	467,807	
Suichuan County 遂川縣 *suìchuān xiàn*	512,109	
Wan'an County 萬安縣 *wàn'ān xiàn*	250,991	
Anfu County 安福縣 *ānfú xiàn*	329,053	
Yongxin County 永新縣 *yǒngxīn xiàn*	393,984	
Jingdezhen City[a] 景德**鎮**市 ***jǐngdézhèn shì***		**1,618,979**
Changjiang District 昌江區 *chāngjiāng qū*	201,363	
Zhushan District 珠山區 *zhūshān qū*	383,453	
Leping City 樂平市 *lèpíng shì*	753,787	
Fuliang County 浮梁縣 *fúliáng xiàn*	280,376	
Jiujiang City 九江市 ***jiǔjiāng shì* [abbrev. 潯 *xún*]**		**4,600,276**
Xunyang District 潯陽區 *xúnyáng qū*	433,122	
Lianxi District 濂溪區 *liánxī qū*	418,339	
Lushan City 廬山市 *lúshān shì*	231,525	
Ruichang City 瑞昌市 *ruìchāng shì*	403,655	
Gongqingcheng City 共青城市 *gòngqīngchéng shì*	194,689	
Chaisang District柴桑區 *cháisāng qū*	312,807	
Wuning County 武寧縣 *wǔníng xiàn*	322,161	
Xiushui County 修水縣 *xiūshuǐ xiàn*	710,620	
Yongxiu County 永修縣 *yǒngxiū xiàn*	316,365	
De'an County 德安縣 *dé'ān xiàn*	167,090	
Duchang County 都昌縣 *dūchāng xiàn*	577,684	
Hukou County 湖口縣 *húkǒu xiàn*	227,462	
Pengze County 彭澤縣 *péngzé xiàn*	284,757	
Pingxiang City 萍**鄉**市 ***píngxiāng shì***		**1,804,805**
Anyuan District 安源區 *ānyuán qū*	553,293	
Xiangdong District 湘東區 *xiāngdōng qū*	304,423	

(continued)

Table 19.4 (continued)

CITIES AND SUBORDINATE SECTORS, POPULATION (2020 CENSUS)	Subordinate district, city and county populations (2020)	Population (2020)
Lianhua County 蓮花縣 *liánhuā xiàn*	216,938	
Shangli County 上栗縣 *shànglì xiàn*	469,957	
Luxi County 蘆溪縣 *lúxī xiàn*	260,194	
Shangrao City 上饒市 ***shàngráo shì***		**6,491,088**
Xinzhou District 信州區 *xìnzhōu qū*	545,134	
Dexing City 德興市 *déxīng shì*	293,596	
Guangfeng District 廣豐區 *guǎngfēng qū*	775,364	
Guangxin District 廣信區 *guǎngxìn qū*	748,265	
Yushan County 玉山縣 *yùshān xiàn*	519,357	
Qianshan County 鉛山縣 *qiānshān xiàn*	386,200	
Hengfeng County 横峰縣 *héngfēng xiàn*	187,326	
Yiyang County 弋陽縣 *yìyáng xiàn*	338,817	
Yugan County 餘干縣 *yúgān xiàn*	840,498	
Poyang County 鄱陽縣 *póyáng xiàn*	1,184,097	
Wannian County 萬年縣 *wànnián xiàn*	357,449	
Wuyuan County 婺源縣 *wùyuán xiàn*	314,985	
Xinyu City 新余市 ***xīnyú shì***		**1,202,499**
Yushui District 渝水區 *yúshuǐ qū*	672,942	
Fenyi County 分宜縣 *fēnyí xiàn*	271,224	
Xiannühu District 仙女湖區 *xiānnǚhú qū*	72,036	
Xinyu High Technology Industrial Zone 新余高新技術產業開發區 *xīnyú gāoxīnjìshù chǎnyè kāifāqū*	186,297	
Yichun City 宜春市 ***yíchūn shì***		**5,007,702**
Yuanzhou District 袁州區 *yuánzhōu qū*	1,121,707	
Fengcheng City 豐城市 *fēngchéng shì*	1,065,641	
Zhangshu City 樟樹市 *zhāngshù shì*	485,649	
Gao'an City 高安市 *gāo'ān shì*	744,694	
Fengxin County 奉新縣 *fèngxīn xiàn*	268,617	
Wanzai County萬載縣 *wànzài xiàn*	486,435	
Shanggao County 上高縣 *shànggāo xiàn*	343,767	
Yifeng County 宜豐縣 *yífēng xiàn*	252,974	
Jing'an County 靖安縣 *jìng'ān xiàn*	121,800	
Tonggu County 銅鼓縣 *tónggǔ xiàn*	116,418	
Yingtan City 鷹潭市 ***yīngtán shì***		**1,154,223**
Yuehu District 月湖區 *yuèhú qū*	287,489	
Guixi City 貴溪市 *guìxī shì*	540,572	
Yujiang County 余江縣 *yújiāng xiàn*	326,162	

[a]Does not include deployed People's Liberation Army (PLA) troops or overseas Chinese (Taiwanese as well as people from Macao, and Hong Kong)

Jiangxi Province (贛 gàn)

Provincial Capital: Nanchang (Table 19.5)

Table 19.5 Jiangxi Province: Permanent Registered (戶籍人口 *hùjí rénkǒu*) Populations. (MCA 2020)

Name	Traditional	Simplified	Population (2012)	Population (2016)	Population (2020)	Area (Sq. Km)
Jiangxi Province	江西省	江西省	46,940,000	48,040,000	50,260,000	167,064
Nanchang City	南昌市	南昌市	5,020,000	5,070,000	5,320,000	7268
Honggutan District[a] (Shajing Subdistrict)	紅谷灘區 (沙井街道)	红谷滩区 (沙井街道)	N/A	N/A	330,000	190
Donghu District (Gongyuan Subdistrict)	東湖區 (公園街道)	东湖区 (公园街道)	590,000	640,000	430,000	57
Xihu District (Chaoyangzhou Subdistrict)	西湖區 (朝陽洲街道)	西湖区 (朝阳洲街道)	440,000	440,000	460,000	46
Qingyunpu District (Sanjiadian Subdistrict)	青雲譜區 (三家店街道)	青云谱区 (三家店街道)	260,000	270,000	270,000	43
Wanli District[b] (Zhaoxian Town)	灣里區 (招賢鎮)	湾里区 (招贤镇)	90,000	80,000	N/A	(254)
Qingshanhu District (Jingdong Town)	青山湖區 (京東鎮)	青山湖区 (京东镇)	810,000	790,000	640,000	214
Nanchang County (Liantang Town)	南昌縣 (蓮塘鎮)	南昌县 (莲塘镇)	1,000,000	1,010,000	1,260,000	1839
Xinjian District (Changling Town)	新建區 (長凌鎮)	新建区 (长凌镇)	730,000	710,000	700,000	2274
Anyi County (Longjin Town)	安義縣 (龍津鎮)	安义县 (龙津镇)	280,000	290,000	310,000	656
Jinxian County (Minhe Town)	進賢縣 (民和鎮)	进贤县 (民和镇)	820,000	840,000	850,000	1952
Jiujiang City	九江市	九江市	5,180,000	5,280,000	5,230,000	18,823
Xunyang District (Gantang Subdistrict)	潯陽區 (甘棠街道)	浔阳区 (甘棠街道)	280,000	290,000	290,000	50
Lianxi District[c] (Shili Subdistrict)	濂溪區 (十里街道)	濂溪区 (十里街道)	N/A	N/A	380,000	503
Lushan District (Nankang Town)	廬山區 (十里街道)	庐山区 (十里街道)	360,000	360,000	N/A	(548)
Lushan City (Nankang Town)	廬山市 (南康鎮)	庐山市 (南康市)	360,000	360,000	280,000	618

(continued)

Table 19.5 (continued)

Name	Traditional	Simplified	Population (2012)	Population (2016)	Population (2020)	Area (Sq. Km)
Ruichang City (Pencheng Subdistrict)	瑞昌市 (湓城街道)	瑞昌市 (湓城街道)	450,000	460,000	460,000	1423
Gongqingcheng City (Chashan Subdistrict)	共青城市 (茶山街道)	共青城市 (茶山街道)	190,000	190,000	120,000	307
Jiujiang County[d] (Shahejie Subdistrict)	九江縣 (沙河街道)	九江县 (沙河街道)	330,000	330,000	N/A	(911)
Chaisang District (Shahe Subdistrict)	柴桑區 (沙河街道)	柴桑区 (沙河街道)	N/A	N/A	340,000	911
Wuning County (Yuning Subdistrict)	武寧縣 (豫寧街道)	武宁县 (豫宁街道)	380,000	390,000	410,000	3507
Xiushui County (Yining Town)	修水縣 (義寧鎮)	修水县 (义宁镇)	820,000	850,000	890,000	4504
Yongxiu County (Tubu Town)	永修縣 (塗埠鎮)	永修县 (涂埠镇)	380,000	390,000	400,000	1940
De'an County (Puting Town)	德安縣 (蒲亭鎮)	德安县 (蒲亭镇)	240,000	240,000	180,000	838
Xingzi County[e] (Nankang Town)	星子縣 (南康鎮)	星子县 (南康镇)	260,000	270,000	N/A	(596)
Duchang County (Duchang Town)	都昌縣 (都昌鎮)	都昌县 (都昌镇)	820,000	830,000	820,000	1988
Hukou County (Shuangzhong Town)	湖口縣 (雙鐘鎮)	湖口县 (双钟镇)	290,000	300,000	300,000	669
Pengze County (Longcheng Town)	彭澤縣 (龍城鎮)	彭泽县 (龙城镇)	380,000	380,000	380,000	1542
Jingdezhen City	景德鎮市	景德镇市	1,630,000	1,680,000	1,700,000	5270
Changjiang District (Xijiao Subdistrict)	昌江區 (西郊街道)	昌江区 (西郊街道)	180,000	170,000	160,000	354
Zhushan District (Shishibu Subdistrict)	珠山區 (石獅埠街道)	珠山区 (石狮埠街道)	280,000	310,000	320,000	76
Leping City (Jiyang Subdistrict)	樂平市 (洎陽街道)	乐平市 (洎阳街道)	890,000	910,000	950,000	1973
Fuliang County (Fuliang Town)	浮梁縣 (浮梁鎮)	浮梁县 (浮梁镇)	280,000	290,000	280,000	2867
Yingtan City	鷹潭市	鹰潭市	1,190,000	1,240,000	1,290,000	3554

(continued)

Table 19.5 (continued)

Name	Traditional	Simplified	Population (2012)	Population (2016)	Population (2020)	Area (Sq. Km)
Yuehu District (Jiangbian Subdistrict)	月湖區 (江邊街道)	月湖区 (江边街道)	220,000	230,000	240,000	137
Guixi City (Huayuan Subdistrict)	貴溪市 (花園街道)	贵溪市 (花园街道)	600,000	620,000	650,000	2480
Yujiang County (Dengbu Town)	余江縣 (鄧埠鎮)	余江县 (邓埠镇)	370,000	390,000	400,000	931.06
Xinyu City	新余市	新余市	1,180,000	1,200,000	1,250,000	3178
Yushui District (Chengnan Subdistrict)	渝水區 (城南街道)	渝水区 (城南街道)	850,000	870,000	900,000	1786
Fenyi County (Fenyi Town)	分宜縣 (分宜鎮)	分宜县 (分宜镇)	330,000	330,000	350,000	1392
Pingxiang City	萍鄉市	萍乡市	1,880,000	1,930,000	2,000,000	3802
Anyuan District (Anyuan Town)	安源區 (安源鎮)	安源区 (安源镇)	450,000	460,000	480,000	212
Xiangdong District (Xiangdong Town)	湘東區 (湘東鎮)	湘东区 (湘东镇)	400,000	410,000	410,000	853
Lianhua County (Qinting Town)	蓮花縣 (琴亭鎮)	莲花县 (琴亭镇)	260,000	270,000	280,000	1062
Shangli County (Shangli Town)	上栗縣 (上栗鎮)	上栗县 (上栗镇)	480,000	490,000	520,000	712
Luxi County (Luxi Town)	蘆溪縣 (蘆溪鎮)	芦溪县 (芦溪镇)	290,000	300,000	310,000	963
Ganzhou City	贛州市	赣州市	9,080,000	9,210,000	9,810,000	39,379
Zhanggong District (Jiefang Subdistrict)	章貢區 (解放街道)	章贡区 (解放街道)	650,000	670,000	770,000	591
Ruijin City (Xianghu Town)	瑞金市 (象湖鎮)	瑞金市 (象湖镇)	660,000	680,000	710,000	2448
Nankang District (Rongjiang Subdistrict)	南康區 (蓉江街道)	南康区 (蓉江街道)	800,000	760,000	860,000	1732
Ganxian District (Meilin Town)	贛縣區 (梅林鎮)	赣县区 (梅林镇)	620,000	630,000	660,000	2993
Xinfeng County (Jiading Town)	信豐縣 (嘉定鎮)	信丰县 (嘉定镇)	730,000	750,000	780,000	2878
Dayu County (Nan'an Town)	大余縣 (南安鎮)	大余县 (南安镇)	310,000	310,000	310,000	1368

(continued)

Table 19.5 (continued)

Name	Traditional	Simplified	Population (2012)	Population (2016)	Population (2020)	Area (Sq. Km)
Shangyou County (Dongshan Town)	上猶縣 (東山鎮)	上犹县 (东山镇)	310,000	310,000	320,000	1544
Chongyi County (Hengshui Town)	崇義縣 (橫水鎮)	崇义县 (横水镇)	210,000	210,000	220,000	2197
Anyuan County (Xinshan Town)	安遠縣 (欣山鎮)	安远县 (欣山镇)	370,000	380,000	410,000	2375
Longnan County (Longnan Town)	龍南縣 (龍南鎮)	龙南县 (龙南镇)	310,000	320,000	340,000	1641
Dingnan County (Lishi Town)	定南縣 (歷市鎮)	定南县 (历市镇)	210,000	210,000	220,000	1316
Quannan County (Chengxiang Town)	全南縣 (城厢鎮)	全南县 (城厢镇)	190,000	190,000	200,000	1521
Ningdu County (Meijiang Town)	寧都縣 (梅江鎮)	宁都县 (梅江镇)	780,000	790,000	850,000	4053
Yudu County (Gongjiang Town)	于都縣 (貢江鎮)	于都县 (贡江镇)	1,020,000	1,050,000	1,120,000	2893
Xingguo County (Lianjiang Town)	興國縣 (瀲江鎮)	兴国县 (潋江镇)	780,000	800,000	860,000	3214
Huichang County (Wenwuba Town)	會昌縣 (文武壩鎮)	会昌县 (文武坝镇)	500,000	510,000	530,000	2722
Xunwu County (Changning Town)	尋烏縣 (長寧鎮)	寻乌县 (长宁镇)	320,000	320,000	330,000	2311
Shicheng County (Qinjiang Town)	石城縣 (琴江鎮)	石城县 (琴江镇)	310,000	320,000	330,000	1582
Shangrao City	上饒市	上饶市	7,400,000	7,600,000	7,890,000	22,777
Xinzhou District (Maojialing Subdistrict)	信州區 (茅家嶺街道)	信州区 (茅家岭街道)	400,000	410,000	440,000	309
Dexing City (Yincheng Subdistrict)	德興市 (銀城街道)	德兴市 (银城街道)	320,000	330,000	340,000	2082
Shangrao County[f] (Xuri Subdistrict)	上饒縣 (旭日街道)	上饶县 (旭日街道)	780,000	800,000	N/A	(2246)
Guangfeng District (Yongfeng Subdistrict)	廣豐區 (永豐街道)	广丰区 (永丰街道)	900,000	920,000	980,000	1378
Guangxin District[g] (Xuri Subdistrict)	廣信區 (旭日街道)	广信区 (旭日街道)	N/A	N/A	730,000	2232

(continued)

Table 19.5 (continued)

Name	Traditional	Simplified	Population (2012)	Population (2016)	Population (2020)	Area (Sq. Km)
Yushan County (Bingxi Subdistrict)	玉山縣 (冰溪街道)	玉山县 (冰溪街道)	600,000	620,000	650,000	1723
Qianshan County (Hekou Town)	鉛山縣 (河口鎮)	铅山县 (河口镇)	450,000	470,000	480,000	2178
Hengfeng County (Xing'an Subdistrict)	横峰縣 (興安街道)	横峰县 (兴安街道)	220,000	220,000	230,000	655
Yiyang County (Yijiang Town)	弋陽縣 (弋江鎮)	弋阳县 (弋江镇)	400,000	410,000	430,000	1592
Yugan County (Yuting Town)	餘干縣 (玉亭鎮)	余干县 (玉亭镇)	1,000,000	1,060,000	1,090,000	2331
Poyang County (Poyang Town)	鄱陽縣 (鄱陽鎮)	鄱阳县 (鄱阳镇)	1,570,000	1,590,000	1,580,000	4215
Wannian County (Chenying Town)	萬年縣 (陳營鎮)	万年县 (陈营镇)	400,000	410,000	440,000	1135
Wuyuan County (Rancheng Subdistrict)	婺源縣 (蚺城街道)	婺源县 (蚺城街道)	360,000	360,000	380,000	2947
Fuzhou City	撫州市	抚州市	4,050,000	4,180,000	4,320,000	18,817
Linchuan District (Qingyun Subdistrict)	臨川區 (青雲街道)	临川区 (青云街道)	1,130,000	1,190,000	1,220,000	2121
Nancheng County (Jianchang Town)	南城縣 (建昌鎮)	南城县 (建昌镇)	320,000	330,000	340,000	1698
Lichuan County (Rifeng Town)	黎川縣 (日峰鎮)	黎川县 (日峰镇)	250,000	250,000	250,000	1729
Nanfeng County (Qincheng Town)	南豐縣 (琴城鎮)	南丰县 (琴城镇)	290,000	300,000	320,000	1909
Chongren County (Bashan Town)	崇仁縣 (巴山鎮)	崇仁县 (巴山镇)	360,000	370,000	390,000	1520
Le'an County (Aoxi Town)	樂安縣 (鰲溪鎮)	乐安县 (鳌溪镇)	360,000	370,000	390,000	2413
Yihuang County (Fenggang Town)	宜黄縣 (鳳岡鎮)	宜黄县 (凤冈镇)	230,000	230,000	240,000	1944
Jinxi County (Xiugu Town)	金溪縣 (秀谷鎮)	金溪县 (秀谷镇)	300,000	310,000	320,000	1358
Zixi County (Hecheng Town)	資溪縣 (鶴城鎮)	资溪县 (鹤城镇)	110,000	110,000	120,000	1251
Dongxiang County (Ligang Town)	東鄉縣 (李崗鎮)	东乡县 (孝岗镇)	460,000	470,000	480,000	1262
Guangchang County (Xujiang Town)	廣昌縣 (盱江鎮)	广昌县 (盱江镇)	240,000	250,000	250,000	1612

(continued)

Table 19.5 (continued)

Name	Traditional	Simplified	Population (2012)	Population (2016)	Population (2020)	Area (Sq. Km)
Yichun City	宜春市	宜春市	5,590,000	5,730,000	6,050,000	18,707
Yuanzhou District (Lingquan Subdistrict)	袁州區 (靈泉街道)	袁州区 (灵泉街道)	1,050,000	1,090,000	1,160,000	2631
Fengcheng City (Hezhou Subdistrict)	豐城市 (河洲街道)	丰城市 (河洲街道)	1,370,000	1,390,000	1,510,000	2845
Zhangshu City (Ganyang Subdistrict)	樟樹市 (淦陽街道)	樟树市 (淦阳街道)	590,000	600,000	610,000	1219
Gao'an City (Ruizhou Subdistrict)	高安市 (瑞州街道)	高安市 (瑞州街道)	820,000	850,000	880,000	2439
Fengxin County (Fengchuan Town)	奉新縣 (馮川鎮)	奉新县 (冯川镇)	320,000	320,000	340,000	1642
Wanzai County (Kangle Subdistrict)	萬載縣 (康樂街道)	万载县 (康乐街道)	510,000	530,000	580,000	1720
Shanggao County (Aoyang Subdistrict)	上高縣 (敖陽街道)	上高县 (敖阳街道)	350,000	370,000	380,000	1350
Yifeng County (Xinchang Town)	宜豐縣 (新昌鎮)	宜丰县 (新昌镇)	290,000	290,000	300,000	1935
Jing'an County (Shuangxi Town)	靖安縣 (雙溪鎮)	靖安县 (双溪镇)	150,000	150,000	150,000	1378
Tonggu County (Yongning Town)	銅鼓縣 (永寧鎮)	铜鼓县 (永宁镇)	140,000	140,000	140,000	1548
Ji'an City	吉安市	吉安市	4,930,000	5,070,000	5,390,000	25,341
Jizhou District (Wenshan Subdistrict)	吉州區 (文山街道)	吉州区 (文山街道)	340,000	350,000	370,000	425
Qingyuan District (Hedong Subdistrict)	青原區 (河東街道)	青原区 (河东街道)	200,000	210,000	230,000	915
Jinggangshan City (Xiaping Town)	井岡山市 (廈坪鎮)	井冈山市 (厦坪镇)	160,000	160,000	170,000	1297
Ji'an County (Dunhou Town)	吉安縣 (敦厚鎮)	吉安县 (敦厚镇)	470,000	490,000	530,000	2117
Jishui County (Wenfeng Town)	吉水縣 (文峰鎮)	吉水县 (文峰镇)	510,000	530,000	570,000	2509
Xiajiang County (Shuibian Town)	峽江縣 (水邊鎮)	峡江县 (水边镇)	170,000	180,000	190,000	1287

(continued)

Table 19.5 (continued)

Name	Traditional	Simplified	Population (2012)	Population (2016)	Population (2020)	Area (Sq. Km)
Xingan[h] County (Jinchuan Town)	新幹縣 (金川鎮)	新干县 (金川镇)	330,000	330,000	350,000	1248
Yongfeng County (Enjiang Town)	永豐縣 (恩江鎮)	永丰县 (恩江镇)	450,000	450,000	490,000	2695
Taihe County (Chengjiang Town)	泰和縣 (澄江鎮)	泰和县 (澄江镇)	550,000	560,000	600,000	2660
Suichuan County (Quanjiang Town)	遂川縣 (泉江鎮)	遂川县 (泉江镇)	560,000	580,000	620,000	3144
Wan'an County (Furong Town)	萬安縣 (芙蓉鎮)	万安县 (芙蓉镇)	300,000	310,000	320,000	2051
Anfu County (Pingdu Town)	安福縣 (平都鎮)	安福县 (平都镇)	390,000	400,000	420,000	2793
Yongxin County (Hechuan Town)	永新縣 (禾川鎮)	永新县 (禾川镇)	500,000	520,000	530,000	2200

[a]Formally established 13 December 2019
[b]Merged into Xinjian County in December 2019
[c]Established in 2016 out of Lianxi district, parts of the latter being made Lushan City
[d]Dissolved in August 2017, establishing Chaisang district
[e]Dissolved in May 2016
[f]Dissolved on 27 June 2019, incorporated into Shangrao city, Guangxin district
[g]Established on 27 June 2019
[h]Before 1957 named 新淦 *xīn'gàn*

References

Bagley, Robert. 1999. Shang archaeology. In *The Cambridge history of ancient China: From the origins of civilization to 221 B.C*, ed. Michael Loewe and Edward L. Shaughnessy, 124–231. New York: Cambridge University Press.

Blench, Roger, Laurent Sagart, and Alicia Sanchez-Mazas, eds. 2005. *The peopling of East Asia: Putting together archaeology, linguistics and genetics*. New York: Routledge.

Ch'en, Vincent, and Matteo Ricci. 1939. Matteo Ricci's contribution to, and influence on, geographical knowledge in China. *Journal of the American Oriental Society*. September. 59(3): 325–359.

Elvin, Mark. 1973. *The pattern of the Chinese past: A social and economic interpretation*. Stanford: Stanford University Press.

Halliday, Jon, and Jung Chang. 2005. *Mao: The unknown story*. New York: Alfred A. Knopf.

Hsieh, Chiao-min, and Jean Kan Hsieh. 1995. *China: A provincial atlas*. New York: Macmillan Publishing.

Jiangxi Province Bureau of Statistics (JPBS). 2021. [Communiqué of the seventh national census of Jiangxi Province, issue no. 2]. 江西省第七次全国人口普查公报(第一号). 26 May. http://www.poyang.gov.cn/pyxtjj/zhengwudongtai4aueux/202105/77f4fd40aa264757abca47b0ff3b6200.shtml.

Laven, Mary. 2011. *Mission to China: Matteo Ricci and the Jesuit encounter with the east*. London: Faber and Faber.

Lo, Yuet Keung. 2006. My second self: Matteo Ricci's friendship in China. *Monumenta Serica* 54: 221–241.

Ministry of Civil Affairs (MCA), People's Republic of China. 2020. [*County/township administration handbook*]. Beijing: China Statistics Press. 中華人民共和國民政部, 中華人民共和國, 鄉鎮行政區劃簡冊.

Shang-Ch'i Guide. 2017. [*Backpacking in China: the most complete collection of self-guided travel for China, 2018*]. Taipei: Shang-Ch'i Shitai publishing. 2018 最完整的中國自助旅遊全集. 台北: 上奇時代.

Sun, Hai. 2006. [*Lin Xinjian's collection of Chinese archaeology: A review*]. Henan: Zhongzhou Classical Publishing. 孙海. 藺新建中國考古集成: 综述. 河南: 中州古籍出版社.

Tan, Qixiang. 1985. *Concise historical atlas of China*. Beijing: China Cartographic Publishing House.

Yang, Zihui. 1995. [*China's historical population statistical data research*]. Beijing: Reform Press. 楊子慧. 中國歷代人口統計資料研究. 北京: 改革出版社.

Zhang, Shunan. 2021. [The 2020 per capita income list of residents in various provinces: Shanghai is the richest, and it has risen sharply]. Finance.people.com. 22 January. 张澍楠. 2020年各省份居民人均收入榜: 上海最有钱, 这地涨得猛. http://finance.people.com.cn/n1/2021/0122/c1004-32008733.html.

Chapter 20
Jilin Province

Abstract Human inhabitation of Jilin and nearby areas go back at least 10,000 years. In addition to the legacy of the Tungusic tribes that made up its earliest known inhabitants, as well as the Mohe (see also Heilongjiang), Jilin had significant influences from ancient and modern Korea. The nomadic Liao (Qidan) and then the Mongols took control of the region, followed by the Jurchen people. Eventually, by the Qing dynasty, Jilin became part of the empire, but tellingly as a "protectorate." As part of the Japanese colonial "Manchukuo" state, with the "New Capital" (Xinjing) where Changchun City used to be, it was reverted to China after World War II. With the defeat of the Nationalists during the Chinese Civil War (1945–49), Changchun was laid siege by the Red Army, leading to about 160,00 civilian deaths. Today, Jilin continues to be heavily influenced by Korean people and their culture, to include its "Yanbian Korean Autonomous Prefecture" of nearly two million people. Being part of China's rustbelt, Jilin (along with other neighboring provinces) has seen a contraction in its resident population, as its younger people look for new opportunities elsewhere in China.

E. Croddy, *China's Provinces and Populations*,
https://doi.org/10.1007/978-3-031-09165-0_20

Jilin Province (吉林省 *jílín shěng*): Abbreviation 吉 (*jí*) (Fig. 20.1)

Jilin Province Population (2020)

1.	**Baicheng City**	**1,551,378**
2.	**Songyuan City**	**2,252,994**
3.	**Changchun City**	**9,066,906**
4.	**Siping City**	**1,814,733**
5.	**Jilin City**	**3,623,713**
6.	**Liaoyuan City**	**996,903**
7.	**Yanbian Chaoxian (Korean) Autonomous Prefecture**	**1,941,700**
8.	**Baishan City**	**951,866**
9.	**Tonghua City**	**1,302,778**

Fig. 20.1 Jilin Province Major Cities (Provincial Capital: Changchun City). (Drawn by the author, after People's Republic of China, Ministry of Civil Affairs. (MCA 2020))

Jilin Province: General Impressions

Also rendered "Chilin" and "Kirin" in the past, the name Jilin (吉林 *jílín*, auspicious forest) is probably from the Manchurian *Girinula* (吉林烏拉 *jílín wūlā*), meaning on the bank of the Sungari or Songhua River (松花江 *songhuā jiāng*). Jilin's more famous geographical features includes the famous Changbai Mountain (長白山 *chángbái shān*). For Korea, it is known as Mount Paektu (Baekdu 백두산; 白頭山 *báitóushān*). Sitting at the base of Changbai Mountain is Liaoyuan City (遼源市 *liáoyuán shì*), and is one of China's largest coal-producing regions.

Bordering on North Korea as it does, Jilin Province also includes the Yanbian Korean Autonomous Prefecture (延邊朝鮮族自治州 *yánbiān cháoxiānzú zìzhìzhōu*), where over 30 percent of the population are ethnic Korean. Yanbian was originally formed on 3 September 1952 out of an agreement reached between North Korea and China, and formally named a prefecture (州 *zhōu*) in 1955. Today, as many as a third to a half of its population speak Korean as well as Chinese, and many storefront signs use Chinese characters accompanied by Korean script (Hangul).

Part of China's "rust belt," Jilin province is home to China's first modern film studio (長春電影製片廠, *chángchūn diànyǐng zhìpiànchǎng*, ca. 1940s), as well as the first Chinese-made truck under the "Liberation" (解放牌 *jiěfàngpái*) badge (CA10) that rolled out of the plant in July 1956 by the China First Automobile Works (FAW) Corporation.[1] It is worth noting that the FAW first began by using Soviet-supplied equipment when Sino-Soviet relations were still warm. In July 2021, it was announced with much fanfare that the FAW plant produced its eight millionth vehicle, a semi-truck (Xinhua 2021).

Of geological interest, Changbai Mountain is volcanic, having erupted three times since the late sixteenth century, the last being April 1702. The mountain features Tianchi Lake (in Korean, 천지 Ch'ŏnji; 天池 tiānchí), said to be the highest volcanic lake (caldera) in the world, bordering China and North Korea. It has a maximum depth of 384 m. Like Scotland's Loch Ness ("Nessie"), Chinese lore also boasts a legendary lake creature here, with sightings going back at least to 1903. An eyewitness account in 1908 reported on a strange animal floating along the surface, golden color with a large flat head, what and local hunters believed to be a dragon. Occasionally, purported sightings of the "Tianchi Monster" (天池怪獸 *tiānchí guàishòu*) make the local television news.

Neolithic Jilin

Excavations at the Da'an City's (大安市 *dà'ān shì*) Houtaomuga site (後套木嘎遺址 *hòutàomùgā yízhǐ*) revealed some of oldest known pottery shards in China's northeast, dating back at least ten thousand years. Significantly, fossilized human bones in Neolithic burial sites at the Shuangta (雙塔遺址 *shuāngtǎ yízhǐ*) site in Taobei District (洮北區 *táoběi qū*), Baicheng City (白城市 *báichéng shì*) are also dated in the vicinity of 10,000 years ago (Kunikita et al. 2017).

[1] 中國第一汽車集團有限公司 *zhōngguó dìyī qìchē jítuán yǒuxiàn gōngsī* or simply "一汽 *yīqì*."

Ancient Jilin History

Along with the neighboring provinces of Liaoning and Heilongjiang, the earliest known peoples to live in Jilin and its surrounding areas have included Korean as well as Tungusic nomadic groups. Going back to the Shang (1600–1046 BCE) and Zhou (1122–256 BCE) dynasties, peoples known as the Sushen (肅慎 *sùshèn*); Huimo (Korean Yemaek 예맥; 濊貊 *huìmò*); the Donghu (東胡); Xianbei (先卑 *xiānbēi*); Mohe (靺鞨 *mòhé*); and the Wuji (勿吉 *wùjí*), all lived at various times in today's Jilin Province.

Related to the bronze-age cultures found in the Liaodong peninsula, remnants of Late Bronze Age people have been found centered around modern-day Jilin City. Early excavations made in the 1930s and later expanded in the 1960s found evidence of what has been called Xituanshan Culture 西團山文化 (*xītuánshān wénhuà*) on a mountain in Chuanying District (船營區 *chuányíng qū*) southwest of Jilin City. Dated from eleventh century to as recent as the second century BCE, initial finds of Xituanshan Culture first expanded radially out west to modern day Nong'an County (農安縣 *nóngān xiàn*) to the north, Huadian City (樺甸市 *huàdiàn shì*) to the south, and Jiahe City (蛟河市 *jiāohé shì*) to the east. More recently, remains of Xituanshan Culture have since been found further out west to Siping City (四平市 *sìpíng shì*), Jilin province. Additional archeological discoveries were found at Saodagou (騷達溝 *sāodágōu*) several kilometers away, revealing a number of tombs that included bronze tools (Byington 2016).

From about second century BCE to 500 CE, Jilin was occupied by the Korean Buyeo (Puyŏ; 부여; 扶餘 *fúyú*) kingdom until it was absorbed by the Goguryeo (高句麗 *gāojùlì*) hegemon. According to classic histories, the State of Buyeo (扶餘國 *fúyú guó*) was bordered by the Yilou people (挹婁 *yìlóu*—also transliterated as I-Lou) to the east, Xianbei nomadic tribes to the west, and the Songhua River (松花江 *sōnghuā jiāng* or Ruoshui 弱水 *ruòshuǐ*) to the north. In 668 CE, the combined forces of the Korean Silla (신라; 新羅 *xīnluó*) kingdom and Chinese Tang dynasty forces defeated Goguryeo. As the Tang dynasty was also engaged in warfare with the Khitan (契丹 *qìdān*) Mongols, the Korean Dae Joyeong (대조영; 大祚榮 *dàzuòróng*), later named King Go (고왕; 高王 *Gāo Wáng*; 698–719), faced off the Tang military punitive expeditions, including those sent by Empress Wu Zetian (武則天 *Wǔ Zétiān*). Dae Joyeong then prevailed at the Battle of Tianmenling (天門嶺之戰 *tiānménlǐng zhīzhàn*) in 698, thereafter creating the kingdom of Balhae (i.e., Bohai; 발해; 渤海 *bóhǎi*).

By 820, the Bohai (Balhae) kingdom stretched from the top of Wonsan Bay in today's North Korea, all the way to the Heilong (Amur) river, west to today's Lishu County (梨樹縣 *líshù xiàn*), and east to the Sea of Japan. Its upper capital, Shangjing (上京 *shàngjīng*), was located in (roughly) today's Mudanjiang City 牡丹江市 (*mǔdānjiāng shì*), Heilongjiang Province. More germane here, its middle capital (中京 *zhōngjīng*) occupied where Dunhua City (敦化市 *dūnhuà shì*), Jilin Province, is today. The Western Capital (西京 *xījīng*) was not far from Hunjiang District (渾

江區 *húnjiāng qū*), while the Eastern Capital (東京 *dōngjīng*) was located near Hunchun City (琿春市 *húnchūn shì*) in today's Yanbian Korean Autonomous Prefecture. Finally, its Southern Capital (南京 *nánjīng*) was where North Korea's Yŏnghŭng bay (영흥만) / 永興灣 *yǒngxīng wān*) is now.

From 907 to 1125, modern-day Jilin and northeastern China was ruled by the Liao (契丹 *qìdān*). Like much of northern China and Mongolian regions that were dominated by nomadic clans, modern-day Jilin was eventually occupied by the Jin (金朝 *jīncháo*; Jurchen) dynasty (1115–1234). By 1227, however, their territory was squeezed by the Mongols to the north and Song Dynasty forces to the south, leaving the Jin territory ranging from Xining (西寧 *xīníng*), Qinghai Province to the central Henan region and the Bohai Gulf. In 1290, the Mongols (Yuan Dynasty) ruled the entire northeast China area.

From 1403–1433, all of Manchuria (to include Jilin and parts of modern-day Russia) was administered under the Nurgan Regional Military Commission (奴兒干都指揮使司 *nú'érgān dūzhǐhuīshǐsī*). Based in the eponymous Nurgan City on the Amur river (in today's Tyr, Russia), the Nurgan Military Commission was a Jurchen-based administration outsourced by the Ming Yongle emperor (永樂帝 *yǒnglèdì*) to manage the northern regions. Control of the Jurchens was always less than tenuous, and the last (and final) Ming dynasty expedition (under Emperor Xuande 宣德帝 *xuāndédì*) to Nurgan was in 1432 (Twitchett and Mote 1998).

After the Ming dynasty (1368–1644), during which time Jilin was still largely a tribute state, the Qing dynasty installed a "Protectorate of Jilin" (or "General of Jilin" 吉林將軍 *jílín jiāngjūn*) in 1757. By 1820, Jilin "subordinated banners" delineated a swath through southern Manchuria, from the Liaodong peninsula to the Sea of Japan. Modern-day Jilin was largely bordered by two of these administrative zones, the Kirin (Jilin) subordinated banner (吉林副都統轄區 *jílín fùdūtǒngxiáqū*) and the Ningguta subordinated banner (寧古塔副都統轄區 *nínggǔtǎ fùdūtǒngxiáqū*). While the latter extended out to the coast of the Sea of Japan, after the Opium Wars and the "unequal treaties" that were signed between China and western powers, Russia acquired all of Jilin's coast (Ussuri Krai or modern Primorsky Krai) in 1860 (Herrman 1966). Hitherto largely composed of the Manchu nationality, more and more Han Chinese, mostly from Shandong Province, were allowed to migrate into modern Jilin Province in the 1900s. These immigrants numbered about 800,000 (Hsieh and Hsieh 1995).

Revolutionary Jilin

During the Republic of China (中華民國 *zhōnghuá mínguó*) era, Jilin City remained the governmental seat of Jilin Province. In 1913 and again in 1929, Jilin was divided into Jilin (吉林縣 *jílín xiàn*) and Yongji (永吉縣 *yǒngjí xiàn*) counties. This would soon be made irrelevant with the occupation of Japanese forces on 21 September 1931 that established the so-called Jilin Provincial Government (吉林省公署 *Kitsurinshō Kōsho*). Controlling all of Manchuria in 1932, Japan established Changchun—renamed Hsinking 新京 (*xīnjīng*)—as the capital of Japan's puppet government, Manchukuo. This occupied "Kingdom" was nominally led by the last emperor of China, (Henry) Pu Yi (溥儀 *pŭ yí*), who died in October 1967 (Dikötter 2013).

Per its Yalta obligations, the Soviet Union invaded Manchuria and defeated Japanese forces there (20 August 1945). Not content with this victory, the Red Army looted industrial equipment and other materials from Changchun, transporting them by rail back to the Soviet Union. When Soviet troops began their withdrawal in mid-March 1946, completing their exit by 3 May, Joseph Stalin called upon Chinese Communist Party (CCP) to take the offensive from Manchuria against the Nationalists. The Soviet Union also ensured that large stocks of left-behind Japanese munitions were given to Chinese communist troops (Heinzig 2015).

Japan also left behind a toxic legacy of chemical weapons, most of these being hastily buried in Manchuria, the majority of these being in Jilin Province. Japan is destroying these abandoned chemical weapons (ACW) per agreement under the Chemical Weapons Convention (1993). The largest remaining ACW caches are in Dunhua city (敦化市 *dūnhuà shì*), Ha'erbaling (哈爾巴嶺 *hā'ĕrbālĭng*), in Yanbian Prefecture. As of 2018, a total of 52,000 ACWs were disposed of, with operations likely to continue through 2022 (MOFA 2019).

For the CCP, the defeat of Nationalist forces in Manchuria was a strategic win, but at horrific cost. Chinese communist forces carried out a brutal siege of Jilin's capital, Changchun, during which some 160,000 civilians died of starvation (Dikötter 2013). With no hope left, on 16 October 1948, Generalissimo Chiang Kai-shek ordered the surrender of Changchun City to the Red Army field commander Lin Biao (林彪 *lín biāo*).

After China's "liberation" in 1949, Jilin Province was much smaller than its present borders. Despite its later enlargement, when it incorporated Baicheng and Tonghua cities (1954), land-locked Jilin never recovered its earlier direct access to the Sea of Japan. In 1969, the Zhelimu League (哲里木盟 *zhélĭmù méng*), once part of Inner Mongolia, was incorporated into Jilin Province, only to be returned to Inner Mongolian boundaries in 1980 (Fig. 20.2; Table 20.1).

1. **Taonan City**
2. **Taobei District**
3. **Zhenlai County**
4. **Da'an City**
5. **Qianguo'erluosi Mongolian Auotnomous County**
6. **Ningjiang District**
7. **Fuyu City**
8. **Yushu City**
9. **Shulan City**
10. **Jiaohe City**
11. **Dunhua City**
12. **Wangqing City**
13. **Antu County**
14. **Yanji City**
15. **Helong City**
16. **Longjing City**
17. **Tumen City**
18. **Hunchun City**
19. **Tongyu County**
20. **Qian'an County**
21. **Nong'an County**
22. **Dehui City**
23. **Jiutai District**
24. **Jilin City**
25. **Changling County**
26. **Shuangliao City**
27. **Gongzhuling City**
28. **Lishu County**
29. **Tiexi District**
30. **Tiedong District**
31. Changchun City
32. **Yitong Manchu Autonomous County**
33. **Yongji County**
34. **Panshi City**
35. **Dongfeng County**
36. **Meihekou City**
37. **Huinan County**
38. **Huadian City**
39. **Xi'an District**
40. **Dongliao County**
41. **Fengshan District**
42. **Jingyu County**
43. **Liuhe County**
44. **Fusong County**
45. **Tonghua County**
46. **Hunjiang District**
47. **Jiangyuan District**
48. **Erdaojiang District**
49. **Dongchang District**
50. **Linjiang City**
51. **Changbai Chaoxian (Korean) Autonomous County**
52. **Ji'an City**

Fig. 20.2 Jilin Province: Subdistricts (Provincial Capital City: Changchun City). (Drawn by the author, after People's Republic of China, Ministry of Civil Affairs. (MCA 2020))

Table 20.1 Population Data: Jilin Province. (JPBS 2010, 2021)

1912	5,540,000
1932	8,280,000
1942	11,910,000
1945	12,000,000
1949	10,084,000
1950	10,295,000
1953	11,336,000
1960	13,971,000
1961	11,951,000
1970	18,604,000
1980	22,107,000
1985	22,980,000
1990	24,658,271
2000	26,273,000
2010	27,462,297
2020	24,073,453

Jilin: Economic and Population Trends

Jilin Province has traditionally been known as part of Manchuria, and has long been known as a strategic source of industrial minerals. Being rich in raw materials and possessing a vital railway transport corridor drew the Imperial Japanese Army to invade Manchuria in the 1930s. In more modern times, Jilin is also known as a significant producer of corn, soybeans and ginseng (the latter having been grown in the region for over 1600 years), as well as sable fur. Unfortunately, as much of its heavy industrial sector has fallen in decline, Jilin's economy, unlike most of the rest of China's 31 provinces and major cities, actually fell in terms of gross domestic product (GDP), totaling USD $221 billion in 2015, but dropping to $191 billion in 2020. For per capita income, Jilin is in the lower third at $4005 (Zhang 2021).

As part of China's rustbelt, Jilin (along with Heilongjiang and Liaoning provinces) also posted a significant drop (12.3%) in overall resident population in 2020 compared with the decade prior. The exodus is likely due to Jilin provincial residents moving to more economically developed regions in China's southeast coast (Leng 2021). This is reflected in the disparity (2,000,000 people) of the *hukou* population of 26,090,000 in 2020 (Table 20.4), compared with the typical resident population that (census) year of about 24,073,000 (Table 20.2). That is, about two million official residents of Jilin Province spend most (if not all) of there time in other Chinese provinces and cities to live and work.

Table 20.2 Jilin Province Population (Residential 常住人口 *chángzhù rénkǒu*) Data. (JPBS 2021)

City	Population (2010)	Population (2020)
Changchun City 長春市 *chángchūn shì*	7,677,089	9,066,906
Jilin City 吉林市 *jílín shì*	4,414,681	3,623,713
Siping City 四平市 *sìpíng shì*	3,386,325	1,814,733
Liaoyuan City 遼源市 *liáoyuán shì*	1,176,645	996,903
Tonghua City通化市 *tōnghuà shì*	2,325,242	1,302,778
Baishan City 白山市 *báishān shì*	1,296,575	951,866
Songyuan City 松原市 *sōngyuán shì*	2,881,082	2,252,994
Baicheng City 白城市 *báichéng shì*	2,033,058	1,551,378
Yanbian Korean Autonomous Prefecture 延邊朝鮮族自治州 *yánbiān cháoxiānzú zìzhì zhōu*	2,271,600	1,941,700
Changbai Mountain Management Committee 長白山管委會[a] *chángbáishān guǎnwěihuì*	N/A	61,146
Meihekou City 梅河口市 *méihékǒu shì*	N/A	509,336
Total	**27,462,297**	**24,073,453**

[a]Full name of governing entity: Jilin province, Changbai Mountain Protection Development Committee (吉林省長白山保護開發管理委員會 *jílínshěng chángbáishān bǎohù kāifā guǎnlǐ wěiyuánhuì*)

Internally, there has been population growth in a relatively new administrative area, the Changbai Mountain Management Committee[2] (see Table 20.2). Since 2005, due to the popularity of Korean (mostly from the southern Republic of Korea) tourism of the Changbai Mountain area, that is, Mount Paektu (Baekdu 백두산; 白頭山 *báitóushān*), Jilin has been developing the Changbai region under the rubric of the Changbai Mountain Protection Development Committee. New infrastructure of the area now supports a number of sporting (e.g., skiing) and luxurious destinations to include hot springs. According to the official Chinese 2020 census, this region had a residential population of over 61,000 people.

Table 20.4 (below) shows the *hukou* (family registered) populations based on PRC Ministry of Civil Affairs data. (Districts listed directly under major cities are government seats, as are those in parentheses). One can compare these data with the census (usual residential populations based on 2010 and 2020 censuses in Tables 20.2 (above) and 20.3 (below):

[2] 吉林省長白山保護開發管理委員會 *jílínshěng chángbáishān bǎohù kāifā guǎnlǐ wěiyuánhuì*.

Table 20.3 Jilin Province: Population Data of Cities and Their Subordinate Sectors. (JPBS 2021)

Selected cities and subordinate sectors, population (2020 CENSUS)[a]	Subordinate district, city and county populations (2020)	Population (2020)
Changchun City 長春市 ***chángchūn shì***		**9,066,906**
Nanguan District 南關區 *nánguān qū*	657,682	
Chaoyang District 朝陽區 *cháoyáng qū*	614,021	
Kuancheng District 寬城區 *kuānchéng qū*	669,148	
Erdao District 二道區 *èrdào qū*	522,453	
Lüyuan District 綠園區 *lǜyuán qū*	714,919	
Shuangyang District 雙陽區 *shuāngyáng qū*	335,723	
Dehui City 德惠市 *déhuì shì*	691,550	
Jiutai City 九台區 *jiǔtái qū*	569,976	
Yushu City 榆樹市 *yúshù shì*	836,098	
Nong'an County 農安縣 *nóng'ān xiàn*	867,274	
Changchun Economic and Technology Development Zone 長春經濟技術開發區 *chángchūn jīngjìjìshù kāifāqū*	429,387	
Changchun Jingyue National High Technology Development Zone 長春淨月國家新技術產業開發區 *chángchūn jìngyuè guójiā xīnjìshù chǎnyè kāifāqū*	408,740	
Changchun New District 長春新區 *chángchūn xīnqū*	502,165	
Changchun Automobile Economic and Technology Development Zone 長春汽車經濟技術開發區 *chángchūn qìchē jīngjìjìshù kāifāqū*	317,978	
Changchun Lotus Mountain Ecology Travel Resort 長春蓮花山生態旅遊度假區 *chángchūn liánhuāshān shēngtàilǚyóudùjiǎ qū*	37,513	
China-Republic of Korea (Changchun) International Cooperation Demonstration Zone 中韓 (長春) 國際合作示範區 *zhōnghán (chángchūn) guójì hézuò shìfànqū*	29,966	
Gongzhuling City[b] 公主嶺市 *gōngzhǔlǐng shì*	862,313	
Siping City 四平市 ***sìpíng shì***		**1,814,733**
Tiexi District 鐵西區 *tiěxī qū*	314,307	
Tiedong District 鐵東區 *tiědōng qū*	313,650	
Shuangliao City 雙遼市 *shuāngliáo shì*	317,758	
Lishu County 梨樹縣 *líshù xiàn*	537,145	
Yitong Manzu (Manchu) Autonomous County 伊通滿族自治縣 *yītōng mǎnzú zìzhìxiàn*	331,873	
Liaoyuan City 遼源市 ***liáoyuán shì***		**996,903**
Longshan District 龍山區 *lóngshān qū*	327,079	
Xi'an District 西安區 *xī'ān qū*	136,337	
Dongfeng County 東豐縣 *dōngfēng xiàn*	307,302	
Dongliao County 東遼縣 *dōngliáo xiàn*	226,185	
Baishan City 白山市 ***báishān shì***		**951,866**
Hunjiang District 渾江區 *húnjiāng qū*	307,982	

(continued)

Table 20.3 (continued)

Selected cities and subordinate sectors, population (2020 CENSUS)[a]	Subordinate district, city and county populations (2020)	Population (2020)
Jiangyuan District 江源區 *jiāngyuán qū*	138,272	
Linjiang City 臨江市 *línjiāng shì*	121,616	
Fusong County 撫松縣 *fǔsōng xiàn*	217,252	
Jingyu County 靖宇縣 *jìngyǔ xiàn*	108,478	
Changbai Chaoxianzu (Korean) Autonomous County 長白朝鮮族自治縣 *chángbái cháoxiānzú zìzhìxiàn*	58,266	
Songyuan City 松原市 ***sōngyuán shì***		**2,252,994**
Ningjiang District 寧江區 *níngjiāng qū*	619,364	
Fuyu City 扶余市 *fúyú shì*	475,017	
Changling County 長嶺縣 *chánglǐng xiàn*	451,620	
Qian'an County 乾安縣 *qián'ān xiàn*	205,542	
Qianguo'erluosi Mengguzu (Qian Gorlos Mongol) Autonomous County 前郭爾羅斯蒙古族自治縣 *qiánguōěrluósī měnggǔzú zìzhìxiàn*	407,385	
Songyuan Economic and Technology Development Zone 松原經濟技術開發區 *sōngyuán jīngjìjìshù kāifāqū*	94,066	
Baicheng City 白城市 ***báichéng shì***		**1,551,378**
Taobei District 洮北區 *táoběi qū*	356,054	
Da'an City 大安市 *dà'ān shì*	270,911	
Taonan City 洮南市 *táonán shì*	307,215	
Zhenlai County 鎮賚縣 *zhènlài xiàn*	217,387	
Tongyu County 通榆縣 *tōngyú xiàn*	281,589	
Jilin Baicheng Economic Development Zone 吉林白城經濟開發區 *jílín báichéng jīngjì kāifāqū*	118,222	
Yanbian Korean Autonomous Prefecture 延邊朝鮮族自治州 ***yánbiān cháoxiānzú zìzhì zhōu***		**1,941,700**
Yanji City 연길시 (*Yŏn'gil-si*) 延吉市 *yánjí shì*	686,136	
Tumen City 도문시 (*Tomun-si*) 圖們市 *túmén shì*	85,248	
Dunhua City 돈화시 (*Tonhwa-si*) 敦化市 *dūnhuà shì*	392,486	
Hunchun City 훈춘시 (*Hunch'un-si*) 琿春市 *húnchūn shì*	239,359	
Longjing City 룡정시 (*Ryongjŏng-si*) 龍井市 *lóngjǐng shì*	129,286	
Helong City 화룡시 (*Hwaryong-si*) 和龍市 *hélóng shì*	117,087	
Wangqing County 왕청현 (*Wangch'ŏng-hyŏn*) 汪清縣 *wāngqīng xiàn*	167,911	
Antu County 안도현 (*Ando-hyŏn*) 安圖縣 *āntú xiàn*	124,187	

[a]Not all district population data from 2020 are available as of 14 January 2022

[b]Gonzhuling city, previously under Siping city, was placed under the jurisdiction of Changchun city on 19 June 2020

Jilin Province (吉)

Provincial Capital: Changchun

Table 20.4 Jiangxi Province: Permanent Registered (戶籍人口 *hùjí rénkǒu*) Populations. (MCA 2020)

Name	Traditional	Simplified	Population (2012)	Population (2016)	Population (2020)	Area (Sq. Km)
Jilin Province	吉林省	吉林省	**27,240,000**	**27,020,000**	**26,090,000**	**190,234**
Changchun City	長春市	长春市	**7,590,000**	**7,560,000**	**7,510,000**	**20,565**
Nanguan District (Nanling Subdistrict)	南關區 (南嶺街道)	南关区 (南岭街道)	660,000	660,000	740,000	497
Chaoyang District (Nanzhan Subdistrict)	朝陽區 (南站街道)	朝阳区 (南站街道)	740,000	730,000	750,000	379
Kuancheng District (Xinfa Subdistrict)	寬城區 (新發街道)	宽城区 (新发街道)	660,000	660,000	650,000	877
Erdao District (Dongsheng Subdistrict)	二道區 (東盛街道)	二道区 (东盛街道)	560,000	550,000	580,000	965
Lüyuan District (Chuncheng Subdistrict)	綠園區 (春城街道)	绿园区 (春城街道)	620,000	640,000	650,000	301
Shuangyang District (Yunshan Subdistrict)	雙陽區 (雲山街道)	双阳区 (云山街道)	390,000	380,000	370,000	1663
Dehui City (Shengli Subdistrict)	德惠市 (勝利街道)	德惠市 (胜利街道)	840,000	830,000	810,000	3096
Jiutai City (Jiutai Subdistrict)	九台區 (九台街道)	九台区 (九台街道)	710,000	700,000	670,000	2875
Yushu City (Huachang Subdistrict)	榆樹市 (華昌街道)	榆树市 (华昌街道)	1,300,000	1,310,000	1,230,000	4691
Nong'an County (Nong'an Town)	農安縣 (農安鎮)	农安县 (农安镇)	1,100,000	1,100,000	1,060,000	5221
Baicheng City	白城市	白城市	2,030,000	2,010,000	1,900,000	25,683
Taobei District (Mingren Subdistrict)	洮北區 (明仁街道)	洮北区 (明仁街道)	510,000	510,000	490,000	2525
Da'an City (Jinhua Subdistrict)	大安市 (錦華街道)	大安市 (锦华街道)	420,000	410,000	380,000	4879
Taonan City (Guangming Subdistrict)	洮南市 (光明街道)	洮南市 (光明街道)	440,000	430,000	410,000	5108

(continued)

Table 20.4 (continued)

Name	Traditional	Simplified	Population (2012)	Population (2016)	Population (2020)	Area (Sq. Km)
Zhenlai County (Zhenlai Town)	鎮賚縣 (鎮賚鎮)	镇赉县 (镇赉镇)	290,000	290,000	260,000	4695
Tongyu County (Kaitong Town)	通榆縣 (開通鎮)	通榆县 (开通镇)	370,000	370,000	360,000	8476
Songyuan City	松原市	松原市	2,900,000	2,890,000	2,750,000	20,159
Ningjiang District (Tuanjie Subdistrict)	寧江區 (團結街道)	宁江区 (团结街道)	590,000	590,000	560,000	1576
Fuyu County[a] (Sanchahe Town)	扶余縣 (三岔河鎮)	扶余县 (三岔河镇)	770,000	N/A	N/A	(5787)
Fuyu City (Hexing Subdistrict)	扶余市 (和興街道)	扶余市 (和兴街道)	N/A	760,000	710,000	4189
Changling County (Changling Town)	長嶺縣 (長嶺鎮)	长岭县 (长岭镇)	640,000	640,000	630,000	5787
Qian'an County (Qian'an Town)	乾安縣 (乾安鎮)	乾安县 (乾安镇)	310,000	310,000	270,000	3522
Qianguo'erluosi Mengguzu (Qian Gorlos Mongol) Autonomous County (Qianguo e'luosi Town)	前郭爾羅斯蒙古族自治縣 (前郭爾羅斯鎮)	前郭尔罗斯蒙古族自治县 (前郭尔罗斯镇)	590,000	590,000	570,000	5085
Jilin City	吉林市	吉林市	4,320,000	4,300,000	4,140,000	27,722
Chuanying District (Desheng Subdistrict)	船營區 (德勝街道)	船营区 (德胜街道)	460,000	460,000	460,000	711
Longtan District (Longhua Subdistrict)	龍潭區 (龍華街道)	龙潭区 (龙华街道)	480,000	470,000	440,000	1209
Changyi District (Xinghua Subdistrict)	昌邑區 (興華街道)	昌邑区 (兴华街道)	620,000	620,000	610,000	865
Fengman District (Taishan Subdistrict)	豐滿區 (泰山街道)	丰满区 (泰山街道)	260,000	260,000	290,000	1032
Panshi City (Dongning Subdistrict)	盤石市 (東寧街道)	磐石市 (东宁街道)	540,000	540,000	510,000	3867
Jiaohe City (Minzhu Subdistrict)	蛟河市 (民主街道)	蛟河市 (民主街道)	450,000	450,000	420,000	6235
Huadian City (Minghua Subdistrict)	樺甸市 (明樺街道)	桦甸市 (明桦街道)	460,000	450,000	420,000	6624
Shulan City (Beicheng Subdistrict)	舒蘭市 (北城街道)	舒兰市 (北城街道)	660,000	660,000	610,000	4554

(continued)

Table 20.4 (continued)

Name	Traditional	Simplified	Population (2012)	Population (2016)	Population (2020)	Area (Sq. Km)
Yongji County (Kouqian Town)	永吉縣 (口前鎮)	永吉县 (口前镇)	390,000	390,000	380,000	2625
Siping City	四平市	四平市	3,400,000	3,360,000	3,190,000	14,323
Tiexi District (Zhanqian Subdistrict)	鐵西區 (站前街道)	铁西区 (站前街道)	280,000	270,000	360,000	778
Tiedong District (Simalu Subdistrict)	鐵東區 (四馬路街道)	铁东区 (四马路街道)	330,000	340,000	320,000	945
Shuangliao City (Liaonan Subdistrict)	雙遼市 (遼南街道)	双辽市 (辽南街道)	420,000	410,000	390,000	3121
Gongzhuling City (Dongsan Subdistrict)	公主嶺市 (東三街道)	公主岭市 (东三街道)	1,090,000	1,080,000	1,030,000	4027
Lishu County (Lishu Town)	梨樹縣 (梨樹鎮)	梨树县 (梨树镇)	800,000	790,000	640,000	2967
Yitong Manzu (Manchu) Autonomous County (Yitong Town)	伊通滿族自治縣 (伊通鎮)	伊通满族自治县 (伊通镇)	480,000	470,000	450,000	2523
Liaoyuan City	遼源市	辽源市	1,230,000	1,230,000	1,170,000	5125
Longshan District (Nankang Subdistrict)	龍山區 (南康街道)	龙山区 (南康街道)	300,000	300,000	300,000	257
Xi'an District (Xiancheng Subdistrict)	西安區 (仙城街道)	西安区 (仙城街道)	180,000	180,000	150,000	172
Dongfeng County (Dongfeng Town)	東豐縣 (東豐鎮)	东丰县 (东丰镇)	400,000	400,000	390,000	2522
Dongliao County (Baiquan Town)	東遼縣 (白泉鎮)	东辽县 (白泉镇)	350,000	350,000	340,000	2174
Tonghua City	通化市	通化市	2,260,000	2,240,000	2,160,000	15,698
Dongchang District (Xinzhan Subdistrict)	東昌區 (新站街道)	东昌区 (新站街道)	320,000	310,000	320,000	547
Erdaojiang District (Dongtonghua Subdistrict)	二道江區 (東通化街道)	二道江区 (东通化街道)	130,000	130,000	120,000	378
Meihekou City (Xinhua Subdistrict)	梅河口市 (新華街道)	梅河口市 (新华街道)	620,000	620,000	590,000	2175
Ji'an City (Liming Subdistrict)	集安市 (黎明街道)	集安市 (黎明街道)	220,000	220,000	210,000	3408

(continued)

Table 20.4 (continued)

Name	Traditional	Simplified	Population (2012)	Population (2016)	Population (2020)	Area (Sq. Km)
Tonghua County (Kuaidamao Town)	通化縣 (快大茂鎮)	通化县 (快大茂镇)	250,000	240,000	240,000	3554
Huinan County (Chaoyang Town)	輝南縣 (朝陽鎮)	辉南县 (朝阳镇)	350,000	350,000	330,000	2277
Liuhe County (Liuhe Town)	柳河縣 (柳河鎮)	柳河县 (柳河镇)	370,000	370,000	360,000	3348
Baishan City	白山市	白山市	1,300,000	1,290,000	1,180,000	17,485
Hunjiang District (Xinjian Subdistrict)	渾江區 (新建街道)	浑江区 (新建街道)	350,000	350,000	330,000	1388
Jiangyuan District (Sunjiapuzi Subdistrict)	江源區 (孫家堡子街道)	江源区 (孙家堡子街道)	250,000	240,000	210,000	1348
Linjiang City (Jianguo Subdistrict)	臨江市 (建國街道)	临江市 (建国街道)	170,000	170,000	150,000	3009
Fusong County (Fusong Town)	撫松縣 (撫松鎮)	抚松县 (抚松镇)	290,000	290,000	280,000	6150
Jingyu County (Jingyu Town)	靖宇縣 (靖宇鎮)	靖宇县 (靖宇镇)	150,000	150,000	130,000	3094
Changbai Chaoxianzu (Korean) Autonomous County (Changbai Town)	長白朝鮮族自治縣 (長白鎮)	长白朝鲜族自治县 (长白镇)	90,000	90,000	80,000	2496
Yanbian Chaoxianzu (Korean) Autonomous Prefecture [Korean name: 연변조선족자치주 **Yŏnbyŏn Chosŏnjok Chach'iju]**	延邊朝鮮族自治州	延边朝鲜族自治州	2,190,000	2,110,000	2,090,000	43,474
Yanji City 연길시 [Yŏn'gil-si] (Xinxing Subdistrict)	延吉市 (新興街道)	延吉市	510,000	520,000	550,000	1731

(continued)

Table 20.4 (continued)

Name	Traditional	Simplified	Population (2012)	Population (2016)	Population (2020)	Area (Sq. Km)
Tumen City 도문시 [Tomun-si] (Xiangshang Subdistrict)	圖們市 (向上街道)	图们市 (向上街道)	130,000	120,000	110,000	1142
Dunhua City 돈화시 [Tonhwa-si] (Minzhu Subdistrict)	敦化市 (民主街道)	敦化市 (民主街道)	480,000	460,000	460,000	11,963
Hunchun City 훈춘시 [Hunch'un-si] (Henan Subdistrict)	琿春市 (河南街道)	珲春市 (河南街道)	230,000	220,000	230,000	4938
Longjing City 룡정시 [Ryongjŏng-si] (Anmin Subdistrict)	龍井市 (安民街道)	龙井市 (安民街道)	180,000	170,000	150,000	2193
Helong City 화룡시 [Hwaryong-si] (Wenhua Subdistrict)	和龍市 (文化街道)	和龙市 (文化街道)	200,000	180,000	170,000	5069
Wangqing County 왕청현 [Wangch'ŏng-hyŏn] (Wangqing Town)	汪清縣 (汪清鎮)	汪清县 (汪清镇)	240,000	230,000	220,000	8944
Antu County 안도현 [Ando-hyŏn] (Mingyue Town)	安圖縣 (明月鎮)	安图县 (明月镇)	220,000	210,000	200,000	7444

[a]Dissolved 24 January 2013, creating Fuyu City

References

Byington, Mark E. 2016. *The ancient state of Puyŏ in Northeast Asia*. Cambridge, MA: Harvard East Asian Monographs.

Dikötter, Frank. 2013. *The Tragedy of liberation: A history of the Chinese revolution: A history of the Chinese revolution, 1945–57*. New York: Bloomsbury Press.

Heinzig, Dieter. 2015. *The Soviet Union and Communist China 1945–1950: The arduous road to the alliance*. New York: Routledge.

Herrman, Albert. 1966. *An historical atlas of China*. Chicago: Aldine Publishing Company.

Hsieh, Chiao-min, and Jean Kan Hsieh. 1995. *China: A provincial atlas*. New York: Macmillan Publishing.

Japan Ministry of Foreign Affairs (MOFA). 2019. *Diplomatic blue book 2019*. https://www.mofa.go.jp/files/000527162.pdf.

Jilin Province Bureau of Statistics (JPBS). 2021. [Reports for Jilin/Changchun seventh national census communiqué 2020]. 8 June. 吉林/长春市第七次全国人口普查公报 2020. https://tjgb.hongheiku.com/12418.html.

———. 2010. [Bulletin of the main data of the sixth national population census in Jilin Province in 2010]. 9 May. 吉林省2010年第六次全国人口普查主要数据公报. https://www.cnstats.org/rkpc/201105/jls-2010-nrmfn.html.

Kunikita, Dai, Wang Lixin, Onuki Shizuo, et al. 2017. Radiocarbon dating and dietary reconstruction of the early Neolithic Houtaomuga and Shuangta Sites in the Song-Nen Plain, Northeast China. *Quaternary International* 441 (B): 62–68.

Leng, Sidney. 2021. China's rust belt population plummeted in last decade, exacerbating regional economic divide. *South China Morning Post*. 9 July. https://www.scmp.com/economy/china-economy/article/3133397/chinas-rust-belt-population-plummeted-last-decade.

Ministry of Civil Affairs (MCA), People's Republic of China. 2020. [*County/township administration handbook*], Beijing: China Statistics Press. 中華人民共和國民政部, 中華人民共和國, 鄉鎮行政區劃簡冊.

Shang-Ch'i Guide. 2017. [*Backpacking in china: the most complete collection of self-guided travel for China, 2018*]. Taipei: Shang-Ch'i Shitai publishing. 2018 最完整的中國自助旅遊全集. 台北: 上奇時代.

Twitchett, Denis, and Frederick W. Mote, eds. 1998. *The Cambridge history of China 8(2). The Ming dynasty 1368–1644*. New York: Cambridge University Press.

Xinhua. 2021. Chinese Automaker FAW Jiefang Produces Eight Millionth Vehicle. *Via Global Times*, 14 July. https://www.globaltimes.cn/page/202107/1228607.shtml.

Zhang, Shunan. 2021. [The 2020 per capita income list of residents in various provinces: Shanghai is the richest, and it has risen sharply]. Finance.people.com. 22 January. 张澍楠. 2020年各省份居民人均收入榜: 上海最有钱, 这地涨得猛. http://finance.people.com.cn/n1/2021/0122/c1004-32008733.html.

References

Chapter 21
Liaoning Province

Abstract Excavations in Liaoning have revealed fossilized remains of an extremely old hominid (ca. 260,000 years ago), as well as remnants of the Hongshan Culture (ca. 3000 BCE). Sharing with Jilin and Heilongjiang a legacy of various nomadic tribes, ancient Korean kingdoms, and especially the Manchu, Liaoning Province was also subjected to Japanese military colonialization until the end of World War II. Following the Chinese Civil War (1945–49), Liaoning, along with the rest of what was once called 'Manchuria,' was heavily influenced by Soviet advisors who pushed for heavy industry (such as steel manufacture). Thus, in recent years, Liaoning has now become part of China's "rustbelt" with a shrinking population (about 2.6% from 2010 to 2020), and now faces the inevitable challenges in the modern economy. With regard to the latter, Liaoning's gross domestic product (GDP) actually fell between 2015 and 2020, although its per capita income of USD $5100 remains above average among mainland China's 31 provinces and major cities.

E. Croddy, *China's Provinces and Populations*,
https://doi.org/10.1007/978-3-031-09165-0_21

Liaoning Province (遼寧省 *liáoníng shěng*): Abbreviation 遼 (*liáo*) (Fig. 21.1)

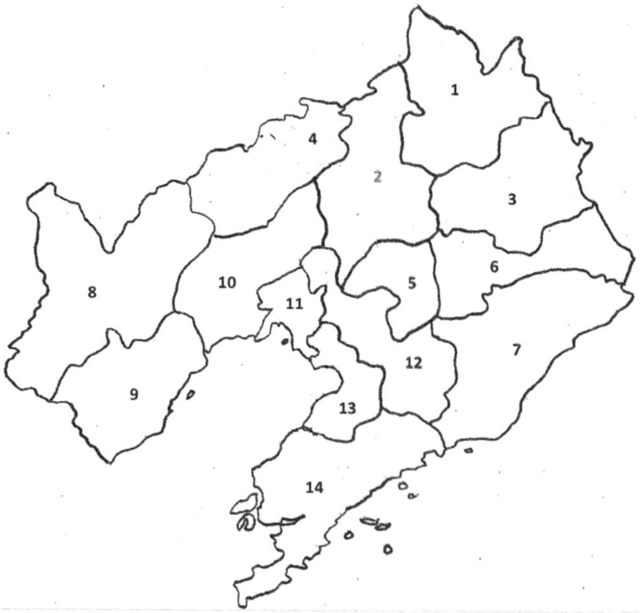

Liaoning Population (2020)

1.	Tieling City	2,388,294
2.	Shenyang City	9,027,781
3.	Fushun City	1,731,864
4.	Fuxin City	1,647,280
5.	Liaoyang City	1,604,580
6.	Benxi City	1,326,018
7.	Dandong City	2,188,436
8.	Chaoyang City	2,872,857
9.	Huludao City	2,434,194
10.	Jinzhou City	2,703,853
11.	Pajin City	1,389,691
12.	Anshan City	3,325,372
13.	Yingkou City	2,328,582
14.	Dalian City	7,450,785

Fig. 21.1 Liaoning Province major cities (Provincial Capital: Shenyang City). (Drawn by the Author after People's Republic of China, Ministry of Civil Affairs. (MCA 2020))

Liaoning Province: General Impressions

Reflecting its Manchu dynastic origins, for many years to the rest of the world the capital of Liaoning (Shenyang City) was known as 'Mukden.' Liaoning was also among the major regions occupied by wartime Japan (1896–1945), and Liaoning's post-war development, as it was during the Japanese occupation, focused on heavy industries (e.g., steel), and, later, was the beneficiary of generous Soviet assistance (1952–60). As it happens across all industrializing economies, Liaoning has recently become more and more of a rustbelt, losing a fairly significant number (well over a million) of its population since 2010, many of these likely moving to other, more dynamic provinces along China's southeast coast east and south.

Liaoning (遼寧 *liáoníng*) is also the name given to China's first operational aircraft carrier, the Type 001, commissioned 25 September 2012. It was named after the province in which it was fitted out (Dalian Shipyard). A second aircraft carrier, also built in Dalian, is an indigenously-produced Type 002, named *Shandong*. A completely different design of aircraft carrier, Type 003, is being built at the Jiangnan shipyard, and is likely to be named *Shanghai*.[1]

Prehistory

In 1984, Professor Lu Zun'e (呂遵諤 lǚ zūn'è) led his Peking University students in an excavation of the Jinniushan (金牛山 *jīnniúshān*) site, eight kilometers south of Dashiqiao City (大石橋市 *dàshíqiáo shì*) in Yingkou City (營口市 *yíngkǒu shì*), Liaoning Province. There, they discovered 58 hominid fossils, including an intact cranium that belonged to a mature female (about 20 years old), the largest such ever found, dated 260,000 years ago. Subsequent analysis of the specimen showed that the female weighed about 80 kilograms (175 lbs). Other mammalian fossils at the dig included monkeys and rhinoceros, indicating this area had a much milder climate than it does today. In the early 1980s, researchers made a spectacular find at the Niuheliang (牛河梁 *niúhéliáng*) archeological site in Chaoyang City (朝陽市 *cháoyáng shì*) near the borders of Lingyuan City (凌源市 *língyuán shì*) and Jianping County (建平縣 *jiànpíng xiàn*). Categorized as a representative of the Hongshan Culture (紅山文化 *hóngshān wénhuà*; 3500–3000 BCE), this excavation revealed a temple-like structure of some 80 square kilometers. Inside were numerous figurines, clay statuettes, and jade adornments, suggesting goddess worship and/or fertility rituals were performed there by a shamanistic society (Underhill and Habu 2006.)

Even before these most recent discoveries, colored pottery and jade implements found at Shaguotun (砂鍋屯 *shāguōtún*) in Huludao City (葫蘆島市 *húlúdǎo shì*, Nanpiao District 南票區 *nánpiào qū*) in the 1920s were critical in characterizing

[1] At the time of this writing, this was my estimation, as Shanghai is a provincial-level entity. It turns out that the third Chinese aircraft carrier has been named Fujian, likely as a strategic warning to Taiwan.

the Chinese Neolithic period (Chang 1977). Dated post-Hongshan Culture (3000–2500 BCE), these cave specimens showed an early farming society. Subsequent analysis of the Shaguotun artifacts categorized them Xiaoheyan ("Small River Bank") Culture (小河沿文化 *xiǎohéyán wénhuà*), named after the location of similar archeological finds at Aohanqi (Aohan Banner, 敖漢旗 *áohànqí*), Chifeng City, Inner Mongolia.

Depending upon the dynastic eras, different names have been used to describe the area of Liaoning Province as we know it today: Under the (legendary) Xia (2070–1600 BCE) and Shang (1600–1046 BCE), the region was known as the State of You (Youzhou 幽州 *yōuzhōu*). In the Warring States (475–221 BCE), it was known as Yan (燕 *yàn*).

Upon the unification of China under Qin Shi Huang, three prefectural areas were established: Liaodong (遼東郡 *liáodōng jùn*), Liaoxi (遼西郡 *liáoxī jùn*), and Youbeiping (右北平郡 *yòuběipíng jùn*) prefectures. In the Eastern Han, ruled by Emperor Andi (漢安帝 *hàn āndì*; 106–25 BCE), Liaodong was a vassal state, occupying an area extending from modern-day Yingkou to Huludao (Xiong 2009). In the spring of 238 CE, the Gongsu clan of the Liaodong Kingdom was defeated by Sima Yi (司馬懿 *Sīmǎ Yì*) of the (Cao) Wei and the Goguryeo (Korean) King. A series of struggles ensued, with pitched battles over territory to include the Liaodong area between the proto-Korean Goguryeo (高句麗 *gāojùlì*) and the Wei. By 414, Goguryeo controlled not only the northern part of the Korean peninsula but southern Manchuria as well. Both Sui and Tang dynasties struggled in their attempts to pacify northeast China as well as Korea. By ca. 700, the Tang dynasty had largely defeated the Goguryeo, maintaining for a short time control over northeastern China as well as part of northern Korea.

By ca. 900 CE, Liaoning was gradually occupied by the Khitan (契丹 *qìdān*) Mongols, forming the center of the Liao dynastic kingdom (916–1125). Administratively, the Liao was broken up into five main regions (道 *dào*), each having a capital (京 *jīng*) government (府 *fǔ*). The eastern part of the Liao dynasty had its governing capital in Liaoyang (東京遼陽府 *dōngjīng liáoyáng fǔ*), one of China's oldest inhabited cities, and remained the capital of the eastern part of the Jin dynasty (1115–1234 CE). The Yuan (Mongol) dynasty established administrative provinces (行省 *xíngshěng*), counties (縣 *xiàn*) as well as capitals of different categories, including Lu (路 *lù*) or "circuits;" Fu (府 *fǔ*); and Zhou (州 *zhōu*) "prefectures." From 1269 to 1287, the Liaoyang circuit (遼陽路*liáoyáng lù*) was the capital of Liaoyang province (遼陽省 *liáoyáng shěng*), its borders being roughly similar to that of modern-day Liaoning.

During the Qing dynasty, the capital moved to Shenyang (Mukden). Now Liaoning's capital, Shenyang, previously called Shengjing (盛京 *shèngjīng*) "Capital on the Rise" (ca. 1625), was named Mukden in 1634 (and still appears this way on older maps, from the Manchu language "to rise", as in "rising capital.") By the end of the Qing dynasty, the northeast region was organized into Fengtian province (奉天行省 *fèngtiān xíngshěng*) in 1907.

As of 1900, the Qing dynasty had designated modern-day Liaoning as Shengjing Province (Herrman 1966). In 1929, under the new Republic of China, the Nationalist government in Nanjing issued order No. 91, declaring that "Liaohe river region shall be ever peaceful," and changed the name of Fengtian to Liaoning Province (遼寧省 *liáoníng sheng*). In April of that year, the notorious Manchurian warlord, Zhang Xueliang (張學良 *Zhāng Xuéliáng*), ostentatiously approved the name change to Liaoning, reportedly because there should be peace (安寧 *ānníng*) across the Liao River (遼河 *liáohé*).

Mukden (Shenyang) was the city where elements of the Imperial Japanese Army trumped up a bombing incident (18 September 1931), blamed it on the Chinese, and used it as a pretext to conquer Manchuria, since referred to in China as the 9.18 Incident. Having reverted to the name of Fengtian under Japanese occupation (Manchukuo) in 1932, following the end of World War II the Republic of China (ROC) officially reestablished the name Liaoning in 1945. Due to the terms of Yalta, in return for its pledge to turn its guns against Japan, the Soviet Union obtained a "lease" on Lushun (旅順 *lǚshùn*), also known as Port Arthur, for a naval base, the Russians returning to Dalian (大連 *dàlián* aka Dalny, Darien) in 1945 (Mason 1997). Soviet military forces finally departed from Lushun and Dalian in 1955 (Shen and Xia 2015).

In the year following the establishment of the People's Republic of China (PRC) on 1 October 1949, China was drawn into six larger administrative areas:

- North China Administrative District (AD): 華北行政區 *huáběi xíngzhèngqū*)
- Northeast AD (東北行政區 *dōngběi xíngzhèngqū*)
- Northwest AD (西北行政區 *xīběi xíngzhèngqū*)
- East China AD (華東行政區 *huádōng xíngzhèngqū*)
- Mid-southern AD (中南行政區 *zhōngnán xíngzhèngqū*) and
- Southwest AD (西南行政區 *xīnán xíngzhèngqū*)

Until 1953, with Shenyang as the capital of the Northeast AD, modern-day Liaoning was divided in Liaodong (遼東省 *liáodōng shěng*; East Liao) and Liaoxi (遼西省 *liáoxī shěng*; West Liao) provinces. In 1954, Liaodong and Liaoxi were finally merged into Liaoning. Five of its major cities, including Shenyang, Luda (旅大市 *lǚdà shì*), Anshan (鞍山市 *ānshān shì*), Fushun (撫順市 *fǔshùn shì*), and Benxi (本溪市 *běnxī shì*) cities were now redrawn into Liaoning.

In 1956, the eastern part of Jehol Province (熱河省 *rèhé shěng*) included five counties:

- Chaoyang (朝陽 *cháoyáng*)
- Jianping (建平 *jiànpíng*)
- Lingyuan (凌源 *língyuán*)
- Jianchang (建昌 *jiànchāng*)
- Beipiao (北票 *běipiào*), and
- Kalaqin Left Wing (喀喇沁左翼 *kālǎqìn zuǒyì*)

All places listed above were eventually drawn inside Liaoning's borders (PRC 2001). From 1969 until 1978, Zhaowuda League (Juu Uda; 昭烏達盟

Table 21.1 Liaoning population estimates. (Yang 1995; LPBS 2021)

2 BCE	1,250,000
1851	2,580,000
1881	4,210,000
1953	18,545,147
1964	26,946,200
1982	35,721,693
1984	36,550,000
1990	39,459,697
2000	41,824,412
2010	43,746,323
2020	42,591,407

zhāowūdáméng) fell within Liaoning Province, but was then later returned to Inner Mongolia in 1979. In 1981, the city previously known as Luda (旅大 *lǚdà*) was renamed (once again) Dalian City. Given the shifting borders and complex interactions with rival powers throughout the region's history, accurate figures for the province's inhabitants are difficult to come by, but the following table (17.1) gives a sense of Liaoning populations throughout history (Table 21.1):

Liaoning's Modern Population Trends

Chinese media reported that in 2015 Liaoning's permanent registered population (戶籍總人口 *hùjízǒng rénkǒu*) was an estimated 42,708,000 (Sohu 2017). This number was roughly on par with internal (China, Ministry of Public Safety) *hukou* population data showing 42,450,000 for the same year (see Table 21.4). By 2020, the decennial census showed a total population of 42,591,407, with a registered population of 41,920,000 (see Table 21.2 and 21.3). While not as dramatic as other provinces in the northeast, Liaoning's population dropped about 2.6% from 2010 to 2020.

Like neighboring Jilin province, Liaoning's economy has slowed, with a gross domestic product (GDP) in 2015 of USD $445 billion, dropping to $390 billion in 2020, but ranks in the upper third of China's 31 provinces and major cities in terms of per capita income of $5091 (Zhang 2021).

Table 21.4 (below) shows the *hukou* (family registered) populations based on PRC Ministry of Civil Affairs data. (Districts listed directly under major cities are government seats, as are those in parentheses). One can compare these data with the census (usual residential populations based on 2010 and 2020 censuses in Tables 21.2 and 21.3 (below):

Table 21.2 Liaoning population (residential 常住人口 *chángzhù rénkǒu*) data. (LPBS (2021)

City	Population (2010)	Population (2020)
Shenyang 瀋陽市 *shěnyáng shì* [Abbrev. 瀋 *shěn*]	8,106,171	9,027,781
Dalian 大連市 *dàlián shì*	6,690,432	7,450,785
Anshan 鞍山市 *ānshān shì*	3,645,884	3,325,372
Benxi 本溪市 *běnxī shì*	1,709,538	1,326,018
Chaoyang 朝陽市 *cháoyáng shì*	3,044,641	2,872,857
Dandong 丹東市 *dāndōng shì*	2,444,697	2,188,436
Fushun 撫順市 *fǔshùn shì*	2,138,090	1,731,864
Fuxin 阜新市 *fùxīn shì*	1,819,339	1,647,280
Huludao 葫蘆島市 *húlúdǎo shì*	2,623,541	2,434,194
Jinzhou 錦州市*jǐnzhōu shì*	3,126,463	2,703,853
Liaoyang 遼陽市 *liáoyáng shì*	1,858,768	1,604,580
Panjin 盤錦市 *pánjǐn shì*	1,392,493	1,389,691
Tieling 鐵嶺市 *tiělǐng shì*	2,717,732	2,388,294
Yingkou 營口市 *yíngkǒu shì*	2,428,534	2,328,582
Shenfu reform and innovation demonstration zone[a] 瀋撫改革創新示範區 *shěnfǔ gǎigé chuàngxīn shìfàn qū*	N/A	171,820
Total	**43,746,323**	**42,591,407**

[a]Formerly established in September 2018, comprises selected areas shared between neighboring Shenyang and Fushun cities

Table 21.3 Liaoning Province: population data of cities and their subordinate sectors. (LPBS 2021)

Cities and subordinate sectors, population (2020 census)	Subordinate district, city and county populations (2020)	Total population (2020)
Shenyang City 瀋陽市 ***shěnyáng shì* [Abbrev.** 瀋 ***shěn*]**		**9,070,093**
Hunnan District 渾南區 *húnnán qū*	798,765	
Shenhe District 瀋河區 *shěnhé qū*	782,628	
Heping District 和平區 *hépíng qū*	730,785	
Dadong District 大東區 *dàdōng qū*	754,952	
Huanggu District 皇姑區 *huánggū qū*	877,287	
Tiexi District 鐵西區 *tiěxī qū*	1,335,935	
Sujiatun District 蘇家屯區 *sūjiātún qū*	524,336	
Shenbei New District 瀋北新區 *shěnběi xīnqū*	619,375	
Yuhong District 于洪區 *yúhóng qū*	1,066,062	
Xinmin City 新民市 *xīnmín shì*	565,634	
Liaozhong County 遼中縣 *liáozhōng xiàn*	395,017	
Kangping County 康平縣 *kāngpíng xiàn*	278,384	
Faku County 法庫縣 *fǎkù xiàn*	340,933	
Dalian 大連市 ***dàlián shì***		**7,450,785**
Xigang District 西崗區 *xīgǎng qū*	305,317	
Zhongshan District 中山區 *zhōngshān qū*	388,564	
Shahekou District 沙河口區 *shāhékǒu qū*	670,310	

(continued)

Table 21.3 (continued)

Cities and subordinate sectors, population (2020 census)	Subordinate district, city and county populations (2020)	Total population (2020)
Ganjingzi District 甘井子區 *gānjǐngzǐ qū*	1,534,722	
Lüshunkou District 旅順口區 *lǚshùnkǒu qū*	355,427	
Jinpu New District 金普新區 *jīnpǔ xīnqū*	1,545,491	
Wafangdian City 瓦房店市 *wǎfángdiàn shì*	818,847	
Pulandian District 普蘭店區 *pǔlándiàn qū*	629,664	
Zhuanghe City 莊河市 *zhuānghé shì*	742,496	
Changhai County 長海縣 *chánghǎi xiàn*	66,824	
Changxing Island 長興島 *chángxīng dǎo*	86,235	
Dalian High Technology Industry Development Park 大連高新技術產業園區 *dàlián gāoxīnjìshù chǎnyèyuánqū*	306,888	
Anshan 鞍山市 ***ānshān shì***		**3,325,372**
Tiedong District[a] 鐵東區 *tiědōng qū*	511,574	
Tiexi District 鐵西區 *tiěxī qū*	309,397	
Lishan District 立山區 *lìshān qū*	406,680	
Qianshan District 千山區 *qiānshān qū*	94,729	
Haicheng City 海城市 *hǎichéng shì*	106,7905	
Tai'an County 台安縣 *tái'ān xiàn*	300,764	
Xiuyan Manzu (Manchu) Autonomous County 岫岩滿族自治縣 *xiùyán mǎnzú zìzhìxiàn*	413,007	
Anshan High Technology Industry Development Park鞍山高新技術產業園區 *ānshān gāoxīnjìshù chǎnyèyuánqū*	122,595	
Benxi 本溪市 ***běnxī shì***		**1,326,018**
Pingshan District 平山區 *píngshān qū*	226,059	
Xihu District 溪湖區 *xīhú qū*	142,982	
Mingshan District 明山區 *míngshān qū*	378,936	
Nanfen District 南芬區 *nánfēn qū*	55,560	
Benxi Manzu (Manchu) Autonomous County 本溪滿族自治縣 *běnxī mǎnzú zìzhìxiàn*	230,850	
Huanren Manzu (Manchu) Autonomous County 桓仁滿族自治縣 *huánrén mǎnzú zìzhìxiàn*	229,953	
Benxi High Technology Industry Development Park 本溪高新技術產業園區 *běnxī gāoxīnjìshù chǎnyèyuánqū*	61,678	
Chaoyang 朝陽市 ***cháoyáng shì***		**2,872,857**
Shuangta District 雙塔區 *shuāngtǎ qū*	463,543	
Longcheng District 龍城區 *lóngchéng qū*	222,065	
Beipiao City 北票市 *běipiào shì*	439,998	
Lingyuan City 淩源市 *língyuán shì*	540,832	
Chaoyang County 朝陽縣 *cháoyáng xiàn*	404,460	
Jianping County 建平縣 *jiànpíng xiàn*	455,826	
Kalaqinzuoyi Mengguzu (Harqin Left Wing Mongol; Harqin Zuoyi Mongol) Autonomous County 喀喇沁左翼蒙古族自治縣 *kālǎqìnzuǒyì měnggǔzú zìzhìxiàn*	346,133	

(continued)

Table 21.3 (continued)

Cities and subordinate sectors, population (2020 census)	Subordinate district, city and county populations (2020)	Total population (2020)
Dandong 丹東市 ***dāndōng shì***		**2,188,436**
Zhenxing District 振興區 *zhènxīng qū*	423,538	
Yuanbao District 元寶區 *yuánbǎo qū*	202,325	
Zhen'an District 振安區 *zhèn'ān qū*	189,995	
Fengcheng City 鳳城市 *fèngchéng shì*	469,376	
Donggang City 東港市 *dōnggǎng shì*	568,566	
Kuandian Manzu (Manchu) Autonomous County 寬甸滿族自治縣 *kuāndiàn mǎnzú zìzhìxiàn*	334,636	
Fushun 撫順市 ***fǔshùn shì***		**1,731,864**
Shuncheng District 順城區 *shùnchéng qū*	336,618	1395246
Xinfu District 新撫區 *xīnfǔ qū*	222,984	
Dongzhou District 東洲區 *dōngzhōu qū*	236,731	
Wanghua District 望花區 *wànghuā qū*	266,749	
Fushun County 撫順縣 *fǔshùn xiàn*	83,125	
Xinbin Manzu (Manchu) Autonomous County 新賓滿族自治縣 *xīnbīn mǎnzú zìzhìxiàn*	217,259	
Qingyuan Manzu (Manchu) Autonomous County 清原滿足自治縣 *qīngyuán mǎnzú zìzhìxiàn*	238,890	
Shen(yang)-Fu(shun) Demonstration Region, Fushun Section 瀋撫示範撫順片區 *shěnfǔ shìfàn fǔshùn piànqū*	129,508	
Fuxin 阜新市 ***fùxīn shì***		**1,647,280**
Xihe District 細河區 *xìhé qū*	273,525	
Haizhou District 海州區 *hǎizhōu qū*	234,029	
Xinqiu District 新邱區 *xīnqiū qū*	66,769	
Taiping District 太平區 *tàipíng qū*	142,171	
Qinghemen District 清河門區 *qīnghémén qū*	51,394	
Zhangwu County 彰武縣 *zhāngwǔ xiàn*	333,643	
Fuxin Mengguzu (Mongol) Autonomous County 阜新蒙古族自治縣 *fùxīn mēnggǔzú zìzhìxiàn*	545,749	
Huludao 葫蘆島市 ***húlúdǎo shì***		**2,434,194**
Longgang District 龍港區 *lónggǎng qū*	294,250	
Lianshan District 連山區 *liánshān qū*	468,110	
Nanpiao District 南票區 *nánpiào qū*	182,135	
Xingcheng City 興城市 *xīngchéng shì*	490,300	
Suizhong County 綏中縣 *suízhōng xiàn*	545,963	
Jianchang County 建昌縣*jiànchāng xiàn*	453,436	
Jinzhou 錦州市***jǐnzhōu shì***		**2,703,853**
Taihe District 太和區 *tàihé qū*	175,098	
Guta District 古塔區 *gǔtǎ qū*	252,209	
Linghe District 淩河區 *línghé qū*	402,038	
Linghai City 淩海市 *línghǎi shì*	412,513	
Beizhen City 北鎮市 *běizhèn shì*	422,289	

(continued)

Table 21.3 (continued)

Cities and subordinate sectors, population (2020 census)	Subordinate district, city and county populations (2020)	Total population (2020)
Heishan County 黑山縣 *hēishān xiàn*	451,206	
Yixian County 義縣 *yìxiàn*	305,996	
Binhai New District 濱海新區 *bīnhǎi xīnqū*	100,068	
Songshan New District 松山新區 *sōngshān xīnqū*	182,436	
Liaoyang 遼陽市 ***liáoyáng shì***		**1,604,580**
Baita District 白塔區 *báitǎ qū*	359,401	
Wensheng District 文聖區 *wénshèng qū*	160,466	
Hongwei District 宏偉區 *hóngwěi qū*	142,491	
Gongchangling District 弓長嶺區 *gōngchánglǐng qū*	80,870	
Taizihe District 太子河區 *tàizǐhé qū*	134,604	
Dengta City 燈塔市 *dēngtǎ shì*	354,617	
Liaoyang County 遼陽縣 *liáoyáng xiàn*	372,131	
Panjin 盤錦市 ***pánjǐn shì***		**1,389,691**
Xinglongtai District 興隆台區 *xīnglóngtái qū*	529,394	
Shuangtaizi District 雙台子區 *shuāngtáizǐ qū*	214,290	
Dawa District (Base District Level) 大洼區本級 *dàwā qūběnjí*	375,716	
Dawa District 大洼區 *dàwā qū*	422,797	
Panshan County 盤山縣 *pánshān xiàn*	223,210	
Tieling 鐵嶺市 ***tiělǐng shì***		**2,388,294**
Yinzhou District 銀州區 *yínzhōu qū*	322,498	
Tieling Economic and Technology Development Zone 鐵嶺經濟技術開發區 *tiělǐng jīngjìjìshù kāifāqū*	527,94	
Qinghe District 清河區 *qīnghé qū*	84,693	
Diaobingshan City 調兵山市 *diàobīngshān shì*	206,058	
Kaiyuan City 開原市 *kāiyuán shì*	460,927	
Tieling County 鐵嶺縣 *tiělǐng xiàn*	324,383	
Xifeng County 西豐縣 *xīfēng xiàn*	225,123	
Changtu County 昌圖縣 *chāngtú xiàn*	711,818	
Yingkou 營口市 ***yíngkǒu shì***		**2,328,582**
Zhanqian District 站前區 *zhànqián qū*	261,439	
Xishi District 西市區 *xīshì qū*	212,913	
Bayuquan District 鮁魚圈區 *bàyúquān qū*	541,113	
Laobian District 老邊區 *lǎobiān qū*	146,748	
Dashiqiao City 大石橋市 *dàshíqiáo shì*	607,098	
Gaizhou City 蓋州市 *gàizhōu shì*	559,271	
Shen(yang)-Fu(shun) reform and innovation demonstration zone[b] 瀋撫改革創新示範區 ***shěnfǔ gǎigé chuàngxīn shìfàn qū***		**171,820**

[a]Includes the scenic area

[b]Formerly established in September 2018, comprises selected areas shared between neighboring Shenyang and Fushun cities

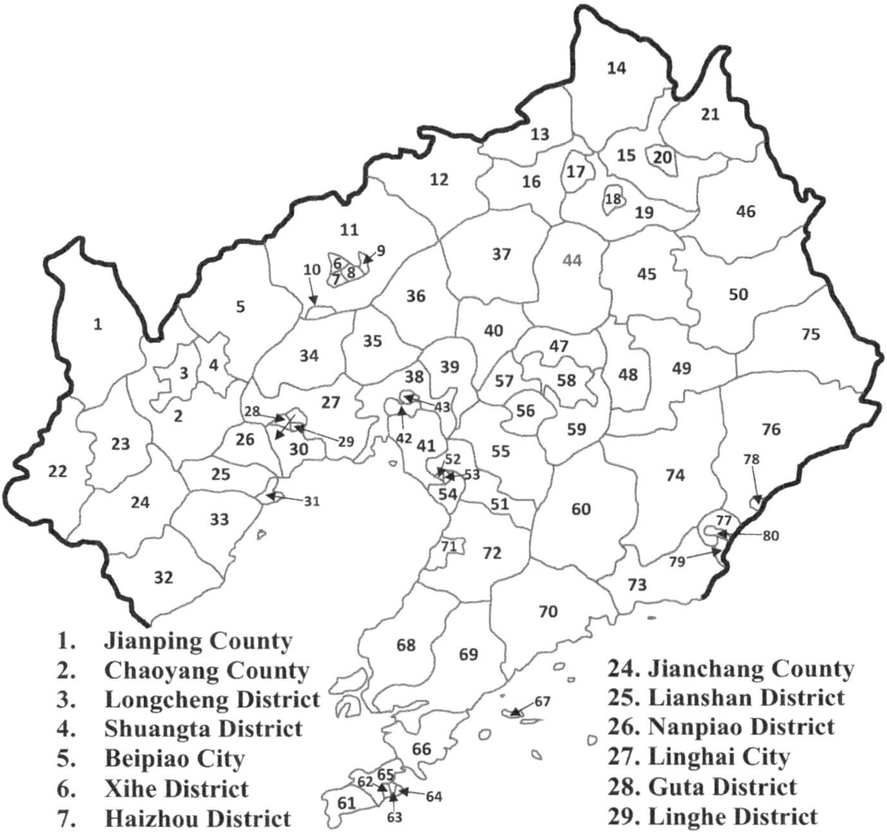

1. **Jianping County**
2. **Chaoyang County**
3. **Longcheng District**
4. **Shuangta District**
5. **Beipiao City**
6. **Xihe District**
7. **Haizhou District**
8. **Taiping District**
9. **Xinqiu District**
10. **Qinghemen District**
11. **Fuxin Mongol Autonomous County**
12. **Zhangwu County**
13. **Kangping County**
14. **Changtu County**
15. **Kaiyuan City**
16. **Faku County**
17. **Diaobingshan City**
18. **Yinzhou District**
19. **Tieling County**
20. **Qinghe District**
21. **Xifeng County**
22. **Lingyuan City**
23. **Kalaqinzuoyi (Harqin Left Wing) Mongol Autonomous County**
24. **Jianchang County**
25. **Lianshan District**
26. **Nanpiao District**
27. **Linghai City**
28. **Guta District**
29. **Linghe District**
30. **Taihe District**
31. **Longgang District**
32. **Suizhong County**
33. **Xingcheng City**
34. **Yixian County**
35. **Beizhen City**
36. **Heishan County**
37. **Xinmin City**
38. **Panshan County**
39. **Tai'an County**
40. **Liaozhong County**

Fig. 21.2 Liaoning Province: Subdistricts (Provincial Capital City: Shenyang City). (Drawn by the Author after People's Republic of China, Ministry of Civil Affairs. (MCA 2020))

41. Dawa District
42. Xinglongtai District
43. Shuangtaizi District
44. Shenyang City
45. Fushun County
46. Qingyuan Manchu Autonomous County
47. Dengta City
48. Benxi City
49. Benxi Manchu Autonomous County
50. Xinbi Manchu Autonomous County
51. Dashiqiao City
52. Xishi District
53. Zhanqian District
54. Laobian District
55. Haicheng City
56. Anshan City
57. Liaoyang County
58. Liaoyang City
59. (Liaoyang County jurisdiction)
60. Xiuyan Manchu Autonomous County
61. Lüshunkou District
62. Shahekou District
63. Xigang District
64. Zhongshan District
65. Ganjingzi District
66. Jinzhou District
67. Changhai County
68. Wafangdian City
69. Pulandian Di
70. Zhuanghe Citystrict
71. Bayuquan District
72. Gaizhou City
73. Donggang City
74. Fengcheng City
75. Huanren Manchu Autonomous County
76. Kuandian Manchu Autonomous County
77. Zhen'an District
78. (Zhen'an District jurisdiction)
79. Zhenxing District
80. Yuanbao District

Fig. 21.2 (continued)

Liaoning Province (遼 *liáo*)

Provincial Capital: Shenyang City

Table 21.4 Liaoning Province: permanent registered (戶籍人口 *hùjí rénkǒu*) populations. (MCA 2020)

Provincial Capital: Shenyang City	Traditional	Simplified	Population (2012)	Population (2016)	Population (2020)	Area (Sq. Km)
Liaoning Province	遼寧省	辽宁省	42,520,000	42,450,000	41,920,000	148,084
Shenyang City	瀋陽市	沈阳市	8,930,000	7,260,000	7,450,000	12,980
Hunnan District (Shenzhong Street)	渾南區 (瀋中大街)	浑南区 (沈中街)	320,000	320,000	410,000	793
Shenhe District (Huangcheng Subdistrict)	瀋河區 (皇城街道)	沈河区 (皇城街道)	1,160,000	720,000	710,000	53
Heping District (Nanshichang Subdistrict)	和平區 (南市場街道)	和平区 (南市场街道)	680,000	640,000	720,000	61

(continued)

Table 21.4 (continued)

Provincial Capital: Shenyang City	Traditional	Simplified	Population (2012)	Population (2016)	Population (2020)	Area (Sq. Km)
Dadong District (Jinqiao Subdistrict)	大東區 (津橋街道)	大东区 (津桥街道)	910,000	700,000	650,000	105
Huanggu District (Huanghe Subdistrict)	皇姑區 (黃河街道)	皇姑区 (黄河街道)	1,120,000	810,000	840,000	67
Tiexi District (Dugong Subdistrict)	鐵西區 (篤工街道)	铁西区 (笃工街道)	1,020,000	890,000	940,000	277
Sujiatun District (Jiefang Subdistrict)	蘇家屯區 (解放街道)	苏家屯区 (解放街道)	430,000	430,000	420,000	781
Shenbeixin District (Xinchengzi Subdistrict)	瀋北新區 (新城子街道)	沈北新区 (新城子街道)	310,000	310,000	330,000	831
Yuhong District (Yingbinlu Subdistrict)	于洪區 (迎賓路街道)	于洪区 (迎宾路街道)	980,000	410,000	480,000	499
Xinmin City (Xinliu Subdistrict)	新民市 (新柳街道)	新民市 (新柳街道)	700,000	690,000	670,000	3315
Liaozhong County (Puxi Subdistrict)	遼中縣 (蒲西街道)	辽中县 (蒲西街道)	520,000	540,000	510,000	1647
Kangping County (Shengli Subdistrict)	康平縣 (勝利街道)	康平县 (胜利街道)	330,000	350,000	340,000	2231
Faku County (Faku Town)	法庫縣 (法庫鎮)	法库县 (法库镇)	450,000	450,000	440,000	2320
Chaoyang City	朝陽市	朝阳市	3,410,000	3,400,000	3,360,000	19,736
Shuangta District (Nanta Subdistrict)	雙塔區 (南塔街道)	双塔区 (南塔街道)	400,000	400,000	410,000	500
Longcheng District (Xinhua Subdistrict)	龍城區 (新華街道)	龙城区 (新华街道)	180,000	210,000	210,000	647
Beipiao City (Nanshan Subdistrict)	北票市 (南山街道)	北票市 (南山街道)	590,000	580,000	560,000	4469
Lingyuan City (Beijie Subdistrict)	淩源市 (北街街道)	凌源市 (北街街道)	650,000	650,000	640,000	3264
Chaoyang County (Chaoyang City Shuangta District Qianjin Subdistrict)	朝陽縣 (朝陽市雙塔區前進街道)	朝阳县 (朝阳市双塔区前进街道)	570,000	560,000	560,000	3751
Jianping County (Hongshan Subdistrict)	建平縣 (紅山街道)	建平县 (红山街道)	590,000	580,000	580,000	4865

(continued)

Table 21.4 (continued)

Provincial Capital: Shenyang City	Traditional	Simplified	Population (2012)	Population (2016)	Population (2020)	Area (Sq. Km)
Kalaqinzuoyi Mengguzu (Harqin Left Wing Mongol; Harqin Zuoyi Mongol) Autonomous County (Dachengzi Subdistrict)	喀喇沁左翼蒙古族自治縣(大城子街道)	喀喇沁左翼蒙古族自治县(大城子街道)	430,000	420,000	420,000	2240
Fuxin City	阜新市	阜新市	1,930,000	1,910,000	1,850,000	10,445
Xihe District (Dongyuan Subdistrict)	細河區(東苑街道)	细河区(东苑街道)	180,000	180,000	200,000	126
Haizhou District (Xinxing Subdistrict)	海州區(新興街道)	海州区(新兴街道)	270,000	270,000	260,000	97
Xinqiu District (Xinglong Subdistrict)	新邱區(興隆街道)	新邱区(兴隆街道)	90,000	90,000	80,000	128
Taiping District (Hongshu Subdistrict)	太平區(紅樹街道)	太平区(红树街道)	170,000	170,000	150,000	108
Qinghemen District (Qinghe Subdistrict)	清河門區(清河街道)	清河门区(清河街道)	70,000	70,000	60,000	105
Zhangwu County (Zhangwu Town)	彰武縣(彰武鎮)	彰武县(彰武镇)	420,000	410,000	400,000	3635
Fuxin Mengguzu (Mongol) Autonomous County (Chengqu Subdistrict)	阜新蒙古族自治縣(城區街道)	阜新蒙古族自治县(城区街道)	730,000	720,000	710,000	6246
Tieling City	鐵嶺市	铁岭市	3,060,000	3,020,000	2,920,000	13,029
Yinzhou District (Gongren Subdistrict)	銀州區(工人街道)	银州区(工人街道)	350,000	340,000	330,000	201
Qinghe District (Hongqi Subdistrict)	清河區(紅旗街道)	清河区(红旗街道)	100,000	100,000	90,000	480
Diaobingshan City (Diaobingshan Subdistrict)	調兵山市(調兵山街道)	调兵山市(调兵山街道)	240,000	240,000	230,000	262
Kaiyuan City (Xincheng Subdistrict)	開原市(新城街道)	开原市(新城街道)	590,000	580,000	560,000	2813

(continued)

Table 21.4 (continued)

Provincial Capital: Shenyang City	Traditional	Simplified	Population (2012)	Population (2016)	Population (2020)	Area (Sq. Km)
Tieling County (Tieling City Yinzhou District Gongren Subdistrict)	鐵嶺縣 (鐵嶺市銀周區工人街道)	铁岭县 (铁岭市银周区工人街道)	390,000	390,000	380,000	2250
Xifeng County (Xifeng Town)	西豐縣 (西豐鎮)	西丰县 (西丰镇)	350,000	340,000	330,000	2699
Changtu County (Changtu Town)	昌圖縣 (昌圖鎮)	昌图县 (昌图镇)	1,040,000	1,030,000	990,000	4324
Fushun City	撫順市	**抚顺**市	2,380,000	2,180,000	2,090,000	11,344
Shuncheng District (Changchun Subdistrict)	順城區 (長春街道)	顺城区 (长春街道)	490,000	430,000	430,000	348
Xinfu District (Yong'antai Subdistrict)	新撫區 (永安台街道)	新抚区 (永安台街道)	360,000	310,000	280,000	113
Dongzhou District (Dalian Subdistrict)	東洲區 (搭連街道)	东洲区 (搭连街道)	370,000	310,000	280,000	604
Wanghua District (Jianshe Subdistrict)	望花區 (建設街道)	望花区 (建设街道)	400,000	380,000	370,000	317
Fushun County (Shiwen Town)	撫順縣 (石文[a]鎮)	抚顺县 (石文鎮)	120,000	120,000	110,000	1754
Xinbin Manzu (Manchu) Autonomous County (Xinbin Town)	新賓滿族自治縣 (新賓鎮)	新宾满族自治县 (新宾镇)	300,000	300,000	290,000	4287
Qingyuan Manzu (Manchu) Autonomous County (Qingyuan Town)	清原滿族自治縣 (清原鎮)	清原满族自治县 (清原镇)	340,000	330,000	320,000	3921
Benxi City	本溪市	本溪市	1,540,000	1,540,000	1,460,000	8413
Pingshan District (Dongming Subdistrict)	平山區 (東明街道)	平山区 (东明街道)	330,000	320,000	290,000	178
Xihu District (Hedong Subdistrict)	溪湖區 (河東街道)	溪湖区 (河东街道)	210,000	210,000	190,000	312
Mingshan District (Xinming Subdistrict)	明山區 (新明街道)	明山区 (新明街道)	330,000	340,000	340,000	413
Nanfen District (Nanfen Subdistrict)	南芬區 (南芬街道)	南芬区 (南芬街道)	80,000	80,000	70,000	615

(continued)

Table 21.4 (continued)

Provincial Capital: Shenyang City	Traditional	Simplified	Population (2012)	Population (2016)	Population (2020)	Area (Sq. Km)
Benxi Manzu (Manchu) Autonomous County (Guanyinge Subdistrict)	本溪滿族自治縣(觀音閣街道)	本溪满族自治县(观音阁街道)	290,000	290,000	280,000	3342
Huanren Manzu (Manchu) Autonomous County (Baguacheng Subdistrict)	桓仁滿族自治縣(八卦城街道)	桓仁满族自治县(八卦城街道)	300,000	300,000	290,000	3553
Liaoyang City	遼陽市	辽阳市	1,830,000	1,810,000	1,750,000	4741
Baita District (Xinghuo Subdistrict)	白塔區(星火街道)	白塔区(星火街道)	210,000	370,000	360,000	24
Wensheng District (Wensheng Subdistrict)	文聖區(文聖街道)	文圣区(文圣街道)	180,000	130,000	130,000	38
Hongwei District (Guanghua Subdistrict)	宏偉區(光華街道)	宏伟区(光华街道)	140,000	140,000	140,000	117
Gongchangling District (Tanghe Town)	弓長嶺區(湯河鎮)	弓长岭区(汤河镇)	90,000	90,000	90,000	288
Taizihe District (Xinhua Subdistrict)	太子河區(新華街道)	太子河区(新华街道)	130,000	150,000	150,000	166
Dengta City (Wanbaoqiao Subdistrict)	燈塔市(萬寶橋街道)	灯塔市(万宝桥街道)	510,000	450,000	440,000	1313
Liaoyang County (Shoushan Town)	遼陽縣(首山鎮)	辽阳县(首山镇)	570,000	480,000	460,000	2795
Anshan City	鞍山市	鞍山市	3,600,000	3,510,000	3,420,000	9252
Tiedong District (Jiefang Subdistrict)	鐵東區(解放街道)	铁东区(解放街道)	620,000	530,000	560,000	135
Tiexi District (Bajiazi Subdistrict)	鐵西區(八家子街道)	铁西区(八家子街道)	370,000	310,000	290,000	147
Lishan District (Lishan Subdistrict)	立山區(立山街道)	立山区(立山街道)	530,000	440,000	400,000	165
Qianshan District (Dong'anshan Town)	千山區(東鞍山鎮)	千山区(东鞍山街道)	100,000	240,000	220,000	344

(continued)

Table 21.4 (continued)

Provincial Capital: Shenyang City	Traditional	Simplified	Population (2012)	Population (2016)	Population (2020)	Area (Sq. Km)
Haicheng City (Dongsi Subdistrict)	海城市 (東四街道)	海城市 (东四街道)	1,080,000	1,090,000	1,070,000	2566
Tai'an County (Bajiaotai Subdistrict)	台安縣 (八角台街道)	台安县 (八角台街道)	380,000	380,000	370,000	1393
Xiuyan Manzu (Manchu) Autonomous County (Fuchang Subdistrict)	岫岩滿族自治縣 (阜昌街道)	岫岩满族自治县 (阜昌街道)	520,000	520,000	510,000	4502
Dandong City	丹東市	丹东市	2,420,000	2,420,000	2,340,000	15,030
Zhenxing District (Zhanqian Subdistrict)	振興區 (站前街道)	振兴区 (站前街道)	430,000	430,000	430,000	80
Yuanbao District (Guangji Subdistrict)	元寶區 (廣濟街道)	元宝区 (广济街道)	190,000	190,000	180,000	81
Zhen'an District (Yalüjiang Subdistrict)	振安區 (鴨綠江街道)	振安区 (鸭绿江街道)	180,000	180,000	170,000	669
Fengcheng City (Fenghuangcheng Subdistrict)	鳳城市 (鳳凰城街道)	凤城市 (凤凰城街道)	580,000	580,000	550,000	5518
Donggang City (Xinxing Subdistrict)	東港市 (新興街道)	东港市 (新兴街道)	610,000	610,000	590,000	2496
Kuandian Manzu (Manchu) Autonomous County (Kuandian Town)	寬甸滿族自治縣 (寬甸鎮)	宽甸满族自治县 (宽甸镇)	430,000	430,000	420,000	6186
Dalian City	大連市	大连市	5,870,000	5,910,000	5,950,000	13,328
Xigang District (Beijing Subdistrict)	西崗區 (北京街道)	西岗区 (北京街道)	300,000	300,000	280,000	26
Zhongshan District (Guilin Subdistrict)	中山區 (桂林街道)	中山区 (桂林街道)	360,000	360,000	360,000	43
Shahekou District (Baishanlu Subdistrict)	沙河口區 (白山路街道)	沙河口区 (白山路街道)	660,000	660,000	630,000	49
Ganjingzi District (Xinzhaizi Subdistrict)	甘井子區 (辛寨子街道)	甘井子区 (辛寨子街道)	760,000	790,000	910,000	491

(continued)

Table 21.4 (continued)

Provincial Capital: Shenyang City	Traditional	Simplified	Population (2012)	Population (2016)	Population (2020)	Area (Sq. Km)
Lüshunkou District (Shuishiying Subdistrict)	旅順口區 (水師營街道)	旅顺口区 (水师营街道)	220,000	220,000	220,000	506
Jinzhou District (Maqiaozi Subdistrict)	金州區 (馬橋子街道)	金州区 (马桥子街道)	750,000	670,000	790,000	1390
Wafangdian City (Gongji Subdistrict)	瓦房店市 (共濟街道)	瓦房店市 (共济街道)	1,020,000	1,000,000	990,000	3791
Pulandian District (Nanshan Subdistrict)	普蘭店區 (南山街道)	普兰店区 (南山街道)	820,000	930,000	820,000	2923
Zhuanghe City (Xinhua Subdistrict)	莊河市 (新華街道)	庄河市 (新华街道)	910,000	910,000	890,000	3900
Changhai County (Dachangshandao Town)	長海縣 (大長山島鎮)	长海县 (大长山岛镇)	70,000	70,000	70,000	119
Yingkou City	營口市	营口市	2,360,000	2,440,000	2,310,000	5262
Zhanqian District (Jianshe Subdistrict)	站前區 (建設街道)	站前区 (建设街道)	270,000	310,000	280,000	82
Xishi District (Desheng Subdistrict)	西市區 (得勝街道)	西市区 (胜利街道)	160,000	220,000	170,000	307
Bayuquan District (Honghai Subdistrict)	鮁魚圈區 (紅海街道)	鲅鱼圈区 (红海街道)	350,000	360,000	380,000	268
Laobian District (Laobian Subdistrict)	老邊區 (老邊街道)	老边区 (老边街道)	130,000	110,000	110,000	273
Dashiqiao City (Qinghua Subdistrict)	大石橋市 (青花街道)	大石桥市 (青花街道)	720,000	720,000	690,000	1379
Gaizhou City (Xicheng Subdistrict)	蓋州市 (西城街道)	盖州市 (西城街道)	730,000	720,000	690,000	2953
Panjin City	盤錦市	盘锦市	1,440,000	1,290,000	1,300,000	4121
Xinglongtai District (Xinghai Subdistrict)	興隆台區 (興海街道)	兴隆台区 (兴隆街道)	510,000	430,000	440,000	975
Shuangtaizi District (Jianshe Subdistrict)	雙台子區 (建設街道)	双台子区 (建设街道)	300,000	210,000	200,000	127
Dawa County (Dawa Town)	大洼縣 (大洼鎮)	大洼县 (大洼镇)	380,000	380,000	N/A	(1355)

(continued)

Table 21.4 (continued)

Provincial Capital: Shenyang City	Traditional	Simplified	Population (2012)	Population (2016)	Population (2020)	Area (Sq. Km)
Dawa District (Dawa Town)	大洼區 (大洼鎮)	大洼区 (大洼镇)	N/A	N/A	390,000	1355
Panshan County (Taiping Town)	盤山縣 (太平鎮)	盘山县 (太平镇)	250,000	270,000	270,000	1664
Jinzhou City	錦州市	锦州市	3,080,000	3,140,000	2,950,000	10,059
Taihe District (Taihe Subdistrict)	太和區 (太和街道)	太和区 (太和街道)	220,000	410,000	360,000	865
Guta District (Bao'an Subdistrict)	古塔區 (保安街道)	古塔区 (保安街道)	250,000	300,000	240,000	68
Linghe District (Longjiang Subdistrict)	淩河區 (龍江街道)	凌河区 (龙江街道)	460,000	410,000	360,000	42
Linghai City (Dalinghe Subdistrict)	淩海市 (大淩河街道)	凌海市 (大凌河街道)	570,000	480,000	500,000	2417
Beizhen City (Beizhen Subdistrict)	北鎮市 (北鎮街道)	北镇市 (北镇街道)	520,000	520,000	500,000	1693
Heishan County (Heishan Subdistrict)	黑山縣 (黑山街道)	黑山县 (黑山街道)	630,000	620,000	590,000	2497
Yixian County (Yizhou Subdistrict)	義縣 (義州街道)	义县 (义州街道)	430,000	400,000	400,000	2477
Huludao City	葫蘆島市	葫芦岛市	2,820,000	2,800,000	2,760,000	10,434
Longgang District (Yuhuang Subdistrict)	龍港區 (玉皇街道)	龙港区 (玉皇街道)	220,000	220,000	240,000	172
Lianshan District (Lianshan Subdistrict)	連山區 (連山街道)	连山区 (连山街道)	640,000	470,000	460,000	1182
Nanpiao District (Jiulong Subdistrict)	南票區 (九龍街道)	南票区 (九龙街道)	140,000	290,000	280,000	1002
Xingcheng City (Wenquan Subdistrict)	興城市 (溫泉街道)	兴城市 (温泉街道)	550,000	550,000	530,000	2103
Suizhong County (Suizhong Town)	綏中縣 (綏中鎮)	绥中县 (绥中镇)	640,000	640,000	640,000	2780
Jianchang County (Jianchang Town)	建昌縣 (建昌鎮)	建昌县 (建昌镇)	630,000	630,000	620,000	3195

[a]Sometimes seen as 紋 but this is incorrect

References

Chang, Kwang-chih. 1977. *The archeology of ancient China*. 3rd ed. New Haven: Yale University Press.

Herrman, Albert. 1966. *An historical atlas of China*. Chicago: Aldine Publishing Company.

Liaoning Province Bureau of Statistics (LPBS). 2021. [*Communiqué of the seventh national census of Liaoning Province 2020*]. 30 May. 辽宁省第七次全国人口普查公报 2020. https://tjgb.hongheiku.com/11664.html.

Mason, Michael G. 1997. *Development and disorder: A history of the third world since 1945*. Hanover: University Press of New England.

Ministry of Civil Affairs (MCA), People's Republic of China. 2020. [*County/township administration handbook*]. Beijing: China Statistics Press. 中華人民共和國民政部, 中華人民共和國, 鄉鎮行政區劃簡冊.

People's Republic of China (PRC). 2001. *Administrative division reform atlas, 1949–1999*. Beijing: China Map Publishers.

Shang-Ch'i Guide. 2017. [*Backpacking in China: The most complete collection of self-guided travel for China, 2018*]. Taipei: Shang-Ch'i Shitai publishing. 2018 最完整的中國自助旅遊全集. 台北: 上奇時代.

Shen, Zhihua, and Yafeng Xia. 2015. *Mao and the Sino–Soviet partnership, 1945–1959: A new history*. Lanham, MD: Lexington Books.

Sohu.com. 2017. [*In 2020, the elderly population in Liaoning will exceed 10 million*]. 8 March. 2020年辽宁老年人口将超千万. https://www.sohu.com/a/128197806_355251.

Underhill, Anne P., and Junko Habu. 2006. Early communities in East Asia: Economic and sociopolitical organization at the local and regional levels. In *Archeology of Asia*, ed. Miriam T. Stark, 134–140. Malden, MA: Blackwell Publishing.

Xiong, Victor Cunrong. 2009. *Historical dictionary of medieval China*. Lanham, MD: Scarecrow Press.

Yang, Zihui. 1995. [*China's historical population statistical data research*]. Beijing: Reform Press. 楊子慧. 中國歷代人口統計資料研究.北京: 改革出版社.

Zhang, Shunan. 2021. [The 2020 per capita income list of residents in various provinces: Shanghai is the richest, and it has risen sharply]. Finance.people.com. 22 January. 张澍楠. 2020年各省份居民人均收入榜: 上海最有钱, 这地涨得猛. http://finance.people.com.cn/n1/2021/0122/c1004-32008733.html.

Chapter 22
Macao Special Administrative Region (SAR)

Abstract Having been part of the Chinese empire since at least the Qin dynasty (ca. 200 BCE), the ancient history and human settlements of Macao are quite similar to that of Hong Kong, to include their administration before European occupation. Although having been returned to Chinese authority from Portugal in 1999, Macao still maintains its old character from early mercantile trade between Europe, Japan, and China, beginning in the sixteenth century, and becoming quite brisk during the 1800s. In addition to being a transit point for various goods to include opium, Macao also served as a transit point for "coolie" labor from China to other countries, many such laborers being refugees from the tumultuous Taiping Rebellion (ca. 1860). Macao also developed a notorious reputation as a free-wheeling center for vice, chiefly gambling but also prostitution. Major immigration waves later occurred during the Sino-Japanese war (1937–1945), the vast majority being Cantonese. Today, Macao has a gross domestic product (GDP) of about USD $54 billion (2021), and a per capita income ($36,350), three times that of Shanghai City.

E. Croddy, *China's Provinces and Populations*,
https://doi.org/10.1007/978-3-031-09165-0_22

Macao (Macau) Special Administrative Region (澳門特別行政區 *àomén tèbié xíngzhèngqū*): Abbreviation 澳 (*ào*) (Fig. 22.1)

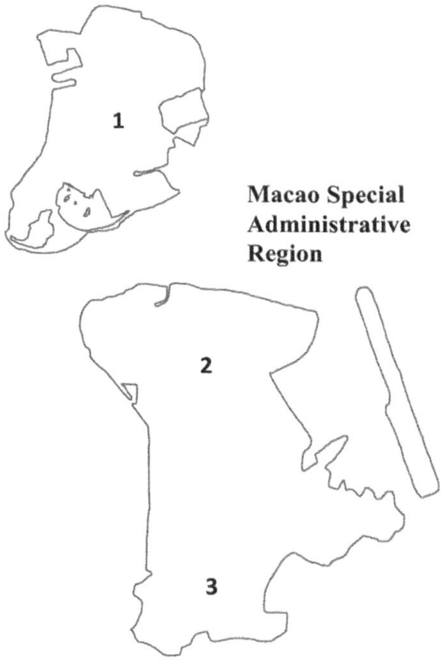

Macao Population (2011)

1. Macao Peninsula (Península de Macau澳門半島 *àomén bàndǎo*)	**469,009**
2. Taipa island (Ilha da Taipa氹仔島 *dànzǎi dǎo*)	**78,497**
3. Coloane (Ilha Coloane路環島 *lùhuán dǎo*)	**4,262**
***Water areas**	**735***

Fig. 22.1 Macao (Portugese: Região Administrativa Especial de Macau) administrative regions. (Drawn by the author, after People's Republic of China, Ministry of Civil Affairs. (MCA 2020))

Macao: General Impressions

A picturesque admixture of Portugal and China. "Las Vegas east," where just about anything goes. Macao is all at once famous and notorious, chiefly for its highly developed gambling industry, as well as its *laissez-faire* attitude towards the sex trade (prostitution is illegal, although running a house of prostitution is technically not).

Macao has officially been part of the People's Republic of China (PRC) since 1999, governed in the form of the Macao Special Administrative Region (SAR) Macao (formerly 'Macau'). Measuring just 29.2 square kilometers, formed by Taipa (氹仔[1] *dàngzǎi*) in the north, Coloane (路環 *lùhuán*) to its immediate south, and an isthmus made from reclaimed landfill, Cotai (路氹城 *lùdàngchéng*), Macao is a densely-populated peninsula (20,800 people per square km).

Until his assassination in Malaysia by North Korean operatives, Macao had been home to the North Korean Kim family's Kim Jong-nam, eldest son of Kim Jong-il.

Macao Prehistory

Excavations at Macao's Hac Sa Wan site (黑沙灣遺址 *hēishāwān yízhǐ*) on Coloane Island (路環 *lùhuán*) revealed pre-Han petroglyphs (similar in some ways to those of the Hawaiian variety), as well as painted pottery dating back to ca. 4500–3500 BCE (Bowman 2000).

When incorporated under the Qin dynasty (ca. 220 BCE), the area in and around Macao was part of the Nanhai Prefecture, Panyu County (南海郡番禺縣 *nánhǎi jùn pānyù xiàn*). Later in 420 CE, it belonged to Xinhui Prefecture, Fengle County (新會郡封樂縣 *xīnhuì jùn fēnglè xiàn*). During the Sui dynasty (ca. 600 CE), Macao fell under a new administered area and name, Bao'an County (寶安縣 *bǎoān xiàn*), and changing again under the Tang (757 CE), this time sub-ordinated to Donguan County (東莞縣 *dōngguǎn xiàn*).

In the time of the Song dynasty (1152 CE), Macao was part of Xiangshan (香山 *xiāngshān*, later 中山 *zhōngshān* in modern times), but was then mostly unpopulated. Small villages eventually grew in number, the locals being involved mostly in fishing and some agriculture (Hao 2011). By the thirteenth Century, what later became Macao (or the later Qing Dynasty 澳門 *àomén*, "Inlet Gate") was then called Haojing'ao (壕鏡澳 *háojìngào*): "Channel Mirror Inlet." Other variants going back into history included: 濠江 *háojiāng*; 海鏡 *hǎijìng*; 鏡海 *jìnghǎi*; and 梳

[1] 氹 = 凼.

打埠 *shūdăbù*. The first people to populate Macao in large numbers were likely the boat (Tanka 疍家 *dànjiā*) people, who had immigrated from Guangdong and Fujian during the Ming Dynasty (ca. 1400).

The name "Macao" itself, tradition has it, comes from the corruption of the name of a temple, Mage Miao (媽閣廟 *māgé miào*), or in Cantonese Ma Kok Miu (*ma5gok3miu6*). In ways that echo how Hong Kong got its name, the Portuguese who had first landed on Macao asked locals where they were, and happened to have been near the Mage Temple. Using the local dialect, its residents responded with "Ma Kok," and heard by the foreigners as something along the lines of "Macao." A competing theory is that Macao was once called "Ama Wan" during the Ming dynasty (阿媽灣 *āmāwān*), which was pronounced in the local patois as "Ah-Ma Gao," but the former explanation (i.e., Ma Kok) has the most support (Pletcher 2011).

Modern History of Macao

Paula Morais breaks down the recent history of Macao into five basic historical stages (Morais 2014):

1557–1849: "Chinese Imperial Territorial Concession".
1849–1887: "Restricted Autonomy".
1987–1999: "Portuguese Territory in Chinese Land".
1999–2009: "Special Administrative Region of the People's Republic of China (PRC").
2009–2049: "PRC Mega-City: Macao-Zhuhai metropolitan area".

Enter Portugal

The culture, architecture, language, and general atmosphere of Macao today is linked to mid-sixteenth century Portuguese influence, chiefly through its role in trading goods between Japan and China. For Portugal, since having seized Goa in India (1510), it was necessary to find a navigable trade route between Melaka (Malacca) and Japan. For if Goa was the center of Portuguese colonial operations, the establishment of a Portuguese trading center on Macao would also allow Christian missionaries a stepping stone into China's interior, using the peninsula-island as a forward operating base. This was particularly the case of the Society of Jesus (Jesuits), who were to utilize Macao as a communications center for its missions worldwide (Laven 2011).

Marriage of Convenience

In ca. 1514, the Portuguese merchant Jorge Alvares captained the first boat to set anchor in the Pearl River (aka Canton River). Two years later, the Italian Rafael Perestrello, sailing from Malacca, reportedly floating on a Chinese Junk, became the second known European to sail to the mouth of the Pearl (Canton) River, albeit no further (Corner 1853). But China, ever suspicious of foreigners, was not keen on Portuguese (or any other Europeans) setting foot on Ming empire soil. Portuguese merchants and marine operators, their reputations known by now well in advance, did not always acquit themselves with intercultural sensitivity, as we have already seen in their activities in and around Canton (Guangzhou). Given their profession that involved high-risk navigation around the world, dealing with sometimes hostile receptions throughout all of Asia, such men of adventurous mercantilism in the sixteenth century were not the retiring type, nor easily deterred by just saying "no" (in any language). And Southern Chinese xenophobia towards Westerners was especially intense, as the Jesuit Matteo Ricci would soon encounter, making his missionary work all the more challenging (Laven 2011).

Some inroads had been made along the Chinese southeast coast to facilitate trade with Portugal. One island, Shuangyu (雙嶼 *shuāng yǔ*), located of the coast of Zhejiang province, was among the earliest. In 1524, a mélange of local Chinese smugglers, Portuguese and Japanese merchants, traded on this island which they referred to as "Liampó," a misnomer, as Portugal mistook this area to be synonymous with the larger Ningbo area. The various products hustled through Shuangyu included those typical of sixteenth century East Asia trade with Europe (and was prohibited to be sold to and from China at that time): Ivory, pearls, rhino horns, spices, precious stones, silk, porcelain, tea, saltpetre, silk, cotton, and state-of-the-art "Portuguese (佛狼機 *fólángjī*) Cannon" This smuggling operation was essentially ended with a military assault by the Ming authorities in 1548 (Jing 2022).

More famously, Shangchuan island (上川島 *shàngchuān dǎo*), one of the largest in the Pearl River estuary, is located 9 kilometers off the coast of Guangdong Province. It was here, named by the Portuguese St. John (São João) Island, where one of the original founding Jesuits, Saint Francis Xavier, died of fever in 1552 while awaiting passage to mainland China proper. As evidence of its role as a proto-trade center, dated before Macao became Portugal's main entrepot for trade with China, shards of Ming-dynasty porcelain were unearthed on Shangchuan island by the Guangdong Provincial Research Institute of Cultural Relics and Archaeology in 2016. Some of these ceramics showed markings of Ming dynasty vintage (大明嘉靖年製 *dàmíng jiājìng niánzhì*), that is: "Great Ming; Jiajing reign (ca. 1522–1566) manufactured" (Xiao 2020).

Also in the Guangdong's Pearl River delta, Lampacau (浪白奧 làngbái'ào) served as a place for the trade of goods for the Portuguese. Its exact location and its name have been obscured by history, but was probably located in or near modern-day Jinwan District (金灣區 *jīnwān qū*), Zhuhai City. The Japanese historian Haneda Masashi (羽田正 *yǔtián zhèng*) tells us that Portugal transitioned to

Lampacau from Shangchuan in the 1554–1555 timeframe before moving on to a more permanent post in Macao (Haneda 2013).

Macao as Mercantile Center and Operating Base for Christian Missionaries in China

While still Chinese sovereign territory, subordinate to then Xiangshan County[2] (香山縣 *xiāngshān xiàn*), China allowed the operation of a Portuguese outpost on Macao in exchange for 500 taels of silver (weighing about 42 pounds), and, later, 515 taels of silver for yearly rent in return for Portugal's help in combatting piracy (Boland-Crewe and Lea 2002). By 1557, Macao had become the first European settlement in China (Bailey 2007). Macao's location near China (but sequestered from Chinese territory by a wall with guards) now served as the main trading post for Portugal (Spence 1984).

Key to the importance of Macao to the Portuguese was China's kibosh on its own direct trade with Japan. Serving as the middleman between Japan and China, Portuguese sailors and their mercantile firms took the risk on the high seas and treacherous, pirate-ridden shoals, making as much as 40% commission in the process (Spence 1984). Adding to Portugal's comparative advantage, China predominantly used silver ingot (tael, the Portuguese word via the Malaysian for the Chinese equivalent of a 兩 *liǎng* or 40 grams of silver) as currency, and was in much demand. Japan, for its part, had a supply of silver from its mines. On the other hand, the Japanese market much sought after Chinese silk, while Europeans also enjoyed porcelain, such as that produced in Jingdezhen, Jiangxi Province, and sold in Canton markets.

Matteo Ricci: Chosen for China

Having established themselves in Macao by 1563, the Society of Jesus had by 1579 built three churches and a school on Macao. It was also in 1579 that the Jesuit Michele Ruggieri had also taken up his post in Macao, having been given written instructions upon his landing to learn the official Chinese language used by the imperial court in Beijing. And, although Ruggieri has since been treated as a second-hand player in the Jesuit mission to China in favor of Matteo Ricci, it should be said that Ruggieri made considerable process in learning the difficult Chinese written language, even writing the first (if basic) Portuguese-Chinese dictionary (Liu 2011).

[2] Renamed Zhongshan island in 1925 in honor of Dr. Sun Yat-sen, i.e., Sun Zhongshan (孫中山 sūn zhōngshān).

Ruggieri's ability to communicate in Chinese when he made visits to Canton (Guangzhou) made him particularly successful in making the first, best impressions upon the local officials. He also brought gifts that were of enormous interest to the Chinese: clocks. Because the clockmaking craftsmen in China were decimated in the twelfth century, and with a burgeoning clock producing industry in Europe at the time of Ruggieri's mission, this could answer the high demand on the Chinese side for improvements to the moribund chronological technology they at hand. (Ironically, giving a clock to a Chinese person in recent times is considered gauche, as the homonym for clock 鐘 *zhōng* sounds like 終 *zhōng*, as in the "end" of a relationship).

As Ruggieri was conducting the all-important preparations for a mission in Chinese territory itself, Matteo Ricci (Chinese name 利瑪竇 *lì mǎdòu*), a highly-educated Jesuit born (1552) in Macerata, Italy, had arrived in Macao in 1582. In addition to having a hospital and a charity organization in place, by this time Macao had a population of at least 5000, including 400–500 Portuguese, all men, as well as nearly four hundred Chinese families (Laven 2011). In 1583, building upon Ruggieri's steady preparation and diplomatic efforts, both he and the newly arrived missionary, Matteo Ricci, were able to get permission to establish a mission residence in Guangdong province the next year.

Macao: 17th Through Nineteenth Centuries

In 1601, Dutch troops unsuccessfully attempted to occupy Macao. Following the war between the Portuguese and the Dutch, the local westerners (including Japanese) built ramparts and establish cannon positions to improve their defenses:

> In 1612, three of the principal men endeavored at Canton, to demonstrate the necessity of walling and fortifying the place, because the Dutch were enemies of both Portuguese and Spain (Ljungstedt 1835).

On 27 November 1623, the Secretary of Macao, Diogo Caldeira Rego, wrote that, in order to strengthen Macao.

> We have worked hard on the Chinese and have bribed ("bountiful presents") them again. Then a few Chinese officials came to inspect the enemy's [i.e., Dutch] fleet and the dead bodies left on the battlefield. They also took the heads of a few dead people to Guangzhou to prove that we were building the walls only to defend the city… In more than a year, a few sections of a long wall were completed. Each section is about two meters long and four meters high. And forts and battlements are above them. Thus almost all of the land is completely encircled (Tang 2015).

During this uneasy relationship between China and the Europeans, the Chinese generally maintained a reluctant and suspicious attitude. The historian Zhidong Hao put most succinctly, that in dealing with western barbarians, "China's strategy in dealing with the Westerners was to keep them as far away as possible." (Hao 2011).

However, the Portuguese possessed, *inter alia*, advanced technology in firearms that the Chinese found attractive, leading to the building of a cannon foundry on Macao (ca. 1625):

> The King of Cochin China sent, in 1651, twenty-five peculs of copper for a large gun to be cast at Macao, where the art was still practiced in the beginning of the eighteenth century. Thus, when China allowed the Portuguese to set foot on their sacred soil, Macao was remote enough to maintain their distance, and still be close enough to facilitate trade with neighboring Canton (Ljungstedt 1835).

The Kangxi emperor (d. 1722) granted foreigners access to mainland Chinese port facilities in 1685. Later (1733), the Yongzheng emperor (13 December 1678 – 8 October 1735) wanted Macao to be the exclusive sole point of foreign trade entry, but he died (1735) before this could be fully implemented. Nonetheless, by 1729, the Portuguese were shipping a variety of goods to include opium through Macao (Hao 2011). By 1744, a governing entity was established called the Macao Coast and Military Authority (澳門防軍民同知 *àomén fángjūn míntóngzhī*), put in charge over Panyu, Shunde, Dongguan and Xiangshan. And, of some interest, the year 1805 marked the first use of western-styled smallpox vaccine (vaccinia) in China, starting with Macao, and subsequently was distributed to the rest of the mainland.

Trade in Macao was such in ca. 1835 that the locals benefited from revenues that drew from commerce:

> The inhabitants of Macao, are burdened neither with a poll tax, nor with taxes on houses, windows,[3] etc. The resources of which the government can dispose, for meeting the expenses, and paying the debt of the city, are all derived from duties, paid on goods, imported principally in ships, belonging to Macao: no export duty is paid by the merchants (Ljungstedt 1835).

The Opium War (1840s) and Treaty of Nanjing led to European imposition upon Chinese sovereignty as reparations. Portugal followed along in this vein, and sensing political weakness on the part of the Qing government, declared Macao a free port in 1845. Macao eventually expelled its remaining Chinese officials, and the territory was formally handed over to Portugal in 1887. By this time, Macao had already become a key port for trade in coolie labor, made up of many unfortunate Chinese who were out of options to make a living. Especially during and after the tumult of the Taiping Revolution (1850–1865), Chinese refugees often traveled through Macao to find safety in other countries. Those Chinese immigrants who sought a living in Macao usually could only make subsistence wages doing menial labor, such as operating rickshaws:

> The rickshaw driver has to pay a lot of rent, a grueling profession he undergoes. Daily he can't make up for his own costs, and with the taxes he has to pay, he's barely standing, unable to keep his belly full (Hao 2011).

[3] Refers to old Europe practice of taxing properties based on the number of windows; this led to the construction of very large windows (or bricking over smaller ones) to reduce their overall number just to avoid this tax.

Macao and the Gambling Industry

Chinese history is replete with spasms of popularized gambling, and when-ever it reached its apogee the government (or court) often promulgated laws to punish this vice. For example, during the Warring States (476 BCE – 221 BCE), the Kingdom of Qi (齊國 *qíguó*), modern day Shandong province, outlawed gambling for the purpose of maintaining the virtue of its high-ranking officials as well as improving the morality of the commoner.

In nineteenth century Macao, however,

> [T]here's myriad gambling, with Fan Tan games, and the collectors take their cut. On the street "Rua Das Estalagens" people mill about like ants, every house lit up through the night (Hao 2011).

With the collapse of the Qing dynasty and the Chinese revolution in 1911, Macao continued to maintain a legal environment for gambling, and this continued following the communist takeover of the mainland (minus Macao). As of 2000, following its handover to China by Portugal (1999), half of Macao SAR's governmental revenues came from taxation on gambling (Boland-Crewe and Lea 2002).

Macao and the Sex Trade

In the late seventeenth century, Macao had also established a reputation as a sex workers' oasis, along with seamstresses, mistresses, and other vendors of the female persuasion. Indeed, Macao, with some 16,000 women out of a population of no more than 20,000, was sometimes referred to as the "City of Women." In the late 1800s, the sex trade in Macao was typified in the following way:

> Macao has any number of houses with prostitutes, hanging around the doors smiling, all dolled up. They swap out their clothing, so you might mistake these brothels for dance halls (Zheng and Wan 2014).

When prostitution was made *de jure* legal in Macao, not surprisingly, its brothels continued to prosper. In the late 1930s, there were some 120 houses of ill-repute and approximately 15,000 sex workers in Macao. The sex trade continues today in Macao, raising concerns about human trafficking. According to the U.S. State Department in 2014:

> The Macao Special Administrative Region of the People's Republic of China is primarily a destination and, to a much lesser extent, a source territory for women and children subjected to sex trafficking and forced labor. Sex trafficking victims originate primarily from mainland China; many are from inland Chinese provinces and travel to the border province of Guangdong in search of better employment. Some are from Mongolia, Vietnam, Ukraine, and Russia. Many trafficking victims fall prey to false advertisements for jobs in casinos and other legitimate employment in Macao, but upon arrival are forced into prostitution.

Foreign and mainland Chinese women are sometimes passed to local organized crime groups, held captive, and forced into sexual servitude. Victims are some-times confined in massage parlors and illegal brothels, where they are closely monitored, forced to work long hours, have their identity documents confiscated, and are threatened with violence. Chinese, Russian, and Thai criminal syndicates are believed to be involved in recruiting women for Macao's commercial sex industry. Children are reportedly subjected to sex trafficking on the premises of casinos in Macao (US State Department 2014).

Populations of Macao Through History

As of 1621, Macao had a population of approximately 8300, with ethnic Chinese making up about 7500 (Deng 1999). All Catholic missions tried to maintain missions in Macao because Portugal held and adhered to the protectorate of its missions in Asia, and, crucially, because Macao played a special role for missionaries seeking entry into China. In the first half of the seventeenth century, Japan had outlawed Christianity, leading many Japanese Christians to move to Macao. At about this time, Macao had a population that included 20,000 Chinese, 2000 Portuguese, as well as 5000 slaves (mostly of African descent).

In 1743, the population in Macao had fallen to 5500, and of those 3500 were Portuguese citizens. By 1825, a contemporary observer estimated there were 22,500 people in Macao, 8000 of these being Chinese (Cremer, 1991). Five years later, Macao's registered population was about 30,000, Portuguese citizens making up 4049 of that number. As for the exclusively Portuguese population, a tabulation from 1834 (total of 5093 across three church parishes) not only revealed their demographics (see Table 22.1) but also the numbers of slaves in their employ:

From 1868 to 1872, the average population of Macao was about 12,000, with 20,000 at its peak. By the early 1900s, Macao had 75,000 people. In 1910, Macao had a total population of 75,866 (Deng 1999). During the Sino-Japanese War period (1937–1945), refugees poured into Macao, bringing the population up to 240,000 in 1939 from about 140,000 the previous year. By 1940, the population of Macao had ballooned to 400,000 (Song 1999). Throughout World War II, due to it having been made neutral territory in the midst of the Sino-Japanese War, so many refugees fled to Macao its population swelled to 600,000 (Pletcher 2011).

Table 22.1 Portuguese population (1834) by Parish, and slaves in each. (Ljungstedt 1834)

Church Parish	White men	White women	Male slaves	Female slaves
Parish of St. Peter	660	1,057	147	383
Parish of St. Lawrence	547	834	257	305
Parish of St. Anthony	280	415	65	143

Modern Macao

In 1951, Portugal formally made Macao its overseas territory. On 25 July 1952, PLA troops clashed with Portuguese troops, resulting in casualties on each side. In 1970, Macao had a population of 249,000, and shrank down to 242,000 by 1981 (Veek et al. 2011). In April 1987, Portugal and the PRC government agreed to the return of Macao to mainland China in 1999, which was finally made official on 20 December of that year. (Also, according to that same agreement, the spelling of Macau was officially changed to Macao.) By this time, the Macao Special Autonomous Region (SAR) had a population of 437,455. China pledged to honor Macao's status as a Special Administrative Region (SAR) for 50 years, while defense and foreign relations were relegated to Beijing. Compared to the transfer of Hong Kong to the PRC in 1997, Macao's return to China was met with much less fanfare. In 2000, Macao SAR had a population of 445,000, and the northern peninsular area was considered to have been the most densely populated region in the world, with 120,000 persons per kilometer.

In ca. 2007, with a population of 465,000, more than 95% of these were Cantonese in origin (Bailey, 2007). In 2008, Macao had 552,000 people; while another source holds 549,000 in that same year (Veek et al. 2011). According to yet another, in 2013 Macao's population was estimated to be 598,200 (Pletcher 2011). Based on official Macao statistical and survey bureau, in 2014 Macao's population was 636,200, and in 2015 increased to 646,800, and an estimated population of 682,500 in first quarter 2021 (GMSAR 2021). (Because Macao and Hong Kong are not traditional subordinate entities to mainland China, there are no *hukou* population data for either SAR.) Population data for Macao from 1993 to 2021 are shown below (Table 22.2).

Table 22.2 Macao population: 1993–2021. (GMSAR 2021)

1993	390,000	
1994	403,600	
1995	415,000	
1996	415,200	
1997	419,400	
1998	425,200	
1999	429,600	
2000	431,500	
2001	436,300	
2002	440,500	
2003	446,700	
2004	462,600	
2005	484,300	
2006	509,900	
2007	531,800	

(continued)

Table 22.2 (continued)

1993	390,000	
2008	543,100	
2009	533,300	
2010	540,600	
2011	552,503	
2012	582,000	
2013	607,500	
2014	636,200	
2015	646,800	
2016	650,834	
2017	653,100	
2018	667,400	
2019	679,600	
2020	683,100	
2021	682,500	

No doubt due to the COVID-19 pandemic and its impact on the travel industry, Macao's gross domestic production (GDP) fell 3.5% in 2020, but made gains in 2021 (6.0%), and should reach USD $53.7 billion. Per capita income in Macao in 2020 was USD $36,350, below that of Hong Kong, but far and away greater than any of China's 31 provinces and major cities, and more than three times than that of Shanghai (WDA 2021).

References

Bailey, Steven K. 2007. *Strolling in Macau: A visitor's guide to Macau, Taipa, and Coloane*. San Francisco: Things Asian Press.

Boland-Crewe, Tara, and David Lea, eds. 2002. *The territories of the People's Republic of China*. London: Europa Publications.

Bowman, John, ed. 2000. *Columbia chronologies of Asian history and culture*. New York: Columbia University Press.

Corner, Julia. 1853. *China pictorial, descriptive, and historical: With some account of Ava and the Burmese, Siam and Anam*. London: Henry G. Bohn.

Cremer, Rolf. 1991. *Macau: City of commerce and culture, continuity and change*. University of California: API Press.

Deng, Kaisong. 1999. [*History of Macao (1840–1949)*]. Zhuhai: Zhuhai Press. 邓开颂. 澳门历史: (1840–1949). 珠海: 珠海出版社.

Government of Macao Special Administrative Region (GMSAR), Department of the Census. 2020. 澳門特別行區政府統計暨普查局. https://www.dsec.gov.mo/zh-MO/.

Government of Macao Special Administrative Region, (GMSAR), Department of the Census. 2021. [*Time Series Database, Population Estimates, Birth and Death Statistics, Marriage and Divorce Statistics*]. 時間序列資料庫, 人口估計、出生及死亡統計、結婚及離婚統計. https://www.dsec.gov.mo/ts/#!/step2/PredefinedReport/zh-MO/1.

Haneda, Masashi. 2013. [*History as seen from the high seas.*] 海から見た歴史. 東京大学出版会. Tokyo: Tokyo University Press.

Hao, Zhidong. 2011. *Macau history and society*. Hong Kong: Hong Kong University Press.

Jing Ming. 2022. 16th Century's Liuheng Shangyu harbor. *Jinri Putuo,* 12 April. 靖茗. 16世纪的六横双屿港. 今日普陀. http://paper.cztvcloud.com/jrpt/pc/content/202204/12/content_220857.html#.

Laven, Mary. 2011. *Mission to China: Matteo Ricci and the Jesuit encounter with the east*. London: Faber and Faber.

Liu, Yu. 2011. The true pioneer of the Jesuit China mission: Michele Ruggieri. *History of Religions*. May. 50(4): 362–383.

Ljungstedt, Sir Andrew. 1835. *An historical sketch of the Portuguese settlements in China, and of the Roman Catholic church and mission in China*. Boston: James Munroe & Co.

Morais, Paula. 2014. Macao's urban identity question, 1557-1999/2009. In *Macao – The formation of a global city*, ed. C.X. George Wei, 156–185. New York: Routledge.

Pletcher, Kenneth, ed. 2011. *The geography of China: Sacred and historic places*. New York: Britannica Educational Publishing.

Song, Shichang. 1999. [*Macao's spring-autumn*]. Beijing: China Taxation Publishing House. 宋世昌. 澳门春秋. 北京: 中国税务出版社.

Spence, Jonathan D. 1984. *The memory palace of Matteo Ricci*. New York: Elisabeth Sifton Books/Viking.

Tang Kaijian. 2015. Japanese Christians in Macau and the Guangdong government's response. In *Setting Off from Macau: Essays on Jesuit History during the Ming and Qing Dynasties*, ed. Kaijian Tang, 90–128. Boston: Brill.

US Department of State. 2014. *Trafficking in Persons Report: Macau.*

Veeck, Gregory, Clifton W. Pannell, Christopher J. Smith, and Youqin Huang. 2011. *China's geography: Globalization and the dynamics of political, economic, and social change*. 2nd ed. New York: Rowman & Littlefield.

World Data Atlas (WDA). 2021. https://knoema.com/atlas/Macau/GDP-per-capita. Accessed 19 Sept 2021.

Xiao, Dashun. 2020. Blue-and-white porcelain on Shangchuan Island: Chinese-Portuguese trade during the Ming dynasty. *The Newsletter* (International Institute for Asian Studies). Summer. No. 86. https://www.iias.asia/the-newsletter/article/blue-and-white-porcelain-shangchuan-island-chinese-portuguese-trade-during.

Zheng, Victor, and Po-San Wan. 2014. *Gambling dynamism: The Macao miracle*. New York: Springer.

Chapter 23
Ningxia

Abstract Archeology of the Hetao Culture shows early inhabitants of Ningxia having lived there at least 25,000 years ago. The Ningxia Hui Autonomous Region is named for its well-known Hui (Moslem) minority in this western province, going back to the Tang dynasty. While not the only province to have significant numbers of the Hui minority, as of 2015 Ningxia had the largest number (2,400,000), forming about a third of Ningxia's total population. Historically, the region of modern Ningxia included the kingdom of the Tanguts, who, among other things, had an even more complex written language than Chinese. Ningxia is also near the bottom of mainland China's 31 provinces and cities in terms of gross domestic product (GDP), and ranks 21st in the same field for per capita income (USD $4000). One area in which Ningxia is looking to boost its economy is wine making, with a goal of producing some USD $3 billion in wine for export by 2035.

E. Croddy, *China's Provinces and Populations*,
https://doi.org/10.1007/978-3-031-09165-0_23

Ningxia Hui Autonomous Region (寧夏回族自治區 *níngxià huízú zìzhìqū*): Abbreviation 寧 (*níng*) (Fig. 23.1)

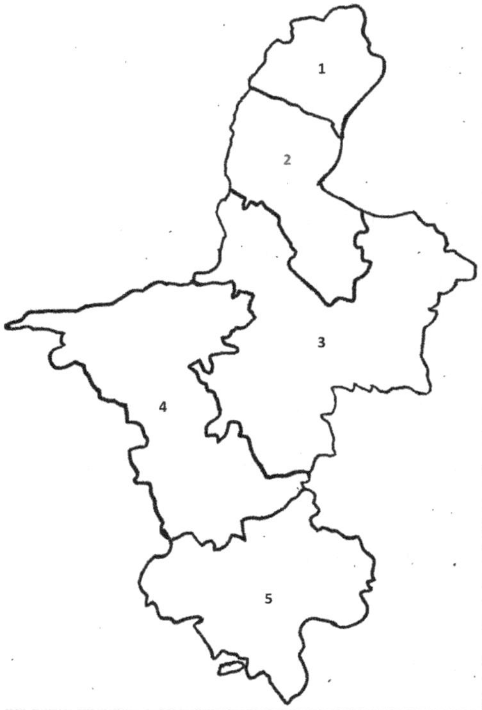

Ningxia Population (2020)

1.	**Shizuishan City**	**751,389**
2.	**Yinchuan City**	**2,859,074**
3.	**Wuzhong City**	**1,382,713**
4.	**Zhongwei City**	**1,067,336**
5.	**Guyuan City**	**1,142,142**

Fig. 23.1 Ningxia Hui Autonomous Region major cities (provincial capital: Yinchuan City). (Drawn by the author, after People's Republic of China, Ministry of Civil Affairs. (MCA 2020))

Ningxia: General Impressions

Traces of the Neolithic Hetao (river) culture (河套文化 *hétào wénhuà*) and the ancient silk road are found in Ningxia, particularly in its capital, Yinchuan City (銀川市 yínchuān shì), where the Tangut Empire (Xixia 西夏 *xīxià*, 1038–1227) once ruled "at the headrest of Qingshan mountain, with its feet resting on the Yellow river." (Shang-Ch'i 2017).[1] It is also where China and Islam share in their cultural history. Ningxia Hui Autonomous Region, the smallest of China's provinces in terms of its geographical area, is China's only provincial-level entity named for its Hui (Muslim) minority. The ancestry of the ethnic minority known as Hui (回 *huí*) goes back to the Tang dynasty. The Hui are the descendants of Arabic, Persian and Central Asians who, while communicating back and forth along the Silk Road, intermarried with Chinese. China previously referred to Muslims (and, at times, practicing Jews and other foreigners during the Yuan) as Huihui (回回 *huí huí*). Having lived in various regions of China, by the Ming dynasty Chinese Muslims (Hui) ultimately became a distinct group. The surname Ma (馬 *mǎ*) is often found among Chinese Muslims, owing to the previously transcribed (and subsequently shortened) name of Sheikh Muhammad (馬合麻沙亦黑 *mǎhémá shāyìhēi*). There are over ten-and-a-half million Hui across China, distributed throughout the northeast (2,200,000), central (1,700,000), and western regions (6,650,000), the latter representing 63% of the total Hui minority population. Of the western provinces, Ningxia has the largest concentration of Hui in China (over 2,400,000) (NPG 2015).

Other Chinese provinces with significant Hui populations include.

- Gansu (1,260,000)
- Xinjiang (980,000)
- Henan (960,000)
- Yunnan (834,000)
- Hebei (700,000)
- Shandong (572,000)

There are also an estimated additional 536,000 ethnic Hui distributed among other areas in mainland China. In Beijing's Niujie subdistrict (牛街街道 *niújiē jiēdào*), for example, this one community is home to about 200,000 ethnic Hui.

Prehistory: Hetao Culture (河套文化 *hétào wénhuà*)

Representing the Neolithic Hetao culture, the Shuidonggou (水洞溝 *shuǐdònggōu*) Paleolithic site in Shuidongcun Village (水洞溝村 *shuǐdònggōu cūn*), Linhe Town (臨河鎮 *línhé zhèn*) has been studied for nearly a century. The Jesuit and paleontologist Pierre Teilhard de Chardin originally published his analytical findings of

[1] "頭枕青山, 腳依黃河" *tóuzhěn qīngshān, jiǎoyī huánghé*.

sediment layers at Shuidonggou in 1925. Based on these and other excavated specimens, archeologists believe hunter-gatherers ("Hetao Man") in the Shuidonggou region were active some 24,000 to 29,000 years ago, and a more permanent human occupation was present there about 5–9 thousand years ago. It is hypothesized that during the intervening years of the last glacial maximum, approximately 22,000 years before present, local animals and plants were insufficient for continuous human inhabitation (Gao et al. 2008).

Ningxia in the Zhou, Warring States, and the Yuan Dynasty

Guyuan City's (固原市 *gùyuán shì*) Yanglang (楊郎 *yangláng*) burial site revealed hundreds of gold, silver, iron, bronze. and bone objects of the Eastern Zhou (770–221 BCE) period, while also showing similarities with Xiongnu (匈奴 *xiōngnú*) styles found in Ordos (鄂爾多斯 *è'ěrduōsī*), Inner Mongolia. Dated to the Warring States-era (ca. 475 BCE), horse sacrifice and other northern Eurasian nomadic traditions were also found in Zhongning County (中寧縣 *zhōngníng xiàn*). (Di Cosmo 1999). Evidence also shows that, in ca. 220 BCE, modern-day Ningxia inhabitants utilized man-made canals to divert water from the Yellow River (Huanghe). (Hsieh and Hsieh 1995).

Ningxia province itself ("peaceful Xia," so named by the Yuan following the Mongol invasion) has its origins in the Xixia (西夏 *xīxià*) Kingdom (1038–1227) of the Tanguts, ruling an expanse encompassing modern-day Gansu, Inner Mongolia and Yinchuan. Before then, during the sixth century CE, a collection of nomads collectively known as the Qiang (羌 *qiāng*) also lived in these western regions.

Xumishan Grottoes

Spanning a time period between ca. 400 and 900 CE, a series of monks and specialized sculptors carved out caves at the Xumishan Grottos (須彌山窟 *xūmíshān kū*). Visible there at great distance is a spectacular sitting Buddha statue standing 20.6 meters (nearly 68 feet) high, hewn into the northern base of the Xumi hillside in the Liupanshan (六盤山 *liùpánshān*) mountain range, Guyuan City. With 162 rooms of various sizes carved into the rock, and over a thousand statues ensconced therein, Xumishan was named after the Sanskrit "Mount Sumeru," the Buddhist concept of a spiritual center of the universe. Having undergone extensive decrepitude over the centuries, including damage from the Haiyuan (海原 *hǎiyuán*) earthquake in 1920, only about ten percent of the caves are in decent shape (Garrity 2009). Some desultory restoration has been done since the 1980s, but it has been haphazard and difficult. Recently (April 2020), work was underway to carry out basic restoration for, among other areas, over 185 square meters of cave murals (*Fanhua* 2020).

The Tanguts

One of the Qiang (羌 *qiāng*) clans was named by the Chinese Dangxiang (黨項), or Dangxiangqiang (黨項羌 *dǎngxiàng qiāng*). The name "Tangut" probably has similar provenance in the name "Dang," although its exact etymology is unclear. Nonetheless, the related Tanguts were a Tibeto-Burmese speaking people who had migrated into northwest China during the Tang, forming the state that was ultimately referred to as the Xixia by the Chinese. The Tanguts called their homeland Minia: "The great state of high and white" (Wood 2002). The Xixia emperor, Li Yuanhao (李元昊 *lǐ yuánhào*), established the first capital in modern day Ningxia, Yinchuan City, then known as Xingqing Prefecture (興慶府 *xīngqìng fǔ*). Li Yuanhao (1004–1048) purportedly ordered the development of a complex Tangut script, and the Academician Yeliren Rong (野利仁榮 *yělìrén róng*) worked to improve upon the written form of Tangut language in ca. 1038.

Written Tangut was employed in conjunction with Chinese ideographs (漢子 *hànzi*), especially for official documents. Even by written Chinese standards, Tangut is a highly complicated script, and one wonders if it was purposefully designed to ensure widespread illiteracy for those without the wealth (and available time) to learn it. If we compare the Chinese numbers first line with the Tangut script for their equivalents, one gets the basic idea:

Chinese: 1, 2, 3, 4, 5, 6, 7, 8, 9, 10: 一 二 三 四 五 六 七 八 九 十
Tangut: 1, 2, 3, 4, 5, 6, 7, 8, 9, 10: 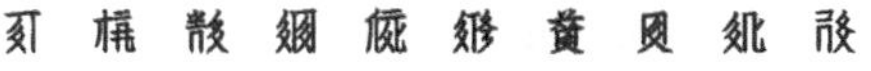

The Tangut script, although used throughout the Xixia state fell into desuetude after the Mongolian invasion. In fact, Chinggis Khan died in summer 1227 during the final campaign to ultimately vanquish the Xixia state (Mote 1999). During the subsequent Yuan dynasty, by 1287 the Mongols, under its administrative provincial (行省 *xíngshěng*) system, included a Ningxia Governmental Circuit (寧夏府路 *níngxià fǔlù*) within Gansu Province (甘肅行省 *gānsù xíngshěng*). Ningxia included within its borders the major prefectural city of Lingzhou (靈州 *língzhōu*), also known by its Mongolian name of Dormägai (朵兒蔑該 *duǒ'érmiègāi*).

By the Ming dynasty, as of 1582, the northern part of today's Ningxia Province was subordinate to Shaanxi Province, named Ningxiawei (寧夏衛 *níngxià wèi*), its north bordered by the "Front Ningxia" (寧夏前衛 *níngxià qiánwèi*), while its western and eastern borders were formed by middle Ningxia (寧夏中衛 *níngxià zhōngwèi*), and rear Ningxia (寧夏後衛 *níngxià hòuwèi*).

In the so-called Dungan Rebellion (Tongzhi Hui Revolt: 同治陝甘回變 *tóngzhì shǎngān huíbiàn*), an uprising that spanned Shaanxi and Gansu provinces, Hui military forces laid siege to Ningxia's Guyuan City in 1863. According to a modern Chinese source, estimates are that over 200,000 Han Chinese were ultimately killed. Months later, the Hui assaulted Ningxia prefecture (寧夏府 *níngxiàfǔ*), and some tens of thousands of Han Chinese were annihilated. In September 1869, the Muslim (Jahriyya) militarist Ma Hualong (馬化龍 *mǎ huàlóng*) attacked Lingzhou City (靈州城 *língzhōu chéng*), today's Lingwu City (靈武市 *língwǔ shì*), which resulted in a commensurate number of deaths. Ultimately defeated by the Qing military in November 1870, the imperial court regained control of the Ningxia area. As of 1882, during the Qing dynasty, Ningxia prefecture remained part of Gansu province.

Depopulation of Western China: 1820–1908

After years of poor agriculture yields, natural disasters (see Table 23.1 below), and the wars (above), there was a substantial drop in population throughout the western prefectures during the nineteenth century. Still a governmental prefecture then, Ningxia (寧夏府 *níngxià fŭ*) saw its population fall from 1,392,815 in 1820, and was reduced further down to no more than 231,000 persons by 1908.

Table 23.1 Natural disasters afflicting Ningxia and neighboring prefectural city-states. (Shi 2000)

Year	Types of weather-related disasters	Severity	Cities, prefectures affected
1821	Drought, hailstorms, flooding	Severe	27 prefectures and counties, including Gaolan (Gansu), Xining (Qinghai), Wuwei (Gansu), Ningxia
1822	Drought, hailstorms, frost	Severe	21 prefectures and counties, including Gaolan (Gansu), Xining (Qinghai), Gaotai (Gansu), Ningxia
1823	Flooding	Moderate	16 prefectures and counties, including Longxi and Lingtai (Gansu)
1824	Drought, hailstorms, flooding	Severe	29 prefectures and counties, including Gaolan, Hezhou (Gansu), Xining, and Wuwei
1825	Flooding and hailstorms	Moderate	25 prefectures and counties, including Gaolan, Ningxia, and Lingzhou
1826	Drought, hailstorms and floods	Moderate	13 prefectures and counties, including Gaolan, Ningxia, and Wuwei
1827	Drought, hailstorm, and floods	Moderate	14 prefectures and counties, including Gaolan, Ningxia and Guyuan (Ningxia)
1828	Hailstorms and floods	Moderate	12 prefectures and counties, including Qinzhou (Gansu), Xining, and Jiezhou (Gansu)
1829	Drought and floods	Moderate	15 prefectures and counties, including Gaolan, Nianbo (Qinghai), and Ningxia
1830	Hailstorms and floods	Moderate	16 prefectures and counties, incliuding Gaolan, Ningxia, and Nianbo
1831	Drought, hailstorms and floods	Severe	21 prefectures and counties, including Gaolan, Wuwei, Guyuan and Nianbo
1832	Drought, hailstorm and floods	Moderate	15 prefectures and counties, including Gaolan, Ningxia and Lingzhou
1833	Drought, hailstorms and insects	Severe	27 prefectures and counties, including Gaolan, Zhangye (Gansu), and Ningxia

(continued)

Table 23.1 (continued)

Year	Types of weather-related disasters	Severity	Cities, prefectures affected
1834	Drought, hailstorms and floods	Severe	27 prefectures and counties, including Gaolan, Pingliang (Gansu), Wuwei and Guyuan
1835	Drought, hailstorms, and floods	Severe	28 prefectures and counties, including Gaolan, Ningxia, and Nianbo
1836	Drought, hailstorm and floods	Severe	24 prefectures and counties, including Gaolan, Wuwei, Nianbo and Guyuan
1837	Drought, hailstorms and floods	Severe	23 prefectures and counties, including Gaolan, Ningxia, Nianbo and Guyuan
1838	Drought, hailstorms and floods	Severe	20 prefectures and counties, including Gaolan, Ningxia, Zhangye and Guyuan
1840	Drought, hailstorms and floods	Moderate	Prefectures and counties, including Gaolan, Ningxia and Guyuan
1841	Hailstorms and frost	Moderate	18 prefectures and counties, including Gaolan, Nianbo and Ningxia
1842	Drought, hailstorms and floods	Severe	26 prefectures and counties, including Gaolan, Nianbo, Wuwei and Ningxia
1843	Drought, hailstorms and floods	Severe	24 prefectures and counties, including Gaolan, Nianbo, Ningxia and Jingzhou (Gansu)
1844	Drought, hailstorms, high winds	Severe	21 prefectures and counties, including Gaolan, Xining, Ningxia and Guyuan
1846	Drought, hailstorms, and floods	Moderate	16 prefectures and counties, including Gaolan, Nianbo, and Guyuan
1847	Drought, floods and frost	Severe	21 prefectures and counties, including Gaolan, Zhangye, Ningxia and Nianbo
1848	Drought, hailstorms and floods	Severe	22 prefectures and counties, including Weiyuan (Gansu), Ningxia, Xining, and Jingzhou
1849	Hailstorms and floods	Moderate	21 prefectures and counties, including Gaolan, Wuwei, Ningxia and Jingzhou

Revolutionary Ningxia

In 1936, the Chinese Communist Party (CCP) established a Yuhai Hui Autonomous Government (豫海回民自治政府 *yùhǎi huímín zìzhì zhèngfǔ*) in the Tongxin (同心縣 *tóngxīn xiàn*) and Haiyuan county (海原縣 *hǎiyuán xiàn*) areas. After the founding of the People's Republic of China (PRC), a country-wide census (1953) counted 3,500,000 ethnic Hui in China, and, as a CCP-friendly history put it, the PRC leadership (Mao Zedong, Zhou Enlai, and Deng Xiaoping) were of a mind to consider larger autonomous entity for the Hui (Wang 2002). After borders were redrawn in Gansu Province (1956–7), on 25 October 1958, the PRC officially designated the Ningxia Hui Autonomous Region.

Ningxia and the Great Leap Forward (1958–61)

Among the regions most impacted during the Great Leap Forward (1958–62), Zhongning county (中寧縣 *zhōngníng xiàn*), with a population of about 11,000 in 1958, recorded 1801 deaths from hunger from the winter of 1959 to spring 1960. In addition, Zhongning county had 2605 cases of edema from starvation, and 8518 of its residents fled the country altogether. Ningxia recorded about 30,000 unnatural deaths from 1958–1962 (Yang 2007).

Ningxia Studios

Designed for both filming historical dramas as well as a tourist destination, the Zhenbeibao West Film Art Center (鎮北堡西部影城 *zhènběibǎo xībù yǐngchéng*), located in Xixia district Xixia District (西夏區 *xīxià qū*), Yinchuan City, Zhenbeibao features simulacra of various scenes throughout China's history. Rediscovered in the 1980s, Zhenbeibao was used for China's burgeoning film industry, and was where director Zhang Yimou filmed *Red Sorghum* (1987), based on the novel of the same name. Built around an abandoned fort (ca. 1500), the Zhenbei Film Center has three main sections depicting Ming dynasty (Mingcheng), Qing dynasty (Qingcheng), and Yinchuan Old Street (ZWFAC 2021). Not as well advertised is the section on the 1966–1976 Cultural Revolution with its "Cultural Revolution Alley" (文革大院 *wéngé dàyuàn*). No less an authoritative source than ChinaToday.com had this to say about Zhebeibao's homage to the Cultural Revolution:

The most popular—and morbid—of the studio sets is the Cultural Revolution Alley. Here, 1960s-style buildings are covered with slogans and murals. Gleeful tourists rent khaki uniforms, wield prop rifles, and stage mock "denunciation sessions," filmed by hired camera crews. Watching live reenactments of such distressing incidents can be disconcerting to the foreign traveler, but it does serve to give a glimpse into the conflicting mix of forgiveness, nostalgia, and amnesia that pervades modern China (*China Today* 2021).

Ningxia Economic and Population Trends

In the recent decade (2010–2020), Ningxia has remained third from the bottom of mainland China's 31 provinces and major cities, with a gross domestic product (GPD) of USD $45 billion in 2015, but rising to $61 billion in 2020. Its per capita income ranks 21st in the same field, just over $4000 in 2020 (Zhang 2021). Among the more promising sectors for foreign trade is the wine industry, as the Helan mountain region possesses excellent terroir for grapevines. By 2035, or so recent planning goes (May 2021), Ningxia hopes to produce over USD $3 billion in wine alone (Cheng 2021).

Albeit starting from a relatively small population, its growth in this area was rather dramatic, increasing more than 14% from 2010–2020 (see Table 23.2; Fig. 23.2).

Table 23.2 Ningxia Hui Autonomous Region population (residential 常住人口 *chángzhù rénkǒu*) data. (NBS 2021)

Cities and subordinate sectors, population (2020 census)	Subordinate district, city and county populations (2010)	Subordinate district, city and county populations (2020)
Yinchuan City 銀川市 ***yínchuān shì***	**1,993,088**	**2,859,074**
Xingqing District 興慶區 *xìngqìng qū*	678,306	808,282
Xixia District 西夏區 *xīxià qū*	329,310	449,559
Jinfeng District 金鳳區 *jīnfèng qū*	282,554	643,952
Yongning County 永寧縣 *yǒngníng xiàn*	218,260	321,618
Helan County 賀蘭縣 *hèlán xiàn*	222,981	341,507
Lingwu City 靈武市 *língwǔ shì*	261,677	294,156
Shizuishan City 石嘴山市 *shízuǐshān shì*	**725,482**	**751,389**
Dawukou District 大武口區 *dàwǔkǒu qū*	286,669	298,292
Huinong District 惠農區 *huìnóng qū*	185,803	178,891
Pingluo County 平羅縣 *píngluó xiàn*	253,010	274,206
Wuzhong City 吳忠市 ***wúzhōng shì***	**1,273,792**	**1,382,713**
Litong District 利通區 *lìtōng qū*	379,346	460,790
Hongsibu District 紅寺堡區 *hóngsìbù qū*	165,016	197,604
Yanchi County 鹽池縣 *yánchí xiàn*	146,560	159,209
Tongxin County 同心縣 *tóngxīn xiàn*	318,153	320,801
Qingtongxia City 青銅峽市 *qīngtóngxiá shì*	264,717	244,309
Zhongwei City 中衛市 ***zhōngwèi shì***	**1,080,832**	**1,067,336**
Shapotou District 沙坡頭區 *shāpōtóu qū*	378,606	399,796
Zhongning County 中寧縣 *zhōngníng xiàn*	312,921	344,022
Haiyuan County 海原縣 *hǎiyuán xiàn*	389,305	333,518
Guyuan City 固原市 ***gùyuán shì***	**1,228,156**	**1,142,142**
Yuanzhou District 原州區 *yuánzhōu qū*	411,854	471,329
Xiji County 西吉縣 *xījí xiàn*	354,321	315,827
Longde County 隆德縣 *lóngdé xiàn*	160,754	109,451
Jingyuan County 涇源縣 *jīngyuán xiàn*	101,026	85,023
Pengyang County 彭陽縣 *péngyáng xiàn*	200,201	160,512
Total	**6,301,350**	**7,202,654**

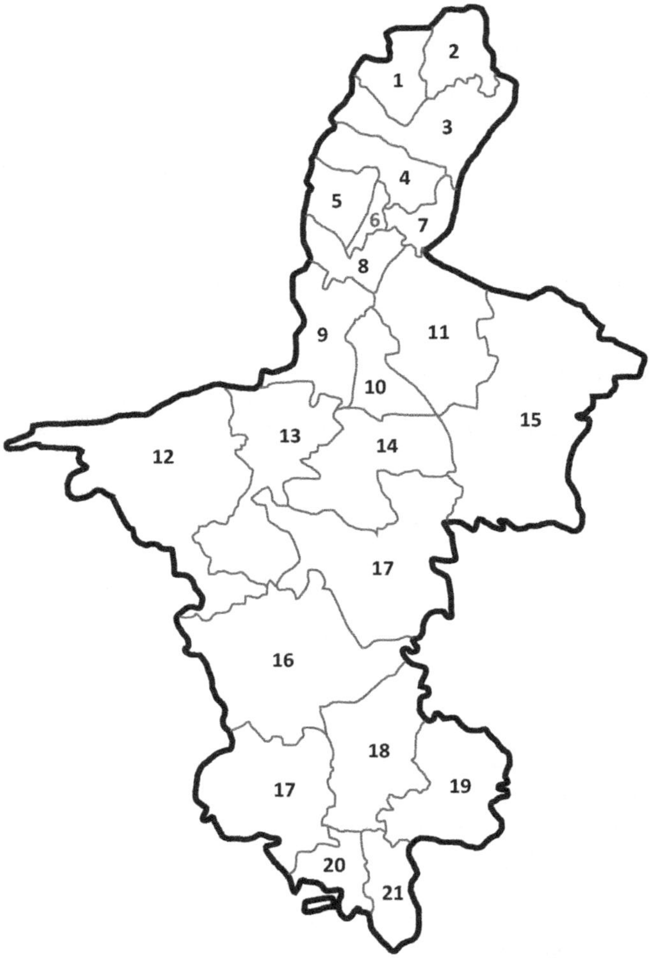

1. **Dawukou District**
2. **Huinong District**
3. **Pingluo County**
4. **Helan County**
5. **Xixia District**
6. **Jinfeng District**
7. **Xingqing District**
8. **Yongning County**
9. **Qingtongxia City**
10. **Litong District**
11. **Lingwu City**
12. **Shapotou District**
13. **Zhongning County**
14. **Hongsibu District**
15. **Yanchi County**
16. **Haiyuan County**
17. **Tongxin County**
18. **Yuanzhou District**
19. **Pengyang County**
20. **Longde County**
21. **Jingyuan County**

Fig. 23.2 Ningxia Hui Autonomous Region: subdistricts (Capital City Governmental Seat: Jinfeng District). (Drawn by the author, after People's Republic of China, Ministry of Civil Affairs. (MCA 2020))

Table 23.3 (below) shows the *hukou* (family registered) populations based on PRC Ministry of Civil Affairs data. (Districts listed directly under major cities are government seats, as are those in parentheses). One can compare these data with the census (usual residential populations based on 2010 and 2020 censuses in Table 23.2 (above):

Ningxia Hui Autonomous Region (寧 *níng*)

Provincial Capital: Yinchuan City

Table 23.3 Heilongjiang Province: permanent registered (戶籍人口 *hùjí rénkǒu*) populations (MCA 2020)

Name	Traditional	Simplified	Population (2012)	Population (2016)	Population (2020)	Area (Sq. Km)
Ningxia Hui Autonomous Region	寧夏回族自治區	宁夏回族自治区	6,430,000	6,590,000	6,840,000	66,400
Yinchuan City	銀川市	银川市	1,590,000	1,680,000	1,930,000	8874
Jinfeng District (Changcheng Zhonglu Subdistrict)	金鳳區 (長城中路街道)	金凤区 (长城中路街道)	200,000	230,000	370,000	345
Xingqing District (Yuhuanggebeijie Subdistrict)	興慶區 (玉皇閣北街街道)	兴庆区 (玉皇阁北街街道)	520,000	540,000	590,000	828
Xixia District (Helanshanxilu Subdistrict)	西夏區 (賀蘭山西路街道)	西夏区 (贺兰山西路街道)	230,000	240,000	240,000	1130
Lingwu City (Dongta Town)	靈武市 (東塔鎮)	灵武市 (东塔镇)	230,000	240,000	250,000	3846
Yongning County (Yanghe Town)	永寧縣 (楊和鎮)	永宁县 (杨和镇)	210,000	220,000	240,000	1194
Helan County (Xigang Town)	賀蘭縣 (習崗鎮)	贺兰县 (习岗镇)	200,000	210,000	240,000	1531
Shizuishan City	石嘴山市	石嘴山市	750,000	760,000	7,400,000	5208
Dawukou District (Renminlu Subdistrict)	大武口區 (人民路街道)	大武口区 (人民路街道)	270,000	270,000	260,000	1213
Huinong District (Beijie Subdistrict)	惠農區 (北街街道)	惠农区 (北街街道)	190,000	190,000	170,000	1361
Pingluo County (Chengguan Town)	平羅縣 (城關鎮)	平罗县 (城关镇)	290,000	30,000	310,000	2634
Wuzhong City	吳忠市	吴忠市	1,390,000	1,420,000	1,440,000	21,420
Litong District (Shengli Town)	利通區 (勝利鎮)	利通区 (胜利镇)	380,000	400,000	420,000	1415

(continued)

Table 23.3 (continued)

Name	Traditional	Simplified	Population (2012)	Population (2016)	Population (2020)	Area (Sq. Km)
Hongsibu District (Hongsibu Town)	紅寺堡區 (紅寺堡鎮)	红寺堡区 (红寺堡镇)	170,000	180,000	180,000	3523
Qingtongxia City (Yumin Subdistrict)	青銅峽市 (裕民街道)	青铜峡市 (裕民街道)	270,000	280,000	280,000	2438
Yanchi County (Huamachi Town)	鹽池縣 (花馬池鎮)	盐池县 (花马池镇)	170,000	170,000	170,000	8377
Tongxin County (Yuhai Town)	同心縣 (豫海鎮)	同心县 (豫海镇)	400,000	390,000	380,000	5667
Guyuan City	固原市	固原市	1,530,000	1,540,000	1,510,000	13,450
Yuanzhou District (Beiyuan Subdistrict)	原州區 (北塬街道)	原州区 (北塬街道)	450,000	460,000	470,000	3501
Xiji County (Jiqiang Town)	西吉縣 (吉強鎮)	西吉县 (吉强镇)	510,000	510,000	500,000	4000
Longde County (Chengguan Town)	隆德縣 (城關鎮)	隆德县 (城关镇)	180,000	180,000	170,000	1268
Jingyuan County (Xiangshui Town)	涇源縣 (香水鎮)	泾源县 (香水镇)	130,000	130,000	120,000	1443
Zhangyang County (Baiyang Town)	彰陽縣 (白陽鎮)	彭阳县 (白阳镇)	260,000	260,000	250,000	3238
Zhongwei City	中衛市	中卫市	1,180,000	1,200,000	1,220,000	17,448
Shapotou District (Binhe Town)	沙坡頭區 (濱河鎮)	沙坡头区 (滨河镇)	400,000	400,000	420,000	6877
Zhongning County (Ning'an Town)	中寧縣 (寧安鎮)	中宁县 (宁安镇)	320,000	340,000	350,000	4193
Haiyuan County (Sanhe Town)	海原縣 (三河鎮)	海原县 (三河镇)	460,000	460,000	450,000	6378

References

Cheng, Evelyn. 2021. China wants to build up its wine country into one that could rival France's Bordeaux. *CNBC.com,* 20 June. https://www.cnbc.com/2021/06/21/china-wine-ningxia-strives-to-be-france-bordeaux-amid-tariffs-on-australia.html.

China Today. 2021. *Ningxia Hui Autonomous Region*. 20 September. http://www.chinatoday.com/city/ningxia.htm.

Cosmo, Di, and Nicola. 1999. The northern frontier in pre-imperial China. In *The Cambridge history of ancient China: From the origins of civilization to 221 B.C*, ed. Michael Loewe and Edward L. Shaughnessy, 885–966. New York: Cambridge University Press.

Fanhua. 2020. [The Xumishan grottoes are being overhauled again! Restoring and protecting the statues and frescoes in the grottoes is a long 'journey of ingenuity']. 3 July. 梵華網. 須彌山石窟再度迎來大檢修!修復保護石窟的造像和壁畫, 是漫長的 '匠心苦旅.' https://www.buddhistdoor.org/tc/news/.

Gao, Xing, Yuan Baoyin, Pei Shuwen, et al. 2008. Analysis of sedimentary-geomorphologic variation and the living environment of hominids at the Shuidonggou Paleolithic site. *Chinese Science Bulletin* 53 (13): 2025–2032.

Hsieh, Chiao-min, and Jean Kan Hsieh. 1995. *China: a provincial atlas*. New York: Macmillan Publishing.

Garrity, Lyn. 2009. Endangered site: Xumishan grottoes, China. *Smithsonian Magazine,* March 2009. https://www.smithsonianmag.com/travel/endangered-site-xumishan-grottoes-china-52045177/.

Ministry of Civil Affairs (MCA), People's Republic of China. 2020. [*County/township administration handbook*]. Beijing: China Statistics Press. 中華人民共和國民政部, 中華人民共和國, 鄉鎮行政區劃簡冊.

Mote, Frederick W. 1999. *Imperial China: 900–1800*. Cambridge, MA: Harvard University Press.

Ningxia Bureau of Statistics (NBS). 2021. [Bulletin of the main data of the seventh national census in Ningxia]. 25 May. 宁夏第七次全国人口普查主要数据公报. http://www.nxnews.net/zt/2018/hy/hywztt/202105/t20210526_7151659.html.

Ningxia Provincial Government (NPG). 2015. [At the end of 2015, the resident population of all districts reached 6.68 million]. 2015年末全区常住人口达668万人. 宁夏自治区人民政府. www.nx.gov.cn. Accessed 21 Sept 2021.

Shang-Ch'i Guide. 2017. [Backpacking in China: the most complete collection of self-guided travel for China, 2018]. Taipei: Shang-Ch'i Shitai publishing. 2018 最完整的中國自助旅遊全集. 台北: 上奇時代.

Shi, Zhixin. 2000. [At the end of the Qing Dynasty, the economy of Gansu was stagnant and the population dropped sharply]. *Researches in Chinese Economic History*. 石志新. 清末甘肃地区经济凋敝和人口锐减. 中国经济史研究. No. 2: 79–86.

Wang, Zhengwei. 2002. [*Hui nationality in Ningxia*]. Beijing: Wuzhou Dissemination Publishers. 王正伟. 宁夏回族. 北京: 五洲傳播出版社.

Wood, Frances. 2002. *The silk road: Two thousand years in the heart of Asia*. Los Angeles: University of California Press.

Yang, Jisheng. 2007. *Tombstone: Record of China's great famine in the 1960s* (Chinese version). 楊繼繩. 墓碑: 中国六十年代大饥荒纪实. https://cdn.jsdelivr.net/gh/easy2view/books/resources/grave-stone.pdf.

Zhang, Shunan. 2021. [The 2020 per capita income list of residents in various provinces: Shanghai is the richest, and it has risen sharply]. Finance.people.com. 22 January. 张澍楠. 2020年各省份居民人均收入榜: 上海最有钱, 这地涨得猛. http://finance.people.com.cn/n1/2021/0122/c1004-32008733.html.

Zhenbeibao West Film Art Center (ZWFAC). Trip.com. https://www.trip.com/travel-guide/attraction/yinchuan/zhenbeibao-west-film-art-center-10558661/. Accessed 20 Sept 2021.

Chapter 24
Qinghai Province

Abstract Archeological discoveries of so-called Majiayao Culture ("horse, house, and kiln") date back to ca. 3000 BCE in modern-day Qinghai Province. Based on a high plateau and bordering on Tibet, with just under six million residents, Qinghai is the least populated of all mainland China's 31 provinces and major cities. Its high altitude lent itself to its pastoral lifestyle, and Qinghai has a complex history of various nomadic peoples, to include the Qiang, Xiongnu and the Mongols. Qinghai is also home to the "40 tribes of Yushu," and it was only by the time of the Nationalist Republic of China (ROC) that Qinghai was formally named. Among the largest of China's provinces in terms of landmass it is also the poorest, with a per capita income of USD $3,700. Nonetheless, the official registered (*hukou*) population is roughly equal to that of residents counted in the 2020 census, leading to the conclusion that Qinghai citizens are not overrepresented in China's "floating population."

E. Croddy, *China's Provinces and Populations*,
https://doi.org/10.1007/978-3-031-09165-0_24

Qinghai Province (青海省 *qīnghǎi shěng*): Abbreviation (青 *qīng*) (Fig. 24.1)

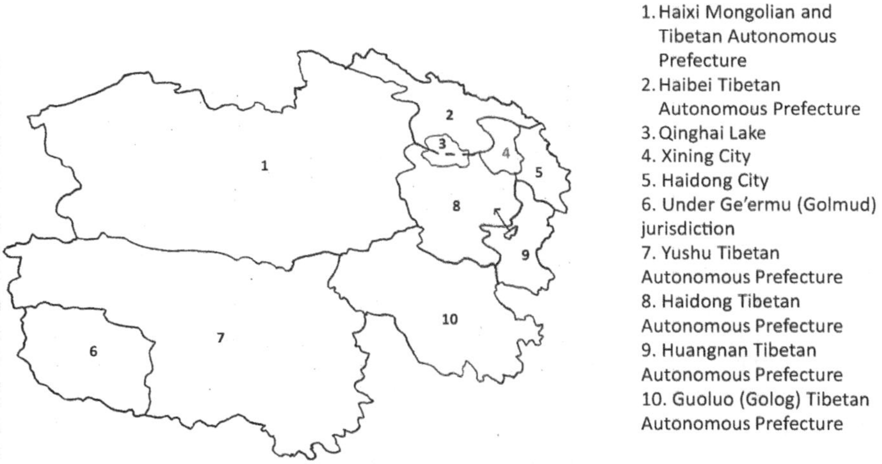

Fig. 24.1 Qinghai province major cities (provincial capital: Xining City). (Drawn by the Author after People's Republic of China, Ministry of Civil Affairs. (MCA 2020))

Qinghai Province: General Impressions

Located on the Tibetan Plateau, or referred to in China as the Qinghai-Tibetan plateau (青藏高原 *qīngzànggāoyuán*), Qinghai province is pastoral and sparsely populated, with the smallest population of all China's provinces, all at a very high altitude (average over 3 km). Qinghai has also been known as Kokonur (Koko Nur or Koko-nor), a corruption of its Mongolian name, Köke Nayur. Going back before 200 BCE in China, there were two contrasting societies in the Qinghai region, separated roughly into western and eastern. The latter developed into a central, stratified polity, while those in the west grew more scattered and less class centric. These features are still seen in the old and new populations in western China, to include Qinghai Province.

Prehistoric Qinghai

Examples of Majiayao Culture—literally, "horse, house, and kiln" (馬家窯文化 *mǎjiāyáo wénhuà*)—that flourished approximately 3300–2100 BCE, are found in a stretch of territory extending east of Qinghai lake, and along the Huanghe (Yellow River 黃河 *huánghé*) as the latter flows towards Gansu province. To date, archaeological excavations of these sites, dating from the Neolithic to the Bronze age, can be found in the following areas:

- Huangyuan County (湟源縣 *huángyuán xiàn*)
- Datong Hui and Tujia Autonomous County (大通回族土族自治縣 *dàtōnghuízú tǔzú zìzhìxiàn*)
- Jianzha County (見扎縣 *jiànzhā xiàn*)
- Xining City (西寧市 *xīníng shì*)
- Xunhua Sala (Salar) Autonomous County (循化撒拉族自治縣 *xúnhuà sālāzú zìzhìxiàn*), and
- Minhe Hui, Tujia Autonomous County (民和回族土族自治縣 *mínhé huízú tǔzú zìzhìxiàn*), *inter alia*

Stone tools in evidence include sickles (鐮 *lián*), axes (斧 *fǔ*), hoes (鋤 *chú*), as well as mortar (臼 *jiù*) and pestles (杵 *chǔ*). In addition to hunting wild deer, antelope, and wild monkeys, these communities domesticated swine, dogs, oxen, and chickens.

The peoples of the Hehuang area, in today's Minhe (Hui and Tujia Autonomous) County, conducted burial practices related to the Gansu Banshan Culture (ca. 2700–2000 BCE). Their domestication of pigs, which is not well suited for a nomadic lifestyle, meant this society likely lived in more permanent settlements. But later on, with changing climate (2000–1000 BCE) and the cooling temperatures of the time, given that ruminants can exist mostly on grass and other plants, raising sheep, not swine, began to make more sense. Perhaps more importantly, ruminants and equids didn't compete nearly as much with human-compatible foodstuffs (as it is in the case of omnivores). More and more, the Hehuang regional inhabitants shifted to herding horse, cattle, and sheep in the higher altitudes. Indeed, from 1700 to 600 BCE, this transition to a more nomadic lifestyle occurred fairly rapidly.

From the Qin to the Han, there were some 150 or more tribes collectively categorized as the Qiang (羌 *qiāng*) who lived in western China (QHDMB 1991). Leading a largely pastoral life, along with hunting and some cultivated agriculture, numerous Qiang tribes lived in the general area of Qinghai Province during the Western Han (ca. 206–24 BCE). The Xiongnu (a people probably related to the Huns) eventually overwhelmed the Qiang tribes that lived in the Hehuang region, a northeastern plateau that runs alongside the Qinghai-Tibetan border.

In 121 BCE, the Western Han dispatched General Huo Qubing (霍去病 *huò qùbìng*) to the west, defeating the Xiongnu, and by 111 BCE, after tackling the Qiang, the Han began to gain control over the eastern part of Qinghai. By this time, under the euphemistic "Protectorate Commandant of the Qiang" (護羌校尉 *hùqiāng xiàowèi*), the Hehuang region was named Jincheng Prefecture (金城郡 *jīnchéng jùn*), and the Han Chinese built the famed Xiping Pavilion (西平亭 *xīpíngtíng*) redoubt in modern-day Xining City. In 61 BCE, after defeating the Xianling Qiang (先零羌 *xiānlíng qiāng*) chieftain, Yang Yu (楊玉 *yang yù*), the Han General Zhao Chongguo (趙充國 *zhào chōngguó*) occupied the Hehuang region, establishing the "Jincheng Dependent State" (金城屬國 *jīnchéngshŭguó*).

Based around the Xiping Pavilion, the region from east of Qinghai Lake to the Gansu border was named Xiping Prefecture in 222 CE. By the early fourth century CE, originating from the erstwhile Xianbei kingdom, the nomadic Tuyuhun (吐谷渾 *tŭgŭhún*) moved in, taking over the Gansu and Qinghai regions. Xiping Prefecture (today's Xining City) remained part of the Former Liang (前涼 *qiánliáng* 314 CE - 376 CE), one of the "16 kingdoms of the five barbarians" (QHDMB 1991).

In 609 CE, the Sui Emperor Yang (楊廣 *yáng guăng*) defeated the Tuyuhun, capturing their leader, and ultimately gained control of modern day Qinghai. During the Sui dynasty, modern-day Qinghai (then Hexi commanderies 河西諸郡 *héxī zhūjùn*) existed as three contiguous prefectures: Xihai (西海郡 *xīhăi jùn*), Heyuan (河源郡 *héyuán jùn*) and Xiping (西平郡 *xīpíng jùn*). Upon the end of the Sui, the Tuyuhun took back control over their territory, but they were under constant threat from Tang dynastic forces. Finally, in 663, the Tibetans (吐蕃 *tŭfān*) conquered the Tuyuhun, ultimately taking over modern-day Xinjiang, Qinghai, Tibet, Gansu and western Sichuan provinces by ca. 820 CE.

During the Northern Song (1103), what was still the main center called Qingtang City (青唐城 *qīngtángchéng*), and what had previously been known as Shanzhou (鄯州 *shànzhōu*), was changed to Xining (西寧 *xīníng* "western peace"). Under the Mongolian (Yuan) empire in the thirteenth century, Xining became part of Gansu province (甘肅行省 *gānsù xíngshĕng*), while the remainder of what was part of the Tibetan territory was relegated to the Xuanwei Shisi (宣慰使司 *xuānwèishĭsī*) administrative area. During the Ming, Xining was changed from a prefecture to a garrison (衛 *wèi*), populated by about six thousand households in 1371.

In ca. 1600, the Qošod (和碩特 *héshuòtè*; Khoshot or Khosot) Mongols, one of four federations from the original Oirats (厄魯特 *èlŭtè*), moved into Qinghai. In 1723, the chieftain of the Khosot Mongols, Lobsang Danjin (羅布藏丹津 *luóbùcáng dānjīn*) believed he had been essentially promised Tibet, but was double-crossed by the Qing government, and so he rebelled (Rawski 1998). The Qing dynasty defeated Lobsang Danjin, and the empire established a Grand Minister Superintendent of Qinghai (青海辦事大臣 *qīnghăi bànshì dàchén*).

In the early nineteenth century, the Qing dynasty province of Qinghai was divided roughly into two regions: The upper Mongolian Oirats (青海厄魯特 *qīnghǎi èlǔtè*) to the north, and the Yushu forty tribes (玉樹等四十族 *yùshù děng sìshízú*) to the south (for a complete listing of the forty tribes see Table 24.1). The latter Yushu forty tribes, including Mongolian (蒙古族 *ménggǔ zú*), Tibetan (藏族 *zàngzú*) and Tusi (土司 *tǔsī*), lived in areas that included today's Yushu Tibetan Autonomous Prefecture (玉樹藏族自治州 *yùshù zàngzú zìzhìzhōu*) and its subordinate Yushu City (玉樹市 *yùshù shì*), as well as the following counties:

- Zaduo (雜多縣 *záduō xiàn*)
- Chenduo (稱多縣 *chēnduō xiàn*)
- Zhiduo (治多縣 *zhìduō xiàn*)

Table 24.1 The "Forty (40) Ethnic Groups" or Tribes of Yushu. (QHDMB 2015)

Ningxia: Yushu forty tribes
阿里克族 *ālǐkè zú*
雍希葉布族 *yōngxīyèbù zú*
蒙古爾津族 *Ménggǔ'ěrjīn zú*
尼木錯族 *nímùcuò zú*
固察族 *gùchá zú*
稱多族 *chēngduō zú*
拉布族*lābù zú*
隆布族 *lóngbù zú*
上隆布族 *shànglóngbù zú*
安圖族 *āntú zú*
阿隆族 *ālóng zú*
列玉族 *lièyù zú*
阿永族 *āyǒng zú*
葉吉族 *yèjí zú*
拉則族*lāzé zú*
典巴族 *diǎnbā zú*
哈秀族 *hāxiù zú*
班右族 *bānyòu zú*
上阿拉克碩族 *shàng'ālākèshuò zú*
下阿拉克碩族 xià'*ālākèshuò zú*
扎武族 *zhāwǔ zú*
布慶族 *bùqìng zú*
拉達族 *lādá zú*
蘇莽族 *sūmǎng zú*
吹靈多拉族 *chuīlíngduōlā zú*
巴彥南稱族*bāyànnánchēng zú*
南稱桑色爾族 *Nánchēngsāngsè'ěr zú*
南稱隆冬族 *nánchēnglóngdōng zú*

(continued)

Table 24.1 (continued)

Ningxia: Yushu forty tribes
南稱綽火爾族 *Nánchēngchuòhuǒ'ěr zú*
洞巴族 *dòngbā zú*
蘇魯克族 *sūlǔkè zú*
下隆壩族 *xiàlóngbà zú*
上隆壩族 *shànglóngbà zú*
上格吉族 *shànggéjí zú*
下格吉族 *xiàgéjí zú*
中格吉族 *zhōnggéjí zú*
玉樹族 *yùshù zú*
噶爾布族 *gá'ěrbù zú*
白利族 *báilì zú*
覺拉族 *juélā zú*

Table 24.2 Breakdown of major Qinghai ethnic groups. (QHDMB 2015)

Qinghai province: major ethnic groups (2010)	Percentage
Han 漢族 (*hànzú*)	~53
Tibetan 藏族 (*zàngzú*)	24.44
Hui (Moslem) 回族 (*huízú*)s	14.83
Tu 土族 / (Monguor) 蒙古爾 (*ménggǔ'ěr*)	3.63
Salar 撒拉族 (*sālā zú*)	1.9
Mongol 蒙古族 (*ménggǔ zú*)	1.77

- Nangqian (囊謙縣 *nángqiān xiàn*) and
- Qumalai (曲麻萊縣 *qūmálái xiàn*)

As of 1840, the Hui (870,000) made up the majority population in Xining Prefecture. In 1853, Qinghai had a total population of about 920,000 (Wang and Lingzhidorje 1998).

From 1915 to 1928, the very capable military leader (and ethnic Hui) Ma Qi (馬麒 *mǎ qí*) governed modern-day Qinghai province. With the title of Gansu, Ningxia and Qinghai Defense Governor,[1] and later their Military Protectorate,[2] Ma Qi and his family essentially served as the military governorship of Gansu, Ningxia and Qinghai. In January 1929, the Republic of China (ROC) government formally established Qinghai Province. At this time, Qinghai had a population of about one million. In July 1932, Ma Qi's son, Ma Bufang (馬步芳 *Mǎ Bùfāng*), repulsed an

[1] 甘邊寧海鎮守使 *gānbiānnínghǎizhèn shǒushǐ.*

[2] 甘邊寧海護軍使 *gānbiānnínghǎi hùjūnshǐ.*

attack by Tibetan troops who had invaded earlier that March (Wang and Gyaincain 1997).

The Sino-Japanese war (1937–45) forced many Chinese to immigrate to Qinghai in order to escape from war torn areas. Qinghai's population grew from about 1.3 million in the 1930s to 1,483,300 by 1949. In the early 1950s, Qinghai had a population of 1.5 million (Rohlf 2016).

Post-1949 Qinghai and the Great Leap Forward (1958–62)

The Chinese Communist Party (CCP) promoted an industrial growth program in 1956 to include the development of Xining city, importing up 700,000 people to the region by 1959. But the disastrous results of the "Great Leap Forward" (1958–1962) led to country-wide starvation, affecting Qinghai to the point that some 570,000 people fled during 1960–1963 (Goodman 2004). Qinghai recorded some 103,000 "unnatural deaths" during those years (Yang 2007). And this doesn't include the large numbers of people who were persecuted by the authorities for their real or (mostly) imagined political crimes. According to one estimate, adding up those who were arrested, jailed, or otherwise repressed by CCP officials from 1958–60 amounted to over four percent of Qinghai's population (108,558 out of total 2,440,000). Regional areas and their population changes during this time also tell a story: Yushu Prefecture (玉樹州 *yùshù zhōu*) had a population of 159,419 in 1957, which dropped to 93,483 (over 40 percent) by 1963. Guoluo (Golog) prefecture (果洛州 *guǒluò zhōu*) in 1953 had its population nearly halved, beginning with 100,000 residents and then losing 48,753 people by 1963 (Li 2012).

In the late twentieth century, Qinghai was regarded as the poorest of all Chinese provinces. In 1999, at least 36 of Qinghai's 46 counties were regarded as "poverty stricken" (Goodman 2004). That said, when compared with the other western provinces in China, Qinghai's economic development has been, at least in relative terms, the fastest, nearly 8% annually from 1982–2000 (Li et al. 2016). As of 2015, Qinghai's per capita income was USD $3,567, climbing to over $3,700 in 2020 (Zhang 2021).

By end of 2014, the total resident population of Qinghai was 5,834,200, and the 2020 (see Table 24.3) census showed continued growth (5,923,957). The permanent (*hukou*) registered population for 2020 recorded 5,870,000 individuals (Table 24.6), this small difference likely reflecting a very low percentage of Qinghai's population choosing to live elsewhere to live, work, and study. Table 24.4 breaks down populations down to district and counties, and Table 24.5 lists officially recognized ethnic groups in Qinghai Province (Fig. 24.2).

Table 24.3 Qinghai province population (residential 常住人口 *chángzhù rénkǒu*) data (QPBS 2021)

Prefecture/county	Population (2010)	Population (2020)
Xining City 西寧市 *xīníng shì*	2,208,708	2,467,965
Haidong City 海東市 *hǎidōng shì*	1,396,846	1,358,471
Haixi Mongol and Tibetan Autonomous Prefecture 海西蒙古族藏族自治州 *hǎixī ménggǔzú zàngzú zìzhìzhōu*	489,338	468,216
Haibei Tibetan Autonomous Prefecture 海北藏族自治州 *hǎiběi zàngzú zìzhìzhōu*	273,304	265,322
Hainan Tibetan Autonomous Prefecture 海南藏族自治州 *hǎinán zàngzú zìzhìzhōu*	441,689	446,996
Huangnan Tibetan Autonomous Prefecture 黃南藏族自治州 *huángnán zàngzú zìzhìzhōu*	256,716	276,215
Yushu Tibetan Autonomous Prefecture 玉樹藏族自治州 *yùshù zàngzú zìzhìzhōu*	378,439	425,199
Guoluo (Golog) Tibetan Autonomous Prefecture 果洛藏族自治州 *guǒluò zàngzú zìzhìzhōu*	181,682	215,573
Total	**5,626,722**	**5,923,957**

Table 24.4 Qinghai province population (residential 常住人口 chángzhù rénkǒu) data. (QPBS 2021)

Cities and subordinate sectors, population (2020 census)	Subordinate district, city and county populations (2020)	Total population (2020)
Xining City 西寧市 ***xīníng shì***		**2,467,965**
Chengzhong District 城中區 *chéngzhōng qū*	325,813	
Chengdong District 城東區 *chéngdōng qū*	489,372	
Chengxi District 城西區 *chéngxī qū*	326,866	
Chengbei District 城北區 *chéngběi qū*	417,701	
Datong Huizu (Hui) and Tu Autonomous County 大通回族土族自治縣 *dàtōng huízú tǔzú zìzhìxiàn*	403,368	
Huangyuan County 湟源縣 *huángyuán xiàn*	109,802	
Huangzhong County 湟中縣 *huángzhōng xiàn*	395,043	
Haidong City 海東市 ***hǎidōng shì***		**1,358,471**
Ping'an District 平安區 *píng'ān qū*	117,883	
Ledu District 樂都區 *lèdū qū*	240,949	
Minhe Huizu Tuzu (Hui and Tu) Autonomous County 民和回族土族自治縣 *mínhé huízú tǔzú zìzhìxiàn*	326,964	
Huzhu Tuzu (Tu) Autonomous County 互助土族自治縣 *hùzhù tǔzú zìzhìxiàn*	337,941	
Hualong Huizu (Hui) Autonomous County 化隆回族自治縣 *huàlóng huízú zìzhìxiàn*	200,474	

(continued)

Table 24.4 (continued)

Cities and subordinate sectors, population (2020 census)	Subordinate district, city and county populations (2020)	Total population (2020)
Xunhua Salazu (Salar) Autonomous County 循化撒拉族自治縣 *xúnhuà sālāzú zìzhìxiàn*	134,260	
Haixi Mongol and Tibetan Autonomous Prefecture 海西蒙古族藏族自治州 ***hǎixī ménggǔzú zàngzú zìzhìzhōu***		**468,216**
Delingha (Delhi) City 德令哈市 *délínghā shì*	88,227	
Ge'ermu (Golmud) City 格爾木市 *gé'ěrmù shì*	221,863	
Mangya (Mangnai) City 茫涯市 *mángyá shì*	18,856	
Wulan (Ulan) County 烏蘭縣 *wūlán xiàn*	31,507	
Dulan County 都蘭縣 *dūlán xiàn*	68,273	
Tianjun County 天峻縣 *tiānjùn xiàn*	23,203	
Dachaidan (Da Qaidam) Administrative Committee 大柴旦行政委員會 *dàcháidàn xíngzhèng wěiyuánhuì*	16,287	
Haibei Tibetan Autonomous Prefecture 海北藏族自治州 ***hǎiběi zàngzú zìzhìzhōu***		**265,322**
Haiyan County 海晏縣 *hǎiyàn xiàn*	37,729	
Qilian County 祁連縣 *qílián xiàn*	48,538	
Gangcha (Gangca) County 剛察縣 *gāngchá xiàn*	40,720	
Menyuan Huizu (Hui) Autonomous County 門源回族自治縣 *ményuán huízú zìzhìxiàn*	138,335	
Hainan Tibetan Autonomous Prefecture 海南藏族自治州 ***hǎinán zàngzú zìzhìzhōu***		**446,996**
Gonghe County 共和縣 *gònghé xiàn*	133,409	
Tongde County 同德縣 *tóngdé xiàn*	60,268	
Guide County 貴德縣 *guìdé xiàn*	105,645	
Xinghai County 興海縣 *xīnghǎi xiàn*	75,833	
Guinan (Mangra) County 貴南縣 *guìnán xiàn*	71,841	
Huangnan Tibetan Autonomous Prefecture 黃南藏族自治州 ***huángnán zàngzú zìzhìzhōu***		**276,215**
Tongren (Rebgong; Rebkong) County 同仁縣 *tóngrén xiàn*	101,519	
Jianzha (Jainca) County 尖扎縣 *jiānzā xiàn*	58,173	
Zeku (Zêkog) County 澤庫縣 *zékù xiàn*	75,659	
Henan Menggu (Mongol) Autonomous County 河南蒙古族自治縣 *hénán mēnggǔzú zìzhìxiàn*	40,864	
Yushu Tibetan Autonomous Prefecture 玉樹藏族自治州 ***yùshù zàngzú zìzhìzhōu***		**425,199**
Yushu City 玉樹市 *yùshù shì*	141,308	
Zaduo (Zadoi) County 雜多縣 *záduō xiàn*	68,759	
Chenduo (Chindu) County 稱多縣*chènduō xiàn*	57,159	

(continued)

Table 24.4 (continued)

Cities and subordinate sectors, population (2020 census)	Subordinate district, city and county populations (2020)	Total population (2020)
Zhiduo (Zhidoi) County 治多縣 *zhìduō xiàn*	34,496	
Nangqian (Nangchen; Nangqên) County 囊謙縣 *nángqiān xiàn*	90,307	
Qumalai (Qumarlêb) County 曲麻萊縣 *qūmálái xiàn*	33,170	
Guoluo (Golog) Tibetan Autonomous Prefecture 果洛藏族自治州 *guǒluò zàngzú zìzhìzhōu*		**215,573**
Maqin (Maqên) County 瑪沁縣 *mǎqìn xiàn*	58,117	
Banma (Baima) County 班瑪縣 *bānmǎ xiàn*	31,794	
Gande (Gadê) County 甘德縣 *gāndé xiàn*	41,046	
Dari (Darlag) County 達日縣 *dárì xiàn*	40,197	
Jiuzhi (Jigzhi) County 久治縣 *jiǔzhì xiàn*	29,929	
Maduo (Madoi) County 瑪多縣 *mǎduō xiàn*	14,490	

Table 24.5 Detailed ethnic minority breakdown (2010 data), Qinghai Province. (QPBS 2015)

Ethnic group	Pinyin	Population
Tibetan 藏族	*zàngzú*	1,375,059
Hui (Moslem) 回族	*huízú*	834,298
Tu 土族 / (Mongol) 蒙古爾	*tǔzú / ménggǔ'ěr*	204,412
Salar 撒拉族	*sālā zú*	107,089
Mongol 蒙古族	*ménggǔ zú*	99,815
Manchu 滿族	*mǎn zú*	8,029
Sarta 東鄉族	*dōngxiāng zú*	6,331
Tujia 土家族	*tǔjiā zú*	1,537
Zhuang 壯族	*zhuàng zú*	980
Miao 苗族	*miáo zú*	911
Bonan 保安族	*bǎoān zú*	904
Yi 彝族	*yí zú*	683
Kazakh 哈薩克族	*hāsàkè zú*	680
Bai 白族	*bái zú*	320
Korean 朝鮮族	*cháoxiǎn zú*	312
Bouyei 布依族	*bùyī zú*	251
Uyghur 維吾爾族	*wéiwúěr zú*	209
Yao 瑶族	*yáo zú*	209
Yugur 裕固族	*yùgù zú*	163
Dong 侗族	*dòng zú*	161

(continued)

Table 24.5 (continued)

Ethnic group	Pinyin	Population
Li 黎族	*lí zú*	139
Xibe 錫伯族	*xībó zú*	128
Qiang 羌族	*qiāng zú*	104
Klau 仡佬族	*gēlǎo zú*	69
She 畲族	*shē zú*	53
Russian 俄羅斯族	*éluōsī zú*	38
Nakhi 納西族	*nàxī zú*	32
Dai 傣族	*dǎi zú*	31
Sui 水族	*shuǐ zú*	30
Dauer 達斡爾族	*dáwò'ěr zú*	26
Lisu 傈僳族	*lìsù zú*	21
Gaoshan 高山族	*gāoshān zú*	20
Wa 佤族	*wǎ zú*	20
Hani 哈尼族	*hāní zú*	17
Mulao 仫佬族	*mùlǎo zú*	15
Hezhen 赫哲族	*hèzhé zú*	11
Gin 京族	*jīng zú*	10
Maonan 毛南族	*máonán zú*	8
Lahu 拉祜族	*lāhù zú*	8
Ewenki/Evenks 鄂溫克族	*èwēnkè zú*	5
Nu 怒族	*nù zú*	5
Jingpo 景頗族	*jǐngpǒ zú*	5
Monba 門巴族	*ménbā zú*	4
Kyrgyz 柯爾克孜族	*kē'ěrkèzī zú*	4
Derung 獨龍族	*dúlóng zú*	4
Tajik 塔吉克族	*tǎjíkè zú*	3
Pumi 普米族	*pǔmǐ zú*	3
Blang 布朗族	*bùlǎng zú*	2
Tatar 塔塔爾族	*tǎtǎěr zú*	2
Uzbek 烏孜別克族 / 烏茲別克族	*wūzībiékè zú*	2
Oroqen 鄂倫春族	*èlúnchūn zú*	2
Deang 德昂族	*déáng zú*	1
Jino 基諾族	*jīnuò zú*	1
Achang 阿昌族	*āchāng zú*	1
Lhoba 珞巴族	*luòbā zú*	0
Other individuals from as of yet unrecognized minority groups		**20**

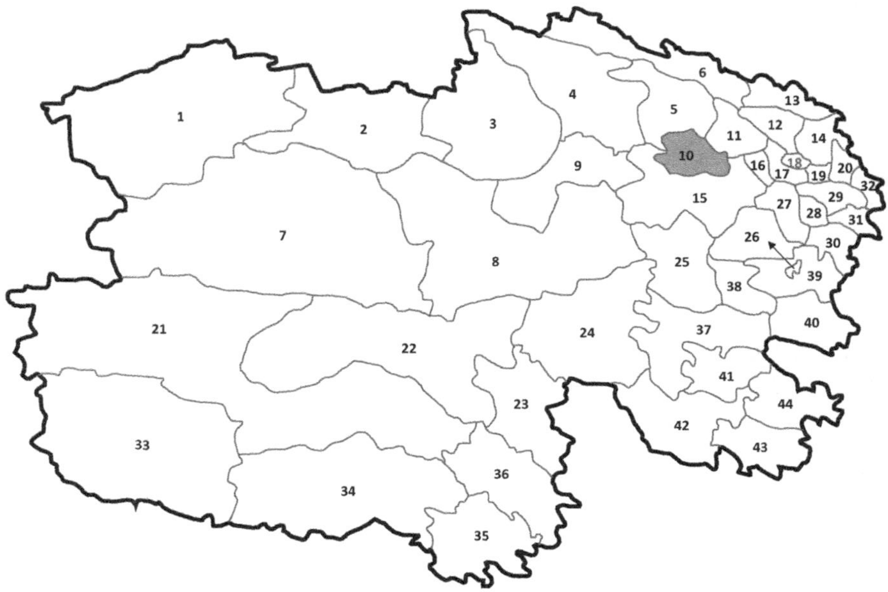

1. Mangya (Mangnai) City
2. (Autonomous prefecture, under direct administration)
3. Delingha City
4. Tianjun County
5. Gangcha County
6. Qilian County
7. Ge'ermu City (Golmud)
8. Dulan County
9. Wulan County
10. Qinghai Lake
11. Haiyan County
12. Datong Hui and Tu Autonomous County
13. Menyuan Hui Autonomous County
14. Huzhu Tu Autonomous County
15. Gonghe County
16. Huangyuan County
17. Huangzhong District
18. Xining City
19. Ping'an District
20. Ledu District
21. Zhiduo County
22. Qumacai County
23. Chenduo (Chindu) County
24. Maduo County
25. Xinghai County
26. Guinan County
27. Guide County
28. Jianzha County
29. Hualong
30. Tongren County
31. Xunhua Sala (Salar) Autonomous County
32. Minhe Hui and Tu Autonomous County
33. (Under Golmud jurisdiction)
34. Zaduo (Zadoi) County
35. Nangqian (Nangqên) County
36. Yushu City
37. Maqin (Maqên) County
38. Tongde County
39. Zeku County
40. Henan Mongol Autonomous County
41. Gande County
42. Dari (Darlag) County
43. Banma (Baima) County
44. Jiuye (Jigzhi) County

Fig. 24.2 Qinghai province: Subdistricts (provincial capital city: Xining City). (Drawn by the Author after People's Republic of China, Ministry of Civil Affairs. (MCA 2020))

Table 24.6 (below) shows the *hukou* (family registered) populations based on PRC Ministry of Civil Affairs data. (Districts listed directly under major cities are government seats, as are those in parentheses). One can compare these data with the census (usual residential populations based on 2010 and 2020 censuses in Tables 24.3 and 24.4 (above):

Qinghai Province (青 *qīng*)

Provincial Capital: Xining City

Table 24.6 Qinghai province: Permanent registered (戶籍人口 *hùjí rénkǒu*) populations. (MCA 2020)

Name	Traditional	Simplified	Population (2012)	Population (2016)	Population (2020)	Area (Sq. Km)
Qinghai Province	青海省	青海省	5,500,000	5,660,000	5,870,000	720,000
Xining City	西寧市	西宁市	1,960,000	1,990,000	2,070,000	7524
Chengzhong District (Qinmajie Subdistrict)	城中區 (欽馬街街道)	城中区 (饮马街街道)	230,000	240,000	250,000	151
Chengdong District (Dazhongjie Subdistrict)	城東區 (大眾街街道)	城东区 (大众街街道)	250,000	250,000	260,000	135
Chengxi District (Wusidajie Subdistrict)	城西區 (五四大街街道)	城西区 (五四大街街道)	210,000	210,000	250,000	57
Chengbei District (Chaoyang Subdistrict)	城北區 (朝陽街道)	城北区 (朝阳街道)	210,000	220,000	230,000	138
Datong Huizu (Hui) and Tu Autonomous County (Qiaotou Town)	大通回族土族自治縣 (橋頭鎮)	大通回族土族自治县 (桥头镇)	450,000	460,000	470,000	3090
Huangyuan County (Chengguan Town)	湟源縣 (城關鎮)	湟源县 (城关镇)	140,000	130,000	13,000	1509
Huangzhong District (Lusha'er Town)	湟中區 (魯沙爾鎮)	湟中区 (鲁沙尔镇)	470,000	480,000	460,000	2444
Haidong City	海東市	海东市	1,610,000	1,680,000	1,730,000	13,202
Ping'an District (Ping'an Town)	平安區 (平安鎮)	平安区 (平安镇)	120,000	130,000	130,000	735
Ledu District (Nianbo Town)	樂都區 (碾伯鎮)	乐都区 (碾伯镇)	280,000	290,000	290,000	2600
Minhe Huizu Tuzu (Hui and Tu) Autonomous County (Chuankou Town)	民和回族土族自治縣 (川口鎮)	民和回族土族自治县 (川口镇)	410,000	430,000	440,000	1890
Huzhu Tuzu (Tu) Autonomous County (Weiyuan Town)	互助土族自治縣 (威遠鎮)	互助土族自治县 (威远镇)	380,000	390,000	400,000	3423
Hualong Huizu (Hui) Autonomous County (Bayan Town)	化隆回族自治縣 (巴燕鎮)	化隆回族自治县 (巴燕镇)	280,000	290,000	310,000	2740
Xunhua Salazu (Salar) Autonomous County (Jishi Town)	循化撒拉族自治縣 (積石鎮)	循化撒拉族自治县 (积石镇)	140,000	150,000	160,000	1814

(continued)

Table 24.6 (continued)

Name	Traditional	Simplified	Population (2012)	Population (2016)	Population (2020)	Area (Sq. Km)
Haibei Zangzu (Tibetan) Autonomous Prefecture (Haiyan County Xihai Town)	海北藏族自治州(海晏縣西海鎮)	海北藏族自治州(海晏县西海镇)	290,000	300,000	300,000	34,443
Haiyan County (Sanjiaocheng Town)	海晏縣(三角城鎮)	海晏县(三角城镇)	40,000	40,000	40,000	4443
Qilian County (Babao Town)	祁連縣(八寶鎮)	祁连县(八宝镇)	50,000	50,000	50,000	14,000
Gangcha (Gangca) County (Shaliuhe Town)	剛察縣(沙柳河鎮)	刚察县(沙柳河镇)	40,000	50,000	50,000	9600
Menyuan Huizu (Hui) Autonomous County (Haomen Town)	門源回族自治縣(浩門鎮)	门源回族自治县(浩门镇)	160,000	160,000	160,000	6400
Hainan Zangzu (Tibetan) Autonomous Prefecture	海南藏族自治州	海南藏族自治州	450,000	460,000	470,000	43,493
Gonghe County (Qiabuqia Town)	共和縣(恰卜恰鎮)	共和县(恰卜恰镇)	130,000	130,000	130,000	16,624
Tongde County (Gabasongduo [Gabasumdo] Town)	同德縣(尕巴松多鎮)	同德县(尕巴松多镇)	60,000	60,000	60,000	4600
Guide County (Heyin Town)	貴德縣(河陰鎮)	贵德县(河阴镇)	110,000	110,000	110,000	3600
Xinghai County (Ziketan Town)	興海縣(子科灘鎮)	兴海县(子科滩镇)	70,000	80,000	80,000	12,183
Guinan (Mangra) County (Mangqu Town)	貴南縣(茫曲鎮)	贵南县(茫曲镇)	80,000	80,000	80,000	6486
Huangnan Zangzu (Tibetan) Autonomous Prefecture	黃南藏族自治州	黄南藏族自治州	260,000	260,000	280,000	17,809
Tongren (Rebgong; Rebkong) County (Longwu [Rongwo] Town)	同仁縣(隆務鎮)	同仁县(隆务镇)	90,000	90,000	100,000	3465
Jianzha (Jainca) County (Maketang Town)	尖扎縣(馬克唐鎮)	尖扎县(马克唐镇)	60,000	60,000	60,000	1600
Zeku (Zêkog) County (Zequ Town)	澤庫縣(澤曲鎮)	泽库县(泽曲镇)	70,000	70,000	80,000	6494

(continued)

Table 24.6 (continued)

Name	Traditional	Simplified	Population (2012)	Population (2016)	Population (2020)	Area (Sq. Km)
Henan Menggu (Mongol) Autonomous County (Youganning Town)	河南蒙古族自治縣 (優干寧鎮)	河南蒙古族自治县 (优干宁镇)	40,000	40,000	40,000	6250
Guoluo (Golog Tibetan) Zangzu Autonomous Prefecture	果洛藏族自治州	果洛藏族自治州	170,000	200,000	200,000	74,367
Maqin (Maqên) County (Dawu Town)	瑪沁縣 (大武鎮)	玛沁县 (大武镇)	50,000	50,000	50,000	13,500
Banma (Baima) County (Sailaitang [Sêraitang] Town)	班瑪縣 (賽來塘鎮)	班玛县 (赛来塘镇)	30,000	30,000	30,000	6452
Gande (Gadê) County (Kequ [Pagqên] Town)	甘德縣 (柯曲鎮)	甘德县 (柯曲镇)	30,000	40,000	40,000	7125
Dari (Darlag) County (Jimai [Gyümai] Town)	達日縣 (吉邁鎮)	达日县 (吉迈镇)	30,000	60,000	40,000	14,495
Jiuzhi (Jigzhi) County (Zhiqingsongduo [Chugqênsumdo] Town)	久治縣 (智青松多鎮)	久治县 (智青松多镇)	20,000	30,000	30,000	8300
Maduo (Madoi) County (Machali Town)	瑪多縣 (瑪查理鎮)	玛多县 (玛查理镇)	10,000	10,000	20,000	24,495
Yushu (Yulshul) Zangzu (Tibetan) Autonomous Prefecture	玉樹藏族自治州	玉树藏族自治州	380,000	400,000	410,000	204,891
Yushu City (Jiegu [Gyêgu] Subdistrict)	玉樹市 (結古街道)	玉树市 (结古街道)	100,000	110,000	110,000	15,413
Zaduo (Zadoi) County (Sahuteng [Qapugtang] Town)	雜多縣 (薩呼騰鎮)	杂多县 (萨呼腾镇)	60,000	60,000	70,000	35,520
Chenduo (Chindu) County (Chengwen Town)	稱多縣 (稱文鎮)	称多县 (称文镇)	60,000	60,000	60,000	14,615
Zhiduo (Zhidoi) County (Jiajiboluo [Gyaijêpozhanggê] Town)	治多縣 (加吉博洛鎮)	治多县 (加吉博洛镇)	30,000	40,000	30,000	80,648

(continued)

Table 24.6 (continued)

Name	Traditional	Simplified	Population (2012)	Population (2016)	Population (2020)	Area (Sq. Km)
Nangqian (Nangchen; Nangqên) County (Xiangda [Xangda] Town)	囊謙縣 (香達鎮)	囊谦县 (香达镇)	100,000	100,000	100,000	12,061
Qumalai (Qumarlêb) County (Yuegai Town)	曲麻萊縣 (約改鎮)	曲麻莱县 (约改镇)	30,000	30,000	30,000	46,634
Haixi Menggu Zangzu (Mongol and Tibetan) Autonomous Prefecture	海西蒙古藏族自治州	海西蒙古族藏族自治州	380,000	400,000	590,000	300,854
Delingha (Delhi) City (Hexi Subdistrict)	德令哈市 (河西街道)	德令哈市 (河西街道)	70,000	80,000	70,000	27,766
Ge'ermu (Golmud) City (Kunlunlu Subdistrict)	格爾木市 (崑崙路街道)	格尔木市 (昆仑路街道)	120,000	130,000	140,000	119,167
Mangya [Mangnai] City (Huatugou Town)	茫涯市 (花土溝鎮)	茫涯市 (花土沟镇)	N/A	N/A	80,000	49,890
Wulan (Ulan) County (Xiligou [Xireg] Town)	烏蘭縣 (希里溝鎮)	乌兰县 (希里沟镇)	100,000	100,000	100,000	44,574
Dulan County (Chahanwusu [Qagan Us] Town)	都蘭縣 (察汗烏蘇鎮)	都兰县 (察汗乌苏镇)	70,000	70,000	70,000	45,265
Tianjun County (Xinyuan Town)	天峻縣 (新源鎮)	天峻县 (新源镇)	20,000	20,000	20,000	25,613

References

Goodman, David S. G. 2004. Qinghai and the emergence of the west: nationalities, communal interaction and national integration. In *China's campaign to 'open up the west': national, provincial and local perspectives*, ed. David S. G. Goodman, 65–85, China Quarterly Special New Issues, No. 5. New York: Columbia University Press.

Li, Jianglin. 2012. *When iron birds fly in the sky: The secret war on the Qinghai-Tibet plateau, 1956–1962*. Taipei: National Central Library. 李江琳. 當鐵鳥在天空飛翔, 1956–1962: 青藏高原上的秘密戰爭. 台北: 國家圖書館.

Li, Zhang, Richard LeGates, and Min Zhao. 2016. *Understanding China's urbanization: The great demographic, spatial, economic, and social transformation*. Massachusetts: Edward Elgar Publishing.

Ministry of Civil Affairs (MCA), People's Republic of China. 2020. [*County/township administration handbook*]. Beijing: China Statistics Press. 中華人民共和國民政部, 中華人民共和國, 鄉鎮行政區劃簡冊.

Modern China: Qinghai (MCQ). 1991. Beijing: Modern China Press, 当代中国的青海. 北京: 当代中国出版社, Vol. 1.

Qinghai Hujing District Management Bureau (QHDMB). 2015. [*Brief history of Qinghai*]. 青海历史简要: 青海湖景区管理局. http://223.220.143.92. Accessed 21 Dec 2021.

Qinghai Province Bureau of Statistics (QPBS). 2021. [Communiqué of the seventh national population census of Qinghai Province, issue no. 2]. 青海省第七次全国人口普查公报(第二号). 16 June. https://epaper.tibet3.com/qhrb/html/202106/16/16a47b85-d996-4320-8d89-972082ecff62.pdf.

Rawski, Evelyn S. 1998. *The last emperors: A social history of Qing imperial institutions*. Berkeley: University of California Press.

Rohlf, Gregory. 2016. *Building new China, colonizing Kokonor: Resettlement to Qinghai in the 1950s*. Boulder: Lexington Books.

Wang, Jiawei, and Nyima Gyaincain. 1997. *The historical status of China's Tibet*. Beijing: Wuzhou Dissemination Publishers.

Wang, Tianjin and Luosang Lingzhidorje. 1998. [*Population and environmental carrying capacity of the Qinghai-Tibet plateau*]. Beijing: China Tibetology Press. 王天津. 洛桑灵智多杰, 青藏高原人口与环境承载力. 北京: 中国藏学出版社.

Yang, Jisheng. 2007. *Tombstone: Record of China's Great Famine in the 1960s* (Chinese version). 楊繼繩. 墓碑: 中国六十年代大饥荒纪实. https://cdn.jsdelivr.net/gh/easy2view/books/resources/grave-stone.pdf.

Zhang, Shunan. 2021. [The 2020 per capita income list of residents in various provinces: Shanghai is the richest, and it has risen sharply]. Finance.people.com. 22 January. 张澍楠. 2020年各省份居民人均收入榜: 上海最有钱, 这地涨得猛. http://finance.people.com.cn/n1/2021/0122/c1004-32008733.html.

Chapter 25
Shaanxi Province

Abstract Shaanxi Province differentiates its English name with neighboring Shanxi province by spelling with an extra "a" to indicate its third tone in Chinese. Shaanxi is home to the oldest hominid discovered in China, Lantian Man, who lived about 1.6 million years ago. Shaanxi is also the site of the Yangshao Culture (ca. 6000 BCE), elements of the Shang (ca. 1500 BCE); the Zhou (ca. 1000 BCE); and the critical stage of Chinese unification under the Qin (221 BCE), which basically led to the modern administration of China's people today. Shaanxi also brings to mind Mao Zedong's revolutionary redoubt in Yan'an, a case study in political and psychological indoctrination through China's own Red Terror. Rich in coal deposits, Shaanxi also enjoys significant tourism revenues (at least during nonepidemic times). Ranking about average in terms of gross domestic product and per capita income (about (USD $4400), Shaanxi's population for both registered (*hukou*, 40.2 million) and 2020 census numbers (39.5 million) of its usual residents are roughly equal.

E. Croddy, *China's Provinces and Populations*,
https://doi.org/10.1007/978-3-031-09165-0_25

Shaanxi Province (陕西省 *shǎnxī shěng*): Abbreviations 陕 (*shǎn*); 秦 (*qín*) (Fig. 25.1)

Fig. 25.1 Shaanxi province major cities (provincial capital: Xi'an). (Drawn by the author, after People's Republic of China, Ministry of Civil Affairs. (MCA 2020))

Shaanxi Province: General Impressions

First things first: The main difference between the pronunciation of neighboring Shanxi (山西 *shānxī*) and Shaanxi (陕西 *shǎnxī*) provinces is their respective tones. In order to avoid confusion, Shaanxi (陕西 *shǎnxī*) is spelled with an extra "a" in English to represent the third tone (*shǎn*). Older references include the transliteration 'Shensi.' Shorthand characters for Shaanxi are Shaan (陕 *shǎn*), and Qin (秦 *qín*), a reference to the founding Qin dynasty. Other short hand characters include Tai (泰 *tài*) or Santai (三泰 *sāntài*.)

Any visitor to Shaanxi province will likely spend all of their time in and around the capital of Xi'an. For when it comes to history, as a Chinese tourism guide puts it, "For 20 years of reform, one looks at Shenzhen; one hundred years of change: Shanghai. When thinking of a thousand years of tumultuous shifts, see Beijing. But for five thousand years of civilization, it's Xi'an" (Shang-Ch'i 2017.) Famously, not far from Xi'an in Lantian County (藍田縣 *lántián xiàn*), in 1974 local well diggers stumbled upon some of the most spectacular of Chinese archeological finds, including the famous terracotta army of the first Qin emperor (Qin Shi Huangdi 秦始皇帝 *qínshǐ huángdì*).

Shaanxi was also the province where the Chinese Communist Party (CCP) set up its fortified enclave in Yan'an (延安 *yán'ān*) during World War II, and where Mao Zedong consolidated his power. In the modern era, Chinese President and General Secretary of the CCP, Xi Jinping (習近平 *Xí Jìnpíng*), has links to Shaanxi Province through his father, Xi Zhongxun (習仲勳 *Xí Zhòngxūn*) who was born in Fuping county (富平縣 *fùpíng xiàn*). As such, Xi Jinping has well-established contacts and relationships with party members ('*guanxi*') from Shaanxi, to include high ranking (Standing Politburo) CCP members Wang Qishan (王岐山 *wáng qíshān*) and Yu Zhengsheng (俞正聲 *yú zhèngshēng*).

Prehistoric Shaanxi

As important was the discovery of Peking man (outside Beijing in Zhoukoudian), perhaps even more significant were the specimens found (1963) of Lantian Man (*Homo erectus lantianensis*, previously named *Sinanthropus lantienensis*), also found in Lantian county. Later analysis in 2014 showed Lantian Man lived about 1.63 million years ago (Holloway 2014).

During the late 1950s, evidence of the Laoguantai Culture (老官台文化 *lǎoguāntái wénhuà*, 6500–5000 BCE) was discovered in Huaxian County (華縣 *huáxiàn*), in Weinan City (渭南市 *wèinán shì*). Laoguantai pottery features Bo (缽 *bō*; alternatively, 鉢 *bō*), and Guan (罐 *guàn*) forms, as well as ceramics with tripod legs and flat bottomed vessels. Some Laoguantai pottery also includes red-banded decor, representing the oldest colored ceramic discovered in China. Some of these artifacts showed influence of the so-called Chengbeixi Culture (城背溪文化 *chéngbèixī wénhuà*), dated ca. 8500–7000 years ago, and were also found at sites in Hubei Province, Yidu City (宜都市 *yídū shì*) (Underhill 2013).

Also discovered during the 1950s, showing its origins in the Laoguantai Culture, the famous Banpo (半坡 *bànpō*) village, just outside Xi'an in Baqiao District (灞橋區 *bàqiáo qū*), was a Neolithic settlement of at least a few hundred individuals.

Based on radiocarbon dating, this stone-age village existed some 5600–6700 years ago. Classified as Yangshao Culture after the village where it was originally categorized (仰韶村 *yǎngsháo cūn*) in Henan Province, these excavations also revealed distinctive, black-striped pottery with textured designs (Zhang 1977). The Banpo society had a relatively advanced form of agriculture, growing millet, cabbage, and raising pigs, dogs, chickens and cattle (Zhang 2005).

Shaanxi, along with other regions in China, also possesses Shang Dynasty (1570–1045 BCE) archeological sites. Some scholars believe the inhabitants of the region of east and west Shaanxi were highly influential in the development of the Shang, later expanding into Shanxi, northern Henan, and southern Hebei (Yuan and Jiao 2007).

Western Zhou (Eleventh Century to 771 BCE)

The Western Zhou began with the conquering of the Shang at Muye (牧野 *mùyě*), modern-day Zhaoge Subdistrict (朝歌街道 *zhāogē jiēdào*), in Qixian County (淇縣 *qíxiàn*). This event was recorded on the famous Li Gui (利簋 *lì guǐ*) bronze vessel, found in Lintong District (臨潼區 *líntóng qū*), and is hitherto the oldest extant inscription of the Zhou ever discovered. The bronze script reads in part:

> King Wu … sacrificed, and was able to make known that he had routed the Shang (Shaugnessy 1991).

Sources conflict, but according to the widely accepted historical record, the Zhou dynasty King Wen (文王 *wén wáng*) founded a capital at Fengjing (豐京 *fēngjīng*), southwest of today's Xi'an Chang'an District (長安區 *cháng'ān qū*) on the west bank of the Feng River (灃河 *fēng hé*). The city was built over a stretch of land that includes Rongsheng Zhuang (容省莊 *róngshěng zhuāng*), Zhangjia Po (張家坡 *zhāngjiā pō*), Mawang Cun (馬王村 *mǎwáng cūn*) and Xiyu Cun (西玉村 *xīyù cūn*) villages. Then, King Wu Wang conquered King Wen, and, finding the Feng capital insufficient for his needs, moved his about 25 km to the east of the Feng River, naming the new capital Hao (鎬京 *hàojīng*). The Hao capital was roughly northwest of today's Chang'an District, along an area that includes Doumen Town (斗門鎮 *dǒumén zhèn*), Pudu (普渡村 *pǔdù cūn*) and Fenghao (豐鎬村 *fēnggǎo cūn*) villages. Although another source has Feng to "the east and [Hao] to the west of the Feng River," the historical map clearly shows Feng just west of the Feng River, and Hao to the east. In any event, no archeological finds to date can definitively link Zhou dynasty clans in that area (Rawson 1999).

In 771 BCE, combined forces of the Shen (申 *shēn*) and the Quan Rong (犬戎 *quǎnróng*) people battled with the Western Zhou, killing King You of Zhou (周幽王

zhōuyōu wáng) and signaled the end of this long-lived reign. The Zongzhou (宗周 *zōngzhōu*) imperial grounds (in the Feng and Hao capital areas) had been rendered uninhabitable due to conflict, and so the remaining Zhou dynasty family moved to Chengzhou (成周 *chéngzhōu*) in modern-day Luoyang City, Henan Province (Hsu 1999). As the Zhou fell into decline and moved east, the vassal state of Qin moved in its place, dominating the Shaanxi region during the Warring States (ca. 475 BCE) period. Considered by the other states to be less cultured, the Qin learned much from the Zhou in terms of learning and rites (Shirokauer and Brown 2013). In 383 BCE, its capital at Liyang (櫟陽 *lìyang*, located in modern-day northern Lintong) became the center of the Qin State. By 350 BCE, Duke Xiao of Qin (秦孝公 *qínxiàogōng*) moved the Qin State capital from Liyang to Xianyang (咸陽 *xiányáng*),[1] and through his minister Shang Yang (商鞅 *shāng yāng*, 390–338 BCE) carried out various reforms. At about this time, the Shaanxi region had a population of about two million (Cao 1986).

The Qin state really began to flourish in 246 BCE with the ascension of Ying Zheng (嬴政 *yíng zhèng*), who later became the infamous "First Emperor of Qin" (秦始皇帝 *qín shǐhuángdì*). Under the leadership of General Meng Tian (蒙恬 *méng tián*), the Qin deployed 300,000 troops to strike at the Xiongnu (匈奴 *xiōngnú*) tribes. With the expansion of the northern border, and using freed prisoners to populate newly acquired territory, these developments added about 350,000 to the the population of the Shaanxi region.

Unification Under the Qin (秦 *qín*)

While relatively short-lived, the unification of China under the Qin Dynasty (221 BC - 206 BC) laid the framework for Chinese rule ever since. The Qin created *de novo* the political administration of Chinese kingdoms, states and provinces. It also modernized the written language, standardized measures, instituted new (albeit often harsh) laws, all measures to centralize the rule of China over its population. This idea of firm, top-to-bottom ideological and administrative control remained through modern times. For example, Mao Zedong famously remarked that his vision of the modern Chinese political system was essentially "Marx plus Qin Shihuangdi" (Yang 2007).

In ca. 195 BCE, due to strategic geographical concerns, the Han Dynasty founded its capital Chang'an (長安 *cháng'ān*) just northwest of modern-day Xi'an City. The logistical and cultural center for connecting the Silk Road, Chang'an then had a population of 146,000. With the flourishing of the Western Han, in 2 CE the

[1] The Xianyang capital was later known to the west as Khumdan, which was so named in the Sogdian language from the Tang dynasty's Nestorian tradition in China, and persisted in Arabic thereafter. Khumdan itself was the transliteration from the older Chinese for Xianyang (*G'em-diang*).

population had increased to 246,200. Historian Xue Pingshuan (薛平拴 *xuē píngshuān*) tells us that at this time in the region of modern-day Shaanxi province there were 902,780 households totaling 3,597,179 people (Yuan 2012). By the end of the Han (ca. 200 CE), the Shaanxi region of today had a population of no less than four million.

With a population of more than 1,400,000, the city of Chang'an was the center of Chinese culture and politics during the Sui and Tang. Indeed, as of 741 CE, Chang'an was the largest metropolis in the world, and was administered by Jingji Prefecture (京畿道 *jīngjīdào*) in modern day Xi'an. At this time, the Jingji capital was known to have been "densely packed with people, with not much in the way of farmland." (Wang 2008).

The origins of the name Shaanxi (陝西 *shǎnxī*) goes back to 997 CE. Its name was derived from the administrative district Shaanxi Lu (陝西路 *shǎnxī lù* "mountain pass") that controlled Guanzhong (關中 *guānzhōng*), which also included Hanzhong (漢中 *hànzhōng*) and Ankang (安康 *ānkāng*). During the Northern Song period (ca. 1000 CE), the Shaanxi region of today had a population of 2,915,000. The formal designation of Shaanxi Prefecture (陝西行省 *shǎnxī xíngshěng*) would have to wait until the Yuan (ca. 1330). But these were very hardscrabble years under the Mongols. With infertile soil and difficult living conditions, in 1393 the area recorded a population of about 1,610,000. Shaanxi returned to political relevancy during the Ming dynasty. The newly named capital (西安府 *xī'ān fǔ*), formerly known as Fengyuan Lu (奉元路 *fèng yuánlù*) during the Yuan, is how modern Xi'an City gets its name.

1556 Earthquake

On 23 January 1556, a probable Richter 8 earthquake, centered at Huaxian County (華縣 *huá xiàn*) killed an estimated 830,000 people. Destroying 101 counties, the giant temblor (remembered as much for its thunderous resonance as the shaking) impacted an area reaching 2700 square kilometers, impacting the neighboring provinces of Gansu, Ningxia, Shanxi and Henan, a total of five provinces and 227 counties. Because the quake occurred around midnight, it caught most people asleep, compounding the numbers of casualties (Xie and Zhang 2005).

Qing Dynasty Shaanxi Populations

In ca. 1650 (beginning of the Qing dynasty), the population of Shaanxi was no larger than 3,600,000. However, with the improving stability and economic development in the Qing dynasty, Shaanxi's population increased dramatically to an estimated 6,700,000 in 1685. Continued growth increased the population by the 41st Qianlong year (1776) to 7,965,000. Shaanxi further experienced a population boom during the Qing, recording about 12,100,000 people in 1850. There was, however, a slight decrease by 1862 in population down to 11,973,000 (Feng 1997).

Dungan Revolt

From about 1862–1878 the Moslem Rebellion (or Dungan Revolt; 同治回變 *tóng-zhìhuíbiàn*), which mostly began as a collection of skirmishes on ethnic lines against the Han Chinese, brought about disastrous conflict in Shaanxi province. Large battles raged between Hui Moslems against the Qing military. The Shaanxi area suffered some 300,000 dead during the first 7 years of the conflict, increasing to half a million dead (including both Han Chinese and Hui) throughout the course of the uprising.

War and Drought

The political and military turmoil resulting the Opium War in the mid-nineteenth century also heavily impacted Shaanxi. The aftermath of unrest and natural disasters eventually brought Shaanxi's population down to eight million in 1910. Then began a severe two-year drought in 1928, accompanied by a severe famine that struck a number of provinces. Subsequently, Shaanxi lost about a third of its population. In 1933, the Republic of China (ROC) assigned the name "Shaanxi Province," with Xi'an being renamed Xijing (西京 *xījīng*: "western capital").

Revolutionary Shaanxi

Decades later, Mao Zedong consolidated his forces in Yan'an (aka Yenan; 延安 *yán'ān*) from 1937 to 1949. This achieved two main practical purposes: to keep the Chinese Communist forces at a safer distance from the invading Japanese, while using only irregular combat operations in the mountains, and to increase Mao's control over the CCP (Pantsov 2012). It also raised thousands of young recruits to join the revolutionary movement, bringing in some 40,000 into Yan'an by 1938. Mao Zedong's political machinations reached their peak intensity during 1942–1944, employing psychological terror as well as physical violence during the so-called Yan'an Rectification Movement.[2]

[2] 延安整風運動 *yánān zhěngfēng yùndòng*.

Shaanxi: Population and Economic Trends

Known for its rich coal reserves, especially in Shenmu City (神木市 *shénmù shì*) and Fugu County (府谷縣 *fŭgŭ xiàn*), Shaanxi is ranked third in terms of coal production after Shanxi and Inner Mongolia. When added together with petroleum and natural gas industries, these account for about a quarter of Shaanxi's gross industrial output as of 2019 (HKTDC 2021).

Because of its resplendent historical sites going back millennia, especially in the capital city of Xi'an, a significant portion of Shaanxi's economy benefits from tourists. In 2014, Shaanxi province reported a total of 252.14 billion Chinese Yuan (US$39 billion) in revenues from tourism, representing an impressive 14% of the province's gross domestic product (GDP: 1,768.9 billion Yuan, US$274 billion). Shaanxi's GDP in 2015 was $282 billion, rising to $407 billion in 2020, ranking it 14th among mainland China's 31 provinces and major cities. Its per capita income was roughly average in this field, about $4435 in 2020 (Zhang 2021).

In 2015 Shaanxi province had total population (including permanent and non-permanent residents) of 37,751,200, and registered permanent population of about 39,260,000 (compared to 38,314,000 in 2010). This gap was roughly the same in 2020, with a census population that year of 39,529,000 (Table 25.1), and a *hukou* (official, registered) population of 40,230,000 (Table 25.3; Fig. 25.2).

Table 25.3 (below) shows the *hukou* (family registered) populations based on PRC Ministry of Civil Affairs data. (Districts listed directly under major cities are government seats, as are those in parentheses). One can compare these data with the census (usual residential populations based on 2010 and 2020 censuses in Tables 25.1 and 25.2 (below):

Table 25.1 Shaanxi province population (residential 常住人口 *chángzhù rénkŏu*) data. (SPBS 2021)

Shaanxi province cities	Population (2010)	Population (2020)
Xi'an City 西安市 *xī''ān shì*	8,467,837	12,952,907
Ankang City 安康市 *ānkāng shì*	2,629,906	2,493,436
Baoji City 寶雞市 *băojī shì*	3,716,731	3,321,853
Hanzhong City 漢中市 *hànzhōng shì*	3,416,196	3,211,462
Shangluo City 商洛市 *shāngluò shì*	2,341,742	2,041,231
Tongchuan City 銅川市 *tóngchuān shì*	834,437	698,322
Weinan City 渭南市 *wèinán shì*	5,286,077	4,688,744
Xianyang City 咸陽市 *xiányáng shì*	4,894,834	3,959,842
Yan'an City 延安市 *yán'ān shì*	2,187,009	2,282,581
Yulin City 榆林市 *yúlín shì*	3,351,437	3,624,750
Yangling Demonstration Zone 楊凌示範區[a] *yánglíng shìfànqū*	201,172	253,871
Total	**37,327,378**	**39,528,999**

[a]Full name is the Yangling Agricultural Hi-tech Industries Demonstration Zone 楊凌農業高新技術產業示範區 *yánglíng nóngyè gāoxīnjìshù chănyè shìfànqū*

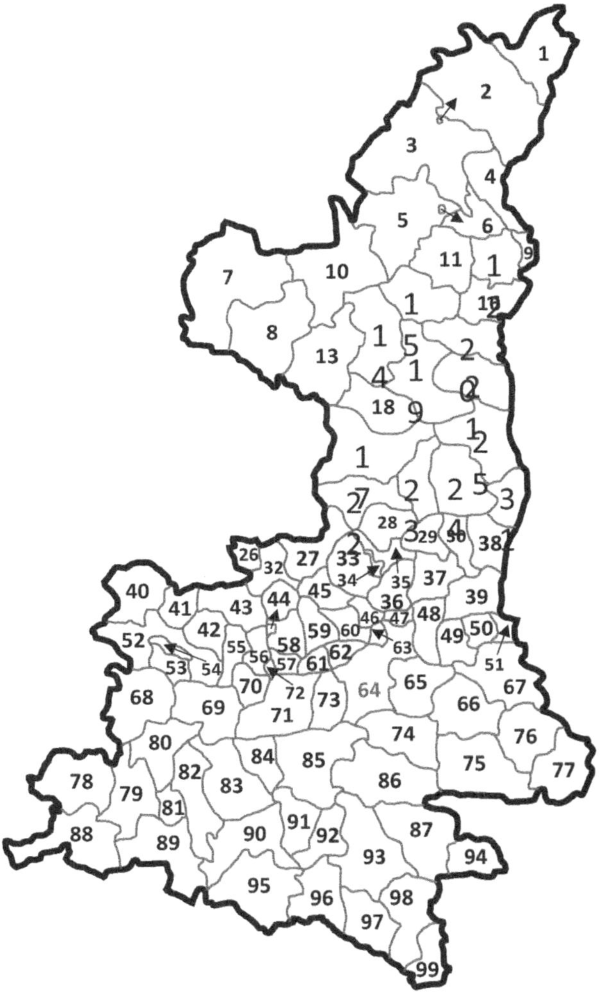

1. Fuyu County
2. Shenmu City
3. Yuyang District
4. Jiaxian County
5. Hengshan District
6. Mizhi County
7. Dingbian County
8. Wuqi County
9. Wubu County
10. Jingbian County
11. Zizhou County
12. Suide County
13. Zhidan County
14. Ansai District
15. Zichang City
16. Qingjian County
17. Fuxian County
18. Ganquan County
19. Baota District
20. Yanchuan County
21. Yanchang County
22. Huangling County
23. Luochuan County
24. Huanglong County
25. Yichuan County
26. Changwu County
27. Xunyi County
28. Yijun County
29. Baishui County
30. Chengcheng County
31. Hancheng City
32. Binzhou City
33. Huizhou District
34. Wangyi District
35. Yintai District
36. Fuping County
37. Pucheng County
38. Heyang County
39. Dali County
40. Longxian County
41. Qianyang County
42. Fengxiang County
43. Linyou County
44. Yongshou County
45. Chunhua County
46. Sanyuan County
47. Yanliang District
48. Linwei District
49. Huazhou District
50. Huayin City
51. Tongguan County
52. Chencang District
53. Weibin District
54. Jintai District
55. Qishan County
56. Fufeng County
57. Wugong County
58. Qianxian County
59. Liquan County
60. Jingyang County
61. Xingping City
62. Xianyang City
63. Gaoling District
64. Xi'an City
65. Lantian County
66. Shangzhou District
67. Luonan County
68. Fengxian County
69. Taibai County
70. Meixian County
71. Zhouzhi County
72. Yangling County
73. Huyi District
74. Zhashui County
75. Shanyang County
76. Danfeng County
77. Shangnan County
78. Lüeyang County
79. Mianxian County
80. Liuba County
81. Hantai District
82. Chenggu County
83. Yangxian County
84. Foping County
85. Ningshan County
86. Zhen'an County
87. Xunyang County
88. Ningqiang County
89. Nanzheng County
90. Xixiang County
91. Shiquan County
92. Hanyin County
93. Hanbin District
94. Baihe County
95. Zhenba County
96. Ziyang County
97. Langao County
98. Pingli County
99. Zhenping County

Fig. 25.2 Shaanxi province: Subdistricts (provincial capital city: Xi'an City). (Drawn by the author, after People's Republic of China, Ministry of Civil Affairs. (MCA 2020))

Table 25.2 Shaanxi province: Population data of cities and their subordinate sectors. (SPBS 2021)

Cities and subordinate sectors, population (2020 census)	Subordinate district, city and county populations (2020)	Total population (2020)
Xi'an City 西安市 ***xī'ān shì***		**12,952,907**
Weiyang District 未央區 *wèiyāng qū*	733,403	
Lianhu District 蓮湖區 *liánhú qū*	1,019,102	
Xincheng District 新城區 *xīnchéng qū*	644,702	
Beilin District 碑林區 *bēilín qū*	756,840	
Baqiao District 灞橋區 *bàqiáo qū*	593,962	
Yanta District 雁塔區 *yàntǎ qū*	1,202,038	
Yanliang District 閻良區 *yánliáng qū*	281,536	
Lintong District 臨潼區 *líntóng qū*	675,961	
Chang'an District 長安區 *cháng'ān qū*	1,090,600	
Lantian County 藍田縣 *lántián xiàn*	491,975	
Zhouzhi County 周至縣 *zhōuzhì xiàn*	504,144	
Huyi District 鄠邑區 *hùyì qū*	459,417	
Gaoling District 高陵區 *gāolíng qū*	416,996	
Xixian New District 西咸新區 *xīxián xīnqū*	1,304,618	
Xi'an High Technology and Industry Development Zone 西安高新技術產業開發區 *xī'ān gāoxīnjìshù chǎnyè kāifāqū*	958,333	
Xi'an Economic and Technology Development Zone 西安經濟技術開發區 *xī'ān jīngjìjìshù kāifāqū*	550,411	
Qujiang New District 曲江新區 *qūjiāng xīnqū*	399,872	
Xi'an Yanliang National Aviation Technology Industry Base ("China Aviation Industrial Base") 西安閻良國家航空高技術產業基地 *xī'ān yánliáng guójiā hángkōnggāojìshù chǎnyè jīdì*	21,748	
Xi'an National Civil Aerospace Industrial Base 西安國家民用航天產業基地 *xī'ān guójiā mínyònghángtiān chǎnyè jīdì*	161,304	
Chanba Ecological Area 滻灞生態區 *chǎnbà shēngtàiqū*	550,015	
Xi'an International Trade and Logistics Park 西安國際港務區 *xī'ān guójìgǎngwù qū*	135,930	
Ankang City 安康市 ***ānkāng shì***		**2,493,436**
Hanbin District 漢濱區 *hànbīn qū*	674,834	
Ankang City Hengkou Demonstration Zone 安康市恒口示範區 *ānkāngshì héngkǒu shìfànqū*	114,290	
Hanyin County 漢陰縣 *hànyīn xiàn*	240,188	
Shiquan County 石泉縣 *shíquán xiàn*	153,221	
Ningshan County 寧陜縣 *níngshǎn xiàn*	59,905	
Ziyang County 紫陽縣 *zǐyáng xiàn*	260,971	
Langao County 嵐皋縣 *lángāo xiàn*	135,006	
Pingli County 平利縣 *pínglì xiàn*	181,286	

(continued)

Table 25.2 (continued)

Cities and subordinate sectors, population (2020 census)	Subordinate district, city and county populations (2020)	Total population (2020)
Zhenping County 鎮坪縣 *zhènpíng xiàn*	47,356	
Xunyang County 旬陽縣 *xúnyáng xiàn*	357,876	
Baihe County 白河縣 *báihé xiàn*	162,774	
Ankang National High and New Technology Industrial Development Zone 安康國家高新技術產業開發區 *ānkāng guójiā gāoxīnjìshù chǎnyè kāifāqū*	105,729	
Baoji Cit y寶雞市 ***bǎojī shì***		**3,321,853**
Jintai District 金台區 *jīntái qū*	460,950	
Weibin District 渭濱區 *wèibīn qū*	585,833	
Chencang District 陳倉區 *chéncāng qū*	479,179	
Fengxiang County 鳳翔區[a] *fèngxiáng qū*	386,156	
Qishan County 岐山縣 *qíshān xiàn*	365,209	
Fufeng County 扶風縣 *fúfēng xiàn*	313,231	
Meixian County 眉縣 *méixiàn*	281,211	
Longxian County 隴縣 *lǒngxiàn*	208,482	
Qianyang County 千陽縣 *qiānyáng xiàn*	99,510	
Linyou County 麟游縣 *línyóu xiàn*	73,297	
Fengxian County 鳳縣 *fèngxiàn*	79,165	
Taibai County 太白縣 *tàibái xiàn*	39,360	
Hanzhong City 漢中市 ***hànzhōng shì***		**3,211,462**
Hantai District 漢台區 *hàntái qū*	618,204	
Nanzheng County 南鄭縣 *nánzhèng xiàn*	466,244	
Chenggu County 城固縣 *chénggù xiàn*	442,035	
Yangxian County 洋縣 *yángxiàn*	345,354	
Xixiang County 西鄉縣 *xīxiāng xiàn*	321,535	
Mianxian County 勉縣 *miǎnxiàn*	344,935	
Ningqiang County 寧強縣 *níngqiáng xiàn*	256,373	
Lüeyang County 略陽縣 *lüèyáng xiàn*	143,989	
Zhenba County 鎮巴縣 *zhènbā xiàn*	210,871	
Liuba County 留壩縣 *liúbà xiàn*	35,325	
Foping County 佛坪縣 *fópíng xiàn*	26,597	
Shangluo City 商洛市 ***shāngluò shì***		**2,041,231**
Shangzhou District 商州區 *shāngzhōu qū*	472,978	
Luonan County 洛南縣 *luònán xiàn*	765,376	
Danfeng County 丹鳳縣 *dānfèng xiàn*	247,259	
Shangnan County 商南縣 *shāngnán xiàn*	203,796	
Shanyang County 山陽縣 *shānyáng xiàn*	359,967	
Zhen'an County 鎮安縣 *zhèn'ān xiàn*	253,786	
Zhashui County 柞水縣 *zhàshuǐ xiàn*	137,709	
Tongchuan City[b] 銅川市 ***tóngchuān shì***		**698,322**

(continued)

Table 25.2 (continued)

Cities and subordinate sectors, population (2020 census)	Subordinate district, city and county populations (2020)	Total population (2020)
Weinan City 渭南市 ***wèinán shì***		**4,688,744**
Linwei District 臨渭區 *línwèi qū*	920,044	
Linwei Main District 臨渭本區 *línwèi běn qū*	723,860	
Weinan High Technology Industry Development Zone 渭南高新技術產業開發區 *wèinán gāoxīnjìshù chǎnyè kāifāqū*	117,520	
Weinan Economic and Technology Development Zone 渭南經濟技術開發區 *wèinán jīngjìjìshù kāifāqū*	78,664	
Huayin City 華陰市 *huáyīn shì*	205,119	
Hancheng City 韓城市 *hánchéng shì*	383,097	
Huazhou District 華州區 *huázhōu qū*	268,620	
Tongguan County 潼關縣 *tóngguān xiàn*	215,317	
Dali County 大荔縣 *dàlì xiàn*	592,888	
Pucheng County 蒲城縣 *púchéng xiàn*	662,603	
Chengcheng County 澄城縣 *chéngchéng xiàn*	304,089	
Baishui County 白水縣 *báishuǐ xiàn*	223,832	
Heyang County 合陽縣 *héyáng xiàn*	360,683	
Fuping County 富平縣 *fùpíng xiàn*	642,452	
Xianyang City[c] 咸陽市 ***xiányáng shì***		**3,959,842**
Qindu District 秦都區 *qíndū qū*	491,631	
Weicheng District 渭城區 *wèichéng qū*	303,516	
Xingping City 興平市 *xīngpíng shì*	463,254	
Sanyuan County 三原縣 *sānyuán xiàn*	357,250	
Jingyang County 涇陽縣 *jīngyáng xiàn*	241,675	
Qianxian County 乾縣 *qiánxiàn*	456,680	
Liquan County 禮泉縣 *lǐquán xiàn*	365,555	
Yongshou County 永壽縣 *yǒngshòu xiàn*	160,230	
Binzhou City 彬州市 *bīnzhōu shì*	300,226	
Changwu County 長武縣 *chángwǔ xiàn*	148,404	
Xunyi County 旬邑縣 *xúnyì xiàn*	211,932	
Chunhua County 淳化縣 *chúnhuà xiàn*	141,756	
Wugong County 武功縣 *wǔgōng xiàn*	317,733	
Yan'an City 延安市 ***yán'ān shì***		**2,282,581**
Baota District 寶塔區 *wǔgōng xiàn*	640,951	
Yanchang County 延長縣 *yáncháng xiàn*	117,965	
Yanchuan County 延川縣 *yánchuān xiàn*	139,713	
Zichang City 子長市 *zǐcháng shì*	217,735	
Ansai District 安塞區 *ānsāi qū*	163,135	
Zhidan County 志丹縣 *zhìdān xiàn*	155,129	
Wuqi County 吳起縣 *wúqǐ xiàn*	146,167	
Ganquan County 甘泉縣 *gānquán xiàn*	76,929	

(continued)

Table 25.2 (continued)

Cities and subordinate sectors, population (2020 census)	Subordinate district, city and county populations (2020)	Total population (2020)
Fuxian County 富縣 *fùxiàn*	142,981	
Luochuan County 洛川縣 *luòchuān xiàn*	201,663	
Yichuan County 宜川縣 *yíchuān xiàn*	112,090	
Huanglong County 黃龍縣 *huánglóng xiàn*	41,198	
Huangling County 黃陵縣 *huánglíng xiàn*	127,015	
Yulin City 榆林市 *yúlín shì*		**3,624,750**
Yuyang District 榆陽區 *yúyáng qū*	967,639	
Shenmu City 神木市 *shénmù shì*	571,869	
Fugu County 府谷縣 *fǔgǔ xiàn*	255,397	
Hengshan District 横山區 *héngshān qū*	283,918	
Jingbian County 靖邊縣 *jìngbiān xiàn*	389,002	
Dingbian County 定邊縣 *dìngbiān xiàn*	339,077	
Suide County 綏德縣 *suídé xiàn*	255,294	
Mizhi County 米脂縣 *mǐzhī xiàn*	141,324	
Jiaxian County 佳縣 *jiāxiàn*	113,035	
Wubu County 吳堡縣 *wúbǔ xiàn*	53,938	
Qingjian County 清澗縣 *qīngjiàn xiàn*	115,645	
Zizhou County 子洲縣 *zǐzhōu xiàn*	138,612	

[a]Formerly a county, made a district on 29 January 2021
[b]Data on subdistrict populations not available as of 25 August 2021
[c]Includes the Yangling Demonstration Zone (楊凌示範區*yánglíng shìfànqū*) population: 253,871

Shaanxi Province (陕 *shǎn*; 秦 *qín*)

Provincial Capital: Xi'an City

Table 25.3 Shaanxi province: permanent registered (戶籍人口 *hùjí rénkǒu*) populations. (MCA 2020)

Name	Traditional	Simplified	Population (2012)	Population (2016)	Population (2020)	Area (Sq. Km)
Shaanxi Province	陝西省	陕西省	**38,740,000**	**39,260,000**	**40,230,000**	**205,629**
Xi'an City (Subprovincial level)	西安市	西安市	**7,820,000**	**7,960,000**	**9,230,000**	**10,106**
Weiyang District (Zhangjiabao Subdistrict)	未央區 (張家堡街道)	未央区 (张家堡街道)	520,000	560,000	890,000	263
Lianhu District (Beiyuanmen Subdistrict)	蓮湖區 (北院門街道)	莲湖区 (北院门街道)	640,000	640,000	730,000	39

(continued)

Table 25.3 (continued)

Name	Traditional	Simplified	Population (2012)	Population (2016)	Population (2020)	Area (Sq. Km)
Xincheng District (Xiyilu Subdistrict)	新城區 (西一路街道)	新城区 (西一路街道)	500,000	500,000	530,000	30
Beilin District (Zhangjiacun Subdistrict)	碑林區 (張家村街道)	碑林区 (张家村街道)	730,000	710,000	720,000	23
Baqiao District (Fangzhicheng Subdistrict)	灞橋區 (紡織城街道)	灞桥区 (纺织城街道)	510,000	520,000	630,000	324
Yanta District (Xiaozhailu Subdistrict)	雁塔區 (小寨路街道)	雁塔区 (小寨路街道)	790,000	810,000	1,180,000	152
Yanliang District (Fenghuanglu Subdistrict)	閻良區 (鳳凰路街道)	阎良区 (凤凰路街道)	250,000	260,000	270,000	244
Lintong District (Lishan Subdistrict)	臨潼區 (驪山街道)	临潼区 (骊山街道)	700,000	710,000	730,000	916
Chang'an District (Weiqu Subdistrict)	長安區 (韋曲街道)	长安区 (韦曲街道)	980,000	1,020,000	1,220,000	1594
Lantian County (Languan Town)	藍田縣 (藍關鎮)	蓝田县 (蓝关镇)	640,000	650,000	660,000	2006
Zhouzhi County (Erqu Town)	周至縣 (二曲鎮)	周至县 (二曲镇)	670,000	670,000	690,000	2946
Huyi District (Ganting Subdistrict)	鄠邑區 (甘亭街道)	鄠邑区 (甘亭街道)	600,000	600,000	630,000	1281
Gaoling District (Luyuan Subdistrict)	高陵區 (鹿苑街道)	高陵区 (鹿苑街道)	290,000	310,000	360,000	288
Yan'an City	延安市	延安市	2,310,000	2,360,000		36,032
Baota District (Baotashan Subdistrict)	寶塔區 (寶塔山街道)	宝塔区 (宝塔山街道)	460,000	460,000		3538
Yanchang County (Qilicun Town)	延長縣 (七里村鎮)	延长县 (七里村镇)	160,000	160,000	150,000	2362
Yanchuan County (Yanchuan Town)	延川縣 (延川鎮)	延川县 (延川镇)	190,000	200,000	190,000	1987
Zichang County[a] (Wayaobu Town)	子長縣 (瓦窯堡鎮)	子长县 (瓦窑堡镇)	270,000	280,000	N/A	(2393)
Zichang City (Wayaobu Subdistrict)	子長市 (瓦窯堡街道)	子长市 (瓦窑堡街道)	N/A	N/A	220,000	2405
Ansai District (Zhenwudong Town)	安塞區 (真武洞鎮)	安塞区 (真武洞镇)	180,000	190,000	200,000	2951

(continued)

Table 25.3 (continued)

Name	Traditional	Simplified	Population (2012)	Population (2016)	Population (2020)	Area (Sq. Km)
Zhidan County (Bao'an Town)	志丹縣 (保安鎮)	志丹县 (保安镇)	150,000	140,000	160,000	3790
Wuqi County (Wuqi Town)	吳起縣 (吳起鎮)	吴起县 (吴起镇)	140,000	140,000	150,000	3789
Ganquan County (Chengguan Town)	甘泉縣 (城關鎮)	甘泉县 (城关镇)	90,000	90,000	90,000	2276
Fuxian County (Chafang Town)	富縣 (茶坊鎮)	富县 (茶坊镇)	150,000	160,000	160,000	4180
Luochuan County (Fengqi Town)	洛川縣 (鳳棲鎮)	洛川县 (凤栖镇)	220,000	220,000	220,000	1791
Yichuan County (Danzhou Town)	宜川縣 (丹州鎮)	宜川县 (丹州镇)	120,000	120,000	120,000	2937
Huanglong County (Shibu Town)	黃龍縣 (石堡鎮)	黄龙县 (石堡镇)	50,000	50,000	50,000	2751
Huangling County (Qiaoshan Town)	黃陵縣 (橋山鎮)	黄陵县 (桥山镇)	130,000	130,000	120,000	2287
Tongchuan City	銅川市	铜川市	850,000	860,000	800,000	3881
Yaozhou District (Yong'anlu Subdistrict)	耀州區 (永安路街道)	耀州区 (永安路街道)	320,000	330,000	340,000	1608
Wangyi District (Hongqijie Subdistrict)	王益區 (紅旗街街道)	王益区 (红旗街街道)	210,000	210,000	180,000	156
Yintai District (Chengguan Subdistrict)	印台區 (城關街道)	印台区 (城关街道)	230,000	230,000	190,000	609
Yijun County (Chengguan Town)	宜君縣 (城關鎮)	宜君县 (城关镇)	90,000	90,000	90,000	1508
Weinan City	渭南市	渭南市	5,600,000	5,650,000	5,460,000	13,033
Linwei District (Sheqiao Subdistrict)	臨渭區 (社橋街道)	临渭区 (杜桥街道)	980,000	980,000	950,000	1262
Huayin City (Taihualu Subdistrict)	華陰市 (太華路街道)	华阴市 (太华路街道)	270,000	270,000	240,000	675
Hancheng City (Xincheng Subdistrict)	韓城市 (新城街道)	韩城市 (新城街道)	400,000	400,000	400,000	1596
Huaxian County (Huazhou Town)	華縣 (華州鎮)	华县 (华州镇)	350,000	N/A	N/A	(1128)
Huazhou District[b] (Huazhou Town)	華州區 (華州鎮)	华州区 (华州镇)	N/A	350,000	320,000	1128
Tongguan County (Chengguan Town)	潼關縣 (城關鎮)	潼关县 (城关镇)	170,000	170,000	150,000	429
Dali County (Chengguan Town)	大荔縣 (城關鎮)	大荔县 (城关镇)	720,000	730,000	720,000	1696

(continued)

Table 25.3 (continued)

Name	Traditional	Simplified	Population (2012)	Population (2016)	Population (2020)	Area (Sq. Km)
Pucheng County (Chengguan Town)	蒲城縣 (城關鎮)	蒲城县 (城关镇)	780,000	790,000	780,000	1582
Chengcheng County (Chengguan Town)	澄城縣 (城關鎮)	澄城县 (城关镇)	400,000	400,000	380,000	1123
Baishui County (Chengguan Town)	白水縣 (城關鎮)	白水县 (城关镇)	290,000	300,000	280,000	988
Heyang County (Chengguan Town)	合陽縣 (城關鎮)	合阳县 (城关镇)	450,000	460,000	450,000	1308
Fuping County (Chengguan Town)	富平縣 (城關鎮)	富平县 (城关镇)	790,000	800,000	790,000	1246
Xianyang City	咸陽市	咸阳市	5,380,000	5,470,000	5,420,000	10,323
Qindu District (Renminlu Subdistrict)	秦都區 (人民路街道)	秦都区 (人民路街道)	490,000	500,000	530,000	259
Yangling District (Yangling Subdistrict)	楊陵區 (楊陵街道)	杨陵区 (杨陵街道)	190,000	190,000	190,000	133
Weicheng District (Weiyang Subdistrict)	渭城區 (渭陽街道)	渭城区 (渭阳街道)	410,000	410,000	420,000	269
Xingping City (Dongcheng Subdistrict)	興平市 (東城街道)	兴平市 (东城街道)	600,000	610,000	600,000	509
Sanyuan County (Chengguan Subdistrict)	三原縣 (城關街道)	三原县 (城关街道)	410,000	420,000	410,000	577
Jingyang County (Jinggan Subdistrict)	涇陽縣 (涇干街道)	泾阳县 (泾干街道)	510,000	530,000	530,000	777
Qianxian County (Chengguan Subdistrict)	乾縣 (城關街道)	乾县 (城关街道)	600,000	600,000	590,000	1000
Liquan County (Chengguan Subdistrict)	禮泉縣 (城關街道)	礼泉县 (城关街道)	490,000	500,000	480,000	1011
Yongshou County (Jianjun Subdistrict)	永壽縣 (監軍街道)	永寿县 (监军街道)	210,000	210,000	210,000	888
Binxian County[c] (Chengguan Town)	彬縣 (城關鎮)	彬县 (城关镇)	350,000	360,000	N/A	(1181)
Binzhou City (Chengguan Subdistrict)	彬州市 (城關街道)	彬州市 (城关街道)	N/A	N/A	360,000	1181

(continued)

Table 25.3 (continued)

Name	Traditional	Simplified	Population (2012)	Population (2016)	Population (2020)	Area (Sq. Km)
Changwu County (Zhaoren Subdistrict)	長武縣 (昭仁街道)	长武县 (昭仁街道)	180,000	190,000	190,000	570
Xunyi County (Chengguan Subdistrict)	旬邑縣 (城關街道)	旬邑县 (城关街道)	280,000	290,000	290,000	1774
Chunhua County (Chengguan Subdistrict)	淳化縣 (城關街道)	淳化县 (城关街道)	200,000	200,000	190,000	983
Wugong County (Puji Subdistrict)	武功縣 (普集街道)	武功县 (普集街道)	450,000	460,000	440,000	392
Baoji City	寶雞市	宝鸡市	3,800,000	3,840,000	3,780,000	18,120
Jintai District (Zhongshandonglu Subdistrict)	金台區 (中山東路街道)	金台区 (中山东路街道)	380,000	390,000	370,000	311
Weibin District (Jinling Subdistrict)	渭濱區 (金陵街道)	渭滨区 (金陵街道)	440,000	440,000	420,000	842
Chencang District (Guozhen Subdistrict)	陳倉區 (虢鎮街道)	陈仓区 (虢镇街道)	600,000	610,000	600,000	2472
Fengxiang County (Chengguan Town)	鳳翔縣 (城關鎮)	凤翔县 (城关镇)	520,000	520,000	520,000	1229
Qishan County (Fengming Town)	岐山縣 (鳳鳴鎮)	岐山县 (凤鸣镇)	470,000	470,000	460,000	855
Fufeng County (Chengguan Subdistrict)	扶風縣 (城關街道)	扶风县 (城关街道)	440,000	450,000	440,000	745
Meixian County (Shoushan Subdistrict)	眉縣 (首善街道)	眉县 (首善街道)	320,000	320,000	330,000	858
Longxian County (Chengguan Town)	隴縣 (城關鎮)	陇县 (城关镇)	260,000	270,000	270,000	2279
Qianyang County (Chengguan Town)	千陽縣 (城關鎮)	千阳县 (城关镇)	130,000	130,000	130,000	999
Linyou County (Jiuchenggong Town)	麟游縣 (九成宮鎮)	麟游县 (九成宫镇)	90,000	90,000	90,000	1708
Fengxian County (Shuangshipu Town)	鳳縣 (雙石鋪鎮)	凤县 (双石铺镇)	100,000	100,000	90,000	3148
Taibai County (Zuitou Town)	太白縣 (嘴頭鎮)	太白县 (嘴头镇)	50,000	50,000	50,000	2716
Hanzhong City	漢中市	汉中市	3,790,000	3,850,000	3,810,000	27,093

(continued)

Table 25.3 (continued)

Name	Traditional	Simplified	Population (2012)	Population (2016)	Population (2020)	Area (Sq. Km)
Hantai District (Zhongshanjie Subdistrict)	漢台區 (中山街街道)	汉台区 (中山街街道)	550,000	560,000	570,000	546
Nanzheng County (Hanshan Subdistrict)	南鄭縣 (漢山街道)	南郑县 (汉山街道)	550,000	560,000	560,000	2808
Chenggu County (Bowang Subdistrict)	城固縣 (博望街道)	城固县 (博望街道)	530,000	540,000	540,000	2217
Yangxian County (Yangzhou Subdistrict)	洋縣 (洋州街道)	洋县 (洋州街道)	440,000	450,000	450,000	3194
Xixiang County (Chengguan Subdistrict)	西鄉縣 (城關街道)	西乡县 (城关街道)	410,000	420,000	420,000	3229
Mianxian County (Mianyang Subdistrict)	勉縣 (勉陽街道)	勉县 (勉阳街道)	420,000	430,000	410,000	2390
Ningqiang County (Hanyuan Subdistrict)	寧強縣 (漢源街道)	宁强县 (汉源街道)	330,000	330,000	320,000	3256
Lüeyang County (Chengguan Subdistrict)	略陽縣 (城關街道)	略阳县 (城关街道)	200,000	200,000	180,000	2826
Zhenba County (Jingyang Subdistrict)	鎮巴縣 (涇洋街道)	镇巴县 (泾洋街道)	290,000	290,000	280,000	3407
Liuba County (Chengguan Subdistrict)	留壩縣 (城關街道)	留坝县 (城关街道)	40,000	40,000	40,000	1951
Foping County (Yuanjiazhuang Subdistrict)	佛坪縣 (袁家莊街道)	佛坪县 (袁家庄街道)	30,000	30,000	30,000	1269
Yulin City	**榆**林市	**榆**林市	3,650,000	3,750,000	3,840,000	42923
Yuyang District (Qingshanlu Subdistrict)	榆陽區 (青山路街道)	榆阳区 (青山路街道)	520,000	550,000	600,000	6797
Shenmu City (Shenmu Subdistrict)	神木市 (神木街道)	神木市 (神木街道)	410,000	420,000	450,000	7481
Fugu County (Fugu Town)	府谷縣 (府谷鎮)	府谷县 (府谷镇)	240,000	240,000	250,000	3202
Hengshan County[d] (Hengshan Town)	橫山縣 (橫山鎮)	横山县 (横山镇)	360,000	N/A	N/A	(4084)

(continued)

Table 25.3 (continued)

Name	Traditional	Simplified	Population (2012)	Population (2016)	Population (2020)	Area (Sq. Km)
Hengshan District (Hengshan Subdistrict)	橫山區 (橫山街道)	横山区 (横山街道)	N/A	370,000	380,000	4299
Jingbian County (Zhangjiapan Subdistrict)	靖邊縣 (張家畔街道)	靖边县 (张家畔街道)	330,000	340,000	360,000	4975
Dingbian County (Dingbian Town)	定邊縣 (定邊街道)	定边县 (定边街道)	330,000	340,000	360,000	6821
Suide County (Mingzhou Town)	綏德縣 (名州鎮)	绥德县 (名州镇)	360,000	370,000	350,000	1853
Mizhi County (Yinzhou Subdistrict)	米脂縣 (銀州街道)	米脂县 (银州街道)	220,000	220,000	220,000	1168
Jiaxian County (Jialu Subdistrict)	佳縣 (佳蘆街道)	佳县 (佳芦街道)	260,000	270,000	270,000	2029
Wubu County (Songjiachuan Subdistrict)	吳堡縣 (宋家川街道)	吴堡县 (宋家川街道)	90,000	90,000	80,000	421
Qingjian County (Kuanzhou Town)	清澗縣 (寬洲鎮)	清涧县 (宽洲镇)	220,000	220,000	210,000	1850
Zizhou County (Shuanghuyu Subdistrict)	子洲縣 (雙湖峪街道)	子洲县 (双湖峪街道)	310,000	320,000	300,000	2027
Ankang City	安康市	安康市	3,040,000	3,060,000	3,040,000	23,535
Hanbin District (Laocheng Subdistrict)	漢濱區 (老城街道)	汉滨区 (老城街道)	1,010,000	1,020,000	1,010,000	3644
Hanyin County (Chengguan Town)	漢陰縣 (城關鎮)	汉阴县 (城关镇)	310,000	310,000	310,000	1365
Shiquan County (Chengguan Town)	石泉縣 (城關鎮)	石泉县 (城关镇)	180,000	180,000	180,000	1516
Ningshan County (Chengguan Town)	寧陜縣 (城關鎮)	宁陕县 (城关镇)	70,000	70,000	70,000	3664
Ziyang County (Chengguan Town)	紫陽縣 (城關鎮)	紫阳县 (城关镇)	340,000	340,000	340,000	2244
Langao County (Chengguan Town)	嵐皋縣 (城關鎮)	岚皋县 (城关镇)	170,000	170,000	170,000	1957
Pingli County (Chengguan Town)	平利縣 (城關鎮)	平利县 (城关镇)	240,000	240,000	230,000	2648
Zhenping County (Chengguan Town)	鎮坪縣 (城關鎮)	镇坪县 (城关镇)	60,000	60,000	60,000	1502
Xunyang County (Chengguan Town)	旬陽縣 (城關鎮)	旬阳县 (城关镇)	450,000	460,000	450,000	3541
Baihe County (Chengguan Town)	白河縣 (城關鎮)	白河县 (城关镇)	210,000	210,000	210,000	1454
Shangluo City	商洛市	商洛市	2,450,000	2,490,000	2,510,000	19,581

(continued)

Table 25.3 (continued)

Name	Traditional	Simplified	Population (2012)	Population (2016)	Population (2020)	Area (Sq. Km)
Shangzhou District (Chengguan Subdistrict)	商州區 (城關街道)	商州区 (城关街道)	550,000	550,000	560,000	2645
Luonan County (Chengguan Subdistrict)	洛南縣 (城關街道)	洛南县 (城关街道)	450,000	460,000	460,000	2833
Danfeng County (Longjuzhai Subdistrict)	丹鳳縣 (龍駒寨街道)	丹凤县 (龙驹寨街道)	300,000	310,000	310,000	2407
Shangnan County (Chengguan Subdistrict)	商南縣 (城關街道)	商南县 (城关街道)	240,000	240,000	250,000	2314
Shanyang County (Chengguan Subdistrict)	山陽縣 (城關街道)	山阳县 (城关街道)	450,000	470,000	470,000	3531
Zhen'an County (Yongle Subdistrict)	鎮安縣 (永樂街道)	镇安县 (永乐街道)	300,000	300,000	300,000	3488
Zhashui County (Qianyou Subdistrict)	柞水縣 (乾佑街道)	柞水县 (乾佑街道)	160,000	160,000	160,000	2363

[a]Dissolved 25 July 2019, creating Zichang city
[b]Established in 2015
[c]Dissolved May 2018, creating Binzhou city
[d]Dissolved in 2015, creating Hengshan district

References

Cao, Zhanquan. 1986. [*Shaanxi provincial gazette: Population records*]. Shaanxi: Sanqin Publishing House. 曹占泉. 陕西省志: 人口志. 陕西: 三秦出版社.

Chang, Kwang-chih. 1977. *The archeology of ancient China*. 3rd ed. New Haven: Yale University Press.

Feng Fukuan. 1997. [*History of the Shaanxi Hui people*]. Shaanxi: Shaanxi People's Press. 冯福宽. 陕西回族史. 陕西: 陕西人民出版社.

HKTDC Research. 2021. *Shaanxi: Market profile*. https://research.hktdc.com/en/data-and-profiles/mcpc/provinces/shaanxi. Accessed 20 Sept 20 2021.

Holloway, April. 2014. New dating of *Homo erectus* skull reclassifies Lantian man as oldest known hominin [sic] in Northeast Asia. *Ancient Origins*. https://www.ancient-origins.net/news-evolution-human-origins/new-dating-homo-erectus-skull-reclassifies-lantian-man-020118.

Hsu, Cho-yun. 1999. The spring and autumn period. In *The Cambridge history of ancient China: From the origins of civilization to 221 B.C*, ed. Michael Loewe and Edward L. Shaughnessy, 545–586. New York: Cambridge University Press.

Rawson, Jessica. 1999. Western Zhou archaeology. In *The Cambridge history of ancient China: From the origins of civilization to 221 B.C*, ed. Michael Loewe and Edward L. Shaughnessy, 352–449. New York: Cambridge University Press.

Ministry of Civil Affairs (MCA), People's Republic of China. 2020. [*County/township administration handbook*]. Beijing: China Statistics Press. 中華人民共和國民政部, 中華人民共和國, 鄉鎮行政區劃簡冊.

Pantsov, Alexander V. 2012. *Mao: The real story*. New York: Simon & Schuster.

Schirokauer, Conrad, and Miranda Brown. 2013. *A brief history of Chinese civilization*. 4th ed. Boston: Wadsworth.

Shaanxi Province Bureau of Statistics (SPBS). 2021. [Bulletin of the main data of the seventh national census of Shaanxi Province, issue no. 2]. 19 May. 陕西省第七次全国人口普查主要数据公报, 第二号. http://tjj.shaanxi.gov.cn/tjsj/ndsj/tjgb/qs_444/202105/t20210528_2177393.html.

Shang-Ch'i Guide. 2017. [*Backpacking in China: the most complete collection of self-guided travel for China, 2018*]. Taipei: Shang-Ch'i Shitai publishing. 2018 最完整的中國自助旅遊全集. 台北: 上奇時代.

Shaughnessy, Edward L. 1991. *Sources of western Zhou history: Inscribed bronze vessels*. Los Angeles: University of California Press.

Underhill, Anne P., ed. 2013. *A companion to Chinese archaeology*. Hoboken: Wiley-Blackwell.

Wang, Mingde. 2008. [*From the age of the Yellow River to the age of the canal: A study on the changes of China's ancient capital*]. Chengdu: Bashu Publishing House; 王明德, 从黄河时代到运河时代: 中国古都变迁研究. 成都:巴蜀书社.

Xie, Lili, and Zhang Jingfa. 2005. [*Global shaking: Earthquake science*]. Beijing: Tsinghua University Press. 谢礼立, 张景发. 颤抖的地球: 地震科学. 北京: 清华大学出版社有限公司.

Yang, Jisheng. 2007. *Tombstone: Record of china's great famine in the 1960s* (Chinese version). 楊繼繩. 墓碑: 中国六十年代大饥荒纪实. https://cdn.jsdelivr.net/gh/easy2view/books/resources/grave-stone.pdf.

Yuan, Zuliang, and Jiao Peimin. 2007. [*China's population through history: beginning Qin volume*]. Beijing: People's Press. 袁祖亮, 焦培民. 中國人口通史:先秦卷, Vol. 2. 北京: 人民出版社.

Yuan, Zuliang. 2007. [*China's population through history: Qin to western Han*]. Beijing: People's Press. 袁祖亮. 中國人口通史: 秦西漢卷, Vol. 3. 北京:人民出版社.

Zhang, Shunan. 2021. [The 2020 per capita income list of residents in various provinces: Shanghai is the richest, and it has risen sharply]. Finance.people.com. 22 January. 张澍楠. 2020年各省份居民人均收入榜: 上海最有钱, 这地涨得猛. http://finance.people.com.cn/n1/2021/0122/c1004-32008733.html.

Zhang, Zhongpei. 2005. The Yangshao period: Prosperity and the transformation of prehistoric society. In *The formation of Chinese civilization: An archaeological perspective*, ed. Kwang-chih Chang et al., 43–84. New Haven: Yale University Press.

Chapter 26
Shandong Province

Abstract Shandong Province, along with Henan, possesses a large share of archeological sites that trace back to the earliest progenitors of Chinese civilization. In addition to evidence of Neolithic human settlements going back to ca. 6500 BCE, Shang dynastic culture spread from Henan to Shandong in ca. 1000 BCE, and, of course, Shandong (the State of Lu) was the birthplace of Confucius (551–479 BCE). The State of Qi (also in present-day Shandong) was among the prominent Warring States (ca. 260 BCE). If the historical data are to be believed, the Mongolian invasion (ca. 1300 CE) led to a steep drop in Shandong's population. In more modern times, Germany held a lease on a part of Shandong in the nineteenth century, while Japan occupied the province along with other large swaths of northern Chinese territory from 1937–1945. Today, Shandong's economy ranks in the upper third of China's 31 provinces and major cities, with a gross domestic product of USD $1.14 billion, and a per capita income of over USD $5,000. Its relatively prosperous economy likely explains its relatively brisk population growth of 6% from 2010–2020.

E. Croddy, *China's Provinces and Populations*,
https://doi.org/10.1007/978-3-031-09165-0_26

Shandong Province (山東省 *shāndōng shěng*): Abbreviation 魯 (*lŭ*) (Fig. 26.1)

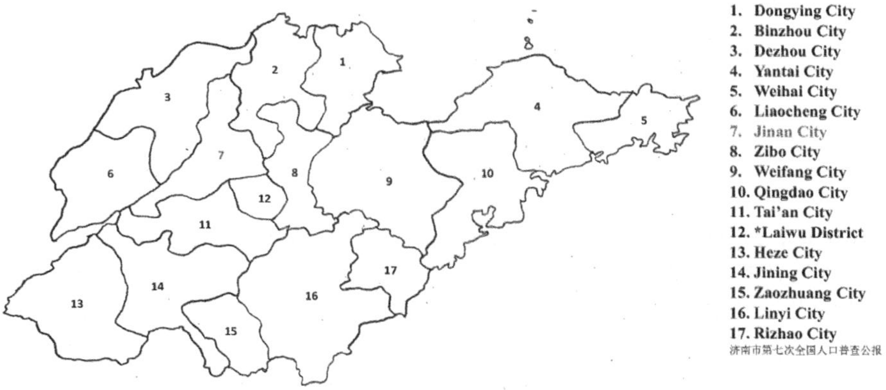

Fig. 26.1 Shandong Province major cities (provincial city: Jinan City). (Drawn by the author, after People's Republic of China, Ministry of Civil Affairs. (MCA 2020))

Shandong Province: General Impressions

Chinese generalize the people of Shandong as being physically tall and strong, and what they lack in gentle speech they make up for in their straight-talking honesty, loyalty, and willingness to help others. (In 2014, military officers of general rank originally born in Shandong are famously over represented in the Chinese People's Liberation Army; perhaps relevant to this fact is that people from Shandong Province are also considered to be among the tallest by average in China.) Shandong provincials do have an accent that can bewilder standard mandarin Chinese speakers, but we are advised that if they slow their speech down a bit, communication shouldn't be a problem (Shang-Ch'i 2017).

Shandong gets its name for its geographical location, being east of the Taihang Mountains (太行山 *tàiháng shān*). In a nod to its ancient kingdom origins, the short character abbreviation for Shandong is Lu 魯 (*lŭ*).

Prehistoric Shandong

In 1981, researchers from Peking University and Yiyuan county (沂源縣 *yíyuán xiàn*) discovered human fossils similar to *Homo erectus pekinensis* in caves at the Eastern base of Qizi'anshan Mountain (騎子鞍山 *qízĭ'ān shān*), Tumen County (土門鄉 *tŭmén xiāng*). According to Chinese sources, the age of these *Homo erectus Yiyuanensis* specimens, which included a cranial cap, teeth, humeral and femoral bone, are estimated to be about 500 thousand years old (Wu et al. 2002).

Discovered in the early 1970s, the oldest known Neolithic settlement of its kind along the Chinese eastern seaboard is the Houli Culture (後李文化 *hòulĭ wénhuà*), found in Houliguanzhuang (後李官莊 *hòulĭguānzhuāng*), Linzi District (臨淄區 *línzī qū*), Zibo City. With provenance going back to 6500–5500 BCE, the Houli Culture showed evidence of milling grain (rice and millet), and was recently discovered at Yuezhuang (月莊 *yuèzhuāng*) in Changqing District (長清區 *chángqīng qū*), Jinan City. Findings at various Houli Cultural sites are replete with a panoply of stone tools, including scythes, adzes, and polishing stones. Dated between 5000–4100 BCE, the Beixin Culture (北辛文化 *bĕixīn wénhuà*) was unearthed (in 1962 and 1964) at Tengzhou City (滕州市 *téngzhōu shì*), and Xisangyuan (西桑園 *xīsāngyuán*) in Yanzhou District (兖州區 *yănzhōu qū*), also in Jining City. Unlike the Houli Culture, the Beixi Culture featured a much larger emphasis on farming, to include growing and processing millet and rice. Significantly, the Beixi Culture practiced animal domestication of cows, pigs, and chickens (Wang 2013).

The remains of the Dawenkou Culture (大汶口文化 *dàwènkŏu wénhuà*), dating back to 5000–3000 BCE, were found in Dawenkou Town (大汶口鎮 *dàwènkŏu zhèn*) in Tai'an City (泰安市 *tài'ān shì*). Like other early farming cultures, this one also featured the domestication of millet. What makes Dawenkou stand out among other Neolithic sites, however, are its distinctive and complex burial structures that used a "two-tier platform" (二層臺 *èrcéngtái*) built with wooden logs. Excavations also found ivory eating utensils as well as complex, colored tripod (鼎 *dǐng*) pottery. Other significant Dawenkou Culture sites include the Neolithic remains at Xixiahou Village (西夏侯村 *xīxiàhóu cūn*), Xizou Town (息陬鎮 *xízōu zhèn*), Qufu City (曲阜市 *qūfù shì*). And nearly 900 burial sites were discovered at Wangyin Village (王因村 *wángyīn cūn*) in Yanzhou District (兗州區 *yǎnzhōu qū*). These yielded large quantities of stone and bone tools as well as pottery (Chang 1999).

It was also in Shandong that, at least according to tradition, the tribes and progeny of the legendary founding emperor Fuxi (ca. 2800 BCE) set up their communities. As the histories relate to us, these included areas within today's Dongping (東平縣 *dōngpíng xiàn*) and Pingyi (平邑縣 *píngyì xiàn*) counties (Yuan and Jiao 2007).

From the Shang to the Zhou

At the time of the Shang Dynasty (ca. 1600–1100 BCE), Chinese culture spread from Henan Province into western Shandong, where the eastern barbarian Dongyi (東夷 *dōngyí*) had once dominated. In 1045 BCE, King Wu (武王 *wǔ wáng*) and his army of some 45,000 soldiers crossed into modern Henan Province, leading to the demolishment of the Shang Dynasty, and the establishment of the (Western) Zhou. The commander of the troops that dealt the Shang its major defeat, Tai Gong Wang (太公望 *tài gōng wàng*), also called Jiang Tai Gong (姜太公 *jiāngtàigōng*), took control of the Qi (齊 *qí*) state, today's Zibo City (淄博市 *zībó shì*). With its capital at Linzi, the State of Qi (齊國 *qíguó*) prospered. In addition to salt and fishing, the State of Qi also produced handicrafts and textiles. During its course, the Zhou Sinicized the eastern Yi ("barbarian") peoples.

Later, Bo Qin (伯禽 *bó qín*), son of Zhou Gong Dan (周公旦 *zhōu gōngdàn*) and the younger brother of King Wu, took control of Lu (魯 *lǔ*) at Qufu City (曲阜市 *qūfùshì*), south of today's Jinan City (Shaugnessy 1999). (Thus the abbreviation Lu 魯 *lǔ* for Shandong Province, a historical reference going back 3,000 years). In the contemporary Poetry Classic, dating back to the Western Zhou dynastic period (1046–771 BCE), there is an ode (from Pi Kung: 閟公 *bìgōng*) to the State of Lu (魯國 *lǔguó*):

> To us belongs T'ai's frowning height[1]For all in Lu the grandest sight. Both Kuei and Mêng[2] we safely keep; To farthest east our sway shall sweep, Till all the states along the sea, To Lu obedient shall be. The tribes of Huai[3] will own our might, Proud to our prince their faith to plight. Such the memorial he shall leave! Such deeds our marquis shall achieve! (Legge 1876)

[1] That is, Mount Taishan.

[2] Famous mountain area in Shandong: Mengshan in Linyi.

[3] Huaiyi, 淮夷 *huáiyí*, probably related to the Dong Yi.

Home of Confucius

The State of Lu was the birthplace of Confucianism. The family of Confucius (孔丘 aka 孔夫子 *kǒng qiū*; *kǒngfū zi*; 551–479 BCE) originated from Xiayi (夏邑 *xiàyì*) in the State of Song (宋國 *songguó*), modern-day Xiayi County (夏邑縣 *xiàyì xiàn*) in neighboring Henan Province. Confucius himself was born in the State of Lu, in Zouyi (陬邑 *zōuyì*), today's Qufu City, Shandong. The State of Qi, also falling within the modern-day borders of Shandong, was among the seven of the Warring States (475–221 BCE), having a population then of about 350,000. Its capital, Linzi (臨淄 *línzī*), was a bustling community, described by a contemporary Su Qin (380–284 BCE) as having an adult male population of 210,000. He also noted that in the busy burg of Linzi, "there were numerous carriages running on the roads each day; as a result, accidents happened periodically." (Zhang 2015).

The State of Chu demolished the State of Lu in 249 BCE; later, the Qin dynasty unified the vying kingdoms, conquering the Chu and Qi states in 223 BCE. During the Qin Dynasty reign, some 54 prefectures (commanderies 郡 *jùn*) were established, five of which administered regions in modern-day Shandong:

- Linzi (臨淄郡 *línzī jùn*)
- Langya (琅邪郡 *lángyá jùn*, present day Huangdao District (黃島區 *huángdǎo qū*)
- Donghai (東海郡 *dōnghǎi jùn*, modern day Tancheng County (郯城縣 *tánchéng xiàn*)
- Jibei (濟北郡 *jǐběi jùn*), southeast of today's Tai'an (泰安 *tài'ān*); and
- Jiaodong (膠東郡*jiāodōng jùn*), southeast of today's Pingdu City (平度市 *píngdù shì*).

Through the early and later Han dynasties (ca. 220 BCE - 220 CE), Shandong had earned a reputation for its fertile soil, fecund enough to support its burgeoning agricultural sector, and was critical for supplying grain to the central empire. Shandong had also become a key source of cloth products for the Silk Road (絲綢之路 *sīchóuzhīlù*), exporting to the western world a large quantity of textiles. (Tan 1985).

Bamboo Writings

Linyi City's Lanshan District (蘭山區 *lánshān qū*) is home to a remarkable discovery of ancient bamboo strips at a Han dynasty tumulus in Yinqueshan:[4]

On 10 April 1972, construction workers stumbled upon what appeared to be a rather ordinary Han dynasty tomb. Upon preliminary inspection by archeologists, it appeared to warrant no further investigation. But this suddenly changed when a worker quite accidentally found a piece of bamboo with Chinese characters written on it. Suspecting it could be a genuine ancient bamboo slip, archeologists confirmed

[4] 銀雀山漢墓竹簡 *yínquèshān, hànmù zhújiǎn*.

the discovery, and as this was in the middle of the chaotic Cultural Revolution, took the precaution of calling in military personnel to secure the site. Further excavation revealed a trove of ancient texts found in these Western Han tombs (dated ca. third century BCE to the first century CE). In addition to pottery and paintings of Han dynasty heritage, this invaluable cache of bamboo strips included the following texts: *The Art of War*, that is, Sun Zi (Sun Tzu), 孫子兵法 *sūnzi bīngfǎ*, said to have been compiled during the Spring and Autumn period (770–476 BC), and a later volume authored by Sun Wu's descendent, Sun Bin (孫臏兵法 *sūn bìn bīngfǎ)* during the Warring States (475 BCE - 221 BCE). In addition, archaeologists at Yinqueshan found the following priceless texts:

- Wei Liao Zi (尉繚子 *wèi liáozi*): "Master Wei Liao," writings on military matters from the Warring States (475–221 BCE);
- Yanzi (晏子 *yànzi*), speeches and other political stories by the prime minister of the State of Qi, Yan Ying (晏嬰 *yàn yīng*);
- Six Stratagems (六韜 *liù tāo*), a treatise that was published in the Warring States; purports to hold the "secrets" to military statecraft of the eleventh century BCE founder of the Zhou dynasty, Lü Shang (吕尚 *lǚ shàng*), also known as Jiang Ziya (姜子牙 *jiāng ziyá*) and Jiang Shang (姜尚 *jiāng shàng*);
- "Shouling" (守令 *shǒulìng*: Keeping Peace and Order), by Tang Le *tang le* (唐勒 *Táng Lè*), a Chu (楚 *chǔ*) State writer from the third century BCE, fragments of which include discussions between Tang Le and Song Yu (宋玉 *sòng yù*) on chariot riding (Knechtges and Chang 2014); as well as other texts on calendars and divining (*Sun-Tzu* 1993).

Under control of the warlord Cao Cao (曹操 *cáo cāo*), modern-day Shandong was controlled by the Kingdom of Wei (魏國 *wèi guó*) during the Three Kingdoms era (220–265 CE). In ca. 400 CE, following the Uprising of the Five Barbarians (五胡亂華 *wǔhúluànhuá*; 304–316), the Xianbei (鮮卑 *xiānbēi*) clan chief Murong De (慕容德 *mùróng dé*) declared himself King of Yan, establishing the Southern Yan (南燕 *nányàn*) capital at Guanggu (廣固 *guǎnggù*). In modern times, the latter was called Yidu (益都 *yìdū*): "Yi Capital." In 1986 it was renamed Qingzhou (青州市 *qīngzhōu shì*), a name that itself goes back to the Western Han (206 BCE - 24 CE). Its borders were similar to those of Shandong Province of today.

With the flourishing of the Sui Dynasty, ca. 600, the Shandong area held over 20% of China's entire population. The chaos following the end of the Sui led to economic hard times for the region, until the Tang Dynasty saw its restoration. However, by ca. 940 CE its economy had largely stalled. As of 1111 CE, as part of the Northern Song (北宋 *běisòng*), the Shandong region was ruled under Jingdong Donglu (京東東路 *jīngdōng dōnglù*). Later, two administrative entities were created: Shandong (East Circuit) Donglu (山東東路 *shāndōng dōnglù*) with its capital at Yidu, and Shandong (West Circuit) Xilu (山東西路 *shāndōng xīlù*), with Dongping Prefecture (東平府 *dōngpíng fǔ*) as its capital on its west. This state of affairs largely remained that way through the year 1200 (Tan 1985).

Yuan Through the Ming

As of 1290 (if the population data from this period are to be believed), the decimation wrought by the Mongol invasion reduced the region of today's Shandong's population from about ten million down to 2.23 million (Lu 1994). The subsequent Ming Dynasty (1368) formally established Shandong Province, which also included Liaodong. By 1644, during the Ming-Qing Transition, Shandong Province was redrawn inside borders that we would recognize today. (Additional population history of Shandong is found in Table 26.1).

Table 26.1 Shandong historical population data. (Lu 1994; SPBS 2021)

Year (CE)	Population
2	1,200,000
281	1,720,000
550	1,890,000
609	7,660,000
713	4,210,000
752	5,660,000
980	2,450,000
1210	10,090,000
1290	2,230,000
1351	2,600,000
1381	5,180,000
1573	5,644,000
1626	7,320,000
1685	2,111,000
1749	24,012,000
1773	26,019,000
1790	23,359,000[a]
1830	30,000,000
1851	33,380,000
1872	35,220,000
1898	37,920,000
1949	45,490,000
1953	48,876,548
1964	55,519,038
1982	74,419,054
1988	80,000,000
1990	84,392,827
2000	89,971,789
2010	95,793,100
2020	101,527,453

[a]Jonathan Spence (Spence 1999) notes that the drop in population in this period was likely due to rebellions and natural disasters.

Modern Shandong: War and Occupation

During the Sino-Japanese War (1895), China's North Sea Fleet was then essentially destroyed when Japan attacked Weihai (威海衛 *wēihǎiwèi*). On 14 November 1897, Germany had obtained a lease on Shandong Province's vital Jiaozhou Bay (膠州灣 *jiāozhōu wān*) and Qingdao City (青島市 *qīngdǎo shì*) for 99 years, but that lease was abruptly ended at the end of World War I (Paine 2003). Famously, Qingdao became the source of the German-styled beer and still operates today. Weihai (Port Edward) was leased to England from 1898 to 1930.

Boxer Rebellion

In the late 1800s, the northwest of Shandong was a hot bed of anti-Christian hostility, especially against foreign missionaries. It was there that was formed a Chinese spiritual martial art organization, the Spirit Boxers (神拳 *shénquán*), the progenitor of the Fists of Righteous Harmony (義和拳*yìhéquán*), later called the Boxer Movement (義和團運動 *yìhétuán yùndòng*). It then evolved into the ultra-violent Boxer Rebellion (義和團起義 *yìhétuán qǐyì*) in 1900. While the German acquisition of Jiaozhou Bay, and the failure of China's nascent reform movement (Hundred Days' Reform, September 1898) motivated the Boxers, a terrible draught and famine were blamed upon the machinations of foreigners. Local rumors, such as unfounded stories about Christian missionaries poisoning wells, triggered violence throughout the countryside (Tiedemann 2010).

World War I and Japanese Occupation

Following the establishment of the Republic of China (ROC) in 1912, five years later it declared war against Germany in 1917, but had no substantive military force. Instead, significant numbers of men from Shandong participated as a labor force, the so-called "Chinese Labour Corps."[5] A total of some 140,000 Chinese served in the Western Front in World War I. Promised to only serve in non-combat roles, digging trenches, hauling materiel and the like, nonetheless about 2,000 Chinese were

[5] 中國勞工旅 *zhōngguó láogōnglǚ*.

killed as a result of warfare, and many were buried in Belgium and France. After the Great War, a very small percentage of these Chinese laborers decided to remain in Europe, and some of these same expats joined the budding Chinese Communist Party in the 1920s (Charlemagne 2010).

In 1922, the Treaty of Washington (華盛頓會議 *huáshèngdùn huìyì*) returned Qingdao and the (German-built) Jiaozhou-Jinan Railroad (膠濟鐵路 *jiāojǐ tiělù*) to the Republic of China. After its invasion of Manchuria, Japan controlled Shandong from the end of 1937 to 1945.

Upon the establishment of the People's Republic of China (PRC) in 1949, Shandong Province was divided for a short time into three separate administrative regions: Bohai to the north (渤海行政區 *bóhǎi xíngzhèngqū*), Jiaodong to the far east (膠東行政區 *jiāodōng xíngzhèngqū*), and Luzhongnan (魯中南行政區 *lǔzhōngnán xíngzhèngqū*) to the south (PRC 2001).

Shandong Economics and Population Trends

In terms of economics, of mainland China's 31 provinces and major cities, Shandong has consistently ranked third in gross domestic product (GDP) during the first two decades of the twenty-first century, totaling USD $977 billion in 2015, and nearly $1.14 billion in 2020. In terms of per capita income, Shandong ranked 8th in 2020 with $5,114 (Zhang 2021).

In 2016, Shandong had total population (including permanent and non-permanent residents) of 98,470,000. By the 2020 census (see Tables 26.2 and 26.3), its population of 101,527,453 showed a 6% increase over 2010, and differed slightly (0.56%) from the permanent (戶籍人口 *hùjí rénkǒu*) population in 2020 of 100,960,000 (Fig. 26.2).

Table 26.4 (below) shows the *hukou* (family registered) populations based on PRC Ministry of Civil Affairs data. (Districts listed directly under major cities are government seats, as are those in parentheses). One can compare these data with the census (usual residential populations based on 2010 and 2020 censuses in Tables 26.2 and 26.3 (below):

Table 26.2 Shandong Province population (residential 常住人口 *chángzhù rénkǒu*) data. (SPBS 2021)

City	Population (2010)	Population (2020)
Jinan City 濟南市 *jǐnán shì* [abbrev. 濟 *jǐ*]	6,814,000	9,202,432
Qingdao City 青島市 *qīngdǎo shì*	8,715,100	10,071,722
Binzhou City 濱州市 *bīnzhōu shì*	3,748,500	3,928,568
Dezhou City 德州市 *dézhōu shì*	5,568,200	5,611,194
Dongying City 東營市 *dōngyíng shì*	2,035,300	2,193,518
Heze City 菏澤市 *hézé shì*	8,287,800	8,795,939
Jining City 濟寧市 *jǐníng shì*	8,081,900	8,357,897
Laiwu City 萊蕪市 *láiwú shì*	1,298,500	N/A
Liaocheng City 聊城市 *liáochéng shì*	5,789,900	5,952,128
Linyi City 臨沂市 *línyí shì*	10,039,400	11,018,365
Rizhao City 日照市 *rìzhào shì*	2,801,100	2,968,365
Tai'an City 泰安市 *tài'ān shì*	5,494,200	5,472,217
Weifang City 濰坊市 *wéifāng shì*	9,086,200	9,386,705
Weihai City 威海市 *wēihǎi shì*	2,804,800	2,906,548
Yantai City 煙台市 *yāntái shì*	6,968,200	7,102,116
Zaozhuang City 棗莊市 *zǎozhuāng shì*	3,729,300	3,855,601
Zibo City 淄博市 *zībó shì* [abbrev. 淄 *zī*]	4,530,600	4,704,138
Total	**95,793,100**	**101,527,453**

Table 26.3 Shandong Province: population data of cities and their subordinate sectors. (SPBS 2021)

Cities and subordinate sectors, population (2020 census)	Subordinate district, city and county populations (2020)	Total population (2020)
Jinan City 濟南市 *jǐnán*[a] *shì* [abbrev. 濟 *jǐ*]		**9,202,432**
Shizhong District 市中區 *shìzhōng qū*	903,714	
Lixia District 歷下區 *lìxià qū*	819,139	
Huaiyin District 槐蔭區 *huáiyīn qū*	675,048	
Tianqiao District 天橋區 *tiānqiáo qū*	718,024	
Licheng District 歷城區 *lìchéng qū*	1,112,022	
Changqing District 長清區 *chángqīng qū*	595,549	
Zhangqiu City 章丘市 *zhāngqiū shì*	1,075,784	
Pingyin County 平陰縣 *píngyīn xiàn*	323,072	
Jiyang County 濟陽縣 *jǐyáng xiàn*	401,826	
Laiwu District 萊蕪區 *láiwú qū*	816,009	
Gangcheng District[b] 鋼城區 *gāngchéng qū*	286,966	
Shanghe County 商河縣 *shānghé xiàn*	527,311	

(continued)

Table 26.3 (continued)

Cities and subordinate sectors, population (2020 census)	Subordinate district, city and county populations (2020)	Total population (2020)
Jinan High Technology Industry Development Zone 濟南高新技術產業開發區 *jǐnán gāoxīnjìshù chǎnyè kāifāqū*	424,047	
Laiwu High Technology Industry Development Zone 萊蕪高新技術產業開發區 *láiwú gāoxīnjìshù chǎnyè kāifāqū*	153,623	
"[Jinan] Prior Zone For Replacing Old Growth Drivers With New Ones" 新舊動能轉換先行區 *xīnjiù dòngnéng zhuǎnhuànxiānxíng qū*	166,031	
Nanbu Mountain Region 南部山區 *nánbùshān qū*	204,267	
Qingdao City 青島市 ***qīngdǎo shì***		**10,071,722**
Shinan District 市南區 *shìnán qū*	486,643	
Shibei District 市北區 *shìběi qū*	1,096,879	
Xihai'an New District 西海岸新區 *xīhǎi'àn xīnqū*	1,903,595	
Laixi City 萊西市 *láixī shì*	720,103	
Laoshan District 嶗山區 *láoshān qū*	502,370	
Chengyang District 城陽區 *chéngyáng qū*	1,109,606	
Licang District 李滄區 *lǐcāng qū*	737,281	
Jiaozhou City 膠州市 *jiāozhōu shì*	987,820	
Jimo District 即墨區 *jímò qū*	1,336,077	
Pingdu City 平度市 *píngdù shì*	1,191,348	
Binzhou City 濱州市 ***bīnzhōu shì***		**3,928,568**
Bincheng District 濱城區 *bīnchéng qū*	629,552	
Huimin County 惠民縣 *huìmín xiàn*	569,975	
Yangxin County 陽信縣 *yángxìn xiàn*	421,502	
Wudi County 無棣縣 *wúdì xiàn*	432,311	
Zhanhua District 沾化區 *zhānhuà qū*	334,948	
Boxing County 博興縣 *bóxīng xiàn*	508,140	
Zouping City 鄒平市 *zōupíng shì*	774,517	
Binzhou Economic and Technology Development Zone 濱州經濟技術開發區 *bīnzhōu jīngjìjìshù kāifāqū*	160,898	
Binzhou High Technology and Industry Development Zone 濱州高新技術產業開發區 *bīnzhōu gāoxīnjìshù chǎnyè kāifāqū*	63,199	
Binzhou Beihai Economic Development Zone 濱州北海經開發區 *bīnzhōu běihǎi jīngjì kāifāqū*	33,526	
Dezhou City 德州市 ***dézhōu shì***		**5,611,194**
Decheng District 德城區 *déchéng qū*	695,310	
Laoling City 樂陵市 *làolíng shì*	559,166	
Yucheng City 禹城市 *yǔchéng shì*	488,014	
Lingcheng District 陵城區 *língchéng qū*	486,794	

(continued)

Table 26.3 (continued)

Cities and subordinate sectors, population (2020 census)	Subordinate district, city and county populations (2020)	Total population (2020)
Pingyuan County 平原縣 *píngyuán xiàn*	419,088	
Xiajin County 夏津縣 *xiàjīn xiàn*	458,112	
Wucheng County 武城縣 *wǔchéng xiàn*	353,721	
Qihe County 齊河縣 *qíhé xiàn*	576,375	
Linyi County 臨邑縣 *línyì xiàn*	473,421	
Ningjin County 寧津縣 *níngjīn xiàn*	473,314	
Qingyun County 慶雲縣 *qìngyún xiàn*	318,105	
Dezhou Economic and Technology Development Zone 德州經濟技術開發區 *dézhōu jīngjìjìshù kāifāqū*	223,316	
Yunhe Economic Development Zone 運河經濟開發區 *yùnhé jīngjì kāifāqū*	86,458	
Dongying City 東營市 ***dōngyíng shì***		**2,193,518**
Dongying District 東營區 *dōngyíng qū*	547,643	
Hekou District 河口區 *hékǒu qū*	197,648	
Kenli District 墾利區 *kěnlì qū*	257,104	
Lijin County 利津縣 *lìjīn xiàn*	238,189	
Guangrao County 廣饒縣 *guǎngráo xiàn*	521,742	
Dongying Economic and Technology Development Zone 東營經濟技術開發區 *dōngyíng jīngjìjìshù kāifāqū*	383,909	
Dongying Harbor Economic Development Zone 東營港經濟開發區 *dōngyínggǎng jīngjì kāifāqū*	47,283	
Heze City 菏澤市 ***hézé shì***		**8,795,939**
Mudan District 牡丹區 *mǔdān qū*	1,098,707	
Caoxian County 曹縣 *cáoxiàn*	1,384,282	
Dingtao District 定陶區 *dìngtáo qū*	540,016	
Chengwu County 成武縣 *chéngwǔ xiàn*	595,159	
Shanxian County 單縣 *shànxiàn*	1,026,555	
Juye County 巨野縣 *jùyě xiàn*	923,923	
Yuncheng County 鄆城縣 *yùnchéng xiàn*	1,120,854	
Juancheng County 鄄城縣 *juànchéng xiàn*	747,972	
Dongming County 東明縣 *dōngmíng xiàn*	760,956	
Heze Economic and Technology Development Zone 菏澤經濟技術開發區 *hézé jīngjìjìshù kāifāqū*	412,353	
Heze High Technology Industry Development Zone 菏澤高新技術產業開發區 *hézé gāoxīnjìshù chǎnyè kāifāqū*	185,162	
Jining City 濟寧市 ***jǐníng shì***		**8,357,897**
Rencheng District 任城區 *rènchéng qū*	1,075,599	
Qufu City 曲阜市 *qūfù shì*	621,971	

(continued)

Table 26.3 (continued)

Cities and subordinate sectors, population (2020 census)	Subordinate district, city and county populations (2020)	Total population (2020)
Yanzhou District 兖州區 *yǎnzhōu qū*	540,662	
Zoucheng City 鄒城市 *zōuchéng shì*	1,166,559	
Weishan County 微山縣 *wēishān xiàn*	613,421	
Yutai County 魚台縣 *yútái xiàn*	420,010	
Jinxiang County 金鄉縣 *jīnxiāng xiàn*	634,144	
Jiaxiang County 嘉祥縣 *jiāxiáng xiàn*	700,149	
Wenshang County 汶上縣 *wènshàng xiàn*	687,544	
Sishui County 泗水縣 *sìshuǐ xiàn*	542,895	
Liangshan County 梁山縣 *liángshān xiàn*	730,683	
Jining Economic and Technology Development Zone 濟寧經濟技術開發區 *jǐníng jīngjìjìshù kāifāqū*	119,887	
Jining High Technology Industry Development Zone 濟寧高新技術產業開發區 *jǐníng gāoxīnjìshù chǎnyè kāifāqū*	334,601	
Taibaihu New District 太白湖新區 *tàibáihú xīnqū*	169,772	
Liaocheng City 聊城市 ***liáochéng shì***		**5,952,128**
Dongchangfu District 東昌府區 *dōngchāngfǔ qū*	1,008,594	
Linqing City 臨清市 *línqīng shì*	794,529	
Yanggu County 陽谷縣 *yánggǔ xiàn*	700,083	
Shenxian County 莘縣 *shēnxiàn*	930,370	
Chiping District 茌平區 *chípíng qū*	517,641	
Dong'e County 東阿縣 *dōng'ē xiàn*	346,053	
Guanxian County 冠縣 *guānxiàn*	719,354	
Gaotang County 高唐縣 *gāotáng xiàn*	455,193	
Liaocheng Economic and Technology Development Zone 聊城經濟技術開發區 *liáochéng jīngjìjìshù kāifāqū*	209,157	
Liaocheng High Technology Industry Development Zone 聊城高新技術產業開發區 *liáochéng gāoxīnjìshù chǎnyè kāifāqū*	149,421	
Liaocheng Jiangbei Shuicheng Tourist Resort 聊城江北水城旅游度假區 *liáochéng jiāngběi shuǐchéng lǚyóudùjià qū*	121,733	
Linyi City 臨沂市 ***línyí shì***		**11,018,365**
Lanshan District 蘭山區 *lánshān qū*	1,844,089	
Luozhuang District 羅莊區 *luózhuāng qū*	679,333	
Hedong District 河東區 *hédōng qū*	908,324	
Tancheng County 郯城縣 *tánchéng xiàn*	885,156	
Lanling County 蘭陵縣 *lánlíng xiàn*	1,104,391	
Ju'nan County 莒南縣 *jǔ'nán xiàn*	841,035	
Yishui County 沂水縣 *yíshuǐ xiàn*	967,570	

(continued)

Table 26.3 (continued)

Cities and subordinate sectors, population (2020 census)	Subordinate district, city and county populations (2020)	Total population (2020)
Mengyin County 蒙陰縣 *mēngyīn xiàn*	485,252	
Pingyi County 平邑縣 *píngyì xiàn*	892,276	
Feixian County 費縣 *fèixiàn*	798,403	
Yinan County 沂南縣 *yínán xiàn*	806,390	
Linshu County 臨沭縣 *línshù xiàn*	586,024	
Linyi High Technology Industry Development Zone 臨沂高新技術產業開發區 *línyí gāoxīnjìshù chǎnyè kāifāqū*	220,122	
Rizhao City 日照市 ***rìzhào shì***		**2,968,365**
Donggang District 東港區 *dōnggǎng qū*	838,176	
Lanshan District 嵐山區 *lánshān qū*	379,308	
Wulian County 五蓮縣 *wǔlián xiàn*	443,600	
Juxian County 莒縣 *jǔxiàn*	973,252	
Rizhao Economic and Technology Development Zone 日照經濟技術開發區 *rìzhào jīngjìjìshù kāifāqū*	168,493	
Rizhao High Technology Industry Development Zone 日照高新技術產業開發區 *rìzhào gāoxīnjìshù chǎnyè kāifāqū*	66,959	
Shanhaitian Tourist Resort山海天旅游度假區 *shānhǎitiān lǚyóudùjiǎ qū*	98,577	
Tai'an City泰安市***tài'ān shì***		**5,472,217**
Taishan District 泰山區 *tàishān qū*	799,971	
Daiyue District 岱岳區 *dàiyuè qū*	675,161	
Xintai City 新泰市 *xīntài shì*	1,272,698	
Feicheng City 肥城市 *féichéng shì*	894,115	
Ningyang County 寧陽縣 *níngyáng xiàn*	668,520	
Dongping County 東平縣 *dōngpíng xiàn*	687,385	
Tai'an High Technology Industry Development Zone 泰安高新技術產業開發區 *tài'ān gāoxīnjìshù chǎnyè kāifāqū*	224,824	
Taishan Famed Scenic Area 泰山風景名勝區 *tàishān fēngjǐngmíngshèng qū*	79,470	
Tai'an City Culaishan Wenhe Scenic Area 泰安市徂徠山汶河景區 *tài'ān shì cúlàishān wènhé jǐngqū*	170,073	
Weifang City 濰坊市 ***wéifāng shì***		**9,386,705**
Kuiwen District 奎文區 *kuíwén qū*	475,103	
Weicheng District 濰城區 *wéichéng qū*	521,368	
Hanting District 寒亭區 *hántíng qū*	334,403	
Fangzi District 坊子區 *fāngzǐ qū*	361,737	
Anqiu City 安丘市 *ānqiū shì*	840,553	

(continued)

Table 26.3 (continued)

Cities and subordinate sectors, population (2020 census)	Subordinate district, city and county populations (2020)	Total population (2020)
Changyi City 昌邑市 *chāngyì shì*	564,501	
Gaomi City 高密市 *gāomì shì*	877,393	
Qingzhou City 青州市 *qīngzhōu shì*	960,882	
Zhucheng City 諸城市 *zhūchéng shì*	1,078,178	
Shouguang City 壽光市 *shòuguāng shì*	1,163,364	
Linqu County 臨朐縣 *línqú xiàn*	806,314	
Changle County 昌樂縣 *chānglè xiàn*	583,799	
Binhai District 濱海區 *bīnhǎi qū*	136,714	
Xiashan District 峡山區 *xiáshān qū*	159,288	
Weifang High Technology Industry Development Zone 濰坊高新技術產業開發區 *wéifāng gāoxīnjìshù chǎnyè kāifāqū*	389,041	
Weifang Economic and Technology Development Zone 濰坊經濟技術開發區 *wéifāng jīngjìjìshù kāifāqū*	134,067	
Weihai City 威海市 ***wēihǎi shì***		**2,906,548**
Huancui District 環翠區 *huáncuì qū*	446,193	
Rongcheng City 榮成市 *róngchéng shì*	714,211	
Rushan City 乳山市 *rǔshān shì*	464,078	
Wendeng District 文登區 *wéndēng qū*	518,583	
Weihai Huoju High Technology Industry Development Zone 威海火炬高新技術產業開發區 *wēihǎi huǒjù gāoxīnjìshù chǎnyè kāifāqū*	336,407	
Weihai Economic and Technology Development Zone 威海經濟技術開發區 *wēihǎi jīngjìjìshù kāifāqū*	280,457	
Weihai Lingang Economic and Technology Development Zone 威海臨港經濟技術開發區 *wēihǎi língǎng jīngjìjìshù kāifāqū*	101,673	
Weihai Nanhai New District 威海南海新區 *wēihǎi nánhǎi xīnqū*	44,946	
Yantai City 煙台市 ***yāntái shì***		**7,102,116**
Laishan District 萊山區 *láishān qū*	389,494	
Zhifu District 芝罘區 *zhīfú qū*	877,237	
Fushan District 福山區 *fúshān qū*	452,553	
Muping District 牟平區 *mùpíng qū*	444,831	
Qixia City 棲霞市 *qīxiá shì*	435,405	
Haiyang City 海陽市 *hǎiyáng shì*	582,711	
Longkou City 龍口市 *lóngkǒu shì*	729,880	
Laiyang City 萊陽市 *láiyáng shì*	794,986	
Laizhou City 萊州市 *láizhōu shì*	824,708	
Penglai City 蓬萊市 *pénglái shì*	434,575	

(continued)

Table 26.3 (continued)

Cities and subordinate sectors, population (2020 census)	Subordinate district, city and county populations (2020)	Total population (2020)
Zhaoyuan City 招遠市 *zhāoyuǎn shì*	543,127	
Changdao Marine Ecological Culture and General Experimental Zone 長島海洋生態文明綜合試驗區 *chángdǎo hǎiyáng shēngtàiwénmíng zōnghé shìyànqū*	37,984	
Yantai Economic and Technology Development Zone 煙台經濟技術開發區 *yāntái jīngjìjìshù kāifāqū*	453,286	
Yantai High Technology Industry Development Zone 煙台高新技術產業開發區 *yāntái gāoxīnjìshù chǎnyè kāifāqū*	91,984	
Shandong Kunyu Mountain National Level Natural Preserve 山東崑嵛山國家級自然保護區 *shāndōng kūnyúshān guójiājí zìránbǎohù qū*	9,355	
Zaozhuang City 棗莊市 ***zǎozhuāng shì***		**3,855,601**
Xuecheng District 薛城區 *xuēchéng qū*	485,637	
Shizhong District 市中區 *shìzhōng qū*	613,015	
Yicheng District 嶧城區 *yìchéng qū*	362,524	
Tai'erzhuang District 台兒莊區 *tái'érzhuāng qū*	305,102	
Shanting District 山亭區 *shāntíng qū*	406,722	
Tengzhou City 滕州市 *téngzhōu shì*	1,574,648	
Zaozhuang High Technology Industry Development Zone 棗莊高新技術產業開發區 *zǎozhuāng gāoxīnjìshù chǎnyè kāifāqū*	107,953	
Zibo City 淄博市 ***zībó shì* [abbrev.** 淄 ***zī*]**		**4,704,138**
Zhangdian District 張店區 *zhāngdiàn qū*	795,837	
Zichuan District 淄川區 *zīchuān qū*	614,158	
Boshan District 博山區 *bóshān qū*	410,643	
Linzi District 臨淄區 *línzī qū*	649,160	
Zhoucun District 周村區 *zhōucūn qū*	353,840	
Huantai County 桓台縣 *huántái xiàn*	489,479	
Gaoqing County 高青縣 *gāoqīng xiàn*	313,130	
Yiyuan County 沂源縣 *yíyuán xiàn*	515,058	
Zibo High Technology Industry Development Zone 淄博高新技術產業開發區 *zībó gāoxīnjìshù chǎnyè kāifāqū*	239,306	
Zibo Economic and Technology Development Zone 淄博經濟技術開發區 *zībó jīngjìjìshù kāifāqū*	278,634	
Wenchanghu District 文昌湖區 *wénchānghú qū*	44,893	

[a]濟 takes third tone in place names (*jǐ*)
[b]Made subordinate to Jinan City in 9 January 2019

1. Ningjin County
2. Leling City
3. Qingyun County
4. Wudi County
5. Zhanhua County
6. Hekou District
7. Decheng District
8. Wucheng County
9. Lingcheng District
10. Linyi County
11. Shanghe County
12. Yangxin County
13. Huimin County
14. Bincheng Districts
15. Lijin County
16. Kenli District
17. Xiajin County
18. Pingyuan County
19. Jiyang County
20. Zouping City
21. Gaoqing County
22. Boxing County
23. Dongying District
24. Guangrao County
25. Linqing County
26. Gaotang County
27. Yucheng City
28. Qihe County
29. Tianqiao District
30. Licheng District
31. **Huaiyin District**
32. **Shizhong District**
33. **Lixia District**
34. **Zhangqiu City**
35. **Zhoucun District**
36. **Gaoqing County**
37. **Huantai County**
38. **Linzi District**
39. **Qingzhou City**
40. **Shouguang City**
41. **Hanting District**
42. **Changyi City**
43. **Laizhou City**
44. **Zhaoyuan City**
45. **Longkou City**
46. **Penglai City**
47. **Changdao County**
48. **Fushan District**
49. **Zhifu District**
50. **Laishan District**
51. **Guanxian County**
52. Shenxian County
53. Dongchangfu District
54. Chiping District
55. Dong'e County
56. Changqing District
57. Taishan District
58. Daiyue District
59. Laiwu District
60. Zichuan District
61. Boshan District
62. Linqu County
63. Changle County
64. Weicheng District
65. Kuiwen District
66. Pingdu City
67. Laixi City
68. Qixia City
69. Muping District
70. Huancui District
71. Yanggu County
72. Pingyin County
73. Feicheng City
74. Xintai City
75. Gangcheng District
76. Yiyuan County
77. Anqiu City
78. Gaomi City
79. Jiaozhou City
80. Laiyang City
81. Jimo City
82. Chengyang District
83. Licang District
84. Shibei District
85. Shinan District
86. Laoshan District
87. Haiyang City
88. Rushan City
89. Wendeng District
90. Rongcheng City
91. Dongping County
92. Juancheng County
93. Yuncheng County
94. Liangshan County
95. Wenshang County
96. Ningyang County
97. Yanzhou District
98. Qufu City
99. Sishui County
100. Pingyi County
101. Mengyin County
102. Yishui County
103. Juxian County
104. Zhucheng City
105. Wulian County
106. Huangdao District
107. Yinan County
108. Junan County
109. Lanshan District
110. Donggang District
111. Dongming County
112. Mudan District
113. Dingtao County
114. Juye County
115. Jiaxiang County
116. Rencheng District
117. Zoucheng City
118. Bixian County
119. Lanshan District
120. Hedong District
121. Caoxian County
122. Chengwu County
123. Shanxian County
124. Jinxiang County
125. Yutai County
126. Tengzhou City
127. Weishan County
128. Shanting District
129. Xuecheng District
130. Shizhong District
131. Yicheng District
132. Tai'erzhuang District
133. Lanling County
134. Luozhuang District
135. Tancheng County
136. Linshu County

Fig. 26.2 Shandong Province: subdistricts (capital city governmental seat: Shizhong District). (Drawn by the author, after People's Republic of China, Ministry of Civil Affairs. (MCA 2020))

Shandong Province (鲁 *lǔ*)

Provincial Capital: Jinan City

Table 26.4 Shandong Province: permanent registered (戶籍人口 *hùjí rénkǒu*) populations. (MCA 2020)

Name	Traditional	Simplified	Population (2012)	Population (2016)	Population (2020)	Area (Sq. Km)
Shandong Province	山東省	山东省	95,360,000	95,870,000	100,960,000	158,219
Jinan City	濟南市	济南市	6,030,000	6,090,000	7,850,000	10,423
Shizhong District (Ganshiqiao Subdistrict)	市中區 (杆石橋街道)	市中区 (杆石桥街道)	570,000	580,000	650,000	280
Lixia District (Yaojia Subdistrict)	歷下區 (姚家街道)	历下区 (姚家街道)	540,000	550,000	680,000	101
Huaiyin District (Xingfu Subdistrict)	槐蔭區 (興福街道)	槐荫区 (兴福街道)	380,000	390,000	440,000	151
Tianqiao District (Wuyingshan Subdistrict)	天橋區 (無影山街道)	天桥区 (无影山街道)	500,000	510,000	530,000	249
Licheng District (Shandalu Subdistrict)	歷城區 (山大路街道)	历城区 (山大路街道)	920,000	930,000	1,030,000	1298
Changqing District (Wenchang Subdistrict)	長清區 (文昌街道)	长清区 (文昌街道)	560,000	560,000	570,000	1178
Zhangqiu City (Mingshui Subdistrict)	章丘市 (明水街道)	章丘市 (明水街道)	1,020,000	1,020,000	1,050,000	1855
Pingyin County (Yushan Subdistrict)	平陰縣 (榆山街道)	平阴县 (榆山街道)	370,000	370,000	370,000	827
Jiyang County (Jibei Subdistrict)	濟陽縣 (濟北街道)	济阳县 (济北街道)	560,000	560,000	590,000	1076
Laiwu District (Fengcheng Subdistrict)	萊蕪區 (鳳城街道)	莱芜区 (凤城街道)	N/A	N/A	990,000	1740
Gangcheng District[a] (Aishan Subdistrict)	鋼城區 (艾山街道)	钢城区 (艾山街道)	300,000	300,000	300,000	506
Shanghe County (Xushang Subdistrict)	商河縣 (許商街道)	商河县 (许商街道)	620,000	620,000	640,000	1162

(continued)

Table 26.4 (continued)

Name	Traditional	Simplified	Population (2012)	Population (2016)	Population (2020)	Area (Sq. Km)
Liaocheng City	聊城市	聊城市	5,970,000	5,940,000	6,450,000	8721
Dongchangfu District (Liuyuan Subdistrict)	東昌府區 (柳園街道)	东昌府区 (柳园街道)	1,060,000	1,150,000	1,280,000	1443
Linqing City (Qingnianlu Subdistrict)	臨清市 (青年路街道)	临清市 (青年路街道)	760,000	760,000	840,000	950
Yanggu County (Qiaorun Subdistrict)	陽谷縣 (僑潤街道)	阳谷县 (侨润街道)	800,000	790,000	830,000	1066
Shenxian County (Yanta Subdistrict)	莘縣 (燕塔街道)	莘县 (燕塔街道)	1,020,000	1,010,000	1,110,000	1420
Chiping County[b] (Zhenxing Subdistrict)	茌平縣 (振興街道)	茌平县 (振兴街道)	600,000	540,000	N/A	(1003)
Chiping District (Zhenxing Subdistrict)	茌平區 (振興街道)	茌平区 (振兴街道)	N/A	N/A	570,000	1003
Dong'e County (Tongcheng Subdistrict)	東阿縣 (銅城街道)	东阿县 (铜城街道)	440,000	400,000	410,000	729
Guanxian County (Qingquan Subdistrict)	冠縣 (清泉街道)	冠县 (清泉街道)	800,000	800,000	880,000	1161
Gaotang County (Yuqiuhu Subdistrict)	高唐縣 (魚邱湖街道)	高唐县 (鱼邱湖街道)	490,000	490,000	520,000	949
Dezhou City	德州市	德州市	5,710,000	5,790,000	5,980,000	10,361
Decheng District (Xinhu Subdistrict)	德城區 (新湖街道)	德城区 (新湖街道)	600,000	610,000	660,000	544
Laoling City (Shizhong Subdistrict)	樂陵市 (市中街道)	乐陵市 (市中街道)	690,000	700,000	720,000	1173
Yucheng City (Shizhong Subdistrict)	禹城市 (市中街道)	禹城市 (市中街道)	520,000	530,000	540,000	992
Lingcheng District (Linqi Subdistrict)	陵城區 (臨齊街道)	陵城区 (临齐街道)	590,000	600,000	600,000	1213
Lingxian[c] County (Ande Subdistrict)	陵縣 (安德街道)	陵县 (安德街道)	590,000	N/A	N/A	(1213)

(continued)

Table 26.4 (continued)

Name	Traditional	Simplified	Population (2012)	Population (2016)	Population (2020)	Area (Sq. Km)
Pingyuan County (Longmen Subdistrict)	平原縣 (龍門街道)	平原县 (龙门街道)	460,000	470,000	480,000	1047
Xiajin County (Yincheng Subdistrict)	夏津縣 (銀城街道)	夏津县 (银城街道)	520,000	530,000	550,000	882
Wucheng County (Guangyun Subdistrict)	武城縣 (廣運街道)	武城县 (广运街道)	390,000	390,000	400,000	748
Qihe County (Yancheng Subdistrict)	齊河縣 (晏城街道)	齐河县 (晏城街道)	620,000	630,000	640,000	1411
Linyi County (Xingdong Subdistrict)	臨邑縣 (邢東街道)	临邑县 (邢侗街道)	540,000	540,000	560,000	1016
Ningjin County (Ningcheng Subdistrict)	寧津縣 (寧城街道)	宁津县 (宁城街道)	470,000	470,000	490,000	833
Qingyun County (Bohailu Subdistrict)	慶雲縣 (渤海路街道)	庆云县 (渤海路街道)	310,000	320,000	340,000	502
Dongying City	東營市	东营市	1,850,000	1,860,000	1,970,000	8617
Dongying District (Shengli Subdistrict)	東營區 (勝利街道)	东营区 (胜利街道)	620,000	620,000	670,000	1187
Hekou District (Hekou Subdistrict)	河口區 (河口街道)	河口区 (河口街道)	210,000	220,000	220,000	2267
Kenli District (Kenli Subdistrict)	墾利區 (墾利街道)	垦利区 (垦利街道)	220,000	220,000	240,000	2331
Lijin County (Lijin Subdistrict)	利津縣 (利津街道)	利津县 (利津街道)	300,000	300,000	310,000	1666
Guangrao County (Guangrao Subdistrict)	廣饒縣 (廣饒街道)	广饶县 (广饶街道)	500,000	500,000	530,000	1166
Zibo City	淄博市	淄博市	4,220,000	4,240,000	4,340,000	5964
Zhangdian District (Mashang Town)	張店區 (馬尚鎮)	张店区 (马尚镇)	730,000	760,000	850,000	360
Zichuan District (Banyanglu Subdistrict)	淄川區 (般陽路街道)	淄川区 (般阳路街道)	670,000	670,000	660,000	960
Boshan District (Chengdong Subdistrict)	博山區 (城東街道)	博山区 (城东街道)	460,000	450,000	440,000	698

(continued)

Table 26.4 (continued)

Name	Traditional	Simplified	Population (2012)	Population (2016)	Population (2020)	Area (Sq. Km)
Linzi District (Jixia Subdistrict)	臨淄區 (稷下街道)	临淄区 (稷下街道)	610,000	610,000	610,000	664
Zhoucun District (Qingnianlu Subdistrict)	周村區 (青年路街道)	周村区 (青年路街道)	320,000	320,000	320,000	306
Huantai County (Suzhen Subdistrict)	桓台縣 (素鎮街道)	桓台县 (索镇街道)	500,000	500,000	500,000	509
Gaoqing County (Tianzhen Subdistrict)	高青縣 (田鎮街道)	高青县 (田镇街道)	370,000	370,000	370,000	831
Yiyuan County (Lishan Subdistrict)	沂源縣 (歷山街道)	沂源县 (历山街道)	560,000	560,000	580,000	1636
Weifang City	**濰**坊市	**潍**坊市	8,730,000	8,800,000	9,140,000	16,138
Kuiwen District (Dongguan Subdistrict)	奎文區 (東關街道)	奎文区 (东关街道)	490,000	500,000	570,000	163
Weicheng District (Yuhe Subdistrict)	濰城區 (於河街道)	潍城区 (于河街道)	360,000	360,000	370,000	270
Hanting District (Hanting Subdistrict)	寒亭區 (寒亭街道)	寒亭区 (寒亭街道)	430,000	430,000	450,000	1301
Fangzi District (Fenghuang Subdistrict)	坊子區 (鳳凰街道)	坊子区 (凤凰街道)	540,000	540,000	550,000	895
Anqiu City (Xin'an Subdistrict)	安丘市 (新安街道)	安丘市 (新安街道)	950,000	950,000	980,000	1712
Changyi City (Kuiju Subdistrict)	昌邑市 (奎聚街道)	昌邑市 (奎聚街道)	580,000	580,000	590,000	1628
Gaomi City (Liquan Subdistrict)	高密市 (醴泉街道)	高密市 (醴泉街道)	870,000	880,000	900,000	1527
Qingzhou City (Wangfu Subdistrict)	青州市 (王府街道)	青州市 (王府街道)	910,000	920,000	950,000	1569
Zhucheng City (Mizhou Subdistrict)	諸城市 (密州街道)	诸城市 (密州街道)	1,080,000	1,090,000	1,120,000	2151
Shouguang City (Shengcheng Subdistrict)	壽光市 (聖城街道)	寿光市 (圣城街道)	1,040,000	1,050,000	1,100,000	1990

(continued)

Table 26.4 (continued)

Name	Traditional	Simplified	Population (2012)	Population (2016)	Population (2020)	Area (Sq. Km)
Linqu County (Chengguan Subdistrict)	臨朐縣 (城關街道)	临朐县 (城关街道)	870,000	880,000	930,000	1831
Changle County (Baodu Subdistrict)	昌樂縣 (寶都街道)	昌乐县 (宝城街道)	610,000	620,000	640,000	1101
Yantai City	煙台市	烟台市	6,500,000	6,520,000	6,540,000	13,654
Laishan District (Huanghailu Subdistrict)	萊山區 (黃海路街道)	莱山区 (黄海路街道)	220,000	220,000	260,000	285
Zhifu District (Xiangyang Subdistrict)	芝罘區 (向陽街道)	芝罘区 (向阳街道)	680,000	680,000	700,000	179
Fushan District (Qingyang Subdistrict)	福山區 (清洋街道)	福山区 (清洋街道)	440,000	450,000	500,000	711
Muping District (Ninghai Subdistrict)	牟平區 (寧海街道)	牟平区 (宁海街道)	450,000	460,000	450,000	1375
Qixia City (Zhuangyuan Subdistrict)	棲霞市 (莊園街道)	栖霞市 (庄园街道)	630,000	620,000	590,000	2016
Haiyang City (Dongcun Subdistrict)	海陽市 (東村街道)	海阳市 (东村街道)	660,000	660,000	640,000	1909
Longkou City (Xinjia Subdistrict)	龍口市 (新嘉街道)	龙口市 (新嘉街道)	630,000	640,000	640,000	901
Laiyang City (Chengxiang Subdistrict)	萊陽市 (城廂街道)	莱阳市 (城厢街道)	870,000	870,000	860,000	1732
Laizhou City (Wenchanglu Subdistrict)	萊州市 (文昌路街道)	莱州市 (文昌路街道)	860,000	860,000	840,000	1928
Penglai City (Dengzhou Subdistrict)	蓬萊市 (登州街道)	蓬莱市 (登州街道)	450,000	450,000	450,000	1129
Zhaoyuan City (Luofeng Subdistrict)	招遠市 (羅峰街道)	招远市 (罗峰街道)	570,000	570,000	560,000	1432
Changdao County (Nanchangshan Subdistrict)	長島縣 (南長山街道)	长岛县 (南长山街道)	40,000	40,000	40,000	57
Weihai City	威海市	威海市	2,530,000	2,540,000	2,570,000	5797
Huancui District (Huancuilou Subdistrict)	環翠區 (環翠樓街道)	环翠区 (环翠楼街道)	650,000	720,000	780,000	991

(continued)

Table 26.4 (continued)

Name	Traditional	Simplified	Population (2012)	Population (2016)	Population (2020)	Area (Sq. Km)
Rongcheng City (Yatou Subdistrict)	榮成市 (崖頭街道)	荣成市 (崖头街道)	670,000	670,000	660,000	1526
Rushan City (Chengqu Subdistrict)	乳山市 (城區街道)	乳山市 (城区街道)	570,000	570,000	550,000	1665
Wendeng District (Tianfu Subdistrict)	文登區 (天福街道)	文登区 (天福街道)	640,000	580,000	570,000	1615
Qingdao City	青島市	青岛市	7,640,000	7,710,000	8,180,000	11,064
Shinan District (Xianggangzhonglu Subdistrict)	市南區 (香港中路街道)	市南区 (香港中路街道)	550,000	550,000	550,000	30
Shibei District (Dunhualu Subdistrict)	市北區 (敦化路街道)	市北区 (敦化路街道)	490,000	870,000	900,000	63
Huangdao District (Yinzhu Subdistrict)	黃島區 (隱珠街道)	黄岛区 (隐珠街道)	310,000	1,160,000	1,300,000	2096
Laoshan District (Zhonghan Subdistrict)	嶗山區 (中韓街道)	崂山区 (中韩街道)	240,000	260,000	310,000	396
Chengyang District (Chengyang Subdistrict)	城陽區 (城陽街道)	城阳区 (城阳街道)	480,000	490,000	550,000	532
Licang District (Licun Subdistrict)	李滄區 (李村街道)	李沧区 (李村街道)	310,000	320,000	400,000	99
Jiaozhou City (Sanlihe Subdistrict)	膠州市 (三里河街道)	胶州市 (三里河街道)	800,000	810,000	860,000	1324
Jimo District (Tongji Subdistrict)	即墨區 (通濟街道)	即墨区 (通济街道)	1,130,000	1,130,000	1,180,000	1780
Pingdu City (Chengguan Subdistrict)	平度市 (城關街道)	平度市 (城关街道)	1,370,000	1,380,000	1,390,000	3176
Laixi City (Shuiji Subdistrict)	萊西市 (水集街道)	莱西市 (水集街道)	740,000	740,000	740,000	1568
Rizhao City	日照市	日照市	2,870,000	2,880,000	3,070,000	5359
Donggang District (Rizhao Subdistrict)	東港區 (日照街道)	东港区 (日照街道)	810,000	870,000	960,000	1266
Lanshan District (Andongwei Subdistrict)	嵐山區 (安東衛街道)	岚山区 (安东卫街道)	420,000	360,000	440,000	646

(continued)

Table 26.4 (continued)

Name	Traditional	Simplified	Population (2012)	Population (2016)	Population (2020)	Area (Sq. Km)
Wulian County (Hongning Subdistrict)	五蓮縣 (洪凝街道)	五莲县 (洪凝街道)	510,000	510,000	510,000	1497
Juxian (Chengyang Subdistrict)	莒縣 (城陽街道)	莒县 (城阳街道)	1,130,000	1,140,000	1,160,000	1950
Linyi City	臨沂市	临沂市	10,730,000	10,840,000	11,800,000	17,192
Lanshan District (Nanfang Subdistrict)	蘭山區 (南坊街道)	兰山区 (南坊街道)	950,000	1,130,000	1,300,000	818
Luozhuang District (Luozhuang Subdistrict)	羅莊區 (羅莊街道)	罗庄区 (罗庄街道)	430,000	610,000	670,000	642
Hedong District (Jiuqu Subdistrict)	河東區 (九曲街道)	河东区 (九曲街道)	660,000	750,000	850,000	834
Tancheng County (Tancheng Subdistrict)	郯城縣 (郯城街道)	郯城县 (郯城街道)	1,040,000	940,000	1,030,000	1195
Lanling County (Bianzhuang Subdistrict)	蘭陵縣 (卞莊街道)	兰陵县 (卞庄街道)	1,290,000	1,300,000	1,450,000	1724
Ju'nan County (Shizilu Subdistrict)	莒南縣 (十字路街道)	莒南县 (十字路街道)	1,010,000	1,020,000	1,070,000	1751
Yishui County (Yicheng Subdistrict)	沂水縣 (沂城街道)	沂水县 (沂城街道)	1,130,000	1,140,000	1,190,000	2414
Mengyin County (Mengyin Subdistrict)	蒙陰縣 (蒙陰街道)	蒙阴县 (蒙阴街道)	550,000	550,000	580,000	1602
Pingyi County (Pingyi Subdistrict)	平邑縣 (平邑街道)	平邑县 (平邑街道)	1,010,000	1,020,000	1,110,000	1823
Feixian County (Feicheng Subdistrict)	費縣 (費城街道)	费县 (费城街道)	980,000	830,000	910,000	1660
Yinan County (Jiehu Subdistrict)	沂南縣 (界湖街道)	沂南县 (界湖街道)	950,000	910,000	980,000	1719
Linshu County (Linshu Subdistrict)	臨沭縣 (臨沭街道)	临沭县 (临沭街道)	660,000	640,000	670,000	1010
Zaozhuang City	棗莊市	枣庄市	3,900,000	3,940,000	4,230,000	4564
Xuecheng District (Lincheng Subdistrict)	薛城區 (臨城街道)	薛城区 (临城街道)	500,000	510,000	580,000	508

(continued)

Table 26.4 (continued)

Name	Traditional	Simplified	Population (2012)	Population (2016)	Population (2020)	Area (Sq. Km)
Shizhong District (Longshanlu Subdistrict)	市中區 (龍山路街道)	市中区 (龙山路街道)	520,000	530,000	590,000	374
Yicheng District (Tanshan Subdistrict)	嶧城區 (壇山街道)	峄城区 (坛山街道)	390,000	390,000	430,000	635
Tai'erzhuang District (Yunhe Subdistrict)	台兒莊區 (運河街道)	台儿庄区 (运河街道)	310,000	310,000	340,000	533
Shanting District (Shancheng Subdistrict)	山亭區 (山城街道)	山亭区 (山城街道)	500,000	510,000	540,000	1019
Tengzhou City (Beixin Subdistrict)	滕州市 (北辛街道)	滕州市 (北辛街道)	1,680,000	1,690,000	1,750,000	1495
Jining City	濟寧市	济宁市	8,430,000	8,500,000	8,910,000	11,191
Shizhong District[d] (Fuqiao Subdistrict)	市中區 (阜橋街道)	市中区 (阜桥街道	590,000	N/A	N/A	(381)
Rencheng District (Fuqiao Subdistrict)	任城區 (阜橋街道)	任城区 (阜桥街道)	530,000	1,140,000	1,240,000	889
Qufu City (Lucheng Subdistrict)	曲阜市 (魯城街道)	曲阜市 (鲁城街道)	640,000	640,000	660,000	815
Yanzhou District (Longqiao Subdistrict)	兖州區 (龍橋街道)	兖州区 (龙桥街道)	630,000	640,000	650,000	648
Zoucheng City (Gangshan Subdistrict)	鄒城市 (鋼山街道)	邹城市 (钢山街道)	1,160,000	1,190,000	1,220,000	1616
Weishan County (Xiazhen Subdistrict)	微山縣 (夏鎮街道)	微山县 (夏镇街道)	720,000	720,000	730,000	1738
Yutai County (Guting Subdistrict)	魚台縣 (谷亭街道)	鱼台县 (谷亭街道)	470,000	470,000	480,000	654
Jinxiang County (Jinxiang Subdistrict)	金鄉縣 (金鄉街道)	金乡县 (金乡街道)	640,000	640,000	680,000	888
Jiaxiang County (Jiaxiang Subdistrict)	嘉祥縣 (嘉祥街道)	嘉祥县 (嘉祥街道)	870,000	870,000	930,000	975
Wenshang County (Zhongdu Subdistrict)	汶上縣 (中都街道)	汶上县 (中都街道)	780,000	780,000	820,000	889

(continued)

Table 26.4 (continued)

Name	Traditional	Simplified	Population (2012)	Population (2016)	Population (2020)	Area (Sq. Km)
Sishui County (Sihe Subdistrict)	泗水縣 (泗河街道)	泗水县 (泗河街道)	620,000	620,000	650,000	1118
Liangshan County (Shuibo Subdistrict)	梁山縣 (水泊街道)	梁山县 (水泊街道)	780,000	790,000	850,000	961
Tai'an City	泰安市	泰安市	5,570,000	5,580,000	5,730,000	7762
Taishan District (Daimiao Subdistrict)	泰山區 (岱廟街道)	泰山区 (岱庙街道)	620,000	620,000	630,000	337
Daiyue District (Zhoudian Subdistrict)	岱岳區 (粥店街道)	岱岳区 (粥店街道)	970,000	970,000	1,000,000	1750
Xintai City (Qingyun Subdistrict)	新泰市 (青雲街道)	新泰市 (青云街道)	1,390,000	1,400,000	1,450,000	1934
Feicheng City (Xincheng Subdistrict)	肥城市 (新城街道)	肥城市 (新城街道)	980,000	980,000	990,000	1277
Ningyang County (Wenmiao Subdistrict)	寧陽縣 (文廟街道)	宁阳县 (文庙街道)	820,000	820,000	840,000	1125
Dongping County (Dongping Subdistrict)	東平縣 (東平街道)	东平县 (东平街道)	790,000	790,000	810,000	1339
Laiwu City[e]	萊蕪市	**莱芜**市	1,270,000	1,260,000	N/A	(2246)
Laicheng District[f] (Fengcheng Subdistrict)	萊城區 (鳳城街道)	莱城区 (凤城街道)	970,000	960,000	N/A	(1740)
Gangcheng District[g] (Aishan Subdistrict)	鋼城區 (艾山街道)	钢城区 (艾山街道)	300,000	300,000	N/A	(506)
Binzhou City	濱州市	**滨**州市	3,790,000	3,810,000	3,970,000	9156
Bincheng District (Shizhong Subdistrict)	濱城區 (市中街道)	滨城区 (市中街道)	640,000	650,000	700,000	1041
Huimin County (Sunwu Subdistrict)	惠民縣 (孫武街道)	惠民县 (孙武街道)	640,000	640,000	650,000	1363
Yangxin County (Xincheng Subdistrict)	陽信縣 (信城街道)	阳信县 (信城街道)	450,000	450,000	470,000	798
Wudi County (Difeng Subdistrict)	無棣縣 (棣豐街道)	无棣县 (棣丰街道)	450,000	460,000	490,000	1586

(continued)

Table 26.4 (continued)

Name	Traditional	Simplified	Population (2012)	Population (2016)	Population (2020)	Area (Sq. Km)
Zhanhua District (Fuguo Subdistrict)	沾化區 (富國街道)	沾化区 (富国街道)	390,000	390,000	400,000	2218
Boxing County (Bochang Subdistrict)	博興縣 (博昌街道)	博兴县 (博昌街道)	490,000	490,000	500,000	900
Zouping City (Huangshan Subdistrict)	鄒平市 (黃山街道)	邹平市 (黄山街道)	730,000	730,000	740,000	1250
Heze City	**菏澤市**	**菏泽市**	9,570,000	9,570,000	10,250,000	12,256
Mudan District (Xicheng Subdistrict)	牡丹區 (西城街道)	牡丹区 (西城街道)	1,530,000	1,500,000	1,650,000	1415
Caoxian County (Caocheng Subdistrict)	曹縣 (曹城街道)	曹县 (曹城街道)	1,560,000	1,590,000	1,700,000	1974
Dingtao District (Tianzhong Subdistrict)	定陶區 (天中街道)	定陶区 (天中街道)	670,000	670,000	710,000	846
Chengwu County (Wenting Subdistrict)	成武縣 (文亭街道)	成武县 (文亭街道)	690,000	700,000	730,000	998
Shanxian County (Beicheng Subdistrict)	單縣 (北城街道)	单县 (北城街道)	1,220,000	1,210,000	1,280,000	1670
Juye County (Fenghuang Subdistrict)	巨野縣 (鳳凰街道)	巨野县 (凤凰街道)	1,010,000	1,010,000	1,100,000	1308
Yuncheng County (Tangta Subdistrict)	鄆城縣 (唐塔街道)	郓城县 (唐塔街道)	1,220,000	1,220,000	1,280,000	1643
Juancheng County (Guquan Subdistrict)	鄄城縣 (古泉街道)	鄄城县 (古泉街道)	860,000	860,000	930,000	1032
Dongming County (Chengguan Subdistrict)	東明縣 (城關街道)	东明县 (城关街道)	810,000	810,000	880,000	1370

[a]Made subordinate to Jinan city in 9 January 2019
[b]Made a district in June 2019
[c]Dissolved in 2014, made Lingcheng district
[d]Dissolved in 2013, incorporated into Rencheng district
[e]Made subordinate to Jinan city in 9 January 2019
[f]Made subordinate to Jinan city in 9 January 2019
[g]Made subordinate to Jinan city in 9 January 2019

References

Chang, Kwang-chih. 1999. China on the eve of the historical record. In *The Cambridge history of ancient China: From the origins of civilization to 221 B.C*, ed. Michael Loewe and Edward L. Shaughnessy, 37–73. New York: Cambridge University Press.

Charlegmagne. 2010. Strange meeting. *The Economist*, 26 April. https://www.economist.com/charlemagne/2010/04/26/strange-meeting.

Shaugnessy, Edward L. 1999. Western Zhou history. In *The Cambridge history of ancient China: From the origins of civilization to 221 B.C*, ed. Michael Loewe and Edward L. Shaughnessy, 292–351. New York: Cambridge University Press.

Knechtges, David R., and Taiping Chang, eds. 2014. *Ancient and early medieval Chinese literature: A reference guide, part two*. Boston: Brill.

Legge, James. 1876. *The Book of Poetry*, 1876. http://www.sacred-texts.com/cfu/bop/index.htm. Accessed 21 Sept 2021.

Lu, Yu. [*Shandong's Population*]. 1994. Jinan, Shandong: Jinan Shandong People's Publishing House, 路遇. 山东人口. 济南: 山东人民出版社.

Ministry of Civil Affairs (MCA), People's Republic of China. 2020. [*County/township administration handbook*]. Beijing: China Statistics Press. 中華人民共和國民政部, 中華人民共和國, 鄉鎮行政區劃簡冊.

Paine, S.C.M. 2003. *The Sino-Japanese War of 1894–1895: Perceptions, power, and primacy*. New York: Cambridge University Press.

People's Republic of China (PRC). 2001. *Administrative division reform atlas, 1949–1999*. Beijing: China Map Publishers.

Shandong Province Bureau of Statistics (SPBS). 2021. [Communiqué of the seventh national census of Shandong Province, issue no. 2]. 21 May. 山东省第七次全国人口普查公报, 第二号. http://tjj.shandong.gov.cn/art/2021/5/21/art_6293_10287511.html.

Shang-Ch'i Guide. 2017. [*Backpacking in China: the most complete collection of self-guided travel for China, 2018*]. Taipei: Shang-Ch'i Shitai publishing. 2018 最完整的中國自助旅遊全集. 台北: 上奇時代.

Spence, Jonathan D. 1999. *The search for modern China*. New York: W. W. Norton & Company.

Sun-Tzu: The Art of War: the first english translation incorporating the recently discovered Yin-ch'üeh-shan texts, translated, with an introduction and commentary, by Roger T. Ames. 1993. New York: Ballantine Books.

Tan, Qixiang. 1985. *Concise historical atlas of China*. Beijing: China Cartographic Publishing House.

Tiedemann, R.G., ed. 2010. *Handbook of Christianity in China, volume 2: 1800 to the present*. Boston: Brill.

Wang, Fen. 2013. The Houli and Beixin cultures. In *A companion to Chinese archaeology*, ed. Anne P. Underhill, 389–410. Malden, MA: Blackwell Publishing.

Wu, Chucai, Zhang Luocheng, and Ji Zixiu. 2002. [*The rise of China's coastal economic low regions*]. Beijing: University of Science and Technology of China Press. 吴楚材, 张落成, 季子修. 中国沿海经济低谷地区的崛起. 北京: 中国科学技术大学出版社.

Yuan, Zuliang and Jiao Peimin. 2007. [*China's population through history: beginning Qin volume*]. Beijing: People's Press; 袁祖亮, 焦培民. 中國人口通史: 先秦卷, Vol. 2. 北京: 人民出版社.

Zhang, Qizhi. 2015. *An introduction to Chinese history and culture*. New York: Springer.

Zhang, Shunan. 2021. [The 2020 per capita income list of residents in various provinces: Shanghai is the richest, and it has risen sharply]. Finance.people.com. 22 January. 张澍楠. 2020年各省份居民人均收入榜: 上海最有钱, 这地涨得猛. http://finance.people.com.cn/n1/2021/0122/c1004-32008733.html.

Chapter 27
Shanghai City

Abstract Known as an international metropolis today, Shanghai has been a household name in the west since at least the 1920s. Part of both the Wu and Yue states in its past, Shanghai as a city had modest beginnings, its name likely from a government liquor tax authority in ca. 1000 CE. Blessed with a deep-water port, by the nineteenth century Shanghai was forced to open its doors to foreign trade, creating foreign enclaves run by their respective countries, to include the French, British, and American. Although under authoritarian rule during the Nationalist period, Shanghai was not just a center for bustling merchants, but was open to new fashions and ideas from abroad. With regard to the latter, Shanghai was also the birthplace of the Chinese Communist Party (CCP) in 1921. Further establishing itself as a cosmopolitan city, Shanghai hosted the world's fair in 2010, and also became the wealthiest of all regions among mainland China's 31 provinces and major cities. Shanghai City's residential population in 2020 reached over 24,800,000, while the official household (*hukou*) registered population that same year was 14,600,000. Thus, a difference of some 10,000,000 individuals indicates Shanghai has among the highest representation of China's "floating populations" in China.

E. Croddy, *China's Provinces and Populations*,
https://doi.org/10.1007/978-3-031-09165-0_27

Shanghai City (上海市 *shànghǎi shì*): Abbreviations 滬; 申 (*hù; shēn*) (Fig. 27.1)

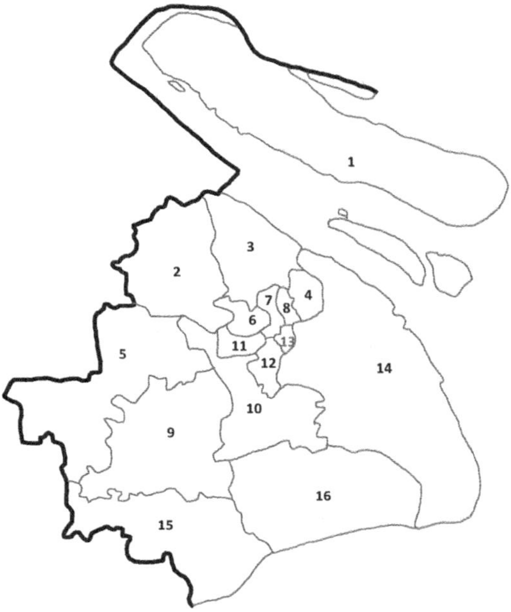

Fig. 27.1 Shanghai City: Subdistricts (Capital City Governmental Seat: Huangpu Distrtict). Drawn by the Author after People's Republic of China, Ministry of Civil Affairs. (MCA 2020)

Shanghai City: General Impressions

(For general history of the region in and around Shanghai see also Zhejiang and Jiangsu Provinces). One thinks of the metropolitan city of Shanghai of today: bright city lights, skyscrapers, financial institutions, an efficient metro system, and a busy port. It also worth recalling that Shanghai has been an international cosmopolitan city going back to the 1920s, complete even back then with streetcars, automobiles, and numerous foreigners (usually living in their own extraterritorial sectors). In either era, Shanghai represents all that a modern city can offer for the modern Chinese citizen and expat alike.

"Shanghai'ed"

The nineteenth century term "to Shanghai" or "Shanghai'ed" referred to the practice of kidnapping sailors, and forcing them to serve on merchant vessels plying the Pacific Ocean. The term probably first was made popular San Francisco in the early 1850s. One story held that there was a saloon-cum-boarding house in San Francisco (in the notorious Barbary Coast district) named Shanghai Kelly's on Pacific Street (now Pacific Avenue, between Drumm and Davis). The proprietor Kelly, once having spotted good candidates to press into service, laced their drink (a mickey), usually a combination shot of Schnapps and opium-laced beer. This incapacitated his victims, who would then fall through a trap door to a skiff waiting below.

While the latter story appears to have been largely fiction, the "crimping" of sailors and forced labor on ships did in fact occur. The demand for sailors to sail from the west coast of the United States to Shanghai often was unmet due to the unpopularity of the cruise itself. Rarely was there a round trip possible, and thus crewmen were forced to take a voyage around the world to return home, a journey that could take at least a year. And the law of the times was of no help: The U.S Supreme Court ruled in 1897 that the 13th Amendment (outlawing slavery) did not apply to sailors, the rationale being they were no more than addled children, and therefore not responsible enough to be masters of their own destiny.

Prehistoric Shanghai

Named after a village in Qingpu District, Shanghai City, the Songze Culture (崧澤文化 *sōngzé wénhuà*) dates from about 5,300 to 6,000 years ago. Excavations revealed water wells, tombs, decorative jade, and evidence of rice cultivation.

Evidence found at the Guangfulin archeological site (廣富林遺址 *guǎngfùlín yízhǐ*) in Songjiang District, Shanghai, shows a relatively sophisticated human settlement, to include agriculture and distinct pottery manufacture, dating back about

5,000 years. This late-stage Liangzhu Culture (良渚文化 *liángzhǔ wénhuà*) ranged from Hangzhou to Shanghai's Maqiao and Qingpu districts, featuring extensive and spectacular jade carvings. Lasting from about 3300–2300 BCE, Liangzhu Culture is unique in having jade inscriptions with a prototypical written language that may be the precursor to those found on oracle bones (Itzstein-Davey et al. 2007).

Historical Sketch of Shanghai

When the Wu (吳 *wú*) kingdom, consisting of modern-day Jiangsu Province and Shanghai, fell to the Yue (越 *yuè*) during the Spring and Autumn (春秋 *chūnqiū*) period (771–476 BCE), the encroachment of the dominant Chu (楚 *chǔ*) state brought the Shanghai area under the control of Lord Chun Shen (d. 238 BCE; 春申君 *chūnshēn jūn*). This is whence the short-hand character shen (申 *shēn*) for Shanghai is derived. Following the Qin (秦 *qín*) conquest over the Chu in 223 BCE, the larger Shanghai-Suzhou area of today was then administered in the prefecture of Kuaiji[1] (會稽郡 *kuàijījùn*). (Hargett 2013). One of its subordinate counties, Liuxian (瞜縣 *liúxiàn*), in today's Kunshan (昆山 *kūnshān*), comprised the boarders of modern-day metropolitan Shanghai City. Liuxian later changed its name to Louxian county (樓縣 *lóuxiàn*) in 207 BCE (Xuan 2006).

While the backstory of the shorthand character Shen (申 *shēn*) is relatively straightforward, the history of another popular character abbreviation for Shanghai, Hu (滬 *hù*), is a bit more convoluted. By the Jin Dynasty (265–400 CE) dynasty, indigenous people who lived along the Wusong River (吳松江 *wúsōng jiāng*), the lower reaches of which runs through Shanghai, employed a bamboo fishing mesh called Hu (扈 hù). In addition, the entry into the open water was called Du (瀆 *dú*), and the general area was thus named Hudu (扈瀆 *hùdú*). Eventually this merged into a single character Hu (滬 *hù*) as a colloquial name for the region, and has since become the more common abbreviated name for Shanghai.

During the Sui and Tang dynasties (ca. 580–905 CE), China's economy expanded to the southeast, and as it did so, the Shanghai region became more dynamic as well. Beginning in the Tang, improvements in farming were made in the practice of field irrigation, and the use of riverine transportation spurred the economic development of the region in and around modern-day Shanghai. Although written records indicated a trading port existed called Qinglong town (青龍鎮 *qīnglóng zhèn*) in 746 CE, physical evidence remained hidden until artifacts were unearthed beginning in 2010. Among them, numerous caches of porcelain and other items showed Qinglong was a significant trading port for shipping pottery wares to northern China, complete with its Qinglong Pagoda[2] (built ca. 821–824 CE) that also served

---

[1] Alternatively "Guiji."

[2] 青龍塔 *qīnglóngtǎ* aka 吉雲禪寺塔 *jíyúnchánsì tǎ*.

as a lighthouse. This trading area was eventually lost to history as it was supplanted by other ports beginning about the Yuan (CCTV 2016).

Transitioning to the Northern Song (北宋 *běisòng*), in 1032 CE, four counties in the Shanghai region were brought under the administration of Xiuzhou (秀州 *xiùzhōu*), including Huating County (華亭縣 *huátíng xiàn*). Within Xiuzhou were established seventeen wine (or liquor) revenue offices (酒務 *jiǔwù*), each responsible for the taxing of alcoholic beverages. And in Huating County one finds the 'Shanghai wine revenue office' (上海務 *shànghǎiwù*), this probably being the first appearance of the place name Shanghai (1077). In 1127, after the Jurchen Jin (金 *jīn*) from the north laid siege to Kaifeng (then known as Bianjing 汴京 *biànjīng*), merchants, farmers, and other key economic players were forced to move southward, leading to the rapid development of the Shanghai region. By 1267, during the southern Song, Shanghai was formally made a "Market Town" (上海鎮 *shànghǎi zhèn*) (Zhu et al. 2008). In the Yuan (Mongol) dynasty (ca. 1271–1368), Shanghai became famous for its textiles, notably cotton. By 1277, Shanghai had also developed into one of China's major shipping and boat yards. In 1292, the aforementioned Huating County (華亭縣 *huátíng xiàn*) was divided, and from it was created Shanghai County (上海縣 *shànghǎi xiàn*). Shanghai then incorporated Huangpu District (黃浦區 *huángpǔ qū*), forming the borders of Shanghai City of today.

As of the late Ming (1368–1644), Shanghai was subordinate to Songjiang Prefecture (松江府 *sōngjiāng fǔ*) within the much larger Nanzhili (南直隸 *nánzhílì*) region which also included modern-day eastern Anhui and Jiangsu (Tan 1996). Due to Japanese (and Chinese) piracy, a wall was built nearly four miles in length and some 20 feet in height to protect Shanghai in 1554.

As of 1820 Songjiang Prefecture was made a prefecture within Jiangsu during the Qing dynasty. Still closed off to direct foreign trade, visiting foreigners nonetheless noted the growing and vibrant city of Shanghai in the early 1830s. Having seen Shanghai for himself, in 1832, Reverend Charles Gutzlaff wrote, "Shanghae (sic) appears to be the greatest emporium of the empire" (Gamble 2003).

During the later stages of the Qing dynasty, the Treaty of Nanking (29 August 1842, 南京條約 *nánjīng tiáoyuē*) forced China to open its ports at Shanghai, along with Guangzhou, Xiamen, Fuzhou, and Ningbo to foreign trade. This led to a large migration of laborers to Shanghai, especially from Canton (Guangzhou City). (Goodman 1995). In 1846, Britain and China signed the "Shanghai Lend-lease,"[3] making Shanghai a foreign concession, cementing its global role as a treaty port. Not just British, but French and American sectors were established within Shanghai, while British and US acquisitions were later combined together into the International Settlement in 1863 (Latourette 1967).

During the chaos of the Taiping Rebellion, Shanghai was a refuge for many, with some 80,000 having moved into the foreign concession areas (Lu 1999).

---

[3] 上海租地章程 *shànghǎizūdì zhāngchéng*.

Business families from Zhejiang's Ningbo also found opportunities and relative safety in Shanghai (Goodman 1995). Eventually, however, the Taiping Rebellion armies found their way to Shanghai in August 1860. The strategic goal of this maneuver was to grab silver ingots, upwards to 1 million ounces that were held within the city vaults, and which could then fund the construction of a modern Taiping rebel navy. To the surprise of the Taiping general, Li Xiucheng (李秀成 *lǐ xiùchéng*; d. 1864) the foreigners in Shanghai did not stand down, but fiercely fought back with firearms and cannon, bringing the Taiping offensive to a halt. Seeking to avenge his losses, in January 1862 Li Xiucheng brought an estimated 15,000 soldiers back to threaten Shanghai. But here again he is ultimately stymied, primarily due to snow and freezing cold weather, "unprecedented in the meteorological annals of Shanghai for its severity and the low range of the thermometer" (Spence 1996).

Throughout its own roaring 1920s and 1930s, Shanghai grew to an international metropolis and a key East Asian financial center. Some 60,000 foreigners lived in Shanghai during the 1920s, more than anywhere else in China. The libertine lifestyle and free-wheeling nature of Shanghai earned it two sobriquets during this Golden Age of Shanghai: "Paris of the East" and, less charitably, the "Whore of the Orient" (Williams and Chan 2003.) For historical population data on Shanghai, see Table 27.1 below.

Table 27.1 Shanghai's population from nineteenth to twentieth century. (Yang 1995)

Year	Population
1880	107,812
1889	168,129
1900	345,276
1905	920,000
1910	1185,859
1911	1,250,000
1936	3,810,000
1949	5,030,000
1952	5,730,000
1958	7,510,000
1959	10,280,000
1965	10,940,000
1977	10,860,000
1980	11,470,000
1985	12,170,000
1990	12,830,000
1992	12,890,000

Birth of the Chinese Communist Party (CCP) in Shanghai (1921)

The People's Republic of China (PRC) celebrates 1 July 1921 as the formation of the Chinese Communist Party (CCP). However, this a convenient date that is not historically correct. It was during the last week of July (23–30) that a 15-person CCP delegation (including Mao Zedong) convened its first congress in Shanghai's French concession. They first began their meeting in a women's school dormitory, and later in a residence of one of the participants (Li Hanjun 李漢俊 *lǐ hànjùn*) in today's Huangpu District (黃浦區 *huángpǔ qū*). Although the latter venue was chosen for its security, it was nonetheless raided by the French police on 30 July. By some miracle (for the CCP, anyway), the French constabulary never discovered the draft of the "Program for the Communist Party of China" that had been haphazardly placed in a desk drawer (Pantsov 2012).

Shanghai Jewish Ghetto

Shanghai's Hongkou ("Honkew") district (虹口區 *hóngkǒu qū*) ghetto became home to some 20,000–30,000 Jews that had fled Nazi Germany since the early 1930s (Erdogan 2016). In 1943, the Japanese, both to protect its inhabitants but also prevent collaboration between them and their Chinese hosts, had forced all Jews living in Shanghai into the small Hongkou ghetto, which was part of the International Settlement (Goldstein 2015).

The sizeable jump in Shanghai's population in the late 1950s can be explained at least in part by a massive influx of farmers who, desperate for relief from Mao Zedong's insistence upon the collectivization of agriculture during the Great Leap Forward (1958–1962), moved to larger cities across China. Even when the *hukou* registration system prohibited such migrations in 1958, up to as many as 15 million peasants sought work (and survival) in urban areas such as Shanghai (Dikötter 2010).

Shanghai World's Fair, Economics, and Population in the Twenty-First Century

In 2010, Shanghai hosted the world's fair ('Expo 2010 Shanghai') from May to October, costing China about $45 billion, and attracted some 73 million visitors. Reflecting the economic power of the fast-growing eastern region of China, the per capita income for urban Shanghai has continued to rank among the highest in China at USD $11,233 in 2020 (Zhang 2021). Shanghai also "punches above its weight" in terms of its gross domestic product (GDP = $602 billion), ranked 10th (behind

Anhui province) of mainland China's 31 provinces and major cities. Continuing to grow in population at a significant pace (8% from 2010–2020), these high wages and economic opportunities draw enormous numbers of "floating populations" to Shanghai. According to the 2020 census (see Tables 27.2, 27.3) with a population of about 24,870,900, its registered permanent (*hukou*) population (Table 27.4) in 2020 was listed as 14,620,000.

Table 27.4 (below) shows the *hukou* (family registered) populations based on PRC Ministry of Civil Affairs data. (Districts listed directly under major cities are government seats, as are those in parentheses). One can compare these data with the census (usual residential populations based on 2010 and 2020 censuses (Table 27.2). For a selected district population (Qingpu) and its subdistricts, see Table 27.3.

Table 27.2 Shanghai population over four decades (Residential 常住人口 *chángzhù rénkǒu*). Data (SCBS 2021)

District or County	Population (1990)	Population (2000)	Population (2010)	Population (2020)
Huangpu District 黃埔區 *huángpǔ qū*	733,200	574,500	429,891	662,030
Nanshi District 南市區 *nánshì qū*	825,924	N/A	N/A	N/A
Luwan District 盧灣區 *lúwān qū*	475,796	328,900	248,779	N/A
Xuhui District 徐匯區 *xúhuì qū*	776,602	1,064,600	1,085,130	1,113,078
Changning District 長寧區 *chángzhù qū*	585,418	702,200	690,571	693,051
Jing'an District 靜安區 *jìngān qū*	486,625	305,400	246,788	975,707
Putuo District 普陀區 *pǔtuó qū*	796,151	1,051,700	1,288,881	1,239,800
Zhabei District 閘北區 *zháběi qū*	712,917	798,600	830,476	N/A
Hongkou District 虹口區 *hóngkǒu qū*	879,658	860,700	852,476	757,498
Yangpu District 楊浦區 *yángpǔ qū*	1,124,454	1,243,800	1,313,222	1,242,548
Minhang District 閔行區 *mǐnháng qū*	158,786	1,217,300	2,429,372	2,653,489
Baoshan District 寶山區 *bǎoshān qū*	658,853	1,228,000	1,904,886	2,235,218
Shanghai County上海縣 *shànghǎi xiàn*	449,331	N/A	N/A	N/A
Jiading County 嘉定縣 *jiādìng xiàn*	536,576	753,100	1,471,231	1,834,258
Chuansha County 川沙縣 *chuānshā xiàn*	645,541	N/A	N/A	N/A

(continued)

Table 27.2 (continued)

District or County	Population (1990)	Population (2000)	Population (2010)	Population (2020)
Nanhui County 南匯縣 *nánhuì xiàn*	705,871	785,100	N/A	N/A
Fengxian County 奉賢縣 *fèngxián xiàn*	526,706	624,300	1,083,463	1,140,872
Songjiang County 松江縣 *sōngjiāng xiàn*	511,547	641,100	1,582,398	1,909,713
Jinshan County 金山縣 *jīnshān xiàn*	554,128	580,400	732,410	822,776
Qingpu County 青浦縣 *qīngpǔ xiàn*	461,578	595,900	1,081,022	1,271,424
Chongming District 崇明區 *chóngmíng xiàn*	736,190	649,800	703,722	637,921
Pudong New District 浦東新區 *pǔdōng xīnqū*	N/A	N/A	5,044,430	5,681,512
Total:	**13,341,852**	**16,737,700**	**23,019,148**	**24,870,895**

Table 27.3 Selected population data: Qingpu District, Shanghai City. (SCBS 2021)

Shanghai City, Qingpu County population (2020 census)[a]	Subordinate subdistrict populations (2020)	Total population (2020)
Qingpu County 青浦縣 *qīngpǔ xiàn*		**1,271,424**
Zhaoxiang Town 趙巷鎮 *zhàoxiàng zhèn*	143,350	
Xujing Town 徐涇鎮 *xújīng zhèn*	198,376	
Xinhua Town 華新鎮 *huáxīn zhèn*	200,124	
Chonggu Town 重固鎮 *chónggù zhèn*	65,695	
Baihe Town 白鶴鎮 *báihè zhèn*	91,130	
Zhujiajiao Town 朱家角鎮 *zhūjiājiǎo zhèn*	94,067	
Liantang Town 練塘鎮 *liàntáng zhèn*	53,929	
Jinze Town 金澤鎮 *jīnzé zhèn*	44,517	
Xiayang Subdistrict 夏陽街道 *xiàyáng jiēdào*	149,517	
Yingpu Subdistrict 盈浦街道 *yíngpǔ jiēdào*	128,691	
Xianghuaqiao Subdistrict 香花橋街道 *xiānghuāqiáo jiēdào*	102,028	

[a]As of 27 August 2021, only Qingpu county had published data on its subdistricts

Shanghai City 滬; 申 (*hù; shēn*)

Table 27.4 Shanghai City: permanent registered (戶籍人口 *hùjí rénkǒu*) populations. (MCA 2020)

Name	Traditional	Simplified	Population (2012)	Population (2016)	Population (2020)	Area (Sq. km)
Shanghai City	上海市	上海市	14,120,000	14,400,000	14,620,000	6340
Huangpu District (Waitan Subdistrict)	黃浦區 (外灘街道)	黄浦区 (外滩街道)	910,000	900,000	830,000	20
Xuhui District (Xujiahui Subdistrict)	徐匯區 (徐家匯街道)	徐汇区 (徐家汇街道)	910,000	920,000	920,000	55
Changning District (Jiangsulu Subdistrict)	長寧區 (江蘇路街道)	长宁区 (江苏路街道)	620,000	630,000	580,000	38
Jing'an District (Jiangninglu Subdistrict)	靜安區 (江寧路街道)	静安区 (江宁路街道)	310,000	1,120,000	930,000	37
Putuo District (Zhenru Town)	普陀區 (真如鎮街道)	普陀区 (真如镇街道)	880,000	880,000	890,000	55
Zhabei District[a] (Tianmuxilu Subdistrict)	閘北區 (天目西路街道)	闸北区 (天目西路街道)	690,000	N/A	N/A	(29)
Hongkou District (Jiaxinglu Subdistrict)	虹口區 (嘉興路街道)	虹口区 (嘉兴路街道)	790,000	790,000	730,000	23
Yangpu District (Pinglianglu Subdistrict)	楊浦區 (平涼路街道)	杨浦区 (平凉路街道)	1,090,000	1,090,000	1,070,000	61
Minhang District (Xinzhuang Town)	閔行區 (莘莊鎮)	闵行区 (莘庄镇)	970,000	1,000,000	1,130,000	371
Baoshan District (Youyilu Subdistrict)	寶山區 (友誼路街道)	宝山区 (友谊路街道)	880,000	910,000	990,000	271
Jiading District (Xinchenglu Subdistrict)	嘉定區 (新成路街道)	嘉定区 (新成路街道)	560,000	570,000	640,000	464
Pudong Xinqu District (Huamu Subdistrict)	浦東新區 (花木街道)	浦东新区 (花木街道)	2,760,000	2,810,000	3,030,000	1210
Jinshan District (Shanyang Town)	金山區 (山陽鎮)	金山区 (山阳镇)	520,000	520,000	520,000	586

(continued)

Table 27.4 (continued)

Name	Traditional	Simplified	Population (2012)	Population (2016)	Population (2020)	Area (Sq. km)
Songjiang District (Fangsong Subdistrict)	松江區 (方松街道)	松江区 (方松街道)	580,000	590,000	640,000	606
Qingpu District (Xiayang Subdistrict)	青浦區 (夏陽街道)	青浦区 (夏阳街道)	460,000	470,000	490,000	670
Fengxian District (Nanqiao Town)	奉賢區 (南橋鎮)	奉贤区 (南桥镇)	520,000	530,000	540,000	687
Chongming District (Chengqiao Town)	崇明區 (城橋鎮)	崇明区 (城桥镇)	690,000	690,000	680,000	1185

[a]Dissolved on 13 October 2015, with the creation of a new Jing'an district

References

CCTV (Online). 2016. Discoveries at Qinglong site shine new light on Shanghai. *Looking China*, 19 December. http://english.cctv.com/2016/12/19/VIDETSMwIhBScdren57TnSTU161219.shtml.

Dikötter, Frank. 2010. *Mao's great famine: The history of China's most devastating catastrophe, 1958–1962*. New York: Walker & Co.

Erdogan, Furkan. 2016. Judaism with Shanghai characteristics. *Global Times*. 6 May, via http://jewishpudong.com/media/pdf/950/cTov9509568.pdf

Gamble, Jos. 2003. *Shanghai in transition: Changing perspectives and social contours of a Chinese metropolis*. New York: Routledge Curzon.

Goldstein, Jonathan. 2015. *Jewish identities in East and Southeast Asia: Singapore, Manila, Taipei, Harbin, Shanghai, Rangoon and Sarabaya*. Berlin: Walter de Gruyter.

Goodman, Bryna. 1995. *Native place, city, and nation: Regional networks and identities in Shanghai, 1853–1937*. Berkeley: University of California Press.

Hanchao, Lu. 1999. *Beyond the neon lights: Everyday Shanghai in the early twentieth century*. Berkeley: University of California Press.

Hargett, James M. 2013. Guaiji? Guiji? Huiji? Kuaiji? Some remarks on an ancient Chinese place-name. *Sino-Platonic Papers* 234: 3–35.

Itzstein-Davey, Freea, Pia Atahan, John Dodson, et al. 2007. A sediment-based record of late glacial and Holocene environmental changes from Guangfulin, Yangtze Delta, eastern China. *The Holocene* 17 (8): 1221–1231.

Latourette, Kenneth Scott. 1967. *The Chinese: Their history and culture*. New York: The Macmillan Company.

Ministry of Civil Affairs (MCA), People's Republic of China. 2020. *County/township administration handbook*. Beijing: China Statistics Press. 中華人民共和國民政部, 中華人民共和國，鄉鎮行政區劃簡冊.

Pantsov, Alexander V. 2012. *Mao: The real story*. New York: Simon & Schuster.

Qixiang, Tan, ed. 1996. *The historical atlas of China, volume VII*. Beijing: China Cartographic Publishing House.

Shanghai City Bureau of Statistics (SCBS). 2021. *Bulletin of the main data of the seventh national population census in Shanghai*, issue no. 2. 19 May. 上海市第七次全国人口普查主要数据公报, 第二号. http://tjj.sh.gov.cn/7rp-pcyw/20210519/f470438f902f4c88af63be0f84c9808f.html

Spence, Jonathan D. 1996. *God's Chinese Son: The Taiping heavenly kingdom of Hong Xiuquan*. New York: W. W. Norton.

Williams, Jack F., and Kam Wing Chan. 2003. Cities of East Asia. In *Cities of the world: World regional urban development*, ed. Stanley D. Brunn, Jack Williams, and Donald J. Zeigler, 3rd ed., 412–455. Boulder, Colorado: Rowman and Littlefield Publishers.

Xuan, Xuan. 2006. *The wonders of Shanghai beach*. Chengdu: Youhui Cultural Communications. 暄暄. 上海灘奇人奇事. 成都: 右灰文化傳播有限公司.

Yang, Zihui. 1995. *China's historical population statistical data research*. Beijing: Reform Press. 楊子慧. 中國歷代人口統計資料研究. 北京: 改革出版社.

Zhang, Shunan. 2021. *The 2020 per capita income list of residents in various provinces: Shanghai is the richest, and it has risen sharply*. Finance.people.com. 22 January. 张澍楠. 2020年各省份居民人均收入榜: 上海最有钱, 这地涨得猛. http://finance.people.com.cn/n1/2021/0122/c1004-32008733.html

Zhu, Guodong, Liu Hong, and Chen Zhiqiang. 2008. *Shanghai migrations*. Shanghai: Shanghai Financial University Press. 朱国栋, 刘红, 陈志强. 上海移民, 上海: 上海财经大学出版社.

Chapter 28
Shanxi Province

Abstract With a population of 10,000 in ca. 2000 BCE, possessing archeological sites representing the Longshan Culture, and traditionally the land of the legendary Emperor Yao (the great), Shanxi was a major part of the Jin (晉*jìn*), and a rival kingdom during the Spring Autumn period (722–403 BCE). Taiyuan (then a prefecture) become a major city and center of industry following the unification of the Qin (221 BCE). As an administrative entity, Shanxi derived its name officially during the Ming dynasty, during which time massive migration out of the province was enforced and its territory divided up during the Manchu Qing. During rule by the Chinese Communist Party (CCP), Shanxi's model town of Dazhai was lauded for emulation for its revolutionary fervor, although much of this was found to be a fabrication. Endowed with large coal deposits, Shanxi's population has declined slightly due to lack of other opportunities, and its gross domestic product (GDP) ranks 21st out of mainland China's 31 provinces and major cities, while its per capita income (USD $3,900) is relatively low as well.

E. Croddy, *China's Provinces and Populations*,
https://doi.org/10.1007/978-3-031-09165-0_28

Shanxi Province (山西省 *shānxī shěng*): Abbreviation 晉 (*jìn*) (Fig. 28.1)

Fig. 28.1 Shanxi Province major cities (Provincial Capital: Taiyuan City). Drawn by the Author after People's Republic of China, Ministry of Civil Affairs. (MCA 2020)

*Shanxi (*山西 **shānxī***) Province: General Impressions*

The capital of Shanxi, Taiyuan (太原 *tàiyuán*) is a treasure-filled city, chockablock with ancient temples and vibrant history (often amidst brutal conflicts) going back to the earliest days of a unified Chinese empire. Shanxi province is also coal country, home to heavy industrial enterprises. The name itself, Shanxi (山西 *shānxī*), refers to its location ("West of the Taihang Mountains" 太行山 *tàiháng shān*), the latter extending for about 400 km through Shanxi and Hebei provinces. Shanxi is also referred to as its single character initialism "jin" (晉 *jìn*). Other names include Sanjin (三晉 *sānjìn*), Shanyou (山右 *shānyòu*), and Hedong (河東 *hédōng*).

Prehistory

The city of Taosi (陶寺 *táosì*), located in Xiangfen County (襄汾縣 *xiāngfén xiàn*), was established in ca. 2300–1900 BCE, and was the center for a late-stage Longshan Culture with a population of about 10,000 (Anderson 2014). Excavations at the Taosi site have revealed ancient variants of primitive writing, curved roof tiles, evidence of solar observation, and primitive musical instruments. A palace structure even contained what is believed to be an underground ice storage facility (Nu 2018). Some archeologists have even linked this ancient city to the ancient capital of the Yao (帝堯 *dì yáo*) emperor.

Legacies of Yao, Shun and Yu

China's legendary founding king, Huang Di (黄帝 *huáng dì*), the Yellow Emperor, was the first of the legendary Five Emperors. Huang Di is credited with developing basic elements of civilization. For it was under the Yellow Emperor that, as it is written in the *Thousand Word Classic* (千字文 *qiānzìwén*), "writing first developed, and clothes were invented." He also is said to have introduced the rule of law and basic governance. On a more spiritual level, the second Emperor Zhuan Xu (顓頊 *zhuān xù*) heralded the separation of Heaven and Earth, and, "after this had been done, order was restored and the *people* returned to virtue" (Chang 1999). The following three emperors then succeeded: Yao, Shun and Yu (堯 *yáo*, 舜 *shùn*, 虞 *yú*), purportedly the founders of the Xia (夏 *xià*) dynasty (ca. twenty-first to sixteenth centuries BCE).

While the Xia is mentioned in the classics (e.g., Mencius and Confucius), its existence predates the use of writing in China (prior ca. 1,800 BCE), thus we lack a verified historical record of a Xia dynastic polity. Some clues to its existence have been found, however, in western Henan and southern Shanxi (Wilkinson 2012). In the latter are old place names that speak to their Xia dynastic origins:

- Yaodu Pingyang (堯都平陽 *yáodū píngyáng*) in today's Linfen City (臨汾市 *línfén shì*);
- Shundu Puban (舜都蒲板 *shùndū púbǎn*), in Yongji City (永濟市 *yǒngjì shì*);
- Yudu Anyi (禹都安邑 *yǔdū'ān yì*) in Xiaxian County (夏縣 *xiàxiàn*), Yuncheng City (運城市 *yùnchéng shì*).
- Temple in Linfen City, Yao Miao (堯廟 *yáomiào*), and the Yaoling mausoleum (堯陵 *yáolíng*);
- The Shun Emperor Plateau (舜王坪 *shùnwángpíng*) in Qinshui (沁水 *qìnshuǐ*), Jincheng City (晉城市 *jìnchéng shì*); and
- The Dragon's Gate (龍門 *lóngmén*; also known as Yu's gateway 虞門口 *Yúménkǒu*) in Hejin (河津 *héjīn*), Yuncheng City. This is where, legend has it, that the great Yu (Da Yu 大虞 *Dà Yú*) of the Xia controlled the floods by widening a gorge to tame the Yellow River.

Shanxi province owes its current abbreviated initialism (晉 *jìn*) to the Jin dynasty, which occupied a large portion of Shanxi's plains, and was the largest of rival states during the Spring and Autumn period (722–403 BCE). Following the Jinyang War (晉陽之戰 *jìnyáng zhīzhàn*; 453 BCE), when the combined Wei (魏 *wèi*), Han (韓 *hán*), and Zhao (趙 *zhào*) armies fought the Jin, the latter was subsequently broken into those three kingdoms.

Taiyuan Prefecture

With the unification of the reign of Qin (221–206 BCE), China was organized into roughly 54 prefectures or commanderies (郡 *jùn*). Among the most prominent of was Taiyuan Prefecture, today's capital of Shanxi. During the Eastern Han (ca. 200 CE), the region of modern-day Shanxi had a population of 1,366,820 people (Yuan and Peimin 2007).

In the Han Dynasty under the Xian Di Emperor (獻帝 *xiàn dì*, 216 CE), Xiongnu (匈奴 *xiōngnú*) nomads occupied large swaths of the Lǚliangshan (吕梁山 *lǚliángshān*) mountains and the Fenhe River (汾河 *fénhé*) valley where they raised horses. The famous military leader and potentate of the Han, Cao Cao (曹操 *cáo cāo*; 155–220) battled the Xiongnu nomads (who had long been among China's main "barbarian" nemeses). In order to divide and to rule, Cao Cao had them arranged his lands into five administrative sections:

- Bingzhou (并州 *bìngzhōu*) now Fenyang (汾陽 *fényáng*)
- Qi (祁 *qí*), now Qixian County (祁縣 *qíxiàn*)
- Puzi (蒲子 *púzi*), now Xianxian County (顯縣 *xiǎnxiàn*)
- Xinxing (新興 *xīnxìng*) now Xinzhou (忻州 *xīnzhōu*); and
- Daling (大陵 *dàlíng*), now Wenshui (文水 *wénshuǐ*)

These areas held a combined population of about several hundred thousand.

Other "Barbarian" Groups

Including the Xiongnu, there were a total of "five barbarian" (五胡 *wǔhú*) regional ethnic groups, the other four being:

- Jie (羯族 *jiézú*); in today's Wuxiang (武鄉 *wǔxiāng*);
- Xianbei (also read Xianbi 鮮卑族 *xiānbēi zú*)
- Tuobabu (拓跋部 *tuòbábù*) head-quarted at Daixian County (代縣 *dàixiàn*); and
- Datong (大同 *dàtóng*)

In addition, there were the neighboring Di (氐 *dī*) and the Qiang (羌 *qiāng*) ethnic minorities who populated modern-day Shaanxi and Gansu provinces. In 304, the Xiongnu leader Liu Yuan (劉淵 *liú yuān*), the first non-Han leader to have an era name (元熙 *yuán xī*), raised an army in modern-day Lishi (離石 *líshí*), proclaiming himself Han emperor (漢趙 *hàn zhào*). In 386 CE, the Xianbei Tuobagui (鮮卑拓跋珪 *xiānbēi tuòbáguī*) established the Northern Wei (北魏 *běiwèi*; 386–534) capital at Pingcheng (平城 *píngchéng*; modern-day Datong City). Buddhism flourished during the later years of the Northern Wei, the court supporting some 30,000 temples and nearly 2 million monks.

In 617, the general Li Yuan (李淵 *lǐ yuān*) at Taiyuan rebelled against the Sui Dynasty. In the years following the establishment of the Tang (618–907), the Shanxi region proved to be a vital economic resource for the empire with its vast amounts of salt. Several internecine and dynastic struggles later, the Shanxi region flourished again during the Northern Song (北宋 *běisòng*, ca. 960). Taiyuan was known far and wide (at least in the Chinese empire) for, among other things, the production of shearing scissors and bronze mirrors.

During the Yuan (Mongol) dynasty (1271–1368), an administrative "Pacification Commission of the Hedong Shanxi Region" (河東山西的宣慰司 *hédōngshānxī dexuānwèisī*) formed the mechanism for centralized control by about the middle of the fourteenth century. Finally, the Ming dynasty (1368–1644) established a Shanxi administrative province (山西行省 *shānxī xíngshěng*) in 1368.

Hongdong County: Dahuaishu Migration

In the Ming dynastic Yongle (永樂 *yǒnglè*) reign (1403–1424), Shanxi Province's southern region, near today's Hongdong County, Dahuaishu (洪洞縣大槐樹 *hóngdòng xiàn dàhuáishù*), was the locus of a massive, forced migration. In contrast to those unlucky enough to be living in the central plains at the beginning of the Ming dynasty, the Shanxi region enjoyed good yearly harvests, and was largely spared from natural disasters. Furthermore, Shanxi was relatively stable, and possessed a flourishing economy. According to Ming historical records, at that time Hebei and Henan combined had a population of some 3,780,000, while Shanxi alone reached about 4 million. In order to revitalize parts of the country which had been devastated from war, poverty, flooding, as well as a host of other problems, the Ming government decided to use Shanxi as a source of human capital.

For a 50-year period (1368–1417), there were 18 major migrations out of Shanxi imposed by imperial fiat, representing the largest organized mass dislocations of a population in China's history. Under the Ming court policy, "families of four will leave one behind; of six, two; of eight, three," and migrants were given travel funds, plowing oxen, seed for planting, carts and food rations, while forgiving their taxes for 3 years. By 1414, each emigrating family was allotted 50 mu (about 8.25 acres) of land. Local records in Hongdong County showed its citizens having been forced to spread out across 19 provinces and autonomous regions throughout China, including Beijing, Tianjin, and Hebei. To get a further sense of scale of the population movements in this region, detailed accounts from the 24th year of the Ming dynasty's Hongwu (洪武 *hóng wǔ*) era (1391) showed Shanxi having a recorded population of 4.38 million. Following the forced migration, it dropped to about 3.1 million. This is consistent with later estimates of over a million people having moved out of Shanxi during this time (CRN 2011).

In 2005, China reported the discovery of a tombstone that recorded details of one of these migratory episodes in Hebei Province, eastern Zhaoxian County (趙縣 *zhàoxiàn*) (ANU 2005). Dating to the Jiajing (嘉靖 *jiājìng*) reign (1521–1567), the epitaph provided recorded proof of the forced migration. It also described how the Zhaoxian County region had been essentially bereft of life following successive natural disasters and extended warfare.

Qing Dynasty

Following the Manchu invasion and Qing dynasty reign in the 1600s, Shanxi was divided into nine main government offices, 16 prefectures and 108 counties. Shanxi led China's commercial industry at that time with the rise of the Shanxi merchants (山西商人 *shānxī shāngrén*).

In 1952, Shanxi expanded into former Chaha'er (察哈爾 *cháhā'ěr*), its new northern border now basically delineated by the Great Wall. Significantly, this area also included the rich coalmining area of Datong (PRC 2001).

The Dazhai Model

In 1964, the community of Dazhai (大寨 *dàzhài*), located in Shanxi's Xiyang County (昔陽縣 *xíyáng xiàn*), was heralded by the Chinese Communist Party (CCP) as a model for modern agriculture in 1964. Thus began a leftist "learn agriculture from Dazhai" (農業學大寨 *nóngyè xuédàzhài*) movement that ran through the end of the 1970s. Dazhai's production figures were later revealed to have been modest, however, and much of its purported Stakhanovite labor by its citizens was largely fabricated (Becker 2000).

Shanxi Population and Economic Trends

With the highest quantity of mined coal in China (over 85 thousand tons in 2019), and ranked third globally in terms of coal reserves, Shanxi is also a major consumer, using 4.2 billion metric tons of coal in 2013 (Coal Hub 2021). Of all of China's coal-producing regions, Shanxi represents among the largest, with significant reserves found in Datong, while the quality of its Yangquan (陽泉 yangquán) anthracite has long been well known. Other significant coal mines in Shanxi include that of Jincheng (晉城 *jìnchéng*) (Wei 2003).

For all its wealth underground, Shanxi is ranked 21st in terms of gross domestic product (GDP) in 2020 at USD $274 billion, and per capita income ($3,921) is in the bottom third (Zhang 2021). With relatively fewer economic opportunities, many choose to uproot and look elsewhere, and thus the population of Shanxi has dropped just over 2% from 2010–2020. This is evidenced in the larger number of permanent (*hukou*) registered population (Table 28.3) of 35,340,000, compared to the 2020 census (Tables 28.1 and 28.2) of all residents (34,915,616). That is, more people of Shanxi choose to live and work elsewhere for a significant amount of time than remain at their home province.

China's premier satellite and missile launch complex, the Taiyuan Satellite Launch Center (太原卫星发射中心 *tàiyuán wèixīngfǎshèzhōngxīn*), has also been known as Base 25 per the China's Commission on Science, Technology and National

Table 28.1 Shanxi population (residential 常住人口 *chángzhù rénkǒu*). Data (SPBS 2021)

City	Population (2010)	Population (2020)
Taiyuan City 太原市 *tàiyuán shì* [abbrev. 并 *bīng*[a]]	4,201,591	5,304,061
Changzhi City 長治市 *chángzhì shì* [abbrev. 潞*lù*]	3,334,564	3,180,884
Datong City 大同市 *dàtóng shì* [abbrev.]	3,318,057	3,105,591
Jincheng City晉城市 *jìnchéng shì* [abbrev. 澤*zé*]	2,279,151	2,194,545
Jinzhong City 晉中市 *jìnzhōng shì*	3,249,425	3,379,498
Linfen City 臨汾市 *línfén shì*	4,316,612	3,976,481
Lüliang City 呂梁市 *lǚliáng shì*	3,727,057	3,398,431
Shuozhou City 朔州市 *shuòzhōu shì*	1,714,857	1,593,444
Xinzhou City 忻州市 *xīnzhōu shì*	3,067,501	2,689,668
Yangquan City 陽泉市 *yángquán shì*	1,368,502	1,318,505
Yuncheng City 運城市 *yùnchéng shì*	5,134,794	4,774,508
Total:	**35,712,111**	**34,915,616**

[a]In this instance as a place name, 并 is first tone *bīng*

Table 28.2 Shanxi Province: population data of selected cities and their subordinate sectors. (SPBS 2021)

Selected cities and subordinate sectors, population (2020 census)	Subordinate district, city and county populations (2020)	Total population (2020)
Taiyuan City 太原市 ***tàiyuán shì* [abbrev. 并 *bīng*]**		**5,304,061**
Gujiao City 古交市 *gǔjiāo shì*	210,757	
Jiancaoping District 尖草坪區 *jiāncǎopíng qū*	530,499	
Jinyuan District 晉源區 *jìnyuán qū*	316,445	
Loufan County 婁煩縣 *lóufán xiàn*	91,208	
Qingxu County 清徐縣 *qīngxú xiàn*	344,472	
Wanbailin District 萬柏林區 *wànbǎilín qū*	951,238	
Xiaodian District 小店區 *xiǎodiàn qū*	1,357,242	
Xinghualing District 杏花嶺區 *xìnghuālǐng qū*	779,479	
Yangqu County 陽曲縣 *yángqū xiàn*	128,483	
Yingze District 迎澤區 *yíngzé qū*	594,238	
Changzhi City 長治市 ***chángzhì shì* [abbrev. 潞*lù*]**		**3,180,884**
Luzhou District潞州區 *lùzhōu qū*	895,280	
Shangdang District 上擋區 *shàngdǎng qū*	319,660	
Tunliu District 屯留區 *túnliú qū*	253,756	
Lucheng District 潞城區 *lùchéng qū*	219,256	
Xiangyuan County 襄垣縣 *xiāngyuán xiàn*	260,081	
Pingshun County 平順縣 *píngshùn xiàn*	115,927	
Licheng County 黎城縣 *líchéng xiàn*	134,186	
Huguan County 壺關縣 *húguān xiàn*	240,109	
Changzi County 長子縣 *chángzǐ xiàn*	298,690	
Wuxiang County 武鄉縣 *wǔxiāng xiàn*	155,386	
Qin County 沁縣 *qìnxiàn*	138,578	
Qinyuan County 沁源縣 *qìnyuán xiàn*	149,975	
Datong City 大同市 ***dàtóng shì* [abbrev. 同*tóng*]**		**3,105,591**
Xinrong District 新榮區 *xīnróng qū*	88,664	
Pingcheng District 平城區 *píngchéng qū*	1,105,699	
Yungang District 雲岡區 *yúngāng qū*	684,753	
Yuzhou District 雲州區 *yúnzhōu qū*	151,087	
Yanggao District 陽高縣 *yánggāo xiàn*	191,981	
Tianzhen County 天鎮縣 *tiānzhèn xiàn*	160,691	
Guangling County 廣靈縣 *guǎnglíng xiàn*	154,253	
Lingqiu County 靈丘縣 *língqiū xiàn*	212,771	
Hunyuan County 渾源縣 *húnyuán xiàn*	237,749	
Zuoyun County 左雲縣 *zuǒyún xiàn*	117,943	
Jincheng City.晉城市 ***jìnchéng shì* [abbrev. 澤*zé*]**		**2,194,545**
Qinshui County 沁水縣 *qìnshuǐ xiàn*	196,528	

(continued)

Table 28.2 (continued)

Selected cities and subordinate sectors, population (2020 census)	Subordinate district, city and county populations (2020)	Total population (2020)
Yangcheng County 陽城縣 *yángchéng xiàn*	350,474	
Lingchuan County 陵川縣 *língchuān xiàn*	204,825	
Zezhou County 澤州縣 *zézhōu xiàn*	414,999	
Gaoping City 高平市 *gāopíng shì*	453,054	
Jinzhong City 晉中市 ***jìnzhōng shì***		**3,379,498**
Yuci District 榆次區 *yúcì qū*	904,518	
Taigu District 太谷區 *tàigǔ qū*	322,099	
Yushe County 榆社縣 *yúshè xiàn*	111,714	
Zuoquan County 左權縣 *zuǒquán xiàn*	144,519	
Heshun County 和順縣 *héshùn xiàn*	121,617	
Xiyang County 昔陽縣 *xīyáng xiàn*	190,861	
Shouyang County 壽陽縣 *shòuyáng xiàn*	200,325	
Qixian County 祁縣 *qíxiàn*	254,535	
Pingyao County 平遙縣 *píngyáo xiàn*	450,697	
Lingshi County 靈石縣 *língshí xiàn*	246,491	
Jiexiu City 介休市 *jièxiū shì*	432,095	
Linfen City[a] 臨汾市 ***línfén shì***		**3,976,481**
Lüliang City 呂梁市 ***lǚliáng shì***		**3,398,431**
Lishi District 離石區 *líshí qū*	456,355	
Wenshui County 文水縣 *wénshuǐ xiàn*	372,580	
Jiaocheng County 交城縣 *jiāochéng xiàn*	226,768	
Xingxian County 興縣 *xīngxiàn*	183,484	
Linxian County 臨縣 *línxiàn*	394,713	
Liulin County 柳林縣 *liǔlín xiàn*	287,969	
Shilou County 石樓縣 *shílóu xiàn*	96,808	
Lanxian County 嵐縣 *lánxiàn*	148,315	
Fangshan County 方山縣 *fāngshān xiàn*	112,692	
Zhongyang County 中陽縣 *zhōngyáng xiàn*	138,498	
Jiaokou County 交口縣 *jiāokǒu xiàn*	95,313	
Xiaoyi County 孝義縣 *xiàoyì xiàn*	477,289	
Fenyang County 汾陽市 *fényáng shì*	407,647	
Shuozhou City 朔州市 ***shuòzhōu shì***		**1,593,444**
Shuocheng District[b] 朔城區 *shuòchéng qū*	565,075	
Pinglu District 平魯區 *pínglǔ qū*	148,212	
Shanyang District 山陽區 *shānyáng qū*	199,505	
Yingxian County 應縣 *yīngxiàn*	243,970	
Youyu County 右玉縣 *yòuyù xiàn*	88,212	
Huairen City 懷仁市 *huáirén shì*	348,470	
Xinzhou City 忻州市 ***xīnzhōu shì***		**2,689,668**
Xinfu District 忻府區 *xīnfǔ qū*	577,089	
dDingxiang County 定襄縣 *dìngxiāng xiàn*	193,997	
Wutai County 五台縣 *wǔtái xiàn*	216,178	

(continued)

Table 28.2 (continued)

Selected cities and subordinate sectors, population (2020 census)	Subordinate district, city and county populations (2020)	Total population (2020)
Daixian County 代縣 *dàixiàn*	178,870	
Fanzhi County 繁峙縣 *fánzhì xiàn*	250,409	
Ningwu County 寧武縣 *níngwǔ xiàn*	136,470	
Jingle County 靜樂縣 *jìnglè xiàn*	119,277	
Shenchi County 神池縣 *shénchí xiàn*	75,757	
Wuzhai County 五寨縣 *wǔzhài xiàn*	100,220	
Kelan County 岢嵐縣 *kělán xiàn*	69,324	
Hequ County 河曲縣 *héqū xiàn*	123,505	
Baode County 保德縣 *bǎodé xiàn*	144,218	
Pianguan County 偏關縣 *piānguān xiàn*	73,382	
Wutaishan Scenery Area 五台山風景區 *wǔtáishān fēngjǐngqū*	17,050	
Yuanping City 原平市 *yuánpíng shì*	413,922	
Yangquan City 陽泉市 ***yángquán shì***		**1,318,505**
Chengqu District 城區 *chéngqū*	225,443	
Kuangqu District 礦區 *kuàngqū*	230,691	
Jiaoqu District 郊區 *jiāoqū*	275,094	
Pingding County 平定縣 *píngdìng xiàn*	306,228	
Yuxian County 盂縣 *yúxiàn*	281,049	
Yuncheng City 運城市 ***yùnchéng shì***		**4,774,508**
Yanhu District 鹽湖區 *yánhú qū*	928,334	
Linyi County 臨猗縣 *línyǐ xiàn*	482,559	
Wanrong County 萬榮縣 *wànróng xiàn*	361,956	
Wenxi County 聞喜縣 *wénxǐ xiàn*	355,269	
Jishan County 稷山縣 *jìshān xiàn*	316,144	
Jiangxian County 絳縣 *jiàngxiàn*	282,230	
Yuanqu County 垣曲縣 *yuánqū xiàn*	226,871	
Xiaxian County 夏縣 *xiàxiàn*	197,772	
Pinglu County 平陸縣 *pínglù xiàn*	205,080	
Ruicheng County 芮城縣 *ruìchéng xiàn*	342,889	
Yongji City 永濟市 *yǒngjì shì*	394,935	
Hejin City 河津市 *héjīn shì*	392,561	

[a]Details on subdistrict population were not available as of 27 August 2021

[b]Includes population (71,744) of the Shuocheng Economic and Technology Development Zone (朔城經濟技術開發區 *shuòchéng jīngjìjìshù kāifāqū*)

Defense Industry (COSTIND). These launch facilities are located in Xinzhou City (忻州市 *xīnzhōu shì*), Kelan County (岢嵐縣 *kělán xiàn*).

Table 28.3 (below) shows the *hukou* (family registered) populations based on PRC Ministry of Civil Affairs data. (Districts listed directly under major cities are government seats, as are those in parentheses). One can compare these data with the census (usual residential populations based on 2010 and 2020 censuses in Tables 28.1 and 28.2 (above) (Fig. 28.2).

Shanxi Province (晉 *jìn*)

Provincial Capital: Taiyuan City

Table 28.3 Guangdong Province: permanent registered (戶籍人口 *hùjí rénkǒu*) populations. (MCA 2020)

Name	Traditional	Simplified	Population (2012)	Population (2016)	Population (2020)	Area (Sq. Km)
Shanxi Province	山西省	山西省	34,740,000	35,010,000	35,340,000	156,698
Taiyuan City	太原市	太原市	3,660,000	3,660,000	3,770,000	6909
Xinghualing District (Julun Subdistrict)	杏花嶺區 (巨輪街道)	杏花岭区 (巨轮街道)	590,000	590,000	610,000	146
Xiaodian District (Xiaodian Subdistrict)	小店區 (小店街道)	小店区 (小店街道)	620,000	620,000	670,000	290
Yingze District (Liuxiang Subdistrict)	迎澤區 (柳巷街道)	迎泽区 (柳巷街道)	520,000	520,000	540,000	105
Jiancaoping District (Chaicun Subdistrict)	尖草坪區 (柴村街道)	尖草坪区 (柴村街道)	360,000	350,000	330,000	296
Wanbailin District (Qianfeng Subdistrict)	萬柏林區 (千峰街道)	万柏林区 (千峰街道)	560,000	560,000	580,000	289
Jinyuan District (Jinyuan)	晉源區 (晉源街道)	晋源区 (晋源街道)	200,000	200,000	210,000	290
Gujiao City (Dongqu Subdistrict)	古交市 (東曲街道)	古交市 (东曲街道)	220,000	220,000	220,000	1,512
Qingxu County (Qingyuan Town)	清徐縣 (清源鎮)	清徐县 (清源镇)	310,000	320,000	340,000	608
Yangqu County (Huangzhai Town)	陽曲縣 (黃寨鎮)	阳曲县 (黄寨镇)	150,000	150,000	150,000	2,084
Loufan County (Loufan Town)	婁煩縣 (婁煩鎮)	娄烦县 (娄烦镇)	130,000	130,000	130,000	1,289
Datong City	大同市	大同市	3,180,000	3,180,000	3,180,000	14,056
Pingcheng District[a] (Xiangyangli Subdistrict)	平城區 (向陽里街道)	平城区 (向阳里街道)	N/A	N/A	750,000	240
Yungang District (Kouquan Township)	雲岡區 (口泉鄉)	云岗区 (口泉乡)	N/A	N/A	660,000	743
Xinrong District (Xinrong Town)	新榮區 (新榮鎮)	新荣区 (新荣镇)	110,000	110,000	100,000	1,090

(continued)

Table 28.3 (continued)

Name	Traditional	Simplified	Population (2012)	Population (2016)	Population (2020)	Area (Sq. Km)
Yunzhou District[b]	雲州區 (西坪鎮)	云州区 (西坪镇)	N/A	N/A	190,000	1,478
Yanggao County (Longquan Town)	陽高縣 (龍泉鎮)	阳高县 (龙泉镇)	290,000	290,000	270,000	1,678
Tianzhen County (Yuquan Town)	天鎮縣 (玉泉鎮)	天镇县 (玉泉镇)	220,000	220,000	230,000	1,629
Guangling County (Huquan Town)	廣靈縣 (壺泉鎮)	广灵县 (壶泉镇)	180,000	180,000	180,000	1,204
Lingqiu County (Wuling Town)	靈丘縣 (武靈鎮)	灵丘县 (武灵镇)	240,000	240,000	250,000	2,732
Hunyuan County (Yong'an Town)	渾源縣 (永安鎮)	浑源县 (永安镇)	360,000	360,000	350,000	1,968
Zuoyun County (Yunxing Town)	左雲縣 (雲興鎮)	左云县 (云兴镇)	150,000	150,000	140,000	1,294
Datong County[c] (Xiping Town)	大同縣 (西坪鎮)	大同县 (西坪镇)	180,000	N/A	N/A	(1,478)
Shuozhou City	朔州市	朔州市	1,600,000	1,620,000	1,630,000	10,626
Shuocheng District (Beicheng Subdistrict)	朔城區 (北城街道)	朔城区 (北城街道)	430,000	440,000	450,000	1,780
Pinglu District (Jingping Town)	平魯區 (井坪鎮)	平鲁区 (井坪镇)	230,000	230,000	230,000	2,315
Shanyin County (Daiyue Town)	山陰縣 (岱岳鎮)	山阴县 (岱岳镇)	240,000	240,000	240,000	1,645
Yingxian County (Jincheng Town)	應縣 (金城鎮)	应县 (金城镇)	310,000	310,000	310,000	1,673
Youyu County (Xincheng Town)	右玉縣 (新城鎮)	右玉县 (新城镇)	110,000	110,000	110,000	1,979
Huairen City (Yunzhong Town)	懷仁市 (雲中鎮)	怀仁市 (云中镇)	280,000	290,000	290,000	1,234
Yangquan City	陽泉市	阳泉市	1,310,000	1,320,000	1,320,000	4,559
Chengqu District (Shangzhan Subdistrict)	城區 (上站街道)	城区 (上站街道)	230,000	230,000	240,000	15
Kuangqu (mining) District (Pingtanjie Subdistrict)	礦區 (平潭街街道)	矿区 (平潭街街道)	250,000	260,000	270,000	12
Jiaoqu District (Yinying Town)	郊區 (蔭營鎮)	郊区 (荫营镇)	210,000	210,000	190,000	627
Pingding County (Guanshan Town)	平定縣 (冠山鎮)	平定县 (冠山镇)	320,000	320,000	320,000	1,391

(continued)

Table 28.3 (continued)

Name	Traditional	Simplified	Population (2012)	Population (2016)	Population (2020)	Area (Sq. Km)
Yuxian County (Xiushui Town)	盂縣 (秀水鎮)	盂县 (秀水镇)	300,000	300,000	310,000	2,514
Changzhi City	長治市	长治市	3,320,000	3,370,000	3,390,000	13,954
Luzhou District (Taihangdongjie Subdistrict)	潞州區 (太行東街街道)	潞州区 (太行东街街道)	N/A	740,000	750,000	344
Shangdang District (Handian Town)	上黨區 (韓店鎮)	上党区 (韩店镇)	N/A	340,000	350,000	482
Lucheng District (Luhua Subdistrict)	潞城區 (潞華街道)	潞城区 (潞华街道)	220,000	230,000	230,000	614
Xiangyuan County (Guhan Town)	襄垣縣 (古韓鎮)	襄垣县 (古韩镇)	260,000	260,000	270,000	1,178
Tunliu District (Linjiang Town)	屯留區 (麟絳鎮)	屯留区 (麟绛镇)	270,000	270,000	280,000	1,190
Pingshun County (Qingyang Town)	平順縣 (青羊鎮)	平顺县 (青羊镇)	160,000	150,000	150,000	1,510
Licheng County (Lihou Town)	黎城縣 (黎侯鎮)	黎城县 (黎侯镇)	170,000	170,000	160,000	1,113
Huguan County (Longquan Town)	壺關縣 (龍泉鎮)	壶关县 (龙泉镇)	290,000	300,000	300,000	1,008
Changzi County (Danzhu Town)	長子縣 (丹朱鎮)	长子县 (丹朱镇)	350,000	360,000	370,000	1,031
Wuxiang County (Fengzhou Town)	武鄉縣 (豐州鎮)	武乡县 (丰州镇)	210,000	210,000	210,000	1,615
Qinxian County (Dingchang Town)	沁縣 (定昌鎮)	沁县 (定昌镇)	170,000	180,000	170,000	1,320
Qinyuan County (Qinhe Town)	沁源縣 (沁河鎮)	沁源县 (沁河镇)	160,000	160,000	160,000	2,549
Jincheng City	晉城市	晋城市	2,160,000	2,180,000	2,210,000	9,425
Chengqu District (Dongjie Subdistrict)	城區 (東街街道)	城区 (东街街道)	350,000	360,000	400,000	143
Gaoping City (Beicheng Subdistrict)	高平市 (北城街道)	高平市 (北城街道)	480,000	480,000	490,000	980
Zezhou County (Nancun Town)	澤州縣 (南村鎮)	泽州县 (南村镇)	500,000	500,000	490,000	2,024
Qinshui County (Longgang Town)	沁水縣 (龍港鎮)	沁水县 (龙港镇)	200,000	210,000	200,000	2,658
Yangcheng County (Fengcheng Town)	陽城縣 (鳳城鎮)	阳城县 (凤城镇)	380,000	380,000	380,000	1,918

(continued)

Table 28.3 (continued)

Name	Traditional	Simplified	Population (2012)	Population (2016)	Population (2020)	Area (Sq. Km)
Lingchuan County (Chongwen Town)	陵川縣 (崇文鎮)	陵川县 (崇文镇)	250,000	250,000	250,000	1,702
Xinzhou City	忻州市	忻州市	3,090,000	3,120,000	3,080,000	25,154
Xinfu District (Xiurong Subdistrict)	忻府區 (秀容街道)	忻府区 (秀容街道)	530,000	540,000	550,000	1,987
Yuanping City (Beicheng Subdistrict)	原平市 (北城街道)	原平市 (北城街道)	490,000	490,000	490,000	2,550
Dingxiang County (Jinchang Town)	定襄縣 (晉昌鎮)	定襄县 (晋昌镇)	220,000	220,000	220,000	851
Wutai County (Taicheng Town)	五台縣 (台城鎮)	五台县 (台城镇)	320,000	320,000	310,000	2,865
Daixian County (Shangguan Town)	代縣 (上館鎮)	代县 (上馆镇)	210,000	210,000	200,000	1,729
Fanshi County (Fancheng Town)	繁峙縣 (繁城鎮)	繁峙县 (繁城镇)	270,000	280,000	280,000	2,373
Ningwu County (Fenghuang Town)	寧武縣 (鳳凰鎮)	宁武县 (凤凰镇)	170,000	170,000	160,000	1,944
Jingle County (E'cheng Town)	靜樂縣 (鵝城鎮)	静乐县 (鹅城镇)	160,000	160,000	160,000	2,037
Shenchi County (Longquan Town)	神池縣 (龍泉鎮)	神池县 (龙泉镇)	100,000	100,000	100,000	1,471
Wuzhai County (Yancheng Town)	五寨縣 (硯城鎮)	五寨县 (砚城镇)	120,000	120,000	110,000	1,388
Kelan County (Lanyi Town)	岢嵐縣 (嵐漪鎮)	岢岚县 (岚漪镇)	80,000	80,000	80,000	1,980
Hequ County (Wenbi Town)	河曲縣 (文筆鎮)	河曲县 (文笔镇)	150,000	150,000	140,000	1,317
Baode County (Dongguan Town)	保德縣 (東關鎮)	保德县 (东关镇)	160,000	170,000	160,000	995
Pianguan County (Xinguan Town)	偏關縣 (新關鎮)	偏关县 (新关镇)	110,000	110,000	100,000	1,667
Jinzhong City	晉中市	晋中市	3,220,000	3,240,000	3,340,000	16,391
Yuci District (Xinjian Subdistrict)	榆次區 (新建街道)	榆次区 (新建街道)	600,000	600,000	630,000	1,318
Taigu District[d] (Mingxing Town)	太谷區 (明星鎮)	太谷区 (明星镇)	N/A	N/A	310,000	1,046
Jiexiu City (Beiguan Subdistrict)	介休市 (北關街道)	介休市 (北关街道)	400,000	410,000	440,000	741

(continued)

Table 28.3 (continued)

Name	Traditional	Simplified	Population (2012)	Population (2016)	Population (2020)	Area (Sq. Km)
Yushe County (Jicheng Town)	榆社縣 (箕城鎮)	榆社县 (箕城镇)	140,000	140,000	150,000	1,700
Zuoquan County (Liaoyang Town)	左權縣 (遼陽鎮)	左权县 (辽阳镇)	160,000	160,000	160,000	2,022
Heshun County (Yixing Town)	和順縣 (義興鎮)	和顺县 (义兴镇)	140,000	140,000	140,000	2,194
Xiyang County (Leping Town)	昔陽縣 (樂平鎮)	昔阳县 (乐平镇)	240,000	240,000	240,000	1,945
Shouyang County (Chaoyang Town)	壽陽縣 (朝陽鎮)	寿阳县 (朝阳镇)	210,000	210,000	210,000	2,116
Taigu County (Mingxing Town)	太谷縣 (明星鎮)	太谷县 (明星镇)	290,000	290,000	N/A	(1,046)
Qixian County (Zhaoyu Town)	祁縣 (昭余鎮)	祁县 (昭余镇)	270,000	270,000	280,000	853
Pingyao County (Gutao Town)	平遙縣 (古陶鎮)	平遥县 (古陶镇)	510,000	520,000	540,000	1,254
Lingshi County (Cuifeng Town)	靈石縣 (翠峰鎮)	灵石县 (翠峰镇)	260,000	260,000	260,000	1,202
Yuncheng City	運城市	运城市	5,030,000	5,130,000	5,130,000	14,183
Yanhu District (Zhongcheng Subdistrict)	鹽湖區 (中城街道)	盐湖区 (中城街道)	660,000	670,000	700,000	1,205
Yongji City (Chengxi Subdistrict)	永濟市 (城西街道)	永济市 (城西街道)	430,000	440,000	440,000	1,208
Hejin City (Chengqu Subdistrict)	河津市 (城區街道)	河津市 (城区街道)	390,000	400,000	400,000	593
Linyi County (Yishi Town)	臨猗縣 (猗氏鎮)	临猗县 (猗氏镇)	550,000	560,000	560,000	1,362
Wanrong County (Jiedian Town)	萬榮縣 (解店鎮)	万荣县 (解店镇)	430,000	440,000	440,000	1,076
Wenxi County (Tongcheng Town)	聞喜縣 (桐城鎮)	闻喜县 (桐城镇)	400,000	410,000	400,000	1,168
Jishan County (Jifeng Town)	稷山縣 (稷峰鎮)	稷山县 (稷峰镇)	350,000	360,000	360,000	686
Xinjiang County (Longxing Town)	新絳縣 (龍興鎮)	新绛县 (龙兴镇)	320,000	330,000	330,000	597
Jiangxian County (Gujiang Town)	絳縣 (古絳鎮)	绛县 (古绛镇)	280,000	290,000	280,000	978
Pinglu County (Shengrenjian Town)	平陸縣 (聖人澗鎮)	平陆县 (圣人涧镇)	250,000	250,000	250,000	1,174

(continued)

Table 28.3 (continued)

Name	Traditional	Simplified	Population (2012)	Population (2016)	Population (2020)	Area (Sq. Km)
Yuanqu County (Xincheng Town)	垣曲縣 (新城鎮)	垣曲县 (新城镇)	230,000	230,000	220,000	1,609
Xiaxian County (Yaofeng Town)	夏縣 (瑤峰鎮)	夏县 (瑶峰镇)	360,000	370,000	360,000	1,351
Ruicheng County (Guwei Town)	芮城縣 (古魏鎮)	芮城县 (古魏镇)	380,000	380,000	380,000	1,176
Linfen City	臨汾市	临汾市	4,380,000	4,280,000	4,330,000	20,301
Yaodu District (Ludong Subdistrict)	堯都區 (路東街道)	尧都区 (解放路街道)	840,000	810,000	820,000	1,307
Houma City (Ludong Subdistrict)	侯馬市 (路東街道)	侯马市 (路东街道)	250,000	240,000	240,000	220
Huozhou City (Kaiyuanjie Subdistrict)	霍州市 (開元街街道)	霍州市 (开元街街道)	310,000	300,000	310,000	765
Quwo County (Lechang Town)	曲沃縣 (樂昌鎮)	曲沃县 (乐昌镇)	230,000	230,000	230,000	437
Yicheng County (Tangxing Town)	翼城縣 (唐興鎮)	翼城县 (唐兴镇)	320,000	310,000	310,000	1,168
Xiangfen County (Xincheng Town)	襄汾縣 (新城鎮)	襄汾县 (新城镇)	500,000	490,000	500,000	1,031
Hongdong County (Dahuaishu Town)	洪洞縣 (大槐樹鎮)	洪洞县 (大槐树镇)	760,000	750,000	770,000	1,495
Guxian (Yueyang Town)	古縣 (岳陽鎮)	古县 (岳阳镇)	90,000	90,000	90,000	1,196
Anze County (Fucheng Town)	安澤縣 (府城鎮)	安泽县 (府城镇)	80,000	80,000	80,000	1,960
Fushan County (Tiantan Town)	浮山縣 (天壇鎮)	浮山县 (天坛镇)	140,000	130,000	130,000	940
Jixian County (Jichang Town)	吉縣 (吉昌鎮)	吉县 (吉昌镇)	110,000	110,000	110,000	1,780
Xiangning County (Changning Town)	鄉寧縣 (昌寧鎮)	乡宁县 (昌宁镇)	240,000	240,000	240,000	2,025
Daning County (Xinshui Town)	大寧縣 (昕水鎮)	大宁县 (昕水镇)	70,000	70,000	70,000	962
Xixian County (Longquan Town)	隰縣 (龍泉鎮)	隰县 (龙泉镇)	110,000	110,000	110,000	1,413
Yonghe County (Zhihe Town)	永和縣 (芝河鎮)	永和县 (芝河镇)	70,000	70,000	70,000	1,214
Puxian County (Pucheng Town)	蒲縣 (蒲城鎮)	蒲县 (蒲城镇)	110,000	110,000	110,000	1,513

(continued)

Table 28.3 (continued)

Name	Traditional	Simplified	Population (2012)	Population (2016)	Population (2020)	Area (Sq. Km)
Fenxi County (Yong'an Town)	汾西縣 (永安鎮)	汾西县 (永安镇)	150,000	140,000	150,000	875
Lüliang City	呂梁市	吕梁市	3,830,000	3,920,000	3,940,000	21,140
Lishi District (Binhai Subdistrict)	離石區 (濱河街道)	离石区 (滨河街道)	280,000	280,000	290,000	1,324
Xiaoyi City (Xinyi Subdistrict)	孝義市 (新義街道)	孝义市 (新义街道)	470,000	490,000	490,000	938
Fenyang City (Taiheqiao Subdistrict)	汾陽市 (太和橋街道)	汾阳市 (太和桥街道)	420,000	420,000	430,000	1,170
Wenshui County (Fengcheng Town)	文水縣 (鳳城鎮)	文水县 (凤城镇)	440,000	450,000	450,000	1,069
Zhongyang County (Ningxiang Town)	中陽縣 (寧鄉鎮)	中阳县 (宁乡镇)	150,000	160,000	160,000	1,439
Xingxian County (Weifen Town)	興縣 (蔚汾鎮)	兴县 (蔚汾镇)	310,000	320,000	290,000	3,169
Linxian County (Linquan Town)	臨縣 (臨泉鎮)	临县 (临泉镇)	630,000	650,000	660,000	2,976
Fangshan County (Gedong Town)	方山縣 (圪洞鎮)	方山县 (圪洞镇)	150,000	150,000	160,000	1,433
Liulin County (Liulin Town)	柳林縣 (柳林鎮)	柳林县 (柳林镇)	330,000	320,000	290,000	3,169
Lanxian County (Dongcun Town)	嵐縣 (東村鎮)	岚县 (东村镇)	190,000	190,000	190,000	1,513
Jiaokou County (Shuitou Town)	交口縣 (水頭鎮)	交口县 (水头镇)	120,000	120,000	120,000	1,260
Jiaocheng County (Tianning Town)	交城縣 (天寧鎮)	交城县 (天宁镇)	220,000	230,000	230,000	1,826
Shilou County (Lingquan Town)	石樓縣 (靈泉鎮)	石楼县 (灵泉镇)	120,000	120,000	120,000	1,735

[a]Created 9 February 2018
[b]Created out of Datong county, 9 February 2018
[c]Datong county dissolved to create Yunzhou district, 9 February 2018
[d]On 6 November 2019, Taigu county was dissolved and made into a district

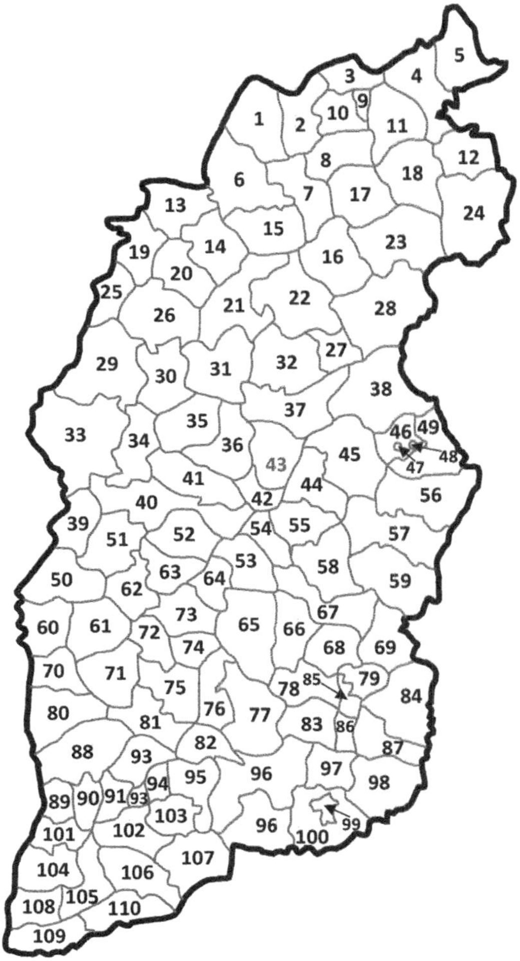

1. Youyu County
2. Zuoyun County
3. Xinrong District
4. Yanggao County
5. Tianzhen County
6. Pinglu District
7. Shanyin County
8. Huairen City
9. Pingcheng District
10. Yungang District
11. Yunzhou District
12. Guangling County
13. Pianguan County
14. Shenchi County
15. Shuocheng District
16. Daixian County
17. Yingxian County
18. Hunyuan County
19. Hequ County
20. Wuzhai County
21. Ningwu County
22. Yuanping City
23. Fanshi County
24. Lingqiu County
25. Baode County
26. Kelan County
27. Dingxiang County
28. Wutai County
29. Xingxian County
30. Lanxian County
31. Jingle County
32. Xinfu District
33. Linxian County
34. Fangshan County
35. Loufan County
36. Gujiao City
37. Yangqu County
38. Yuxian County
39. Liulin County
40. Lishi District
41. Jiaocheng County
42. Qingxu County
43. Taiyuan City
44. Jinzhong City
45. Shouyang County
46. Jiaoqu District
47. Kuangqu (Mining district)
48. Chengqu District
49. Pingding County
50. Shilou County
51. Zhongyang County
52. Fenyang City
53. Pingyao County
54. Qixian County
55. Taigu District
56. Xiyang County
57. Heshun County
58. Yushe County
59. Zuoquan County
60. Yonghe County
61. Xixian County
62. Jiaokou County
63. Xiaoyi City
64. Jiexiu City
65. Qinyuan County
66. Qinxian County
67. Wuxiang County
68. Xiangyuan County
69. Licheng County
70. Yonghe County
71. Puxian County
72. Fenxi County
73. Lingshi County
74. Huozhou City
75. Hongdong County
76. Guxian County
77. Anze County
78. Tunliu District
79. Lucheng City
80. Jixian County
81. Yaodu District
82. Fushan County
83. Changzi County
84. Pingshun County
85. Luzhou District
86. Shangdang District
87. Huguan County
88. Xiangning County
89. Hejin City
90. Jishan County
91. Xinjiang County
92. Xiangfen County
93. Houma City
94 Quwo County
95. Yicheng County
96. Qinshui County
97. Gaoping City
98. Lingchuan County
99. Chengqu District
100. Zezhou County
101. Wanrong County
102. Wenxi County
103. Jiangxian County
104. Linyi County
105. Yanhu District
106. Xiaxian County
107. Huanqu County
108. Yongji City
109. Ruicheng County
110. Pinglu County

Fig. 28.2 Shanxi Province: Subdistricts (Provincial Capital: Taiyuan City). Drawn by the Author after People's Republic of China, Ministry of Civil Affairs. (MCA 2020)

References

Anderson, E.N. 2014. *Food and environment in early and medieval China*. Philadelphia: University of Pennsylvania.

Australian National University (ANU). China Heritage Project. 2005. *China Heritage Newsletter*. No. 2.

Becker, Jasper. 2000. *The Chinese*. New York: The Free Press.

Chang, Kwang-chih. 1999. China on the eve of the historical record. In *The Cambridge history of ancient China: From the origins of civilization to 221 B.C.*, ed. Michael Loewe and Edward L. Shaughnessy, 37–73. York: Cambridge University Press.

China Reader News (CRN). 2011. *Demystifying the great population migration in the early Ming dynasty: how many people's hometown is Dahuaishu in Hongdong, Shanxi?* 揭秘明初人口大遷徙:多少人故鄉在山西洪洞大槐樹? 中華讀書報. 27 October. http://www.szhfg.com/history/3162.html

Ministry of Civil Affairs (MCA), People's Republic of China. 2020. *County/township administration handbook*. Beijing: Statistics Press. 中華人民共和國民政部, 中華人民共和國, 鄉鎮行政區劃簡冊.

Nu, He. 2018. Taosi: An archaeological example of urbanization as a political center in prehistoric China. *Archeological Research in Asia* 14: 20–32.

People's Republic of China (PRC). 2001. *Administrative division reform atlas, 1949–1999*. Beijing: China Map Publishers.

Shanxi Province Bureau of Statistics (SPBS). 2021. *Communiqué of the seventh national census of Shanxi Province*, 27 May. 山西省第七次全国人口普查公报. http://ty.bendibao.com/news/2021527/52548.shtm

The Coal Hub. 2021. *Top 3 provinces contribute 70% of China's coal output in Jan-May*. https://thecoalhub.com/top-3-provinces-contribute-70-of-chinas-coal-output-in-jan-may.html. Accessed 21 Sept 2021.

Wei, Wanjun. 2003. Current issues of China's coal industry: The case of Shanxi. In *Proceedings of the 15th Annual Conference of the Association for Chinese Economics Studies Australia (ACESA)*, October.

Wilkinson, Endymion. 2012. *Chinese history: A new manual*. Cambridge, MA: Harvard University Press.

Yuan, Zuliang, and Jiao Peimin. 2007. *China's population through history: Eastern Han volume*. Beijing: People's Press. 袁祖亮, 焦培民. 中國人口通史: 東漢卷. Vol. 4. 北京:人民出版社.

Zhang, Shunan. 2021. *The 2020 per capita income list of residents in various provinces: Shanghai is the richest, and it has risen sharply*. Finance.people.com. 22 January. 张澍楠. 2020年各省份居民人均收入榜: 上海最有钱, 这地涨得猛. http://finance.people.com.cn/n1/2021/0122/c1004-32008733.html

Chapter 29
Sichuan Province

Abstract Archeological evidence shows human activity in Sichuan going back some 20,000 years, perhaps even earlier. Long known as "a land of plenty," among its more striking physical features include being surrounded by mountains, and this in many ways spared Sichuan during times of political violence throughout the Chinese empire. Classically, Sichuan is referred to as Shu (蜀 *shŭ*), a reference to the old kingdom. Going back to when Chongqing was part of the Sichuan (but now its own provincial-level city), one also sees Sichuan Province represented by the single character for river: (川 *chuān*), such as that found in the names of restaurants that serve spicy dishes (e.g., noodles). Prosperous through the Southern Song, and the first known to have issued paper currency, the Mongolian invasion brought Sichuan significant death and displacement of its population. Despite having a relatively high gross domestic product (GDP) when compared with mainland China's 31 provinces and major cities, Sichuan's per capita income (USD $4,125) is average, and likely helps to explain why significant numbers of its official registered residents live outside their *hukou* registry.

E. Croddy, *China's Provinces and Populations*,
https://doi.org/10.1007/978-3-031-09165-0_29

Sichuan Province 四川省 (*sìchuān shěng*): Abbreviations 川 (*chuān*); 蜀 (*shǔ*) (Fig. 29.1)

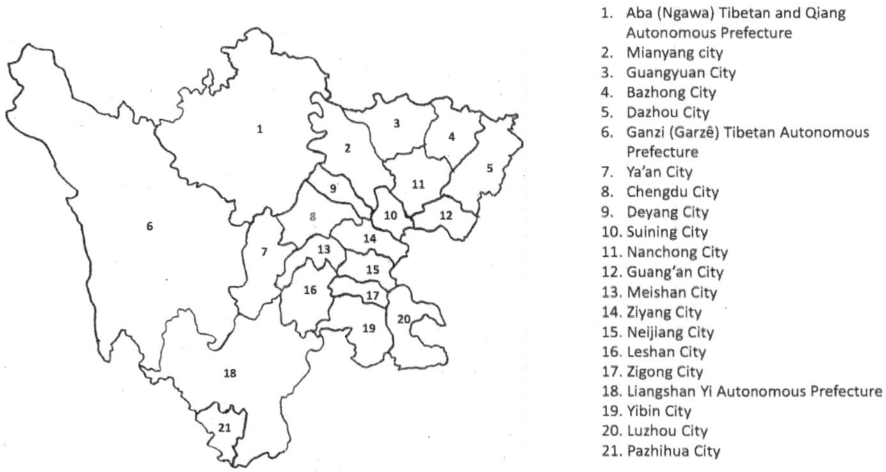

Fig. 29.1 Sichuan Province major cities and prefectures (Provincial Capital: Chengdu). (Drawn by the Author after People's Republic of China, Ministry of Civil Affairs (MCA 2020))

Sichuan Province: General Impressions

Sichuan is the home of its native pandas; the Leshan Buddha (樂山大佛 *lèshāndàfó*); and, for better or worse, Chinese Communist Party (CCP) founder and leader Deng Xiaoping. Its capital (Chengdu City) is famed for its cuisine, to include *mala* (numbing and spicy) hot pot (麻辣火鍋 *málà huǒguō*). Anywhere you go where Chinese food is served, the shorthand character (川 *chuān*) immediately tells you "Sichuan" has some influence there, and that spicey ingredients are also likely involved.

According to ancient records going back to the Shang dynasty, the area that includes modern-day Sichuan was referred to as Ba and Shu (巴 *bā*; 蜀 *shǔ*). Thus, in addition to (川 *chuān*) there is also the commonly used short character abbreviation 蜀 (*shǔ*).

There are two prevailing explanations for the name Sichuan (四川 *sìchuān*). The more conventional version is Sichuan is named after the four major rivers in the region: Minjiang 岷江 (*mín jiāng*), Tuojiang 沱江 (*tuó jiāng*), Jialingjiang 嘉陵江 (*jiālíng jiāng*) and Wujiang烏江 (*wū jiāng*), all previously known as chuan (川*chuān*; rivers), thus, Sichuan (四川four rivers). (Hsieh and Hsieh 1995).[1]

A more convoluted etymology is that during the Northern Song, a provincial (lu) entity, Chuanxia Lu (川峽路 *chuānxiá lù*) was further divided into four: Yizhou Lu (益州路 *yìzhōu lù*), Zizhou Lu (梓州路 *zǐzhōu lù*), Lizhou Lu (利州路 *lìzhōu lù*), and Kuizhou Lu (夔州路 *kuízhōu lù*). Altogether these were referred to as the "river-gorge four-provinces" (川峽四路), then shortened to Sichuan Lu (四川路 *sìchuān lù*), and thus the name. But this explanation is problematic, as the name Chuaxia Lu is not found in China's historical atlas, and in the Northern Song (1111 CE) there were four provincial areas (Lu) occupying modern-day Sichuan that do not with the "river gorge four provinces" story. While we can find Zizhou Lu (梓州路 *zǐzhōu lù*), Lizhou Lu (利州路 *lìzhōu lù*), and Kuizhou Lu (夔州路 *kuízhōu lù*), the historical atlas does not list Yizhou Lu (益州路 *yìzhōu lù*) (Tan 1996). One can only conclude that the "four major river" story makes the most sense.

Prehistoric Sichuan

While not precisely dated, some 5000 stone tools were found at the Fulin Culture site (富林文化遺址 *fùlín wénhuà yízhǐ*), Hanyuan County (漢源縣 *hànyuán xiàn*), Sichuan. Estimates place these in the late Paleolithic, approximately 20,000 years ago. The famous discovery of the Ziyang human skull (uncovered during construction of the Chengdu-Chongqing Railway in 1951) revealed a very old specimen of *Homo sapiens*, but determining its precise date range (7000–37,000 years ago) has been problematic (Olsen et al. 1992).

Discoveries of ancient Chinese civilization in Sichuan Province occurred relatively recently, notably a *hangtu* (夯土 *hāngtǔ*) rammed earth wall) city uncovered

---

[1] Hsieh and Hsieh posit the Changjiang (Yangtze) river was included in these.

at Sanxingdui (三星堆 *sānxīngduī*) in Sichuan in 1980. This site, located in Guanghan City (廣漢市 *guǎnghàn shì*) and dating back to 1200 BCE, challenged the centrality of Chinese civilization as being primarily in the central plain (e.g., Henan). Along with discoveries made of ancient communities at Xingan County[2] (新干縣 *xīngān xiàn*), Jiangxi Province, this mounting archeological evidence forced Chinese historians to adjust their traditional assessment of China having "multiple centers of innovation jointly ancestral to Chinese civilization." And while some of its pottery appeared to have some contact with Erligang culture, the specimens found at Sanxingdui, which included sacrificial pits (albeit no human remains), as well as unique, bronze statues and other artifacts, all appear to be largely *sui generis*. The connection between these finds and the subsequent Shu (蜀 *shǔ*) state has been postulated but as of yet unproven (Bagley 1999).

Located about 25 miles from Sanxingdui, the artifacts found at the Jinsha (金沙 *jīnshā*) site in Chengdu City's Qingyang District (青羊區 *qīngyáng qū*) include highly sophisticated jade work, stone, ivory, porcelain and bronze. This was indeed the Shu dynastic capital, having relocated from Sanxingdui during the period of late Shang to the Spring-Autumn period (ca. 1200–650 BCE). Jinsha has been considered by some to be the most important pre-Qin Dynast archeological site in all of China.

By the Warring States period (475–221 BCE), two separate kingdoms of Ba and Shu (巴 *bā*, 蜀 *shǔ*) had been established: The Ba state was basically located in modern-day Chongqing City (重慶市 *chóngqìng shì*), while the Shu (蜀 *shǔ*) people were centered at Chengdu City (成都市 *chéngdū shì*). The ancient people of the Ba extended to Yichang City (宜昌市 *yíchāng shì*) and the Three Gorges (三峽 *sānxiá*) area (Hubei Province). Artifacts which included pottery and bronze weapons from the Ba were discovered in Ganjinggou (干井溝 *gānjǐng gōu*), Zhongxian County (忠縣 *zhōngxiàn*), Chongqing City (Xu 1984). Discoveries at Qingjiang, Yidu City (宜都市 *yídū shì*) in Yichang showed evidence of linkages between the Shang and the Ba, notably a characteristic Shang-style bronze lei (罍 *léi*) vessel (Lu and Wenming 2005). Harkening back to Shang dynasty origins, the capital of Chengdu originally had its city walls erected according to the Shamanistic fortune telling via pyromancy, heating tortoise shells and divining their cracks to determine the most auspicious method of their architecture (Gernet 1962).

The Ba and Shu intermingled sufficiently to have developed an almagmated Bashu Culture (巴蜀文化 *bāshǔ wénhuà*). In 316 BCE, the King of Shu set off to conquer his younger brother, Jiameng (葭萌 *jiā méng*), the Marquis of Ju (苴侯 *jū hóu*), near modern-day Jiang'e County (劍閣縣 *jiàngé xiàn*). Having fled to the neighboring Ba Kingdom, and being on good terms with the King of Qin, the Duke of Ju called upon the Qin for assistance. Using this as a pretext, Generals Zhang Yi (張儀 *Zhāng Yí*) and Sima Cuo (司馬錯 *Sīmǎ Cuò*) arrived, eventually bringing not just the Shu, but also the Ju and Ba kingdoms into the Qin kingdom. Thus, during

[2] Previously known as 新淦 *xīn'gàn*.

the Eastern Han (ca. 200 CE), Shu (蜀郡 *shǔ jùn*) and Ba (巴郡 *bā jùn*) prefectures subsequently appear.

Perhaps because it was protected by steep terrain that nearly surrounds the entire region, the Sichuan basin was largely spared much of the chaotic impact from the Qin and Han dynastic transitions. Indeed, there was relatively rapid social, economic, and cultural development in this "land of plenty" (or "Heaven's Pantry"; 天府之國 *tiānfǔ zhīguó*), an expression still being used to describe Sichuan today. Later, during the Three Kingdoms era, Sichuan was the locus of the Shuhan (蜀漢 shǔ hàn) State (221–263 CE), which vied for power amongst neighboring powers and kingdoms.

Having solidified its borders and polity during its Pre-Shu (924) and Later Shu (954) era, benevolent rule and administration led to another period of relative prosperity. While home to multiple small-scale peasant uprisings, none would lead to serious calamity. With its continued economic growth, Sichuan distinguished itself by issuing the first paper currency (1021 CE) called *Jiaozi* (交子 *jiāozi*), then later replaced by paper bills (錢引 *qiányǐn*), the value of which being backed up by iron metal (von Glahn 2013). The general region of Sichuan and environs comprised about 24% of the total population of the Southern Song, and about one-quarter of its overall economic output.

However, the Mongolian invasions (1231) put an end to all of that, with mass slaughter and destruction leading to massive population loss, this being especially the case in Sichuan (Xiao 2009). The Yuan occupation and the destruction it wrought led to Sichuan devolving into a veritable wasteland for the next 300 years. If Sichuan had 2,640,000 households in 1175, by 1242 this number had dropped to 120,000, only to partially recover decades later, with an estimated population of 775,000 in 1278. As the region became incorporated within the Yuan ruling structure, by 1330 Sichuan was given its prefectural name (四川行省 *sìchuān xíngshěng*). Steady population growth brought Sichuan to about 1,340,000 people in 1371, and in the Ming dynasty (1578) had a population of 3,102,073.

Sichuan suffered immensely again during the end of the Ming dynasty, when the 1621 Tusi (土司 *tǔsī*) native official rebellion (奢安之亂 *shē'ān zhīluàn*) cast the region into chaos. Then, in 1644, the peasant rebel warlord Zhang Xianzhong (張獻忠 *zhāng xiànzhōng*), having razed parts of Sichuan on five separate campaigns, captured Chengdu, after which Ming forces laid siege to the city for 2 years. Qing military forces then entered Sichuan in 1646, leading to a period of lawlessness, multiple factions fighting one another in a civil war. For several years onward, the common saying was "brigands everywhere … if they didn't get around to chopping of heads, disease would take care of the rest." And, "through warfare, famine, epidemics and wild beasts, the population of Shu (Sichuan) dropped by over half." During the fractious 60 years between 1621 and 1680, as China dealt with multiple calamities, Sichuan was hit particularly hard. Those who survived were often amputees, missing ears and noses. Using adjusted statistics from 1670, Sichuan had a population about 620 thousand, whereas a hundred years before (1578) the province recorded 3,102,703 residents (Tian 2011).

Other regional national disasters heavily impacted both Hubei and Hunan. In desperation, refugees from the latter provinces were forced to emigrate to other area, including Sichuan. These late seventeenth century Qing court measures to encourage citizens to move to Sichuan, called "filling out Sichuan with the Huguang region" (湖廣填四川 *húguǎngtián sìchuān*), increased its population of 400,000 in 1720 to 955,000 in 1790 (Tian 2011) (Tables 29.1 and 29.2).

Table 29.1 Sichuan Province populations: Qing Dynasty to 1953. (Cao 2003)

Sichuan regions	1776	1795	1820	1910	1953
Chongqing Fu[a] 重慶府 *chóngqìngfǔ*	1,333,000	2,744,000	3,649,000	6,927,000	10,606,000
Luzhou 瀘州 *lúzhōu*	307,000	496,000	735,000	1,621,000	2,365,000
Xuyong Ting 敘永廳 *xùyǒngtīng*	117,000	199,000	283,000	656,000	716,000
Shunqing Fu 順慶府 *shùnqìngfǔ*	1,022,000	1,210,000	1,718,000	3,164,000	4,853,000
Tongchuan Fu 潼川府 *tóngchuān fǔ*	705,000	1,163,000	1,802,000	4,526,000	6,769,000
Zizhou 資州 *zīzhōu*	375,000	619,000	959,000	2,667,000	3,603,000
Baoning Fu 保定府 *bǎodìngfǔ*	534,000	773,000	1,197,000	2,931,000	4,496,000
Youyang Zhou 酉陽州 *yǒuyángzhōu*	257,000	448,000	622,000	1,028,000	1,460,000
Suiding Fu 綏定府 *suīdìngfǔ*	310,000	699,000	1,083,000	2,623,000	3,294,000
Taiping Ting 太平廳 *tàipíngtīng*	N/A	96,000	140,000	N/A	416,000
Kuizhou Fu 夔州府 *kuízhōufǔ*	429,000	918,000	1,303,000	2,158,000	3,734,000
Zhongzhou 忠州府 *zhōngzhōufǔ*	309,000	473,000	698,000	1,393,000	2,138,000
Shizhu Ting 石柱廳 *shízhùtīng*	66,000	75,000	108,000	33,000	322,000
Mianzhou 綿州 *miánzhōu*	347,000	633,000	806,000	1,335,000	1,673,000
Chengdu Fu 成都府 *chéngdūfǔ*	1,624,000	1,806,000	2,565,000	4,121,000	5,902,000
Qiongzhou 邛州 *qióngzhōu*	279,000	266,000	390,000	707,000	862,000
Long'an Fu 龍安府 *lóng'ānfǔ*	280,000	251,000	326,000	576,000	651,000
Meizhou 眉州 *méizhōu*	289,000	318,000	424,000	691,000	855,000
Jiading Fu 嘉定府 *jiādìngfǔ*	818,000	840,000	1,132,000	2,196,000	2,810,000
Xuzhou Fu 敘州府 *xùzhōufǔ*	881,000	1,301,000	1,769,000	3,049,000	3,920,000
Yazhou Fu 雅州府 *yǎzhōufǔ*	315,000	492,000	626,000	1,007,000	1,264,000
Ningyuan Fu 寧遠府 *níngyuǎnfǔ*	380,000	835,000	1,045,000	1,649,000	2,070,000
Maozhou 茂州 *màozhōu*	114,000	49,000	53,000	63,000	69,000
Lifan Ting 理番廳 *lǐfāntīng*	24,000	17,000	18,000	33,000	24,000
Maogong Ting 懋功廳 *màogōngtīng*	N/A	31,000	39,000	35,000	83,000
Songpan Ting 松潘廳 *sōngpāntīng*	19,000	59,000	75,000	64,000	152,000
Total	**11,134,000**	**16,811,000**	**23,565,000**	**45,253,000**	**65,108,000**

Table 29.2 Sichuan city and county populations: 1812 and 1953. (Cao 2003)

City/County	1812	1953
Chengdu 成都 *chéngdū*	386,397	856,713
Huayang 華陽 *huáyáng*	389,656	415,511
Shuangliu 雙流 *shuāngliú*	181,797	175,272
Wenjiang 溫江 *wēnjiāng*	270,998	194,193
Xinfan 新繁 *xīnfán*	222,658	129,986
Jintang 金堂 *jīntáng*	222,808	636,808
Xindu 新都 *xīndū*	177,458	131,284
Pixian County 郫縣 *píxiàn*	236,659	225,506
Chongning 崇寧 *chóngníng*	183,570	100,020
Guanxian County 灌縣 *guànxiàn*	251,266	341,529
Pengxian 彭縣 *péngxiàn*	230,418	401,234
Jianzhou 簡州 *jiǎnzhōu*	256,536	1,123,799
Chongqing 崇慶 *chóngqìng*	228,565	429,454
Xinjin 新津 *xīnjīn*	193,581	172,792
Hanzhou 漢州 *hànzhōu*	229,485	323,656
Shifang 什防 *shífáng*	174,652	244,262
Total:	**3,836,504**	**5,902,019**

Sichuan expanded its territory dramatically in 1955, when Xikang Province (西康省 *xīkāng shěng*) was made part of Sichuan. A few years later, the Qing dynasty walls of Chengdu, built ca. 1700, met the same fate as Beijing's city walls. Mao Zedong, after seeing them in 1958, reportedly said "We've knocked down Beijing's city walls. These walls are unsightly and obstruct traffic. City walls are backward; dismantling them is progressive." Thus, Mao Zedong having spoken, the Chengdu walls were destroyed (Yang 2012).

The Disaster of the Great Leap Forward Years (1958–1962)

As a consequence of its relatively large population but also smaller portion of arable land, Sichuan was among the hardest hit during the Great Leap Forward (1958–62), with an estimated eight (low end estimate) million to 12 million deaths from starvation. In many cases, deaths also resulted from unimaginably brutal violence. Then a county under Sichuan provincial administration, Chongqing accounted for a majority of its overall deaths (6,420,000).

Following the Sino-Soviet split (1960), Mao Zedong undertook a warlike footing in order to prepare for a future conflict, establishing the so-called "Third Line (front)," moving industries and strategic centers of gravity inland away from potential strikes from the Soviet Union (and the United States). One such building effort included Sichuan in 1964, with Chongqing as the center, increasing its population to about 22,400,000 over the next decade.

Wenchan Earthquake

On 12 May 2008, a 7.9 Richter scale earthquake struck Sichuan, with its epicenter Wenchuan County (汶川縣 *wènchuān xiàn*), leading to the deaths of 69,188 people, 18,440 were unaccounted for, and 374,177 injured.

Sichuan Province Economics and Population Trends

Sichuan has, at least based on Chinese state-provided statistics, enjoyed a decent economy, with a gross domestic product (GDP) of USD $467 billion in 2015, and $756 billion in 2020, ranked sixth out of all mainland China's provinces and major cities. Its per capita income in 2020 was roughly average among this same group, about $4125 (Zhang 2021). Sichuan has also steadily grown in population, about 4% from 2010 to 2020 (see Table 29.3). In contrast with the census (2020)

Table 29.3 Sichuan Province (Residential 常住人口 *chángzhù rénkǒu*) data. (SPBS 2021)

City	Population (2010)	Population (2020)
Chengdu City 成都市 *chéngdū shì* [abbrev. 蓉 *róng*]	14,047,625	20,937,757
Mianyang City 綿陽市 *miányáng shì*	4,613,862	4,868,243
Guangyuan City 廣元市 *guǎngyuán shì*	2,484,125	2,305,657
Nanchong City 南充市 *nánchōng shì*	6,278,622	5,607,565
Bazhong City 巴中市 *bāzhōng shì*	3,283,771	2,712,894
Dazhou City 達州市 *dázhōu shì*	5,468,092	5,385,422
Ya'an City 雅安市 *yǎ'ān shì*	1,507,264	1,434,603
Deyang City 德陽市 *déyáng shì*	3,615,759	3,456,161
Suining City 遂寧市 *suìníng shì*	3,252,551	2,814,196
Guang'an City 廣安市 *guǎng'ān shì*	3,205,476	3,254,883
Meishan City 眉山市 *méishān shì*	2,950,548	2,955,219
Ziyang City 資陽市 *zīyáng shì*	3,665,064	2,308,631
Leshan City 樂山市 *lèshān shì*	3,235,756	3,160,168
Neijiang City 內江市 *nèijiāng shì*	3,702,847	3,140,678
Zigong City 自貢市 *zìgòng shì*	2,678,898	2,489,256
Yibin City 宜賓市 *yíbīn shì*	4,472,001	4,588,804

(continued)

Table 29.3 (continued)

City	Population (2010)	Population (2020)
Luzhou City 瀘州市 *lúzhōu shì*	4,218,426	4,254,149
Panzhihua City 攀枝花市 *pānzhīhuā shì*	1,214,121	1,212,203
Ganzi Tibetan Autonomous Prefecture 甘孜藏族自治州 *gānzī zàngzú zìzhìzhōu*	1,091,872	1,107,431
Aba (Ngawa) Tibetan and Qiang Autonomous Prefecture 阿壩藏族羌族自治州 *ābà zàngzú qiāngzú zìzhìzhōu*	898,713	822,587
Liangshan Yi Autonomous Prefecture 涼山彝族自治州 *liángshān yízú zìzhìzhōu*	4,532,809	4,858,359
Total	**80,418,200**	**83,674,866**

population of all residents (83,674,866), this is substantially lower than the permanent (*hukou*) registered population that year of 91,210,000 (Table 29.5). One can only include that a substantial number of Sichuanese spend significant amounts of time outside their province for work, study, etc., a state of affairs that has existed since at least 1995, when Sichuan led mainland China with 6.1 million out-migrants (Jia 1998).

Ethnic Minorities

According to findings from the PRC's national census (2010), Sichuan is home to no fewer than 56 ethnic groups (including Han Chinese), altogether amounting to 4,908,000 individuals of different groups. The following seven are the major ethnic nationalities in Sichuan (SNN 2011):

- Yi (彝族 *yízú*)
- Tibetan (藏族 *zàngzú*)
- Qiang (羌族 *qiāngzú*)
- Hui (回族 *huízú*)
- Tujia (土家族*tŭjiāzú*)
- Mongolian (蒙古族 *ménggŭzú*), and
- Li-Su (Lisaw 傈僳族 *lìsùzú*) (Fig. 29.2)

Table 29.5 (below) shows the *hukou* (family registered) populations based on PRC Ministry of Civil Affairs data. (Districts listed directly under major cities are government seats, as are those in parentheses). One can compare these data with the census (usual residential populations based on 2010 and 2020 censuses in Table 29.3 (above) and 29.4 (below):

Table 29.4 Sichuan Province: population data of cities and their subordinate sectors. (SPBS 2021)

Cities and subordinate sectors, population (2020 census)	Subordinate district, city and county populations (2020)	Total Population (2020)
Chengdu City 成都市 ***chéngdū shì* [abbrev.** 蓉 ***róng*]**		**20,937,757**
Sichuan Tianfu New District 四川天府新區 *sìchuān tiānfǔ xīnqū*	866,233	
Chengdu Dongbu New District 成都東部新區 *chéngdū dōngbù xīnqū*	379,096	
Chengdu High Technology Industry Development Zone 成都高新技術產業開發區 *chéngdū gāoxīnjìshù chǎnyè kāifāqū*	1,257,541	
Jinjiang District 錦江區 *jǐnjiāng qū*	902,933	
Qingyang District 青羊區 *qīngyáng qū*	955,954	
Jinniu District 金牛區 *jīnniú qū*	1,265,398	
Wuhou District 武侯區 *wǔhóu qū*	1,206,568	
Chenghua District 成華區 *chénghuá qū*	1,381,894	
Longquanyi District 龍泉驛區 *lóngquányì qū*	1,346,210	
Qingbaijiang District 青白江區 *qīngbáijiāng qū*	490,091	
Xindu District 新都區 *xīndū qū*	1,558,466	
Wenjiang District 溫江區 *wēnjiāng qū*	967,868	
Shuangliu District 雙流區 *shuāngliú qū*	1,465,785	
Pidu District 郫都區 *pídū qū*	1,390,913	
Xinjin District 新津區 *xīnjīn qū*	363,591	
Jianyang District 簡陽區 *jiǎnyáng qū*	738,169	
Dujiangyan District 都江堰區 *dūjiāngyàn qū*	710,056	
Pengzhou City 彭州市 *péngzhōu shì*	780,399	
Qiongxia City 邛峽市 *qióngxiá shì*	602,973	
Chongzhou City 崇州市 *chóngzhōu shì*	735,723	
Jintang County 金堂縣 *jīntáng xiàn*	800,371	
Dayi County 大邑縣 *dàyì xiàn*	515,962	
Pujiang County 蒲江縣 *pújiāng xiàn*	255,563	
Mianyang City 綿陽市 ***miányáng shì***		**4,868,243**
Fucheng District 涪城區 *fúchéng qū*	1,298,524	
Youxian District 游仙區 *yóuxiān qū*	561,379	
Anzhou District 安州區 *ānzhōu qū*	372,962	
Santai County 三台縣 *sāntái xiàn*	955,811	
Yanting County 鹽亭縣 *yántíng xiàn*	370,739	
Zitong County 梓潼縣 *zǐtóng xiàn*	276,996	
Beichuan Qiangzu Autononous County 北川羌族自治縣 *běichuān qiāngzú zìzhìxiàn*	174,132	
Pingwu County 平武縣 *píngwǔ xiàn*	126,357	
Jiangyou City 江由市 *jiāngyóu shì*	731,343	
Guangyuan City 廣元市 ***guǎngyuán shì***		**2,305,657**
Lizhou District 利州區 *lìzhōu qū*	621,978	

(continued)

Table 29.4 (continued)

Cities and subordinate sectors, population (2020 census)	Subordinate district, city and county populations (2020)	Total Population (2020)
Zhaohua District 昭化區 *zhāohuà qū*	134,202	
Chaotian District 朝天區 *cháotiān qū*	126,506	
Wangcang County 旺蒼縣 *wàngcāng xiàn*	330,108	
Qingchuan County 青川縣 *qīngchuān xiàn*	156,387	
Jiange County 劍閣縣 *jiàngé xiàn*	423,859	
Cangxi County 蒼溪縣 *cāngxī xiàn*	512,617	
Nanchong City 南充市 ***nánchōng shì***		**5,607,565**
Shunqing District 順慶區 *shùnqìng qū*	834,294	
Gaoping District 高坪區 *gāopíng qū*	570,415	
Jialing District 嘉陵區 *jiālíng qū*	531,825	
Nanbu County 南部縣 *nánbù xiàn*	817,235	
Yingshan County 營山縣 *yíngshān xiàn*	620,480	
Peng'an County 蓬安縣 *péng'ān xiàn*	461,485	
Yilong County 儀隴縣 *yílǒng xiàn*	729,141	
Xichong County 西充縣 *xīchōng xiàn*	420,023	
Langzhong City 閬中市 *làngzhōng shì*	622,667	
Bazhong City 巴中市 ***bāzhōng shì***		**2,712,894**
Bazhong District[b] 巴中區 *bāzhōng qū*	651,534	
Enyang District 恩陽區 *ēnyáng qū*	345,728	
Tongjiang County 通江縣 *tōngjiāng xiàn*	521,875	
Nanjiang County 南江縣 *nánjiāng xiàn*	467,609	
Pingchang County 平昌縣 *píngchāng xiàn*	658,644	
Bazhong Economic Development Zone 巴中經濟開發區 *bāzhōng jīngjì kāifāqū*	67,504	
Dazhou City達州市***dázhōu shì***		**5,385,422**
Tongchuan District 通川區 *tōngchuān qū*	905,678	
Dachuan District 達川區 *dáchuān qū*	899,728	
Wanyuan City 萬源市 *wànyuán shì*	406,685	
Xuanhan County 宣漢縣 *xuānhàn xiàn*	954,090	
Kaijiang County 開江縣 *kāijiāng xiàn*	414,310	
Dazhu County 大竹縣 *dàzhú xiàn*	841,960	
Quxian County 渠縣 *qúxiàn*	917,508	
Dazhou High Technology Industrial Park 達州高新技術產業園區 *dázhōu gāoxīnjìshù chǎnyè yuánqū*	45,463	
Ya'an City 雅安市 ***yǎ'ān shì***		**1,434,603**
Yucheng District 魚城區 *yúchéng qū*	368,909	
Mingshan District 名山區 *míngshān qū*	254,632	
Yingjing County 滎經縣 *yíngjīng xiàn*	131,491	
Hanyuan County 漢源縣 *hànyuán xiàn*	285,558	
Shimian County 石綿縣 *shímián xiàn*	114,116	

(continued)

Table 29.4 (continued)

Cities and subordinate sectors, population (2020 census)	Subordinate district, city and county populations (2020)	Total Population (2020)
Tianquan 天全縣 *tiānquán xiàn*	132,033	
Lushan County 蘆山縣 *lúshān xiàn*	99,824	
Baoxing County 寶興縣 *bǎoxīng xiàn*	48,040	
Deyang City 德陽市 ***déyáng shì***		**3,456,161**
Jingyang District 旌陽區 *jīngyáng qū*	828,189	
Luojiang District 羅江區 *luójiāng qū*	209,088	
Zhongjiang County 中江縣 *zhōngjiāng xiàn*	946,019	
Guanghan City 廣漢市 *guǎnghàn shì*	626,132	
Shifang City 什邡市 *shífāng shì*	406,775	
Mianzhu City 綿竹市 *miánzhú shì*	439,958	
Suining City 遂寧市 ***suìníng shì***		**2,814,196**
Chuanshan District 船山區 *chuánshān qū*	832,863	
Anju District 安居區 *ānjū qū*	431,310	
Pengxi County 蓬溪縣 *péngxī xiàn*	430,344	
Daying County 大英縣 *dàyīng xiàn*	387,299	
Shehong City 射洪市 *shèhóng shì*	732,380	
Guang'an City 廣安市 ***guǎng'ān shì***		**3,254,883**
Guang'an District 廣安區 *guǎng'ān qū*	744,115	
Qianfeng District 前鋒區 *qiánfēng qū*	232,255	
Yuechi County 岳池縣 *yuèchí xiàn*	742,747	
Wusheng County 武勝縣 *wǔshèng xiàn*	555,897	
Lingshui County 鄰水縣 *línshuǐ xiàn*	707,537	
Huaying City 華鎣市 *huáyíng shì*	272,332	
Meishan City 眉山市 ***méishān shì***		**2,955,219**
Dongpo District 東坡區 *dōngpō qū*	904,412	
Pengshan District 彭山區 *péngshān qū*	328,236	
Renshou County 仁壽縣 *rénshòu xiàn*	1,110,017	
Hongya County 洪雅縣 *hóngyǎ xiàn*	295,744	
Danling County 丹棱縣 *dānlíng xiàn*	148,820	
Qingshen County 青神縣 *qīngshén xiàn*	167,990	
Ziyang City 資陽市 ***zīyáng shì***		**2,308,631**
Yanjiang District 雁江區 *yànjiāng qū*	867,119	
Anyue County 安岳縣 *ānyuè xiàn*	950,939	
Dongzhi County 東至縣 *dōngzhì xiàn*	490,573	
Leshan City 樂山市 ***lèshān shì***		**3,160,168**
Shizhong District 市中區 *shìzhōng qū*	814,597	
Shawan District 沙灣區 *shāwān qū*	144,931	
Wutongqiao District 五通橋區 *wǔtōngqiáo qū*	237,933	
Jinkouhe District 金口河區 *jīnkǒuhé qū*	38,727	
Qianwei County 犍為縣 *qiánwéi xiàn*	416,673	

(continued)

Table 29.4 (continued)

Cities and subordinate sectors, population (2020 census)	Subordinate district, city and county populations (2020)	Total Population (2020)
Jingyan County 井研縣 *jǐngyán xiàn*	280,641	
Jiajiang County 夾江縣 *jiājiāng xiàn*	305,441	
Muchuan County 沐川縣 *mùchuān xiàn*	192,313	
Ebian Yizu Autonomous County 峨邊彝族自治縣 *ébiān yízú zìzhìxiàn*	121,554	
Mabian Yizu Autonomous County 馬邊彝族自治縣 *mǎbiān yízú zìzhìxiàn*	188,251	
Emeishan City 峨眉山市 *éméishān shì*	419,107	
Neijiang City 內江市 ***nèijiāng shì***		**3,140,678**
Shizhong District 市中區 *shìzhōng qū*	337,106	
Dongxing District 東興區 *dōngxīng qū*	681,439	
Weiyuan County 威遠縣 *wēiyuǎn xiàn*	547,059	
Zizhong County 資中縣 *zīzhōng xiàn*	845,579	
Neijiang Economic Development Zone 內江經濟開發區 *nèijiāng jīngjì kāifāqū*	87,914	
Neijiang High Technology Industry Development Zone 內江高新技術產業開發區 *nèijiāng gāoxīnjìshù chǎnyè kāifāqū*	72,681	
Longchang City 隆昌市 *lóngchāng shì*	568,900	
Zigong City 自貢市 ***zìgòng shì***		**2,489,256**
Ziliujing District 自流井區 *zìliújǐng qū*	481,981	
Gongjing District 貢井區 *gòngjǐng qū*	226,704	
Da'an District 大安區 *dà'ān qū*	291,645	
Yantan District 沿灘區 *yántān qū*	297,365	
Rongxian District 榮縣 *róngxiàn*	469,488	
Fushun County 富順縣 *fùshùn xiàn*	722,073	
Yibin City 宜賓市 ***yíbīn shì***		**4,588,804**
Cuiping District 翠屏區 *cuìpíng qū*	887,359	
Nanxi District 南溪區 *nánxī qū*	332,976	
Xuzhou District 敘州區 *xùzhōu qū*	938,157	
Jiang'an County 江安縣 *jiāng'ān xiàn*	424470	
Changning County 長寧縣 *chángníng xiàn*	327,904	
Gaoxian County 高縣 *gāoxiàn*	380,893	
Gongxian County 珙縣 *gǒngxiàn*	339,200	
Junlian County 筠連縣 *yúnlián xiàn*	332,805	
Xingwen County 興文縣 *xīngwén xiàn*	380,036	
Pingshan County 屏山縣 *píngshān xiàn*	245,184	
Luzhou City 瀘州市 ***lúzhōu shì***		**4,254,149**
Jiangyin District 江陽區 *jiāngyáng qū*	761,576	
Naxi District 納溪區 *nàxī qū*	354,846	
Longmatan District 龍馬潭區 *lóngmǎtán qū*	479,697	

(continued)

Table 29.4 (continued)

Cities and subordinate sectors, population (2020 census)	Subordinate district, city and county populations (2020)	Total Population (2020)
Luxian County 瀘縣 *lúxiàn*	764,362	
Hejiang County 合江縣 *héjiāng xiàn*	688,731	
Xuyong County 敘永縣 *xùyǒng xiàn*	552,979	
Gulin County 古藺縣 *gǔlìn xiàn*	651,958	
Panzhihua City 攀枝花市 ***pānzhīhuā shì***		**1,212,203**
Dongqu District 東區 *dōngqū*	411,427	
Xiqu District 西區 *xīqū*	129,406	
Renhe District 仁和區 *rénhé qū*	265,562	
Miyi County 米易縣 *mǐyì xiàn*	227,011	
Yanbian County 鹽邊縣 *yánbiān xiàn*	178,797	
Ganzi Tibetan Autonomous Prefecture 甘孜藏族自治州 ***gānzī zàngzú zìzhìzhōu***		**1,107,431**
Kangding City 康定市 *kāngdìng shì*	126,785	
Luding County 瀘定縣 *lúdìng xiàn*	84,204	
Danba County 丹巴縣 *dānbā xiàn*	49,872	
Jiulong County 九龍縣 *jiǔlóng xiàn*	53,738	
Yajiang County 雅江縣 *yǎjiāng xiàn*	51,162	
Daofu (Dawu) County 道孚縣 *dàofú xiàn*	53,378	
Luhuo County 爐霍縣 *lúhuò xiàn*	47,185	
Ganzi (Garzê) County 甘孜縣 *gānzī xiàn*	72,698	
Xinlong County 新龍縣 *xīnlóng xiàn*	45,698	
Dege County 德格縣 *dégé xiàn*	88,542	
Baiyu County 白玉縣 *báiyù xiàn*	59,524	
Shixian County 石縣 *shíxiàn*	103,633	
Bada County 色達縣 *sèdá xiàn*	64,681	
Litang County 理塘縣 *lǐtáng xiàn*	67,293	
Batang County 巴塘縣 *bātáng xiàn*	49,967	
Xiangcheng County 鄉城縣 *xiāngchéng xiàn*	31,407	
Daocheng County 稻城縣 *dàochéng xiàn*	32,916	
Derong County 得榮縣 *déróng xiàn*	24,748	
Aba (Ngawa) Tibetan and Qiang Autonomous Prefecture 阿壩藏族羌族自治州 ***ābà zàngzú qiāngzú zìzhìzhōu***		**822,587**
Ma'erkang (Barkam) County 馬爾康市 *mǎ'ěrkāng shì*	58,390	
Wenchuan County 汶川縣 *wènchuān xiàn*	82,971	
Lixian County 理縣 *lǐxiàn*	36,926	
Maoxian County 茂縣 *màoxiàn*	95,361	
Songpan County 松潘縣 *sōngpān xiàn*	66,937	
Jiuzhaigou County 九寨溝縣 *jiǔzhàigōu xiàn*	66,055	
Jinchuan County 金川縣 *jīnchuān xiàn*	58,068	

(continued)

Table 29.4 (continued)

Cities and subordinate sectors, population (2020 census)	Subordinate district, city and county populations (2020)	Total Population (2020)
Xiaojin County 小金縣 *xiǎojīn xiàn*	64,813	
Heishui County 黑水縣 *hēishuǐ xiàn*	44,564	
Rangtang County 壤塘縣 *rǎngtáng xiàn*	44,679	
Aba (Ngawa) County 阿壩縣 *ābà xiàn*	80,467	
Ruo'ergai (Zoigê) County 若爾蓋縣 *ruò'ěrgài xiàn*	76,712	
Hongyuan County 紅原縣 *hóngyuán xiàn*	46,644	
Liangshan Yi Autonomous Prefecture 涼山彝族自治州 *liángshān yízú zìzhìzhōu*		**4,858,359**
Xichang City 西昌市 *xīchāng shì*	955,041	
Muli Zangzu (Tibetan) Autonomous County 木里藏族自治縣 *mùlǐ zàngzú zìzhìxiàn*	122,944	
Yanyuan County 鹽源縣 *yányuán xiàn*	340,898	
Dechang County 德昌縣 *déchāng xiàn*	216,533	
Huili County 會理縣 *huìlǐ xiàn*	390,531	
Huidong County 會東縣 *huìdōng xiàn*	346,082	
Ningnang County 寧南縣 *níngnán xiàn*	184,293	
Puge County 普格縣 *pǔgé xiàn*	180,052	
Butuo County 布拖縣 *bùtuō xiàn*	185,553	
Jinyang County 金陽縣 *jīnyáng xiàn*	170,063	
Zhaojue County 昭覺縣 *zhāojué xiàn*	252,435	
Xide County 喜德縣 *xǐdé xiàn*	158,139	
Mianning County 冕寧縣 *miǎnníng xiàn*	369,166	
Yuexi County 越西縣 *yuèxī xiàn*	301,865	
Ganluo County 甘洛縣 *gānluò xiàn*	205,991	
Meigu County 美姑縣 *měigū xiàn*	238,624	
Leibo County 雷波縣*léibō xiàn*	240,149	

Sichuan Province (川 *chuān*); (蜀 *shǔ*)

Provincial Capital: Chengdu

Table 29.5 Sichuan Province: permanent registered (戶籍人口 *hùjí rénkǒu*) populations. (MCA 2020)

Name	Traditional	Simplified	Population (2012)	Population (2016)	Population (2020)	Area (Sq. Km)
Sichuan Province	四川省	四川省	90,010,000	90,970,000	91,210,000	490,000
Chengdu City	成都市	成都市	11,480,000	11,710,000	14,760,000	14,312
Wuhou District (Jiangxijie Subdistrict)	武侯區 (漿洗街街道)	武侯区 (浆洗街街道)	940,000	980,000	1,290,000	75
Qingyang District (Xinhuaxilu Subdistrict)	青羊區 (新華西路街道)	青羊区 (新华西路街道)	570,000	600,000	710,000	66
Jinjiang District (Shuyuannanjie Subdistrict)	錦江區 (書院南街街道)	锦江区 (书院南街街道)	420,000	450,000	600,000	61
Jinniu District (Fuqin Subdistrict)	金牛區 (撫琴街道)	金牛区 (抚琴街道)	720,000	730,000	770,000	108
Chenghua District (Mengzhuiwan Subdistrict)	成華區 (猛追灣街道)	成华区 (猛追湾街道)	640,000	670,000	780,000	110
Longquanyi District (Longquan Subdistrict)	龍泉驛區 (龍泉街道)	龙泉驿区 (龙泉街道)	590,000	600,000	710,000	557
Qingbaijiang District (Hongyang Subdistrict)	青白江區 (紅陽街道)	青白江区 (红阳街道)	410,000	410,000	420,000	379
Xindu District (Xindu Subdistrict)	新都區 (新都街道)	新都区 (新都街道)	680,000	700,000	800,000	497
Wenjiang District (Liucheng Subdistrict)	溫江區 (柳城街道)	温江区 (柳城街道)	370,000	380,000	490,000	277
Dujiangyan City (Guankou Subdistrict)	都江堰市 (灌口街道)	都江堰市 (灌口街道)	610,000	610,000	620,000	1208
Pengzhou City (Tianpeng Town)	彭州市 (天彭鎮)	彭州市 (天彭镇)	800,000	800,000	800,000	1420
Qionglai City (Linqiong Subdistrict)	邛崍市 (臨邛街道)	邛崃市 (临邛街道)	660,000	660,000	650,000	1384

(continued)

Table 29.5 (continued)

Name	Traditional	Simplified	Population (2012)	Population (2016)	Population (2020)	Area (Sq. Km)
Chongzhou City (Chongyang Subdistrict)	崇州市 (崇陽街道)	崇州市 (崇阳街道)	670,000	670,000	660,000	1090
Jianyang City[c] (Jiancheng Subdistrict)	簡陽市 (射洪壩街道)	简阳市 (射洪坝街道)	N/A	N/A	1,510,000	2214
Jintang County (Zhaozhen Subdistrict)	金堂縣 (趙鎮街道)	金堂县 (赵镇街道)	880,000	890,000	900,000	1156
Shuangliu District (Dongsheng Subdistrict)	雙流區 (東升街道)	双流区 (东升街道)	920,000	960,000	1,320,000	1032
Pixian County (Pitong Subdistrict)	郫縣 (郫筒街道)	郫县 (郫筒街道)	510,000	520,000	N/A	(438)
Pidu District[d] (Pitong Subdistrict)	郫都區 (郫筒街道)	郫都区 (郫筒街道)	510,000	520,000	630,000	438
Dayi County (Jinyuan Subdistrict)	大邑縣 (晉原街道)	大邑县 (晋原街道)	520,000	510,000	510,000	1327
Pujiang County (Heshan Subdistrict)	蒲江縣 (鶴山街道)	蒲江县 (鹤山街道)	260,000	260,000	270,000	583
Xinjin County (Wujin Subdistrict)	新津縣 (五津街道)	新津县 (五津街道)	310,000	310,000	320,000	330
Guangyuan City	廣元市	广元市	3,110,000	3,110,000	3,010,000	16,310
Lizhou District (Dongba Subdistrict)	利州區 (東壩街道)	利州区 (东坝街道)	480,000	480,000	490,000	1534
Zhaohua District (Yuanba Town)	昭化區 (元壩鎮)	昭化区 (元坝镇)	N/A	240,000	230,000	1437
Yuanba District[e] (Yuanba Town)	元壩區 (元壩鎮)	元坝区 (元坝镇)	240,000	N/A	N/A	(1437)
Chaotian District (Chaotian Town)	朝天區 (朝天鎮)	朝天区 (朝天镇)	210,000	210,000	200,000	1613
Wangcang County (Donghe Town)	旺蒼縣 (東河鎮)	旺苍县 (东河镇)	460,000	460,000	440,000	2976
Qingchuan County (Qiaozhuang Town)	青川縣 (喬莊鎮)	青川县 (乔庄镇)	240,000	240,000	230,000	3216
Jiange County (Xiasi Town)	劍閣縣 (下寺鎮)	剑阁县 (下寺镇)	690,000	690,000	650,000	3204
Cangxi County (LingjiangTown)	蒼溪縣 (陵江鎮)	苍溪县 (陵江镇)	790,000	790,000	760,000	2330

(continued)

Table 29.5 (continued)

Name	Traditional	Simplified	Population (2012)	Population (2016)	Population (2020)	Area (Sq. Km)
Mianyang City	綿陽市	绵阳市	5,430,000	5,450,000	5,360,000	20,257
Fucheng District (Chengxiang Subdistrict)	涪城區 (城廂街道)	涪城区 (城厢街道)	680,000	690,000	740,000	554
Youxian District (Fule Subdistrict)	游仙區 (富樂街道)	游仙区 (富乐街道)	540,000	550,000	560,000	1017
Jiangyou City (Zhongba Town)	江油市 (中壩鎮)	江油市 (中坝镇)	880,000	890,000	860,000	2721
Santai County (Tongchuan Town)	三台縣 (潼川鎮)	三台县 (潼川镇)	1,480,000	1,470,000	1,410,000	2660
Yanting County (Yunxi Town)	鹽亭縣 (雲溪鎮)	盐亭县 (云溪镇)	600,000	600,000	550,000	1646
Anxian County (Huagai Town)	安縣 (花荄鎮)	安县 (花荄镇)	440,000	440,000	N/A	(1182)
Anzhou District[f] (Huagai Town)	安州區 (花荄鎮)	安州区 (花荄镇)	N/A	N/A	440,000	1182
Zitong County (Wenchang Town)	梓潼縣 (文昌鎮)	梓潼县 (文昌镇)	380,000	390,000	380,000	1444
Beichuan Qiangzu (Qiang) Autonomous County (Yongchang Town)	北川羌族自治縣 (永昌鎮)	北川羌族自治县 (永昌镇)	240,000	240,000	230,000	3083
Pingwu County (Long'an Town)	平武縣 (龍安鎮)	平武县 (龙安镇)	190,000	180,000	180,000	5950
Deyang City	德陽市	德阳市	3,880,000	3,920,000	3,870,000	5911
Jingyang District (Jingdong Subdistrict)	旌陽區 (旌東街道)	旌阳区 (旌东街道)	660,000	680,000	700,000	648
Shifang City (Fangting Subdistrict)	什邡市 (方亭街道)	什邡市 (方亭街道)	430,000	440,000	430,000	820
Guanghan City (Luocheng Town)	廣漢市 (雒城鎮)	广汉市 (雒城镇)	600,000	610,000	600,000	549
Mianzhu City (Jiannan Town)	綿竹市 (劍南鎮)	绵竹市 (剑南镇)	510,000	510,000	500,000	1246
Luojiang District (Wan'an Town)	羅江區 (萬安鎮)	罗江区 (万安镇)	250,000	250,000	250,000	448
Zhongjiang County (Kaijiang Town)	中江縣 (凱江鎮)	中江县 (凯江镇)	1,430,000	1,430,000	1,390,000	2200
Nanchong City	南充市	南充市	7,510,000	7,600,000	7,280,000	12,514

(continued)

Table 29.5 (continued)

Name	Traditional	Simplified	Population (2012)	Population (2016)	Population (2020)	Area (Sq. Km)
Shunqing District (Zhongcheng Subdistrict)	順慶區 (中城街道)	顺庆区 (中城街道)	640,000	650,000	660,000	556
Gaoping District (Baita Subdistrict)	高坪區 (白塔街道)	高坪区 (白塔街道)	590,000	600,000	600,000	806
Jialing District (Huohua Subdistrict)	嘉陵區 (火花街道)	嘉陵区 (火花街道)	690,000	700,000	690,000	1179
Langzhong City (Qili Subdistrict)	閬中市 (七里街道)	阆中市 (七里街道)	870,000	880,000	830,000	1878
Nanbu County (Shubei Subdistrict)	南部縣 (蜀北街道)	南部县 (蜀北街道)	1,310,000	1,320,000	1,250,000	2229
Yingshan County (Sui'an Subdistrict)	營山縣 (綏安街道)	营山县 (绥安街道)	940,000	950,000	910,000	1633
Peng'an County (Xiangru Town)	蓬安縣 (相如鎮)	蓬安县 (相如镇)	700,000	710,000	680,000	1334
Yilong County (Xinzheng Town)	儀隴縣 (新政鎮)	仪陇县 (新政镇)	1,110,000	1,130,000	1,080,000	1791
Xichong County (Jincheng Town)	西充縣 (晉城鎮)	西充县 (晋城镇)	660,000	660,000	600,000	1108
Guang'an City	廣安市	广安市	4,650,000	4,970,000	4,620,000	6344
Guang'an District (Nonghui Subdistrict)	廣安區 (濃洄街道)	广安区 (浓洄街道)	1,250,000	1,010,000	900,000	1032
Qianfeng District[g] (Qianfeng Town)	前鋒區 (大佛寺街道)	前锋区 (大佛寺街道)	N/A	530,000	370,000	504
Huaying City (Shuanghe Subdistrict)	華鎣市 (雙河街道)	华蓥市 (双河街道)	360,000	360,000	360,000	466
Yuechi County (Jiulong Town)	岳池縣 (九龍鎮)	岳池县 (九龙镇)	1,180,000	1,190,000	1,160,000	1457
Wusheng County (Yankou Town)	武勝縣 (沿口鎮)	武胜县 (沿口镇)	840,000	850,000	820,000	966
Linshui County (Dingping Town)	鄰水縣 (鼎屏鎮)	邻水县 (鼎屏镇)	1,020,000	1,030,000	1,020,000	1919
Suining City	遂寧市	遂宁市	3,810,000	3,760,000	3,650,000	5326
Chuanshan District (Kaixuan Subdistrict)	船山區 (凱旋街道)	船山区 (凯旋街道)	690,000	700,000	700,000	618

(continued)

Table 29.5 (continued)

Name	Traditional	Simplified	Population (2012)	Population (2016)	Population (2020)	Area (Sq. Km)
Anju District (Fenghuang Subdistrict)	安居區 (鳳凰街道)	安居区 (凤凰街道)	810,000	800,000	770,000	1258
Pengxi County (Pu'an Subdistrict)	蓬溪縣 (普安街道)	蓬溪县 (普安街道)	740,000	710,000	690,000	1251
Shehong City (Taihe Subdistrict)	射洪市 (太和街道)	射洪市 (太和街道)	N/A	N/A	960,000	1496
Shehong County[h] (Zi'ang Subdistrict)	射洪縣 (子昂街道)	射洪县 (子昂街道)	1,020,000	1,010,000	N/A	(1496)
Daying County (Yanjing Subdistrict)	大英縣 (鹽井街道)	大英县 (盐井街道)	530,000	540,000	540,000	703
Neijiang City	內江市	內江市	4,250,000	4,270,000	4,120,000	5386
Shizhong District (Chengdong Subdistrict)	市中區 (城東街道)	市中区 (城东街道)	530,000	530,000	510,000	388
Dongxing District (Dongxing Subdistrict)	東興區 (東興街道)	东兴区 (东兴街道)	880,000	890,000	880,000	1181
Weiyuan County (Yanling Town)	威遠縣 (嚴陵鎮)	威远县 (严陵镇)	750,000	750,000	710,000	1289
Zizhong County (Chonglong Town)	資中縣 (重龍鎮)	资中县 (重龙镇)	1,310,000	1,310,000	1,250,000	1734
Longchang County (Guhu Subdistrict)	隆昌縣 (古湖街道)	隆昌县 (古湖街道)	780,000	790,000	770,000	794
Leshan City	樂山市	乐山市	3,530,000	3,550,000	3,510,000	12,759
Shizhong District (Haitang Subdistrict)	市中區 (海棠街道)	市中区 (海棠街道)	590,000	600,000	640,000	825
Shawan District (Yinhe Subdistrict)	沙灣區 (銀河街道)	沙湾区 (银河街道)	190,000	190,000	180,000	610
Wutongqiao District (Zhugen Town)	五通橋區 (竹根鎮)	五通桥区 (竹根镇)	320,000	320,000	300,000	473
Jinkouhe District (Yonghe Town)	金口河區 (永和鎮)	金口河区 (永和镇)	50,000	50,000	50,000	598
E'meishan City (Shengli Subdistrict)	峨眉山市 (勝利街道)	峨眉山市 (胜利街道)	430,000	430,000	430,000	1181
Qianwei County (Yujin Town)	犍為縣 (玉津鎮)	犍为县 (玉津镇)	570,000	570,000	560,000	1375

(continued)

Table 29.5 (continued)

Name	Traditional	Simplified	Population (2012)	Population (2016)	Population (2020)	Area (Sq. Km)
Jingyan County (Yancheng Subdistrict)	井研縣 (研城街道)	井研县 (研城街道)	420,000	420,000	400,000	841
Jiajiang County (Qingyi Subdistrict)	夾江縣 (青衣街道)	夹江县 (青衣街道)	350,000	350,000	350,000	749
Muchuan County (Muxi Town)	沐川縣 (沐溪鎮)	沐川县 (沐溪镇)	260,000	260,000	250,000	1408
Ebian Yizu (Yi) Autonomous County (Shaping Town)	峨邊彝族自治縣 (沙坪鎮)	峨边彝族自治县 (沙坪镇)	150,000	150,000	150,000	2395
Mabian Yizu (Yi) Autonomous County (Minjian Town)	馬邊彝族自治鎮 (民建鎮)	马边彝族自治县 (民建镇)	200,000	210,000	220,000	2304
Zigong City	自貢市	自贡市	3,270,000	3,290,000	3,230,000	4382
Ziliujing District (Dangui Subdistrict)	自流井區 (丹桂街道)	自流井区 (丹桂街道)	350,000	360,000	400,000	153
Da'an District (Longjing Subdistrict)	大安區 (龍井街道)	大安区 (龙井街道)	460,000	460,000	430,000	399
Gongjing District (Xiaoxi Subdistrict)	貢井區 (筱溪街道)	贡井区 (筱溪街道)	300,000	300,000	290,000	417
Yantan District (Yantan Town)	沿灘區 (沿灘鎮)	沿滩区 (沿滩镇)	390,000	390,000	360,000	468
Rongxian County (Xuyang Town)	榮縣 (旭陽鎮)	荣县 (旭阳镇)	700,000	700,000	670,000	1609
Fushun County (Fushi Town)	富順縣 (富世鎮)	富顺县 (富世镇)	1,070,000	1,080,000	1,070,000	1336
Luzhou City	瀘州市	泸州市	5,030,000	5,060,000	5,100,000	12,232
Jiangyang District (Dashanping Subdistrict)	江陽區 (大山坪街道)	江阳区 (大山坪街道)	640,000	650,000	680,000	649
Naxi District (Anfu Subdistrict)	納溪區 (安富街道)	纳溪区 (安富街道)	480,000	490,000	470,000	1150
Longmatan District (Lianhuachi Subdistrict)	龍馬潭區 (蓮花池街道)	龙马潭区 (莲花池街道)	350,000	350,000	370,000	333
Luxian County (Yuchan Subdistrict)	瀘縣 (玉蟾街道)	泸县 (玉蟾街道)	1,090,000	1,090,000	1,070,000	1525

(continued)

Table 29.5 (continued)

Name	Traditional	Simplified	Population (2012)	Population (2016)	Population (2020)	Area (Sq. Km)
Hejiang County (Hejiang Town)	合江縣 (合江鎮)	合江县 (合江镇)	900,000	910,000	900,000	2414
Xuyong County (Xuyong Town)	敘永縣 (敘永鎮)	叙永县 (叙永镇)	720,000	720,000	720,000	2977
Gulin County (Gulin Town)	古藺縣 (古藺鎮)	古蔺县 (古蔺镇)	850,000	850,000	880,000	3184
Yibin City	宜賓市	宜宾市	5,390,000	5,470,000	5,520,000	13,271
Cuiping District (Beicheng Subdistrict)	翠屏區 (北城街道)	翠屏区 (北城街道)	810,000	820,000	850,000	1,501
Nanxi District (Nanxi Subdistrict)	南溪區 (南溪街道)	南溪区 (南溪街道)	420,000	430,000	430,000	704
Xuzhou District (Baixi Subdistrict)	敘州區 (柏溪街道)	叙州区 (柏溪街道)	N/A	N/A	1,020,000	2,570
Yibin County[i] (Baixi Town)	宜賓縣 (柏溪鎮)	宜宾县 (柏溪镇)	1,020,000	1,030,000	N/A	(2940)
Jiang'an County (Jiang'an Town)	江安縣 (江安鎮)	江安县 (江安镇)	550,000	560,000	560,000	894
Changning County (Changning Town)	長寧縣 (長寧鎮)	长宁县 (长宁镇)	450,000	460,000	460,000	996
Gaoxian County (Qingfu Town)	高縣 (慶符鎮)	高县 (庆符镇)	530,000	530,000	490,000	1323
Yunlian County (Yunlian Town)	筠連縣 (筠連鎮)	筠连县 (筠连镇)	420,000	430,000	450,000	1256
Gongxian County (Xunchang Town)	珙縣 (巡場鎮)	珙县 (巡场镇)	420,000	430,000	430,000	1150
Xingwen County (Gusong Town)	興文縣 (古宋鎮)	兴文县 (古宋镇)	460,000	470,000	490,000	1373
Pingshan County (Pingshan Town)	屏山縣 (屏山鎮)	屏山县 (屏山镇)	310,000	310,000	310,000	1,504
Panzhihua City	攀枝花市	攀枝花市	1,120,000	1,120,000	1,080,000	7440
Dongqu District (Dadukou Subdistrict)	東區 (大渡口街道)	东区 (大渡口街道)	320,000	310,000	290,000	167
Xiqu District (Qingxiangping Subdistrict)	西區 (清香坪街道)	西区 (清香坪街道)	150,000	150,000	130,000	124
Renhe District (Renhe Town)	仁和區 (仁和鎮)	仁和区 (仁和镇)	220,000	230,000	230,000	1727
Miyi County (Panlian Town)	米易縣 (攀蓮鎮)	米易县 (攀莲镇)	220,000	220,000	220,000	2153

(continued)

Table 29.5 (continued)

Name	Traditional	Simplified	Population (2012)	Population (2016)	Population (2020)	Area (Sq. Km)
Yanbian County (Tongzilin Town)	鹽邊縣 (桐子林鎮)	盐边县 (桐子林镇)	210,000	210,000	210,000	3269
Bazhong City	巴中市	巴中市	3,880,000	3,940,000	3,680,000	12,292
Bazhou District (Dongcheng Subdistrict)	巴州區 (東城街道)	巴州区 (东城街道)	1,380,000	820,000	790,000	1407
Enyang District (Dengke Subdistrict)	恩陽區[j] (登科街道)	恩阳区 (登科街道)	N/A	610,000	570,000	1159
Tongjiang County (Nuojiang Town)	通江縣 (諾江鎮)	通江县 (诺江镇)	770,000	770,000	730,000	4116
Nanjiang County (Nanjiang Town)	南江縣 (南江鎮)	南江县 (南江镇)	680,000	690,000	660,000	3383
Pingchang County (Tongzhou Subdistrict)	平昌縣 (同州街道)	平昌县 (同州街道)	1,050,000	1,050,000	950,000	2227
Dazhou City	達州市	达州市	6,860,000	6,920,000	6,660,000	16,605
Tongchuan District (Dongcheng Subdistrict)	通川區 (東城街道)	通川区 (东城街道)	430,000	580,000	590,000	901
Dachuan District[k] (Sanliping Subdistrict)	達川區 (三里坪街道)	达川区 (三里坪街道)	N/A	1,200,000	1,170,000	2245
Wanyuan City (Taiping Town)	萬源市 (太平鎮)	万源市 (太平镇)	590,000	600,000	570,000	4065
Daxian County[l] (Nanwai Town)	達縣 (南外鎮)	达县 (南外真)	1,360,000	N/A	N/A	(2695)
Xuanhan County (Dongxiang Town)	宣漢縣 (東鄉鎮)	宣汉县 (东乡镇)	1,300,000	1,330,000	1,290,000	4271
Kaijiang County (Xinning Town)	開江縣 (新寧鎮)	开江县 (新宁镇)	600,000	610,000	590,000	1033
Dazhu County (Zhuyang Subdistrict)	大竹縣 (竹陽街道)	大竹县 (竹阳街道)	1,100,000	1,120,000	1,090,000	2077
Quxian County (Qujiang Town)	渠縣 (渠江鎮)	渠县 (渠江镇)	1,480,000	1,480,000	1,340,000	2013
Ziyang City	資陽市	资阳市	5,020,000	5,060,000	3,460,000	5757
Yanjiang District (Yulian Subdistrict)	雁江區 (玉蓮街道)	雁江区 (玉莲街道)	1,090,000	1,100,000	1,080,000	1632
Jianyang City[m] (Jiancheng Subdistrict)	簡陽市 (簡城街道)	简阳市 (简城街道)	1,470,000	1,480,000	N/A	(2214)

(continued)

Table 29.5 (continued)

Name	Traditional	Simplified	Population (2012)	Population (2016)	Population (2020)	Area (Sq. Km)
Lezhi County (Tianchi Town)	樂至縣 (天池鎮)	乐至县 (天池镇)	850,000	860,000	810,000	1425
Anyue County (Yueyang Town)	安岳縣 (岳陽鎮)	安岳县 (岳阳镇)	1,600,000	1,620,000	1,580,000	2700
Meishan City	眉山市	眉山市	3,490,000	3,500,000	3,450,000	7134
Dongpo District (Suci Subdistrict)	東坡區 (蘇祠街道)	东坡区 (苏祠街道)	850,000	860,000	880,000	1331
Renshou County (Wenlin Subdistrict)	仁壽縣 (文林街道)	仁寿县 (文林街道)	1,590,000	1,600,000	1,540,000	2606
Pengshan District (Fengming Town)	彭山區 (鳳鳴鎮)	彭山区 (凤鸣镇)	340,000	330,000	330,000	465
Hongya County (Hongchuan Town)	洪雅縣 (洪川鎮)	洪雅县 (洪川镇)	350,000	350,000	350,000	1896
Danling County (Danling Town)	丹棱縣 (丹棱鎮)	丹棱县 (丹棱镇)	160,000	160,000	160,000	449
Qingshen County (Qingzhu Subdistrict)	青神縣 (青竹街道)	青神县 (青竹街道)	200,000	200,000	190,000	387
Ya'an City	雅安市	雅安市	1,540,000	1,560,000	1,530,000	15,303
Yucheng District (Qingjiang Subdistrict)	雨城區 (青江街道)	雨城区 (青江街道)	350,000	350,000	340,000	1070
Mingshan District (Mengyang Town)	名山區 (蒙陽鎮)	名山区 (蒙阳镇)	270,000	280,000	280,000	614
Yingjing County (Yandao Town)	滎經縣 (嚴道鎮)	荥经县 (严道镇)	150,000	150,000	150,000	1782
Hanyuan County (Fulin Town)	漢源縣 (富林鎮)	汉源县 (富林镇)	320,000	330,000	320,000	2388
Shimian County (Xinmian Subdistrict)	石棉縣 (新棉街道)	石棉县 (新棉街道)	120,000	120,000	120,000	2678
Tianquan County (Chengxiang Town)	天全縣 (城廂鎮)	天全县 (城厢镇)	150,000	150,000	150,000	2491
Lushan County (Luyang Subdistrict)	蘆山縣 (蘆陽街道)	芦山县 (芦阳街道)	120,000	120,000	120,000	1166
Baoxing County (Muping Town)	寶興縣 (穆坪鎮)	宝兴县 (穆坪镇)	60,000	60,000	60,000	3114

(continued)

Table 29.5 (continued)

Name	Traditional	Simplified	Population (2012)	Population (2016)	Population (2020)	Area (Sq. Km)
Aba Zangzu (Ngawa Tibetan) and Qiangzu (Qiang) Autonomous Prefecture	阿壩藏族羌族自治州	阿坝藏族羌族自治州	900,000	930,000	900,000	85,131
Ma'erkang (Barkam) County[n] (Ma'erkang Town)	馬爾康縣 (馬爾康鎮)	马尔康县 (马尔康镇)	60,000	N/A	N/A	(6639)
Ma'erkang (Barkam) City (Ma'erkang Town)	馬爾康市 (馬爾康鎮)	马尔康市 (马尔康镇)	N/A	60,000	50,000	6633
Wenchuan County (Weizhou Town)	汶川縣 (威州鎮)	汶川县 (威州镇)	100,000	100,000	90,000	4084
Lixian County (Zagunao Town)	理縣 (雜谷腦鎮)	理县 (杂谷脑镇)	50,000	50,000	40,000	4318
Maoxian County (Fengyi Town)	茂縣 (鳳儀鎮)	茂县 (凤仪镇)	100,000	110,000	110,000	3903
Songpan County (Jin'an Town)	松潘縣 (進安鎮)	松潘县 (进安镇)	70,000	80,000	70,000	9339
Jiuzhaigou County (Nanping Town)	九寨溝縣 (南坪鎮)	九寨沟县 (南坪镇)	70,000	70,000	70,000	5290
Jinchuan (Quqên) County (Jinchuan Town)	金川縣 (金川鎮)	金川县 (金川镇)	70,000	70,000	70,000	5550
Xiaojin County (Meixing Town)	小金縣 (美興鎮)	小金县 (美兴镇)	80,000	80,000	80,000	5571
Heishui County (Luhua Town)	黑水縣 (蘆花鎮)	黑水县 (芦花镇)	60,000	60,000	60,000	4154
Rangtang (Camtang; Zamtang) County (Rangke [Zamkog] Town)	壤塘縣 (壤柯鎮)	壤塘县 (壤柯镇)	40,000	40,000	50,000	6836
Aba (Ngawa) County (Aba Town)	阿壩縣 (阿壩鎮)	阿坝县 (阿坝镇)	70,000	80,000	80,000	10,435
Ruo'ergai (Zoigê) County (Dazhasi Town)	若爾蓋縣 (達扎寺鎮)	若尔盖县 (达扎寺镇)	80,000	80,000	80,000	10,620
Hongyuan County (Qiongxi Town)	紅原縣 (邛溪鎮)	红原县 (邛溪镇)	40,000	50,000	50,000	8398

(continued)

Table 29.5 (continued)

Name	Traditional	Simplified	Population (2012)	Population (2016)	Population (2020)	Area (Sq. Km)
Ganzi (Garzê) Zangzu (Tibetan) Autonomous Prefecture	甘孜藏族自治州	甘孜藏族自治州	1,070,000	1,110,000	1,100,000	152,629
Kangding County (Lucheng Town)	康定縣 (爐城鎮)	康定县 (炉城镇)	110,000	N/A	N/A	(11,486)
Kangding City (Lucheng Town)	康定市 (爐城鎮)	康定市 (炉城镇)	N/A	110,000	110,000	11,486
Luding County (Luqiao Town)	瀘定縣 (瀘橋鎮)	泸定县 (泸桥镇)	90,000	90,000	90,000	2165
Danba County (Zhanggu Town)	丹巴縣 (章谷鎮)	丹巴县 (章谷镇)	60,000	60,000	60,000	4656
Jiulong County (Ga'er Town)	九龍縣 (呷爾鎮)	九龙县 (呷尔镇)	60,000	70,000	60,000	6766
Yajiang County (Hekou Town)	雅江縣 (河口鎮)	雅江县 (河口镇)	50,000	50,000	50,000	7558
Daofu (Dawu) County (Xianshui Town)	道孚縣 (鮮水鎮)	道孚县 (鲜水镇)	60,000	60,000	60,000	7053
Luhuo (Draggo; Zhaggo) County (Xindu Town)	爐霍縣 (新都鎮)	炉霍县 (新都镇)	50,000	50,000	50,000	4601
Ganzi (Garzê) County (Ganzi Town)	甘孜縣 (甘孜鎮)	甘孜县 (甘孜镇)	70,000	70,000	70,000	7303
Xinlong County (Rulong Town)	新龍縣 (茹龍鎮)	新龙县 (茹龙镇)	50,000	50,000	50,000	8570
Dege (Dêgê) County (Gengqing Town)	德格縣 (更慶鎮)	德格县 (更庆镇)	80,000	80,000	90,000	11,025
Baiyu County (Jianshe Town)	白玉縣 (建設鎮)	白玉县 (建设镇)	50,000	50,000	60,000	10,386
Shiqu (Sêrxü) County (Niga Town)	石渠縣 (尼呷鎮)	石渠县 (尼呷镇)	90,000	110,000	100,000	24,944
Seda (Sêrtar) County (Seke [Sêrkog] Town)	色達縣 (色柯鎮)	色达县 (色柯镇)	50,000	50,000	60,000	9332
Litang County (Gaocheng Town)	理塘縣 (高城鎮)	理塘县 (高城镇)	60,000	70,000	70,000	13,677
Batang County (Xiaqiong Town)	巴塘縣 (夏邛鎮)	巴塘县 (夏邛镇)	50,000	50,000	50,000	7852
Xiangcheng County (Xiangbala Town)	鄉城縣 (香巴拉鎮)	乡城县 (香巴拉镇)	30,000	30,000	30,000	5016

(continued)

Table 29.5 (continued)

Name	Traditional	Simplified	Population (2012)	Population (2016)	Population (2020)	Area (Sq. Km)
Daocheng County (Jinzhu Town)	稻城縣 (金珠鎮)	稻城县 (金珠镇)	30,000	30,000	30,000	7323
Derong (Dêrong) County (Songmai Town)	得榮縣 (松麥鎮)	得荣县 (松麦镇)	30,000	30,000	30,000	2916
Liangshan Yizu (Yi) Autonomous Prefecture	涼山彝族自治州	凉山彝族自治州	4,790,000	4,990,000	5,300,000	60,423
Xichang City (Beicheng Subdistrict)	西昌市 (北城街道)	西昌市 (北城街道)	620,000	640,000	680,000	2655
Yanyuan County (Yanjing Town)	鹽源縣 (鹽井鎮)	盐源县 (盐井镇)	380,000	390,000	390,000	8388
Dechang County (Dezhou Subdistrict)	德昌縣 (德州街道)	德昌县 (德州街道)	200,000	210,000	220,000	2284
Huili County (Chengbei Subdistrict)	會理縣 (城北街道)	会理县 (城北街道)	460,000	460,000	460,000	4527
Huidong County (Huidong Subdistrict)	會東縣 (魚城街道)	会东县 (鱼城街道)	410,000	420,000	430,000	3227
Ningnan County (Ningyuan Town)	寧南縣 (寧遠鎮)	宁南县 (宁远镇)	190,000	190,000	200,000	1667
Puge County (Puji Town)	普格縣 (普基鎮)	普格县 (普基镇)	170,000	180,000	220,000	1905
Butuo County (Temuli Town)	布拖縣 (特木里鎮)	布拖县 (特木里镇)	170,000	180,000	220,000	1685
Jinyang County (Tiandiba Town)	金陽縣 (天地壩鎮)	金阳县 (天地坝镇)	180,000	190,000	210,000	1587
Zhaojue County (Xincheng Town)	昭覺縣 (新城鎮)	昭觉县 (新城镇)	280,000	300,000	340,000	2699
Xide County (Guangming Town)	喜德縣 (光明鎮)	喜德县 (光明镇)	210,000	220,000	230,000	2206
Mianning County (Gaoyang Subdistrict)	冕寧縣 (高陽街道)	冕宁县 (高阳街道)	370,000	390,000	410,000	4423
Yuexi County (Yuecheng Town)	越西縣 (越城鎮)	越西县 (越城镇)	320,000	340,000	370,000	2257
Ganluo County (Xinshiba Town)	甘洛縣 (新市壩鎮)	甘洛县 (新市坝镇)	210,000	220,000	240,000	2156

(continued)

Table 29.5 (continued)

Name	Traditional	Simplified	Population (2012)	Population (2016)	Population (2020)	Area (Sq. Km)
Meigu County (Bapu Town)	美姑縣 (巴普鎮)	美姑县 (巴普镇)	240,000	260,000	280,000	2573
Leibo County (Jincheng Town)	雷波縣 (錦城鎮)	雷波县 (锦城镇)	250,000	260,000	280,000	2932
Muli Zangzu (Tibetan) Autonomous County (Qiaowa Town)	木里藏族自治縣 (喬瓦鎮)	木里藏族自治县 (乔瓦镇)	130,000	140,000	140,000	13,252

[a]Chongqing City was made an independent municipality in 1997
[b]Does not include the Bazhong Economic Development Zone
[c]Made subordinate to Chengdu in 2016
[d]Created out of Pixian county on 24 November 2016
[e]Renamed Zhaohua district in March 2013
[f]Changed from Anxian county to Anzhou district 20 May 2016
[g]Established in 2013
[h]County made a city on 12 July 2019
[i]Dissolved in 2018, establishing Xuzhou district
[j]Created in 2013, taking parts of Bazhou district
[k]Made a district in 2013
[l]Made a district in 2013
[m]Made subordinate to Chengdu in 2016
[n]Made into a city in 2013

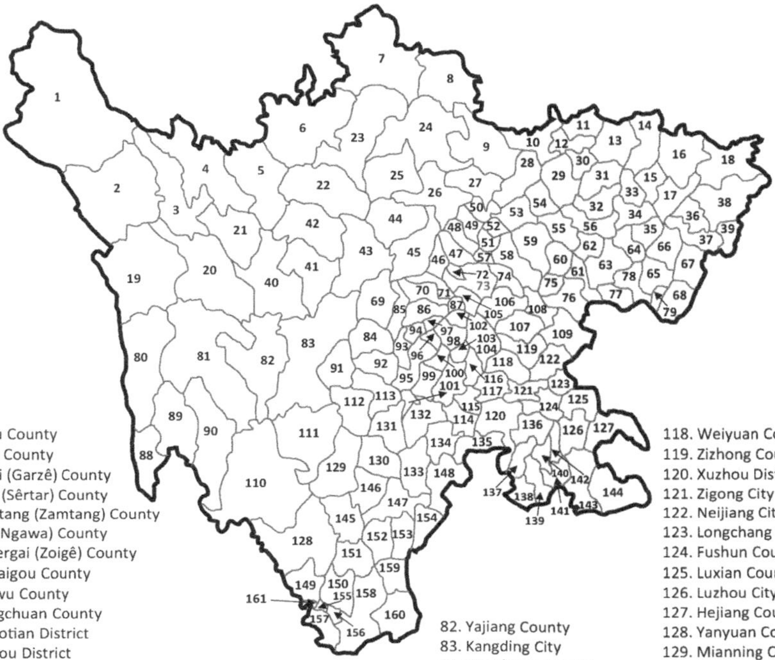

1. Shiqu County
2. Dege County
3. Ganzi (Garzê) County
4. Seda (Sêrtar) County
5. Rangtang (Zamtang) County
6. Aba (Ngawa) County
7. Ruo'ergai (Zoigê) County
8. Jiuzhaigou County
9. Pingwu County
10. Qingchuan County
11. Chaotian District
12. Lizhou District
13. Wangcang County
14. Nanjiang County
15. Sezhou District
16. Tongjiang County
17. Pingchang County
18. Wanyuan City
19. Baiwu County
20. Xinlong County
21. Luhuo (Draggo) County
22. Ma'erkang (Barkam) City
23. Hongyuan County
24. Songpan County
25. Heishui County
26. Maoxian County
27. Beichuan Qiang Autonomous County
28. Jiangyou City
29. Jiange County
30. Zhaohua District
31. Cangxi County
32. Langzhong City
33. Siyang District
34. Yilong County
35. Yingshan County
36. Tongchuan District
37. Dachuan District
38. Xuanhan County
39. Kaijiang County
40. Daofu County
41. Danba County
42. Jinchuan County
43. Xiaojin County
44. Lixian County
45. Wenchuan County
46. Dujiangyan City
47. Pengzhou City
48. Shifang City
49. Mianzhu City
50. Anzhou District
51. Deyang City
52. Luojiang District
53. Mianyang City
54. Zitong County
55. Yanting County
56. Nanbu County
57. Guanghan City
58. Zhongjiang County
59. Santai County
60. Shehong City
61. Pengxi County
62. Xichong County
63. Nanchong City
64. Peng'an County
65. Guang'an City
66. Quxian County
67. Dazhu County
68. Linshui County
69. Baoxing County
70. Dayi County
71. Chongzhou City
72. Pidu District
73. Chengdu City
74. Jintang County
75. Daying County
76. Anju District
77. Wusheng County
78. Yuechi County
79. Huaying City
80. Batang County
81. Litang County
82. Yajiang County
83. Kangding City
84. Tianchuan County
85. Lushan County
86. Qionglai City
87. Xinjin County
88. Derong County
89. Xiangcheng County
90. Daocheng County
91. Luding County
92. Yingjing County
93. Ya'an City
94. Mingshan County
95. Hongya County
96. Danling County
97. Pujiang County
98. Meishan City
99. E'meishan City
100. Jiajiang County
101. Leshan City
102. Pengshan District
103. Qingshen County
104. Renshou County
105. Shuangliu District
106. Jianyang City
107. Yanjiang District
108. Lezhi County
109. Anyue County
110. Muli Tibetan Autonomous County
111. Jiulong County
112. Shimian County
113. Hanyuan County
114. Muchuan County
115. Qianwei County
116. Jingyan County
117. Rongxian County
118. Weiyuan County
119. Zizhong County
120. Xuzhou District
121. Zigong City
122. Neijiang City
123. Longchang County
124. Fushun County
125. Luxian County
126. Luzhou City
127. Hejiang County
128. Yanyuan County
129. Mianning County
130. Yuexi County
131. Ganluo County
132. Ebian Yi Autonomous County
133. Meigu County
134. Mabian Yi Autonomous County
135. Pingshan County
136. Yibin City
137. Gaoxian County
138. Junlian County
139. Gongxian County
140. Changning County
141. Xingwen County
142. Jiang'an County
143. Xuyong County
144. Gulin County
145. Xichang City
146. Xide County
147. Zhaojue County
148. Leibo County
149. (Renhe District jurisdiction)
150. Mixi County
151. Dechang County
152. Puge County
153. Butuo County
154. Jinyang County
155. Dongqu District
156. Yanbian County
157. Renhe District
158. Huili County
159. Ninnan County
160. Huidong County
161. Xiqu District

Fig. 29.2 Sichuan Province: subdistricts (Provincial Capital City: Chengdu City). (Drawn by the Author after People's Republic of China, Ministry of Civil Affairs. (MCA 2020))

References

Bagley, Robert. 1999. Shang archaeology. In *The Cambridge history of ancient China: From the origins of civilization to 221 B.C*, ed. Michael Loewe and Edward L. Shaughnessy, 124–231. New York: Cambridge University Press.

Cao, Shuji. 2003. Population of Sichuan separate prefectures in mid-Qing dynasty—looking at 1812 data. *Chinese Economic History Research*. 曹树基. 清代中期四川分府人口: 以 1812 年数据为心. 中国经济史研究. No. 1: 92–105.

Gernet, Jacques. 1962. *Daily life in China: On the eve of the Mongol invasion*, 1250–1276. Stanford: Stanford University Press.

Hsieh, Chiao-min, and Jean Kan Hsieh. 1995. *China: a provincial atlas*. New York: Macmillan Publishing.

Jia, T. 1998. An analysis of the situation of China's floating population. *China's Population Today* 15: 13–14.

Lu, Liancheng, and Yan Wenming. 2005. Society during the three dynasties. In *The formation of Chinese civilization: An archaeological perspective*, ed. Kwang-chih Chang et al., 202–247. New Haven: Yale University Press.

Ministry of Civil Affairs (MCA), People's Republic of China. 2020. *County/township administration handbook*. Beijing: China Statistics Press. 中華人民共和國民政部, 中華人民共和國,鄉鎮行政區劃簡冊.

Olsen, John W., W. John, and Sari Miller-Antonio. 1992. The Palaeolithic [sic] in southern China. *Asian Perspectives* 31 (2): 144–145; 151.

Sichuan News Network (SNN). 2011. *All 56 ethnic groups in the country are distributed in Sichuan, and the Yi, Tibetan and Qiang ethnic groups are among the top three ethnic minorities*. 4 July. 全国56个民族在四川均有分布 彝藏羌族居少数民族前三位," 四川新闻网. http://www.民族宗教网.中国/html/report/217984-1.htm.

Sichuan Province Bureau of Statistics (SPBS). 2021. *Communiqué of the seventh national population census of Sichuan Province*, Issue No. 2. 26 May. 四川省第七次全国人口普查公报, 第二号. http://tjj.sc.gov.cn/scstjj/tjgb/2021/5/26/68cf8ce902a44c389e72591bd5a31ca2.shtml.

Tan, Qixiang, ed. 1996. *The historical atlas of China, volume VI*. Beijing: China Cartographic Publishing House.

Tian, Kai. 2011. *Reconstruction and change of local urban landscape in the Qing dynasty: Chengdu as research center in the 17th–19th century*. Chengdu: Sichuan Publishing Group. 田凯. 清代地方城市景观的重建与变迁: 以17-19世纪成都为研究中心. 成都: 四川出版集团.

von Glahn, Richard. 2013. Cycles of silver in chinese monetary history. In *The economy of lower Yangzi delta in late imperial China: Connecting money, markets and institutions*, ed. Billy Kee Long So, 221–254. New York: Routledge.

Xiao, Jiansheng. 2009. *Reflections on Chinese civilization*. Hong Kong: New Century Press. 蕭建生. 中國文明的反思. 香港: 新世紀出版社.

Xu, Wenbin. 1984. *Collection of historical and archaeological works of Chongqing municipal museum*. Chongqing City: Shapingba District Educational Bureau. 徐文彬. 重庆市博物馆历史考古文集. 重庆市: 沙坪坝区教育局.

Yang, Jisheng. 2012. *Tombstone: the great Chinese famine, 1958–1962*. Trans. Stacy Mosher and Guo Jian. New York: Farrar, Straus and Giroux.

Zhang, Shunan. 2021. *The 2020 per capita income list of residents in various provinces: Shanghai is the richest, and it has risen sharply*. Finance.people.com. 22 January. 张澍楠. 2020年各省份居民人均收入榜: 上海最有钱, 这地涨得猛. http://finance.people.com.cn/n1/2021/0122/c1004-32008733.html.

Chapter 30
Tianjin City

Abstract Built upon a salt mine monopoly in ca. 200 BCE, Tianjin City today is a major port city that, along with Shanghai, Beijing and Chongqing now has provincial-level status. Now with the largest manmade harbor in all of China at Xingang (literally 'new harbor'), Tianjin ("Shanghai of the north") has long been a key maritime link to not only Beijing but for all of China. Supplying large amounts of salt through the Tang dynasty (ca. 700 CE), it continues to produce this vital product today. Long considered a militarily significant city, it was subjected to foreign military invasion about 125 years after Qing Dynasty made Tianjin a prefecture in 1725. In 2015, Tianjin City made international news when a massive chemical explosion, due to improper storage of hazardous materials, leveled large sections of the Binhai New District area, killing at least 165 people. As a city, Tianjin still ranks well in terms of gross domestic product (GDP) when compared to mainland China's 31 provinces and major cities. But it is its relatively high per capita income (USD $6800, as of 2020), however, that probably drives many Chinese residents of other regions to move there for job opportunities.

E. Croddy, *China's Provinces and Populations*,
https://doi.org/10.1007/978-3-031-09165-0_30

Tianjin City (天津市 *tiānjīn shì*): Abbreviation (津 *jīn*) (Fig. 30.1)

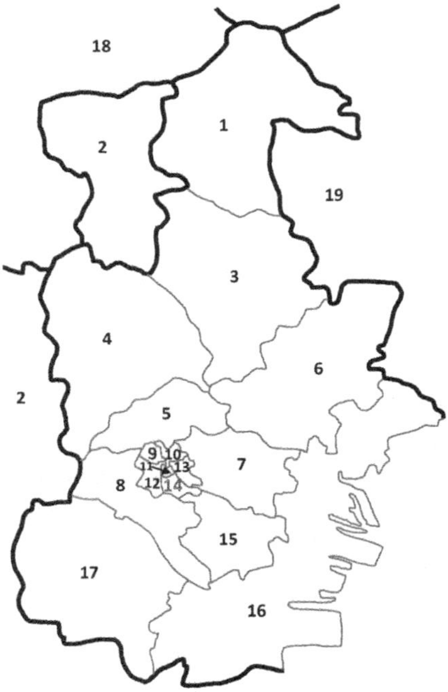

1. Jixian County
2. * (Hebei Province) Langfang City
3. Baodi District
4. Wuqing District
5. Beichen District
6. Ninghe District
7. Dongli District
8. Xiqing District
9. Hongqiao District
10. Hebei District
11. Heping District
12. Nankai District
13. Hedong District
14. Hexi District
15. Jinnan District
16. Binhai Xinqu (new district)
17. Jinghai District
18. * Beijing City
19. * (Hebei Province) Tangshan City

Fig. 30.1 Tianjin city subdistricts (Capital City Governmental Seat: Hexi District). (Drawn by the Author after People's Republic of China, Ministry of Civil Affairs, MCA 2020)

Tianjin City: General Impressions

By the end of the Qing dynasty, a popular saying described the character of people living in the three main cities: "Beijing City people are slick talkers; Tianjin City people have the gift of gab, while those in Baoding City are government errand runners" (Sohu.com 2020) Traditionally, Tianjin city was looked upon as the first line defense of Beijing. Nowadays, as a Chinese travel guide notes, even though it is located close as it is to the capital of Beijing, Tianjin's culture is decidedly different, where even in a big city one can be relaxed. Tianjin is also well regarded for its richly endowed folk art scene to include its own version of rhythmic story telling (天津快板 *tiānjīn kuàibǎn*) (Shang-Ch'i 2017).

Located on the Bohai Gulf, occupying salty marshes and wetlands Tianjin ("Emperor's Ford") has long been key for transportation during China's riverine (漕運 *cáoyùn*) period of development (e.g., Sui and Yuan dynasties). An abundance of coal and fish also made Tianjin a vital economic hub in its own right. Tianjin City (see also Beijing section) is one of the three metropolises that will eventually comprise the future "Jing-Jin-Ji" megacity, combining Beijing (京 *jīng*), Hebei (冀 *jì*) and Tianjin (津 *jīn*) into political-economic zone of over 130 million people by ca. 2030.

Historical Sketch of Tianjin

As mentioned in the Guan Zi (管子 *guǎnzǐ*), the Bohai region during the Spring and Autumn period (770–476 BCE) was well known as a bountiful source of salt (Bun 2001). In ca. 100 BCE, the Western Han dynasty established a salt monopoly in the Wuqing area, northwest of present-day Tianjin City. By the year 2 CE, this region had a population of about 64,000, but a combination of war and famine in the sixth century brought its population down to 9000. By the Sui dynasty (ca. 600 CE) and the building of the Beijing-Hangzhou canal, the Sanhe tributary (三合岔河 *sānhé chàhé*) contributed greatly to the area's now flourishing economic development (China.com 2019).

Nearby Lutai (蘆台 *lútái*) and Baodi (寶坻 *bǎodǐ*) became significant salt field and storage areas, respectively, by the Tang dynasty (618–907 CE). Even today, Tianjin represents at least 25% of all Chinese sea salt produced every year, notably at the Changlu (長蘆 *chánglú*) salt fields. At this time, the region of modern-day Tianjin had a population of about 82,000. In addition to this profitable industry, Tianjin also became an important port for moving grain and silk up and down China's coast, as well as to shore up and supply food in the defense of the north against "barbarians" (Lee 2005).

In the Yuan Dynasty (thirteenth century), a military center at Haijin township (海津鎮 *hǎijīnzhèn)* was established, forming a defensive redoubt at the meeting of southern and northern Great Canals. Its population then hovered around 62,000 (Hsieh and Hsieh 1995). A vital port for transportation of goods by the Ming dynasty, the Tianjin area, since ancient times known as Zhigu (直沽 *zhígū*), continued to serve as a significant military stronghold.

Sources differ as to the origins of the more modern name Tianjin. Some report that it was named by the famous minister Qu Yuan (屈原 *qūyuán*, d. 278 BCE), or it was from a reference to an astronomical constellation. But most popular is the story that, in 1404, the Ming Yongle emperor Zhu Di (朱棣 *zhū dì*) bestowed the name upon the newly-constructed Tianjin Garrison (天津衛 *tiānjīnwèi*) the 'Emperor's ford (天子津渡 *tiānzǐjīndù*),' in honor of his passage on his way to overthrow his nephew. By 1406, the military population of Tianjin reached about 16,800 (Bun 2001).

By the Qing dynasty, Tianjin was raised to the level of a prefecture (州 *zhōu*) in 1725. The Opium Wars in the nineteenth century led to a Franco-British assault on Tianjin in 1858, representing yet another "humiliating" episode in China's relations with the West. This onerous and punitive invasion of Chinese territory concluded with the infamous "Treaty of Tianjin," compelling the imperial Qing government to open its lands and port facilities to foreign trade in 1860. Decades later, the Boxer Rebellion targeted foreign settlements in 1900, attacking Christian missionaries and other civilians, resulting in the Battle of Tientsin (Tianjin) or Relief of Tientsin. The weakened and vacillating Qing dynastic court essentially gave support to the Boxers in these assaults, and Chinese troops participated in fighting against eight foreign nations, including Japanese, French, British, German, and American forces. These foreign nations ultimately rallied together to lift the siege.

The perfidy of the Chinese imperial court and the viciousness of the Boxers were answered by numerous atrocities committed by Western troops, to include American, French, Germans and Russians, who looted, raped and pillaged Chinese towns and villages. In contrast, Japanese soldiers acquitted themselves slightly more honorably (van de Ven 2006). Savage fighting also spilled over in Beijing, and Boxers slaughtered Chinese Christians there. (In the middle of all of this chaos, a young Herbert Hoover, who had been in Tianjin as a mining engineer, was forced to contend with these harrowing events.) The old city walls that survived for centuries were largely destroyed by the time of the Boxer Rebellion, and now form the foundation for Tianjin's modern roadways (Hsieh and Hsieh 1995).

Today, Chinese military leadership reminds its audiences that the route of foreign depredations, be they the 1840 Opium Wars or the Japanese invasion in the 1930s, often utilized maritime assaults against the Tianjin region, which would then immediately threaten the Beijing capital area. Thus the strategic nature of this very important city for the Chinese (Wu 2003). Going back to the Ming dynasty, a relatively large portion of Tianjin's population were made up by imperial soldiers. The estimates below give us a basic idea of this martial population from the seventeenth to the twentieth centuries (Tables 30.1 and 30.2):

By 1840, Tianjin had a population of about 200,000, and as the port opened to international commerce the number of its inhabitants increased to 300,000 by 1860. Previously subordinate to the Chinese (CCP) government since the 1949 founding of the PRC, Tianjin was put under the jurisdiction of Hebei province until 1967.

Modern Tianjin City

On 7 April 1970, Tianjin undertook its own development of an underground subway, called "Project 7047", for the year, 1970, month (4), and day (7) for the founding of current Tianjin metro rail system. In 1973, five of the current Tianjin subordinate entities were formally placed under Tianjin City jurisdiction: Jizhou, Baodi, and Wuqing districts, as well as Jinghai and Ninghe counties (薊縣 *jìxiàn*, 寶坻 *bǎodǐ*, 武清 *wǔqīng*, 靜海 *jìnghǎi*, 寧河 *nínghé*). The devastating Tangshan City earthquake on 28 July 1976 greatly impacted Tianjin as well. Tianjin City suffered over 24,000 dead, and 700,000 people made homeless.

It was only by 1984 (following China's reforming and opening up) that Tianjin's economic development got underway in earnest, albeit nowhere to the degree of

Table 30.1 Green Banner troops stationed at Tianjin, Qing dynasty (Gao 2002)

1686	30,700
1727	33,938
1758	44,348
1785	39,402
1812	42,532
1821	41,689
1849	41,355
1887	44,992

Table 30.2 Historical population data, Tianjin (Gao 2002)

Year	Number of households	Total population
1903	64,693	326,552
1904	72,720	377,634
1905	65,452	339,871
1906	63,472	356,503
1928	170,686	869,139
1929	178,865	884,226
1930	179,676	864,477
1933	188,867	1,110,567
1934	221,180	1,021,671
1935	229,449	1,071,072
1936	227,228	1,081,072
1937	237,608	1,132,263
1938	237,009	1,114,029
1939	256,923	1,232,004
1940	261,448	1,274,792
1941	267,532	1,210,150
1942	285,482	1,426,098
1943	299,951	1,524,365
1944	336,618	1,800,039
1945	322,583	1,759,513
1947[a]	333,416	1,710,910
1948	377,483	1,860,818

[a]1946 data unavailable

China's southern special economic zones. In 1994, Tianjin City undertook a strategic economic development program, and, by 1995, the master plan for the development of the Tianjin Binhai New Area (天津濱海新區 *tiānjīn bīnhǎi xīnqū*) was approved, making it one of the largest economic development initiatives in China. At this time the area of Tianjin occupied 11,000 km^2, while today it is estimated at about 12,000 km^2.

In 2010, the Binhai New District contributed to over half of Tianjin City's entire GDP. In 2011, Chinese developers anticipated that the Tianjin Binhai New District would increase its gross development product (GDP) an average of 20%, and could total a trillion Yuan by 2015. Then chief of the Binhai New District told the China Daily that.

> To better hone the economic structure and transform the development pattern, we must seek growth by cultivating three internationally leading hubs in the Tianjin Binhai New Area—namely, in the aerospace and aviation, the petrochemical, and the alternative energy industries. (Wang and Xiaozheng 2011)

In 2015, Tianjin City had a published gross domestic product (GDP) of USD $256 billion, but had fallen to $219 billion in 2020, ranking 23rd out of mainland China's 31 provinces and major cities, just below Inner Mongolia. But in terms of per capita income, Tianjin came in at fourth at $6820 (Zhang 2021). Tianjin City's population growth (7.2%) has been relatively robust, with a permanent (*hukou*) registered population of 10,820,000 in 2020 (Table 30.5). Based on the 2020 census (Table 30.4) of its typical residential population (13,866,000), this suggests a great number of Tianjin's residents originally hail from other regions in China (and elsewhere).

Tianjin City population statistics for the years between the founding of the PRC and the year 2020 are below (Table 30.3).

12 August 2015 ("8.12") Tianjin Binhai New District (Area) Explosion

Close to midnight (Beijing local time) on 12 August 2015, two large explosions ripped apart the Ruihai (瑞海 *ruìhǎi*) hazardous materials storage facility at the Binhai New District harbor complex, killing 165 people. Improperly stored nitrocellulose, in combination with nearby ammonium nitrate fertilizer at the Ruihai shipyard, contributed to the massive destruction of the Binhai district area. The first blast registered 15 tons of TNT equivalent, while the second triggered an explosion of about 430 tons TNT (Gui et al. 2016). Damage to buildings (broken walls, windows) extended two kilometers in radius from the epicenter.

While the exact cause of the disaster has yet to be fully understood, poor handling and storage of hazardous materials were likely the source. (Similar disasters have occurred elsewhere, such as the Texas City explosion in April 1947, in which nitrate fertilizer accidentally detonated). Adding to the concern of residents and the Chinese government, about 700 tons of sodium cyanide were also stored near the site of the explosion at the time. People's Liberation Army (PLA) anti-chemical troops (防化兵 *fánghuàbīng*) were called in to assist with monitoring for chemical hazards and for remediation.

Table 30.3 Tianjin city population 1953–2010 (TCBS 2012)

Year	Population (total)
1953	2,693,831
1982	7,764,141
1990	8,785,402
2000	9,848,731
2010	12,938,224

Table 30.4 Tianjin city population (Residential 常住人口 *chángzhù rénkǒu*) data (TCBS 2021)

Tianjin subordinate districts and counties[a]	Population (2010)	Population (2020)
Heping District 和平區 *hépíng qū*	273,466	355,000
Hedong District 河東區 *hédōng qū*	860,852	858,787
Hexi District 河西區 *héxī qū*	870,632	822,174
Nankai District 南開區 *nánkāi qū*	1,018,196	890,422
Hebei District 河北區 *héběi qū*	788,368	647,702
Hongqiao District 紅橋區 *hóngqiáo qū*	531,526	483,130
Dongli District 東麗區 *dōnglì qū*	569,955	857,027
Xiqing District 西青區 *xīqīng qū*	684,690	1,195,124
Jinnan District 津南區 *jīnnán qū*	593,063	928,066
Beichen District 北辰區 *běichén qū*	669,031	909,643
Wuqing County 武清縣 *wǔqīng xiàn*	949,413	1,151,313
Baodi County 寶坻縣 *bǎodǐ xiàn*	799,057	722,367
Binhai New District 濱海新區 *bīnhǎi xīnqū*	2,482,065	2,063,718
Ninghe County 寧河縣 *zhùhé xiàn*	416,143	395,314
Jinghai County 靜海縣 *jìnghǎi xiàn*	646,978	787,106
Jizhou District 薊州區 *jìzhōu qū*	784,789	795,516
Total	**12,938,224**	**13,866,009**

[a]Population data for subdistricts not available as of 29 August 2021

Table 30.5 shows the *hukou* (family registered) populations based on PRC Ministry of Civil Affairs data. (Districts listed directly under major cities are government seats, as are those in parentheses). One can compare these data with the census (usual residential populations based on 2010 and 2020 censuses in Table 30.4.

Tianjin City (津 *jīn*) and Subdistricts

Table 30.5 Tianjin city: permanent registered (戶籍人口 *hùjí rénkǒu*) populations (MCA 2020)

Name	中文	Simplified	Population (2012)	Population (2016)	Population (2020)	Area (km²)
Tianjin City	天津市	天津市	9,900,000	9,960,000	10,820,000	11,903
Hexi District (Dayingmen Subdistrict)	河西區 (大營門街街道)	河西区 (大营门街道)	800,000	800,000	850,000	37
Heping District (Xiaobailou Subdistrict)	和平區 (小白樓街街道)	和平区 (小白楼街道)	400,000	400,000	440,000	10
Hedong District (Dawangzhuangjie Subdistrict)	河東區 (大王莊街街道)	河东区 (大王庄街道)	710,000	740,000	870,000	39
Nankai District (Changhongjie Subdistrict)	南開 (長虹街街道)	南开区 (长虹街道)	860,000	850,000	870,000	39
Hebei District (Wanghailou Subdistrict)	河北區 (望海樓街道)	河北区 (望海楼街道)	630,000	620,000	630,000	27
Hongqiao District (Xiyuzhuangjie Subdistrict)	紅橋區 (西於莊街街道)	红桥区 (西于庄街道)	540,000	520,000	510,000	21
Dongli District (Zhangguizhuangjie Subdistrict)	東麗區 (張貴莊街街道)	东丽区 (张贵庄街道)	350,000	360,000	400,000	460
Xiqing District (Yangliuqing Town)	西青區 (楊柳青鎮)	西青区 (杨柳青镇)	370,000	380,000	440,000	545
Jinnan District (Xianshuigu Town)	津南區 (鹹水沽鎮)	津南区 (咸水沽镇)	410,000	420,000	490,000	401
Beichen District (Guoyuanxincunjie Subdistrict)	北辰區 (果園新村街街道)	北辰区 (果园新村街道)	370,000	380,000	430,000	478
Wuqing District (Yunhexijie Subdistrict)	武清區 (運河西街街道)	武清区 (运河西街道)	870,000	860,000	990,000	1570
Baodi District (Baoping Subdistrict)	寶坻區 (寶平街道)	宝坻区 (宝平街道)	670,000	680,000	730,000	1523
Binhai New District (Xingang Subdistrict)	濱海新區 (新港街道)	滨海新区 (新港街道)	1,120,000	1,160,000	1,380,000	2270
Jizhou District (Wenchangjie Subdistrict)	薊州區 (文昌街街道)	蓟州区 (文昌街道)	830,000	840,000	870,000	1593
Ninghe District (Lutai Town)	寧河區 (蘆台鎮)	宁河娶区 (芦台镇)	380,000	390,000	410,000	1414
Jinghai District (Jinghai Town)	靜海區 (靜海鎮)	静海区 (静海镇)	560,000	580,000	610,000	1476

References

Bun, Kwan Man. 2001. *The salt merchants of Tianjin: State-making and civil society in late imperial China*. Honolulu: University of Hawai'i Press.

China.com. 2019. *Brief introduction of Tianjin*. April 11. http://www.china.org.cn/china/2019-04/11/content_74669254.htm.

Gao, Yanlin. 2002. [Tianjin population study: 1404–1949]. Tianjin: Tianjin People's Press. 高艳林. 天津人口研究: 1404–1949. 天津: 天津人民出版社.

Gui, Fu, Jianhao Wang, and Mingwei Yan. 2016. Anatomy of Tianjin port fire and explosion: Process and causes. *Process Safety Progress* 35 (3): 216–220.

Hsieh, Chiao-min, and Jean Kan Hsieh. 1995. *China: A provincial atlas*. New York: Macmillan Publishing.

Lee, Khoon Choy. 2005. *Pioneers of modern China: Understanding the inscrutable Chinese*. River Edge: World Scientific.

Ministry of Civil Affairs (MCA), People's Republic of China. 2020. [County/township administration handbook]. Beijing: China Statistics Press. 中華人民共和國民政部, 中華人民共和國, 鄉鎮行政區劃簡冊.

Shang-Ch'i Guide. 2017. [Backpacking in China: The most complete collection of self-guided travel for China, 2018]. Taipei: Shang-Ch'i Shitai Publishing. 2018 最完整的中國自助旅遊全集. 台北: 上奇時代.

Sohu.com. 2020. [Capital slick talking, ingratiating gab, and running dogs of Baoding prefecture: What does this Beijing saying mean?]. May 11. 京油子卫嘴子, 保定府的狗腿子, 这句北京俗语是什么意思? https://www.sohu.com/a/394509293_118889.

Tianjin City Bureau of Statistics (TCBS). 2012. [Bulletin of the main data of the sixth national population census in Tianjin in 2010]. February 28. 天津市 2010 年第六次全国人口普查主要数据公报. http://www.stats.gov.cn/tjsj/tjgb/rkpcgb/dfrkpcgb/201202/t20120228_30405.html.

———. 2021. [Bulletin on the main data of the seventh national population census in Tianjin in 2020, no. 2]. May 21. 天津市 2020 年第七次全国人口普查主要数据公报, 第 2 号. http://stats.tj.gov.cn/tjsj_52032/tjgb/202105/t20210521_5457330.html.

van de Ven, Hans. 2006. Robert Hart and Gustav Detring during the Boxer Rebellion. *Modern Asian Studies* 40 (3): 631–662.

Wang, Yu, and Rong Xiaozheng. 2011. Tianjin Binhai new area to propel development. *China Daily*. January 17. http://www.chinadaily.com.cn/m/tianjin/e/2011-01/17/content_11871945.htm.

Wu, Ningxian. 2003. *A survey of Chinese military geography*. Changsha: National Defense Technology University Press.

Zhang, Shunan. 2021. [The 2020 per capita income list of residents in various provinces: Shanghai is the richest, and it has risen sharply]. Finance.people.com. January 22. 张澍楠. 2020年各省份居民人均收入榜: 上海最有钱, 这地涨得猛. http://finance.people.com.cn/n1/2021/0122/c1004-32008733.html.

Chapter 31
Tibet

Abstract Evidence of human activity in Tibet goes back at least four thousand years. Beginning about 500 BCE, the Zhangzhung Kingdom reportedly lasted for over a thousand years, until the Tibetan Kingdom was established in ca. 600 CE. While paying tribute to the conquering Mongols of the Yuan dynasty (ca. 1200 CE), Tibet historically remained relatively autonomous, remaining so throughout the Ming, with Buddhist sectarian warfare erupting in the seventeenth century. Conquered and administered under the Qing, republican China allowed Tibet uneven autonomy, until finally being brought under repressive rule under the Chinese Communist Party. By the twentieth century, Beijing's policy of developing the western provinces through migration has caused real or perceived Han chauvinism towards Tibetans, leading to occasions of violent protests. Among China's poorest provinces among the mainland's 31 provinces and major cities, it falls last in terms of gross domestic product (GDP) and second last in per capita income.

E. Croddy, *China's Provinces and Populations*,
https://doi.org/10.1007/978-3-031-09165-0_31

Tibet Autonomous Region (西藏自治區 *xīzàng zìzhìqū*): Abbreviation (藏 *zàng*) (Fig. 31.1)

Fig. 31.1 Tibet Major cities and Prefectures (Provincial City: Lhasa City). Drawn by the Author after People's Republic of China, Ministry of Civil Affairs. (MCA 2020)

Tibet: General Impressions

High in altitude, rich in Buddhist culture, and generally under the constant oppressive thumb of the Chinese Communist Party (CCP), the so-called Tibet Autonomous Region (西藏自治區 *xīzàng zìzhìqū*) is one of the most spectacular and unique places in the world. The capital city of Lhasa (拉薩 *lāsà*) is written using the Chinese character transcription of the Tibetan for "Land of the Gods" (*Lha Sa*). Classical Tibetan refers to Tibet as "Bod," although modern pronunciation is closer to "p'ö."

The precise origins of the Chinese name Xizang (西藏 *xīzàng*) for Tibet are somewhat controversial. And while it is certainly true that that Tibet is mentioned in Sui dynasty (581–618 CE) sources, there is no support for the name "Tubo." Upon the founding of Tibet (629 CE), Tang sources referred to the kingdom to the west as Tufan (吐蕃 *tǔfān* in ca. 634). As Endymion Wilkinson writes,

> Tufan is referred to in medieval Türkic sources as *Tubbat* and medieval Arabic sources as *al-Tibbat* (from the Mongolian word transcribed into Chinese as Tubote (土伯特 *tǔbótè*) from which Tibet in English and other Western languages is derived. It referred to greater Tibet. Tobote, however, did not become the standard name for Tibet in Chinese itself. The Mongols divided greater Tibet into separate units, outside the administration of China, establishing an Office for the Pacification of central and southern Tibet proper, naming it Wusizang (烏思藏 *wūsīzàng*), from the Tibetan toponyms *dBus* (center), the Lhasa area; and *gTsang* (short for *gTsangbu* for river), the valley of the Upper Yalu river. The Ming used Xifan (西番 *xī fán*) or the newer Wusizang (also Weizang 衛藏 *wèi zàng*) for Tibet proper (Wilkinson 2012).

Thus, the English name itself, Tibet, makes its own circuitous journey from eastern and western contacts. But the Chinese name, Xizang also goes though some of its own linguistic hurdles. As the Qing dynasty came to power, the Manchu language transliterated Weizang (衛藏 *wèi zàng*) as "*wargi Dzang*." *Wargi* is similar to the

Manchurian word for "western," thus later named "Western Dzang," i.e., Xizang (西藏 *xīzàng*).

Prehistoric Tibet

Earliest Neolithic evidence of human habitation has been found at Karuo (Karub) Town (卡若鎮 *kǎruò zhèn*) in Qamdo (Chamdo) City (昌都市 *chāngdū shì*). Specimens excavated there have been dated between 4000–2000 BCE, and include painted and textured pottery vessels. Its prehistoric inhabitants hunted local deer as well as the small Tibetan antelope, and may have raised pigs. The Qugong Culture (曲貢文化 *qūgòng wénhuà*) site, located about three miles north of Lhasa, includes over thirty graves in one cemetery. Based on this evidence, it is estimated a community of substantial size thrived there in ca. 1750 BCE. This settlement also relied heavily both on hunting and domesticating animals. Pre-Buddhist sites dated 400–100 BCE have also been found at Sasongtang (薩松塘墓群 *sàsōngtáng mùqún*) and Gebusailu (格布塞魯墓群 *gébùsāilǔ mùqún*) cemeteries. Excavations in two ancient burial complexes revealed bone, bronze, and iron objects (Aldenderfer and Zhang 2013).

The historical (and somewhat legendary) kingdom of Zhangzhung (Shangshung)[1] in the western regions of Tibet reportedly lasted from 500 BCE to 625 CE. Tibet, at least during the early Qin state era (ca. 230 BCE), was regarded by the Chinese as being inhabited by barbarian tribes, what the Chinese called the Qiang (羌 *qiāng*), or Xiqiang (西羌 *xīqiāng*, i.e., western), and Faqiang (髮羌 *fǎqiāng*: literally, the "Hairy" Qiang), among others.

While we are less certain of the exact parameters of Zhangzhung, the founding of the Tibetan empire begins with Namri Songsten (囊日論贊 *nángrì lùnzàn*), who forcefully consolidated rival and neighboring clans in 608 CE. After Namri Songsten was murdered (poisoned) in 618 CE, his son Songsten Gampo (松贊干布 *sōngzàn gānbù*), born in Mozhugonka County (墨竹工卡縣 *mòzhúgōngkǎ xiàn*; aka Maizhokunggar; Meldro Gungkar), Gyama (甲瑪鄉 *jiǎmǎ xiāng*) Township, took charge at the tender age of thirteen (Peissel 2002). Most famously, Songsten Gampo is credited with having brought Buddhism to Tibet, and he was later held to be the embodiment of the bodhisattva Avalokiteśvara.

The legend has it that the Tibetan emperor dispatched Thonmi Sambhota (along with other young scholars) to India (633 CE) to learn their script. Upon his return, so the story goes, Thonmi Sambhota devised the written Tibet language and systematized its grammar. Remnants of the birthplace of Thonmi Sambhota have reportedly been discovered in Lhünzê County (隆子縣 *lóngzi xiàn*), Lhünzê town (隆子鎮 *lóngzi zhèn*). By this time, the capital of Tibet had been established at Luosuo City

[1] Also Xang Xung; Chinese transcribed: 象雄 (*xiàngxióng*).

(邏些城 *luósuòchéng*), in modern-day Lhasa. The Tibetan kingdom would grow ever westward, rivalling the Tang dynastic empire: to modern-day Afghanistan to the west, north to the Hami City oasis (哈密市 *hāmì shì*), Xichang to the east, and southward to the Indian border.

The traditional histories have it that Songsten Gampo personally led an assault on the Chinese city to the east, Songzhou (松州 *sōngzhōu*), located in modern-day Sichuan, Songpan County (松潘縣 *sōngpān xiàn*). Meanwhile, Tibet was also reaching out to the Chinese imperial court, sending diplomatic envoys to Chang'an. Ultimately defeated by Tang armies in September 638, Songsten Gampo (after giving substantial tribute) arranged to marry the Chinese princess Wen Cheng (641), establishing a détente of sorts between the two empires. Indeed, peace largely reigned for over 10 years until the passing of Songsten Gampo (d. 649). (Lin 2015).

From about 650 CE, conflict resumed between the Tibetans and the Tang emperor Wu Zetian (武則天 *wǔ zétiān*), while the distraction of the An Lushan Rebellion (安史之亂 *ānshǐ zhīluàn*; 755–763) gave Tibet an opportunity to expand its borders, even occupying the Chinese capital of Chang'an (長安 *cháng'ān*), albeit for just about 2 weeks. The Tibetan occupation of northern territories included modern-day Dunhuang (敦煌 *dūnhuáng*), Gansu Province, in 787 CE (Norbu 2001). (Tibetan language and many other priceless documents were preserved there in the famous Dunhuang grottoes, and were accidentally uncovered there in June 1900.)

Balkanization of Tibet began under the "anti-Buddhist" Langdarma (838 CE–842 CE), who persecuted Buddhists and was finally assassinated by a monk. While a Buddhist revival occurred in the mid-10th century, Tibet would remain fissiparous until the Mongolian period (Kapstein 2000). The Song dynasty (ca. eleventh century) made use of Tibetan warriors to combat its nomadic rivals (barbarian vs. barbarian), while employing Tibetan territory in the west to keep the rival Tanguts (Xixia 西夏 *xīxià*) at bay. Tibetan regions then included Amdo (安多 *ānduō*), modern-day Qinghai province, and Kham (康 *kāng*).

In 1207, after the Mongols had begun their assault on the neighboring Tanguts (*Xixia*), Tibet made the strategically astute decision to provide tribute to Chingghis Khan. Later, Sakya Pandita (d. 1251), born to the powerful Khön family and a famed Buddhist scholar himself, arranged again to negotiate a modus vivendi with the Mongolian Khan, Godan (Khodan; 1206–1251), the grandson of Chinnghis. Under this arrangement, Tibet maintained considerable autonomy (unusual for a subject of the Yuan empire), and was administered under the Yuan "Commission for Buddhist and Tibetan Affairs" (宣政院 *xuānzhèngyuàn*). (Norbu 2001).

Apart from administrative functions and conducting population surveys, such as one in 1268: "130,000 households" (Zhang and Jingxuan 1999), the Mongols largely left the rule of Tibetan territory to the monasteries, which existed under the patronage of powerful families (Stein 2013). An unbroken succession of 19 Sakya rulers continued from 1251 to 1358. Afterward, from the end of Yuan and during the Ming dynasty (1368 until 1642), Tibet was essentially an independent kingdom, but ruled as much by lay officials than religious orders.

Tibet in the seventeenth century was marked by intra-Buddhist, sectarian warfare. On the one side was the Kamarpa or "Red Hat" sect, backed by the King of Tsang (Karma Tenkyong) of west-central Tibet. Their rival was the expansionist Gulugpa (Gelukpa) sect of the Dalai Lamas, or the "Yellow Hats." With the 5th Dalai Lama (Ngwang Lozang Gyatso; 1617–1682) in ascendancy, and considered to be the incarnate lama of the Gelugpa sect, he requested the Qoshot (alt. Koshot, 和碩特 *héshuòtè*) Mongol Gushri Khan to smite his Red Hat rivals. Starting with Lhasa (1638), Gushri Khan conquered the Tsang region by 1642 (Grunfeld 2015), whereupon the 5th Dalai Lama began his reign over Tibet. In that same year and already looking forward, the "Great Fifth" Dalai Lama sent a delegation as friendly emissary to the Manchurian court in Shenyang (then known as Mukden, or 盛京 *shèngjīng*), Liaoning Province. Manchu invasion and Qing dynastic rule (1644–1911) held Tibet as more of a satrap than a subordinated province. As for Tibet's relationship with the Manchurian court, an authority on the subject has this to say:

> [T]here can be no question regarding the subordination of Tibet to Manchu-ruled China following the chaotic era of the sixth and seventh Dalai Lamas in the first decades of the 18th century… By mid-19th century, if not earlier, Manchu Chinese influence was miniscule (Goldstein 1989).

Tibet remained an autonomously-ruled entity with Qoshot Mongolian support. But the interloping action of Qoshot Mongol Lajang Khan (1707), and controversy of the true identity of the 7th Dalai Lama irked the Tibetans, who asked the Djungar Mongols to get rid of Lajang Khan. [The Djungar or Zunghar (from *züüngar* 準噶爾 *zhǔngáěr*, Mongolian "left hand") originally descended from the Eleuths (Oirat 厄魯特蒙古 *èlǔtè ménggǔ*; or Altai (western) Mongolians)]. After they attacked Lhasa in 1717, Lajang was killed and chaos ensued. The Manchus were finally able to send a military force capable of defeating the Djungar Mongols in 1720. Significantly, the Manchurians then installed the 7th Dalai Lama, Kelzang Gyatso (1708–1758).

From October 1720 onward, Chinese control over Tibet was more pronounced and integrated, leaving a garrison of about 3000 troops in Lhasa. Manchurian interest in Tibet was piqued and challenged in 1723 when the Qoshot Mongols, possibly in cahoots with the Dalai Lama, attempted a return to power. Qing imperial military forces ruthlessly put this revival down (Brook 2010). From 1724, the Manchus ruled Tibet much like the Mongolians, allowing for substantial local autonomy while controlling its military and administrative functions. Tibet in 1737 had a population of about 8 million (Guo 2016).

Responding once again to outsider threats, this time from the south, Tibet was attacked twice by Nepal-based Gurkhas in the late eighteenth century, the second time in 1791. The invaders had made their way to Rikaze City (日喀則市 *rìkāzé shì*). The Qing sent a division sized force (up to as many as 15,000 troops), pushing the Gurkhas within about ten miles outside Kathmandu, Nepal.

During the Sino-Sikh War (1841–1842), Tibet was invaded from Ladakh. Both Chinese and Tibetan forces were able to repulse the attack by the Sikhs, but overextended themselves in Ladakh, leading to the Treaty of Chushul (September 1842) which reestablished the antebellum borders (Guo 2016).

British Invasion

A century later, in ca. 1902, Lord Curzon, British Governor-General of India, was convinced that Russia had designs on Tibet:

> I am myself a firm believer in the existence of a secret understanding, if not a secret treaty, between Russia and China about Tibet: and as I have before said, I regard it as a duty to frustrate this little game while there is still time (Grunfeld 2015).

Based on such rumors that China might cede Tibet to Russia (threatening bordering colonial India), Britain launched a military expedition against Tibet in 1903 (Lal 2008). The leader of this military adventure was Sir Francis Younghusband, who eventually made his way to Lhasa in August 1904. With the Dalai Lama having already absconded to Mongolia, and the decrepit Qing Dynasty unable to do much about it in any case, Britain managed to work out an indemnity arrangement under the Anglo Chinese Treaty (1906). Within this agreement, China still retained Tibet but the British held trading and other extraterritorial rights, such as trading posts in the following areas:

Table 31.1 Tibetan populations: seventeenth and eighteenth century estimates. (Yang and Changwen 2005)

Year	Population
1661	1,159,980
1685	1,200,422
1724	1,269,170
1749	1,315,296
1757	1,330,407
1762	1,339,940
1767	1,349,542
1786	1,386,657
1787	1,388,639
1788	1,390,610
1789	1,392,639
1790	1,394,600
1791	1,491,401
1812	1,489,281
1819	1,487,156
1829	1,485,034

- Gartok (噶大克 *gádàkè*; now Gar County (噶爾縣 *gá'ěr xiàn*), Garyarsa Town (噶爾雅沙鎮 *gáěryăshā zhèn*)
- Gyangzê Town (江孜鎮 *jiāngzī zhèn*); and
- Dromo County (Yadong 亞東縣 *yàdōng xiàn*)

As it happened, Younghusband never did find any evidence of Sino-Russian collusion regarding Tibet (Grunfeld 2015).

Qing Dynasty control over Tibet solidified with the occupation of Lhasa by General Zhong Yin (鍾穎 *zhōngyǐng*) in February 1910. However, with the 1911 overthrow of the Qing dynasty, Tibet regained its self-proclaimed independence (in 1913) after the 13th Dalai Lama returned, who ruled Tibet until 1933. The Republic of China and other nations (including Britain) claimed Tibet was part of China. In 1935, Tibet had a population of about 3,720,000 (Guo 2016).

Tibet was its own entity during the chaos of the Sino-Japanese war and the post-World War II Chinese civil conflict. In fall 1950, Mao Zedong's People's Liberation Army (PLA) forces were ordered to attack after Tibet failed to answer entreaties to "peaceful liberation," that is, the subjugation of Tibet to China once and for all. On 7 October 1950, the PLA attacked Chamdo (昌都 *chāngdū*), ultimately defeating the independent Tibetan state.

In a plaintive letter, written on behalf of the Tibetans by the Indian representative in Lhasa (14 November 1950):

> The slender tie that Tibet maintained with China after the 1911 revolution became less justified when China went underwent a further revolution and turned into a full-fledged Communist state. There can be no kinship or sympathy between such divergent creeds as those espoused by China and Tibet. [However], Tibet recognizes that she is in no position to resist. It is thus that she agreed to negotiate on friendly terms with the Chinese government… The problem is simple. The Chinese claim Tibet as part of China (Goldstein 2007).

Suing for peace, the Tibetans signed the "Seventeen-Point Agreement on the Peaceful Liberation of Tibet" on 23 May 1951. Distraught at this turn of events, the 14th (and still in exile) Dalai Lama (Tenzin Gyatso b. 1935) could only observe from afar in Dromo (aka Yadong 亞東 *yàdōng*) near the Indian border. For the first time in over a millennium, Tibet was forced to sign away her independence and formally recognize Chinese suzerainty (Goldstein 1997).

1959 Tibetan Uprising

Following rumors the PLA was plotting to kidnap the Dalai Lama, anti-Chinese communist agitation among Tibetans reached the tipping point. Beginning on 10 March 1959, protests in Lhasa developed into armed rebellion. The PLA crushed the Tibetan uprising after weeks of fighting against Tibetan rebels, and the 14th Dalai Lama fled to India.

The Great Leap Forward (1958–1962) did not have the same impact upon Tibet as it did other provinces in China. Due to its remote location, it was able to escape much of the forced communalization that went on in the rest of China. Thus, the scale of hunger and tragedy of the Great Leap Forward was not as pronounced in Tibet (Yang 2007). Records from that time (1960) indicate that food rations actually increased for Tibetans while the rest of China lacked food. Indeed, favoring food deliveries to Tibet may have been done as a means to solidify and pacify Tibet following the rebellion of 1959 (Wemheuer 2014).

In the early twenty-first century, Tibetan hostility towards Chinese governmental policies as well as anti-Han (and Hui) sentiment surfaced upon the 49th anniversary of the March 1959 uprising. Exacerbating tensions, China's policy of opening up the west for economic development (西部大開 *xībùdàkāi*) has brought a large influx of Han Chinese into Tibet, leading to claims of Han chauvinism against local Tibetans (Dickson 2016). On the morning of the 14th March 2008, monks from Ramoche temple (小昭寺 *xiǎozhāo sì*) in Lhasa turned over a patrol vehicle, and that afternoon fights broke out. Widespread Tibetan violence ensued against ethnic Han-owned businesses. Hundreds of Chinese were killed both during the riot, and as many as a hundred Tibetans were killed after China's paramilitary response (Smith 2010).

Tibetan Population and Economy

In 2013, Tibet had a resident population of 3,175,500, up from just over 3 million in 2010. By 2020 it totaled 3,648,100, with a registered permanent (*hukou*) population of 3,320,000 that same year (Table 31.2). To the extent that this difference in number reflects the movement of Tibetans out of their homeland to find opportunities in other regions of China, the poor state of Tibetan economic figures no doubt plays a role. Economically it ranked last in 2015 and 2020, with a gross domestic product (GDP) of USD $16 billion and $30 billion, respectively. Its per capita income of $3381 ranks second last of mainland China's 31 provinces and major cities (Zhang 2021) (Tables 31.3 and 31.4).

Table 31.5 (below) shows the *hukou* (family registered) populations based on PRC Ministry of Civil Affairs data. (Districts listed directly under major cities are government seats, as are those in parentheses). One can compare these data with the census (usual residential populations based on 2010 and 2020 censuses in Tables 31.3 and 31.4 (below):

Table 31.2 Population data for Tibet. (Ma 2007)

1912	1,660,000
1919	1,594,600
1925	1,538,000
1928	1,509,700
1931	1,481,300
1936	1,434,300
1946	1,000,000
1952	1,150,000
1953	1,270,000
1955	1,274,000
1956	1,274,000
1957	1,274,000
1958	1,274,000
1959	1,190,000–1,228,000
1960	1,269,800
1961	1,298,700
1962	1,301,700
1963	1,323,800
1964	1,346,700
1965	1,371,200
1966	1,396,700
1967	1,424,100
1968	1,451,600
1969	1,480,500
1970	1,512,000
1971	1,553,800
1972	1,592,800
1973	1,629,200
1974	1,661,200
1975	1,691,100
1976	1,724,000
1977	1,756,200
1978	1,788,200
1979	1,828,200
1980	1,852,800
1981	1,859,600
1982	1,892,500
1983	1,931,400
1984	1,966,800
1985	1,994,800

(continued)

Table 31.2 (continued)

1986	2,024,900
1987	2,079,500
1988	2,123,100
1989	2,159,100
1990	2,180,500
1991	2,217,800
1992	2,252,700
1993	2,288,800
1994	2,319,800
1995	2,355,500
1996	2,393,000
1997	2,427,400
1998	2,453,900
1999	2,477,200
2000	2,512,300
2001	2,537,000
2002	2,554,400
2003	2,592,100
2004	2634,400
2005	2,675,500
2006	2,685,800

Table 31.3 Tibet population (2010 and 2020 Census Data). (TBS 2021)

Prefecture/County	Population (2010)	Population (2020)
Lhasa City 拉薩市 *lāsà shì*	559,423	867,891
Changdu (Qamdo) City 昌都市 *chāngdū shì*	657,505	760,966
Rikaze City (Xigazê/Shigatse) 日喀則市 *rìkāzé shì*	703,292	798,153
Shannan City (Lhoka) 山南市 *shānnán shì*	328,990	354,035
Linzhi (Nyingchi) City林芝市 *línzhī shì*	195,109	238,936
Ali (Ngari) Prefecture 阿里地區 *ālǐ dìqū*	95,465	123,281
Naqu (Nagqu) Prefecture 那曲地區 *nàqū dìqū*	462,382	504,838
Total	**3,002,166**	**3,648,100**

Table 31.4 Tibet: population data of cities and their subordinate sectors. (SPBS 2021) (Fig. 31.2)

Cities and subordinate sectors, population (2020 census)	Subordinate district, city and county populations (2020)	Total population (2020)
Lhasa City 拉薩市 ***lāsà shì***		**867,891**
Chengguan District 城關區 *chéngguān qū*	473,586	
Duilongdeqing (Doilungdêqên) District 堆龍德慶區 *duīlóngdéqìng qū*	91,065	
Dazi (Dagzê) District 達孜區 *dázī qū*	32,318	
Linzhou (Lhünzhub) County 林周縣 *línzhōu xiàn*	50,596	
Dangxiong (Damxung) County 當雄縣 *dāngxióng xiàn*	47,900	
Nimu (Nyêmo) County 尼木縣 *nímù xiàn*	29,989	
Qushui (Qüxü) County 曲水縣 *qūshuǐ xiàn*	41,851	
Mozhugongka (Maizhokunggar) County 墨竹工卡縣 *mòzhúgōngkǎ xiàn*	49,511	
Lhasa National Economic and Technology Development Zone 拉薩國家經濟技術開發區 *lāsà guójiā jīngjìjìshù kāifāqū*	11,804	
Xizang (Tibet) Cultural Tourism Innovation Park 西藏文化旅游創意園區 *xīzàng wénhuà lǚyóuchuàngyìyuánqū*	4689	
Lhasa Liuwu High Technology Zone 拉薩柳梧高新區 *lāsà liǔwú gāoxīnqū*	34,582	
Changdu (Qamdo) City 昌都市 ***chāngdū shì***		**760,966**
Karuo (Karub) District 卡若區 *kǎruò qū*	148,511	
Jiangda (Jomda) County 江達縣 *jiāngdá xiàn*	92,800	
Leiwuqi (Riwoqê) County 類烏齊縣 *lèiwūqí xiàn*	58,856	
Dingqing (Dêngqên) County 丁青縣 *dīngqīng xiàn*	98,677	
Chaya (Zhag'yab) County 察雅縣 *cháyǎ xiàn*	57,065	
Zuogong (Zogang) County 左貢縣 *zuǒgòng xiàn*	46,608	
Mangkang (Markam) County 芒康縣 *mángkāng xiàn*	79,001	
Luolong (Lhorong) County 洛隆縣 *luòlóng xiàn*	53,185	
Bianba (Banbar) County 邊壩縣 *biānbà xiàn*	42,716	
Gongjue (Gonjo) County 貢覺縣 *gòngjué xiàn*	40,009	
Basu (Baxoi) County 八宿縣 *bāsù xiàn*	43,538	
Rikaze City (Xigazê/Shigatse) 日喀則市 ***rìkāzé shì***		**798,153**
Sangzhuzi (Samzhubzê) District 桑珠孜區 *sāngzhūzī qū*	158,290	
Nanmulin (Namling) County 南木林縣 *nánmùlín xiàn*	83,531	
Jiangzi (Gyangzê) County 江孜縣 *jiāngzī xiàn*	68,650	
Dingri (Tingri) County 定日縣 *dìngrì xiàn*	58,173	
Sajia (Sa'gya) County 薩迦縣 *sàjiā xiàn*	48,766	
Lazi (Lhazê) County 拉孜縣 *lāzī xiàn*	56,355	
Angren (Ngamring) County 昂仁縣 *ángrén xiàn*	55,108	
Xietongmen (Zhetongmön) County 謝通門縣 *xiètōngmén xiàn*	45,573	
Bailang (Bainang) County 白朗縣 *báilǎng xiàn*	44,564	
Renbu (Rinbung) County 仁布縣 *rénbù xiàn*	33,530	
Kangma (Kangmar) County 康馬縣 *kāngmǎ xiàn*	20,864	

(continued)

Table 31.4 (continued)

Cities and subordinate sectors, population (2020 census)	Subordinate district, city and county populations (2020)	Total population (2020)
Dingjie (Dinggyê) County 定結縣 *dìngjié xiàn*	20,362	
Zhongba County 仲巴縣 *zhòngbā xiàn*	26,897	
Yadong (Dromo; Chomo) County 亞東縣 *yàdōng xiàn*	15,449	
Jilong (Gyirong) County 吉隆縣 *jílóng xiàn*	17,536	
Nielamu (Nyalam) County 聶拉木縣 *nièlāmù xiàn*	17,009	
Saga County 薩嘎縣 *sàgā xiàn*	16,220	
Gangba (Kamba) County.崗巴縣 *gǎngbā xiàn*	11,276	
Shannan City (Lhoka) 山南市 ***shānnán shì***		**354,035**
Naidong (Nêdong) County 乃東區 *nǎidōng qū*	81,608	
Zhanang (Chanang) County 扎囊縣 *zānáng xiàn*	36,656	
Gongga (Konggar) County 貢嘎縣 *gònggā xiàn*	53,701	
Sangri County 桑日縣 *sāngrì xiàn*	18,041	
Qiongjie (Qonggyai) County 瓊結縣 *qióngjié xiàn*	15,199	
Qusong (Qusum) County 曲松縣 *qūsōng xiàn*	12,962	
Cuomei (Comai) County 措美縣 *cuòměi xiàn*	12,132	
Luozha (Lhozhag) County 洛扎縣 *luòzā xiàn*	19,865	
Jiacha (Gyaca) County 加查縣 *jiāchá xiàn*	23,534	
Longzi (Lhünzê) County 隆子縣 *lóngzǐ xiàn*	33,570	
Cuona (Cona) County 錯那縣 *cuònà xiàn*	13,932	
Langkazi (Nagarzê) County 浪卡子縣 *làngkǎzǐ xiàn*	32,835	
Linzhi (Nyingchi) City 林芝市 ***línzhī shì***		**238,936**
Bayi District 巴宜區 *bāyí qū*	84,254	
Gongbujiangda (Gongbo'gyamda) County 工布江達縣 *gōngbùjiāngdá xiàn*	32,874	
Milin (Mainling) County 米林縣 *mǐlín xiàn*	26,176	
Motuo (Mêdog) County 墨脱縣 *mòtuō xiàn*	14,889	
Bomi (Bomê) County 波密縣 *bōmì xiàn*	34,858	
Chayu (Zayü) County 察隅縣 *cháyú xiàn*	28,237	
Langxian (Nang) County 朗縣 *lǎngxiàn*	17,648	
Ali (Ngari) Prefecture 阿里地區 ***ālǐ dìqū***		**123,281**
Pulan (Burang) County 普蘭縣 *pǔlán xiàn*	12,242	
Zhada (Zanda) County 札達縣 *zhádá xiàn*	8454	
Ga'er (Gar) County 噶爾縣 *gá'ěr xiàn*	31,052	
Ritu (Rutog) County 日土縣 *rìtǔ xiàn*	11,167	
Geji (Gêgyai) County 革吉县 *géjí xiàn*	18,012	
Gaize (Gêrzê) County 改則縣 *gǎizé xiàn*	25,327	
Cuoqin (Coqên) 措勤縣 *cuòqín xiàn*	17,027	
Naqu (Nagqu) Prefecture 那曲地區 ***nàqū dìqū***		**504,838**
Seni District 色尼區 *sèní qū*	104,490	
Jiali (Lhari) County 嘉黎縣 *jiālí xiàn*	38,797	
Biru County 比如縣 *bǐrú xiàn*	72,618	
Nierong (Nyainrong) County 聶榮縣 *nièróng xiàn*	35,163	

(continued)

Table 31.4 (continued)

Cities and subordinate sectors, population (2020 census)	Subordinate district, city and county populations (2020)	Total population (2020)
Anduo (Amdo) County 安多縣 *ānduō xiàn*	39,683	
Shenzha (Xainza) County 申扎縣 *shēnzā xiàn*	21,768	
Suoxian (Sog) County 索縣 *suǒxiàn*	52,923	
Bange (Baingoin) County 班戈縣 *bāngē xiàn*	39,309	
Baqing (Baqên) County 巴青縣 *bāqīng xiàn*	56,200	
Nima (Nyima) County 尼瑪縣 *nímǎ xiàn*	33,006	
Shuanghu County 雙湖縣 *shuānghú xiàn*	10,881	

1. Ritu (Rutog) County
2. Gaize (Gêrzê) County
3. Nima (Nyima) County
4. Shuanghu County
5. Anduo (Amdo) County
6. Nierong (Nyainrong) County
7. Baqing (Baqên) county
8. Naqu (Nagqu) County
9. Biru County
10. Suoxian (Sog) County
11. Jiali (Lhari) County
12. Bianba (Banbar) County
13. Dingqing (Dêngqên) County
14. Luolong (Lhorong) County
15. Louwuqi (Riwoqê) County
16. Karuo (Karub) District
17. Chaya (Chagyab) County
18. Jiangda (Jomda) County
19. Gongjue (Gongjo) County
20. Zhada (Zanda) County
21. Ga'er (Gar) County
22. Geji (Gê'gyai) County
23. Zhongba County
24. Cuoqin (Coqên) County
25. Angren (Ngamring) County
26. Shenzha (Xainza) County
27. Bange (Baingoin) County
28. Dangxiong (Damxung) County
29. Linzhou (Lhünzhub) County
30. Mozhugongka (Maizhokunggar) County
31. Gongbujiangda (Gongbo'gyamda) County
32. Bayi District
33. Bomi (Bomê) County
34. Milin (Mainling) County
35. Motuo (Mêdog) County
36. Basu (Baxoi) County
37. Zuogong (Zogang) County
38. Mangkang (Markham) County
39. Chayu (Zayü) County
40. Xietongmen (Xaitongmoin) County
41. Nanmulin (Namling) County
42. Nimu (Nyêmo) County
43. Duilongdeqing (Doilungdêqên) District
44. Chengguan District
45. Dazi (Dagzê) County
46. Gongga (Gonggar) County
47. Zhanang (Chanang) County
48. Qiongjie (Qonggyai) County
49. Naidong (Nêdong) County
50. Kangma (Kangmar) County
51. Langkazi (Nagarzê)) County
52. Luozha (Lhozhag) County
53. Cuomei (Comai) County
54. Sangri County
55. Qusong (Qusum) County
56. Jiacha (Gyaca) County
57. Langxian (Nang) County
58. Longzi (Lhünzê) County
59. Cuona (Cona) County
60. Pulan (Burang) County
61. Saga county
62. Jilong (Gyirong) County
63. Nielamu (Nyalam) County
64. Dingri (Tingri) County
65. Lazi (Lhazê) County
66. Sajia (Sa'gya) County
67. Sangzhuzi District
68. Bailang (Bainang) County
69. Renbu County
70. Dingjie (Dinggyê) County
71. Gangba (Gamba) County
72. Jiangzi (Gyantse) County
73. Yadong (Dromo) County

Fig. 31.2 Tibet subdistricts (Capital City Governmental Seat: Chengguan District). Drawn by the Author after People's Republic of China, Ministry of Civil Affairs. (MCA 2020)

Xizang (Tibet) Autonomous Region (藏 *Zàng*)

Provincial Capital: Lasa (Lhasa)

Table 31.5 Tibet: permanent registered (戶籍人口 *hùjí rénkǒu*) populations. (MCA 2020)

Name	Traditional	Simplified	Population (2012)	Population (2016)	Population (2020)	Area (Sq. Km)
Xizang (Tibetan) Autonomous Region	西藏自治區	西藏自治区	2,940,000	3,100,000	3,320,000	1,194,047
Lasa (Lhasa) City	拉薩市	拉萨市	490,000	500,000	550,000	31,662
Chengguan (Chingoinqü) District (Jibenggang [Jebumgang] Subdistrict)	城關區 (吉崩崗街道)	城关区 (吉崩岗街道)	180,000	200,000	220,000	523
Linzhou (Lhünzhub) County (Gandanquguo [Gandainqonkor] Town)	林周縣 (甘丹曲果鎮)	林周县 (甘丹曲果镇)	60,000	60,000	60,000	4512
Dangxiong (Damxung) County (Dangquka [Damquka] Town)	當雄縣 (當曲卡鎮)	当雄县 (当曲卡镇)	50,000	50,000	50,000	12,000
Nimu (Nyêmo) County (Tarong [Tarrong] Town)	尼木縣 (塔榮鎮)	尼木县 (塔荣镇)	30,000	30,000	30,000	3275
Qushui (Qüxü) County (Qushui Town)	曲水縣 (曲水鎮)	曲水县 (曲水镇)	40,000	30,000	40,000	1680
Duilongdeqing (Doilungdêqên) County[a] (Dongga [Donggar] Town)	堆龍德慶縣 (東嘎鎮)	堆龙德庆县 (东嘎镇)	50,000	N/A	N/A	(2679)
Duilongdeqing (Doilungdêqên) District (Dongga [Donggar] Town)	堆龍德慶區 (東嘎鎮)	堆龙德庆区 (东嘎镇)	N/A	50,000	60,000	2679
Dazi (Dagzê) County (Deqing [Dêqên] Town)	達孜縣 (德慶鎮)	达孜县 (德庆镇)	30,000	30,000	30,000	1373
Mozhugonka (Maizhokunggar; Meldro Gungkar) County (Gongka [KUNGGAR] Town)	墨竹工卡縣 (工卡鎮)	墨竹工卡县 (工卡镇)	50,000	50,000	60,000	5620

(continued)

Table 31.5 (continued)

Name	Traditional	Simplified	Population (2012)	Population (2016)	Population (2020)	Area (Sq. Km)
Naqu (Nagqu) Prefecture	那曲地區	那曲地区	450,000	490,000	540,000	369,674
Seni District (Naqu Town)	色尼區 (那曲鎮)	色尼区 (那曲镇)	100,000	110,000	110,000	15,305
Jiali (Lhari) County (Azha [Arza] Town)	嘉黎縣 (阿扎鎮)	嘉黎县 (阿扎镇)	30,000	30,000	40,000	13,338
Biru County (Biru Town)	比如縣 (比如鎮)	比如县 (比如镇)	60,000	70,000	80,000	11,429
Nierong (Nyainrong) county (Nierong Town)	聶榮縣 (聶榮鎮)	聂荣县 (聂荣镇)	30,000	30,000	40,000	10,258
Anduo (Amdo) County (Panna [Pagnag] Town)	安多縣 (帕那鎮)	安多县 (帕那镇)	40,000	40,000	40,000	22,000
Shenzha (Xainza) County (Shenzha Town)	申扎縣 (申扎鎮)	申扎县 (申扎镇)	20,000	20,000	20,000	62,414
Suoxian (Sog) County (Yala [Yakla] Town)	索縣 (亞拉鎮)	索县 (亚拉镇)	50,000	50,000	50,000	5892
Bange (Baingoin) County (Pubao [Pubu] Town)	班戈縣 (普保鎮)	班戈县 (普保镇)	40,000	40,000	40,000	29,600
Baqing (Baqên) County (Laxi [Lhashé] Town)	巴青縣 (拉西鎮)	巴青县 (拉西镇)	50,000	50,000	60,000	10,301
Nima (Nyima) County (Nima Town)	尼瑪縣 (尼瑪鎮)	尼玛县 (尼玛镇)	40,000	40,000	30,000	72,500
Shuanghu County[b] (Duoma [Domar] Township)	雙湖縣 (多瑪鄉)	双湖县 (多玛乡)	N/A	10,000	10,000	116,637
Changdu (Chamdo; Qamdo) City	昌都市	昌都市	660,000	730,000	770,000	110,154
Karuo (Karub) District (Chengguan Town)	卡若區 (城關鎮)	卡若区 (城关镇)	N/A	110,000	120,000	10,652
Changdu County[c] (Chengguan Town)	昌都縣 (城關鎮)	昌都县 (城关镇)	100,000	N/A	N/A	(10,652)
Jiangda (Jomda) County (Jiangda Town)	江達縣 (江達鎮)	江达县 (江达镇)	90,000	100,000	100,000	13,200
Gongjue (Konjo; Gonjo) County (Moluo [Bolo] Town)	貢覺縣 (莫洛鎮)	贡觉县 (莫洛镇)	40,000	50,000	50,000	6256

(continued)

Table 31.5 (continued)

Name	Traditional	Simplified	Population (2012)	Population (2016)	Population (2020)	Area (Sq. Km)
Leiwuqi (Riwoqê, Riwoche) County (Sangduo [Samdo] Town)	類烏齊縣 (桑多鎮)	类乌齐县 (桑多镇)	50,000	50,000	60,000	5879
Dingqing (Dêngqên) County (Dingqing Town)	丁青縣 (丁青鎮)	丁青县 (丁青镇)	60,000	80,000	90,000	12,955
Chaya (Chagyab; Zhag'yab) County (Yanduo [Yêndum] Town)	察雅縣 (煙多鎮)	察雅县 (烟多镇)	60,000	60,000	70,000	8413
Basu (Baxoi) County (Baima Town)	八宿縣 (白瑪鎮)	八宿县 (白玛镇)	40,000	500,000	50,000	12,564
Zuogong (Zogang) County (Wangda [Woinbodoi] Town)	左貢縣 (旺達鎮)	左贡县 (旺达镇)	50,000	50,000	50,000	11,726
Mangkang (Markham) County (Gatuo [Gartog] Town)	芒康縣 (嘎托鎮)	芒康县 (嘎托镇)	90,000	90,000	90,000	11,431
Luolong (Lhorong) County (Zituo [Zito] Town)	洛隆縣 (孜托鎮)	洛隆县 (孜托镇)	40,000	50,000	60,000	8184
Bianba (Banbar) County (Caoka [Coka] Town)	邊壩縣 (草卡鎮)	边坝县 (草卡镇)	40,000	40,000	40,000	8894
Linzhi (Nyingchi) Prefecture	林芝地區	林芝地区	180,000	N/A	N/A	(116,175)
Linzhi (Nyingchi) City	林芝市	林芝市	N/A	180,000	200,000	116,175
Bayi District[d] (Shuangyonglu Subdistrict)	巴宜區 (雙擁路街道)	巴宜区 (双拥路街道)	N/A	40,000	50,000	10,237
Linzhi (Nyingchi) County (Bayi Town)	林芝縣 (八一鎮)	林芝县 (八一镇)	40,000	N/A	N/A	(10,237)
Gongbujiangda (Gongbo'gyamda) County (Gongbujiangda Town)	工布江達縣 (工布江達鎮)	工布江达县 (工布江达镇)	30,000	30,000	30,000	11,650
Milin (Mainling) County (Milin Town)	米林縣 (米林鎮)	米林县 (米林镇)	20,000	20,000	20,000	9471
Motuo (Mêdog) County (Motuo Town)	墨脫縣 (墨脫鎮)	墨脱县 (墨脱镇)	10,000	10,000	10,000	34,000

(continued)

Table 31.5 (continued)

Name	Traditional	Simplified	Population (2012)	Population (2016)	Population (2020)	Area (Sq. Km)
Bomi (Bomê) County (Zhamu [Zhamog; Zhamo] Town)	波密縣 (扎木鎮)	波密县 (扎木镇)	30,000	30,000	30,000	14,972
Chayu (Zayü) County (Zhuwagen [Drowagön] Town)	察隅縣 (竹瓦根鎮)	察隅县 (竹瓦根镇)	30,000	30,000	30,000	31,659
Langxian (Nang) County (Langzhen Town)	朗縣 (朗鎮)	朗县 (朗镇)	20,000	20,000	20,000	4186
Shannan (Lhoka) Prefecture	山南地區	山南地区	340,000	360,000	360,000	79,699
Naidong (Nêdong) County (Zedang [Zêtang] Town)	乃東區 (澤當鎮)	乃东区 (泽当镇)	60,000	60,000	60,000	2211
Zhanang (Chanang) County (Zhatang [Chatang] Town)	扎囊縣 (扎塘鎮)	扎囊县 (扎塘镇)	40,000	40,000	40,000	2157
Gongga (Konggar; Gonggar) County (Jixiong [Gyixong] Town)	貢嘎縣 (吉雄鎮)	贡嘎县 (吉雄镇)	50,000	50,000	50,000	2283
Sangri County (Sangri Town)	桑日縣 (桑日鎮)	桑日县 (桑日镇)	20,000	20,000	20,000	2634
Qiongjie (Qonggyai) County (Qiongjie Town)	瓊結縣 (瓊結鎮)	琼结县 (琼结镇)	20,000	20,000	20,000	1030
Qusong (Qusum) County (Qusong Town)	曲松縣 (曲松鎮)	曲松县 (曲松镇)	20,000	20,000	20,000	1936
Cuomei (Comai) county (Cuomei Town)	措美縣 (措美鎮)	措美县 (措美镇)	10,000	10,000	20,000	4530
Luozha (Lhozhag) County (Luozha Town)	洛扎縣 (洛扎鎮)	洛扎县 (洛扎镇)	20,000	20,000	20,000	5570
Jiacha (Gyaca) County (Anrao [Ngarrab] Town)	加查縣 (安饒鎮)	加查县 (安绕镇)	20,000	20,000	20,000	4493
Longzi (Lhünzê) County (Longzi Town)	隆子縣 (隆子鎮)	隆子县 (隆子镇)	30,000	40,000	40,000	9809
Cuona (Cona) County (Cuona Town)	錯那縣 (錯那鎮)	错那县 (错那镇)	10,000	20,000	20,000	34,937

(continued)

Table 31.5 (continued)

Name	Traditional	Simplified	Population (2012)	Population (2016)	Population (2020)	Area (Sq. Km)
Langkazi (Nagarzê) County (Langkazi Town)	浪卡子縣 (浪卡子鎮)	浪卡子县 (浪卡子镇)	40,000	40,000	40,000	8109
Rikaze (Shigatse) Prefecture	日喀則地區	日喀则地区	710,000	N/A	N/A	(182,000)
Rikaze (Shigatse) City	日喀則市	日喀则市	N/A	750,000	800,000	182,000
Rikaze City[e] (Chengnan Subdistrict)	日喀則市 (城南街道)	日喀则市 (城南街道)	110,000	N/A	N/A	(3700)
Sangzhuzi (Samzhubzê) District (Chengnan Subdistrict)	桑珠孜區 (城南街道)	桑珠孜区 (城南街道)	N/A	110,000	120,000	3700
Nanmulin (Namling) County (Nanmulin Town)	南木林縣 (南木林鎮)	南木林县 (南木林镇)	80,000	80,000	90,000	8300
Jiangzi (Gyangzê; Gyantze; Gyantse) County (Jiangzi Town)	江孜縣 (江孜鎮)	江孜县 (江孜镇)	70,000	70,000	70,000	3800
Dingri (Tingri) County (Xiege'er [Xêgar] Town)	定日縣 (協格爾鎮)	定日县 (协格尔镇)	50,000	50,000	60,000	14,000
Sajia (Sa'gya) County (Sajia Town)	薩迦縣 (薩迦鎮)	萨迦县 (萨迦镇)	50,000	50,000	50,000	6400
Lazi (Lhazê) County (Quxia [Quxar] Town)	拉孜縣 (曲下鎮)	拉孜县 (曲下镇)	50,000	60,000	60,000	4400
Angren (Ngamring) County (Kaga [Kaika] Town)	昂仁縣 (卡嘎鎮)	昂仁县 (卡嘎镇)	50,000	60,000	60,000	27,600
Xietongmen (Xaitongmoin; Zhetongmön) County (Kaga [Kaika; Chabkha; Qiaga] Town)	謝通門縣 (卡嘎鎮)	谢通门县 (卡嘎镇)	50,000	50,000	50,000	14,000
Bailang (Bainang) County (Luojiang [Norbukyungzê] Town)	白朗縣 (洛江鎮)	白朗县 (洛江镇)	50,000	50,000	50,000	2500
Renbu (Rinbung) County (Dejilin [Dê'gyiling] Town)	仁布縣 (德吉林鎮)	仁布县 (德吉林镇)	30,000	40,000	40,000	2100

(continued)

Table 31.5 (continued)

Name	Traditional	Simplified	Population (2012)	Population (2016)	Population (2020)	Area (Sq. Km)
Kangma (Kangmar) County (Kangma Town)	康馬縣 (康馬鎮)	康马县 (康马镇)	20,000	20,000	20,000	5400
Dingjie (Dinggyê) County (Jiangga [Gyangkar] Town)	定結縣 (江嘎鎮)	定结县 (江嘎镇)	20,000	20,000	20,000	5300
Zhongba County (Larang [Labranggosa] Township)	仲巴縣 (拉讓鄉)	仲巴县 (拉让乡)	20,000	20,000	30,000	45,900
Yadong (Dromo; Chomo) County (Xiasima [Xarsingma] Town)	亞東縣 (下司馬鎮)	亚东县 (下司马镇)	10,000	10,000	10,000	5100
Jilong (Gyirong) County (Zongga Town)	吉隆縣 (宗嘎鎮)	吉隆县 (宗嘎镇)	10,000	20,000	20,000	9300
Nielamu (Nyalam) County (Nielamu Town)	聶拉木縣 (聶拉木鎮)	聂拉木县 (聂拉木镇)	20,000	20,000	20,000	7700
Saga County (Jiajia [Gya'gya] Town)	薩嘎縣 (加加鎮)	萨嘎县 (加加镇)	10,000	10,000	20,000	12,400
Gangba (Kamba, Gamba) County (Gangba Town)	崗巴縣 (崗巴鎮)	岗巴县 (岗巴镇)	10,000	10,000	10,000	4100
Ali (Ngari) Prefecture	阿里地區	阿里地区	90,000	100,000	110,000	304,683
Ga'er (Gar) County (Shiquanhe Town)	噶爾縣 (獅泉河鎮)	噶尔县 (狮泉河镇)	20,000	20,000	20,000	18,087
Pulan (Burang) County (Pulan Town)	普蘭縣 (普蘭鎮)	普兰县 (普兰镇)	10,000	10,000	10,000	12,539
Zhada (Zanda) County (Tuolin [Toding; Tholing; Toling] Town)	札達縣 (托林鎮)	札达县 (托林镇)	10,000	10,000	10,000	24,580
Ritu (Rutog) County (Ritu Town)	日土縣 (日土鎮)	日土县 (日土镇)	10,000	10,000	10,000	71,963
Geji[f] (Gêgyai; Gê'gyai) county (Geji Town)	革吉縣 (革吉鎮)	革吉县 (革吉镇)	10,000	20,000	20,000	55,287
Gaize (Gêrzê) County (Gaize Town)	改則縣 (改則鎮)	改则县 (改则镇)	20,000	20,000	30,000	99,324

(continued)

Table 31.5 (continued)

Name	Traditional	Simplified	Population (2012)	Population (2016)	Population (2020)	Area (Sq. Km)
Cuoqin (Coqên) County (Cuoqin Town)	措勤縣 (措勤鎮)	措勤县 (措勤镇)	10,000	10,000	20,000	22,903

[a]Made a district in October 2015
[b]Established November 2012
[c]Made into Karuo (Karub) district in November 2014
[d]On 16 March 2015, Linzhi prefecture and Linzhi county were dissolved making Linzhi city, and established Bayi district
[e]On 26 June 2014, Rikaze (Shigatse) prefecture was made a city, and the original lower level Rikaze (Shigatse) city was named Sangzhumu district
[f]Other names include Napug (那坡 *nàpō*)

References

Aldenderfer, Mark, and Zhang Yinong. 2013. In *The Tibetan history reader*, ed. Gray Tuttle and Kurtis R. Schaeffer, 3–48. New York: Columbia University Press.

Brook, Timothy. 2010. Tibet and the Chinese world-empire. In *Empires and autonomy: Moments in the history of globalization*, ed. Stephen Streeter, John Weaver, and William D. Coleman, 24–40. Vancouver: University of British Columbia Press.

Dickson, Bruce. 2016. *The dictator's dilemma: The Chinese communist party's strategy for survival*. New York: Oxford University Press.

Goldstein, Melvyn C. 1989. *A history of modern Tibet, 1913–1951: The demise of the Lamaist state*. Berkeley: University of California Press.

———. 1997. *The snow lion and the dragon: China, Tibet, and the Dalai Lama*. Berkeley: University of California Press.

———. 2007. *A history of modern Tibet, volume 2: The calm before the storm, 1951–1955*. Berkeley: University of California Press.

Grunfeld, Tom A. 2015. *The making of modern Tibet, revised edition*. New York: Routledge.

Guo, Rongxing. 2016. *China's regional development and Tibet*. Singapore: Springer.

Kapstein, Matthew T. 2000. *The Tibetan assimilation of Buddhism: Conversion, contestation, and memory*. New York: Oxford University Press.

Lal, Dinesh. 2008. *Indo-Tibet-China conflict*. Delhi: Kalpaz Productions.

Lin, Guanqun. 2015. *Research on the tubo prime minister system in Tang dynasty*. Taipei: Linking Publishing. 林冠群. 唐代吐蕃宰相制度之研究. 台北: 聯經初出版社.

Ma, Rong. 2007. *Population structure and changes in the Tibet autonomous region—An analysis of the recent census data*. Paper presented at the International Conference on "Tibet Autonomy" at Harvard University.

Ministry of Civil Affairs (MCA), People's Republic of China. 2020. *County/township administration handbook*. Beijing: China Statistics Press, 中華人民共和國民政部, 中華人民共和國，鄉鎮行政區劃簡冊.

Norbu, Dawa. 2001. *China's Tibet policy*. Richmond: Curzon Press.

Peissel, Michel. 2002. *Tibet: The secret continent*. New York: St. Martin's Press.

Smith, Warren W. 2010. *Tibet's last stand? The Tibetan uprising of 2008 and China's response*. Boulder: Rowman & Littlefield.

Stein, R.A. 2013. The evolution of monastic power. In *The Tibetan history reader*, ed. Gray Tuttle and Kurtis R. Schaeffer, 196–210. New York: Columbia University Press.

Tibet Bureau of Statistics. 2021. *Communiqué on main data of the seventh national population census of the Tibet autonomous region*, 20 May. 西藏自治区第七次全国人口普查主要数据公报. http://tjj.xizang.gov.cn/xxgk/tjxx/tjgb/202105/t20210520_202889.html

Wemheuer, Felix. 2014. *Famine politics in Maoist China and the Soviet Union*. New Haven: Yale University Press.

Wilkinson, Endymion. 2012. *Chinese history: A new manual*. Cambridge, MA: Harvard University Press.

Yang, Jisheng. 2007. *Tombstone: record of China's great famine in the 1960s*, August 2007 (Chinese version). 楊繼繩 ，墓碑: 中国六十年代大饥荒纪实. https://cdn.jsdelivr.net/gh/easy2view/books/resources/grave-stone.pdf.

Yang, Huajun, and Chen Changwen. 2005. History and analysis of Tibetan population statistics. *Chinese Tibetan Studies*. 杨华军,陈昌文. 西藏人口统计的历史和分析. 中国藏学 3: 136–143.

Zhang, Shunan. 2021. *The 2020 per capita income list of residents in various provinces: Shanghai is the richest, and it has risen sharply*. Finance.people.com. 22 January. 张澍楠. 2020年各省份居民人均收入榜: 上海最有钱, 这地涨得猛. http://finance.people.com.cn/n1/2021/0122/c1004-32008733.html.

Zhang, Jian, and Qi Jingxuan. 1999. *China's ethnic and religious policies in past dynasties*. Beijing: Capital Normal University Press. 张践, 齐经轩. 中国历代民族宗教政策. 北京: 首都师范大学出版社.

Chapter 32
Xinjiang

Abstract Archeology has characterized Neolithic settlements in China's "New Border" area, Xinjiang, that date about 10,000 years ago. In both its geography and early populations, and exemplified by the well-preserved mummies, such as the "Beauty of Xiaohe" and the (Caucasian) "Beauty of Loulan," Xinjiang can be accurately described as Eurasian. Modern-day Xinjiang was part of the Han dynasties "western" protectorate, and the rise of the Uyghur rule in this region began in ca. seventh century CE. By the Qing (eighteenth century), further efforts were made in making Xinjiang a permanent part of the Chinese empire, with Han migration being promoted well into revolutionary China under the Chinese Communist Party (1949 onwards). In the face of real or perceived resistance by the Uyghur population in the early twenty-first century, the Chinese government has imposed a strict policy of detaining an unknown but very large number—at least in the hundreds of thousands—of Xinjiang Muslims into detention facilities. Xinjiang's economy in 2020 was ranked 24th in terms of gross domestic product (GDP) among mainland China's 31 provinces and major cities, and per capita income near the bottom of about USD $3700.

E. Croddy, *China's Provinces and Populations*,
https://doi.org/10.1007/978-3-031-09165-0_32

Xinjiang Uyghur Autonomous Region (新疆維吾爾自治區 *xīnjiāng wéiwú'ěr zìzhìqū*): Abbreviation (新 *xīn*) (Fig. 32.1)

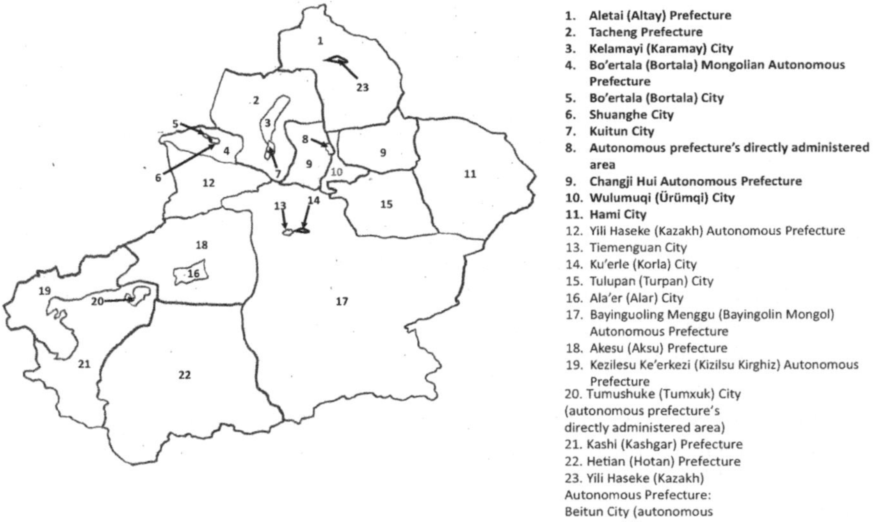

Fig. 32.1 Xinjiang Major Regions (Provincial Capital: Ürümqi City). (Drawn by the Author after People's Republic of China, Ministry of Civil Affairs (MCA 2020))

Xinjiang: General Impressions

With its vast regions of arid desert, surrounded by an incredible mountain scape to include the Tianshan and Kunlun ranges, Xinjiang holds the mystique of its very name, "new frontier," which was given to it by the Qing dynasty in the eighteenth century. Going back even further into ancient history, the capital Ürümqi (Mongolian word for "beautiful pastures") was a key transportation and logistical hub for those travelling along the ancient silk road.

Its formal name, Xinjiang Uyghur Autonomous Region, as in other so-called "autonomous regions" in mainland China, belies the fact that the Uyghur people have no ability to determine their own past, present or future. The Chinese Communist Party (CCP) wields enormous, terrible power over them, carrying out the rampant persecution of the majority ethno-religious group, the Uyghurs, an ongoing and unremitting atrocity that includes destruction of cultural relics, torture, rape, forced labor and sterilizations (US Department of State 2021).[1]

Prehistory

Going back 20,000 years ago, the climate was wetter in present-day Xinjiang province, particularly in and around the southern reaches of the Tarim basin (Altishahr; 塔里木盆地 *tălĭmùpéndì*). Along with evidence of stone tools and basic hunter-gatherer activity in Khotan (和田 *hétián*), there are also ruins of ancient human settlements in Xinjiang dating to the Neolithic period (ca. 10,000 years ago). These communities operated a basic agricultural economy and processed grain.

The archeological record shows large numbers of people migrated into Xinjiang around 2000 BCE (Milward 2007). Well-preserved remains of Eurasian people dating back some 4000 years have been found at the Xiaohe site (小河墓地 *xiăohé mùdì*) in the Tarim basin, Ruoqiang County, Lop Nur (羅布泊鎮 *luóbùbó zhèn*), south of the Kongque River (孔雀河 *kŏngquè hé*). This archaeological site is also called Ördek's Necropolis, named after the local who assisted the Swedish investigator, Folke Bergman, in locating the burial grounds in 1934. At the Xiaohe bronze-age site, towards the end of 2000, the famed "Beauty of Xiaohe" (小河公主 *xiăohé gōngzhŭ*), a naturally-preserved mummy about 3800 years old, as well as many other remains (some 300 gravesites) were "rediscovered." Based on DNA studies of additional bodies found at Xiaohe, it would appear that these were people of mixed Western European and Siberian ancestry who originally migrated from the Kazakh steppes (Kilgrove 2015).

In addition, the Caucasian female "Beauty of Loulan" (樓蘭美女 *lóulán mĕinǚ*) of the Gumugou Culture (古墓溝文化 *gŭmùgōu wénhuà*) was discovered along the northern side of the Kongque river in 1980. She was probably about 45 years of age with light brown hair, and belonged to a group of people that weaved wool garments, tattooed their skin, and demonstrated knowledge of medicinal herbs. Of the some-odd 300 skulls found in grave sites throughout southern Xinjiang, based on a samples dating from the nineteenth Century BCE to about 300 CE, nearly 90 percent of these showed Caucasian morphology while the remainder were Mongoloid (Baumer 2012). Researchers have also uncovered bronze-age burial sites in 2012 at the Adunqiaolu (阿敦喬魯 *ādūnqiáolŭ*) site. Named from the Mongolian *Aduun*

[1] See the following statement on 22 March 2021 by the US Department of State: "We, the Foreign Ministers of Canada and the United Kingdom, and the United States Secretary of State, are united in our deep and ongoing concern regarding China's human rights violations and abuses in Xinjiang. The evidence, including from the Chinese Government's own documents, satellite imagery, and eyewitness testimony is overwhelming. China's extensive program of repression includes severe restrictions on religious freedoms, the use of forced labour, mass detention in internment camps, forced sterilisations, and the concerted destruction of Uyghur heritage."

Chuluu (meaning "stones scattered as horse herds"), this archaeological site is located outside Wenquan County (Arixang), in Bortala (Bo'ertala) Mongol Autonomous Prefecture (博爾塔拉蒙古自治州 *bó'ěrtālā ménggǔ zìzhìzhōu).* Dating back to the nineteenth through seventeenth centuries BCE, the *Aduun Chuluu* site contains "family tombs" to include that of two children each buried in their own stone-slab sarcophagus. Over the 20 tombs surveyed, researchers have found pottery as well as bronze earrings and bronze mirrors.

From about 700–490 BCE, an ancient people associated with the Saka Culture (Scythian) exploited copper mines in Nilka County (尼勒克縣 *nílèkè xiàn*). Dating to about 550–250 BCE, burial sites found in Xiata (夏塔 *xiàtǎ*), Zhaosu County (昭蘇縣 *zhāosū xiàn*) typified those of the Wu Sun (烏孫 *wū sūn*) people who were also Caucasian (Europoid) in their morphology. The cemetery included numerous iron, gold, and bronze objects. Han dynasty maps showed the Wu Sun having occupied western Xinjiang, having originally fled the Gansu region from the Xiongnu (匈奴 *xiōngnú*) invasions (Di Cosmo 1999).

By the second century BCE, another group of people had arrived in Xinjiang, referred to by the Chinese as the Yuezhi (月氏 *yuèzhī*). The Yuezhi had been known to have trafficked in jade via Xinjiang as early as 600 BCE. Han dynasty (ca. 200 BCE - 200 CE) records the Yuezhi as supplying horses to the Chinese. (For population estimates for the Han period in modern-day Xinjiang see Table 32.1). The Xiongnu nomadic warriors pushed the Yuezhi out to the western border near Kazakhstan (176 BCE), scattering the remainder to other regions (e.g., Sichuan). At this time, the region now known as Xinjiang became the key route for the Silk Road, a term originally coined by Ferdinand von Richtofen in the late nineteenth century. For his part, the archeologist and explorer Aurel Stein noted (ca. 1900) that "[Xinjiang] served as the channel for that interchange of the early civilizations of India, China, and the Hellenized west of Asia" (Hansen 2012).

The Western Han (ca. 200 BCE) historical map shows the Xinjiang region of today as the "Western Region Protectorate" (西域都護府 *xīyùdūhù fǔ*). The oasis of Guizi (龜茲 *guīzī*) was located roughly in the center of the province in today's Kuqa County (庫車縣 *kùchē xiàn*). The Xiongnu, possibly related to the Huns, built a military garrison state in the Lake Bosten (博斯騰湖 *bósīténg hú*) area, making the

Table 32.1 Western Han Dynasty (ca. 206 BCE–220 CE), estimates of Xinjiang population. (Yuan 2012)

Western Han Dynasty Population of Today's Xinjiang	Households	Total population
Ruoqiang 婼羌 *ruòqiāng*	450	1750
Shanshan 鄯善 *shànshàn*	1570	14,100
Qiemo 且末 *qiěmò*	230	1610
Xiaowan 小宛 *xiǎowǎn*	150	1050
Jingjue State 精絕國 *jīngjuéguó*	480	3360
Ronglu State 戎盧國 *rónglúguó*	240	1610

(continued)

Table 32.1 (continued)

Western Han Dynasty Population of Today's Xinjiang	Households	Total population
Xumi State 圩彌國 *xūmíguó*	3340	20,040
Qule 渠勒 *qúlè*	310	2170
Yutian State 於闐國 *yútiánguó*	3300	19,300
Pishan State 皮山國 *píshānguó*	500	3500
Wuhao State 烏秏國 *wūhàoguó*	490	2733
Xiye State 西夜國 *xīyèguó*	350	4000
Puli State 蒲犁國 *púlíguó*	650	5000
Yinai State 依耐國 *yīnàiguó*	125	670
Wulei State 無雷國 *wúléiguó*	333	2333
Sundu State 損毒國 *sǔndúguó*	380	1100
Shache State 莎車國 *shāchēguó*	2339	16,373
Shule State 疏勒國 *shūlèguó*	1510	18,647
Weitou State 尉頭國 *wèitóuguó*	300	2300
Wu Sun 烏孫 *wūsūn*	60,000	365,000
Gumo 姑墨 *gūmò*	3500	24,500
Wensuo (Onsu) State 溫宿國 *wēnsùguó*	2200	8400
Guizi 龜茲 *guīzī* (now 庫車 *kùchē*; Kucha)	6970	81,317
Wulei 烏壘 *wūlěi*	110	1200
Quli 渠犁 *qúlí*	130	1480
Weixu State 危須國 *wéixūguó*	700	4900
Yanqi (Karasahr) State 焉耆國 *yānqíguó*	4000	32,100
Wutanzili State 烏貪訾離國 *wūtānzīlíguó*	41	231
Beilu State 卑路國 *bēilùguó*	227	1387
Beiluhou State 卑路後國 *bēilùhòuguó*	462	1137
Yulishi State 郁立師國 *yùlìshīguó*	190	1145
Shanhuan State 單桓國 *shānhuánguó*	27	194
Puleihou State 蒲類後國 *púlèihòuguó*	100	1070
Yuli 尉犁 *yùlì*	1200	9600
Xiqiemi 西且彌 *xīqiěmí*	332	1926
Dongqiemi 東且彌 *dōngqiěmí*	191	1948
Jie State 劫國 *jiéguó*	99	500
Guhu State 孤胡國 *gūhúguó*	55	264
Shan State 山國 *shānguó*	450	5000
Cheshiqian (front) State 車師前國 *chēshīqiánguó*	700	6050
Cheshihou (rear) State 車師後國 *chēshīhòuguó*	595	4774
Cheshiduwei State 車師都尉國 *chēshīdōuwèiguó*	40	333
Cheshihoucheng State 車師後城長國 *chēshīhòuchéngchángguó*	154	960
Bailongdui 白龍堆 *báilóngduī*	700	6050
Total	**98,645**	**679,094**

Tarim Basin its sovereign territory by 130 BCE. The Han were able to seize the eastern part of Xinjiang which was known to western history as Kroraina, but for the Chinese was known as Loulan (樓蘭 *lóulán*) as of 108 BCE. Located on the north side of Lop Nur Later, this area was then renamed Shanshan (鄯善 *shànshàn*) by the Chinese in 77 BCE.

Today, the People's Republic of China (PRC) claims Xinjiang Province back to 60 BCE. But in fact, throughout its history, Chinese control over its western region was often tenuous. For example, from about 200–300 CE the Chinese Wei and Jin empires claimed it had outposts under the auspices of the Shanshan (鄯善 *shàn-shàn*) Kingdom. However, in 399 CE the itinerant monk Faxian (法顯 *fǎxiǎn*) reported that he himself saw no Chinese in Shanshan (Milward 2007).

Rise of the Uyghurs and the Origins of the Hui

Very old Chinese histories refer to the modern-day "Uyghur" (維吾爾 *wéiwú'ěr*) people as Huigu (回鶻 *huígú*) or Huihe (回紇 *huíhé*), these meaning "united." In 390 CE, China referred to them as "Yuanhe (袁紇 *yuánhé*)," describing one of the smaller nomadic tribes that "lived in the marshes." It was in that year the Chinese emperor "launched a western expedition, situated in Luhunhai [鹿渾海 *lùhúnhǎi*, about 250 km west of modern-day Ulaanbaatar, Mongolia], attacking the Yuanhe (aka Huihe 回紇 *huíhé*) tribe of Gaoche [高車 *gāochē*] and plundering more than 200,000 head of men and livestock" (Wang 2018). Although the term Hui Hui 回回 *huíhuí*) generally was used when referring to foreigners, especially those who followed Islam and Judaism, it has since become an official ethnic category for the Hui (回族 *huízú*), i.e., Chinese Muslims.

Having grown much stronger by 646 CE, the Huihe leader, Tumitu (吐迷度 *tǔmídù*), declared himself Khan of the Huihe people. About a century later, the Huihe leader of the Yaghlakar (藥羅葛 *yàoluógé*) clan, after eliminating the later Turkestan Khanate (後突厥汗國 *hòu tújué hànguó*) in 744, named himself Khan, or Kutlug I Bilge Kagan (Köl Bilgä Qaγan 骨咄祿闕伽毗可汗 *gúduòlù quēqié kĕhàn*). He established his khanate at Khangai mountain area in central Asia, at the upper reaches of the Orkhon river (鄂爾渾河 *è'ěrhún hé*) in Mongolia (Tian 2001).

In 788 CE, the Khan Dunmohe (頓莫賀 *dùnmòhè*) famously sent an official party to the Tang court, asking that the official name of his nation of people be changed from Huihe (回紇 *huíhé*) to Huigu (回鶻 *huígú*). At that time, the north-central sector of Huigu (回鶻 *huígú*) in Asia ran west, from today's Yining (Ghulja) City (伊寧市 *yīníng shì*), through Ulaanbaator, capital of modern Mongolia, and all the way north to Nerchinsk in Russia. By ca. 800 CE, imperial China had sufficient administrative control of Xinjiang, governing it from Kuqa (*Kuçar*; 龜茲 *guīzī*), modern day Kuche county (庫車縣 *kùchē xiàn*), then already a very important oasis. At this time, the Uyghur nation (Khaganate) still controlled most of northern Xinjiang, while the ascendant Tibetans were in control of the south. As the latter two powers fell into decline, in the eleventh century western Xinjiang was occupied by the Turkic Kara-Khanid Khanate. What was left of Uyghur kingdom now occupied modern-day Turfan (吐魯番 *tǔlǔfān*) and Ürümqi (烏魯木齊 *wūlǔmùqí*).

By 1209, the Uyghurs submitted tribute (in the form of taxes) to the Mongols. As of 1225, under the Yuan dynastic system, Xinjiang was subsumed within the Chagatai Khanate (察合台汗國 *cháhétái hànguó*), and were nominally ruled by Chinggis (Genghis) Khan's second son, Chagatai. The Ming dynasty, having overthrown and pushed the Mongols back to their steppes, largely left the western region to govern itself as a tribute state. During this time, from ca. 1484–1509, the Eastern Turkestan region was held by the Ili Baliq (亦力把里 *yìlìbǎlǐ*) Khanate, with its capital near today's Yining (Ghulja) City (伊寧市 *yīníng shì*).

The continued fractious nature of Xinjiang kingdoms and states remained largely outside the direct control of the Chinese imperial court until 1759, when the Qing empire finally incorporated Xinjiang as a province. Estimates are that Xinjiang in the early 1800s had a total population of about one million (Clarke 2011).

In ca. 1840 a series of natural disasters led to an influx of the Kyrgyz (then known in Chinese 黠戛斯 *xiájiásī*), a nomadic group from the northwest, which brought in about 100,000 people into the Huigu Khanate. The pushed the Uyghurs west towards the Gansu region. Later, Muslim revolts in Shaanxi and Gansu ultimately led to the Qing court losing control of Xinjiang in 1864, as the province came under control of the Khanate of Koqand (based in present-day Uzbekistan) as well as Russia. From the Chinese revolution (1911) to the founding of the PRC (1949), Xinjiang was still largely an autonomous region, "ruled by Chinese but not really by China," as one wag put it (Chaudhuri 2016).

Sinicized Xinjiang

Efforts by China to increase ethnic Han Chinese migration to Xinjiang go back at least to the Qing dynasty (1884), but has been especially concerted since 1949. In 1940, the Han Chinese population in Xinjiang was about 190,000, which was about the same number found in the early nineteenth century. From 1949 to 1953, in addition to substantial numbers of People's Liberation Army (PLA) soldiers, large numbers of professionals (engineers, medics, as well as college-educated people and political cadres) emigrated to Xinjiang. By 1955, Xinjiang's total population was 5,117,800. During the desperate years of the Great Leap Forward (1958–62) and the famine that resulted, some 50,000 people tried to escape the Ili (伊犁 *yīlí*) region to Kazakhstan to find relief. As was typical, China's policy during the Great Leap Forward was to dissuade such movements of people, and the PLA was ordered to close the border. This instigated riots among locals, including Uyghurs and Kazakhs, resulting in the beating of government cadres. At the same time, even more desperate and starving people in neighboring provinces sought relief by moving into Xinjiang in 1959–1960, which led to a flood of 800,000 Han Chinese immigrants (Bovindgon 2014).

Aksai Chin Disputed Area

In order to move troops from Xinjiang to Tibet, in late 1950 the PRC utilized the Aksai Chin (阿克賽欽 *ākè'sàiqīn*) region as a crossing point, which was a desolate expanse claimed by India (part of the Jammu and Kashmir). By 1957, Stakhanovite Chinese laborers had completed a nearly 1300-mile strategic highway that ran through Aksai Chin. This construction continued apparently without the knowledge (nor much interest) by the government of India (Ray 2011). But Sino-Indian relations soured to the point that in 1962 Chinese forces fought Indian troops over the disputed Aksai Chin region. This highway No. 219 begins in Kargilik County (葉城縣 *yèchéng xiàn*), Xinjiang Province, and ends in Lhazê County (拉孜縣 *lāzī xiàn*) in Tibet. It is still a disputed area today between the two most populated countries on earth.

By 1973, Xinjiang had a population of ten million, about 35% of whom were ethnic Han Chinese. In ca. 2005, the Uyghur population was 46% of the total population of Xinjiang (9.5 million). Other significant minority groups in Xinjiang are represented by Hui, Mongolian, Kyrghyz, Uzbek, Xibo, Kazakh, Tatar, Tadjik, Russian, and Manchu (see Table 32.2). (Hayes 2012).

In Xinjiang Province today, the majority of the Han Chinese primarily live in more affluent areas, while locals, notably Uyghurs, predominate in the poorer rural regions. Recent tensions created by Han immigration to Xinjiang are voiced and expressed by opinions such as (Han) "the minority people here are very rude," and "the Han always have the idea that they are the masters of the Uyghur people" (Webber 2012). And as a reflection of the late Sinification of Xinjiang, most people in Xinjiang did not speak Chinese until more recent times (Millward 2007). Even so, as of 2010, a lack of Mandarin-speaking teachers meant that only 42 percent of Xinjiang students were being taught in the Chinese language. Current goals, probably unrealistic, hoped to achieve fluency in mandarin among all students in Xinjiang by 2020. As has been the trend, the CCP has been forcing schools in Xinjiang to replace Uyghur language and teaching only mandarin (OpIndia 2021).

Persecution of the Muslim Uyghur Population

Based on China's own statistics, 99.7% of Xinjiang's ethnic minority populations, notably the Uyghurs but also other related groups, are practicing Muslims (Ma 2014). Beginning in 2014, China instituted a "war on terror" upon its own Muslim population, largely in Xinjiang province, but has since gone on to spread across other provinces (Myers 2019). From about 2017 to 2020, based on policy enunciated by Chinese Communist Party Chairman and President Xi Jinping, hundreds of detention centers, administratively termed "Xinjiang Vocational Education and

Table 32.2 Ethnic Breakdown of Xinjiang Province (2008). (Reed and Raschke 2010)

Ethnic group	Population
Uyghur	9,650,629
Han Chinese	8,239,245
Kazakh	1,483,883
Hui	942,956
Kyrgyz	181,862
Mongol	177,120
Tajik	44,824
Xibo	42,444
Manchu	25,626
Uzbek	16,138
Russian	11,609
Daur	6678
Tatar	4728
Other	124,158
Total:	**20,951,900**

Training Centers"[2] have been built in and around Xinjiang to forcefully monitor and control its Uyghur population. According to a recent study,

> Since 2017, hundreds of thousands of Uyghur Muslims (out of a population of about 11 million) have moved through holding cells in the Xinjiang prison system before being handed long sentences or indefinite internment in concentration camps that push 'transformation through education' (Ahmed 2022).

According to the Australian Strategic Policy Institute (ASPI), these facilities are grouped in the following categories:

Tier 1: Suspected lower security re-education camps
Tier 2: Suspected dedicated re-education camps
Tier 3: Suspected detention centers
Tier 4: Suspected maximum-security prisons (Ruser 2020)

Using commercial satellite imagery, ASPI found over 380 suspected "vocational education and training centers" as of 2020. Of those characterized as Tier 4 (suspected maximum-security prisons), these were located in the following areas, and in some places listed there is more than one such facility (Ruser 2020):

- Akchi county (阿合奇縣 *āhéqí xiàn*), Kizilsu Kirghiz Autonomous Prefecture (克孜勒蘇柯爾克孜自治州 *kèzīlèsūkēěrkèzī zìzhìzhōu*)
- Akto county (阿克陶縣 *ākètáo xiàn*), Kizilsu Kirghiz Autonomous Prefecture (克孜勒蘇柯爾克孜自治州 *kèzīlèsūkēěrkèzī zìzhìzhōu*)

[2] 新疆職業技能教育配訓中心 *xīnjiāng zhíyè jìnéng jiàoyù pèixùn zhōngxīn.*

- Altay city (阿勒泰市 *ālètài shì*), Altay Prefecture (region) 阿勒泰地區 (*ālètài dìqū*)
- Arishang (Arixang) county (溫泉縣 *wēnquán xiàn*), Bortala Mongol Autonomous prefecture (博爾塔拉蒙古自治州 *bóěrtălā měnggŭ zìzhìzhōu*)
- Atush city (阿圖什市 *ātúshí shì*), Kizilsu Kirghiz Autonomous Prefecture (克孜勒蘇柯爾克孜自治州 *kèzīlèsūkēěrkèzī zìzhìzhōu*)
- Baghrash county (博湖縣 *bóhú xiàn*), Bayingolin Mongol Autonomous Prefecture (巴音郭楞蒙古自治州 *bāyīnguōléng měnggŭzìzhìzhōu*)
- Bay county (拜城縣 *bàichéng xiàn*), Aksu Prefecture (region) 阿克蘇地區 (*ākèsū dìqū*)
- Beitun town (北屯鎮 *běitún zhèn*), Beitun city (北屯市 *běitún shì*)
- Bortala city (博樂市 *bólè shì*), Bortala Mongol Autonomous prefecture (博爾塔拉蒙古自治州 *bóěrtălā mēnggŭ zìzhì zhōu*)
- Bügür county (輪台縣 *lúntái xiàn*), Bayingolin Mongol Autonomous Prefecture (巴音郭楞蒙古自治州 *bāyīnguōléng měnggŭzìzhìzhōu*)
- Burchin country (布爾津縣 *bùěrjīn xiàn*), Altay Prefecture (region) 阿勒泰地區 (*ālètài dìqū*)
- Burultoqay county (福海縣 *fúhăi xiàn*), Altay Prefecture (region) 阿勒泰地區 (*ālètài dìqū*)
- Chaghantoqay (裕民縣 *yùmín xiàn*), Tarbaghatay prefecture (region) (塔城地區 *tăchéng dìqū*)
- Chapchal-Xibe autonomous county (察布查爾錫伯自治縣 *chábùcháěr xībó zìzhì xiàn*), Ili Kazakh Autonomous prefecture (*yīlí hāsàkè zìzhìzhōu*)
- Chaqiliq county (若羌縣 *ruòqiāng xiàn*), Bayingolin Mongol Autonomous Prefecture (巴音郭楞蒙古自治州 *bāyīnguōléng měnggŭzìzhìzhōu*)
- Cherchen county (且末縣 *qiěmò xiàn*), Bayingolin Mongol Autonomous Prefecture (巴音郭楞蒙古自治州 *bāyīnguōléng měnggŭzìzhìzhōu*)
- Chira county (策勒縣 *cèlè xiàn*), Hotan prefecture (region) (和田地區 *hétián shì*)
- Fukang city (阜康市 *fùkāng shì*), Changji (Sanji) Hui Autonomous Prefecture (昌吉回族自治州 *chāngjí huízú zìzhìzhōu*)
- Ghulja city (伊寧市 *yīníng shì*), Ili Kazakh Autonomous prefecture (*yīlí hāsàkè zìzhìzhōu*)
- Guma county (皮山縣 *píshān xiàn*), Hotan prefecture (region) (和田地區 *hétián shì*)
- Hejing county (和靜縣 *héjìng xiàn*), Bayingolin Mongol Autonomous Prefecture (巴音郭楞蒙古自治州 *bāyīnguōléng měnggŭzìzhìzhōu*)
- Hotan City (和田市 *hétián shì*), Hotan prefecture (region) (和田地區 *hétián shì*)
- Jeminey county (吉木乃縣 *jímùnăi xiàn*), Altay Prefecture (region) 阿勒泰地區 (*ālètài dìqū*)
- Jing county (精河縣 *jīnghé xiàn*), Bortala Mongol Autonomous prefecture (博爾塔拉蒙古自治州 *bóěrtălā měnggŭ zìzhìzhōu*)
- Karakash county (墨玉縣 *mòyù xiàn*), Hotan prefecture (region) (和田地區 *hétián shì*)

- Karashahar Hui Autonomous county (焉耆回族自治縣 *yānqí huízú zìzhìxiàn*), Bayingolin Mongol Autonomous Prefecture (巴音郭楞蒙古自治州 *bāyīnguōléng měnggǔzìzhìzhōu*)
- Kargilik county (葉城縣 *yèchéng xiàn*), Kashgar prefecture (region) 喀什地區 *kāshí dìqū*)
- Kelpin county (柯坪縣 *kēpíng xiàn*), Aksu Prefecture (region) 阿克蘇地區 (*ākèsū dìqū*)
- Kériye county (于田縣 *yútián xiàn*), Hotan prefecture (region) (和田地區 *hétián shì*)
- Koboksar Mongol Autonomous county (和布克賽爾蒙古自治縣 *hébùkèsàiěr mēnggǔ zìzhì xiàn*), Tarbaghatay prefecture (region) (塔城地區 *tǎchéng dìqū*)
- Koktogay county (富蘊縣 *fùyùn xiàn*), Altay Prefecture (region) 阿勒泰地區 (*ālètài dìqū*)
- Konasheher county (疏附縣*shūfù xiàn*), Kashgar prefecture (region) 喀什地區 *kāshí dìqū*)
- Korgas city (霍爾果斯市 *huòěrguǒsī shì*), Ili Kazakh Autonomous prefecture (*yīlí hāsàkè zìzhìzhōu*)
- Korla City (庫爾勒市 *kùěrlè shì*), Bayingolin Mongol Autonomous Prefecture (巴音郭楞蒙古自治州 *bāyīnguōléng měnggǔzìzhìzhōu*)
- Kucha county (庫車縣 *kùchē xiàn*), Aksu Prefecture (region) 阿克蘇地區 (*ākèsū dìqū*)
- Kunes county (新源縣 *xīnyuán xiàn*), Ili Kazakh Autonomous prefecture (*yīlí hāsàkè zìzhìzhōu*)
- Kuytun city (奎屯市 *kuítún shì*), Ili Kazakh Autonomous prefecture (*yīlí hāsàkè zìzhìzhōu*)
- Lop county (洛浦縣 *luòpǔ xiàn*), Hotan prefecture (region) (和田地區 *hétián shì*)
- Manas county (瑪納斯縣 *mǎnàsī xiàn*), Changji (Sanji) Hui Autonomous Prefecture (昌吉回族自治州 *chāngjí huízú zìzhìzhōu*)
- Maralbeshi county (巴楚縣 *bāchǔ xiàn*), Kashgar prefecture (region) (喀什地區 *kāshí dìqū*)
- Maytagh district (獨山子區 *dúshān zǐqū*), Karamay city (克拉瑪依市 *kèlāmǎyī shì*)
- Mekit county (麥蓋提縣 *màigětí xiàn*), Kashgar prefecture (region) (喀什地區 *kāshí dìqū*)
- Midong district (米東區 *mǐdōng qū*), Ürümchi city (烏魯木齊市 *wūlǔmùqí shì*)
- Mongolkure county (昭蘇縣 *zhāosū xiàn*), Ili Kazakh Autonomous prefecture (*yīlí hāsàkè zìzhìzhōu*)
- Mori Kazakh Autonomous county (木壘哈薩克自治縣 *mùlěihāsàkè zìzhì xiàn*), Changji (Sanji) Hui Autonomous Prefecture (昌吉回族自治州 *chāngjí huízú zìzhìzhōu*)
- Niya county (民豐縣 *mínfēng xiàn*), Hotan prefecture (region) (和田地區 *hétián shì*)

- Onsu (Wensu) county (溫宿縣 *wēnsù xiàn*), Aksu Prefecture (region) 阿克蘇地區 (*ākèsū dìqū*)
- Peyziwat county (伽師縣 *jiāshī xiàn*), Kashgar prefecture (region) (喀什地區 *kāshí dìqū*)
- Poskam county (澤普縣 *zépǔ xiàn*), Kashgar prefecture (region) (喀什地區 *kāshí dìqū*)
- Qitai county (奇台縣 *qítái xiàn*), Changji (Sanji) Hui Autonomous Prefecture (昌吉回族自治州 *chāngjí huízú zìzhìzhōu*)
- Qumul (region) prefecture (哈密地區 *hāmì dìqū*)
- Saybagh district (沙依巴克區 *shāyībākè qū*), Ürümchi city (烏魯木齊市 *wūlǔmùqí shì*)
- Shanshan (Piqan) county (鄯善縣 *shànshàn xiàn*), Tupan prefecture (region) (吐魯番地區 *tǔlǔfān dìqū*)
- Shawan county (沙灣縣 *shāwān xiàn*), Tarbaghatay prefecture (region) (塔城地區 *tǎchéng dìqū*)
- Shuanghe city (雙河市 *shuānghé shì*)
- Shuimogou district (水磨溝區 *shuǐmògōu qū*), Ürümchi city (烏魯木齊市 *wūlǔmùqí shì*)
- Tashqorghan Tajik Autonomous county (塔什庫爾干塔吉克自治縣 *tǎshíkùěrgān tǎjíkè zìzhì xiàn*), Kashgar prefecture (region) (喀什地區 *kāshí dìqū*)
- Tianshan district (天山區 *tiānshān qū*), Ürümchi city (烏魯木齊市 *wūlǔmùqí shì*)
- Tiemenguan city (鐵門關市 *tiěménguān shì*)
- Toli county (托里縣 *tuōlǐ xiàn*), Tarbaghatay prefecture (region) (塔城地區 *tǎchéng dìqū*)
- Toqsu county (新和縣 *xīnhé xiàn*), Aksu Prefecture (region) 阿克蘇地區 (*ākèsū dìqū*)
- Toqsun county (托克遜縣 *tuōkèxùn xiàn*), Tupan prefecture (region) (吐魯番地區 *tǔlǔfān dìqū*)
- Toutunhe district (頭屯河區 *tóutúnhé qū*), Ürümchi city (烏魯木齊市 *wūlǔmùqí shì*)
- Tumshuq city (圖牧舒克市 *túmùshūkè shì*)
- Turpan city (吐魯番市 *tǔlǔfān shì*), Turpan prefecture (region) (吐魯番地區 *tǔlǔfān dìqū*)
- Uchturpan county (烏什縣 *wūshí xiàn*), Aksu Prefecture (region) 阿克蘇地區 (*ākèsū dìqū*)
- Uchturpan county (烏什縣 *wūshí xiàn*), Aksu Prefecture (region) 阿克蘇地區 (*ākèsū dìqū*)
- Xinshi district (新市區 *xīnshì qū*), Ürümchi city (烏魯木齊市 *wūlǔmùqí shì*)
- Yarkant county (莎車縣 *shāchē xiàn*), Kashgar prefecture (region) 喀什地區 *kāshí dìqū*)
- Yengisar county (英吉沙縣 *yīngjíshā xiàn*), Kashgar prefecture (region) 喀什地區 *kāshí dìqū*)

- Yopurgha county (岳普湖縣 yuèpǔhú xiàn), Kashgar prefecture (region) (喀什地區 *kāshí dìqū*)

Xinjiang and Islam

Xinjiang once was home to some 24,000 mosques. Over a three-year period (approximately 2017–2020), analysts at the Australian Strategic Policy Institute) estimate that the Chinese government has destroyed thousands of these, perhaps leaving behind fewer than 15,000 mosques as of 2020, with many of these being damaged. Based on satellite imagery analysis by Earthrise Alliance and Agence France-Presse (AFP), by early 2020 over a hundred historical Uyghur cemeteries had been razed, most during the time span of 2018–2020. Of these was among the most famous and revered, the Sultanim graveyard (蘇爾坦墓園 *sūěrtǎn mùyuán*), which was over 1000 years old, located in downtown Hotan city (Khotan; 和田市 *hétián shì*). It was paved over to make a parking lot in ca. 2019 (Sintash 2019).

Based on China's national census (see Table 32.3) in 2010, of the total population of Xinjiang (21,810,000) those identifying as Moslems numbered some 13,000,000. These numbers further broke down to Uyghurs (10,001,302), Kazakh (1,418,278), Hui (983,015), Kyrgyz (180,472), Dongxiang (Sarta; 61,613), Tajik (47,261), Uzbek (10,114), Salar (3728), Tatar (3242), and Bao'an (568). Not only did Muslims make up more than half the population of Xinjiang, they also comprised half of all Moslems throughout China. Chinese media reporting listed the following populations in Xinjiang Province (total: 23,225,400) as of 2013 (Table 32.4):

Xinjiang's Population and Economy

Xinjiang's population increased 18.5% from 2010 to 2020. Its permanent registered (*hukou*) population (see Table 32.5) for 2020 was 22,830,000, significantly lower than the 2020 census figure of 25,852,345. Xinjiang's economy has long been near the bottom third of 31 provinces and major cities, ranked 24th in terms of gross domestic product (GDP) of USD $214 billion in 2020, up from $145 billion in 2015. Near bottom rank was Xinjiang's per capita income in 2020 of $3708 (Zhang 2021).

Table 32.5 (below) shows the *hukou* (family registered) populations based on PRC Ministry of Civil Affairs data. (Districts listed directly under major cities are government seats, as are those in parentheses). One can compare these data with the census (usual residential populations based on 2010 and 2020 censuses in Table 32.3 (below):

Table 32.3 Xinjiang population (residential 常住人口 *chángzhù rénkǒu* data). (XBS 2021)[a]

Prefecture/County	Population (2010)	Population (2020)
Yili Hasake Autonomous Prefecture 伊犁哈薩克自治州 *yīlí hāsàkè zìzhìzhōu*	2,482,627	2,848,393
Ürümchi (Urumqi) 烏魯木齊市 *wūlǔmùqí shì*	3,110,280	4,054,369
Karamay (Kelamayi) City 克拉瑪依市 *kèlāmǎyī shì*	391,008	490,348
Turpan City 吐魯番市 *tǔlǔfān shì*	622,679	693,988
Hami City 哈密市 *hāmì shì*	572,400	673,383
Altay Prefecture 阿勒泰地區 *ālètài dìqū*	603,280	668,587
Tacheng Prefecture 塔城地區 *tǎchéng dìqū*	1,219,212	1,138,638
Kashi Prefecture 喀什地區 *kāshí dìqū*	3,979,362	4,496,377
Aksu Prefecture 阿克蘇地區 *ākèsū dìqū*	2,370,887	2,714,422
Hotan Prefecture 和田地區 *hétián dìqū*	2,014,365	2,504,718
Bortola Mongol Autonomous Prefecture 博爾塔拉蒙古自治州 *bó'ěrtǎlā měnggǔ zìzhìzhōu*	443,680	488,198
Changji Hui (Moslem) Autonomous Prefecture 昌吉回族自治州 *chāngjí huízú zìzhìzhōu*	1,428,592	1,613,585
Kizilsu Kirghiz Autonomous Prefecture 克孜勒蘇柯爾克孜自治州 *kèzīlèsū kē'ěrkèzī zìzhìzhōu*	525,599	622,222
Bayingolin Mongol Autonomous Prefecture 巴音郭楞蒙古自治州 *bāyīnguōlèng měnggǔ zìzhìzhōu*	1,278,492	1,613,979
(Other autonomous, directly-subordinate regions)	770,871	1,231,138
Total	**21,813,334**	**25,852,345**

[a]Subdistrict population data for 2020 were unavailable as of 30 August 2021

Table 32.4 Xinjiang ethnic group populations (2013) (Baidu.com 2013)

Uyghur	11,271,900, or about 49%;
Han Chinese	8,595,100, or 37%;
Kazakh	1,598,700, or about 7%;
Hui (Muslim)	1,058,500, or 4.5%;
Kyrgyz	202,400, or about 1%;
Mongolian	185,300, or about 1%;
Tajik	50,100, or 0.2%;
Xibo	43,500, or about 0.2%;
Russian	12,000, or 0.05%;
Uzbek	18,500, or 0.08%
Tatar	5100, or 0.02%;
Manchu	28,100, or about 0.12%;
Daur	6900, or 0.03%;
Other	149,400, or 0.64%

Xinjiang Uyghur Autonomous Region (新 *xīn*)

Capital: Ürümqi (Wulumuqi)

Table 32.5 Xinjiang: Permanent Registered (戶籍人口 *hùjí rénkǒu*) populations. (MCA 2020)

Name	Traditional	Simplified	Population (2012)	Population (2016)	Population (2020)	Area (Sq. Km)
Xinjiang Uyghur Autonomous Region	新疆維吾爾自治區	新疆维吾尔自治区	21,640,000	22,260,000	22,830,000	1,660,000
Wulumuqi (Ürümqi; Urumqi) City	烏魯木齊市	乌鲁木齐市	2,420,000	2,580,000	2,220,000	13,788
Tianshan District (Xingfulu Subdistrict)	天山區 (幸福路街道)	天山区 (幸福路街道)	550,000	580,000	460,000	171
Shayibake (Saybagh) District (Yangzijianglu Subdistrict)	沙依巴克區 (揚子江路街道)	沙依巴克区 (扬子江路街道)	520,000	540,000	470,000	422
Xinshi District (Beijinglu Subdistrict)	新市區 (北京路街道)	新市区 (北京路街道)	530,000	560,000	510,000	263
Shuimogou District (Shuimogou Subdistrict)	水磨溝區 (水磨溝街道)	水磨沟区 (水磨沟街道)	270,000	300,000	230,000	278
Toutunhe District (Huochexizhan Subdistrict)	頭屯河區 (火車西站街道)	头屯河区 (火车西站街道)	140,000	230,000	200,000	276
Dabancheng District (Dabancheng Town)	達坂城區 (達坂城鎮)	达坂城区 (达坂城镇)	40,000	40,000	30,000	4759
Midong District (Gumudi Town)	米東區 (古牧地鎮)	米东区 (古牧地镇)	280,000	270,000	280,000	3407
Wulumuqi (Ürümqi) County (Wulumuqi City, Shuimogou District, Nanhunanlu Subdistrict)	烏魯木齊縣 (烏魯木齊市水磨溝區南湖南路街道)	乌鲁木齐县 (乌鲁木齐市水磨沟区南湖南路街道)	90,000	60,000	50,000	4212
Kelamayi (Karamay) City	克拉瑪依市	克拉玛依市	290,000	300,000	310,000	7734
Kelamayi District (Kunlunlu Subdistrict)	克拉瑪依區 (昆侖路街道)	克拉玛依区 (昆仑路街道)	180,000	190,000	210,000	3431

(continued)

Table 32.5 (continued)

Name	Traditional	Simplified	Population (2012)	Population (2016)	Population (2020)	Area (Sq. Km)
Dushanzi (Maytag; Maytagh) District (Xininglu Subdistrict)	獨山子區 (西寧路街道)	独山子区 (西宁路街道)	60,000	60,000	60,000	400
Baijiantan District (Zhongxinglu Subdistrict)	白鹼灘區 (中興路街道)	白碱滩区 (中兴路街道)	40,000	40,000	40,000	1272
Wu'erhe (Urho) District (Liushujie Subdistrict)	烏爾禾區 (柳樹街街道)	乌尔禾区 (柳树街街道)	10,000	10,000	10,000	2229
Autonomous Region Subordinate, County-Level Administrative Units	自治區直轄縣級行政單位	自治区直辖县级行政单位				
Shihezi City (Hongshan Subdistrict)	石河子市 (紅山街道)	石河子市 (红山街道)	630,000	620,000	590,000	457
Ala'er (Alar) City (Jinyinchuanlu Subdistrict)	阿拉爾市 (金銀川路街道)	阿拉尔市 (金银川路街道)	190,000	190,000	170,000	5266
Tumushuke (Tumxuk; Tumshuq) City (Qiganquele Subdistrict)	圖牧舒克市 (齊干卻勒街道)	图木舒克市 (齐干却勒街道)	160,000	170,000	170,000	2003
Wujiaqu City (Renminlu Subdistrict)	五家渠市 (人民路街道)	五家渠市 (人民路街道)	90,000	90,000	100,000	742
Beitun City (Beitun Town)	北屯市 (北屯鎮)	北屯市 (北屯镇)	80,000	80,000	80,000	911
Tiemenguan City[a] (Xingjianglu)	鐵門關市 (興疆路)	铁门关市 (兴疆路)	N/A	50,000	40,000	590
Shuanghe City[b] (Hongxing Erlu)	雙河市 (紅星二路)	双河市 (红星二路)	N/A	90,000	50,000	742
Kekedala (Kokdala) City[c] (Xingfulu)	可克達拉市 (幸福路)	可克达拉市 (幸福路)	N/A	80,000	80,000	979.71
Kunyu City[d] (Kunyu Boulevard)	昆玉市 (昆玉大道)	昆玉市 (昆玉大道)	N/A	N/A	50,000	1008
Huyanghe City[e] (Guangming Donglu)	胡楊河市 (光明東路)	胡杨河市 (光明东路)	N/A	N/A	80,000	678

(continued)

Table 32.5 (continued)

Name	Traditional	Simplified	Population (2012)	Population (2016)	Population (2020)	Area (Sq. Km)
Kashi (Kashgar) Prefecture	喀什地區	喀什地区	4,030,000	4,210,000	4,630,000	111,741
Kashi City (Wusitang Boyi (Boyei) Subdistrict)	喀什市 (吾斯塘博依街道)	喀什市 (吾斯塘博依街道)	470,000	640,000	650,000	791
Shufu (Konaxahar; Konasheher) County (Tuokezhake Town)	疏附縣 (托克扎克鎮)	疏附县 (托克扎克镇)	330,000	260,000	280,000	2986
Shule County (Shule Town)	疏勒縣 (疏勒鎮)	疏勒县 (疏勒镇)	340,000	340,000	380,000	2207
Yingjisha (Yengisar; Yengisheher; Yengi) County (Yingjisha Town)	英吉沙縣 (英吉沙鎮)	英吉沙县 (英吉沙镇)	270,000	290,000	310,000	3421
Zepu (Poskam) County (Zepu Town)	澤普縣 (澤普鎮)	泽普县 (泽普镇)	200,000	210,000	220,000	1000
Shache (Yarkant; Yarkand) County (Shache Town)	莎車縣 (莎車鎮)	莎车县 (莎车镇)	800,000	790,000	890,000	9037
Yecheng (Kargilik) County (Kageleke Town)	葉城縣 (喀格勒克鎮)	叶城县 (喀格勒克镇)	450,000	470,000	550,000	28,929
Maigaiti (Makit; Mekit) County (Maigaiti Town)	麥蓋提縣 (麥蓋提鎮)	麦盖提县 (麦盖提镇)	250,000	260,000	270,000	11,023
Yuepuhu (Yopurga; Yopurgha) County (Yuepuhu Town)	岳普湖縣 (岳普湖鎮)	岳普湖县 (岳普湖镇)	160,000	160,000	180,000	3166
Jiashi (Peyziwat) County (Baren Town)	伽師縣 (巴仁鎮)	伽师县 (巴仁镇)	390,000	410,000	460,000	6601
Bachu (Maralbexi; Maralbashi) County (Bachu Town)	巴楚縣 (巴楚鎮)	巴楚县 (巴楚镇)	330,000	340,000	380,000	18,491
Tashiku'ergan (Tashkurgan; Taxkorgan; Toxkhürghon; Tashqorghan) Tajike (Tajik) Autonomous County (Tashiku'ergan Town)	塔什庫爾干塔吉克自治縣 (塔什庫爾干鎮)	塔什库尔干塔吉克自治县 (塔什库尔干镇)	40,000	40,000	40,000	24,089

(continued)

Table 32.5 (continued)

Name	Traditional	Simplified	Population (2012)	Population (2016)	Population (2020)	Area (Sq. Km)
Akesu (Aksu) Prefecture	阿克蘇地區	阿克苏地区	2,370,000	2,400,000	2,560,000	126,760
Akesu City (Yingbazha Subdistrict)	阿克蘇市 (英巴扎街道)	阿克苏市 (英巴扎街道)	490,000	500,000	550,000	13,647
Wensu (Onsu) County (Wensu Town)	溫宿縣 (溫宿鎮)	温宿县 (温宿镇)	250,000	250,000	270,000	14,376
Kuche (Kuqa; Kucha) County[f] (Kuche Town)	庫車縣 (庫車鎮)	库车县 (库车镇)	470,000	470,000	N/A	(14,529)
Kuche (Kuqa; Kucha) City (Xincheng Subdistrict)	庫車市 (新城街道)	库车市 (新城街道)	N/A	N/A	490,000	14,529
Shaya (Shayar; Xayar) County (Shaya Town)	沙雅縣 (沙雅鎮)	沙雅县 (沙雅镇)	250,000	260,000	260,000	31,887
Xinhe (Toksu; Toqsu) County (Xinhe Town)	新和縣 (新和鎮)	新和县 (新和镇)	170,000	170,000	190,000	5831
Baicheng (Bay) County (Baicheng Town)	拜城縣 (拜城鎮)	拜城县 (拜城镇)	230,000	230,000	240,000	15,917
Wushi (Uqturpan; Uchturpan) County (Wushi Town)	烏什縣 (烏什鎮)	乌什县 (乌什镇)	210,000	220,000	230,000	9065
Awati (Awat) County (Awati Town)	阿瓦提縣 (阿瓦提鎮)	阿瓦提县 (阿瓦提镇)	250,000	250,000	270,000	12,593
Keping (Kalpin; Kelpin) County (Keping Town)	柯坪縣 (柯坪鎮)	柯坪县 (柯坪镇)	50,000	50,000	60,000	8915
Hetian (Hotan) Prefecture	和田地區	和田地区	2,050,000	2,130,000	2,530,000	247,938
Hetian City (Nu'erbage Subdistrict)	和田市 (奴爾巴格街道)	和田市 (奴尔巴格街道)	320,000	330,000	410,000	466
Hetian County (Hetian City Gujiangbake Subdistrict)	和田縣 (和田市古江巴格街道)	和田县 (和田市古江巴格街道)	270,000	280,000	360,000	41,302
Moyu (Qaraqash; Karakash; Karakax)[g] County (Kalakashi Town)	墨玉縣 (喀拉喀什鎮)	墨玉县 (喀拉喀什镇)	520,000	540,000	650,000	25,420

(continued)

Table 32.5 (continued)

Name	Traditional	Simplified	Population (2012)	Population (2016)	Population (2020)	Area (Sq. Km)
Pishan County (Guma Town)	皮山縣 (固瑪鎮)	皮山县 (固玛镇)	260,000	270,000	320,000	38,921
Luopu (Lop) County (Luopu Town)	洛浦縣 (洛浦鎮)	洛浦县 (洛浦镇)	240,000	250,00	300,000	14,104
Cele (Qira; Chira) County (Cele Town)	策勒縣 (策勒鎮)	策勒县 (策勒镇)	150,000	160,000	170,000	31,592
Yutian (Keriya; Kériye) County (Mugala Town)	于田縣 (木尕拉鎮)	于田县 (木尕拉镇)	250,000	260,000	290,000	39,373
Minfeng (Niye) County (Niya Town)	民豐縣 (尼雅鎮)	民丰县 (尼雅镇)	40,000	40,000	40,000	56,760
Tulufan (Turpan) Prefecture	吐魯番地區	吐鲁番地区	630,000	N/A	N/A	(70,049)
Tulufan (Turpan) City[h]	吐魯番市	吐鲁番市	N/A	630,000	630,000	70,049
Tulufan City (Laochenglu Subdistrict)	吐魯番市 (老城路街道)	吐鲁番市 (老城路街道)	280,000	N/A	N/A	(13,690)
Gaochang District (Laochenglu Subdistrict)	高昌區 (老城路街道)	高昌区 (老城街道)	N/A	280,000	290,000	13,690
Shanshan (Pichan; Piqan)[i] County (Shanshan Town)	鄯善縣 (鄯善鎮)	鄯善县 (鄯善镇)	230,000	230,000	220,000	39,759
Tuokexun (Toksun; Toqsun) County (Tuokexun Town)	托克遜縣 (托克遜鎮)	托克逊县 (托克逊镇)	120,000	120,000	120,000	16,600
Hami (Kumul; Qumul) Prefecture[j]	哈密地區	哈密地区	570,000	590,000	N/A	(138,919)
Hami City	哈密市 (東河區街道)	哈密市 (东河区街道)	**N/A**	**N/A**	**560,000**	**138,919**
Hami City[k] (Donghequ Subdistrict)	哈密市 (東河區街道)	哈密市 (东河区街道)	450,000	470,000	N/A	(81,794)
Yizhou District (Donghequ Subdistrict)	伊州區 (東河區街道)	伊州区 (东河区街道)	N/A	N/A	430,000	81,794
Yiwu (Aratürük) County (Yiwu Town)	伊吾縣 (伊吾鎮)	伊吾县 (伊吾镇)	20,000	20,000	20,000	19,821

(continued)

Table 32.5 (continued)

Name	Traditional	Simplified	Population (2012)	Population (2016)	Population (2020)	Area (Sq. Km)
Balikun Hasake (Barköl Kazakh) Autonomous County (Balikun Town)	巴里坤哈薩克自治縣 (巴里坤鎮)	巴里坤哈萨克自治县 (巴里坤镇)	100,000	100,000	110,000	37,304
Kezilesu Ke'erkezi (Kizilsu Kyrghiz) Autonomous Prefecture	克孜勒蘇柯爾克孜自治州	克孜勒苏柯尔克孜自治州	540,000	550,000	620,000	70,896
Atushi (Artux; Atush) City (Guangminglu Subdistrict)	阿圖什市 (光明路街道)	阿图什市 (光明路街道)	240,000	250,000	290,000	15,698
Aketao (Akto) County (Aketao Town)	阿克陶縣 (阿克陶鎮)	阿克陶县 (阿克陶镇)	200,000	200,000	230,000	24,535
Aheqi (Akqi; Akchi) County (Aheqi Town)	阿合奇縣 (阿合奇鎮)	阿合奇县 (阿合奇镇)	40,000	40,000	50,000	11,545
Wuqia (Ulugqat) County (Wuqia Town)	烏恰縣 (烏恰鎮)	乌恰县 (乌恰镇)	60,000	60,000	60,000	19,118
Bo'ertala Menggu (Bortala; Bartala Mongol) Autonomous Prefecture	博爾塔拉蒙古自治州	博尔塔拉蒙古自治州	480,000	520,000	480,000	26,100
Boleshi (Bortala) City (Qingdeli Subdistrict)	博樂市 (青得里街道)	博乐市 (青得里街道)	260,000	270,000	260,000	7802
Alashankou City[1] (Alatao Subdistrict)	阿拉山口市 (阿拉套街道)	阿拉山口市 (阿拉套街道)	N/A	40,000	10,000	1204
Jinghe (Jing) County (Jinghe Town)	精河縣 (精河鎮)	精河县 (精河镇)	140,000	140,000	140,000	11,189
Wenquan (Arixang; Arishang) County (Bogeda'er Town)	溫泉縣 (博格達爾鎮)	温泉县 (博格达尔镇)	80,000	70,000	70,000	5905
Changji Huizu (Hui) Autonomous Prefecture	昌吉回族自治州	昌吉回族自治州	1,420,000	1,400,000	1,390,000	73,659
Changji City (Yan'anbeilu Subdistrict)	昌吉市 (延安北路街道)	昌吉市 (延安北路街道)	390,000	370,000	390,000	7981
Fukang City (Bofeng Subdistrict)	阜康市 (博峰街道)	阜康市 (博峰街道)	170,000	170,000	160,000	8545

(continued)

Table 32.5 (continued)

Name	Traditional	Simplified	Population (2012)	Population (2016)	Population (2020)	Area (Sq. Km)
Hutubi County (Hutubi Town)	呼圖壁縣 (呼圖壁鎮)	呼图壁县 (呼图壁镇)	220,000	220,000	210,000	9518
Manasi (Manas) County (Ma'nasi Town)	瑪納斯縣 (瑪納斯鎮)	玛纳斯县 (玛纳斯镇)	170,000	170,000	170,000	9154
Qitai County (Qitai Town)	奇台縣 (奇台鎮)	奇台县 (奇台镇)	240,000	240,000	240,000	16,709
Jimusa'er (Jimsar) County (Jimusa'er Town)	吉木薩爾縣 (吉木薩爾鎮)	吉木萨尔县 (吉木萨尔镇)	140,000	140,000	140,000	8170
Muleihasake (Mori Kazakh) Autonomous County (Mulei Town)	木壘哈薩克自治縣 (木壘鎮)	木垒哈萨克自治县 (木垒镇)	90,000	90,000	90,000	13,582
Bayinguoling Menggu (Bayingolin Mongol) Autonomous Prefecture	巴音郭楞蒙古自治州	巴音郭楞蒙古自治州	1,310,000	1,370,000	1,240,000	471,140
Ku'erle (Korla) City (Sayibage Subdistrict)	庫爾勒市 (薩依巴格街道)	库尔勒市 (萨依巴格街道)	530,000	550,000	470,000	6038
Luntai (Bügür; Bugur) County (Luntai Town)	輪台縣 (輪台鎮)	轮台县 (轮台镇)	110,000	120,000	120,000	14,185
Yuli (Lopnur) County (Yuli Town)	尉犁縣 (尉犁鎮)	尉犁县 (尉犁镇)	110,000	110,000	110,000	59,251
Ruoqiang (Qarkilik; Charkliq; Chaqiliq) County (Ruoqiang Town)	若羌縣 (若羌鎮)	若羌县 (若羌镇)	30,000	30,000	30,000	199,222
Qiemo (Qarqan; Cherchen) County (Qiemo Town)	且末縣 (且末鎮)	且末县 (且末镇)	60,000	60,000	70,000	138,680
Hejing County (Hejing Town)	和靜縣 (和靜鎮)	和静县 (和静镇)	190,000	200,000	180,000	34,984
Heshuo (Hoxud) County (Tewulike Town)	和碩縣 (特吾里克鎮)	和硕县 (特吾里克镇)	70,000	80,000	70,000	12,754
Bohu (Bagrax; Baghrash) County (Bohu Town)	博湖縣 (博湖鎮)	博湖县 (博湖镇)	60,000	60,000	60,000	3597

(continued)

Table 32.5 (continued)

Name	Traditional	Simplified	Population (2012)	Population (2016)	Population (2020)	Area (Sq. Km)
Yanqi (Qarasheher; Karasahr; Karashar; Karashahar) Huizu (Hui) Autonomous County (Yanqi Town)	焉耆回族自治縣 (焉耆鎮)	焉耆回族自治县 (焉耆镇)	150,000	160,000	130,000	2429
Yili Hasake (Ili Kazakh) Autonomous Prefecture	伊犁哈薩克自治州	伊犁哈萨克自治州	4,490,000	4,720,000	2,750,000	267,343[m]
Yining (Ghulja; Gulja) City (Ailanmubage Subdistrict)	伊寧市 (艾蘭木巴格街道)	伊宁市 (艾兰木巴格街道)	470,000	520,000	570,000	730
Kuitun (Küytun; Kuytun) City (Tuanjielu Subdistrict)	奎屯市 (團結路街道)	奎屯市 (团结路街道)	310,000	300,000	210,000	910
Huo'erguosi (Khorgas; Korgas) City[n] (Longhailu)	霍爾果斯市 (隴海路)	霍尔果斯市 (陇海路)	N/A	90,000	60,000	1909
Yining (Gulja) County (Jiliyuzi Town)	伊寧縣 (吉里於孜鎮)	伊宁县 (吉里于孜镇)	420,000	430,000	430,000	4386
Huocheng County (Shuiding Town)	霍城縣 (水定鎮)	霍城县 (水定镇)	400,000	410,000	280,000	2930
Gongliu (Tokkuztara) County (Gongliu Town)	鞏留縣 (鞏留鎮)	巩留县 (巩留镇)	200,000	200,000	200,000	4124
Xinyuan (Künas; Kunes) County (Xinyuan Town)	新源縣 (新源鎮)	新源县 (新源镇)	300,000	320,000	320,000	7583
Zhaosu (Mongolküre; Mongolkure) County (Zhaosu Town)	昭蘇縣 (昭蘇鎮)	昭苏县 (昭苏镇)	180,000	190,000	180,000	10,465
Tekesi (Tekes) County (Tekesi Town)	特克斯縣 (特克斯鎮)	特克斯县 (特克斯镇)	160,000	170,000	170,000	8080
Nileke (Nilka) County (Nileke Town)	尼勒克縣 (尼勒克鎮)	尼勒克县 (尼勒克镇)	180,000	190,000	180,000	10,130

(continued)

Table 32.5 (continued)

Name	Traditional	Simplified	Population (2012)	Population (2016)	Population (2020)	Area (Sq. Km)
Chabucha'erxibo (Qapqal Xibe; Qapqal; Chapchal) Autonomous County (Chabucha'er Town)	察布查爾錫伯自治縣 (察布查爾鎮)	察布查尔锡伯自治县 (察布查尔镇)	190,000	190,000	130,000	4126
Tacheng (Tarbaghatay) Prefecture	塔城地區	塔城地区	1,030,000	1,050,000	990,000	94,876
Tacheng (Qoqek) City (Heping Subdistrict)	塔城市 (和平街道)	塔城市 (和平街道)	170,000	170,000	160,000	4007
Wusu (Usu) City (Hongqiao Subdistrict)	烏蘇市 (虹橋街道)	乌苏市 (虹桥街道)	220,000	230,000	220,000	14,379
Emin (Dorbiljin) County (Emin Town)	額敏縣 (額敏鎮)	额敏县 (额敏镇)	220,000	220,000	210,000	9147
Shawan County (Sandaozi Town)	沙灣縣 (三道河子鎮)	沙湾县 (三道河子镇)	210,000	220,000	200,000	12,460
Tuoli (Toli) County (Tuoli Town)	托里縣 (托里鎮)	托里县 (托里镇)	100,000	100,000	90,000	19,992
Yumin (Qagantokay; Chaghantoqay) County (Halabula Town)	裕民縣 (哈拉布拉鎮)	裕民县 (哈拉布拉镇)	60,000	60,000	60,000	6107
Hebukesai'er Menggu (Hoboksar; Koboksar Mongol) Autonomous County (Hebukesai'er Town)	和布克賽爾蒙古自治縣 (和布克賽爾鎮)	和布克赛尔蒙古自治县 (和布克赛尔镇)	50,000	50,000	50,000	28,784
Aletai (Altay) Prefecture	阿勒泰地區	阿勒泰地区	650,000	660,000	660,000	117,078
Aletai (Altay) City (Jinshanlu Subdistrict)	阿勒泰市 (金山路街道)	阿勒泰市 (金山路街道)	230,000	230,000	230,000	10,819
Bu'erjin (Burqin; Burchin) County (Bu'erjin Town)	布爾津縣 (布爾津鎮)	布尔津县 (布尔津镇)	70,000	70,000	70,000	10,369
Fuyun (Koktokay) County (Ku'e'erqisi Town)	富蘊縣 (庫額爾齊斯鎮)	富蕴县 (库额尔齐斯镇)	90,000	100,000	100,000	32,327

(continued)

Table 32.5 (continued)

Name	Traditional	Simplified	Population (2012)	Population (2016)	Population (2020)	Area (Sq. Km)
Fuhai (Burultokay; Burultoqay) County (Fuhai Town)	福海縣 (福海鎮)	福海县 (福海镇)	70,000	70,000	70,000	32,442
Habahe (Kaba) County (Akeqi Town)	哈巴河縣 (阿克齊鎮)	哈巴河县 (阿克齐镇)	90,000	90,000	90,000	8186
Qinghe (Qinggil) County (Qinghe Town)	青河縣 (青河鎮)	青河县 (青河镇)	60,000	60,000	60,000	15,790
Jimunai (Jeminay; Jeminey) County (Tuoputiereke Town)	吉木乃縣 (托普鐵熱克鎮)	吉木乃县 (托普铁热克镇)	40,000	40,000	40,000	7145

[a]Established December 2012
[b]Established 2014
[c]Established March 2015
[d]Established 2016
[e]Established November 2019
[f]Kuche county made a city in November 2019
[g]National Geographic holds "Katakax" but this appears to be in error. *Atlas of China*, Washington, DC: National Geographic, 2008, p. 119
[h]Established March 2015, along with Gaochang district
[i]From another name transliterated from 皮羌 (*píqiāng*)
[j]Dissolved in 2016 to form a larger, municipal-level Hami City
[k]County-level city of Hami dissolved, renamed Yizhou district in 2016
[l]Established 2012
[m]Area also includes that of Tacheng and Aletai prefectures
[n]Established 2014

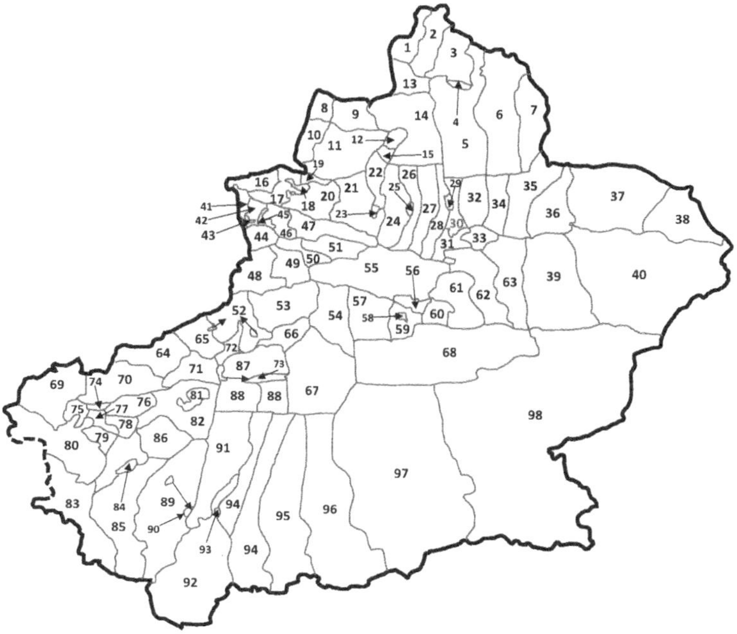

1. Habahe (Kaba) County
2. Bu'erjin (Burqin) County
3. Aletai (Altay) City
4. Beitun City
5. Fuhai County
6. Fuyun County
7. Qinghe County
8. Tacheng City
9. Emin (Dorbiljin) County
10. Yumin County
11. Tuoli (Toli) County
12. Wu'erhe (Urho) District
13. Jimunai (Jeminay) County
14. Hebukesai'er (Hoboksar) Mongol Autonomous County
15. Baijiantan District
16. Wenquan County
17. Bole (Bortala) City
18. Shuanghe City
19. Alashankou City
20. Jinghe County
21. Wusu (Usu) City
22. Kelamayi (Karamay) District
23. Dushanzi District
24. **Shawan County**
25. **Shihezi City**
26. **Manasi (Manas) County**
27. **Hutubi County**
28. **Changji City**
29. **Wujiaqu City**
30. **Wulumuqi (Ürümqi) City**
31. **Wulumuqi (Ürümqi) County**
32. **Fukang City**
33. **Dabancheng District**
34. Jimusa'er (Jimsar) County
35. Qitai County
36. Muleihasake (Mori Kazakh) Autonomous County
37. Balikun (Barköl Kazakh) Autonomous County
38. Yiwu (Aratürük) County
39. Shanshan County
40. Yizhou District
41. Huo'erguosi (Khorgas) City
42. Huocheng County
43. Kekedala (Kokdala) City
44. Chabucha'erxibo (Qapqal Xibe) Autonomous County
45. Yining (Ghulja) City
46. Yining (Ghulja) County
47. Nileke (Nilka) County
48. Zhaosu (Mongolküre) County
49. Tekesi (Tekes) County
50. Gongliu (Tokkuztara) County
51. Xinyuan County
52. **Wensu County**
53. **Baicheng County**
54. **Kuche (Kuqa) City**
55. **Hejing County**
56. **Yanqi Hui Autonomous County**
57. **Luntai County**
58. **Tiemenguan City**
59. **Ku'erle (Korla) City**
60. **Bohu County**
61. **Heshuo (Hoxud) County**
62. **Tuokexun (Toksun) County**
63. **Gaochang District**
64. **Aheqi (Akqi) County**
65. **Wushi (Uqturpan) County**
66. **Xinhe County**
67. **Shaya (Xayar) County**
68. **Yuli (Lopnur) County**
69. **Wuqia (Ulugchat) County**
70. **Atushi (Artux) City**
71. **Keping (Kalpin) County**
72. **Akesu (Aksu) City**
73. **Ala'er (Alar) City**
74. **Kashi (Kashgar) City**
75. **Shufu County**
76. **Jiashi (Peyziwat) County**
77. **Shule County**
78. **Yuepuhu (Yopurga) County**
79. **Yingjisha (Yengisar) County**
80. **Aketao (Akto) County**
81. **Tumushuke (Tumxuk) City**
82. **Bachu (Maralbexi) County**
83. **Tashiku'ergan (Taxkorgan) Tajik Autonomous County**
84. **Zepu (Poskam) County**
85. **Yecheng (Kargilik) County**
86. **Maigaiti (Makit) County**
87. **Awati (Awat) County**
88. **(Subordinate to Akesu City)**
89. **Pishan County**
90. **Kunyu City**
91. **Moyu (Karakax) County**
92. **Hetian (Hotan) County**
93. **Hetian (Hotan) City**
94. **Luopu (Lop) County**
95. **Cele (Qira) County**
96. **Yutian (Keriya) County**
96. Minfeng (Niye) County
97. Qiemo (Qarqan) County
98. Ruoqian (Qarkilik) County

Fig. 32.2 Xinjiang: Subdistricts (Provincial Capital City: Ürümqi City). (Drawn by the Author after People's Republic of China, Ministry of Civil Affairs (MCA 2020))

References

Ahmed, Zaneb. 2022. Revolution and state formation as oasis storytelling in Xinjiang. In *Xinjiang year zero*, ed. Darren Byler, Ivan Franceschini, and Nicholas Loubere, 31–40. Canberra: Australian University Press.

Baidu.com. 2013. *International religions: China's favorable Islamic development situation*. 国际宗教:中国伊斯兰教发展形势喜人各省穆斯林人口排行. Accessed 9 Mar 2013.

Baumer, Christoph. 2012. *The history of Central Asia: The age of the steppe warriors*. New York: I.B. Tauris.

Bovingdon, Gardner. 2014. Xinjiang. In *Politics in China: An introduction*, ed. William A. Joseph, 2nd ed., 428–451. New York: Oxford University Press.

Chaudhuri, Debasish. 2016. China's policy in Xinjiang, 1948-1978. In *Xinjiang—China's Northwest Frontier*, ed. K. Warikoo, 56–81. New York: Routledge.

Clarke, Michael E. 2011. *Xinjiang and China's rise in Central Asia—A history*. New York: Routledge.

Di Cosmo, Nicola. 1999. The northern frontier in pre-imperial China. In *Xinjiang—China's Northwest Frontier*, ed. Michael Loewe and Edward L. Shaughnessy, 885–966. New York: Cambridge University Press.

Hansen, Valerie. 2012. *The silk road: A new history*. New York: Oxford University Press.

Hayes, Anna. 2012. Uighur transnationalism in contemporary Australia: Exile, sanctuary, community and future. In *Cultures in refuge: Seeking sanctuary in modern Australia*, ed. Anna Hayes and Robert Mason, 179–193. New York: Routledge.

Killgrove, Kristina. 2015. DNA reveals these red-haired Chinese mummies come from Europe and Asia. *Forbes*, 18 July. https://www.forbes.com/sites/kristinakillgrove/2015/07/18/these-red-haired-chinese-mummies-come-from-all-over-eurasia-dna-reveals/?sh=1fbc6e523e2c.

Ma, Zhengliang. 2014. Analysis of Chinese Muslim population trends. *Journal of Guizhou University Art Edition* (sic). 馬正亮. 中國穆斯林人口發展分析. 貴州大學學報 (社會科學版) 32(3):98–106.

Millward, James A. 2007. *Eurasian crossroads: A history of Xinjiang*. New York: Columbia University Press.

Ministry of Civil Affairs (MCA), People's Republic of China. 2020. *County/township administration handbook*. Beijing: China Statistics Press. 中華人民共和國民政部, 中華人民共和國,鄉鎮行政區劃簡冊.

Myers, Steven Lee. 2019. A crackdown on Muslims is spreading beyond Xinjiang. *The New York Times*. 23 September. Section A, p. 8.

OpIndia. 2021. *'Mandarin only': China removes Uyghur language as medium of instruction in Xinjiang*. 1 February. https://www.opindia.com/2021/02/china-xinjiang-province-uyghur-language-students-not-allowed-mandarin-only/.

Ray, Jayanta Kumar. 2011. *India's foreign relations, 1947–2007*. New Delhi: Routledge.

Reed, J. Todd, and Diana Raschke. 2010. *The ETIM: China's Islamic militants and the global terrorist threat*. Santa Barbara: Praeger.

Ruser, Nathan. 2020. *Documenting Xinjiang's detention system*. Australian Strategic Policy Institute (ASPI), September 2020. https://cdn.xjdp.aspi.org.au/wp-content/uploads/2020/09/25125443/documenting-xinjiangs-detention-system.cleaned.pdf.

Sintash, Bahram K. 2019. *Demolishing faith: The destruction and desecration of Uyghur mosques and shrines*. Uyghurism.com and the Uyghur Human Rights Project. https://docs.uhrp.org/pdf/UHRP_report_Demolishing_Faith.pdf.

Tian, Weijiang. 2001. *Xinjiang history*. Beijing: Wuzhou Media Publishing House. 田卫疆. 新疆历史. 北京: 五洲傳播出版社.

US Department of State, Joint Statement on Xinjiang. 2021. 22 March. https://www.state.gov/joint-statement-on-xinjiang/.

Wang, Xiaofu. 2018. A new study on Mouyu Qaghan's conversion to Manichaeism. In *Great journeys across the Pamir mountains: A festschrift in honor of Zhang Guangda on his eighty-fifth birthday*, ed. Huai Yuchen and Xinjiang Rong, 111–127. Boston: Brill.

Webber, Michael John. 2012. *Making capitalism in rural China*. Northhampton: Edgar Elgar Publishing.

Xinjiang Bureau of Statistics (XBS). 2021. *Communiqué of the Seventh National Census of Xinjiang Uygur Autonomous Region*. 14 June. 新疆维吾尔自治区第七次全国人口普查公报. http://kr.china-embassy.org/chn/xwxx/t1884235.htm.

Yuan, Zuliang. 2012. *China's population through history: Qin to Western Han*. Beijing: People's Press. 袁祖亮,中國人口通史: 秦西漢卷 Vol. 3, 北京: 人民出版社.

Zhang, Shunan. 2021. *The 2020 per capita income list of residents in various provinces: Shanghai is the richest, and it has risen sharply*. Finance.people.com. 22 January. 张澍楠. 2020年各省份居民人均收入榜: 上海最有钱, 这地涨得猛. http://finance.people.com.cn/n1/2021/0122/c1004-32008733.html.

Chapter 33
Yunnan

Abstract Home to the oldest hominid ever discovered in China, *Homo erectus Yuanmouensis*, named after Yuanmou County, Yunnan is tropical, tobacco-growing country. Originating with the Dian Kingdom (279 BCE), and from which Yunnan derives its abbreviated name, famed Chinese military strategist, Zhuge Liang led campaigns to pacify the region of modern-day Yunnan. Rich with copper and silver, under the Yuan dynasty, Yunnan received its administrative name (1276), while its population (especially from Han Chinese migrations) increased rapidly through the Ming. Today, economically, Yunnan's key cash crop is tobacco, although as a province it ranks in the bottom ten of mainland China's 31 provinces and major cities in terms of gross domestic product (GDP), and 28th in per capita income (USD $3600). From 2010–2020, Yunnan's population has grown about 2.7%, and the official family registered (*hukou*) population differs from the 2020 census residential population by about 600,000, indicating Yunnan does not significantly contribute to China's "floating population."

E. Croddy, *China's Provinces and Populations*,
https://doi.org/10.1007/978-3-031-09165-0_33

Yunnan Province (雲南省 *yúnnán shěng*): Abbreviations 云 (*yún*); 滇 (*diān*) (Fig. 33.1)

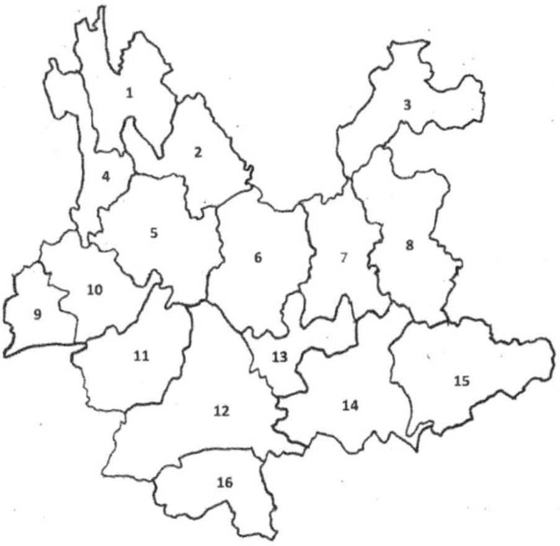

1. Diqing Tibetan Autonomous Prefecture
2. Lijiang City
3. Zhaotong City
4. Nujiang Lisu Autonomous Prefecture
5. Dali Bai Autonomous Prefecture
6. Chuxiong Yi Autonomous Prefecture
7. Kunming City
8. Qujing City
9. Dehong Dai and Jingpo Autonomous Prefecture
10. Baoshan City
11. Lincang City
12. Pu'er City
13. Yuxi City
14. Honghe Hani and Yi Autonomous Prefecture
15. Wenshan Zhuang and Miao Autonomous Prefecture
16. Xishuangbanna Dai Autonomous Prefecture

Fig. 33.1 Yunnan province major cities and prefectures (provincial capital: Kunming City). (Drawn by the Author after People's Republic of China, Ministry of Civil Affairs. (MCA 2020))

Yunnan Province: General Impressions

In some ways, one can compare Yunnan somewhat closely to that of states in the United States southeast region (e.g. North Carolina): a region replete with large tobacco and cotton farms, not as economically developed as the northeast, and generally possessing a large rural sector. And then there is the warm, tropical weather. As a Chinese tourist guidebook describes visiting the provincial capital of Kunming city: "No matter where you come from, and regardless of the season, what you feel most is the ever-spring and brilliant sunlight" (Shang-Ch'i 2017). With significant influences from its many ethnic groups, even within such a varied landscape that is Chinese cooking, Yunnanese or Dian (滇菜 *diān cài*) cuisine is especially unique. (The simplified abbreviation for Yunnan, Dian (滇 *diān*), has been in use since 1413). Yunnan is also known for its tea, and of China's many famous tea varieties, Pu'er (普洱市 *pŭ'ĕr*) being among them, and large quantities of Pu'er tea are produced in Xishuang, Lincang, and Baoshan.

Prehistoric Yunnan

Yunnan is home to (as far as it is known) the oldest specimen of *Homo erectus* ever discovered in China (possibly Asia). It was named *Homo erectus Yuanmouensis* after its place of discovery, Yuanmou County (元謀縣 *yuánmóu xiàn*), in Chuxiong Yi Autonomous Prefecture (楚雄彝族自治州 *chǔxióngyízú zìzhìzhōu*). Not without controversy, research indicates "Yuanmou Man" is 1.7 million years old (Zhu et al. 2008). In 1976, a humanoid cranial specimen was found at Longtanshan Mountain (龍潭山 *lóngtánshān*), Dayuxiang Township (大漁鄉 *dàyú xiāng*), in Kunming City. "Kunming Man" lived approximately 30,000 years ago. The Laohu Cave (老虎洞 *lǎohǔ dòng*) site, located in Shidian County (施甸縣 *shīdiàn xiàn*), was first excavated in 1987. Dating back to about 18,500 years ago (using carbon-14), researchers have uncovered numerous stone tools such as hammers and scrapers. Other Paleolithic sites in Yunnan include:

- Cituo Cave (刺托洞 *cìtuō dòng*), Fuyuan County, (富源縣 *fùyuán xiàn*), dated ca. 40,000 years ago
- Dabanqiao (大板橋 *dàbǎn qiáo*), Kunming City, Guandu district (官渡區 *guāndù qū*), ca 10,000 years old
- The Zhangkou Cave site (張口洞 *zhāngkǒu dòng*), located in Kunming City's Yiliang County, Jiuxiang Township (宜良縣九鄉 *yíliáng xiàn, jiǔ xiāng*) is dated about 10,000–15,000 years ago

Yunnan's Ancient Past

The Dian Kingdom (滇國 *diānguó*), located next to Dian Lake (滇池 *diānchí*) and near modern-day Kunming city, has its origins dating back to the Warring States period. In 279 BCE, the Chu Kingdom General Zhuang Qiao (莊蹻 *zhuāng qiāo*) led a military campaign in southern China that included today's Guizhou Province and further down south to Kunming City. His triumphant journey back home, however, was interrupted by the invasion of Chu by the Qin (277 BCE). He then decided to remain, establishing the Dian Kingdom, and he was enthroned as King Zhuang (莊王 *zhuāng wáng*). In the Western Han (221–207 BCE), modern-day Yunnan province was administered within the Ailao State (哀牢 *āiláo*) in today's Myanmar (Burma), then under the larger Yizhou Inspectorate (益州刺史部南部 *yìzhōu cìshǐbù nánbù*). An entity known as Yunnan (雲南 *yúnnán*) was one of the major cities in the Yizhou Prefecture (益州郡 *yìzhōu jùn*) (Tan 1996). In 109 BCE, during the Eastern Han, Yunnan of today formed the main center of the Yizhou Inspectorate in and around modern-day Puning City (普寧市*pǔníng shì*). This was evinced by its official seal (滇王之印 *diānwáng zhī yìn*) that was found in the King of Dian's tomb (dated 206–25 BCE) at the Shizhaishan site (石寨山古墓群 *shízhàishān gǔmùqún*) in Jinning District (晉寧區 *jìnníng qū*). Located about 40 kilometers south of Kunming, the Shizhaishan tomb excavation also revealed an ornately designed bronze plaque fashioned with etched symbols similar to Egyptian hieroglyphics. These symbols on the metallic surface depict people being taken captive, enumerating livestock, containers and other items. Each of these pictographs are accompanied by a numeric system of circles and dashes representing tens and ones, respectfully (Smith, 2013). The precise meaning of many of its other inscriptions have yet to be deciphered.

The famed strategist and statesman Zhuge Liang (諸葛亮 *zhūgé liàng*; 181–234 CE) led pacification campaigns against the indigenous peoples of Yunnan in 225 CE. Famously, Zhuge Liang captured and released his nemesis, Meng Huo (孟獲 *mèng huò*), over and over several times until the latter capitulated, and Zhuge Liang's forces then finally seized the lake of Dian (滇池 *diānchí*) region. In ca. 320 CE, the Cuan clan (爨氏 *cuàn shì*) moved in and occupied modern-day Yunnan. Following that, Cuan Chen (爨琛 *cuàn chēn*) ruled the area for the next four centuries. By ca. 600, the Nanning Region (南寧地區 *nánníng dìqū*), which was similar in size and dimensions of today's Yunnan province, was ruled by the Nanning Governorship (南寧州總管府 *nánníngzhōu zǒngguǎnfǔ*). Its regional localities took on names reflecting the dominance of the Cuan clan of the times, to include East (東爨 *dōng cuàn*) and West Cuan (西爨 *xī cuàn*). At about this same time there was established Kunming Prefecture (昆明府 *kūnmíng fǔ*). Having crushed the Cuan hegemon at last in 748, the Tang dynasty established Nanzhao (南詔 *nánzhào*), expanding its territorial holdings into modern-day Burma, Laos and Vietnam. In 779 CE, the monarch of Nanzhao, Yi Mouxun (異牟尋 *yì móuxún*; 754–808 CE), moved its capital to the oddly-named Yangjumie City (陽苴咩城 *yángjūmiē chéng*), also known as Purple City (紫城 *zǐ chéng*). The remains of this old city were later discovered buried under the ancient walls of modern-day Dali.

During the Tang dynasty, Nanzhao was divided into a number of martial governorships, such as the Lishui (麗水節度 *lìshuǐ jiédù*), Yongchang (永昌節度 *yǒngchāng jiédù*), and Tonghai (通海都督 *tōnghǎidū dū*), as well as a southern grouping called the "ten tribes, those with blackened teeth."[1] In 937, Duan Siping (段思平 *Duàn Sīpíng*), himself of Bai ethnicity, conquered the region of Yunnan, establishing the Dali Kingdom (大理國 *dàlǐ guó*), its capital located in today's Dali City (大理市 *dàlǐshì*) in Dali Bai (Bo) Autonomous Prefecture (大理白族自治州 *dàlǐ báizú zìzhìzhōu*). This would last until 1253, when Kublai Khan (忽必烈 *hūbìliè*) sent his military to conquer Dali, splitting it up into five sectors:

- Chahanzhang Peoples' Chiefdom (茶罕章管民官 *cháhǎnzhāng guǎnmínguān*);
- Hacizhang (哈刺章 *hācì zhāng*)
- Yachi (鴨齒 *yāchǐ*)
- Chituge'er (赤突哥兒 *chìtúgē'ér*) and

[1] 黑齒等十部落 *hēichǐděng shíbùluò*.

- Jinchi (金齒 *jīnchǐ*)

While the Yuan dynasty (ca. 1270 CE) established its own military command structure, much of the pre-Mongolian administrative structure remained in place. The place names at this time reflected not only Mongolian but also Tibetan influences: Hacizhang (哈刺章 *hācì zhāng*), the Yuan Dynasty name for Dali City, was originally transliterated from the Mongolian word for "black", while Chahan, located opposite to modern day Lijiang, meant "white." The Yachi region, on the other hand (today's Kunming City) derives its name from how Mongolians heard the local Naxi (Nakhi) tribe's accent when referring to Kunming: "*yichi*," meaning "south." Another interesting moniker was given to an area located in modern-day Anshun City, Chituge'er (赤秃哥兒 *chìtūgē'ér*), which is from the Mongolian word for "ghost." Throughout the changes it went while under the Mongolian (Yuan) rule, the Dali capital, Hacizhang, remained as ever an important political, cultural and economic stronghold.

The province of Yunnan (雲南行省*yúnnán xíngshěng*) was formally established in 1276. Yunnan's first governor, residing in Zhongqing Lu (中慶路 *zhōngqìng lù*, today's Kunming) was a Muslim, originally born in Bhukara (Uzbekistan): Sayyid Ajjal Shams al-Din Omar, rendered in Chinese as Saidianchi-Shansiding (賽典赤·贍思丁 *sàidiǎnchì shànsīdīng*). In addition to Mongolians, large numbers of other Central Asians, referred to by the Chinese as Semuren (色目人 *sèmùrén*), moved to Yunnan, who originally formed the Hui minority that exist there today.

Yunnan prospered greatly from its bountiful sources of copper and silver. Upon the end of the Yuan, the Ming Dynasty brought more and more Han Chinese to Yunnan, its population growing from 200,000 to 1,400,000 by 1661, when the last Ming emperor, Zhu Youlang (朱由榔 *zhū yóuláng*), fled to the province for safety. Still on the run from the Qing court, Zhu Youlang was captured in Burma the year after, and summarily strangled to death (typical form of execution in those days) in Kunming.

The Panthay Hui People Rebellion

The Panthay (a Burmese-Shan word for Moslem) were Hui rebels who rose up against the Qing Dynasty from 1856–1874. At least a million people died during this conflict. Its leader, Du Wenxiu (杜文秀 *dù wénxiù*), a Han Chinese convert to the Islamic faith, governed Yunnan for 16 years and was seated in Dali City. He was eventually overthrown by the Qing, committing suicide by poison (possibly an opium overdose) in 1872.

Following the Wuchang Uprising led by Sun Yat-sen's organization of revolutionaries, Yunnan was separated from the Qing Dynasty on 30 October 1911, an event locally referred to as the Chongjiu Uprising (重九起義 *chóngjiǔ qǐyì*), named after the traditional lunar calendar date. One of the key military leaders of the Chongjiu Uprising, Tang Jiyao (唐繼堯 *táng jìyáo*) became governor-warlord of Yunnan Province from 1913–27, followed by Long Yun (龍雲 *lóng yún* 1928–1945). In October 1945, Generalissimo Chiang Kai-shek turned against Long Yun and had him overthrown. The Yunnan-Burma road was built during the Sino-Japanese War (1937–1945), becoming the main overland connection between China and the outside world. During its invasion of Yunnan in 1942 and its occupation of Burma, the Japanese army infamously cutoff these Yunnan-Burmese corridors.

Great Leap Forward (1958–1962)

For those in Yunnan suffering under the Maoist collective nightmare of the Great Leap Forward, and unlike for those living in other provinces, there was an option to escape the famine by dint of Yunnan's long border with Burma (Myanmar) and Laos. Nonetheless, Yunnan's northwest prefecture, Lijiang (麗江府 *lìjiāng fǔ*), could not escape the ravages of Mao Zedong's man-made catastrophe. As elsewhere throughout China during this period, exaggerated food production quotas exacerbated the famine. For example, a Lijiang prefectural[2] gazette (中甸縣誌 *zhōngdiàn xiàn zhì*) reported 22,780,000 kilos of food, but the figure reported to Party officials was twice that (47,000,000 kilos). Due to these fraudulant ration supply figures, nearly 8% of persons living in Zhongdian county in 1960 starved, leading to 2037 deaths that year. From 1957 to the end of 1961, Lijiang Prefecture's population fell by about 87,000 people during the famine (Yang 2007).

Yunnan's Economy and Population Trends

In some ways resembling the economies of other southern regions such is that of the United States, Yunnan Province is China's largest tobacco producing region. This is certainly saying something, as mainland China is the largest tobacco growing country in the world. To get a sense, in ca. 2010, 45% of Yunnan's tax revenues came from its tobacco industry (Norton 2011).

Ranking in the bottom ten in terms of economic output, in 2015 Yunnan had a nominal gross domestic product (GDP) of USD $213 billion in 2015, and $381

[2] Now Shangri-La City 香格里拉市 *xiānggélǐlā shì*, part of Diqing Tibetan Autonomous Prefecture 迪慶藏族自治州 díqìngzàngzú zìzhìzhōu.

billion, ranked 18th out of mainland China's 31 provinces and major cities. Yunnan was ranked 28th in terms of per capita income of $3,623 (Zhang, 2021). With a 2020 population (census) of 47,209,277 (see Tables 32.1 and 32.2), rising 2.7% overall since 2010, its residential population is somewhat lower than its permanent (*hukou*) registered population that year of 47,690,000 (Table 32.3).

Yunnan's Ethnic Groups

Over 15 million of Yunnan's residents belong to 25 (out of 56) of China's officially recognized ethnic groups (including the Han majority). Of these, the following ethnic minorities in Yunnan number over one million: Yi (4,050,000), Hani (1,660,000), Bai (1,570,000), Lisu (1,260,000), Miao (1,203,000) and Dai (1,160,000). Of those groups numbering more than 100,000 are the Zhuang (nearly one million), Lahu (490,000), Wa (430,000), Naxi (310,000), Yao (190,000), Jingpo (148,000), Tibetan (143,000), and Bulang (120,000); nine groups that number over 10,000 individuals include the Bouyei (55,000), Achang (40,000), Nu (37,000), Jinuo (21,000), Hui (27,000), Pumi (20,000), De'ang (20,000), and Manchurian (14,000). The Mongolian, Shui, and Derong (Dulong) make up the remaining, with about 6–10 thousand individuals each (Xixi 2019).

Table 33.3 (below) shows the *hukou* (family registered) populations based on PRC Ministry of Civil Affairs data. (Districts listed directly under major cities are government seats, as are those in parentheses). One can compare these data with the census (usual residential populations based on 2010 and 2020 censuses in Tables 33.1 and 33.2 (below):

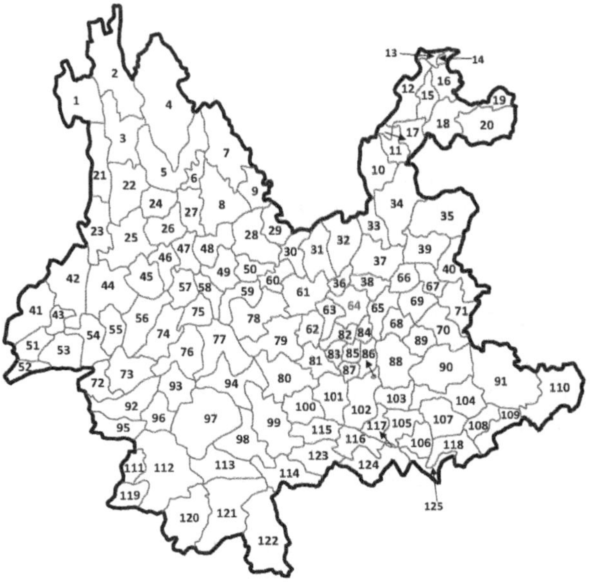

1. Gongshan Derong and Nu Autonomous County
2. Deqin (Dêqên) County
3. Weixi Lisu Autonomous County
4. Xianggelila (Shangri-La) City
5. Yulong Naxizu (Nakhi) Autonomous County
6. Gucheng District
7. Ninglang Yi Autonomous County
8. Yongsheng County
9. Huaping County
10. Qiaojia County
11. Ludian County
12. Yongshan County
13. Suijiang County
14. Shuifu City
15. Daguan County
16. Yanjin County
17. Zhaoyang District
18. Yiliang County
19. Weixin County
20. Zhenxiong County
21. Fugong County
22. Lanping Bai and Pumi Autonomous County
23. Lushui City
24. County Jianchuan
25. Yunlong County
26. Eryuan County
27. Heqing County
28. Dayao County
29. Huaping County
30. Yuanmou County
31. Wuding County
32. Luquan Yi and Miao Autonomous County
33. Dongchuan District
34. Huize County
35. Xuanwei City
36. Fumin County
37. Xundian Hui and Yi Autonomous County
38. Songming County
39. Zhanyi District
40. Fuyuan County
41. Yingjiang County
42. Tengchong City
43. Lianghe County
44. Longyang District
45. Yongping County
46. Yangbi Yi Autonomous County
47. Dali City
48. Binchuan County
49. Yangyun County
50. Yao'an County
51. Longchuan County
52. Ruili City
53. Mangshi City
54. Longling County
55. Shidian County
56. Changning County
57. WeishanYi and Hui Autonomous County
58. Midu County
59. Nanhua County
60. Mouding County
61. Lufeng County
62. Yimen County
63. Anning City
64. Kunming City
65. Yiliang County
66. Malong District
64. Kunming City
65. Yiliang County
66. Malong District
67. Qilin District
68. Shilin Yi Autonomous County
69. Luliang County
70. Shizong County
71. Luoping County
72. Zhenkang County
73. Yongde County
74. Fengqing County
75. Nanjian Yi Autonomous County
76. Yunxian County
77. Jingdong Yi Autonomous County
78. Chuxiong City
79. Shuangbai County
80. Xinping Yi and Dai Autonomous County
81. Eshan Yi Autonomous County
82. Jinning District
83. Hongta District
84. Chengjiang City
85. Jiangchuan District
86. Huaning County
87. Tonghai County
88. Mile City
89. Luxi County
90. Qiubei County
91. Guangnan County
92. Gengma Da and Wa (Va) Autonomous County
93. Linxiang District
94. Zhenyuan Yi, Hani and Lahu Autonomous County
95. Cangyuan Wa (Va) Autonomous County
96. Shuangjiang Lahu, Wa (Va), Bulang (Blang) and Dai Autonomous County
97. Jinggu Dai and Yi Autonomous County
98. Ning'er Hani and Yi Autonomous County
99. Mojiang Hani Autonomous County
100. Yuanjiang Hani, Yi and Dai Autonomous County
101. Shiping County
102. Jianshui County
103. Kaiyuan City
104. Yanshan County
105. Mengzi City
106. Pingbian Miao Autonomous County
107. Wenshan City
108. Xichou County
109. Malipo County
110. Funing County
111. Ximeng Wa (Va) Autonomous County
112. Lancang Lahu Autonomous County
113. Disrict Simao
114. Jiangcheng Hani and Yi Autonomous County
115. Honghe County
116. Yuanyang County
117. Gejiu City
118. Maguan County
119. Menglian Dai, Lahu, and Va (Wa) Autonomous County
120. Menghai County
121. Jinghong City
122. Mengla County
123. Lüchun County
124. Jinping Miao, Yao and Dai Autonomous County
125. Hekou Yao Autonomous County

Fig. 33.2 Yunnan province: subdistricts (provincial capital: Kunming City). (Drawn by the Author after People's Republic of China, Ministry of Civil Affairs. (MCA 2020))

Table 33.1 Yunnan province population (residential 常住人口 *chángzhù rénkǒu*) data. (YPBS 2021)

City/Region	Population (2010)	Population (2020)
Kunming City 昆明市 *kūnmíng shì*	6,432,000	8,460,088
Qujing City 曲靖市 *qūjìng shì*	5,855,000	5,765,775
Yuxi City 玉溪市 *yùxī shì*	2,304,000	2,249,502
Baoshan City 保山市 *bǎoshān shì*	2,506,000	2,431,211
Zhaotong City 昭通市 *zhāotōng shì*	5,213,000	5,092,611
Lijiang City 麗江市 *lìjiāng shì*	1,245,000	1,253,878
Pu'er City 普洱市 *pǔ'ěr shì*	2,543,000	2,404,954
Lincang City 臨滄市 *líncāng shì*	2,430,000	2,257,991
Dehong Dai and Jingpo Autonomous Prefecture 德宏傣族景頗族自治州 *déhóng dǎizú jǐngpōzú zìzhìzhōu*	1,211,000	1,315,709
Nujiang Lisu Autonomous Prefecture 怒江傈僳族自治州 *nùjiāng lìsùzú zìzhìzhōu*	534,000	552,694
Diqing Tibetan Autonomous Prefecture 迪慶藏族自治州 *díqìng zàngzú zìzhìzhōu*	400,000	387,511
Dali Bai (Bo) Autonomous Prefecture 大理白族自治州 *dàlǐ báizú zìzhìzhōu*	3.456,000	3,337,559
Chuxiong Yi Autonomous Prefecture 楚雄彝族自治州 *chǔxióng yízú zìzhìzhōu*	2,684,000	2,416,747
Honghe Hani and Yi Autonomous Prefecture 紅河哈尼族彝族自治州 *hónghé hānízú yízú zìzhìzhōu*	4,501,000	4,478,422
Wenshan Zhuang Autonomous Prefecture 文山壯族苗族自治州 *wénshān zhuàngzú miáozú zìzhìzhōu*	3,518,000	3,503,218
Xishuangbanna Dai Autonomous Prefecture 西雙版納傣族自治州 *xīshuāng bǎnnà dǎizú zìzhìzhōu*	1,134,000	1,301,407
Total	**45,966,000**	**47,209,277**

Table 33.2 Yunnan province: population data of cities and their subordinate sectors. (YPBS 2021)

Cities and subordinate sectors, population (2020 census)	Subordinate District, city and county populations (2020)	Total population (2020)
Kunming City 昆明市 ***kūnmíng shì***		**8,460,088**
Wuhua District 五華區 *wǔhuá qū*	1,143,085	
Panlong District 盤龍區 *pánlóng qū*	987,955	
Guandu District 官渡區 *guāndù qū*	1,602,279	
Shanxi District 西山區 *xīshān qū*	960,746	
Dongchuan District 東川區 *dōngchuān qū*	260,774	
Chenggong District 呈貢區 *chénggòng qū*	649,501	
Jinning District 晉寧區 *jìnníng qū*	346,268	

(continued)

Table 33.2 (continued)

Cities and subordinate sectors, population (2020 census)	Subordinate District, city and county populations (2020)	Total population (2020)
Fuming County 富民縣 *fùmín xiàn*	149,506	
Yiliang County 宜良縣 *yíliáng xiàn*	384,875	
Shilin Yizu Autonomous County 石林彝族自治縣 *shílín yízú zìzhìxiàn*	240,827	
Chongming County 崇明縣*chóngmíng xiàn*	410,929	
Luquan Yizu Miaozu Autonomous County 祿勸彝族苗族自治縣 *lùquàn yízú miáozú zìzhìxiàn*	378,881	
Xundian Huizu Yizu Autonomous County 尋甸回族彝族自治縣 *xúndiàn huízú yízú zìzhìxiàn*	460,739	
Anning County 安寧縣 *ānníng xiàn*	483,753	
Qujing City 曲靖市 ***qūjìng shì***		**5,765,775**
Qilin District 麒麟區 *qílín qū*	996,279	
Zhanyi District 沾益區 *zhānyì qū*	405,305	
Malong District 馬龍區 *mǎlóng qū*	193,137	
Luliang County 陸良縣 *lùliáng xiàn*	599,266	
Shizong County 師宗縣 *shīzōng xiàn*	376,902	
Luoping County 羅平縣 *luópíng xiàn*	535565	
Fuyuan County 富源縣 *fùyuán xiàn*	675,229	
Huize County 會澤縣 *huìzé xiàn*	794,279	
Xuanwei City 宣威市 *xuānwēi shì*	1,189,813	
Yuxi City 玉溪市 ***yùxī shì***		**2,249,502**
Hongta District 紅塔區 *hóngtǎ qū*	588,738	
Jiangchuan District 江川區 *jiāngchuān qū*	253,295	
Tonghai County 通海縣 *tōnghǎi xiàn*	289,891	
Huaning County 華寧縣 *huáníng xiàn*	190,425	
Yimen County 易門縣 *yìmén xiàn*	151,671	
Eshan County 峨山縣 *éshān xiàn*	143,903	
Xinping County 新平縣 *xīnpíng xiàn*	262,771	
Yuanjiang County 元江縣 *yuánjiāng xiàn*	195,647	
Chengjiang City 澄江市 *chéngjiāng shì*	173,161	
Baoshan City 保山市 ***bǎoshān shì***		**2,431,211**
Longyang District 隆陽區 *lóngyáng qū*	903,081	
Shidian County 施甸縣 *shīdiàn xiàn*	293,022	
Tengchong City 騰沖市 *téngchōng shì*	642,481	
Longling County 龍陵縣 *lónglíng xiàn*	272,769	
Changning County 昌寧縣 *chāngníng xiàn*	319,858	
Zhaotong City 昭通市 ***zhāotōng shì***		**5,092,611**
Zhaoyang District 昭陽區 *zhāoyáng qū*	911,766	
Ludian County 魯甸縣 *lǔdiàn xiàn*	398,447	
Qiaojia County 巧家縣 *qiǎojiā xiàn*	462,173	
Yanjin County 鹽津縣 *yánjīn xiàn*	317,463	

(continued)

Table 33.2 (continued)

Cities and subordinate sectors, population (2020 census)	Subordinate District, city and county populations (2020)	Total population (2020)
Daguan County 大關縣 *dàguān xiàn*	209,116	
Yongshan County 永善縣 *yǒngshàn xiàn*	349,157	
Suijiang County 綏江縣 *suíjiāng xiàn*	135,468	
Zhenxiong County 鎮雄縣 *zhènxióng xiàn*	1,349,795	
Yiliang County 彝良縣 *yíliáng xiàn*	503,376	
Weixin County 威信縣 *wēixìn xiàn*	352,318	
Shuifu City 水富市 *shuǐfù shì*	103,532	
Lijiang City 麗江市 ***lìjiāng shì***		**1,253,878**
Gucheng District 古城區 *gǔchéng qū*	288,787	
Yulong Naxizu (Nakhi) Autonomous County 玉龍納西族自治縣 *yùlóng nàxīzú zìzhìxiàn*	224,039	
Yongsheng County 永勝縣 *yǒngshèng xiàn*	336,832	
Huaping County 華坪縣 *huápíng xiàn*	159,695	
Ninglang Yizu Autonomous County 寧蒗彝族自治縣 *nínglàng yízú zìzhìxiàn*	244,525	
Pu'er City 普洱市 ***pǔ'ěr shì***		**2,404,954**
Simao District 思茅區 *sīmáo qū*	416,188	
Ning'er District 寧洱區 *níng'ěr qū*	162,711	
Mojiang County 墨江縣 *mòjiāng xiàn*	281,554	
Jingdong County 景東縣 *jǐngdōng xiàn*	303,109	
Jinggu County 景谷縣 *jǐnggǔ xiàn*	277,417	
Zhenyuan County 鎮沅縣 *zhènyuán xiàn*	179,503	
Jiangcheng County 江城縣 *jiāngchéng xiàn*	111,033	
Menglian County 孟連縣 *mènglián xiàn*	144,693	
Lancang County 瀾滄縣 *láncāng xiàn*	441,455	
Ximeng County 西盟縣 *xīméng xiàn*	87,291	
Lincang City 臨滄市 ***líncāng shì***		**2,257,991**
Linxiang District 臨翔區 *línxiáng qū*	370,947	
Fengqing County 鳳慶縣 *fèngqìng xiàn*	385,420	
Yunxian County 雲縣 *yúnxiàn*	389,180	
Yongde County 永德縣 *yǒngdé xiàn*	328,864	
Zhenkang County 鎮康縣 *zhènkāng xiàn*	172,879	
Shuangjiang Lahuzu Wazu Bulangzu Daizu (Lahu, Va, Blang and Dai) Autonomous County 雙江拉祜族佤族布朗族傣族自治縣 *shuāngjiāng lāhùzú wǎzú bùlǎngzú dǎizú zìzhìxiàn*	164,756	
Gengma Daizu Wazu (Dai and Va) Autonomous County 耿馬傣族佤族自治縣 *gěngmǎ dǎizú wǎzú zìzhìxiàn*	285,683	
Cangyuan Wazu (Va) Autonomous County 滄源佤族自治縣 *cāngyuán wǎzú zìzhìxiàn*	160,262	

(continued)

Table 33.2 (continued)

Cities and subordinate sectors, population (2020 census)	Subordinate District, city and county populations (2020)	Total population (2020)
Dehong Dai and Jingpo Autonomous Prefecture 德宏傣族景頗族自治州 ***déhóng dǎizú jǐngpōzú zìzhìzhōu***		**1,315,709**
Mangshi City 芒市 *mángshì*	439,931	
Ruili City 瑞麗市 *ruìlì shì*	267,638	
Longchuan County 隴川縣 *lǒngchuān xiàn*	181,364	
Yingjiang County 盈江縣 *yíngjiāng xiàn*	292,508	
Lianghe County 梁河縣 *liánghé xiàn*	134,268	
Nujiang Lisu Autonomous Prefecture 怒江傈僳族自治州 ***nùjiāng lìsùzúzìzhìzhōu***		**552,694**
Lushui City 瀘水市 *lúshuǐ shì*	203,977	
Fugong County 福貢縣 *fúgòng xiàn*	114,372	
Gongshan County 貢山縣 *gòngshān xiàn*	38,471	
Lanping County 蘭坪縣 *lánpíng xiàn*	195,874	
Diqing Tibetan Autonomous Prefecture 迪慶藏族自治州 ***díqìng zàngzú zìzhìzhōu***		**387,511**
Xianggelila (Shangri-La) City 香格里拉市 *xiānggélǐlā shì*	186,412	
Deqin (Dêqên) County 德欽縣 *déqīn xiàn*	54,736	
Weixi County 維西縣 *wéixī xiàn*	146,363	
Dali Bai (Bo) Autonomous Prefecture 大理白族自治州 ***dàlǐ báizú zìzhìzhōu***		**3,337,559**
Dali City 大理市 *dàlǐ shì*	771,128	
Yangbi County 漾濞縣 *yàngbì xiàn*	97,610	
Xiangyun County 祥雲縣 *xiángyún xiàn*	406,642	
Binzhou County 賓川縣 *bīnchuān xiàn*	341,319	
Midu County 彌渡縣 *mídù xiàn*	261,205	
Nanjian County 南澗縣 *nánjiàn xiàn*	192,942	
Weishan County 巍山縣 *wēishān xiàn*	267,474	
Yongping County 永平縣 *yǒngpíng xiàn*	164,613	
Yunlong County 雲龍縣 *yúnlóng xiàn*	182,977	
Eryuan County 洱源縣 *ěryuán xiàn*	248,147	
Jianchuan County 劍川縣 *jiànchuān xiàn*	160,471	
Heqing County 鶴慶縣 *hèqìng xiàn*	243,031	
Chuxiong Yi Autonomous Prefecture 楚雄彝族自治州 ***chǔxióng yízú zìzhìzhōu***		**2,416,747**
Chuxiong City 楚雄市 *chǔxióng shì*	631,530	
Lufeng City 祿豐市 *lùfēng shì*	366,512	
Shuangbai (Shuangbo) County 雙柏縣 *shuāngbǎi xiàn*	133,884	
Mouding County 牟定縣 *móudìng xiàn*	149,437	
Nanhua County 南華縣 *nánhuá xiàn*	203,704	
Yao'an County 姚安縣 *yáo'ān xiàn*	164,165	

(continued)

Table 33.2 (continued)

Cities and subordinate sectors, population (2020 census)	Subordinate District, city and county populations (2020)	Total population (2020)
Dayao County 大姚縣 *dàyáo xiàn*	228,961	
Yongren County 永仁縣 *yǒngrén xiàn*	97,985	
Yuanmou County 元謀縣 *yuánmóu xiàn*	201,510	
Wuding County 武定縣 *wǔdìng xiàn*	239,059	
Honghe Hani and Yi Autonomous Prefecture 紅河哈尼族**彝**族自治州 ***hónghé hānízú yízú zìzhìzhōu***		**4,478,422**
Gejiu City 個舊市 *gèjiù shì*	419,314	
Kaiyuan City 開遠市 *kāiyuǎn shì*	323,031	
Mengzi City 蒙自市 *mēngzì shì*	585,976	
Mile City 彌勒市 *mílè shì*	538,083	
Pingbian Miaozu Autonomous County 屏邊苗族自治縣 *píngbiān miáozú zìzhìxiàn*	129,448	
Jianshui County 建水縣 *jiànshuǐ xiàn*	534,205	
Shiping County 石屏縣 *shípíng xiàn*	271,951	
Luxi County 瀘西縣 *lúxī xiàn*	389,138	
Yuanyang County 元陽縣 *yuányáng xiàn*	359,155	
Honghe County 紅河縣 *hónghé xiàn*	284,607	
Jinping Miaozu Yaozu Daizu (Miao, Yao, and Dai) Autonomous County 金平苗族瑤族傣族自治縣 *jīnpíng miáozú yáozú dǎizú zìzhìxiàn*	331,377	
Lüchun County 綠春縣 *lǜchūn xiàn*	210,166	
Hekou Yaozu Autonomous County 河口遙族自治縣 *hékǒu yáozú zìzhìxiàn*	101,971	
Wenshan Zhuang Autonomous Prefecture 文山壯族苗族自治州 ***wénshān zhuàngzú miáozú zìzhìzhōu***		**3,503,218**
Wenshan City 文山市 *wénshān shì*	623,772	
Yanshan County 硯山縣 *yànshān xiàn*	476,587	
Xichou County 西疇縣 *xīchóu xiàn*	203,630	
Malipi County 麻栗坡縣 *málìpō xiàn*	243,587	
Maguan County 馬關縣 *mǎguān xiàn*	318,704	
Qiubei County 丘北縣 *qiūběi xiàn*	468,172	
Guangnan County 廣南縣 *guǎngnán xiàn*	771,948	
Funing County 富寧縣 *fùníng xiàn*	396,818	
Xishuangbanna Dai Autonomous Prefecture 西雙版納**傣**族自治州 ***xīshuāng bǎnnà dǎizú zìzhìzhōu***		**1,301,407**
Jinghong City 景洪市 *jǐnghóng shì*	642,737	
Menghai County 勐海縣 *měnghǎi xiàn*	353,720	
Mengla County 勐臘縣 *měnglà xiàn*	304,950	

Yunnan Province (滇 *diān*; 雲 *yún*)

Provincial Capital: Kunming

Table 33.3 Yunnan Province: Permanent registered (戶籍人口 *hùjí rénkǒu*) populations. (MCA 2020)

Name	Traditional	Simplified	Population (2012)	Population (2016)	Population (2020)	Area (Sq. Km)
Yunnan Province	雲南省	云南省	45,280,000	45,760,000	47,690,000	394,029
Kunming City	昆明市	昆明市	5,350,000	5,420,000	5,690,000	21,473
Chenggong District (Longcheng Subdistrict)	呈貢區 (龍城街道)	呈贡区 (龙城街道)	190,000	190,000	220,000	541
Panlong District (Tuodong Subdistrict)	盤龍區 (拓東街道)	盘龙区 (拓东街道)	510,000	520,000	570,000	340
Wuhua District (Huashan Subdistrict)	五華區 (華山街道)	五华区 (华山街道)	640,000	630,000	650,000	398
Guandu District (Guanshang Subdistrict)	官渡區 (關上街道)	官渡区 (关上街道)	540,000	560,000	590,000	552
Xishan District (Xiyuan Subdistrict)	西山區 (西苑街道)	西山区 (西苑街道)	500,000	510,000	560,000	791
Dongchuan District (Tongdu Subdistrict)	東川區 (銅都街道)	东川区 (铜都街道)	310,000	310,000	320,000	1674
Anning City (Lianran Subdistrict)	安寧市 (連然街道)	安宁市 (连然街道)	270,000	270,000	280,000	1313
Jinning District (Kunyang Subdistrict)	晉寧區 (昆陽街道)	晋宁区 (昆阳街道)	280,000	280,000	290,000	1391
Fumin County (Yongding Subdistrict)	富民縣 (永定街道)	富民县 (永定街道)	150,000	150,000	150,000	1030
Yiliang County (Kuangyuan Subdistrict)	宜良縣 (匡遠街道)	宜良县 (匡远街道)	420,000	450,000	440,000	1880
Songming County (Songyang Subdistrict)	嵩明縣 (嵩陽街道)	嵩明县 (嵩阳街道)	290,000	300,000	310,000	1442
Shilin Yizu (Yi) Autonomous County (Lufu Subdistrict)	石林彝族自治縣 (鹿阜街道)	石林彝族自治县 (鹿阜街道)	240,000	240,000	250,000	1777
Luquanyizumiaozu (Yi and Miao) Autonomous County (Pingshan Subdistrict)	祿勸彝族苗族自治縣 (屏山街道)	禄劝彝族苗族自治县 (屏山街道)	470,000	470,000	490,000	4378

(continued)

Table 33.3 (continued)

Name	Traditional	Simplified	Population (2012)	Population (2016)	Population (2020)	Area (Sq. Km)
Xundianhuizuyizu (Hui and Yi) Autonomous County (Rende Subdistrict)	尋甸回族彝族自治縣 (仁德街道)	寻甸回族彝族自治县 (仁德街道)	540,000	540,000	570,000	3966
Qujing City	曲靖市	曲靖市	6,270,000	6,370,000	6,640,000	29,855
Qilin District (Nanning Subdistrict)	麒麟區 (南寧街道)	麒麟区 (南宁街道)	700,000	710,000	760,000	1442
Xuanwei City (Wanshui Subdistrict)	宣威市 (宛水街道)	宣威市 (宛水街道)	1,480,000	1,510,000	1,550,000	6257
Malong District (Tongquan Subdistrict)	馬龍區 (通泉街道)	马龙区 (通泉街道)	200,000	210,000	210,000	1751
Zhanyi District (Xiping Subdistrict)	沾益區 (西平街道)	沾益区 (西平街道)	420,000	430,000	440,000	2910
Fuyuan County (Zhong'an Subdistrict)	富源縣 (中安街道)	富源县 (中安街道)	780,000	790,000	830,000	3348
Luoping County (Luoxiong Subdistrict)	羅平縣 (羅雄街道)	罗平县 (罗雄街道)	610,000	610,000	650,000	3116
Shizong County (Danfeng Subdistrict)	師宗縣 (丹鳳街道)	师宗县 (丹凤街道)	410,000	420,000	440,000	2858
Luliang County (Zhongshu Subdistrict)	陸良縣 (中樞街道)	陆良县 (中枢街道)	660,000	670,000	690,000	2096
Huize County (Gucheng Subdistrict)	會澤縣 (古城街道)	会泽县 (古城街道)	1,010,000	1,020,000	1,060,000	6077
Yuxi City	玉溪市	玉溪市	2,130,000	2,140,000	2,230,000	15,285
Hongta District (Yuxinglu Subdistrict)	紅塔區 (玉興路街道)	红塔区 (玉兴路街道)	420,000	430,000	450,000	1004
Jiangchuan County[a] (Dajie Subdistrict)	江川區 (大街街道)	江川区 (大街街道)	270,000	N/A	N/A	(850)
Jiangchuan District (Dajie Subdistrict)	江川區 (大街街道)	江川区 (大街街道)	N/A	280,000	280,000	850
Chengjiang County[b] (Fenglu Subdistrict)	澄江縣 (鳳麓街道)	澄江县 (凤麓街道)	160,000	140,000	N/A	(773)
Chengjiang City (Fenglu Subdistrict)	澄江市 (鳳麓街道)	澄江市 (凤麓街道)	N/A	N/A	180,000	773

(continued)

Table 33.3 (continued)

Name	Traditional	Simplified	Population (2012)	Population (2016)	Population (2020)	Area (Sq. Km)
Tonghai County (Xiushan Subdistrict)	通海縣 (秀山街道)	通海县 (秀山街道)	280,000	280,000	290,000	721
Huaning County (Ningzhou Subdistrict)	華寧縣 (寧州街道)	华宁县 (宁州街道)	210,000	210,000	210,000	1313
Yimen County (Longquan Subdistrict)	易門縣 (龍泉街道)	易门县 (龙泉街道)	170,000	170,000	170,000	1571
E'shan Yizu (Yi) Autonomous County (Shuangjiang Subdistrict)	峨山彝族自治縣 (雙江街道)	峨山彝族自治县 (双江街道)	150,000	150,000	160,000	1972
Xinpingyizudaizu (Yi and Dai) Autonomous County (Guishan Subdistrict)	新平彝族傣族自治縣 (桂山街道)	新平彝族傣族自治县 (桂山街道)	270,000	270,000	280,000	4223
Yuanjianghanizu (Hani), Yizu Daizu (Yi and Dai) Autonomous County (Honghe Subdistrict)	元江哈尼族彝族傣族自治縣 (紅河街道)	元江哈尼族彝族傣族自治县 (红河街道)	200,000	210,000	210,000	2858
Baoshan City	保山市	保山市	2,530,000	2,550,000	2,640,000	19,637
Longyang District (Lancheng Subdistrict)	隆陽區 (蘭城街道)	隆阳区 (兰城街道)	900,000	910,000	940,000	5011
Shidian County (Dianyang Town)	施甸縣 (甸陽鎮)	施甸县 (甸阳镇)	340,000	340,000	350,000	2009
Tengchong County[c] (Tengyue Town)	騰衝縣 (騰越鎮)	腾冲县 (腾越镇)	650,000	N/A	N/A	(5845)
Tengchong City (Tengyue Town)	騰衝市 (騰越鎮)	腾冲市 (腾越镇)	N/A	660,000	690,000	5845
Longling County (Longshan Town)	龍陵縣 (龍山鎮)	龙陵县 (龙山镇)	290,000	290,000	300,000	2884
Changning County (Tianyuan Town)	昌寧縣 (田園鎮)	昌宁县 (田园镇)	350,000	350,000	350,000	3888
Zhaotong City	昭通市	昭通市	5,720,000	5,820,000	6,250,000	23,021
Zhaoyang District (Fenghuang Subdistrict)	昭陽區 (鳳凰街道)	昭阳区 (凤凰街道)	830,000	850,000	940,000	2240
Ludian County (Wenping Town)	魯甸縣 (文屏鎮)	鲁甸县 (文屏镇)	430,000	430,000	470,000	1519
Qiaojia County (Baihetan Town)	巧家縣 (白鶴灘鎮)	巧家县 (白鹤滩镇)	570,000	590,000	620,000	3245

(continued)

Table 33.3 (continued)

Name	Traditional	Simplified	Population (2012)	Population (2016)	Population (2020)	Area (Sq. Km)
Yanjin County (Yanjing Town)	鹽津縣 (鹽井鎮)	盐津县 (盐井镇)	390,000	390,000	400,000	2096
Daguan County (Cuihua Town)	大關縣 (翠華鎮)	大关县 (翠华镇)	280,000	280,000	290,000	1802
Yongshan County (Xiluodu Town)	永善縣 (溪落渡鎮)	永善县 (溪落渡镇)	450,000	460,000	480,000	2833
Suijiang County (Zhongcheng Town)	綏江縣 (中城鎮)	绥江县 (中城镇)	170,000	170,000	170,000	882
Zhenxiong County (Wufeng Subdistrict)	鎮雄縣 (烏峰街道)	镇雄县 (乌峰街道)	1,500,000	1,540,000	1,680,000	3785
Yiliang County (Jiaokui Town)	彝良縣 (角奎鎮)	彝良县 (角奎镇)	580,000	590,000	630,000	2884
Weixin County (Zhaxi Town)	威信縣 (扎西鎮)	威信县 (扎西镇)	420,000	420,000	450,000	1416
Shuifu City (Yunfu Subdistrict)	水富市 (雲富街道)	水富市 (云富街道)	100,000	100,000	110,000	319
Lijiang City	麗江市	丽江市	1,200,000	1,190,000	1,230,000	21,219
Gucheng District (Xi'an Subdistrict)	古城區 (西安街道)	古城区 (西安街道)	150,000	150,000	160,000	1127
Yongsheng County (Yongbei Town)	永勝縣 (永北鎮)	永胜县 (永北镇)	400,000	390,000	410,000	5099
Huaping County (Zhongxin Town)	華坪縣 (中心鎮)	华坪县 (中心镇)	160,000	160,000	160,000	2266
Yulong Naxizu (Nakhi) Autonomous County (Huangshan Town)	玉龍納西族自治縣 (黃山鎮)	玉龙纳西族自治县 (黄山镇)	220,000	220,000	220,000	6521
Ninglang Yizu (Yi) Autonomous County (Daxing Town)	寧蒗彝族自治縣 (大興鎮)	宁蒗彝族自治县 (大兴镇)	270,000	270,000	280,000	6206
Pu'er City	普洱市	普洱市	2,480,000	2,510,000	2,540,000	45,385
Simao District (Simao Town)	思茅區 (思茅鎮)	思茅区 (思茅镇)	220,000	220,000	240,000	4093
Ning'er Hanizu Yizu (Hani and Yi) Autonomous County (Ning'er Town)	寧洱哈尼族彝族自治縣 (寧洱鎮)	宁洱哈尼族彝族自治县 (宁洱镇)	190,000	190,000	190,000	3670
Mojiang Hanizu (Hani) Autonomous County (Lianzhu Town)	墨江哈尼族自治縣 (聯珠鎮)	墨江哈尼族自治县 (联珠镇)	370,000	370,000	370,000	5459

(continued)

Table 33.3 (continued)

Name	Traditional	Simplified	Population (2012)	Population (2016)	Population (2020)	Area (Sq. Km)
Jingdong Yizu (Yi) Autonomous County (Jinping Town)	景東彝族自治縣(錦屏鎮)	景东彝族自治县(锦屏镇)	360,000	370,000	370,000	4532
Jinggu Daizu Yizu (Dai and Yi) Autonomous County (Weiyuan Town)	景谷傣族彝族自治縣 (威遠鎮)	景谷傣族彝族自治县 (威远镇)	310,000	320,000	320,000	7777
Zhenyuan Yizu Hanizu Lahuzu (Yi, Hani and Lahu) Autonomous County (Sile Town)	鎮沅彝族哈尼族拉祜族自治縣(思樂鎮)	镇沅彝族哈尼族拉祜族自治县(恩乐镇)	210,000	210,000	210,000	4223
Jiangcheng Hanizu Yizu (Hani and Yi) Autonomous County (Menglie Town)	江城哈尼族彝族自治縣(勐烈鎮)	江城哈尼族彝族自治县(勐烈镇)	110,000	110,000	120,000	3476
Menglian Daizu Lahuzu Wazu (Dai, Lahu and Wa) Autonomous County (Nayun Town)	孟連傣族拉祜族佤族自治縣(娜允鎮)	孟连傣族拉祜族佤族自治县(娜允镇)	130,000	130,000	130,000	1957
Lancang Lahuzu (Lahu) Autonomous County (Menglang Town)	瀾滄拉祜族自治縣(勐朗鎮)	澜沧拉祜族自治县(勐朗镇)	490,000	500,000	490,000	8807
Ximeng Wazu (Wa) Autonomous County (Mengsuo Town)	西盟佤族自治縣(勐梭鎮)	西盟佤族自治县(勐梭镇)	90,000	90,000	90,000	1391
Lincang City	臨滄市	**临沧**市	2,340,000	2,370,000	2,410,000	24,469
Linxiang District (Fengxiang Subdistrict)	臨翔區(鳳翔街道)	临翔区(凤翔街道)	310,000	320,000	330,000	2652
Fengqing County (Fengshan Town)	鳳慶縣(鳳山鎮)	凤庆县(凤山镇)	440,000	440,000	440,000	3451
Yunxian County (Aihua Town)	雲縣(愛華鎮)	云县 (爱华镇)	440,000	450,000	450,000	3760
Yongde County (Dedang Town)	永德縣(德黨鎮)	永德县(德党镇)	350,000	350,000	360,000	3296
Zhenkang County (Nansan Town)	鎮康縣(南傘鎮)	镇康县(南伞镇)	180,000	180,000	180,000	2642
Shuangjiang Lahuzu Wazu Bulangzu Daizu (Lahu, Va, Blang, and Dai) Autonomous County (Mengmeng Town)	雙江拉祜族佤族布朗族傣族自治縣(勐勐鎮)	双江拉祜族佤族布朗族傣族自治县(勐勐镇)	170,000	170,000	180,000	2292

(continued)

Table 33.3 (continued)

Name	Traditional	Simplified	Population (2012)	Population (2016)	Population (2020)	Area (Sq. Km)
Gengma Daizu Wazu (Dai and Wa) Autonomous County (Gengma Town)	耿馬傣族佤族自治縣 (耿馬鎮)	耿马傣族佤族自治县 (耿马镇)	280,000	290,000	300,000	3837
Cangyuan Wazu (Wa) Autonomous County (Mengdong Town)	滄源佤族自治縣 (勐董鎮)	沧源佤族自治县 (勐董镇)	170,000	170,000	170,000	2539
Dehong Daizu Jingpozu (Dai and Jingpo) Autonomous Prefecture	德宏傣族景頗族自治州	德宏傣族景颇族自治州	1,140,000	1,140,000	1,220,000	11,526
Mangshi City (Menghuan Subdistrict)	芒市 (勐焕街道)	芒市 (勐焕街道)	370,000	370,000	400,000	2987
Ruili City (Mengmao Town)	瑞麗市 (勐卯鎮)	瑞丽市 (勐卯镇)	130,000	130,000	140,000	1020
Lianghe County (Zhedao Town)	梁河縣 (遮島鎮)	梁河县 (遮岛镇)	170,000	170,000	170,000	1159
Yingjiang County (Pingyuan Town)	盈江縣 (平原鎮)	盈江县 (平原镇)	290,000	290,000	310,000	4429
Longchuan County (Zhangfeng Town)	隴川縣 (章鳳鎮)	陇川县 (章凤镇)	180,000	180,000	190,000	1931
Nujiang Lisuzu (Lisu) Autonomous Prefecture	怒江傈僳族自治州	怒江傈僳族自治州	520,000	530,000	560,000	14,703
Lushui City (Liuku Town)	瀘水市 (六庫鎮)	泸水市 (六库镇)	170,000	180,000	190,000	2938
Fugong County (Shangpa Town)	福貢縣 (上帕鎮)	福贡县 (上帕镇)	100,000	100,000	120,000	2804
Gongshan Dulongzu (Derung) and Nu Autonomous County (Cikai Town)	貢山獨龍族怒族自治縣 (茨開鎮)	贡山独龙族怒族自治县 (茨开镇)	40,000	40,000	40,000	4506
Lanping Baizu Pumizu (Bai and Pumi) Autonomous County (Jinding Town)	蘭坪白族普米族自治縣 (金頂鎮)	兰坪白族普米族自治县 (金顶镇)	210,000	210,000	220,000	4455
Diqing (Dêqên) Tibetan Autonomous Prefecture	迪慶藏族自治州	迪庆藏族自治州	350,000	360,000	370,000	23,870

(continued)

Table 33.3 (continued)

Name	Traditional	Simplified	Population (2012)	Population (2016)	Population (2020)	Area (Sq. Km)
Xianggelila (Shangri-La) City (Jiantang Town)	香格里拉市 (建塘鎮)	香格里拉市 (建塘镇)	140,000	150,000	150,000	11,613
Deqin (Dêqên) County (Shengping Town)	德欽縣 (升平鎮)	德钦县 (升平镇)	60,000	60,000	60,000	7596
Weixi Lisuzu (Lisu) Autonomous County (Baohe Town)	維西傈粟族自治縣 (保和鎮)	维西傈僳族自治县 (保和镇)	150,000	150,000	160,000	4661
Dali Baizu (Bai) Autonomous Prefecture	大理白族自治州	大理白族自治州	3,530,000	3,570,000	3,640,000	29,459
Dali City (Xiaguan Town)	大理市 (下關鎮)	大理市 (下关镇)	610,000	610,000	640,000	1468
Xiangyun County (Xiangcheng Town)	祥雲縣 (祥城鎮)	祥云县 (祥城镇)	470,000	470,000	480,000	2498
Binchuan County (Jinniu Town)	賓川縣 (金牛鎮)	宾川县 (金牛镇)	350,000	360,000	370,000	2627
Midu County (Micheng Town)	彌渡縣 (彌城鎮)	弥渡县 (弥城镇)	330,000	330,000	330,000	1571
Yongping County (Bonan Town)	永平縣 (博南鎮)	永平县 (博南镇)	180,000	180,000	190,000	2884
Yunlong County (Nuodeng Town)	雲龍縣 (諾鄧鎮)	云龙县 (诺邓镇)	210,000	210,000	210,000	4712
Eryuan County (Zibihu Town)	洱源縣 (茈碧湖鎮)	洱源县 (茈碧湖镇)	290,000	290,000	300,000	2961
Jianchuan County (Jinhua Town)	劍川縣 (金華鎮)	剑川县 (金华镇)	180,000	180,000	180,000	2318
Heqing County (Yunhe Town)	鶴慶縣 (雲鶴鎮)	鹤庆县 (云鹤镇)	270,000	280,000	280,000	2395
Yangbi Yizu (Yi) Autonomous County (Cangshanxi Town)	漾濞彝族自治縣 (蒼山西鎮)	漾濞彝族自治县 (苍山西镇)	100,000	110,000	110,000	1957
Nanjian Yizu (Yi) Autonomous County (Nanjian Town)	南澗彝族自治縣 (南澗鎮)	南涧彝族自治县 (南涧镇)	230,000	230,000	230,000	1802
Weishan Yizu (Yi and Hui) Huizu Autonomous County (Nanzhao Town)	巍山彝族自治縣 (南詔鎮)	巍山彝族回族自治县 (南诏镇)	310,000	320,000	320,000	2266
Chuxiong Yizu (Yi) Autonomous Prefecture	楚雄彝族自治州	楚雄彝族自治州	2,620,000	2,600,000	2,650,000	29,258

(continued)

Table 33.3 (continued)

Name	Traditional	Simplified	Population (2012)	Population (2016)	Population (2020)	Area (Sq. Km)
Chuxiong City (Lucheng Town)	楚雄市 (鹿城鎮)	楚雄市 (鹿城镇)	510,000	510,000	540,000	4482
Shuangbai County (Tuodian Town)	雙柏縣 (妥甸鎮)	双柏县 (妥甸镇)	160,000	150,000	150,000	4045
Mouding County (Gonghe Town)	牟定縣 (共和鎮)	牟定县 (共和镇)	200,000	200,000	200,000	1494
Nanhua County (Longchuan Town)	南華縣 (龍川鎮)	南华县 (龙川镇)	240,000	240,000	240,000	2343
Yao'an County (Dongchuan Town)	姚安縣 (棟川鎮)	姚安县 (栋川镇)	210,000	210,000	210,000	1803
Dayao County (Jinbi Town)	大姚縣 (金碧鎮)	大姚县 (金碧镇)	280,000	280,000	280,000	4146
Yongren County (Yongding Town)	永仁縣 (永定鎮)	永仁县 (永定镇)	110,000	110,000	110,000	2189
Yuanmou County (Yuanma Town)	元謀縣 (元馬鎮)	元谋县 (元马镇)	220,000	210,000	220,000	1803
Wuding County (Shishan Town)	武定縣 (獅山鎮)	武定县 (狮山镇)	270,000	270,000	280,000	3322
Lufeng County (Jinshan Town)	祿豐縣 (金山鎮)	禄丰县 (金山镇)	420,000	420,000	420,000	3631
Honghe Hanizu (Hani and Yi) Yizu Autonomous Prefecture	紅河哈尼族彝族自治州	红河哈尼族彝族自治州	4,410,000	4,480,000	4,660,000	32,930
Mengzi City (Wenlan Town)	蒙自市 (文瀾鎮)	蒙自市 (文澜镇)	370,000	380,000	420,000	2228
Gejiu City (Chengqu Subdistrict)	個舊市 (城區街道)	个旧市 (城区街道)	390,000	390,000	380,000	1597
Kaiyuan City (Lebaidao Subdistrict)	開遠市 (樂白道街道)	开远市 (乐白道街道)	280,000	280,000	290,000	2009
Lüchun County (Daxing Town)	綠春縣 (大興鎮)	绿春县 (大兴镇)	230,000	230,000	250,000	3167
Shiping County (Yilong Town)	石屏縣 (異龍鎮)	石屏县 (异龙镇)	310,000	310,000	320,000	3090
Mile City (Miyang Town)	彌勒市 (彌陽鎮)	弥勒市 (弥阳镇)	520,000	540,000	550,000	4004
Jianshui County	建水縣 (臨安鎮)	建水县 (临安镇)	520,000	530,000	550,000	3940
Luxi County (Zhongshu Town)	瀘西縣 (中樞鎮)	泸西县 (中枢镇)	420,000	420,000	450,000	1674
Yuanyang County (Nansha Town)	元陽縣 (南沙鎮)	元阳县 (南沙镇)	420,000	440,000	460,000	2292

(continued)

Table 33.3 (continued)

Name	Traditional	Simplified	Population (2012)	Population (2016)	Population (2020)	Area (Sq. Km)
Honghe County (Yisa Town)	紅河縣(迤薩鎮)	红河县(迤萨镇)	320,000	330,000	350,000	2034
Jinping Miaozu Yaozu Daizu (Miao, Yao and Dai) Autonomous County (Jinhe Town)	金平苗族瑤族傣族自治縣(金河鎮)	金平苗族瑶族傣族自治县(金河镇)	380,000	380,000	390,000	3677
Hekou Yaozu (Yao) Autonomous County (Hekou Town)	河口瑤族自治縣(河口鎮)	河口瑶族自治县(河口镇)	90,000	90,000	90,000	1313
Pingbian Miaozu (Miao) Autonomous County (Yuping Town)	屏邊苗族自治縣(玉屏鎮)	屏边苗族自治县(玉屏镇)	160,000	160,000	160,000	1905
Wenshan Zhuangzu Miaozu (Zhuang and Miao) Autonomous Prefecture	文山壯族苗族自治州	文山壮族苗族自治州	3,710,000	3,710,000	3,960,000	32,239
Wenshan City (Wolong Subdistrict)	文山市(臥龍街道)	文山市(卧龙街道)	480,000	480,000	520,000	3064
Yanshan County (Jiangna Town)	硯山縣(江那鎮)	砚山县(江那镇)	490,000	490,000	53,000	3888
Xichou County (Xisa Town)	西疇縣(西灑鎮)	西畴县(西洒镇)	260,000	260,000	260,000	1545
Malipo County (Mali Town)	麻栗坡縣(麻栗鎮)	麻栗坡县(麻栗镇)	290,000	290,000	300,000	2395
Maguan County (Mabai Town)	馬關縣(馬白鎮)	马关县(马白镇)	380,000	370,000	390,000	2755
Qiubei County (Jinping Town)	丘北縣(錦屏鎮)	丘北县(锦屏镇)	520,000	530,000	570,000	5150
Guangnan County (Liancheng Town)	廣南縣(蓮城鎮)	广南县(莲城镇)	840,000	850,000	920,000	7983
Funing County (Xinhua Town)	富寧縣(新華鎮)	富宁县(新华镇)	440,000	440,000	460,000	5459
Xishuangbanna Dai Autonomous Prefecture	西雙版納傣族自治州	西双版纳傣族自治州	940,000	960,000	1,010,000	19,700
Jinghong City (Yunjinghong Subdistrict)	景洪市(允景洪街道)	景洪市(允景洪街道)	400,000	410,000	430,000	7133

(continued)

Table 33.3 (continued)

Name	Traditional	Simplified	Population (2012)	Population (2016)	Population (2020)	Area (Sq. Km)
Menghai County (Menghai Town)	勐海縣 (勐海鎮)	勐海县 (勐海镇)	320,000	320,000	330,000	5511
Mengla County (Mengla Town)	勐臘縣 (勐臘鎮)	勐腊县 (勐腊镇)	220,000	230,000	240,000	7056

[a]Made a district in 2015
[b]Chengjiang made a city in November 2019
[c]Made a city in 2015

References

Ministry of Civil Affairs (MCA), People's Republic of China. 2020. [*County/township administration handbook*]. Beijing: China Statistics Press. 中華人民共和國民政部, 中華人民共和國, 鄉鎮行政區劃簡冊.

Norton, Chris. 2011. Yunnan's tobacco dilemma: Revenue vs health. Gokunming.com 23 May. https://www.gokunming.com/en/blog/item/2239/yunnans-tobacco-dilemma-revenue-vs-health.

Shang-Ch'i Guide. 2017. [*Backpacking in China: the most complete collection of self-guided travel for China, 2018*]. Taipei: Shang-Ch'i Shitai publishing. 2018 最完整的中國自助旅遊全集. 台北: 上奇時代.

Smith, Adam D. 2013. Are writing systems intelligently designed? In *Agency in ancient writing*, ed. Joshua Englehardt, 71–94. Boulder: University Press of Colorado.

Tan, Qixiang, ed. 1996. *The historical atlas of China,* Volume I. Beijing: China Cartographic Publishing House.

Xixi Net. 2019. [Do you know all of the 25 minority groups in Yunnan?] 云南有25个少数民族, 你都知道吗?11 September. http://m.news.xixik.com/content/58a41c75062760d7/.

Yang, Jisheng. 2007. *Tombstone: Record of China's great famine in the 1960s* (Chinese version). 楊繼繩, 墓碑: 中国六十年代大饥荒纪实. https://cdn.jsdelivr.net/gh/easy2view/books/resources/grave-stone.pdf.

Yunnan Province Bureau of Statistics (YPBS). 2021. [*Bulletin of the main data of the seventh national census in Yunnan Province*]. 15 May. 云南省第七次全国人口普查主要数据公报. http://yn.people.com.cn/n2/2021/0515/c378439-34726806.html.

Zhang, Shunan. 2021. [The 2020 per capita income list of residents in various provinces: Shanghai is the richest, and it has risen sharply]. Finance.people.com. 22 January. 张澍楠. 2020年各省份居民人均收入榜: 上海最有钱, 这地涨得猛. http://finance.people.com.cn/n1/2021/0122/c1004-32008733.html.

Zhu, R.X., A.R. Potts, Y.X. Pan, et al. 2008. Early evidence of the genus *Homo* in East Asia. *Journal of Human Evolution* 55 (6): 1075–1085.

Chapter 34
Zhejiang Province

Abstract With archeological excavations showing Neolithic communities in modern-day Zhejiang having thrived over seven thousand years ago, they also revealed that modern cultivars of rice (i.e., *Oryza sativa*) were originally developed in this region. In addition, with Hemudu and Majiabang cultures represented in the lower regions of the Changjiang (Yangtze) river, these challenge the centrality of Chinese civilization growing from the central plains, indicating it actually grew out of multiple foci all across China. The land where the kingdoms of Wu and Yue once contended for power, connecting the Zhejiang center of commerce with the great canal in ca. 600 CE placed this region in a much more viable position. Eventually, Hangzhou City became an internationally-recognized metropolis (e.g., by Marco Polo) during the Yuan (ca. 1280 CE). During the Ming-Qing transition, the population of Zhejiang dropped significantly due to violence and disease, but largely recovered by 1776. Following both twentieth century revolutions, and for many years now, Zhejiang has remained in the top five of 31 mainland provinces and major cities in terms of gross domestic product (GDP), and in 2020 was ranked fourth in per capita income (USD $8250).

E. Croddy, *China's Provinces and Populations*,
https://doi.org/10.1007/978-3-031-09165-0_34

Zhejiang Province (浙江省 *zhèjiāng shěng*): Abbreviation 浙 (*zhè*) (Fig. 34.1)

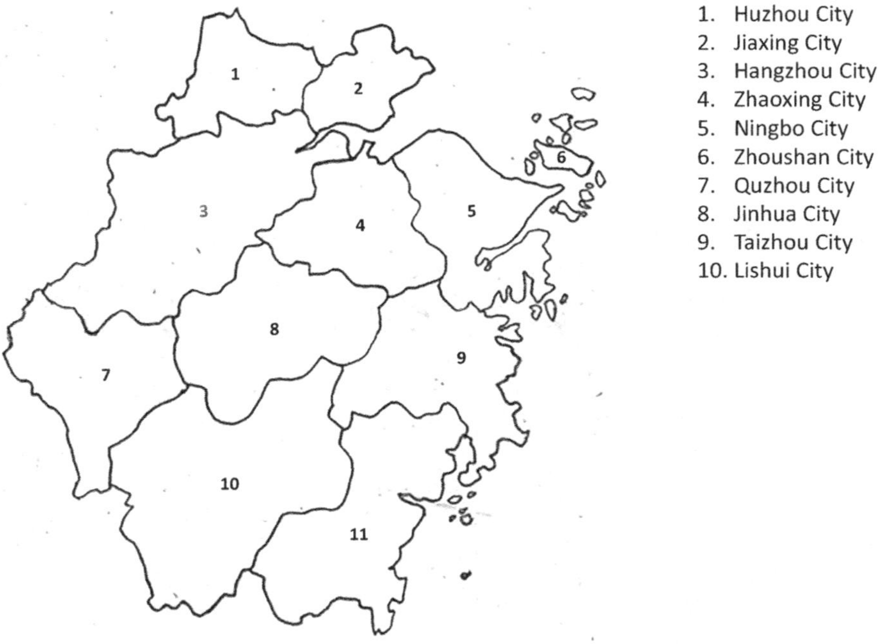

Fig. 34.1 Zhejiang province major cities (provincial capital: Hangzhou City). (Drawn by the Author after People's Republic of China, Ministry of Civil Affairs. (MCA 2020))

Zhejiang Province: General Impressions

When it comes to Zhejiang province, its historic capital city of Hangzhou first comes to mind, the fame of which going back to the Tang dynasty, and a polis that greatly impressed the Venetian Marco Polo centuries later. And then there is the textile industry of great renown, and is why Hangzhou City (杭州市 *hángzhōu shì*) has been called the "capital of silk cloth" (絲綢之府 *sīchóuzhīfǔ*). (Shang-Ch'i 2017).

Zhejiang gets its name after the river (浙江 *zhèjiāng*), formerly known as Qiantang River (錢塘河 *qiántáng hé*), its source being located in the Huangshan mountain region in Anhui Province. Some have suggested that the name Zhejiang is derived from "winding" river (Hsieh and Hsieh 1995), but it is more likely a from a combination of old phonetic Wu (吳 *wú*) dialect (which is still spoken in Zhejiang) and other, written Chinese components. Other short hand references to Zhejiang also include the variant 淛 (*zhì*).

Prehistory

Neolithic pottery fragments found at the Shangshan site in Pujiang County (浦江縣 *pŭjiāng xiàn*) may be nearly 10,000 years old. Within those shards were found rice husks and other plant material, suggesting rudimentary rice cultivation. At the Kuahuqiao archeological site (跨湖橋遺址 *kuàhúqiáo yízhǐ*) in Xiaoshan District (蕭山區 *xiāoshān qū*), researchers have also found evidence of rice farming going back some 7700 years, showing a transition from wild to domesticated strains. The site also includes a dugout canoe (about 8000 years old) as well as pottery (Bar-Yosef 2012). This (along with other evidence) supports the contention that China's Yangtze (Changjiang) river valley is the original source of modern cultivated rice (*Oryza sativa*) (Gross and Zhao 2014). The two varieties, *Oryza sativa Japonica* (short, sticky) and *Oryza sativa Indica* probably bifurcated around 5000 BCE (Anderson 2014).

Additional evidence of Neolithic rice agriculture was found in northern Zhejiang Province, dated approximately 4000 BCE, including the Hemudu (河姆渡文化 *hémŭdù wénhuà*) near Yuyao city (余姚市 *yúyáo shì*) and the Majiabang cultures (馬家浜文化 *măjiābāng wénhuà*) in Jiaxing City (嘉興市 *jiāxìng shì*). River and lakeshore dwellings of these cultures held intricately-decorated pottery with distinctively black (Hemudu) and brown (Majiabang) coloration, as well as textured rope markings. Remnants of kernels, husks and straw at the excavated Hemudu sites showed an emphasis on agriculture, and tools made from bone were used to plant rice in paddies. Evidence also showed domestication of dogs, water buffalo and especially swine. Bone was used to fashion simple flute whistles and wood-crafted drums were also discovered at the Hemudu Culture settlements (Yan 2005). Significantly, these finds point to a divergence in the traditional thought regarding the rise of Chinese civilization. In the 1960s, the general theory was China developed in the basic central plain, e.g., Henan and Shaanxi Provinces, and then expanded radially outwards. By the 1980s, however, the developing archeological record, to include the Neolithic finds at Hemudu and Majiabang in the lower Changjiang (Yangtze) River, further challenged this assumption. Instead of starting from a central point, the historian Su Bingqi uses the expression a "star-filled sky (滿天星斗 *mǎntiānxīngdǒu*)" to describe multiple foci of early societies across China, ultimately leading to the growth of the earliest Chinese civilization (Chang 1999).

Among the earliest excavations and the first in Southern China (1936–1938) was discovered a Neolithic tradition, the Liangzhu Culture (良渚文化 *liángzhŭ wénhuà*; 3400–2250 BCE), named after Liangzhu Town (良渚鎮 *liángzhŭzhèn*), Yuhang District (餘杭區 *yúháng qū*), about 20 km outside Hangzhou City. Liangzhu culture features elaborate shamanistic burial sites, including ritual jade *yue*-styled (鉞 *yuè*) axes. Garnering the most attention, however, were large jade *bi* (璧 *bì*) discs and jade *cong* (琮 *cóng*) cylinders which were unearthed from burial sites. The latter may have had some cosmological significance (Wilkinson 2012). Specimens of Liangzhu human bones were tested in 2007, and genetic analysis revealed links to

Austronesian (e.g., Taiwanese aboriginals, New Zealand Maori) and Thai-related peoples (see also chapter on Republic of China, Taiwan).

Bronze Age to Early Recorded History

As far back as eleventh century BCE, non-Han people living in the Yangtze (Changjiang River) region developed into an organized society, possessing bronze metal technology, thus possessing a rudimentary means to defend themselves against Han Chinese invasion. By the sixth century BCE, northern Zhejiang was mentioned in the old histories of the Wu (吳 *wú*), and referred to its people of the Yue (越 *yuè*), meaning "The Beyond," and who lived in the capital of Kuaiji[1] (會稽 *kuàijī*) near today's Shaoxing City (紹興市 *shàoxìng shì*) (von Falkenhausen 1999). The Chinese histories generally described them as the "Hundred Yue" (百越 *bǎiyuè*), a non-Chinese group of peoples who lived mostly along the coast.

In 1965, excavations were carried out in Jiangling County (江陵縣 *jiānglíng xiàn*) that uncovered numerous Chu State tombs and other stunning artifacts. Among these was the Goujian Sword, dated 510 BCE, inscribed with the legend "Sword for Personal Use by Goujian, King of Yue.[2]" Gou Jian himself was said to have family lineage going back to the legendary Great Yu (大虞 *dàyú*) of the Xia (夏 *xià*) (Wagner 1996).

In the fifth century BCE, the King of Wu, Fu Chai (夫差 *fú chāi*), ultimately achieved what his father could not by defeating the King of Yue, Gou Jian (勾踐 *gōu jiàn*) in 494 BCE. Two decades later, and after a three-year siege, in the Yue conquered the Wu (ca. 475 BCE) (Hsu 1999). A succession of Yue kings followed, to include the grandson of Goujian, Yue King Zhu Gou (朱句 *zhū jù*), who moved the capital to Suzhou (Jiangsu Province). Several of these generations of Yue continued until they fell to the Chu (楚 *chǔ*) state. When the Chu occupied Suzhou (306 BCE), the Yue State retreated, eventually holding up at a redoubt to the east near the Qiantang River (錢塘河 *qiántáng hé*).

Following the unification and domination by the Qin (221 BCE), an administrative prefecture in the region was established, called the Kuaiji Commandery (會稽郡 *kuàijī jùn*). The Kuaiji commandery now administered the defeated Wu and Yue in the southern Changjiang river region, a territory consisting of modern-day southeastern Anhui, Shanghai and northern Zhejiang.

In 207 CE, the warlord Cao Cao (曹褋 *cáo cào*) effectively ruled northern China, and he then set his eyes southward. During 220–280 CE (Three Kingdoms) two warlords, Yan Baihu (嚴白虎 *yán báihǔ*) and Wang Lang (王朗 *wáng lǎng*), effectively controlled Zhejiang until Sun Quan (孫權 *sūn quán*) and Sun Ce (孫策 *sūn cè*) took control. Defeated in the famous Battle of the Red Cliffs (赤壁之戰 *chìbì*

[1] Alternatively "Guiji."

[2] "越王勾踐自作用劍" *yuèwáng gōujiàn zìzuòyòng jiàn*.

zhīzhàn), Cao Cao retreated, leaving the victorious Sun Quan to maintain his sovereignty over the Zhejiang area, i.e., the State of Wu (吳國 *wú guó*) in 229 CE. The Wu ultimately fell to the Jin (晉 *jìn*) Dynasty in 280 CE.

With the "Uprising of the (Five) Barbarian Tribes (五胡亂華 *wǔhúluànhuá*; 304–316) against the Jin, chaos ensued in northern China. Its balkanization led to the establishment of the so-called Sixteen States, and a flood of northerners moved south. Some of these Han Chinese immigrants found their way to modern-day Zhejiang. Through the end of the Eastern Jin (420 CE), the Zhejiang region was administered by a series of famous courts with very recognizable Chinese surnames today: Song (宋 *sòng*), Qi (齊 *qí*), Liang (梁 *liáng*), and Chen (陳 *chén*), among others.

Sui Through the Tang

The building of the great canal in the Sui Dynasty (ca. 600 CE) connected the modern-day Zhejiang region to China's imperial central authority in Luoyang, Henan Province. During this period, as of 612 CE, the following prefectures and counties were founded that later would form today's Zhejiang's modern cities (Table 34.1).

In 626 CE, the Tang armies invaded modern-day Zhejiang. From about this time forward, the Jiangsu and Zhejiang regions prospered, the latter supplying much of the north with foodstuffs. During the An Lushan (安祿山 *ānlùshān*) rebellion (755 CE; 安史之亂 *ānshǐzhīluàn*), as people fled south due to widespread turmoil, additional migrations from the north continued into the coastal region including today's Zhejiang.

The Two Zhe Circuit (兩浙路 *liǎngzhèlù*) ca. 1000 CE

In the northern Song period, an administrative area known as the Two Zhe Circuits (兩浙路 *liǎngzhèlù*) were established, the term 路 (*lù*) replacing 道 (*dào*) in 997 CE, comprised of fourteen prefectures, including two military (軍 *jūn*) ones. (Military prefectures once played a defensive role such as in the prior Tang, but later were essentially the same as other prefectural administrations):

- Suzhou 蘇州 *sūzhōu*
- Changzhou 常州 *chángzhōu*
- Runzhou 潤州 *rùnzhōu* [now Zhenjiang 鎮江 *zhènjiāng*]
- Hangzhou 杭州 *hángzhōu*
- Huzhou 湖州 *húzhōu*
- Xiuzhou 秀州 *xiùzhōu* [now Jiaxing 嘉興 *jiāxīng*]
- Yuezhou 越州 *yuèzhōu* [today's Shaoxing 紹興 *shàoxīng*, and thus its modern abbreviation 越 *yuè*]

Table 34.1 Sui dynasty administrative areas and modern Zhejiang equivalents. (Baike 2021)

Sui Dynasty administrative area (612 CE)	Counties	Modern-day Zhejiang cities
Kuaiji Commandery 會稽郡 *kuàijī jùn*	Kuaiji County 會稽縣 *kuàijī xiàn*	Shaoxing City 紹興市 *shàoxīng shì*
Dongyang Commandery東陽郡 *dōngyáng jùn*	Jinhua County 金華縣 *jīnhuá xiàn*	Jinhua City 金華市 *jīnhuá shì*
Sui'an Commandery 遂安郡 *suìān jùn*	Zhishan County 雉山縣*zhìshān xiàn*	Near Tuohuawu, Chun'an County 淳安縣駝花塢 *chúnān xiàn tuóhuāwù*
Xuhang Commandery 徐杭郡 *xúháng jùn*	Qiantang County 錢唐縣 *qiántáng xiàn*	Hangzhou City 杭州市 *hángzhōu shì*
Yongjia Commandery 永嘉郡 *yǒngjiā jùn*	Kuocang County 括蒼縣 *kuòcāng xiàn*	Lishui City 麗水市 *lìshuǐ shì*

- Mingzhou 明州 *míngzhōu* [today's Ningbo 寧波 *níngbō*]
- Taizhou 台州 *táizhōu*
- Wuzhou 婺州 *wùzhōu* [today's Jinhua 金華 *jīnhuá*, and thus its modern abbreviation 婺 *wù*]
- Quzhou 衢州 *qúzhōu*
- Muzhou 睦州 *mùzhōu* [today's Jiande 建德 *jiàndé*]
- Wenzhou 溫州 *wēnzhōu*
- Chuzhou 處州 *chǔzhōu* [today's Lishui 麗水 *lìshuǐ*, and thus its modern abbreviation 處 *chǔ*]
- Jiangyin military prefecture 江陰軍 *jiāngyīn jūn*
- Shun'an military prefecture 順安軍 *shùnān jūn*

Over the next decade, this area was combined, split up, recombined, and finally in ca. 1130 CE split into the 'Two-Zhe West Circuits,' 兩浙西路 (*liǎngzhè xīlù*) and the 'Two-Zhe East Circuits 兩浙東路 (*liǎngzhè dōnglù*).

Twelfth Century Descriptions of Zhejiang

A contemporary assessment of the population in the Zhejiang region was written by Lü Zuqian (呂祖謙 *lǚ zǔqiān*) in 1167, who enumerated the numbers of local households according to their classes, from well-to-do (first rank) to the landless (fifth rank) living in Yanzhou Prefecture (嚴州 *yánzhōu*). At that time, Yanzhou comprised six counties, including modern-day Tonglu County (桐廬縣 *tónglú xiàn*), Chun'an County (淳安縣 *chúnān xiàn*), and Jiande City (建德市 *jiàndé shì*):

> For a total of six counties, there are only 10,718 adult males belonging to households of the first to fourth ranks. There are 71,479 adult males belonging to households of the fifth rank owning taxable property. Although nominally they own taxable property, most of them only pay in fractional amounts, and it is as if they owned nothing. They are not capable of being self-sufficient. There are altogether 40,198 adult males belonging to households without taxable property. They possess not a scrap of land, not one foot of a rafter or a house. They

> turn from this occupation to that in hunger and cold, unable to make plans in the morning for the selfsame evening. This prefecture [Yanzhou] has charge of 122,393 adult males, and of these those in the fifth rank of household owning taxable property and without property amount to 111,675 adult males (Elvin 1973).

The city of Hangzhou grew into a glorious and commercially-vibrant metropolis. When Marco Polo visited Hangzhou it was described to him by the Yuan court as being a "temporary residence," or a *Xingcai* (行在 *xíngzài*). This name was later corrupted by Westerners as "Quinsay or Kinsay." For his part, Marco Polo called it "the finest and noblest city in the world." During the Yuan (ca. 1280 CE), the Two Zhe Lu state was combined with the Two Huai River State into Jianghuai Administrative Province.[3] As before, the new ruling dynasty was heavily dependent upon Zhejiang for rice that continued to be shipped north in the form of tax payments (Hsieh and Hsieh, 1995).

During the Ming, in 1368 the modern-day Zhejiang region was wholly subordinated under the Provincial Executor (承宣布政使司 *chéngxuānbù zhèngshǐsī*), and in 1381 a provincial entity was formed. This Zhejiang Executor (浙江承宣布政使司 *zhèjiāngchéng-xuānbù zhèngshǐsī*) included 11 states, one prefecture and 75 counties. Today's Jiaxing and Huzhou became prominently famous for their raw silk products, and prospered with the advent of international commerce.

At this time there was a marked difference in the social structure of southern Zhejiang (referred to as "Zhe East' 浙東 *zhèdōng*) from that of the north. According to the militarist-scholar Yu Que (余闕 *yú quē*), who lived from 1303–1358:

> Zhedong lay in ancient times with the kingdom of the Yue (越 *yuè*). Its land is divided into small units. There are no very rich or poor persons. In its hilly valleys there live people whose dwelling-houses occupy a sixth of an acre [i.e., one mu] of land, and whose fields amount to one and two-thirds of an acre, the property having been handed down intact from one generation to the next. The land is not fertile[4]; and these humble folk have to toil for their living. Even persons of quality are modest and frugal, being imbued with respect for the *Book of Odes* and the *Book of Documents*. They are unlike the men of Wu [i.e., northern Zhejiang and southern Jiangsu] with their high-handed, land-grabbing great families whose harvests each year amount to several million measures, while none of the poor have anything at all to store away (Elvin 1973).

Zhejiang province continued to grow in population, with about 11 million in 1393, and 23.6 million in 1630. However, with the onset of the Ming-Qing dynastic transition, the people of Zhejiang were heavily impacted by warfare due to Manchurian invasions and the inevitable epidemics that followed. Its population subsequently plummeted to seven million as of 1661. In the beginning years of the Qing Kangxi reign (ca. 1670), the imperial court changed the existing Zhejiang executor,[5] simply calling the area Zhejiang Province. By 1776, Zhejiang had recovered much of its population to about 22.4 million (Zhao 2015).

---

[3] 江淮等處行中書省 *jiānghuái děngchǔ xíngzhōngshūshěng*.

[4] Literally barren: 瘠 *jí*.

[5] 浙江承宣布政使司 *zhèjiāng chéngxuānbù zhèngshǐsī*.

In 1840, the Opium War brought English guns to bear on Dinghai on the Zhoushan (舟山) archipelago. China's terms of surrender led to the Jiangning Treaty (江寧條約 *jiāngníng tiáoyuē* or Treaty of Nanking), forcing Ningbo to open its ports to European access and commerce.

Taiping Rebellion (1850–1864)

The Confucianist-leaning population of Zhejiang was anathema to Taiping Rebellion ideology, and served to increase the viciousness of Taiping army attacks, especially in 1861. Zhejiang suffered a significant portion of casualties, and according to estimates over 96% of the populations in Wukang, Xiaofeng and Anji were all but wiped out. In contrast, Zhejiang was later able to avoid most of the ravages of the Boxer Rebellion (1900) by participating in a Southeast Provincial Mutual Defense Agreement (東南互保 *dōngnánhùbǎo*) with neighboring provinces. Following the revolution against the Manchus, and the revolutionary Hangzhou New Army uprising in November 1911, Zhejiang declared its independence from the Qing.

Wartime Zhejiang

During the Sino-Japanese War in the 1930s, Zhejiang formed a major (Third) theatre, employing delay tactics and a scorch earth policy against the Japanese. Along with other eastern areas of China, Zhejiang province suffered greatly:

As a token answer to avenge the Japanese attack on Pearl Harbor, on 18 April 1942 the United States conducted a daring mission to bomb Tokyo using long range bombers, the famous "Doolittle Raid." A significant part of this plan included preparing areas for B-25 bombers to find safe and immediate landing after their attack on Japan, mainly in Zhejiang. Only having been given notice a week before the bombers were to be launched, the leader of Free China, Chiang Kai-shek, asked the United States for a delay to prepare against expected Japanese reprisals against the Chinese. He was denied. In the best English-language biography thus far on Chiang Kai-shek, Jay Taylor writes what happened next:

> After the raid, Chiang sent an angry message to [George] Marshall reporting that in reprisal, Japanese troops had attacked the coastal areas of China where locals had rescued the American fliers. 'The Japanese,' Chiang said, 'slaughtered every man, woman and child in these areas—let me repeat, every man, woman and child.' In the resulting battles in Zhejiang and Jiangxi, Chiang committed thirty-four divisions against the Japanese and suffered 30,000 casualties. All of [Claire] Chennault [of the Flying Tigers] airfields in East China were destroyed. The Doolittle raid, brave as it was, did scant damage in Tokyo and, as Chiang had feared, caused great harm for China (Taylor 2011).

At the end of the Chinese civil war, People's Liberation Army (PLA) Third Field Army made their way into Zhejiang and had reached Ningbo by May 1949. The

Zhejiang government moved to Zhoushan, administering the outer Zhejiang islands that were still held by Nationalist troops. By May 1950, about 125,000 Kuomintang (KMT) troops and 20,000 civilians had fled to Taiwan. And although the PLA had by this time "liberated" much of mainland China, there were still Nationalist holdouts in the Zhejiang southeastern Dachen Islands (大陳列島 *dàchén lièdǎo*), the Taizhou archipelago (台州列島 *táizhōu lièdǎo*), and Yijiangshan Island (一江山島 *yījiāng shāndǎo*). In its first true joint-PLA operation, led by Marshal Zhang Aiping, Chinese communist forces assaulted Yijiangshan Island in January 1955, and the United States Navy 7th Fleet assisted in rescuing the retreating Nationalists (Li 2003).

Zhejiang Economy and Population: Past and Present

Hangzhou City is still famed as a source of Chinese silk products, and its attraction for tourism, for both local Chinese and international alike goes back centuries. And not only is Shaoxing City (紹興市) famous for its representative Zhejiang cuisine, but is also the home of the original Shaoxing rice wine, its fermentation process involving a ferment, *qu (麴 qú)*, similar to the Japanese *koji*, and has remained much the same since the ancient Zhou dynasty (ca. 1000 BCE) (Huang 2000). Jinhua City is not only famous for its rice, but for its ham (金華火腿 *jīnhuá huǒtuǐ*), produced in a similar fashion to the Italian *prosciutto di parma* (Leistner 2000).

Following Deng Xiaoping's reforms in 1978, exemplified by cities like Wenzhou and shipbuilding at Ningbo, Zhejiang participated in a growing economy, with Shaoxing and Wuyi leading in terms of consumer goods and light manufacturing. This has since resulted in unqualified success, as Zhejiang Province remained in the top five of all mainland China's 31 provinces and major cities in terms of gross domestic production (GDP): USD $665 billion in 2015, and $1.005 billion in 2020. As of 2020, Zhejiang was also fourth in terms of per capita income ($8249) (Zhang 2021). As a consequence, Zhejiang's residential population (see Table 34.2) has grown apace (18.6% from 2010–2020), just behind Guangdong, with a 2020 population (census) of about 64,568,000, dwarfing that of the permanent (*hukou*) registered population that year of 50,000,000 (Table 34.4). Such a disparity demonstrates the strong pull of economic growth and opportunity for mainland Chinese, especially for those in less-developed provinces (Table 34.3; Fig. 34.2).

Table 34.4 (below) shows the *hukou* (family registered) populations based on PRC Ministry of Civil Affairs data. (Districts listed directly under major cities are government seats, as are those in parentheses). One can compare these data with the census (usual residential populations based on 2010 and 2020 censuses in Tables 34.2 and 34.3 (below):

Table 34.2 Zhejiang province population data. (ZPBS 2021)

City	Population (2010)	Population (2020)
Hangzhou 杭州市 *hángzhōu shì* [abbrev. 杭 *háng*]	8,700,400	11,936,010
Ningbo City 寧波市 *níngbō shì* [abbrev. 甬 *yǒng*]	7,605,700	9,404,283
Huzhou City 湖州市 *húzhōu shì*	2,893,500	3,367,579
Jiaxing City 嘉興市 *jiāxīng shì* [abbrev. 禾 *hé*]	4,501,700	5,400,868
Jinhua City 金華市 *jīnhuá shì* [abbrev. 婺 *wù*]	5,361,600	7,050,683
Lishui City 麗水市 *líshuǐ shì* [abbrev. 處 *chǔ*]	2,117,000	2,507,396
Quzhou City 衢州市 *qúzhōu zhì*	2,122,700	2,276,184
Shaoxing City 紹興市 *shàoxīng shì* [abbrev. 越 *yuè*]	4,912,200	5,270,977
Taizhou City 台州市 *tāizhōu shì*	5,968,800	6,622,888
Wenzhou City 溫州市 *wēnzhōu shì* [abbrev. 甌 *ōu*]	9,122,100	9,572,903
Zhoushan City 舟山市 *zhōushān shì*	1,121,300	1,157,817
Total	**54,426,900**	**64,567,588**

Table 34.3 Zhejiang Province: population data of cities and their subordinate sectors. (ZPBS 2021)

Cities and subordinate sectors, population (2020 census)	Subordinate district, city and county populations (2020)	Total population (2020)
Hangzhou 杭州市***hángzhōu shì* [abbrev. 杭 *háng*]**		**11,936,010**
Shangcheng District 上城區 *shàngchéng qū*	1,323,467	
Gongshu District 拱墅區 *gǒngshù qū*	1,120,985	
Xihu District 西湖區 *xīhú qū*	1,089,229	
Binjiang District 濱江區 *bīnjiāng qū*	503,859	
Xiaoshan District 蕭山區 *xiāoshān qū*	2,011,699	
Yuhang District 余杭區 *yúháng qū*	1,226,673	
Linping District 臨平區 *línpíng qū*	1,175,841	
Qiantang District 錢塘區 *qiántáng qū*	769,150	
Fuyang District 富陽區 *fùyáng qū*	832,017	
Lin'an District 臨安區 *lín'ān qū*	634,555	
Tonglu County 桐廬縣 *tónglú xiàn*	453,106	
Chun'an County 淳安縣 *chún'ān xiàn*	328,957	
Jiande City 建德市 *jiàndé shì*	442,709	
Xihu Scenic Famed Area 西湖風景名勝區 *xīhú fēngjǐngmíngshèng qū*	23,763	

(continued)

Table 34.3 (continued)

Cities and subordinate sectors, population (2020 census)	Subordinate district, city and county populations (2020)	Total population (2020)
Ningbo City 寧波市 ***níngbō shì* [abbrev. 甬*yǒng*]**		**9,404,283**
Haishu District 海曙區 *hǎishǔ qū*	1,041,285	
Jiangbei District 江北區 *jiāngběi qū*	488,885	
Beilun District 北侖區 *běilún qū*	829,448	
Zhenhai District 鎮海區 *zhènhǎi qū*	510,462	
Yinzhou District 鄞州區 *yínzhōu qū*	1,609,555	
Fenghua District 奉化區 *fènghuà qū*	577,505	
Xiangshan County 象山縣 *xiàngshān xiàn*	567,665	
Ninghai County 寧海縣 *nínghǎi xiàn*	695,958	
Yuyao City 余姚市 *yúyáo shì*	1,254,032	
Cixi City 慈溪市 *cíxī shì*	1,829,488	
Huzhou City 湖州市 ***húzhōu shì***		**3,367,579**
Wuxing District 吳興區 *wúxīng qū*	712,595	
Nanxun District 南潯區 *nánxún qū*	542,889	
Deqing County 德清縣 *déqīng xiàn*	548,568	
Anji County 安吉縣 *ānjí xiàn*	586,409	
Changxing County 長興縣 *chángxīng xiàn*	673,776	
Nantaihu New District 南太湖新區 *nántàihú xīnqū*	303,342	
Jiaxing City 嘉興市 ***jiāxīng shì* [abbrev. 禾 *hé*]**		**5,400,868**
Nanhu District 南湖區 *nánhú qū*	624,655	
Xiuzhou District 秀洲區 *xiùzhōu qū*	556,971	
Jiaxing Economic and Technology Development Zone 嘉興經濟技術開發區 *jiāxīng jīngjìjìshù kāifāqū*	337,028	
Jiashan County 嘉善縣 *jiāshàn xiàn*	648,160	
Haiyan County 海鹽縣 *hǎiyán xiàn*	456,775	
Haining City 海寧市 *hǎiníng shì*	1,076,199	
Pinghu City (includes harbor district) 平湖市 *pínghú shì*	671,326	
Tongxiang City 桐鄉市 *tóngxiāng shì*	1,029,754	
Jinhua City 金華市 ***jīnhuá shì* [abbrev. 婺 *wù*]**		**7,050,683**
Wucheng District[a] 婺城區 *wùchéng qū*	957055	
Jinyi New District (Jindong District) 金義新區 *jīnyì xīnqū* (金東區 *jīndōng qū*)	506,935	
Lanxi City 蘭溪市 *lánxī shì*	574,801	
Yiwu City 義烏市 *yìwū shì*	1,859,390	

(continued)

Table 34.3 (continued)

Cities and subordinate sectors, population (2020 census)	Subordinate district, city and county populations (2020)	Total population (2020)
Dongyang City 東陽市 *dōngyáng shì*	1,087,950	
Yongkang City 永康市 *yǒngkāng shì*	964,203	
Wuyi County 武義縣 *wǔyì xiàn*	462,462	
Pujiang County 浦江縣 *pǔjiāng xiàn*	460,726	
Pan'an County 磐安縣 *pán'ān xiàn*	177,161	
Lishui City 麗水市 ***líshuǐ shì* [abbrev.** 處 ***chǔ*]**		**2,507,396**
Liandu District 蓮都區 *liándū qū*	562,116	
Qingtian County[b] 青田縣 *qīngtián xiàn*	509,053	
Jinyun County 縉雲縣 *jìnyún xiàn*	405,318	
Suichang County 遂昌縣 *suìchāng xiàn*	194,395	
Songyang County 松陽縣 *sōngyáng xiàn*	204,880	
Yunhe County 雲和縣 *yúnhé xiàn*	129,216	
Qingyuan County 慶元縣 *qìngyuán xiàn*	142,551	
Jingning County 景寧縣 *jǐngníng xiàn*	111,011	
Longquan City 龍泉市 *lóngquán shì*	248,866	
Quzhou City 衢州市 ***qúzhōu zhì***		**2,276,184**
Kecheng District 柯城區 *kēchéng qū*	528,847	
Qujiang District 衢江區 *qújiāng qū*	373,920	
Longyou County 龍游縣 *lóngyóu xiàn*	360,229	
Jiangshan City 江山市 *jiāngshān shì*	494,412	
Changshan County 常山縣 *chángshān xiàn*	259,966	
Kaihua County 開化縣 *kāihuà xiàn*	258,810	
Shaoxing City 紹興市 ***shàoxīng shì* [abbrev.** 越 ***yuè*]**		**5,270,977**
Yuecheng District 越城區 *yuèchéng qū*	1,020,037	
Keqiao District 柯橋區 *kēqiáo qū*	1,098,859	
Shangyu District 上虞區 *shàngyú qū*	839,747	
Zhuji City 諸暨市 *zhūjì shì*	1,218,072	
Shengzhou City 嵊州市 *shèngzhōu shì*	675,226	
Xinchang County 新昌縣 *xīnchāng xiàn*	419,036	
Taizhou City 台州市 ***tāizhōu shì***		**6,622,888**
Jiaojiang District 椒江區 *jiāojiāng qū*	826,074	
Huangyan District 黃岩區 *huángyán qū*	707,453	
Luqiao District 路橋區 *lùqiáo qū*	628,934	
Linhai City 臨海市 *línhǎi shì*	1,114,146	
Wenling City 溫嶺市 *wēnlǐng shì*	1,416,199	

(continued)

Table 34.3 (continued)

Cities and subordinate sectors, population (2020 census)	Subordinate district, city and county populations (2020)	Total population (2020)
Yuhuan City 玉環市 *yùhuán shì*	644,014	
Tiantai County 天台縣 *tiāntái xiàn*	474,411	
Xianju County 仙居縣 *xiānjū xiàn*	431,888	
Sanmen County 三門縣 *sānmén xiàn*	379,469	
Wenzhou City 溫州市 ***wēnzhōu shì* [abbrev. 甌*ōu*]**		**9,572,903**
Lucheng District 鹿城區 *lùchéng qū*	1,167,164	
Longwan District 龍灣區 *lóngwān qū*	475,706	
Ouhai District 甌海區 *ōuhǎi qū*	963,238	
Dongtou District 洞頭區 *dòngtóu qū*	107,027	
Yongjia County 永嘉縣 *yǒngjiā xiàn*	869,548	
Pingyang County 平陽縣 *píngyáng xiàn*	863,166	
Cangnan County 蒼南縣 *cāngnán xiàn*	843,959	
Wencheng County 文成縣 *wénchéng xiàn*	288,168	
Taishun County 泰順縣 *tàishùn xiàn*	265,973	
Rui'an City 瑞安市 *ruì'ān shì*	1,520,046	
Yueqing City 樂清市 *yuèqīng shì*	1,453,090	
Longgang City 龍港市 *lónggǎng shì*	464,695	
Oujiangkou Industrial Cluster District 甌江口產業集聚區 *ōujiāngkǒu chǎnyè jíjùqū*	41,780	
Zhenan Industiral Cluster District 浙南產業集聚區 *zhènán chǎnyè jíjùqū*	249,343	
Zhoushan City 舟山市 ***zhōushān shì***		**1,157,817**
Dinghai District 定海區 *dìnghǎi qū*	358,720	
Putuo District 普陀區 *pǔtuó qū*	347,634	
Daishan County 岱山縣 *dàishān xiàn*	207,982	
Shengsi County 嵊泗縣 *shèngsì xiàn*	66,903	
Xincheng (New Town) 新城 *xīnchéng*	169,164	
Putuo Shan 普陀山 *pǔtuó shān*	7,414	

[a]Includes population (477,938) of the Jinhua Economic and Technology Development Zone (金華經濟技術開發區 *jīnhuá jīngjìjìshù kāifāqū*)

[b]The residential population of Qingtian County includes 146,108 overseas Chinese

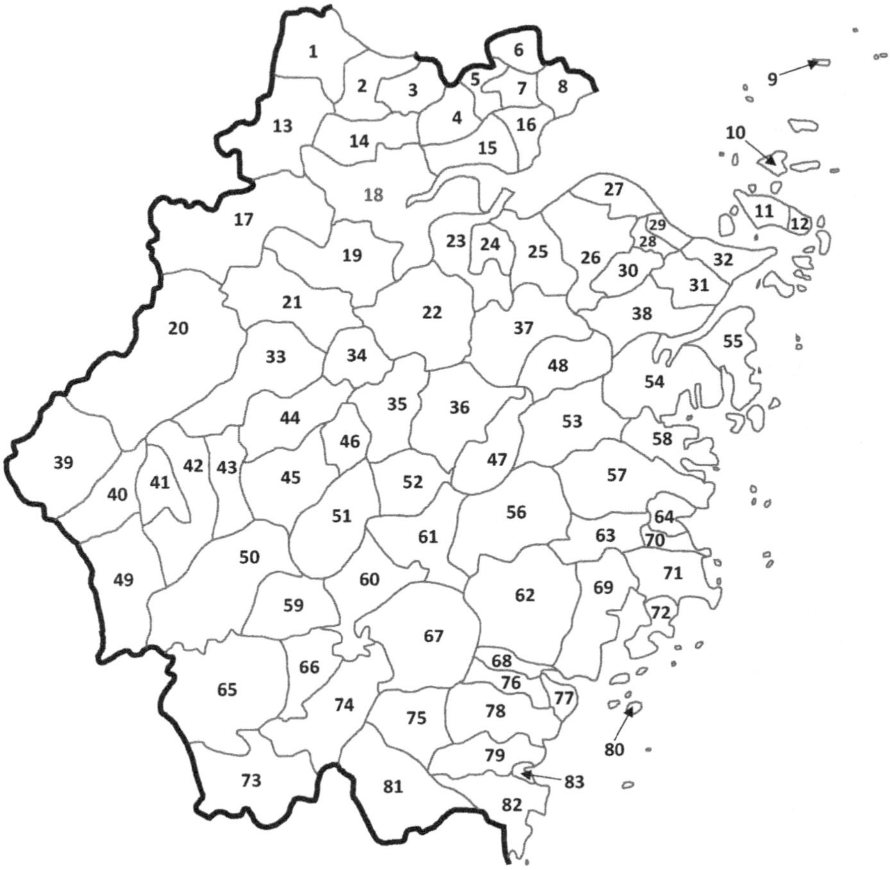

1. Changxing County
2. Wuxing District
3. Nanxun District
4. Tongxiang City
5. Xiuzhou District
6. Jiashan County
7. Nanhu District
8. Pinghu City
9. Shengsi County
10. Daishan County
11. Dinghai District
12. Putuo District
13. Anji County
14. Deqing County
15. Haining City
16. Haiyan County
17. Lin'an District
18. Hangzhou City
19. Fuyang District
20. Chun'an County
21. Tonglu County
22. Zhuji City
23. Keqiao District
24. Yuecheng District
25. Shangyu District
26. Yuyao City
27. Cixi City
28. Jiangbei District
39. Zhenhai District
30. Haishu District
31. Yinzhou District
32. Beilun District
33. Jiande City
34. Pujiang County
35. Yiwu City
36. Dongyang City
37. Shengzhou City
38. Fenghua City
39. Kaihua County
40. Changshan County
41. Kecheng District
42. Qujiang District
43. Longyou County
44. Lanxi City
45. Wucheng District
46. Jindong District
47. Pan'an County
48. Xinchang County
49. Jiangshan City
50. Suichang City
51. Wuyi County
52. Yongkang City
53. Tiantai County
54. Ninghai County
55. Xiangshan County
56. Xianju County
57. Linhai City
58. Sanmen County
59. Songyang County
60. Liandu District
61. Jinyun County
62. Yongjia County
63. Huangyan District
64. Jiaojiang District
65. Longquan City
66. Yunhe County
67. Qingtian County
68. Lucheng District
69. Leqing City
70. Luqiao District
71. Wenling City
72. Yuhuan City
73. Qingyuan County
74. Jingning She Autonomous County
75. Wencheng County
76. Ouhai District
77. Longwan District
78. Rui'an City
79. Pingyang County
80. Dongtou District
81. Taishun County
82. Cangnan County
83. Longgang City

Fig. 34.2 Zhejiang province: subdistricts (provincial capital city: Hangzhou City). (Drawn by the Author after People's Republic of China, Ministry of Civil Affairs. (MCA 2020))

Zhejiang Province (浙 *zhè*)

Provincial Capital: Hangzhou City

Table 34.4 Henan province: permanent registered (戶籍人口 *hùjí rénkǒu*) populations. (MCA 2020)

Name (government seat)	Traditional	Simplified	Population (2012)	Population (2016)	Population (2020)	Area (Sq. Km)
Zhejiang Province	浙江省	浙江省	47,480,000	47,980,000	50,000,000	103,493.4
Hangzhou City	杭州市	杭州市	6,890,000	7,030,000	7,740,000	16,596
Gongshu District (Hushu Subdistrict)	拱墅區 (湖墅街道)	拱墅区 (湖墅街道)	310,000	320,000	380,000	88
Shangcheng District (Qingbo Subdistrict)	上城區 (清波街道)	上城区 (清波街道)	330,000	330,000	320,000	18
Xiacheng District (Wulin Subdistrict)	下城區 (武林街道)	下城区 (武林街道)	400,000	410,000	410,000	31
Jianggan District (Caihe Subdistrict)	江幹區 (采荷街道)	江干区 (采荷街道)	450,000	460,000	600,000	210
Xihu District (Lingyin Subdistrict)	西湖區 (靈隱街道)	西湖区 (灵隐街道)	630,000	650,000	740,000	263
Binjiang District (Xixing Subdistrict)	濱江區 (西興街道)	滨江区 (西兴街道)	150,000	170,000	260,000	73
Yuhang District (Linping Subdistrict)	余杭區 (臨平街道)	余杭区 (临平街道)	860,000	890,000	1,100,000	1222
Xiaoshan District (Chengxiang Subdistrict)	蕭山區 (城廂街道)	萧山区 (城厢街道)	1,220,000	1,240,000	1,320,000	1163
Lin'an District[a] (Jincheng Subdistrict)	臨安區 (錦城街道)	临安区 (锦城街道)	530,000	530,000	540,000	3124
Fuyang District (Fuchun Subdistrict)	富陽區 (富春街道)	富阳区 (富春街道)	650,000	660,000	680,000	1808
Jiande City (Xin'anjiang Subdistrict)	建德市 (新安江街道)	建德市 (新安江街道)	510,000	510,000	510,000	2364

(continued)

Table 34.4 (continued)

Name (government seat)	Traditional	Simplified	Population (2012)	Population (2016)	Population (2020)	Area (Sq. Km)
Tonglu County (Chengnan Subdistrict)	桐廬縣 (城南街道)	桐庐县 (城南街道)	400,000	400,000	420,000	1780
Chun'an County (Qiandaohu Town)	淳安縣 (千島湖鎮)	淳安县 (千岛湖镇)	450,000	460,000	460,000	4452
Huzhou City	湖州市	湖州市	2,600,000	2,620,000	2,670,000	5794
Wuxing District (Yuehe Subdistrict)	吳興區 (月河街道)	吴兴区 (月河街道)	600,000	610,000	630,000	872
Nanxun District (Nanxun Town)	南潯區 (南潯鎮)	南浔区 (南浔镇)	490,000	490,000	490,000	716
Changxing County (Zhicheng Subdistrict)	長興縣 (雉城街道)	长兴县 (雉城街道)	620,000	630,000	640,000	1388
Deqing County (Wukang Town)	德清縣 (武康鎮)	德清县 (武康镇)	430,000	430,000	440,000	936
Anji County (Changshuo Subdistrict)	安吉縣 (昌碩街道)	安吉县 (昌硕街道)	460,000	460,000	470,000	1882
Jiaxing City	嘉興市	嘉兴市	3,400,000	3,460,000	3,600,000	3915
Nanhu District (Dongpeng Subdistrict)	南湖區 (東栅街道)	南湖区 (东栅街道)	470,000	480,000	520,000	426
Xiuzhou District (Xincheng Subdistrict)	秀洲區 (新城街道)	秀洲区 (新城街道)	360,000	370,000	400,000	542
Pinghu City (Danghu Subdistrict)	平湖市 (當湖街道)	平湖市 (当湖街道)	490,000	490,000	500,000	536
Haining City (Xiashi Subdistrict)	海寧市 (硤石街道)	海宁市 (硖石街道)	660,000	670,000	700,000	681
Tongxiang City (Wutong Subdistrict)	桐鄉市 (梧桐街道)	桐乡市 (梧桐街道)	670,000	680,000	700,000	723
Jiashan County (Luoxing Subdistrict)	嘉善縣 (羅星街道)	嘉善县 (罗星街道)	380,000	390,000	400,000	504
Haiyan County (Wuyuan Subdistrict)	海鹽縣 (武原街道)	海盐县 (武原街道)	370,000	380,000	380,000	503
Zhoushan City	舟山市	舟山市	970,000	970,000	970,000	1440

(continued)

Table 34.4 (continued)

Name (government seat)	Traditional	Simplified	Population (2012)	Population (2016)	Population (2020)	Area (Sq. Km)
Dinghai District (Changguo Subdistrict)	定海區 (昌國街道)	定海区 (昌国街道)	380,000	380,000	400,000	569
Putuo District (Shenjiamen Subdistrict)	普陀區 (沈家門街道)	普陀区 (沈家门街道)	320,000	320,000	320,000	459
Daishan County (Gaoting Town)	岱山縣 (高亭鎮)	岱山县 (高亭镇)	190,000	190,000	180,000	326
Shengsi County (Caiyuan Town)	嵊泗縣 (菜園鎮)	嵊泗县 (菜园镇)	80,000	80,000	80,000	86
Ningbo City	寧波市	宁波市	5,740,000	5,770,000	6,030,000	9365
Haishu District (Jiangxia Subdistrict)	海曙區 (江厦街道)	海曙区 (江厦街道)	300,000	300,000	630,000	595
Jiangdong District[b] (Baizhang Subdistrict)	江東區 (百丈街道)	江东区 (百丈街道)	280,000	280,000	N/A	(38)
Jiangbei District (Zhongma Subdistrict)	江北區 (中馬街道)	江北区 (中马街道)	240,000	240,000	260,000	218
Beilun District (Xinqi Subdistrict)	北侖區 (新碶街道)	北仑区 (新碶街道)	380,000	380,000	420,000	585
Zhenhai District (Zhaobaoshan Subdistrict)	鎮海區 (招寶山街道)	镇海区 (招宝山街道)	230,000	230,000	260,000	218
Yinzhou District (Shounan Subdistrict)	鄞州區 (首南街道)	鄞州区 (首南街道)	810,000	830,000	900,000	814
Cixi City (Baishalu Subdistrict)	慈溪市 (白沙路街道)	慈溪市 (白沙路街道)	1,040,000	1,040,000	1,060,000	1154
Yuyao City (Lanjiang Subdistrict)	余姚市 (蘭江街道)	余姚市 (兰江街道)	830,000	830,000	840,000	1346
Fenghua City (Jinping Subdistrict)	奉化市 (錦屏街道)	奉化市 (锦屏街道)	480,000	480,000	480,000	1268
Ninghai County (Yuelong Subdistrict)	寧海縣 (躍龍街道)	宁海县 (跃龙街道)	610,000	620,000	630,000	1880
Xiangshan County (Dandong Subdistrict)	象山縣 (丹東街道)	象山县 (丹东街道)	540,000	540,000	550,000	1172

(continued)

Table 34.4 (continued)

Name (government seat)	Traditional	Simplified	Population (2012)	Population (2016)	Population (2020)	Area (Sq. Km)
Shaoxing City	紹興市	绍兴市	4,390,000	4,400,000	4,470,000	8256
Yuecheng District (Tashan Subdistrict)	越城區 (塔山街道)	越城区 (塔山街道)	650,000	740,000	760,000	498
Keqiao District (Keqiao Subdistrict)	柯橋區 (柯橋街道)	柯桥区 (柯桥街道)	N/A	640,000	680,000	1041
Zhuji City (Jiyang Subdistrict)	諸暨市 (暨陽街道)	诸暨市 (暨阳街道)	1,070,000	1,070,000	1,090,000	2311
Shangyu District (Baiguan Subdistrict)	上虞區 (百官街道)	上虞区 (百官街道)	780,000	780,000	780,000	1403
Shengzhou City (Shanhu Subdistrict)	嵊州市 (剡湖街道)	嵊州市 (剡湖街道)	730,000	730,000	730,000	1790
Shaoxing County[c] (Keqiao Subdistrict)	紹興縣 (柯橋街道)	绍兴县 (柯桥街道)	720,000	N/A	N/A	(1196)
Xinchang County (Nanming Subdistrict)	新昌縣 (南明街道)	新昌县 (南明街道)	440,000	440,000	430,000	1213
Quzhou City	衢州市	衢州市	2,510,000	2,520,000	2,580,000	8837
Kecheng District (Xin'an Subdistrict)	柯城區 (信安街道)	柯城区 (信安街道)	430,000	430,000	440,000	609
Qujiang District (Zhangtan Subdistrict)	衢江區 (樟潭街道)	衢江区 (樟潭街道)	400,000	400,000	410,000	1748
Jiangshan City (Shuangta Subdistrict)	江山市 (雙塔街道)	江山市 (双塔街道)	600,000	600,000	620,000	2018
Changshan County (Tianma Subdistrict)	常山縣 (天馬街道)	常山县 (天马街道)	330,000	340,000	340,000	1099
Kaihua County (Huabu Town)	開化縣 (華埠鎮)	开化县 (华埠镇)	350,000	350,000	360,000	2224
Longyou County (Longzhou Subdistrict)	龍游縣 (龍洲街道)	龙游县 (龙洲街道)	400,000	400,000	400,000	1139
Jinhua City	金華市	金华市	4,660,000	4,710,000	4,890,000	10,919
Wucheng District (Chengzhong Subdistrict)	婺城區 (城中街道)	婺城区 (城中街道)	620,000	620,000	650,000	1388

(continued)

Table 34.4 (continued)

Name (government seat)	Traditional	Simplified	Population (2012)	Population (2016)	Population (2020)	Area (Sq. Km)
Jindong District (Duohu Subdistrict)	金東區 (多湖街道)	金东区 (多湖街道)	310,000	320,000	340,000	657
Lanxi City (Lanjiang Subdistrict)	蘭溪市 (蘭江街道)	兰溪市 (兰江街道)	660,000	670,000	660,000	1310
Yongkang City (Dongcheng Subdistrict)	永康市 (東城街道)	永康市 (东城街道)	570,000	580,000	620,000	1049
Yiwu City (Choucheng Subdistrict)	義烏市 (稠城街道)	义乌市 (稠城街道)	740,000	750,000	820,000	1103
Dongyang City (Wuning Subdistrict)	東陽市 (吳寧街道)	东阳市 (吴宁街道)	820,000	830,000	850,000	1739
Wuyi County (Hushan Subdistrict)	武義縣 (壺山街道)	武义县 (壶山街道)	340,000	340,000	350,000	1577
Pujiang County (Puyang Subdistrict)	浦江縣 (浦陽街道)	浦江县 (浦阳街道)	390,000	390,000	400,000	900
Pan'an County (Anwen Town)	磐安縣 (安文鎮)	磐安县 (安文镇)	210,000	210,000	210,000	1196
Taizhou City	台州市	台州市	5,830,000	5,920,000	6,050,000	9413
Jiaojiang District (Haimen Subdistrict)	椒江區 (海門街道)	椒江区 (海门街道)	510,000	520,000	550,000	276
Huangyan District (Dongcheng Subdistrict)	黃岩區 (東城街道)	黄岩区 (东城街道)	600,000	600,000	620,000	988
Luqiao District (Lubei Subdistrict)	路橋區 (路北街道)	路桥区 (路南街道)	440,000	450,000	460,000	274
Linhai City (Gucheng Subdistrict)	臨海市 (古城街道)	临海市 (古城街道)	1,160,000	1,180,000	1,200,000	2171
Wenling City (Taiping Subdistrict)	溫嶺市 (太平街道)	温岭市 (太平街道)	1,190,000	1,210,000	1,220,000	836
Sanmen County (Haiyou Subdistrict)	三門縣 (海游街道)	三门县 (海游街道)	430,000	440,000	450,000	1072
Tiantai County (Chicheng Subdistrict)	天台縣 (赤城街道)	天台县 (赤城街道)	580,000	590,000	600,000	1426

(continued)

Table 34.4 (continued)

Name (government seat)	Traditional	Simplified	Population (2012)	Population (2016)	Population (2020)	Area (Sq. Km)
Xianju County (Fuying Subdistrict)	仙居縣 (福應街道)	仙居县 (福应街道)	500,000	500,000	520,000	1992
Yuhuan City[d] (Yucheng Subdistrict)	玉環市 (玉城街道)	玉环市 (玉城街道)	420,000	430,000	440,000	378
Wenzhou City	溫州市	温州市	7,880,000	7,990,000	8,290,000	11,784
Lucheng District (Wuma Subdistrict)	鹿城區 (五馬街道)	鹿城区 (五马街道)	710,000	730,000	780,000	294
Longwan District (Yongzhong Subdistrict)	龍灣區 (永中街道)	龙湾区 (永中街道)	340,000	320,000	340,000	228
Ouhai District (Louqiao Subdistrict)	甌海區 (婁橋街道)	瓯海区 (娄桥街道)	410,000	420,000	460,000	615
Rui'an City (Anyang Subdistrict)	瑞安市 (安陽街道)	瑞安市 (安阳街道)	1,190,000	1,220,000	1,250,000	1278
Longgang City (Zhenqianlu)	龍港市 (鎮前路)	龙港市 (镇前路)	N/A	N/A	380,000	122
Yueqing City (Chengdong Subdistrict)	樂清市 (城東街道)	乐清市 (城东街道)	1,240,000	1,270,000	1,310,000	1174
Yongjia County (Beicheng Subdistrict)	永嘉縣 (北城街道)	永嘉县 (北城街道)	950,000	960,000	980,000	2674
Wencheng County (Daxue Town)	文成縣 (大峃鎮)	文成县 (大峃镇)	380,000	390,000	410,000	1294
Pingyang County (Kunyang Town)	平陽縣 (昆陽鎮)	平阳县 (昆阳镇)	870,000	870,000	890,000	1042
Taishun County (Luoyang Town)	泰順縣 (羅陽鎮)	泰顺县 (罗阳镇)	360,000	360,000	370,000	1762
Dongtou County[e] (Bei'ao Subdistrict)	洞頭區 (北嶴街道)	洞头区 (北岙街道)	130,000	N/A	N/A	(151)
Dongtou District (Bei'ao Subdistrict)	洞頭區 (北嶴街道)	洞头区 (北岙街道)	N/A	150,000	150,000	151
Cangnan County[f] (Lingxi Town)	蒼南縣 (靈溪鎮)	苍南县 (灵溪镇)	1,130,000	1,300,000	N/A	(1272)
Lishui City	麗水市	丽水市	2,590,000	2,620,000	2,700,000	17,298
Liandu County (Wanxiang Subdistrict)	蓮都縣 (萬象街道)	莲都区 (万象街道)	390,000	390,000	410,000	1502

(continued)

Table 34.4 (continued)

Name (government seat)	Traditional	Simplified	Population (2012)	Population (2016)	Population (2020)	Area (Sq. Km)
Longquan City (Longyuan Subdistrict)	龍泉市 (龍淵街道)	龙泉市 (龙渊街道)	290,000	290,000	290,000	3059
Jinyun County (Wuyun Subdistrict)	縉雲縣 (五雲街道)	缙云县 (五云街道)	450,000	460,000	470,000	1482
Qingtian County (Hecheng Subdistrict)	青田縣 (鶴城街道)	青田县 (鹤城街道)	510,000	520,000	560,000	2484
Yunhe County (Fuyun Subdistrict)	雲和縣 (浮雲街道)	云和县 (浮云街道)	110,000	110,000	110,000	978
Suichang County (Miaogao Subdistrict)	遂昌縣 (妙高街道)	遂昌县 (妙高街道)	230,000	230,000	230,000	2539
Songyang County (Xiping Subdistrict)	松陽縣 (西屏街道)	松阳县 (西屏街道)	240,000	240,000	240,000	1406
Qingyuan County (Songyuan Subdistrict)	慶元縣 (松源街道)	庆元县 (松源街道)	200,000	210,000	210,000	1898
Jingning Shezu (She) Autonomous County (Hongxing Subdistrict)	景寧畲族自治縣 (紅星街道)	景宁畲族自治县 (红星街道)	170,000	170,000	170,000	1950

[a]Converted from a city to a district in July 2017
[b]Merged with Yinzhou district in 2016
[c]Dissolved in October 2013, forming Keqiao district
[d]Made a city in April 2017
[e]Made a district in July 2015
[f]Dissolved in August 2019, establishing Longgang city

References

Anderson, E.N. 2014. *Food and environment in early and medieval China*. Philadelphia: University of Pennsylvania.

Baike (Encyclopedia). 2021. [Sui dynastic political administration]. 隋朝行政区划. https:www.baike.com. Accessed 15 Aug 2021.

Bar-Yosef, Ofer. 2012. From foraging to farming in western and eastern Asia. In *Biodiversity in agriculture: Domestication, evolution, and sustainability*, ed. Paul Gepts, Thomas R. Famula, Robert L. Bettinger, et al., 57–91. New York: Columbia University Press.

Chang, Kwang-chih. 1999. China on the eve of the historical record. In *The Cambridge history of ancient China: From the origins of civilization to 221 B.C*, ed. Michael Loewe and Edward L. Shaughnessy, 37–73. New York: Cambridge University Press.

Elvin, Mark. 1973. *The pattern of the Chinese past: A social and economic interpretation*. Stanford: Stanford University Press.

Gross, Briana L., and Zhijun Zhao. 2014. Archaeological and genetic insights into the origins of domesticated rice. *Proceedings of the National Academy of Sciences* 111 (17): 6190–6197.

Hsieh, Chiao-min, and Jean Kan Hsieh. 1995. *China: A provincial atlas*. New York: Macmillan Publishing.

Hsu, Cho-yun. 1999. The spring and autumn period. In *The Cambridge history of ancient China: From the origins of civilization to 221 B.C*, ed. Michael Loewe and Edward L. Shaughnessy, 545–586. New York: Cambridge University Press.

Huang, H.T. 2000. *Science and civilisation in China*. Volume 6, Biology and Biological Technology, Part V: Fermentations and Food Science. Cambridge: Cambridge University Press.

Leistner, Lothar. 2000. Use of combined preservative factors in foods of developing countries. In *Microbiological safety and quality of food*, ed. Barbara Lund, Tony C. Baird-Parker, and Grahame W. Gould, vol. 1, 457–485. Gaithersburg: Aspen Publishers.

Li, Xiaobing. 2003. PLA attacks and amphibious operations during the Taiwan strait crises of 1954–55, and 1958. In *Chinese warfighting: The PLA experience since 1949*, ed. Mark A. Ryan, David Michael Finkelstein, and Michael A. McDevitt, 143–172. Armonk, New York: M.E. Sharpe.

Ministry of Civil Affairs (MCA), People's Republic of China. 2020. [*County/township administration handbook*]. Beijing: China Statistics Press. 中華人民共和國民政部, 中華人民共和國, 鄉鎮行政區劃簡冊.

Shang-Ch'i Guide. 2017. [*Backpacking in China: the most complete collection of self-guided travel for China, 2018*]. Taipei: Shang-Ch'i Shitai Publishing. 2018 最完整的中國自助旅遊全集. 台北: 上奇時代.

Taylor, Jay. 2011. *[蔣] the generalissimo: Chiang Kai-shek and the struggle for modern China*. Cambridge: The Belknap Press of Harvard University Press.

von Falkenhausen, Lothar. 1999. The waning of the bronze age: Material culture and social developments, 770-481 B.C. In *The Cambridge history of ancient China: From the origins of civilization to 221 B.C*, ed. Michael Loewe and Edward L. Shaughnessy, 450–544. New York: Cambridge University Press.

Wagner, Donald B. 1996. *Iron and steel in ancient China*. New York: E.J. Brill.

Wilkinson, Endymion. 2012. *Chinese history: A new manual*. Cambridge, MA: Harvard University Press.

Yan, Wenming. 2005. The beginning of farming. In *The formation of Chinese civilization: An archaeological perspective*, ed. Kwang-chih Chang et al., 27–42. New Haven: Yale University Press.

Zhang, Shunan. 2021. [The 2020 per capita income list of residents in various provinces: Shanghai is the richest, and it has risen sharply]. Finance.people.com. 22 January. 张澍楠. 2020年各省份居民人均收入榜: 上海最有钱, 这地涨得猛. http://finance.people.com.cn/n1/2021/0122/c1004-32008733.html.

Zhao, Dingxin. 2015. *The Confucian-legalist state: A new theory of Chinese history*. New York: Oxford University Press.

Zhejiang Provincial Bureau of Statistics (ZPBS). 2021. [*Bulletin of the main data of the seventh population census of Zhejiang Province*]. 13 May. 浙江省第七次人口普查主要数据公报. https://tjj.zj.gov.cn/art/2021/5/13/art_1229129205_4632764.html.

Chapter 35
Republic of China (Taiwan)

Abstract Archeological studies suggest activity by *Homo sapiens* on Taiwan island goes back some 25,000 years. Analysis of the oldest of human fossils on Taiwan, Liangdao Man, supports the intriguing (and well-founded) theory that Taiwan was the original staging place for the Austronesian diaspora across the Pacific, reaching across Southeast Asia to Madagascar. With its own indigenous cultures long having inhabited Taiwan, and following immigration of Han Chinese from the mainland, Taiwan sequentially became a haven for pirates, a Dutch colonial satrap, part of the Qing dynastic empire, and then colonized within Japan's "Greater East Asia Co-Prosperity Sphere" from 1895 to the end of World War II. Defeated by the Chinese Communist Red Armies, the Nationalist government of Chiang Kai-shek moved to Taipei in 1949, irrevocably altering the nature of the Taiwanese population and society, and not necessarily always for the better. However, what was once known as "Formosa" has since transitioned from an authoritarian dictatorship under martial law to now a full-fledged civil democracy, and is now considered a model of economic development in Asia.

E. Croddy, *China's Provinces and Populations*,
https://doi.org/10.1007/978-3-031-09165-0_35

Republic of China (Taiwan; 中華民國臺灣 *zhōnghuá mínguó táiwān*) Abbreviation: 台/臺 (*tái*) (Fig. 35.1)

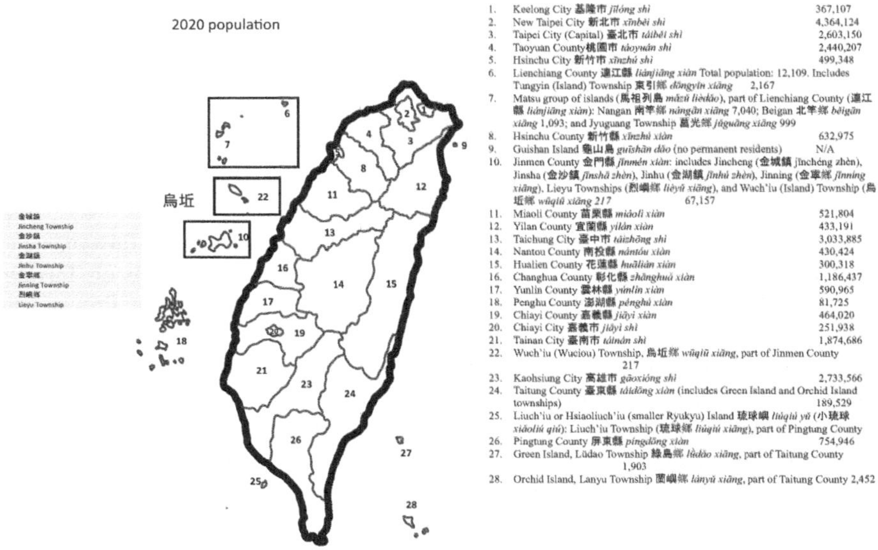

Fig. 35.1 Taiwan: Cities, counties, and Administered Islands (TCDC 2020). Population (2020): 23,561,236. Map Drawn by the author after administrative maps, Republic of China (Taiwan)

Republic of China (ROC), Taiwan: General Impressions

Since the end of the dictatorial regimes of both Chiang Kai-shek (蔣介石 *jiǎng jièshí*) and his son, Chiang Ching-kuo (蔣經國 *jiǎng jīngguó*), the Republic of China (ROC) on Taiwan has grown into a modern, pluralistic, multicultural, and liberal democratic state. It is Chinese in organization and language, having prominent, residual Japanese architectural and cultural influences, but also strong Western modes of thinking, and in style. Overall, however, there is a distinct Taiwanese spirit, maintained in the widely spoken dialect (Minnan 閩南語 *mǐnnányǔ* or *Taigi* 台語 *táiyǔ*), with a very proud and independent polity. Although mainland China claims Taiwan to be province under its jurisdiction, the authorities (and a large plebiscite) on Taiwan beg to differ. While 5% of Taiwanese want formal independence right way, with 1.5% responding in recent poll that they urgently desire unification with mainland China, the vast majority of the Taiwanese public favor the status quo (Zhao 2021). This generally has reflected the views of the Taiwanese people for decades now.

It is also important to note that, especially since resuming links between mainland China and Taiwan in 2008, large numbers of Taiwanese have been living and working in the People's Republic of China (PRC), amounting to approximately 1.2 million as of late 2020 (Li 2020). This represented nearly 5% of Taiwan's total population. However, with the advent of the severe acute respiratory syndrome coronavirus 2 (SARS-CoV-2) epidemic, decreased economic opportunities (in large part due to US trade tariffs against mainland Chinese imports), weaker salary offerings, and worsening China-Taiwan relations in the 2 years since, this number of Taiwanese expats desiring to live and work in China is expected to fall (TN 2020).

Names for Taiwan: "Formosa"

As is the case of Hong Kong and Macao, place names in European languages of distant lands often owe their origins not from within but after encounters with the West. In the case of Taiwan, for many years (and occasionally today), it was referred to usually as "Formosa." The standard explanation begins with Portuguese mercantile fleets, sailing as they did from their trading post in Macao (澳門 *àomén*) south of China, all the way north to Japan. In the course of these travels, they often passed through the Taiwan strait and near the Penghu group of islands known as the Pescadores (from the Portuguese *Os Baixos dos Pescadores*). (The latter islands had earlier been recorded by the Yuan dynasty historian Ma Duanlin (馬端臨 mǎ duānlín, 1254–1323) as "彭湖" *pénghú*).[1]

Along this navigation route, according to the textbook story, Portuguese sailors witnessed the grandeur and beauty of Taiwan main island, calling it "Formosa," or beautiful island (*Ilha Formosa*). Indeed, the map drawn by the Portuguese cartographer Lopo Homem in 1554 clearly calls out Taiwan as "*I. Fremosa*," its earliest known Western appellation. This was later corrected by his son, Diogo Homem, who followed in his father's footsteps as a map maker, rendering it "*I. Fermosa*" (TNM 2016). However, the modern historian Kaim Ang (翁佳音 *wēng jiāyīn*) struggled to find records of contemporary Portuguese sailors having used the name "Formosa" to refer to Taiwan (Weng 2006). Based on the accounts of an Iberian boat captain and his passengers[2] of a shipwreck that famously landed on Taiwan in 1582, it appears that it was the Spanish who officially used the name *As Ilhas Fermosas* when referring to the main island. Forty years prior, Portuguese navigators routinely used "*Lequeo pequeno*" to refer to Taiwan, and "*Ilhla Formosa*" was actually the

[1] Modern characters: 澎湖 *pénghú*.

[2] One of them another, Spaniard, Father Alonso Sánchez, had a young Filipino boy onboard who was able to communicate with the aborigines that they ran into, and managed to secure supplies. But eventually the survivors had to repel attacks from the "swarms" of local aborigines, and is the etymological source of the aboriginal tribe "Siraya."

Portuguese cognomen for Okinawa. When the Dutch established its colony on Taiwan (1624), the Western world began to refer to Taiwan as Formosa, and is occasionally still seen rendered into Chinese phonetics as 福爾摩沙 (*fúěrmóshā*) (Everington 2017).

Etymological Origins of Chinese Name for Taiwan (臺灣 *táiwān*)

Despite the confusing history concerning the name Formosa, it is the model of simplicity compared to the origins of the (Chinese) name for Taiwan. The most commonly accepted explanation is that the name "Taiwan" (in the Chinese language) developed from a corruption of local pronunciation of the name used to refer to a very localized area: 大員 (*dàyuán*) or 大圓 (*dàyuán* = "Big Round"). The Ming-dynasty history (1603) of Taiwan compiled by Chen Di (陳第 *chén dì*), *Records of Barbarian East* (東番記 *dōngfānjì*), for example, makes mention of a place called Dayuan 大員 (*dàyuán*), among others. Located in a harbor of modern-day Tainan city, this locale had long been known for its oval-shaped sandbars running north and south along the coastal port, seven of which being numbered as Kunshen "鯤鯓 (*kūnshēn*)" (as they resembled breaching whales). These sandbars made boat loading and alighting much easier for transporting goods and personnel. It was at "Whale No. 1" (一鯤鯓 *yīkūnshēn*) where the Dutch found most strategically viable, and is where they built Fort Zeelandia (安平古堡 *ānpíng gǔbǎo*). Significantly, another local name for "Whale No. 1" was Dayuan 大員 (*dàyuán*). At the same time, the local Siraya (西拉雅 *xīlāyǎ*) aboriginal tribe had their own name for their village in that area, rendered into Chinese as "大灣社" (*dàwānshè*): Big Bay Village (Zhao 2012).

At that time, among the local plains tribes, the aforementioned Chinese name of Dayuan 大員 (*dàyuán*) was colloquially known in dialect as "*tâi-uân.*" No doubt in conjunction with the use of the Sirayan name for their local village (大灣社" *dàwānshè*), this eventually morphed into (variously) "台窩灣" (*táiwōwān*; compare the old Dutch rendering of *Taijowan*), and then Taiwan (臺灣/台灣 *táiwān*) (Tai 2020). How it was that the character/meaning of 臺/台 "platform" was used has yet to be satisfyingly explained. (As for the other proposed intended meaning of "terraced bay," this appears to have no foundation.)

Much less plausible, but worthy of note, is the suggestion that its name originated from a pejorative used to refer to Taiwan centuries ago: "enraging" (埋冤 *máiyuān*), due to the difficult, dangerous, and disease-ridden conditions experienced by Chinese immigrants. *Maiyuan* then morphed linguistically from local dialect to "Taiwan." Further supporting the latter assertion, this was one of the reasons why Koxinga changed the name from the inauspicious sounding Taiwan to Tungtu (東都 *dōngdū*), and his son then changed this to Tungning (東寧 *dōngníng*) in 1664 (Su 2015).

Prehistoric Taiwan

In 2008, fishermen operating along Taiwan's offshore islands of Penghu (澎湖 *pénghú* aka Pescadores, Penghu County 澎湖縣 *pénghú xiàn*) retrieved a hominid jawbone that had been resting some 90 m below. The anglers sold their find to a local curio shop, whereupon a fossil collector, Tsai Kun-yu (蔡坤玉 *cài kūnyù*), then purchased it. Later realizing that he possessed something of great archeological value, Tsai Kun-yu generously donated it to the Taichung City (台中市 *táizhōng shì*) National Museum of Natural Science (國立自然科學博物館 *guólì zìrán kēxué bówùguǎn*). In 2015, it was given a prospective name, *Homo tsaichangensis* (蔡張人 *cài zhāngrén* or 澎湖原人 *pénghú yuánrén*), after the prospector (Tsai) and the lead scientist Chun-hsiang Chang (張鈞翔 *zhāng jūnxiáng*) who first characterized this "Penghu 1" (right) mandible. Despite having nearly complete molars, however, there was not enough extant tissue (collagen) to carry out traditional carbon dating techniques (Chang et al. 2015). While believed to represent a new and as of yet unclarified species of early *Homo* species, with a rough estimate in age of 190,000–250,000 years ago, its features are similar to that of the giant ape also found in China, *Gigantopithecus blacki* (a possible range of 2.6 million to 11,000 years ago), fossils of which having also been found in Hubei province.

Changbin Culture (長濱文化 *chángbīn wénhuà*)

In 1968, Taiwan National University anthropologist Wen-Hsun Sung (宋文薰 *sòng wénxūn*) and geologist Ch'ao-Ch'i Lin (林朝棨 *lín cháoqǐ*) led an archeological team to investigate the sea-coastal "Eight Immortals Cave" (八仙洞 *bāxiāndòng*), located in Taidong county, Changbin Township (台東縣長濱鄉 *táidōngxiàn, chángbīn xiāng*). It was there that they found Taiwan's first and oldest Paleolithic site, later named Changbin Culture (長濱文化 *chángbīn wénhuà*) by the archeologist Li Chi (李濟 *lǐ jì*). Further excavations at additional caves (such as 崑崙洞 *kūnlún dòng* and 乾元洞 *qiányuán dòng*) found accumulated charcoal layers, lending them to Carbon-14 dating, and were found to be as old as 15,000 years. Subsequent studies and dating techniques have pushed the dates of human inhabitation in this area to about 25,000 years ago (Basian 2009).

At first, only Changbin Culture stone tools and some signs of hunting and fishing were in evidence, but later, in 1988, at the Xiaoma cave in Taidong County, Chenggong Township (成功鎮 *chénggōng zhèn*),[3] Taiwan's first pre-Neolithic skeleton was found. Originally buried in a squatting position bones were removed but remained unstudied at the Taiwan National University for many years. It was only

[3] Taiwan census data uses the English "township" to represent 鎮 here, thus we will use this translation for Taiwanese place names throughout.

much later that a thorough analysis was finally performed, specifically the cranial size of the skeleton, as well as carbon-dating of collocated sea shells. The probable female skeleton was dated to about 6000 years ago. Fascinatingly, this human was not of Austronesian background, but rather, according the Matsumura et al.: "The short stature, short limbs, and small cranial size of the Xiaoma individual indicate a close affinity to Negrito (Ayta) groups in the Philippines" (Matsumura et al. 2021). Indeed, there are references in old Formosan indigenous tribal (Austronesian) lore that spoke of a people who were short in stature, and whose pigment was much darker than others.

Liangdao Man: Ancient Patriarch of the Austronesians?

In December 2011, a construction crew stumbled upon the Liangdao Man burial remains, located on Liang Island in the Taiwan offshore Matsu (馬祖 *mǎzǔ*) group, administered under Lienchiang County (連江縣 *liánjiāng xiàn*). Among many things notable about this site, in addition to the nearly complete skeleton of a male, was the "fetal position" style in which he was buried, similar to that seen among Taiwan's aboriginal population until about a hundred years ago. Carbon-14 dating suggests "Liangdao Man," who was about 160 cm tall and 30 years of age when he died, lived between 7500–8000 years ago. Albert Min-Shan Ko (葛明軒 *gé míngxuān*) and colleagues examined the DNA from thigh and foot bones from Lingdao Man, and were not only able to deduce that he was from mainland China's coastal region, but that he is "the oldest genetic relative of aboriginal Formosans." Ko et al. were able to characterize Liangdao Man's mitochondrial DNA profile as belonging to Haplogroup E, a genetically-inherited type not typically found in China, but predominantly found among Austronesian-speaking peoples ranging from Taiwan, to Guam, and to Easter Island. Albert Ko believes that Liangdao Man fits the hypothesis that the migration of Austronesians, originating from coastal China (modern-day Zhejiang and Fujian provinces), arrived in northern Taiwan about six thousand years ago. And, according to this "Austronesian dispersal hypothesis" (or, more colloquially, the "Express train from Taiwan"), these peoples went on to migrate southward, leaving Taiwan about two thousand years later, going on to populate such areas as Southeast Asia, Oceania, and all the way to Madagascar (Ko et al. 2014).

As for the linguistic connections among the proto-Austronesian source of languages of Taiwan and other populations in Southeast Asia, scholars have looked at their vocabulary having to do with "rice" and/or "millet," both grains having been cultivated in Taiwan for some five millennia (Tsang et al. 2017). Table 35.1 provides some examples of these related word origins and their similarities found among aboriginal Taiwanese, Philippines, and Indonesia:

As Albert Ko concludes, based on both DNA evidence and linguistic patterns shared by Austronesians, "there is multidisciplinary evidence to suggest a direction of expansion from the southeastern coast of mainland China to northern Taiwan and then to southern Taiwan."[4]

Dabenkeng Culture (大坌坑文化 *dàbènkēng wénhuà*)

Among the most studied among Taiwan's archeological sites and dated roughly to 4000–2200 BCE, Dabenkeng Culture shows a wide range of diverse pottery styles and earliest forms of agriculture on Taiwan. Not only are many features of Danbenkeng Culture consistent with that of migrations from China's coast several millennia ago, but they also appear to also be the source of the Austronesian-speaking peoples that have inhabited Taiwan since ancient times, as well as the Polynesian diaspora throughout Southeast Asia and the Pacific. (Table 35.2 shows Paleolithic and Neolithic site distribution throughout Taiwan).

The first archeological evidence of "Tapenk'eng" (Dabenkeng) culture was discovered on 28 June 1958 by Sheng Ch'ing-yi[5] (盛清沂 *shèng qīngyí*), a member of the Commission for Historic Research of (then) Taipei Prefecture (Chang 1969). Located in (now) New Taipei City, Bali District (八里區 *bālǐqū*), further examinations found large quantities of stone tools (e.g., axes), and cord-marked pottery shards. Dabenkeng is also the earliest known culture in Taiwan that practiced agriculture, as evidenced at the Nan-kuan-li (南關里 *nánguānlǐ*) archeological site on the southern part of Taiwan, Tainan City, Southern Taiwan Science Park.[6] At the Nan-kuan-li eastern site, Chen-Hwa Tsang (臧振華 *zāng zhènhuá*) and colleagues

Table 35.1 Reconstructed proto-Austronesian terms related to rice/millet and their distribution. (Blust 2017)

Word	Meaning	Taiwan	Philippines	Indonesia (west)	Indonesia (east)
*pajay	Rice plant; field rice	✓	✓	✓	✓
*beCeŋ	Millet (prob. foxtail)	✓	✓	✓	✓
*qani	To harvest (e.g., rice)	✓	✓	✓	✓
*paspas	Thresh by beating	✓	✓	✓	✓
*qaSelu	Pestle	✓	✓	✓	✓
*lepaw	Granary	✓	✓	✓	✓
*qeCah	Rice husk	✓	✓	✓	
*bayu	To pound rice	✓	✓	✓	✓

[4] Albert Min-Shan Ko, personal communication, 5 December 2021.

[5] Kwang-Chih Chang renders his name Sheng Ch'ing-ch'i. Elsewhere Sheng Qingyi.

[6] 南部科學工業園區 *nánbù kēxué gōngyèyuánqū*.

Table 35.2 Geographical dispersal of Paleolithic-Neolithic Taiwan. (Hung and Carson 2014)

Era	Approximate Date(s)	Culture (文化 *wénhuà*), characteristics	Geography
Paleolithic	25,000–4000 BCE	N/A	
Early Neolithic	4000–2200 BCE	Pottery, cord marked Dabenkeng (大坌坑 *dàbènkēng*)	Main Taiwan island, along the coast
Mid-Neolithic	2600–1500 BCE	Pottery, fine cord and red markings:	
		Hsunt'angp'u (訊塘埔 *xùntángpǔ*)	Northwest
		Niumat'ou (牛罵頭 *niúmàtóu*)	Central-west
		Niuch'outzu (牛稠子 *niúchóuzǐ*)	Southwest
		Fushan (富山 *fùshān*)	Southeast
		Hongmaokang (紅毛港 *hóngmáogǎng*)	Middle of north and central-west
Late Neolithic	1500–300 BCE	Pottery (plain, some adorned):	
		Yuanshan (圓山 *yuánshān*)	Northwest
		Chihshanyan (芝山岩 *zhīshānyán*)	Taipei
		Wanshan (丸山 *wánshān*)	Northeast
		Yingp'u (營埔 *yíngpǔ*)	Central-west
		Tamalin (大罵璘 *dàmàlín*)	Puli basin (埔里盆地 *pǔlǐpéndì*), Central Taiwan
		Tahu (大湖 *dàhú*)	Southwest
		Fengpitou (鳳鼻頭 *fèngbítóu*)	Southwest
		Huakangshan (花崗山 *huāgǎngshān*)	Central-west
		Peinan (卑南 *bēinán*)	Southeast

analyzed an abundance of ancient charred grains, showing a combination of rice-millet farming was well underway approximately 5000 years ago (Tsang et al. 2017). Other Dabenkeng cultural sites include those in Tainan County, Bajia Village, in Guiren Township (歸仁鄉八甲村 guīrénxiāng bājiǎcūn), and Taipei's Yuanshan in Zhongshan District (中山區圓山 zhōngshānqū).

As to the progenitors of these Dabenkeng-related cultures, a connection can be made to mainland China's Zhejiang Province: the Hemudu Culture (河姆渡文化 *hémǔdù wénhuà*), notably the similarities in pottery styles; and, the Majiabang Culture (馬家浜文化 *mǎjiābāng wénhuà*), sharing both of their habitation patterns as well as pottery. Kwang-Chih Chang also found mainland Chinese Longshan Culture (龍山文化 *lóngshān wénhuà*) to be closely related to that of Dabenkeng culture, such as that found at the Fengpitou site, located in Kaohsiung City's Xiaogang District (小港區鳳鼻頭 *xiǎogǎngqū fèngbítóu*). The latter's discovery goes back to the

Japanese colonial period in 1944 (Chang 1969). In contrast with other Dapengkeng-related cultures, Fengpitou showed evidence of early migrations from today's Fujian province.

Tsochen Man (左鎮人 *zuǒzhèn rén*): An Historical Recalculation

In the summer of 1970, Kuo Teh-ling (郭德鈴 *guō délíng*), a fossil enthusiast in his spare time, typically scoured river beds for interesting rocks and specimens in the small valley of the nearby Tsai-Liao Creek (菜寮溪 *càiliáoxī*) in Tsochen District (左鎮區 *zuǒzhèn qū*), Tainan County (臺南縣 *táinán xiàn*). Typhoons typically hit Taiwan from year to year, but these disastrous events sometimes led to positive results, as the storms lift off layers of sediment revealing valuable fossils below. Among these, Mr. Kuo collected gray-red fossils of unknown provenance. Then, about 2 years later, Wen-Hsun Sung (宋文薰 *sòng wénxūn*) and colleagues visited the Tsai-Liao creek in Tsochen, while also taking the opportunity to see Kuo Teh-ling's collection. Those self-same grey-red fossils caught their eyes. Suspecting they were hominid, after conducting further research, they called this discovery "Tsochen Man." First dated about 20 thousand years ago, this *Homo sapiens* was thought to be similar to that of "Upper Cave Man" (Shandingdong Man 山頂洞人 *shāndǐngdòngrén*) found in Zhoukoudian, Beijing (Yang and An 2005). Based on the surrounding area and other fossils found, there were likely groups of at least several dozen living in the nearby area. No doubt Tsochen Man's predecessors likely crossed the land bridge from modern-day Fujian province to Taiwan. Tsochen Man was originally dated to be as old as 30,000 years. Most recently, however, based on recent Carbon-14 dating conducted by U.S. and Australian laboratories, this date has been dramatically recalculated to no more than 3000 years ago (CAN 2016).

The Iron Age Shihsanhang Culture (十三行文化 *shísānháng wénhuà*)

In the autumn of 1955, Taiwanese Air Force (TAF) Major Pan Ko-yung (潘克泳 *pān kèyǒng*) was flying his jet aircraft over Kuanyin Mountain (觀音山 *guānyīnshān*) in today's New Taipei City, Wugu District (五股區), and not far from Bali where the Dabenkeng Cultural excavations were also found. To Maj. Ko's astonishment, his magnetic compass detected a very strong anomaly, suggesting a large amount of iron deposits below. The aforementioned Taiwanese geologist Ch'ao-ch'i Lin and his colleagues were dispatched to investigate. What they found were indeed pieces of iron, but these were the remnants of human-based activity, and were very old. In addition, there were numerous stone implements and pottery shards. Further excavations revealed some key finds, such as stylized bronze knife handles and pots, glass jewelry, as well as stylized ceramics. The area in which these were found (Dinggu Village) was once called Shihsanhang (十三行 *shísānháng*), its name derived from a Qing dynasty era business center where 13 mercantile (商家 *shāngjiā*) houses once operated (行 *háng*). (Another story has is that when Han Chinese came over from the mainland hundreds of years ago, usually bachelors, thirteen of these single men took it upon themselves to clear out land here to make their homestead and livelihoods. There is yet another possibility, that the name is a phonetic corruption of a name from local Taiwanese dialect). The dates of the relics found at Shihsanhang range from about 2000 to 500 years ago. The presence of whale and shark bones indicated capability of long-range fishing by what Taiwanese archeologists believe were the ancestors of the indigenous Ketagalan aboriginal tribe (TMC 2015). More recent (2007) finds in mid-southeastern Taiwan's Taroko (太魯閣 *tàilǔgé*) National Park, Hualien County (花蓮縣 *huālián xiàn*), showed signs of gold prospecting having been conducted there by people of the Shihsanhang Culture some 1000 years ago. In addition, two funerary sites with their complete skeletons were uncovered in Congde Community (崇德社區 *chóngdé shèqū*), in Hualien's Xiulin Township (秀林鄉 *xiùlínxiāng*) (Lax 2009).

Taiwan as Seen by the Ancient Chinese

*"Barbarian Isle" (*夷洲 **yízhōu***)*

Three Kingdoms: In the second year of the Yellow Dragon (黃龍) reign year (230 CE), Emperor Sun Quan (孫權 *sūn quán*) dispatched a 10,000-man strong force, led by General Zhuge Zhi (諸葛直 *zhūgé zhí*), to "Barbarian Isle" (夷洲 *yízhōu*) and "Island Real" 亶洲 (*dǎnzhōu*), bringing back several thousand prisoners from Yi Zhou. Most believe those islands referred to Taiwan. During the same period, China's Danyang (丹陽郡 *dānyángjùn*) prefectural chief and military commander, Shen Ying (沈瑩; 3–280 CE), described Yizhou in the *Chronicles of Lands Across the Water* (臨海水土志 *línhǎishuǐtǔ zhì*), a treatise compiled from about 268–280 CE: "A land without frosty snow, evergreen grass and trees, surrounded all sides by mountains … Barbarian [men] all have their heads shaved on top, and ears pierced, but the females are not so adorned … living in thatched houses made from water reeds. In their fecund soil they grow various grains [lit: the five grains], and have multiple types of fish to eat. Deer bone are used to make spears for battle, and they sharpen blue-green stone to fashion arrowheads and axe blades" (Thompson 1964). He also wrote of their headhunting and cannibalism.

Liuqiu (琉球 *liúqiú*)

By 612 CE, Taiwan appeared on the Sui (隋) Dynasty's maps as Liuqiu (琉球 *liúqiú*) or elsewhere referred to as Liuqiu Kingdom (琉球國 *liúqiúguó*). During the early years of Emperor Sui Yangdi's (隋煬帝 *suíyángdì*) reign (604–618), he dispatched commander Zhu Kuan (朱寬 *zhū kuān*)—twice—to conduct an expedition to Liuqiu, but because they were unable to communicate with the locals, Zhu Kuan only took one native back home along with the latter's battle kit. Unfazed, in ca. 610, Sui Yangdi ordered another campaign, tasking Chen Ling (陳稜 *chén líng*) and Zhang Zhenzhou (張鎮州 *zhāng zhènzhōu*) to lead troops to do battle with Liuqiu. Setting off from modern-day Chaozhou in Guangdong, the local villagers in Liuqiu were completely overwhelmed, and several thousand men and women were taken prisoner. Scholars believe that these initial expeditions took place in or around modern-day Lugang township, Changhua County (彰化縣鹿港鎮 *zhānghuàxiàn lùgǎngzhèn*), and subsequent battles occurred in Taiwan's northwestern Daxi River area (大甲溪 *dàjiǎxī*). Apart from these incidents, however, throughout the intervening dynasties, Taiwan's contact with Chinese officialdom was rare.

Yuan Dynasty (1271–1368) Penghu and Liuqiu (Taiwan) Islands

During Mongolian rule of China, observers from the mainland made their own chronicles of the peoples living on Penghu, which was then administered under Fujian's Jinjiang County, in Quanzhou Prefecture. In his Brief *Accounts of the Island Barbarians* (島夷誌略 *dǎoyí zhìlüè*; 1349), Wang Ta-yüan (汪大淵 *wāng dàyuān*) noted that the people on Penghu, "make their houses by thatching grass. They boil sea [water] to get salt, and ferment millet to make liquor. They gather fish, shrimp, snails, and clams to supplement their [staple of grain. Their] goats multiply into flocks of several tens of thousands." (Thompson 1964). The Yuan Dynasty (from about 1280–1294) collected taxes on the salt produced there, but reportedly exacted no other financial revenues or in-kind labor.

As for the main island of Liuqiu itself, which was most certainly the main island of Taiwan, Wang Ta-yüan (Wang Dayuan) further recounts:

> It is a vast land, with forests of huge trees. The name of [some important] moutains are Ts'ui-lu (翠麓 *cuìlù*), Chung-man (重慢 *chóngmàn*), Fu-t'ou (斧頭 *fǔtóu*), and Ta-chih (大峙 *dàzhì*). The men and women bind up their hair. They make their garments from colored cloth. They boil sea water to get salt, and ferment sugarcane juice to make liquor. Should a person from another country offend them, they [kill him and] cutting off the raw flesh, eat it [or, cut the flesh off while he is still alive and eat it], and they take his head and hang it on a wooden pole (Thompson 1964).

As of 1330 CE, late Yuan dynasty, Taiwan was still called Liuqiu on imperial maps.

Ming Dynasty (14th Through Mid-17th Centuries), and the "Eastern Barbarians": Dongfan (東番 *dōngfān*)

From the early Ming dynasty, as far as the Chinese imperial court was concerned, Taiwan was known as that land of Eastern Barbarians (東番 *dōngfān*). According to the *History of the Ming* (明史 *míngshǐ*), in the early 1400s, when the eunuch admiral Cheng Ho (鄭和 *zhèng hé*) commanded his grand flotilla along the coastal waters, he was accustomed to "barbarian" countries falling over themselves in providing tribute to the imperial court. Not so on Taiwan. Regarding the "Eastern Barbarians" with utmost contempt, it is said that Cheng Ho (Zheng He) demanded the natives he found wear bells around their necks as if they were dogs. However, the locals did not necessarily take it the way it was intended, as these "dog bells" were passed down centuries later as cherished heirlooms. It was not that long after this that Ming Dynasty China had given up on their administrative post on the Penghu islands, bringing all of its people back to the mainland (Wills 1999).

"Chicken Coop Mountain": 雞籠山 (*jīlóngshān*)

In the Ming era, according to *History of the Ming* (明史 *míngshǐ*) which was compiled in 1739, Jilongshan or "Chicken Coop Mountain" (雞籠山 *jīlóngshān* or 雞頭籠 *jītóulóng*) was yet another moniker used by the Chinese for Taiwan. In this case, Jilongshan was described as a place of "high mountains, large marshes, many settlements scattered everywhere, all without a prince. Some fifteen villages, some with a thousand, others less with some five hundred individuals" (Thompson 1964). Jilongshan essentially described the northern part of Taiwan, roughly today's Jioufen (九份 *jiǔfèn*) and Jinguashih (金瓜石 *jīnguāshí*), both located in New Taipei City's Ruifang District (瑞芳區 *ruìfāngqū*). Yet another name for Taiwan in this time period, Beigang (北港 *běigǎng*),[7] likely referred to an area that includes Yunlin County's Beigang Township (雲林縣北港鎮 *yúnlínxiàn běigǎngzhèn*) and Xingang Township in today's Chiayi County (新港鄉 *xīngǎngxiāng*).

Tungning (Dongning 東寧 *dōngníng*; Minnanyu Dialect: *Tang-lêng*)

Defeating the Dutch at Fort Zeelandia in 1661 (see also below), Koxinga immediately changed the name of Taiwan to Tungtu Mingjing (東都明京 *dōngdū míngjīng*): The Eastern Capital of the Ming Dynasty. Following the ouster of the Dutch, and

[7] Other variations of this name also included Bengang (笨港 *bèngǎng*), Wanggang (魍港 *wǎnggǎng*), and Wengang (蚊港 *wéngǎng*).

during the reign-era of Koxinga, i.e., Cheng Ch'eng-kung (鄭成功 *zhèng chénggōng*), another name was attached to the Tainan area by his son, Cheng Ching (鄭經 *zhèng jīng*) in 1664: Tung-ning (Dongning (東寧 *dōngníng*) "Eastern Peace," or the Kingdom of Tungning (東寧王國 *dōngníng wángguó*). At this time, Cheng Ching had retreated from the Chinese coastal areas of Jinmen (金門 *jīnmén*; Kinmen; aka Quemoy) and Amoy (廈門 *xiàmén*) (Liu and Huang 2009). Dongning became yet another moniker for all of Taiwan island until the defeat of the Zheng clan in 1683 by Qing military forces.

Taiwan: Imperial Past to Modern Times

> Piecing together the history of Taiwan's population before 1895 is a difficult task. There is no reliable record to show even the number of people on the island before the twentieth century. Prior to 1600, Taiwan was sparsely occupied by a few tribes of 'savages' of origins that are unknown–George W. Barclay (Barklay 1954).

Until the arrival of the Dutch and their precise (even if incomplete) population counts (often for tax collecting purposes), there are no reliable numbers for the inhabitants of Taiwan. As noted earlier, personal accounts have given some details, but the only references include that of the Ming historical record, where visitors saw 15 villages in their tour of Taiwan (雞籠山 *jīlóngshān*), each varying in size from 1000 people to around 5–6 hundred individuals in each. What's more, this latter observation was likely cribbed from the aforementioned *Records of Barbarian East* (東番記 *dōngfānjì*). Up until about 1600, Taiwan had been visited by, and perhaps at least temporarily been home to, various Chinese and Japanese fishermen, smugglers, and assorted pirates. Before this time, permanent activity by Han Chinese or Japanese people on Taiwan has not been recorded with any specificity (Zhou 2010). This is despite the fact that, despite a kibosh on emigration to Taiwan by Chinese during the Ming, it nonetheless occurred. Still, if figures of later seventeenth century are to be believed, until the advent of European colonialists, at various times anywhere between 50,000–100,000 individuals (nearly all aboriginal peoples) lived on Taiwan.

Dutch Colonialization

After having tried but failed to obtain a foothold in the Penghu islands in 1604, the Chinese authorities advised the defeated Dutch to set up their trading adventure on Taiwan main island. When the Dutch first arrived on at modern-day Tainan in 1622, in addition to the indigenous tribes they had already met, they estimated there were up to 1500 mainland (Han) Chinese living on Formosa (see Table 35.3). Other sources suggest that at least 20,000 Chinese were already living in Taiwan when the Dutch arrived (Wills 1999).

Table 35.3 Dutch East India company figures on aboriginal villages under its Jurisdiction. (Zhou 2010)

Year	Villages	Households	Population (total)
1647	246	13,619	62,849
1648	251	13,955	63,861
1650	315	15,249+	68,657+

It was in modern-day Tainan, southern Taiwan, where the Dutch built their Fort Zeelandia at a large sandbar (see also above), later known as Anping (安平 *ānpíng*), in 1624. Two years later, Spain set up their own colony on Taiwan in the north, establishing their operations at Tamsui (淡水 *dànshuǐ*) and "Quelung" (Keelong 基隆 *jīlóng*) (Chiu 2008). And the year 1626 was a critical one, as famine in mainland China forced thousands of Chinese to move to Taiwan (Stamps 1977). However, various pressures remained against Han Chinese emigration, such as Ming dynasty laws against maritime trade, competition with Japanese interests, taxes, and local resistance from aboriginal Taiwanese. The result was that only about 7–8 hundred Chinese individuals emigrated to Taiwan through 1634.

Dutch East India Company on Taiwan

From about 1625–1641, with a force of only about 200–600 made up mostly of sailors and soldiers, the *Verenigde Oostindische Compagnie* (Dutch East India Company) had a relatively small footprint given the amount of territory it would later claim. Over the years, the villages the Dutch claimed sovereignty over climbed to top 315 villages in 1650. If anything, the Dutch East India Company left a rich field of documentation, including precise (if sometimes problematic in overall accuracy) accounting of aboriginal villages and their populations. First, however, we look at how the various indigenous Taiwanese were characterized throughout history.

China's Differentiation of Taiwan's Indigenous Tribes: "Raw" and "Cooked" Barbarians

Dongfan (東番 *dōngfān*), the term initially used by China to describe the southern, Austronesian-speaking Taiwanese natives, first appeared in 1574. Also abbreviated simply as (番 *fān*), this word in ancient times had the connotation of being valorous in battle. By the Sui and Tang dynasties, however, it was used to describe different national groups or races, and, eventually, became a pejorative term (Hong 2009).

Under the Qing, the Chinese used the term *Fan* (番 *fān*), roughly meaning "barbarian," while separating the aborigines on Formosa in two main categories: *Shengfan* (生番 *shēngfān*) meaning "raw" or "uncivilized;" and *Shoufan* (熟番 *shóufān*) "cultured" or "civilized" barbarians. Generally speaking, cultured barbarians were those plains aborigines who lived in low, flat country along the west coast. Over the decades, they already had extensive interaction with Han Chinese, as well as a tenuously peaceful relationship with colonial invaders, and learned how to farm with ox and plow. As for those *Shengfan* "raw savages" (生番 *shēngfān*), these were aborigines who lived in the mountains, and were usually feared. As Lan Dingyuan wrote in 1732, with regard to the Taiwanese aborigines:

> The natives barbarians of Taiwan are of two kinds: Those that live deep in the mountains, having yet to be civilized: These are the raw savages (生番 *shēngfān*), who have not been domesticated nor civilized, all wearing deer skins to cover themselves, digging up taro roots to eat in the mountains, and in which bows, arrows, and throwing spears are where they excel. The various inhabitants of the plains, the people follow the rules and labor under them, these are the cultured barbarians (熟番 *shóufān*), who carry out agriculture and get along with others, just like any other people. The only difference are those characteristics such as having long or cropped hair, ear piercing, tattoos, and types of clothing (Hung 2009).

Other terms to differentiate the main categories of Taiwanese aboriginals included "Plains savages" (平埔番 *píngpǔfān*), or mountain savages (山番 *shānfān*) and/or high mountain savages (高山番 *gāoshānfān*) (Hong 2009).

Growth of Han Chinese Population in Dutch Ruled Formosa

From their initial landings and operations on Taiwan (1622), the Dutch observed that more and more (Han) Chinese had not just been conducted extensive trade with the aboriginal Taiwanese, but began to set up permanent residences, while also learning to communicate with the locals in their dialects. According to Dutch East India Company statistics, and research estimates by the Taiwan-based scholar Chiang Shu-sheng (江樹生 *jiāng shùshēng*), Table 35.4 shows the approximate numbers of Han Chinese living permanently in Taiwan from 1640 to 1661.

After 1635, the following conditions promoted an increase in Han Chinese emigration to Taiwan:

- Improved Chinese-Dutch relations, better business relationships being made between both countries, as well as pacification of aborigines;
- Influx of Han women (1646): Up until this time only males had emigrated from mainland China, but now they were allowed and even encouraged to bring significant others;
- Chaos and conflict at home (1648), famine and spiraling food costs, also drove many to emigrate from Fujian Province to Taiwan (Hsu 2019)

Table 35.4 Estimates of Han Chinese Living in Taiwan under Dutch Rule: 1640–1661. (Zhou 2010)

Year	Han Chinese population in Taiwan (est)	Tax-paying individuals
1640	3568	2593
1641	4000	2922
1642	4500	3287
1643	9584	7000
1644	N/A	N/A
1645	N/A	N/A
1646	13,500	10,000
1647	N/A	N/A
1648	17,500	12,782
1649	15,000	12,000
1650	15,000	10,811
1651	19,716	14,400
1652	17,500	12,782
1653	13,500	10,629
1654	14,200	10,372
1655	15,492	11,315
1656	18,730	13,680
1657	15,177	11,085
1658	22,500	14,229
1659	27,500	20,086
1660	27,500	20,086
1661	27,500	20,086

Meanwhile, Spain continued establishing its own foothold in northern Taiwan. By 1640 there were 50 Spanish troops, 30 Filipinos, 200 slaves, and 130 Chinese posted in the Keelong redoubt. Spanish activity in Taiwan was initially spurred by a real or perceived threat by Holland to its interest in the Philippines (Knapp 1999). By 1642, however, the Dutch had overwhelmed the Spanish garrison, and Spain ceased since then to have a significant presence in Taiwan.

With famine on mainland China (ca. 1648) having abated in 1649, many withdrew from Taiwan, bringing the number of Han Chinese down to 15,000. However, when the Dutch planted sugar cane on Formosa, this attracted more Chinese. The drop in population on Taiwan from 1652–1653 appears to be the result of the chaos and violence following the local Taiwanese Kuo Huai-yi (郭懷一 *guō huáiyī*) tax revolt (1652) against the Dutch. The latter conflict led to the death of about 4000 Han Chinese (Zhou 2010).

Koxinga: Zheng Ch'eng-kung (鄭成功 *zhèng chénggōng*)

Loyal to the Ming dynasty in the face of the Qing (Manchu) invasion, the scion of a very influential and wealthy financial organization, a pirate, and, in his later days, a madman, Cheng Ch'eng-kung (鄭成功 *zhèng chénggōng)* was born to a Japanese mother, spending the first 6 years of his life in Japan. He was soon sent to Nanjing for schooling. It was his early love of traditional Chinese classics that helped form his hostility to non-Chinese invaders, i.e., the Qing Manchus. As such, Cheng Ch'eng-kung differentiated the truly "Chinese" (華 *huá*) from the "barbarian" (夷 *yí*) (Xing 2010). Indeed, at the age of 21, and having once been in the presence of the Ming Longwu (隆武帝 *lóngwǔdì*) emperor, Cheng Ch'eng-kung made such an impression that he was bequeathed a title, Kuohsingyeh (國姓爺 *guóxìngyé*)—Lord of the Imperial Surname. In the Minnanyu (Fujianese) dialect pronunciation, this name was corrupted into Koxinga.[8]

To get a sense of how Koxinga (Cheng Ch'eng-kung) harried the incoming Qing dynastic regime, desperate measures were instituted in response. The most desperate means to defend against Koxinga's pirating forces was the "Great Clearance" (遷界令 *qiānjièlíng* = "order to shift the boundary"). Enacted at various times, the "Great Clearance" was carried out with particular intensity in 1661 as a means to deny Koxinga and his forces easy access to coastal populations. This meant entire communities from Shandong and Hebei provinces to Guangdong were ordered to evacuate to interior areas. This ukase not only prohibited maritime travel, but enforced this extreme policy by destroying homes and laying fallow to farmlands. As a consequence, homeless and destitute populations decided to move to other regions such as Hong Kong and Taiwan (Roy 2003).

Koxinga, imbued with "down with the Qing, and restore the Ming" (反清復明 *fǎnqīng fùmíng*) fervor, and maintaining that Taiwan had always been Chinese territory, Cheng Ch'eng-kung's forces landed at "Tayouan" (that is, modern-day Tainan, then known as 大員 *dàyuán*) in 1661, forcing Dutch surrender in February 1662. Fort Zeelandia was renamed upon Koxinga's victory: because Cheng Ch'eng-kung (鄭成功 *zhèng chénggōng*) was born in modern-day Anhai Township (安海鎮 *ānhǎizhèn*), Fujian Province, a place that was also known in antiquity as Anping, Koxinga renamed Fort Zeelandia "Anping township" (安平鎮 *ānpíngzhèn*) (Xing 2010).

At about the time Cheng Ch'eng-kung captured Taiwan, there were as many as 50,000 Han Chinese living on Taiwan (lower estimate: 27,500). Koxinga dispatched some 25,000 soldiers (using roughly 200 ships) to lay siege to Fort Zeelandia, forcing Dutch capitulation. Now, with the Cheng family's encouragement of mainland immigration, during 1650 to 1680 the Han Chinese population on Taiwan grew to an estimated 100,000–250,000 (see Table 35.4).

---

[8] He was also conferred the grand and official martial title of "Generalissimo who commands surrender and quells rebellions" (招討大將軍 *zhāotǎo dàjiāngjūn*).

Not long after gaining control of Taiwan, Koxinga died in June 1662 at the age of 37. It was said that he died of malaria, a parasitical disease that has been ever present in that region. (There was also strong circumstantial evidence that he suffered from syphilis as well, which may have also helped to explain his erratic behavior before he passed). His son, Cheng Ching (鄭經 *zhèng jīng*) took over the enterprise of running Tungning, which soon became the scene of lascivious disputes and a power struggle within the Zheng family (鄭氏 *zhèng shì*). The existence of the Zheng-run administration of Taiwan continued under an uneasy truce with the Qing government, agreeing to tributary status under Beijing's terms. For the Qing, its officials were not anxious to conquer Taiwan in any event, fearing an expensive and drawn-out quagmire. This reticence lasted until 1683, when a former Zheng loyalist, Admiral Shih Lang (施琅 *shī láng*), convinced the Qing court of Taiwan's strategic value, referring to it as a "defense shield for several southeastern [Chinese] provinces." After defeating Tungning's navy at Penghu, and by encouraging Cheng military personnel to defect, the Cheng regime finally capitulated. The third and final king, Cheng Ko-shuang (鄭克塽 *zhèng kèshuǎng*), was allowed to live out the rest of his life of ease in Beijing (Roy 2003).

Taiwan Under Qing Dynasty Rule (1683–1895)

In Kangxi 23 Year (1684), the Qing dynasty formally established in their maps Taiwan Prefecture (臺灣府 *táiwān fǔ*) subordinate to Fujian Province, dividing the prefecture into three counties: Taiwan County (台灣縣 *táiwān xiàn*), Fengshan County (鳳山縣 *fèngshān xiàn*), and Zhuluo County (諸羅縣 *zhūluó xiàn*), the latter counties comprising some two-thirds of the island. After this subordination, we find more precise population figures of Chinese living in Taiwan. Its first prefect, Chiang Yüying (蔣毓英 *jiǎng yùyīng*), in office from 1684–1688, compiled a gazetteer of Taiwan prefecture, arriving at a total of 116,665 Han Chinese (Zhou 2010). When totaled in combination with plains aborigines (平埔族 *píngpǔzú*), the population was estimated in 1684 to be about 130,000 (Shepherd 1999).

Hakka Chinese Emigration from China to Taiwan

Now forming at least 15 percent of Taiwan's population today, the Hakka are a Chinese minority with their own language and unique circumstances of origin. There is good evidence the Hakka—the Cantonese pronunciation of their Chinese name "guest people" (客家 *kèjiā*)—first emerged from Henan province, moving south in 419 CE due to persecution by the imperial authorities (Manthorpe 2009). Hakka later formed a significant part the Chinese who first emigrated to Taiwan during the time of Dutch rule (ca. 1630), many having fled from local unrest in Guangdong Province (Barclay 1954).

When the Qing conquered Taiwan in 1683, immigration from mainland China was encouraged, but it was really only after the death of Admiral Shi Lang in 1696, and the relaxation of rules against maritime activity in the region, that large numbers arrived in Taiwan. Many of these immigrants were from coastal cities in Guangdong (Huizhou 惠州 *huìzhōu*) and Fujian (Chaozhou 潮州 *cháozhōu*). According to a comment in a notice against grain smuggling (1711), "over a hundred thousand of people from Fujian and Guangdong each year are making the perilous journey" to Taiwan (Yin 2021). It was among these immigrants that many Hakka Chinese arrived to their new home. The earliest documentation of Hakka people in Taiwan appears in county records of 1711–1720, where it is remarked that their community was the source of social unrest. As it happened, it had much to do with local officials and Fujianese businessmen trying to squeeze out the Hakka from their area of competing interests.

In the late nineteenth century, foreign observers made note of the Hakka population in Taiwan:

> The Hakkas, or Chinese immigrants, not being the agricultural [Fujianese] men, form a strongly marked and important feature of the Formosan population. They have many thriving villages on these border marches, where they live independent of the Chinese administration. Up to 1874 many of the large Hakka villages would not even allow an official to enter their fortified precincts (Notes 1888).

With their diaspora extending throughout Southeast Asia as well as many other countries beyond, in Taiwan the Hakka have since gained a collective reputation for their devotion to hard work, learning, and respect for the written word (Tseng 2020). According to Taiwan's 2020 census, of all Taiwan nationals aged 6 years and older, about 330,000 people spoke Hakka primarily in the household, and about 864,000 spoke it as a secondary language, totaling about 5.5 percent of this population who speak the Hakka dialect (MOI 2021).

Late Qing Taiwan Population

The Republic of China (Taiwan) Academia Sinica (中央研究院 *zhōngyāng yánjiūyuàn*), has estimated populations of Taiwan during the later Qing period, including snapshot data for 1811 and 1893. See Fig. 35.2 and 35.3 for respective years, below. Table 35.5 shows populations from the Qing dynasty to the first decade of Japan's occupation of Taiwan (1684–1905) (AST 2021).

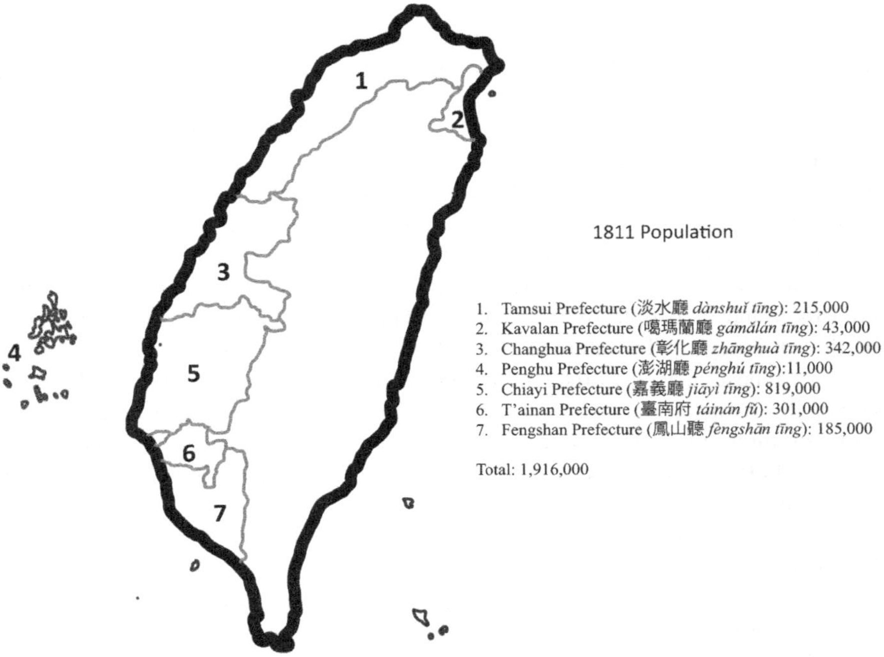

Fig. 35.2 Population of Taiwan (1811). (AST 2021)

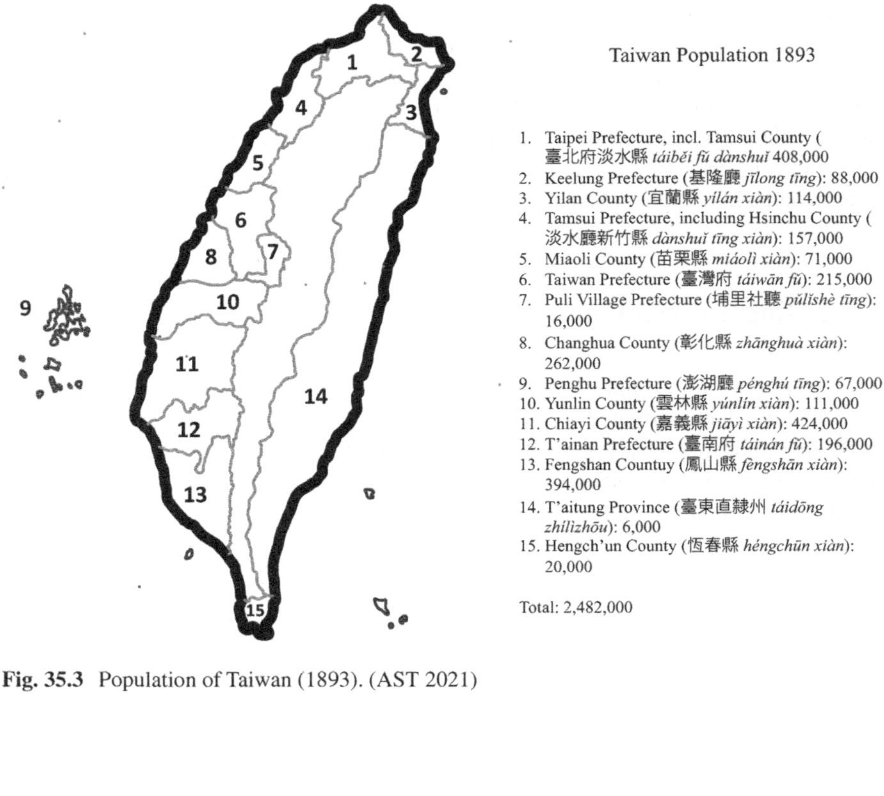

Fig. 35.3 Population of Taiwan (1893). (AST 2021)

Table 35.5 Taiwan population under the Qing dynasty and first decade of Japanese colonialization. (Shepherd 1999)

Year	Population in Taiwan: estimates are of Han Chinese and plains aborigines (only)
1684	130,000
1700	187,000
1735	415,000
1756	660,147
1777	839,803
1824	1,328,069
1893–1895	2,545,731
1903–1905	2,973,280

Japanese Colonialization of Taiwan: Takasago-koku (高砂國)[9]

In an effort to expand its empire, Japan referred to modern-day Taiwan as Takasago-koku (高砂國 *gāoshāguó*), originally named as such by the Japanese feudal warlord Toyotomi Hideyoshi (豐臣秀吉 *fēngchén xiùjí)* in ca. 1593. Later, in a desperate throw to burnish his credentials, the vice-governor of Nagasaki (and Christian) Murayama Tōan (村山等安 *cūnshān děngān*) led a naval expedition against Taiwan in 1616 Turnbull 2021). [(Of note, at this time there were reportedly some 160 Japanese individuals living in villages north of modern-day Tainan (Zhou 2010)]. Commanding a flotilla of between 11–13 junks, before they could make landfall his fleet was blunted (in historically ironic fashion) by a typhoon, and were forced to land along the Fujian coast. Following the Sino-Japanese war (1895) and China's capitulation under terms of the Treaty of Shimonoseki (Chinese: 馬關條約 *mǎguāntiáoyuē*), the Qing court ceded all of Taiwan island to Japan. Now called Takasago-koku (高砂國 *gāoshāguó*), Japan pursued its colonial policy of assimilation, *dōka* (同化 *tónghuà*), and set about registering the residents on Taiwan based on whether or not they were born on the island, and those who were immigrants. Until Japan's surrender in 1945, Taiwan was subjected to a combination of harsh, repressive measures to control its population, especially the indigenous peoples on the island. For example, the Japanese instituted laws that included the all-encompassing 1898 "Bandit Punishment Ordinance," and the 1904 "Fine and Flogging" law that applied specifically to local Taiwanese. Japanese reprisals and punitive measures against Taiwanese resistance resulted in over 12,000 "bandit-rebels" being killed or executed from 1898–1902, and violently put down six consecutive uprisings during 1907–1915 (Lamley 1999). (Table 35.6 provides Japanese named prefectures and population data for occupied Taiwan as of 1915).

[9] Japanese Kanji: 高砂国.

Table 35.6 Taiwan under Japanese administration: populations (1915). (PDT 2021)

Name (Prefecture)	Chinese	Population	Area (km^2)
Taihoku-chō	臺北廳 *táiběi tīng*	523,502	1,692
Giran-chō	宜蘭廳 *yílán tīng*	143,912	711
Tōen-chō	桃園廳 *táoyuán tīng*	231,409	985
Shinchiku-chō	新竹廳 *xīnzhú tīng*	327,164	1,705
Taichū-chō	臺中廳 *táizhōng tīng*	592,577	2,271
Nantō-chō	南投廳 *nántóu tīng*	126,223	1,275
Kagi-chō	嘉義廳 *nántóu tīng*	566,158	3,250
Tainan-chō	臺南廳 *táinán tīng*	569,292	2,345
Akō-chō	阿緱廳 *āgōu tīng*	259,441	2,202
Taitō-chō	臺東廳 *táidōng tīng*	36,997	1,204
Karenkō-chō	花蓮港廳 *huāliángǎng tīng*	45,521	1,316
Hōko-chō	澎湖廳*pénghú tīng*	57,726	127
Name (Prefecture)	**Chinese**	**Population**	**Area (km^2)**

It is also worth noting Taiwan's role that played in Japanese military operations, serving as, among other things, a staging area for bombing campaigns against Luzon, Philippines (Lamley 1999). As imperial subjects, an estimated 80,000 Taiwanese fought in uniform for the Japanese imperial army/navy, with an additional 126,000 serving in non-combat positions, and about 30,300 died during the war (Roy 2003).

Improvements in Taiwan's Public Health Under Japanese Rule

Throughout its colonial administration, Japan meted out punishments in the form of military assaults (in at least one case, using chemical warfare) against the Taiwanese. But it is also worth noting that Japanese themselves who colonized Formosa did not have it easy. In the very first stages of occupying the island, Japan did not encounter very stiff resistance, recording 154 deaths from combat. But due to endemic tropical diseases on Taiwan, Japan listed some 4000 deaths due to illness in its first several months of occupation, and 27,000 were hospitalized. Even if to serve Japan's "Greater East Asia Co-Prosperity Sphere" (*Dai Tōa Kyōeiken*大東亞共榮圈 *dàdōngyà gòng róngquān*), the Japanese also built much-needed infrastructure, helping to stage Taiwan's future economic success, as well as public health improvements, and a routinized, educational system. Notably, beginning in 1898, the first civilian governor of Taiwan under the Japanese, Count *Gotō Shinpei* (後藤新平 *hòuténg xīnpíng*), who himself had received extensive medical training, set about improving general hygiene on Taiwan. By 1905, significant improvements had been

Table 35.7 Mortality, Taiwan, 1906–1943. (Barclay 1954)

Years	Deaths per 1000 persons
1906–10	33.4
1911–15	28.6
1916–20	31.0
1921–25	25.0
1926–30	22.1
1931–35	21.1
1936–40	20.6
1941–43	18.5

made in tackling, among other afflictions, bubonic plague, smallpox, and cholera on Taiwan (Barclay 1954). Except for the years 1915–1920, during which malaria and the global influenza impacted Taiwan, through nearly the end of World War II, there was a steady and overall decrease in mortality on Formosa (see Table 35.7 above).

Wushe (Musha) Incident (霧社事件 *wùshè shìjiàn*)

Unlike the previous Qing policy that employed a more assimilating and conciliatory tone with the Formosan aboriginals, Japan decidedly used repressive and persecutive measures in dealing with Taiwanese natives. Especially under the fifth governor-general of Taiwan, Sakuma Samata (佐久間左馬太 *zuǒjiǔjiān zuǒmǎtài*), Japan instituted a five-year plan to "manage the natives" (*riban* = 理蕃 *lǐfán*) which involved kinetic military operations (Ye 2017). These reached their apogee with the attack against the Seediq tribe (賽德克族 *sàidékè zú*), but in fairness it was in response to deadly violence instigated against the Japanese. While having shown some success in pacification of the aboriginals, especially Seediq tribe, the Japanese were also exploiting the locals for labor, and were generally repressive in their administration. In October 1930, tensions rose to a peak when the chief of the tribe, Mona Rudao (莫那·魯道*mònà lǔdào*), held a wedding reception for his son, Daho Mona (達多·莫那 *dáduō mònà*) at Mahebo Village (馬赫坡社 *mǎhèpō shè*), then in Taichung Prefecture (*Taichū-shū* = 台中州 *táizhōng zhōu*), Renai township, Nantou county (南投縣仁愛鄉 *nántóu xiàn rénài xiāng*). When the groom took offense by a visiting Japanese police officer at the event, a fight ensued. Later that month, when hundreds of Japanese gathered at the nearby Wushe Public School (霧社公學校 *wùshè gōngxuéxiào*) for a sporting event, Chief Mona Rudao led over 300 Seediq warriors (along with hundreds of others) in an attack on Japanese while they were performing a flag raising ceremony. Slashing and beheading their victims, a total of 134 Japanese were slaughtered, including women and children, as well as two local Taiwanese who were in Japanese-styled garb. The Japanese authorities responded with a large military contingent to include aircraft, forcing the rebels into the mountains. As the Seediq holed up inside redoubts, the Japanese resorted to using chemical warfare, most likely employing tear gas (chloroacetophenone, or CN), and ultimately 644 of the rebelling aboriginals died, about half by suicide (Thornton 2005). Following this disturbing incident, the Japanese administrators decided to moderate their repressive policies against the aboriginals. The 2011 film *Warriors of the Rainbow: Seediq Bale* (賽德克·巴萊 *sàidékè bālái*) depicts this episode of Taiwan's history (Fig. 35.4; Tables 35.8 and 35.9).

Japan's Kaohsiung: From "Beat Dog" to "Lofty and Heroic"

The name of modern-day Kaohsiung (高雄 *gāoxióng*) is a holdover from Japan's occupation of Taiwan in the first half of the twentieth century. Originally named "Takow" from the Qing dynasty name of the coastal city, Takou (打狗 *dǎgǒu*), the latter is said to be the phonetic rendering of the plains aboriginal Makatao (馬卡道 *mǎkǎdào*) word for *Bambusa blumeana* (thorny bamboo; 刺竹 *cìzhú*) that grew in the area (Huang 1994).[10] But because the Chinese characters 打狗 (*dǎgǒu*) literally mean "beat dog," the Japanese colonizers felt that this was undignified. Japan renamed the area instead as "lofty and heroic" (高雄 *gāoxióng*), or, in the Japanese reading, *Takao*, and has since been the name of the large port city of Kaohsiung City.

End of World War II and the Status of Taiwan ("Formosa")

The verbiage of the Allied 1943 Cairo declaration, as accepted by Chiang Kai-shek (蔣介石 *jiǎng jièshí*), stated that "all the territories Japan has stolen from the Chinese, such as Manchuria, Formosa, and the Pescadores [Penghu], shall be restored to the Republic of China" (Roy 2003), In September 1945, following the end of hostilities and Japan's surrender, some 170,000 Japanese military personnel remained on Taiwan, as well as about 1300 US prisoners of war (POWs). A formal Act of Surrender by the Japanese was held in Nanking (Nanjing) on 9 September 1945, with Commander-in-Chief of the Chinese Army, General Ho Ying-ch'in (何應欽 *hé yīngqīn*), and Lieutenant General Okamura Yasuji (岡村寧次 *gāngcūn níngcì*), the Japanese forces commander in Central China, representing each side.

[10] Other sources say it means "bamboo forest" in the aboriginal language. In a sense, both are correct: Plains aborigines in the area had long ago planted thorny bamboo in the shape of walls in order to defend themselves against Japanese brigands, forming a veritable bamboo forest.

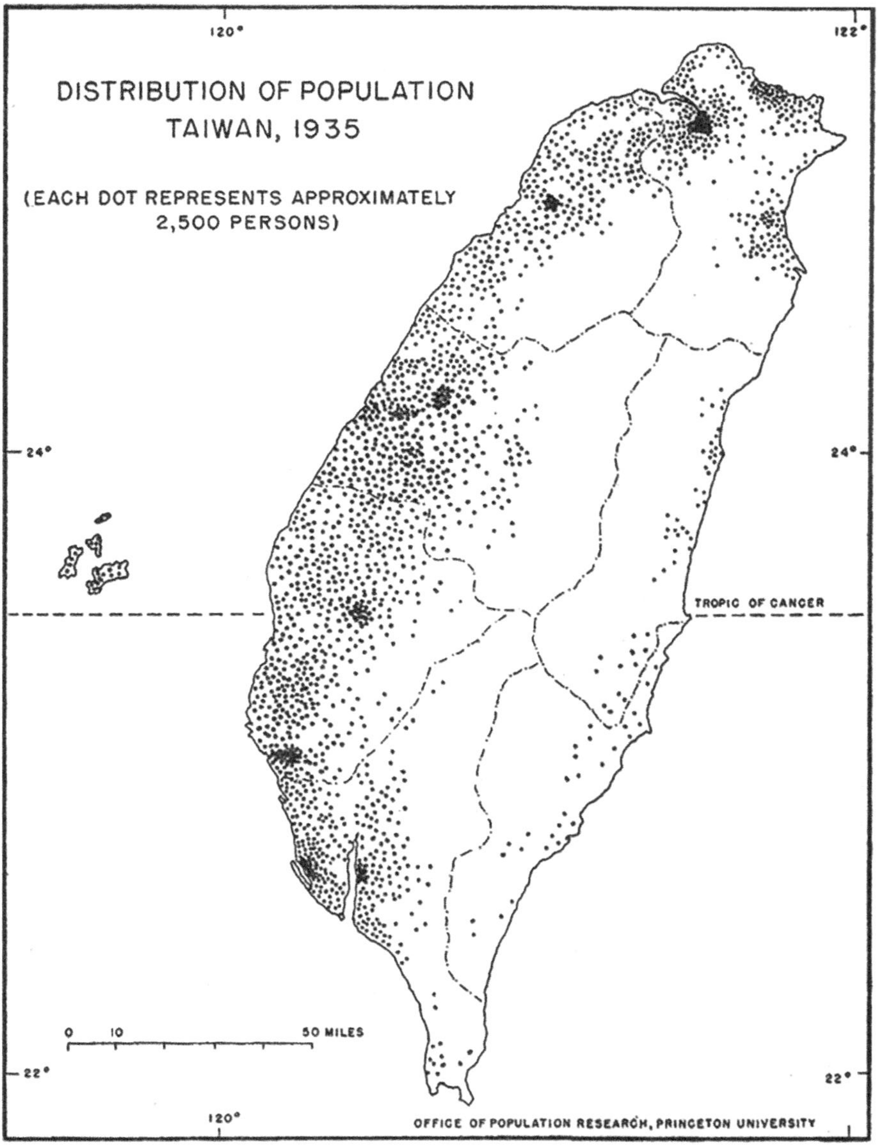

Fig. 35.4 Taiwan (1935) Population map (each dot = 2500 people) (Barclay 1954). (Reprinted courtesy of the Office of Population Research, Princeton University)

Table 35.8 Taiwan population under Japanese colonial rule: 1941. (PDT 2021)

Prefecture	Chinese	Population	Area (km^2)
Taihoku-shū	台北州 *táiběi zhōu*	1,140,530	4594
Shinchiku-shū	新竹州 *xīnzhú zhōu*	783,416	4570
Taichū-shū	台中州 *táizhōng zhōu*	1,303,709	7383
Tainan-shū	台南州 *táinán zhōu*	1,487,999	5421
Takao-shū	高雄州 *gāoxióng zhōu*	857,214	5722
Karenkō-chō	花蓮港廳[a] *huāliángǎng tīng*	147,744	4629
Taitō-chō	台東廳 *táidōng tīng*	86,852	3515
Hōko-chō	澎湖廳 *pénghú tīng*	64,620	127

[a]Kanji = 庁

Table 35.9 Population of Taiwan 1897–1943, including Japanese on Island. (Zhou 2010)

Year	Han Chinese	Aborigines (plains and mountain)	Japanese	Other
1897	2,699,122	82,100+	16,321	N/A
1905	2,890,485	272,433	57,333	9136
1915	3,231,927	180,404	137,229	18,225
1920	3,371,358	179,697	166,621	24,836
1930	4,118,772	141,711*	232,298	46,691
1939	5,367,461**	157,439	323,148	47,726
1943	5,910,328	224,080	396,674	54,759

[a]Probably Mountain ("Raw savages" 生番 *shēngfān*) only
[b]Likely includes "Cultured savages" (熟番 *shóufān*)

Significantly, throughout the Act of Surrender, Taiwan ("Formosa") is not specifically mentioned as being part of the Republic of China (ROC): it simply stated that all Japanese military forces were to surrender to the authorities as represented by the Supreme Commander for the Allied Powers (General McArthur) and Generalissimo Chiang Kai-shek (蔣介石 *jiǎng jièshí*), which was based on the former's General Order No. 1. The latter was previously signed as the instrument of Japan's surrender on 17 August 1945:

> The senior Japanese commanders and all ground, sea, air and auxiliary forces within China (excluding Manchuria), Formosa and French Indo-China north of 16 north latitude shall surrender to Generalissimo Chiang Kai-shek (SCAP 1945).

But of course the fighting was not really over, as the struggle for the future of China continued with a civil war between the Chinese Communist Party (CCP), represented by Mao Zedong, and the ROC, represented by the Nationalists, under the party of Kuomintang (國民黨 *guómíndǎng*), or KMT. While at first welcomed by the Taiwanese, when Nationalist troops began arriving on Taiwan in October 1945, disappointment and resentment followed with the establishment of a military-led government under Chiang Kai-shek (Roy 2003). When the Chinese communist forces would gain the upper hand, the massive influx of KMT troops landing on Taiwan led to disastrous social disruption and tragedy. The increase in population numbers are shown below (Table 35.10).

Table 35.10 Taiwan population: 1946–1951. (Zhou 2010)

Year	Overall Population	Taiwan (本省人 *běnshěngrén*) Local population	Mainland (外省人 *wàishěngrén*) Chinese
1946	6,097,117	6,059,139	37,978
1947	6,497,734	6,436,444	61,290
1948	6,807,601	6,678,969	128,632
1949	7,396,931	6,980,234	414,697
1950	7,554,399	7,029,459	524,940
1951	7,869,247	7,268,557	600,690

28 February 1947: "228 Incident"

Named after the date's abbreviation, the 28th day of the second month (February) of 1947, the "228 Incident" (二二八事件 *èrèrbā shìjiàn*) refers to the spark that ignited an orgy of violence committed by KMT troops against Taiwanese citizens. It began on the day before, when a widow (Lin Chiang-mai 林江邁 *lín jiāngmài*) was (illegally, according to the monopolistic regulations on tobacco and alcohol selling cigarettes in front of a tea shop on Nanjing West Road (南京西路 *nánjīng xīlù*) in Taipei. Having confiscated her cigarettes and cash, the enforcement agents pistol whipped her when she resisted. An angry crowd descended on the scene, and one of the officers shot and killed an onlooker. On 28 February, about two thousand protestors converged on the headquarters of the Monopoly Bureau, and then proceeded to the Provincial Governor's Office,[11] which is now the Executive Yuan (行政院 *xíngzhèngyuàn*) in Taipei. The guards at their post shot at the crowd, killing two, sparking further unrest throughout the city, with fights breaking out between locals (本省人 *běnshěngrén*) and outsiders (外省人 *wàishěngrén*, i.e., recent transplants from mainland provinces). Despite Chiang Kai-shek and the local governor, Chen Yi (陳儀 *chén yí*), having urged restraint at first, by mid-March 1928 Taiwan was placed under martial law. The Nationalists deployed regular army troops and armed police from the mainland to restore order. Essentially given orders to "exterminate traitors" (徹底肅奸 *chèdǐsùjiān*) and to "clear out the townships" (清鄉 *qīngxiāng*), pacification took the form of KMT soldiers pacifying the country "by indiscriminately shooting anyone in the streets" Rubinstein 1999). Well-researched estimates have arrived at numbers between 8 thousand and 28 thousand people were ultimately killed. The table below shows a wide disparity of casualty figures from differing sources, from the equally improbable 190 to tens of thousands of fatalities due what transpired following the "228 Incident:" (Table 35.11)

Understandably, the atrocities that occurred after the 228 Incident made the tenuous relationship between the "local" (本省人 *běnshěngrén*) Taiwanese and "outside provincial" (外省人 *wàishěngrén*) mainland Chinese immigrants (not to mention the aboriginal tribes) into an extremelty hostile one. Even more so, as the steady

[11] 行政長官公署 *xíngzhèngzhǎngguān gōngshǔ*.

Table 35.11 Estimates of Casualties from the "228 Incident". (TNL 2016)

Source	Reported Casualty estimates from the "228 Incident"
Yang Liang-kung (楊亮功 *yáng liànggōng*) report	190 killed; 1,761 wounded
Pai Ch'ung-hsi (白崇禧 *bái chóngxǐ*) report	1,860 killed and wounded
New York Times, Nanjing special wire reporting	2,200 killed
Taiwan Garrison Command Headquarters	3,200 killed
Defense Security Command	6,300 killed
Ho Han-wen (何漢文 *hé hànwén*), Control Yuan committee member	7,000-8,000 killed
New York Times, foreign correspondent	10,000 killed
Taiwan Luhu Group of Six Commission (臺灣旅滬六團體 *táiwān lǚhù liùtuántǐ*) "Taiwan Incident Report"	Over 10,000 dead
Chiang Wei-ch'uan (蔣渭川 *jiǎng wèichuān*), head of Department of Civil Affairs	17,000-18,000 killed
Japan, *Mainichi Shimbun*, investigative research office	Ten thousand to multiple tens of thousands killed
George Henry Kerr, vice-council, US Embassy, Taipei	20,000 or more killed
Executive Yuan official report (Taiwan)	18,000 to 28,000 killed

stream of mainland Chinese moving to Taiwan became a flood, now defeated, Chiang Kai-shek officially moved the capital to Taipei on 7 December 1949. In addition to maintaining a one-party dictatorship, the ROC government on Taiwan curtailed civil and political rights, maintained extensive censorship, and even banned the Taiwanese dialect, forcing the educational and political system to use mandarin Chinese only. The allowance and teaching of Taiwanese (Minnan) dialect only became routinized in the 1990s, and the Taiwan Ministry of the Interior concluded in 1993 that the prohibition of the local dialect(s) was an historical injustice (Klöter 2004; Table 35.12).

Republic of China (Taiwan): Modern Times

Under strict martial law under both Chiang Kai-shek and his successor and son, Chiang Ching-kuo (蔣經國 *jiǎng jīngguó*), in many ways Taiwan was not that different from a Leninist authoritarian system. Even when martial law was lifted in 1987, it took another 5 years before country-wide elections were held, and the first presidential campaign (with opposition parties participating) being held in 1996. Nonetheless, from 1949 through the 1980s, and certainly when compared to mainland China, even with restrictions against opposition parties, censorship, and illiberal treatment of dissenting views, Taiwan was less repressive (relatively speaking). Critically, the KMT government fostered growing economy, making Taiwan one of the "four tigers" in East Asia, the other three being South Korea,

Table 35.12 Taiwan regional censuses from 1956–2000. (TPC 2021)[a]

Republic of China year (counting from original 1911 revolution, e.g., ROC national year 45 = 1956	International date of census	Population Total[b]
National Year 45: First Taiwan-Fujian regional census	16 Sep 1956	9,367,661
National Year 55: Second Taiwan-Fujian regional census	16 December 1966	13,505,463
National Year 59 Taiwan-Fujian Regional Population Census (5% sampling)	16 December 1970	14,769,702
National Year 64 Taiwan-Fujian Regional Population Survey (5% sampling)	16 December 1975	16,279,356
National Year 69 Third Taiwan-Fujian Regional Census	28 December 1980	18,029,798
National Year 79 Fourth Taiwan-Fujian Regional Census	16 December 1990	20,393,628
National Year 89 Third Taiwan-Fujian Regional Census	16 December 2000	22,300,929

[a]For 2000, census included: Taiwan, Penghu, Jinmen, Matsu regions, as well as Taiwan government officials and dependents serving overseas; it also included foreign registered populations, including workers, overseas Chinese, but did not include foreign government officials posted in Taiwan as well as their dependents

[b]For years 1956 through 1990, scope of census included: Taiwan, Penghu, Quemoy (Jinmen), Matsu; Included deployed naval, air, and ground military units, as well as foreign-deployed defense attaches, their dependents, and overseas Chinese; but did not include foreign governments' defense attaches and their dependents

Singapore, and Hong Kong. Combining a free-market economy with a government-led industrial policy focusing upon agriculture, light industries, consumer products, and most recently, high-technology (computer chip design and manufacturing), Taiwan had a gross domestic product (GDP) valued at about USD $62 billion (based on purchasing power parity) in 1980, growing to $205 billion in 1990, then more than doubling by 2000 ($481 billion), and reaching over $668 billion in 2020 (EOC 2021). In terms of per capital income, Taiwan's increase in personal wealth (USD $24,400) is even more striking, especially when compared with even the most prosperous regions (e.g., Shanghai, less than $10,000) in the PRC (ROC 2021). In 2021, despite the challenges presented by the COVID-19 pandemic, Taiwan's economy grew nearly 6.3 percent, much of this growth being spurred by exports (Huaxia 2022). However, as often seen in rapidly developing industrialized countries, in 2021 Taiwan's population shrank by about 185,000 to 23,375,314 compared to the year prior, or nearly 0.8 percent (Everington 2022; Table 35.13).

Official Recognition of Taiwanese Aboriginal Groups (原住民 *yuánzhùmín*)

Previously referred to as "Mountain People" (山地人 *shāndìrén*) or "high mountain" (高山族 *gāoshānzú*) tribes, the ROC government on Taiwan has made important strides in recognizing the rights and dignity of all Taiwanese aborigines. In 2016, for example, Taiwanese President Tsai Ing-wen (蔡英文 *cài yīngwén*) made

Table 35.13 Taiwan: 2010, 2015, and 2020 populations. (MOI 2021)

City/County	Population (2010)	Population (2015)	Population (2020)
New Taipei City 新北市 *xīnběi shì*	3,897,367	3,970,644	4,030,954
Taipei City 臺北市 *táiběi shì*	2,618,772	2,704,810	2,602,418
Taoyuan City 桃園市 *táoyuán shì*	2,002,060	2,105,780	2,268,807
Taichung City 臺中市 *táizhōng shì*	2,648,419	2,744,445	2,820,787
Tainan City 臺南市 *táinán shì*	1,873,794	1,885,541	1,874,917
Kaohsiung City 高雄市 *gāoxióng shì*	2,773,483	2,778,918	2,765,932
Yilan County 宜蘭縣 *yílán xiàn*	460,486	458,117	453,087
Hsinchu County 新竹縣 *xīnzhú xiàn*	513,015	542,042	570,775
Miaoli County 苗栗縣 *miáolì xiàn*	560,968	563,912	542,590
Changhua County 彰化縣 *zhānghuà xiàn*	1,307,286	1,289,072	1,266,670
Nantou County 南投縣 *nántóu xiàn*	526,491	509,490	490,832
Yunlin County 雲林縣 *yúnlín xiàn*	717,653	699,633	676,873
Chiayi County 嘉義縣 *jiāyì xiàn*	543,248	519,839	499,481
Pingtung County 屏東縣 *píngdōng xiàn*	873,509	841,253	812,658
Taitung County 臺東縣 *táidōng xiàn*	230,673	222,452	215,261
Hualien County 花蓮縣 *huālián xiàn*	338,805	331,945	324,372
Penghu County 澎湖縣 *pénghú xiàn*	96,918	102,304	105,952
Keelong City 基隆市 *jīlóng shì*	384,134	372,105	367,577
Hsinchu City 新竹市 *xīnzhú shì*	415,344	434,060	451,412
Chiayi City 嘉義市 *jiāyì shì*	272,390	270,366	266,005
Chinmen (Kinmen aka Quemoy) 金門縣 *jīnmén xiàn*	97,364	132,799	140,597
Lienjiang County 連江縣 *liánjiāng xiàn*	9944	12,547	13,279
Total	**23,162,123**	**23,492,074**	**23,561,236**

a public apology, offering the following to the aboriginal people on Taiwan, "I express to you our deepest apology. For the four centuries of pain and mistreatment you have endured, I apologize to you on behalf of the government" (Silversmith 2016). A year later, in June 2017, the Taiwan government, in order to "achieve historical justice, further preserve and promote the indigenous languages, and guarantee that the languages are used and passed down," issued the Indigenous Languages Development Act (Zeldin 2017). As of 2022, Taiwan officially recognizes 16 aboriginal tribes, and in 2020 these numbered a total of 576,792 aborigines, roughly half being plains (平地原住民 *píngdì yuánzhùmín*) aboriginals (269,966), and the larger half residing in mountainous (山地原住民 *shāndì yuánzhùmín*) areas (306,826). Table 35.14 breaks down the major, recognized aboriginal tribes and their populations (see Fig. 35.5 and Table 35.14):

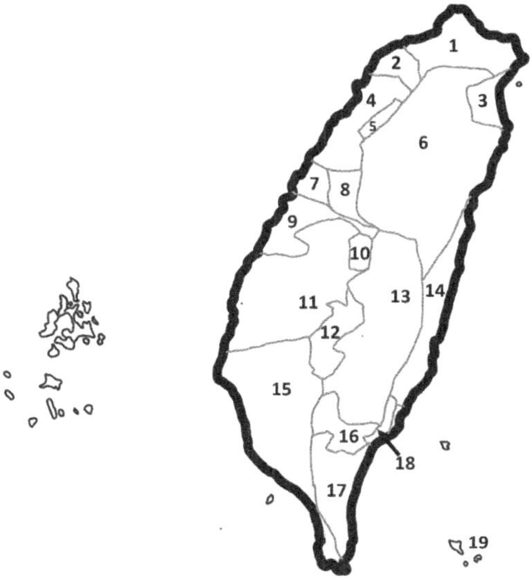

1. Basay 巴賽
2. Kulon 龜崙
3. Ketagalan 凱達格蘭
4. Taokas 道卡斯
5. Saisiyat 賽夏
6. Atayal 泰雅 (includes Seediq 賽德克 and Taroko 太魯閣)
7. Papola 巴布拉
8. Pazih 巴則海
9. Babuza 巴布薩 (sometimes seen as 貓霧捒)
10. Thao 邵
11. Hoanya 洪雅
12. Tsou 鄒
13. Bunun 布農
14. Amis 阿美
15. Siraya 西拉雅
16. Rukai 魯凱
17. Paiwan 排灣
18. Pinuyumayan 卑南
19. Yami 雅美

Fig. 35.5 Geographical dispersion of Taiwanese aboriginal tribes. (Taiwan Aries 2011)

Table 35.14 Taiwanese aboriginal tribes and populations (officially recognized), 2020. (MOI 2021)

Amis (阿美族 *āměizú*)	213,368
Atayal (泰雅族*tàiyǎzú*)	92,014
Paiwan (排灣族 *páiwānzú*)	102,625
Bunun (布農族*bùnóngzú*)	59,497
Pinuyumayan (卑南族*bēinánzú*)	14,512
Rukai (魯凱族 *lǔkǎizú*)	13,462
Cou aka Tsou (鄒族 *zōuzú*)	6698
Saisiyat (賽夏族 *sàixiàzú*)	6735
Yami (雅美族 *yǎměizú*)	4680
Thau or Thao (邵族*shàozú*)	816
Kebalan aka Kavalan or Kuvalan (噶瑪蘭族 *gámǎlánzú*)	1494
Truku aka Taroko (太魯閣族 *tàilǔgézú*)	32,292
Sakizaya (撒奇萊雅族 *sāqíláiyǎzú*)	984
Seediq aka Sediq aka Seejiq (賽德克族 *sàidékèzú*)	10,436
Hla'alua (拉阿魯哇族 *lā'ālǔwāzú*)	413
Kanakanavu (卡那卡那富族 *qiǎ'nàqiǎ'nàfùzú*)	355

South China Sea and Taiwan's Claims

As a carryover from the earliest days of the ROC, technically, Taiwan has a similar "nine-dash line" claim around islands in the South China Sea. In fact, Taiwan administers (primarily uninhabited) off shore islands in the region, to include Dongsha (東沙島 *dōngshādǎo*) or Pratas island, subordinate to Kaohsiung City, Cijin District (高雄市旗津區 *gāoxióng shì, qíjīn qū*), located over 400 km southeast of Taiwan. In addition, Taiwan has occupied Itu Aba, or Taiping island (太平島 *tàipíngdǎo*), the largest of the Spratley group of islands, also subordinate to Cijin District under its southern-most section of Chunghsingli (中興里 *zhōngxīnglǐ*). Unlike mainland China, however, Taiwan has chosen to take a more passive view with regard to its historical map claims over the South China Sea (for a bilingual Chinese-English listing of South China Sea atolls and islands see chapter on Hainan, Table 10.4).

Finally, there is along running territorial dispute regarding uninhabited islands located 170 km northeast of Taiwan. Shared among three claimants, Japan; over what it calls the Senkaku islands: 尖閣群島 (*Senkaku-guntō*); the People's Republic of China (what it refers to as Diaoyu islands 釣魚島 *diàoyúdǎo*); and Taiwan, what the latter calls Diaoyutai (釣魚臺 *diàoyútái*).

References

Academia Sinica, Taiwan (AST). 2021. [*Qing dynasty Taiwan population statistics*]. 清代臺灣人口統計. http://thcts.ascc.net/themes/rc10.php. Accessed 24 Dec 2021.

Barclay, George W. 1954. *Colonial development and population in Taiwan*. Princeton: Princeton University Press.

Basian cave artifacts go back 25,000 years. 2009. *Taiwan Today*. 25 July. https://michaelturton.blogspot.com/2009/07/basian-cave-artifacts-go-back-25000.html?m=1.

Blust, Robert. 2017. Historical linguistics and archaeology: An uneasy alliance. In *New perspectives in Southeast Asian and Pacific prehistory*, ed. Philip J. Piper, Hirofumi Matsumura, and David Bulbeck, 275–292. Canberra: Australian National University Press.

Chang, Chun-Hsiang, Yousuke Kaifu, and Masanaru Takai, et al. 2015. The first archaic *homo* from Taiwan. *Nature Communications* 6(6037). https://doi.org/10.1038/ncomms7037.

Chang, Kwang-Chih. 1969. *Fengpitou, Tapenkeng, and the prehistory of Taiwan*. New Haven: Department of Anthropology, Yale University Press.

Chiu, Hsin-hui. 2008. *The colonial 'civilizing process' in Dutch Formosa, 1624–1662*. Boston: Brill.

CNA (Taiwan News). 2016. [After Tsochen Man case overturned, Changbin culture is earliest in Taiwan.] 5 January. 左鎮人翻案後, 長濱文化台灣最早. https://www.cna.com.tw/news/first-news/201601050121.aspx.

Economy of Taiwan (EOC). 2021. https://en.wikipedia.org/wiki/Economy_of_Taiwan. Accessed 31 Dec 2021.

Everington, Keoni. 2017. Island named 'Formosa' by Portuguese may not be Taiwan: Scholar. *Taiwan News*, 13 November 13. https://www.taiwannews.com.tw/en/news/3296323.

Hong, Liwan. 2009. [*'Shufan' social network and collective consciousness: historical changes of the Pingpu ethnic group in central Taiwan (1700–1900)*]. Taiwan Studies Series. Taipei:

Linking Publishing. 洪麗完. 熟番社會網絡與集體意識:臺灣中部平埔族群歷史變遷 (1700–1900). 臺灣研究叢刊. 台北: 聯經出版.
Hsu, Hsue-chi. 2019. [*Home or homeland: Moving in and out of Taiwan*]. Taipei: Taiwan National University Press. 許雪姬. 來去台灣. 台北: 國立臺灣大學出版中心.
Huang, Junjie. 1994. [*Collected essays on Kaohsiung history and culture*]. Vol. 1. Kaohsiung City: Chen Chung-he Wengci Charitable Foundation. 黃俊傑, 高雄歷史與文化論集, 高雄市: 陳中和翁慈善基金會.
Huaxia (ed). 2022. Taiwan reports 6.28 pct economic growth in 2021. *Xinhua,* 29 January. http://www.xinhuanet.com/english/20220129/a6f5876025c54f129c1a4cdf3a45bdaa/c.html.
Hung, Hsiao-chun, and Mike T. Carson. 2014. Foragers, fishers and farmers: Origins of the Taiwanese Neolithic. *Antiquity* 88: 1115–1131.
Klöter, Henning. 2004. Language policy in the KMT and DPP eras. *China Perspectives*. November–December. https://doi.org/10.4000/chinaperspectives.442.
Knapp, Ronald G. 1999. The shaping of Taiwan's landscapes. In *Taiwan: A new history*, ed. Murray A. Rubinstein, 3–26. Armonk, New York: M.E. Sharpe.
Ko, Albert Min-Shan, Chung-Yu Chen, Fu Qiaomei, et al. 2014. Early Austronesians: Into and out of Taiwan. *The American Journal of Human Genetics* 94: 426–436. https://doi.org/10.1016/j.ajhg.2014.02.003.
Lamley, Harry J. 1999. Taiwan under Japanese rule, 1895-1945: The vicissitudes of colonialism. In *Taiwan: A new history*, ed. Murray A. Rubinstein, 201–260. Armonk, New York: M.E. Sharpe.
Lax, Kevin. 2009. 1000 years ago Shisanhang culture people came to Taroko to prospect for gold. *National Parks of Taiwan,* 24 September. https://np.cpami.gov.tw/news/271-english/news/taroko/2215-2009-07-24-15-15-41.html
Li, Lixin. 2020. [Three reasons why Taiwanese businessmen no longer love China]. *The Economist*, 24 November. 李立心. 3大原因, 台商不再愛中國. 經濟學人. https://www.cw.com.tw/article/5102878.
Li, Wenliang. 2019. [*The Hakka that made Taiwan*]. Taipei: Taiwan National University Press. 李文良. 成為臺灣的客家人. 台北: 台大出版社中心.
Liu, Chenggao, and Huang Liangxiong. 2009. [*Taiwan's historical stories*]. Taipei: Linking Publishing. 劉城高, 黃良雄. 台灣史話. 台北: 聯經編輯部.
Manthorpe, Jonathan. 2009. *Forbidden nation: A history of Taiwan*. New York: St. Martin's Griffin.
Matsumura, Hirofumi, Guangmao Xie, and Lan Cuong Nguyen, et al. 2021. Female craniometrics support the 'two-layer model' of human dispersal in Eastern Eurasia. *Nature* (Scientific Reports), 11: https://doi.org/10.1038/s41598-021-00295-6.
Ministry of the Interior (MOI), Taiwan database. 2021. https://www.moi.gov.tw/cl.aspx?n=4406. Accessed 28 Dec 2021.
Ministry of the Interior (MOI), Taiwan. 2021. Hakka and Aboriginal Committee. [Ethnic groups]. 9 March. 客家委員會, 原住民族委員會. 族群. https://www.ey.gov.tw/state/99B2E89521FC31E1/2820610c-e97f-4d33-aa1e-e7b15222e45a.
The News Lens (TNL). 2016. [Exactly how many people died? six and a half minutes to tell you what happened following 2–28″]. 28 February. 到底死了多少人?6分半告訴你 '228之後' 發生了什麼事. https://www.thenewslens.com/article/37136.
Notes from parliamentary papers, No. 2: races of Formosa. 1888. *The Archaeological Review* 1(3): 182–183.
Political divisions of Taiwan (PDT), 1895–1945. 2021. *Wikipedia*. https://en.wikipedia.org/wiki/Political_divisions_of_Taiwan_(1895%E2%80%931945). Accessed 30 Dec 2021.
Republic of China (ROC), Taiwan. 2022. *Taiwan statistical yearbook* (database). https://eng.stat.gov.tw/ct.asp?xItem=41878&ctNode=2815&mp=5. Accessed 31 Dec 2021.
Roy, Denny. 2003. *Taiwan: A political history*. Ithaca, New York: Cornell University Press.
Rubinstein, Murray A. 1999. Between assimilation and independence: Taiwanese political aspirations under nationalist Chinese rule, 1945–1948. In *Taiwan: A new history*, ed. Murray A. Rubinstein, 267–311. Armonk, New York: M.E. Sharpe.

Shepherd, John R. 1999. The island frontier of the Ch'ing: 1684-1780. In *Taiwan: A new history*, ed. Murray A. Rubinstein, 107–132. Armonk, New York: M.E. Sharpe.

Silversmith, Shondiin. 2016. Taiwan's indigenous people finally get an official apology. *The World.* 3 August. https://theworld.org/stories/2016-08-03/taiwans-indigenous-people-finally-get-official-apology.

Stamps, Richard B. 1977. New light on Taiwan's prehistory. *Asian Perspectives* 20 (2): 183–190.

Su, Huang-Lan. 2015. *Writing "Taiwanese": The Péh-oē-jī romanization and identity construction in Taiwan, 1860s–1990s*. PhD dissertation. Graduate College of the University of Illinois at Urbana-Champaign.

Supreme commander for the allied powers (SCAP). 1945. *General order number one*. 2 September. http://www.taiwandocuments.org/surrender05.htm. Accessed 29 Dec 2021.

Tai, Pao-tsun. 2020. [*Does 'Formosa' refer to Taiwan specifically? Where did the name 'Taiwan' start?*]. National Taiwan University. 18 May. 戴寶村, 福爾摩沙是專指臺灣? 臺灣名稱從何開始? https://www.youtube.com/watch?v=k4qLHydCaNo.

Taiwan Academia Sinica (TAS). 2020. [*Qing dynasty population statistics*]. 清代臺灣人口統計. http://thcts.ascc.net/themes/rc10.php. Accessed 24 Dec 2021.

Taiwan Aries. 2011. [General knowledge of Taiwan's aboriginal people]. 22 October. 台灣原住民.分布常識. http://ariesgogogo.blogspot.com/2011/10/blog-post_22.html.

Taiwan centers for disease control (TCDC). 2020. https://www.cdc.gov.tw/Category/Page/ej2Gth-VV2Pag0EVMBNpqyw. Accessed 31 Dec 2021.

Taiwan Ministry of Culture (TMC). 2015. *Shihsanhang museum of archaeology*. 20 July https://www.moc.gov.tw/en/information_251_77420.html.

Taiwan National Museum (TNM). 2016. *Taiwan in maps*. https://kangxitaiwanmap.ntm.gov.tw/stories.html. Accessed 9 Dec 2021.

Taiwan News (TN). 2020. *Taiwanese workers in China long for home*. 9 January. https://www.taiwannews.com.tw/en/news/3853491.

Taiwan population censuses (TPC). 2021. 臺灣人口普查. https://zh.wikipedia.org. Accessed 1 Dec 2021.

Thompson, Laurence G. 1964. The earliest Chinese eyewitness accounts of the Formosan aborigines. *Monumenta Serica* 23: 163–204.

Thornton, Rod. 2005. Wushe incident. In *Weapons of mass destruction: An encyclopedia of worldwide policy, technology, and history*, ed. Eric A. Croddy, James J. Wirtz, and Jeffrey A. Larsen, vol. 334. Santa Barbara: ABC-CLIO.

Tsang, Chen-Hwa, Kuang-Ti Li, Tze-Fu Hsu, et al. 2017. Broomcorn and foxtail millet were cultivated in Taiwan about 5000 years ago. *Botanical Studies* 58 (3): 1–10.

Tseng, Yung-hsien. 2020. [*From left to right, sixty years: Oral History of Tseng Yung-hsien*]. Taipei: Academia Historia Office. 從左到右六十年:曾永賢先生訪談錄, 台北: 國史館.

Turnbull, David. 2021. *The lost Samurai: Japanese mercenaries in South East Asia, 1593–1688*. Yorkshire: Frontline Books.

Weng, Jiayin (Kaim Ang). 2006. [The Portuguese and 'Formosa': comparing the shipwreck of 1582]. *History Monthly*. 翁佳音. 葡萄牙人與 '福爾摩沙'—並論1582年的船難. 歷史月刊. 220. May. http://blog.udn.com/mobile/history3/302534. Accessed 9 Dec 2021.

Wills, John E., Jr. 1999. The seventeenth-century transformation: Taiwan under the Dutch and the Cheng regime. In *Taiwan: A new history*, ed. Murray A. Rubinstein, 84–106. Armonk, New York: M.E. Sharpe.

Xing, Hang. 2010. *Between trade and legitimacy, maritime and continent: the Zheng organization in seventeenth-century East Asia*. PhD dissertation. University California at Berkeley.

Yang, Lihui, and Deming An, with Jessica Anderson. 2005. Handbook of Chinese mythology. New York: Oxford University Press.

Ye, Ruiping. 2017. *Colonisation and aboriginal land tenure: Taiwan during the Qing period (1684–1895) and the Japanese period (1895–1945)*. PhD thesis, Victoria University of Wellington, Faculty of Law.

Yin, Chang-Yi. 2021. [*Hakka and the Liudui history in Taiwan*]. 尹章義, 臺灣客家與六堆史研究, 台北: 蘭台出版社.

Zeldin, Wendy. 2017. Taiwan: new indigenous languages act. *Global Legal Monitory.* (U.S. Library of Congress). 21 June. https://www.loc.gov/item/global-legal-monitor/2017-06-21/taiwan-new-indigenous-languages-act/.

Zhao, Iris. 2021. An increasing number of Taiwanese people want independence, but they're in no rush. *ABC News*, 10 December. https://www.abc.net.au/news/2021-12-11/taiwan-independence-vs-unification-china-taiwanese-australians/100670574.

Zhao, Juling. 2012. [*Taiwan's story of its development: The southern region*]. Taipei: Tianwei Culture Publishing. 趙莒玲, 臺灣開發故事: 南部地區, 台北: 天衛文化.

Zhou, Wanyao. 2010. [*Population problems in Taiwan history* (second draft)]. Taiwan database for empirical legal studies research communication]. 周婉窈, 臺灣史上的人口問題(二稿). 臺灣法實證研究資料庫研究通訊. Issue 11. http://tadels.law.ntu.edu.tw/wp-content/uploads/2020/02/communication100515.pdf.

Chapter 36
China's Population: Past and Future

Abstract China's rulers of the past traditionally favored having more children, and this included Mao Zedong himself. Malthusian warnings that geometric population growth will necessarily outstrip food supplies found their way to China in the late nineteenth century. However, both Kuomintang (KMT) and rival Chinese Communist Party (CCP) intellectuals did not immediately favor family planning efforts, and this state of affairs continued even after the establishment of the People's Republic of China (PRC) in 1949. It took the death of Mao and the ascendency of Deng Xiaoping to formally promote family planning in China, beginning with a moderate "late, far apart, and few" policy, to a strict, "one-child policy" in the late 1970s. Intended to support China's economic reforms, with a target of quadrupling per capita income from 1980 to 2000, the one-child policy had deleterious consequences for Chinese society at large, not the least of which being a growing elderly population that will require more and more social services in the near future. A discussion of Taiwan follows, which includes data on its own demographic challenges and the (im)plausible future of "One China."

Move Over, Malthus

In the reign year of Qianlong 58 (乾隆 *qiánlóng*), or 1793, in the Western chronology, George Leonard Staunton, Secretary to the British mission in its representations to the Chinese Imperial (Qing) court, heard something astounding. Staunton was accompanying his boss, Lord Macartney, the first British envoy to Beijing, on a diplomatic visit to Tianjin. His interlocutor was "Chow-ta-Zhin," that is, 'His Excellency Chow,' or in the Mandarin dialect, 喬大人 (*qiáo dàrén*). His personal name was Qiao Renjie (喬人傑 *qiáo réjié*). Born (1740) to a poor family in today's Qingxu County (清徐縣 *qīngxú xiàn*), Shanxi province, Qiao Renjie's was a classic story of a humble but very bright student who, having passed rigorous national exams, steadily rose through the ranks of imperial government service. Now a high-ranking official (responsible for the all-important salt monopoly) in the Tianjin circuit (天津道 *tiānjīn dào*), he personally accompanied the Macartney Mission for

E. Croddy, *China's Provinces and Populations*,
https://doi.org/10.1007/978-3-031-09165-0_36

several months. Staunton, who had learned passable Chinese from Jesuit passengers who sailed with him to China, discovered from speaking with Qiao Renjie that the population of the Chinese empire stood then at 333 million. (While this was slightly above official numbers for that year, about 310.5 million, it was within the margin of error). Staunton was also told that these population figures were provided by provincial taxation authorities ("tithing men"), with their accumulated data then being assembled and tabulated in a "great register in Pekin." The very idea of a population of 333 million was mindboggling for the British legation, and economists back home were nonplussed as well.

In 1798, Thomas Robert Malthus (1766–1834) had published his first, short version of his now (in)famous *An Essay on the Principle of Population*. It is difficult to overstate the impact of Malthusian thinking, both in its short- and long-term effects, on how Western and other intellectuals were to view growth in populations. In the case of England, alarmed at the prospect that food will never support a geometrically increasing number of people (the Malthusian thesis in a nutshell), the British Parliament hastened to pass the Census Act in 1800 (UKONS 2016). When Malthus learned of the 333 million people living in China, he compared that to the populations of England and Wales (8.9) million, as well as Scotland (1.6 million). Even when allowing for China's larger geographical size, Malthus still was amazed at such a densified population (Bashford 2019).

In a later expanded edition of his book, while admiring the industriousness and diligence of its agricultural sector, Malthus related the real poverty suffered by so many of China's citizens. Quoting the French Jesuit, Jean-Baptiste Du Halde (d. 1743), who had collated numerous accounts by foreigners in their visits to China:[1]

> Yet it must be owned, that, notwithstanding the great sobriety and industry of the inhabitants of China, the prodigious number of them occasions a great deal of misery. There are some so poor that, being unable to supply their children with common necessaries, they expose them in the streets. In the great cities, such as Pekin and Canton, this shocking sight is very common (Malthus 1826).

Quoting another Jesuit and missionary to China, Joseph Henri Marie de Prémare, Malthus highlights the following which also alludes to the ubiquity of infanticide:

> It is well known, that extreme misery impels people to the most dreadful excesses. A spectator in China, who examines things closely, will not be surprised that mothers destroy or expose many of their children; that parents sell their daughters for a trifle; that the people should be interested; and that there should be such a number of robbers. The surprise is, that nothing still more dreadful should happen; and that in the times of famine which are here but too frequent, millions of people should perish with hunger, without having recourse to those dreadful extremities, of which we read examples in the histories of Europe (Malthus 1826).

It was indeed the practice of infanticide in China, explained (if not excused) by crushing poverty that drove families to drown or expose their newborn infants to the elements, that Malthus believed was the major "check" against Chinese overpopulation. But he believed it still would not be enough to avoid catastrophic famine,

[1] Rendered "Duhalde" in Malthus' writings.

which, based on Malthusian calculations, inevitably will occur as populations outstrip the ability to feed them (Bashford 2019).

And, to be fair, in times before improved agricultural techniques became widespread, and the (truly) great leap forward in the green revolution led by Norman Borlaug (1970s), as China's population rose so did the occasion for devastating famines. (Whether or not these were correlations versus causations is an open question). A historical review with approximate death tolls follows in Table 36.1.

Malthusian warnings of the inevitable immiseration and poverty of growing populations greatly impacted the thinking of Western intellectuals, and continues to influence the political and academic circles of today.

But little of Malthus' treatise reached China until the 1880s. Indeed, throughout China's history, the imperial emphasis has been on the fertility of its subjects, and the overall objective of Chinese rulers was to promote childbirth. But by the late nineteenth century, even before the 1911 revolution, there was now Chinese interest in Western Enlightenment thinking and values. Chinese academics who studied in the West, to include the United States, came back with an enthusiasm for the Malthusian-based analysis of China's massive population. In 1920, published under the banner of none other than China's most famous leftist intellectual, Chen Duxiu (陳獨秀 *chén dúxiù*), the economist Ku Meng-yu (顧孟余 *gù mèngyú*) baldly stated that Malthus was right, and that "population is the key to social problems" (Wang et al. 2016). The American family-planning proponent (and eugenicist) Margaret Sanger visited China in 1922, and the famous Chinese thinker Hu Shi (胡適 *hú shì*) was her interpreter during her speech at Peking University. Her pamphlet on "Family Limitation" was translated into Chinese, and apparently was a hit. Sanger later remarked about this experience:

> If anyone wishes to refute Malthusian theory, it is worthwhile before wasting his time, to take a trip to China, for there the population question with all the horrors that Malthus depicted, is vindicated (Wang et al. 2016).

In contrast, Sun Yat-sen, his fellow stalwart Kuomintang (KMT) Nationalists, as well as their rival communist adherents (Mao Zedong et al), were against Malthusian-based schemes aimed at limiting China's population (Wang et al. 2016). For the Marxists, after all, it was not the population per se, but the inadequate distribution of goods and services that was the root of all poverty.

Mao Zedong himself set the tone just before the 1949 revolution, which was to carry great weight in China until his death in 1976. In response to US Secretary of State Dean Acheson, who doubted that China would be able to feed herself, Mao responded (September 1949):

> Of all things in the world, people are the most precious. Under the leadership of the Communist Party, as long as there are people, every kind of miracle can be performed. We are refuters of Acheson's counter-revolutionary theory. We believe that revolution can change everything, and that before long there will arise a new China with a big population and a great wealth of products, where life will be abundant and culture will flourish. All pessimistic views are utterly groundless (Wang et al. 2016).

Table 36.1 Historical listing of famines and approximate deaths (where known) in China. (CWE 2021)

Name	Timeframe	Est. population of China	Region(s)	Background and context	Approximate deaths
N/A	875–884	43,000,000	All China	Peasant rebellion/	N/A
N/A	1333–1337	60,000,000	All China	General famine	N/A
N/A	1630–1631	150,000,000	Northwest China	Chaos during dissolution of the Ming	N/A
N/A	1810–1811; 1846; 1849	350,000,000; 425,000,000	All China	N/A	45 million; numbers maybe affected by tax avoidance and thus not appearing on census rolls
N/A	1850–1873	430,000,000–380,000,000	All China	Nian and Taiping rebellions	10–30 million
Great Famine of the Northwest	1876–1879	435,000,000	Northwest China	Drought	9–13 million
N/A	1896–1897	400,000,000	Northwest China	Boxer rebellion and other social unrest	N/A
Great Qing Famine	1907	450,000,000	Central China coast, plains, and Guangdong	N/A	25 million
Northern Famine of 1920–1921	1920–1921	450,000,000	Henan, Shandong, Shanxi, and Hebei provinces	N/A	500,000
China Famine of 1928–1930	1928–1930	442,000,000	Northwest China	Drought	3 million
Famine of 1936–1937	1936–1937	480,000,000	Sichuan and Gansu provinces	N/A	Uncertain, possibly as many as 5 million
Famine of 1942–1943	1942–1943	520,000,000	Mostly Henan province	Sino-Japanese War	2–3 million
Great Famine of China	1959–1961	690,000,000	All China	Mao Zedong's 'Great Leap Forward'	At least 35 million

In 1954, however, China's leaders took stock of China's growing population and had second thoughts. While open talk of birth control and family planning remained taboo, Zhou Enlai gave a signal of sorts when he delivered the following at the 1956 Eighth Congress of the Chinese Communist Party:

> To protect women and children and to have a well-bred young generation so as to promote national health and prosperity, it is advisable to enforce adequate birth control. The health authorities should be made responsible for coordinating efforts at carrying out propaganda in favor of birth control and initiating effective measures (Chai 1977).

Mao Zedong's vainglorious and catastrophic Great Leap Forward (GLF) program (beginning in 1958) was to end all talk of family planning. Kicking off the GLF in January 1958, Mao said, "For now, a large population is better" (Wang et al. 2016). And if this would spell the end of any efforts to control population growth, there was another factor that likely encouraged Chinese families to have even more children: the introduction of the *hukou* (戶口 *hù kǒu*) registration system.

By 1958, when the *hukou* system was officially implemented in China, the imposition of socialism under Mao, eternally hostile against capitalism and private property, had already led to wanton privation and economic ruin. There were no financial incentives remaining once the state had acquired the land and the means of production. However, the state did provide goods and services, such as they were, to be distributed "each according to their need." Ideology, trumpeted by Mao Zedong ("the more people, the stronger we are") only encouraged families to have more children. From a much more practical standpoint, however, a family now found it advantageous to have more children in order to increase their subsidized allotments from the state. Thus, researchers Howden and Yang explain that China's rapid rise in population from 1949 to 1979 resulted from families seeking more benefits from the state, especially during times of shortages, and achieving this by having more children. That it had the blessing of the Great Helmsman himself, Mao Zedong, certainly played a significant role as well (Howden and Yang 2015).

Still resistant to family planning measures, nonetheless in December 1973 China enacted a non-coercive *wanxishao* policy, encouraging Chinese families to have children later, i.e., (晚 *wǎn*), spaced apart (稀 *xī*), and fewer (少 *shǎo*) of them. This reasonable measure had great effect, bringing the average household down to just under three children when this directive was tested in selected Chinese populations. However, now anticipating a large uptick in population because of the increase in births during the 1960s (see also above), in 1978 a leading group on the question decided that "one is best, two at most." (Greenhalgh 2005).

One-Child Policy Set in Motion

> The movement for planning owes its present strength largely to the fact that, while planning is in the main still an ambition, it unites almost all the single-minded idealists, all the men and women who have devoted their lives to a single task. The hopes they place in planning,

> however, are the result not of a comprehensive view of society but rather of a very limited view and often the result of a great exaggeration of the importance of the ends they place foremost. –F.A. Hayek (Hayek 1944).

Marshall Zhu De (朱德 *zhū dé*), arguably the most important general in Mao Zedong's Red Army, was born (1886) into a poverty-stricken home in Sichuan Province. In his memoirs, Zhu De recalls that his father, a stern man, drowned at least five of his siblings in order to keep the family alive (Colville 2021). Fellow Sichuanese Deng Xiaoping (登小平 *dēng xiǎopíng*), another key founder of the CCP's revolutionary army, was no doubt familiar with such sad stories. However, Deng Xiaoping, who later ordered the military crackdown on student protests in Tiananmen (1989), was not a sentimentalist, and it was economic growth and setting targets that were now on his mind. This was made abundantly clear during his high-visibility tour of Sichuan in early September of 1980. Deng Xiaoping, now undisputed leader, was adamant in achieving his "Four Modernizations," that is of industry, agriculture, national defense, and science and technology, which would then create the conditions for a robust, growing economy (Olsen 2015). Population control was key to this effort:

> In birth planning, we must definitely keep propagating that every couple has only one child. We cannot make concessions here. There is no hope for the Four Modernizations, should this lever be broken. It is of major important for the national economy (Sharping 2003).

Because it all came down to economics, it necessarily had to do with mathematics. With a goal set in having a population of 1.2 billion in the year 2000, looking to achieve by then a *per capita* income of USD $1000 (four times that of 1980), it was simply a matter of dividing by as low a number possible to achieve this goal, to wit, keeping the number of children down to one per family. Although never written as national law, an 'Open Letter' to the CCP and Communist Youth League served as the ukase, and in 1982 family planning along these lines was made "basic state policy" (Wang et al. 2012).

Although the one-child policy had some leniencies and ethnic minorities were exempt, its overall strict and uncompromising application led to decades of crippling financial fines against families who decided to have additional children, the abandonment of newborn girls to an uncertain fate in a state-run adoption system, countless sex-selective terminations of pregnancy, as well as forced abortions and sterilizations. Tragically, as demonstrated by other East Asian countries who employed much more modest programs in family planning, China's economic development was not likely to have been sidetracked by the much more moderate *wanxishao* guidelines of the mid-1970s. But even when it was shown that Chinese cities that used more relaxed regimen of two children per family still achieved moderate economic growth and, importantly, a more reasonable sex ratio of births, such data were ignored, and the one-child policy continued unchanged (Olsen 2015).

In a remarkable assessment of China's one-child policy, demographers Feng Wang, Cai Yong and Gu Baochang wrote the following in 2012:

> History will remember China's one-child policy as the most extreme example of state intervention in human reproduction in the modern era. History will also likely view this policy as a very costly blunder, born of the legacy of a political system that planned population numbers in the same way that it planned the production of goods. It showcases the impact of a policymaking process that, in the absence of pubic deliberations, transparency, debate, and accountability, can do permanent harm to the members of a society (Wang et al. 2012).

China's Future Populations

In 2009, an internal document meant for reading at the highest level of leadership in the PRC, looked back over the previous 50 years of the nation's founding, and the pressing needs for the future. One article, "Food crisis: fact or fiction?" looked at China's "great successes having since turning back from monumental errors." The author, Wang Zhongxue (王中學 *wáng zhōngxué*), a professor at Beijing Aerospace University, reminded the readers about the tragedy of the GLF, and the lessons learned: "If you are to govern, first you must have enough food." In a graph, Wang Zhongxue notes the specific year of 1956 when, 7 years after the revolution and establishment of the PRC, the average food production per person in China was about 307 kg per person. In 1960, at its nadir (and apex of suffering during the GLF), the average was only about 217 kg per person. While China had largely solved its food problem by the 1990s, Wang Zhongxue had his own Malthusian angst about whether or not "food production will keep up with the rate of population increases," and whether famine could strike China again? At the time of its writing, China was anticipating a population of 1.5 billion by the year 2040, in which case Wang Zhongxue pointedly asks, "How much food will we need?" (Wang 2009).

Still, from the widest aperture possible when looking at China's past century, the most remarkable story is its rise from dire poverty in 1978 to present day. Nowadays, food shortages only appear in China when the government decides to close down entire cities, to include Shanghai (nearly 25 million people) and Baotou, Inner Mongolia (2.7 million people). These recent draconian measures were taken in order to control COVID outbreaks (April 2022), leaving millions of citizens uncertain of how to obtain daily necessities. Under normal circumstances, however, with its massive economy, plus the availability of food produced both in domestic and international markets, it unlikely that China will ever be "the sick man of Asia," nor will it ever go hungry, even if pockets of desperately poor still remain.

For China, it will be the demographics of its people, namely, the aged, that will present its greatest challenge. Despite having revised the one-child policy to three, there are no signs that Chinese families will increase the number of children in any way to have a large effect. In addition to the imbalance of males over females, a severely imbalanced ratio that is not expected to ameliorate over the next few decades, China's population growth will continue to shrink. With an anticipated peak of 1.4 billion people by 2040, the fertility rate in China for every female over her lifespan has already dropped now to 1.3 children, whereas the replacement level was 2.1 during the early 1990s. In addition to a contraction in population growth, the graying of China's population will continue apace, and by 2040 some 25% of China's population will be 65 or older. With its current policies of low immigration (and blessed with long life expectancies), there is nothing on the horizon that will significantly change this demographic trend (Eberstadt 2021).

Republic of China (Taiwan)

In tandem with trends seen in developing countries, Taiwan saw its first ever contraction in its population by 0.18% in 2020 compared to the year earlier (Chen et al. 2022). Although Taiwan has relaxed its immigration and permanent status rules in order to attract talent from overseas, as well as increasing child-care credits, its national demographic landscape also portends an ever-growing elderly population. If China will have a quarter of its population over 65 years of age in 2040, and Japan will be even higher (35%), Taiwan is anticipated to reach about 30% of that same demographic. In looking at the population trends and forecasting for economic development, the Taiwanese economist Yuan-Ho Hsu recommends (and with Hayekian caution):

> [P]olicy measures that increase the size of working-age population by means of encouraging continuous immigration or encouraging the increase in total fertility ... However, this measure is the most complicated one because it may trigger social and political tensions between interest groups. The implementation of such measure needs through and delicate planning (Hsu 2017).

Yet one more critical trend to consider with regard to the future of Taiwan, mainland China, and their relationship across the strait. As the Taiwanese grow older, those who have traditionally adhered to the KMT's policy towards a future unification with China are being more and more outnumbered by a generation that does not see formal unification of China and Taiwan in their future. By the same token, since 1994, Taiwanese supporting *de jure* Taiwanese independence ("as soon as possible") have never polled larger than 8% of those surveyed, while in 2021 only 6% favored moving towards unification (NCCU 2021). As these demographic and cultural trends solidify into a truly Taiwanese identity, unless it carries out a military invasion (something China has long threatened to do), the PRC is unlikely to ever achieve unification with Taiwan.

References

Bashford, Alison. 2019. Malthus and China. *The Historical Journal* 63 (1): 63–89.
Chai, Sunglin. 1977. *Population and population policy in Mainland China*. Taipei: Asia and the World Forum Monograph Series, No. 6.
Chen, Chun-hua, Pan Tzu-yu and Evelyn Kao. 2022. Taiwan's population declines for second straight year: MOI. *Focus Taiwan*, 10 January. https://focustaiwan.tw/society/202201100018.
Chinese Wiki-Encyclopedia (CWE). 2021. *List of famines in China*. 中国饥荒名单-维基百科. https://wikichi.icu/wiki/List_of_famines_in_China#cite_note-li1982-9.
Colville, Alex. 2021. Zhu was first: the rise and fall of commander-in-chief Zhu De. *SupChina*, 10 May. https://supchina.com/2021/05/10/zhu-was-first-the-rise-and-fall-of-commander-in-chief-zhu-de/.
Eberstadt, Nicholas. 2021. The China Challenge: a demographic predicament will plague the mainland for decades. *Discourse*, 9 June. https://www.discoursemagazine.com/culture-and-society/2021/06/09/the-china-challenge-a-demographic-predicament-will-plague-the-mainland-for-decades/.
Greenhalgh, Susan. 2005. Missile science, population science: The origins of China's one-child policy. *The China Quarterly* 182: 253–276.
Hayek, F.A. 1944. *The road to serfdom*. New York: Routledge.
Howden, David, and Yang Zhou. 2015. Why did China's population grow so quickly? *The Independent Review* 20 (2): 227–248.
Hsu, Yuan-Ho. 2017. Population aging, labor force participation, and economic growth. *Journal of Business & Economic Policy* 4 (1): 119–129.
Malthus, Thomas Robert. 1826. *An essay on the principle of population*. Vol. 1. 6th ed. London: John Murray.
National Chengchi University (NCCU), Election Study Center. 2021. *Changes in the unification-independence stances of Taiwanese as tracked in surveys by election study center [sic], NCCU (1994–2021)*. https://esc.nccu.edu.tw/upload/44/doc/6963/Tondu202112.jpg.
Olsen, Alexa. 2015. A brutality born of helplessness. *Foreign Policy*, 3 November. https://foreignpolicy.com/2015/11/03/a-brutality-born-of-helplessness-china-one-child-policy-western-population-bomb-fearmongering/.
Sharping, Thomas. 2003. *Birth control in China, 1949–2000: Population policy and demographic development*. New York: RoutledgeCurzon.
United Kingdom, Office for National Statistics (UKONS). 2016. *The modern census*, 16 January. https://www.ons.gov.uk/census.
Wang, Zhongxue. 2009. Food crisis: Fact or fiction? In *Zhongnanhai: New high-level think tank*, vol. 1, 254–264. Beijing: China Wealth Management Forum. 王中學. 糧食危機: 真實的還是虛擬的. 中南海高層新智囊. [內部資料].
Wang, Feng, Yong Cai, and Gu. Baochang. 2012. Population, policy, and politics: How will history judge China's one-child policy? *Population and Development Review* 38: 115–129.
Wang, Zhihe, Ming Yang, Jiaming Zhang, and Jiang Chang. 2016. Was the one-child-policy every needed? *The American Journal of Economics and Sociology* 75 (4): 929–979.

The manufacturer's authorised representative in the EU is Springer Nature Customer Service Centre GmbH, Europaplatz 3, 69115 Heidelberg, Germany. If you have any concerns regarding our products, please contact ProductSafety@springernature.com

Printed and bound by CPI Group (UK) Ltd, Croydon, CR0 4YY
30/09/2026
02225237-0020